The New York Times BOOK OF THE DEAD

had an amazing fecundity of imagination that permitted him to metamorphize a mood or an idea into a work of art with bewildering quickness. He was, in André Malraux's phrase, "the archwizard of modern art," a man who, as a painter alone, produced well over 6,000 pictures. Some he splashed off in a few hours; others took weeks.

In 1969, his 88th year, he produced out of his volcanic energy a total of 165 paintings and 45 drawings, which were exhibited at the Palace of the Popes in Avignon, France. Crowding the walls of that venerable structure, the Picasso array drew exclamatory throngs and moved Emily Genauer, the critic, to say, "I think Picasso's new pictures are the fire of heaven."

Explaining the source of this energy Picasso said as he neared 90, "Everyone is the age he has decided on, and I have decided to remain 30."

The painter was so much known for works that blurred or obliterated conventional distinctions between beauty and ugliness and for depersonalized forms that he was accused of being an antihumanist. That appraisal disturbed him, for he regarded himself, with all his vagaries, as having created new insights into a seen and unseen world in which fragmentation of form was the basis for a new synthesis.

A Bull From a Bicycle Seat

"What is art?" a visitor once asked him. "What is not?" he replied. And he substantiated this point once by combining a bicycle seat and a pair of handlebars to make a bull's head.

"Whatever the source of the emotion that drives me to create, I want to give it a form that has some connection with the visible world, even if it is only to wage war on that world," he explained to Françoise Gilot, who was one of his mistresses and herself a painter.

"Otherwise," he continued, "a painting is just an old grab bag for everyone to reach into and pull out what he himself has put in. I want my paintings to be able to defend themselves, to resist the invader, just as though there were razor blades on all surfaces so no one could touch them without cutting his hands. A painting isn't a market basket or a woman's handbag, full of combs, hairpins, lipstick, old love letters

sand possibilities of interpreting my canvas. I want there to be only one and in that one to some extent the possibility of recognizing nature, even distorted nature, which is, after all, a kind of struggle between my interior life and the external world as it exists for most people.

"As I've often said, I don't try to express nature; rather, as the Chinese put it, to work like nature. And I want that internal surge — my creative dynamism — to propose itself to the viewer in the form of traditional painting violated."

In the long course of upending traditionalism, Picasso became a one-man history of modern are. In every phase of its turbulent (and often violent) development he was either a daring pioneer or a gifted practitioner. The sheer variousness of his creations reflected his probings of modern art for ways to communicate the multiplicity of its expressions; and so Picasso could not be categorized as belonging to this or that school, for he opened and tried virtually all of them.

In his peripateticism he worked in oils, water-colors, pastels, gouaches, pencil and ink drawings and aquatints he etched, made lithographs, sculptured, fashioned ceramics, put together mosaics and constructed murals.

One of his masterpieces was "Guernica," painted in 1937 and on loan for many years to the Museum of Modern Art in New York. An oil on canvas 11¼ feet high and 25½ feet long, it is a majestic, stirring indictment of the destructiveness of modern war. By contrast, another masterpiece was a simply and perfectly drawn white pigeon, "The Dove," which was disseminated around the world as a symbol of peace. But masterpiece or something not so exalted, virtually all Picasso were interesting and provocative. Praised or reviled, his work never evoked quiet judgments.

A Different View

The artist, however, held a different view. "There is no such thing as bad Picasso," he said, "some are less good than others."

Exhibitions of his work, especially in his later years, were sure-fire attractions. The mention of his name

The New York Times

BOOK

of the

DEAD

‹‹‹‹ *320 Print and 10,000 Digital Obituaries of Extraordinary People* ››››

Edited by WILLIAM McDONALD

Black Dog & Leventhal Publishers
Hachette Book Group
1290 Avenue of the Americas
New York, NY 10104

www.hachettebookgroup.com

www.blackdogandleventhal.com

First Edition: October 2016

Black Dog & Leventhal Publishers is an imprint of Hachette Books, a division of Hachette Book Group. The Black Dog & Leventhal Publishers name and logo are trademarks of Hachette Book Group, Inc.

The publisher is not responsible for websites (or their content) that are not owned by the publisher.

The Hachette Speakers Bureau provides a wide range of authors for speaking events. To find out more, go to www.HachetteSpeakersBureau.com or call (866) 376-6591.

Print book interior design by Lorie Pagnozzi

Library of Congress Cataloging-in-Publication Data

Names: McDonald, William.
Title: The New York Times book of the dead : 320 print and 10,000 digital
    obituaries of extraordinary people / edited by Bill McDonald (obituaries
    editor for The New York Times).
Other titles: New York times.
Description: First edition. | New York, NY : Black Dog & Leventhal, 2016 |
    Includes bibliographical references and index.
Identifiers: LCCN 2016023114 | ISBN 9780316395472 (hardcover) | ISBN
    9781478913429 (audio download) | ISBN 9780316395465 (ebook)
Subjects: LCSH: Biography—20th century. | Biography—19th century. |
    Biography—21st century. | United States—Biography. | Obituaries. |
    Obituaries—United States. | BISAC: HISTORY / United States / General. |
    BIOGRAPHY & AUTOBIOGRAPHY / General. | HISTORY / World.
Classification: LCC CT120 .N455 2016 | DDC 920.02—dc23 LC record available
    at https://lccn.loc.gov/2016023114

ISBN: 978-0-31639-547-2

Printed in Malaysia

IM

10 9 8 7 6 5 4 3 2

CONTENTS

tenzoon van Rosevelt, as the name was then spelled, came to this country in 1649. His son, Nicholas, was an Alderman of the Leislerian party; John Roosevelt, Cornelius C. Roosevelt, and James Roosevelt also served as Aldermen, and James J. Roosevelt was in turn Alderman, Assemblyman, Congressman and, Supreme Court Justice.

But although his name is Dutch, in his veins were mingled Irish, Scotch and Huguenot blood; and his mother was a Southerner. She was Martha Bulloch, daughter of James Stevens Bulloch, a major in Chatham's battalion, and a granddaughter of General Daniel Stewart of Revolutionary fame. His father, Theodore Roosevelt, Sr., organized a number of New York regiments in the civil war and was one of the leaders in organizing the Sanitary Commission and other work for the soldiers. He was a practical philanthropist and the works he accomplished for the poor were legion. When he died in 1878 flags flew at half mast all over the city and rich and poor followed him to the grave.

The second Theodore Roosevelt was born in this city Oct. 27, 1858. He was graduated from Harvard in 1880, and after a year spent in travel and study in Europe he plunged at once into that field of activity which he never afterward forsook—politics. He was an officeholder almost continuously from 1882 until he retired from the Presidency in 1909. The only intermission came during his life as a rancher after he retired from the Legislature.

As a boy he was puny and sickly; but with that indomitable determination which characterized him in every act of his life, he entered upon the task of transforming his feeble body not merely into a strong one, but into one of the strongest. How well he succeeded everybody knows. This physical feebleness bred in him nervousness and self-distrust, and in the same indomitable way he set himself to change his character as he changed his body and to make himself a man of self-confidence and courage. He has told the story himself in his autobiography:

"When a boy I read a passage in one of Marryat's books which always impressed me. In this passage the captain of some small British man-of-war is explaining to the hero how to acquire the quality of fearlessness. He says that at the outset almost every man is frightened when he goes into action, but that the course to follow is for the man to keep such a grip on himself that he can act just as if he was not frightened. After this is kept up long enough it changes from pretense to reality, and the man does in very fact become fearless by sheer dint of practicing fearlessness when he does not feel it. (I am using my own language, not Marryat's.) This was the theory upon which I went. There were all kinds of things of which I was afraid at first, ranging from griz-

laws and brutalities. He was warned by cautious friends that other Commissioners had tried the same thing and had failed; that the force was so honeycombed with petty jealousies and favoritism and blackmail, that the board could never ascertain the truth about what the men were doing. Roosevelt smiled and said: "Well, we will see about that," and see about it he did literally, for he personally sought the patrolmen on their beats at unexpected hours of the night, interviewed them as to their duties, and whenever one was found derelict he was promptly reprimanded or dismissed. The plan had a sudden and wholesome effect, for no roundsman, no sergeant, or police captain knew at what hour the Commissioner might turn up and catch him napping.

When he went into the Police Board and insisted on enforcing the excise laws literally, Chief Byrnes said, "It will break him. He will have to yield in time. He is only human."

At the height of his unpopularity a monster parade was organized to show New York's disgust with his policy. It paraded with such signs as "Send the Police Czar to Russia." A perfunctory invitation, or, perhaps, a sarcastic one, had been sent to him, and to everybody's astonishment he arrived early and took his seat on the reviewing stand.

Among the foremost of the paraders was a German, who looked back with pride on the great host behind him. Waving his hand, he shouted in a stentorian voice:

"Nun, wo ist der Roosevelt?" ("Where is Roosevelt now?")

A beaming face with a bulldog grin looked down from the stand.

"Hier bin ich. Was willst du, kamarad?" ("Here I am. What do you want, comrade?")

The German stopped, paralyzed with astonishment. Then an answering grin overspread his own face.

"Hurrah for Roosevelt!" he shouted. His followers took up the cry, and those who came to scoff remained to cheer.

In April, 1897, through the influence of his old friend, Senator Lodge, he was appointed Assistant Secretary of the Navy. He became convinced that war with Spain was inevitable and promptly proceeded to make provision for it. For command of the Asiatic Fleet certain politicians were pushing an officer of the respectable, commonplace type. Roosevelt determined to get the appointment for Commodore Dewey, who was this officer's junior, and who had no political backing, but whose career Roosevelt had been watching. He enlisted the services of Senator Redfield Proctor, whom he knew to be close to the President, checkmated the politicians and secured the appointment which resulted in so much glory for the American Navy.

Mr. Roosevelt also set about at once to secure a better equipment for the navy, and to him belongs credit for the drill of officers and men in target practice, the results of which were soon after made manifest. Soon after he became Assistant Secretary he asked for the sum of $800,000 for "practical target" shooting. That was considered a pretty large sum, and only a few months later he asked for $600,000 more. He was asked what had become of the first appropriation and replied that it had all been shot away, adding that very likely the same thing would happen to the new appropriation if it was granted. And the same thing did hap-

INTRODUCTION BY WILLIAM McDONALD

The headline appeared on the front page of The New York Times on April 17, 1865:

OUR GREAT LOSS

The Assassination of President Lincoln

DETAILS OF THE FEARFUL CRIME

Measured against the national calamity it described, the headline was relatively small, occupying the page's upper left corner over one long, narrow column of type. The tone was more mournful than excited, more a comforting hand on the shoulder than an urgent clutching of the lapels. The reporting that followed was sober, unhurried—so much so that The Times thought it prudent to tell its readers quickly, in the third paragraph, that in Washington "all business in the departments was suspended during the day."

Still, as we read it now, our imaginations are stirred by the account. We can never know what it was like for Americans of that distant year to learn the shocking news that Lincoln had been assassinated. But by reading the very words that they did, we can, for a moment, suspend our superior 21st-century knowledge of the event and put ourselves in the mid-19th-century shoes of a populace hungry for whatever information could be had about "the horrible crime," as The Times called it.

It's a time-transcending experience that may be found throughout this book, for each obituary here is largely what appeared in print after the momentous death occurred. (I say "largely" because most of these have been abridged somewhat so that all might fit snugly between the covers.)

An even fuller experience awaits readers who may wish to plumb the searchable online archive of obituaries to which the purchase of this book provides access— a deep well of more than 10,000, unabridged, that have appeared in The Times since its first issue, on Sept. 18, 1851.

Think about that date for a moment. As the obituaries editor of The Times, I admit that I may harbor a certain bias born of institutional pride, but I can think of precious few news organizations still in operation today that can boast of a legacy reaching back that far— that could mine their archives to present so vast a historical lineup, from Daniel Webster to David Bowie. And few news organizations, I would venture, have been as conscious of contributing to the historical record as The Times. Thumbing through these pages will attest to that; the book is a veritable portrait gallery of some of the most luminous personalities to have left their mark on the world since before the American Civil War.

As that 10,000-strong online archive suggests, however, "The Book of the Dead" does not purport to be comprehensive; the historical figures who have shaped the world since the early decades of the 19th century number vastly more than the 350 or so presented here. A fuller roster might fill a 10-volume set. But the ones who are included—heroes and villains alike—are indisputably deserving, for good or ill.

They're not unlike the people who appear in Times obituaries on any given day. In both cases, book and newsprint, they're the chosen few. Their accomplishments, their prominence, their impact on society elevate them to a rarefied plane. As we say on the obit desk, "They rise."

That is not to suggest that in life they were necessarily better than you or me, just more consequential, broadly speaking; not necessarily more worthy of our esteem as human beings, just more newsworthy.

The parade of giants portrayed in this book has something else in common with the daily run of notables featured on the obituary page: They rose above their competition, their fellow deceased. They were judged as simply having a greater claim on our attention than others, even if by a hair. The choosing is a necessary practicality: Even the most conscientious news organization has only so many hands and so much time in the day to produce these short-form biographies. And a book like this has only so many pages in which to accommodate them. Reasonable arguments are routinely made for many accomplished candidates who nevertheless fail to make the cut in the newspaper, just as sound cases could be made for the hundreds of history shapers who are not accounted for in these pages. But the inn has only so many rooms. Many worthy subjects had to be turned away, often reluctantly. (And, for production reasons, none who died after June 3, 2016, could be included.)

Like the daily obituary page, this book is a mirror on the past—a wide rearview mirror. A lone obituary tells a life story, but when gathered with others on a broadsheet page or in a bound volume, they may collectively reflect the society that shepherded those lives to the forefront in the first place.

One will notice that most of the people who appear in these pages are white and male. One may notice a similar imbalance in the newspaper, though lately, I'm happy to say it's diminishing as the more overtly discriminatory past recedes ever further from view. But the bias is undeniable, and it, too, is historical: It reflects the prejudices and injustices of an earlier era. To single out the movers and shakers of history—Western history in any case—one must inevitably draw from those who controlled the levers of power, and that group, as we know, was composed mostly of white men.

But history is also a tale of barriers breached. Many stories in this book tell of men and women who overcame racism, sexism, anti-Semitism and other forms of bigotry to help shape their world and, by their achievements, repudiate those very "isms." Harriet Tubman, Martin Luther King and Cesar Chavez are just a few. (In some cases white men themselves could be counted among the disadvantaged, strivers who climbed the social ladder and succeeded with little but their own native intelligence and grit. See Lincoln.)

Obituaries by definition evoke the past, and when written decades or centuries ago, they echo those lost worlds in their diction, their vocabulary, their styles of punctuation and capitalization, and their tone, be it eloquent, turgid, blunt or florid. "The rays of the morning sun fell across the cottage porch upon a family waiting only for death," The Times reported in its melodramatic account of the death of Ulysses S. Grant in 1885. One pleasure of this book is that as a time portal it lets you hear the past as well.

It also lets you chart the evolution, by stops and starts, of the obituary as a journalistic form. In the early days of The Times, the obit was often little more than a bulletin-board notice, a few paragraphs to inform readers of the fact of death, not to rehearse the entire life. "The London Times announces the death of the distinguished author of 'Democracy in America'; an event for which previous reports of his rapidly declining health had prepared us," The Times wrote in 1859 about the death of Alexis de Tocqueville.

Later obits offered abbreviated biographies, often carrying a eulogistic tone. Others suggested that political sympathies may have been at play. President Grant's last breath elicited a long, fevered report from his deathbed as well as a crushing biography of more than 40,000 leaden words, his great rival, Gen. Robert E. Lee, received a fraction of that total and, it seems, the back of the hand when The Times, stalwart of the Union, lamented that "so gifted" a military man had "cast his lot with traitors" in their "wicked plot to tear asunder the Republic."

The obituary took a more standardized form in the early decades of the 20th century. Typically a brief wire service report announcing the news would be plunked on top of an obituary written in advance by an anonymous Times staff member. But the treatment from one day or one year to the next was not always even-handed. J.P. Morgan received a gargantuan obituary; the legendary pitcher Cy Young something well short of a column. Only later did bylines appear, notably that of Alden Whitman, who gained a measure of fame as a writer of elegant advance obituaries, often traveling to interview his subjects for posthumous publication. And only later were the word lengths of obituaries reliable measures of the subjects' significance, at least in the judgment of the editors.

The pages of The Times through much of its history have abounded with underplayed obituaries. Gustav Mahler's, focusing on his conducting, was modest. ("Noted Also as Composer," the headline said.) Karl Marx was buried on page 3 in 1883, 600 words sufficing. James Dean merited 133 words. The death of Jackson Pollock did make the front page in 1955, although he took something of a back seat, as it were, in a subdued account. The headline said: "8 Killed in 2 L. I. Auto Crashes; Jackson Pollock Among Victims."

Often the attenuation was readily explainable. James Dean was not yet a legend when he died. (But still, only 133 words?) Neither was Herman Melville, whom The Times described as "a man who is so little known, even by name, to the generation now in the vigor of life." (The paper nevertheless gave his obit a respectable 1,000 words, though that was less than a third of what it granted an important but arguably lesser literary lion, J.D. Salinger, 119 years later.)

More striking are the outright omissions. You will not find in this book obituaries about Vincent van Gogh, Paul Gauguin or Paul Cézanne; about Soren Kierkegaard, Franz Kafka or Anton Chekhov; about Charlotte Bronte, Emily Dickinson or Sylvia Plath— for the simple reason that none were ever published. And the reason they weren't, as best as can be determined, is that those now illustrious products of the 19th century were not widely known, if known at all, at the time of their deaths. Reputations grew only posthumously. Emily Dickinson's poetry went unpublished in her lifetime, and so went the news of her death. The stature of Kierkegaard and Chekhov did not become apparent until the early 20th century.

On the other hand, I'm not sure there was any excuse for dispensing with Jim Morrison, one of the dominant rock stars of his era, with only 300-odd words when he died at 27 in 1971, to much of the world's shock.

But no one has ever called journalism a science. Its rules and standards, its attitudes and perspectives— not to mention its technology— have changed as the larger society it mirrors has. Journalism continues to evolve, in all its various precincts, including the obituary beat. Never in the history of The Times has the obit been used so winningly as a vehicle for narrative storytelling as it is now, as vividly demonstrated by some of the more recent obits in this book— Yogi Berra's, for example, or Maya Angelou's. Where once there was a lone Alden Whitman to compose artful obituaries in advance, today he has many heirs; the obits desk has become home for some of The Times's finest writers, and they are continuing to reshape this venerable form, attracting legions of readers, young and old, many of whom spread the words through social media. An obituary like David Bowie's may draw an online readership in the millions.

In time the written obit may become the foundation for still undreamt of ways in which a life story may be told, whether in the multimedia digital ether or in the sensory frontiers of virtual reality. But in whatever shape it takes, I suspect the obit will hold to its fundamental mission, as it was performed throughout much of this book: to recall in full a life of consequence, to illuminate the past that molded it, and to show how the path one person took helped lead us to where we, the inheritors, are now.

rre, Mao insisted in letters and
eches that have since reached the
side world that he had been suspi-
s of Marshal Lin as early as 1966
had used him only to help get
of Mr. Liu.

or several years after Marshal Lin's
th, the redoubtable Mr. Chou, a
ster administrator and conciliator,
ed the visibly aging Mao lead the
ntry and embark on what seemed
stained period of economic growth.

Mr. Chou's death from cancer in
uary 1976 left the daily leadership
the hands of Mr. Teng, the former
ty Secretary General, whom Mr.
ou resurrected in 1973, evidently
h Mao's approval, and installed as
ior Deputy Prime Minister and like-
uccessor.

An Even Quicker Fall

Mr. Teng then fell victim to Mao's
picions even more quickly than had
Liu and Marshal Lin. Only three
nths after Mr. Chou's demise, Mr.
g was stripped of his posts, casti-
ed once again as a "capitalist-roader
hin the party" and accused by Mao
misinterpreting his personal direc-
es by overstressing economic devel-
ment.

n these later years there were some
o thought that Mao appeared as an
g autocrat, given more and more
whim. His invitation last winter to
Nixon to revisit Peking, the scene

*Mao reviewing troops of Ei
base in northwest China afte*

period when Mao and others in the
newly organized Chinese party were
groping for a way to power, and Stalin,
from the distance of Moscow gave
them orders that repeatedly led them
into disaster.

Stalin and his representatives from
the Communist International who
served as advisers in China—Mao
dubbed them "imperial envoys"—first
directed the Communists to ally with
Chiang Kai-shek's Nationalists. Then,
after Generalissimo Chiang turned on
the Communists in 1927, massacring
thousands, Stalin ordered the party to
anticipate a "revolutionary upsurge" in
the cities by the (largely nonexistent)
proletariat.

Mao was shorn of his posts and
power in the early 1930's as a result
of direct Soviet interference. It was
only after the Communists were forced
to begin the Long March in 1934, after
more errors in strategy, that Mao won
command because of his genius for or
ganizing and leading peasant guerrillas
in a revolution in the countryside.

His First Journey Abroad

When Mao traveled triumphantly to
Moscow—it was his first journey

Some Quotations From Chairman Mao

A man's head is not like a scallion, which will grow again if you
cut it off; if you cut it off wrongly, then even if you want to correct
your error, there is no way of doing it. (1956)

Our nation will never again be an insulted nation. We have stood
up. (1949)

The Red Army is like a furnace in which all captured soldiers are
melted down and transformed the moment they come over. In China
not only the masses of workers and peasants need democracy, but
the army needs it even more urgently. (1928)

The popular masses are like water, and the army is like a fish.
How then can it be said that when there is water, a fish will have
difficulty in preserving its existence? An army which fails to maintain
good discipline gets into opposition with the popular masses, and thus
by its own action dries up the water. (1938)

h Route Army in Yenan, his
he epic Long March that took

Thereafter the Russians continued to build up their army, navy and air force along the Chinese frontier until a fourth of their troops were stationed in the area.

Mao spent hours lecturing every visiting head of state on the danger of Soviet expansionism—hegemonism, as he termed it. His belief that Soviet "social-imperialism" was the greatest threat to peace enabled him to take a more sanguine view of the United States and helped bring about the gradual improvement in relations after 1972.

An Austere Style

Although Mao commanded enormous authority—in 1955, in a casual talk with local officials, he overturned the provisions of the five-year plan fixed only a day before by the National People's Congress—he avoided the trappings of high office. He rarely appeared in public, perhaps to preserve a sense of awe and mystery, and he eschewed fancy dress or medals, in conformity with the simple standard he himself had set during his guerrilla days. Whatever the occasion, he wore only a plain gray tunic buttoned to the neck and trousers to match that came to be called a Mao suit in the West and for a period in the 1970's became a fashion craze.

Edgar Snow, the American journalist who in 1936 became the first Westerner to meet Mao, felt that his style owed much to the simplicity, if not roughness and crudeness, of his peasant upbringing. He had the "personal habits of a peasant, plain speaking and plain living," Mr. Snow reported after a visit to the Communists' guerrilla headquarters in Shensi, near Yenan. Mao was completely indifferent to personal appearance; he lived in a two-room cave like other peasants "with bare, poor, map-covered walls." His chief luxury was a mosquito net, Mr. Snow found, and he owned only his blankets and two cotton uniforms.

"Mao's food was the same as everybody's, but being a Hunanese he had the southerner's ai-la, or love of pepper," Mr. Snow wrote. "He even had

more than a year, starting
the most difficult terrain

trooped to Yenan in the 1940's dur an optimistic interlude when Washi ton hoped to bring Mao and Chia together to fight the Japanese, inev bly were impressed by Mao's obvi earnestness and by his willingness sacrifice personal comfort for the p suit of an ideal. In these he contras all too clearly with the corruption indifference of most Nationalist le ers.

Some of Mao's dedication, toughn and reserve may also have been product of his bitter personal expe ences along the road to power. His ter and his second wife, Yang Kai-were executed in 1930 by Gene hiang; a younger brother was kil fighting a rear-guard action during ... another younger brot ... executed ... Sinkiang, a ... st son ... illed in the rean War. Another son, according Red Guard sources during the Cultu Revolution, was said to have gone n because of the way he was brou up by a "bourgeois" family after mother was executed.

Mao also had several close brus with death. In 1927, when he was ganizing peasants and workers Hunan, he was captured by local p Kuomintang—that is, pro-Nationalis militiamen, who marched him back their headquarters to be shot. Just sight of their office, Mao broke lo and fled into a nearby field, where hid in tall grass until sunset.

"The soldiers pursued me, and for some peasants to help them search me," he related to Mr. Snow. "Ma times they came very near, once twice so close that I could almost h touched them, but somehow I esca discovery. At last when it was d they abandoned the search."

Mindful of Cost to Family

He was certainly mindful of the c of the revolution to his family friends. In a talk in 1964 with

BENJAMIN DISRAELI

December 21, 1804–April 19, 1881

LONDON—The Earl of Beaconsfield, after an illness of less than a month, died at an early hour this morning.

He was first attacked during the last week of March, with gout and violent asthmatic symptoms, both of which troubles were soon alleviated by his skillful medical attendants. Since his prostration, bulletins giving reports of his condition have been issued several times each day. Early this morning his physicians were at his bedside, but the utmost exertions of the medical gentlemen failed to have effect, and the great statesman expired peacefully. He was perfectly conscious to the last.

Among the Jews who were driven out of Spain at the close of the fifteenth century, when the inquisition and other persecutions forced from that land the most industrious and active races that lived in it, were the ancestors of Lord Beaconsfield. They found a home and opportunities to restore their fortune in Venice. While living in Spain they had been forced to adopt a Christianized surname, but as soon as the shores of Venice were touched the name was changed to D'Israeli, a designation which unmistakably indicated the race to which they belonged.

They remained in Venice more than 200 years before one of the family sent his youngest son to England to seek his fortune. He married and settled in Enfield, a few miles from London. His only child, Isaac, was the father of Lord Beaconsfield. Isaac married in 1802 the daughter of George Basevi, a Justice of the Peace in Sussex, who bore him four children, of whom Benjamin (Dec. 21, 1804) was the second.

It does not appear that Isaac D'Israeli took even ordinary care to perfect the education of his boy. Universal testimony declares that the son was remarkably precocious and of very bright mind, but he was sent to a boarding-school in Winchester, to the house of a Unitarian minister, and to an attorney's office instead of to Harrow, Rugby, Oxford or Cambridge. Lord Beaconsfield, in many ways so remarkable, is singularly so in this, that he was one of the few eminent English statesmen who had not been at Oxford or Cambridge.

Rarely has a literary success so sudden as the young Mr. Disraeli's occurred in literature. He was only 22 years of age when "Vivian Grey" was launched anonymously into the London world. Vivian Grey, the character, was the author himself, who remained anonymous. The novel depicted the course of a young man of genius and ambition who was without friends and aspired to political honors. On its title page was this prophetic quotation: "Why, then, the world's mine oyster, Which I with sword will open—." It was a sufficient index of his subsequent career.

Flushed with the success of "Vivian Grey," the young author went abroad, returning to find himself a lion in the society of London.

Count D'Orsay drew a picture of him during this period which represents a very handsome man, such as might ornament and delight any London drawing-room. His hair was of silken blackness and fell in ringlets about his neck and forehead; his dress coat was of black velvet, lined with white satin, and he carried an ivory-handled cane, inlaid with gold, and ornamented with a tassel of black silk.

Men laughed at his affectation, and generally held him in low esteem, but women approved of his peculiarities, and the more discerning of them predicted that time would see him a great man.

England, in 1831, was in the last stage of the struggle for Parliamentary reform. Then began the public life of this remarkable man who was to astonish and puzzle the world for 50 years. A son of Earl Grey, then the Premier, had been put forward in the Borough of High Wycombe, as a candidate for Parliament, and the young Mr. Disraeli entered into the contest against him. His nomination was proposed by a Radical, and a Tory seconded it, but the united votes of the two parties failed to elect him.

A second candidature, and a third, ended in like manner.

This latter was the occasion of his famous quarrel with [the Irish member of Parliament Daniel] O'Connell. O'Connell had allied himself with the Whigs, in spite of the fact that the Whigs had formerly treated him with great contempt, and thus appeared in the forefront against Mr. Disraeli, who singled him out for an attack as an "incendiary," a "traitor," and a "liar in word and action."

O'Connell's retort is known everywhere. "He," said the Irishman, "possesses just the qualities of the impenitent thief who died upon the cross, whose name, I verily believe, must have been Mr. Disraeli. For aught I know, the present Mr. Disraeli is descended from him, and with the impression that he is, I now forgive the heir-at-law of the blasphemous thief who died upon the cross."

Mr. Disraeli's first reply to this was a challenge to O'Connell's son, Morgan. Bridled in this effort, he retorted in a letter to the London Times which was regarded at the time as fuss and fury. He got to have a reputation of being a vain and frothy young man, in too great a hurry to succeed.

With the beginning of Victoria's reign the public life of Benjamin Disraeli took a sudden turn. In accordance with constitutional usage, the accession of a new sovereign to the throne was followed by a general election, and in this Mr. Disraeli—through stupid conduct on the part of the Whigs, it is often maintained—found himself in Parliament, the junior member from Maidstone.

Parliament reassembled in November, 1837, and three weeks had not passed before the young member delivered his maiden speech.

It was on the Irish election petitions, and in direct reply to O'Connell, whom he had now come, as he promised, "to meet at Philippi." Again and again he was interrupted, and finally was compelled to sit down amid laughter and jeers. His last words were these: "I have begun several things many times, and I have often succeeded at last. I will sit down now, but the time will come when you will hear me."

As early as 1839 he had expressed himself on the subject of electoral reform. In July, he astonished certain classes by a declaration that denounced the tendency of Government to centralization and the monopoly of power in the hands of the middle classes. To the lower classes he appealed to yield up the Government to the upper, declaring that "the aristocracy and the laboring class constituted the nation."

Mr. Disraeli's power in England as a leader of the Tory Party dates from 1847. The sudden death of Lord George Bentinck, a year later, left him the acknowledged head of the Protectionists. Out of failures by the Whigs on free trade measures, he gathered strength, and the year 1852 found him far advanced in the esteem of Parliament, where he became Chancellor of the Exchequer and leader of the House of Commons. When Parliament assembled in November, and the conflict over free trade soon arose, [William] Gladstone, his rival, won the day.

Out of power, Mr. Disraeli remained in his place in the House, and on all occasions, when his patriotism was appealed to, gave Lord Palmerston his loyal and earnest support.

With the changes of 1858, which more or less had their origin in the Orsini conspiracy against the life of Napoleon III, Mr. Disraeli was intimately associated. There had been in France loud complaints against England for permitting a conspiracy to be hatched on her own soil against a neighboring power, and certain published statements indicated that the French Government was of like feeling on the subject.

Under these circumstances, Lord Palmerston moved for leave to bring in a bill relating to conspiracy to murder. Lord Palmerston's proposal became extremely unpopular, and Mr. Disraeli, reading public feeling that had so intensified itself against the bill, declared against it.

The Spring of 1859 found Mr. Disraeli again in office as Chancellor of the Exchequer and leader of the House. But Mr. Disraeli and his colleagues were soon out of power again over the contentious issue of Parliamentary reform.

Lord Palmerston's sudden death in October, 1865, when the returns of a general election had scarcely ceased to be received, left the Government without a head. Lord Russell was called upon, but in less than a year he resigned and Lord Derby formed an Administration with Mr. Disraeli again leader in the House. During the recess of 1866–67 it became known that the ministry had decided to introduce a Reform bill.

Six Reform bills since 1852 had been introduced, and all had failed. This one did not, and in August, 1867, it received the Queen's signature. Mr. Disraeli's work for it was of a tremendous order. He was not only the author of the bill, but his speeches numbered 310. By this law the right of suffrage was extended to all house-holders in a borough and to every person in a county who had a freehold of 40s. It enfranchised nearly a million of men.

Following its passage came Mr. Disraeli's elevation to the Premiership, and the first question that met him was Irish disestablishment. A long debate ended in his defeat: he refused to abandon his position, and Parliament was dissolved. The new election showed a strong majority for the Opposition, and in December, 1868, Mr. Disraeli and his colleagues resigned in favor of Gladstone.

Gradually the Gladstone Ministry was living out its lease of power. Matters went on until February, 1874, when it found a majority of 50 against it and fell. Mr. Disraeli was called upon to form a new Cabinet, and then saw himself for the first time strong in a majority on which he could rely, and possessed of the personal confidence of the Queen.

From this time on his great career is a matter of vivid public recollection, and needs only to be indicated briefly here. England had fallen into disrepute among the nations; her want of participation in the policy of Europe was a subject of ridicule. Under him, she laid aside her insular character and obtained position as a military power in Europe; she acquired Cyprus and gained authority in Asiatic Turkey.

Victoria did not transfer her seat of empire from London to Delhi, as he had foretold that she might do, but he made her Empress of India; he summoned Indian troops into Europe to support England; he made Asia Minor acknowledge her sway, and in buying the Suez Canal shares he secured the short way to India. After all this, he was voted out of power again, and his old rival came in. He went into retirement and wrote "Endymion" to find a publisher at £10,000.

Mr. Disraeli, about the year 1840, was married, his wife being the widow of his old friend, Wyndham Lewis, who was the senior member for Maidstone when he was the junior. She was more than ten years his elder, and brought him a large fortune. It was a singularly happy union for both. He has more than once owned his great indebtedness to her. She had an enthusiastic interest in all his undertakings, and was the soul of devotion to all his purposes. In 1868, when a Peerage was offered him, he declined it for himself, but prayed that the Queen would make his wife Countess of Beaconsfield, and she bore that title until she died in 1873.

OTTO VON BISMARCK

April 1, 1815–July 30, 1898

BERLIN—Prince Bismarck died shortly before 11 o'clock this evening. Details of his death are obtained with difficulty because of the lateness of the hour, the isolation of the castle, and the endeavors of attendants of the family to prevent publicity of what they consider private details.

The death of the ex-Chancellor at the age of 83 comes as a surprise to all Europe. There was apprehension when the sinking of the Prince was first announced. But when the daily bulletins chronicled improvement in his condition and told of his devotion to his pipe, the public accepted his doctor's assertion that there was no reason why Bismarck should not reach the age of 90 years.

The Saturday papers in Europe dismissed Bismarck with a paragraph, while his condition was overshadowed in the English papers by the condition of the Prince of Wales's knee.

The Bismarck family, with its estate at Friedrichsruh, traces its lineage back to the 13th century. The present title, that of Fürst von Bismarck, dates from 1871. This title will be borne by Bismarck's eldest son, known up to now as Count Herbert.

The news of the death of Prince Bismarck became known throughout New York City early in the evening. At all places where Germans congregate, at clubs, meetings, and in numerous East Side cafés, the subject was talked of all evening.

"Bismarck is dead," said Gerthue Maaf, one of the oldest members of the Liederkranz club, "but only in the body. His fame is imperishable as the stars."

The old-fashioned Prussian country house in which Otto von Bismarck, the future consolidator of Germany, saw the light on the 1st of April, 1815, has become a place of pilgrimage for tourists of all nations. His birth just when all Germany was rising to meet the last effort of Napoleon have made some persons picture him as a modern Hannibal, self-vowed from his cradle to eternal enmity against France.

Although the active, bright-eyed child of course had little idea of his own future greatness, there is little doubt that the surroundings of young Otto's boyhood left a deep and lasting trace upon his mind. As a child he would hear old country gentlemen telling of the wasted lands that marked Napoleon's destroying march through conquered Prussia in 1806 and the tremendous retribution that avenged this havoc seven years later when the Fatherland arose against the tyrant. He would listen to men from Berlin, Frankfurt, or Cologne lamenting the fatal dissensions which made the great German race almost a cipher in the politics of Europe.

He would later see the proofs of the weakness produced by Germany's fragmentary condition, while at the same time his keen eye would detect the latent strength which might make her invincible, could those fragments be wielded into one compact whole.

While her future leader was climbing trees and leaping ditches, Germany was passing through the most momentous period of her modern history. The movement which cleared German soil of its French invaders in 1813 and dethroned Napoleon a few months later was a victory for the Teutonic race. The conquerors began to ask themselves why they should not be united permanently.

It was in the crisis of this great national excitement that Bismarck's public career began.

This great apostle of unquestioned authority was always intolerant of authority himself. His Saxon Boswell, Dr. Moritz Busch, has chronicled the first flashes of that haughty and indomitable spirit which would one day trample in the dust the pride of Austria and France. Being called to account while a student at Gottingen for some breach of university rules, Bismarck swaggered into the presence of the horrified President with a rakish student cap and a sorely stained velvet jacket, an enormous bulldog at his heels.

Such actions, coupled with his reckless exposure of himself to all weathers and his wild gallops across country at the imminent risk of his neck, earned him the nickname of "Mad Bismarck," and made many prim old gentlemen regard him as a harum-scarum lad who would come to no good.

Toward the end of 1833 he quitted the University of Gottingen for that of Berlin, and in June, 1835, he was admitted to the bar.

In 1847 he made his first appearance in the Parliament of Berlin as delegate of the nobility of his district. Into a circle of solemn mediocrities burst like a thunderbolt this dashing, fiery rebel. "I come among these nonentities like pepper," said he, with grim enjoyment.

This was no exaggeration. The towering figure, the massive head thrown haughtily back, the brawny arms folded defiantly, the stern, piercing eye, the deep, challenging voice, and the crushing sarcasm, became well known in Berlin. Enemies multiplied as rapidly as acquaintances, and the new delegate quickly became, as he himself declared, "the best-hated man in all Prussia."

This was hardly surprising. The popular excitement, which would culminate in the great tidal wave of popular movements of 1848, had reached its height. Between such a man and such a movement there could be no sympathy. No one could have been a more typically complete aristocrat than this scion of a house of secondary rank, whose own mother had belonged to the bourgeois class. Throughout his career, all popular movements were anathema to Bismarck.

Bismarck seemed to hold that the King ought to do what he pleased without letting his people say anything at all. In early 1848 he asserted that "the world could never hope for any lasting peace until all large cities, those hotbeds of democracy and constitutionalism, were swept from the face of the earth."

In this period Bismarck beheld many things worthy of note. France had again proclaimed herself a republic. Austria was sitting sullenly amid the ruins of her ancient system. Russia was casting her mighty shadow across the whole of Europe. Germany lay a formless heap of incoherent atoms, each with its own toy sovereign and its own army of half a dozen men.

While the pillars of the world were shaking around him, Bismarck was enjoying one of the few intervals of quiet happiness which checkered his stormy life. Few sweeter love stories have been told than that which ended on the 28th of July, 1847, in the union of gentle Johanna von Puttkammer with the bearded giant whose name was a by-word throughout all Prussia.

It is fortunate that so many of Bismarck's letters to his wife remain to show the man as he really was. Anyone who had seen him only as the world sees him might stand amazed at the hearty, boyish merriment, the simple, childlike faith, the heartfelt tenderness revealed by this man whom 99 persons out of 100 regard as an apostle of "blood and iron."

Yet even while the future Chancellor of the German Empire was helping his new bride up Swiss hillsides and rowing her over Italian lakes, there were signs across Europe of the mighty events that would come 20 years later, among them a suggestion of universal suffrage and a rupture between Prussia and Austria.

Amid these warring influences one man stood forward. That man was Otto von Bismarck, who would mastermind the wars that unified the German states, a unification that did not include Austria, into a powerful German Empire under Prussian leadership.

One can understand Bismarck's opposition to "German unity" at a time when that unity meant the subordination of his native Prussia and all the other States of Northern Germany to that ill-corded bundle of Czechs, Hungarians, Croats, Poles, and Ruthenians, which called itself the Austrian Empire.

In 1861 the death of his insane brother made the Prince Regent King in fact as well as in name. The new sovereign was a sworn friend of Bismarck, and one of his first acts was to appoint to the Premiership the man whom he now knew to be as great in mind as in body.

This was the beginning of the end. Austria, perceiving too late that the substance had fallen to Prussia, grew angry and menacing. She shifted her center of gravity to the eastward and ceased to be a German power.

Any ordinary man would have been carried away by this astounding triumph and by the sudden change from universal hatred to the adoration of all Prussia. But Bismarck saw that France must follow Austria before the Prussian Kingdom could become the German Empire.

All this time the secret maturing of his mighty project went steadily on. "In the streets of Paris," wrote a traveler who saw Bismarck at the Paris Exhibition of 1867, "the tawny hair beneath the peaked helmet, the long, sweeping, reddish-brown mustache, the stern eyes, the ruddy, blonde complexion, the strange, grim expression soon became familiar. He bore himself haughtily and silently amid the fantastic festivities of Paris."

In truth, his next entrance into "the metropolis of the universe" three years later was no smiling matter. France struggled longer than Austria, but in vain, and the same month that witnessed the surrender of Paris saw the coronation at Versailles of "William I, Emperor of Germany."

Throughout that conflict Bismarck's proverbial energy outdid itself. "Often," says Dr. Busch, "when just out of bed, he began to think and work, to read and annotate dispatches, to study the newspapers, give instructions to the Councilors and other colleagues, put questions on the most various State problems, and even write or dictate.

"Then came the study of maps, the correction of papers that he had ordered to be prepared, the jotting down of ideas with the well-known big pencil, the composition of letters, the news to be telegraphed or sent to the papers for publication, and amid all this the reception of unavoidable visitors.

"Not till 2 or even 3 P.M. did the Chancellor, in places where a halt of any length was made, allow himself, a little breathing time, and then he generally took a ride in the neighborhood. Then to work again until dinner at 5 or 6 P.M., and in an hour and a half at latest he was back at his writing table, where midnight often found him reading or noting down his thoughts."

The Emperor's coronation was likewise that of Bismarck. But, like Napoleon and the Czar Nicholas, Bismarck lived too long. His later years were one incessant and fruitless struggle with the problems of political economy that had overmatched Frederick the Great and the revolutionary spirit that had defied even the autocrats of Russia.

When the enforcement of his arbitrary system of political economy drove yearly across the sea myriads of those sturdy laborers who were the lifeblood of Germany, Bismarck sought to enable these emigrants to become colonists without ceasing to be German citizens.

The "Iron Chancellor" began that series of annexations which established Germany in New-Guinea and the Samoan Isles, and extended the shadow of her imperial flag over 750 miles of coast along Western and Southwestern Africa. Bismarck clung to the idea of founding another German empire abroad.

"Once a German, always a German," said he. "When a man can cast away his nationality like a worn-out coat, I have nothing more to say to him."

When the aged Kaiser died, it was suspected that Bismarck's ascendency under the Emperor Frederick would be less than it had been under William, but he remained Chancellor and held his former place as the foremost figure in European diplomacy.

Finally Frederick died and his son William came to the throne. Matters went from bad to worse until March 18, 1890, when Bismarck finally resigned.

The personal character of this remarkable man remains a subject of dispute, thanks to the extravagant praises of his friends on one side and the calumnies of his foes on the other. In his domestic relations his worst enemies can find nothing to blame, but they denounced his public acts as those of a tyrannical, bloodthirsty man.

Tyrannical he was, but a hard-hearted man would not have stood with tears in his eyes beside the body of his favorite dog, or have all but lost his own life in saving that of his drowning servant. And a bloodthirsty man would have reveled in the horrors of war instead of doing his utmost to alleviate them.

QUEEN VICTORIA

May 24, 1819–January 22, 1901

COWES, ISLE OF WIGHT—Queen Victoria is dead. The greatest event in the memory of this generation, almost the most stupendous change in England that could be imagined, has taken place quietly, almost gently.

The end of this splendid career came at exactly 6:30 yesterday in a simply furnished room in Osborne House. This most respected of all women, living or dead, lay in a great four-posted bed. Within view of her dying eyes there hung a portrait of the Prince Consort.

A few minutes later the inevitable element of materialism stepped into this pathetic chapter of international history, for the Court ladies went busily to work ordering their mourning from London.

For several weeks the Queen had been failing. On Wednesday she suffered a paralytic stroke, accompanied by intense weakness. It was her first illness in all her 81 years, and she would not admit she was sick.

Albert Edward, Prince of Wales for more than 59 years, is now Edward VII of the United Kingdom of Great Britain and Ireland, and Emperor of India.

The reign of Queen Victoria, who came to the throne in 1837, was the longest in English history; indeed, it was one of the longest in the history of Europe. Victoria's more than half century of reign began when she was a grown-up woman and legally of age.

In a greater sense, however, was this reign a memorable one in English history. Literary endeavor and the search for knowledge in no other single reign, save that of Elizabeth, made such splendid contributions to the stock of new facts and written words that men will not let die. The scientific results achieved by the mind of man in the age of Victoria stand alone as the wonder and blessing of mankind.

No former sovereign reigned over so extensive a British Empire. In her time vast areas were added in Africa, India, and the Pacific, so that it was never quite so true as in her time that the British Empire was one on which the sun never set.

Though the royal house to which Queen Victoria belonged was that of Hanover, from the house of Stuart Victoria claimed her crown.

In Kensington Palace on the 24th of May, 1819, was born the future Queen of England.

When the child was six months old she was taken by her parents to Sidmouth, on the Devonshire coast, and here the Duke, her father, soon met his death. He had come home one day with his feet wet, and had stopped to play with his daughter before changing his boots. A fatal inflammation of the lungs ensued.

For many years, Victoria's position as heir apparent was doubtful. Even so late as 1830, the life of William IV stood between her and the throne.

Victoria had not been brought up with any assurance that she was heir to the throne. Strict orders were in force that no one should speak to her on the subject.

But when William IV became King nearing 65 years of age, statesmen then saw as all but inevitable that this little girl, who was 12 years old, was to be the future Queen.

It was thought time for her to know her position. The story told is that her governess conveyed the information by placing in one of her books a genealogical table. Examining it, the Princess said to the governess, "I see I am nearer the throne than I thought."

In England 18 is the age at which a royal Princess reaches her majority. Victoria passed this period on May 24, 1837. Less than a month afterward, on June 20, at 2:20 A.M., the King breathed his last. Immediately after this a carriage containing the Archbishop of Canterbury and the Lord Chamberlain departed for Kensington Palace. What followed has been described in the "Diary" of Miss Wynn:

"They knocked, they rang, they thumped for a considerable time before they could arouse a porter at the gate. They rang the bell and desired that the attendant of the Princess Victoria might be sent to inform her royal Highness that they requested an audience on business of importance.

"The attendant stated that the Princess was in such a sweet sleep that she could not disturb her. They then said: 'We are come on business of State to the Queen, and even her sleep must give way to that.' In a few moments she came into the room in a white nightgown and shawl, her nightcap thrown off and her hair falling upon her shoulders, her feet in slippers, tears in her eyes, but perfectly collected."

It was arranged that a Council should be held that day at Kensington. In Greville's "Diary" the following account of this Council is given, and Greville was not a man given to emotion:

"Never was anything like the first impression she produced, or the chorus of praise and admiration which it raised about her manner and behavior, and certainly not without justice. It was very extraordinary, and something far beyond what was looked for. Her extreme youth and inexperience, and the ignorance of the world concerning her, naturally excited intense curiosity to see how she would act on this trying occasion.

"She was plainly dressed and in mourning. After she had read her speech and taken the oath for the security of the Church of Scotland, the Privy Councilors were sworn, and, as these old men knelt before her swearing allegiance and kissing her hand, I saw her blush up to the eyes, and this was the only sign of emotion that she evinced."

On the following day occurred the ceremony of the proclamation, when the Queen made her appearance at the open window in St. James's Palace. At Kensington a range of apartments were set apart for her use, and there she lived until she left for Buckingham Palace.

She opened the first Parliament of her reign in November, and the following June she was formally crowned in Westminster Abbey. Harriet Martineau, an eye-witness, has described that scene with much felicity.

"The throne," says she, "covered, as was its footstool, with cloth of gold, stood on an elevation of four steps in the center of the area.

"About 9 the first gleams of the sun started into the Abbey, and presently traveled down to the peeresses Each lady shone out as a rainbow. The brightness, vastness, and dreamy magnificence of the scene produced a strange effect of exhaustion and sleepiness."

Albert, Prince Consort of England, was the second son of Ernest, Duke of Saxe-Coburg-Gotha, and was three months younger than Victoria.

Prince Albert first saw the Princess Victoria in the Spring of 1836, when he made a visit to England. The two are believed to have parted reluctantly. Victoria, in a letter to her uncle, begged him to "take care of the health of one now so dear to me."

Albert well understood how the strict etiquette of the Court obliged the Queen to take the initiative, and hence, on his second visit, in October, 1839, when the purpose of his visit was clearly understood, he waited anxiously for some sign of the Queen's decision in his favor. This he had the happiness to obtain on the second evening of his visit, at a ball, when she gave him her bouquet, and he received a message from her that she desired to speak with him on the following day.

In the following year occurred the wedding.

One of the most charming domestic pictures that royal lives have afforded is furnished in the married life of Albert and Victoria. Prince Albert was a man of honest purposes and devoted affections; he was endowed with noble ambitions guided by intelligence. Painting, etching, and music were accomplishments that afforded amusement to both, and the Prince was a man of taste and skill in landscape gardening. He loved a country life and early hours. To these tastes the Queen learned to conform.

The difficulties encountered at the outset of this union were incident to the peculiar relations of the Queen and Prince. Head of the family though the Prince was in his position as husband, his place in public affairs was necessarily subordinate. The common judgment is that he bore himself with good sense and dignity in this trying situation. The Queen, however, soon showed her determination that in all matters not affairs of State, the Prince was to exercise paramount authority.

The Queen became the mother of nine children. At the time of her first jubilee, which was celebrated with extraordinary splendor on a perfect June day in 1887, the Queen had thirty-one grandchildren and six great-grandchildren.

The domestic life of the Queen for the 20 years her husband lived was singularly happy. Fate seemed to shower upon her every blessing to which a woman could aspire.

In the eighteen-sixties came the illness of the Prince Consort. In December 1861 he breathed his last.

Victoria's life after her husband died was one of quiet seclusion. Her people saw little of her, and the projects honoring his memory were, for the most part, the only ones in which she manifested particular interest. In London the colossal Albert Memorial was erected, and in 1867 the Queen laid the foundation stone of the Albert Hall of Arts and Sciences.

In 1863 the Prince of Wales completed his 21st year, and was married.

In 1877 a new eminence was acquired by the Queen. She was made Empress of India.

When Victoria assumed the Crown, English statesmen had been for some years occupied with measures of electoral reform.

Under the reform bill passed in 1832, 56 boroughs in England, containing populations of less than 2,000 each, were disfranchised, 30 others were reduced to one member only, and 42 new ones were created. These boroughs which had been disfranchised were rotten boroughs. A new era in Parliamentary government was about to open.

Later on in her reign reform bills became familiar subjects in Parliamentary life.

Reform acts of 1884 and 1885 have been pronounced "the most extensive reform ever attempted in England." They applied to Scotland as well as England, and were extended to Ireland. England thenceforth has possessed practically universal suffrage.

Also an issue during Victoria's reign were the Corn Laws, which imposed tariffs on imported grain, thus raising food prices and prompting opposition from city residents.

Save for the war with China, begun in 1839, England had no war on her hands until the portentous cloud arose on the Bosporus in 1853.

The war in China was a war for trade. The precise occasion for declaring war was the Chinese demand for the surrender of opium. Peace was not formally secured until July, 1843. By the terms of this treaty England was to receive from China the sum of $21,000,000, and Hongkong was ceded to her in perpetuity.

The war in the Crimea was an outgrowth of designs respecting Turkey long entertained by Russia.

A dispute arose between Russia and France as to the possession of the holy places in Palestine. A commission appointed by Turkey decided in favor of Russia. Further claims on Turkey were then made by Russia.

The Sultan of Turkey then appealed to his allies, and the English and French fleets advanced for his protection. By September of 1853 English and French ships were in the Dardanelles; in October Turkey had declared war against Russia.

Operations in the Crimea began with the landing of the armies of the allies in September, 1854. They forced the Russians to retreat to Sebastopol, and in October the attack on the fortress was begun.

The incidents of this celebrated siege need only be named here. They include the battle of Balaklava, with the charge of the light cavalry, which Tennyson has celebrated; Florence Nightingale's work in the hospitals, tales of great suffering from cold weather, the death of the Czar Nicholas, and the peace treaty concluded in March, 1856.

England lost in this war nearly 24,000 men. Those killed in action and who died of wounds numbered 3,500; cholera caused the death of 4,244, and other diseases nearly 16,000.

One year later there occurred in India the first incidents of that famous mutiny, the suppression of which would tax the best energies of England's administrators and soldiers for more than two years.

A result of this mutiny was the formal transfer of the direct Government of India from the East India Company to the British Crown. In November, 1858, Victoria was proclaimed in the principal places of India, and thus became the sovereign to that country. The proclamation of Victoria as Empress of India occurred in May, 1876.

Had the reign of Victoria no other great achievements besides those of cheap postage and rapid travel by steam, it would still deserve to be ranked among the great epochs of English civilization. Later years, however, have seen the penny-postage system superseded by the telegraph—even a telegraph that connects continents otherwise divided by great oceans—and still later ones have seen the telephone disputing with the telegraph its claims to usefulness in the service of man.

Connected by a natural link with these inventions has also been the expansion of the iron industries of England. In 1837 the total yearly output of crude iron in England was only about 1,000,000 tons. Now it is over 8,000,000 tons. Twenty years after 1837 an invention was applied in iron manufactures which has wrought great changes in the world. This was Sir Henry Bessemer's process for making steel by blowing air into molten pig iron. This process has caused the price of steel to be greatly reduced, so that steel now competes with iron for many purposes.

If we turn now to the literature of this reign a noble and lasting output will be found, including books produced by men of science, like Darwin, who have given us books as epoch-making as any the mind of man ever produced. It is not for contemporaries to say if the verse of Tennyson and the prose of Macaulay, Carlyle, and Thackeray will live on, but the chances are good for a reasonable degree of immortality.

The poetry of Mrs. Browning almost exclusively belongs to this reign, and so does that of her husband. Matthew Arnold's first success, the poem on Cromwell, dates from 1843. Swinburne was born in the year of Victoria's accession. Dickens's first volume, "Sketches by Boz," came out in 1836. Ere the genius of George Eliot should become known twenty years were to elapse. Carlyle had written many of his essays, but was still waiting for the day when literature should raise him above actual want.

NICHOLAS II
OF RUSSIA

May 18, 1868–July, 17 1918

LONDON—Nicholas Romanoff, ex-Czar of Russia, was shot July 16, according to a Russian announcement by wireless today.

The central executive body of the Bolshevist Government announces that it has important documents concerning the former Emperor's affairs, including his own diaries and letters from the monk Rasputin, who was killed shortly before the revolution. These will be published in the near future, the message declares.

The text of the Russian wireless message reads in part:

"At the first session of the Central Executive Committee, elected by the fifth Congress of the Councils, a message was made public that had been received by direct wire from the Ural Regional Council concerning the shooting of the ex-Czar Nicholas Romanoff.

"Recently Yekaterinburg, the capital of the Red Urals, was seriously threatened by the approach of Czechoslovak hands, and a counterrevolutionary conspiracy was discovered, which had as its object the wresting of the ex-Czar from the hands of the council's authority. In view of this fact, the President of the Ural Regional Council decided to shoot the ex-Czar, and the decision was carried out on July 16.

"The wife and the son of Nicholas Romanoff have been sent to a place of security.

"Documents concerning the conspiracy which was discovered have been forwarded to Moscow by a special messenger. It had been recently decided to bring the ex-Czar before a tribunal to be tried for his crimes against the people, and only later occurrences led to delay in adopting this course."

There have been rumors since June 24 that ex-Czar Nicholas of Russia had been assassinated. The first of these stated that he had been killed at Yekaterinburg by Red Guards. This report was denied later, but this denial was closely followed by a Geneva dispatch saying that Nicholas had been executed by the Bolsheviki after a trial at Yekaterinburg. This report seemed to be confirmed by advices to Washington from Stockholm.

The next report was what purported to be an intercepted wireless message from M. Tchicherin, the Bolshevist Foreign Minister, in which it was stated that Nicholas was dead. Still another report was to the effect that he had been bayonetted by a guard while being taken from Yekaterinburg to Perm. Of all these reports there was no direct confirmation.

There seemingly is no question that yesterday's dispatch is authentic. It comes in the form of a Russian wireless dispatch, and as the wireless plants of Russia are under the control of the Bolsheviki, it appears that it is an official version of the death of the former Emperor.

NIKOLAI LENIN

April 22, 1870–January 21, 1924

MOSCOW—Nikolai Lenin died last night at 6:50 o'clock. The immediate cause of death was paralysis of the respiratory centers due to a cerebral hemorrhage.

Lenin was 54 years old. He belonged to the class known as the small nobility. He was brought up in the Orthodox faith and educated to be a professor. His father was a State Councilor. The family name was Ulianoff. "Lenin" is a pen name. Lenin's wife, Nadjeduda Constantinova Krupshata, was with him at the end. —*Walter Duranty*

While Russia declined into economic ruin, while millions starved to death within short distances of rich lands which were formerly the greatest wheat producing regions of Europe; while civilization disappeared and some districts fell even into cannibalism; while the country with the greatest agricultural resources in the world had to be fed from abroad; while preventable disease made havoc such as has been unknown for centuries—all this time Lenin easily held his power in Russia, and even kept international followers, who pleaded with their own countries to follow the example of Russia.

The Russian masses seemed to have the same feeling toward Lenin which they had formerly had toward the "Little Father." They used to revere the Czar and to find excuses for him while hating his functionaries. In the same way the ordinary Russian found no fault with Lenin and laid the ruin of the country to those around him and to circumstances that he could not control.

While the peasant and workingmen had a superstitious reverence for Lenin, those who were nearer to him had a loyalty founded on their knowledge of his absolute disinterestedness and the intensity of his convictions. They felt that he worked hard, lived ascetically, scorned riches and was inspired by a fierce enthusiasm unmixed with baser motives.

The fact that his doctrines did not work had been several times reported to be a contributing cause to his fatal illness. No amount of fanaticism could blind him to the fact that they had not worked out right. He had readjusted those doctrines and temporarily suspended some of his axioms, in the hope of reviving industry and keeping the people fed during the interim caused by some inexplicable delay in the arrival of Utopia.

For every one legally assassinated in the French Revolution, he had caused the judicial murder of hundreds—all, of course, for the good of Russia. This was frankly admitted and defended as an essential step in clearing the stage for the communistic millennium. The age of blood was to be a preliminary to the age of gold.

His greatest disappointment was the failure of the international movement, the inability of Communists in other countries to overthrow their Governments and put the world under the rule of Soviets in the early stages of the revolution.

But temporizing with "capitalistic" Governments has been allowable, under Lenin's system of conduct, from the beginning. Lenin was deliberately placed in Russia by the German General Staff in 1917 to put Russia out of the war. He was in Geneva when the Czar's Government broke down. His transportation across Germany was arranged by the German high command as a strategic maneuver.

Lenin was perfectly willing to accept this help from a capitalist Government. He believed that the Russian revolution he foresaw would be followed by uprisings of the proletariat all over the world, the German revolution being one of the first. But the event proved that the Germans had calculated correctly. Lenin did put Russia out of the war. He did not succeed in his hope of a proletarian triumph in Germany. The German revolution came later from military and economic causes, not as a result of Soviet infection.

At two periods in his career Lenin was the most important man in Russia. The earlier time was during the attempted revolution of 1905. He left his mark on Russia heavily in 1905, because the insurrection

which he then led checked the steps which had been taken to put Russia on a constitutional basis. Lenin was a perfect specimen of the doctrinaire in 1905, as in 1917. His devotion to dogma would not permit him to look with favor on half measures. At a later period he was ready to barter and trade in practical measures, but he would hear of no compromise where a political dogma was involved.

Already in 1905 Lenin and the Social Democratic Party, which he founded, had worked out the theory of government by a small revolutionary minority, commanding the majority and working in their interest.

The first Soviet was formed in Petrograd in 1905 after the granting of the Constitution. It was to the activity of this Soviet and the influence of Lenin that Russia owed the gradual curtailment of the Constitution granted by the Czar in 1905. The actual uprising by the followers of Lenin was quickly suppressed, but it gave reactionaries the argument that any concessions offered to the Russian people would cause revolt, and that the safety of the Government lay in the practice of despotism according to the old rules.

When he was 17 years old, Lenin's brother Alexander was executed for complicity in a terrorist plot against the life of Alexander III. In the same year Lenin finished his course in the Simbirsk Gymnasium and entered the Kazan University. He was banished from Kazan a few months later for taking part in a students' riot.

His offense was overlooked, however, and in 1891 he was a student in the University of St. Petersburg, where he studied law and economics. He also studied in Germany.

In 1895, arrested in St. Petersburg as a dangerous Socialist, he was exiled to Siberia for three years. In 1900 he went abroad. Living much of the time in Switzerland, he was the head of the group of exiled and condemned revolutionists of Russia and other countries. Of Lenin's life in Switzerland, M. J. Olgin wrote:

"A smoky back room in a little café in Geneva; a few score of picturesque-looking Russian revolutionary exiles, men and women, seated around uncovered tables over glasses of beer or tea; at the head of the table a man in his forties, talking in a slow yet impassioned manner; and now and then an exclamation of disapproval, an outburst of indignation among a part of the audience, which would be instantly parried by a flashing remark of the speaker, a striking home with unusual trenchancy and venom—this is how I see now in my imagination the leader of the Bolsheviki, the great Inquisitor of the Russian social democracy, Nicolai Lenin.

"There is nothing remarkable in the appearance of this man—a typical Russian with rather irregular features; a stern but not unkindly expression; something crude in manner and dress, recalling the artisan rather than the intellectual and the thinker. You would ordinarily pass by a man of this kind without noticing him at all. Yet, had you happened to look into his eyes or to hear his public speech, you would not be likely to forget him.

"His eyes are small, but glow with compressed fire; they are clever, shrewd and alert; they seem to be constantly on guard, and they pierce you behind half-closed lids."

With the overthrow of the Czar the Russian revolutionaries returned to Russia. [Alexander] Kerensky [head of the Russian Provisional Government] fell in November, and Lenin and [Leon] Trotsky set up the "dictatorship of the proletariat," maintaining themselves in power by the slaughter of tens of thousands as counterrevolutionaries.

Maxim Gorky described the work of Lenin as an experiment in a laboratory, with the exception of the fact that it was performed on a living thing, and that, if the experiment did not have the expected success, the outcome would be death.

An almost complete stoppage of production, chaos in the transportation system, famine in the big cities, then in the country districts, all accompanied the Bolshevist régime almost from the beginning—effects largely due, according to outside observers, to the belief that work was no longer a necessity, but that all could live off those richer than themselves.

Spasmodic efforts to bring back production by introducing martial law with the nationalization of industries, compelling workers to do a hard day's work at peril of their lives, were announced from time to time, but proved not to be enduring or of wide application.

Lenin's literary output, explaining and recommending the Russian system to the rest of the world, went on unabated, in spite of the Russian collapse. The real condition of starvation and ruin in Russia was denied, and the reports of it attributed to the malice of the capitalist press.

Lenin as he was in the third year of his absolute dictatorship was described by H. G. Wells as follows in an article printed in The New York Times:

"I had come expecting to struggle with a doctrinaire Marxist. I found nothing of the sort. I had been told that Lenin lectured people; he certainly did nothing of the sort on this occasion. Much has been made of his laugh in the descriptions—a laugh which is said to be pleasing at first and afterward to become cynical.

"Lenin has a pleasant, quick-changing brownish face, with a lively smile and a habit (due, perhaps, to some defect in focusing) of screwing up one of his eyes as he pauses in his talk. He is not very much like the photographs you see of him, because he is one of those persons whose change of expression is more important than their features."

In addressing the Russian Assembly of Political Education in 1921, Lenin, for the first time, made a partial admission of defeat and error.

"In part," he said, "under the influence of military problems which were showered upon us and of the seemingly desperate condition in which the republic found itself under the influence of these circumstances, we made the mistake of deciding to pass immediately to communistic production and distribution.

"We decided that the peasants, according to the system of requisition of surplus, would give us the needed quantity of bread, and we should distribute it to the factories and workshops and arrive at communistic production and distribution. I cannot say that we drew up thus definitely and clearly any such plan, but we acted in that spirit.

"This, I am sorry to say, is a fact. I am sorry because an experience which did not take long has convinced us of the mistakenness of the proceeding, which was in contradiction to what we had previously written in regard to the transition from capitalism to socialism, and has convinced us that without passing through a phase of socialistic supervision and control you cannot rise even to the first degree of communism."

Attempts of the Soviet Government to interest American capitalists and manufacturers in Russia had failed, both because of lack of support from the American Government and because an exploring party of American manufacturers came to the conclusion that Russia had nothing with which to pay them except promises. When hope to tempt this country to resume trade was at an end, the Soviet Government pleaded for provisions, which resulted in the sending of the American Relief Administration to Russia and the feeding of millions in that way.

There has been little news about Lenin from Russia in the last few months until recently, when there have been hints of discussion among the Communists as to his successor.

SUN YAT-SEN

November 12, 1866–March 12, 1925

PEKING—Dr. Sun Yat-sen, the South China leader, died this morning at 58 years of age.

Dr. Sun for some time had been suffering from cancer of the liver.

As the Southern leader yesterday was slowly passing into his final sleep, his headquarters in Canton announced that his troops had occupied Swatow, in the Province of Kwangtung, whence all the rebel leaders were said to have fled without giving battle.

The name of Dr. Sun Yat-sen first began to be heard in Chinese political affairs in the late 1880's, when his vigorous pronouncements against the Manchu emperors of China reached beyond the boundaries of his native land. Since that time few men in public life have known more ups and downs, more victories, more defeats, than Dr. Sun, who won the title of the "Father of the Republic."

To Dr. Sun was given the credit for having engineered the uprising by which the people retired the Manchus and proclaimed the republic in 1912.

When the revolution broke out prematurely in the Yangtze Valley in October, 1911, Dr. Sun was in England. He hurried back and was chosen head of the revolutionary Republican headquarters at Nanking, the rebels designating him "Provisional President of the Republic."

Actually and officially he never was President of China, as the Manchus had merely appointed Yuan Shi-kai, as Premier in Peking, to mediate with the rebels. The result was the formal establishment of the republic in February, 1912, with Yuan Shi-kai as President, and Dr. Sun's organization, by agreement, was disbanded.

Yuan served as President until his death in June, 1916, which occurred soon after his futile attempt to become emperor, an empty title he bestowed upon himself for 100 days. He was succeeded by Vice President Li Yuan-hung.

Again in 1921 the remnant of the original Chinese Republican Parliament of 1913, never having received any further mandate to sit, besides having been dissolved by Yuan Shi-kai, met in Canton and "elected" Sun Yat-sen "President of China." The real President of China was then Hsu Shin-ch'ang, and he was in no way superseded by Dr. Sun.

However, Dr. Sun and his associates took control of affairs in South China, with headquarters in Canton, and they have administered an area with a population of about 40,000,000 people ever since. The total population of China is estimated to be 400,000,000.

Out of this assumption of power in the South grew what is called the "Republic of South China," which, however, has never been recognized by any Government in the world.

Since 1922 the Sun group has been fighting, on the battlefield and in political councils, with General Chen Chiung-min, for control of the South, resulting in constant pillage, murder and turmoil there.

Dr. Sun's father was a Christian farmer in Kuangtung Province, where Sun Yat-sen was born in 1866. Under the tutelage of Dr. Kerr of an American mission school, he learned English rapidly and took up the study and practice of medicine.

A political career had a stronger appeal to him than the profession of medicine, and with the launching of the Young China Party his active work in the affairs of his country began. One of the exciting incidents in his career came in October, 1896, while he was in London. While outside the Chinese Legation he was kidnapped. The intention, it was learned afterward, was to smuggle him to China, where there was a price on his head.

He was confined in the basement of the legation, but he was able to smuggle out a letter addressed to his former teacher, Sir James Cantle, who took the note to the Foreign Office. His liberation was effected by policemen sent to the legation by Lord Salisbury.

At the first opportunity Dr. Sun appeared openly in China. This opportunity came in 1911, as outlined above.

Perhaps his narrowest escape was in Canton in 1905. One of his plots to assassinate the Manchu officials and seize the city was betrayed, and a round-up of the leaders was set in motion. Dr. Sun fled with a band of hostile soldiers at his heels. Suddenly a door opened and he was drawn inside. The door closed as mysteriously as it had opened, and the pursuers passed on. A friendly servant in the house of a prominent mandarin had made the rescue. There, days later, the fugitive watched from a window of that same house as fifteen of his followers were put to death.

—Associated Press

LEON TROTSKY

November 7, 1879–August 21, 1940

By Arnaldo Cortesi

MEXICO CITY—After twenty-six hours of an extraordinarily tenacious fight for life, Leon Trotsky died at 7:25 P.M. today of wounds inflicted upon his head with a pickaxe by an assailant in his home yesterday.

Almost his last words, whispered to his secretary, were:

"Please say to our friends I am sure of the victory of the Fourth International. Go forward!"

The 60-year-old exile's losing struggle for existence continued all last night and all day today.

The assassin, Jacques Mornard van den Dreschd, for months an intimate of the Trotsky household, had a declaration written in French on his person when he was arrested yesterday. Police said that in it he told of having quarreled with his leader when Mr. Trotsky tried to induce him to go to Russia to perform acts of sabotage.

The declaration adds that the writer decided to kill Mr. Trotsky because the latter did everything in his power to prevent van den Dreschd from marrying Sylvia Ageloff of Brooklyn, who had introduced the two men to each other.

Questioned by police, Miss Ageloff declared she introduced "Frank Jackson," as she knew him, to Mr. Trotsky in perfect good faith not knowing he had any designs on the former Soviet War Commissar's life.

The assassin, who entered Mexico posing as a Canadian, Frank Jackson, now is said to have been born in Teheran, Iran, son of a Belgian diplomat.

With remarkable fortitude, Mr. Trotsky, despite his very severe wound, was able to grapple with his as-

sailant and then run from the room in which he was attacked, shouting for help. He did not collapse until his wife and his guards had rushed to his aid.

The devotion of Mrs. Trotsky filled everyone who saw her with pity. This small, white-haired, retiring woman was the first to run to her husband's aid and to grapple with his assailant. She did not leave Mr. Trotsky's bedside for a single minute.

Joseph Hansen, one of Mr. Trotsky's American secretaries, issued a written account of the attack. It said, in part:

"Trotsky knew the assassin, Frank Jackson, personally for more than six months. Jackson enjoyed Trotsky's confidence because of his connection with Trotsky's movement in France and the United States. Jackson visited the house frequently. At no time did we have the least ground to suspect he was an agent of the GPU (Russian secret police).

"He entered the house on Aug. 20 at 5:30 o'clock. He met Mr. Trotsky in the patio near the chicken yard, where he told Trotsky he had written an article on which he wished his advice. Trotsky agreed as a matter of course and walked with him to the dining room, where they met Mrs. Trotsky.

"Trotsky then invited Jackson into the study but without previously notifying his secretaries. The first indication of something wrong was the sound of terrible cries and a violent struggle in Trotsky's study.

"The assassin apparently struck Trotsky from behind with a miner's pick or alpenstock—the point penetrating into the brain. Instead of dropping unconscious as the assassin had evidently planned, Trotsky still retained consciousness and struggled with the assailant. As he lay bleeding on the floor later, he described the struggle to Mrs. Trotsky and Secretary Hansen. He told Hansen: 'Jackson shot me with a revolver. I am seriously wounded. I feel that this time it is the end.'

"Hansen tried to convince him it was only a surface wound and could not have been caused by a revolver because nobody heard a shot, but Trotsky replied: 'No, I feel here (pointing to his heart) that this time they have succeeded.'"

Leon Trotsky, whose real name was Leba Bronstein, was born of Jewish parents in 1879 in a small town in Kherson, Russia, near the Black Sea. His father was a chemist. He received his education in the local schools, but did not attend the university. He was expelled from school at the age of 15 for desecrating a sacred icon, an image of the Orthodox Russian Church, thus giving an early indication of his radical temperament, which led him throughout his life to attack religion as well as the other factors in the existing order of things.

While still in his teens Trotsky became a revolutionist, and began to write articles, make speeches and help in the organization of revolutionary movements. He became a disciple of Karl Marx, and gradually formulated the communistic ideas which he and Lenin later were to put into practice in Russia.

Trotsky was arrested when the 1905 rebellion was put down and was exiled to Siberia. But he escaped after six months on a false passport made out in the name of Trotsky, said to have been the name of a guard. This was the way in which Trotsky got the name which has become known throughout the world ever since.

When the war started, Trotsky was editing a newspaper in Berlin, where he had found many friends among the radicals and had had help in writing a history of the first Russian revolution. Exiled from Germany as a "dangerous anarchist," he found refuge in Vienna.

Next he went to Zurich, Switzerland, and then on to Paris. He began the publication of a radical sheet called Our World, but it was suppressed, and Trotsky was expelled from France. He was escorted to the Spanish frontier, but was arrested. On his release he sailed for New York with his wife and two sons, Leo and Sergius.

Trotsky and his family arrived here on the steamship Monserrat from Barcelona, Spain, on Jan. 14, 1917, and they went to live in a three-room apartment on Vyse Avenue, the Bronx. He found work as an editorial writer on the Russian radical daily Novy Mir. While he was here he predicted that the war would result in revolution among the working classes in the warring countries.

Following the overthrow of the Czar, Trotsky and his family returned to Russia. On his arrival in Petrograd he joined Lenin and the other Maximalists, or Bolsheviki, in the Left Wing of the Russian Socialists. They first supported the Kerensky government, but gradually broke away on the issue of peace. The November revolution, in which the Kerensky government was overthrown, brought Lenin and Trotsky to the top.

Trotsky became Lenin's right-hand man, taking the post of Minister of Foreign Affairs and then Minister of War. It was in the latter capacity that his monumental achievement of reorganizing and directing the Red Army took place.

The numerical strength of the army he organized was about 1,500,000. In four years of almost constant fighting on various fronts it defeated the forces under Yudenitch, Kolchak, Denikin, the "White Army" of Wrangel in the Crimean, and the Polish Army.

Once the army was functioning smoothly Trotsky was able to turn his efforts to other fields. In 1919 he started to reorganize the railroad system, but his severe tactics alienated the employees and Lenin ultimately removed him in summary fashion. It was the first of many rumored quarrels with Lenin. When Lenin became incapacitated by illness in 1923, Trotsky was expected to step into Lenin's shoes. His failure to do so ultimately caused his political ruin.

While Lenin was unable to carry on his work, the All-Russian Congress named a triumvirate to take his place. It consisted of Kameneff, Zinovleff and Stalin, who was later to prove Trotsky's conqueror in the struggle for power.

Lenin died in January, 1924, and the inevitable fight for control of the Communist party began almost immediately after. It soon became evident that the triumvirate was too strong for Trotsky. A year later he was removed as chairman of the Revolutionary War Council, which meant his automatic dismissal as Minister of War and the beginning of the end of his political career.

The crux of his opposition, then and afterward, was on the question of "right" and "left." Trotsky always stood for communism in the strict sense of the word, without compromise. Russia should have nothing to do with capitalistic systems of government or economics, he believed; the "world revolution" should be fostered; the well-to-do peasants should not be favored at the expense of the poorer.

In January, 1925, Trotsky went to the Caucasus, ostensibly for his health but really as an exile. Within four months he regained much of his old power and seemingly healed the breach with Stalin.

But it was only a brief truce. The mills of Stalin kept grinding and did not stop until Trotsky was deprived of every office and honor. When the tenth anniversary of the establishment of the Soviet was celebrated, in November, 1927, and a great parade of the Red Army was held in Moscow, Trotsky, who had organized the army and was once its beloved idol, stood in the street with other spectators, almost unnoticed, and watched it march by.

If the news emanating from Russia in January, 1929, is to be trusted, Trotsky, who had been exiled to Siberia, was, in fact, preparing for a return to power by means of a revolution. On Jan. 23 it was announced that 150 followers of Trotsky had been arrested and after summary trial sent into "rigorous isolation" in a number of prisons as "enemies of the proletarian dictatorship" for plotting a civil war against the State.

In the days succeeding the wholesale arrests, rumors came thick and fast that Trotsky was en route to Turkey, whence he had been banished. Official Moscow kept silent, but on Feb. 1 The New York Times correspondent definitely announced that the decision to send Trotsky out of the country had been taken.

Thus Trotsky, who in 1917 was being hailed as the "Napoleon of the Revolution," ended, like Robespierre, a victim of the very forces he had done so much to create.

On Feb. 6, 1929, he arrived at Constantinople with his family, and busied himself with writing his memoirs and pamphlets by the hundred. It was during this stay that he wrote his voluminous "History of the Russian Revolution," a work that bitterly attacked

Stalin and sought to prove that there were two great men of New Russia—Lenin and Trotsky.

His daughter, Zinaide Wolkow, committed suicide in a Berlin rooming house in 1933. Trotsky blamed it on Stalin, because the dictator had refused to admit her to citizenship in the Soviet land.

In July, 1933, he arrived at Marseilles and received sanctuary through the French Government. Less than a year later he was expelled because he had "not observed the duties of neutrality."

Trotsky, accompanied by his family, arrived in Oslo in June, 1935. In August, 1936, after a period of comparative quiet, he was again in the midst of turmoil, emanating from the trial of sixteen Bolsheviks in Moscow, the so-called Zinovieff-Kameneff trial. They were accused of conspiring with Trotsky to assassinate Stalin and other Soviet leaders and restore capitalism in Russia. Tried in absentia, Trotsky was pictured as the villain of the alleged conspiracy.

The verdicts of guilty were founded wholly upon confessions of the accused, which Trotsky denounced as false, characterizing the trial as a frame-up. He demanded an impartial investigation of the charges and threatened to sue a Communist paper in Norway for libel because it repeated these accusations as proven. The Norwegian Government, however, forbade him to bring the suit.

After the trial the Soviet Government demanded Trotsky's expulsion from Norway, and although Norway declined to accede to the demand, it finally declined to renew his residence permit. Eventually the Mexican Government permitted him to come to Mexico on condition that he would not interfere in Mexican affairs.

He had no sooner taken up residence in a villa outside Mexico City than his peace was again disturbed by another treason trial in Moscow, this time of 17 Bolsheviks accused of counterrevolutionary activities. They, too, confessed, involving Trotsky as their leader.

For weeks he supplied the American and world press with statements and articles refuting the charges, accusing Stalin of trying to liquidate the Communist party and the revolution and establish a Red fascism in Russia.

To the last moment of his life Trotsky remained a stormy petrel, clinging to his extreme Communist ideas, particularly his theory of permanent revolution. Few men have ever provoked such hatred in some and such devotion in others as Trotsky. Whatever history's verdict upon him may be, it will not fail to record that he helped fill some of its most colorful pages.

BENITO MUSSOLINI

July 29, 1883–April 28, 1945

MILAN—Benito Mussolini came back last night to the city where his fascism was born. He came back on the floor of a closed moving van, his dead body flung on the bodies of his mistress and twelve men shot with him. All were executed yesterday by Italian partisans. The story of his final downfall, his flight, his capture and his execution is not pretty, and its epilogue in the Piazza Loretto here this morning was its ugliest part. It will go down in history as a finish to tyranny as horrible as any ever visited on a tyrant.

As if he were not dead or dishonored enough, at least two young men in the crowd broke through and aimed kicks at his skull. One glanced off. But the other landed full on his right jaw and there was a hideous crunch that wholly disfigured the once-proud face.

Mussolini wore the uniform of a squadrist militiaman. It comprised a gray-brown jacket and gray trousers with red and black stripes down the sides. He wore black boots, badly soiled, and the left one hung half off as if his foot were broken. His small eyes were open and it was perhaps a final irony that this man who had thrust his chin forward for so many official photographs had to have his yellowing face propped up with a rifle butt to turn it into the sun for the only two Allied cameramen on the scene. —*Milton Bracker*

Benito Mussolini, founder of Fascism and for more than 20 years the ruler of Italy in all but name, was the first of the modern totalitarian dictators to achieve power, as he was the first of them to lose it.

His career, from its beginnings in obscurity to its end, was unfailingly colorful and dramatic. Never was this more true than in his downfall, which served to provide one of the great turning points of the World War for which he bore such a heavy burden of responsibility.

Although the Fascist regime had been badly shaken by the Axis defeats in North Africa and the loss of the Italian Empire on that continent, it was the invasion of Sicily by the Anglo-American forces under Gen. Dwight D. Eisenhower that set in motion the chain of events that culminated in the overthrow of Il Duce.

Mussolini was born on July 29, 1883, in the hamlet of Dovia, Province of Forli. His parents were miserably poor. As a boy he was unruly, turbulent and aggressive. On completing his elementary education he became a teacher, but soon tired of this life. He wandered through Switzerland, Germany, France and Austria, working as a bricklayer, station porter, weaver and butcher's boy. In the evenings he attended various universities, or studied alone.

Returning to Italy he became prominent as a Socialist agitator in Forli. He founded the newspaper Lotta di Classe—Class Struggle—which became the local Socialist organ.

Mussolini stood trial for his active stand against the Italo-Turkish war, but was acquitted. His oration in his own defense helped win him national recognition as the leader of the left wing of the Socialist party, the place he held when the first World War broke out.

Within a few months he swung violently away from his radical position to one of active championing of Italian entry into the war on the side of the Allies. For this he was denounced as a traitor by his former Socialist comrades, who contended, probably truly, that he had been subsidized by Allied propagandists.

After Italy declared war on May 23, Mussolini, assigned to the Bersaglieri, made an exemplary soldier. He was wounded several times and repeatedly mentioned in dispatches.

After the war Mussolini secretly allied himself with the most reactionary elements. He founded the Fasci di Combattimento in Milan in March, 1919, for the avowed purpose of fighting the widespread unrest. The movement received a great impetus when the Italian Government sent Italian troops to fire upon Gabriel d'Annunzio and his followers in Fiume.

This move sent thousands of volunteers flocking to the standards of Fascismo. When the anarcho-syndicalists, with some help from the Communists, occupied a number of Italian factories, the Fascisti turned on them fiercely and, when the strike collapsed quickly, set up a fanfare about how they had saved Italy from a Red revolution. Actually, some historians believe the alleged strikes were deliberately fomented by a provocateur.

By the autumn of 1922 the Fascist party claimed more than 1,000,000 members. On Oct. 24 of that year, Mussolini issued this ultimatum to the Government:

"Either the government of the country is handed to us peaceably or we shall take it by force, marching on Rome and engaging in a struggle to the death with the politicians now in power."

Four days later the black-shirted legions began the march on Rome from their headquarters in Milan, discreetly followed by Mussolini in a sleeping car. The Cabinet declared martial law, but King Victor Emmanuel refused to sign the decree. The Cabinet resigned and the King asked Mussolini to form a government.

He first formed a coalition Cabinet, although the Fascists were, of course, dominant. He himself took the posts of Minister of War and Minister of the Interior, and demanded a grant of extraordinary power from the Chamber of Deputies to balance the budget, solve the labor problem and revise Italy's foreign policy.

Within a month he used these powers to make himself dictator. He began a drastic overhaul of the entire governmental machinery, displacing old government employees by members of his own black-shirted militia. He boasted that he would make Italy powerful, prosperous and efficient and would make the dreams of Mazzini and Garibaldi come true.

He and his unruly young Blackshirts were ruthless in grinding down these opponents, raiding political meetings and newspapers, burning buildings, disciplining obstreperous opponents with beatings and forced doses of castor oil.

Mussolini and his regime met its first great crisis in June, 1924, when Giacomo Matteotti, leader of the Socialist party and the only outstanding politician who continued publicly to defy the dictator within Italy, disappeared. Well-known Fascists were arrested as his kidnappers. When Matteotti's murdered body was found later in the summer, a world-wide storm of indignation broke.

For a time Mussolini seemed in danger of falling, but he used the crisis ruthlessly as a means of extending his power. He abandoned all pretense of a coalition government and substituted one that was frankly Fascist. Under fascism the Government regimented every aspect of the life of the Italian people and their industry.

Although Mussolini did not regard himself as a "good" Catholic, he made enough concessions to the Roman Catholic Church to keep it friendly toward him.

Mussolini's foreign policy was ultra-nationalistic and ultra-militaristic. As early as 1923, in the Corfu incident, the Italian fleet had bombarded the Greek island of Corfu in a dispute over the murder of four Italian commissioners. Greece appealed to the League of Nations, but Mussolini refused to recognize the right of the League to interfere.

More than a decade later he again defied the League and risked war with Great Britain when he began the carefully planned conquest of Ethiopia, which shattered the Four-Power Pact of 1933, in which Great Britain, France, Germany and Italy undertook to guarantee the peace of Europe for ten years.

Mussolini took advantage of border clashes between his troops and the Ethiopians as a pretext for the invasion, which began on Oct. 2, 1935. The Ethiopians were overwhelmed.

In May, 1936, the Council of the League of Nations refused Mussolini's request to drop the sanctions that it had imposed, whereupon the Italian delegation walked out of the Council chamber. Friction continued between the British and Italian Governments, and British fleets were stationed in the Mediterranean. After several weeks' tension, however, the British withdrew their ships. Later the League of Nations likewise dropped its sanctions.

Hardly had this dispute been settled when the Spanish Civil War broke out. Although Italy joined the other

Western European powers in a non-intervention pact, Mussolini at first covertly and later openly sent men, arms and money to aid the rebel forces.

The hatred of Britain that Mussolini felt as the result of the sanctions policy was ameliorated little if at all by the effort at appeasement that followed the advent of Neville Chamberlain to power. This led eventually to the outstanding event of Italian foreign policy under Mussolini—the formation of the celebrated Axis with Germany, at first a secret and then an avowed declaration of solidarity.

The first important fruit of that agreement was the occupation of Austria by German troops in March, 1938. Afterward, Mussolini exchanged telegrams pledging continued friendship with Hitler.

In the succeeding crisis over Czechoslovakia, Mussolini and Hitler were again found side by side. During the days of greatest tension Mussolini called upon France and England to abandon this smaller democracy.

Despite his truculence, Prime Minister Chamberlain of Great Britain turned to Mussolini to use his good offices to keep Hitler from marching into the territory of the Sudeten Germans. Mussolini persuaded Hitler to meet Mr. Chamberlain and Premier Daladier at the Munich conference, at which Czechoslovakia was partitioned.

Soon, Mussolini took a more and more pronounced pro-Nazi attitude. His henchmen set up a cry for Corsica and Tunisia, French possessions with large Italian populations. He introduced a series of anti-Semitic measures and speeded up preparations for the war that seemed inevitable.

When it came, with the German invasion of Poland on Sept. 1, 1939, Mussolini was silent. It was not until Sept. 23 that he declared his intention of maintaining Italy's neutrality. This position he maintained, although with marked indications of pro-German sympathy, until the German onslaught crushed the French Army. Mussolini took his country into the war on June 10, 1940, two days before the Germans reached Paris. [Prime Minister] Churchill likened his action to that of a jackal.

The course of the war soon showed that Mussolini had gravely miscalculated. Although he shared in the easy triumph over France, he received little of the spoils he had anticipated. In the autumn Italian armies invaded Greece and suffered such heavy reverses that Germany had to come to their assistance.

In North Africa, meanwhile, his forces were shattered by numerically inferior British armies. Italian air power and Navy proved unequal to the tasks that were placed upon them.

In June, 1941, Mussolini obediently followed the Fuehrer into war against Russia, and on Dec. 11 declared war on the United States.

As defeat followed defeat for Italian arms in the year and a half that followed, Mussolini appeared less and less often on his favorite balcony. The terrific blow dealt his troops by the British at El Alamein; the heavy bombings of Italian industrial cities by the Royal Air Force, and the American landings in North Africa in November, 1942, combined to crush the spirits of his followers.

Then came the Allied invasion of Sicily, the collapse of Italian and German forces, along with the end of Mussolini's power, and finally the grisly scene in the Piazza Loretto.

ADOLF HITLER

April 20, 1889–April 30, 1945

LONDON—Adolf Hitler died this afternoon, the Hamburg radio announced tonight, and Grand Admiral Karl Doenitz, proclaiming himself the new Fuehrer by Hitler's appointment, said that the war would continue.

Crowning days of rumors about Hitler's health and whereabouts, the Hamburg radio said that he had fallen in the battle of Berlin at his command post in the Chancellery.

Early this evening the Germans were told that an important announcement would be broadcast tonight. There was no hint of what was coming. The stand-by announcement was repeated at 9:40 P.M.

A few minutes later the announcer said: "Achtung! Achtung! In a few moments you will hear a serious and important message to the German people." Then the news was given to the Germans and the world after the playing of the slow movement from Bruckner's Seventh Symphony, commemorating Wagner's death.

Appealing to the German people for help, order and discipline, Doenitz eulogized Hitler as the hero of a lifetime of service to the nation. "It is my first task," Doenitz added, "to save Germany from destruction by the advancing Bolshevist enemy. For this aim alone the military struggle continues."—*Sydney Gruson*

Adolf Hitler, one-time Austrian vagabond who rose to be the dictator of Germany, "augmenter of the Reich" and the scourge of Europe, was, like Lenin and Mussolini, a product of the First World War.

The same general circumstances, born of the titanic conflict that carried Lenin, a bookish professional revolutionist, to the pinnacle of power in the Empire of the Czars and cleared the road to mastery for Mussolini in the Rome of the Caesars, also paved the way for Hitler's domination in the former mighty Germany of the Hohenzollerns.

Like Lenin and Mussolini, Hitler came out of the blood and chaos of 1914–18, but of the three he was the strangest phenomenon. Lenin, while not known to the general public, had for many years before the Russian Revolution occupied a prominent place as leader and theoretician of the Bolshevist party. Mussolini was a widely known Socialist editor, orator and politician before making his bid for power. Hitler was nothing, and from nothing he became everything to most Germans.

Lenin dreamed of world revolution. Mussolini thundered of the coming world victory of Fascism. Hitler actually challenged the earth to combat by unleashing another war of nations.

Before the climax of a career unparalleled in history, he had subdued nine nations, defied and humiliated the greatest powers of Europe, and created a social and economic system that subjected scores of millions to his will in all basic features of social, political, economic and cultural life.

Sixty-five million Germans yielded to the blandishments and magnetism of this slender man of medium height, whose fervor and demagogy swept everything before him with outstretched arms as the savior and regenerator of the Fatherland.

Austria, with 7,000,000 inhabitants, succumbed helplessly to his invasion. More than 2,000,000 Germans in the Sudeten country were added to his domain when he threatened to invade Czechoslovakia, and 10,000,000 Czechs and Slovaks were tied to his chariot wheel, their nation stripped of its defenses, their State destroyed, while all of Central Europe trembled before what appeared to be the irresistible advance of the goose-stepping Nazi hordes of his adopted country.

For more than six years after his advent to power in January, 1933, there seemed to be no one who would dare to challenge Hitler's progress from victory to victory until he met resistance from Poland, backed by the Anglo-French alliance.

Shortly after his dismemberment and subjugation of Czechoslovakia, Hitler was reported to have said, "My time is short." His blow against Poland and challenge to France and England less than a year later were taken as indications that he had sensed that time was against him, that he had unleashed forces of hatred and opposition throughout the world that might eventually destroy him.

Those who had hoped that success at home and extension of his power abroad would make him more circumspect had abandoned that hope when, in violation of his promise to respect the integrity of Czechoslovakia, he marched on Prague and reduced that nation to a German protectorate.

The worldwide condemnation of his methods was fed by the system of terrorism he had established at home and in the countries he had conquered, the jailing of scores of thousands in prisons and concentration camps, the secret murder of opponents and those suspected of opposition, the ruthless destruction of the Jews and the persecution of the Catholic and Protestant Churches in his drive for nazification of the nation.

The deteriorating social, political and economic conditions, as they developed in post-war Germany, supplied the springboard for Hitler's leap to power in 1933.

But an understanding of Hitler's conduct has been sought by students of the man in the study of his youth and family history.

Many who watched Hitler from the time when he first made his appearance on the political scene noticed his megalomania, his gambler's readiness to take risks, his habit of wild exaggeration and inability to grasp the full implications of things he said and did. It was this failure to measure the significance of his words and deeds that was considered responsible for the coolness he displayed at critical moments after violent outbursts of thought and temper, although on occasions he was reported to fall into tears and hysterics.

At the same time, however, he possessed an uncanny shrewdness in his estimate of the psychology of masses and individuals, and developed to a fine degree the art of swaying their emotions. The success he achieved in this field enhanced his contempt for the people, whom he called a "flock of sheep and blockheads," a "mixture of stupidity and cowardice."

This contempt for the people and his unbounded capacity for hatred, which found expression in his merciless treatment of opponents and persecution of the Jews, according to psychologists who have studied the man's career closely, emanated in Hitler from the frustrations of his youth.

Hitler was born in an inn at Braynau, Austria, close to the German frontier, April 20, 1889. His father was Alois Schickelgruber, a peasant who later entered the customs service. His third wife, who was also his niece and ward and twenty years younger than her husband, was the future dictator's mother.

Hitler had no love for his father and resented his insistence that he prepare for the Government service. At the age of 14, after his father's death, Hitler went to live with his mother at Linz. There he stayed until he was 19, pampered by his mother, who catered to his habit of idling.

Upon her death he found himself alone, quite unprepared for the battle of life. He betook himself to Vienna, where he was denied admission to the Academy of Arts.

From 1909 to the outbreak of the First World War, Hitler led a wretched existence. For awhile, he lived in a "flophouse." He spent nights on park benches. He earned a precarious living by painting picture postcards and doing minor carpenter work.

Nevertheless, he considered himself to be an artist of talent and yearned passionately to make an impression, to know everything, to master the world.

His greatest passion was for politics. A shy and beaten youth, Hitler would become transformed as soon as conversation turned on matters political. His tongue would loosen and a torrent of words would rush from his lips. Jeered at by acquaintances, he wept.

The one thing that gave him hope was the disintegration of the Austro-Hungarian Empire. Considering himself a German, he felt superior to those around him. For the Slavs he felt contempt. For the Jews he felt hatred. As for the workers, he believed them to be not much better.

Long before he had dreamed of achieving power he had developed the principles that nations were destined to hate, oppose and destroy one another; that the law of history was the struggle for survival between peoples; that the Germans were chosen by destiny to rule over others, and that the great mass of the people were mediocrities destined to be dominated by a higher social type.

In 1913, Hitler left for Munich, where he barely managed to earn his keep.

Then came the war. It lifted Hitler into a state of exaltation.

Accepted in the German Army, he felt a sense of great things to come. At the front, where he served as a dispatch carrier, he was friendless. His services were recognized by his superiors, however, and he was rewarded with the Iron Cross.

He was gassed, and the end of the war found him in a hospital in Pomerania. He viewed with pain the collapse of the German Empire. Enraged at the revolutionists, bitter at the Kaiser and Field Marshal von Hindenburg because of their failure to suppress the revolution, he felt that his day would come.

Though officially demobilized, he remained in the service of the Reichswehr. His work was in the political intelligence division. In those days the Reichswehr had already begun to dream of revenge. Many officers and former officers attached themselves to various conspiratory "free corps" organizations, formed for political purposes and the spreading of terrorism.

Hitler acted as a spy for these "free corps" bands. He established relations with influential military circles both inside and outside the Reichswehr.

In 1919 Hitler was assigned to keep an eye on a little band calling itself the German Labor party. This party developed ultimately into the German National Socialist party, the organization forged by Hitler as the instrument for the achievement of power.

By force of eloquence, ruthless methods and daring ideas, Hitler forged ahead in the movement founded by the little band, stirring audiences with the promise of new power and greatness to come.

He was treated as a circus performer but persevered.

His strategy was based on a simple principle: to obtain the support of powerful elements in the army, industry and finance and to buttress that with support among the masses. He addressed himself first to the middle classes and managed to obtain some assistance from elements among the workers disappointed in the revolution.

He also put forward his slogans of extreme nationalism and racism. Believing the mission of national and social regeneration was to be realized by what he called a vigorous minority, a desperate elite, he gathered around him a group of intellectuals, officers, former officers, penurious students and ambitious youths without prospects in the Germany of that time.

Army generals, active and retired, regarded him with suspicion because of his lowly origin and demagogic appeals to the middle classes. They joined him openly after he had made an impression and showed that his chances of success were not to be minimized.

On Nov. 8, 1923, in Munich, in what became known as "the beer-cellar Putsch," Hitler forced his way into an assembly of high-ranking Bavarian generals, Ministers, Government officials and politicians in Munich City Hall and fired a shot into the air, announcing that his revolution had begun. He called for a march on Berlin. Those present were taken aback. They had made him promise that he would not use violence that might endanger their own positions. They promptly proclaimed Hitler a traitor to the State.

There followed a skirmish next day between several thousand of Hitler's followers and the police and troops. The police fired and thousands of Nazis scattered in all directions.

Hitler was caught and tried for treason. The sentence was five years' imprisonment in a fortress. He served only a few months and was paroled, returning to political activity.

It seemed as if Hitler's cause was irretrievably lost. Hitler appeared to go into retirement. He was at work on "Mein Kampf," begun in prison, but continued quietly to rebuild his shattered group.

Within the next seven years he obtained a huge following, which came to number 3,000,000. His army consisted of the Storm Troops, who wore brown shirts, and the Black Guards, representing more carefully picked formations, wearing black shirts. These troops attacked Jews, broke up meetings of the opposition, staged street brawls with Communists and republicans, beat up leaders of other parties and, in general, conducted a reign of terror with which the authorities found it increasingly difficult to cope.

An atmosphere of disorder was created with the intent of feeding popular demand for a "strong hand." All this was staged with tremendous dramatic effect by the able propaganda organization directed by Dr. Joseph Goebbels.

With a positive genius for political strategy, Hitler amalgamated the support of the most powerful elements, the army and industrialists, with the enthusiasm and blind approval of his masses.

But it was not until 1930 that Hitler emerged definitely as a mighty political power in Germany. In the elections that fall, he received 6,000,000 votes and captured 107 seats.

It was one of the greatest upsets in the turbulent history of the struggling German Republic. The factor that gave his movement this great impetus was the economic crisis that broke over the world in 1929 and struck Germany with particular severity.

The crisis fed with unprecedented force the extremist elements on the right and on the left. The armies of Hitlerism and communism made it increasingly difficult for the democratic republic to function.

Outmaneuvering opponents and allies, exercising ruthless brutality, Hitler became Chancellor on Jan. 30, 1933, with the proviso that new Reichstag elections were to be called so he could seek the approval of the electorate.

The Reichstag was dissolved and the Nazis unleashed a flood of propaganda eclipsing anything that had gone before, terrorizing the electorate and crippling the campaign activities of other parties.

One of the most shocking events in the history of the Nazi regime came on the evening of Feb. 27, 1933, a week before the elections, when the Reichstag building suddenly went up in flames. The fire, it was determined, was of incendiary origin. Hitler announced that Communists were the incendiaries. Masses of people believed him.

The burning of the Reichstag produced a profound impression. Indeed, in the elections he won his greatest victory, but with only 43 percent of the votes cast.

After the election Hitler proceeded at full steam toward establishment of his dictatorship. Decrees vested the Government with dictatorial power. Hitler then proceeded to destroy the last vestiges of opposition.

There were mass arrests of Socialists, Communists, liberals, Catholics and others, many of whom were taken to concentration camps, where they were maltreated in brutal fashion.

At the same time, a wave of anti-Semitic outrages spread. Decrees depriving Jews of civil rights, of property and the right to work in various professions were issued. These found expression later in even severer form in the Nuremberg laws.

One of the most shocking episodes of the early period of the Hitler regime was the burning of the books of outstanding German and foreign authors in the streets and public squares of leading cities. The spectacle served to emphasize the divorce of Nazi Germany from Western civilization.

On Dec. 1, 1933, a decree proclaimed the "unity of the Nazi party and the State," meaning that all labor organizations, youth organizations, universities, schools, parties and individuals had lost their identity and were merged, so far as the Nazis were concerned, in the State.

But his position was not yet entirely secure, not even in his own party, where the so-called left wing, led by Captain Ernst Roehm, leader of the Storm Troopers, regarded themselves as the real force that carried the Nazi party to victory.

On June 30, 1934 and the following day, under Hitler's personal direction, Roehm and his associates were murdered.

The nation was treated to another surprise on Aug. 2, 1934. President von Hindenburg died on his estate in Prussia. Within a space of a few hours, Hitler announced that he had taken over the powers of President in addition to those of Chancellor and proclaimed himself Fuehrer. He won an overwhelming victory in a plebiscite soon after.

From that moment Hitler embarked upon his bold program in the domain of internal and foreign affairs, a program that made Germany once more a great military power, leading to reoccupation and militarization of the Rhineland, the annexation of Austria, the occupation of Czechoslovakia, the seizure of Memel, Danzig and the Polish Corridor, the destruction of Poland, the seizure of Denmark and Norway, the conquest of Holland, Belgium, Luxembourg, France and the Balkans, the invasion of Russia, and the long domination of the European Continent by Nazi Germany.

It all ended, however, in the confirmation of Napoleon's dictum: "Empires die of indigestion."

With the fall of Hitler's empire under the blows of Allied arms, Germany fell to the lowest estate experienced by any nation in modern times.

That was Hitler's contribution to the history of the "master race."

EVA PERÓN

May 7, 1919–July 26, 1952

BUENOS AIRES—Señora Doña Maria Eva Duarte de Perón, wife of President Juan D. Perón, who had made herself one of the most powerful women in the history of Argentina and of the New World, died tonight at 8:25 o'clock. She had long been ill.

According to the Argentine Who's Who, she was 30 years old. [Biographical material not currently published in Argentina gave Señora Perón's age as 33, her date of birth May 17, 1919.]

The people of Argentina, who had been celebrating masses for the recovery of the First Lady, who was called "the spiritual chief of the nation," were well prepared for the event. During the course of the day the Sub-Secretariat of Information had issued three bulletins in rapid succession that clearly indicated the end was near.

President Perón, who was at her bedside when she died, had been staying nearly all week close to his wife in the Presidential Residence.

Señora Perón was operated upon last November for cancer. Her last public appearance was on June 4, when, looking extremely pale and worn, she attended the ceremony at which General Perón was inaugurated to succeed himself as President—largely through her help.

At the bedside when she died were, besides President Perón, a dozen of her relatives and close political friends. They included her mother, Señora Juana Ibarguren de Duarte; three sisters, and her brother.

Throughout Argentina, Perónista groups had tried to outdo each other in paying homage to the First Lady. The eloquence of the oratory in the Congress was typified in a speech by a Senator who said Señora Perón not only combined the best virtues of Catherine the Great of Russia, Queen Elizabeth I of England, Joan of Arc and Isabella of Spain, but had also multiplied these virtues in herself to the infinite.

Earlier a law had been adopted calling for the erection of a huge bronze marble statue of Señora Perón in the center of this city and replicas of it in all provincial and territorial capitals. The powerful General Confederation of Labor decreed that the 6,000,000 trade union members give up their wages on Aug. 22 to help finance this project. This decree was conservatively estimated to yield more than $1,250,000, and business and agricultural interests were also to be tapped for donations.

Aug. 22 was to be known as Renunciation Day, because on that date in 1951 Señora Perón announced

that she would not be a candidate for Vice President in the year's elections.

In reference to this event, the role played by the Argentine Army has rarely been mentioned. It is commonly understood that the Army chiefs could not countenance a possibility of a woman becoming Commander in Chief of the armed forces. The Army leaders confronted President Perón on this point with unaccustomed unanimity, and Señora Perón's announcement that she was not a candidate followed.

Nevertheless Señora Perón not only maintained but increased the tremendous power she had acquired in state affairs. Her influence did not abate during the course of her illness and she dictated appointments from her sickbed.

Ambitious, ruthless, untiring, clever and strikingly beautiful, Maria Eva Duarte de Perón had in large measure many of the qualities needed to lift her in a dozen short years from obscurity to fame, wealth and power on the unpredictable currents of Argentine political life.

The child of a poor village landowner who had been separated from his first wife, she rose meteorically through a brief radio and motion picture career to become the first lady of her land and one of the most influential women in the Western hemisphere.

Señora Perón's ascent and her important role in governmental affairs and propaganda were all the more remarkable for the contrast that they presented to the conservative social traditions of Latin America, where women previously were seldom seen, and never heard, in public life.

No less than her husband, Señora Perón was a controversial figure. To her supporters, among whom were the many recipients of her highly publicized charities, she approached the stature of a dazzling goddess. She was "la dama de la esperanza," the lady of hope.

For her opponents, political and social, however, there were not words strong enough to express their dislike and envy of this blonde upstart, who seemed to have virtually taken over the country.

The controversial aspect of the role of Señora Perón was by no means limited to Argentina. She became a truly international figure, a worldwide topic of conversation and invariably a subject of conjecture.

Countless anecdotes—factual as well as apocryphal—pointed this up. The inevitably humorless way in which she lent herself to the promulgation of absolute Perónismo was never better illustrated than on the day she had to undergo minor surgery.

One of the Buenos Aires newspapers owned outright by the Government ran a front-page box, allegedly describing the moment that she was being wheeled into the operating room.

"Before they put me to sleep," she was quoted as having said, "if I do not awake—Viva Perón!"

She was born May 7, 1919, in Los Toldos, a village of Buenos Aires province, youngest of five children of Juan Duarte and Juana Ibarguren. Her father died while she was still a child, and her mother moved to the near-by town of Junin and opened a boarding house.

After two years of high school, still in her mid-teens, the slim blonde girl went to Buenos Aires on her own to seek an acting career. Through characteristic persistence, she was able to land a permanent job with Radio Belgrano, a major station, after several fruitless excursions into both radio and motion pictures.

It was in 1943 that she met at a studio party Col. Juan D. Perón, a 49-year-old widower who was Under-Secretary of the War Ministry and a rising figure on the political scene. Both evidently were impressed, for a close association resulted, and they were married secretly in October, 1945.

Even before her marriage, Evita, as she preferred to be known, began to broaden her interests to suit those of her future husband. While he was becoming the champion of the "decamisados," originally the shirtless, and later the shirtsleeved ones, as Minister of Labor, she helped organize a radio employee's union and undertook her first campaigns for the underprivileged.

When Colonel Perón was forced to resign from the Government in October, 1945, Señorita Duarte was dismissed from her radio post. Within a week, however, he had returned to power, and four months later he was elected President and took Señora Perón, then 26, to the executive mansion as his wife.

She set up offices in the Ministry of Labor and Social Welfare, there holding daily audiences and distributing food, medicine and money to petitioners.

Although Señora Perón insisted repeatedly that she was interested only in social work, political observers began to credit her with influence in Government affairs that was second only to her husband's if indeed that.

In 1947 Señora Perón made a tour of Europe that was considered highly significant politically. She was feted with great enthusiasm in Madrid and decorated by Generalissimo Francisco Franco. In Rome she had an audience with Pope Pius XII, and was the subject of several leftist demonstrations. She was received by President Vincent Auriol in Paris, but canceled plans to visit England.

One of Señora Perón's several legislative triumphs was won in September, 1947, when a bill giving women the right to vote in Argentina was approved.

Early in 1951 the Peróns started a high-pressure campaign to have themselves drafted as a husband and wife team to run the country. By late August they had "agreed" to "accept" the nominations for President and Vice President of the Perónista party.

After taking four days to make up her mind, Evita told a demonstration audience of 250,000 in Plaza Moreno that she and her husband would "do what the people want." Then on the last day of the month, she changed her mind and declined the nomination.

In a choked voice on the same broadcast on which she had announced her decision, Señora Perón said she had hoped history would say: "There was a woman alongside General Perón who took to him the hopes and needs of the people to satisfy them, and her name was Evita."

JOSEPH STALIN

December 18, 1878–March 5, 1953

By Harrison E. Salisbury

Moscow—Premier Joseph Stalin died yesterday in the Kremlin at the age of 73, it was announced officially this morning. He had been in power 29 years.

[He was actually 74. Baptismal and school records discovered decades later showed that the birth year given in his official biography was incorrect.]

The announcement was made in the name of the Central Committee of the Communist party, the Council of Ministers and the Presidium of the Supreme Soviet.

Calling on the Soviet people to rally firmly around the party and the Government, the announcement asked them to display unity and the highest political vigilance "in the struggle against internal and external foes."

His death brought to an end the career of one of the great figures of modern times—a man whose name stands second to none as the organizer and builder of the great state structure the world knows as the Soviet Union.

The Soviet leader began his life in the simple mountain village of Gori deep in poverty-stricken Georgia. He rose to head the greatest Russian state that has ever existed.

His death from general circulatory and respiratory deficiency occurred just short of four days after he had been stricken with a brain hemorrhage in his Kremlin apartment.

A medical certificate revealed that in the last hours Mr. Stalin's condition grew worse rapidly, with heavy and sharp circulatory and heart collapses. His breathing grew superficial and sharply irregular. His pulse rate rose to 140 to 150 a minute and at 9:50 P.M., "because of a growing circulatory and respiratory insufficiency, J. V. Stalin died."

Pravda appeared this morning with broad black borders around its front page, which was devoted entirely to Mr. Stalin. The layout included a large photograph of the Premier, the announcement by the Government, the medical bulletin and the announcement of the formation of a funeral commission headed by Nikita S. Khrushchev, secretary of the Central Committee of the party. [No announcement was made of a successor.]

The announcement of Mr. Stalin's death was made to the Soviet people by radio early this morning. The announcement was early enough so that persons going to work had heard the news before leaving their homes.

This correspondent circled the Kremlin several times during the evening and early morning. The great red flag flew as usual over the Supreme Soviet Presidium building behind Lenin's Tomb. The city was quiet and sleeping, and in Red Square all was serene.

Throngs of Muscovites made their way to Red Square this morning and stood in silent tribute to their lost leader.

The Hall of Columns, where Mr. Stalin's body will lie in state so that millions of Soviet citizens can throng past the bier and pay their last respects, is one of the most beautiful buildings in Moscow and one of the architectural jewels of Europe.

A great forty-foot portrait of Mr. Stalin in his gray generalissimo's uniform was erected today on the front of the building. It was framed in heavy gilt.

Joseph Stalin became the most important figure in the political direction of one-third of the people of the world. He was one of a group of hard revolutionaries that established the first important Marxist state and, as its dictator, he carried forward its socialization and industrialization with vigor and ruthlessness.

During the Second World War, Stalin personally led his country's vast armed forces to victory. When Germany was defeated, he pushed his country's frontiers to their greatest extent and fostered the creation of a buffer belt of Marxist-oriented satellite states from Korea across Eurasia to the Baltic Sea. Probably no other man ever exercised so much influence over so wide a region.

In the late nineteen-forties, when an alarmed world saw no end to the rapid advance of the Soviet Union and her satellites, there was a hasty and frightened grouping of forces to form a battle line against the Marxist advance, with the United States the keystone in the arch of non-Marxist states.

Stalin took and kept the power in his country through a mixture of character, guile and good luck. He outlasted his country's intellectuals, if, indeed, he did not contrive to have them shot, and he wore down the theoreticians and dreamers. He could exercise great charm when he wanted to. President Harry Truman once said in an unguarded moment:

"I like old Joe. Joe is a decent fellow, but he is a prisoner of the Politburo."

Leon Trotsky, Stalin's brilliant and defeated adversary, regarded him as an intellectual nonentity who personified "the spirit of mediocrity" that impregnated the Soviet bureaucracy. Lenin, who valued Stalin highly as a party stalwart, characterized him as "crude" and "rough" and as a "cook who will prepare only peppery dishes."

But those who survived the purges hailed Stalin as a supreme genius.

His role as Russia's leader in the war brought him the admiration and high praise of Allied leaders, including President [Franklin D.] Roosevelt and [British Prime Minister] Winston Churchill.

When most of the Government machinery and the diplomatic corps were moved to Kuibyshev in December, 1941, in expectation of the imminent capture of Moscow, Stalin remained in the Kremlin to direct the operations that finally hurled the Nazi hordes from the frontyard of the capital.

With the turn of the tide against the Germans, Stalin proclaimed himself marshal of the Soviet Union and later generalissimo. He was portrayed in the Soviet and foreign press as the supreme commander responsible for overall strategy. To what extent this was true will have to be determined by the future historian, but that his role in the conduct of the war was paramount is undeniable.

Long before he dreamed of becoming the supreme autocrat of Russia, he had displayed the steel in his character as a political prisoner under the Czarist regime. A fellow prisoner gave an illustration of Stalin's grit. This was in 1909, in the prison at Baku. In punishment [for] rioting by the prisoners, the authorities ordered that they be marched in single file between two lines of soldiers who proceeded to shower blows upon them with rifle butts. With head high, a book under his arm, Stalin walked the gantlet without a whimper, his face and head bleeding, his eyes flashing defiance.

Joseph Vissarionovich Djugashvili, later to become famous under his revolutionary name of Joseph Stalin, was born in the Georgian village of Gori Dec. 21, 1879.

His father was an impoverished and drunken shoemaker who made him sullen and resentful by regular beatings. His mother, Ekaterina, a peasant's daughter, was a woman of singular sweetness, patience and strength of character who exercised great influence on her son. She called him Soso (Little Joe) and lived to see him dictator of the world's largest empire.

When he was six or seven, young Stalin contracted smallpox, which left him pock-marked for life. Through the efforts of his mother, he entered a church school at nine. He was remembered there as a bright, self-assertive boy who loved argument and who flew into a fury with those who did not agree with him.

His revolutionary apprenticeship was served as an organizer of the Tiflis transportation workers. He helped stage street demonstrations and distribute revolutionary leaflets.

In April, 1899, he received his first baptism of fire at a demonstration he helped organize in the heart of the city. The demonstration was drowned in blood by Cossacks, and he went into hiding for a year to escape the police.

In April, 1902, he was arrested and lodged in the Batum prison, from which he was transferred to Kutais. While in prison he learned of the meeting in London, in 1903, of the second congress of the Russian Social Democratic party, at which the party split into Bolsheviks and Mensheviks, extremists and moderates, an event that subsequently determined the course of the Russian Revolution.

Stalin allied himself with Nikolai Lenin, leader of the Bolsheviks. Trotsky was against Lenin, although in 1917, after the revolution, he joined Lenin and became his principal lieutenant in the October Revolution and in the establishment of the Soviet regime.

On July 9, 1903, while in prison in Kutais, Stalin was sentenced to three years of exile to Siberia. There he received his first letter from Lenin in response to one concerning Bolshevist policy and tactics. Determined to escape, Stalin made his way safely to Irkutsk at the end of the year. From there he proceeded to Baku, in the Caucasus, where he experienced his second baptism of fire as leader of a strike of oil workers, part of a wave of strikes that was the harbinger of the Revolution of 1905.

Shortly after the outbreak of a general strike, which was the key element in that revolution, Stalin met Lenin for the first time at a party conference in Tammerfors, Finland.

Stalin was repeatedly imprisoned and exiled, and repeatedly escaped unbowed, each time resuming his revolutionary activity and his communications with Lenin. After 20 years of revolutionary activity, Stalin, exiled in Siberia once again, found himself at a dead end.

Then came the news of the First World War in 1914, the war that Lenin predicted would bring the downfall of the Russian autocracy and world revolution.

Stalin was transferred to Atchinsk, on the Trans-Siberian Railway, and it was there he first received word of the revolution of March 12, 1917. Almost

the very first act of the Provisional Revolutionary Government was to order the release of all political prisoners. Among the many thousands who profited by this decree, signed by Alexander Kerensky, head of the Provisional Government, was Joseph Stalin.

It was not until April 16, 1917, that Lenin arrived in Petrograd after his famous journey in a sealed car provided by the German General Staff. The journey led across Germany to Stockholm and through Finland. A month later Trotsky arrived from America.

Trotsky lost no time in associating himself with Lenin in his demand for the overthrow of the Provisional Government, conclusion of an immediate peace, a sweeping Socialist program and advocacy of world revolution.

In the October Revolution Stalin took a relatively modest part. The minutes of the Central Committee of the party for Oct. 23, two days before the coup d'etat, show clearly that Lenin and Trotsky took the lead in demanding approval of the uprising.

During the civil war after the Bolshevik revolution, Stalin and Trotsky were at loggerheads. Repeatedly Trotsky called him to order, and on various occasions Lenin had to intervene to make peace between them.

Already during Lenin's illness, which lasted about two years, Stalin began preparing for his leadership of the party and of the Government. This he ultimately achieved by utilizing his new position as General Secretary of the party in building a party machine loyal to him.

After Lenin's death, authority was vested by the party in the hands of a triumvirate, consisting of Stalin, Zinoviev and Kamenev. In the bitter factional polemics that ensued, Stalin, regarded as the spokesman for the center, played the left against the right and vice versa and eventually defeated both, as well as Trotsky.

In 1936, during the period of purges, Stalin proclaimed a new Constitution for Russia, with promises of universal secret suffrage and freedom of the press, speech and assembly. It was interpreted to maintain the dictatorship and to stabilize the revolution.

Not since the days of Peter the Great, who sought to westernize Russia by force, had the country witnessed so violent a transformation.

In 1929 Stalin began predicting a second world war and avowed that his purpose was to keep Russia clear of the conflict. Despite this policy, with the advent of Hitler to power he joined in collective security measures. He abruptly abandoned his advocacy of collective security in 1939, when he about-faced and signed a mutual nonaggression pact with Nazi Germany.

It led to World War II, into which Russia later was drawn by Hitler's attack on her. This onslaught forged a Soviet alliance with the West, an alliance that ultimately enlarged the Soviet sphere.

The press prepared the Soviet public on Stalin's 69th anniversary for the grim reality that years had left their impress even on "the teacher and inspirer of the world proletariat." Pictures were published showing that his hair had whitened.

When he turned 70, his anniversary was celebrated in grand fashion. It was the first occasion in which Stalin had permitted public participation in his private life; hence little was known about his personal affairs.

He married twice. His first wife was Ekaterina Svanidze, who died after a long illness in 1907. They had a son, Jacob, whose fate has been unknown since he became a German prisoner during World War II.

In 1919 the Premier married Nadya Alliluyeva, the 17-year-old daughter of his old revolutionary crony, Sergei Alliluyev. She died in 1932 under mysterious circumstances. They had two children. The son, Vassily, is now a lieutenant-general in the Soviet Air Force. All that became known of the daughter was her name, Svetlana, and her intellectual interests.

POPE JOHN XXIII

November 25, 1881–June 3, 1963

ROME—Pope John XXIII, champion of world peace and a tireless fighter for the union of all Christian churches, died in the Vatican tonight while Cardinals and other prelates and several of his relatives prayed around his sickbed. He was 81 years old.

John XXIII was the 261st Pope to sit on the throne that was first occupied by the Apostle Peter. In the four years, seven months and six days of his reign he conquered the hearts of people throughout the world. Few other Popes before him were so universally admired.

The Pope's death came at 7:49 P.M. (2:49 P.M. Eastern daylight time). After a long struggle the Pope developed peritonitis, brought on by a stomach tumor.

In his last words, addressed to the assembled Cardinals and prelates around his sickbed, the Pope said:

"Ut unum sint." They are Latin words meaning "That they may be one." The words were originally spoken by Jesus after the Last Supper.

Those around the bedside included the Pope's three brothers—Giuseppe, Alfredo and Zaverio Roncalli—and his widowed sister, Assunta.

Mass for the Pope was said at an altar in an adjoining room while male nurses at the Pope's bedside prepared him to receive the sacrament of extreme unction and absolution. This rite is performed in much the same way as it would be for any layman, except that the Pope does not receive absolution for carnal sins.

While the Pope's sister and his personal secretary, Msgr. Loris Capovilla, sobbed aloud, everyone present recited prayers. Cardinal Fernando Cento, the Grand Penitentiary, bent over the Pope. Then he straightened and said to the assembled company: "Vere Papa mortuus est" ("In truth the Pope is dead").—*Arnaldo Cortesi*

Pope John XXIII saw himself first and always as a simple priest. In his first speech after he became Patriarch of Venice in 1953 he said:

"I come from humble origins. . . . Providence moved me from my native village and made me travel the roads of the world in the east and the west, bringing me in contact with people of different religions and different ideologies, into contact with acute and threatening social problems, and preserved in me the calm and equilibrium of investigation and appraisal."

In this role Pope John set himself to preserve the simple parish virtues of the Roman Catholic Church in a world menaced by atheistic Communism, which exploited militant racism and petty nationalism and tribal discord such as shook Africa in the early years of his reign.

A great event in the reign of Pope John began on Oct. 11, 1962, when he opened the 21st Ecumenical Council in the Vatican amid scenes of great pomp and splendor. In opening the assembly, the Pope called for the "visible unity in truth of all the followers of Christ." Such councils are convened by Popes to provide advice on matters of great religious importance. The first Ecumenical Council was convened in 325. The latest one before the 1962 Council was in 1869–70.

On April 10, 1963, Pope John issued his encyclical "Pacem in Terris" ("Peace on Earth"), and few communications from a Pope have had as much impact on the world.

In an obvious allusion to Communism, Pope John declared that great historical movements could not be identified simply with philosophical teachings that may have been false. The movements that arise from these teachings, he said, can come to "contain elements that are positive and deserving of approval." In moving words, the Pope pleaded for universal peace, and "Pacem in Terris" was acclaimed by people of many faiths and beliefs.

Angelo Giuseppe Roncalli became the 261st Supreme Pontiff of the Roman Catholic Church in 1958. A short, stout man of 76, he had white hair and was slightly bent with age. He had a large hawk nose, a bright smile and eyes keen with study and contemplation. His easy and natural amiability had endeared him to all sorts and conditions of men. He liked a good dinner and was believed to be the first Pope to smoke cigarettes.

He was born Nov. 25, 1881, in a cold and uncomfortable 200-year-old house of thick gray stone in the Lombardy village of Sotto il Monte, five miles from Bergamo.

Angelo Roncalli's father, Giovanni Roncalli, was a landless sharecropper. Eventually he saved enough money to buy the farm that he worked. In later years the future Pope John wrote of his childhood:

"We were poor but happy. We did not realize that we lacked anything, and, in truth, we didn't. Ours was a dignified and happy poverty."

Since the fifteenth century, the family had worshiped God in the region's village churches, such as the one in Sotto il Monte, where Angelo was baptized late at night on the day he was born. On that night the village was shaken by a storm and the priest had grumbled mildly at being kept out of bed, but the Roncallis believed in prompt baptism, just in case. Angelo was the third child in a family of thirteen children.

When he was 11, Angelo entered the seminary at Bergamo; he said some years later that he had never wanted to be anything but a priest. He won a scholarship for study at the Seminario Romano in Rome, sometimes called the Apollinaire.

He was ordained a priest on Aug. 10, 1904, in the church of Santa Maria in Rome, and celebrated his first mass the next day in St. Peter's Basilica.

Bergamo, a magnet to Angelo Roncalli for many years, drew him to his first task after he became a priest secretary to the new bishop, Giacomo Radini-Tedeschi.

Because Bergamo was near Milan, it was natural that Don Angelo should have many occasions to go there, particularly to visit the famous Ambrosiana Library. Msgr. Achille Ratti, who was to become Pope Pius XI, was then prefect of the library and he formed a good opinion of the young priest.

In 1925 the Pope named Msgr. Roncalli an Archbishop, charged with protecting the interests of the small Roman Catholic minority in Bulgaria. In 1935 he became Apostolic Delegate to Turkey and Greece and took up residence in Istanbul.

Toward the end of World War II, Archbishop Roncalli was named Papal Nuncio in Paris and head of the Vatican diplomatic mission to the victorious Government of Brig. Gen. Charles de Gaulle.

It was a delicate task. He did what he could to mitigate the fury of the avenging de Gaulle forces and of the Communists against the partisans of the defeated Vichy Government. He also aided the hundreds of German Roman Catholic divinity students who were military prisoners of war in France.

About the same time, he was approached by Franz von Papen, German Ambassador to Turkey, who later wrote that while Msgr. Roncalli "could see no alternative to a German defeat," he "forwarded to the Vatican my pleas that the Allies should realize the difference between the Hitler regime and the German people."

On Jan. 12, 1953, at the age of 71, Msgr. Roncalli was elevated to the College of Cardinals by Pope Pius XII and was named Patriarch of Venice. He soon became a familiar figure as he went about the canals in a police launch. He never used a gondola. He said that he was a modern prelate and that the gondola was old-fashioned.

Pius died on Oct. 9, 1958, and 19 days later, on the 11th or 12th ballot, the College of Cardinals elected Cardinal Roncalli as his successor. On Nov. 4, 1958, he was crowned Pope in impressive ceremonies at St. Peter's.

Pius XII had been a lean, intense man with an air of great asceticism who once told of having seen a vision of Jesus by his bedside. His successor entered briskly into possession of the papacy, moved the furniture about and changed a good many customs, including the custom that the Pope eats alone. Pope John usually ate with members of his immediate administrative household, and the atmosphere was somewhat less ethereal than it had been under his predecessor.

On the day after Christmas in the first year of his reign, Pope John visited the prisoners in Rome's Regina Coeli prison.

"Since you could not come to me, I came to you," he told them. He recalled to the men that a member of his family had once been under arrest for poaching.

When he ascended the throne of St. Peter, Pope John indicated that an attempt to heal the rift begun in 1054 between the Eastern Catholic Church and the Roman Catholic Church would be one of his aims.

The Vatican reacted cautiously in 1960 to the presidential candidacy of Senator John F. Kennedy, the second Roman Catholic, after Gov. Alfred E. Smith of New York, to receive the nomination of a major party. The Vatican refrained from making any reference to Senator Kennedy's religion. Spokesmen let it be known that under no circumstances would the Vatican attempt to bring pressure of any kind on Catholics to vote for Senator Kennedy or on Mr. Kennedy himself should he be elected.

The constant menace of nuclear warfare distressed Pope John, who appealed to nations to put aside the means of nuclear war. He also took great interest in scientific development, such as the penetration of space.

During his reign the Vatican's relations with some Communist countries showed signs of improving. In

April, 1963, he sent a representative to Poland and Hungary to try to pave the way for an accord.

Vatican officials stressed that the Pontiff was not easing his anti-Communist position. They said he was merely trying to make conditions less oppressive for Roman Catholics living behind the Iron Curtain.

On Aug. 7, 1960, in a radio allocution from Castel Gandolfo, his summer residence, the Pope made this plea to Christ for intercession to save the world from physical and moral destruction:

"Divine Redeemer, who for the life of the world does daily on our altars offer to the eternal Father the sacrifice of the body and blood, protect the human race from the dangers of death!"

Two and one-half months after his coronation, Pope John elevated 23 Cardinals, and in March, 1960, he created eight more. This latter group included the first Negro Cardinal, the first Filipino and the first Japanese.

Pope John had a keen sense of togetherness with his staff, and one of his first acts as Pope was to give Vatican workers a substantial pay raise.

He handled the bulk of his daily business in his office in the library overlooking St. Peter's Square. On his desk was a crucifix and a picture of the Madonna. On a separate table was a white telephone, Extension 101. The phone was for outgoing calls. Nobody telephones directly to the Pope.

After a brief rest after lunch, Pope John often took a short walk in the Vatican gardens. He sometimes watched a television program for a few minutes in the evening and usually returned to his desk for work before retiring.

The Pontiff's daily routine illustrated the fact that he retained all the simplicity of life of his predecessor, but not all of the austerity.

WINSTON CHURCHILL

November 30, 1874–January 24, 1965

By Anthony Lewis

LONDON—Sir Winston Churchill is dead.

The great figure who embodied man's will to resist tyranny passed into history this morning at his home. He was 90 years old.

His old friend and physician, Lord Moran, gave the news to the world after informing Queen Elizabeth II and Prime Minister Harold Wilson.

The announcement was read at 8:35 A.M. to members of the press standing in the rain at the entrance to Hyde Park Gate, the small street south of Kensington Gardens where Sir Winston had lived for so long.

Lord Moran had come to the house at 7:18. A few minutes earlier Sir Winston's son, Randolph, had driven up. Also there at the end were Lady Churchill and their daughter, Sarah, and Randolph's son, Winston.

Another daughter, Mary, Mrs. Christopher Soames, also survives Sir Winston. Other survivors are 10 grandchildren and three great-grandchildren, the last born just two days ago.

The world had been watching and waiting since Jan. 15, when it was announced that Sir Winston had suffered a stroke. Medical experts said that only phenomenal tenacity and spirit of life could enable a man of 90 to hold off death so long in these circumstances.

But then those were the qualities that had made Winston Churchill a historical figure in his lifetime. His pluck in rallying Britain to victory in World War II saved not only this country but, in all likelihood, free nations everywhere.

Sir Winston will be given a state funeral, the first commoner so to be honored since the death of William Ewart Gladstone in 1898. The body will lie in state in Westminster Hall for several days. Services will be held in St. Paul's Cathedral.

Today was the anniversary of the death of Sir Winston's father, Lord Randolph Churchill, a somewhat eccentric Tory politician. He died in 1894.

For virtually everyone in Great Britain, Sir Winston's death will be a wrenching personal loss and a symbolic break with a past whose glories seem already faded.

For the world, too, it is the end of an age.

Sir Winston will always be remembered as the great war leader who defied Hitler. But he was more than that, a personality larger than life, an extraordinary man in language and character as well as war and politics.

He was the linchpin of the Grand Alliance of 26 nations that vanquished the Axis powers in 1945 after nearly six years of war. For him as for his countrymen his finest hour came in 1940 when Britain stood alone, beleaguered at sea and in the air.

He employed all his skill as an orator to rally British pride and courage, and all his ability as a statesman to get arms and sustenance from abroad. With almost all of Europe under or about to fall under the Nazi jackboot, it was Sir Winston who flung this challenge at the enemy:

"We shall not flag, or fail. We shall go on to the end, we shall fight in France, we shall fight on the seas and oceans, we shall fight with growing confidence and growing strength in the air, we shall defend our island, whatever the cost may be, we shall fight on the beaches, we shall fight on the landing grounds, we shall fight in the fields and in the streets, we shall fight in the hills;

we shall never surrender, and even if, which I do not for a moment believe, this island or a large part of it were subjugated and starving, then our empire beyond the seas, armed and guarded by the British fleet, would carry on the struggle, until, in God's good time, the new world, with all its power and might, steps forth to the rescue and the liberation of the old."

As the late President John F. Kennedy said in 1963, in conferring upon Sir Winston an honorary citizenship of the United States, "He mobilized the English language and sent it into battle."

Quite apart from his fame as a world statesman and global strategist, he won distinction as an artist and fame as a historian, notably of Great Britain, and author. He was awarded the Nobel Prize in Literature in 1953. A special citation paid tribute to his oratory.

In 1953, Queen Elizabeth II, the last of the six British sovereigns he served, conferred upon him the highest order of chivalry that can come to a commoner: Knight Companion of the Order of the Garter.

Sir Winston's paramount place in history lay in providing the leadership and ensuring the cohesion of the three great wartime allies—Britain, the Soviet Union and the United States. He was a warm friend of Franklin D. Roosevelt and a tactfully candid collaborator with Josef Stalin.

He was constantly on the go—to Washington, to Moscow, to the various fronts and to the conferences of the Big Three at Teheran, Yalta and finally Potsdam.

It was in the middle of this postwar conference in 1945 that he learned that the British people had turned out his Government at the polls. As leader of the Opposition for the next six years he fought Socialism at home and Communism abroad; in 1951 he became Prime Minister a second time.

His was among the first voices to warn of the dangers of Soviet expansionist exploitation of the peace, as it had been among the first to cry out against the hidden danger of Hitlerism.

On March 5, 1946, he delivered his famous speech at Fulton, Mo. Although he spoke no longer as head of a government, his words were flashed around the world.

Introduced by President Harry S. Truman, he said: "From Stettin on the Baltic to Trieste in the Adriatic, an iron curtain has descended across the Continent. Behind that line lie all the capitals of the ancient states of central and eastern Europe—Warsaw, Berlin, Prague, Vienna, Budapest, Belgrade, Bucharest and Sofia—all these famous cities and the populations around them lie in what I must call the Soviet sphere and are all subject in one form or another not only to Soviet influence but to a very high, and in many cases increasing, measure of control from Moscow."

Winston Leonard Spencer Churchill was born on Nov. 30, 1874, at Blenheim Palace, built for his illustrious ancestor the first Duke of Marlborough. His father, who had a distinguished political career, was the third son of the seventh Duke of Marlborough. His mother was the former Jennie Jerome of New York.

Winston was an undersized, emotional child. He adored his brilliant father, who, however, was convinced by his son's school failures that the boy was retarded. The child saw little of his mother and became deeply attached to his nurse, Mrs. Everest. When he became one of the greatest figures of his age, Mrs. Everest's picture was over his desk.

After attendance at a small private school, where he was brutally caned, Winston was sent to Harrow. He twice failed his entrance examinations to the Royal Military College at Sandhurst and was finally admitted to the "cavalry class," a sort of scholastic back door for young gentlemen wealthy enough to provide their own horses.

After graduating in 1894, he became a lieutenant in the Fourth (Queen's Own) Hussars. There being no active service at the moment, he went to Cuba as a war correspondent, without giving up his commission.

In 1897–98 he fought in India and the Sudan as a war correspondent-officer, a dual role then permitted. Returning to England, he found he lacked the Latin or Greek required for Oxford, and decided to enter politics forthwith. But he was badly defeated in a hopeless race for the House of Commons.

In 1899, not yet 25, he took the field in his fifth campaign, in South Africa. Captured and interned by Boers, he managed to escape in a characteristic burst of skill and good luck; the Boers offered a reward for his capture, saying he had a "small, hardly noticeable mustache, talks through his nose and cannot pronounce the letter S properly."

Back again in England, Sir Winston stood again for Parliament and this time was elected, taking his seat on Jan. 23, 1901. Thus began a stormy tenure that saw him switch parties twice, from Conservatives to Liberals and back again; serve in Cabinet posts of increasing importance; and play a central role in a succession of crises, from the labor strife of the 1910's through World War I, the postwar demobilization and the Irish civil war.

As First Lord of the Admiralty in World War I, he became a strong and controversial advocate for naval action in the Mediterranean. The resulting British-French expedition to the Dardanelles ended catastrophically at the battle of Gallipoli, in 1915–16. But by that time Churchill had already resigned from the Government, serving at his own request as an infantry officer in France.

In the 1920's, after his return to Parliament, he developed serious differences with his fellow Conservative Stanley Baldwin, the bland, pipe-smoking Prime Minister, who believed that the British people wanted peace at almost any price. Churchill believed that the

nation should be aroused to the dangers of a second world war.

In the Churchill of the early 1930's, portly, middle-aged and at times pugnacious, dignity joined with youthful high spirits to make the figure the world was to know in World War II.

Sir Winston lived handsomely in the international world of fashion and politics. He smoked expensive cigars and drank the best brandy. He knew many of the world's most interesting people.

In 1937, the first coalition Government of Neville Chamberlain came to power, but pacifist sentiment was strong and Churchill was not asked to join the Cabinet.

At 6 P.M. Sept. 3, 1939, seven hours and 45 minutes after Britain had declared war on Germany, a wireless flash told British men-of-war in all parts of the world:

"Winston is back."

Churchill was made First Lord of the Admiralty, his post in 1914 at the outbreak of the World War I.

On May 10, 1940, Germany invaded the Netherlands and Belgium and the distraught Neville Chamberlain resigned as Prime Minister. King George VI invited Churchill to form a new Government.

In his memoirs Churchill wrote:

"I was conscious of a profound sense of relief. At last I had authority to give direction over the whole scene."

Churchill, who was then 65, possessed a capacity for work seldom equaled. He drove his associates with memorandums that crackled. It was usually: "Pray let me know by 4 P.M. today on one sheet of paper . . ."

On May 11 the formation of his National Coalition Government was announced, and on May 13 he told Parliament grimly that "I have nothing to offer but blood, toil, tears and sweat."

Britain had not been in such peril since the Spanish Armada. A French military leader predicted that Britain was going to have her "neck wrung like a chicken." Later, Churchill remarked: "Some neck. Some chicken!"

On June 18, when it had become apparent that France was capitulating to the German invaders, Churchill broadcast a message of courage and defiance. His concluding sentence will be long remembered:

"Let us therefore brace ourselves to our duties, and so bear ourselves that, if the British Empire and its Commonwealth last for a thousand years, men will still say, 'This was their finest hour.'"

Not long afterward, the Germans launched their long-expected air attack against Britain. It was anyone's bet whether Britain's air force could stave off defeat, but by the end of October it was clear that it had done so.

Meanwhile, Churchill sought to convince the United States that its interests demanded that it join Britain in the war. Toward this end he was greatly aided by the presence of President Roosevelt, a cultivated, European-minded statesman and a strong Anglophile.

When the Japanese attack at Pearl Harbor on Dec. 7, 1941, ensured the entrance of the United States on Britain's side, Churchill's relief was great. As he wrote later, "Being saturated and satiated with emotion and sensation, I went to bed and slept the sleep of the saved and thankful."

Still, reversals throughout 1941 stirred Parliamentary opposition to the Prime Minister. On Jan. 27, 1942, a three-day secret debate began in the House of Commons. The House finally voted confidence in the Government by 461 to 1.

President Roosevelt sent Churchill his congratulations. "It is fun to be in the same decade with you," the President cabled.

As the tide of battle turned in favor of the Allies, Churchill met several times with his Big Three counterparts—President Roosevelt and Premier Stalin, notably at Teheran and Yalta—to clarify war aims and plan a postwar world order.

On May 7, 1945, the Prime Minister proclaimed the end of European hostilities in a broadcast to the British people. But just a few weeks later his coalition Government broke up, and the Tories were defeated in the national election. Six years later, with Labor clinging to a tenuous majority, Churchill forced an election and was returned to power as Prime Minister, but with a majority of only 16 seats.

Long sick of war and its horrors, Sir Winston would have liked to crown his career with the creation of a structure for durable and lasting world peace. But a succession of conferences of great powers fell considerably short of his hopes. On April 2, 1955, he called upon Queen Elizabeth II at Buckingham Palace and received her permission to submit his resignation as Prime Minister.

He retained his seat in the House of Commons until just prior to last October's general election, when he announced, nearing 90, that he would not stand again. Having been elected uninterruptedly since 1924, he had become the "Father of the House of Commons."

Apart from his political and literary gifts, Churchill was widely known as an enthusiastic amateur painter. His touch on canvas was softer than that of Hitler, who also had sought relaxation at the easel. Hitler, who had once striven to be an architect, tended to hold to a hard drawn line. Sir Winston liked the soft touch of the French impressionists. For several years his paintings were reproduced as Christmas cards.

HO CHI MINH

May 19, 1890–September 2, 1969

HONG KONG—President Ho Chi Minh of North Vietnam died yesterday morning in Hanoi at the age of 79.

A Hanoi radio report said he succumbed after a heart attack.

[Vietnamese leaders later asserted that they falsified the date of Ho's death. A statement said that because the death—on Sept. 2—fell on Vietnam's National Day, the party leadership announced that he died a day later "to prevent the date of Uncle Ho's death from coinciding with a day of great national rejoicing."—*The Associated Press*

By Alden Whitman

Among 20th-century statesmen, Ho Chi Minh was remarkable for the tenacity and patience with which he pursued his goal of Vietnamese independence and for his success in blending Communism with nationalism.

From his youth Ho espoused freedom for the French colony of Vietnam. He persevered through years when his chances of success were so minuscule as to seem ridiculous. Ultimately, he organized the defeat of the French in 1954 in the historic battle of Dienbienphu, which occurred nine years after he was named President of the Democratic Republic of Vietnam.

After the supposed temporary division of Vietnam at the 17th parallel by the Geneva Agreement of 1954, and after that division became hardened by United States support of Ngo Dinh Diem in the South, Ho led his countrymen in the North against the onslaughts of American military might.

Ho was also an inspiration for the National Liberation Front, or Vietcong, which operated in South Vietnam in the long, bloody and costly conflict against the Saigon regime and its American allies.

In the war, Ho maintained an exquisite balance in his relations with the Soviet Union and the People's Republic of China, Communist countries that were his principal suppliers of war goods.

To the 19 million people north of the 17th parallel and to millions below it, the small, frail figure of Ho, with its long ascetic face, straggly goatee and luminous eyes, was that of a patriarch, the George Washington of his nation.

He was universally called "Uncle Ho." His popularity was such that it was generally conceded that Vietnam would have been unified under his leadership had the countrywide elections pledged at Geneva taken place. As it was, major segments of South Vietnam were effectively controlled by the National Liberation Front despite the presence of hundreds of thousands of American troops.

Intelligent, resourceful and dedicated, Ho created a favorable impression on many who dealt with him, among them Harry Ashmore of the Center for the Study of Democratic Institutions and former editor of The Arkansas Gazette.

"Ho was a courtly, urbane, highly sophisticated man with a gentle manner and without personal venom," Mr. Ashmore recalled after a visit in 1967. At the meeting Ho wore his characteristic high-necked white pajama type of garment and rubber sandals.

Ho reminded Mr. Ashmore that he had once visited the United States. "I think I know the American people," Ho said, "and I don't understand how they can support their involvement in this war. Is the Statue of Liberty standing on her head?"

Ho was an enormously pragmatic Communist, a doer rather than a theoretician. And like Mao Tsetung, a fellow Communist leader, Ho composed poetry, some of it quite affecting. One poem, written when he was a prisoner of the Chinese Nationalists, is called "Autumn Night" and includes this passage:

Innocent, I have now endured a whole
* year in prison.*
Using my tears for ink, I turn my
thoughts into verses.

Ho's rise to power and world eminence was not a fully documented story, in part because he used a dozen aliases, of which Ho Chi Minh (which can be translated as Ho, the Shedder of Light) was but one. Another reason was his reluctance to disclose biographical information

The most reliable evidence indicates he was born May 19, 1890, in Kimlien, a village in central Vietnam. It is generally accepted that his birth name was Nguyen Tat Thanh.

His father was only slightly better off than the area's rice peasants, but he passed examinations that gave him a job in the imperial administration just when the French rule was beginning.

An ardent nationalist, Ho's father joined anti-French secret societies. Young Ho got his first underground experience as his father's messenger in the anti-French network. Shortly, the father lost his Government job and became a traditional healer. Ho's mother was believed to have been of peasant origin.

Ho attended the village school and high school at the Lycee Quoc-Hoc in the old imperial capital of Hue. He then decided to go to Europe. As a step toward that goal, he went to a trade school in Saigon, where he learned the duties of a kitchen boy and pastry cook's helper, skills in demand by Europeans of that day.

He signed aboard a ship as a kitchen boy. In his travels, he visited Marseilles and ports in Africa and North America. Explaining the significance of these voyages for Ho's education as a revolutionary, the late Bernard Fall, an American authority of Vietnam, wrote in "The Two Vietnams":

"His contacts with the white colonizers on their home grounds shattered any of his illusions as to their 'superiority,' and his association with sailors from Brittany, Cornwall and the Frisian Islands—as illiterate and superstitious as the most backward Vietnamese rice farmer—did the rest."

With the advent of World War I, Ho went to live in London, where he worked as a cook's helper under Escoffier, the master chef, at the Carlton Hotel. Sometime during the war, Ho journeyed to the United States, and around 1918 he returned to France and lived in the Montmartre section of Paris.

At the Versailles Peace Conference of 1919 Ho emerged as a self-appointed spokesman for his native land. Seeing the possibility of Vietnam's independence, Ho, dressed in a hired black suit and bowler hat, traveled to the Palace of Versailles to present his case. He was not received, although he offered a program for Vietnam that included basic freedoms and equality between the French rulers and the native population.

When the Versailles Conference failed to settle colonial issues, Ho's faith was transferred to Socialist action. He became a founding member of the French Communist party because he believed that the Communists were willing to promote national liberation.

With that decision, Ho's career took a turn. For one thing, he became the French party's resident expert on colonial affairs. He also gravitated to Moscow, then the nerve center of world Communism. He went there first in 1922 for the Fourth Comintern Congress, where he met Lenin and became a member of the Comintern's Southeast Asia Bureau.

Moscow was his base for years. He attended the University of the Toilers of the East, receiving training in Marxism and the techniques of agitation and propaganda.

In 1925 Ho was dispatched to Canton, China, to help Chiang Kai-shek, then in Communist favor as an heir of Sun Yat-sen. Once in Canton, Ho set about spreading the spirit of revolution in the Far East. He organized Vietnamese refugees into the Vietnam Revolutionary Youth Association and set up the League of Oppressed Peoples of Asia, which became the South Seas Communist party, the forerunner of various national Communist groups, including his Indochinese Communist party of 1930.

In July, 1927, when Chiang turned on his Communist allies, Ho fled to Moscow. He later traveled among Vietnamese exiles and published newspapers that were smuggled over the border into Vietnam.

In 1930, Ho helped organize the Indochinese Communist party, which became the Vietnamese Communist party and later the Vietnamese Workers party. In that year, a peasant rebellion erupted in Vietnam, which the Communists backed.

Ho was back in China in 1938 as a communications operator with Mao Tse-tung's Eighth Route Army. Subsequently, he found his way south and entered Vietnam in 1940 for the first time in 30 years. The timing was ideal. The Japanese had taken control of the Indochinese Peninsula, and the French administrators agreed to cooperate with the Japanese. With great daring and imagination, Ho took advantage of World War II to piece together a coalition of Vietnamese nationalists and Communists into what was called the Vietminh, or Independence Front.

The Vietminh created a 10,000-man guerrilla force that battled the Japanese in the jungles. Ho's actions projected him onto the world scene as the leading Vietnamese nationalist and an ally of the United States against the Japanese.

In 1942 Ho was sent to Kunming. He was arrested there by Chiang Kai-shek's men and jailed until September, 1943.

On his release, according to Mr. Fall, he helped form a large Vietnamese freedom group. One result was that in 1944 Ho accepted a portfolio in the Provisional Republican Government of Vietnam. Ho's Vietminh took over Hanoi in 1945, and it was in this period that he took the name Ho Chi Minh.

With the end of World War II, Ho proclaimed the independence of Vietnam, but it took nine years for his declaration to become an effective fact. Under the Big Three Agreement at Potsdam, the Chinese Nationalists occupied Hanoi and northern Vietnam. The French arrived to reclaim Saigon and the country's southern portion. Ho's nationalist coalition was strained under pressure of these events.

Forming a new guerrilla force around the Vietminh, Ho and his colleagues dealt summarily with dissidents unwilling to fight for independence. As the Chinese withdrew from the north and the French advanced from the south, Ho negotiated with the French to save his nationalist regime.

In 1946 Ho agreed to let the Democratic Republic of Vietnam become a part of the French Union as a free state within the Indochina federation. The French recognized Ho as chief of state and promised a plebiscite in the South on the question of a unified Vietnam under Ho.

By the start of 1947, the agreement had broken down, and Ho's men were fighting the French Army. The Vietminh guerrillas held the jungles and villages, the French the cities. For seven years the war raged as Ho's forces gathered strength.

On May 8, 1954, the French forces were decisively defeated at Dienbienphu. The Indochina war ended officially in July at a cost to the French of 172,000 casualties and to the Vietminh of perhaps three times that many.

The cease-fire accord was signed in Geneva July 21, 1954. By that time the United States, fearful of Communist expansion in Asia, was involved in Vietnam on the French side.

The Geneva Accord divided Vietnam at the 17th parallel, creating a North and a South Vietnam. It removed the French administration and provided for all-Vietnam elections in 1956.

But the United States declined to sign the Geneva Accord, and South Vietnam refused to hold the elections. The United States built up its military mission in Saigon to counter continued guerrilla activity of the National Liberation Front.

Beginning in 1964, thousands of American troops were poured into South Vietnam to battle the Vietcong and then bomb North Vietnam. The halt of American bombing in 1968 finally led to the peace negotiations in Paris, but fighting in South Vietnam continued.

Throughout, Ho was confident of victory. Even in early 1967 he told Mr. Ashmore, "We have been fighting for our independence for more than 25 years, and of course we cherish peace, but we will never surrender our independence to purchase a peace with the United States or any party."

CHARLES DE GAULLE

November 22, 1890–November 9, 1970

PARIS—Gen. Charles de Gaulle died last night of a heart attack, the French Government announced today. He would have been 80 years old on Nov. 22.

The announcement said General de Gaulle succumbed at his country home in the village of Colombey-les-Deux-Eglises.

The General, the French hero of World War II, took over the government in 1958, when France was near civil war and the army was in revolt in Algeria.

For 11 years he ruled as a strongman, repeatedly going to the people in referenda to make certain he had their backing. Each time he won until the spring of 1969, when he lost what he considered a crucial referendum on administrative reform.

De Gaulle, who is survived by two children, then withdrew entirely from French political life. More than the end of a singular political reign, it was the end of an era.—*United Press International*

By Alden Whitman

That era started on June 18, 1940, when an obscure temporary brigadier general, having escaped to London from a battered and disorganized France about to capitulate to Nazi Germany, exhorted his countrymen to continue in a war that he perceived would evolve into a world conflict.

"Must we abandon all hope?" the 49-year-old officer asked in his speech in a British Broadcasting Corporation studio. "Is our defeat final and irremediable? To those questions I answer—No!"

And he added: "Whatever happens, the flame of French resistance must not and shall not die."

It seemed ludicrous to some that de Gaulle, with a mere 100,000 francs and a handful of volunteers, could put together a Free French cause, but the general exuded total faith in himself.

"When leaders fail," he wrote, "new leaders are projected upward out of the eternal spirit of France: from Charlemagne to Joan of Arc to Napoleon, Poincare and Clemenceau. Perhaps this time I am one of those thrust into leadership by the failure of others."

De Gaulle's certainty that he was France ("Je suis la France," he declared in 1940) sustained him through many mutations of fortune before the country's liberation in 1944; and it emboldened him when he was shaping the Fifth Republic, decolonizing the empire, and freeing Algeria. His certainty also contributed to his blindness to the domestic economic disaffections that turned public opinion against him.

His hauteur permitted him to stride into the pantheon of heroes in August, 1944, as he led a Paris liberation parade from the Arch of Triumph to Notre Dame. Cheered by two million people in an explosion of national fervor, he experienced his finest hour. It was the hauteur, too, that exasperated Allied leaders during the war. "The Cross of Lorraine [de Gaulle's emblem] was the heaviest cross I have ever had to bear," Winston Churchill once bristled.

Charles Andre Joseph Marie de Gaulle was born Nov. 22, 1890, in Lille. His father, Henri, was lay headmaster of a Jesuit College in Paris when his son was born. Charles's mother, Jeanne Maillot-Delannoy, was intensely patriotic.

In 1910 the young man entered Saint-Cyr, the officer-training academy, and two years later joined the 33rd Infantry Regiment at Arras commanded by Col. Henri-Philippe Petain.

The lives of the two men became ironically entwined. Early in World War II, when de Gaulle founded the Resistance, his old colonel, then head of the collaborationist Vichy regime, had him condemned to death for desertion. When the tables were turned after the war, Petain was condemned to death for treason, and de Gaulle, the provisional President-Premier of France, commuted his sentence to life imprisonment.

In World War I, de Gaulle was wounded and captured by the Germans at Verdun.

In 1925 Petain attached his friend to his secretariat in the Supreme War Council. Two years later de Gaulle became a major and served in the Rhineland and the Middle East. He returned to France in 1932, became a lieutenant colonel and was named secretary to the High Council of National Defense.

De Gaulle's career up to this point had not been brilliant. One reason was his spit-and-polish personality; another was his book, "Vers l'armee de metier" ("Toward a Modern Army"), published in 1934. The book disparaged the Maginot Line, a supposedly impregnable fortress system along the French-German border. Equally upsetting to reigning military minds was de Gaulle's proposal for a modernized army with an elite mobile tank force at its head.

When World War II broke out, de Gaulle was a colonel in command of a tank regiment in Metz. When Hitler, after chewing up Poland, turned on France, the debacle that de Gaulle had foreseen took place: The Maginot Line was turned and northern France was overrun by Nazi tanks.

On June 5, 1940, Premier Paul Reynaud brought him into the Cabinet as Under Secretary of Defense. About then he came to his momentous decision. Concluding that events made it evident that Britain would remain in the war and that the conflict would become worldwide, he decided that he would try to organize French resistance based on the nation's colonies.

After the discomfited French Government fled to Bordeaux and prepared to sue for an armistice, de Gaulle took flight to London. Assuming there the epic task of organizing a resistance, he was recognized by the British Government "as the leader of all the Free French, wherever they may be, who will rally to him in defense of the Allied cause."

With a mystique already sprouting around him, de Gaulle was able, by claiming to embody France, to draw into his cause the governors of French Equatorial Africa, Chad and the French Cameroons. A month later, in June, 1941, the Soviet Union's entrance into the war produced two important developments: direct Free French contact with the Russians and the start of an active Resistance in France, now organized by the French Communist party.

Meanwhile, de Gaulle organized, in September, 1941, the French National Committee, a virtual government in exile, with himself as chairman. Roosevelt, meanwhile, sought a more compliant alternative to de Gaulle. W. Averell Harriman, the diplomat, summed up official feeling when he wrote: "Unfortunately de Gaulle is thinking more of how he is going to rule France than of ways of liberating her. That is his great flaw. Also, he is extremely vain and imagines himself a sort of Joan of Arc."

De Gaulle meanwhile met with Roosevelt in Washington. One result was Washington's recognition of his committee as "qualified to exercise the administration of France." He went on to establish his personal authority in a tremendous outburst of emotional frenzy that convulsed Paris when he led a triumphal march from the Arch of Triumph to the Cathedral of Notre Dame on Aug. 26, 1944.

Paris had been liberated the day before by the efforts of armed Parisians, Gen. Jacques Leclerc's Second Armored Division and American troops. But de Gaulle, smartly turned out in his military best, was the person on whom the hero's mantle seemed to fall.

In the days that followed, de Gaulle created a moderate Government of National Unanimity, which lasted for 14 months.

In October, 1945, the French, disavowing the Third Republic, elected a Constituent Assembly. With its convocation, which foreshadowed the Fourth Republic, de Gaulle became a parliamentary executive. He resigned in January, 1946, but emerged from "retirement" in April, 1947, to call for formation of a Rally of the French People—a party against parties.

At first he attracted thousands to the Rally as he inveighed against the Communists and the trade unions. But he overplayed his hand by issuing an ultimatum to the National Assembly that sought an immediate general election.

By 1954, his Rally was in disarray, and in July, 1955, he announced his retirement from public life. From then until the middle of 1958, he lived at Colombey, where he completed "The War Memoirs of Charles de Gaulle."

The "tempest" that brought de Gaulle back to public life and to power, was the war in Algeria, underway since 1954. The Fourth Republic, already stung by the loss of Indochina, was bedeviled by the conflict against the Algerian Nationalists. By 1958 some 35,000 French troops were in Algeria trying to contain 15,000 insurgents.

The crisis came in May, when Europeans in Algeria seized Government offices with the aid of army officers. De Gaulle was invested as Premier of France on June 1 and given decree powers for six months with the right within that time to submit a new Constitution.

He moved to dismantle the French Algerians' Committees of Public Safety. A Constitution for the Fifth Republic that placed power in a President rather than in Parliament was ratified by 80 percent of the voters, and in December de Gaulle was elected President for a seven-year term that began Jan. 8, 1959.

He transferred to France 1,500 army officers associated with the French Algerian diehards. Nevertheless, in January, 1960, there was an army-led insurrection in Algiers, which was contained with the arrest of the ringleaders and the cashiering of some rightist generals.

That November de Gaulle suggested an independent Algeria, a proposal endorsed in a referendum in France and Algeria in January, 1961. Orderly progression to independence was thwarted, however, by the rise of the Secret Army Organization and the obduracy of many French Algerians. Terrorism spread into France, while the violence in Algeria culminated in rebellion there in April, 1961.

De Gaulle acted with firmness and energy. The revolt collapsed, and three of its four leaders went into hiding while the fourth was jailed. In September, 1962, an independent Algerian regime was established, and within a year about 750,000 French Algerians emigrated to metropolitan France.

Once the Algerian problem was solved, de Gaulle was able to flex French muscle in Europe and around the world. A mighty ingredient of the "new" France was her development of an atomic bomb in 1960.

De Gaulle's first term as President of the Fifth Republic expired in January, 1966. He was elected to a second term, but only after a runoff. The principal attack on him came from the Left, temporarily united under Francois Mitterrand.

It was domestic discontent that eventually brought him down. Expenses for items like membership in the nuclear "club" cost millions of francs. This meant austerity at home at a time when a nation of chiefly small shopkeepers and farmers was struggling to transform itself into a more modern country.

The transition brought with it tensions in every segment of society. There were dislocations in the countryside as corporate farming increased. In the cities supermarkets began to appear, dooming neighborhood grocery stores.

In education, more students than ever before crowded the universities and studied under curriculums that were irrelevant to the times. In an effort to accommodate the influx of students, satellites of older universities were set up, as at Nanterre, outside Paris.

It was at Nanterre that open rebellion against de Gaulle broke out in the spring of 1968. The issue was reform of education. Students at the school occupied a classroom on March 22, and were routed by the police. The number of militant students grew and the authorities closed the university in early May. Thereupon a group from Nanterre met with a Sorbonne group to plan a joint protest.

From this beginning sprang "the events of May," a month-long clash of social, economic and political forces that generated a near-revolution. The Sorbonne students went on strike, and were clubbed by the police. The turmoil spread to the provinces, and soon the children of bourgeois parents were battling not just oppressive education but government itself.

The students' spirit of audacity spread to the workers, who had their own discontents, and soon there were factory sit-ins. All France seemed engaged in crisis demonstrations and strikes.

De Gaulle eventually tried to resolve the crisis, first by acting to pacify the 10 million striking workers with pay increases, then by cracking down further on the students. Finally, on May 30, he dissolved the National Assembly and warned the country that he would restore law and order with all the means at his disposal.

Immediately after he spoke, hundred of thousands of his adherents thronged the Place de la Concorde in Paris to voice their support. Leftist elements, including the Communists, backed down from the barricades, deciding to take their chances in the National Assembly elections made necessary by de Gaulle's dissolution of that body. The "days of May" were over.

De Gaulle won a big victory in the elections. By the fall of 1968 he seemed more in control than ever. However, as Georges Pompidou, then the Premier, remarked shortly after the student-worker insurgency, "Things would never be quite the same again."

The proof that de Gaulle had lost the adherence of his people came over a minor issue—the future regional structure of France and the role of its Senate. The matter was to be settled in a referendum in April, 1969, that at first created only slight interest.

Then de Gaulle injected himself. The result of the voting was to be a test of public confidence. The general was persuaded, until the returns were indubitable, that he would triumph. Retiring once more to Colombey, he set to writing his memoirs.

NIKITA KHRUSHCHEV

April 15, 1894–September 11, 1971

Moscow—Nikita S. Khrushchev, who ruled the Soviet Union with a dramatic flair for more than a decade before his ouster seven years ago by the current, more conservative Kremlin leaders, died today of a heart attack. He was 77 years old.

Word of Mr. Khrushchev's death in a Kremlin hospital about noon was relayed to Western newsmen by friends of his family and confirmed informally by the Foreign Ministry in reply to queries.

As of 9 P.M. Moscow time—some nine hours later—there had been no official announcement of the death of the stocky man who became the head of the Soviet Communist party after Stalin's death in 1953 and who spent the next 11 years seeking to blacken the reputation and expose the crimes of the former dictator.

Because of the news blackout, ordinary Russians had no knowledge of the death of the man who made "peaceful coexistence" part of the world vocabulary. In 24 hours, the word, however, will have spread throughout Moscow as people with short-wave radios tell their friends the news being reported from abroad.

After his forced resignation in what amounted to a Kremlin coup in October, 1964, Mr. Khrushchev lived in virtual isolation and was rarely mentioned in Soviet publications.—*Bernard Gwertzman*

By Alden Whitman

Late in the afternoon of Friday, Feb. 24, 1956, a short, rotund, round-headed, gleamingly bald, baggy-suited man stepped to the microphone at the concluding session of the 20th Congress of the Communist party of the Soviet Union, from which all foreign delegates and reporters had been excluded.

It was well after midnight when the session adjourned, and what the delegates had heard in Nikita Sergeyevich Khrushchev's 20,000-word speech was nothing less than a documented, count-by-count indictment of Josef Stalin, then dead about three years and who for a quarter-century had been held up to the Soviet people, Communist and non-Communist, and to Communists throughout the world as the infallible genius-leader of his country who had advanced it unerringly toward Socialism.

What some delegates may have suspected but refused to credence, Mr. Khrushchev, the First Secretary (chief) of the Soviet party, laid bare with whiplash candor—that Stalin had brought about the deaths of thousands of innocent persons; that he had ruled the party and the country by terror and torture; that he had been pusillanimous in World War II; that he had become increasingly vainglorious to the point even of writing his own encomiums, and that he had set up "serious obstacle[s] in the path of Soviet social development."

Thus, the burden of the speech was to put the blame for the evils of Stalinism on Stalin's personal shortcomings, while seeking to make clear that the dictator's associates, including many of those on the Congress podium—and the speaker himself—had been powerless to alter those terrible events.

This extraordinary speech marked the start of a 10-year de-Stalinization of Soviet life.

In speaking out with such uncompromising bluntness, Mr. Khrushchev exhibited some of the brash daring that characterized his 10 years (from 1954 to 1964) as one of the world's most powerful men. The risk was obvious. Could Stalin's reputation be denigrated without destroying the structure of the system that had made him possible?

Apart from presiding over the vast changes that flowed from de-Stalinization, Mr. Khrushchev put new emphasis on the bread-and-butter goals of Communism. ("And what sort of Communist society is it that has no sausage?" he often asked.)

Moreover, he championed a policy of peaceful coexistence between Socialist and capitalist states. He also accepted some national differences among Socialist countries, as in the mixed economies of Poland and Yugoslavia; but not in Hungary, where he dealt with attempted revolt in 1956 as counterrevolution.

Mr. Khrushchev introduced a new style into Soviet politics. Whereas Stalin was reclusive, his successor was a tireless traveler and speaker who became intimately acquainted with the cities, towns and villages of his country. Just as he journeyed about his own country, so he traveled extensively in the world outside.

Some of the very extrovert traits that gave Mr. Khrushchev his human dimensions accounted for his downfall. By nature an impatient and impulsive man, he promised his people more than he could deliver. Economic and bureaucratic dislocation contributed heavily to his ouster. And not the least of those who turned against him were the bureaucrats whose traditional ways and power relationships he threatened.

Another ingredient in Mr. Khrushchev's ouster was the failure of his gamble in the Cuban missile crisis of 1962. Many in the Kremlin believed that the affair was a first-class miscalculation.

He was damaged also by the American U-2 spy plane incident in 1960 and the subsequent breakup of a Paris summit meeting with President Eisenhower. Mr. Khrushchev had insisted to his colleagues that President Eisenhower was a reasonable man and that statesmen could promote international amity through personal understandings. This homespun theory was severely strained when the U-2 was shot down over the Soviet Union and Mr. Eisenhower took the responsibility.

Ranged against him, too, were powerful voices in the army who were dismayed by his schemes to achieve defense at the lowest possible cost.

Mr. Khrushchev also caused alarm by the escalation of his quarrel with Mao Tse-tung, the Chinese leader. The Soviet leader's China policy seemed to many Soviet and other Communists to threaten the fraternal spirit of world Communism.

And there was Mr. Khrushchev's willfulness as well as an increasing tendency to take the spotlight. His enemies accused him of both lack of foresight and building a cult of personality.

His shortcomings more than outweighed his virtues in the eyes of his colleagues, and he was pensioned off in October, 1964. But it was a measure of the changes he had wrought that he was voted out of office, not shot, and that some of his key policies, such as peaceful coexistence and arms limitation and emphasis on Soviet consumer needs, were taken up by his successors.

He was uncomfortable with intellectuals and impatient with abstract theory. It was as a practical man that Mr. Khrushchev rose from lowly beginnings to the top in the Communist hierarchy.

He was born April 17, 1894, in Kalinovka, a poor village in Kursk Province, where Great Russia borders on the Ukraine. His father, he said, was a farmer who worked in the coal mines in the winter.

When the Revolution began in 1917, Mr. Khrushchev was active in practical measures in its defense and was a member of the Rutchenkovo Soviet.

In the civil war he fought as a member of the Red Guards. When it ended, he returned to Rutchenkovo as a party organizer.

His climb up the party ladder began in earnest in 1922, when he was sent to the Don Technical College at Yuzovka to remedy his lack of formal education and to become acquainted with Marxism.

At the college he was named party secretary, a post of considerable importance. On graduation, Mr. Khrushchev was appointed party secretary at Petrovo-Marinsky, a mining district in the Ukraine, where he distinguished himself for his bustling, firsthand knowledge of the mines.

He moved up in the party apparatus, first to Kharkov, then to Kiev and finally to Moscow, becoming second in command of the Moscow city party in 1933 and its chief in 1934. He gained membership in the party's Central Committee the same year, making him one of the hundred or so most powerful men in the Soviet Union, and in 1935 he became party leader for the entire Moscow region.

Mr. Khrushchev's principal job was in the modernization of Moscow and especially in the construction of its subway, for which he received his first Order of Lenin.

His time in Moscow coincided with what has been called the Soviet Union's "Iron Age," when heavy industry and industrial construction were stressed. It was also a period of forced collectivization of agriculture, in which hundreds of thousands of peasants died, and of the "show trials" in which Stalin's opponents were obliged to confess to horrendous crimes before they were executed. Of the 139 members of the Central Committee elected with Mr. Khrushchev in 1934, about 100 were arrested and shot by 1938.

Having survived the worst of the purges, Mr. Khrushchev was elected to the Politburo in 1938 and dispatched to the Ukraine as first secretary of the party there. His toughness is said to have been unrelenting in successfully managing the Ukrainian economy.

After the Nazi invasion in June, 1941, Mr. Khrushchev not only represented the party at the front but also directed partisan warfare behind the German lines. He took part in the initial severe setbacks of the Soviet Army in the Ukraine and in the triumphant stand at Stalingrad in 1942. For his efforts at Stalingrad, he was made a lieutenant general, and he marched with the Red army as it retook the Ukraine in 1943.

After the war Mr. Khrushchev was in charge of rebuilding the Ukraine, the most damaged of any area in Europe. In 1949 he was brought to Moscow as head of the party organization and as one of the Central Committee secretariat, which ran the party day by day.

Until Stalin's death in 1953, Mr. Khrushchev lived a somewhat precarious existence, he indicated in his speech in 1956. On other occasions he related that Stalin had forced him to dance a peasant dance and to sit in a puddle of beer. More seriously, the two differed about agriculture. Whereas Stalin was content to sweat the peasants, Mr. Khrushchev seemed genuinely concerned to increase party control over the farms, to create more efficient production units and to raise the standards of living. Mr. Khrushchev was relieved of supervision over farming.

Georgi M. Malenkov was Stalin's immediate successor, but in the wheeling and dealing he was either forced or persuaded to drop his job as principal party secretary while retaining the Soviet Premiership. This gave Khrushchev his opening, for he took over virtual control of the party organization—machinery that he knew best of all.

Mr. Khrushchev and Mr. Malenkov engaged in a duel for power with agriculture one of the main points of difference. By 1955, Mr. Khrushchev had strengthened his position sufficiently to strike down Mr. Malenkov. He accomplished this in part by getting army support. In the new alignment, Marshal Nikolai A. Bulganin was Premier and Mr. Khrushchev was the party leader. Together they were known as "B & K" and they consolidated power.

Meantime, in 1955, "B & K" made three journeys abroad, in which Mr. Khrushchev displayed his energies and his extroversions to an astonished world. One important trip was to Belgrade, where he apologized to Marshal Tito, the Yugoslav Communist leader, for Stalin's expulsion of him from the Communist world in 1948. The reconciliation was never complete, but there was a general accommodation.

Later, "B & K" went to Geneva, where they met President Eisenhower and the leaders of France and Britain and reiterated Soviet commitment to peaceful coexistence.

One of his greatest foreign policy victories was in the Mideast. In 1955 he arranged an arms deal with Egypt that opened the way for large-scale expansion of Soviet influence among the Arab peoples. He was also successful in wooing such countries as India and Indonesia.

Although Mr. Khrushchev was clearly the chief Soviet leader from 1954, his position was vastly enhanced by his speech at the party Congress in 1956. By emphasizing the corrective steps the party had taken since 1953, and was prepared to take, the speech cast Mr. Khrushchev in a favorable light. Eventually, it contributed to the routing of hard-liners.

Restiveness first showed itself in Poland in October, 1956, when the Poles proposed to install as party leader Wladislaw Gomulka, a "nationalist" Communist whom Stalin had jailed. Mr. Khrushchev threatened the use of force to prevent a Polish defection. Mr. Gomulka, however, stood his ground and won out after pledging to keep Poland within the Moscow bloc.

Immediately thereafter trouble broke out in Hungary. A de-Stalinized government under Imre Nagy announced that Hungary would leave the Warsaw Pact, the Eastern counterpart of the North Atlantic Treaty Organization.

This, to Mr. Khrushchev's mind, amounted to counterrevolution, and the Nagy regime was crushed with Soviet tanks. The difference between Poland and Hungary appeared to be that the Poles were willing to remain within the Soviet orbit.

Mr. Khrushchev's triumph over his Kremlin foes was complete in 1957, when he became both Premier and party leader—the same dual role occupied by Stalin.

For more than six years he ruled without serious challenge. He grew cocky and domineering with his colleagues, unable to believe, until it was too late, that he could be deposed.

In these six years, Mr. Khrushchev had his diplomatic ups and downs with the United States. One of the ups was his visit to the United States in 1959, which followed a "debate" with Vice President Richard M. Nixon in Moscow over the relative merits of capitalism and Communism. The impromptu exchange took place in a model kitchen at the American Exhibition there.

Arriving in the United States, the Soviet leader got a decidedly mixed reception. Mr. Khrushchev, however, came bearing olive branches, saying if "the two biggest countries in the world" could develop amicable relations, "peace on earth will be more stable and durable."

The U-2 spy plane episode and the questionable result of the Cuban missile crisis weakened his support among Soviet leaders, as did his appearance in 1960 at the United Nations General Assembly. While Harold Macmillan, the British Prime Minister, was addressing the Assembly, Mr. Khrushchev interrupted him with heckling shouts and table-thumping.

Oblivious to decorum, he took off his right shoe, brandished it at one speaker and then pounded it on his desk. And he referred to a Philippine delegate as a stooge and a jerk. After 25 days, he returned home.

The end to the Cuban adventure also cost Mr. Khrushchev dearly in his worsening quarrel with Mao Tse-tung, who saw it as yet another example of his inability to deal with American "imperialism." But Mr. Khrushchev and his Soviet colleagues were unwilling to go on the offensive against the United States.

As bitterness with China escalated, Mr. Khrushchev was faced with discontent at home. Harvests were poor; grain had to be imported from the United States, and in 1962 meat and butter prices were raised.

All of these things came to a boil in October, 1964, when members of the Politburo were quietly called to a meeting, with Leonid I. Brezhnev in the chair. Mr. Khrushchev was on holiday in the Black Sea. The vote went against him both in the Politburo and in the Central Committee. It was all over quickly and without fanfare.

DAVID BEN-GURION

October 16, 1886–December 1, 1973

TEL AVIV—David Ben-Gurion, a founding father of modern Israel and its first Premier, died today at the age of 87. He succumbed at 11:06 A.M. local time (4:06 A.M. New York time) to a brain hemorrhage that had struck him two weeks ago.

Because of the Sabbath, the Government withheld an official announcement until sundown tonight.

Premier Golda Meir convened the Cabinet for a memorial meeting in Jerusalem tonight.

The start of a funeral service on Monday will be marked by sirens throughout the country and two minutes of silence will be observed. In Jerusalem work will stop for an hour during the service.

The coffin will then be flown for burial to Sde Boker, the collective settlement in the Negev where Mr. Ben-Gurion made his home after he retired temporarily from the premiership in 1953.

An official announcement tonight said that public participation in the funeral would be restricted because of the emergency situation after the October war.

In recent years Mr. Ben-Gurion concentrated on his literary work. At the time of his stroke, he was preparing his memoirs for the year 1937.

By Homer Bigart

David Ben-Gurion symbolized the tough little state of Israel. Short, round, with a nimbus of white hair flaring angrily from a massive head, "B-G," as he was known to many, attained world leadership by firmly concentrating on the achievement of a dream.

That dream, the birth and triumphant survival of a Jewish homeland amid a sea of hostile Arabs, led Mr. Ben-Gurion through a lifetime of turmoil.

He was chairman of the Jewish Agency, the executive body of the World Zionist Organization, through the critical years of rising Arab nationalism, of Nazism, of World War II and of the postwar diplomatic struggle between Britain and the Jews of Palestine.

When Britain finally gave up the Palestine mandate, it was Mr. Ben-Gurion who proclaimed the Jewish state.

This was his moment of supreme test. For on that same day, May 14, 1948, the Arab armies began their invasion of the fledgling state.

Exhilarated by the challenge, the 62-year-old leader put on battle dress and assumed the direction of military operations. He was de facto Premier and Minister of Defense.

To Mr. Ben-Gurion fell most of the credit for having won the first Jewish campaign since that of Judas Maccabaeus 2,000 years before.

He became an almost mystical figure to many Zionists: the wise patriarch who embodied all the traditional virtues and who would ultimately lead Israel to triumph over the ring of Arab enemies.

But he embittered millions of others. He alarmed the United Nations and ensured the continued hatred of the Arab states by adopting a policy of swift and ruthless retaliation for Arab raids on Israel. Although an armistice was arranged by the United Nations, technically Jordan, Lebanon, Syria and Egypt remained at war with Israel, and border incidents were frequent after the war of 1948–49.

Mr. Ben-Gurion also alienated many American Jews by insisting that all true Zionists must live in Israel. Disturbed by the influx of Oriental Jews, which he feared would transform Israel into "just another Levantine state," Mr. Ben-Gurion dreamed of a vast migration of Jews from the Soviet Union and the United States.

With the 1967 and 1973 wars and increased United States aid, the old man's idea of Zionism came to be the accepted one. By 1970, American immigration to Israel was reaching 10,000 a year.

At home, Mr. Ben-Gurion managed to roil elements of the population, even members of his own Mapai party, by methods that often seemed autocratic. He never enjoyed sharing authority, and he chafed under Israel's system of proportional representation, which assures religious parties of representation in the government.

The Mapai party, although dominant, was never able to win a clear majority in the Knesset, or Parliament; this was a cause of the formation of 11 coalition governments in Israel, including the provisional government that was set up in April, 1948. In March, 1949, Mr. Ben-Gurion became Premier in the first regularly constituted Government of Israel.

These political marriages into coalitions were usually brief and stormy. The Socialist Mapai had little in common with the small left-wing labor parties and religious groups that were persuaded to join coalitions in exchange for concessions in legislation or for a ministerial post or two.

Mr. Ben-Gurion resigned several times, but his retirements to Sde Boker were fleeting except for one interval: In December, 1953, he turned over his office and leadership, explaining that he felt "tired, tired, tired."

In February, 1955, he was called to Jerusalem to resume the post of Minister of Defense, which he had held throughout his Premiership. He also assumed leadership of the Mapai and again became Premier in November, 1955.

Under Mr. Ben-Gurion, Israel adopted a policy that led to war. There had been a flurry of frontier incidents. Israel complained that the United Nations truce supervision teams were futile instruments for checking Arab commando raids. Mr. Ben-Gurion mounted large-scale retaliatory operations aimed at destroying what he called guerrilla bases across the frontier.

In December, 1955, after Syrians had fired on Israeli fishing craft in the Sea of Galilee, Mr. Ben-Gurion ordered his army into Syrian territory. A network of Syrian coastal positions was blown up, and 50 Syrian soldiers were killed.

Tensions continued to rise, and during the summer of 1956 he told his Parliament that the greatest menace to Israel was an impending attack by "the Egyptian Fascist dictator," President Gamal Abdel Nasser. He proclaimed: "We will never start a war."

Two weeks later, in complicity with France and Britain, he launched a "preventive war" to knock out President Nasser's army.

Mr. Ben-Gurion's objective was the fall of President Nasser and the signing of a peace treaty with Egypt.

The invasion by the three nations was on the verge of success.

Then the roof fell in. President Dwight D. Eisenhower was furious at Britain and France for having committed open aggression while the West was reaping moral capital over the Hungarian revolt. So the United States supported United Nations demands that the invading forces vacate Egypt promptly and unconditionally.

Confronted also by threats of Soviet intervention, Britain and France withdrew their forces in 27 days.

Mr. Ben-Gurion defied the world for weeks, flouting six successive General Assembly orders to get out of Egypt. But when President Eisenhower cut short a vacation to warn of "pressure" if Israel failed to cooperate, the tough little Premier knew the game was up.

The collapse of the Sinai adventure was the bleakest moment in Mr. Ben-Gurion's career.

Israel's man of decision was born in Plonsk, Poland, on Oct. 16, 1886. His name was David Green, and his father was Avigdor Green, an unlicensed lawyer who wore a silk top hat and a frock coat rather than the fur hat and caftan traditionally worn by the men of his community. David was to adopt the pen name "Ben-Gurion" as a journalist in Jerusalem. He thought it had a resonant Old Testament ring—it was the name of one of the last defenders of Jerusalem against the Roman legions. The Hebrew word "Ben" means "Son of," and "Gurion" means "Lion Cub."

Mr. Ben-Gurion's formal education did not go much beyond the Plonsk Jewish schools, but he acquired an excellently stocked mind through wide reading, particularly in history. He achieved a brilliant reputation as a linguist through his mastery of English, Russian, Greek, Yiddish, Turkish, French and German. He read but did not speak Arabic. He also studied Spanish.

In 1906, kindled by Theodor Herzl's aim for a Jewish commonwealth, David Green was one of a group of young Plonsk Jews who went to Palestine. Of his first night there he wrote in a letter to his father: "I did not sleep. I was amid the rich smell of corn. I heard the braying of donkeys and the rustle of leaves in the orchards. Above were massed clusters of stars against the deep blue firmament. My heart overflowed with happiness."

The Balfour Declaration of 1917 established the principle of a Jewish homeland in Palestine, and in 1922 the British were entrusted by the League of Nations with a mandate for Palestine.

Mr. Ben-Gurion spent years campaigning for the union of Palestine's labor parties, and in 1930 the Mapai was formed. In 1935 he became chairman of the Jewish Agency, the executive body of Zionism.

British policy became clearly pro-Arab, and in 1939 the British Government issued a White Paper that limited Jewish immigration to Palestine and land purchases there, and was aimed at ensuring a permanent minority status for the Jews there.

When Britain declared war on Germany, the Jews in Palestine pledged support against the common enemy but continued their resistance to the British policy.

In 1945 he visited displaced-persons camps in Germany, and the next year told a conference of survivors: "We shall not rest until the last one of you who so desires shall join us in the land of Israel to build the Jewish state together with us."

After the United Nations, on Nov. 29, 1947, resolved to partition Palestine into Jewish and Arab states, Mr. Ben-Gurion assumed the security portfolio of the Jewish Agency Executive.

For 15 years Mr. Ben-Gurion made most of the decisions for Israel. The most fateful were to come after he had returned to Jerusalem in 1955 and had begun leading the nation on a more adventurous path.

Mr. Ben-Gurion was a profound student of the Bible. His speeches were enriched with references to the heroes and prophets of the Old Testament. He had had little formal education, but his intellectual curiosity led him, at 56, to learn Greek so he could read the Septuagint, the Greek version of the Old Testament. At 68 his interest turned to the Dialogues of Buddha, and he began learning Sanskrit to understand them fully.

He already knew enough yoga to stand on his head, and photos of Mr. Ben-Gurion in bathing trunks, inverted on the Mediterranean sands, invoked wry comment. Friends insisted, however, that Hazaken—the Old Man—as he was affectionately called, was sharper-witted upside down than most of his opponents right side up.

Eventually Mr. Ben-Gurion suffered the bitter fate that overtakes a statesman who has been around too long. He became a bore to his people, and they rejected him. He remained in the Knesset until 1970—at the end as a member of the splinter party Rafi.

In his last years Mr. Ben-Gurion aged considerably. His white hair seemed to grow wispier, and his thoughts sometimes rambled. He spent much of his time in his cluttered study at Sde Boker, living among his books and in the past. There was a large portrait of his wife, a map of Israel, a vase of desert roses among the awards and mementos. On his desk, there was always a Bible and a bottle of apple juice.

CHIANG KAI-SHEK

October 31, 1887–April 5, 1975

TAIPEI, Taiwan, Sunday, April 6—Chiang Kai-shek, the President of Nationalist China and the last survivor of the Big Four Allied leaders of World War II, died of a heart attack here last night. He was 87 years old.

By Alden Whitman

Twenty-two years after rising to the leadership of China in a bloody coup against the Communists in 1927, Chiang Kai-shek lost power in 1949 in the Communist revolution. Thrust aside by the convulsion that shook half a billion people and an ancient culture, he spun out his long life on the small island of Taiwan in the East China Sea. There he presided sternly over a martial group of 2 million Nationalist refugees and about 11 million Taiwanese.

At first he talked aggressively of returning to the mainland by force; but as that possibility faded he waited hopefully for the Communist regime to collapse and for the Chinese to welcome him back.

That did not happen. The People's Republic of China grew in might, displacing Chiang's regime in the United Nations in 1971 and winning diplomatic recognition by 1972 from all the major powers except the United States. And even this country, as a result of President Nixon's visit to Peking in 1972, all but dropped Chiang diplomatically.

During his years as China's leader, Chiang ruled a restive country, beset by intractable domestic strife and Japanese invaders. Although China had a national government for these two decades, there was so much political, social and economic turmoil, so much Japanese aggression, that national unity was more fiction than reality.

Nonetheless, Chiang was the visible symbol of China; a member, with Franklin D. Roosevelt, Winston Churchill and Josef Stalin, of the Big Four; his nation's supreme commander in World War II; and the principal architect of a domestic policy that aimed, however unsuccessfully, at internal stability.

Chiang faced Herculean tasks once his National Government at Nanking was recognized by the Western powers in November, 1928. He sought political unification by force of arms rather than attacking fundamental social and economic problems. Only later, and under enormous pressure, did he turn his attention to rebuffing the Japanese.

The choice proved unwise, for his campaigns and his battles with local satraps permitted the Communists to befriend the peasantry, harness the forces of social revolution that had been gathering since 1911 and, ultimately, to align themselves with a nascent nationalism in the anti-Japanese war.

Had China been more than a geographical expression in the nineteen-twenties, Chiang might have imposed a viable government on it. But the weaknesses of the social system were such that his regime was enmeshed in corruption and guile.

Yet to many Americans Chiang was a heroic and embattled figure, the embodiment of a "new" China struggling to adapt politically and culturally to the 20th century. He was widely pictured as indomitable and as a bulwark against Communism in Asia.

From the nineteen-forties onward, Chiang's chief promoters were collectively known as the China Lobby. It included Mrs. Claire Chennault, widow of the Flying Tiger leader; William Loeb, the New Hampshire publisher; and Henry R. Luce, the publisher of Time, Life and Fortune, whose periodicals published eulogistic articles about Chiang and optimistic assessments of the situation in China.

From 1945 to 1949, the China Lobby pressured Congress and the Administration for military and economic aid to Chiang, much of which was reported to have been pocketed by his generals. The lobby savaged Foreign Service officers who had long warned of Chiang's fatal shortcomings.

Although it seemed evident to many that his Taiwan regime was not a world power, it retained not only its membership in the United Nations but also its seat as a permanent member of the Security Council until 1971. The United States consistently voted against the admission of the People's Republic to the United Nations, and it was widely supported in this policy by Americans who saw desertion of Chiang as a betrayal of an old ally.

Another aspect of Chiang that appealed to many in this country was his conversion to Protestantism—he joined the Methodist Church in 1931—and his professed devotion to New Testament ideals. Unlike some of his associates, Chiang Kai-shek, whose given name can be rendered in English as "Firm Rock," led an austere and frugal life.

Chiang clung to a traditional belief in a system of personal loyalty, in which the subject was loyal to the ruler, the son to the father, the younger to the older. This led to situations where he imputed disloyalty to his critics; it also led to his reliance on a very small circle of advisers.

Chiang was born in the waning years of the Manchu Dynasty, on Oct. 31, 1887, at Fenghua, Chekiang Province, 100 miles south of Shanghai. He was the son of a petty salt merchant and his "second wife," or concubine. His father died when he was nine, and Chiang had a grim childhood.

Yet somehow he got into the Paoting Military Academy, where he did well enough to be sent to Japan in 1907 for two years of advanced instruction. There he became acquainted with Chinese revolutionaries, including, it is said, Dr. Sun Yat-sen, a founder of modern China.

Chiang joined a secret society that was the forerunner of the Kuomintang, the Nationalist party, which he dominated after Dr. Sun's death in March, 1925. When revolts broke out in China in October, 1911, Chiang resigned from the Japanese Army (he had signed up as an officer), returned to the mainland and took the field against the Manchu forces.

At some point he apparently had a falling out with Dr. Sun and went into private business in Shanghai. But around 1921 or 1922, Chiang returned to military-political life as chief of staff of Dr. Sun's Canton-based regime. Rickety and in constant clash with warlords and with the shadowy official government in Peking, this regime sought and received military and political help from the newly established Soviet Union.

Chiang was sent to Moscow to help organize this assistance. Scores of Soviet advisers went to China and became influential in the Kuomintang. Chiang, as another consequence of the mission, organized a military academy that trained officers for the Kuomintang army.

With Dr. Sun's death the bond between Communists and Chiang's more conservative group in the Kuomintang dissolved. In a tragedy of plot and counterplot, Chiang slaughtered thousands of Communists and workers in Canton and Shanghai and, in 1927–28, organized his own National Government at Nanking.

According to some China specialists, Chiang was materially helped by Shanghai financial interests and landowners. In return, he excluded left-wing elements and Communists from the new National Revolutionary Government. The bargain was cemented by his marriage to the American-educated Soong Mei-Ling. Members of her powerful banking family were given key Government and party posts.

With the coup that brought Chiang to power, the Chinese Communist party was shattered. Its leaders and some members fled the coastal cities and found refuge in the mountains. Over the next few years Chiang, with the advice of imported Nazi generals, sought to eliminate the Communists. But after breaking free of an attempt to trap them, the Communists conducted the epic Long March to safety in the northwest.

Chiang's regime became a loose coalition of military chieftains bound to Chiang by pledges of personal loyalty. His programs seemed irrelevant in the face of Japanese aggression. Alarmed by the possibility that the Japanese would strike southward, the northern warlords rebelled in 1936.

In theory up to then, these warlords, principally Marshal Chang Hsueh-Liang, were battling the Communists in Shensi; but, in fact, little blood was being shed. Chiang arrived in Sian, Marshal Chang's capital in December, 1936, to investigate and was arrested on Chang's orders.

Chang presented his nominal superior with a series of demands that included immediate cessation of the civil war against the Communists in favor of a general policy of armed resistance to Japan. Some insurgents wanted to execute Chiang, but he was saved by the intervention of the Communist leader Chou En-lai. Chiang capitulated and was released.

The Japanese struck south from Peking in 1937–38. The ferocity of the onslaught, while it held the united front together for a time, drove Chinese troops out of key coastal cities and obliged the Government to shift its capital from Nanking to the smaller interior city of Chungking.

With United States entry into World War II in late 1941, American strategists saw China as a potentially effective front against Japan. However, Chiang's relations with Americans were less than cordial, especially those with Gen. Joseph W. Stilwell, who was sent to Chungking in 1942 as Chiang's chief of staff.

General Stilwell, who loved the Chinese and spoke their language, was President Roosevelt's choice to be commander of Chinese and American forces in China. But Chiang and the outspoken general, whose nickname was "Vinegar Joe," fell out. In his report to the War Department, General Stilwell said that Chiang sought to "dominate rather than unify and lead" China. (In private, General Stilwell called Chiang "the peanut.")

By 1944, with the military situation in China in disarray save in the Communist-controlled areas, President Roosevelt cabled Chiang urging that General Stilwell be given command of the Nationalist troops. "With further delay, it may be too late to avert a military catastrophe," the President said.

However, according to "Stilwell and the American Experience in China," by Barbara Tuchman, Chiang intended to stay out of the war "no matter how much of east China was lost, until the Allies should defeat Japan and he could emerge on the winning side."

Chiang interposed conditions, among them control of millions of American Lend-Lease supplies lest any arms get into the hands of the Communists, whose efficient troops General Stilwell wanted to use against the Japanese. The Communists, Mrs. Tuchman wrote, were willing to fight under the general, but not under Chiang.

Chiang wanted effective authority over the general in strategy and tactics. Chiang feared, according to Mrs. Tuchman, that if the Americans succeeded in imposing Stilwell on him "they might do likewise in the matter of the Communists." The result was Chiang's demand for General Stilwell's recall, to which a weary President Roosevelt acceded.

Chiang's hold on the Nationalist leadership was prolonged by Japan's surrender. In December, 1945, President Truman sent Gen. George C. Marshall to China to unify and pacify the country. On Jan. 10, 1946, a cease-fire was signed, but it was quickly breached, and before long there was civil war. With 3 million troops to Mao Tse-tung's 1 million, Chiang gained the early upper hand, but by the spring of 1947 it was clear where the initiative lay.

As Communist forces were overrunning the country, the State Department issued a 1,054-page White Paper, writing off Nationalist China. "A large proportion of the military supplies furnished the Chinese armies by the United States . . . has fallen into the hands of the Chinese Communists through the military ineptitude of the Nationalist leaders, their defections and surrenders, and the absence among their forces of the will to fight," Secretary of State [Dean] Acheson wrote.

The generalissimo resigned as President on Jan. 1, 1949. Soon, he retreated to Taiwan, where he imposed tight military and police control. On March 1, 1950, he announced that he had resumed the Presidency of China. Inaugurated for a fourth term in 1966, he vowed that one day he would return to the mainland "and establish on the ruins a new country of unity and freedom."

FRANCISCO FRANCO

December 4, 1892–November 20, 1975

MADRID—Generalissimo Francisco Franco died early today after 36 years of dictatorial rule over Spain. He was 82 years old.

The death of the Chief of State, who led rightist military forces to victory in the Spanish Civil War that ended in 1939, came at 4:30 A.M. at the La Paz Hospital. He had been rushed there on Nov. 7 from the Pardo Palace for surgery to stop internal bleeding.

His designated successor, Prince Juan Carlos de Borbón, 37, will be sworn in as King of Spain within 48 hours.

General Franco's death came while most Spaniards were sleeping and few were aware of the event for several hours. The death was ascribed to toxic shock produced by peritonitis.—*Henry Giniger*

By Alden Whitman

One of the most durable, canny and empirical of modern dictators, Francisco Paulino Hermenegildo

Teódulo Franco y Bahamonde became master of Spain as a result of a military conspiracy, a dash of luck, timely help from foreign corporations, the influence of the Roman Catholic hierarchy and crucial armed assistance from Hitler and Mussolini.

At the close of his long and sternly authoritarian rule, he could look back on 36 years of an imposed stability that rested on a policy of suppression of fundamental democratic rights. But it was also a stability that gave Spain a rising standard of living, industrial growth and an important alliance with the United States.

His regime, exceedingly harsh at the outset, was moderated somewhat from the middle of the nineteen-fifties into a condition of relative calm. Contributing to this was the memory of the Civil War, a renewal of which none of his organized opponents wanted to provoke.

There were outbursts against Franco, but these were put down. One of the last such episodes occurred in September, 1975, when five convicted Basque terrorists were executed despite protests from most of Western Europe and appeals for clemency from Pope Paul VI.

Coming to power after victory in a civil war that had devastated Spain, Franco clinched his grip on an impoverished and backward country by systematic terror. Then, by clever diplomacy, he took Spain through World War II as a nonbelligerent while averring his attachment to the Fascist powers. Exercising patience, he waited out years of international ostracism after the war, from which he was rescued by a United States decision in 1950 to acquire military bases in the country as a move in the cold war with the Soviet Union.

Now esteemed by the West, he was able in 1955 to have his nation admitted to the United Nations, which had expressly barred Spain in 1946 in a resolution asserting that "in origin, nature, structure and general conduct, the Franco regime is a Fascist regime."

After his diplomatic resurrection, Franco began to loosen the rigors of dictatorship. Foreign investment was encouraged, tourism was promoted, wage levels inched upward. By 1962 per capita income for the nation's 33 million people reached $300 a year and then quadrupled by 1972.

Most authoritarian restrictions remained. There was no press freedom; no trade unions were permitted; only one political party was allowed; the armed forces were omnipresent.

The technique of his rule was to spread power among rival factions—big business and its technocrats, landowners, the church, his own Falange party, the army—and to control their respective gains and losses of strength. He was thus the indispensable arbiter of all major decisions.

Franco was very much the product of 19th-century Spain and the tradition that sons of military officers should follow the father's profession. He was born Dec. 4, 1892, at El Ferrol, on the Galician coast, the son of Nicolás Franco, a naval officer, and Pilar Bahamonde

Franco. It is widely believed, although skirted officially, that Sephardic Jews were among his ancestors.

Commissioned a second lieutenant in the army in 1910 (the Naval Academy had no openings), he became in rapid succession its youngest captain, major, colonel and general. His star continued rising after Spain's incompetent monarchy was replaced in 1931 by a predominantly right-wing Republican Government.

In February, 1936, Spain elected a Popular Front Government, which was dominated by moderates and Socialists. As soon as the election returns were posted, a generals' plot against the Republic took shape. Franco, after some hesitation, joined the conspiracy.

That July, a private British plane carried Franco from the Canaries to Teután in Spanish Morocco, where he was to take command of Moorish and Spanish troops.

To get them to the Spanish mainland despite a Republican naval blockade, Franco accepted a German offer, authorized by Hitler and his Air Force chief, Hermann Goering, to supply some 20 heavy transport planes.

Nazi support, in the form of munitions and men, was to continue throughout the Civil War. The Nationalist rebels also received important support from the Italian dictator Benito Mussolini and from some elements of American business.

For a time, however, it seemed that the plotters might fail. When the three leading generals died—two killed in plane crashes, one captured and executed by the Government—Franco became the Nationalist leader.

The conflict was waged on both sides with great ferocity. One of history's most publicized experiments in calculated terror occurred in the Basque town of Guernica on market day, April 26, 1937. Aviators of the Nazi Condor Legion, in complicity with the Nationalist command, dropped high-explosive bombs on the townspeople, then machine-gunned them in flight. A total of 1,654 persons were killed and 889 wounded.

When the fighting ended in 1939, Franco ordered shot nearly all captured Republican officers, and his prisons contained thousands of so-called "Reds," many of whom were also executed.

World War II, which began in the fall of 1939, put Franco in a difficult position. His sympathies were with Hitler and Mussolini, but his nation was too desolated to join the fighting. Meeting with Mussolini in Italy in February, 1941, he affirmed an "identity of views" between Spain and Italy. Later that month he wrote Hitler:

"I consider as you do yourself that the destiny of history has united you with myself and with the Duce in an indissoluble way."

Shortly after the American troop landings in North Africa in November, 1942, President Franklin D. Roosevelt told Franco that the Allies harbored no aggressive intentions toward Spain. In reply, Franco cited the "relations of friendship which unite our people and which should be preserved."

After the war, nonetheless, the Allies put Franco temporarily beyond the pale, and the United States and many other nations withdrew their ambassadors or ministers from Madrid.

The diplomatic boycott of Franco Spain ended in fact if not in name in November, 1950—a consequence of the cold war between the United States and the Soviet Union, in which Spain occupied a geographically important place.

Several months before the boycott was lifted, Congress approved a $62.5 million loan to Spain. In 1951 the United States installed an Ambassador in Madrid, and in 1952 Franco declared that "Spain is now sought after by those who in years past scorned our offer to cooperate against Communism."

The following year Spain allowed the United States to use "a number of Spanish air and naval bases for the defense of Western Europe and the Mediterranean." The United States poured into Spain more than $1.5 billion in economic assistance and more than $500 million in military help over the next decade.

For all the pervasiveness of his power, Franco—Caudillo "by the Grace of God," Generalissimo of the Armies of Land, Sea and Air, and Chief of State for life—was among the least majestic of modern rulers.

Standing but 5 feet 3 inches tall, he looked gnomish even in his general's gold-trimmed, olive drab uniform with red silk sash. Unlike Hitler or Mussolini, he never harangued multitudes or stirred them to fervor. He spoke publicly no more than three or four times a year, in a high voice with a slight lisp. His round, mustached face was immobile, and his brown eyes were appraising and chill.

On public occasions, he waved in his stiff, almost timid manner and forced a smile here and there; but there seemed to be almost no rapport between him and the population. Crowds regarded him as more of an institution than as a person.

At El Pardo, the former royal hunting lodge on the outskirts of Madrid where Franco lived and worked, his ormolu-mounted desk and a nearby table were piled with reports and memorandums, virtually all of them unread. "When the piles become too high," he once told Prince Juan Carlos, "I have everything taken out from the bottom and burned."

Franco was celebrated for his secretiveness. "Not even his collar knows what he is thinking," an associate once remarked. It was not uncommon for a subordinate, even a minister, to leave an audience convinced that he had made a splendid impression and the next morning to receive a letter from Franco thanking him for his services and informing him that he had been replaced.

Franco was much flattered by the controlled press, radio and television. It was not unusual for him to be ranked above Augustus, Charles V and Napoleon. About 50 towns caught the spirit of this sycophancy and added his name.

He also had constructed a Pharaonic tomb, in which he wanted to be buried. Called the Valley of the Fallen and dedicated to the Civil War dead, it is situated close to the Escorial, near Madrid. Carved out of living rock, the interior is a basilica, one of the world's largest, and is surmounted by a cross 500 feet tall. Franco took a detailed interest in its construction, which covered 15 years and cost millions. Irreverent Spaniards called it "Franco's folly," but it became a major tourist attraction.

An avid sportsman, the dictator liked to shoot mountain goats, deer, rabbits and partridges. His bag of these birds sometimes reached 300 a day.

Franco's cruelty was that of the centurion, impersonal and efficient. Once, inspecting troops as a colonel of the Spanish Foreign Legion, he had food thrown in his face by a legionnaire protesting its quality. It spattered his uniform, but his facial expression did not change, nor did he say a word. He merely took out his handkerchief, wiped off the food and continued the inspection. Returning to his office, he calmly called an officer, pointed out the offender and said: "Take that soldier out and execute him."

Franco's home life was simple. He dined with his family as often as possible, and lightly to keep his girth down. He was virtually a teetotaler, limiting himself to a glass of wine or beer at a meal. There was no hint of personal scandal in his private life. He had married Carmen Polo y Martínez Valdés, a young woman of good Asturian family, in 1923.

If Franco felt any reaction to criticism or had any self-doubt, it was not observable. Indeed, he had a Moslem-like fatalism, the "maktoob" ("It is written") of the Moroccan rifleman. Horses were shot beneath him. Once a bullet struck a flask from which he was drinking. Leading an assault in 1916, he was shot through the abdomen, but recovered uneventfully.

A similar fatalism, or impassivity, seemed to attend Franco in moments of domestic tension as, for example, when the five Basque terrorists were executed in September. Although the Vatican and most Western European countries protested or asked for clemency, he had the sentences carried out.

The executions also led to speeches at the United Nations and to threatened economic sanctions by the Common Market. The regime, however, did not appear to be swayed.

MAO TSE-TUNG

December 26, 1893–September 9, 1976

PEKING—Mao Tse-tung, the pre-eminent figure of the Chinese Communist revolution and the leader of his country since 1949, died today at the age of 82.

His death, at 12:10 A.M. after a long illness, left uncertain the question of who was to succeed him. There is no designated heir, nor is there anyone among his subordinates who commands the awe and reverence with which he was regarded among the 800 million Chinese.

Funeral music followed today's announcement broadcast over the Peking radio, and 2,000 people gathered in the vast Tien An Men Square, many wearing black armbands, some weeping. Flags fluttered at half staff.

While the official announcement did not specify the illness, which had kept Mao out of the public eye for months, it was widely believed that the chairman had been suffering from Parkinson's disease. —*Reuters*

By Fox Butterfield

Mao Tse-tung, who began as an obscure peasant, died one of history's great revolutionary figures.

Born at a time when China was racked by civil strife, beset with terrible poverty and encroached on by more advanced foreign powers, he lived to fulfill his boyhood dream of restoring it to its traditional place as a great nation.

With incredible perseverance and consummately conceived strategy, he harnessed the forces of agrarian discontent and nationalism to turn a tiny band of peasants into an army of millions, which he led to victory throughout China in 1949 after 20 years of fighting. Along the way the army fought battles as big as Stalingrad and suffered through a heroic march as long as Alexander's.

Then, after establishing the Chinese People's Republic, Mao launched a series of sweeping, sometimes convulsive campaigns to transform a semifeudal, largely illiterate and predominantly agricultural country encompassing a fifth of the world's population into a modern, industrialized socialist state. By the time of his death China had manufactured its own nuclear bombs and guided missiles and had become a major oil producer.

With China's resurgence, Mao also charted a new course in foreign affairs, putting an end to a century of humiliation under the "unequal treaties" imposed by the West. Finally, in 1972, even the United States abandoned its 20 years of implacable hostility when President Richard M. Nixon journeyed to Peking, where he was received by a smiling Mao.

At the same time Mao brooked no opposition to his control. To consolidate his new regime in the early 50's he launched a campaign in which hundreds of thousands were executed. In the late 50's, despite criticism from other party leaders, he ordered the Great Leap Forward, ultimately causing widespread disruption and food shortages. Throughout his years in power he toppled one party rival after another. In the Cultural Revolution of the 1960's he risked throwing the country into chaos.

While China achieved enormous economic progress under Mao, some critics felt his constant political campaigns and his emphasis on conformity finally reduced many Chinese to a dispirited, anxious mass ready to go along with the latest shift in the political wind.

One of the most remarkable personalities of the 20th century, Mao was an infinitely complex man—by turns shrewd and realistic, then impatient and a romantic dreamer, an individualist but also a strict disciplinarian. His motives seemed a mixture of the humanitarian and the totalitarian. He himself once commented that he was "part monkey, part tiger," and perhaps after all he was riven with the same contradictions that he was fond of analyzing in the world around him.

A Chinese patriot, a combative revolutionary, a fervent evangelist, a Marxist theorist, a soldier, a statesman and poet, above all Mao was a moralist who deeply believed, as have Chinese since Confucius, that man's goodness must come ahead of his mere economic progress. Angered by the insults of imperialism, he wanted to tear China down to make it stronger. He envisioned creating in China an egalitarian, revolutionary utopia in which mass enthusiasm provided the motive force.

"I have witnessed the tremendous energy of the masses," Mao wrote in 1958 in the midst of the Great

Leap Forward. "On this foundation it is possible to accomplish any task whatsoever." The two sentences are a striking summary of his thought.

Unlike many great leaders, Mao never exercised, or sought, absolute control over day-to-day affairs. But the man who rose from humble beginnings in a Hunan village became virtually sovereign, if not a living god, to the Chinese. His very words were the doctrine of the state. Printed in millions of little red plastic-bound books as "Quotations from Chairman Mao Tse-tung," they were taken to possess invincible magic properties.

Although Mao was a devoted Leninist who stressed the need for a tightly organized and disciplined party, he came to cast himself above his party and sought to replace it with a personal cult when it thwarted him.

Despite awesome power and prestige, in the later years of his life—from about 1960 onward—he seemed obsessed by anxieties that the Chinese revolution was in danger of slipping back into the old elitism and bureaucratic ways of imperial China.

To revitalize China, to cleanse the party and to ensure that the revolution survived him, Mao launched the Great Proletarian Cultural Revolution in 1966. As he conceded later, it had consequences even he did not foresee.

Hundreds of thousands of youngsters were mobilized as Red Guards. Often unruly, given to fighting among themselves, they roamed the country and humiliated and chastised Mao's opponents in the party after his call to "bombard the headquarters."

After two years of turmoil, economic disruption and even bloodshed, order was finally restored. But Mao had severely undermined the critical and long-standing unity of the party, forged in the 1930's during the epochal Long March—an anabasis of 6,000 miles that took the fledgling army over mountains, rivers and wastelands from Kiangsi, in South China, to Shensi, in the northwest.

Foremost among those purged in the Cultural Revolution were Liu Shao-chi, head of state, and Teng Hsiao-ping, the Secretary General of the party, who were labeled "capitalist roaders." Defense Minister Lin Piao, Mao's "close comrade in arms and successor," died in a plane crash in Mongolia in 1971 and was later accused of plotting to kill Mao.

Mao made his last public appearance in 1971; in published photographs since then he often looked like a sick man. His apparent difficulty in controlling the movement of his hands and face and his slurred speech stirred speculation that he had suffered a stroke or had Parkinson's disease.

In recent years Mao had also been preoccupied with China's monumental quarrel with the Soviet Union, one of the pivotal developments of the postwar world.

Although few outsiders perceived it until the quarrel surfaced in the early 1960's, it is clear now that the trouble had its origin in the earliest contact between the Chinese Communists and the Russians in the 1920's. It was a period when Mao and others in the newly organized

Chinese party were groping for a way to power, and Stalin, from the distance of Moscow, gave them orders that repeatedly led them into disaster.

Mao was shorn of his posts and power in the early 1930's as a result of direct Soviet interference. It was only after the Communists were forced to begin the Long March in 1934, after more errors in strategy, that Mao won command because of his genius for organizing and leading peasant guerrillas in a revolution in the countryside.

Although Mao was to try the Soviet model of economic development, with its emphasis on heavy industry, by the mid-1950's he came to have doubts about it, and a history of uneasy relations descended into bitter wrangling and eventually open armed clashes.

Mao spent hours lecturing every visiting head of state on the danger of Soviet expansionism—hegemonism, as he termed it. His belief that Soviet "social-imperialism" was the greatest threat to peace enabled him to take a more sanguine view of the United States.

Although Mao commanded enormous authority, he shunned the trappings of might. He seldom appeared in public, perhaps to preserve a sense of awe and mystery, and he eschewed fancy dress or medals, in conformity with the simple standard he himself had set during his guerrilla days. Whatever the occasion, he wore only a plain gray tunic buttoned to the neck and trousers to match; it came to be called a Mao suit in the West and for a period in the 1970's became a fashion craze.

Some of Mao's dedication, toughness and reserve may have also been the product of his bitter personal experiences along the road to power. His sister and his second wife were executed in 1930 by the Nationalist leader, Generalissimo Chiang Kai-shek; a brother was killed in the Long March; another brother was executed in 1943 in Sinkiang, and Mao's eldest son was killed in the Korean War. (Mao was married four times, and is survived by his wife of 38 years, Chiang Ching, an outspoken, sometimes vitriolic woman who claimed the mantle of his most faithful disciple.)

Mao "never hesitated to employ violence whenever he believed it necessary," in the words of his biographer Stuart Schram. As Mao himself put it, in one of the most celebrated passages in his writing, about the peasant uprising he led in the late 1920's:

"A revolution is not the same as inviting people to dinner or writing an essay or painting a picture or embroidering a flower. . . . A revolution is an uprising, an act of violence whereby one class overthrows the authority of another. To put it bluntly, it was necessary to bring about a brief reign of terror in every rural area."

Mao Tse-tung was born in a tile-roofed house surrounded by rice fields and low hills in Shaoshan, a village in Hunan Province, in central China, on Dec. 26, 1893. His father, Mao Jen-sheng, was a tall, sturdily built peasant, industrious and thrifty, despotic and high-handed. Through hard work, saving and some small trading he raised himself from being a landless former soldier to what his son later described as the status of a "rich peasant."

Mao's mother, Wen Chi-mei, was a hardy woman who worked in the house and fields. A Buddhist, she exhibited a warm-hearted kindness toward her children much in contrast to her husband's patriarchal sternness. During famines, when her husband was not watching, she would give food to the poor who came begging.

The China into which Mao was born was a restive empire on the point of its final breakup. The mandarins who governed on behalf of the emperor in Peking seemed helpless to stop either the internal decay or the foreign incursions. China had no industry, and its peasants, 85 percent of the population, were mired in poverty and ignorance, subject to the constant threat of starvation and extortionate demands by landlords.

At age six Mao was set to work in the rice fields by his father, who frequently beat him and his two younger brothers and gave them only the most meager food, never meat or eggs. At 16, over his father's opposition, Mao enrolled in a modern school in a busy market town, where his real intellectual and political development began. In newspapers he learned of the nationalistic late 19th-century reformers, and in a book, "Great Heroes of the World," he read about Washington and Napoleon.

In 1918, at the age of 24, he set off for Peking. The timing was critical. The Manchu Dynasty had finally collapsed in 1911. It was a period when intellectuals were turning from one Western "ism" to another in search of the latest and most potent elixir to revive their nation. In Mao's case, as he later wrote, he arrived just when "the salvos of the October Revolution" in Russia were bringing Marxism to China.

Over the next few years he threw himself into organizing radical student groups and editing two popular journals that were suppressed by the local warlord government. In 1921, Mao and 11 other delegates met in Shanghai to form the Chinese Communist Party; filled with a new sense of zeal, he returned to Hunan, where, in orthodox Marxist fashion, he set about organizing labor unions and strikes. He had found his true vocation as a revolutionary.

At first the Communists were allied with the ruling Nationalists, but in 1927 the Nationalist leader, General Chiang, turned on the Communists and massacred thousands of them.

That fall Mao led a small band of supporters up into the Chingkangshan Mountains. It was a storybook setting: a range of precipitous mountains populated only by a few simple villages and groups of bandits. By allying with these bandits and drawing on the peasants, whom he rewarded by reducing rents, Mao built his band of 1,000 soldiers into 100,000 by 1934.

On Oct. 15, 1934, the vastly outnumbered Communist army broke through the Nationalist lines and began the Long March. Only 20,000 would reach the new base area in Shensi, in northwest China, over a year and 6,000 miles later. Yet for all its hardships, the march both saved and strengthened the Communists, giving them a legend of invincibility, a guerrilla ethic, a firm discipline and unity, and a new leader—Mao.

The most decisive stroke by Mao at this time was his genius in making the Communists, rather than the Nationalists, the incarnation of Chinese resistance to the Japanese, who had invaded the country in 1931. He was able to expand Communist areas across the whole of North China under the guise of fighting the Japanese, and by the end of the war, in 1945, Communist troops had grown into a formidable force of a million men covering an area inhabited by 100 million people.

In the civil war between Communists and the Nationalist Kuomintang, which broke out in 1946, General Chiang was vastly overconfident. He had American backing, apparent neutrality on the part of Stalin, who was not eager to see Mao win, and a four-to-one numerical advantage. But his army was racked by corruption, punishing inflation and an incompetent officer corps.

By the middle of 1947 the Nationalists' advantage had been reduced to two to one, and by mid-1948 the two sides were almost even. Nationalist generals began surrendering in packs, and within a year it was all over.

The supreme moment came on Oct. 1, 1949, when Mao, at age 55, stood on the high balcony of Tien An Men, the Gate of Heavenly Peace in Peking through which tribute-bearers had once come to prostrate themselves before the emperors, and proclaimed the People's Republic of China.

Processions had filled the square in front of the scarlet brass-studded gate. The air was chilly with the wind from the Gobi. Mao, wearing a drab cloth cap and a worn tunic and trousers, stood with his comrades Chou En-lai and Chu Teh. Below them the immense throng shouted: "May Mao Tse-tung live 10,000 years!"

Yet to the end, Mao remained uncertain of what would follow him. As he told the American journalist Edgar Snow in 1965, in 1,000 years even Marx and Lenin might "appear rather ridiculous."

Last year, in a poem addressed to the dying Chou En-lai, he put it more poignantly:

Now that the country has become red,
who will be its guardian?
Our mission, unfinished, may take a
thousand years.
The struggle tires us, and our hair
is gray.

The poem concludes: "You and I, old friends, can we just watch our efforts be washed away?"

ANWAR EL-SADAT

December 25, 1918–October 6, 1981

CAIRO—President Anwar el-Sadat of Egypt was shot and killed today by a group of men in military uniforms who hurled hand grenades and fired rifles at him as he watched a military parade commemorating the 1973 war against Israel.

The assassins' bullets ended the life of a man who earned a reputation for making bold decisions in foreign affairs, a reputation based largely on his decision in 1977 to journey to the camp of Egypt's foe, Israel, to make peace.

Regarded as an interim ruler when he came to power in 1970 on the death of Gamal Abdel Nasser, Mr. Sadat, 62, forged his own regime and ran Egypt single-handedly. He was bent on moving his impoverished country into the late 20th century, a drive that led him to abandon an alliance with the Soviet Union and embrace the West.

That rule ended abruptly and violently today. As jet fighters roared overhead, the killers sprayed the reviewing stand with bullets while thousands of horrified people looked on. —*William E. Farrell*

By Eric Pace

"Sadat! Sadat!" tens of thousands of Cairenes chanted at the grinning figure in the open limousine.

"Sadat! The man of peace!" It was the night of Nov. 21, 1977. President Anwar el-Sadat had just returned from his epochal journey to Jerusalem. Egypt's people were giving their frenzied approval to what his trip had achieved, an Egyptian-Israeli thaw that set the stage for the peace treaty of 1979.

What made Mr. Sadat into such a catalytic force in Middle Eastern history was a display of courage and flexibility that transformed what had seemed to be an average Arab officer-turned-potentate. Unlike all other Arab leaders, he was daring enough to do what had been unthinkable in the anguished world of Arab politics, extend the hand of peace to the Israeli foe, and proclaimed his willingness to accept Israel's existence as a sovereign state. Then, along with Presidents Carter and Reagan and Prime Minister Menachem Begin of Israel, he succeeded in keeping the rapprochement alive.

But he also drew outpourings of hatred from Palestinians and other Arabs who saw him as a traitor to their struggles against Israel. And he was unable to quash dissidence in his impoverished, seething homeland.

Eleven days before Mr. Sadat made his trip to Jerusalem, he said in Cairo that he was willing to go to "the ends of the earth" in the cause of peace. The Israeli Government made known that he was welcome in Jerusalem, and after complex negotiations he flew there, although a state of war still existed between the two nations. Hours later, he told the hushed Israeli Parliament, "If you want to live with us in this part of the world, in sincerity I tell you that we welcome you among us with all security and safety."

Mr. Sadat's flexibility, he said later, stemmed from his solitary confinement as a political prisoner in Cairo Central Prison in 1947 and 1948. "My contemplation of life and human nature in that secluded place taught me that he who cannot change the very fabric of his thought will never be able to change reality and will never, therefore, make any progress," he wrote in his memoirs, "In Search of Identity." His willingness to make such a change led to the treaty that he and Prime Minister Begin signed at the White House on March 26, 1979. Before reaching agreement the two men had drawn-out negotiations, for which they were the joint winners of the Nobel Peace Prize in 1978.

The treaty provided that Israel return to Egypt in phases the entire Sinai Peninsula, which the Israelis had seized in the 1967 war. It also envisioned internal autonomy for the Palestinian Arabs of the West Bank of the Jordan River under continued Israeli control. The Egyptian and Israeli Governments were helped by the Nixon and Carter Administrations.

Henry A. Kissinger, after many meetings with Mr. Sadat, wrote that the Egyptian leader "possessed that combination of insight and courage which marks a great statesman," adding, "He had the boldness to go to a war no one thought he could sustain; the moderation to move to peace immediately afterward; and the wisdom to reverse attitudes hardened by decades."

In dealings with Israel and the United States, Mr. Sadat strove to create a harmonious mood that would make it difficult for others to disagree with him. His most audacious use of that technique was the Jerusalem visit.

That gesture and the treaty with Israel brought him hatred and vituperation from many Arab leaders. There was particular outrage because the treaty provided no timetable for full self-determination for the West Bank Palestinians that would lead to an independent Palestinian state.

Self-determination was originally Mr. Sadat's minimum demand; when he settled for less, he found himself virtually isolated in the Arab world. Saudi Arabia's leaders cut back their aid to Egypt, a move that made Egypt more dependent than ever on support from the United States. Mr. Sadat won moral and political support from Washington and large-scale economic and military aid, and in 1975 became the first Egyptian President to make a state visit to the United States.

Many of the 40 million Egyptians, having gone through four painful and expensive wars with Israel, were enthusiastic about the peace treaty. Throngs of well-wishers waved signs and threw rose petals in celebration.

Under the treaty, Israel's withdrawal of its civilian and military forces from Sinai was to be carried out over three years. Two-thirds of the area was to be handed back within nine months after the exchange of formal ratification documents. In return for the Israeli pullback, Mr. Sadat agreed to establish peace. After the nine-month withdrawal was finished, the two Governments were to take up "normal and friendly relations." The early withdrawals were completed, and the final phase is scheduled for next April.

"This is certainly one of the happiest moments of my life," Mr. Sadat, deeply moved, said at the signing ceremony.

Another of his major shifts in policy was his departure from Nasser's longstanding pro-Soviet stance. In July 1972 he ordered the withdrawal of the 25,000 Soviet military specialists and advisers in Egypt.

The changes in the relationship with Washington and Moscow were made after Mr. Sadat had concluded that the Arabs could not achieve a satisfactory end to their confrontation with Israel as long as they were allied closely with the Soviet Union while Israel had the all-out support of the United States.

He was able to make such sharp policy shifts in part because for much of his later tenure as President his power did not seem to be seriously challenged at home. A career officer and longtime confidant of Nasser, he was named Vice President in 1969, and was made President by a rubber-stamp vote of members of the Arab Socialist Union, the only legal political organization. He consolidated and enlarged his power in the spring of 1971 when he forestalled what he said was a coup and arrested his opponents.

Mr. Sadat was widely popular with the Egyptian people, with whom he felt an almost mystic bond. He proudly called himself "a peasant born and brought up on the banks of the Nile." Early in his presidency, he eliminated many police-state controls that Nasser had relied on to keep himself in power in the years after the officers' revolt that brought down the monarchy in 1952. In 1973 Mr. Sadat did much to build national self-respect when he ordered Egyptian troops to cross the Suez Canal; they quickly overran the heavily fortified Israeli positions on the east bank. That confidence lingered, although the Israelis counterattacked, putting a large tank force on the west bank.

Mohammed Anwar el-Sadat was born Dec. 25, 1918, in Mit Abul Kom, a cluster of mud-brick buildings between Cairo and Alexandria. He was one of the 13 children of Mohammed el-Sadat, a Government clerk, and his part-Sudanese wife, a heritage manifest in the boy's skin, darker than the average Egyptian's.

Young Anwar's first schooling was at the hands of an Islamic cleric, who instilled in him a deep faith in Islam.

Like other idealistic Egyptians of his generation, Mr. Sadat wanted his country freed of the control of Britain, which had maintained troops there since the late 19th century. Deciding to become an officer, he gained admission to the Royal Military Academy. Graduating in 1938, he was assigned to an installation near the capital, and there became active in the formation of an organization of officers who wanted to mount an armed revolt against the British presence.

When World War II broke out, Captain Sadat made contact with Nazi agents in Cairo. When they were arrested, they implicated their contact. Captain Sadat was jailed, but ultimately escaped from prison.

In 1950 he was reinstated in the army. He was soon promoted, thanks to help from the dissident officers' clandestine network, which had been growing in size and power under the leadership of an old friend, Lieutenant Colonel Nasser.

The colonel summoned Major Sadat to a rendezvous in Cairo on July 22, 1952, saying the long-awaited uprising, now focused on King Farouk, would take place soon. Nasser did not appear, but that evening Major Sadat found a note from him saying that operations would begin that night and directing him to join the revolutionaries.

"My heart leapt," Mr. Sadat recalled. "I tore off my civilian clothes and threw on my uniform. In five minutes I was at the wheel of my car."

At army headquarters, where the rebels had taken control, Nasser told Mr. Sadat to take over the Cairo radio at dawn and broadcast the announcement of the coup. The revolution led to the exile of Farouk, the withdrawal of British troops from Egypt and the emergence of Nasser as President.

Mr. Sadat was named Vice President, and upon Nasser's death of a heart attack he automatically became Acting President. With his grin, fancy suits and frequent hollow-sounding vows to wage war on Israel, he did not seem to be a strong and purposeful leader. But he enhanced his popularity by displaying an intuitive sense of what the people wanted. He cut back the powers of the hated secret police, ousted the Soviet military experts, and early in 1973 decided to go to war against Israel.

After Moscow approved a limited Egyptian invasion of Sinai and more Soviet arms arrived, Mr. Sadat ordered the attack on Oct. 6. Egyptian troops surged across the canal, and Syrian troops struck Israel from their side. In the fighting that followed, the Syrians were thrown back and the Israelis counterattacked fiercely, encircling Suez and carving out a bridgehead west of the canal.

The war spurred Washington to work to ease tensions in the Middle East. Mr. Sadat was visited by Mr. Kissinger, and, Mr. Sadat wrote, the two began "a relationship of mutual understanding culminating and crystallizing in what we came to describe as a 'peace process.'" Mr. Kissinger worked out a disengagement agreement between Egypt and Israel that allowed the Egyptians to take back a strip of Sinai.

The agreement, signed in January 1974, was followed by a second limited Egyptian-Israeli accord in September 1975.

Mr. Sadat then decided that a new approach was needed. He made the trip to Jerusalem, and told the Israeli Parliament that Egypt's willingness to "welcome you among us" amounted to "a decisive historical change," although he continued to insist that the Israelis withdraw from occupied Arab land and recognize what he called the rights of the Palestinians. He set in motion the first high-level Egyptian-Israeli peace talks.

But deadlock prevailed until Mr. Sadat met with Mr. Begin and President Carter in September 1978 at the Camp David conference called by Mr. Carter. Two weeks of talks produced signed agreements on what was called "a framework for peace."

Mr. Carter flew to Jerusalem and then to Cairo on March 13, 1979, with compromise proposals to break yet another deadlock. Later that month Mr. Sadat and Mr. Begin signed the treaty, ending 30 years of Egyptian-Israeli confrontation. "Let us work together," Mr. Sadat said, paraphrasing the Prophet Isaiah, "until the day comes when they beat their swords into plowshares and their spears into pruning hooks." In protest, 17 Arab nations adopted political and economic sanctions against his Government.

Mr. Sadat's popularity also benefited from an improving economy, which had seemed on the brink of disaster after Egypt's catastrophic defeat in the 1967 war.

President Sadat's relations with the Americans and the Israelis remained relatively harmonious in the months after the signing of the treaty. That good will paid off when Mr. Begin returned a 580-square-mile tract of Sinai to Egypt ahead of schedule. Yet no real progress was made in months of Egyptian-Israeli negotiations on home rule for the Palestinians in the West Bank and the Gaza Strip.

Early in 1980 Mr. Sadat held inconclusive talks with Mr. Begin. Israeli forces withdrew from more of Sinai, leaving two-thirds of the area evacuated. The Israeli-Egyptian border was declared open.

As the new decade got under way, President Sadat seemed confident of his policies, but Cairo's isolation in the Arab world was galling, and the almost total reliance on Washington for food, aid and weapons was a source of concern. Inflation was running at a rate of 30 percent a year, there were signs of increasing repression, and Israel's policy of multiplying settlements on the occupied West Bank intensified pessimism.

Mr. Sadat is the father of three daughters from his first wife, from whom he was divorced, and four from his second wife, Jihan.

In the final months of his life, there were repeated expressions of internal opposition to his rule. In June a Government prosecutor reported a plot to overthrow him.

On Aug. 3, Egypt and Israel signed an agreement establishing an international peace-keeping force in Sinai to police their peace treaty. On Aug. 25 and 26, Mr. Sadat and Mr. Begin met yet again to try to resolve problems that had delayed normalization of relations.

Then Mr. Sadat turned his attention to internal affairs. He cracked down hard, detaining 1,600 opponents, mostly Moslem militants, and then asserted that all of Egypt's internal indiscipline had come to a halt.

In Israel, however, a long-time observer of Mr. Sadat was already raising the possibility that his work might be snuffed out. The Israeli Chief of Staff, Lieut. Gen. Raphael Eitan, said bleakly, "There are troubles in Egypt, and it is possible that President Sadat will go and everything will come to an end."

HIROHITO

April 29, 1901–January 7, 1989

By Susan Chira

TOKYO—Emperor Hirohito, the last of the World War II leaders and Japan's longest-reigning monarch, died today at the Imperial Palace. He was 87 years old.

In his 62-year reign, the Emperor presided over the most tumultuous era in Japan's modern history, although like most of the 123 emperors before him, he watched more than he acted. During his reign, his nation embraced militarism, conquered much of Asia, waged war on the Allied Powers, suffered the world's first atomic bombing, and painfully rebuilt, rising in just four decades to become the world's most vibrant economic power.

Hirohito's death came after more than a year of declining health. He had been confined to his bed for more than three months.

Because Japanese tradition decrees that the Chrysanthemum Throne may not be empty, Crown Prince Akihito, Hirohito's 55-year-old son, became Japan's 125th Emperor.

Shoichi Fujimori, the grand steward of the Imperial Household Agency, announced the Emperor's death at 7:55 A.M. and revealed that Hirohito had been suffering from cancer of the duodenum, a section of the small intestine.

The Emperor's chief physician, Akira Takagi, told reporters this morning that doctors had known Hirohito had cancer in September 1987, after they had operated on his pancreas, the first operation ever performed on a Japanese emperor. But, he said, the doctors lied about that fact to prevent the Emperor from learning that he had cancer. In Japan, cancer patients are usually not told that they have the disease.

As news of Hirohito's death spread, many Japanese throughout Tokyo put flags outside their homes and businesses. An elderly woman hoisted a flag to half-staff outside a sushi shop, radio stations played classical music and a crowd gathered near the Imperial Palace. A large contingent of riot police officers were deployed to guard against anti-Imperial demonstrations or the possibility that avid followers might commit suicide.

According to the Japanese television network NHK, the state funeral will not follow the Shinto rituals performed when the Emperor Taisho, Hirohito's father, died. Because Japan has since adopted a new, democratic Constitution, the Government wants to distinguish all the ceremonies surrounding Hirohito's death and Akihito's ascension from the past, when Shinto was the state religion.

But many traditions are being honored. This morning at the Imperial Palace, Prime Minister Noboru Takeshita, members of his Cabinet, the speakers of both houses of the legislature and other officials, clad in morning coats, watched the brief and ancient ritual that passes to the new Emperor two of Japan's sacred treasures—a sword and a jewel—along with the Imperial seal and the seal of state.

Japanese are now mourning the end of an era: Showa, or Enlightened Peace, the title by which Hirohito will henceforth be known. That was the title chosen for Hirohito's reign when he succeeded his father, the Emperor Taisho, at the age of 25 on Dec. 25, 1926.

When Hirohito ascended the throne, his subjects revered him as a descendant of Amaterasu, the sun goddess who, according to Japanese mythology, created the Japanese archipelago from the drops of water that fell from her spear. Fueled by militarist propaganda that drew on these myths, more than 2 million soldiers died in his name.

But on Aug. 15, 1945, that myth was shattered as his subjects, hearing his voice for the first time, listened as he announced Japan's surrender on the radio and called on the Japanese to "endure the unendurable." In a second precedent-shattering announcement five months later, he told his countrymen that the people were sovereign and the Emperor was not divine.

Thus Akihito becomes the first Emperor to be installed since Japan was transformed into a constitutional democracy under the American Occupation at the end of World War II. The new Emperor is only the fourth in 120 years since Japan opened itself to the world, abandoned feudalism and began its industrial drive under his great-grandfather, the Emperor Meiji.

Hirohito's long illness left his nation prepared for his death. Until the last two years, he had been vital, pursuing his avocation as a marine biologist, walking in his garden, and waving at the public a few times a year from the balcony at the Imperial Palace.

He appeared to rally from the pancreas operation in September 1987. But last year, he began to grow thinner and had to cancel several public appearances. On the night of Sept. 19 he vomited blood, and the nation began a tense, televised vigil. Crews of reporters camped out at the Imperial Palace, reporting his temperature, blood pressure, pulse, and respiration rate throughout his final illness.

As the Emperor's condition worsened, Government officials canceled trips abroad, public figures put off weddings and other celebrations, and cities around the country canceled autumn festivals. For a while, Japan seemed suspended in time, forced to face the prospect of life without the only emperor most of the nation had ever known.

MOBUTU SESE SEKO

October 14, 1930–September 7, 1997

By Howard W. French

Mobutu Sese Seko, Zaire's longtime dictator and the last of a generation of cold war rulers who grew fabulously rich by providing a bulwark against Communism, died in exile yesterday in Rabat, Morocco, after a long battle with prostate cancer. He was 66 years old.

Mr. Mobutu was chased from power in May after a seven-month rebellion led by a lifelong opponent, Laurent Desire Kabila. Throughout his rule, Mr. Mobutu swore that he would never be known as a former President, but only as the late President. He often said that before him there was no Zaire, and that his country would not survive him either.

Mr. Kabila's army put a lie to Mr. Mobutu's first claim, but history ironically proved the second boast true. Hours after Mr. Mobutu fled, the victorious rebel leader proclaimed himself President. In his first official act, Mr. Kabila renamed the country the Congo, restoring the title used by Belgian colonists and changed by Mr. Mobutu in 1971.

France, Mr. Mobutu's close ally to the end, refused to give him asylum. Similarly, Togo, a West African state ruled by another longtime dictator, Gnassingbe Eyadema, asked Mr. Mobutu and his entourage to leave just days after the exiled leader landed there.

Finally, Morocco took Mr. Mobutu in. Just before his death, he was reportedly visited by his wife, Bobi Ladawa, and his son Kongulu Mobutu. He is also survived by several other children.

After seizing power in a 1965 coup, Mr. Mobutu formed one of the continent's archetypal one-party states. He built his political longevity on violence, cunning and the use of state funds to buy off enemies. The chosen symbols of his power became a trademark leopard-skin cap and wooden walking stick, carved with the figure of an eagle at the top. His systematic looting of the national treasury and major industries gave birth to the term "kleptocracy."

Mr. Mobutu's rise from obscurity was due in no small part to the help of Washington and other Western powers who saw in him a valuable ally against instability and Communist encroachment in Central Africa. Playing this strategic card, Mr. Mobutu allowed his huge country to be used as a staging ground for supporting Western client states and anti-Communist guerrilla movements.

In turn, Mr. Mobutu was able to call on his Western allies to help put down rebellions. His aid in the effort to contain Soviet influence in Africa, and his country's status as a repository of immense mineral wealth, earned him direct contacts with every American President from Dwight D. Eisenhower to George H. W. Bush.

But by the 1990's, with much of Africa and the rest of the world swept up in a new spirit of democratic politics, Mr. Mobutu's Western backers had begun to see him as an embarrassing dinosaur. Finally, Washington began to shun him, denying him visas to visit the United States and encouraging him to organize free national elections.

During his long public life, Mr. Mobutu rose from colonial police informer, journalist and army sergeant to chief of staff of his country's armed forces, military dictator and ultimately President.

He changed his name from Joseph Desire Mobutu to Mobutu Sese Seko Kuku Ngbendu waza Banga, which, according to most translations, means "the all-powerful warrior who, because of his endurance and inflexible will to win, will go from conquest to conquest leaving fire in his wake." (According to an alternative translation, the name meant "the rooster that watches over all the hens.")

Likewise, the name Congo was changed to Zaire, an old Portuguese corruption of a local name for the country's greatest river. European-derived place names were replaced with African names; the capital, Leopoldville, was renamed Kinshasa.

Mr. Mobutu's drive for "authenticity" meant that Zairians were forbidden to use Christian names, to bleach their skin and straighten their hair, or play most kinds of foreign music on the radio. Initially, his ideology also carried a strong component of economic nationalism, and in 1973 the Government began taking over foreign-owned industries and plantations.

The distribution of those assets among the President's closest domestic allies instantly created a class of nouveaux riches, but within two years it had also nearly brought a once prosperous economy to a crash.

For Mr. Mobutu, the most important aspect of his ideology was to legitimize his absolute rule by reference to supposedly traditional African political values. According to him, Africa's ancestral culture was incompatible with Western-style democracy.

As long as Mr. Mobutu was courted by Western powers, and prices for Zaire's immense supplies of copper, cobalt and diamonds remained high, his strategy seemed to succeed. Mr. Mobutu amassed a fortune of as much as $5 billion, which enabled him to buy mansions around the world and go on extended vacations and shopping trips.

Mr. Mobutu was born on Oct. 14, 1930, in the northern town of Lisala in what was then the Belgian Congo. Born out of wedlock to a traditional chief of the Ngbaka ethnic group and Mama Marie Madeleine Yemo, he was adopted in infancy by Alberic Gbemani, a cook for local Belgian missionaries who had married his mother.

The young Mobutu was tutored in French and other subjects by missionaries, who helped place him in schools. When he was 20 he joined the colonial army, known as the Force Publique, working as a journalist and rising to sergeant.

Leaving active duty in 1956, he went to work as a columnist for the Leopoldville newspaper L'Avenir. In 1959 he was sent by the colonial administration to study in Brussels. He was able to attend the Brussels Roundtable Conference on Congo Independence and is widely believed to have funneled information to Belgian intelligence on behind-the-scenes discussions.

He returned to Leopoldville just in time for pro-independence riots that swept the capital and accelerated Belgium's timetable for handing over power. At independence in 1960, Mr. Mobutu was called on by the new Prime Minister, Patrice Lumumba, to serve as his army chief of staff. Mr. Lumumba, a left-leaning, fiery African nationalist, had shocked the Belgian delegation in his independence day speech by decrying the brutality and humiliation suffered by Africans at the hands of Europeans.

The speech's biggest surprise, however, was Mr. Lumumba's announcement of the revocation of the Belgian officer corps that commanded the Force Publique, a 25,000-member corps that had hitherto included no African officers. The measure thrust the country into a period of turbulence and secession attempts.

Mr. Mobutu's political savvy seemed to make him ideal for the job of chief of staff of the armed forces, but it was not long before he betrayed the man who had appointed him.

On Sept. 14, 1960, Mr. Mobutu, by then a colonel, "suspended" the country's political institutions. The move came as the Congo was in the throes of a civil war with the copper-rich province of Katanga, now called Shaba, seeking to break away from the new-born country, and with Prime Minister Lumumba and the President, Joseph Kasavubu, locked in a power struggle.

The United Nations Secretary General, Dag Hammarskjold, died in a mysterious airplane crash in 1961 as he attempted to fly into Katanga to settle the crisis.

Colonel Mobutu is widely believed to have been strongly encouraged by Washington, acting through the Central Intelligence Agency. Once Colonel Mobutu took over, Washington supplied him with cash to pay his soldiers and an American-piloted jet for travel around the country.

Mr. Lumumba sought refuge at the United Nations mission in Leopoldville, which for more than two months was surrounded by Colonel Mobutu's soldiers. Mr. Lumumba escaped from the capital on Nov. 27, 1960, and tried to rejoin his loyalists but was captured and tortured by Colonel Mobutu's agents. He was flown to Katanga to be handed over to the secessionist leader, Moise Tshombe, his sworn enemy.

Mr. Lumumba was killed under mysterious circumstances, and his body was never found.

Mr. Mobutu formally restored power to civilian authorities in 1961, but worked with the C.I.A. to put down regional rebellions. On Nov. 24, 1965, Mr. Mobutu, by then a lieutenant general, seized power again. The pretext for the coup was renewed squabbling between President Kasavubu and the country's Prime Minister, Mr. Tshombe. Like Mr. Lumumba, Mr. Tshombe, who went into exile after the coup, was killed under mysterious circumstances.

A year after his coup, Mr. Mobutu founded the Popular Movement of the Revolution. Membership was obligatory for all Zairians. By 1971, when he organized his first national elections, his group had, in effect, become a state within a state. He ran unopposed in the presidential election.

Mr. Mobutu adopted the title of Marshal and launched grandiose public works projects intended to transform Zaire into an economic powerhouse. He was courted anew by Western capitals and their countries' construction firms and banks. But the debt crisis brought on by costly borrowing and the collapse of copper prices ultimately crippled Mr. Mobutu's rule.

In 1975, he again consolidated his links with Washington by cooperating with the C.I.A. in launching an assault on the Angolan capital, Luanda. The incursion of the Zairian Army was aimed at helping a pro-Western guerrilla force, the National Front for the Liberation of Angola, seize the capital on the eve of independence from Portugal. Instead, Cuban support enabled a rival group, the Popular Movement for the Liberation of Angola, to halt the march and rout Mr. Mobutu's troops who had been sent to assist the attack.

Mr. Mobutu spent most of the 1980's wrestling with economic problems brought on in part by his looting of national resources. By the end of the decade, with the demise of Communism in most of the world, he had been stripped of any strategic importance. In 1990, when democratization swept much of Africa, he responded by ordering a massacre of university students.

After the killings, Belgium, Zaire's largest source of aid, cut off assistance, demanding democratic reforms. Soon, the United States and France joined in. In April 1990, Mr. Mobutu announced the opening of the country to multiparty politics and acceded to the organization of a "national conference," which sought to limit his powers. It eventually imposed a Prime Minister chosen from the opposition, Etienne Tshisekedi wa Mulumba, and called for national elections.

Mr. Mobutu took up residence on a yacht moored on the Zaire River. Later, he left the capital, moving to his palace in Gbadolite, nearly 1,000 miles to the north. In September 1991, after rioting in the capital, he bowed to opposition demands that he name Mr. Tshisekedi, his long-standing opponent, as Prime Minister.

Mr. Mobutu dismissed Mr. Tshisekedi only 12 days later, after the new Prime Minister tried to establish control over the Central Bank. Rioting again erupted in January 1993, when Mr. Mobutu's introduction of new bank notes to cope with triple-digit inflation angered soldiers. The renewed violence, in which the French Ambassador to Zaire was killed in his office, intensified international pressure on Mr. Mobutu to carry out reforms.

In October 1996, the Alliance of Democratic Forces for the Liberation of the Congo, a newly formed Zairian militia backed by Rwanda, Uganda, Angola and others, routed Government forces in a string of eastern Zairian cities. By then, Mr. Mobutu was being treated in Switzerland for cancer.

Returning belatedly to his country to face the crisis, Mr. Mobutu complained that he had been "stabbed in the back" by his neighbors. But the tables had merely been turned on a man who had spent his career playing kingmaker.

POPE JOHN PAUL II

May 18, 1920–April 2, 2005

VATICAN CITY—Pope John Paul II died Saturday night, succumbing finally to years of illness endured painfully and publicly, ending an extraordinary, if sometimes polarizing, 26-year reign that remade the papacy.

He died at 9:37 p.m. in his apartment three stories above St. Peter's Square, as tens of thousands of the faithful gathered within sight of his lighted window. People wept and knelt on cobblestones as the news of his death spread across the square, bowing their heads to a man whose long and down-to-earth papacy was the only one that many young and middle-aged Catholics remembered. For more than 10 minutes, not long after his death was announced, the crowd simply applauded him.

Suffering for a decade from Parkinson's disease, the 84-year-old pope had deteriorated to the point where he seemed, as his spokesman once said, to be "a soul pulling a body."

In his last public appearance, from his window on Wednesday, he looked weak and gaunt, unable to pronounce a blessing to the crowd. Still recovering from a tracheotomy, a pope known for his great ability as a communicator could hardly speak. —*Ian Fisher*

By Robert D. McFadden

On the night of Oct. 16, 1978, a vast, impatient throng in floodlit St. Peter's Square cheered wildly as white smoke curled from a chimney atop the Sistine Chapel, signaling the election of a new pope.

Cardinal Pericle Felici emerged minutes later to introduce Cardinal Karol Wojtyla of Poland, the first non-Italian pope since 1523. But even he had trouble pronouncing the name—voy-TEE-wah. Hardly anyone, it seemed, knew who he was. Then a powerfully built man with slightly stooped shoulders and a small smile on his angular face stepped onto the central balcony of St. Peter's Basilica. Cheers faded into silence. The crowd waited.

He stood at the balcony rail, looking out, a Polish stranger in the fresh white robes of the pope. And there were tears in his eyes as he began to speak.

"I have come," he said in lightly accented Italian, "from a faraway country—far away, but always so close in the communion of faith."

There were scattered cheers, and they grew louder as he went on.

"I do not know whether I can express myself in your—in our—Italian language," he said, pausing.

The crowd roared appreciatively, and the laughter swelled into resounding cheers.

"If I make mistakes," he added, beaming suddenly, "you will correct me."

Tumult erupted.

The cheers went on and on, and then grew into rhythmic waves that broke on the basilica facade and echoed across the square:

"Viva il Papa!

"Viva il Papa!

"Viva il Papa!"

It was to be the longest and most luminous pontificate of the 20th century, the second longest in the history of the church, a 26-year era that would witness sweeping political changes around the world. And John Paul was to be a different kind of pope: complex, schooled in confrontation, theologically intransigent but deftly politic, full of wit and daring, energy and physically expressive love.

More than outgoing, he was all-embracing—a bear-hugging, larger-than-life man of action who had climbed mountains, performed in plays, written books and seen war.

He saw himself as a spiritual figure who transcended geographical and ideological boundaries. And he saw it as his mission to deliver a clear set of Catholic ideas and to foster peace and human dignity through the power of faith and the practical efforts of well-meaning nations.

At the dawn of the millennium and in the twilight of his papacy, he also saw it as his duty to issue a daring, unprecedented apology for the errors of his church and individual Catholics over the last 2,000 years, a catalog of sins that included historic injustices against Jews, women, indigenous peoples, immigrants and the poor.

John Paul's extraordinary effort to cleanse his church's conscience, along with his global travels, his challenges to human rights violations around the world, his attacks on the economic injustices of capitalism and his steadfast resistance to changes in church teachings on birth control, priestly celibacy, the ordination of women and other issues were among the fundamental traits of his pontificate.

But they were not his only legacies. He played a major role in the collapse of Communism, instilling its adversaries with confidence. His very election boosted the spirit of believers in Eastern Europe, for whom the appeal "Be not afraid!"—repeated three times during the sermon he preached at his installation on Oct. 22, 1978—had a special meaning.

On that first papal visit to Poland, in 1979, he scolded the officially atheistic Communist government for treating people "merely as a means of production." In retrospect, the visit was widely seen as a detonator of the Solidarity labor movement's challenge to Poland's Communist government and ultimately of the changes that swept the Soviet Union and Eastern Europe a decade later.

He went to Ireland and confronted zealots of the Irish Republican Army and their Protestant foes: "On my knees I beg you to turn away from the path of violence and to return to the ways of peace." He went to Auschwitz and asked, "How far can cruelty go?" And he went to the United Nations in New York and spoke to world leaders of peace for "all the men and women living on this planet."

At the time of his election as 264th bishop of Rome in 1978, John Paul was almost unknown outside the church hierarchy and his native Poland.

There had never been a Slavic pope. To a College of Cardinals stunned by the death of his predecessor, John Paul I, after only a month's reign, Cardinal Wojtyla proved an attractive candidate—theologically orthodox yet a man of personal dynamism and proven political skills who could reach out to Eastern Europe and the third world. At 58, he could be expected to have a long pontificate. Still, his election, on the eighth ballot, met with almost universal astonishment.

The new pope had been an athlete and outdoorsman all his life, a soccer player, backpacker, camper, boater and long-distance runner. He was solidly built and vigorous, with a bullish neck and strong, stooped shoulders that hinted of his youth as a laborer and factory worker. He moved with a deliberate, confident step.

He was 5 feet 10 inches tall and weighed 175 pounds. His eyes were dark and deeply expressive, sometimes wide with mirth, sometimes narrowed to slits of concentration. His hands were big, creased, workman's hands that swept the air in gestures of mildness or came together, poised to pray.

He liked a glass of wine with meals. He wrote many of his own speeches longhand. He liked to chat, to joke and to laugh heartily. He loved to swim and had a pool built at the summer palace at Castel Gandolfo.

To many Catholic leaders, the church was under siege when John Paul became pope. The reforms of the Second Vatican Council in the early 1960's had not halted the tide of secularization in the church's heartland, Western Europe.

The cultural tumult of the late 60's only reinforced the appeal of revolutionary Marxism, the sexual revolution and other challenges to Catholic tradition. Many theologians viewed his predecessor Paul VI's tenure, from 1963 to 1978, as a period of drift and uncertainty.

John Paul agreed that much of the church was in disarray, and he was convinced that he could unify and reinvigorate it. To carry out what some called his "restoration," he approved a revised Code of Canon Law and a new "universal catechism," setting limits on ambiguities and further liberalization in the wake of Vatican II.

He issued 14 encyclicals, or papal instructions, that largely reinforced conservative church doctrine. He orchestrated a campaign against abortion rights, contraception and other measures endorsed by feminists and population experts. He reaffirmed the doctrine that women could not be ordained as priests, saying the matter was not even open to debate.

He was criticized inside and outside the church for his opposition to "liberation theology," a school of thought that blended biblical themes with Marxist economics and served as a justification for the Catholic clergy's involvement in political struggles for the poor in Latin America and other parts of the third world.

No one doubted the power of John Paul's voice or the depth of the feelings he evoked. But many Catholics—especially in America and Western Europe—were distressed by his opposition to change, even in the face of crisis. The depth of distress was never more profound than in the priest-pedophile scandals in America.

As the scandals unfolded, with hundreds of priests implicated in thousands of cases of abuse, the pope in April 2002 acknowledged the suffering and offered what was taken by many to be an apology. Calling the abuse criminal and "an appalling sin in the eyes of God," he said, "To the victims and their families wherever they may be, I express my profound sense of solidarity and concern."

But he sent conflicting signals as well, suggesting that American bishops had gone too far in recommending the removal of any priest who had ever sexually abused a minor.

Aside from the sex scandals, many American Catholics said the church and the pope were out of touch. Women, blacks, Hispanics, homosexuals and even some priests and nuns urged him to be more sensitive to their needs. He usually voiced sympathy, but urged the supplicants to remain faithful to church teachings.

John Paul's relations with Jews were both troubled and pathbreaking. He was the first pope to pray in a synagogue, the first to acknowledge the failure of individual Catholics to act against the Holocaust, the first to call anti-Semitism a sin "against God and man," and the first to make an official papal visit to the Holy Land.

The pope wrote an apostolic letter in 1989 evoking Christian sorrow over the Holocaust, and in 1998—a decade after promising to do so—issued a historic document apologizing for the failure of many Catholics to protect Jews during the reign of the wartime pope, Pius XII.

While the Vatican viewed the document as groundbreaking, many Jewish groups rejected it because it praised Pius's "quiet diplomacy" and did not cite his failure to speak out against the Holocaust. Papal aides said such criticisms stung the pope, who spoke often of a common Christian-Jewish biblical heritage.

His six-day journey to the Holy Land in March 2000 was widely seen as a personal triumph and high point of his reign—a poignant blend of sacred and secular gestures delicately balanced in a land revered by all the Abrahamic faiths: Judaism, Islam and Christianity.

In Tel Aviv, he was received as one of the most important visitors in Israel's history, and his presence in Jerusalem later was hailed by Israeli leaders as nothing less than a Christian affirmation of the Jewish right to a homeland.

For Palestinian leaders, his presence was also a symbolic triumph. He went to Yasir Arafat's home in Bethlehem and to a squalid Palestinian refugee camp; Mr. Arafat called his visit a ringing endorsement of Palestinian nationalist aspirations.

His first journey [as pope] to Poland, in June 1979, proved to be one of his most important trips. From the moment he arrived and knelt to kiss the Polish earth until his tearful departure nine days later, his homecoming was a succession of thundering triumphs.

From Warsaw to Auschwitz to Krakow, in 36 public appearances, he clasped old friends in headlocks, sang hymns and folk songs with his people, offered Masses for throngs that stretched across hillsides, and without directly attacking the government repeatedly challenged its authority. "The exclusion of Christ from the history of man is an act against man," he told vast crowds in Warsaw.

Coal miners, housewives, university students, young people in blue jeans—13 million people of every age and description—turned out to see him.

At Auschwitz, where a million people, mostly Jews, had been killed by the Nazis, he spoke of this place "built on hatred and contempt for man in the name of an insane ideology."

Months later, the pope's role as a moral leader was reinforced by a journey to Ireland and the United States. His outdoor Mass in Dublin drew 1.2 million people. Then, for two whirlwind days in New York City, he addressed the United Nations, offered Mass at Yankee Stadium and engaged in a playful dialogue with young people rallying at Madison Square Garden. He waded into enormous, friendly crowds, hugging and kissing people. He visited a church in Harlem, rode in a rain-soaked ticker-tape parade on lower Broadway and addressed many thousands at Battery Park and Shea Stadium.

At the Battery in a pouring rain, he said: "I address a special word to the leaders of the Jewish community, whose presence here honors me greatly. Shalom! Peace be with you."

John Paul's life as a robust, traveling teacher-pope appeared to have been altered on May 13, 1981, when a 23-year-old Turk, Mehmet Ali Agca, shot him as he rode in an open car before 10,000 people in St. Peter's Square. Wounded in the abdomen, right arm and left hand, he underwent five hours of surgery, and part of an intestine was removed.

Investigators searching Mr. Agca's past learned that he was a murderer who had escaped from a Turkish prison in 1979 and had ties to a neo-Nazi group, the Gray Wolves; later he said the shooting was a Soviet-inspired plot involving Bulgarian and Turkish agents. But no conspiracy was ever proved.

The pope recovered, and his health remained strikingly good until July 1992, when he was hospitalized for a stomach problem that led to the discovery and removal of a colon tumor the size of an orange.

Over the 1990s, he grew frail and began to have difficulty walking, even with a cane. Privately, officials said he had Parkinson's disease and crippling arthritis. By 2002, his hands shook so much he could not hold his speeches, and his speech was slurred. Some Vatican officials privately expressed hope that he would be forced to settle down, travel less and get more involved in running the church. But John Paul was determined to continue his busy life.

Spiritually, Karol Jozef Wojtyla was never far from the land of his birth. He was born on May 18, 1920, in Wadowice, 30 miles southwest of Krakow, the second of two children. His mother, Emilia Kaczorowska Wojtyla, of Lithuanian descent, died when he was nine. His father, Karol Wojtyla, was a sergeant in the Polish Army.

Karol was a good student in elementary and secondary schools and played goalkeeper on his school soccer team. When he was 18, his father, who had retired with a small pension, moved the family from Wadowice to Krakow. (Karol's brother, Edmund, a doctor, died before the outbreak of World War II.)

After high school, Karol enrolled at Jagiellonian University in Krakow. But in 1939, the invading Nazis closed the university and he took a job in a stone quarry to help his ailing father make ends meet. (The father died in 1941.)

Outside work, he fell in with other young intellectuals and helped start an underground drama group, the Rhapsodic Theater. He had a rich baritone voice and liked to sing popular songs at parties, accompanying himself on the guitar; he also wrote plays and poetry.

He studied for the priesthood clandestinely in occupied Krakow, taking underground Jagiellonian University courses and attending others at the Spiritual Seminary directed by Krakow's archbishop, Adam Stefan Sapieha, who became his patron. For the rest of the war, he lived in the basement of the archbishop's fortress-like palace.

He was ordained a priest on Nov. 1, 1946. As the Communists took power in postwar Poland, Arch-bishop Sapieha urged his protégé to continue post-graduate studies abroad. Father Wojtyla was sent to Rome, where he enrolled at the Angelicum, a college operated by the Dominican order.

In two years he had earned a doctorate in philosophy. Returning home, he was assigned to a village parish in Niegowic, in southern Poland, then back to Krakow. In 1953, he earned a second doctorate, in moral theology; a year later he won a chair in social ethics at Catholic University in Lublin, a post he would retain until he became pope.

His reputation grew as he rose rapidly through the ranks. On Jan. 13, 1964, Pope Paul VI made him archbishop of Krakow; he addressed Vatican Council fathers in Rome on eight occasions during Vatican II. On June 26, 1967, the pope elevated him to the College of Cardinals.

At that time, Poland's Communist government regarded him as moderate and flexible. But over the years he became a tough, vocal and eloquent opponent of the government and preached Christian alternatives to Marxism.

In 1969, Cardinal Wojtyla made his first trip to the United States, visiting Polish-American communities in 15 cities. He returned in 1976, this time visiting 16 cities, including Cambridge, Mass., where Thomas E. Crooks, director of Harvard's summer school, recalled being "floored by the sheer physical presence" of the man.

"He exuded such a combination of power and acceptance," Mr. Crooks continued. "He had this smile on his face and a look in his eye that said, 'You're wonderful. And I'm wonderful, too.' We had dinner with him later, and late that evening I told myself, 'This man ought to be pope.'"

John Paul's literary output was prodigious. Besides his encyclicals, he was the author of at least seven books and more than 300 scholarly articles and essays. His last book, "Memory and Identity," published this year, discussed freedom, patriotism and European integration. He also wrote a great deal of poetry, collected in two volumes.

In his homeland, he left a major monument to his faith and perseverance: the starkly modern Church of Our Lady, Queen of Poland, at Nowa Huta, east of Krakow. While Communist authorities had long opposed the project, voluntary contributions were raised, and scarce building materials were scraped together. Somehow construction permits were obtained and volunteer workers took turns at the building site.

It took more than a decade, but the project was dedicated in 1977. In a homily at the time, the future pope declared that men had a right to more than a job and a living wage.

"There are more profound rights of the human spirit that cannot be violated," he said. "These are the rights of freedom of the human spirit, freedom of human conscience, freedom of belief and freedom of religion."

SADDAM HUSSEIN

April 28, 1937–December 30, 2006

BAGHDAD—Saddam Hussein, the dictator who led Iraq through three decades of brutality, war and bombast before American forces chased him from his capital city and captured him in a filthy pit near his hometown, was hanged just before dawn Saturday during the morning call to prayer.

The final stages for Mr. Hussein, 69, came with terrible swiftness after he lost the appeal, five days ago, of his death sentence for the killings of 148 men and boys in the northern town of Dujail in 1982. He had received the sentence less than two months before from a special court set up to judge his reign as the almost unchallenged dictator of Iraq.

His execution at 6:10 a.m. was announced on state-run Iraqiya television. Witnesses said 14 Iraqi officials had attended the hanging, at the former military intelligence building in northern Baghdad, now part of an American base. Those in the room said that Mr. Hussein was dressed entirely in black and carrying a Koran and that he was compliant as the noose was draped around his neck.

Before the rope was slipped around his neck, according to a witness, he was asked if he was afraid. "No," he said without visible emotion. "Anyone who takes this route should not be afraid."

At President George W. Bush's ranch in Crawford, Tex., a White House spokesman, Scott Stanzel, said Mr. Bush had gone to bed before the execution took place and was not awakened. Asked why Mr. Bush had gone to sleep before hearing the news, he said Mr. Bush "knew that it was going to happen."

In a statement written in advance, Mr. Bush said Mr. Hussein "was executed after receiving a fair trial—the kind of justice he denied the victims of his brutal regime." —*Marc Santora, James Glanz and Sabrina Tavernise*

By Neil MacFarquhar

BAGHDAD—The hanging of Saddam Hussein ended the life of one of the most brutal tyrants in recent history. The despot, known as Saddam, had oppressed Iraq for more than 30 years, unleashing devastating regional wars and reducing his oil-rich nation to a claustrophobic police state.

For decades it seemed that his unflinching hold on Iraq would endure, particularly after he lasted through disastrous military adventures against Iran and then Kuwait, where an American-led coalition routed his military in 1991.

His conviction that he was destined by God to rule Iraq forever was such that he refused to accept that he would be overthrown in April 2003, even as American tanks penetrated the Iraqi capital, Baghdad, in a war that has become a bitterly contentious occupation.

Underneath all the socialist oratory, the Koranic references, the tailored suits and the invocations of Iraq's glorious history, Mr. Hussein held onto the ethos of a village peasant who believed that the strongman was everything. While Mr. Hussein was in power, his statue guarded the entrance to every village, his portrait watched over each government office, and he peered down from at least one wall in every home.

Throughout his rule, he unsettled the ranks of the Baath Party with bloody purges and packed his jails with political prisoners. In one of his most brutal acts, he rained poison gas on the Kurdish village of Halabja, killing an estimated 5,000 of his own citizens suspected of being disloyal and wounding 10,000 more.

Aside from his secret police, he held power by filling the government's upper ranks with members of his extended clan. Their feuds became the stuff of gory public soap operas. Mr. Hussein once sentenced his elder son, Uday, to be executed after he beat Mr. Hussein's food taster to death in front of scores of horrified party guests, but later rescinded the order. The husbands of his two eldest daughters were gunned down after they defected and then inexplicably returned to Iraq.

Continual wars sapped Iraq's wealth and decimated its people. In 1980, Mr. Hussein dragged his country into a disastrous attempt to overthrow the new Islamic government in neighboring Iran. By the time the war ended in stalemate in 1988, more than 200,000 Iraqis were dead and hundreds of thousands wounded. Iran suffered a similar toll.

He invaded Kuwait in August 1990, only to be expelled by an American-led coalition in the Persian Gulf war seven months later. His defeat in Kuwait, followed by more than a decade of confrontations with the West over his suspected weapons programs, ultimately led to his overthrow.

Saddam Hussein was born on April 28, 1937, in a mud hut near the village of Tikrit, northwest of Baghdad. He was raised by a clan of landless peasants, his father apparently deserting his mother before his birth.

"His birth was not a joyful occasion, and no roses or aromatic plants bedecked his cradle," his official biographer, Amir Iskander, wrote.

Mr. Hussein's first role in the rough world of Iraqi politics came in 1959, at age 22, when the Baath Party assigned him and others to assassinate Abdul Karim Kassem, the despotic general ruling Iraq. Violence was a quick way for a young man who grew up fatherless in an impoverished village to get ahead; bloodshed became the major theme of his life.

Mr. Hussein married his first cousin in 1963, and the couple had five children. His wife, three daughters and a dozen grandchildren survive him. His sons, Uday and Qusay, along with Qusay's son, Mustapha, died in July 2003 during a gun battle with American forces in a villa in the city of Mosul.

The first years of Saddam Hussein's marriage coincided with political tumult in Iraq before the assassination of King Faisal II in 1958 and the July 1968 putsch that brought the Baath Party to power.

Mr. Hussein's main role in his early 30s was organizing the party's militia, the seed of the dreaded security apparatus. In November 1969, he was appointed vice president and deputy chairman of the Revolutionary Command Council, as the cabinet was known. He remained head of the intelligence and internal security agencies, in effect controlling Iraq.

The Arab Baath Socialist Party had been formed in the 1930s to push a secular, socialist creed as the ideal path to achieving Arab unity. But that dogma proved an excuse for the imprisonment, exile or execution of all potential rivals. No other Arab despot matched the savagery of Mr. Hussein as he went about bending all state institutions to his whim.

His opening act, in January 1969, was hanging about 17 so-called spies for Israel in a Baghdad square. Hundreds of arrests and executions followed as the civilian wing of the Baath Party eclipsed the Iraqi military.

Mr. Hussein saw his first opportunity for Iraq to dominate the region in the turmoil that swept neighboring Iran after its 1979 Islamic revolution. In September 1980, he believed that by invading Iran he could inspire Iranians of Arab origin to revolt against their Persian rulers. Instead, they resisted fanatically, and Iraq fared badly in the war.

Nevertheless, the fear that an Islamic revolution would spread to an oil producer with estimated reserves second only to Saudi Arabia's tipped the United States and its allies toward Baghdad, and they provided weapons and technology.

The war lasted eight years until Iran accepted a cease-fire in July 1988, with both sides terrorizing each other's civilian populations by rocketing major cities. But the March 1988 mustard gas attack on the Iraqi village of Halabja by its own government was perhaps the most gruesome incident.

Mr. Hussein ended the Iran-Iraq war with 1 million men under arms. By then Iraq had embarked on acquiring a homegrown arsenal of nuclear, chemical and biological weapons.

His next target was another neighbor, Kuwait. On Aug. 2, 1990, his army swiftly occupied that tiny, immensely wealthy emirate and installed a puppet government, provoking an international crisis.

The United Nations imposed a trade embargo and economic sanctions. The United States and eventually 33 other nations deployed forces to the region and warned of a wider war if Mr. Hussein did not withdraw.

Even before the war ended, President George H. W. Bush encouraged the Iraqi people to overthrow Hussein. The ground offensive against Iraq ended after 100 hours.

For the next decade, Mr. Hussein refused United Nations weapons inspectors the access required to catalog and destroy Iraq's unconventional weapons.

The United Nations maintained economic sanctions against Iraq until 1996, when some oil exports were allowed to pay for food and medicine. To end the sanctions, Baghdad offered at least five "full, final and complete" weapons disclosures, which the United Nations dismissed as incomplete.

After the August 1995 defection of Mr. Hussein's two sons-in-law and his two eldest daughters to Jordan, the Iraqi government apparently became worried that Lt. Gen. Hussein Kamel al-Majid, a son-in-law and the minister in charge of weapons development, would disclose all he knew. Six months later, the general and his brother declared that they had accepted amnesty and returned. Within days they died in a shootout.

Mr. Hussein tried to control his public image and his security. He dyed his hair black. Each of his 20 palaces was kept fully staffed, with meals prepared daily as if he were in residence to disguise his whereabouts. He was so phobic about germs that top generals summoned to meet him were often ordered to strip to their underwear, and their clothes were then X-rayed.

Under Mr. Hussein, imprisonment, torture, mutilation and execution were frequent occurrences for those who dabbled in anything vaguely political. There was no freedom of expression and no freedom to travel. Contact with foreigners was proscribed.

Evidence from inside Iraq after the invasion confirmed what United Nations weapons inspectors had anticipated, that Mr. Hussein had abandoned the attempt to develop nuclear, biological and chemical weapons after his 1991 defeat.

The controversy over whether Iraq was still developing unconventional weapons stemmed in part from Mr. Hussein's desire to convince different audiences of different things, a study by the Defense Department concluded. He wanted the West to believe that he had ended the program, which he had. Yet he wanted to frighten enemies like Israel by claiming that he possessed the weapons.

Some critics of George W. Bush's administration argued that the accusations over unconventional weapons were a smoke screen, that government hawks were determined to topple Mr. Hussein to reassert American power. Richard Clarke, a former national security adviser to three presidents, described in his 2004 book "Against All Enemies" the scene in the White House right after the Sept. 11, 2001, attacks against the United States, with President Bush and other senior officials trying to link Mr. Hussein directly to Al Qaeda, Osama bin Laden's organization. No link was ever established.

By 2003, Iraq's military was anemic, weakened by sanctions and changes in command. But Mr. Hussein did not take the threat of regime change seriously. He so believed his own publicity about his success in fighting the first Gulf War that he used it as a blueprint for the second. The collapse came so quickly that Mr. Hussein was still issuing orders to units that had ceased to exist.

After an April 9 sighting in public, he disappeared, apparently using up to 30 hiding places and the aid of loyal tribesmen to escape capture.

In December 2003, his location was divulged by a clan member captured in a raid on a Baghdad house. Less than 11 hours later, 600 American soldiers and Special Operations forces supported by tanks, artillery and Apache helicopter gunships surrounded two farmhouses in Ad Dwar, a village southeast of Tikrit. Mr. Hussein was discovered lying at the bottom of an eight-foot-deep hole.

Mr. Hussein often tried to draw parallels between himself and the famous leaders of Mesopotamia, the earliest civilization in the region.

He had the ancient walls of the former capital, Babylon, reconstructed using tens of thousands of newly fired bricks. An archaeologist had once shown him bricks stamped with the name of Nebuchadnezzar II in 605 B.C. After the reconstruction, the small Arabic script on thousands of bricks read in part, "In the reign of the victorious Saddam Hussein, the president of the Republic, may God keep him, the guardian of the great Iraq and the renovator of its renaissance and the builder of its great civilization, the rebuilding of the great city of Babylon was done."

MARGARET THATCHER

October 13, 1925–April 8, 2013

By Joseph R. Gregory

Margaret Thatcher, the "Iron Lady" of British politics, who set her country on a rightward economic course, led it to victory in the Falklands war and helped guide the United States and the Soviet Union through the cold war's difficult last years, died on Monday in London. She was 87.

Her spokesman, Tim Bell, said she died of a stroke at the Ritz Hotel. Queen Elizabeth II authorized a ceremonial funeral with military honors—a notch below a state funeral—at St. Paul's Cathedral in London.

Mrs. Thatcher was the first woman to become prime minister of Britain and the first to lead a major Western power in modern times. Hard-driving and hardheaded, she led her Conservative Party to three straight election wins and held office for 11 years—May 1979 to November 1990—longer than any other British politician in the 20th century.

The strong economic medicine she administered to a country sickened by inflation, budget deficits and industrial unrest brought her wide swings in popularity, culminating with a revolt among her own cabinet ministers in her final year and her shout of "No! No! No!" in the House of Commons to any further integration with Europe.

But by the time she left office, the principles known as Thatcherism—the belief that economic freedom and individual liberty are interdependent, that personal responsibility and hard work are the only ways to national prosperity, and that the free-market democracies must stand firm against aggression—had won many disciples. Even some of her strongest critics accorded her a grudging respect.

At home, Mrs. Thatcher's political successes were decisive. She broke the power of the labor unions and forced the Labour Party to abandon its commitment to nationalized industry, redefine the role of the welfare state and accept the importance of the free market.

Abroad, she won new esteem for a country that had been in decline since its costly victory in World War II. But during her first years in power, even many Tories feared that her election might prove a terrible mistake.

In October 1980, 17 months into her first term, Mrs. Thatcher faced disaster. More businesses were failing and more people were out of work than at any time since the Great Depression. Racial and class tensions smoldered. Even her close advisers worried that her push to stanch inflation, sell off nationalized industry and deregulate the economy was devastating the poor, undermining the middle class and courting chaos.

At the Conservative Party conference that month, the moderates grumbled that they were being led by a free-market ideologue oblivious to life on the street and the exigencies of realpolitik. With electoral defeat staring them in the face, cabinet members warned, now was surely a time for compromise.

But in an address to the party, she played on the title of Christopher Fry's popular play "The Lady's Not for Burning" in insisting that she would press forward with her policies. "You turn if you want to," she told the faltering assembly. "The lady's not for turning."

Her resolve did the trick. A party revolt was thwarted, the Tories hunkered down, and Mrs. Thatcher went on to achieve great victories. She turned the Conservatives, long associated with the status quo, into the party of reform. Her policies revitalized British business, spurred industrial growth and swelled the middle class.

But her third term was riddled with setbacks. Dissension over monetary policy, taxes and Britain's place in the European Community caused her government to give up hard-won gains against inflation and unemployment. By the time she was ousted in another Tory revolt—this one over her resistance to expanding Britain's role in a European Union—the economy was in a recession and her reputation tarnished.

To her enemies she was—as Denis Healey, chancellor of the Exchequer in Harold Wilson's government, called her—"La Pasionaria of Privilege," a woman who railed against the evils of poverty but who was callous and unsympathetic to the plight of the have-nots.

Mrs. Thatcher's relentless hostility to the Soviet Union and her persistent call to modernize Britain's nuclear forces fed fears of nuclear war and even worried moderates in her own party. But her rapport with the new Soviet leader, Mikhail S. Gorbachev, and her friendship with President Ronald Reagan made Mrs. Thatcher a vital link between the White House and the Kremlin in their tense negotiations to halt the arms race of the 1980s.

Though she was the first woman to lead a major political party in the West, she rubbed many feminists the wrong way. "The battle for women's rights has largely been won," she declared. "I hate those strident tones we hear from some women's libbers."

She relished being impolitic. "You don't follow the crowd," she said. "You make up your own mind."

Margaret Hilda Roberts was born on Oct. 13, 1925, in Grantham, Lincolnshire, 100 miles north of London. Her family lived in a cold-water flat above a grocery store owned by her father, Alfred, who was also a Methodist preacher and local politician. She was reared by her parents to follow the tenets of Methodism: personal responsibility, hard work and traditional moral values.

She was admitted to Somerville College, Oxford, in 1943. She earned a master's degree in chemistry from the University of Oxford, worked as a chemical researcher, studied law and entered Conservative politics.

She married Denis Thatcher, a well-to-do businessman and former artillery officer in 1951. In August 1953, Mrs. Thatcher gave birth to twins, Mark and Carol, who survive her, along with grandchildren. (Sir Denis died in 2003.)

In 1951 the Tories began a 13-year run in power. But in exchange for support on foreign affairs, they compromised with the unions and accepted the government's growing role in the marketplace. This "policy of consensus" was successful. Harold Macmillan, seeking re-election in 1959, the year that Mrs. Thatcher was elected to the House of Commons, said, "Most people have never had it so good."

In 1964, the Tories, exhausted by scandal, a souring economy and internal divisions, lost power to Harold Wilson's Labour Party. The Tories regained power in 1970 and the Conservative leader, Edward Heath, appointed Mrs. Thatcher secretary for education. She fought budget cuts in the university system and pushed with zeal to rebuild schools in poor areas.

But it was her effort to restrict a free-milk program for schoolchildren that made her a national figure. Though poor children were exempt from the cutbacks, and the previous Labour government had also reduced free milk in schools, the opposition leapt to the attack. When Mrs. Thatcher argued in Parliament that the cuts would help finance more worthwhile programs, she was jeered. The tabloids labeled her "Thatcher the Milk Snatcher."

The government stood firm on the milk issue. But as the economy worsened, Mr. Heath retreated, imposing wage and price controls as inflation surged and igniting strikes. His U-turn angered the Tory right, and by winter 1974 Mr. Wilson was back in power.

The following December, Mrs. Thatcher, in what many regarded as an act of political gall, declared her candidacy for the Conservative leadership and triumphed on Feb. 11, 1975.

As Labour ran the country, she fought to reshape her party. Mrs. Thatcher and her allies asserted that the Tory policy of consensus had allowed the country to lurch leftward. She called for an all-out attack on inflation, pledged to denationalize basic industry and promised to curb union power.

By the mid-1970s, Britain was the sick man of Europe. In late 1978 and early '79, strikes paralyzed Britain. As the "winter of discontent" dragged on, Prime Minister James Callaghan, of the Labour Party, failed to survive a no-confidence vote and called an election for May 3.

On election day the Tories walked away with 43.9 percent of the vote. Labour received 37 percent and the Liberals 13.8 percent. It was the largest swing to the right in postwar history.

For Mrs. Thatcher and the country, the beginning of her leadership was painful. Income tax cuts balanced by rising gasoline duties and sales taxes fueled inflation. Unemployment spread as she slashed subsidies to faltering industries. Tight money policies drove up interest rates to as high as 22 percent, strengthening the pound, hobbling investment at home and hurting competitiveness overseas. A record 10,000 businesses went bankrupt.

Saying it would take years to cure Britain of the havoc wrought by socialism, Mrs. Thatcher warned, "Things will get worse before they get better."

In the summer of 1981, discontent boiled over into days of rioting in many areas, shocking the nation. In the face of national shame over the violence, she was forced to give way.

Mrs. Thatcher later said that 1981 was her worst year in office. But by the spring of 1982, things were looking up. Inflation was falling; so was the value of the pound, which gave a boost to Britain's exports and, along with tax cuts, began to feed economic growth.

In foreign affairs, she won some small victories. Standing up to the European Community, she argued that her country paid out much more to the organization than it got back in benefits, and won a significant reduction in contributions. Though her rhetoric and style had caught the world's eye, she had yet to stake a position as a world leader.

Then in 1982 Mrs. Thatcher ordered a Royal Navy fleet to the Falkland Islands in the South Atlantic, where British settlers had lived since the 1920s and which Argentina had invaded on April 2. In a 10-week war, the

British retook the islands. The victory cemented Mrs. Thatcher's reputation as a leader to be reckoned with.

Her political fortunes were enhanced by squabbling among her opponents. Far-left factions and militant union leaders were gaining strength in the Labour Party as economic discontent and tensions with the Soviet Union grew.

In 1980, Mrs. Thatcher and President Jimmy Carter had agreed to deploy American intermediate-range cruise missiles in Britain in response to a Soviet buildup in Eastern Europe. Under Mr. Reagan the next year, the United States, with Mrs. Thatcher's support, persuaded other European allies to deploy the missiles. The arms buildups ignited demonstrations across Western Europe.

After Mrs. Thatcher called an election in June 1983, the Conservatives won 397 of the 650 seats in Parliament, the biggest swing in voting since Labour's landslide victory against Churchill in 1945. The working class voted heavily for the Conservatives.

It was an axiom of British politics that one never picked a quarrel with the pope or the National Union of Mineworkers. Mrs. Thatcher flouted it. In 1984 the government announced plans to shut down several coal mines and to eliminate 20,000 of the industry's 180,000 jobs.

The Marxist president of the union, Arthur Scargill, called a walkout on March 6, 1984. The strike was violent. It finally ended in March 1985, after 362 days, without a settlement.

Mrs. Thatcher now pushed harder to fulfill her vision of "popular capitalism." The sale of state-owned industries shifted some 900,000 jobs into the private sector. More than 1 million public housing units were sold to their occupants.

Across the Atlantic, Mr. Reagan cheered Britain's turnaround, and the Reagan-Thatcher axis became, in the words of Hugo Young, "the most enduring personal alliance in the Western world throughout the 1980s."

She vigorously supported the United States' fight against terrorism. In April 1986, after terrorist attacks in Western Europe, the United States sought permission to launch American warplanes from bases in Britain for attacks on Libya. Mrs. Thatcher granted it. The bombing destroyed the living quarters of the Libyan leader, Col. Muammar el-Qaddafi.

Mrs. Thatcher's support for the mission outraged many Britons. But she said that terrorism demanded a united response.

In the 1980s, the Soviet Union was rife with political disillusion and economic chaos. The Reagan administration sought to add pressure by moving ahead with high-tech weapons, including plans for the Strategic Defense Initiative, the space-based defense system known as Star Wars, which would in theory enable the United States to intercept incoming nuclear missiles.

Mr. Gorbachev was unalterably opposed to Star Wars, as were many in the West. Mrs. Thatcher was ambivalent. But in December 1984, she helped draft a position on Star Wars, later adopted by Mr. Reagan, that assured the Soviets that the program would enhance nuclear deterrence, not undercut it, and that it would not get in the way of arms control talks.

Nevertheless, it did. The negotiations fell apart.

The president's position infuriated his critics. But many people in NATO and the Pentagon were relieved. "The fact is that nuclear weapons have prevented not only nuclear war but conventional war in Europe for 40 years," Mrs. Thatcher said in a speech.

Mrs. Thatcher did not fare so well in other battles. In the face of popular opposition, she retreated from plans to privatize the water industry and the National Health Service, replace college grants with a student loan program, cut back pensions and revamp the social security system. But the economy worked in her favor. When she called an election for June 1987, the Tories were returned to power.

That October, Wall Street crashed. In the following months, disagreements among the Tories over Britain's future in the European Community and a series of other events forced Mrs. Thatcher to surrender hard-fought gains.

To make the local authorities more accountable for the way they spent tax money, Mrs. Thatcher pushed through a measure that replaced property taxes with a "poll tax" on all adult residents of a community. The tax was intended to make everyone, not just property owners, pay for local government services. In practice, the measure was manifestly unfair and deeply unpopular. In March 1990, protests flared into riots.

Within her own party, there was a growing feeling that the Iron Lady had become a liability and she was supplanted by a protégé, John Major, the chancellor of the Exchequer. She resigned on Nov. 28, 1990.

In retirement, she continued to call for firmness in the face of aggression. She backed the war to oust the Iraqi leader, Saddam Hussein.

By then Mrs. Thatcher had begun to show signs of the dementia, which would become, to much criticism, the focus of "Iron Lady," a 2011 film about her with Meryl Streep in the title role.

Tony Blair's victory over Mr. Major in 1997 seemed in a curious way to emphasize the success of Mrs. Thatcher's policies. Mr. Blair's platform promised to liberate business from government restrictions, end taxes that discouraged investment and reduce dependence on the state.

Mrs. Thatcher's legacy, "in most respects, is uncontested by the Blair government," Hugo Young, her biographer, said in a 1999 interview. "It made rather concrete something she once said: 'My task will not be completed until the Labour Party has become like the Conservative Party, a party of capitalism.'"

NELSON MANDELA

July 18, 1918–December 5, 2013

By Bill Keller

Nelson Mandela, who led the emancipation of South Africa from white minority rule and served as his country's first black president, becoming an international emblem of dignity and forbearance, died Thursday. Mr. Mandela, who died at home, was 95.

The South African president, Jacob Zuma, announced Mr. Mandela's death.

Mr. Mandela's quest for freedom took him from the court of tribal royalty to the liberation underground to a prison rock quarry to the presidential suite of Africa's richest country. When his first term of office was up, he cheerfully handed over power to an elected successor, the country still gnawed by crime, poverty and corruption but a democracy, remarkably at peace.

The question most often asked about Mr. Mandela was how, after whites had humiliated his people, tortured and murdered many of his friends, and cast him into prison for 27 years, he could be so evidently free of spite.

The government he formed when he finally won the chance was an improbable fusion of races and beliefs, including many of his former oppressors. Mr. Mandela overcame a personal mistrust to share both power and a Nobel Peace Prize with the white president who preceded him, F.W. de Klerk. And as president, from 1994 to 1999, he devoted much energy to moderating the bitterness of his black electorate and reassuring whites fearful of vengeance.

The explanation for his absence of rancor, at least in part, is that Mr. Mandela was that rarity among revolutionaries: a capable statesman, comfortable with compromise and impatient with the doctrinaire.

When the question was put to Mr. Mandela in an interview for this obituary in 2007—after such barbarous torment, how do you keep hatred in check?—his answer was almost dismissive: Hating clouds the mind. Leaders cannot afford to hate. Some who worked with him said this apparent magnanimity came easily to him because he always regarded himself as superior to his persecutors.

In his five years as president, Mr. Mandela lost some luster at home as he strained to hold together a divided populace and turn a fractious liberation movement into a credible government.

Some blacks, including Winnie Madikizela-Mandela, Mr. Mandela's former wife, complained that he had moved too slowly to narrow the vast gulf between the impoverished black majority and the more prosperous white minority. Some whites said he

had failed to control crime, corruption and cronyism. Undoubtedly Mr. Mandela had become less attentive to the details of governing, turning over the daily responsibilities to the deputy who would succeed him in 1999, Thabo Mbeki.

But few among his countrymen doubted that without his authority and political shrewdness, South Africa might well have descended into civil war long before it reached its imperfect state of democracy.

Mr. Mandela was deep into a life prison term when he caught the notice of the world as a symbol of the opposition to apartheid, literally "apartness" in the Afrikaans language, a system of racial gerrymandering that stripped blacks of their citizenship and relegated them to reservation-style "homelands" and townships. Around 1980, exiled leaders of the foremost anti-apartheid movement, the African National Congress, decided that this eloquent lawyer was the perfect hero to humanize their campaign against the system that denied 80 percent of South Africans any voice in their own affairs. "Free Nelson Mandela," already a liberation chant within South Africa, became a pop-chart anthem in Britain.

Mr. Mandela noted in his 1994 autobiography, "Long Walk to Freedom," that this congregation made him the world's best-known political prisoner without knowing precisely who he was. In South Africa, though, and among those who followed the country's affairs closely, Nelson Mandela was already a name to reckon with.

He was born Rolihlahla Mandela on July 18, 1918, in Mvezo, a village of cows, corn and mud huts in the hills of the Transkei, a former British protectorate in the south. His given name, he enjoyed pointing out, translates colloquially as "troublemaker." He received his more familiar English name from a teacher when he began school at age seven.

His father, Gadla Henry Mphakanyiswa, was a chief of the Thembu people, a subdivision of the Xhosa nation. When Nelson was an infant, his father was stripped of his chieftainship. Nine years later, on the death of his father, young Nelson was taken into the home of the paramount chief of the Thembu.

Some close friends would attribute his regal self-confidence to his upbringing in a royal household. Unlike many black South Africans, Mr. Mandela never seemed to doubt that he was the equal of any man. "The first thing to remember about Mandela is that he came from a royal family," said Ahmed Kathrada, a member of his inner circle. "That always gave him a strength."

The enlarging of Mr. Mandela's outlook began at Methodist missionary schools and the University College of Fort Hare, then the country's only residential college for blacks. Studying law at Fort Hare, he fell in with Oliver Tambo, another leader-to-be of the liberation movement. The two were suspended for a student protest in 1940.

Mr. Mandela then ran away to the black metropolis of Soweto, following other young blacks who had left mostly to work in the gold mines around Johannesburg. There he was directed to Walter Sisulu, a spark plug in the African National Congress. Mr. Mandela soon impressed the activists with his ability to win over doubters. "His starting point is that 'I am going to persuade this person no matter what,'" Mr. Sisulu said. "That is his gift. He will go to anybody, anywhere, with that confidence."

Mr. Mandela opened the first black law partnership in South Africa with Mr. Tambo. Impatient with the seeming impotence of their elders in the African National Congress, Mr. Mandela, Mr. Tambo, Mr. Sisulu and other militants also organized the A.N.C. Youth League. Five years later, the young rebels engineered a generational takeover of the African National Congress.

During his years in Soweto, Mr. Mandela married a nurse, Evelyn Ntoko Mase, and they had four children, but the marriage ended abruptly. Not long afterward he met Nomzamo Winifred Madikizela, a stunning, strong-willed young social worker. Mr. Mandela married her in 1958.

In 1961, Mr. Mandela led the African National Congress onto a new road of armed insurrection. He became the first commander of a motley liberation army, grandly named Umkhonto we Sizwe, or Spear of the Nation. The A.N.C.'s armed activities were mostly confined to committing occasional acts of terrorism against civilians.

South Africa's rulers were determined to put Mr. Mandela and his comrades out of action. In 1956, he and scores of other dissidents were arrested on charges of treason. After an acquittal, Mr. Mandela went underground. Upon his capture he was charged with inciting a strike and leaving the country without a passport. His trial resulted in a three-year sentence, but it was just a warm-up for the main event.

Next Mr. Mandela and eight other A.N.C. leaders were charged with sabotage and conspiracy to overthrow the state. It was called the Rivonia trial, for the name of the farm where the defendants had conspired and where incriminating documents were found—many in Mr. Mandela's handwriting—outlining a violent campaign to bring down the regime. At Mr. Mandela's suggestion, the defendants turned the trial into a moral drama that would vindicate them in the court of world opinion. They admitted that they had engaged in sabotage and tried to lay out a political justification for their acts. The four-hour speech with which Mr. Mandela opened the defense's case was one of his most eloquent, and in the view of his biographer, Anthony Sampson, it established him as the leader of both the A.N.C. and the international movement against apartheid.

Mr. Mandela described his evolution from the temptations of black nationalism to the politics of multiracialism. He acknowledged that he was the commander of Spear of the Nation, but asserted that he had turned to violence only after nonviolent resistance had been foreclosed. He likened his alliances with Communists to Churchill's cooperation with Stalin against Hitler. He finished with a coda of his convictions that would endure as an oratorical highlight of South African history.

"I have fought against white domination, and I have fought against black domination," he told the court. "I have cherished the ideal of a democratic and free society in which all persons will live together in harmony and with equal opportunities. It is an ideal for which I hope to live for and to see realized. But my lord, if it needs be, it is an ideal for which I am prepared to die."

Under considerable pressure from liberals at home and abroad to spare the defendants, the judge acquitted one and sentenced Mr. Mandela and the others to life in prison.

Mr. Mandela was 44 when he was manacled and put on a ferry to the Robben Island prison. He would be 71 when he was released.

The routine at Robben Island was one of isolation, boredom and petty humiliations. By day the men were marched to a limestone quarry, where the fine dust stirred up by their labors glued their tear ducts shut.

But for Mr. Mandela and others, Robben Island was a university. In whispered conversations and polemics handed from cellblock to cellblock, the prisoners debated everything from Marxism to circumcision.

Mr. Mandela learned Afrikaans, the language of the dominant whites. He honed his skills as a leader, negotiator and proselytizer, and not only the factions among the prisoners but also some of the white administrators found his charm and iron will irresistible. He credited his prison experience with teaching him the tactics and strategy that would make him president. Almost from his arrival he assumed a kind of command.

Mr. Mandela said he regarded his prison experience as a major factor in his nonracial outlook. He said prison tempered any desire for vengeance by exposing him to sympathetic white guards who smuggled in newspapers and extra rations, and to moderates within the National Party government who approached him in hopes of opening a dialogue.

Above all, prison taught him to be a master negotiator. Mr. Mandela's decision to begin negotiations with the white government was one of the most momentous of his life. With an overture to Kobie Coetsee, the justice minister, and a visit to President P. W. Botha, Mr. Mandela, in 1986, began what would be years of negotiations on the future of South Africa.

In the last months of his imprisonment, he was relocated to Victor Verster Prison outside Cape Town, where the government could meet with him conveniently. He lived in a warden's bungalow and had access to a swimming pool and a chef.

From the moment they learned of the talks, Mr. Mandela's allies in the A.N.C. were suspicious, and their worries were not allayed when the government allowed them to confer with Mr. Mandela in the warden's house. There, Mr. Mandela explained his view that the enemy was morally and politically defeated and the country ungovernable. His strategy, he said, was to give the white rulers every chance to retreat in an orderly way. He was preparing to meet President de Klerk, who had just taken over from Mr. Botha.

In February 1990, Mr. Mandela walked out of prison into a world that he knew little. The African National Congress was now torn by factions. The white government was also split.

Over the next four years Mr. Mandela would be embroiled in a laborious negotiation with both the white government and his own fractious alliance. While he had languished in prison, a campaign of civil disobedience was under way. No one participated more enthusiastically than his wife, Winnie Mandela.

She was jailed and banished with her children to a remote Afrikaner town. When she was released in 1984, she surrounded herself with young thugs who terrorized, kidnapped and killed blacks she deemed hostile to the cause. Yet only in 1995 did he finally file for divorce.

He later fell in love with Graça Machel, an activist for humanitarian causes. They married on Mr. Mandela's 80th birthday. She survives him, as do his two daughters by Winnie Mandela and a daughter by his first wife.

Two years after Mr. Mandela's release from prison, black and white leaders met for negotiations that would lead to an end of white rule. Mr. Mandela and the white president, Mr. de Klerk, maneuvered toward a peaceful transfer of power.

Two years into the negotiations, the two men were jointly awarded the Nobel Peace Prize, but a year after becoming president, with Mr. de Klerk as deputy president, Mr. Mandela said he still suspected Mr. de Klerk of complicity in the murders of countless blacks by police and army units.

Eventually, though, Mr. Mandela and his negotiating team found their way to the grand bargain that assured free elections in exchange for promising opposition parties a share of power and a guarantee that whites would not be subjected to reprisals.

During the elections in April 1994, the African National Congress won 62 percent of the vote, ensuring that Mr. Mandela, as party leader, would be named president. Mr. Mandela was sworn in as president on May 10, and he accepted office with a speech of shared patriotism, summoning South Africans' communal exhilaration in their land and their common relief at being freed from the world's disapproval. "Never, never and never again shall it be that this beautiful land will again experience the oppression of one by another and suffer the indignity of being the skunk of the world," he declared.

Mr. Mandela's instinct for compromise in the interest of unity was evident in the 1995 creation of the Truth and Reconciliation Commission, devised to balance justice and forgiveness in a reckoning of the country's history. The panel offered amnesties for anyone who testified fully on the crimes committed during the apartheid period, and the process was generally counted a success. There was a limit, though, to how much Mr. Mandela could paper over the gulf between white privilege and black privation. He was careless in his relationships with those whose continued investment he saw as vital to South Africa's economy. Corruption and cronyism blossomed.

The South African journalist Mark Gevisser, in his biography of Mr. Mandela's successor as president, Thabo Mbeki, wrote: "The overriding legacy of the Mandela presidency—of the years 1994 to 1999—is a country where the rule of law was entrenched in an unassailable Bill of Rights, and where the predictions of racial and ethnic conflict did not come true. These feats, alone, guarantee Mandela his sanctity. But he was a far better liberator and nation-builder than he was a governor."

to announce the launching of an American satellite, a puny device compared to the Russians' sputnik. In the years that followed, with the illusion of American technological superiority shattered, there was growing criticism of the United States space program.

On the domestic scene the President faced a direct challenge to Federal authority that grew out of resistance to the Supreme Court's ruling, in 1954, that racial segregation in the public schools was unconstitutional.

Riots in Little Rock

Gov. Orval E. Faubus of Arkansas called out the Arkansas National Guard in September, 1957, to prevent Negro students from entering the Little Rock Central High School. When a Federal District Court injunction forced him to withdraw the Guard, rioting broke out and the Negroes had to leave school.

Eisenhower ordered Federal troops to Little Rock, where they restored order. In this crisis Eisenhower spoke up for obedience to Federal law and the courts, but he avoided a direct commitment to the morality of integration.

During 1957, however, he signed the first major bill since Reconstruction to protect the constitutional rights of minorities. The bill created a Civil Rights Commission to investigate denials of minority rights.

Although the President's handling of the explosive Little Rock situation was applauded in the North and West, his prestige generally dropped with the downturn in the national economy. Starting late in 1957 and accelerating in 1958, the slump brought to an end the period of high employment and prosperity that marked Eisenhower's first term.

Some observers attributed the decline of Eisenhower's influence to his being the first President whose tenure was limited to two terms by the 22d Amend-

AMERICAN
LEADERS

HENRY CLAY

April 12, 1777–June 29, 1852

WASHINGTON—How the concerns of life and death intermingle! Amid the hot contention of political strife, a slow, dull sound, filling every ear, brings the long expected annunciation that Henry Clay is no more. The greatest of American Senators has passed to the silent land, and each one who hears has a grief or a hope of his own. Last night bonfires illumined every street; shouts of anticipated victory and hoarse murmurs of defiance went up together; we seemed on the eve of a time, when

> The midnight brought the signal sound of
> strife;
> The morn, the marshaling in arms; the
> day,
> Battle's magnificently stern array!

But the morn brought only "the death in life," its solemn silence and its awful gloom. The curtains were gathered around the dying couch of Henry Clay, and at 11 o'clock darkness had set its seal upon his eyes forever. This does but deepen the sadness of my heart, and consecrates my humble sorrow; for while moving with all this stirring life, and talking coldly of politics and its chances, a little thing that had twined among the tendrils of my inmost nature and nestled there was torn rudely from me. I see now its tiny hand and wavy hair, beckoning and leading the way to that unknown shore where the great and humble must together lie. But pardon this outburst.

The eulogies upon Mr. Clay will not be biographies; for none need be told where he was born, or what he has done. The facts of his life are engraven on the public memory. During the long months of his final illness the Nation's heart has been to him a "Storied urn, an animated bust," on which his "fame and elegy" are written. A niche is reserved for him in the temple consecrated to American statesmanship, eloquence and genius, opposite to Jefferson, Franklin, the elder and younger Adams, and Patrick Henry.

Mr. Clay was surrounded, in dying, by all that could inspire hope and alleviate sorrow. His son, several affectionate friends and physicians, and his spiritual consoler, Dr. Butler, of the Episcopal Church, were present. His last words were these, addressed to Dr. Butler: "Don't leave me; I am dying, I am gone." Instantly after speaking these words, he sank back and expired.

It is well known that Henry Clay received his early education in a log schoolhouse. At the age of 14 he went into a store, from which he soon after entered a law office as copyist, where at first his awkward manners, unhandsome face, and pepper-and-salt dress brought upon him jeers and jokes from his fellow clerks, who soon found it, however, their interest, as well as their pleasure, to treat him with respect.

The following toast, given in 1843, at a Fourth of July dinner in Virginia, by Mr. R. Hughes, illustrates some traits in his character and history:

"He walked barefooted, and so did I—he went to mill and so did I—he was good to his mamma and so was I. I know him like a book, and love him like a brother."

Mrs. Watkins, the mother, died in 1827. Mr. Clay was always a man of deep feelings, and sustained heavy afflictions during life in the loss of his children. Two of his daughters, born in 1800 and 1816, died in infancy. Two other daughters, born in 1809 and 1813, died at the age of 14. The first of these died at Ashland; the other, in 1825, while on her way to Washington. On hearing of this fresh bereavement, Mr. Clay fainted, and did not leave his room for many days.

Mr. Clay always showed himself prompt to sympathize with persons in distress, and ever ready to aid the helpless. He often volunteered his legal services to rescue persons from slavery whom he believed to be unjustly held in bondage, and he never allowed any person to go undefended on account of poverty. He once found a poor Irishman named Russell, who had been lynched and beaten by a gang of persons calling themselves Regulators, and who had compelled him to abandon his house and property. Mr. Clay promptly interfered on his behalf, volunteered his services at great personal risk, and broke up the gang. Many other instances are recorded, of his having undertaken the defense of persons in distress—widows and orphans, who had not the means to employ other counsel.

Mr. Clay was as magnanimous as he was brave. He was quite as ready to acknowledge a fault as to resent an insult. In 1816, while he and Mr. [John] Pope were opposing candidates for Congress, Mr. Clay took offense at something which had been said by some of Mr. Pope's friends and attacked him in the streets of Lexington. The next morning, satisfied he was wrong, he made an apology to the gentleman, and at a public gathering made the same acknowledgment. The magnanimity of the act, and the grace with which it was done, commended him anew to public favor.

Mr. Clay's voice was one of remarkable compass, melody and power. It has often been remarked by spectators in the galleries of the Senate chamber that his ordinary tones in conversing at his desk could be heard more distinctly than the voices of other Senators who might be speaking at the time. He used this wonderful organ with powerful effect. His manner in speaking was marvelously graceful, full of action and energy, yet never for an instant failing in dignity, and admirably adapted to the special topic or mood of the moment.

Many persons are still living in Kentucky who heard his earliest popular harangues in that State, when he was merely a stripling—and according to their testimony, these efforts were marked by the same features which distinguished his maturer exertions. His arguments and appeals before juries in criminal cases, were long remembered as wonderful specimens of forensic eloquence.

No man, probably, ever had more of that quick penetration of intellect which enabled him instantly to seize the strong points of a case than Mr. Clay. His power over a jury was even more remarkable, and instances were frequent where he secured the acquittal of persons charged with murder, against the clearest evidence, simply through his resistless appeals to the sympathies of the jury. It is stated that no person put in peril of his life through the criminal code was ever defended by Mr. Clay without being saved.

In one case, a man named Willis, accused of a peculiarly atrocious murder, Mr. Clay succeeded in dividing the jury. Upon the second trial, Mr. Clay startled the audience by claiming a verdict on the sole ground that no man could be put in peril of his life twice for the same offense. The Court forbade the use of that argument, whereupon Mr. Clay took his papers and left the room, declaring he could not go on under such ruling. Finding the whole responsibility thus thrown upon him, the judge sent for him and invited his return. Mr. Clay came back, pressed that point, and secured an immediate acquittal on that ground alone.

Mr. Clay, as prosecuting attorney, once secured the conviction of a slave for murder, in a case where if he had been free, it would have been only manslaughter. He was so affected by the result that he resigned his commission in disgust.

We could fill column after column with such anecdotes. They all tend to illustrate the traits in the character of Mr. Clay, which were conspicuous throughout his life.

DANIEL WEBSTER

January 18, 1782–October 24, 1852

Daniel Webster, Secretary of State in the Government of the United States, died yesterday morning at 3 o'clock at his home in Marshfield, Massachusetts.

Thus has closed the most illustrious career which has yet graced the civil history of this Republic.

Daniel Webster was born in the town of Salisbury, New Hampshire, on the 18th of January, 1782. His age, at his death, was seventy years.

Ebenezer Webster, the father of the Great Statesman, was born in Kingston, New Hampshire, and served in the French War of 1763. He later commenced a settlement on a branch of the Merrimack River, eventually called Salisbury, and served in the state legislature and as a judge. His second wife, Abigail Eastman, was the mother of Daniel.

While still young, Daniel Webster was daily sent two miles and a half to school, in the middle of Winter, and on foot. In his 14th year, he was placed in Phillips' Academy at Exeter, N.H.

In 1797, Daniel entered Dartmouth College. Upon graduation, he returned home, determined to adopt the profession of the law.

He was married in June, 1808, to Grace Fletcher. They had four children, of whom one survives.

Soon after the Declaration of War against England, Mr. Webster entered public life.

Mr. Webster took his seat in Congress in May, 1813, and was placed by Henry Clay, Speaker of the House, upon the Committee of Foreign Affairs. He delivered his maiden speech on 10th June, 1813, and in it a young man previously unknown in political circles made an indelible impression.

Great Britain then insisting upon her right of search in vessels belonging to the United States, and the mother country and her daughter were again embroiled in war.

Of the speeches of Mr. Webster on the Embargo, the politician Edward Everett said: "His speeches on these questions raised him to the front rank of debaters. He manifested upon his entrance into public life that variety of knowledge, familiarity with the history and traditions of the Government and self possession on the floor, which in most cases are acquired by time and long experience."

Mr. Webster was reelected to the House of Representatives in August, 1814. In the Fall of 1822, he again took his seat in the House, this time representing the City of Boston.

DANIEL WEBSTER.

Early in the session, the subject of the Revolution in Greece came before the House. Mr. Webster presented the following resolution: "That provision ought to be made by law, for defraying the expense incident to the appointment of an Agent or Commissioner to Greece."

In his famous speech in support of this resolution, Mr. Webster showed himself a discriminating judge of the laws that govern the relations of nations. In sympathy for the struggling Greeks, he was not surpassed by any men of his time. He uttered a trumpet-toned remonstrance against the tyranny which sought their degradation. The "Greek Speech" will be remembered as long as American oratory has a place among the records of history.

In November, 1826, Mr. Webster was again solicited to represent his district in the House, but a vacancy occurred in the Senate, and Mr. Webster was chosen to fill that post.

Toward the close of 1827, a domestic affliction was visited upon Mr. Webster, in the loss of his wife, which prevented him from taking his seat until January, 1828.

Gen. [Andrew] Jackson was elected to the Presidency in the fall of 1828, and Mr. Calhoun, as Vice-President, occupied the Chair of the Senate.

In the Senatorial career of Mr. Webster, it is difficult to embrace all the great movements in which he took part.

One event in which Mr. Webster won laurels for himself was the part he took in the great controversy between the North and South—between the national views of the Constitution which he had often vindi-

cated, and the doctrines of state rights, which had been enforced by Mr. Calhoun.

The first session of the 21st Congress opened in December, 1829. Attention was directed to the topic of the public lands. Both the North and the South sought to secure the political alliance of the Western states. Mr. Foote of Connecticut introduced a resolution proposing to limit the sale of public lands.

It has been alleged that this resolution was the starting point of a crusade against New England, and especially Mr. Webster.

The incidents that followed are so vividly presented in one of the chapters of Mr. March's Reminiscences that we transfer it to our columns.

"It was on Tuesday, January the 26th, 1830, that the Senate resumed the consideration of Foote's Resolution. As early as 9 o'clock of this morning crowds poured into the Capitol, in hot haste; at 12 o'clock, the hour of meeting, the Senate Chamber was filled to its utmost capacity. The very stairways were dark with men, who hung on to one another, like bees in a swarm.

"Mr. Webster was never more self possessed. The calmness of superior strength was visible everywhere; in countenance, voice and bearing. A deep-seated conviction of the extraordinary character of the emergency, and his ability to control it, seemed to possess him."

Who can ever forget the tremendous burst of eloquence with which the orator spoke of the Old Bay State or his tones of pathos:

"Mr. President, I shall enter on no encomium upon Massachusetts. There she is—behold her, and judge for yourselves. There is her history: the world knows it by heart. The past, at least, is secure. There is Boston, and Concord, and Lexington, and Bunker Hill—and there they will remain forever. The bones of her sons, falling in the great struggle for independence, now lie mingled with the soil of every State, from New England to Georgia, and there they will lie forever. And, sir, where American Liberty raised its first voice, and where its youth was nurtured and sustained, there it still lives, in the strength of its manhood and full of its original spirit."

No one ever looked the orator as he did. His swarthy countenance lighted up with excitement, he appeared amid the smoke, the fire, the thunder of his eloquence, like Vulcan in his armory forging thoughts for the Gods!

His voice penetrated every corner of the Senate as he pronounced these words:

"When my eyes shall be turned to behold, for the last time, the sun in heaven, may I not see him shining on the broken and dishonored fragments of a once glorious Union; on States dissevered, discordant, belligerent! on a land rent with civil feud, or drenched, it may be, in fraternal blood! Let their last feeble and lingering glance rather behold the gorgeous ensign of the Republic, now known and honored throughout the earth, still full high advanced, its arms and trophies streaming in their original luster, not a stripe erased nor polluted, not a single star obscured, bearing for its motto no such miserable interrogatory as, 'What is all this worth?' Nor those other words of delusion and folly, 'Liberty first, and Union afterwards;' but everywhere, spread all over in characters of living light, blazing on all its ample folds, as they float over the sea and over the land, and in every wind under the whole heavens, that other sentiment, dear to every American heart, Liberty and Union, now and forever, one and inseparable!"

Mr. Webster's "great speech," as it is universally known, produced a sensation. The debate continued for weeks, but the argument had been exhausted.

Mr. Webster continued to take an active part in the debates of the Senate throughout the administration of General Jackson and his successor.

The 22nd Congress was faced with an issue of pressing importance. In South Carolina discontent under the Tariff [acts] had greatly increased. Large manufacturing interest had grown up in the Northern and Central States, while the South had not experienced similar benefits.

The South turned against the principle of protection, and its constitutionality had been denied. Mr. Calhoun had asserted the right of any State to nullify laws which she might consider unconstitutional. Mr. Webster had always maintained the supremacy of the Constitution and the Supreme Court of the United States as the final interpreter of its provisions.

Gen. Jackson was reelected President in the Fall of 1832; and the people of South Carolina were roused into the most intense excitement against the North and the protective policy. The Legislature declared the Tariff acts unconstitutional, and advised all citizens to put themselves in military array.

A bill was proposed that gave the President power to put down any armed resistance to the revenue laws of the United States. Upon this bill, and resolutions which he introduced, embodying his views on the right of a State to annul laws of Congress, Mr. Calhoun made the ablest argument ever advanced in support of his position.

Mr. Webster immediately entered upon a reply. In it he laid down the following propositions:

> I. That the Constitution of the United States is not a compact between the people of the several States in their sovereign capacities, but a Government creating direct relations between itself and individuals.
> II. That no State authority has power to dissolve those relations.
> III. That there is a supreme law, consisting of the Constitution of the United States, acts of Congress, and treaties.
> IV. That an attempt by a State to nullify an Act of Congress is a usurpation on the powers of the General Government and a violation of the Constitution.

The inauguration of Gen. [Benjamin] Harrison, in 1841, was the inauguration of a new era in the life of Mr. Webster, the one in which he became Secretary of State.

At the opening of the Congress of 1845, Mr. Webster resumed his seat in the Senate. He found under discussion some of the gravest questions that ever agitated the country.

The settlement of the Oregon boundary dispute was effected during the first year of Mr. Polk's administration, by a division of the territory to which both England and the United States laid claim. A bill passed the House of Representatives to organize a Government for the territory thus acquired. When it reached the Senate, it was amended, by making the Missouri Compromise a part of it—excluding Slavery above, and admitting it below, the parallel of 36° 30' north latitude.

On the 12th of August, 1848, Mr. Webster insisted upon the right of Congress to exclude slavery from this territory, and against any further extension of slave territory.

"The Southern States have peculiar laws, and by those laws there is property in slaves," he said. "The real meaning, then, of Southern gentlemen, in making this complaint, is, that they cannot go into the territories of the United States carrying with them their own peculiar local law—a law which creates property in persons. This demand I, for one, shall resist."

The bill passed with a clause forever excluding slavery from the territory.

Mr. Webster has achieved high distinction in three walks of life. Surpassed by few in the eloquence of his appeals to the jury, as a lawyer he stands unrivaled. As a statesman, no American except Alexander Hamilton can maintain a comparison with him. He loved his country, and he reverenced the Constitution. But Mr. Webster has achieved the highest rank as a literary man. All the products of his pen and the utterances of his tongue will be studied and admired by future ages.

And great as Mr. Webster was in all these spheres of intellectual activity, he was equally great in the department of conversation. We cannot imagine a richer contribution to the literature of America and the world than would be a record of Mr. Webster's conversations upon topics of public concern.

ABRAHAM LINCOLN

February 12, 1809–April 15, 1865

WASHINGTON—Abraham Lincoln died this morning at 22 minutes after 7 o'clock.

Official notice of the death of the late President Abraham Lincoln was given by the heads of departments this morning to Andrew Johnson, Vice-President. Mr. Johnson appeared before the Hon. Salmon P. Chase, Chief Justice of the United States, and took the oath of office, as President of the United States.

All business in the departments was suspended during the day.

It is now ascertained with reasonable certainty that two assassins were engaged in the horrible crime, Wilkes Booth being the one that shot the President, who was attending a performance at Ford's Theatre, and the other, a companion of his, whose name is not known.

It appears from a letter found in Booth's trunk that the murder was planned before the 4th of March, but fell through then because the accomplice backed out until "Richmond could be heard from." Booth and his accomplice were at the livery stable at 6 o'clock last evening, and left there with their horses about 10 o'clock.

It would seem that they had for several days been seeking their chance, but it was not carried into effect until last night.

The murderers have not yet been apprehended. One of them has evidently made his way to Baltimore. The other has not yet been traced.

Two gentlemen, who went to the Secretary of War, Edwin Stanton, to apprize him of the attack on Mr. Lincoln, met at the residence of the former a man muffled in a cloak, who, when accosted by them, hastened away.

It had been the intention of Mr. Stanton to accompany Mr. Lincoln to the theatre, and occupy the same box, but the press of business prevented.

It seems evident that the aim of the plotters was to paralyze the country by at once striking down the head, the heart and the arm of the country.

As soon as the dreadful events were announced in the streets, Superintendent Richards and his assistants were at work to discover the assassin. Every road leading out of Washington was picketed, and every possible avenue of escape was guarded. Steamboats about to depart down the Potomac were stopped.

The Daily Chronicle says:

"As it is suspected that this conspiracy originated in Maryland, the telegraph flashed the mournful news to Baltimore, and all the cavalry was immediately put upon active duty. Every precaution was taken to prevent the escape of the assassin. Several persons were called to testify, and the evidence as elicited before an informal tribunal, and not under oath, was conclusive to this point:

"The murderer of President Lincoln was John Wilkes Booth. His hat was found in the private box, and identified by several persons who had seen him within the last two days, and the spur which he dropped by accident, after he jumped to the stage, was identified as one of those which he had obtained from the stable where he hired his horse.

"Booth has played more than once at Ford's Theatre, and is acquainted with its exits and entrances."

Secretary of State Seward was also shot that evening, at his home, and the person who shot him left behind him a slouched hat and a rusty navy revolver.

Maunsell B. Field, assistant to the Secretary of the Treasury Department, gave this account of events:

"On Friday evening, April 14, 1865, I was reading the evening paper in Willard's Hotel, at about 10½ o'clock, when I was startled by the report that an attempt had been made a few minutes before to assassinate the President at Ford's Theatre.

"Immediately I proceeded to the scene of the alleged assassination. I found considerable crowds on

the streets leading to the theatre, and a very large one in front of the theatre and the house directly opposite, where the President had been carried after the attempt upon his life.

"I obtained ingress to the house. I was informed that the President was dying; but I was desired not to communicate his condition to Mrs. Lincoln, who was in the front parlor. She appeared hysterical, and exclaimed over and over: "Oh, why didn't he kill me?"

"I returned to Willard's, it now being 2 o'clock in the morning, and remained there until between 3 and 4 o'clock, when I again went to the house where the President was. I proceeded at once to the bedroom on the parlor floor in which the President was lying.

"The bed was a double one, and the President lay diagonally across it. The pillows were saturated with blood. There was a patchwork coverlet thrown over the President, which was only so far removed as to enable the physicians in attendance to feel the arteries of the neck or the heart. The President was breathing regularly, and did not seem to be suffering.

"Among the persons present in the room were the Secretary of War, the Secretary of the Navy, the Postmaster-General, the Attorney-General, the Secretary of the Treasury, the Secretary of the Interior, the Assistant-Secretary of the Interior, Capt. Robert Lincoln, the President's son, and Maj. John Hay.

"For several hours the breathing continued regularly. But about 7 o'clock a change occurred, and the breathing was interrupted at intervals, which became longer and more frequent. But not till 22 minutes past 7 o'clock in the morning did the flame flicker out.

"The President's eyes after death were not entirely closed. I closed them myself with my fingers, and one of the surgeons brought pennies and placed them on the eyes, and subsequently substituted for them silver half-dollars.

"In fifteen minutes there came over the mouth a smile that seemed almost an effort of life. I had never seen upon the President's face an expression more genial.

"About fifteen minutes before the decease, Mrs. Lincoln came into the room, and threw herself upon her dying husband's body. She was allowed to remain there only a few minutes, when she was removed in a sobbing condition.

"Presently her carriage came up, and she was removed to it. She was in a state of tolerable composure until she reached the door, when, glancing at the theatre opposite, she repeated several times: 'That dreadful house! That dreadful house!'"

* * *

The corpse of the late President has been laid out in the northwest wing of the White House. It is dressed in the suit of black clothes worn by him at his late Inauguration. A placid smile rests upon his features. White flowers have been placed over the breast.

The corpse of the President will be laid out in state in the east room on Tuesday, to give the public an opportunity to see once more the features of him they loved so well.

The catafalque upon which the body will rest will be placed there. The catafalque will be lined with fluted white satin, and the outside will be covered with black velvet. Steps will be placed at the side to enable the public to get a perfect view of the face.

The funeral ceremonies of the late President will take place on Wednesday next. The procession will form at 11 o'clock, and the religious service will commence at noon. The procession will move at 2 P.M.

The remains will be taken to Mr. Lincoln's home at Springfield, Illinois.

The funeral car is to be a magnificent affair. The body of the car will be covered with black cloth from which will hang festoons of cloth fastened by rosettes of white and black satin over bows of white and black velvet. The bed of the car, on which the coffin will rest, will be eight feet from the ground, and over this will rise a canopy draped with black velvet.

A silver plate upon the coffin over the breast bears the following inscription:

ABRAHAM LINCOLN. SIXTEENTH PRESIDENT OF THE UNITED STATES, Born July 12, 1809. Died April 15, 1865.

A few locks of hair were removed from the President's head for the family previous to the remains being placed in the coffin.

The Extra Star has the following:

"Developments have been made within the past twenty-four hours, showing the existence of a deep laid plot of a gang of conspirators to murder President Lincoln and his Cabinet. We have reason to believe that Secretary Seward received an intimation from Europe that something of a very desperate character was to transpire at Washington; and it is more than probable that the intimation had reference to the plot of assassination.

"The pickets encircling this city on Friday night to prevent the escape of the parties who murdered President Lincoln were fired upon at several points by concealed foes.

"It was ascertained some weeks ago that the late President had received several private letters warning him that an attempt would probably be made upon his life. But to this he did not seem to attach much, if any, importance."

* * *

Abraham Lincoln was a great man, great intellectually. This was not universally admitted, but a brief glance at his career was sufficient to establish it. He was born in the humblest walks of life, had no advantages of education, had not been aided by any of those adventitious circumstances which assist so many others, and yet had gradually risen until he had reached the highest position in the State.

He had been a leading lawyer, a member of the Legislature of his own State, a member of Congress, the leader of his party in a memorable struggle for the Senatorship, and finally a successful candidate for the Presidency of the party that monopolizes the intelligence of the country. In his speeches delivered in his contest with Frederick Douglass are passages as noble and sublime as ever fell from the lips of any statesman in the country.

His lecture delivered in New York City, in the Cooper Union, in the midst of the learning and refinement of the metropolis, was universally admitted to be the ablest of the campaign. He was the first statesman to enunciate the great truth that the country could not exist partly slave and partly free.

In the discharge of his office, he bore himself with such a burden as no other President had ever borne, deciding questions the most difficult, giving gracious audience to the highest and the lowest, holding firmly the helm of affairs amid the stormiest seas, and conducting all to a successful issue.

The course of Mr. Lincoln for the past four years proves the possession of high intellectual endowments. Few men had ever had such opportunities to benefit their race. No other man since Washington had enjoyed such an opportunity of performing great services for his country.

The emancipating of the slaves was the golden attribute on which his future fame would rest. The Emancipation Proclamation will carry down his fame to the last syllable of recorded time. This had secured him the blessing of those who were ready to perish, and ensured for him such a preeminence among the great and good that he can never be forgotten.

The assassination has embalmed him in the grateful and lasting remembrance of mankind. He was above all a good man, an honest man. The country may well be thankful that one so scrupulous and conscientious was at the helm in these stormy times. He loved his fellow men. With the poor negro he was a demi-god. The bitterest tears shed over his grave will be by the race from whose manacled limbs he struck the fetters, and for whom he did so much.

THEODORE ROOSEVELT

October 27, 1858–January 6, 1919

OYSTER BAY, L.I., —Theodore Roosevelt, former President of the United States, died this morning at his home on Sagamore Hill.

His physicians said that the cause of death was a clot of blood which detached itself from a vein and entered the lungs.

A contributing cause was the fever he contracted during his explorations in Brazil, when he discovered the River of Doubt in 1914. This fever left a poison in the blood.

Colonel Roosevelt, who was 60, was working hard as late as Saturday, dictating articles and letters. He spent Sunday quietly, but looked and felt well, until shortly before 11 o'clock.

Colonel Roosevelt had no idea that he was seriously ill, and was full of plans for the future. When asked about his health by visitors, his reply was a vigorous "Bully!"

The village of Oyster Bay was stunned by the news. Colonel Roosevelt was appreciated by the village as a world figure, but he also was as much of a fellow townsman as the village blacksmith.

When Colonel Roosevelt returned from his South American journey, he gave the first account of his discoveries in an address at the local church, months ahead of the announcement of the discovery of the mysterious Brazilian River, now the Rio Teodoro, in a magazine. He was a village institution in the role of Santa Claus at the Cove Neck School, near Sagamore Hill.

Five airplanes from Quentin Roosevelt Field flew in "V" formation over Sagamore Hill in the afternoon and dropped wreaths of laurel about the house.

Only members of Colonel Roosevelt's family and his intimate friends knew how deeply he suffered because of the death of Quentin, his youngest son, who was killed in combat in France on July 14. This is believed to have been a contributing cause of his death.

When the news was confirmed, Colonel Roosevelt, who had always declared that families should accept cheerfully the sacrifice of their sons in the war, issued a statement in which he said that he and Mrs. Roosevelt took pride in his death.

At his death Colonel Roosevelt carried in his body the bullet which was fired by Schrank, at Milwaukee, during the Presidential campaign of 1912, which nearly resulted in Colonel Roosevelt's death because he went on and delivered his speech immediately after the attack.

Of all the accidents which Colonel Roosevelt went through, that which left the worst effects happened in South America. He tore his leg when he was thrown from a boat while descending the River of Doubt and the wound became badly infected. While ill from this he suffered an attack of fever.

Colonel Roosevelt was also partially blind and partially deaf. The sight of his left eye was destroyed while he was in the White House in a boxing match. The hearing of one ear was destroyed by an abscess. He was ordered by his physicians to give up violent exercise, but this advice he would not follow.

Mr. Roosevelt came from one of the oldest Dutch-American families. The founder of the family, Claes Martenzoon van Rosevelt, as the name was then spelled, came to this country in 1649.

His mother, Martha Bulloch, was a Southerner. His father, Theodore Roosevelt, Sr., was a philanthropist and the works he accomplished for the poor were legion.

The second Theodore Roosevelt was born in this city Oct. 27, 1858. He was graduated from Harvard in 1880, and was an officeholder almost continuously from 1882 until he retired from the Presidency in 1909.

As a boy he was puny and sickly; but with that indomitable determination which characterized his every act, he transformed his feeble body not merely into a strong one, but into one of the strongest. This physical feebleness bred in him nervousness and self-distrust, and in the same indomitable way he set himself to make himself a man of self-confidence and courage.

"When a boy," he wrote in his autobiography, "I read a passage in one of Marryat's books which always impressed me. In this passage the captain of some small British man-of-war is explaining to the hero how to acquire the quality of fearlessness. He says that at the outset almost every man is frightened when he goes into action, but that the course to follow is for the man to keep such a grip on himself that he can act just as if he was not frightened. After this is kept up long enough it changes from pretense to reality, and the man does in very fact become fearless by sheer dint of practicing fearlessness when he does not feel it.

"This was the theory upon which I went. There were all kinds of things of which I was afraid at first, ranging from grizzly bears to 'mean' horses and gunfighters; but by acting as if I was not afraid I gradually ceased to be afraid."

After graduation he took up the study of law, but did not stay at it long. He entered politics, and at the age of 23 was elected to the Legislature. Within a year he was the Republican leader in the lower house. With a little band of men like himself, he fought for reform legislation, which at that time was generally regarded as a silk stocking freak. His biggest achievement was forcing an investigation of the crooked machine government of New York City, in which he acted as Chairman of the Investigating Committee, making a recalcitrant Legislature pass bills reforming some of the more flagrant abuses uncovered by the committee.

He served three terms in the Legislature, and in his third year came the great fight that split the Republican Party over the nomination of [James] Blaine for President. Roosevelt fought Blaine to the last ditch and, young as he was, was elected one of the four delegates-at-large to the National Convention, where he fought for the nomination of George F. Edmunds.

When Blaine was nominated, Mr. Roosevelt went off to become a rancher on the Little Missouri. At first the ranchers were disposed to laugh at the "four-eyed dude," but they changed their opinion when they found that no work was too hard for him, no hardship too severe.

Mr. Roosevelt next attracted notice as a hunter of big game. Small game had no attraction for him, and it is doubtful whether he ever shot a rabbit. Only when the beast had some chance against the hunter did sport appeal to him, and the game that seemed most to his taste was the grizzly bear of the Rockies.

In 1880 President Harrison appointed him Civil Service Commissioner. For six years his constant warfare with the spoilsmen kept up as unending commotion among the politicians. He thought nothing of antagonizing even the greatest leaders in the Senate.

When he became President of the Commission, 14,000 Government offices were under civil service rules; when he left in 1895 to run the New York police, 40,000 offices were under civil service rules.

The election of Mayor [William Lafayette] Strong was caused by the Lexow exposures of police corruption in New York, and the new Mayor realized that the problem of police management would be the crucial one of his administration. He urged Mr. Roosevelt to become President of the New York Police Board.

Mr. Roosevelt was warned that the force was so honeycombed with favoritism and blackmail that the board could never ascertain the truth about what the men were doing. Roosevelt smiled and said: "Well, we will see about that," and he personally sought the patrolmen on their beats at unexpected hours of the night, and whenever one was found derelict he was reprimanded or dismissed.

In April, 1897, he was appointed Assistant Secretary of the Navy. He became convinced that war with Spain was inevitable and proceeded to make provision for it. For command of the Asiatic Fleet, Mr. Roosevelt determined to get the appointment for Commodore [George] Dewey and secured the appointment which resulted in so much glory for the American Navy.

When the Spanish War broke out, Mr. Roosevelt resigned from the Navy Department to organize the famous Rough Riders. He did not feel justified in taking command of men, so he became Lieutenant Colonel. Before the campaign was over he felt warranted in taking the Colonelcy. The story of his prowess at Santiago is too well remembered to need rehearsing here.

When the war was over the soldiers were left in Cuba because of the slow arrangements of the War Department for transporting them home. The danger of pestilence among the Americans was great, and it was then that Col. Roosevelt demanded that the soldiers be taken home at once.

When they arrived at Montauk Point someone asked the Colonel about the state of his health. "I'm feeling as fit as a bull moose," he replied. The simile would furnish a name to a political party.

He returned to the United States to find himself a popular idol, with a universal demand for his nomination for Governor of New York. He was elected by a majority of 18,000.

As Governor he consulted with [Thomas] Boss Platt, but the results of these consultations were what Roosevelt wanted and not what Platt wanted. Platt led an unhappy life while Roosevelt was Governor, and determined not to stand for another two years of it. He resorted to the expedient of kicking him upstairs into the Vice Presidency—little dreaming that he was paving the way to an elevation to the Presidency that would make Roosevelt even more of a thorn in Platt's flesh.

Roosevelt was elected Vice President in 1900, but before the regular session of the Senate could meet, McKinley had been shot and Roosevelt was President. He was inaugurated at Buffalo Sept. 14, 1901.

The new President at once pledged himself to carry out President McKinley's policies, and began by inviting the McKinley Cabinet to remain. Then three weeks after his inauguration, he invited Booker T. Washington, who was visiting the White House, to remain to luncheon. The South was up in arms in a moment, and the specter of social equality began to stalk, and it was long before Mr. Roosevelt could live down the impression that he was unfriendly to the South.

Economic questions at once engaged the President's attention. In 1902 he settled the great anthracite coal strike by the unprecedented step of summoning the contending leaders to Washington and using the power of his personality and his office to influence them to a settlement and then by appointing the Coal Strike Commission.

In his message to Congress in 1902, he urged legislation for the control of trusts. About this time action was begun in the Federal courts against violations of the Sherman law, and Attorney General [Henry]

Knox was pressing a suit to dissolve the Northern Securities Company.

Roosevelt jammed through Congress the so-called Elkins bill, which really was a Roosevelt bill and was designed to end the system of giving rebates to favored corporations who had to ship over this or that railroad. In addition, Roosevelt forced the creation of the Bureau of Corporations and invested it with authority to investigate all the corporate concerns in the country.

It was during his first administration that the Panama Canal was made possible. A treaty was eventually negotiated with the new Republic of Panama, and in May, 1904, the Canal Commission secured full control of the Panama Canal Zone and began operations.

He was nominated for President unanimously by the Republican Convention in 1904. Toward the close of the campaign he employed his famous "square deal" term, saying: "All I ask is a square deal. Give every man a fair chance."

In the election that year he received the largest popular and Electoral vote ever given to a President up to that time.

In his first year he performed one of the greatest public acts of his career—the settlement of the Russo-Japanese war. For this the President received the Nobel Peace Prize. But he himself has always said that his greatest contribution to the cause of peace was sending the American fleet to the Pacific in 1907, an act he believed averted war between Japan and the United States.

In 1905 he began fighting for the regulation of railroad rates. In 1900 he had forced the Hepburn bill through Congress in the face of such bitter opposition from his own party that he was obliged to form an alliance with the Democrats. The latter charged bitterly that he threw them aside like a squeezed lemon when they had served his purpose. But he had no hesitation in breaking with the leaders of his own party, and had the satisfaction of putting his bill through.

His popularity now was at its greatest height, and by merely saying the word he could have had a third term. But on the night of his election in 1904 he had announced that he would under no circumstances accept another nomination.

He undertook to secure the nomination of his friend, William H. Taft, the Secretary of War.

Taft was nominated, and the President virtually took charge of his campaign. He planned, as soon as Taft was inaugurated, to leave the country and bury himself in Africa. But between the election and the inauguration a coolness had already sprung up between them.

Roosevelt perceived that Taft intended to change the Roosevelt policies and remove Roosevelt's friends from office. The accounts that reached him as he emerged from the African jungle put the matter beyond a doubt, and when he reached the United States in June 1910, he was already an enemy of Taft.

The insurgent or progressive element in the Republican Party planned early in 1911 to defeat the renomination of President Taft, and it was decided to put forward Robert M. La Follette as the candidate. But a large element among the progressives wanted the nomination of Roosevelt.

At last, early in 1912, seven progressive Governors united in a demand that Roosevelt become a candidate. His answer was, "My hat is in the ring."

President Taft went on the stump to defeat Roosevelt, but his own State [Ohio] went against him. When the Republican Convention met in Chicago, the bitterness between the factions was so great that predictions of rioting in the convention were made. [Taft ultimately received the nomination.]

The night the convention adjourned, Roosevelt's followers proceeded to Orchestra Hall, where he was informally placed in nomination as a bolting candidate. But a real convention was held later, in August, at which the Progressive Party was formally created and Roosevelt was nominated for President.

The Colonel immediately began a stumping tour that took him through nearly every State in the Union. When Election Day arrived it was found that his achievement was something stupendous. Though his party was not born until two months after the regular party conventions, he had put the old Republican Party out of the running. Taft carried only the two small States of Utah and Vermont, while the Progressive Party had carried the great States of California, Michigan, Minnesota, Pennsylvania, and South Dakota. Roosevelt had over 4,000,000 votes.

[The Democratic nominee, Woodrow Wilson, won the election with a plurality of votes, defeating Roosevelt, Taft and the Socialist Party nominee, Eugene V. Debs.]

While the campaign was going on Col. Roosevelt was shot by a crank named John Schrank just as he was going to deliver a speech in Milwaukee. With astonishing courage, the Colonel insisted on going on with his speech. Then he was rushed to a hospital.

About this time Col. Roosevelt was invited to go to Argentina and deliver some lectures on economic problems. He accepted the invitation, and then decided that he would go into the hinterland and do some exploring and hunting.

He sailed on Oct. 4, 1913, and returned May 19, 1914, much weakened by jungle fever and after having had a narrow escape from death. It was while he was on his voyage of exploration up the Duvida River, which he discovered. He was so weakened by the fever that he could not go on. The party was almost without rations, reduced to five crackers each per day.

"This looks like the last for me, Doctor," said the ex-President to Dr. Cajaziera. "If I'm to go, it's all right. You see that the others don't stop for me." But he pulled through.

The Progressive Party was visibly going to the dogs in 1914. The pitiful figure they cut in the election of 1914 made it evident that as a party they had no future.

Then came our entrance into the war. "I and my four sons will go," announced the Colonel. His four sons went, one of them to death, but he could not. The Administration was hostile to his proposal that he raise a division of volunteers, of which he would be brigadier general. This was the bitterest disappointment of his life.

Mr. Roosevelt was twice married. His first wife was Alice Hathaway Lee, who died in 1884. The only child of this marriage was Alice, the clever and attractive girl who became the wife of Congressman Nicholas Longworth.

In 1886 he married Edith Kermit Carow, and they had five children, Ethel, Theodore Jr., Kermit, Archibald and Quentin. The family life of the Roosevelts was ideal.

As an author Mr. Roosevelt has been prolific. His books include "The Winning of the West," "Hunting Trips of a Ranchman," "History of the Naval War of 1812," "Life of Thomas Hart Benton," "History of New York," "The Wilderness Hunter," "American Ideals," "The Rough Riders," and "The Strenuous Life."

WOODROW WILSON

December 28, 1856–February 3, 1924

WASHINGTON—Woodrow Wilson, 28th President of the United States, a commanding world figure and chief advocate of the League of Nations, is dead. He died at 11:15 o'clock this morning, after being unconscious for nearly twelve hours.

Mrs. Wilson, Miss Margaret Wilson, Joseph Wilson, a brother, and Admiral Grayson, his physician, were at the bedside.

Mr. Wilson's last word was "Edith," his wife's name. In a faint voice he called for her yesterday afternoon when she had left his bedside for a moment. His last sentence was spoken on Friday, when he said: "I am a broken piece of machinery. When the machinery is broken—"I am ready."

Mrs. Wilson held his right hand as his life slowly ebbed away.

Thomas Woodrow Wilson (he dropped the first name early in life) was born on Dec. 28, 1856, at Staunton. Va., where his father, the Rev. Joseph Ruggles Wilson, was pastor of the Presbyterian Church. Not long after his birth the family moved to Augusta, Ga. Those who knew Woodrow Wilson well thought

that he got his first stimulus to political thinking under the impressions of the reconstruction period.

He attended Princeton and entered the Law School of the University of Virginia and in 1882 he began to practice in Atlanta, but for law as a trade he appeared to have no aptitude. So he pursued a career in academia, eventually serving Princeton twelve years as professor and for eight more as President.

In his years as professor he wrote both books and magazine articles, and came into demand as a public speaker. He expressed a tenacious adherence to the idea that the place of the executive in the American Government was as the representative of the whole people, responsible for the advocacy before Congress of the greater policies, which could not be entrusted to a body whose members were concerned with local interests, nor to standing committees, impregnable to criticism and managed largely by log-rolling.

In the years leading up to 1912, the country at large was interested in him as a new and forceful representative of the popular political ideas, who was not handicapped by any accumulation of political enemies.

The public had seen him fight at Princeton with the "aristocracy" of the clubs, and with moneyed men on the Board of Trustees, and regarded the battles as a dramatization of the struggle against "special privilege," which was then agitating the country.

In a sense, his entry into New Jersey politics was a sort of minor-league "try-out" which might fit him for fast company. Wilson, a Democrat, won the Governorship by 49,000 votes in a State which had usually been Republican in recent years.

Before the end of 1911 the Wilson-for-President movement was well under way all over the United States.

He won the nomination at Baltimore the next June. With the Republicans divided, the election went as was generally expected; Wilson was a minority President, to be sure, but he had a plurality of more than 2,000,000 over Roosevelt and nearly 3,000,000 over Taft, and he swept the electoral college with 435 votes to Roosevelt's 88 and Taft's 8. The election also gave the Democrats a heavy majority in Congress.

On March 4, 1913, he was inaugurated as President. He soon triumphed on the issues of tariff and currency reform, changes in anti-trust laws and the creation of the Federal Trade Commission.

The outbreak of the European war in August, 1914, seems to have surprised our Government. At the moment it seemed to call only for the formalities of a neutrality proclamation and a general tender of good offices for mediation toward peace.

While the President was criticized by those who were beginning to think that the war was our business, there was spreading among others the conviction that, whether it was our business or not, it might yet spread so far that we would become involved in it. And America was visibly unready for any war more formidable than an excursion into Mexico. The preparedness movement was countered by organized pacifist activities, with which almost from the first the pro-German faction allied itself.

The President treated the preparedness movement with disdain. He styled some of its advocates "nervous and excitable."

There was now a growing prospect that even neutrality might not keep America from uncomfortable entanglements with the warring powers. This danger did not become acute, however, until the Germans on Feb. 4, 1915, declared British waters a war zone and announced the first submarine campaign. The American Government warned that if American vessels were sunk or American citizens killed, it would hold the German Government to "strict accountability."

"Strict accountability," however, had no terrors for the Germans. The submarines began to kill American citizens. With each new episode more Americans turned against the Germans, and the counter-activities of the pacifists and German agents increased.

Complaints against the failure to make the Germans check the submarines were increasing, chiefly in Republican papers, when the Lusitania was sunk on May 7, with the loss of more than 1,200 lives, including upward of a hundred Americans.

There was now a general feeling that something would be done. However, in a speech, the President invented another of the phrases which his opponents have constantly recalled.

"There is such a thing," he said, "as a man being too proud to fight; there is such a thing as a nation being so right that it does not need to convince others by force that it is right."

Still, he sent a note to the German Government warning that the Administration would not "omit any word or act" necessary to defend the rights of Americans.

The country drew a long breath and prepared for whatever might happen. There was violent protest from the professional leaders of Irish and German racial groups and from the pacifists, but the mass of the articulate part of the population seemed ready for war if that must be.

The German answer was a series of evasions and exculpations. Meanwhile more American lives had been lost by the torpedoing of passenger ships, and the pressure of the American Government obtained from Germany on Sept. 1 a promise to torpedo no more passenger liners without warning. And for a time there were no more.

The partisan bitterness shown by pro-German elements in 1915 had been a revelation of unsuspected national disunity. In the weeks when war seemed an overnight possibility the President had contemplated the condition of the national defenses, and had seen that they were not adequate. He soon undertook a tour to stir up public interest in an improvement of military and naval defenses.

By 1916 Wilson was renominated at St. Louis by acclamation, and the platform gave his record full endorsement.

A significant episode in the convention was the keynote speech of Martin H. Glynn, built upon the theme. "He kept us out of war."

Wilson went on to defeat Charles E. Hughes, with 277 electoral votes to Hughes's 254, and a popular plurality of nearly 600,000.

The Democrats still held a majority of 12 in the Senate; in the lower house they had only 212 Representatives to 213 Republicans, with a corporal's guard of scattering members holding the possibly decisive votes. But the President-Premier, leader of the party, had received a vote of confidence.

The President had been thinking about the proper terms for ending the war, and arrangements that might be made to remove the possibility of a similar catastrophe hereafter. The world was already talking of a League of Nations.

During all of 1916 the chief aim of the President's foreign policy seemed to be to keep America in the position to play the leading part in a peace conference after the peace, and, if need be, take the initiative in bringing the belligerents to the peace table. The difficulty with the belligerents was that something was constantly happening to give one or the other side the hope of victory in a few months more. Moreover, the section of American opinion which favored the Allies was convinced that they must win in the end, and talk of mediation was suspected as being advantageous to Germany.

But the issue of peace or war had already been decided. On Jan. 9 the Germans resumed its policy of unlimited submarine warfare.

On Feb. 3, the President announced that he had broken diplomatic relations with Germany.

A note from Germany to Mexico, endeavoring to enlist Mexican and Japanese aid in the case of war with America, was intercepted by secret agents and published semi-officially. It convinced many who had hitherto been hard to persuade that war was near.

American merchantmen were attacked by submarines. After dissent in the Senate, the President armed the ships by executive order.

The country was waking up. Former pacifists and pro-Germans now stood firmly in support of the President's policy. On April 2 the President appeared before Congress and asked for a declaration that the acts of the German Government constituted war against the United States. Neutrality was no longer possible, he declared.

"We have no quarrel with the German people," he said, but their Government had shown itself to be "the natural foe of liberty." So America would fight for the freedom of all peoples, the German people included; "the world must be made safe for democracy."

It was the most famous of all his famous phrases. The logical dilemma had been solved; the President had found a new and transcendent issue.

Both houses passed the declaration of war by overwhelming majorities. A conscription bill went through Congress by a considerable majority.

The year ended with the allied cause in a rather bad way. The collapse of the Russian armies and the Bolshevist revolution had removed the eastern front. It was evident that the opening of 1918 would see bloodshed more copious than any previous year.

It was during this time, on Jan. 8, 1918, that Wilson gave an address to a joint session of Congress, embodying his Fourteen Points, which detailed his vision of a just peace, one that would allow the League of Nations to settle future conflicts peaceably.

In the Spring American soldiers began to go to France by the tens and hundreds of thousands, and by July 4 a million were on their way. By the end of Summer their intervention had turned the tide. German leaders now began to think of mediation by President Wilson.

In New York on Sept. 27, the President declared in a speech that the League of Nations must be a part of the peace settlement, "in a sense the most essential part."

A new German Chancellor, Max of Baden, on Oct. 4 appealed to the President to call a conference at once. Step by step the Germans, their armies drawing nearer the old frontier every day, were driven to more concessions. On Oct. 12 they promised that the Fourteen Points would be accepted flatly. Two days later the President informed them that there must be an armistice whose terms would "assure the present supremacy" of the allied armies in the field.

On Nov. 5 the Allies informed the President that they accepted the Fourteen Points, with reservations. On Nov. 11 hostilities ceased.

President Wilson thus played the principal part in bringing the war to an end. It left him exalted in the opinion of Europe to a position such as no American ever before enjoyed. But he was not so generally exalted at home.

In the election of 1918, the country went Republican. Opponents of the Administration won a majority of 39 in the lower House, and a majority of two in the Senate, which would have to ratify the President's treaty of peace.

A few days after the armistice was signed, when talk of the Peace Conference had begun, it was intimated in Washington that Lloyd George and Clemenceau wanted the President to come to the meeting. The sentiment of the American public, so far as could be judged from newspaper expression, was strongly against this. Nevertheless, the President decided to go.

He was leaving home after an election in which he had issued an unprecedented challenge and had been defeated. But he enjoyed a triumphal progress through Western Europe. Everywhere the masses of the people received him as the man who had given voice to their aspirations and led them out of the wilderness of war.

There was reason in this. The Fourteen Points and the other Wilson principles which had been accepted as a basis of peace were not so precise as to be incapable of varying interpretations.

Every nation in Europe believed that its program was founded on the principles of Wilson, and that Wilson had come to the peace conference to fight for precisely that.

The Peace Conference opened on the 18th of January. The history of its conflicts is too well known to need repetition. The European powers pressed their own ideas as to what the terms of surrender meant. Some American liberals, when the peace terms were eventually published, denounced the President for his "surrender to European imperialism."

The Wilson who had been the world's idol in December was now only the head of one of many States in conference. Every decision of Mr. Wilson in favor of any particular measure set a body of opinion against him.

Republican leaders at home blamed the President for the collapse of allied unity. Their opposition to the League of Nations, as President Wilson presented, also was growing. As early as Jan. 4, two weeks before the Conference met, Senator Lodge had said that the peace treaty ought to be first and the League discussion taken up later.

On the 14th of February the President read the text of the League covenant to the conference, which adopted it. A few days later the President started for home.

On the night of March 3 Senator Lodge announced that 37 Republican Senators were opposed to the acceptance of the League covenant in the form in which it stood.

Twenty-four hours later, at a meeting in New York, the President declared that the League was inextricably interwoven with the treaty and that he did not intend to bring the corpse of a treaty back from Paris. On the next day he sailed back to the Peace Conference.

The League covenant was somewhat modified to meet Republican suggestions and on June 28 the treaty was signed.

But he could not overcome opposition at home and the treaty was not ratified.

In the 1920 election, the Democratic nominee, Governor James M. Cox of Ohio, fought valiantly for the League, but was plainly willing to compromise on reservations that did not destroy the principles. Woodrow Wilson did not shift his position. But his health had suffered so much that he could not have taken part in the fight if he had wanted to.

The old scenes had changed. The Democratic Party of 1920 was not the party of 1912. Those who had fought in the front ranks in 1912 were most of them out of sight, and the final appeal to the country of the President-Premier for the ratification of a policy to which he had given four years of constant struggle was in the hands of an outsider, the Republican Warren G. Harding.

OLIVER WENDELL HOLMES

March 8, 1841–March 6, 1935

WASHINGTON—Oliver Wendell Holmes, retired Associate Justice of the Supreme Court of the United States, where he served for 29 years, died this morning at his Washington home of bronchial pneumonia.

Death came at 2:15 o'clock to the great liberal of the Supreme Court and soldier of the Union, who would have been 94 years old Friday.

Since he retired on Jan. 12, 1932, Justice Holmes had spent nearly all of his days in his unostentatious little red brick house on I Street. There, in a mellow study running nearly from front to back of the dwelling, its walls lined with books, he read, dictated letters and received intimate friends.

He had waited for the end, his friends said, without fear or melancholy. When he left the bench he told his associates that "for such little time as may be left" he would treasure their friendship as "adding gold to the sunset."

While he delved now and then into his law books, he loved a detective story or a tale with a humorous turn. He chuckled over the absurdities of P. G. Wodehouse's starchy Englishmen. But he would turn now and then to a classic, with whose pages he was familiar years ago.

Although the culture that he gained from classic literature was always with him, he resorted often to quaint words and sentences, products, perhaps, of his New England upbringing. Most of his distinguished legal friends, one 65 years old, were known to him as just "young fellers."

This was a symbol of the inherent democracy that led him to sit for hours and talk with a country flagman in the little railway station at Beverly Farms [in Massachusetts], where the justice spent many of his Summers. The flagman, incidentally, told a friend that the justice was the most unaffected man he ever knew.

He was such a stickler for the forms and ceremonies, for the dignity of the Supreme Court, that it was hard for those who did not know him to realize the great justice's fresh, simple and amusing mental outlook. Despite all the reminiscences of his liberal findings in the court, his war exploits, his dignity, his personal charm, it is his sense of humor that seems to come first to the mind.

One authentic story concerns the play, "Of Thee I Sing," with its flippancy toward the Supreme Court. It seems that in the scene where the court announces that the First Lady has borne a son, one character was to chant: "Brandeis and Holmes dissent."

Eventually the line was deleted for fear of offending the aged justice, but when he heard of this he laughed heartily and said he wished that the sentence had been retained.

Mr. Holmes lived longer than any of the other 75 men who have sat upon the Supreme Court bench. He was the oldest man ever to have sat on the Supreme Court. Only eight justices served longer terms than his 29 years, among them John Marshall and Stephen J. Field, each of whom served 34 years.

As Justice Holmes grew old he became a figure for legend. Eager young students of history and the law made pilgrimages to Washington merely that they might remember at least the sight of him on the bench. Others so fortunate as to be invited to his home were apt to consider themselves thereafter as men set apart.

A group of leading jurists and liberals filled a volume of essays in praise of him, and on the occasion of its presentation Chief Justice [Charles] Hughes said: "The most beautiful and the rarest thing in the world is a complete human life, unmarred, unified by intelligent purpose and uninterrupted accomplishment, blessed by great talent employed in the worthiest activities, with a deserving fame never dimmed and always growing. Such a rarely beautiful life is that of Mr. Justice Holmes."

He was born on March 8, 1841, in Boston. His father, Dr. Oliver Wendell Holmes, was of New England's ruling caste, and the atmosphere of his home was at once Brahminical, scientific and literary. The boy started each day at the breakfast table where a bright saying won a child a second helping of marmalade.

The boy was prepared for Harvard by E. S. Dixwell of Cambridge. Well-tutored, he made an excellent record in college. His intimacy with Mr. Dixwell's household was very close. His tutor's daughter, Fanny Dixwell, and he fell in love and later they were married. (She died in 1929.)

After Fort Sumter was fired on, President Lincoln called for 75,000 volunteers. Holmes, 20 years old and shortly to be graduated from Harvard with the class of '61, walked down Beacon Hill with an open Hobbes's

"Leviathan" in his hand and learned that he was commissioned in the 20th Massachusetts Volunteers.

The regiment was ordered South and into action at Ball's Bluff in Virginia. There were grave tactical errors, and the Union troops were driven down the cliff on the Virginia shore and into the Potomac. Men trying to swim to safety were killed and wounded men drowned.

Lieutenant Holmes, with a bullet through his breast, was placed in a boat with dying men and ferried through saving darkness to the Maryland shore. For convalescence he was returned to Boston. On his recovery he returned to the front.

At Antietam a bullet pierced his neck and again his condition was critical. Dr. Holmes, on learning the news, set out to search for his son. He found him already convalescent and brought him back to Boston.

Back at the front, the young officer was again wounded. A bullet cut through tendons and lodged in his heel. This wound was long in healing and Holmes was retired to Boston with the brevet ranks of Colonel and Major.

The emergency of war over, his life was his own again. He finally turned to law, although it was long before he was sure that he had taken the best course.

"It cost me some years of doubt and unhappiness," he said later, "before I could say to myself: 'The law is part of the universe—if the universe can be thought about, one part must reveal it as much as another to one who can see that part. It is only a question if you have the eyes.'"

Philosophy and William James helped him find his legal eyes while he studied in Harvard Law School and James, a year younger, was studying medicine. But while James went on, continuing in Germany his search for the meanings of the universe, Holmes decided that "maybe the universe is too great a swell to have a meaning," that his task was to "make his own universe livable."

He took his LL.B. in 1866 and went to Europe to climb some mountains. Early in 1867 he was admitted to the bar. In 1870 he was made editor of the American Law Review.

Two years later, on June 17, 1872, he married Fanny Bowditch Dixwell and in March of the next year became a member of the law firm of Shattuck, Homes & Munroe. In that same year, 1873, his important edition of Kent's Commentaries appeared.

His papers, particularly one on English equity, which bristled with citations in Latin and German, showed that he was a master scholar. It was into these early papers that he put the fundamentals of an exposition of the law that he was later to deliver in lectures at Harvard and to publish under the title, "The Common Law." In this book, to quote Benjamin N. Cardozo, he "packed a whole philosophy of legal method into a fragment of a paragraph."

The part to which Judge Cardozo referred reads: "The life of the law has not been logic; it has been experience. The felt necessities of the time, the prevalent moral and political theories, intuitions of public policy avowed or unconscious, even with the prejudices which judges share with their fellow men, have had a great deal more to do than the syllogism in determining the rules by which men should be governed. The law embodies the story of a nation's development through many centuries, and it cannot be dealt with as if it contained only the axioms and corollaries of a book of mathematics."

Holmes was only 39 years old when Harvard called him back to teach in her Law School, and 41 when he became an Associate Justice on the Massachusetts Supreme Court bench. He was Chief Justice on the Commonwealth bench when, in 1901, Theodore Roosevelt noted that Holmes's "labor decisions" were criticized by "some of the big railroad men and other members of large corporations."

For Roosevelt, that was "a strong point in Judge Holmes's favor." In 1902, President Roosevelt appointed Judge Holmes to the Supreme Court of the United States, an appointment that was confirmed by the Senate immediately and unanimously.

A great struggle between the forces of Roosevelt and the elder J. P. Morgan began on March 10, 1902, when the government filed suit in Federal Court charging that the Great Northern Securities Company was "a virtual consolidation of two competing transcontinental lines," whereby not only would "monopoly of the interstate and foreign commerce, formerly carried on by them as competitors, be created," but, through use of the same machinery, "the entire railway systems of the country may be absorbed, merged, and consolidated."

In April, 1903, the lower court decided for the government and the case went to the Supreme Court. On March 14, 1904, the High Court found for the government, with Justice Holmes writing in dissent.

He held that the Sherman act did not prescribe the rule of "free competition among those engaged in interstate commerce," as the majority held. It merely forbade "restraint of trade or commerce." He asserted that the phrases "restraint of competition" and "restraint of trade" did not have the same meaning; that "restraint of trade," which had "a definite and well-established significance in the common law, means and had always been understood to mean, a combination made by men engaged in a certain business for the purpose of keeping other men out of that business."

The objection to trusts was not the union of former competitors, but the sinister power exercised by the combination in keeping rivals out of the business, he said. It was the ferocious extreme of competition with others, not the cessation of competition among the partners, which was the evil feared.

"Much trouble," he continued, "is made by substituting other phrases, assumed to be equivalent, which are then argued from as if they were in the act."

From the opinions and other writings of Justice Holmes the following lines are some that stand out: "The best test of truth is the power of the thought to get itself accepted in the competition of the market. . . . That, at any rate, is the theory of our Constitution. It is an experiment, as all life is an experiment."

Soon after he resigned on Jan. 12, 1932, he sent a message to the Federal Bar Association: "I cannot say farewell to life and you in formal words. Life seems to me like a Japanese picture which our imagination does not allow to end with the margin. We aim at the infinite, and when our arrow falls to earth it is in flames."

LOUIS BRANDEIS

November 13, 1856–October 5, 1941

WASHINGTON—Louis Dembitz Brandeis, retired Associate Justice of the Supreme Court and one of the greatest liberals in the history of that tribunal, died at his residence here at 7:15 o'clock this evening.

Justice Brandeis, whose name was often linked in dissents with that of the late Justice Oliver Wendell Holmes, would have been 85 years old on Nov. 13. He had a heart attack on Wednesday and had been in a coma before the end. At his bedside were Mrs. Brandeis and their two daughters. Mrs. Brandeis received from President Roosevelt a message of condolence.

In frail health during the last two years, he devoted himself largely to consideration of the problems of Jews, whose plight during the European war and under the Nazi persecutions affected him intensely.

More than 82 years old at the time of his retirement, Justice Brandeis was nevertheless marked for his logic, surprising intellectual energy, and extraordinary ability to obtain the basic facts in legal controversies. But his physical strength was decreasing, and after a siege of grippe in January, 1939, he decided to leave the bench where he had sat so long.

When Justice Oliver Wendell Holmes died, in 1935, the mantle of judicial liberalism long since had been wrapped about the lean shoulders of Louis Dembitz Brandeis, like his mentor an outstanding apostle of dissent. He already had spent a long lifetime in pursuit of justice, both real and in the abstract, before he was appointed to the highest court of the land by Woodrow Wilson in 1916.

Throughout the years that followed he continued to pursue it, handing down decision after decision that sparkled with the integrity of his mind, the breadth of his learning and great human qualities which the exactitudes of legalism were never able to dull.

He had been appointed against the wishes of a united front which used every weapon at its command to keep him from donning the black silken robes of an Associate Justice of the Supreme Court of the United States. But when, ten years after he had passed man's allotted span, his aquiline face still peered down from the august bench, men and women in every walk of life, including some of his most bitter former enemies, joined in paying him tribute as one of America's best-loved citizens.

In one of his best-known dissenting opinions, Justice Brandeis expressed those qualities which endeared him even to those who, spurred on by President Roosevelt in 1937, felt that an age limit of 70 years should be imposed upon the members of the Court. He read this decision in a quiet, almost colorless voice on March 21, 1932, while Herbert Hoover was still President and the New Deal had not been broached.

"Some say that our present plight is due, in large measure, to the discouragement to which social and economic invention has been subjected," he said. "I cannot believe that the framers of the Fourteenth Amendment, or the States which ratified it, intended to leave us helpless to correct the evils of technological unemployment and excess productive capacity which the march of invention and discovery have entailed. There must be power in the States and the nation to remold through experimentation our economic practices to meet changing social and economic needs.

"To stay experimentation within the law in things social and economic is a grave responsibility. Denial of the right to such experimentation may be fraught with serious consequences to the nation. It is one of the happy incidences of the Federal system that a single courageous State may, if its citizens choose, serve as a laboratory; and try novel social and economic experiments without risk to the rest of the country. This court has the power to stay such experimentation. We may strike down the statute embodying it on the ground that, in our opinion, it is arbitrary, capricious or unreasonable; for the due-process clause has been held applicable to substantive law as well as to matters of procedure. But in the exercise of this power we should be ever on guard, lest we erect our prejudices into legal principles.

"If we would guide by the light of reason, we must let our minds be bold."

Behind these words lay three-quarters of a century

in which Justice Louis Brandeis had steadfastly endeavored to guide by the light of reason and in which he had been characterized by the boldness of his mind.

Justice Brandeis arbitrated the 1910 garment strike in New York, which affected 70,000 workers and $180,000,000 worth of business; he drove Secretary of the Interior Richard A. Ballinger from office in the Indian "land-grab" scandals of the Taft administration, and he fought zealously the battle of the small entrepreneur, summarizing his economic philosophy in the famous phrase, "the curse of bigness."

It was said of the Justice that he matured early and never had a chance to change his mind about the fundamentals. In 1905 he said: "Democracy is only possible—industrial democracy—among people who think . . . and that thinking is not a heaven-born thing. It is a gift men make and women make for themselves. It is earned, and it is earned by effort."

Outside the legal sphere, this son of German exiles who fled their native land after the failure of the Revolution of 1848 achieved the respect of men of all faiths by his stern adherence to his own religious beliefs. Often called America's outstanding Jew, he became a leader of the Zionist movement, devoting time, energy and money to this cause.

His wide learning, revealed in more than one decision where his footnotes refer not only to scores of law texts, dozens of newspaper and magazine articles ranging from The Nation to The Nation's Business, but to a wide array of books both ancient and modern and, in one instance to a book still in manuscript, set him apart from his brethren on the bench.

Justice Brandeis was born in Louisville, Ky., on Nov. 13, 1856. The spirit of Jackson and the frontier still hovered over the Kentucky in which this German-Jewish lad grew up in comfort derived from his father's grain business. His maternal grandfather had been a leader in a Polish revolution in 1830; his father was an outspoken Union sympathizer in a hostile land, and his mother had risked her life to bring succor to Northern soldiers.

When his parents took up residence abroad, he entered the Annen Realschule at Dresden, where he studied for three years. He returned to America and received his Bachelor of Laws degree from Harvard in 1877.

His social consciousness was developing all the time, and, while his law practice was lucrative, he found time for matters that satisfied his conscience more than his pocketbook. He was "people's counsel" in behalf of the Oregon and Illinois women's ten-hour law, the California eight-hour law and the Oregon State minimum wage law between 1900 and 1907, all models of social legislation by the State. He fought the Oregon law through half a dozen courts with dogged persistence before he was successful.

Another case which brought Mr. Brandeis to the attention of the country was his defense of Louis R. Glavis, who had been dismissed as investigator for the Department of the Interior in 1910. Mr. Glavis had revealed a "land-grab," and the scandal reflected upon the integrity of his chief, Secretary Ballinger. Mr. Brandeis's vehement cross-examination not only caused the resignation of Mr. Ballinger but caught President Taft in some uncomfortable positions because of his attempt to shield the Secretary of the Interior.

A storm broke out when, in 1913, Woodrow Wilson selected Mr. Brandeis as his Attorney General, an appointment that was withdrawn when the cry of "radical" was raised. This storm, however, was nothing to that which broke when, in 1916, Mr. Wilson named him to the Supreme Court.

Leaders of the bar raged. Mr. Taft, recalling the Ballinger episode, fought the appointment. Businessmen and public utilities representatives came to Washington to argue against the former "people's crusader," the man who knew the "curse of bigness." Arrayed against him were men of the school of social and economic thought later characterized by Franklin D. Roosevelt as the "economic royalists." Every former president of the American Bar Association stood against him.

The fight raged from January until June, but Mr. Brandeis was confirmed finally by the Senate.

As a justice he did not revise his economic doctrines but, in the words of Max Lerner, he stood by his guns that "wherever monopoly has taken the place of former competitive units, he wishes to restore and maintain competition; where, in a competitive situation, unfair practices threaten the competitive equilibrium, he wishes to curb them and so maintain the plane of competition; where competition is impossible or undesirable, due to the nature of the industry, he wishes to pattern the system of control as closely as possible upon . . . putative competition."

In October, 1938, Justice Brandeis was stirred out of his judicial seclusion. Forgetting the robes of office, he turned his attention and thereby the attention of many other Americans to the plight of the Jews of the world.

Making one of his rare public appearances, the venerable Brandeis, white of hair but still steady of gait and unflinching of mind, went to the White House.

There for more than two hours he was closeted with President Roosevelt. Neither announced what was discussed; none doubted that the question of Jewish refugees from Nazi Germany was the topic. Some commentators went as far as to suggest that Mr. Roosevelt's stand against Hitler after the Munich pact stemmed from this talk.

Justice Brandeis's first public utterance on Zionism was in the form of an interview in The Jewish Advocate, a Boston daily newspaper. He began by stating that there was no room anywhere for "hyphenated Americans," and spoke of the obligations of Jews to American institutions. Under a complete democracy, he said, there should be an elimination of class distinction.

Always Mr. Brandeis sought to approach the Jewish problem without abandoning the essential Americanism of his methods. When the Zionist leadership failed to agree with his methods, he broke with Zionism until 1938.

In his private life Mr. Brandeis was simple, even austere. His Washington home was a model of un-ostentation and long the gathering place of leaders in many realms of endeavor. Hosts of social workers, lawyers, and executives turned to him for advice.

Justice Brandeis had a musty office above his living quarters, crowded with books, where his secretary worked. He worked downstairs, in a small, almost bare room. There he wrote, in pencil, his decisions. During 1936, when 80, he wrote sixteen decisions.

Mr. Brandeis married the former Alice Goldmark of New York on March 23, 1891. They had two daughters, Susan (Mrs. Jacob H. Gilbert) and Elizabeth (Mrs. Stephen Raushenbush).

FRANKLIN D. ROOSEVELT

January 30, 1882–April 12, 1945

WASHINGTON—Franklin Delano Roosevelt, War President of the United States and the only Chief Executive in history who was chosen for more than two terms, died at 4:35 P.M. today at Warm Springs, Ga. He was 63.

The President, stricken by a cerebral hemorrhage, died on the eighty-third day of his fourth term and in an hour of high triumph. The armies and fleets under his direction as Commander in Chief were at the gates of Berlin and the shores of Japan's home islands as Mr. Roosevelt died, and the cause he led was nearing the conclusive phase of success.

Less than two hours after the official announcement, Harry S. Truman of Missouri, the Vice President, took the oath as the 32nd President.

No President of the United States has died in circumstances so triumphant and yet so grave. World War II, which the United States entered in Mr. Roosevelt's third term, still was being waged at his death, and in the Far East the enemy's resistance was still formidable.

Mr. Roosevelt was regarded by millions as indispensable to winning the war and making a lasting peace, and for this reason he was elected to a fourth term in 1944.

Upon the announcement of his death, crowds gathered across from the executive mansion, and the tears that were shed were not to be seen only on the cheeks of women.

The spoken tributes paid by members of Congress also testified to the extraordinary impression Mr. Roosevelt made on his times. Senator Robert A. Taft of Ohio, a constant adversary on policy, called him "the greatest figure of our time."

The internal crisis which existed at the time of his first inauguration, on March 4, 1933, when the nation's economic system was faltering and its financial organism paralyzed by fear, was followed in his third term by the global war during which he and Winston Churchill emerged as leaders of the English-speaking world.

The years between were packed with swift and drastic social and economic changes that made Mr. Roosevelt the most controversial figure in American history. Beloved by millions, hated by others, he did more to mold the future of the nation he headed, and the world he lived in, than anyone else.—*Arthur Krock*

The early life of Franklin Delano Roosevelt was typical of a member of a family of wealth and social position. His birthplace was a mansion on the Roosevelt estate, overlooking the Hudson River near Hyde Park.

He was born on Jan. 30, 1882, the only child of James and Sara Delano Roosevelt. His father's family was of Dutch descent and made its first appearance in America in 1654. The Delanos, his mother's family, were of Flemish origin and had emigrated to Massachusetts even earlier.

James Roosevelt, a distant cousin of President Theodore Roosevelt and a former railroad president, retired early to lead the life of a country gentleman. Like Franklin D., his father and grandfather before him had been Democrats.

At 14, Franklin Roosevelt entered Groton to prepare for Harvard, where he was editor and president of The Harvard Crimson. After graduation from the Columbia Law School he worked as a law clerk, later establishing his own law partnership. While still a law student, he married his sixth cousin, Miss Anna Eleanor Roosevelt,

the favorite niece of President [Theodore] Roosevelt. The couple had five children.

The year 1910 was a turning point in politics in this State, when after a generation of Republican rule at the Capitol the Democrats took over control of the executive and legislative branch. Roosevelt, then only 28, successfully ran for State Senator from his home district, and was re-elected two years later.

He quickly attracted nationwide attention by assuming the leadership of a group of insurgents in the Legislature which revolted against Tammany Hall.

Tammany Hall opposed the nomination of Woodrow Wilson for President. Anti-Tammany Democrats favored Mr. Wilson. At the 1912 Democratic National Convention, Mr. Roosevelt was active in behalf of Mr. Wilson, who was elected in that year. His reward was appointment as Assistant Secretary of the Navy. The World War broke out in 1914, fifteen months after that appointment.

In the Presidential contest of 1920, the Democrats nominated Gov. James M. Cox of Ohio. Mr. Roosevelt drew second place, but the ticket was defeated.

In August, 1921, came Mr. Roosevelt's tragic illness of infantile paralysis, which at first threatened to end his career and possibly his life, but later came to be regarded as the turning point from which he began his upward climb to the White House. He was swimming near his summer home at Campobello, New Brunswick, when he was stricken. The next day he felt a

stiffness. On the second morning his leg muscles were paralyzed.

For months his life was despaired of. After an epic fight for health he began to recover. The optimism which was a cardinal trait in his makeup, along with his courage, were powerful allies in the battle. He was paralyzed from the waist down. It was almost a year before he could move about with the aid of crutches.

It was at this time that he "discovered" Warm Springs, Ga., and the health-giving qualities of its waters. Gradually he regained in part the use of his legs and could move about with the aid of canes and steel braces. The process of recovery, however, took years, and he never fully recovered the use of his lower limbs.

The foundations of Mr. Roosevelt's political career were laid while he convalesced. In the three years he was absent from the public scene, from 1921 to 1924, he maintained close contact with the key figures in the Democratic party.

In September of 1928 Mr. Roosevelt was persuaded to seek the Democratic nomination for Governor of New York. He was nominated, and upon his election quickly demonstrated his huge capacity for work and his consummate skill as a politician.

At the Democratic National Convention in Chicago in 1932, when the nation, then under the leadership of Herbert Hoover, was in the throes of the Great Depression, Mr. Roosevelt was nominated for

President. At the close of the Presidential contest Mr. Roosevelt carried 42 States.

About three weeks before his inauguration, on Feb. 15, 1933, Mr. Roosevelt had a narrow escape from death at the hand of an assassin in Miami, Fla. Mr. Roosevelt was delivering an open-air address when an anarchist named Giuseppe Zangara fired several shots into the multitude, with the design to kill the President-elect. Zangara was convicted and executed.

Between Jan. 1, 1930, and March 3, 1933, the day before Mr. Roosevelt became President, 5,504 banks, with a total of deposits of $3,432,000,000, had closed their doors. The country was in the grip of fear bordering on panic.

In his first inaugural address, directed to a nation ravaged by the greatest depression in history, President Roosevelt demonstrated that he had a considered plan for the nation's recovery. His outstanding declaration was that "The only thing we have to fear is fear itself." That memorable address set the pattern for most of the accomplishments of his first term and for many of the events in his later administrations.

He attacked the selfish interests, "the unscrupulous money changers," to whom he attributed the economic depression. He asserted that these interests having "fled from their high seats in the temple of our administration," there was no recourse other than to have the Government assume the task of putting men to work, by direct recruiting if necessary.

He then called the Congress into extraordinary session on March 9. Within the next one hundred days the Congress, at his urging, enacted more legislation than in any like period in American history.

This legislation included:

Ratification by Congress of all the steps taken by the President in proclamations dealing with the banking crisis, including the ending of gold as a medium of exchange, and later steps taking the country off the gold standard.

Legalization of 3.2 percent beer before the repeal of the Eighteenth Amendment.

The first Federal farm-subsidy measure under which the Agricultural Adjustment Administration was set up, giving the Government the right to pay subsidies to farmers for not producing, plus a law to refinance farm mortgages with Federal aid.

The Civilian Conservation Corps law, in which the younger generation of the unemployed were employed in forestry and conservation work.

The Tennessee Valley Authority, under which the vast potential of water power in the Tennessee Valley was developed as a governmental enterprise.

The first Securities and Exchange Commission law, under which the issuance of securities by corporations became subject to governmental regulation.

The Home Owners Loan Corporation Act, under which hundreds of thousands of private homes were saved for their owners by the Government taking over and refinancing the mortgages at a low rate of interest.

The National Recovery Administration, designed to permit industries to govern themselves and prevent ruinous competition so higher wages could be paid.

During the winter of 1933 President Roosevelt started his first national work relief program, headed by Harry L. Hopkins, Federal Emergency Relief Administrator, to transfer 4,000,000 unemployed from direct relief to work relief. This was known as the Civil Works Administration to distinguish it from the Public Works Administration, under Secretary of the Interior Harold L. Ickes, which made relief secondary to the construction of large-scale public works.

The "hundred days" of Congress vested in a President for the first time in a period of peace powers virtually dictatorial in essence and broad in scope, which wrought changes of a fundamental and revolutionary character in the American plan of government.

The first measures proposed to Congress were passed by practically unanimous vote, and Mr. Roosevelt's policies won widespread approval throughout the country. His willingness to assume responsibility and his exhibition of unprecedented courage at a time of grave crisis compelled universal admiration and were reflected in a revival of hope and confidence while also producing a rise in the price of securities on the exchanges.

President Roosevelt was inaugurated for his second term on Jan. 20, 1937.

Emergency relief continued to be one of the most pressing problems confronting the President. Business was improving, but employment indices were not keeping up with this improvement, and labor-management strife and riots bordering on open warfare shook the nation.

Addressing a joint session of Congress on Jan. 6, 1938, President Roosevelt voiced his dissatisfaction with the attitude of the United States Supreme Court in declaring unconstitutional certain New Deal measures, and he resolved to curb the Court's power. The nation was not, however, prepared for the drastic program of Federal judiciary reform announced by the President on Feb. 5, which precipitated a crisis such as the government had not known since the Civil War.

The battle raged for five months. Conservative Democrats and Republicans were ranged against Presidential prestige and power. In the midst of the strife, Justice Willis Van Devanter, one of the oldest justices and most often under attack as a "reactionary," retired. The Court reversed itself, turning to a "more liberal interpretation of the Constitution." It upheld the Wagner Labor Relations Act and social security legislation. On July 22, by a vote of 70 to 20, the judicial reform bill was killed in the Senate. Mr. Roosevelt had lost the battle, but he had won the war. Death, retirement and resignation permitted him to appoint more justices than had any other President.

In his frequent press conferences, which continued throughout his 12 years in office, President Roosevelt, more than any other Executive in the nation's history, achieved a direct contact with the press and public. His quick wit and complete control of the situation, as he sat with his inevitable cigarette cocked in a holder, made these verbal sparring matches the best show in Washington.

He also had a gift for vivid phrases that crystallized his policies for the multitude. In accepting his first nomination for the Presidency, he pledged himself to "a new deal for the American people."

He coined an almost equally well-known phrase when in his first inaugural he declared he would dedicate the nation to the policy of "the good neighbor." Eight years later, when he grimly resolved that this nation should furnish arms to Britain, he turned again to the simile of the good neighbor lending a garden hose to fight a fire.

His efforts on behalf of legislation designed to improve the social and economic lot of the less fortunate sections of the country were waged to the declaration that "I see one-third of a nation ill-housed, ill-clad, ill-nourished."

The President also possessed unusual personal charm, which held to him many associates who questioned the wisdom of some of his policies. His distinguished bearing, made familiar to millions of people by countless newsreel and newspaper pictures, was an asset. So was his richly timbred speaking voice, carried by radio into millions of American homes in countless fireside chats and formal addresses.

As delegates to the Democratic National Convention met in Chicago in July of 1940, the President's silence on his third-term aspirations remained unbroken. Nonetheless, he was nominated on the first ballot. While the convention was still in session, Mr. Roosevelt, in a dramatic radio address from the White House, announced his decision to run again, citing the national crisis of the war abroad. Another whirlwind tide of Roosevelt votes came on election day, Nov. 5.

As the overshadowing world crisis developed, President Roosevelt increasingly turned his attention to international affairs. As the war clouds grew blacker over Europe he did what he could to dispel them.

He chose a policy of defiance against the dictators and aggressor nations, denunciation of efforts at appeasement and the extension of all-out material and moral support to the embattled democracies, which were locked in a death-grapple with the Axis powers that would lead to the Japanese attack on Pearl Harbor on Dec. 7, 1941.

When the long-dreaded war broke out in Europe, Mr. Roosevelt promised that all his efforts would be devoted to keeping this nation at peace.

His first step was to call a special session of Congress for amendment of the Neutrality Act. He successfully argued that by repealing the arms embargo and substituting a "cash and carry" provision for the sale of American arms to nations defending themselves, this country could keep the war far from its shores.

When the war leaped into sudden flame in April, 1940, with the German invasion of Denmark and Norway, Mr. Roosevelt denounced the Nazis. The following month, when the German armies overran the Low Countries and France, he called upon the United States to embark upon a defense program of unprecedented magnitude.

Meanwhile he sought to extend to the faltering French nation, and then to the imperiled British, every assistance within his power. He rushed to the British vast quantities of arms and munitions. He arranged a trade of 50 over-age American destroyers to Britain in return for the right to lease air and naval bases on British possessions from Newfoundland to British Guinea.

He also asked Congress for authority and funds to aid the victims of aggression, saying that the most useful role for the United States was to be an "arsenal" for the democracies.

After the attack on Pearl Harbor, President Roosevelt faced the task of providing the leadership for conversion of a peace economy into an efficient war economy capable of delivering the necessary war materials. This required total mobilization of American resources, out of which rose the most powerful war economy of the time.

The President extended the draft to the group between 20 and 44, and ordered seemingly impossible production goals. The program involved a vast dislocation of the civilian economy, a labor shortage that led to a food shortage, and a vast series of governmental organizations, directives, and decrees.

Yet the first 18 months of the war saw production reach miraculous heights. It also saw the armed forces head toward the goal of 11,000,000 men; it saw fathers drafted, and the age limits lowered to take in 18- and 19-year-olds.

By the spring of 1944, many Democratic State organizations were calling for Mr. Roosevelt's renomination for a fourth term.

As the Republicans were preparing to nominate Governor Dewey for President in Chicago, the nation was stirred in early June of 1944 by the landing of American forces in Normandy, France.

Governor Dewey was nominated on June 28. On July 11 President Roosevelt announced that he would accept a nomination for a fourth term.

Democrats argued that Roosevelt was needed to win the peace, that Dewey lacked experience in foreign affairs, and that the rejection of the President would give aid and comfort to the enemy. When the votes were counted, Mr. Roosevelt became the first four-term President in American history, winning 36 States.

JOSEPH McCARTHY

November 14, 1908–May 2, 1957

By W. H. Lawrence

WASHINGTON—Senator Joseph R. McCarthy, who built a global reputation on anti-Communist investigations, died tonight of a liver ailment at the age of 47.

The Wisconsin Republican's death at 6:02 P.M. ended one of the most controversial careers in modern United States politics.

At its peak, from about 1950 to 1954, he wielded more power than any other Senator, and his activities gave a new word, "McCarthyism," to the English language. He charged that Presidents Roosevelt and Truman had not done all they could to root Communists from Government and that their Administrations marked more than 20 years of "treason."

Later he amended his charge to "21 years," thus bringing in the Eisenhower Administration.

But after the Senate voted in December, 1954, to condemn his tactics his political power waned. He seldom was in his Senate seat and his advice, seldom offered, was little heeded.

Washington was shocked by the Senator's sudden death. Friend and foes joined in expressions of regret.

One of the first came from the White House, where President and Mrs. Eisenhower sent to Mrs. McCarthy an expression of their "profound sympathies . . . on the grievous personal loss she has sustained."

Vice President Richard M. Nixon issued a statement in which he said:

"Years will pass before the results of his work can be objectively evaluated, but his friends and many of his critics will not question his devotion to what he considered to be the best interests of his country."

Senator McCarthy, who began his political career as a Democrat but shifted to the Republican party, was a little-known Senator until February, 1950, when he jumped into the limelight on the anti-Communist issue.

His contention, in a speech at Wheeling, W. Va., was that he held in his hand a list of card-carrying Communists on the payroll of the State Department. Challenged to prove it, he maintained before a special Senate committee that the Truman Administration had withheld the proof he needed.

When the Democratic committee majority ruled against him, he charged "whitewash" and helped in the campaign that defeated Senator Tydings for re-election later that year.

He parlayed one charge after another into great political power. "McCarthyism" meant one thing to his friends and another to his foes. His friends prized the new word as meaning a determined effort to root Communists from government and industry. His enemies thought the same word meant "character assassination" on charges that were more frequently false than true.

Senator McCarthy would have been up for re-election in 1958, and this would have confronted President Eisenhower with a difficult political situation. He was one of three Republicans—the others were Senators William E. Jenner of Indiana and George W. Malone of Nevada—who the President publicly had said could not be counted on for help in advancing the Administration's legislative program.

However, tonight a close acquaintance of Mr. McCarthy said that the Senator had wondered whether he would be able to run again, apparently because of his poor health and his lessened political power.

When the Senator was running for his second term in 1952, General Eisenhower was a candidate for the Presidency for the fire time. One of the most celebrated incidents of that campaign was General Eisenhower's deletion from a Milwaukee speech of a paragraph of praise for his old Army friend, General of the Army George C. Marshall. General Marshall had been a target of Senator McCarthy.

In recent months Senator McCarthy seldom was on the Senate floor, and his once powerful voice had virtually no influence on his colleagues. He cast the only negative vote against confirmation of President Eisenhower's nomination of William J. Brennan of New Jersey to be an Associate Justice of the Supreme Court.

One of his foes involved in the Army-McCarthy case was Brig. Gen. Ralph W. Zwicker, recently confirmed by an overwhelming vote for a second star as a major general despite Senator McCarthy's active opposition.

Senator McCarthy's last appearance as an investigator was as a member of the Select Committee on Improper Activities in the Labor or Management Field, which conducted the inquiry into the leadership of the Teamsters Union.

The ineffectual role that the Senator played in the Senate caucus room where he once had held the spotlight emphasized how he had lost his standing both with the public and the Senate.

His questioning had lost its former sharpness. On several days he wandered in, took off on questions apart from the main issue, and after 15 or 20 minutes of repetitive questioning—during which his colleagues scarcely concealed their annoyance—he would give up, and then leave the hearing room.

On many days he never showed up. Several times his appearances provoked a buzz of comment on his condition. He had a ghastly color. He was plainly ill. On one occasion he sat for a while, gazing vacantly, and seemed to arouse himself by breaking into the questioning.

ELEANOR ROOSEVELT

October 11, 1884–November 7, 1962

Mrs. Franklin D. Roosevelt died last night.

The former First Lady, famous as the wife and widow of the 32rd President of the United States and an international figure in her own right, died at 6:15 P.M. in her home at 55 East 74th Street. She was 78 years old.

The woman who was a noted humanitarian, author and columnist, delegate to the United Nations and active force in the Democratic party was mourned by people over the world.

President Kennedy called her "one of the great ladies in the history of this country." Mayor Wagner ordered flags on city buildings flown at half-staff.

Mrs. Roosevelt succumbed four weeks after her birthday, which was Oct. 11, and six weeks after she entered a hospital with anemia and a lung infection.

She will be buried next to her husband, who died on April 12, 1945, in the rose garden of the Roosevelt home in Hyde Park, N.Y.

Shortly after the first signs of illness, she went to the Columbia-Presbyterian Medical Center, on Sept. 26. She marked her 78th birthday in the hospital and went home to convalesce on Oct. 18.

Three of Mrs. Roosevelt's children were at the apartment last night: her daughter, Mrs. Anna Roosevelt Halsted, and her sons Franklin Jr. and John. Her son Elliott was flying here from Miami. Her son James arrived early today from California, where he won re-election to the House of Representatives in Tuesday's elections.

During her illness, Mrs. Roosevelt had only one visitor who was not a member of the family—Adlai E. Stevenson, the United States representative at the United Nations. Mrs. Roosevelt had worked closely with Mr. Stevenson in the United Nations for many years, and she had asked him to talk with her about the Cuban crisis.

Besides her five children, Mrs. Roosevelt is survived by 19 grandchildren and 15 great-grandchildren.

Mrs. Franklin D. Roosevelt was more involved in the minds and hearts and aspirations of people than any other First Lady in history. By the end of her life she was one of the most esteemed women in the world.

During her 12 years in the White House she was sometimes laughed at and sometimes bitterly resented. But during her last years she became the object of almost universal respect.

Again and again, she was voted "the world's most admired woman" in international polls. When she entered the halls of the United Nations, representatives from all countries rose to honor her. She had become not only the wife and widow of a towering President but a noble personality in herself.

She was as indigenous to America as palms to a Florida coastline, and as the nation's most peripatetic woman, she brought her warmth, sincerity, zeal and patience to every corner of the land and to much of the world.

After a career as mistress of the White House that shattered precedents with a regularity never approached by Abigail Adams and Dolley Madison, and after her husband's death, President Harry S. Truman appointed Mrs. Roosevelt in 1945 a delegate to the General Assembly.

The esteem in which Mrs. Roosevelt was held in this country was immense, despite intense criticism that some observers believed stemmed from persons who differed politically and ideologically with her husband. She was accused of stimulating racial prejudices, of meddling in politics, talking too much, traveling too much, being too informal and espousing causes critics felt a mistress of the White House should have left alone.

On the other hand, she was hailed by countless numbers as their personal champion in a world first depression-ridden, then war-torn and finally maladjusted in the postwar years. She was a symbol of the new role women were to play in the world.

The more important chroniclers of Mr. Roosevelt's days in the White House have noted few instances in which it could be established that her counsels were of first importance in changing the tide of affairs. Nor did President Roosevelt always confide in his wife where matters of state were concerned.

There were, however, many known incidents in which Mrs. Roosevelt was able to direct the President's attention to such matters as injustices done to racial or religious minorities in the armed services or elsewhere in the Government.

With characteristic feminine candor, Mrs. Roosevelt always insisted that she had to do what she felt was right.

She got along well with the State Department until the Palestine issue arose. In February and March of 1948 she publicly opposed American policy that maintained an arms embargo on shipment of arms to Israelis. She also came out in favor of partitioning Palestine into Jewish and Arab states.

While often critical of Soviet tactics, Mrs. Roosevelt consistently urged the United States to continue efforts to end the cold war by negotiation. She also advocated the abandonment of nuclear weapons tests and called for United States recognition of Red China.

Mrs. Roosevelt never lost interest in the Democratic party. She addressed its national convention in 1952 and 1956, and both years campaigned for Mr. Stevenson. At the 1960 convention in Los Angeles, she pressed unsuccessfully for a Stevenson-Kennedy ticket and seconded Mr. Stevenson's nomination.

Anna Eleanor Roosevelt was born to Elliott and Anna Hall Roosevelt in New York on Oct. 11, 1884. Theodore Roosevelt, the 25th President, was her uncle. The families of both her parents were prominent socially, the Roosevelts a wealthy family of Dutch descent and the Halls of the same family as

Philip Livingston, the English-descended signer of the Declaration of Independence.

When Eleanor was eight her mother died, and the young girl went to live with her maternal grandmother, Mrs. Valentine G. Hall. Her father died a year and a half later.

She was taught at home by tutors for the most part, and she recalled later in her autobiography, "This Is My Story," that her real education did not begin until she went abroad at the age of 15.

She remained abroad for three years, studying languages, literature and history, perfecting her French and Italian, and spending her vacations traveling on the Continent and absorbing European culture.

At the age of 18 she was brought back to New York for her debut. "It was simply awful," she said in a public discussion once. "It was a beautiful party, of course, but I was so unhappy, because a girl who comes out is so utterly miserable if she does not know all the young people."

She was relieved of her misery within two years by meeting Franklin Delano Roosevelt, who had graduated from Harvard in 1904 and had come to New York to attend the Columbia Law School. He found Miss Roosevelt good company.

The two Roosevelts were distant cousins; they had met first when he was four years old and she two; and they got along easily together. Their relatives approved so highly that the marriage followed naturally. President [Theodore] Roosevelt came from the White House to New York on March 17, 1905, to give the bride in marriage.

Mrs. Roosevelt had her first brush with politics and government in 1911 after Mr. Roosevelt had been elected a State Senator and the family moved to Albany. In 1920 she saw more of the political scene when her husband was a candidate for the Vice Presidency on the democratic ticket with James M. Cox, who ran for President against Warren G. Harding.

The next year poliomyelitis struck her husband, and Mrs. Roosevelt attended him and encouraged him for three years until it was evident that any further recovery would come slowly through the remainder of his life.

It was at this point that Mrs. Roosevelt emerged seriously in search of a career. She took part in political discussion with other women after several years of suffrage, and pointed out in those early years, prophetically perhaps, that "women were not utilizing their opportunity to elevate politics."

She became a director of the Foreign Policy Association and of the City Housing Corporation. In addition, she became a syndicated newspaper columnist, edited a magazine and judged contests.

On March 4, 1933, her husband was inaugurated as the 32nd President, and Eleanor Roosevelt began her 12 years as the First Lady. At the White House she established a weekly conference with the press, the first of its kind ever held by a First Lady, and attended only by women journalists.

Except for the formal occasions and official events, the White House under Mrs. Roosevelt's influence had a gay informality about it, with grandchildren and an odd assortment of dogs scampering through its halls. Visitors were frequent and, she once laughingly remarked, "We call it a hotel."

In 1939 the nation noted a change in Mrs. Roosevelt's newspaper writings. Until then she had devoted the bulk of her space to women. Her columns began discussing the Works Progress Administration, United States neutrality and other current topics, with the result that political observers noted that what she had to say either anticipated or supplemented the President's statements. Concomitantly, she found herself more and more in the field of controversy.

The same year Mrs. Roosevelt announced in her column her resignation from the Daughters of the American Revolution because the society had refused the use of Constitution Hall in Washington for a concert by Marian Anderson, the Negro contralto.

Mrs. Roosevelt's work with the United Nations kept her name before the public for a number of years after the death of her husband. She brought a rare combination of toughness and idealism to its halls. The fact that her lofty objectives were viewed by "realists" as being impossible to attain did not deter her from fighting for them.

Mrs. Roosevelt played an important part in drafting the Covenant on Human Rights, designed to establish basic civil rights of peoples throughout the world.

JOHN F. KENNEDY

May 29, 1917–November 22, 1963

DALLAS—President John Fitzgerald Kennedy was shot and killed by an assassin today.

He died of a wound in the brain caused by a rifle bullet that was fired at him as he was riding through downtown Dallas in a motorcade.

Vice President Lyndon Baines Johnson, who was riding in the third car behind Mr. Kennedy's, was sworn in as the 36th President of the United States 99 minutes after Mr. Kennedy's death.

Mr. Johnson is 55 years old; Mr. Kennedy was 46.

Shortly after the assassination, Lee H. Oswald, 24, who once defected to the Soviet Union and who has been active in the Fair Play for Cuba Committee, was arrested. Tonight he was accused of the killing.

Gov. John B. Connally Jr. of Texas, who with his wife was riding in the same car with Mr. Kennedy, was severely wounded.

The killer fired the rifle from a building just off the motorcade route. A Dallas television reporter reported that as the shots rang out he saw a rifle extended from a window of the Texas Public School Book Depository.

Mr. Kennedy apparently was hit by the first of what witnesses believed were three shots. He was driven at high speed to Dallas's Parkland Hospital, where he died without regaining consciousness.

President Kennedy was shot at 12:30 P.M., Central Standard Time. He was pronounced dead at 1 P.M. and Mr. Johnson was sworn in at 2:39 P.M.

Mr. Johnson, who was uninjured in the shooting, took his oath in the Presidential jet plane as it stood on the runway at Love Field. The body of Mr. Kennedy was aboard.

Standing beside Mr. Johnson was Mrs. Kennedy. She had been sitting next to her husband in the motorcade, and her stockings were spattered with her husband's blood.

Mr. Johnson was sworn in by Federal Judge Sarah T. Hughes of the Northern District of Texas in the private Presidential cabin in the rear of the plane.

As Judge Hughes read the oath of office, her eyes were red from weeping. Mr. Johnson's hands rested on a leather-bound Bible as Judge Hughes read and he repeated: "I do solemnly swear that I will perform the duties of the President of the United States to the best of my ability and defend, protect and preserve the Constitution of the United States."

Those 34 words made Lyndon Baines Johnson, one-time farm boy and schoolteacher of Johnson City, the President.

At 2:46 P.M., seven minutes after Mr. Johnson had become President and 106 minutes after Mr. Kennedy had become the fourth American President to succumb to an assassin's wounds, the jet took off for Washington.—*Tom Wicker*

John Fitzgerald Kennedy gave few signs in his youth that he might some day head for the Presidency.

He was born on May 29, 1917, in Brookline, a Boston suburb. By 1926 the business interests of his father, Joseph P. Kennedy Sr., were concentrated in New York, and the family moved to Bronxville.

John attended Choate, an exclusive boys' school in Wallingford, Conn., graduating in 1935, when he was 18. He was tall, thin, good-looking and energetic. He had decided to break with family tradition and go to Princeton rather than Harvard, where his father had studied and where his older brother, Joseph Jr., was already carving out an important career. However, John had a recurrence of jaundice in December and left Princeton. In the autumn of 1936 he entered Harvard.

His first two years at Harvard were undistinguished. He got slightly better than a C average. He also suffered a back injury that would plague him later on. Toward the end of 1937 his father was named Ambassador to the Court of St. James's by President Roosevelt.

Ambassador Kennedy took the side of the supporters of Prime Minister Neville Chamberlain, backed the Munich agreement, in which Chamberlain allowed Hitler to annex the German-speaking Sudetenland in Czechoslovakia in exchange for promises of peace, and expressed views regarded by his critics as those of isolationism and appeasement.

John Kennedy's final year at Harvard was the best of his educational career. He was determined to be graduated with honors. His grades improved to a B average. But his principal achievement was the writing of a thesis, "Appeasement at Munich." His basic point was that the Munich Pact should not be the object of criticism. Rather, he wrote that underlying factors, such as the state of British opinion and the condition of Britain's armaments, had made "surrender" inevitable.

In June, 1940, John Kennedy was graduated cum laude in political science.

The precise moment when John Kennedy determined to run for the Presidency of the United States may never be determined.

Some historians believe that a campaign for the Presidency was implicit in his decision in late 1945 to embark upon a political career. They point out that he took over, in effect, the projected ambitions of his late older brother, Joseph Jr., who had been killed on a bombing mission in the war. John went on to represent his Massachusetts district in Congress from 1947 to 1953 and serve in the Senate from 1953 to 1960.

To some, the Kennedy ambition for the Presidency stemmed from a frustrated drive originally possessed by his father and transmitted first to his son Joe and then to his son Jack.

In any case, it seems certain that John Kennedy's decision to seek the nation's highest office stemmed from his own year of deep crisis, 1954 to 1955.

He spent most of that period in and out of hospital beds. He underwent surgery several times at grave risk of his life to correct his chronic and painful back injury. During his months of illness and recuperation, he turned his mind to a task that intimately linked his personal and political interests. This was the writing of the book "Profiles in Courage," published in 1956.

Before he picked up the political mantle of his older brother, John Kennedy had been headed for a career as a writer. On the eve of World War II he had turned his college political science thesis into a book called "Why England Slept," an analysis of what led England into World War II.

With "Profiles in Courage" he fused his literary and political aspirations. The book described notable examples of political courage in America. John Quincy Adams, Daniel Webster, Sam Houston and Robert A. Taft were some of the men portrayed.

The book became a best-seller and won a Pulitzer Prize in biography, an honor that helped place the author in a leading position among Presidential possibilities. There was one discordant note. Rumors circulated that the book had been ghost-written by his close friend and political aide, Theodore C. Sorenson.

By early 1956 Mr. Kennedy had become a national figure. In view of his age and the political situation—the renomination of Adlai E. Stevenson as the Democratic Presidential nominee was virtually certain—Senator Kennedy set his sights on the Vice-Presidential nomination. He took the spotlight at the convention, placing Mr. Stevenson in nomination. But on the third ballot he was swamped for the Vice-Presidency by Senator Estes Kefauver of Tennessee.

Mr. Kennedy then turned full-time attention to Presidential politics. In 1957 he began to build a national legislative record in the Senate. He backed aid for Poland and India. He called for the independence of Algeria. He published incisive critiques of United States foreign policy in the quarterly "Foreign Affairs."

And he demonstrated his political appeal in 1958 when he ran for a second term in what proved to be a rough campaign. Mr. Kennedy won with a winning margin of 874,608 votes, the biggest in Massachusetts history.

From that time forward Presidential politics seemed almost completely to preoccupy Senator Kennedy. Behind him was a well organized and seasoned political staff built around the Kennedy family. His brother Robert was campaign manager. His principal aides were the group of close friends and associates he had gathered over the years.

The first task was to obtain the nomination. Senator Kennedy faced Senator Hubert H. Humphrey of Minnesota in two key primaries, first in Wisconsin and then in West Virginia. In Wisconsin, Mr. Kennedy won the state but Mr. Humphrey put up a good showing. In the Wisconsin primary Mr. Kennedy had wanted to demonstrate two things—his ability to run well in the agricultural Middle West and his ability to overcome the "Catholic issue."

When Mr. Kennedy began his quest for the Presidency, the issue of his religion loomed larger than ever. Overhanging the prospects of a Roman Catholic candidate was the memory of the candidacy of Alfred E. Smith, a Catholic Democrat who ran a disastrous race against Herbert Hoover in 1928.

Senators Kennedy and Humphrey were rematched in the West Virginia primary. Here Mr. Kennedy encountered voters who were hard-bitten in their opposition to any candidate of the Catholic faith. But he won a big victory that drove Mr. Humphrey out of the race and was hailed by Kennedy supporters as conclusive evidence that the Al Smith defeat no longer overhung his campaign chances.

By the time the Democratic National Convention opened in Los Angeles in July, political observers were certain that Mr. Kennedy had put together a winning combination, even though Senator Lyndon B. Johnson of Texas was still in the field against him and Mr. Stevenson hoped for a third nomination.

Mr. Kennedy won easily on the first ballot, then asked for and got Mr. Johnson's acceptance as his running mate.

The major innovation of the campaign, which pitted Mr. Kennedy against Vice President Richard M. Nixon, were four national television debates between the two candidates. The first, on Sept. 26 in Chicago, proved the most important. Many observers later felt that this encounter had been the turning point of the campaign.

Kennedy partisans credited this debate with clearing away a major issue that had been raised against their candidate, that of youth, inexperience and immaturity. But after the first and subsequent debates, the Republicans conceded that the issue lost most of its bite because Senator Kennedy had presented himself as an assured, mature figure with a wealth of information about government and policy at his fingertips.

Moreover, Mr. Nixon appeared thin, tired and nervous. In contrast. Mr. Kennedy was ebullient and self-confident and radiated health and energy.

But the religious issue refused to be laid to rest—until Mr. Kennedy appeared before a group of Protestant ministers in Houston. The group was apparently convinced that a Catholic, with allegiance to the pope, could not act with independence in the White House.

Mr. Kennedy confronted his accusers in a dramatic hour-long session, which was televised nationally. The high point was his declaration that he would resign the Presidency if he ever thought that his religious beliefs would not permit him to make a decision in the national interest.

On Election Day, Nov. 8, Mr. Kennedy awaited the election results at his home in Hyannis Port, Mass., where the Kennedy clan had gathered and where his wife was awaiting the birth of their second child (the youngster, John F. Kennedy Jr., was born Nov. 25). Twenty-four hours later, on the morning of Nov. 9, Mr. Nixon conceded the election to Mr. Kennedy after one of the closest votes in national history.

The Administration of John F. Kennedy was marked by a breathless series of major events—the abortive Bay of Pigs invasion, the Berlin Wall, riots at the University of Mississippi and other places in the battle for civil rights, and the Cuban showdown. But from the moment Premier Nikita S. Khrushchev announced the dismantling of the missile bases and withdrawal of the missiles from Cuba in October, 1962, a period of comparative relaxation in cold war tensions began, a generally tranquil time internationally.

For 13 months the nation has been living without fear of imminent war. In this period the President was able to turn his main attention to domestic issues such as civil rights and the lagging economy.

His inaugural address was only 1,355 words long—one of the shorter introductory messages of recent American Presidents.

"Now the trumpet summons us again," he declared, "not as a call to bear arms, though arms we need—not as a call to battle, though embattled we are—but a call to bear the burden of a long twilight struggle year in and year out, 'rejoicing in hope, patient in tribulation'—a struggle against the common enemies of man: tyranny, poverty, disease and war itself."

And in what became his most celebrated passage, he implored: "And so, my fellow Americans: ask not what America will do for you—ask what you can do for your country."

His legislative program had an exceptionally difficult time in Congress, and the lack of results on major items reduced his popular support. At his last White House news conference, a week ago, the President publicly accepted what had become a foregone conclusion: the legislative achievements of this session of Congress would be among the most meager ever.

Congress had not yet taken up the civil rights bill. Other items on the President's program that were still languishing were education and health insurance for the aged under Social Security. The Administration's tax bill, promising lower taxes to stimulate economic recovery, was stalled in the Senate Finance Committee.

President Kennedy had promised to reinvigorate the domestic economy, to "get the country moving again." In April he appointed an Appalachian Regional Commission, which is now drawing up a massive program of Federal aid for a ten-state swath of chronic poverty running from the Pocono Mountains of Pennsylvania to northern Alabama.

The President's relations with the business community had improved considerably since the spring of 1962, when he raised hackles by forcing the steel companies to hold the price line. At that time he made a withering attack on United States Steel and other leading corporations, which had increased steel prices $6 a ton.

The President called the price rise "a wholly unjustifiable and irresponsible defiance of the public interest." Privately, he called the industry leaders "sons of bitches." Big Steel backed down.

The civil rights front became suddenly grimmer in late 1962. In October, a Negro named James Meredith, grandson of a slave and a nine-year veteran of the Air Force, sought to register at the University of Mississippi.

The university town of Oxford was torn by rioting. A mob attacked United States marshals who were guarding Mr. Meredith.

Gov. Ross Barnett pleaded with the President by telephone: "Get Meredith off the campus . . . I can't protect him."

"Listen, Governor," the President shouted, "we're not moving anybody anywhere until order is restored. . . . You are not discharging your responsibility, Governor. . . . There is no sense in talking any more until you do your duty. . . . There are lives in jeopardy. . . . I'm not in a position to do anything, to make any deals, to discuss anything until law and order is restored and the lives of the people are protected. Good-by."

President Kennedy slammed down the phone, and ordered Federal troops into Oxford.

There was also disorders [sic] in Birmingham where on Sunday morning, Sept. 15, 1963, a dynamite explosion shook the 16th Street Baptist Church in Birmingham's downtown Negro section. Rescuers found the bodies of four girls beneath a pile of debris.

President Kennedy called the affair a consequence of the "public disparagement of law and order." He appeared to mean Alabama's Governor, George C. Wallace, a segregationist who had tried to block integration at the University of Alabama in Tuscaloosa.

The President had promised a broad civil rights program. He was forced to appeal for a softening of a bill drafted by a bipartisan group of Northern liberals in the House. But the watered-down bill was still considered the broadest civil rights program ever recommended to Congress.

ROBERT F. KENNEDY

November 20, 1925–June 6, 1968

Los Angeles—Senator Robert F. Kennedy, the brother of a murdered President, died at 1:44 A.M. today of an assassin's shots.

The New York Senator, who was 42, had been wounded more than 20 hours earlier.

Among those at his side when he died were his wife, Ethel, and his sister-in-law, Mrs. John F. Kennedy, whose husband was assassinated 4 1/2 years ago in Dallas.

The man accused of shooting Mr. Kennedy early yesterday in a pantry of the Ambassador Hotel was identified as Sirhan Bishara Sirhan, 24, who was born in Palestinian Jerusalem of Arab parentage and lived in the Los Angeles area.

Eight bullets from a .22-caliber revolver were fired into a throng of Democratic rally celebrants in the hotel. The shots came moments after Senator Kennedy had made a speech celebrating his victory in yesterday's Democratic Presidential primary in California.—*Gladwin Hill*

By Alden Whitman

In his brief but extraordinary political career, the Massachusetts-born Robert Francis Kennedy was Attorney General of the United States under two Presidents and Senator from New York. In those offices he exerted an enormous influence on the nation's domestic and foreign affairs, first as the closest confidant of his brother, President John F. Kennedy, and after Mr. Kennedy's assassination in 1963 as the immediate heir to his New Frontier policies.

The Kennedy name, which John had made magical, devolved on Robert, enabling him to win a Senate seat from a state with which he had minimal association. The Kennedy aura also permitted him to campaign this year for the Democratic Presidential nomination and gain important victories in the primaries. Wherever he went he drew crowds by evoking, through his Boston accent, his gestures and his appearance, a remarkable likeness to his elder brother.

Mr. Kennedy called forth sharply opposed evaluations of himself. Some found him charming, brilliant and sincerely devoted to the welfare of his country. Others saw him as calculating, overly ambitious and ruthless.

Those who praised him regarded his candidacy for his party's Presidential nomination as proof of his selflessness. They quoted his announcement on March 16, in which he said:

"I do not run for the Presidency merely to oppose any man but to propose new policies. I run because I am convinced that this country is on a perilous course."

Those who questioned his motives noted that his candidacy was posed only four days after the New Hampshire primary, in which Senator Eugene J. Mc-Carthy had demonstrated the political vulnerability of President Johnson.

Mr. Kennedy's partisans tended to ignore or discount his inconsistencies. Even many voters who expressed reservations about him were certain that, in public office, he would do "the right thing." This belief was underlined, especially among Negroes and the poor, because of the earnestness with which he pleaded their cause.

Describing the reaction of one ghetto throng in California, Tom Wicker wrote in The New York Times of June 2:

"The crowds surge in alarmingly; children leap and shriek and grown men risk the wheels of Kennedy's car just to pound his arm or grasp his hand. Moving through the sleazy back streets of Oakland, he repeatedly stopped traffic; for six blocks along East 14th Street, his car could barely creep along."

Contrasting with such frenzied warmth was what

Fortune magazine called "the implacable hostility toward him in the business community."

Mr. Kennedy was an indefatigable campaigner, able to put in a 16-hour day of stress and tension and then sleep briefly before going through another strenuous day. And he played with as much concentration as he worked. He was a vigorous touch football participant, a hardy skier, a pacesetting mountain climber and a swimmer who would plunge into the cold Pacific surf on an Oregon beach.

Mr. Kennedy often conceded that he was aggressive, explaining semi-humorously: "I was the seventh of nine children. And when you come from that far down, you have to struggle to survive."

Robert Kennedy was born Nov. 20, 1925, in Brookline, Mass., a suburb of Boston, the son of Joseph and Rose Fitzgerald Kennedy. His father was already amassing a fortune in the stock market and other enterprises. His mother was the daughter of John F. (Honey Fitz) Fitzgerald, who served in the House of Representatives and was Mayor of Boston.

When Robert was born, his brother Joseph Jr. was 10 and John was 8. (Edward was born in 1932.) Thus Robert passed his early years as the little brother, with two older brothers and five sisters. "He was the smallest and thinnest, and we feared he might grow up puny and girlish," his mother recalled. "We soon realized there was no fear of that."

Although Robert as a youth was overshadowed by his older brothers, he displayed grim determination to succeed. After graduation from Harvard, he went to law school at the University of Virginia, graduating in 1951. That same year he joined the criminal division of the Department of Justice in Washington.

He resigned in 1952 to manage the campaign of his brother John for United States Senator from Massachusetts, a campaign notable for the Kennedy organization's painstaking attention to detail and the vast amount of money spent. Mr. Kennedy's first venture into the public limelight occurred in 1953, when he was named an assistant counsel to the Senate Permanent Subcommittee on Investigations.

His immediate superior was Roy M. Cohn, the group's chief counsel. Above them both was Senator Joseph R. McCarthy, Republican of Wisconsin, whose name was soon attached to the committee. It rapidly acquired a malodorous reputation among liberals, intellectuals and civil libertarians for its chivvying of witnesses in its investigations of asserted Communist conspiracies and plots in the Government.

By February, 1954, Mr. Kennedy was counsel to the Democratic minority. The following year he succeeded Mr. Cohn as chief counsel and staff director when Senator John L. McClellan, Democrat of Arkansas, became committee chairman.

Senator McClellan then chose Mr. Kennedy as chief counsel of the Senate Select Committee on Improper Activities in the Labor or Management Field when it was organized in January, 1957. Mr. Kennedy began a headline-making inquiry into the affairs of the International Brotherhood of Teamsters, then under the presidency of Dave Beck. Beck was later imprisoned for filing false income tax returns.

Mr. Kennedy's sharp questioning of Beck before the Senate Rackets Committee, as the McClellan group was known, brought the accusation that he was antilabor. This charge was compounded when he investigated James R. Hoffa, Beck's successor, in 1958.

Hoffa, who was convicted and jailed for jury tampering and misuse of union funds, disliked Mr. Kennedy, calling him "a ruthless monster." Later, when he was Attorney General, Mr. Kennedy continued his investigation of the 1,700,000-member teamsters union, causing Hoffa to charge that he was engaged in a vendetta. Mr. Kennedy left the rackets committee in 1959 to manage his brother's campaign for the Presidency.

In this role, Robert Kennedy never bothered to hide his political muscle. Answering one politician's complaint, he said:

"I'm not running a popularity contest. It doesn't matter if they [the politicians] like me or not. Jack can be nice to them. I don't try to antagonize people, but somebody has to be able to say no. If people are not getting off their behinds and working enough, how do you say that nicely? Every time you make a decision in this business you make somebody mad."

In the election campaign that followed, against Richard M. Nixon, the Republican candidate, Mr. Kennedy proved as drivingly perfectionist as he had been during the primary.

Mr. Kennedy also advised his brother on tactics, and according to his biographer, Lawrence J. Quirk, he was responsible for John Kennedy's intervention in the Martin Luther King case. As Mr. Quirk related it, this is what happened:

"The Rev. Martin Luther King was arrested for staging a sit-in at a department store in Atlanta, and was forthwith sentenced to four months of hard labor in a Georgia penitentiary. This event occurred a scant week before the election.

"Bobby saw to it that J.F.K. called Mrs. King to offer comfort. Then Bobby called the judge who had sentenced Dr. King. Shortly afterward, the Negro leader was freed on bail, and a member of the King family declared, 'I've got a suitcase of votes, and I'm going to take them to Mr. Kennedy and dump them in his lap.'"

After John Kennedy defeated Mr. Nixon in 1960, he appointed his brother Attorney General. Robert Kennedy was reluctant at first, sensitive to the likely charge of nepotism.

John Kennedy, however, wanted his brother in the Cabinet as an absolutely loyal and dependable confidant. In public, when criticism of the appointment mounted, the President explained his choice almost flippantly. "I can't see that it's wrong to give him a little legal experience before he goes out to practice law," he said.

Mr. Kennedy's term as Attorney General touched many sensitive areas of the nation's life—civil rights, immigration, crime, labor legislation, defense of the poor, juvenile delinquency and the Federal judiciary.

In the opinion of his staff—and he recruited a brilliant group that included Byron R. White, now a Supreme Court justice, and Nicholas deB. Katzenbach, now Deputy Secretary of State—Mr. Kennedy was imaginative and inspiring. His relationship with J. Edgar Hoover, director of the Federal Bureau of Investigation, was reportedly more formal than cordial.

Conspicuously active in civil rights, Mr. Kennedy, among other achievements, exerted the Federal force that permitted James H. Meredith, a black student, to enroll in the University of Mississippi in 1962.

In foreign affairs, he was an especially close adviser to the President. He investigated the Central Intelligence Agency after the Cuban Bay of Pigs fiasco in 1961. In the Cuban missile crisis the next year he opposed a pre-emptive air strike on Cuba and advocated the policy of restrained toughness that allowed the Soviet Union to retreat gracefully.

Mr. Kennedy was lunching at his home in McLean, Va., on Nov. 22, 1963, when he was informed of his brother's assassination in Dallas. He was at the airport when the Presidential plane landed in Washington with the President's body, his widow, Jacqueline, and the new President, Lyndon B. Johnson.

The assassination plunged Mr. Kennedy into a deep grief that amounted virtually to melancholy. His face was a mask; sadness enveloped his eyes; he seemed to have shrunk physically, and he often walked alone, his hands dug into his jacket pockets. For the remainder of his life, thoughts of his dead brother were never far from the surface of his mind. When his lassitude lifted, he set out to replan his political life.

For a time in 1964 there was speculation that he might be President Johnson's running mate that fall. Whatever hopes he had were dispelled when Mr. Johnson ruled out all Cabinet members as Vice-Presidential material. Displeased, Mr. Kennedy resigned to run for the Senate from New York and won the nomination without difficulty. His opponent was Senator Kenneth B. Keating, the incumbent Republican, whom Mr. Kennedy defeated by 800,000 votes.

In the Senate he forged a position slightly to the left of Mr. Johnson on the problems of the poor and the cities. He also sought to develop moderately "dovish" views on the war in Vietnam, but his opposition to Mr. Johnson on this issue remained cautious. He held back from contesting the Presidential nomination of 1968 until after the New Hampshire primary on March 12 showed the extent of voter disaffection with the war.

Thereafter, however, he fought keenly for the nomination, winning major primaries in Indiana, Nebraska and California. Campaigning with him was his wife, the former Miss Ethel Skakel, who is expecting their 11th child.

DWIGHT D. EISENHOWER

October 14, 1890–March 28, 1969

WASHINGTON—Dwight David Eisenhower, 34th President of the United States, died peacefully at 12:25 P.M. today at Walter Reed General Hospital after a long fight against coronary heart disease. He was 78 years old.

Death came to the five-star General of the Army and hero of World War II as members of his immediate family stood at his bedside.

The former President's doctors gave no immediate cause of death, presumably because they considered this unnecessary. His damaged heart—scarred by seven attacks and weakened by recent episodes of congestive heart failure—finally gave out.

In all corners of the earth where the name Eisenhower was associated with victory in war and a tireless crusade for peace, great men and small were moved by the passing of the man whose rise from a farm boy in Kansas to supreme Allied commander and conqueror of the Axis powers and President of the United States was a story of devotion to duty.

Trained to command, he welded together the greatest military coalition in history by the tactic of conciliation. After he became President in 1952 he ended the war in Korea, and he refused to give fighter planes to the French forces in Vietnam because he was fearful the United States might become directly involved as a result.

As President he governed effectively through the sheer force of his popularity among average Americans of both major parties, and it was the average American who was the real source of his power.

His critics at home accused him of playing too much golf and of garbling syntax at his news conferences. But the voters loved him and twice elected him President by the largest pluralities ever recorded at the time.

In his infectious grin and his highly expressive face, most Americans thought they saw in "Ike" a dim reflection of themselves.

President Nixon, who had been notified of the death of his former chief moments after the event, left the White House at 12:50 P.M. and was sped to the hospital behind a motorcycle escort. He was accompanied by Mrs. Nixon and their eldest daughter, Tricia.

General Eisenhower's brother Milton S. of Baltimore, former president of John Hopkins University, arrived at the hospital just ahead of the Presidential party. The other surviving brother, Edgar N., lives in Tacoma, Wash.

The Eisenhower family was in a third-floor suite adjoining that of General Eisenhower. Among them were David Eisenhower, the general's grandson, and his wife, the former Julie Nixon, daughter of the President. They had remained in an anteroom while the former President's wife, Mamie, his son, John, and the latter's wife, Barbara, remained at his bedside until the end.—*Felix Belair Jr.*

Dwight D. Eisenhower was born in Denison, Tex., on Oct. 14, 1890. He was of German descent. His ancestors belonged to evangelical groups from which evolved the Mennonite sect.

The future President's father, David Eisenhower, failed in grocery and banking ventures in Kansas. He then moved his family to Texas, where he got a job as a mechanic in Denison. In 1892, when Dwight was two years old, the family returned to Abilene.

His father could not afford to send Dwight to college. The youth, however, took an examination for the United States Military Academy and entered West Point on July 1, 1911.

At West Point, Cadet Eisenhower won his Army "A" in baseball and football. Neither his scholastic record nor deportment was of the best. A steady shower of demerits had rained down on him. He graduated with a standing of 61st in a class of 164.

He did not fight overseas in World War I but he rose steadily over the decades in the peacetime Army and was promoted to the temporary rank of brigadier general on Sept. 29, 1941.

On Dec. 14, 1941, seven days after the Japanese

attacked Pearl Harbor, Gen. George C. Marshall, then the Army's Chief of Staff, called Eisenhower to Washington.

Although he had never commanded troops in battle, he was recognized as a specialist in operations planning and organization. He also had made a reputation as a tactician in the large-scale Louisiana maneuvers of 1941.

Soon he became Chief of Operations for the Army. In June 1942, he was designated Commanding General, European Theater of Operations.

He flew to London and began planning the invasion of French North Africa. One objective was to encourage harmony among British, French and United States officers at headquarters. Relations with the British and French had to be handled delicately.

He directed the troop landings at Casablanca, Oran and Algiers on Nov. 7. The following day he was named Allied Commander in Chief, North Africa.

The fighting at first went badly. United States troops were green and their commanders untried.

After the Allied defeat at Kasserine Pass, Eisenhower relieved Maj. Gen. Lloyd R. Fredenall, ranking United States commander in the field.

The tide turned. In May, 1943, the mass surrender of German and Italian forces in Tunisia brought Eisenhower's first military campaign to a successful end. North Africa was liberated.

He also directed the invasions of Sicily and Italy and the combined operations leading to the conquest of Sicily and reducing Italy to a state of military impotence.

In December, 1943, President Roosevelt announced Eisenhower's selection as Supreme Allied Commander for the invasion of Western Europe.

On June 6, 1944, he directed the landings on the Normandy beaches in France. One vital decision that Eisenhower alone had to make was whether to postpone the invasion because of bad weather. It already had been postponed once.

The weather prediction looked bad for June 6. But Eisenhower had studied meteorology and decided to go ahead. The silent travail he underwent in making this decision has been described by Lieut. Gen. Walter Bedell Smith, then his chief of staff. Writing after the war, General Smith related:

"The silence lasted for five full minutes while General Eisenhower sat on a sofa before a bookcase that filled the end of the room. I never realized before the loneliness and isolation of a commander at a time when a momentous decision has to be taken, with full knowledge that the failure or success rests on his judgment alone. He sat there quietly, not getting up to pace with quick strides as he often does. He was tense, weighing every consideration. . . . Finally he looked up and tension was gone from his face. He said briskly, 'Well, we'll go.'"

Weather conditions still were far from favorable.

Heavy swells on the Channel beset the troops with seasickness. Yet they were able to complete the landings.

By September the Allied invasion from the west had reached German soil and was battering against the strongly fortified Siegfried Line.

Eisenhower was elevated by President Roosevelt to the temporary rank of General of the Army on Dec. 20, 1944.

About this time the Allied campaign met a serious but temporary reverse. Just before Christmas, 1944, Field Marshal Karl von Rundstedt opened a surprise counteroffensive into Belgium and Luxembourg. In their last desperate drive, the German troops broke through a weak point in the United States lines and plunged deep into the Ardennes Forest. This became known as the Battle of the Bulge.

But the Nazis then were gradually beaten back and the Bulge was wiped out.

The end followed quickly. In the spring of 1945 American troops took 317,000 prisoners and broke the back of German resistance in the Ruhr.

On April 23, United States troops met the Russians in the Torgau area on the Elbe River. The Allies smashing from the west and the Russians from the east had crushed Hitler's once mighty legions. The unconditional surrender of Germany was accepted by Eisenhower on May 7, 1945, at Allied headquarters in a schoolhouse at Rheims, France.

In Paris more than 1 million persons thronged the streets through which he rode in a triumphal procession. At Washington more than 1 million persons turned out in the streets for him. New York gave him a ticker-tape parade.

On June 7, 1948, he became president of Columbia University. While there, however, he was called back into uniform on several occasions.

Eisenhower's final leave of absence from Columbia came in 1950. By that time the threat of aggression from the Soviet Union had become so obvious that nations of the North Atlantic area had formed the North Atlantic Treaty Organization to prepare defense armaments. These nations asked President Truman to let Eisenhower command its military forces. The President consented.

Military leadership of the victorious Allied forces invested Dwight David Eisenhower with an immense popularity, almost amounting to devotion, that twice elected him President of the United States. His enormous political success was largely personal, for he was not basically a politician dealing in partisan issues and party maneuvers. What he possessed was a superb talent for gaining the respect and affection of the voters as the man suited to guide the nation through cold war confrontations with Soviet power and to lead the country to prosperity.

Eisenhower's entrance into politics was reluctant. But in 1952, he entered the fray for the Republican

Presidential nomination and defeated Senator Robert A. Taft of Ohio, the "Mr. Republican" of the party's conservative wing.

As a Vice-Presidential candidate the convention chose Senator Richard M. Nixon of California, a man known then for his conservative views.

Eisenhower's concepts of loyalty and integrity were tested in the general election against Gov. Adlai E. Stevenson of Illinois. One episode involved Senator Joseph R. McCarthy, Republican of Wisconsin. The general was persuaded to delete from a campaign speech a defense of General of the Army George C. Marshall, his Army mentor, whom Senator McCarthy had impugned as a traitor. Political advisers had told Eisenhower that he needed McCarthy's support to win the election.

Eisenhower defeated Stevenson soundly, polling 33,936,252 popular votes and 442 votes in the Electoral College; his opponent received 27,314,992 popular votes and 89 electoral votes.

Eisenhower began his first term as a symbol of international goodwill as well as of national high purpose. He had traveled to Korea, where a truce was soon effected. At home the government climate was benign and the press was friendly, even protective, as a seeming new era opened.

Oddly, Old Guard Republicans, long entrenched in Congress, were among the most vocal critics, because the first Republican Administration in 20 years did not make a clean break with the New and Fair Deals.

Under Eisenhower, the nation maintained its international leadership even if, at times, its course seemed uncertain and erratic. The Administration had high hopes that, with the Korean truce, psychological warfare would give the West an ascendancy in the battle of ideologies. But when Stalin died in 1953, and again when revolt flared three years later in Hungary and elsewhere behind the Iron Curtain, there was no master plan ready to capitalize on developments.

To many Americans, however, events abroad seemed remote. Anxieties centered rather on the President, who suffered two major illnesses.

The first, on Sept. 24, 1955, was diagnosed as a coronary thrombosis, a clot in the artery of the heart. It sent the President to the hospital for seven weeks. The second occurred eight and a half months later and was diagnosed as ileitis, an inflammation of the lower part of the small intestine. Eisenhower underwent a successful operation the next day.

Despite his health troubles, Eisenhower decided to run for re-election in 1956. At the peak of his popularity, he conducted a restricted campaign. He made few radio and television speeches and undertook only two campaign swings.

Stevenson, again the Democratic choice, hammered away at the "break-down of leadership." Eisenhower insisted that his Administration had brought "sense and order" to Washington.

The election results gave him 35,582,236 votes, a record up to that time, and 457 electoral votes. Stevenson's popular vote was 26,031,322, his electoral total 73.

Difficult and fateful problems confronted Eisenhower in his second term.

There was mob violence over school integration in the South, and in September, 1957, the President was obliged to send troops to Little Rock, Ark., to enforce court-ordered school desegregation.

Business slumped sharply in the winter of 1957–58. In July, 1959, a steel strike dealt the economy another blow. The national debt climbed higher than ever.

The Soviet Union achieved a stunning scientific success, with strong military implications, when it orbited the first man-made earth satellite in October, 1957.

The perilous stalemate between the Soviet Union and the West over Berlin continued.

Tensions in the Far East reached a peak when the President was forced to cancel a visit to Japan because of anti-American rioting there.

The widening rift between Cuba and the United States brought a threat of Soviet intervention that led Eisenhower to declare that he would never "permit the establishment of a regime dominated by international Communism in the Western Hemisphere."

The demands of the times would have taxed the energy of the healthiest of men, and they were especially heavy for Eisenhower. His health was further compromised in 1957, when he suffered an occlusion of a small branch of the middle cerebral artery on the left side. He was left with a mild aphasia (difficulty in speaking) and he was not pronounced recovered until March 1, 1958.

The President's popularity began a perceptible decline soon after he took his second oath of office.

Some observers attributed the decline to his being the first President whose tenure was limited to two terms by the 22nd Amendment. Others felt that the President was delegating too many functions to subordinates.

This view appeared to be reinforced in 1958 when Sherman Adams, the stern Assistant to the President who presided over the White House offices, came under investigation for alleged intervention with Federal agencies in behalf of his friends. He resigned.

In the elections that November, the Republicans lost 47 House seats and 13 of 21 contested Senate seats. The Democrats controlled Congress by the widest margins since the Roosevelt landslide of 1936.

Few realized it until well afterward, but the elections were the nadir of Eisenhower's political fortunes. By the spring of 1959 some observers were talking about "the new Ike," while others insisted that it was only the re-emergence of the old Ike who had so fired the country's imagination in 1952.

One sign of change was in the field of personal diplomacy and involved a visit to the United States by Premier Nikita S. Khrushchev of the Soviet Union in September, 1959. Informal talks resulted in what was termed "the spirit of Camp David," a thaw in the cold war in which peaceful coexistence was to replace bellicosity.

The Camp David spirit persisted until May 1960, when a summit meeting in Paris was blasted by the disclosure that the United States was using a U-2 photo-reconnaissance plane over the Soviet Union.

Ten days before the meeting on May 5, Khrushchev announced that an American plane had been shot down over the Soviet Union. He withheld details. The State Department unequivocally denied any "deliberate attempt to violate Soviet air space."

This denial had scarcely been made when the Russians produced Francis Gary Powers, the U-2 pilot, and the confession that he had been on a spying mission across Russian territory.

Moscow's revelations forced Washington to admit that it had engaged in U-2 espionage for the last four years. For this Eisenhower took full responsibility.

Khrushchev demanded that the United States end its U-2 project, ban future flights and punish those "directly guilty." Eisenhower made only one concession, saying the espionage flights had been suspended and "are not to be resumed."

It was clear that the last chance had gone for the President, in the final months of his term, to strengthen hopes for peace.

On Jan. 17, Eisenhower delivered a televised farewell address that contained a warning that has echoed down through the years.

Noting that a vast military establishment and a huge arms industry had developed in the United States, Eisenhower said:

"In the councils of government, we must guard against the acquisition of unwarranted influence, whether sought or unsought, by the military-industrial complex. The potential for the disastrous rise of misplaced power exists and will persist."

J. EDGAR HOOVER

January 1, 1895–May 2, 1972

WASHINGTON—J. Edgar Hoover, who directed the Federal Bureau of Investigation for 48 years and built it into a dominant and controversial force in American law enforcement, died during the night from the effects of high blood pressure.

Mr. Hoover, who at 77 still held the F.B.I. firmly within his control, had worked a full day yesterday. He was found by his housekeeper this morning, slumped on the floor of his bedroom in his home in northwest Washington.

The strong-willed and demanding bachelor ruled the bureau from the day—May 14, 1924—when he took over a small, politics-ridden agency, through the eras of its most famous exploits. Yet toward the end, he became the target of critics who thought he rode roughshod over civil liberties and slighted the old F.B.I. role of spy-catching.

The mandatory retirement age for F.B.I. directors is 70, but President Johnson waived it, as did President Nixon, who this morning praised Mr. Hoover's "unparalleled devotion and ability and dedication." Major figures across the political spectrum joined in the admiration.

But Dr. Benjamin Spock, the antiwar activist, called Mr. Hoover's death "a great relief, especially if his replacement is a man who better understands democratic institutions and the American process."—*Fred P. Graham*

By Christopher Lydon

When J. Edgar Hoover ambled through the Mayflower Hotel after one of his ritual fruit salad–and–coffee lunches late last year, he passed almost unnoticed. The once ruddy face was puffy and pale. The brushed-back, gray-brown hair was straight and thin—not the wiry dark curls of a few years ago. Behind his glasses, his dark brown eyes looked fixed, and he seemed to be daydreaming.

In one of his rare reflections on mortality a few years ago, Mr. Hoover told a reporter, "The greatest enemy is time." Time's advances against this seemingly indestructible official had become obvious. But then, Mr. Hoover was

always more human than he or the myth admitted.

Mr. Hoover's power was a compound of performance and politics, publicity and personality. The centralized fingerprint file and the crime laboratory are landmarks in the application of science to police work. The National Police Academy has trained the leadership elite of local forces throughout the country. Mr. Hoover's recruitment of lawyers and accountants set a world standard of professionalism.

His bureau rounded up the gangsters in the nineteen-thirties. It made the once epidemic crime of kidnapping a rarity. It arrested German saboteurs within days after their submarines landed them on the Atlantic Coast.

Not a New Dealer at heart, he had nonetheless dazzled President Franklin D. Roosevelt with his celebrated success against kidnappers. Roosevelt's assignment of counterespionage duties to the F.B.I. as war loomed in 1936 expanded the bureau's size and heightened Mr. Hoover's prestige.

But when the Republicans won the White House again in 1952, Mr. Hoover's loyalty swung to the new team. Mr. Hoover always understood the subtle currents of power among officials in Washington better than almost anyone. The more awesome his power grew, the more plainly Mr. Hoover would state that

there was nothing "political" about it, that the F.B.I was simply a "fact-finding agency" that "never makes recommendations or draws conclusions."

Mr. Hoover's reappointment was virtually the first decision John F. Kennedy announced on the day after his election in 1960. The Hoover-Kennedy relationship started out cordially, based apparently on Mr. Hoover's long acquaintance with the President's father, the late Joseph P. Kennedy. Robert Kennedy had urged the President-elect to retain Mr. Hoover; and when John Kennedy weighed assignments for his brother, Mr. Hoover urged him to follow his instinct and make Robert the Attorney General.

Later, Robert Kennedy and Mr. Hoover fought over the assignment of agents to civil rights and organized crime cases. Mr. Hoover was not used to having a boss who could block his access to the White House.

Robert Kennedy never forgave Mr. Hoover for the cold telephone call that brought the first word of his brother's assassination. Mr. Hoover's voice, Robert Kennedy told William Manchester, the author, was "not quite as excited as if he were reporting the fact that he had found a Communist on the faculty of Howard University."

Until Representative Hale Boggs of Louisiana, the House majority leader, criticized Mr. Hoover in the

House last spring as a "feudal baron" and a wiretapper, the F.B.I. director had been sacrosanct in Congress.

Mr. Hoover insisted that he did not tap the phones or "bug" the offices of Congressmen, and Mr. Boggs failed notably to prove the contrary. But Mr. Hoover always had other ways to keep critics in line.

The late Senator Kenneth D. McKellar, a Tennessee Democrat and chairman of the Senate Appropriations Committee, harassed Mr. Hoover from time to time in the nineteen-thirties, and in the spring of 1936 drew the blushing testimony that the director of the F.B.I. had never made an arrest.

Less than a month later, as if by magic, Mr. Hoover led a raid in New Orleans that captured Alvin (Kreepy) Karpis, a star of the Ma Barker mob. By his own account, Mr. Hoover rushed up to the unsuspecting Karpis as he sat in a car, threatened him with a gun, then snapped out the order to "put the cuffs on him, boys." (In his recently published memoirs, Karpis contends that Mr. Hoover "hid until I was safely covered by many guns.")

When Senator McKellar tried to cut $225,000 out of the F.B.I. budget that year, Senator Arthur H. Vandenberg of Michigan denounced him as "a miser whose parsimony would cause the threat of kidnapping to hang once more over every cradle in America." Mr. Hoover's full budget request was then passed by a resounding voice vote. Since then, the Senate has never questioned the F.B.I. budget, which has also sailed through the House.

While Mr. Hoover's primary genius might well have been publicity, the director never held a news conference. Instead, he relied on Walter Winchell, the Broadway gossip columnist, who traveled with an F.B.I. escort and carried an item about "G-man Hoover" almost every day.

Mr. Hoover promoted "junior G-man" clubs for boys, and sold two and a half million copies of "Masters of Deceit," a book on Communism. His "ten most wanted" list made seedy drifters into headline material. In the age of television, he shrewdly reserved the right to select the actor (Efrem Zimbalist Jr.) who would represent the F.B.I. in millions of living rooms.

Even after political potshots at the director became fashionable in recent years, a Gallup Poll for Newsweek magazine last spring showed that 80 percent of those who had any opinion about Mr. Hoover rated his performance "good" or "excellent."

Mr. Hoover's personality, as well as his office, always inspired fear. Francis Biddle, President Roosevelt's Attorney General in the early nineteen-forties, sensed that behind Mr. Hoover's "absolute self-control" was "a temper that might show great violence if he did not hold it on leash, subject to the domination of a will that is the master of his temperament."

When the Warren commission was investigating President Kennedy's assassination and said that the F.B.I. had not shared its intelligence fully with the Secret Service, Mr. Hoover lashed out at what he called "a classic example of Monday morning quarterbacking."

And when the Rev. Dr. Martin Luther King Jr. said that Southern blacks could not turn to their local F.B.I. offices with any assurance of sympathy or zeal for civil rights, Mr. Hoover called Dr. King "the most notorious liar in the country."

Later, Mr. Hoover had his staff invite newsmen to hear the taped record of F.B.I. bugs in Dr. King's hotel rooms as evidence that "moral degenerates" were leading the civil rights movement. (Mr. Hoover's lifelong practice was to entertain Attorneys General and Presidents with spicy details about the secret lives of famous people.)

John Edgar Hoover was born in Washington on New Year's Day in 1895, the youngest of three children of Dickerson N. Hoover, an easygoing Federal official, and the former Annie M. Scheitlin. Mrs. Hoover instilled in her son an intense discipline and stern sensitivity to moral issues.

As a boy, he was known as "Speed," a reference, apparently, to his agile mind, rattling speech and efficiency as a grocery delivery boy. Unable to make the high school football team, he concentrated on the military drill team, of which he became captain, and public speaking.

He was class valedictorian, and the University of Virginia offered him a liberal arts scholarship. But Mr. Hoover feared that his living expenses would be a burden on his father. He took a $30-a-month clerk's job at the Library of Congress and enrolled at George Washington University, where he was able to win his law degree in three years. With a master's degree in 1917, Mr. Hoover passed the bar and moved into a $1,200-a-year job at the Department of Justice.

His first assignment in "counter-radical activities" came at the end of President Wilson's second term, the era of the "Red raids" under Attorney General A. Mitchell Palmer. Years later, Mr. Hoover said he "deplored" the hysterical dragnet arrests of thousands of innocent aliens in 1919 and 1920, but the record is clear that, as the head of the new General Intelligence Division at the Justice Department, he was responsible for planning the raids, if not their execution.

Under President Harding, the Bureau of Investigation had become "a private secret service for corrupt forces within the Government," according to Alpheus T. Mason, the historian. When Harlan Fiske Stone became Attorney General under President Coolidge in 1924, he determined to rebuild the bureau after the image of Scotland Yard. Secretary of Commerce Herbert Hoover, an untainted holdover from the Harding Administration, recommended J. Edgar (no relation) as director.

Attorney General Stone offered him the job. With confidence and cunning that were very much in character, Mr. Hoover, then only 29, said he would accept the assignment only if appointments to the bureau were divorced from outside politics and if he would have sole control over merit promotions.

Thus the modern bureau—renamed the Federal Bureau of Investigation in 1935—was born.

From the start, Mr. Hoover's personal grip was the organizing principle. Women were not allowed to smoke on the job. No one got a coffee break. The unofficial uniform for an agent came to include a white shirt and dark suit.

Agents quaked at the thought of the director's disapproval, expressed typically in the bright blue ink of Mr. Hoover's stub pen in the margins of their memorandums. Once, it was said, when an assistant's memorandum so filled the page that Mr. Hoover barely had room for a comment, he wrote. "Watch the borders," and his puzzled but obedient aides dispatched agents to patrol the Canadian and Mexican borders for a week.

The few changes in Mr. Hoover's daily routine were forced on him. His friend Clyde Tolson, the F.B.I.'s associate director, was not well enough to walk the last few blocks to the office in recent days, so their morning strolls along Constitution Avenue were abandoned. The old Harvey's Restaurant was razed, so Mr. Hoover and Mr. Tolson had lunch instead at the Mayflower Hotel.

Yet there were continuities in his life: the Jack Daniel's whiskey before dinner, the Miami vacation in December, the July break in California, the passion for horse racing. Above all, there was the friendship with Mr. Tolson, a fellow bachelor with whom Mr. Hoover had lunch and dinner six days a week.

Perhaps the most widely asked question was why Mr. Hoover stayed on. The men around him pointed to his egotism and to the lack of family and other interests. "For him the bureau is everything," one said.

HARRY S. TRUMAN

May 8, 1884–December 26, 1972

KANSAS CITY—Harry S. Truman, the 33rd President of the United States, died this morning. He was 88 years old.

Mr. Truman, an outspoken and decisive Missouri Democrat who served in the White House from 1945 to 1953, succumbed at 7:50 A.M., Central Standard Time, in Kansas City's Research Hospital and Medical Center.

He had been a patient there for the last 22 days, struggling against lung congestion, heart irregularity, kidney blockages, failure of the digestive system and the afflictions of old age.

In the more than seven years he was President, from the time Franklin Delano Roosevelt's death suddenly elevated him from the Vice-Presidency until he himself was succeeded by Dwight David Eisenhower, Mr. Truman left a major mark as a world leader.

He brought mankind face to face with the age of holocaust by ordering atomic bombs dropped on Japan, sent American troops into Korea to halt Communist aggression in Asia, helped contain Communism in Europe by forming the North Atlantic Treaty Organization and speeded the postwar recovery of Europe through the Marshall Plan.

His domestic record was somewhat less dramatic, for his proposals and ideas were often premature. He ended up on the losing side of fights other Presidents later won—Federal health care, equal rights legislation, low-income housing.

His other legacies were perhaps less tangible but no less remembered—the morning walk, the "give 'em hell" campaign that nipped Thomas E. Dewey at the wire, the desk plaque that proclaimed "The buck stops here!" and the word to the timid and indecisive: "If you can't stand the heat, you better get out of the kitchen."

At the time of his death, Mr. Truman's wife, Bess, 87, was at their home in Independence, having spent most of yesterday at the hospital. Mr. Truman's only child, Mrs. Clifton Daniel of New York, also was at the home. She flew to Kansas City last night for a brief visit with her father.

The room in which the former President died is on the sixth floor of Research Hospital, a 500-bed facility he helped dedicate in 1963. The room cost $59.50 a day. In Mr. Truman's case it was paid for by private medical insurance and Medicare.

Long an advocate of Federal health plans, Mr. Truman held Medicare Card No. 1. He had not been able to push such a plan through during his own Presidency, but Lyndon B. Johnson was more successful and came to

Independence in 1965 to sign the Medicare act in the Truman Library, enrolling the former President as the first member.

It was a final political victory for Harry S. Truman.—*By B. Drummond Ayres Jr.*

By Alden Whitman

At 7:09 P.M. on April 12, 1945, Harry S. Truman, the Vice President of the United States, was elevated by the sudden death of Franklin D. Roosevelt to the Presidency of the United States. He lacked a month of being 61 years old, and he had been Vice President for only 83 days.

For Truman, a hitherto minor national figure with a pedestrian background as a Senator from Missouri, the awesome moment came without his having intimate knowledge of the nation's tremendously intricate war and foreign policies. These he had to become acquainted with and to deal with instantly, for on him alone, a former haberdasher and politician of unspectacular scale, devolved the Executive power of one of the world's mightiest nations.

The drama and significance of his accomplishments—ending one war, helping to rebuild a ravaged Europe, and waging war in Korea while maintaining a stable economy—were, of course, not readily predictable when Truman took office, but there was an element of theatricality in the way he was notified that the burden had fallen on him.

He had entered the office of Speaker Sam Rayburn for a chat. Writing to his mother and sister a few days later, he said: ". . . as soon as I came into the room Sam told me that Steve Early, the President's confidential press secretary, wanted to talk with me. I called the White House, and Steve told me to come to the White House 'as quickly and as quietly' as I could."

He arrived there at 5:25 P.M. and was taken by elevator to Mrs. Franklin D. Roosevelt's study on the second floor.

"Harry," she said quietly, "the President is dead."

Fighting off tears, he asked, "Is there anything I can do for you?"

With her characteristic empathy, Mrs. Roosevelt replied, "Is there anything we can do for you? For you are the one in trouble now."

The person on whom the Executive power of the United States was so abruptly thrust was, in appearance, not distinctive. He stood 5 feet 8 inches tall. He had broad, square shoulders, an erect carriage, a round, apple-cheeked face, a long, sharp nose, deep blue eyes that peered through steel-rimmed glasses, and thin gray-white hair that was neatly parted and carefully brushed.

Apart from the plain eyeglasses, the most catching feature of Truman's face were his thin lips, which could be clamped in grimness or parted, over even teeth, in an engaging smile. He seemed a typical small-city businessman, pleasant and substantial, more at home on Main Street than on Pennsylvania Avenue.

His formal education had ended with high school, and he had been in business from time to time, but mostly he had been in politics. He was a county official from 1922 until his election to the Senate in 1934.

In creating and carrying out his policies, Truman built a reputation for decisiveness and courage, echoed by the sign on his desk: "The buck stops here."

With the war in Europe near its end, Truman had immediately to deal with Soviet intentions to impose Communist regimes in Eastern Europe and possibly to exploit the economic breakdown in Western Europe. Simultaneously he had to seek military and political solutions in the war against Japan. Both situations involved Soviet-American relations, and both gave initial shape to decades of strife between the world's two major powers.

In the foreground of Truman's dealings with Josef Stalin, at Potsdam and afterward, was the atomic-bomb project. Started in the deepest secrecy in the early days of World War II, it was on the verge of producing its first explosive when Truman became President.

Truman was unaware and unprepared when Secretary of War Henry L. Stimson explained the atomic project to him on April 25, 1945, 13 days after he had become President, and told him of the then presumed fantastic power of an atomic bomb. Apart from its staggering military potential, what impressed the President were its implications for American diplomacy and world peace.

At the same time, it was assumed by Truman and Stimson and virtually everyone connected with the project that the bomb would be employed as a matter of course to shorten the Japanese war.

"I did not like the weapon," he said, "but I had no qualms, if in the long run millions of lives could be saved."

Against his critics—and there were many in [later] years—he took the responsibility for the atomic havoc inflicted on Hiroshima and Nagasaki. The bombs, he maintained, did shorten the war and did save millions of American and Japanese battlefield casualties.

Japan surrendered Aug. 14, 1945, after the atomic-bomb toll at Hiroshima and Nagasaki had exceeded a total of 100,000 lives and after the Russians had stormed into Manchuria.

The global war was ended and a new and different era was emerging. The Truman domestic program, given to Congress on Sept. 6, 1945, called for full employment, increased minimum wages, private and public housing programs, a national health program, aid to education, Negro job rights, higher farm prices and continuation of key wartime economic controls.

Truman's foreign program was to combat Communist expansion and to strengthen what he called the free world.

There was outstanding success in Europe, thanks to the Truman Doctrine, inaugurated in 1947. In that year Britain, for lack of money, had to halt her subventions to Greece and Turkey, nations under heavy Communist pressure. With great dispatch, Truman convinced Congress it should extend cash help. This historic action, he said later, was "the turning point" in damming Soviet expansion in Europe, because it "put the world on notice that it would be our policy to support the cause of freedom wherever it was threatened."

The Truman Doctrine was the logical base for the Marshall Plan, enunciated by Secretary of State Marshall in the summer of 1947. Under it, the United States invited all European nations to cooperate in their economic recovery with billions of dollars in American backing.

Truman was born at 4 P.M. May 8, 1884, in a small frame house at Lamar, Mo. He was the firstborn of John Anderson Truman and Mary Ellen Young Truman. The initial "S" was a compromise between Shippe and Solomon, both kinsman's names.

When Harry was six, the family moved to Independence. It was there that Harry, whose mother had taught him his letters by five, went to school. He made friends, one in particular. "She had golden curls . . . and the most beautiful blue eyes," he said of Bess Wallace, the childhood sweetheart who was to become his wife.

Truman entered into politics in 1922, when he was elected a judge of the Jackson County Court. He proved conscientious, vigorous and industrious, both as a campaigner and as an administrator.

In 1934, running on a pro-Roosevelt program, he won a Senate seat. The time Truman spent in the Senate he recalled as "the happiest 10 years of my life." He spoke seldom on the floor, and then briefly, without ostentation; his voting record was New Deal.

When Roosevelt sought his fourth term, Truman had no serious thought of himself as Vice-Presidential material. But Roosevelt decided to drop Vice President Henry A. Wallace and chose Truman.

"A gone goose" was how Clare Boothe Luce described Harry S. Truman in 1948. There was a generalized voter discontent over inflation and high taxes, but he won the nomination. Republicans, emphasizing "it is time for a change," had chosen Gov. Thomas E. Dewey of New York as their candidate.

Truman's campaign, during which he repeatedly denounced "that no good, do nothing 80th Congress," covered 31,700 miles, and it included 256 speeches—16 in one day once. More than 12 million people turned out to see him.

"I simply told the people in my own language," he said later, "that they had better wake up to the fact that it was their fight."

Election eve, Truman was in Missouri. He awoke

twice during the night, to listen to Hans von Kaltenborn's clipped, slightly Teutonic-voiced radio analyses of the returns. These showed Truman ahead in the popular vote, but he couldn't possibly win, the commentator insisted. (For years afterward Truman delighted in imitating Kaltenborn's remarks, just as he enjoyed poking fun at The Chicago Tribune, which "elected" Dewey in its early-edition headline.)

Internal security problems preoccupied legislators and the public for the remainder of Truman's time in office, becoming acute when Senator Joseph R. McCarthy, Republican of Wisconsin, began to accuse the State Department of harboring Communists and to charge that the Administration was "soft" on party members and sympathizers.

Beset on the home front, Truman was soon fatefully involved again in the Far East, where Japan was obliged to give up her 40-year suzerainty over Korea. The peninsula was divided for occupation purposes between the United States and the Soviet Union, with American forces supervising the area south of the 38th Parallel.

On Saturday, June 24, 1950, the North Koreans invaded. Truman requested an immediate special meeting of the United Nations Security Council, seeking a declaration that the invasion was an act of aggression under the United Nations Charter.

With North Korean forces rapidly penetrating southward, the President ordered Gen. Douglas MacArthur to use American air and naval forces to aid the South Koreans. Within the next few days, under nominal United Nations command, American ground troops entered the conflict.

Early in the conflict there were two developments that deeply affected the fighting and brought Truman into collision with MacArthur. The general was optimistic: the Chinese Communists would not enter Korea and the fighting would end by Thanksgiving, he predicted. But the Chinese did enter the conflict, sending thousands of "volunteers" into North Korea. The Communist forces eventually beat back the American and United Nations troops to the 38th Parallel, where a front was established that lasted until the truce of 1953.

Truman's policy was to continue to confine the fighting to Korea, to avoid escalation. MacArthur, on the other hand, wanted to strike directly at the Chinese. In March, 1951, MacArthur wrote to Representative Joseph W. Martin Jr., the House Republican leader, criticizing the President's policy. A month later Truman discharged MacArthur for insubordination.

In the midst of the Korean conflict there was a crude attempt to assassinate the President. On Nov. 1, 1950, when the Trumans were living in Blair House while the White House was under repair, two men got out of a taxicab, and one drew a pistol and fired at a guard. The other ran toward the front door of Blair House.

In a few minutes, Griselio Torresola, a Puerto Rican extremist, lay dead, and a guard was mortally wounded. The second would-be assassin, Oscar Collazo, was shot in the chest. He was subsequently convicted of murder and sentenced to die, but the President commuted the penalty in 1952 to life imprisonment.

Truman's second term, like his first, was marked by greater harmony on foreign policy—especially economic and military aid to Europe—than on domestic affairs.

Truman strove to keep the economy stable, a determination that he dramatized by seizing the steel industry on April 8, 1952, to avert a strike and a price rise. Steel challenged the seizure and was upheld by the Supreme Court on the ground the President had exceeded his authority.

Truman's intimates and advisers, who had watched him mature in office, praised him above all for his forthrightness. He himself, reviewing his actions, said:

"I have tried my best to give the nation everything I had in me. There are probably a million people who could have done the job better than I did, but I had the job, and I always quote an epitaph on a tombstone in a cemetery in Tombstone, Arizona: 'Here lies Jack Williams. He done his damndest.'"

LYNDON B. JOHNSON

August 27, 1908–January 22, 1973

By Albin Krebs

SAN ANTONIO—Lyndon Baines Johnson, 36th President of the United States, died today of an apparent heart attack suffered at his ranch in Johnson City, Tex.

Although his vision of a Great Society dissolved in the morass of war in Vietnam, Mr. Johnson, 64, left a legacy of progress and innovation in civil rights, Social Security, education and housing.

The Texan who began his career in public life in 1937 with his election to Congress as an ardent New Dealer, a career that led him to the majority leadership of the Senate and the Vice-Presidency, was thrust into the Presidency on Nov. 22, 1963, when an assassin's bullet took the life of President [John F.] Kennedy in Dallas.

He won election in 1964 to a full term as President with the greatest voting majority ever accorded a candidate, but was transformed by the Vietnam war into the leader of a divided nation.

Amid rising personal unpopularity, in the face of lingering war and racial strife at home, Mr. Johnson surprised the nation on March 31, 1968, with a television speech in which he announced, "I shall not seek, and I will not accept, the nomination of my party for another term as your President."

Although the nation was frustrated and angry about the war in Vietnam and troubled by racial strife, most Americans had assumed that Mr. Johnson would run for re-election in 1968.

In his speech, Mr. Johnson announced that he had ordered a major reduction in the bombing of Communist North Vietnam and called for peace talks. Then he said he would not be a candidate for another term.

With those electrifying words, Mr. Johnson in effect admitted the shattering of a dream he had cherished, since Nov. 22, 1963, when an assassin's bullet killed his predecessor and made him President, that he would restore peace to the American people.

He set forth those goals in a ringing speech before a joint session of Congress on March 15, 1965.

"This is the richest and most powerful country which ever occupied this globe," he said. "The might of past empires is little compared to ours. But I do not want to be the President who built empires, or sought grandeur, or extended dominion.

"I want to be the President who educated young children to the wonders of their world.

"I want to be the President who helped to feed the hungry and to prepare them to be taxpayers instead of tax-eaters.

"I want to be the President who helped the poor to find their own way and who protected the right of every citizen to vote in every election.

"I want to be the President who helped to end hatred among his fellow men and who promoted love among the people of all races, all regions and all parties.

"I want to be the President who helped to end war among the brothers of this earth."

Less than two years after the day in Dallas when John F. Kennedy was shot, and less than a year after he had been chosen President in his own right, Mr. Johnson found himself trapped in a bloody and incredibly costly war that would seemingly never end.

The budgets of his Administration were mortgaged to that war, and its unpopularity drained his political strength. Moreover, the cities of America were ravaged by decay and racial dissension, and the white majority responded with anger, fear and vindictiveness. By the time he left office on Jan. 20, 1969, the name of Lyndon Johnson had become inextricably linked with war and its consequences.

Those who knew him would also remember that the essential Lyndon Johnson was a dynamo of a man who worked himself and those around him like Texas field hands. He was constantly on the telephone, ordering, threatening, wheeling and dealing.

He was often a cruel man, capable of great rages and monumental castigations of anyone who dared cross him.

By the time he had decided to leave the Presidency, the man who had been fond of saying, "Let us reason together," had found fewer and fewer of his fellow Americans reasoning along his lines. Vast numbers of the people wanted someone else to be their President.

It had seemed unlikely that Lyndon Baines Johnson would even attain the Presidency. His career had been clouded by charges of vulgarism, by his disputed election to the Senate in 1948, by his ownership of lucrative Government-regulated television broadcasting rights, and by the tangled affairs of his protégé, Robert G. Baker. Moreover, he was a Texan, and no Southerner had occupied the White House since Woodrow Wilson, a Virginian, had left it in 1921. But the fact that he would go into politics seemed certain from the start.

Mr. Johnson's father, his father's father and his mother's father all served in the Texas Legislature. It was said that on Aug. 27, 1908, Mr. Johnson's rancher grandfather, Sam Johnson Sr., rode on horseback around Johnson City proclaiming that "a United States Senator was born this morning—my grandson."

Lyndon Johnson was born in the three-room Johnson home at Hye, near the village of Johnson City, in the hills of southwest Texas. He was the eldest of five children of Samuel Ealy Johnson Jr. and Rebekah Baines. The Johnson family was extremely poor.

In February, 1927, he entered Southwest Texas

State Teachers College at San Marcos and graduated in three years. His first full-time job was teaching at Sam Houston High School in Houston, where many of his students were Mexican-Americans.

While teaching in Houston, Mr. Johnson worked as a volunteer in the 1931 Congressional campaign of Richard M. Kleberg Sr., an owner of the mammoth King Ranch. When Mr. Kleberg won election to the House, the tall, gangling Mr. Johnson, then 22, went to Washington with him as his legislative assistant.

Lyndon Johnson hit Capitol Hill in those Depression days like a Texas tornado, seeking drought relief, unemployment relief, anything for the folks back home. Mr. Johnson had the help of Sam Rayburn, soon to become the powerful Speaker of the House.

In September, 1934, he met Claudia Alta Taylor, nicknamed Lady Bird. They were married on Nov. 17, 1934, and had two daughters, Lynda Bird, now Mrs. Charles S. Robb, and Luci Baines, now Mrs. Patrick J. Nugent. His wife and daughters survive him.

In 1935, Mr. Johnson was appointed Texas state director of the National Youth Administration. And his chance to run for office came in 1937 when the United States Representative from his district, James P. Buchanan, died.

When the ballots were counted, Lyndon Johnson had piled up twice as many votes as his nearest opponent. He had won the first of his six House terms handily.

He won re-election easily in 1938, and in 1940 he breezed through to a second full term without formal opposition.

Meanwhile, Mr. Johnson obtained more than his share of public works projects for his district. Among these was a flood-control and electricity-generating dam-and-spillway system for the Pedernales River, which runs through what is now the LBJ Ranch at Johnson City.

In 1941, after the death of Senator Morris Sheppard, he announced that he planned to run for the vacant Senate seat. Mr. Johnson lost the race by 1,311 votes to the colorful former Gov. W. Lee (Pappy) O'Daniel.

In 1942 a virtually bankrupt radio station in Austin came up for sale, and the Johnsons bought the station for $17,500. The assets of the station, KTBC, and later KTBC-TV, were by 1964 listed at $3.2 million.

By 1948, Mr. Johnson was ready for another try at the Senate. He faced a formidable opponent in former Gov. Coke Stevenson. In the runoff that became required after the Democratic primary, Mr. Johnson squeaked to victory by a margin of 87 votes of 988,295 cast.

There were accusations of ballot-box irregularities, But in the general election he defeated his Republican opponent by a 2-to-1 margin. For years, Mr. Johnson was derisively called "Landslide Lyndon" and there were persistent charges that the election had been "fixed."

In the Senate, Mr. Johnson cultivated the veteran Senator Richard Russell of Georgia, and in 1951 Mr. Johnson was elected majority whip, a testament to his growing capacity to wield influence.

The Democrats lost majority control in the Senate in the 1952 election, which brought Dwight D. Eisenhower into the White House. Mr. Johnson became Democratic minority leader. At 44, he was the youngest man ever to hold that position.

The Republicans lost control of both houses of Congress in 1954 and Mr. Johnson became majority leader in the Senate. His achievements as majority leader became a legend in Washington. Mr. Johnson exhibited an uncanny ability to know precisely what chances a given bill had for passage.

He was proud of having piloted through the Senate, in 1957, the first civil rights bill since Reconstruction, and in 1960 he helped beat back a filibuster aimed at blocking an expanded civil rights measure.

Mr. Johnson withheld the announcement of his decision to seek the Presidential nomination in 1960 until shortly before the opening of the convention in Los Angeles.

Senator John F. Kennedy was the nominee, and his selection of Mr. Johnson as his running mate came as a surprise. But Mr. Kennedy knew he could benefit from Mr. Johnson's presence on the Democratic ticket, which ultimately triumphed over the Republican team of Richard M. Nixon and Henry Cabot Lodge by the smallest vote margin in this century.

Mr. Johnson accompanied Mr. Kennedy to Texas on Nov. 21, 1963. The following day Mr. Johnson and his wife rode in a motorcade through Dallas behind an open limousine bearing John and Jacqueline Kennedy and Gov. John Connally of Texas. Lee Harvey Oswald fired three shots from a window of the Texas Book Depository, and John Fitzgerald Kennedy was assassinated.

Thirteen minutes after the President was pronounced dead, Mr. Johnson was hustled into an unmarked police car and driven to Love Field, where Air Force One, the Presidential jet, was waiting. Mr. Johnson took the oath of office in the plane's cramped executive suite. At his right stood his wife, Lady Bird, to his left the grief-stricken Jacqueline Kennedy.

At Andrews Air Force Base, near Washington, when Air Force One rolled to a halt, Mr. Johnson stepped forward and read the nation a few words of reassurance from a white card, ending: "I will do my best. That is all I can do. I ask for your help—and God's."

Five days later the new Chief Executive stood before a joint session of Congress and said, "Let us continue." He made it apparent that what he meant was passage of Mr. Kennedy's entire legislative program, including civil rights laws and a tax reduction to stimulate the economy.

In his first 15 months in office Mr. Johnson best demonstrated the qualities for which he hoped to be remembered—by masterly managing the transition of power from the slain President to himself, by breaking legislative logjams of decades' duration, and by persuading the world of the strength and continuity of American institutions.

Action on a tax-cut bill occurred only weeks after Mr. Johnson became President.

In July, 1964, Mr. Johnson signed into law the most sweeping civil rights bill since Reconstruction days. The measure, which had been submitted to Congress in June, 1963, by Mr. Kennedy, outlawed discrimination in places of public accommodation, publicly owned facilities, employment and Federally-aided programs.

To get the legislation he wanted, the President used what came to be known in Washington as "the Johnson treatment," a combination of cajolery, flattery, concession, and arm-twisting threats.

Early in his Administration, the President declared what he called a "war on poverty." He traveled to the distressed Appalachia area to dramatize the need for an antipoverty drive for which he asked Congress to appropriate $1 billion.

He first spoke of the Great Society, the phrase with which he sought to identify his Administration, in May of 1964.

"I ask you to march with me along the road to the future," he said, "the road that leads to the Great Society, where no child will go unfed and no youngster will go unschooled . . . where every human being has dignity and every worker has a job; where education is blind to color and unemployment is unaware of race; where decency prevails and courage abounds."

Mr. Johnson's record in the months after Mr. Kennedy's assassination left no doubt that he would be his party's nominee in the 1964 election. He chose as his running mate Sen. Hubert H. Humphrey of Minnesota.

Much campaign oratory was devoted to arguments as to whether Mr. Johnson's Republican opponent, Barry Goldwater, the conservative Senator from Arizona, might plunge the nation into atomic holocaust. The Democrats charged that a President Goldwater might escalate the United States participation in the fighting in Vietnam, while Mr. Johnson would seek peace in Southeast Asia.

On Election Day, 1964, it became quickly apparent that Mr. Johnson had received a record-breaking majority of 61 percent of the popular vote.

Mr. Johnson took the oath of office for his full term in the Presidency on Jan. 20, 1965. His 1,500-word inaugural address was one of the shortest in history.

The President believed that many of his dreams for a better America could become reality, for the voters had given him not only a landslide victory but also a Congress dominated by Democrats. That Congress soon began to enact far-reaching programs, among them Medicare for the elderly, a massive program of Federal aid to elementary and secondary schools, new safeguards for Negro voting rights, reform of the immigration laws, grants for the "model cities" development program, and increased funds for the antipoverty program. All these and tax cuts too were realized by the President, with the help of the 89th Congress.

The problems of South Vietnam had plagued both President Dwight D. Eisenhower and President Kennedy. They sent military advisers to help the South Vietnamese army combat the Communist rebels, the Vietcong, who were armed by Communist North Vietnam. But President Johnson committed American troops to a long and costly land war in South Vietnam.

The stage for his escalation of the war was set in August, 1964, after Communist PT boats had attacked United States destroyers in the Gulf of Tonkin. Mr. Johnson obtained Congressional approval of a resolution granting him full support for "all necessary action to protect our armed forces." In February, 1965, there were about 20,000 American servicemen in South Vietnam.

At that time, Mr. Johnson learned that the Saigon Government stood in danger of collapse and the Vietcong were on the march. He authorized what became daily air bombardment of North Vietnam. By November, 1965 there were 160,000 American troops in Vietnam.

Three years after the escalation had begun, the number of troops in Vietnam soared past a half million. By the end of January, 1969, two weeks after Mr. Johnson left office, more than 31,000 Americans had been killed in Vietnam and nearly 435,000 had been wounded.

The financial cost of the war went from $103 million in 1965 to an estimated $28.8 billion for the 1969 fiscal year.

A large and vocal minority of Americans disagreed, sometimes violently, with Mr. Johnson's pursuit of the war in Vietnam. Some came to hate him and the war passionately.

Everywhere he turned, at home and abroad, Lyndon Johnson ran headlong into the limitations set for him by the war, which sapped both money and governmental energy from addressing the decay of the cities and the revolt of the Negroes in the ghettos.

Only a week after Mr. Johnson had signed the Voting Rights Act of 1965, rioting engulfed the Watts Negro ghetto of Los Angeles. Newark, Detroit and other cities were in open rebellion for several days in 1967, and after the assassination in April, 1968, of the Rev. Dr. Martin Luther King Jr., the nonviolent civil rights leader, rioting took place in dozens of cities.

Behind the riots lay the decay of the cores of the nation's major cities and pervasive patterns of discrimination that kept poor Negroes imprisoned there. Behind the angry white response lay the deterioration of much of the quality of life in middle-class America, despite a booming economy.

As the nation sank deeper and deeper into the horror of Vietnam, the President's popularity continued to wane. The intellectual community found him vulgar and untrustworthy. Much of the press treated him as crude and temperamental.

In his own party, opponents of the Vietnam war and critics of his domestic failures were getting growing attention. Two Democratic Senators, Eugene J. McCarthy of Minnesota and Robert F. Kennedy of New York (who was assassinated in June, 1968), had entered state primaries.

On Jan. 20, 1969, Mr. Johnson turned over the Presidency to Mr. Nixon, the Republican who defeated Vice President Hubert H. Humphrey in the 1968 election.

EARL WARREN

March 19, 1891–July 9, 1974

By Anthony Lewis

WASHINGTON—Earl Warren, who as Chief Justice of the United States presided over extraordinary constitutional change, died tonight at Georgetown University Hospital. He was 83 years old.

He had entered the hospital a week ago with what was diagnosed as coronary insufficiency and congestive heart failure—his third hospitalization with heart problems this year.

Mrs. Warren, the former Nina Meyers, was with him. Other survivors are his sons James, Earl Jr. and Robert, and daughters Virginia (Mrs. John Charles Daly), Dorothy (Mrs. Harry Van Knight) and Nina (Mrs. Stuart Brien).

President Nixon said in a statement: "America has lost one of her finest public servants."

Mr. Warren was Attorney General of California for four years, Governor for 12 and the Republican candidate for Vice President in 1948. But his long political career was entirely overshadowed by his nearly 16 years as Chief Justice, from 1953 to 1969.

The school segregation case, Brown v. Board of Education, was the best-known symbol of those years. Decided on May 17, 1954, just eight months after Mr. Warren took his seat, the case held segregated schools unconstitutional, overruling the 60-year-old separate-but-equal doctrine. Later cases applied the new rule to all racial barriers imposed by law.

The Chief Justice's role in the Brown case was hidden by the Supreme Court tradition of secrecy in deliberation. But many students of the period believe that he had a crucial role in achieving unanimity on the Court.

The Warren Court also interpreted the Constitution to provide many new rights for those suspected of accused of crime, including the landmark case of Miranda v. Arizona in 1966. The Court held that all arrested persons had a right to see a lawyer before being questioned by the police—a free lawyer if they could not pay for one—and had to be advised of that right.

Chief Justice Warren once said that he regarded the apportionment cases as more important than those dealing with either race or criminal defendants' rights.

Precedents had barred Federal courts from even considering challenges to legislative districts that were gerrymandered or grossly unequal in population. Then, in 1962, the Court turned away from that history and said that Federal judges could consider apportionment cases.

Two years later, in a massive opinion by the Chief Justice, the Court held that every house of every state legislature had to be districted substantially on the basis of equal population. The result was the redistricting, in a short time, of almost all American state legislatures.

These cases made Earl Warren a highly controversial figure, very likely the most controversial judge of the century. Southern segregationists ran campaigns to "impeach Earl Warren." Liberals honored him more than they did most Presidents.

From his seat on the bench Chief Justice Warren would often indicate a distaste for something that the Federal Government or a state had done to some individual. He would ask counsel, as if the latter were personally responsible, "Was that fair?"

By Alden Whitman

Presiding over the Supreme Court for 16 years, Earl Warren championed the Constitution as the vigorous protector of the individual rights and equality of all Americans.

Reflecting the dynamics of social change in the nation (and profoundly affecting them), Mr. Warren's Court, amid much dispute, elaborated a doctrine of fairness in such areas as criminal justice, voting rights, legislative districting, employment, housing, transportation and education. In so doing, the Chief Justice contributed greatly to a reshaping of the country's social and political institutions.

"I would like the Court to be remembered as the people's court," he remarked on his retirement. This was a quite different attitude from his earlier law-and-order views as a California prosecutor; but Mr. Warren had become more liberal with age and perspective. "On the Court I saw [things] in a different light," he once explained.

The impact of the Warren Court was cumulative, and Mr. Warren's stature grew perceptibly over 16 years. The parts that constituted the whole were embodied in a series of decisions that had the collective effect of reinforcing popular liberties. Among these were rulings that:

> *Outlawed school segregation.*
> *Enunciated the one-man, one-vote*
>   *doctrine.*
> *Made most of the Bill of Rights binding on*
>   *the states.*
> *Curbed wiretapping.*
> *Upheld the right to be secure against*
>   *"unreasonable" searches and*
>   *seizures.*
> *Buttressed the right to counsel.*
> *Underscored the right to a jury trial.*
> *Barred racial discrimination in voting, in*
>   *marriage laws, in the use of public*
>   *parks, airports and bus terminals and*
>   *in housing sales and rentals.*
> *Extended the boundaries of free speech.*

Many observers believed that the desegregation rulings, starting with Brown v. Board of Education of Topeka in 1954, were the Warren Court's most important because they led to a readjustment of long-standing racial imbalances in the country.

Mr. Warren himself, however, regarded the redistricting cases as the most significant. The essence of Mr. Warren's (and the Court's) position on one man, one vote—a doctrine that transformed the political map of the nation—was set forth in Reynolds v. Sims.

At issue was whether factors other than equal representation of voters could be considered in electing state legislators. Assuming that members of one house would be elected from districts of equal populations, could members of the other house represent geographical areas of varying densities in order to assure a voice to sparsely settled localities and minority interests?

Because to do so would give some persons more influence than others, Mr. Warren replied with a firm "no." "Legislators represent people, not trees or acres," he wrote.

As a result of this and other rulings, states redrew their legislative districts, and many reviewed Congressional boundaries.

Ranking just below redistricting in Mr. Warren's estimation came the school desegregation rulings that started with the Brown case. This historic decision was one of 45 in which the Warren Court overruled prior Supreme Court holdings and set in motion profound changes in the country's racial relations.

Mr. Warren's handling of the Brown case to achieve unanimity illustrated the qualities that made him, in the minds of many lawyers, an outstanding Chief Justice. Describing what happened, he said:

"Ordinarily, the Justices, at our Friday conferences stated their positions, offered debate and then voted. But in Brown we were all conscious of the case, so I held off a vote from conference to conference while we discussed it. If you'll remember, Brown was argued in the fall of 1953, and I did not call for a vote until the middle of the following February, when I was certain we would be unanimous. We took one vote, and that was it."

Speaking for the Court, Mr. Warren brushed aside the "separate but equal" doctrine of Plessy v. Ferguson that had been in effect for 58 years. "We conclude," he wrote, "that in the field of public education the doctrine of 'separate but equal' has no place."

From the Brown decision flowed a score or more of holdings by the Court and by inferior courts that collectively struck down racial inequalities in most areas of public life. As a result, parks, swimming pools, bus terminals and housing were desegregated.

Ranking third in Mr. Warren's mind was a group of criminal cases that expanded protection for the rights of the accused. "Then we come to the Miranda case," he said, "and the question arises: If he's entitled to a lawyer when his lawyer is present, when is he first entitled to a lawyer?"

More than many Chief Justices, Mr. Warren removed himself from partisanship and political activity, but in one instance he felt obliged to take on, albeit reluctantly, an extra-judicial task. That was the chairmanship of the so-called Warren Commission, which investigated the assassination of President Kennedy in November, 1963, and concluded that Lee Harvey Oswald, acting alone, had shot the President.

In taking the post, Mr. Warren yielded to the importunings of President Johnson. The 10 months of the commission's work were "the unhappiest time of my life," he said, adding that "to review the terrible happenings of that assassination every day [was] a traumatic experience.

Mr. Warren was born in Los Angeles on March 19, 1891, the son of Methias H. (Matt) Warren and Crystal Hernlund Warren. His mother was a native of Sweden and his father was born in Norway.

The family moved to Bakersfield, where, after a number of years Matt Warren slipped into the way of an eccentric who did not live with his family. He was bludgeoned to death in 1938, and the case was never solved.

Earl attended public schools in Bakersfield and went to the University of California, getting a Bachelor of Letters degree in 1912 and a doctorate in jurisprudence in 1914.

He practiced law for several years, served as an infantry first lieutenant in World War I, and began his public career as Deputy City Attorney for Oakland, Calif. Then he became a Deputy District Attorney for Alameda County. As the County's District Attorney, from 1925 to 1938, he emerged as a racket-busting prosecutor.

Mr. Warren was Republican national committeeman when he ran successfully for California Attorney General in 1938. In four years in the post, he kept in the public eye with an occasional raid on gambling dens, but most of his work was administrative. Nonetheless, he appeared frequently around the state, usually with his wife, the former Mrs. Nina Palmquist Meyers, a widow, whom he had married in 1925.

In 1942 Mr. Warren ran for Governor and won by defeating the favored Democratic nominee, Governor Culbert L. Olson. He was re-elected twice. In 1948, he was selected to run for the Vice-Presidency with Gov. Thomas E. Dewey of New York. They lost to Harry S. Truman and Alben W. Barkley.

He was a big, fair-haired man, at 6 feet and 215 pounds, called Pinky in his youth, who loved spectator sports and outdoor life, and whose suits were always double-breasted blue serge. He could call hundreds of people by name, but he had few close friends, preferring to spend free time with his family.

In his early years, Mr. Warren was instinctively attracted to the kind of conservative thinking that made him a favorite of California's regular Republicans.

Mr. Warren's opportunity for a Court seat came in 1953 when Chief Justice Fred M. Vinson, a lackluster jurist, died, and President Eisenhower nominated the Californian. He was sworn in on Oct. 5.

In June, 1968, Mr. Warren was stunned by the assassination of Robert F. Kennedy. He later told a friend

of reading with astonishment that a few hours before the assassination, people stood two and three deep along the highway into Los Angeles from the airport. He had seen many politicians travel that route, and he knew that no such assemblage had ever greeted a candidate before. He took it as a sign that the nation was reaching out for younger leaders and new ideas.

On June 13, he wrote President Johnson and tendered his resignation "at your pleasure." A few days later, in his first public news conference as Chief Justice, he explained that "at the age of 77, this was a good time to retire."

It was Mr. Warren's tendency to interpret the Constitution in terms of the result he found desirable that drew the most criticism. The result, critics said, was to transform the Supreme Court into a perpetual constitutional convention, updating the Constitution to square with the liberal majority's concept of what the law ought to be.

Mr. Warren's admirers answered that a half-century had passed since Charles Evans Hughes had conceded that the Constitution is what the judges say it is, and that the Supreme Court must, because it is supreme, "make" law.

At a time of great social upheaval, sensitive issues were being placed before the Court, and it was argued that the Justices' duty was to decide those issues.

For Mr. Warren, the outcome almost always reflected idealism, fairness and equality—and the decisions made him a revered figure to many Americans and people around the world.

THURGOOD MARSHALL

July 2, 1908–January 24, 1993

By Linda Greenhouse

WASHINGTON—Thurgood Marshall, pillar of the civil rights revolution, architect of the legal strategy that ended the era of official segregation and the first black Justice of the Supreme Court, died today. He was 84 years old.

A Court's spokeswoman said Justice Marshall died of heart failure at Bethesda Naval Medical Center in Maryland.

Thurgood Marshall was a figure of history well before he began his 24-year service on the Supreme Court on Oct. 2, 1967. During more than 20 years as director-counsel of the NAACP Legal Defense and Educational Fund, he was the principal architect of the strategy of using the courts to provide what the political system would not: a definition of equality that assured black Americans the full rights of citizenship.

His greatest legal victory came in 1954 with the Supreme Court's decision in Brown v. Board of Education, which declared an end to the "separate but equal" system of racial segregation then in effect in the public schools of 21 states.

Despite the years of turmoil that followed the unanimous decision, the Court left no doubt that it was bringing an end to the era of official segregation in public institutions. The Court continued to confront issues involving the legacy of segregation even after Justice Marshall retired.

As a civil rights lawyer, Mr. Marshall devised the legal strategy that brought the school desegregation issue before the Court, and he argued the case himself in the plain-spoken manner that was the hallmark of his courtroom style. Asked by Justice Felix Frankfurter what he meant by "equal," Mr. Marshall replied, "Equal means getting the same thing, at the same time, and in the same place."

Mr. Marshall, who was born and reared in Baltimore, was excluded from the all-white law school at the University of Maryland. Later he brought successful lawsuits that integrated that school and other state university systems. He received his legal education at the law school of Howard University in Washington, D.C., the nation's pre-eminent black university, where he graduated first in his class in 1933.

"To do what he did required a heroic imagination," Paul Gewirtz, one of Justice Marshall's former law clerks and a professor at Yale Law School, wrote in a tribute.

"He grew up in a ruthlessly discriminatory world," Mr. Gewirtz continued, "a world in which segregation of the races was pervasive and taken for granted, where lynching was common, where the black man's inherent inferiority was proclaimed widely and wantonly. Thurgood Marshall had the capacity to imagine a radically different world, the imaginative capacity to believe that such a world was possible, the strength to sustain that image in the mind's eye and the heart's longing, and the courage and ability to make that imagined world real."

Yet Justice Marshall was not satisfied with what he had achieved, believing that the Constitution's promise of equality remained unfulfilled.

For much of his Supreme Court career, as the Court's majority increasingly drew back from affirmative action and other remedies for discrimination that he believed were still necessary to combat the nation's legacy of racism, Justice Marshall used dissenting opinions to express his disappointment and anger.

In 1978, in the Bakke case, in which the Court found it unconstitutional for a state-run medical school to reserve places in the entering class for black and other minority students, Justice Marshall filed a separate opinion tracing the black experience in America.

"In light of the sorry history of discrimination and its devastating impact on the lives of Negroes," he wrote, "bringing the Negro into the mainstream of American life should be a state interest of the highest order. To fail to do so is to insure that America will forever remain a divided society."

He dissented in City of Richmond v. Croson, a 1989 ruling in which the Court declared unconstitutional a municipal ordinance setting aside 30 percent of public contracting dollars for companies owned by blacks or other minorities. The Court majority called the program a form of state-sponsored racism that was as offensive as a policy officially favoring whites.

In his dissenting opinion, Justice Marshall said that in reaching that conclusion "a majority of this Court signals that it regards racial discrimination as largely a phenomenon of the past, and that government bodies need no longer preoccupy themselves with rectifying racial injustice."

He added: "I, however, do not believe this nation is anywhere close to eradicating racial discrimination or its vestiges."

Justice Marshall's most powerful voice was in dissent, and not only in the area of racial discrimination. Like his friend and closest ally, Justice William J. Brennan Jr., Justice Marshall believed that the death penalty was unconstitutional under all circumstances. He wrote more than 150 dissenting opinions in cases in which the Court had refused to hear death penalty appeals.

In an article published after his retirement, Kathleen M. Sullivan, a Harvard Law School professor, called Justice Marshall "the great dissenter," adding, "With his departure goes part of the conscience of the Court—a reminder of the human consequences of legal decisions."

The phrase "first black Supreme Court Justice" scarcely encompassed the unusual range of legal experience that Justice Marshall brought to the Court.

By the time President Lyndon B. Johnson named him to succeed Justice Tom C. Clark, who had retired, Mr. Marshall had argued 32 cases before the Court and won 29 of them. He argued 18 of these cases as Solicitor General of the United States, the Federal Government's chief advocate in the Supreme Court. President Johnson had named him to that position in 1965, two years before nominating him to the Supreme Court.

From 1961 to 1965, Thurgood Marshall was a Federal appeals court judge, named by President John F. Kennedy to the United States Court of Appeals for the Second Circuit, in Manhattan. He wrote 112 opinions on that court, none of which was overturned on appeal.

In the courtroom Justice Marshall's face was an inscrutable mask. But those who knew him well said that behind the mask was a man with an earthy sense of humor, a spellbinding storyteller with an anecdote from his own long life for every occasion.

Thurgood Marshall was born in Baltimore on July 2, 1908. His mother, Norma, was a teacher. His father, William Marshall, had worked as a Pullman car waiter. A great-grandfather had been taken as a slave from the Congo to the Eastern Shore of Maryland, where the slaveholder eventually freed him.

Mr. Marshall was named for his paternal grandfather, who had chosen the name "Thoroughgood" when he enlisted as a private in the Union Army during the Civil War. His grandson later explained that he adopted the spelling "Thurgood" in grade school because he "got tired of spelling all that out."

In his high school years, he worked as a delivery boy after classes. He waited on tables to help pay the tuition at Lincoln University in Chester, Pa., where he became a star debater and graduated with honors in 1930.

His mother wanted him to become a dentist, a lucrative career for a black professional in those days, but he was determined to become a lawyer. Enrolling at Howard University Law School meant a long daily commute from Baltimore because he could not afford housing at the school. His mother pawned her wedding and engagement rings to pay the entrance fees.

At Howard he met a man who would influence the course of his life, Charles Hamilton Houston, then the law school's vice dean. Mr. Houston, a Harvard Law School graduate who later served as chief counsel to the National Association for the Advancement of Colored People and became the first black lawyer to win a case before the Supreme Court, imbued his students with the goal of using the law to attack institutional racism.

After earning his law degree Mr. Marshall opened a law office in Baltimore. His courtroom victories, including his successful challenge to segregation at the University of Maryland Law School, began to be noticed, and in 1936 Mr. Houston, by then the chief counsel of the N.A.A.C.P., recruited him for a job on the organization's legal staff in New York. Two years later, when Mr. Houston returned to Washington, Mr. Marshall succeeded to the chief counsel's title.

Pursuing a long-range strategy to eradicate segregation, the two men concentrated first on graduate and professional schools. As successes mounted, they turned their attention to segregation in public elementary and high schools.

"Under Marshall, the N.A.A.C.P.'s legal staff became the model for public interest law firms," wrote Mark Tushnet, one of the Justice's biographers. "His commitment to racial justice led him and his staff to develop ways of thinking about constitutional litigation that have been enormously influential far beyond the areas of segregation and discrimination."

In its public school cases, the initial focus of the N.A.A.C.P., and later of the NAACP Legal Defense and Educational Fund, was to seek to equalize the resources available to the all-black schools in segregated systems. Mr. Marshall persuaded the organization's board to abandon that approach and refuse any cases that did not challenge the fact of segregation itself.

By 1961, when President Kennedy named him to the Federal appeals court, Thurgood Marshall was the nation's best-known black lawyer. Six years later, President Johnson said that placing Judge Marshall on the Supreme Court was "the right thing to do, the right time to do it, the right man and the right place."

Liberals still dominated the Court in the closing years of Chief Justice Earl Warren's tenure, and Justice Marshall fit in comfortably with such colleagues as Justices Brennan and William O. Douglas.

But the ideological landscape changed. By the time Justice Marshall announced his retirement, on June 27, 1991, he had served longer than all but one of the sitting Justices, Byron R. White, and was more liberal than any of them.

One of his best-known dissents was a 63-page opinion in a 1973 case, San Antonio School District v. Rodriguez. The majority in that case held that the Constitution's guarantee of equal protection was not violated by the property tax system used by Texas and most other states to finance public education. Under the system, districts with generous tax bases can afford to provide better schools than less wealthy districts.

In his dissenting opinion, Justice Marshall accused the majority of an "unsupportable acquiescence in a system which deprives children in their earliest years of the chance to reach their full potential as citizens."

He argued that the right to an education should be regarded as a "fundamental" constitutional right, and that state policies that have the effect of discriminating on the basis of wealth should be subject to searching judicial scrutiny.

"In my judgment," he wrote, "the right of every American to an equal start in life, so far as the provision of a state service as important as education is concerned, is far too vital to permit state discrimination on grounds as tenuous as those presented by this record."

Justice Marshall's first wife, the former Vivien Burey, whom he married in 1929, died in February 1955. That December he married Cecilia Suyat, known as Cissy. They had two sons.

Justice Marshall, a few days shy of his 83rd birthday, gave health as the reason for his retirement at the end of the 1990–1991 term. At a news conference the next day he was asked, "What's wrong with you, sir?"

"What's wrong with me?" Justice Marshall replied. "I'm old. I'm getting old and coming apart."

RICHARD NIXON

January 9, 1913–April 22, 1994

Richard Milhous Nixon, the 37th President of the United States, who was the only President in more than two centuries of American history to resign from office, died last night of a stroke at New York Hospital–Cornell Medical Center. He was 81 years old.

Mr. Nixon's daughters, Julie Nixon Eisenhower and Tricia Nixon Cox, were at his bedside.—*R. W. Apple Jr.*

By John Herbers

To millions of Americans, Richard Nixon was the most puzzling and fascinating politician of his time. He was a highly intelligent man whose talents, especially in international affairs, were deeply respected. Yet he was so motivated by hatreds and fears that he abused his powers and resorted to lies and cover-ups.

Almost constantly in the public eye from the time he entered politics in 1946, he propelled himself into a career that culminated a generation later when he became the first President to travel to Communist China and the first to resign from office. His career was a tumultuous roller-coaster ride of victory, crisis, defeat, revival, triumph, ruin and re-emergence as an elder statesman who traveled widely and wrote copiously. "No one," he told an interviewer in 1990, "had ever been so high and fallen so low."

Mr. Nixon never received the accolades he would have earned had he not resigned the Presidency in the face of certain impeachment for the cover-up of a political burglary of Democratic offices in the Watergate complex and other illegal acts of domestic espionage. Still, he never confessed to the "high crimes and misdemeanors" of which he was accused in articles of impeachment, which were approved by the House Judiciary Committee and precipitated his resignation in 1974.

"When the President does it, that means it is not illegal," he told David Frost in a celebrated television interview three years after he was pardoned by his successor, Gerald R. Ford.

So strong was the stigma of the Watergate scandals that it tended to obscure Mr. Nixon's accomplishments. In foreign affairs these included establishing relations with Communist China and initiating nuclear arms control treaties with the Soviet Union.

Yet his accomplishments were marred by his methods and motives. Carrying out the "peace with honor" agreement to end the long, divisive war in Southeast Asia took five years from the time he was elected to office on a peace pledge—years in which American society was scarred by riots against bombings and incursions into new territory.

By the end of 1968, 30,610 Americans had died in the war, and another 27,557 over the next five years.

Then came Watergate. Watergate in its broadest sense—not only the burglary of Democratic headquarters and subsequent efforts at a cover-up, but also the corruption of Federal agencies for illegal purposes—had such an impact on politics and government that it remains a promontory on the landscape of American history.

"Though he was a remote and private man, we had all been drawn into his life story," Garry Wills, author of "Nixon Agonistes," wrote after the resignation. "Decade by decade, crisis by crisis, we were unwilling intruders on his most intimate moments—we saw him cry, sweat, tremble, saw him angry, hurt, vindictive. The tapes even let us eavesdrop on those embarrassing conversations."

The future President was born Jan. 9, 1913, in Yorba Linda, Calif., near Los Angeles. His father, Francis Anthony Nixon, worked in the Quaker community of Whittier, where he met Hannah Milhous. They were married in 1908, and Frank bought a general store and filling station.

"It was not an easy life, but it was a good one," Richard Nixon, the second of the couple's five sons, recalled in his memoirs.

He daydreamed of faraway places, worked hard to win good grades, and attended a strict Quaker church. One brother died when Richard was 12, another when he was 20.

After graduating from Whittier College and Duke University Law School in Durham, N.C., he returned to California to practice law. He also acted in a little theater group, where he met Thelma Catherine Ryan, a schoolteacher called Pat, and they married two years later.

After serving in the Navy in World War II, he was asked by a committee of California Republicans if he were interested in running for Congress against the incumbent, the liberal Jerry Voorhis. Mr. Nixon won the primary, and in the general election he developed a technique he would use time and again: discredit your opponent. Mr. Nixon won the election and headed for Washington.

The Alger Hiss case made Richard Nixon a national celebrity. In 1948, Mr. Hiss, a former State Department official, was accused by Whittaker Chambers, a former Communist and an editor at Time magazine, of having given Mr. Chambers secret Government documents for delivery to the Soviet Union. Mr. Hiss denied the charges before the House Committee on Un-American Activities, and the matter might have been dropped had Mr. Nixon not pursued it as head of a special subcommittee. Mr. Chambers produced from a pumpkin on his Maryland farm microfilm of documents that he said had been given to him by Mr. Hiss. Mr. Hiss was convicted in 1950.

In 1950, Mr. Nixon faced off against Rep. Helen Gahagan Douglas, a liberal Democrat, for a California Senate seat. He set out to discredit her loyalty, attacking her as "the pink lady," insinuating that she had Communist sympathies. It was in this contest that Mr. Nixon, the winner, was first called "Tricky Dick."

Dwight D. Eisenhower, a war hero running for President as a moderate Republican, picked Richard Nixon as his running mate in 1952, but the campaign was barely under way when newspapers disclosed that wealthy California businessmen had raised a fund of $18,235 to defray Nixon's political expenses.

Many demanded that Mr. Nixon resign from the ticket on ethical grounds, but Eisenhower gave him the opportunity to state his case on national television, and Mr. Nixon maintained that he had done nothing wrong.

His best remembered remarks were in reference to his wife and a dog named Checkers. "Pat and I have the satisfaction that every dime that we've got is honestly ours," he said. "I should say this—that Pat doesn't have a mink coat. But she does have a respectable Republican cloth coat."

Then he said a man in Texas had given the family a cocker spaniel. "And our little girl, Tricia, the six-year-old, named it Checkers. And you know, the kids love the dog, and I just want to say this right now, that regardless of what they do about it, we're going to keep it."

Public response was positive, and he remained on the ticket.

Mr. Nixon proved an active Vice President, visiting 56 countries. His 1958 trip to South America turned out to be one of the "Six Crises" he would recall in his book of that title, with crowds erupting in an anti-Nixon frenzy. There followed the celebrated "kitchen debate" with the Soviet leader, Nikita S. Khrushchev, in 1959 while Mr. Nixon was in Moscow to open an American exhibit at a fair. In the kitchen of a model home, the two leaders debated the relative merits of the capitalist and Soviet systems.

After the Eisenhower-Nixon ticket won again in 1956, Mr. Nixon groomed himself for the 1960 Presidential nomination. Once nominated, he chose Henry Cabot Lodge of Massachusetts as his running mate. The Democratic ticket was Senator John F. Kennedy of Massachusetts and Senator Lyndon B. Johnson of Texas.

The campaign went badly from the beginning, and Eisenhower did not help. Asked to cite a major idea of Mr. Nixon's that the Administration had adopted, he replied, "If you give me a week, I might think of one."

Nor was Nixon at his best in the four television debates with Mr. Kennedy. He declined the use of makeup: his dark beard made him resemble the shadowy figure that cartoonists had often depicted.

The outcome was extraordinarily close. In the popular vote Mr. Kennedy led by 113,000 out of 68.8 million cast. Many Republicans believed that Democratic machines in Chicago and Texas had stolen the election for Mr. Kennedy.

At the age of 48, Mr. Nixon returned to California and entered the 1962 race for Governor against the incumbent, Pat Brown, but lost. That night he made an angry speech that included the line, "You won't have Nixon to kick around anymore, because, gentlemen, this is my last press conference."

He moved to New York and became a partner in a Wall Street law firm. On Jan. 31, 1968, he announced his candidacy for the Presidency. That November Mr. Nixon won the popular vote and got 301 electoral votes to 191 for Vice President Hubert H. Humphrey and 46 for Gov. George C. Wallace of Alabama, on a third-party ticket.

As president, Mr. Nixon backed safety and health protection for workers, and agreed to legislation to pour billions into cleaning up the nation's air and waters. He also reshaped the Supreme Court with four appointments: Warren E. Burger as Chief Justice, and three Associate Justices, candidates chosen for their ideology, particularly on such issues as tough law enforcement. The Court was transformed from the "liberal Warren Court" into a body that was attuned to conservative causes.

Most of Mr. Nixon's energies, however, were spent in foreign affairs, and it was his actions in that field that led to his greatest accomplishments and, in the view of some, to his undoing. His faltering efforts to end the Vietnam War brought out what H. R. Haldeman, his chief aide, called his "dark side"—paranoia about enemies real and imagined and violent temper tantrums.

American casualties mounted while the heavy costs fed inflation at home and drained money from domestic programs. Opposition to American involvement grew, and the White House and the Presidency came under unprecedented siege. On one occasion, half a million protesters descended on Washington.

In many ways the seeds of the Nixon scandals were sown in the debate over Vietnam, because the public opposition, demonstrations and leaks of classified information about the war caused the President and his aides to become, in Mr. Nixon's word, "paranoiac" about their detractors.

Mr. Nixon was particularly disturbed when, on June 13, 1971, The New York Times began printing the findings of a 7,000-page government study of American involvement in Southeast Asia. The Justice Department sought to stop further publication, but in a historic decision, the Supreme Court ruled that doing so would violate the First Amendment.

The President then began building a system of covert investigative and protective actions outside the normal legal channels he distrusted. His aides' deeds ranged from burglaries and wiretaps to the compiling of a White House "enemies list" that included the names of many officials and journalists.

While Mr. Nixon and the nation were under great stress over Vietnam, he carried out diplomatic feats on a scale unmatched before or since.

Since the creation of the Communist Government in China, the United States had maintained the fiction that the Nationalist government of Chiang Kaishek on Taiwan was the legitimate Government of all China. But in February 1972, after his chief foreign policy adviser, Henry Kissinger, had laid the groundwork in secret negotiations, Mr. Nixon made a historic, five-day trip to Beijing that inaugurated a new era in international diplomacy.

Then in May of that year came the first of three summit meetings that Mr. Nixon held with Leonid I. Brezhnev and other Soviet leaders. The major achievement was an agreement in 1972 to limit the use of the defensive weapons known as antiballistic missiles.

Then, on June 17, 1972, five men employed by the Committee for the Re-election of the President were arrested in a burglary at the Democratic National Committee headquarters in the Watergate complex

in Washington, and two others were later arrested. White House officials, including the President, dismissed the burglary as the work of overzealous campaign workers, and the defendants said no one close to Mr. Nixon had been involved.

Mr. Nixon went on to an overwhelming victory in November over Senator George McGovern, a liberal from South Dakota. The President took 60.7 percent of the popular vote, losing only Massachusetts and the District of Columbia.

Not long after his inauguration for a second term, an agreement was signed in Vietnam, on Jan. 27, 1973, ending the longest war in United States history.

The United States had never experienced another period like the one from March 1973 to August 1974, when the overriding concern about the Government was whether the President and his closest aides had ordered a burglary, sought to cover up their role in it, and had engaged in other illegal acts.

No President had been forced from office in the history of the Republic. And no President had ever been so exposed to public view, thanks to Mr. Nixon's tape-recording system, which laid bare intimate conversations in the Oval Office for national scrutiny, providing the evidence of wrongdoing that caused his downfall.

Although the burglary of the Democratic headquarters at the Watergate complex took place in June 1972, not until the following March would the scandal began to unfold. At that time, Judge John J. Sirica of Federal District Court threatened long jail terms for the defendants.

James W. McCord, who had been convicted on burglary charges, promised to tell all in return for leniency, and he implicated John W. Dean 3rd, the White House counsel. Mr. Dean told his story in televised hearings before the select committee of the Senate that was investigating the matter. He told of White House involvement in Watergate from the day of the burglary onward and of Mr. Nixon's knowledge of a cover-up and his participation in it.

During this period Mr. Nixon dismissed Mr. Haldeman and Mr. Ehrlichman, prime targets in the investigation, and announced that Defense Secretary Elliot L. Richardson, a moderate Republican, would become Attorney General and have the authority to name a special Watergate prosecutor.

Then, on July 16, Alexander P. Butterfield, a former aide, disclosed that Mr. Nixon had secretly taped conversations in his Oval Office. There began a series of struggles by Congressional committees and prosecutors to obtain the tapes for evidence, with Mr. Nixon insisting that the President's private counsels were protected to maintain the efficient operation of government.

As the dispute continued through September, a parallel crisis erupted involving Vice President Spiro T. Agnew, a former Governor of Maryland. In July

1973, Federal prosecutors accused Mr. Agnew of taking money from contractors who had solicited business with Maryland and said the practice continued when he was Vice President.

On Oct. 10, Mr. Agnew agreed to resign, and Mr. Nixon appointed Representative Gerald R. Ford of Michigan as Vice President.

Then on Oct. 20, 1973, came the "Saturday Night Massacre." After Archibald Cox, the special Watergate prosecutor, refused to support a Nixon plan for access to the White House tapes, the President ordered Attorney General Richardson to dismiss Mr. Cox. The Attorney General refused, and resigned. His deputy, William D. Ruckelshaus, refused, and was dismissed. Finally Solicitor General Robert H. Bork, appointed Acting Attorney General, dismissed Mr. Cox.

The President relented on the subpoenaed tapes, after disclosing that two tapes were missing and a third contained an 18 1/2-minute "gap," and he announced that a new special prosecutor, Leon Jaworski, would be appointed.

At an editors' convention in Orlando, Fla., on Nov. 17, 1973, Mr. Nixon said: "People have got to know whether or not their President is a crook. Well, I'm not a crook."

On March 1, 1974, the Federal grand jury indicted seven former Nixon aides in connection with Watergate, including Mr. Haldeman, Mr. Ehrlichman and former Attorney General John N. Mitchell, who had run the '72 campaign. It was later disclosed that the grand jury named Mr. Nixon an unindicted co-conspirator.

In April, he announced that he would make public edited transcripts of White House conversations concerning Watergate. The tapes and other evidence showed in detail aspects of the "dark side" of the Nixon Presidency that had been concealed from public view. They included:

• *Mr. Nixon's involvement in the cover-up. He proposed paying hush money to the Watergate defendants to keep them from implicating the White House and ordered a halt to the F.B.I.'s investigation.*

• *Illegal burglaries. Mr. Nixon was so disturbed by leaks of official information that a "plumbers group" was set up in the White House to plug them.*

• *Invasion of privacy. White House officials had tapped the telephones of journalists and officials suspected of unauthorized disclosures.*

• *Corruption of Government agencies. Mr. Nixon and his aides drew the F.B.I. and the Central Intelligence Agency into the Watergate cover-up.*

• *"Dirty tricks." Although sabotage of an opponent's campaign had been common in American politics for years, operations set up by the Nixon White House and his election committee exceeded anything known in the past.*

• *Abuse of campaign funds. Some of the money for Mr. Nixon's re-election was diverted to "dirty tricks" and used as "hush money" for the Watergate burglars.*

In late July, with millions of Americans watching on television, the House Judiciary Committee deliberated articles of impeachment. At the end of the month the committee charged that "in violation of his constitutional duty to take care that the laws be faithfully executed," Richard Nixon had "prevented, obstructed and impeded the administration of justice." It seemed almost certain that the full House would impeach the President, and his chances of avoiding conviction by the Senate seemed slim.

The same week, the Supreme Court ordered the President to turn over to Judge Sirica the records of 64 [tape recorded] conversations. In early August he released the tapes that came to be known as the "smoking gun"—recordings of conversations with Mr. Haldeman on June 23, 1972, six days after the Watergate burglary, showing conclusively that Mr. Nixon had ordered a halt to the F.B.I. investigation.

At 9 P.M. on Aug. 8, the President announced on television that he would resign the next day. After a tearful farewell to the staff, he and Mrs. Nixon boarded Air Force One and flew home to San Clemente.

On Sept. 8, President Ford granted Mr. Nixon an unconditional pardon for all Federal crimes he "committed or may have committed or taken part in" while in office, saying a trial would distract the nation from healing the wounds caused by the scandal.

JACQUELINE KENNEDY ONASSIS

July 28, 1929–May 19, 1994

By Robert D. McFadden

Jacqueline Kennedy Onassis, the widow of President John F. Kennedy and of the Greek shipping magnate Aristotle Onassis, died of cancer of the lymphatic system yesterday at her apartment in New York City. She was 64 years old.

Mrs. Onassis, who had enjoyed robust good health nearly all her life, began being treated for non-Hodgkin's lymphoma in January.

In recent years Mrs. Onassis had lived quietly, working at Doubleday; joining efforts to preserve historic New York buildings; spending time with her children; getting away to her estates in New Jersey, at Hyannis, Mass., and on Martha's Vineyard; and going about town with Maurice Tempelsman, a financier who had become her closest companion. She almost never granted interviews on her past, and for decades she had not spoken publicly about Mr. Kennedy, his Presidency or their marriage.

Although she was one of the world's most famous women—an object of fascination to generations of Americans and the subject of countless articles and books about the Kennedy years, the terrible images of the President's 1963 assassination in Dallas, and her made-for-tabloids marriage to the wealthy Mr. Onassis—she was a quintessentially private person, poised and glamorous but shy and aloof.

They were qualities that spoke of her upbringing in the wealthy Bouvier and Auchincloss families, of mansion life in East Hampton and Newport, commodious apartments in New York and Paris, Miss Porter's finishing school and Vassar College. She was only 23, working as an inquiring photographer for a Washington newspaper, when she met John F. Kennedy, the young bachelor Congressman from Massachusetts, at a dinner party in 1952. A year later, after Mr. Kennedy had won a seat in the United States Senate and was already being discussed as a Presidential possibility, they were married at Newport, R.I.

After Mr. Kennedy won the Presidency in 1960, there were a thousand days that seemed to raise up a nation mired in the cold war. There were babies in the White House for the first time in this century, and Jackie Kennedy transforming her new home into a place of elegance and culture.

She redecorated the mansion with early 19th-century furnishings, museum-quality paintings and objets d'art, creating a sumptuous celebration of Americana that 56 million television viewers saw in 1961 as the First Lady gave a guided tour broadcast by the three television networks.

She also threw elegant parties, with guests lists including Nobel laureates and distinguished artists, musicians and intellectuals.

Americans became familiar with the whispering quality of her voice, with the head scarf and dark glasses at

the taffrail of the yacht Honey Fitz on a summer evening on the Potomac, with the bouffant hair and the
barefoot romp with her children on a Cape Cod beach.

Arriving in France, a stunning figure in her pillbox
hat and wool coat as she rode with the President in an
open car, she enthralled crowds that chanted "Vive
Jacqui" on the road to Paris. When the state visit
ended, an amused President Kennedy said, "I am the
man who accompanied Jacqueline Kennedy to Paris."

But the images of Mrs. Kennedy that burned most
deeply were those in Dallas on Nov. 22, 1963: her
lunge across the open limousine as the assassin's bullets struck, the Schiaparelli pink suit stained with her
husband's blood, her stunned face in the blur of the
speeding motorcade, the anguish at Parkland Memorial Hospital as the doctors gave way to the priest, and
finally, the black-veiled widow who walked beside her
husband's coffin and reminded 3-year-old John Jr. to
salute. She was 34 years old.

A week later, it was Mrs. Kennedy who bestowed
the epitaph of Camelot upon a Kennedy Presidency,
which, while flawed in the minds of many, had for
many Americans come to represent something magical and mythical. It happened in an interview with
Theodore H. White, the Kennedy confidant who was
then writing for Life magazine.

The conversation, he said in a 1978 book, "In
Search of History," swung between history and her
husband's death, and while none of J.F.K.'s political
shortcomings were mentioned—stories about his liaisons with women were then known only to insiders
—Mrs. Kennedy seemed determined to "rescue Jack
from all these 'bitter people' who were going to write
about him in history."

She told him that the title song of the musical
"Camelot" had become "an obsession with me" lately.
She said that at night before bedtime, her husband had
often played it, or asked her to play it, on a Victrola in
their bedroom. Mr. White quoted her as saying:

"And the song he loved most came at the very end
of this record, the last side of Camelot, sad Camelot.
. . . 'Don't let it be forgot, that once there was a spot,
for one brief shining moment that was known as
Camelot.'"

Five years later, Mrs. Kennedy shattered her almost
saintly image by announcing plans to marry Mr.
Onassis. It was a field day for the tabloids, a shock
to members of her family and a puzzlement to the
public. The prospective bridegroom was much shorter
than the bride, and more than 28 years older, a canny
businessman and not even American.

The couple were married in 1968, and for a time the
world saw a new, more outgoing Jacqueline Kennedy
Onassis. But within a few years there were reported
fights over money and accounts that each was being
seen in the company of others. While the couple was
never divorced, the marriage was widely regarded as
over long before Mr. Onassis died in 1975.

Jacqueline Bouvier was born on July 28, 1929, in
East Hampton, L.I., to John Vernou Bouvier 3rd
and Janet Lee Bouvier. A sister, Caroline, known as
Lee, was born four years later. From the beginning,
the girls knew the trappings of considerable wealth
at the family's Long Island estate and its apartment
on Park Avenue in Manhattan. The Bouviers were
divorced in 1940, and in 1942 Mrs. Bouvier married
Hugh D. Auchincloss, who, like Mr. Bouvier, was a
stockbroker.

From her earliest days, Jacqueline Bouvier attracted attention, as much for her intelligence as for
her beauty. John H. Davis, a cousin who wrote "The
Bouviers," a family history, described her by saying
that she possessed a "fiercely independent inner life
which she shared with few people and would one day
be partly responsible for her enormous success."

At 15, Jacqueline picked Miss Porter's School in
Farmington, Conn., an institution that along with academic offerings emphasized good manners and the art
of conversation. When she graduated, her yearbook
said her ambition in life was "not to be a housewife."

Jacqueline entered Vassar College in 1947, not long
after she was named "Debutante of the Year" by Igor
Cassini, who wrote for the Hearst newspapers under
the byline Cholly Knickerbocker and who described
her as a "regal brunette who has classic features and
the daintiness of Dresden porcelain."

In 1949, for her junior year at Vassar, she applied
to a program that would let her study for a year in
France. Mrs. Onassis would later recall her stay in
Paris as "the high point in my life, my happiest and
most carefree year."

When the year was up she decided to transfer to
George Washington University in Washington, from
which she graduated in 1951. While she was finishing
the work for her degree, she won Vogue magazine's
Prix de Paris contest, with an essay on "People I
Wish I Had Known." Her subjects were Oscar Wilde,
Charles Baudelaire and Sergei Diaghilev.

In Washington, she got a job as an inquiring photographer at The Washington Times-Herald, assigned
to do a light feature in which people were asked about
a topic of the day. Among the questions she asked
were: "Do you think a wife should let her husband
think he's smarter than she is?"

In May 1952 she met Mr. Kennedy, who would soon
capture the Senate seat held by Henry Cabot Lodge, and
the couple were married Sept. 12, 1953, in Newport.

There were trials in her personal life. In 1955 she
suffered a miscarriage, and in 1956 she had a stillborn
child. But in 1957 Caroline Bouvier Kennedy was
born. Three years later she gave birth to John F. Kennedy Jr. A third child, Patrick Bouvier Kennedy, lived
only 39 hours and died less than four months before
President Kennedy's assassination in 1963.

After Mr. Kennedy was elected President in 1960,
the mystique around Mrs. Kennedy began to grow

rapidly, especially after she and her husband made the state visit to France in 1961. Her elegance and fluency in French captured their hearts, and at a glittering dinner at Versailles she seemed to mesmerize President Charles de Gaulle.

Returning home, Mrs. Kennedy began to make her plans to redecorate the White House. Her social skills were also much in evidence, and her parties spectacular. The cello of Pablo Casals, string trios and quartets and whole orchestras filled the rooms with glorious sound.

"I think she cast a particular spell over the White House that has not been equaled," said Benjamin C. Bradlee, former executive editor of The Washington Post, who was a friend of the Kennedys. "She was young. My God, she was young. She had great taste, a sense of culture, an understanding of art. She brought people like Andre Malraux to the White House who never would have gone there. As personalities, they really transformed the city."

To some, Jacqueline Kennedy seemed to fall from grace as her year of mourning ended. She was photographed wearing a miniskirt and escorted to social gatherings by prominent bachelors like Frank Sinatra. To some Americans she was no longer just the grieving widow of their martyred President.

In 1964 she moved to an apartment on Fifth Avenue, but New York was not all she had hoped it would be. The photographer Ron Galella seemed to be everywhere, taking thousands of photographs of her. The preparation and publication of "The Death of a President," William Manchester's account of the assassination of President Kennedy, turned into an unexpected battle.

Mr. Manchester received permission from the Kennedy family to do an authorized work on the assassination, and Mrs. Kennedy, in a rare departure from her usual practice, agreed to be interviewed. But she subsequently tried to get a court injunction to stop the publication of the book. The case was settled in 1967.

The next year, Mr. Onassis and Mrs. Kennedy announced that they would be married. The ceremony was held on Oct. 20, 1968. She then became Mistress of Skorpios, the Aegean island that Mr. Onassis owned. But within a few years, there were reports that the couple were arguing and the marriage foundered. When Mr. Onassis died in 1975, Mrs. Onassis was in New York.

Mrs. Onassis began her career in publishing in 1975, when her friend Thomas Guinzburg, then the president of Viking Press, offered her a job as a consulting editor. In 1978 she joined Doubleday, where she was eventually promoted to senior editor and produced books on performing arts and other subjects. Books she published included Bill Moyers's "Healing and the Mind" and Edvard Radzinsky's "The Last Tsar: The Life and Death of Nicholas II."

In the years following Mr. Onassis's death, she built a 19-room house on 375 acres of oceanfront land on Martha's Vineyard.

Mrs. Onassis, who is survived by her daughter, Caroline Kennedy Schlossberg; a son, John F. Kennedy Jr.; her sister, and three grandchildren, did not marry again. In the last few years, Mr. Tempelsman, a Belgian-born industrialist and diamond merchant, had been her frequent companion.

RONALD REAGAN

February 6, 1911–June 5, 2004

By Marilyn Berger

Ronald Wilson Reagan, a former film star who became America's 40th president, the oldest to enter the White House but imbued with a youthful optimism rooted in the traditional virtues of a bygone era, died yesterday at his home in Los Angeles. He was 93.

In 1994, he disclosed that he had Alzheimer's disease. "I now begin the journey that will lead me into the sunset of my life," he wrote. "I know that for America there will always be a bright dawn ahead." He died with his wife, Nancy, and his three children by his side.

When he entered the White House, Mr. Reagan was a vigorous 69-year-old who promised a new beginning for a nation battered by Vietnam, damaged by Watergate and humiliated by the taking of hostages in Iran. In his first term, he restored much of America's faith in itself and in the presidency.

But halfway through his second term, his administration was plunged into turmoil. Contrary to official policy, his subordinates sold arms to Iran as ransom for hostages in Lebanon and diverted profits from the sales to the rebels fighting the Marxist Sandinistas governing Nicaragua. A Congressional investigating committee concluded that the affair had been "characterized by pervasive dishonesty and secrecy."

Until the Iran-contra affair, Mr. Reagan enjoyed tremendous popularity. He used it to push many of his major programs through Congress. And despite the Iran-contra affair, he crowned his two terms with a nuclear arms agreement with the Soviet Union.

It was Mr. Reagan's good fortune that during his time the Soviet Union was collapsing. His supporters have argued that his tough policies were the coup de grâce; his detractors attributed the end to 45 years of the American policy of containment.

The historian Michael R. Beschloss said the cold war ended more quickly under Mr. Reagan than it would have had President Jimmy Carter been re-elected. "With Reagan," he said, "the Soviets could no longer con themselves into thinking they would prevail in the cold war because the American people had lost their will and strength and lost their taste for confronting Soviet aggression."

Ronald Reagan never lost his ability to make Americans feel good about themselves. "America is back," he told them. Gliding gracefully across the national stage with his lopsided grin, he escaped blame for political disasters for which any other president would have been excoriated. He became known as the Teflon president.

Ronald Reagan offered an America of boundless opportunity. And indeed, under his presidency came an end to the inflation of the Carter years, along with an economic boom. But huge deficits, brought on partly by tax cuts and increases in military spending, made a mockery of his campaign pledge to balance the budget.

Ronald Reagan was born at home in an apartment above a store in Tampico, a village in northwestern Illinois, on Feb. 6, 1911. His father, John Edward Reagan, was a clerk in a general store. Ronald Reagan later described him as a hearty Irish Roman Catholic who was restless, ambitious and an alcoholic. His mother, Nelle Wilson Reagan, was a gentle Scotch-Irish Protestant who passed on to her children her religious faith and her interest in amateur theater. The family was poor, but Mr. Reagan recalled many years later that he had never been troubled by any sense of need.

He and his older brother, Neil, moved with their parents from one small Illinois town to the next. They eventually settled in Dixon, where his father managed a shoe store. Ronald played football at Northside High School. He was not an especially attentive student but managed to get fairly good grades. He left Dixon to attend Eureka College, a small Christian school near Peoria. By his own account, he was concerned mainly with maintaining his eligibility for football and with acting in school productions.

With the nation mired in the Depression, he returned to Dixon in 1932. He admired President Roosevelt, who used his command of radio to steady a nation in despair, and a former teacher urged Mr. Reagan to try his hand at radio. He landed jobs broadcasting football and baseball games.

In 1937, Mr. Reagan looked up an old friend who had been in several movies. She arranged a meeting with an agent, and soon Warner Brothers offered a seven-year contract beginning at $200 a week.

In three years he landed the role of George Gipp, Notre Dame's legendary Gipper, in "Knute Rockne—All American." The film, with its heroic deathbed scene, provided Mr. Reagan with a line he came to use to inspire supporters: "Win one for the Gipper."

He made 50 movies, a number of them about World War II. Poor eyesight had kept him from the front, and he spent his years in the Army making training films. He wrote later of wanting nothing more after the war than a good rest and time with his wife, the actress Jane Wyman; in fact, they had both been in Hollywood throughout the war.

His flights of imagination remained vivid when he went to the White House. In 1983 he told Prime Minister Yitzhak Shamir of Israel that as part of his war duties he had been assigned to film the Nazi death camps.

He liked to tell a story about a pilot in World War II who told his crew to bail out of their crippled bomber. When the wounded tail gunner said he could not move, the pilot replied, "Never mind, son, we'll ride it down together." When he told the story to a meeting of the Congressional Medal of Honor Society, he added that the pilot was awarded the Medal of Honor posthumously. In fact, no medal was ever awarded for such an incident. The story came from a movie script.

Mr. Reagan had married Miss Wyman in 1940. They had a daughter, Maureen, and adopted a son, Michael. They divorced in 1948. In 1952, Mr. Reagan married Nancy Davis. An actress who was the daughter of a Chicago surgeon, she became his political partner and adviser. They had two children, Patricia and Ronald.

Called before the House Un-American Activities Committee in 1947 to testify about Communist influence in the movie industry, Mr. Reagan refused to name names. But the historian Garry Wills said the Federal Bureau of Investigation file on Mr. Reagan disclosed that he had named people in secret.

In 1952 the Music Corporation of America offered Mr. Reagan the role of host on General Electric Theater. In 1964, having changed his party registration from Democratic to Republican, he burst onto the political stage, delivering a fiery anti-Communist, anti-government speech at a fund-raiser for Barry Goldwater, the Republican presidential candidate.

Wealthy backers formed a committee to initiate Mr. Reagan's successful 1966 candidacy for California governor. When Mrs. Reagan did not like the governor's mansion, the friends bought the Reagans a house in Sacramento, just as they would buy the couple a house in Los Angeles after they left the White House.

In Sacramento, Mr. Reagan found a Democratic legislature unwilling to adopt his proposals to cut the state payroll. He signed a succession of tax increases to erase the state's deficit. In his two terms, the budget more than doubled and the number of state employees grew by 34,000.

In 1975, he left Sacramento to write a column and deliver radio commentary. In 1968 he briefly ran in the presidential primaries. Eight years later he nearly wrested the nomination from President Gerald R. Ford. And on July 16, 1980, in Detroit, the Republican National Convention nominated him for president.

A week before the election Mr. Reagan and Mr. Carter faced each other in a televised debate. "Are you better off than you were four years ago?" Mr. Reagan asked the audience.

At the time, the nation was powerless to liberate 52 Americans held hostage by Iran since November 1979. At home, consumer prices had risen 12.4 percent in one year, and in October 1980 a million and a half more people were out of work than in January. On Nov. 4, Mr. Reagan won an overwhelming victory.

Unlike his predecessor, Mr. Reagan was a 9-to-5 president. He left details to subordinates and relied on 3-by-5 index cards they gave him for information he needed at meetings. Even with the cards, he sometimes got his facts wrong.

Mr. Reagan's first term was marked by charges against more than a dozen officials in his administration of improper financial dealings. When top Justice Department officials resigned in March 1988, criticizing Attorney General Edwin Meese's ethics, there were widespread calls for the attorney general's resignation, which Mr. Meese tendered the following August.

On March 30, 1981, the president was leaving a Washington hotel where he had addressed a union convention. John W. Hinckley Jr., a 25-year-old college dropout, emerged from a crowd and shot him and three other people with a .22-caliber pistol. A bullet penetrated Mr. Reagan's left lung.

"Honey, I forgot to duck," he was reported to have told Mrs. Reagan when she arrived at the hospital. Less than a month later, he addressed Congress to urge passage of his economic program.

He made an equally quick recovery from surgery in 1985. On July 12, he entered a hospital for removal of a noncancerous polyp in his colon. But doctors found a previously unsuspected growth in his large intestine. Doctors removed a malignant polyp. Mr. Reagan returned to the White House a week later.

"Reaganomics" was the idea that a cut in taxes would stimulate economic growth, generating higher revenues and making the deficit disappear. In the 1980 Republican primaries, George Bush, who would become Mr. Reagan's vice president, called the idea "voodoo economics." And Mr. Reagan's own director of the budget, David A. Stockman, suggested that the president was simply proposing a repackaging of economics to favor the rich, whose gains would ultimately trickle down.

Despite widespread criticism, Mr. Reagan sold the program to Congress, both a tax cut and a $28 billion increase in the military budget.

The administration cut back on job training, food stamps, welfare, Medicaid and other social programs. Despite the many budget cuts, the deficit kept growing. By the middle of 1982, with a recession continuing and deficit projections soaring, Mr. Reagan grudgingly agreed to a $98.6 billion increase in excise and other taxes.

After the 1981–82 recession, he presided over the longest economic expansion in history. Then, on

Oct. 19, 1987, the stock market suffered the most severe single-day decline up to that point, dropping 508 points. The meltdown highlighted the administration's failure to deal with the budget and trade deficits and the failure of supply-side economics to encourage investment and productivity. The president and Congress agreed to a deficit-reduction package.

Some economists credit Mr. Reagan with helping to bring about beneficial changes in tax policy. Others point to the huge budget deficits. Prof. James Tobin, a Nobel Prize-winning economist at Yale University, went so far as to say that the Reagan legacy was "a crippled federal government."

On Nov. 8, 1984, Mr. Reagan, declaring it was "morning in America," scored one of the biggest victories in American political history, winning 525 electoral votes to 13 for his Democratic opponent, Walter F. Mondale.

Mr. Reagan, who said over and over that "government is not the solution; government is the problem," had pledged to put an end to the "adversary relationship" between government and business. Banking regulations were loosened, contributing later to the savings and loan scandals. The Justice Department reined in its antitrust division, and its civil rights division led a campaign against court-ordered measures to correct discrimination.

The battle against terrorism was a cornerstone of the Reagan foreign policy. On Aug. 19, 1981, American planes shot down two Libyan jets over the Gulf of Sidra in a dispute with the Libyan leader, Col. Muammar el-Qaddafi. In April 1986, Mr. Reagan ordered the bombing of Tripoli to punish Colonel Qaddafi for his supposed role in a terrorist attack on a discothèque in West Germany that killed an American soldier.

The "Reagan Doctrine" was the name given to the policy of supporting forces fighting Soviet-backed governments in Afghanistan, Nicaragua and Angola. The administration supported the contras fighting to overthrow the Sandinista government of Nicaragua. In El Salvador, the Reagan administration supported the government against a Marxist insurgency. In October 1983, Mr. Reagan sent American forces to Grenada to rescue American students and to evict a government that he called "leftist thugs."

In 1987, he ordered American warships to the Persian Gulf to protect Kuwaiti tankers under attack by Iran. Thirty-seven American sailors were killed by a missile fired from an Iraqi plane at an American frigate. A year later, a Navy warship shot down an Iranian airliner after mistaking it for an attacking fighter jet, killing all 290 people on board.

In 1984, Mr. Reagan delivered a memorable speech at Normandy to mark the 40th anniversary of D-Day. But a year later, it became known that Nazi storm troopers were buried at a cemetery he was scheduled to visit in West Germany. He rejected advice to cancel the stop and created an uproar when he said the German soldiers buried there were victims of Nazism, "just as surely as the victims in the concentration camps."

By late 1986, the president had become obsessed by the hostages held in Lebanon by allies of Iran. Two national security advisers, Robert C. McFarlane and Vice Adm. John M. Poindexter, and a National Security Council staff assistant, Lt. Col. Oliver L. North of the Marines, were emboldened by his concern.

Publicly, Mr. Reagan had condemned Iran as an outlaw state. Yet his own security council staff concocted a secret plan to supply weapons to Iran as ransom for the American hostages. Profits from the sales were earmarked for the contras.

When the secret operation was first reported, Mr. Reagan declared that "we did not, repeat, did not trade arms or anything else for hostages." Later, he backtracked, telling the nation: "My heart and my best intentions still tell me that is true, but the facts and the evidence tell me it is not."

The facts and evidence outlined by a commission led by former Senator John G. Tower, and later in the majority report of a Congressional committee, showed that Mr. Reagan had approved shipments of weapons to Iran months before his first public denial. The findings of the Tower commission left open the question of whether Mr. Reagan had the vigor to recover from prostate surgery and the ability to reverse his lifelong habit of detachment.

On March 4, 1987, Mr. Reagan appeared on television. He outlined actions to correct flaws in White House operations and said he accepted "full responsibility" for the Iran-contra affair. Yet even after Mr. Poindexter and Mr. North were indicted, Mr. Reagan described Mr. North as a hero and said he believed his former aides were not guilty. (Mr. North and Mr. Poindexter were convicted of various felonies, but the verdicts were overturned on appeal.)

Mr. Reagan had promised in his 1980 campaign that his top strategic priority would be to close "the window of vulnerability" through which he believed the Soviet Union could launch a nuclear first strike. On March 23, 1983, he announced plans for a system of space-based defenses that would make nuclear weapons obsolete. Former Defense Secretary James R. Schlesinger said the program, which came to be called "Star Wars," was nothing but "a collection of technical experiments and distant hopes," even though the president treated it "as if it were already a reality."

Nevertheless, minutes of Politburo meetings show that Soviet Premier Mikhail Gorbachev was, in the words of a Russian scholar, "obsessed" by the proposal, which he feared would escalate the arms race.

Mr. Reagan and Mr. Gorbachev met in Reykjavik,

Iceland, in October 1986. Mr. Reagan proposed the elimination of all ballistic missiles by 1996. Mr. Gorbachev proposed the elimination of all strategic nuclear weapons, a proposal that, to the consternation of his aides, Mr. Reagan accepted.

In February 1987, Mr. Gorbachev announced the Soviet Union's willingness to sign an agreement to eliminate Soviet and American medium-range missiles in Europe within five years. The intermediate-range nuclear force treaty was signed the next December.

Politicians and historians differ widely in assessing Ronald Reagan's presidency. "Most of the time he was an actor reading lines," said the former House Speaker Thomas P. O'Neill Jr., Democrat of Massachusetts. "I hate to say it about such an agreeable man, but it was sinful that Ronald Reagan ever became president."

Kenneth Lynn, professor of history at the Johns Hopkins University, said Mr. Reagan "fulfilled a restorative function we desperately needed." But others contend that Mr. Reagan will not rank among great presidents. "He was too late, too little and too lame when it came to human rights abuses at home and abroad," said Thomas Cronin, the McHugh Professor of American Institutions at Colorado College.

When Mr. Reagan was asked in a television interview how he thought history would remember him, he said he had tried to help Americans "get back that pride, and that patriotism, that confidence, that they had in our system. And I think they have."

ANTONIN SCALIA

March 11, 1936–February 13, 2016

By Adam Liptak

Justice Antonin Scalia, whose transformative legal theories, vivid writing and outsize personality made him a leader of a conservative intellectual renaissance in his three decades on the Supreme Court, was found dead Saturday at a resort in West Texas. He was 79.

A spokeswoman for the U.S. Marshals Service, which sent personnel to the scene, said there was no information to indicate the death was the result of anything other than natural causes.

Justice Scalia began his service on the Court as an outsider known for caustic dissents that alienated even potential allies. But his theories, initially viewed as idiosyncratic, gradually took hold, and not only on the right and not only in the courts.

He was, Judge Richard A. Posner wrote in The New Republic in 2011, "the most influential justice of the last quarter century."

Justice Scalia was a champion of originalism, the theory of constitutional interpretation that seeks to apply the understanding of those who drafted and ratified the Constitution. In his hands, originalism generally led to outcomes that pleased political conservatives, but not always: His approach was helpful to criminal defendants in cases involving sentencing and the cross-examination of witnesses.

Justice Scalia also disdained the use of legislative history—statements from members of Congress about the meaning and purposes of laws—in the judicial interpretation of statutes. He railed against vague laws that did not give potential defendants fair warning of what conduct was criminal, and he was sharply critical of Supreme Court opinions that did not provide lower courts and litigants with clear guidance.

All of these views took shape in dissents. Over time, they came to influence and in many cases dominate the debate at the Supreme Court, in lower courts, among lawyers and in the legal academy.

By the time he wrote his most important majority opinion—finding that the Second Amendment protects an individual right to bear arms—even the dissenters were engaged in trying to determine the original meaning of the Constitution, the approach he had championed.

That 2008 decision, District of Columbia v. Heller, also illustrated a second point: Justice Scalia in his later years was willing to bend a little to attract votes from his colleagues. In Heller, the price of commanding a majority appeared to be including a passage limiting the practical impact of the decision.

With the retirement of Justice John Paul Stevens in 2010, Justice Scalia became the longest-serving member of the current Court. By then, he was routinely writing for the majority in the major cases, including ones on the First Amendment, class actions and arbitration.

He was an exceptional stylist who labored over his opinions and took pleasure in finding precisely the right word or phrase. The author of a majority opinion could be confident that a Justice Scalia dissent would not overlook any shortcomings. His opinions were read by lawyers and civilians for pleasure and instruction.

At oral argument, Justice Scalia took professorial delight in sparring with the advocates before him. He seemed to play to the crowd in the courtroom.

His sometimes withering questioning helped transform what had been a sleepy bench when he arrived into one that Justice Roberts has said has become too active, with the justices interrupting the lawyers and each other.

Some of his recent comments from the bench were raw and provocative. In an affirmative action case in December, he said that some minority students may be better off at "a less advanced school, a slower-track school where they do well."

Justice Scalia was a man of varied tastes, with a fondness for poker, opera and hunting. His friends called him Nino.

He seldom agreed with Justice Ruth Bader Ginsburg on the important questions that reached the court, but the two for years celebrated New Year's Eve together. Not long after Justice Elena Kagan, another liberal, joined the court, Justice Scalia took her skeet shooting.

Antonin Gregory Scalia was born on March 11, 1936, in Trenton, New Jersey, to Salvatore Scalia and the former Catherine Panaro. He was their only child and was showered with attention from his parents and their siblings, none of whom had children of their own.

Justice Scalia and his wife, the former Maureen McCarthy, had nine children.

"We were both devout Catholics," Justice Scalia told Joan Biskupic for her 2009 biography, "American Original." "And being a devout Catholic means you have children when God gives them to you, and you raise them."

Young Antonin was an exceptional student, graduating as valedictorian from Xavier High School in Manhattan, first in his class at Georgetown and magna cum laude at Harvard Law School.

He practiced law for six years in Cleveland before accepting a position teaching law at the University of Virginia in 1967. Four years later, he entered government service, first as general counsel of the Office of Telecommunications Policy and then as chairman of the Administrative Conference of the United States, an executive branch agency that advises federal regulators.

In 1974, President Richard M. Nixon nominated him to be assistant attorney general in charge of the Office of Legal Counsel, an elite unit of the Justice Department that advises the executive branch. He was confirmed by the Senate not long after Nixon resigned. In 1977, he returned to the legal academy, joining the law faculty at the University of Chicago.

Mr. Scalia turned down a seat on the federal appeals court in Chicago in the hope of being nominated instead to the U.S. Court of Appeals for the District of Columbia Circuit, whose docket, location and prestige appealed to him. The first opening on the D.C. Circuit in the Reagan years went to another prominent conservative law professor, Robert H. Bork. But the second one, in 1982, went to Mr. Scalia.

In 1986, after Chief Justice Warren Burger announced his intention to retire, President Ronald Reagan nominated Judge Scalia to the Supreme Court. Though his conservative views were well known, he was confirmed by the Senate by a 98–0 vote. He may have benefited from the fact that the liberal opposition was focused on the nomination of Justice William H. Rehnquist, who was already on the Court, to succeed Burger as chief justice.

Justice Scalia's commitment to the doctrine of originalism made him uncomfortable with some of the Supreme Court's most important precedents. He appeared to have reservations about Brown v. Board of Education, which struck down segregation in public schools as a violation of the 14th Amendment's guarantee of equal protection.

Brown, decided in 1954, is widely considered the towering achievement of the Court led by Chief Justice Earl Warren. But for originalists, the Brown decision is problematic. The weight of the historical evidence is that the people who drafted, proposed and ratified the 14th Amendment from 1866 to 1868 did not believe themselves to be doing away with segregated schools.

In remarks at the University of Arizona in 2009, Justice Scalia suggested that Brown reached the right result as a matter of policy but was not required by the Constitution. He added that the decision did not refute his theory.

"Don't make up your mind on this significant question between originalism and playing it by ear on the basis of whether, now and then, the latter approach might give you a result you like," Justice Scalia said.

Justice Scalia took pains to say that he would not follow his theory wherever it would take him. "I am a textualist," he said. "I am an originalist. I am not a nut."

In a C-Span interview in 2009, Justice Scalia reflected on his role and legacy, sketching out a modest conception of the role of a Supreme Court justice.

"We don't sit here to make the law, to decide who ought to win," he said. "We decide who wins under the law that the people have adopted. And very often, if you're a good judge, you don't really like the result you're reaching."

He was a simple, in some ways almost naïve, man, and it was in the quality of logical directness perhaps that his chief genius lay. To a peculiar degree he was the embodiment of America in the era of industrial revolution. Starting as a Midwestern farm boy, he became a mechanic, went into business for himself, and was finally one of the wealthiest men. It was the American success story. The world was horse-drawn when he entered it. When he departed it was a world of powered wheels. He was a man of many contradictions. He was a pacifist and yet it was the tremendous impact of his pioneering and development of the mass-production technique that when multiplied by the hundredfold throughout the country, made us supreme over the enemy in war. For without that conveyor belt we could never have become the arsenal of democracy, in guns, planes, ships and other vehicles of war that spelled victory. And without that same assembly-line, labor, which often denounced Henry Ford, would not have enjoyed

phy had some of the qualities of Ben Franklin. "Our help does not come from Washington, but from ourselves," he was saying back in 1922.

A great liberator, he made it possible for the farmer to come to town, and to bring his wife and children there, for a brief escape from drudgery and the monotony of limited horizons. He helped to make us a nation of travelers, opening up a world that had been confined to horseback and the wagon wheel. To those who argue that this release would have come through the ingenuity of others, it may be said that he at least greatly hastened it and he made it universal, for he changed the automobile from a racing toy that was for the rich alone to a Model T that could sell, brand new and painted black only, for about $300. If he made the workman a cog, he at the same time gave him wages and leisure time to enable him to be a person while outside the factory gates.

His was a single-minded devotion to the fundamentals as he saw them: hard work, the simple virtues, self-reliance, the good earth. He profited by producing what was new, but also treasured that which was bygone. A

TITANS OF
BUSINESS

CORNELIUS VANDERBILT

May 27, 1794–January 4, 1877

Commodore Vanderbilt died at his residence, No. 10 Washington place, yesterday morning, after having been confined to his rooms for about eight months. The immediate cause of his death was exhaustion, brought on by long suffering from a complication of chronic disorders.

Shortly after daylight his family were summoned to his bedside to bid him farewell. He was too weak to say much, but expressed much gratification at having them around him, and after they had been with him a short time requested them to join in singing his favorite hymns. Prayer was then offered, in which he tried to join, and shortly afterward, gradually becoming weaker and weaker, he quietly passed away without a struggle. His death, which had been long expected in financial circles, had little or no effect on the stock market, although the announcement of it created a decided impression throughout the City.

It is estimated that Commodore Vanderbilt left property to the amount of $100,000,000, principally in shares of the New-York Central and Hudson River Road and other railway corporations; but, although it is known that he left a will, it is not known how he has disposed of his wealth. The funeral services will take place at the Church of the Strangers on Sunday at 10:30 A.M., and the remains will then be carried to Staten Island and deposited in the family vault in the Moravian churchyard, near New Dorp.

Cornelius Vanderbilt was born on the 27th day of May, in the year 1794, on a farm on Staten Island. His father was a well-to-do agriculturist. The produce of the farm was sent to the New York markets in a periagua daily, and the young Cornelius took especial delight in navigating this craft, which has now disappeared from our waters. He worked also on the farm, and studied in the Winter days, but his delight was on the sea, and while he was a mere boy he was acknowledged to be the most fearless sailor and the steadiest helmsman on the bay. All his thoughts and instincts were bent in that direction. His one dream was of having a periagua of his own, and sailing it as a ferry-boat between Staten Island and New York. In 1810 he persuaded his mother to give him $100 for the purchase of a boat, and his hand closed firmly upon the tiller which for the next half century was to be to him a veritable scepter.

He was but sixteen, but he had no difficulty in obtaining passengers for his ferry-boat. For the young man was tall, vigorous, broad of shoulder, bright of eye, possessed of a complexion that any belle might envy, and having a very sweet and engaging smile, which all the cares of a very extraordinary and busy life never effaced from his countenance. There was plenty of occupation for him, for the times favored his business. England, plunged in the Napoleonic war, was furious with the services which America, as a neutral State, was able to perform for the French Emperor, and it was obvious that a war must sooner or later settle the power of a neutral flag to protect a cargo. Forts were built on different parts of the bay and on Staten Island, and in the transportation of material Cornelius Vanderbilt was so fair and moderate in his pretensions as to obtain the greater share of the business.

Young Cornele, as everybody called him, was the first person thought of when anything very dangerous or very disagreeable had to be done. When the winds were high, and the sight was blinded with driving sleet and snow, and the waves raged like angry wolves, if an important message had to be sent from the forts to the headquarters in the City, young Cornele was sent for.

In this carrying business he was so successful and made so much money that he thought of starting a home for himself. He married, in December, 1813, Miss Sophia Johnson, of Port Richmond, Staten Island, and expanded his transactions, as if the consciousness that he had given hostages to fortune in the shape of a young, beloved wife had spurred him to increased boldness. Between ship-building and ship-owning, when he balanced his books on the 31st December, 1817, being then twenty-three years and six months old, he found himself the master of $9,000 in hard cash.

Had Cornelius Vanderbilt been an ordinary thinker he would have gone on in this path. He would have sailed and built and chartered vessels and have made a great fortune. But he was an extraordinary thinker, and even in the midst of his young flush of triumph in naval construction there was one thing that troubled him. This was steam.

Fulton was beginning to sail his first regular boat up the Hudson, and some applauded and some derided the invention. The shipping men, as a class, pooh-poohed the whole thing, and very plausibly showed that in consequence of the cumbrous machinery and bulk of fuel, the new invention could not possibly he utilized for carrying freight, which was perfectly true at that time.

But as young Vanderbilt reasoned the thing out in his own mind, he came to the conclusion that the future belonged to the steam-boats. So he renounced the coasting business, sold his interest in different vessels, and built so many magnificent steamers that the public christened him the Commodore, just as the soldiers of the First Napoleon had nicknamed him the Little Corporal. His boats were faster and better, they were more comfortable for passengers, and more commodious for freight than any which had hitherto been seen.

The war of the slaveholders' rebellion brought the Commodore as a chosen counselor to the President of the nation. The Merrimac iron ram of the Confederates had wrought such havoc with the Union fleet as filled loyal men's hearts with gloom. Naval men were unanimous upon the point that if the ram could be fought and smashed there was but one man that could do it, and his name was Cornelius Vanderbilt.

To this man came a telegram asking for his presence in Washington. He came to the house of the Secretary of War, and was greeted with enthusiasm. "Will you," said Stanton, "see the President?" "Certainly," was the reply, and to the President's presence the pair went. "Now," said Mr. Lincoln, "can you stop that rebel ram, and for how much money will you do it?"

The Commodore answered, "I think I can, Mr. President, but I won't do it for money. I do not want the people of this country to look upon me as one who would trade upon her necessities and make blood-money out of her wounds."

Mr. Lincoln shook his head, and evidently thought that the Commodore was a Confederate sympathizer, for he said: "What's the use of further talking! You won't do anything for us, I see."

Vanderbilt said: "I don't know about that, Mr. President. I place myself and all my resources at your disposition without pay." Joyfully the patriotic proposal was accepted, and in 36 hours the Vanderbilt, with the Commodore in command, was at its station in Hampton Roads.

His reputation as a skillful pilot was known to everyone, and when he said that he would run down the Merrimac as a hound runs down a wolf, and, striking her amidships, would send her to the bottom, they all believed that he would do it, and looked admiringly at his huge steamer, the shadow of whose black hull loomed upon the water like the reflection of a great cloud.

"How can we help you?" said the chief officer. "Only by keeping severely out of my way when I am hunting the critter," was the amusing response, at which every one laughed. But the coursing match never came off. The Merrimac's Captain, who had been in Vanderbilt's employ, and knew his antagonist, declined to come out from his hiding place. Nor did the Confederates dare again to send her up the Roads.

Well before the exigencies of war sought him out, Commodore Vanderbilt had turned his tireless brain to consider the inevitable decline of American shipping, and to discover what form of enterprise was the most capable of development. At the war's end, he was nearly 71 years of age, but hale and hearty as a youngster of 20. The world accepted him as the greatest steam-boat man that ever lived, but they did not comprehend that he was great at everything, not to be judged by ordinary rules or average mental measuring rods.

And so he turned his attention to railroads, swiftly buying up the Hudson River and Harlem roads in New York, dismissing incapable and dishonest officers, introducing reforms, and in an incredibly short time making these roads a paying institution, a sound investment security. In 1867 the leading shareholders of the competing New-York Central appealed to the Commodore to "select such a Board of Directors as shall seem to you to be entitled to their confidence."

Now began a series of improvements in the railroad system of the City of New York which fairly transformed it. Commencing with the consolidation of the Hudson River and Central, and the leasing of the long line of the Harlem, Mr. Vanderbilt projected the building of the Forty-second Street Depot, and in due order followed the introduction of steel rails, the laying of a quadruple track from one end of the line to the other, and the wonderful engineering feat of sinking the City part of the track and arching it over for the prevention of accidents, and the improvement of that fine district along Fourth Avenue. The speed of the trains was so greatly increased that to go from New York to Albany in four hours became a common occurrence, yet the distance is fully 150 miles.

In his private life the Commodore was always distinguished by three things—overwhelming affection for his family and his friends, hatred of ostentation, and love of solid comfort. He had lived for many years past in a great double brick house on Washington Place, handsomely furnished, but without the least pretension.

His first wife died in the early part of 1868, which left the Commodore alone in his big house, for all his ten surviving children were married, and some of them had grandchildren even. So in the Fall of 1869 the house on Washington Place received a new mistress, a very handsome and accomplished Southern lady, from Mobile, Ala., formerly a Miss Crawford. The master of the house was all his life surrounded

by friends who repaid his affection by a love "this side idolatry," as Ben Jonson said of Shakespeare. Iron in opposition, he was in private life entirely governed by his affections, nor did age take from him the sweet smiling look of his boyhood.

The eldest son, William H. Vanderbilt, will perhaps take his father's place as a railroad man. He is as much master of the facts of every department as the chief of it, and he is a model of hard-working industry. No man possesses the technique of railroad management in as full a measure as he, and he is training up his sons in the same path.

So the Vanderbilt lines will probably be managed by Vanderbilt scions for generations to come, to the great content of all interested. It is a fair prophecy that the line will not lose one cent by the death of Cornelius Vanderbilt, for the system which he created will live long after him. And herein was displayed another proof of the transcendent powers of his genius, since he so vitalized the Vanderbilt lines and infused such energy into them that they will retain the effects for 50 years to come.

J. PIERPONT MORGAN

April 17, 1837–March 31, 1913

ROME—J. Pierpont Morgan died at the Grand Hotel here five minutes after noon today.

His last words were addressed to his son-in-law, Mr. Herbert Satterlee, to whom he said, "You bet I will pull through."

J. Pierpont Morgan had been the leading figure in American finance for almost as long as the present generation could remember and was often described as the biggest single factor in the banking business of the world. The story of his life is indissolubly intertwined with the periods of expansion in this country in the world of railroads, industrial organization, and banking power.

The pinnacle of his power was reached in the panic of 1907 when he was more than 70 years old. He was put at the head of the forces that were gathered together to save the country from financial disaster, and men like John D. Rockefeller and E. H. Harriman put themselves and their resources at his disposal. Secretary of the Treasury [George B.] Cortelyou, coming to New York to deposit Government funds to help support the tottering financial structure, recognized Mr. Morgan's leadership and acted on his advice in every particular.

Unlike many of the men of great wealth in this country. Mr. Morgan, who was born in Hartford on April 17, 1837, did not have the incentive of poverty to spur him on. He was heir to a fortune estimated at $5,000,000 to $10,000,000.

The decade from 1880 to 1890 was characterized by the most extensive and destructive competition between the railroad systems of the country, and it was during this period that J. P. Morgan developed the policy regarding railroad affairs that he stood forever after. It found its concrete expression in the famous West Shore deal in 1885, which ended a period of warfare almost without parallel between the New York Central and the West Shore Railroad.

At the opening of the new century Mr. Morgan was the largest financial figure on this side of the water, if not in the world. He had gathered around him a notable group of men, including George F. Baker, President of the First National Bank, with which Morgan had more intimate relations than with any other institution.

Big things began to happen with the opening of 1901, and J. P. Morgan was the biggest figure in the doing of them. In January it was announced that he had bought the Jersey Central Railroad and turned it over, with its valuable coal properties, to the Reading. Soon came word that the Pennsylvania Coal Company, the Hillside Coal Company, and others had been bought and turned over to the Erie, two acquisitions which brought the control of the anthracite traffic practically within the Morgan sphere of influence.

Then came news that Andrew Carnegie was going to start a steel plant at Conneaut, Ohio, to manufacture "merchant pipe" in competition with Mr. Morgan's Federal Steel Company and John W. Gates's American Steel and Wire Company.

Here was a denial of the principle which Mr. Morgan had worked for in the railroad field for 20 years. The Steel Corporation was launched in February to take over the Carnegie Steel Company, the Federal Steel, the American Steel and Wire, the American Tin Plate, the American Steel Hoop, and the American Sheet Steel.

This United States Steel enterprise was as notable an example of J. P. Morgan's optimism as anything in his life. It was capitalized on the expectation that the conditions of the most prosperous year in the country's history would continue indefinitely. When the depression of 1903 came along, and the steel stocks dropped off, a banker asked Mr. Morgan what he thought about it.

"I am not concerned with the stock market conditions of the Steel stocks" was the gruff reply, "but I can tell you that the possibilities of the steel business are just as great as they ever were."

When the first rumblings were heard of the storm that would become the furious panic of October, 1907, Mr. Morgan was regarded by many as already out of active life. He was 70 years old and when in this country spent most of his time at his home and library uptown, while J. P. Morgan, Jr., and the other partners in the firm carried on its business.

"Morgan is out of it" was a common view in Wall Street. "He is old and tired and his reputation has suffered. We must look elsewhere for leadership."

How erroneous these ideas were it took but a few weeks to show. While nearly all the captains of finance in Wall Street were lying awake nights in the Spring of 1907, wondering how much longer they could stand the strain, Mr. Morgan was in Europe paying fabulous prices for works of art.

In March came the first signs of panic in the stock market. Worldwide financial disturbance followed a phenomenal break on the New York Stock Exchange. The decline continued until, on March 14, there was a terrific collapse, to be followed by the October panic, caused by the collapse of F. Augustus Heinze's pool in United Copper shares.

Mr. Morgan had been quietly studying the situation. He sat at his desk nearly every day and listened to reports, but said nothing. He was still studying the situation when the panic came.

The National Bank of Commerce, one of the chief Morgan banks, gave notice that after Oct. 22 it would no longer clear checks for the Knickerbocker Trust Company. On the night of Oct. 21 the leading bankers held a conference with Mr. Morgan at his house, and it was reported that he had refused to extend any aid to the trust companies that were on the ragged edge.

The next day the Knickerbocker Trust closed, after paying out $8,000,000 to depositors. That night there was another conference over the affairs of the Trust Company of America, and the next morning a run on that institution started.

Secretary of the Treasury Cortelyou was sent to New York to help afford relief to the banking situation. On Oct. 23 Mr. Morgan and other bankers met Secretary Cortelyou at the Manhattan Hotel, and the Secretary agreed to add $25,000,000 to the Government's deposits.

Again the situation pointed to Mr. Morgan as the only possible leader. Government funds could be deposited only in National banks, not trust companies, and in any case, Mr. Cortelyou explained, he could not give relief to individual banks but had to deal with the situation as a whole. One man who could superintend the whole field was needed, and Mr. Morgan was the man.

When he entered his office the next morning his power was absolute. He was the arbiter between the banks, the trust companies and the National Treasury. His was the power to say who should and should not borrow money. Stock speculation was brought to an end by his fiat. In the days that followed John D. Rockefeller came to him with an offer of $10,000,000 in bonds to be used in securing Government deposits for the afflicted banks. His office was crowded with men like E. H. Gary, head of the Steel Corporation, with $75,000,000 in cash, and James Stillman, representing the untold millions of Standard Oil.

On that first day, with Mr. Morgan fully in the saddle, the Hamilton Bank and the Twelfth Ward Bank closed. The run on the Trust Company of America went on. The streets in the financial district were filled with frenzied throngs. All that day Mr. Morgan sat at his desk, listening to reports, which he received with short, gruff comments.

On the next day, Oct. 24, a run started in the Lincoln Trust Company, and behind this and the Trust Company of America Mr. Morgan determined to make his stand. As securities were thrown into the vortex of the Stock Exchange by frightened investors and by banking institutions that had to liquidate their holdings to meet the demands of the money-hungry lines before their doors, call money on the Exchange soared to incredible heights. Finally no money was to be had at any price.

In the afternoon, R. H. Thomas, President of the Exchange, went to President Stillman of the National City Bank and told him that $25,000,000 was needed to prevent the closing of the Exchange. What followed was recounted by Mr. Thomas:

"Mr. Stillman replied, 'Go right over and tell Mr. Morgan about it.' I went to the office of J. P. Morgan & Co. The place was filled with an excited crowd. After a time Mr. Morgan came out from his private office and said to me, 'I'm going to let you have $25,000,000. Go over to the Exchange and announce it.'"

The next day some of the smaller banks closed while the run on the two trust companies kept up. Another money pool of $10,000,000 was made up in Morgan's office. By the end of the week the Government deposits amounted to $32,000,000.

Conferences were held at Mr. Morgan's house on Sunday, Nov. 3, and at the Waldorf, some of them lasting till 5 in the morning. Plans were made for saving the Lincoln Trust and the Trust Company of America.

That the panic immediately ended is a matter of history.

J. P. Morgan was married twice. His first wife was Amelia Sturges, who died in 1862. In 1865 he married Frances Louise Tracy, who survives him. They had four children, all of whom survive him.

The town house of J. P. Morgan, at Madison Avenue and 36th Street, is notable because of the attractive gardens lying between it and that of J. P. Morgan, Jr., at 37th Street. Including the Morgan building, which houses the Morgan private library and art treasures, this is one of the most attractive groupings of private residences in the heart of the city.

The favorite Summer home of Mr. Morgan was his estate, Cragston, at Highland Falls [N.Y.]. Whenever Mr. or Mrs. Morgan sailed abroad, hampers of the things produced there were sent to the ship. On their trips from here to Cragston the Morgans usually traveled on the Morgan yacht, the Corsair.

Mr. Morgan's youngest child, Miss Anne T. Morgan, helped establish a restaurant for workers in the Brooklyn Navy Yard, which sought to provide them with good and moderate-priced food.

Frequently reports have had it that Miss Morgan was to marry. To a friend Miss Morgan said: "I have not yet met a man whose wife I'd rather be than the daughter of J. Pierpont Morgan."

ANDREW CARNEGIE

November 25, 1835–August 11, 1919

LENOX, MASS.—Andrew Carnegie died at Shadow Brook of bronchial pneumonia at 7:10 o'clock this morning.

Mr. Carnegie was about his estate, apparently in his usual health, on Friday morning with Mrs. Carnegie and his daughter, Mrs. Roswell Miller. Friday evening he complained of difficulty in breathing, but seemed to have nothing worse than a cold.

On Saturday morning he felt fairly well and walked about his home, but during the day he seemed to grow weaker. He grew rapidly worse through Sunday. Mr. Carnegie was in his 84th year.

Of recent days the old man, who was a great lover of flowers, had been fond of being wheeled in a chair into his garden, where he passed many hours. He always wore in the buttonhole of his homespun sack suit a sprig of sweet verbena, which was his favorite plant.

Andrew Carnegie was born Nov. 23, 1835, in Dunfermline, a little manufacturing town in Fifeshire, Scotland, at that time noted for its weaving. His father and his ancestors for a long way back had been weavers, and at the time of Andrew's birth the elder Carnegie owned three or four hand looms, one of which he operated himself. Andrew was to have been a weaver, too, but new inventions were soon to abolish the industry, and William Carnegie, his father, was the last of the weaving line.

Andrew earned his first penny by reciting Burns's long poem, "Man Was Made to Mourn," without a break. There is a story that in Sunday school, being called upon to recite Scripture text, he astonished the assembly by giving this: "Look after the pence, and the pounds will take care of themselves."

Estimates of Mr. Carnegie's wealth made yesterday put it at possibly $500,000,000. When he retired in 1901 he sold his securities of the Carnegie Steel Company to the United States Steel Corporation for $303,450,000 in bonds of that company. He was possessed of large interests in addition to those bonds. When he started in 1901 to endow his great benefactions, he made inroads into his capital for several years in gifts to libraries for peace propaganda, and to other philanthropic causes.

The fortune of $303,450,000 in 5 percent bonds, if allowed to increase by the accumulation of interest and reinvestment since 1901, would amount to about a billion dollars today, but his numerous benefactions prevented this. According to financial authorities, however, the ironmaster's ambition to die poor was not realized, and, despite the scale of his philanthropies, it was believed that his fortune was at his death as large as it ever was.

When he was 12 years old the steam looms drove his father, the master weaver, out of business, and, reduced to poverty, the family emigrated to America. There were four, the parents and two boys, Andrew and Thomas. They settled at Allegheny City, Penn., across the river from Pittsburgh, in 1848. The father and Andrew found work in a cotton factory, the son as bobbin boy. His pay was $1.20 in this, his first job. He was soon promoted to be engineer's assistant, and he stoked the boilers and ran the engine in the factory cellar for 12 hours a day.

It was at this time, he afterward said, that the inspiration came for his subsequent library benefactions. Colonel Anderson, a gentleman with a library of about 400 books, opened it to the boys every weekend and let them borrow any book they wanted. "Only he who has longed as I did for Saturdays to come," he said, "can understand what Colonel Anderson did for me and the boys of Allegheny. Is it any wonder that I resolved if ever surplus wealth came to me, I would use it imitating my benefactor?"

At 14, he became a telegraph messenger and soon learned telegraphy. It was the first step upward. "My entrance into the telegraph office," said Carnegie, "was a transition from darkness to light—from firing a small engine in a dark and dirty cellar into a clean office with bright windows and a literary atmosphere, with books, newspapers, pens, and pencils all around me. I was the happiest boy alive."

He became an operator. When the Pennsylvania Railroad put up a telegraph wire of its own, he became clerk under Divisional Superintendent Thomas A. Scott. At that time telegraphy was still new. The dots and dashes were not read by sound, but were all impressed on tape, and Carnegie is said to have been the third operator in the United States to read messages by sound alone. Scott told the President of the road that he "had a little Scotch devil in his office who would run the whole road if they'd only give him a chance."

Colonel Scott became General Superintendent of the Pennsylvania in 1858 and Vice President in 1860, taking Carnegie along with him at each rise. In May, 1861, the Civil War had broken out and Scott was appointed Assistant Secretary of War in charge of military railroads and telegraphs, and again he took Carnegie with him. Carnegie was now Superintendent of the Western division of the road, and did not want to go to Washington, but Scott insisted.

Mr. Carnegie was placed in charge of the Government telegraph communications. He went to Annapolis and opened communications which the Confederates had interrupted. He started out on the first locomotive which ran from Annapolis to Washington. While passing Elbridge Junction he noticed that the wires had been pegged down by the enemy. He stopped the engine, jumped down beside the wires, and cut them. One of them sprang up and gave him a wound in the cheek, the scar of which remained with him all through life.

Soon, he began to lay the foundation of his wealth. He gained an interest in a small company that made the first sleeping cars and made a profit of about $200,000. He put $40,000 in a company formed for the development of an untried piece of oil land. The company struck oil, and the share remaining to him was worth a quarter of a million.

He invested in iron works in 1863 and two years later became part of a combination called the Union Iron Mills.

It was just at the right time. The Civil War had just ended and the great expansion was beginning. The new concern made great profits, and Carnegie proposed further ventures. It was the era of the building of railroads and the development of the West. Steel rails had become worth $80 to $100 a ton.

By this time Andrew Carnegie was recognized as the leader of this Napoleonic combination, which, with every new success, reached out further. He introduced the Bessemer steel process, which had been a success in England, in his own mills and became principal owner of the Homestead and Edgar Thomson Steel Works and other large plants as head of the firms of Carnegie, Phipps & Co. and Carnegie Brothers & Co.

In 1899 the interests were consolidated in the Carnegie Steel Company, which in 1901 was merged in the United States Steel Corporation, when Mr. Carnegie retired from business.

In 1888 he married Louise Whitefield, who was 20 years his junior. They had one child, Margaret, born in 1897. Mr. and Mrs. Carnegie spent their honeymoon on the Isle of Wight, and then they went to Scotland, where they leased a castle and occupied it for ten years. In 1897, the year of Margaret's birth, Mr. Carnegie bought Skibo Castle [in Scotland], and since then it has been their regular Summer home from May to October. Mrs. Carnegie's chief philanthropic interest has been to work among the thousand-odd tenants of the estate.

The only great clash with labor which occurred while Mr. Carnegie was in business was the Homestead strike of 1892. He was in Europe at the time, and came in for much criticism for not returning and for letting the trouble go to a finish without any action by him.

He sold out to the Steel Corporation for $420,000,000, and in his testimony before the Stanley Committee in 1912, referring to this bargain, he exclaimed, "What a fool I was! I have since learned from the inside that we could have received $100,000,000 more from Mr. Morgan if we had placed that value on our property."

His famous utterance about "dying disgraced" appeared in an article in the North American Review in 1898, in which he said:

"The day is not far distant when the man who dies leaving behind him millions of available wealth, which were free for him to administer during life, will pass away 'unwept, unhonored, and unsung,' no matter to what use he leaves the dross which he cannot take with him. Of such as these the public verdict will be, 'The man who dies thus rich dies disgraced.'"

In 1907 he was the central figure of the dedication of the Carnegie Institute at Pittsburgh, which had cost him $6,000,000.

In "Problems of Today," a book published in 1907, Mr. Carnegie expressed some views on wealth which are unusual in a millionaire. He declared socialism, viewed upon its financial side, to be just, and said, "A heavy progressive tax upon wealth at death of owner is not only desirable, it is strictly just."

Mr. Carnegie did not believe in alms-giving. His idea was to help others help themselves, which was why he said, of his gifts of organs to churches, "I now only give one-half the cost, the congregations first provide the other." As for beggars, he was proud of his indifference to them: "I never give a cent to a beggar, nor do I help people of whose record I am ignorant; this at least is one of my really good actions."

He conceived the original idea of forming a corporation for the purpose of paying out money. It was the Home Trust Company, and it was simply his disbursing office. Its headquarters were in New York.

What is believed to have been one of the last

letters written by Mr. Carnegie, in which he expressed his gratification at the proposed League of Nations, was made public here yesterday by Charles C. James, a broker, to whom the communication was addressed.

"I rejoice in having lived to see the day," said Mr. Carnegie's letter, "when, as Burns puts it, 'man to man the world o'er shall brothers be and a' that.' I believe this happy condition is assured by the League of Nations and that civilization will now march steadily onward, with no more great wars to mar its progress."

JOHN D. ROCKEFELLER

July 8, 1839–May 23, 1937

By Paul Crowell

ORMOND BEACH—John D. Rockefeller Sr., who wanted to live until July 9, 1939, when he would have rounded out a century of life, died at 4:05 A.M. here today at The Casements, his Winter home, a little more than two years from his cherished goal.

Death came suddenly to the founder of the great Standard Oil organization. Less than 24 hours before the aged philanthropist died in his sleep, his son, John D. Rockefeller Jr., had been assured that nothing about his father's condition should cause concern.

John Davison Rockefeller was the richest man in the world at the height of his active career. Starting his business life as a poor boy in an office, with little formal education and no capital, he became the pioneer of efficient business organization and the modern corporation, the most powerful capitalist of his age, and the greatest philanthropist and patron of higher education, scientific research and public health in history.

It was estimated after Mr. Rockefeller retired from business that he had accumulated close to $1,500,000,000 out of the earnings of the Standard Oil trust and other investments, probably the greatest amount any private citizen ever accumulated by his own efforts.

His 1918 income tax returns indicated that his taxable income was then $33,000,000 and his total fortune probably more than $800,000,000.

Mr. Rockefeller, who had been the greatest "getter" of money in the country during the years he was exploiting its oil resources, became, after his retirement, the world's greatest giver. He gave even more than Andrew Carnegie, whose philanthropies amounted to $350,000,000.

Not until Mr. Rockefeller's death was it disclosed that between 1855 and 1934 he had made gifts to charitable and educational organizations totaling $530,853,632.

Of this sum, $182,851,480 went to the Rockefeller Foundation, $129,209,167 to the General Education Board, $73,985,313 to the Laura Spelman Rockefeller Memorial in New York City and $59,931,891 to the Rockefeller Institute for Medical Research.

The life story of the man who started with nothing and accumulated and gave away so much is the outstanding example of the romance of American business.

He was born in Richford, a village in Tioga County, near Oswego, N.Y., on July 8, 1839. His father was William Avery Rockefeller, a country doctor and farmer. His mother was Eliza Davison. He had two brothers.

The story of his first business experience is told in "Random Reminiscences of Men and Events," the only book Mr. Rockefeller ever published.

"When I was 7 or 8 years old," he wrote, "I engaged in my first business enterprise with the assistance of my mother. I owned some turkeys, and she presented me with the curds from the milk to feed them. I took care of the birds myself and sold them all in businesslike fashion. My receipts were all profits, as I had nothing to do with the expense account, and my receipts were kept as carefully as I knew how."

The great gifts Mr. Rockefeller made to charity and his active interest in the church can also be traced to the lessons he learned early on. His parents taught him to make small gifts to the church and to the poor, even when he was a small boy.

He kept from boyhood an account of every cent he received and spent and gave away. The first of these account books, which later became famous as "Ledger A," contained a record of everything. It showed that as a boy Rockefeller had given a cent to his Sunday school every Sunday. In one month there were entries of 10 cents to foreign missions, 12 cents to the Five Points Mission in New York, and 35 cents to his Sunday school teacher for a present.

Mr. Rockefeller discovered the secret of making money his slave at the age of 14. He had saved $50 from his turkey sales, other small enterprises and the performance of chores. Lending this at 7 percent, he received the principal and interest back at the end of a year. About the same time, he received $1.12 for three days of back-breaking labor, digging potatoes for a neighbor. On entering the two transactions in his ledger he realized that his pay for this work was less than one-third the annual interest on his $50, and he resolved to make as much money work for him as he could.

The Rockefeller family moved to a farm near Cleveland in 1853. Mr. Rockefeller spent a year and a half at the Cleveland High School. There he met Laura Celestina Spelman, whom he later married. He briefly attended a business college, learning bookkeeping and the fundamentals of commercial transactions.

At the age of 15 he joined the Erie Street Baptist Church, which had a $2,000 mortgage about to be foreclosed. Young Rockefeller stood at the door of the church begging contributions every Sunday until he raised enough to pay the debt. Two years later he was made a trustee of the church and was superintendent of the Sunday school for 30 years.

He got his first job on Sept. 26, 1855, at the age of 16. His first employers were Hewitt & Tuttle, who had a wholesale produce commission warehouse on the lakefront. At first he was a clerk and assistant bookkeeper. Ledger A showed that he received $50 for more than three months' work, out of this paying his landlady and washerwoman.

In 1858, he went into the commission business for himself in partnership with Maurice B. Clark, an Englishman. Each put $2,000 into the business. He was the firm's junior partner.

"We were prosperous from the beginning," Mr. Rockefeller later told his Bible class. "We did a business of $450,000 the first year. Our profit was not large—I think about $4,400."

Mr. Rockefeller was always "a great borrower," as he said himself. He kept expanding his business and borrowed large sums to finance it.

He drove sharp bargains and continued to live frugally, saving money and putting it back into his business, so that he was prepared to seize the opportunity

which came after oil was discovered in Pennsylvania in 1859.

Mr. Rockefeller went into the oil business in 1862. He and his partner, Clark, invested in a refinery planned by Samuel Andrews, who had learned how to refine the crude oil. A new firm was organized under the name of Andrews, Clark & Co. Although he would become the world's best-known oil man, Rockefeller was so unknown that his name did not even appear in the firm.

Andrews, Clark & Co. built a small refinery on the bank of Kingsbury Run, near Cleveland, in 1863. In 1865 the partnership was dissolved and the plant offered at auction. Mr. Rockefeller bought it for $72,500 and organized the new firm of Rockefeller & Andrews. In 1867 this firm absorbed an oil refinery established by William Rockefeller, and took in as partners William Rockefeller and Henry M. Flagler.

This was the first of the long series of reorganizations and mergers that led to the formation of the great Standard Oil Trust. In 1870, when he was 31 years old, Mr. Rockefeller organized the original Standard Oil Company, with William Rockefeller, Andrews, Flagler and Steven V. Harkness. Mr. Rockefeller was president of the company.

By 1872 nearly all the refining companies in Cleveland had joined the Standard Oil Company. The company soon was refining 29,000 barrels of crude oil a day and making 9,000 barrels a day in its cooper shop. It owned several hundred thousand barrels of oil tankage and warehouses for storing refined oil.

Early conditions in the oil industry were so unstable that many companies were ruined by sharp fluctuations in the market. Mr. Rockefeller began preaching to his local competitors that they might be wiped out unless they had some mutual organization for protection, and inviting them to come into Standard Oil. Within two years nearly all of the petroleum refiners in Cleveland were members of the company.

The Pittsburgh refiners also merged into the Standard Oil combination, as did refiners in Philadelphia, New York, New Jersey, New England, Pennsylvania and West Virginia.

In 1882 Mr. Rockefeller organized the Standard Oil Trust, holding the stocks of all these companies as well as of the original Standard Oil Company. Mr. Rockefeller was growing richer and more powerful every day.

In the Standard Oil Trust Mr. Rockefeller created a new form of commercial enterprise that marked the beginning of an era of modern industrial monopoly. Pipeline companies and other companies for gathering, distributing and marketing petroleum products around the world were organized, all working for the benefit of the trust.

Mr. Rockefeller effected great savings in the business. Standard Oil built its own pipelines, bought its own tank cars for transporting oil in train loads, and established its own depots and warehouses. It made its own barrels in its own shops, and bought whole forests of timber.

The name of Rockefeller spread around the world. His agents and steamships with their cargoes of oil invaded every port. His great corporation had established itself in control of oil production and distribution in America. Mr. Rockefeller began investing his profits in other industries, including iron, steamships and railroads. At the height of his career he directed the affairs of 33 oil companies and indirectly influenced hundreds of other companies. The original Standard Oil Company had assets of $55,000,000; the combined capitalizations of the corporations in which he was interested ran into the billions.

People began to denounce him as a menace and call the Standard Oil an octopus. The anti-trust movement began, and muckraking grew in fashion, with Rockefeller and Standard Oil as the chief targets.

Ida M. Tarbell wrote a book, "The History of the Standard Oil Company," in which she attacked the business methods with which Mr. Rockefeller had created the Oil Trust. He was accused of crushing competition, getting rich on rebates from railroads, bribing men to spy on competing companies, making secret agreements, and coercing rivals to join the Standard Oil Company.

Mr. Rockefeller insisted that the Standard Oil was a good trust and that he had made his money honestly and honorably.

"Sometimes things are said about us that are cruel and they hurt," he once said. "But I am never a pessimist. I never despair. I believe in man and the brotherhood of man and am confident that everything will come out for the good of all in the end."

The Rockefellers had five children. Those living are Alta and John D. Rockefeller Jr.

At one time he had five homes. His town house was at 4 West 45th St. The 3,000-acre estate at Pocantico Hills, called Kikuit, was his favorite residence. Several years ago he bought an estate at Ormond Beach, Fla.

Mr. Rockefeller was friendlier to strangers in his later years. He distributed shiny new dimes among children he found playing in the street and to singers on the ferry between Tarrytown and Nyack.

HENRY FORD

July 30, 1863–April 7, 1947

DETROIT—Henry Ford, noted automotive pioneer, died at 11:40 tonight at the age of 83. He had retired a little more than a year and a half ago from active direction of the great industrial empire he founded in 1903.

Death came at his estate in suburban Dearborn, not far from where he was born in 1863. Mr. Ford was reported to have been in excellent health when he returned only a week ago from his annual winter visit to his estate in Georgia.

There were many reports that he had given up his leadership at the insistence of other members of his family, particularly the widow of his only son, Edsel B. Ford, who was said to be dissatisfied with the course of company affairs. After resigning as president late in 1945, Mr. Ford spent time at the Ford engineering laboratory.

He leaves a widow, the former Clara Bryant, whom he married in 1887, and two grandsons, Henry 2nd, who had assumed control of the company after Mr. Ford's retirement, and Benson. —*The Associated Press*

Henry Ford was the founder of modern American industrial mass production methods, built on the assembly line and the belt conveyor system, which no less an authority than Marshal Joseph Stalin testified were the foundation for an Allied military victory in the Second World War. He was the apostle of an economic philosophy of high wages and short hours that had immense repercussions on American thinking.

He lived to see the Ford Motor Company produce more than 29 million automobiles before the war forced the conversion of its gigantic facilities. Then he directed its production of more than 8,000 four-engine bombers, as well as tanks, tank destroyers, jeeps and amphibious jeeps, transport gliders, trucks, engines and much other equipment.

Struck a cruel blow shortly before his 80th birthday by the death of his only son, Edsel, on May 26, 1943, Mr. Ford remained at the helm as the company reached the peak of its war production.

Mr. Ford was born on July 30, 1863, on a farm nine miles west of Detroit, the eldest of six children. His mother died when he was 12 years of age. He went to school until he was 15. He worked on the farm after school hours and during vacations.

His mechanical bent first showed itself early. When he was 13 he took a watch apart and put it together again so that it would work. He had to do this secretly at night, after he had finished his chores, because his father wanted to discourage his mechanical ambitions. In 1879, at the age of 16, he ran away from home. Walking all the way to Detroit, almost penniless, he went to work as an apprentice in a machine shop.

Returning to his father's farm, he spent his spare time for several years endeavoring to evolve a practical farm tractor of relatively small size and cost. He succeeded in building a steam tractor with a one-cylinder engine, but was unable to devise a boiler light enough to make the tractor practicable.

Convinced that the steam engine was unsuited to light vehicles, he turned to the internal combustion engine, which he had read about in English scientific periodicals, as a means of locomotion for the "horse-less carriage" of which he and other automobile inventors had dreamed.

In 1890 he got a job as engineer and machinist with the Detroit Edison Company at $45 a month, and moved to Detroit. He set up a workshop in his backyard and continued his experiments after hours.

He completed his first "gasoline buggy" in 1892. It had a two-cylinder engine, which developed about four horsepower, and he drove it 1,000 miles. The first, and for a long time the only automobile in Detroit, it was too heavy to suit Mr. Ford, who sold it in 1896 for $200, to get funds to experiment on a lighter car. Later, when he became successful, he repurchased his first car for $100 as a memento.

Meanwhile, he had become chief engineer of the electric company at $125 a month. His superiors offered to make him general superintendent, but only on condition that he give up gasoline and devote himself entirely to electricity. He quit his job on Aug. 15, 1899.

Mr. Ford persuaded a group of men to organize the Detroit Automobile Company to manufacture his car. The company made and sold a few cars on his original model, but after two years Mr. Ford broke with his associates over a fundamental issue. He envisioned the mass production of cars that could be sold in large quantities at small profits, while his backers were convinced that the automobile was a luxury, to be produced in small quantities at large profits per unit.

Renting a one-story brick shed in Detroit, Mr. Ford spent 1902 experimenting with two-cylinder and four-cylinder engines. He built two racing cars, each with a four-cylinder engine developing 80 horsepower. One of the cars, with the celebrated Barney Oldfield at its wheel, won every race in which it was entered.

The publicity helped Mr. Ford to organize the Ford Motor Company, which was capitalized at $100,000, although actually only $28,000 in stock was subscribed. Eventually, he and his son bought out the minority stockholders for $70 million and became sole owners.

In 1903 the Ford Motor Company sold 1,708 two-cylinder, eight-horsepower automobiles. Its operations were soon threatened, however, by a suit for patent infringement brought by the Licensed Association of Automobile Manufacturers, who held the rights to a patent obtained by George B. Selden of Rochester, N.Y., in 1895, covering the combination of a gasoline engine and a road locomotive. Mr. Ford won the suit when the Supreme Court held that the Selden patent was invalid.

For several years, Mr. Ford was balked by the lack of a steel sufficiently light and strong. By chance one day, picking up the pieces of a French racing car that had been wrecked at Palm Beach, he discovered vanadium steel, which had not yet been manufactured in the United States.

With this material he began the era of mass production. He concentrated on a single type of chassis, the celebrated Model T, and specified that "any customer can have a car painted any color he wants, so long as it is black." By 1925, the company was producing almost 2 million Model T's a year.

In January 1914, he established a minimum pay rate of $5 a day for an eight-hour day. Up to then, the average wage throughout his works had been $2.40 a nine-hour day.

To reduce costs and eliminate intermediate profits on raw materials and transportation, Mr. Ford purchased his own coal mines, iron mines and forests, his own railways and his own lake and ocean steamships. The phenomenal success of the new system made Mr. Ford not only fabulously rich, but internationally famous.

In the winter of 1915–16 he was convinced by a group of pacifists that the warring nations in Europe were ready for peace and that a dramatic gesture would end the war. Mr. Ford chartered an ocean liner with the avowed purpose of "getting the boys out of the trenches by Christmas," and sailed from New York on Dec. 4, 1915, with a curiously assorted group of companions. The mission failed to achieve anything. "We learn more from our failures than from our successes," he said.

When the United States declared war on Germany in April, 1917, Mr. Ford placed the industrial facilities of his plants at the disposal of the Government, although he had previously refused orders from belligerent countries.

Mr. Ford retired as active head of the Ford Motor Company in 1918, at the age of 55, turning over the presidency to Edsel and announcing his intention of devoting himself to the development of his farm tractor, and to the publication of his weekly journal, The Dearborn Independent.

In 1919 Mr. Ford sued The Chicago Tribune for libel, because of an editorial that accused him of having been pro-German during the war. The jury awarded him a mere six cents, and only after counsel for the defense had subjected him to a pitiless cross-examination which revealed him to be almost without knowledge of subjects outside his own field. (It would not be unfair to say that, despite his vast wealth and industrial expertise, Mr. Ford remained in some ways a simple man. He believed in hard work and utilitarian education and was opposed to the use of tobacco and liquor. He tried in vain from time to time to interest the younger generation in old-fashioned dances and fiddlers.)

His activities as publisher of The Dearborn Independent involved him in another libel suit. The weekly published a series of articles, which were widely criticized as anti-Semitic. Aaron Sapiro, a Chicago lawyer, sued on the ground that his reputation as an organizer of farmers' cooperative marketing organizations had been damaged by articles asserting that a Jewish conspiracy was seeking to control American agriculture.

On the witness stand, Mr. Ford disclaimed animosity toward Jews. It was brought out that, although a column in the paper was labeled as his, he did not write it nor did he read the publication. Mr. Ford settled the suit without disclosing the terms, discontinued the paper and made a public apology.

The 1921 depression brought the company its most severe financial crisis. Investment bankers were convinced that he would have to go to them "hat in hand," and an officer of one large New York bank journeyed to Detroit to offer Mr. Ford a loan on the condition that a representative of the bankers be appointed treasurer of his company. Mr. Ford silently handed him his hat.

Mr. Ford loaded up Ford dealers throughout the country with all the cars they could handle and compelled them to pay cash. Then, by purchasing a railroad of his own, and by other economies, he cut one-third from the time his raw materials and finished products were in transit.

He realized more money from the sale of Liberty bonds, from by-products and from collections from Ford agents in foreign countries. On April 1, consequently, he had far more than he needed to wipe out the indebtedness. The crisis over, Mr. Ford severed all connections with the banks, except as a depositor. He made a practice of carrying tremendous amounts on deposit. Bankers reported that he invariably drove a hard bargain in placing these funds, often demanding a special rate of interest.

In 1924, the Ford company had manufactured about two-thirds of all the automobiles produced in this country, but by 1926 the Chevrolet, manufactured by the General Motors Corporation, had become a serious competitor.

Mr. Ford closed his plants late in 1926 while he experimented with a six-cylinder model. He abandoned the Model T the next year, substituting the Model A. The new model proved popular, and the Ford Motor Company continued to expand. In 1928 Mr. Ford organized the British Ford Company, and subsequently began operations in other European countries.

Mr. Ford had long regarded Soviet Russia as a potential market. By agreeing to aid in the construction of an automobile factory at Nizhni-Novgorod, and by providing technological assistance in the development of the automobile industry in the Soviet Union, Mr. Ford sold $30 million worth of products to Russia.

After the stock market collapse of October 1929, he was one of the business and industrial leaders who were summoned to the White House by President Hoover. Unlike some industrialists who favored deflation of wages, Mr. Ford argued that the maintenance of purchasing power was of paramount importance.

Although his company lost heavily in the worst of the Depression, Mr. Ford maintained his wage policy until the autumn of 1932, when the company announced a downward readjustment from "the highest executive down to the ordinary laborer." As the Depression waned, he reverted to his high-wage policy and in 1935 established a minimum of $6 a day.

Mr. Ford opposed the New Deal, and he refused to sign the automobile code of the National Recovery Administration, which stipulated that employees had a right to organize. In 1936 he supported Gov. Alf M. Landon. Despite President Roosevelt's triumphant re-election, Mr. Ford remained antagonistic to unions.

The United Automobile Workers began a drive to organize Ford workers. The opening blow was a sit-down strike in the Ford plant in Kansas City, ended only by the promise of officials there to [meet] with the union, a step the company had never taken before. Mr. Ford charged that international financiers had gained control of the unions.

On May 26, 1937, a group of UAW organizers were distributing organizing literature outside the Ford plant at River Rouge, when they were set upon and badly beaten. The union charged that the beatings were administered by company police. The company denied this.

The National Labor Relations Board found the company guilty of unfair labor practices. In April 1941, the UAW called a strike in the Ford plants, and the NLRB held an election. When the votes were counted, the UAW had won about 70 percent of the votes. Mr. Ford signed a contract that gave the union virtually everything for which it had asked.

Mr. Ford opposed American entry into World War II and refused to manufacture airplane motors for Great Britain. But as the pressure for re-armament grew, he felt compelled to build planes for the United States. Ground was broken on April 18, 1941, for the Willow Run plant, and the first of the 30-ton B-24-E bombers came off its assembly line a little more than a year later. Eventually the factory, well over a half-mile long, was turning out bombers at the rate of one an hour.

Notwithstanding his earlier opposition to unions, Mr. Ford said in a September 1944 interview that he wanted his company to pay the highest wages in the automobile industry: "If the men in our plants will give a full day's work for a full day's pay, there is no reason why we can't always do it. Every man should make enough money to own a home, a piece of land and a car."

HOWARD HUGHES

December 24, 1905–April 5, 1976

By James P. Sterba

HOUSTON—Howard R. Hughes died today as mysteriously as he had lived.

The reclusive 70-year-old billionaire was on the way from Acapulco, Mexico, to a hospital for emergency treatment. A physician accompanying him said Mr. Hughes died at 1:27 P.M. in a chartered jet flying over south Texas.

A Hughes spokesman said the cause of death was a "cerebral vascular accident." This is otherwise known as a stroke.

Two years ago one of Howard R. Hughes's many lawyers appeared before a Federal court in Los Angeles in one of the many cases involving the reclusive billionaire.

Asked to explain the failure of his client to appear, the attorney, Norbert Schlei, said Mr. Hughes was "a man to whom you cannot apply the same standards as you can to you and me."

He got no dispute on that point from judge or jury, although the case ended in one of the few setbacks Mr. Hughes ever encountered in court—a $2,823,333 defamation award to his former aide Robert A. Maheu.

Mr. Hughes had a role in a different kind of drama in 1974 as he and the Central Intelligence Agency teamed up to recover a sunken Soviet submarine from the Pacific Ocean floor. The submarine, which sank 750 miles northwest of Hawaii in 1968, held nuclear warheads and code books, and Mr. Hughes, at the behest of the C.I.A., commissioned the construction of a ship called the Glomar Explorer and a mammoth barge to retrieve the vessel. The project was conducted under the ruse of deep-sea research.

[The salvage attempt brought up half the submarine. The half containing the warheads and code books broke off during the operation and dropped three miles to the bottom again.]

No recent episode in Mr. Hughes's life galvanized the attention of the world like the extraordinary sequence of events stemming from the announcement by McGraw-Hill and Life magazine on Dec. 7, 1971, that they planned to publish an "autobiography" of Mr. Hughes, as told to a little-known American writer named Clifford Irving.

Mr. Irving claimed to have met secretly with his subject more than 100 times for tape-recorded discussions and came forward with a 230,000-word manuscript entitled "The Autobiography of Howard Hughes."

McGraw-Hill gave him $750,000 for it—a $100,000 advance and $650,000 in checks made out to "H. R. Hughes," as payment to Mr. Hughes for his "cooper-

ation." Mr. Irving's wife, Edith, using the name Helga R. Hughes, deposited the checks in a Swiss bank. McGraw-Hill sold excerpt rights to Life.

In an extraordinary telephone news conference, Mr. Hughes denounced the work as a hoax, sued to halt publication and promised to prove Mr. Irving was a fake. (He also charged that his aide, Mr. Maheu, "stole me blind," leading to the aforementioned defamation verdict.)

Eventually, Edith Irving was exposed as the "Helga R. Hughes" who appeared in Switzerland. Evidence mounted that Mr. Irving's manuscript resembled published and unpublished materials produced by others. In mid-February of 1972, Life and McGraw-Hill conceded the work was a hoax and canceled publication. Mr. Irving and his wife pleaded guilty and served jail sentences for their deception.

The news conference over the Irving affair was one of the rare instances in recent decades when the voice of Howard Hughes was heard in a relatively public setting. Normally, he saw only his round-the-clock male attendants (he favored Mormons because they did not smoke or drink) and his wife, Jean Peters, the actress he married in 1957. They were divorced in 1971 after a lengthy separation.

Mr. Hughes wasn't always a recluse. Back in the nineteen-thirties, when he was setting air speed records and was a maverick Hollywood producer, the newspapers were full of photographs of a lean and smiling Mr. Hughes posing with Jane Russell, Lana Turner, Ava Gardner and other film and cafe society beauties.

Mr. Hughes set several air speed records and in 1938 flew around the world in 91 hours—a feat for which he was voted a Congressional medal. He never bothered to pick it up, however, and years later President Harry S. Truman found it in a White House desk and mailed it to him.

There were a number of explanations for Mr. Hughes's reclusiveness, including his deafness, his shyness and a fear of germs that extended to separate refrigerators for himself and his wife, separate copies of magazines and newspapers and an unwillingness to shake hands.

In an interview about 25 years ago Mr. Hughes denied that he was eccentric: "I am not a man of mystery. These stories grow like Greek myths. . . . I have no taste for expensive clothes. Clothes are something to wear and automobiles are transportation. If they merely cover me up and get me there, that's sufficient."

After Mr. Hughes had settled in Nevada in 1966 and had invested more than $125 million in casinos and real estate, Gov. Paul Laxalt let it be known that he would like to speak with him. Shortly thereafter Mr. Hughes—or a voice that identified itself as his—telephoned the Governor. Mr. Hughes, according to Mr. Laxalt, was an occasional telephoner, and the two men sometimes conversed for an hour.

Shortly after his arrival in Las Vegas, Mr. Hughes bought the operating contracts of the Desert Inn for $13.25 million, and later the property as well. One story was that he had acted when the owners requested him to leave his $250-a-day suite to make way for already-booked guests. Another explanation was that the deal enabled Mr. Hughes to multiply his millions with relative tax freedom, given Nevada's absence of state income or inheritance taxes.

A third, and perhaps complementary, explanation was that Mr. Hughes envisioned a huge regional airport that would transform Las Vegas into a terminal for the Southwest and California.

Through 1969, Mr. Hughes had invested about $150 million in Las Vegas properties. In addition, he bought Air West with 9,000 route miles in eight Western states, Canada and Mexico. The acquisition cost Mr. Hughes $150 million, but it put him back in the air travel business, which he had left when he sold his controlling interests in Trans World Airlines and Northeast.

Mr. Hughes operated through Mr. Maheu, a strapping ex-F.B.I. agent, and scores of subordinates, most of whom never saw him.

The anchor of Mr. Hughes's fortune was the Hughes Tool Company, which manufactures and leases rock and oil drills. He owned, moreover, the Hughes Aircraft Company in California, which manufactures electronic devices as well as planes and holds many Government contracts.

Howard Robard Hughes Jr. was born on Christmas Eve, 1905, in Houston. He was shy and serious as a boy and showed mechanical aptitude early. He attended two preparatory schools. He also took courses at Rice Institute in Houston and the California Institute of Technology. He obtained no degree.

Mr. Hughes's father was a mining engineer who developed the first successful rotary bit for drilling oil wells through rock. When his mother died in 1922, Howard Hughes inherited 50 percent of the company. On his father's death in 1924, he received 25 percent. He took control of the company at 18, and two years later bought out the remaining family interest.

At 19, Mr. Hughes married Ella Rice, a member of the family that founded Rice Institute. The marriage lasted four and a half years.

Meanwhile, Mr. Hughes had shifted his interest to Hollywood, where he set forth, characteristically, in lone-wolf style, to become a movie producer. His first film was called "Swell Hogan," and it was so bad it was never released.

But then came "Hell's Angels," starring Jean Harlow. Filmed in 1930 at a cost of $4 million, it was then the most expensive movie ever made. Much of the cost resulted when the picture was made over for sound, which had come into general use when it was half finished. Mr. Hughes wrote, produced and directed this film, which grossed $8 million.

Mr. Hughes turned out about a dozen pictures in the late twenties and early thirties. By then, he had become intrigued with aviation. He learned to fly during the filming of "Hell's Angels" and was seriously injured when his plane, of World War I vintage, crashed.

In 1943 he was injured when an experimental two-engine flying boat crashed and sank in Lake Mead. And in 1946 he crashed on the first flight of his XF-11, a high-speed, long-range airplane. His chest and left lung were crushed; he also suffered a skull fracture and had nine broken ribs. During his recovery, he designed a new type of hospital bed.

Mr. Hughes's aviation achievements were overshadowed for a time by a notable failure—the Hughes flying boat. This eight-engine seaplane, built of plywood, was conceived by Mr. Hughes during World War II, when a shortage of metal dictated the use of alternate materials. The Spruce Goose, as it was dubbed by the press, was designed to carry troops. It had a wing spread of 320 feet, a hull three stories high and a tail assembly eight stories tall.

The Government put $18 million into the plane, and Mr. Hughes said he had invested $23 million. The craft flew only once—on Nov. 2, 1947, when, with Mr. Hughes at the controls, it got about 70 feet off the water for a one-mile run.

Before the war was over, Mr. Hughes had returned to independent motion-picture production. The occasion was a film that proved to be his most controversial, "The Outlaw," starring Mr. Hughes's personal discovery, Jane Russell.

Filmed in 1941–42, the western was denied a seal of approval by the Motion Picture Association of America because of greater exposure of Miss Russell than was customary. Shown in San Francisco in 1943, the picture ran into a storm of protest and censorship and was temporarily withdrawn. In 1946, it was put into general distribution, with Mr. Hughes reaping both profits and publicity.

Two years later, Mr. Hughes bought a controlling interest in the Radio-Keith-Orpheum Corporation for $8,825,000. Under Mr. Hughes, R.K.O. was constantly in the red and he was accused in one of the many stockholder suits of running the studio with "caprice, pique and whim." In 1954, he bought up the outstanding stock of R.K.O. But by mid-1955 he was tired of the movies and sold his studio interest.

In his later years Mr. Hughes was engaged in a long-running battle over Trans World Airlines, which he lost control of in 1961 to creditors who had financed the purchase of jets for the line. The new trustee management and Mr. Hughes sued each other, but Mr. Hughes refused to appear in court. Then on April 9, 1966, came the surprise news that he was selling his 78 percent interest in T.W.A. for about $546 million.

Characteristically, Mr. Hughes had no comment.

RAY KROC

October 5, 1902–January 14, 1984

By Eric Pace

Ray A. Kroc, the builder of the McDonald's hamburger empire, who helped change American business and eating habits by deftly orchestrating the purveying of billions of small beef patties, died yesterday in San Diego. He was 81 years old and lived in La Jolla, Calif.

Mr. Kroc, who also owned the San Diego Padres baseball team, died of a heart ailment at Scripps Memorial Hospital in San Diego. At his death he was senior chairman of McDonald's.

Mr. Kroc, a former piano player and salesman of paper cups and milkshake machines, built up a family fortune worth $500 million or more through his tireless, inspired tinkering with the management of the McDonald's drive-ins and restaurants, which specialize in hamburgers and other fast-food items.

He was a pioneer in automating and standardizing operations in the fiercely competitive fast-food industry. He concentrated on swiftly growing suburban areas, where family visits to the local McDonald's became something like tribal rituals.

He started his first McDonald's outside Chicago in 1955, and the chain now has 7,500 outlets in the United States and 31 other countries and territories, registering more than $8 billion in sales in 1983. Three-quarters of its outlets are run by franchiseholders. It is the United States' largest food service organization in sales and number of outlets.

What made Mr. Kroc so successful was the variety of virtuoso refinements he brought to fast-food retailing. He carefully chose the recipients of his McDonald's franchises, seeking managers who were skilled at personal relations; he relentlessly stressed quality, banning from his hamburgers such filler materials as soybeans.

Mr. Kroc also made innovative use of part-time teenage help; he struggled to keep costs down to make McDonald's perennially low prices possible, and he applied complex team techniques to food preparation that were reminiscent of professional football.

After McDonald's had made him a major figure on the business scene, Mr. Kroc became influential in the sports world by buying the San Diego Padres for $10 million in 1974.

The new and eager team owner was notably outspoken: After his club botched a game in 1974, he used the San Diego Stadium public address system to tell the team's fans, "I suffer with you; I've never seen such stupid ball playing in my life."

In the major leagues of American business, Mr. Kroc's career was unusual because its enormous success was so late in coming. He was in his 50's when he went into the hamburger business, making himself president of the McDonald's Corporation in 1955. In 1968 he became chairman, and he took the title of senior chairman in 1977, when McDonald's purveyed more than $3.7 billion worth of fast-food fare, outselling its archcompetitor, the Pillsbury-owned Burger King, by 4 to 1.

McDonald's shares were a Wall Street favorite in the early 70's. By January 1973, investors who bought them when first offered in the mid-1960's had seen their wealth multiply more than sixtyfold.

Over the years, Mr. Kroc was repeatedly involved in controversy. The authors Max Boas and Steve Chain charged in a 1976 book, "Big Mac: The Unauthorized Story of McDonald's," that McDonald's had exploited its employees by forcing them to take lie-detector tests and by appropriating their tips. The architecture of McDonald's outlets was sometimes criticized, as was the nutritional content of the food. But one critic, the nutritionist Jean Mayer, once said, "I am nonfanatical about McDonald's; as a weekend treat, it is clean and fast."

In 1972 Senator Harrison A. Williams Jr., Democrat of New Jersey, suggested that there was a link between the more than $200,000 that Mr. Kroc had contributed to President Nixon's re-election campaign and the Nixon Administration's position on teen-age wage limits, a matter of prime importance to McDonald's.

Mr. Kroc cut a commanding figure, his thin hair brushed straight back, his custom-made blazers impeccable, his eyes constantly checking his restaurants for cleanliness. He sought followers who, like him, were driven by an unending urge to build and excel.

"We want someone who will get totally involved in the business," he once said. "If his ambition is to reach the point where he can play golf four days a week or play gin rummy for a cent a point, instead of a tenth, we don't want him in a McDonald's restaurant."

Understandably, many McDonald's executives decorated their offices with scrolls inscribed with his favorite inspirational dictum:

Nothing in the world can take the place of persistence. Talent will not; nothing is more common than unsuccessful men with talent. Genius will not; unrewarded genius is almost a proverb. Education will not; the world is full of educated derelicts. Persistence and determination alone are omnipotent.

Mr. Kroc established the McDonald's headquarters in Oak Brook, a few miles from the Chicago suburb of Oak Park, where he was born Oct. 5, 1902, the son of an unsuccessful real estate man whose family came from Bohemia in what is now Czechoslovakia.

Ray Albert Kroc did not graduate from high school. In World War I, like his fellow Oak Parker, Ernest Hemingway, he served as an ambulance driver. Then, after holding various jobs, including playing piano in a jazz band, he spent 17 years with the Lily Tulip Cup Company. But by 1941, "I felt it was time I was on my own," Mr. Kroc once recalled, and he became the exclusive sales agent for a machine that could prepare five milkshakes at a time.

Then, in 1954, Mr. Kroc heard about Richard and Maurice McDonald, the owners of a fast-food emporium in San Bernadino, Calif., that was using his mixers. As a milkshake specialist, Mr. Kroc later explained, "I had to see what kind of an operation was making 40 at one time."

"I went to see the McDonald operation," Mr. Kroc went on in a memoir published in The New York Times, and suddenly insights gained during his years in the paper-cup business and the milkshake machine business mingled fruitfully in his mind.

"I can't pretend to know what it is—certainly, it's not some divine vision," he said of his touch in business. "Perhaps it's a combination of your background and experience, your instincts, your dreams. Whatever it was, I saw it in the McDonald operation, and in that moment, I suppose, I became an entrepreneur. I decided to go for broke."

Mr. Kroc talked to the McDonald brothers about opening franchise outlets patterned on their restaurant, which sold hamburgers for 15 cents, french fries for 10 cents and milkshakes for 20 cents.

They later worked out a deal whereby he was to give them a small percentage of the gross of his operation. Mr. Kroc's first restaurant opened in 1955 in Des Plaines, another Chicago suburb. Five years later, there were 228 restaurants, and in 1961 he bought out the brothers.

In choosing franchise owners, Mr. Kroc looked, as he explained it in 1971, "for somebody who's good with people; we'd rather get a salesman than an accountant or even a chef."

Among the license holders were a member of the House of Representatives from Virginia, a chemist, a golf professional, dentists, lawyers and even a former Under Secretary of Labor.

McDonald's poured hundreds of millions of dollars into advertising. One head of another fast-food company said in 1978 that consumers were "so preconditioned by McDonald's advertising blanket that the hamburger would taste good even if they left the meat out."

Mr. Kroc was also unremittingly intense in training his franchise owners at "Hamburger University" in Elk Grove, Ill., where a course led to a "Bachelor of Hamburgerology with a minor in french fries." Instructors taught how to clean grills, flip a hamburger and tell when one was done. "It starts turning brown around the edge."

Mr. Kroc met his wife, Joan, in a restaurant in 1956 when he and she had other spouses. They were married in 1968, and she went on to found and become the head of Operation Cork, a national program to help the families of alcoholics.

Mr. Kroc suffered a stroke in December 1979. His survivors include his wife, a brother, a sister, a stepdaughter and four granddaughters.

STEVE JOBS

February 24, 1955–October 5, 2011

By John Markoff

Steven P. Jobs, the visionary co-founder of Apple who helped usher in the era of personal computers and then led a cultural transformation in the way music, movies and mobile communications were experienced in the digital age, died on Wednesday. He was 56.

The death was announced by Apple, the company Mr. Jobs and his high school friend Stephen Wozniak started in 1976 in a suburban California garage. A friend of the family said the cause was complications of pancreatic cancer.

Mr. Jobs had waged a long and public struggle with the disease, remaining the face of the company even as he underwent treatment, introducing new products for a global market in his trademark blue jeans even as he grew gaunt and frail. He finally stepped down in August.

By then, having mastered digital technology and capitalized on his intuitive marketing sense, Mr. Jobs had largely come to define the personal computer industry and an array of digital consumer and entertainment businesses centered on the Internet. He had also become a very rich man, worth an estimated $8.3 billion.

Eight years after founding Apple, Mr. Jobs led the team that designed the Macintosh computer, a breakthrough in making personal computers easier to use. After a 12-year separation from the company, prompted

by a bitter falling-out with his chief executive, John Sculley, he returned in 1997 to oversee the creation of one innovative digital device after another—the iPod, the iPhone and the iPad. These transformed not only product categories like music players and cellphones but also entire industries, like music and mobile communications.

During his years outside Apple, he bought a tiny computer graphics spinoff from the director George Lucas and built a team of computer scientists, artists and animators that became Pixar Animation Studios. It made the full-length computer-animated film a mainstream art form enjoyed by children and adults worldwide.

Mr. Jobs was neither a hardware engineer nor a software programmer, nor did he think of himself as a manager. He considered himself a technology leader, choosing the best people possible, encouraging and prodding them, and making the final call on product design.

It was an executive style that had evolved. In his early years at Apple, his meddling maddened colleagues, and his criticism could be caustic and even humiliating. But he grew to elicit extraordinary loyalty.

To his understanding of technology he brought an immersion in popular culture. His worldview was shaped by the '60s counterculture in the San Francisco Bay Area, where he had grown up, the adopted son of a Silicon Valley machinist. When he graduated from high school in Cupertino in 1972, he said, "the very strong scent of the 1960s was still there."

After dropping out of Reed College, a stronghold of liberal thought in Portland, Ore., in 1972, Mr. Jobs led a countercultural lifestyle himself. He told a reporter that taking LSD was one of the two or three most important things he had done in his life.

Apple's very name reflected his unconventionality. In an era when engineers and hobbyists tended to describe their machines with model numbers, he chose the name of a fruit, supposedly because of his dietary habits at the time.

Coming on the scene just as computing began to move beyond the walls of research laboratories and corporations in the 1970s, Mr. Jobs saw that computing was becoming personal—that it could do more than crunch numbers and solve scientific and business problems—and that it could even be a force for social and economic change. And at a time when hobbyist computers were boxy wooden affairs with metal chassis, he designed the Apple II as a sleek, low-slung plastic package intended for the den or the kitchen. He was offering not just products but a digital lifestyle.

He put much stock in the notion of "taste," a word he used frequently. Great products, he said, were a triumph of taste, of "trying to expose yourself to the best things humans have done and then trying to bring those things into what you are doing."

Regis McKenna, a marketing executive who helped shape the Apple brand in the late 1970s, said Mr. Jobs's genius lay in his ability "to strip away the excess layers of business, design and innovation until only the simple, elegant reality remained."

Steven Paul Jobs was born in San Francisco on Feb. 24, 1955, and surrendered for adoption by his biological parents, Joanne Carole Schieble and Abdulfattah Jandali, a graduate student from Syria. He was adopted by Paul and Clara Jobs. The elder Mr. Jobs moved his family down the San Francisco Peninsula to Mountain View and then to Los Altos in the 1960s.

Mr. Jobs developed an early interest in electronics. He met Mr. Wozniak while attending Homestead High School in neighboring Cupertino.

The spark that ignited their partnership came from an article in the October 1971 issue of Esquire magazine. The article, "Secrets of the Little Blue Box," by Ron Rosenbaum, detailed an underground hobbyist culture of young men known as phone phreaks who were illicitly exploring the nation's phone system.

Inspired, Mr. Wozniak and Mr. Jobs collaborated on building and selling blue boxes, devices that were widely used for making free—and illegal—phone calls. They raised a total of $6,000 from the effort.

After enrolling at Reed College in 1972, Mr. Jobs left after one semester, but remained in Portland for another 18 months auditing classes.

Leaving school freed his curiosity to follow his interests. "I didn't have a dorm room," he said in his 2005 Stanford speech, "so I slept on the floor in friends' rooms, I returned Coke bottles for the five-cent deposits to buy food with, and I would walk the seven miles across town every Sunday night to get one good meal a week at the Hare Krishna temple. I loved it. And much of what I stumbled into by following my curiosity and intuition turned out to be priceless later on."

In 1974, he took a job as a technician at Atari, the video game manufacturer. He left after several months and traveled to India, returning to Atari that fall. In 1975, he and Mr. Wozniak, then working as an engineer at Hewlett-Packard, began attending meetings of the Homebrew Computer Club, a hobbyist group that met at the Stanford Linear Accelerator Center in Menlo Park, Calif. Personal computing had been pioneered at research laboratories adjacent to Stanford, and it was spreading to the outside world.

"What I remember is how intense he looked," said Lee Felsenstein, a computer designer who was a Homebrew member. "He was everywhere, and he seemed to be trying to hear everything people had to say."

Mr. Wozniak designed the original Apple I computer simply to show it off to his friends at the Homebrew. It was Mr. Jobs who had the inspiration that it could be a commercial product.

In early 1976, he and Mr. Wozniak, using their own money, began Apple with an initial investment of $1,300; they later gained the backing of a former Intel executive, A. C. Markkula, who lent them $250,000.

In April 1977, Mr. Jobs and Mr. Wozniak introduced Apple II at the West Coast Computer Faire in San Francisco. Apple created a sensation, straddling the business and consumer markets by building a computer that could be customized for specific applications.

Sales skyrocketed to $600 million in 1981, the year the company went public. By 1983 Apple was in the Fortune 500. No company had ever joined the list so quickly.

The Apple III, introduced in May 1980, had a host of technical problems, and Mr. Jobs shifted his focus to an office workstation computer code-named Lisa.

By then Mr. Jobs had made his much-chronicled 1979 visit to Xerox's research center in Palo Alto, where he saw the Alto, an experimental personal computer system that foreshadowed modern desktop computing. The Alto, controlled by a mouse pointing device, was one of the first computers to employ a graphical video display, which presented the user with a view of documents and programs, adopting the metaphor of an office desktop.

"It was one of those sort of apocalyptic moments," Mr. Jobs said of his visit in a 1995 oral history interview for the Smithsonian Institution. "I remember within 10 minutes of seeing the graphical user interface stuff, just knowing that every computer would work this way someday."

In 1981 he joined a small group of Apple engineers pursuing a separate project, a lower-cost system code-named Macintosh. The machine was introduced in January 1984 and trumpeted during the Super Bowl telecast by a 60-second commercial, directed by Ridley Scott, that linked I.B.M., then the dominant PC maker, with Orwell's Big Brother.

A year earlier Mr. Jobs had lured Mr. Sculley to Apple to be its chief executive. A former Pepsi-Cola chief executive, Mr. Sculley helped Mr. Jobs introduce a number of new computer models, including an advanced version of the Apple II and later the Lisa and Macintosh desktop computers. Through them Mr. Jobs popularized the graphical user interface, which, based on a mouse pointing device, would become the standard way to control computers.

But when the Lisa failed commercially and early Macintosh sales proved disappointing, the two men became estranged and a power struggle ensued. Mr. Jobs left Apple in 1985.

That September he announced a new venture, NeXT Inc. The aim was to build a workstation computer for the higher-education market. Although NeXT never became a significant computer industry player, it had a huge impact: a young programmer, Tim Berners-Lee, used a NeXT machine to develop the first version of the World Wide Web in 1990.

In 1986, Mr. Jobs spent much of his fortune—$10 million—on acquiring Pixar, a struggling graphics supercomputing company owned by the filmmaker George Lucas.

There was little market at the time for computer-animated movies. But that changed in 1995, when the company, with Walt Disney Pictures, released "Toy Story." That film's box-office receipts ultimately reached $362 million, and when Pixar went public in a record-breaking offering, Mr. Jobs emerged a billionaire. In 2006, the Walt Disney Company agreed to purchase Pixar for $7.4 billion. The sale made Mr. Jobs Disney's largest single shareholder, with about 7 percent of the company's stock.

His wife and his sister, the novelist Mona Simpson, survive him, as do his two daughters and a son with Ms. [Laurene] Powell, another daughter from a relationship with Chrisann Brennan, and another sister.

In 1996, after unsuccessful efforts to develop next-generation operating systems, Apple, with Gilbert Amelio now in command, acquired NeXT for $430 million. The next year, Mr. Jobs returned to Apple as an adviser. He became chief executive again in 2000.

Once in control of Apple again, Mr. Jobs set out to reshape the consumer electronics industry. He pushed the company into the digital music business, introducing iTunes and then the iPod MP3 player. The music arm grew rapidly, reaching almost 50 percent of the company's revenue by June 2008.

In 2005, Mr. Jobs announced that he would end Apple's business relationship with I.B.M. and Motorola and build Macintosh computers based on Intel microprocessors.

Apple began selling the iPhone in June 2007. It sold 11.6 million of the handsets in 2008. By the end of 2010, the company had sold almost 90 million units.

As the gravity of his illness became known, he was increasingly hailed for his genius. If he had a motto, it may have come from "The Whole Earth Catalog," a 1960s counterculture publication that he said had deeply influenced him as a young man. The book, he said in his commencement address at Stanford in 2005, ends with the admonition "Stay Hungry. Stay Foolish."

"I have always wished that for myself," he said.

Steve Lohr contributed reporting.

He was Malcolm Little, alias Big Red, a marijuana-smoking, cocaine - sniffing, zoot - suited, hip - talking hoodlum when he went to prison in 1946.

When he went free seven years later he was Malcolm X, an ascetic, a Black Muslim, a highly articulate man who hated the white world—a world he never made, but by whose standards he said he had lived.

Yesterday the Black Nationalist leader, who broke away last year from the Black Muslims of Elijah Muhammad, was shot dead as he prepared to speak at a rally in Harlem.

"Christianity took me to prison and Islam brought me out," Malcolm X used to say. He had no apologies for his criminal record, he said, "because it was all done when I was part of the white man's Christian world."

He was born in Omaha, on May 19, 1925, the son of the Rev. Earl Little, a 6-foot, 4-inch man who preached the back - to - Africa movement of Marcus Garvey, a Jamaican Negro who died in 1940.

His mother was a West Indian whose father was white. From this "white devil" grandfather Malcolm X got his reddish-brown complexion and reddish-brown hair.

Told of Hate

"I hate every drop of that white rapist's blood that is in me," Malcolm once wrote.

The Little family, including 11 children, moved to Lansing, Mich. Malcolm's earliest vivid

merly Elijah Poole. The core o his teaching was the superiorit of the black man, who was th first man on earth; the white came later, a "devil" race.

Malcolm began to correspon with Elijah Muhammad, an when he left prison he was Black Muslim. He no longe bore the surname of Little, be cause, as with nearly all Amer can Negro surnames, it be longed to the white slav owners.

He went to Chicago, when Elijah Muhammad had his hea quarters and as eagerly as had entered the "cool" wor he entered the ascetic work He gave up pork, tobacco, a cohol, marijuana, cocain gambling, dancing, movie sports and promiscuity.

Elijah Muhammad recogniz almost at once that he had Malcolm a man of intelligen and authority. He sent him speaking tours around the cou try, and eventually Malcol came to New York to ta over Mosque No. 7, then a sma voiceless and ineffectual grou

In ordinary conversation was quiet, pleasant, articula and even humorous. His acce was Midwestern. On the pub platform his quality was co fury; his eyes burned behi horn-rimmed glasses. In a fe years he built up Mosque Sev In 1958 he married a memb of the mosque, Sister Betty and they had four children.

He Was Once a Racist

By his own admission, he h once been a racist, an advoc

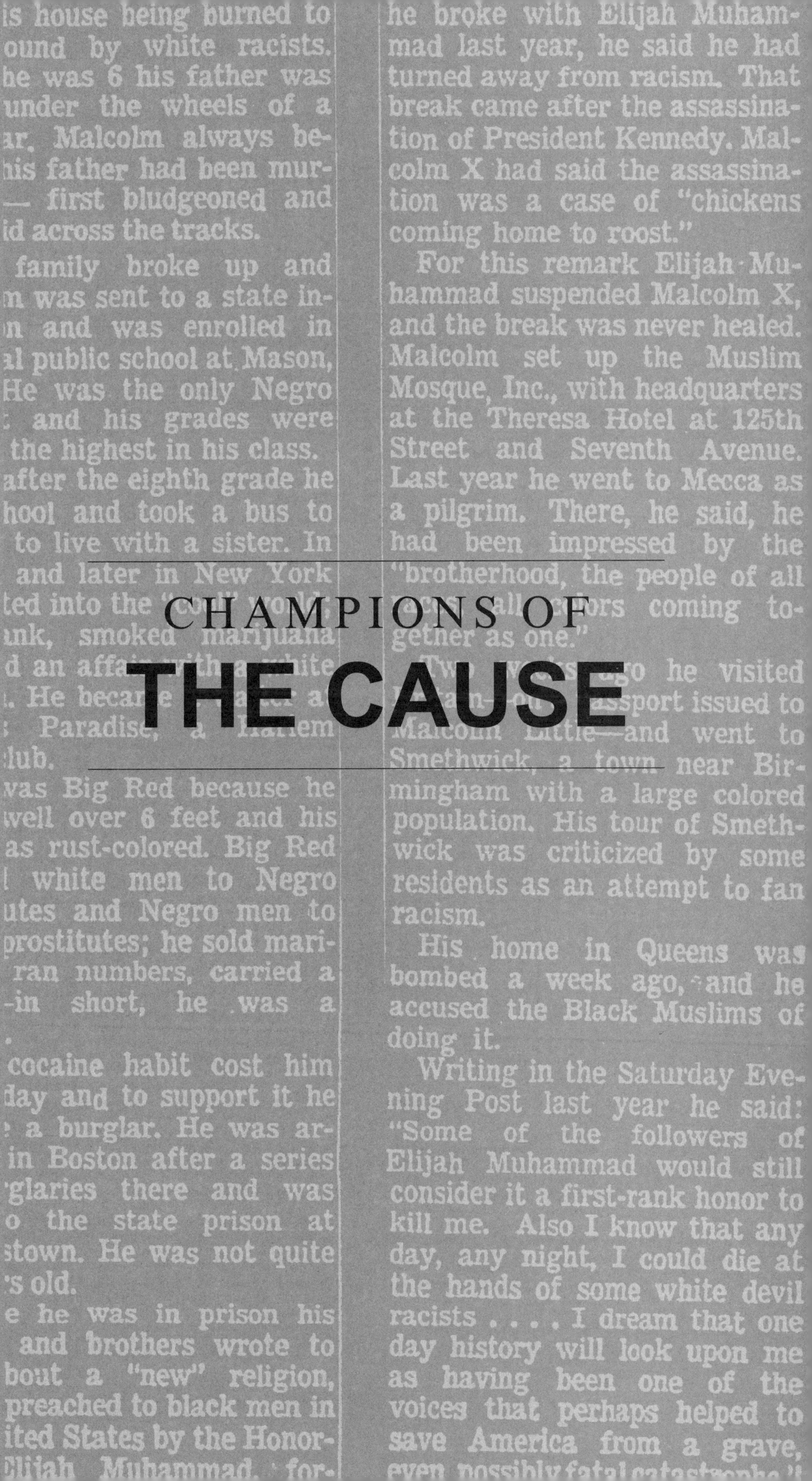

is house being burned to
ound by white racists.
he was 6 his father was
under the wheels of a
ar. Malcolm always be-
his father had been mur-
— first bludgeoned and
id across the tracks.

family broke up and
m was sent to a state in-
n and was enrolled in
al public school at Mason,
He was the only Negro
: and his grades were
the highest in his class.
after the eighth grade he
hool and took a bus to
to live with a sister. In
and later in New York
ted into the
ink, smoked marijuana
d an affair with a white
. He became a waiter a
: Paradise, a Harlem
lub.
was Big Red because he
well over 6 feet and his
as rust-colored. Big Red
l white men to Negro
utes and Negro men to
prostitutes; he sold mari-
ran numbers, carried a
-in short, he was a
.

cocaine habit cost him
day and to support it he
: a burglar. He was ar-
in Boston after a series
glaries there and was
o the state prison at
stown. He was not quite
's old.
e he was in prison his
and brothers wrote to
bout a "new" religion,
preached to black men in
ited States by the Honor-
Elijah Muhammad, for-

he broke with Elijah Muhammad last year, he said he had
turned away from racism. That
break came after the assassination of President Kennedy. Malcolm X had said the assassination was a case of "chickens
coming home to roost."

For this remark Elijah Muhammad suspended Malcolm X,
and the break was never healed.
Malcolm set up the Muslim
Mosque, Inc., with headquarters
at the Theresa Hotel at 125th
Street and Seventh Avenue.
Last year he went to Mecca as
a pilgrim. There, he said, he
had been impressed by the
"brotherhood, the people of all
colors coming to-
gether as one."

Two weeks ago he visited
with an old passport issued to
Malcolm Little—and went to
Smethwick, a town near Birmingham with a large colored
population. His tour of Smethwick was criticized by some
residents as an attempt to fan
racism.

His home in Queens was
bombed a week ago, and he
accused the Black Muslims of
doing it.

Writing in the Saturday Evening Post last year he said:
"Some of the followers of
Elijah Muhammad would still
consider it a first-rank honor to
kill me. Also I know that any
day, any night, I could die at
the hands of some white devil
racists . . . . I dream that one
day history will look upon me
as having been one of the
voices that perhaps helped to
save America from a grave
even possibly fatal catastrophe

CHAMPIONS OF
THE CAUSE

DRED SCOTT

ca. 1799–September 17, 1858

It is not well to let the great pass away without note and worthy honor. Dred Scott is dead in St. Louis. That illustrious personage carried his case to the Supreme Court, not doubting, we may believe, that the adverse decision he encountered will meet with reversal, and that he will be at once admitted to a better freedom and more equal citizenship. It is only now and then that we are called to regret the loss of the truly eminent.

Dred is of these. His name will live when those of Clay, and Calhoun, will be wholly forgotten. Posterity will make inquiry about the subject of that great leading case, decisive of human right, upon which the fate of the Union was in his day presumed to depend. So let the noted Negro have his obituary and monument with the rest.

Dred Scott died at a very advanced age. Longer ago than anybody can remember, he was born, in Virginia, on the property of the Blow family, which we may judge to be connected with the first families. Captain Peter Blow, while our hero was of tender years, moved away from the home of his race to Missouri, carrying Dred with him; and there succumbed to the common fate.

After accepting the claims of several reputable gentlemen to the ownership of his soul, the Negro, in 1834, came into the hands of Dr. Emerson, a surgeon in the Army, who carried him to Rock Island, in Illinois, and subsequently to Fort Snelling, in the Northwest Territory. At the latter point, in 1836, the Negro married Harriet, another chattel of the migratory surgeon, by whom he had two children, Eliza and Lizzie, who still live.

Dr. Emerson, in 1838, settled down in Missouri, where some dozen years ago he died, leaving the slaves in trust to Mr. John F. A. Sandford, the executor of his will, and the defendant in the famous suit. It is ten years ago since Dred brought suit for his freedom, and that of his wife and family, in the Circuit Court of St. Louis, on the ground of their owner having voluntarily taken them to soil declared free by the ordinance of 1787 and then to soil acquired by treaty with Louisiana, north of 36° 30', and therefore free by the terms of the Missouri Compromise.

His claim was held valid by the local Court, but upon appeal it was denied by the Supreme Court of the State, which sent the case back to the lower tribunal. It passed thence into the Circuit and the Supreme Courts of the United States, where, at the December term of 1856, it was finally decided against Dred and his pretensions.

The majority of the Court were of opinion that "A negro held in Slavery in one State, under the laws thereof, and taken by his master, for a temporary residence, into a State where Slavery is prohibited by law, and thence into a Territory acquired by treaty, where Slavery is prohibited by act of Congress, and afterwards returning with his master into the same Slave State, and resuming his residence there, is not such a citizen of that State as may sue there in the Circuit Court of the United States, if by the law of that State a negro under such circumstances is a Slave."

This decision extinguished the hopes of the hapless Dred. The freedom he sighed for was not, however, so remote as he supposed. Shortly after the judgment, his owner proceeded, to consummate the emancipation of the Negro and his family. The owner was the Hon. Calvin C. Chaffee of Massachusetts. But, as under the laws of Missouri the act of emancipation can only be performed by a citizen of that State, the four items of personal property were made over to Mr. Taylor Blow, a son of Capt. Peter Blow, who, on the 26th of May, 1857, gave liberty to the happy captives.

The transaction was probably as gratifying as it was becoming to Mr. Blow, who a half century before had been a playmate of the colored hero. Charitable hands have smoothed the later path of Dred and his Harriet, so that a freedom so tardily come by has not been attended by its usual abuse and suffering.

Few men who have achieved greatness have won it so effectually as this black champion. He belongs to a class whose names are accidentally but ineffably associated with memorable facts in history. The "Dred Scott Decision" is to be classed with the "Lex Julia" and the "Code Napoleon," to which chance rather than merit has attached names, which they shall perpetuate indefinitely. It shall always be remembered that in the person of the old Negro who died yesterday the highest tribunal of America decided that an African was not a man, and could not therefore be a citizen of the United States.

JOHN BROWN

May 9, 1800–December 2, 1859

John Brown has paid the penalty of his crime. He was executed yesterday, according to appointment, with due solemnity and under an imposing display of the military strength of the State of Virginia.

The event created a good deal of feeling throughout the country. Our columns contain notices of meetings and other indications of sympathy, held in various sections of the Northern States. In this City, two churches were opened for public service. No other public demonstrations took place here, and even at these churches the attendance was not large.

In other places, only a small minority of the people took part in these public proclamations of sympathy. It is but just to add, however, that hundreds and thousands of persons, in this City and throughout the North, were deeply moved by personal sympathy for Brown, but were still too thoroughly convinced of the legal justice of his execution to make any outward show of their commiseration.

There is not any general sympathy in the North with Brown's invasion of Virginia or with the object which took him there. But there is a wide and profound conviction in the public mind that he was personally honest and sincere, that he deemed his motives honorable and righteous, and that he believed himself to be doing a religious duty.

We do not believe that one-tenth of the people of the Northern States would deny that he merited the penalty which has overtaken his offense. But we have just as little doubt that most of them pity his fate and respect his memory, as that of a brave, conscientious and misguided man.

Now that the curtain has fallen upon this tragedy, we trust the public feeling will resume a healthier tone, especially in the Southern States, where it has risen to a perilous heat. We take it for granted that the authorities of Virginia will not deem it necessary to continue their formidable display of military force, or further agitate the public mind by apprehensions of invasion.

We can make just allowance for the circumstances which have surrounded them, and for the distrust and dread they have evinced. But the mass of the people in the North cannot understand and do not appreciate either. Knowing how narrow and feeble is the sympathy felt at the North for such movements as that of Brown, our people deem it weak and puerile for the South to clothe herself in military array against imaginary dangers. At this moment, throughout the North, the conviction is well-nigh universal that the Virginians have been needlessly panic-stricken, or that they have been victimized by political demagogues, who have sought to promote their own selfish ends by playing upon the fears and resentments of the mass of the people.

So far as this outbreak of violent sentiment has been the work of partisans, it is useless to protest against it. Some of these men aim at disunion, and they avail themselves of every opportunity to stimulate the distrust, resentment and hatred of the two sections towards each other. Others among them aim only at the ascendancy of their own sectional party, and they use these incidents merely to unite the South and coerce the North into conformity to their desires.

As these men are thoroughly and recklessly selfish in their aims, no considerations of the public good would check their insane endeavors. It is their determination to goad the South into the conviction that the whole North is bent on waging war upon Slavery in the Southern States, and that John Brown's troop was only the advanced guard of the general army. They represent the Northern people as all Abolitionists, all fanatics, all reckless of Southern rights and interests.

Whatever ministers to this belief is lavishly used for that purpose; whatever corrects it is ignored or discredited. The diatribes of our Abolition orators and journalists are greedily copied in Southern prints and put forward as illustrations of Northern sentiment, while the conservative declarations which emanate from our pulpits, our rostrums and our presses are unnoticed. We cannot wonder that the people of the South come to regard every Northern man as their enemy.

The remedy, we believe, lies with the conservatives of the South. They must give signs to the North that reason and patriotic feeling have not wholly fled from the Southern States, and that the Union is worth preserving. If the whole South desires disunion, she can probably have it. If she expects her own condition to be bettered by it, a brief experiment will dispel that delusion.

BRIGHAM YOUNG

June 1, 1801–August 29, 1877

SALT LAKE CITY—Brigham Young died at 4 o'clock this afternoon at the age of 76.

He was born at Whittingham, Windham County, Vt., on the 1st of June, 1801. His father, John Young, was a farmer in different circumstances, with a family of five sons and six daughters, Brigham being the fourth son and ninth child. At the age of 16 John Young joined the Revolutionary Army, and served in three campaigns under Gen. Washington.

In 1785 he married Nabby, a daughter of Phineas and Susannah Howe, the mother of Brigham, and settled down as a farmer in Hopkinton, Middlesex County, Mass.

In the earlier years of his life, Brigham Young worked with his father on the farm in Sherburn, Chenango County, N.Y., whither his father had removed in 1804. Brigham afterward learned the trade of painter and glazier, an occupation which he followed till he was 31 years of age, when the whole current of his life was changed in consequence of his conversion to Mormonism.

In 1833 he was converted by Samuel H., a brother of Joseph Smith. At Kirtland, Ohio, where he joined the Saints, he became intimate with Joseph Smith, was ordained an Elder, and began to preach, his shrewdness, knowledge of character, and strength of

will quickly acquiring for him some measure of that influence and power in the Church which afterward became so absolutely overwhelming.

On the 14th of February, 1835, Brigham was ordained one of the Twelve Apostles of the Church, of whom he became President in the following year, on the apostasy of Thomas B. Marsh. The persecution of the Mormons soon came, and Joe Smith and Brigham Young fled for their lives.

After many hairbreadth escapes and trials they succeeded in rallying together the brethren and sisters who had not apostatized, and they founded a new Mormon colony in Missouri, Brigham securing a still greater share of influence and power. Again persecution came upon the Saints, and they returned to Illinois. In 1840 Brigham was sent to England as a missionary. He commenced preaching in Liverpool immediately, issued an edition of the Book of Mormon, and started a periodical called the Millennial Star.

In 1844 came the riot at Nauvoo, the shooting of Smith, the scattering of the Twelve Apostles, and the assumption of the Mormon Presidency by Sidney Rigdon. Brigham was in Boston at the time; but he hurried off to Nauvoo immediately, knowing well that his opportunity had arrived. Four persons were ambitious of the Mormon Presidency, though, according to Mormon law, it belonged of right to Rigdon. Brigham, however, secured this position for himself by a bold coup d'état.

He summoned the people together, denounced the

other aspirants and their adherents as children of the devil—especially Rigdon—and even went so far as to curse Rigdon and hand him over "to the buffetings of Satan for a thousand years." It silenced all his enemies. In his new office, he set to work to complete the great temple; he built a mansion house, and in increasing the prosperity of Nauvoo, increased his own popularity and power.

Even before the completion of the temple, in 1845, Brigham foresaw the necessity of a migration further westward. In 1846, thousands of the Saints left their homes—all of them poor and many of them destitute—to seek an indefinite home somewhere in the Rocky Mountains.

They crossed the Mississippi on the ice in February, with about as vague an idea of the locality of their ultimate destination as the Israelites had of the land of Canaan, except that they were assured by Brigham that it was to be a land flowing with milk and honey. In the following Winter the Mormons established themselves at Kanesville, now Council Bluffs, in Iowa.

In the Spring of 1847 an expedition, consisting of Brigham and 143 men, left Kanesville. On the 24th of July they reached Salt Lake. Brigham determined to move the entire body of the Church there, a gigantic undertaking.

To carry this intention into effect he felt that he must have more power. That could only be obtained by his assumption of the attributes of Smith, as the Prophet, Seer, and Revelator of the Mormon people. This he did on the 24th of December, 1847, during the delivery of one of the most remarkable and impassioned sermons he ever preached. Women screamed, and fainted, the male Saints wept, and all exclaimed, "The mantle of Joseph has fallen upon Brigham!" When quiet was restored Brigham Young was elected "President of the Church of Jesus Christ of Latter Day Saints in all the World."

In 1848, Brigham moved his people to Salt Lake. His restless energy kept down any more marked demonstrations of discontent, and when they at last reached Salt Lake he kept them so hard at work that they had little time to complain.

The termination of the Mexican war gave Brigham Young the opportunity of securing for his people the protection and recognition of the United States Government, and of adding to the glory, importance, and stability of his own position. A Mormon convention was held on the 15th of March, 1849, the Constitution of the proposed State of Deseret was drawn up, and delegates were sent to Washington to ask that Deseret might be admitted into the Union.

The question was brought up in Congress, and eventuated on the 9th of September, 1850, in the grant of a Territorial Government under the name of Utah. Brigham Young was appointed by President Fillmore to be the first Governor of the new Territory for a term of four years. The Tabernacle was built, and the Mormons began to see prosperity in the future.

Socially, the Mormons were no better off than a horde of peasants, bound to obey the bidding of the suzerain. This is directly shown in the action of the first Utah Territorial Legislature. After passing a code of laws for the government of the Territory, and sending innumerable memorials to Congress, mostly asking for appropriations of public moneys, that body divided up the canons, ferries, pasture lands, woodlands, water privileges, and all the most valuable parts of the State domain among the most prominent of the saints, Brigham Young always coming in for the lion's share.

By tricks and stratagems, Brigham Young succeeded in ridding the Mormon Territory of all Federal authorities, till at last Utah was virtually in a state of rebellion against the Federal Government. The Mormon war of 1857 was the result. In the Summer of 1857, President Buchanan dispatched 3,000 troops to Utah. Brigham Young retaliated by issuing a proclamation which was substantially a declaration of war against the United States, and which placed the Territory of Utah under martial law; at the same time every man who could bear arms was drilled as a soldier.

The "Army of Utah" reached the scene of its operations late in the Fall, and went into encampment. During the Winter negotiations were brought about by Col. [Thomas] Kane, a quasi-Mormon, between Brigham and the Government, which ended in Gov. [Alfred] Cumming visiting Salt Lake City, being received by Brigham with a hypocritical show, and having the Territorial records and papers placed in his possession. In the meantime Federal soldiers were in the city, and Brigham, in the face of such a humiliation, promulgated an order, purporting to come direct from the Almighty, commanding the people to leave their homes and migrate to the South.

They halted at Provo, 50 miles from Salt Lake City. Six days later Mr. Buchanan sent Commissioners to Utah with a proclamation of pardon. They arrived at Salt Lake City on the 7th of June, 1858, and a conference was held, resulting in Brigham agreeing to receive peaceably the civil officers of the Government. On the 5th of July the Mormons were ordered to return to their homes, and the Mormon war was brought to a close without any bloody encounter on the battlefield.

In 1862 Stephen S. Harding, of Indiana, was appointed Governor of Utah by Mr. Lincoln, and in his first message to the Territorial Legislature he gave great offense to Brigham Young and the Mormons by his denunciations of polygamy. The message was suppressed by the Legislature by the order of Brigham, but was afterward printed and published by order of the United States Senate. Brigham and the Mormons were furious.

Meetings were held, the most inflammatory speeches were made by Brigham and others, and an insolent message was dispatched to Mr. Lincoln, requesting him to recall the Governor and other Federal officers.

Mr. Lincoln's hands were fully occupied at the time, and Brigham achieved a decided victory, making him more powerful than ever. He became still more arbitrary and still more reckless in his greed for wealth, and unscrupulous as to his actions and relations. He developed to the last degree the great idea of Mormonism—that "the iniquity of the preacher makes no difference in the principle; that the vices of the administrator cannot affect the acceptability of the ordinance if he only possesses the priesthood."

During the war of the rebellion Brigham and his coadjutors remained almost entirely quiescent, though having a leaning toward secession. Though not a slave Territory, Utah was committed to the purchasing and holding of slaves, by an act passed by the Territorial Legislature on Jan. 31, 1852.

But during the last 10 years, Brigham has principally occupied himself in carrying out as far as possible his favorite idea that Utah contained the elements of everything needed by civilized man, and that by the establishment of manufactories and the production of silk and cotton, both of which have been started, the Mormon Territory might be independent of the world. His great aim was to prevent the Saints from trading with the Gentiles.

The last years of Brigham Young's life were sorely tried by the action directed by the United States Courts against polygamy.

Brigham Young's family relations are matters of common notoriety. He married early in life in his own State of Vermont, but was soon left a widower with two daughters, both of whom subsequently embraced the Mormon faith and contracted polygamic marriages. Shortly after his wife's death he married Mary Ann Angell, who was, as he claimed in his answer to the petition for divorce and alimony of his 19th wife—Ann Eliza—his only lawful wife. She bore Brigham five children.

Lucy Decker Soely was his first wife in "plurality," and the first child, Brigham Heber, was the first-born in Mormon polygamy. Amelia Folsom was the favorite wife of his old age. She occupied till his death a queenly position among the Saints. In all, Brigham Young is credited with having been married or sealed to 40 wives, the majority of whom lived, with their children, a life of drudgery, impecuniosity, and misery.

In appearance, Brigham Young resembled much a New England farmer, as he originally was. He was of rather large figure, broad-shouldered and stooping slightly; hair light in color, somewhat narrow forehead, gray eyes (the lid of one drooping), fleshy cheeks, imperfect teeth, rather sharp-pointed nose, peaked chin, and generally somewhat irregular features.

Illiterate, yet not without talent; fluent in speech, and still without the first elements of the genius of an orator, he held his listeners easily, combining in his preaching a forcible pretension to heavenly revelation with a thorough knowledge of the willing subserviency of one part of his audience and the fervid superstition of the remainder.

WILLIAM LLOYD GARRISON

December 12, 1805–May 24, 1879

William Lloyd Garrison expired at 11 o'clock last night, at the Westmoreland Apartment-house in New York, where he has been lying in a critical condition for the last week.

His physician, Dr. Leonard Weber, defined Mr. Garrison's illness as nervous prostration consequent upon paralysis of the bladder and kidney trouble of long standing. Only his four sons and his daughter were present around his death-bed.

The active public life of William Lloyd Garrison began in 1828, when he established the Journal of the Times in Bennington, Vt., in which he announced his intention to labor, so long as he had strength, for the gradual emancipation of every slave in the Republic, and it may be said to have closed with the last number of the Liberator, on the 1st of January, 1866.

When he began his career as an advocate of emancipation the Missouri Compromise was eight years old. The second Adams was in the third year of his term, and the questions which the statesmen of the day believed to be of the highest and most lasting importance were the currency, banks, the tariff, internal improvements.

In this arid political wilderness a voice was raised, crying out that liberty, not low tariffs or high, the rights of man and not the issue of paper money, were the things to which the country must turn its mind if it would live and not die.

Mr. Garrison was born in the little coast town of Newburyport, Mass., on the 12th of December, 1805 His father abandoned his wife and the children to lead a life of dissipation, giving good cause for Mr. Garrison's life-long hatred of intemperance. After an abortive effort to learn the shoe-maker's trade at Lynn, where his mother had removed, young Garrison was happily apprenticed in 1818—at the age of 13—to the printer of the Newburyport Herald.

He remained with his employer for eight years, gradually learning the art of composition, and offering contributions to the local journals. Garrison early formed the habit of polemic and proselyting writing. He had little conception of a newspaper, but a keen sense of the value of an organ of personal expression.

His first independent effort was made at 22, as the proprietor and editor of the Newburyport Free Press. It was a dead failure within a year. He journeyed to Boston, where, after a severe struggle with poverty, he made his way to be editor of the National Philanthropist, in whose columns he first set his hand publicly in favor of total abstinence. He soon quitted this field, however, to take part with a friend, in 1828, in editing the Journal of the Times.

The first phase of work for the oppressed negroes which enlisted Mr. Garrison's support was the scheme of the Colonization Society, the object of which was to found a black Republic on the shore of Africa to which negroes could be removed. Its advocates were numerous and eloquent in the South, and in the North they painted the evils and wrongs of slavery in vivid colors.

On the 4th of July, 1828, he delivered the annual address before the society in Boston. It was almost the last time that for at least 30 years he was to receive general approbation in his own country. Shortly after, he met Benjamin Lundy, an amiable, but withal courageous Quaker, who had constituted himself a preacher of liberty. One of his instrumentalities was a journal called the Genius of Universal Emancipation.

In 1828 this wandering publication was settled in Baltimore, and from that city Mr. Lundy journeyed on foot all the way to Vermont to invite Mr. Garrison to come and aid in its management. Mr. Garrison went, but, as he said, "I wasn't much help to him, for he had been all for gradual emancipation, and as soon as I began to look into the matter I became convinced that immediate abolition was the doctrine to be preached, and I scattered his subscribers like pigeons."

Garrison was not long in discovering that it was far from a dove-like community into which he had come. He had been in Baltimore but a few months when, learning that a vessel was about to sail for New Orleans with a cargo of slaves, he denounced the act as one of "domestic piracy."

He was promptly indicted for libel, tried, convicted (doubtless fairly enough as Maryland laws then were),

and sentenced to a fine of $1,000 and imprisonment until it was paid. The incident created a good deal of excitement in the North, and John G. Whittier, then an admirer of Henry Clay, wrote to that gentleman urging him to pay the fine.

It is said that Mr. Clay was about to do so when he was anticipated by Mr. Arthur Tappan, of this City, who released Mr. Garrison after seven weeks' imprisonment. He left his cell devoted heart and soul to the cause of "immediate emancipation" as "the right of the slave and the duty of the master."

He wrote from prison an open letter to the Judge who had sentenced him. "So long as a good Providence gives me strength and intellect," he said, "I will not cease to declare that the existence of slavery in this country is a foul reproach to the American name; nor will I hesitate to proclaim the guilt of kidnappers, slavery abettors, or slave-owners, wherever they may reside or however high they may be exalted.

"I expect and I am willing to be persecuted, imprisoned, and bound for advocating the rights of my colored countrymen; and I should deserve to be a slave myself if I shrank from that danger."

He first went to Washington, intending to establish a paper there, but he made up his mind that the field where his labor was most needed was in the North. On the 1st of January, 1831, he published the first number of the Liberator. His only associate was Mr. Isaac Knapp, like himself, a printer. Too poor to hire an office, they got the friendly foreman of the Christian Examiner to give them the use of his type in payment for their labor, and then, after their day's task was over, they labored far into each night on the Liberator.

"A greater revolution was to be effected in the free States—and particularly in New England—than [in] the South," Mr. Garrison said. "I found contempt more bitter, opposition more active, detraction more relentless, prejudice more stubborn, and apathy more frozen than among slaveholders themselves."

And he thus explained the temper with which he entered on his work: "I am aware that many object to the severity of my language; but is there not cause for severity? I will be as harsh as truth and as uncompromising as justice. On this subject I do not wish to think or speak, or write with moderation. I am in earnest. I will not equivocate, I will not excuse. I will not retreat a single inch. And I will be heard."

He soon received convincing evidence that he was heard. James Foster (colored), of Philadelphia, sent him $50 and the names of 25 subscribers. This was his first recognition. His next was quite different. The Vigilance Association of Columbia, S.C., offered "a reward of $1,500 for the apprehension and conviction of any white person detected in circulating in that State the newspaper called the Liberator."

The corporation of Georgetown, D.C., passed an ordinance against any free person of color taking it from the Post Office, the penalty being $20 fine or 30 days' imprisonment. The Legislature of Georgia passed an act offering a reward of $5,000 for the arrest, prosecution, and conviction of the editor or publisher of "a certain paper called the Liberator."

During 1831 Mr. Garrison made an effort to start a National Anti-Slavery Society, but at first his views as to immediate and unconditional emancipation were unacceptable. Later, on the 1st of January, 1832, he succeeded, with 11 others, in completing an organization, of which he was chosen President, a position he held almost continuously for 33 years.

The society plied every corner of the land with tracts and pamphlets. It sought expression in the newspapers. It established branches throughout the North. It held numerous meetings, and its members frequently delivered public addresses.

On Oct. 2, 1833, a meeting of the Anti-Slavery Society was broken up by a mob. Luckily for him, Mr. Garrison was not well known, and actually accompanied the men who were looking for him to give him a coat of tar and feathers.

Entering again on the work which he had laid out for himself, he attracted the attention of many of the leading men of the country. But his unqualified denunciation, his unflinching use of opprobrious epithets, his unsparing criticism of everybody and everything not in harmony with his view of right, frightened most of those to whom he appealed.

In 1834, Mr. Garrison married Helen Eliza Benson, of Brooklyn, Conn. She too was an ardent abolitionist. [She died in 1876.]

Gradually he yielded to the logic which demanded that a Union which existed in name only should cease to exist at all. He declared that the "most important question" for the Anti-slavery Party was "the duty of making the repeal of the union between the North and the South the grand rallying point until it be accomplished or slavery cease to pollute our soil."

In 1845, Massachusetts politics were stirred by the audacious scheme of the annexation of Texas, to furnish new territory for slavery. The Abolitionists joined in the opposition, but with no thought of limiting their efforts to ordinary political measures. An Anti-annexation Convention was held in Faneuil Hall in January, 1845.

Mr. Garrison urged that it should be declared that "if our protest and remonstrance shall be disregarded, and Texas be annexed, then shall the committee of the convention call another at the same place; that then and there Massachusetts shall declare the Union of these States dissolved, and invite all the States that may be disposed to reunite with her as a Republic based truly upon the grand principles of the Declaration of Independence."

The Abolitionists' proposals were voted down, though there was considerable sentiment in favor.

Mr. Garrison, who also spoke in favor of women's suffrage, recognized the hand of God in the course of events which made the Proclamation of Emancipation a war measure. On the 18th of December, 1865, the 13th Amendment to the Constitution was proclaimed. And on the 1st of January following, Mr. Garrison issued the last number of the Liberator.

SOJOURNER TRUTH

ca. 1797–November 26, 1883

Sojourner Truth, the well-known colored lecturer, died at Battle Creek, Mich., yesterday. For almost three-quarters of a century she delivered lectures from the East to the West upon temperance, politics, and the woman's rights question.

She was born a slave, in the State of New York, and spent the early part of her life—until 1817, when slavery was abolished in this State—in hard work in the fields of her many masters. Her parents were brought from the coast of Guinea, and sold as slaves on arriving in the United States.

Her real name—or that which had been given to her by her first master—was Isabella Hardenburg, but, becoming dissatisfied with it, it is said that she went out into a wilderness and prayed to the Lord to give her an appropriate name. After praying for some time she heard, she said, the name "Sojourner" whispered to her, as she was to travel "up and down," and afterward "Truth" was added to it to signify that she should preach nothing but truth to all men.

Sojourner had a tall, masculine-looking figure—she was almost 6 feet high—and talked in a deep, guttural, powerful voice that made many people who heard her think that she was a man, and was imposing upon them by masquerading as a woman. Upon one occasion, while she was preaching to an audience, doubts as to her sex were freely expressed, and she satisfied them that she was a woman. She could neither read nor write, but on her lecturing tours took with her her grandson, who attended to her business affairs.

Sojourner knew many prominent men—her favorite statesman being Abraham Lincoln—and her narratives and descriptions of those whom she had known showed that she had judged their characters exceedingly well. During her later life, or for the past 10 years, her avowed object in traveling around was to obtain names to a petition which she intended presenting to the Government, asking that a portion of the public lands in the West be set apart for the establishment of a negro colony, where she proposed that the negro youth should be educated.

Sojourner undoubtedly did a great deal of good work during her lifetime, for she was instrumental in reclaiming hundreds of men and women from a bad life and by her own life set a splendid example to the colored population.

FREDERICK DOUGLASS

ca. February 1818–February 20, 1895

WASHINGTON—Frederick Douglass dropped dead in the hallway of his residence on Anacostia Heights this evening at 7 o'clock. He had been in the highest spirits, and apparently in the best of health, despite his 78 years, when death overtook him.

This morning he was driven to Washington, accompanied by his wife. She left him at the Congressional Library, and he continued to Metzerott Hall, where he attended the sessions of the Women's Council in the forenoon and the afternoon, returning to Cedar Hill, his residence, between 5 and 6 o'clock. After dining, he had a chat in the hallway with his wife about the doings of the council. He grew very enthusiastic in his explanation of one of the events of the day, when he fell upon his knees, with hands clasped.

Mrs. Douglass, thinking this was part of his description, was not alarmed, but as she looked he sank lower and lower, and finally lay stretched upon the floor, breathing his last. Realizing that he was ill, she raised his head, and then understood that he was dying. She rushed to the front door with cries for help. Some men who were nearby quickly responded, and attempted to reassure the dying man. One of them called Dr. J. Stewart Harrison, and while he was injecting a restorative into the patient's arm, Mr. Douglass passed away, seemingly without pain.

Mr. Douglass had lived for some time at Cedar Hill with his wife. He had two sons and a daughter, the children of his first wife, living here.

The last hours of his life were given in attention to one of the principles to which he has devoted his energies since his escape from slavery. This morning he drove into Washington from his residence, about a mile out from Anacostia, a suburb just across the eastern branch of the Potomac, and at 10 o'clock appeared at Metzerott Hall, where the Women's National Council is holding its triennial. Mr. Douglass was a member of the National Women's Suffrage Association, and had always attended its conventions.

When the meeting had been called to order by Mrs. May Wright Sewall, the President of the Council, she appointed Miss Susan B. Anthony and the Rev. Anna H. Shaw to escort him to the platform.

Miss Anthony and Mr. Douglass formed an intimate friendship when both resided in Rochester, N.Y., and that friendship had continued for many decades.

Frederick Douglass has been often spoken of as the foremost man of the African race in America. Though born and reared in slavery, he managed, through his own perseverance and energy, to win for himself a place that made him beloved by all members of his own race in America and won for himself the esteem and reverence of all fair-minded persons, both in this country and in Europe.

He became well known, early in his career, as an orator upon subjects relating to slavery. He had become known before the Civil War also as a journalist. So highly were his opinions valued that he was often consulted by President Lincoln, after the war began, upon questions relating to the colored race. He held important offices almost constantly from 1871 until 1891.

Mr. Douglass, perhaps more than any other man of his race, was instrumental in advancing the work of banishing the color line.

The exact date of his birth is unknown. It was about the year 1817. His mother was a negro slave and his father was a white man. Mr. Douglass's birthplace was on the Eastern Shore of Maryland. He was reared as a slave on the plantation of Col. Edward Lloyd. He was sent, when 10 years old, to one of Col. Lloyd's relatives in Baltimore. Here he was employed in a shipyard.

Mr. Douglass, according to his own story, suffered deeply while under the bonds of slavery. His superior intelligence rendered him keenly sensitive to his condition. He learned his letters, it is said, from the carpenters' marks on planks and timbers in the shipyard. He used to listen while his mistress read the Bible, and he asked her to teach him to read it for himself.

It was while here that he heard of the abolitionists, and began to formulate plans for escaping to the North. He made his escape from slavery Sept. 3, 1838, and came to New York. Thence he went to New Bedford, where he married. He supported himself for several years by day labor on the wharves and in the workshops.

He made a speech in 1841 at an anti-slavery convention, held at Nantucket, that made a favorable impression, and he became the agent of the Massachusetts Anti-Slavery Society. He then traveled four years through New England, lecturing against slavery.

He went to England in 1845, where his lectures in behalf of the slave won a great deal of attention. Mr. Douglass often met with many unpleasant experiences while traveling about, owing to the prejudice against his race. On one occasion, when the passengers on a boat would not allow him to enter the cabin, his friend Wendell Phillips refused to leave him, and the two men spent the night together on deck.

William Lloyd Garrison had also become interested in young Mr. Douglass, and before Mr. Douglass went to England had done all he could to assist him in gaining an education.

On returning from England Mr. Douglass founded Frederick Douglass's Paper, a weekly journal, at Rochester. The title was changed to The North Star. He continued its publication for several years.

Mr. Douglass and John Brown were friends, and had the same objects in view. Mr. Douglass, however, did not approve of Brown's plan for attacking Harper's Ferry, and the men parted two weeks before the attack.

Mr. Douglass was in Philadelphia the night the Harper's Ferry episode occurred. It became plain to him immediately afterward that he could scarcely hope to escape being implicated in the trouble, and at the earnest solicitation of his friends he made his way to Canada. He went to Quebec, and thence to England, where he remained six or eight months. He afterward returned to Rochester, and again took charge of his paper.

Mr. Douglass urged upon President Lincoln, when the Civil War began, the employment of colored troops and the proclamation of emancipation. Permission for organizing such troops was granted in 1863, and Mr. Douglass became active in enlisting men to fill the colored regiments, notably the 54th and the 55th Massachusetts.

Mr. Douglass returned to the lecture field after slavery had been abolished. He attracted great crowds wherever he went. His appearance on the platform was imposing. His height was over 6 feet and his weight was 200 pounds. His complexion was swarthy rather than black. His head was covered with a great shock of white hair. A large head, low forehead, high cheekbones, and large mouth, with gleaming white teeth, were some of the noticeable characteristics of his appearance. As a speaker he was characterized by his earnestness. He made but few gestures and used simple language.

He received the appointment in 1871 as Assistant Secretary to the commission to San Domingo, and on his return from that mission President [Ulysses S.] Grant appointed him one of the Territorial Council of the District of Columbia. He was elected Presidential Elector at Large for the State of New York in 1872.

Mr. Douglass was appointed United States Marshal for the District of Columbia in 1876, and retained that office till 1881, when he became Recorder of Deeds in the District of Columbia.

President Harrison made Mr. Douglass Minister to Haiti in 1889. He resigned this office in August, 1891. Mr. Douglass's administration in Haiti was not entirely satisfactory, and unfavorable reports of the affairs of his office had reached Washington. The Haitians did not take kindly to Mr. Douglass, because of his race.

Mr. Douglass wrote several books that have met with considerable sale. Among them are "Narrative of My Experience in Slavery," 1844; "My Bondage and My Freedom," 1855; and "Life and Times of Frederick Douglass," 1881.

Of recent years he has been prominent in all movements having in view the social and political advancement of women.

Frederick Douglass was married twice, his second wife being Miss Pitts, a white woman from New York State. For a time this lost him some case among the people of his own race, but his personal standing and overpowering intellectuality quickly dissipated the sentiment that some sought to disseminate to his discredit.

There is no end of stories about Mr. Douglass. One of his most marked characteristics was his intense dislike of being spoken of as Fred Douglass. It is told of him that one day, when in the East Room of the White House, on overhearing a woman say, "There's Fred Douglass," he turned to her, bowed, and said, "Frederick Douglass, if you please."

In addressing a colored school, March 24, 1893, at Easton, Md., Mr. Douglass said:

"I once knew a little colored boy whose mother and father died when he was but six years old. He was a slave and had no one to care for him. He slept on a dirt floor in a hovel, and in cold weather would crawl into a mealbag head foremost and leave his feet in the ashes to keep them warm. Often he would roast an ear of corn and eat it to satisfy his hunger, and many times has he crawled under the barn or stable and secured eggs, which he would roast in the fire and eat.

"That boy did not wear pantaloons, as you do, but a tow linen shirt. Schools were unknown to him, and he learned to spell from an old Webster's spelling book and to read and write from posters on cellar and barn doors, while boys and men would help him. He would then preach and speak, and soon became well known. He became Presidential Elector, United States Marshal, United States Recorder, United States diplomat, and accumulated some wealth. He wore broadcloth and didn't have to divide crumbs with the dogs under the table. That boy was Frederick Douglass.

"What was possible for me is possible for you. Don't think because you are colored you can't accomplish anything."

SUSAN B. ANTHONY

February 20, 1820–March 13, 1906

ROCHESTER—Miss Susan B. Anthony died at 12:40 o'clock this morning. The end came peacefully. Miss Anthony had been unconscious for more than 24 hours. Only her wonderful constitution kept her alive.

Dr. M. S. Ricker, her physician, said Miss Anthony died of heart disease and pneumonia.

Miss Anthony was taken ill while on her way home from the National Suffrage Convention in Baltimore. She stopped in New York, where a banquet was to be given Feb. 20 in honor of her 86th birthday, but she had an attack of neuralgia and hastened home.

On Wednesday she said to her sister: "Write to Anna Shaw immediately, and tell her I desire that every cent I leave when I pass out of this life shall be given to the fund which Miss Thomas and Miss

trousers gathered at the ankles. So great an outcry arose against the innovation that she was forced to abandon it.

Miss Anthony was born at South Adams, Mass., on Feb. 15, 1820. Daniel Anthony, her father, a liberal Quaker, was a cotton manufacturer. Susan Anthony was instructed at home and then sent to finish her education at a Friends' boarding school in Philadelphia. At 17 she received a dollar a week with board by teaching in a private family. She continued to teach until 1852.

Miss Anthony had become impressed with the idea that women were suffering great wrongs, and when she abandoned teaching, she determined to enter the lecture field.

People of today can scarcely understand the strong prejudices Miss Anthony had to live down. In 1851 she called a temperance convention in Albany, admittance to a previous convention having been refused to her because it was not the custom to admit women. The Women's New York State Temperance Society was organized the following year. Through Miss Anthony's exertions and those of Mrs. Stanton, women soon came to be admitted to educational and other conventions, with the right to speak, vote, and act upon committees.

Miss Anthony's active participation in the movement for woman suffrage started in the fifties. As early as 1854 she arranged conventions throughout the State and bombarded the Legislature with messages and appeals. She was active in obtaining the passage of the act of the New York Legislature in 1860 giving married women the possession of their earnings and the guardianship of their children. During the war she was devoted to the Women's Loyal League, which petitioned Congress in favor of the 13th amendment. She was also interested in the 14th amendment, seeking the omission of the word "male."

To test the application of the 14th and 15th amendments, she cast ballots in the State and Congressional election in Rochester in 1872. She was indicted and ordered to pay a fine, but the order was never enforced.

Miss Anthony succeeded Mrs. Stanton as President of the National Woman Suffrage Association in 1892. This office she held until February, 1899. For years she averaged 100 lectures a year. She engaged in eight different State campaigns for a Constitutional amendment enfranchising women, and hearings before committees of practically every Congress since 1869 were granted to her.

Garrett are raising for the cause. I have given my life and all I am to it, and now I want my last act to be to give it all I have, to the last cent."

Miss Shaw, a women's suffrage leader, said:

"On Sunday, about two hours before she became unconscious, I talked with Miss Anthony, and she said: 'To think I have had more than 60 years of hard struggle for a little liberty, and then to die without it seems so cruel.'"

Susan Brownell Anthony was a pioneer leader of the cause of woman suffrage, and worked tirelessly for what she considered the best interests of womankind. In recent years her age made it impossible for her to continue active participation in all the movements for the enfranchisement of women with which she had been connected, but she was at the time of her death the Honorary President of the National Woman Suffrage Association, the society she and Elizabeth Cady Stanton organized in 1869.

Miss Anthony possessed a firm but pleasing face, clear hazel eyes, and dark hair which she wore combed over the ears and bound in a coil at the back. She paid much attention to dress and advised those associated in the movement for woman suffrage to be punctilious in all matters pertaining to attire. For a time in the fifties she wore a bloomer costume, consisting of a short skirt and Turkish

FLORENCE NIGHTINGALE

May 12, 1820–August 13, 1910

LONDON—Florence Nightingale, the famous nurse of the Crimean war, and the only woman who ever received the Order of Merit, died yesterday afternoon at her London home. Although she had been an invalid for a long time, rarely leaving her room, her death was unexpected.

During recent years, owing to her feebleness and advanced age, Miss Nightingale had received but few visitors. On May 12 last, she celebrated her 90th birthday, and was the recipient of a congratulatory message from King George.

Not even the death of a royal personage could have called forth more universal expressions of regret and tributes of love and affection than appear in the English papers.

"The Queen of Nurses" and "The Soldier's Friend" are titles which have stuck to Florence Nightingale since her memorable service in behalf of the wounded and dying in the Crimean war. Though she had been an invalid since she returned from the Levant in the stirring times following the heroic struggle of the British in the Russian Empire, she retained her mental faculties to the last.

Florence Nightingale, the daughter of William Shore Nightingale, a wealthy English landowner in Florence, Italy, was born in that city in 1820 and from that city she took her given name. When a mere child, she returned with her parents to England, where she lived on her father's estate of Lea Hurst, Derbyshire. She was highly educated, being thoroughly at home in the French, German, and Italian languages. Her inclination toward philanthropy manifested itself early in life and she did much for her poor neighbors.

She began her life work by entering as a pupil in the Lutheran Hospital of Pastor Fleidner at Kaiserwerth, near Düsseldorf-on-the-Rhine. Here she acquitted herself in such a manner as to draw the highest praise from her teacher. In the early fifties she returned to London and devoted herself to labor in a hospital for sick governesses. Soon after the greatest undertaking of her life was thrust upon her.

The Crimean war had opened. England was engaged in the formidable task of trying to clip the claws of the Russian bear. Thousands of Englishmen were sent away to the Black Sea, where the rigors of Winter on that iron coast were such that the campaign almost failed through the breakdown of the chain of supplies, while in 1854 there were 18,000 men in the military hospitals.

In the first stage of the Crimean not a woman nurse was employed in any of the military hospitals, for the class of women who had in the past been employed was so notoriously bad that the War Office decided not to send any women nurses to the Crimea. After the battle of the Alma, however, the country rang with indignation at the neglected condition of the sick and wounded soldiers. Stirred into action, Sir Sydney Herbert, Secretary for War, wrote to Miss Nightingale saying that she was the one woman to take charge of the organization of a corps of nurses. A few days later she sailed for the Crimea with 34 nurses.

The women arrived just after the battle of Inkerman. There were 4,000 men in the hospitals, some wounded, but most of them sick.

Few veterans of the war of the Crimea are still alive, yet some remember the sweet and sympathetic face of Florence Nightingale, and were never tired of telling about her noble work in the hospitals. It was not only in the details of nursing, but in the gentle and watchful care for his comfort that Miss Nightingale made herself a beautiful memory to the soldier. She lent her aid to the surgeons when strong men turned away in horror, and sustained the courage of the wounded by her appeals to the ties which bound them to home.

Nor was it in the hospitals alone that her unselfish energy and untiring devotion were felt. There was an invalids' kitchen, where appetizing food for the sick who could not eat ordinary fare was provided under Miss Nightingale's eye. She provided also laundries, where clean linen could be obtained. In company with the army Chaplains she established a library and a school room. She personally attended to the correspondence of the wounded, and in many ways fully earned the title conferred upon her by the soldiers—"The Angel of the Crimea."

For a year and a half she labored in this field until her work there was no longer necessary. In August, 1856, she returned to Lea Hurst. She arrived when she was least expected and eluded those who would have honored her.

The Queen, however was not to be denied. She sent for Miss Nightingale to visit her at Balmoral and decorated her with her own hand.

Miss Nightingale made herself still more popular by refusing to keep a gift of $250,000 from the English Government for her own needs, turning it over for the establishment of St. Thomas's Hospital. In this is the Nightingale Training School for Nurses.

Miss Nightingale at this time was the heroine of the hour. Poems were written in her honor, songs and pianoforte pieces were dedicated to the "good angel of Derbyshire," playbills displayed her name beside that of Hamlet, grocers put her portrait on their bags as an advertisement, broadsheet ballads on "The Nightingale" were the fashion in Seven Dials, and young ladies in ringlets played the "Nightingale Varsoviana" in drawing-room circles.

Although Miss Nightingale's health was never robust after her Crimean experience, she contrived to write much that was of value. Her "Hospital Notes" have been remarkably successful, and her "Notes on Nursing" have had a circulation reaching into the hundreds of thousands.

In her youth Miss Nightingale had a great desire to study medicine, but the profession was closed to women. The injustice of the exclusion ranged her on the side of those who later started the propaganda for opening the professions to women.

CLARA BARTON

December 25, 1821–April 12, 1912

WASHINGTON—Miss Clara Barton, founder of the American Red Cross Society, died this morning at her home in Glen Echo, Md. The cause of her death was chronic pneumonia.

Miss Barton, who celebrated her 90th birthday anniversary Dec. 25, was President for 23 years of the Red Cross Society, which was established in this country through her efforts. She retired in May, 1904, on account of factional quarrels within the organization. But long before the society was founded she had become famous for her work on battlefields in the Civil War and the Franco-Prussian war.

She was born in North Oxford, Mass., on Christmas Day, 1821. She began teaching school at sixteen. In 1853 she visited relatives in Washington, D.C., and was persuaded to take charge of a division of the Patent Office, whose work had been disorganized by betrayal of secret information regarding patents. In a

short time she had transformed her department into a model of efficiency and discretion.

Miss Barton was in Washington when the first blood of the war was shed. The soldiers killed and injured in the Baltimore riot were from her own State. Her great career as a nurse began when she saw 40 of the soldiers, wounded at Baltimore, taken to the infirmary in Washington. After visiting them and giving what aid she could, she distributed thousands of baskets of food to the soldiers.

During the Peninsula campaign, she made daily trips down the river, leaving Washington in a boat carrying a cargo of provisions and returning with a load of wounded men, for whom she cared at her own expense. She also wrote letters home for the wounded under her charge.

Her father died in 1861, leaving her an ample fortune. On his death bed they discussed her plan of going to the front and attending soldiers on the battlefield. Her father said: "Go, if you feel it your duty to go. I know what soldiers are, and I know that every soldier will respect your errand."

She had difficulty getting a hearing from officers to whom she first applied for a pass beyond the army lines. She finally met a friend in Assistant Quartermaster General [Edmund] Rucker, who gave her means of transportation and the freedom to go to the relief of soldiers in battle whenever she wished. She spent large sums on a train of army wagons loaded with provisions and medical supplies.

Before the war ended she was appointed Superintendent of the 10th Army Corps Hospital, near City Point. Shortly before he was assassinated, President Lincoln appointed her to trace captured Union troops who were missing after prisoners of war had been exchanged. Of the 1,300 graves of soldiers who died at Andersonville Prison, she was able to identify all except 400.

In 1869 she went to Europe to rest. While she was at Berne she was called upon by representatives of the International Committee of Relief. They asked her to take part in their convention, which led to the organization of the International Red Cross Society. While she was in Europe the Franco-Prussian war broke out, and she went to the front and served as she had done during the Civil War.

In 1877 a few men and women in Washington had formed an American National Committee of the Red Cross. It was incorporated under the title of the American Association of the Red Cross, and Miss Barton was appointed President by President [James A.] Garfield. At her suggestion the work of the society was broadened to include, in addition to work on the battlefield, the object of relieving suffering in times of great National calamity. In 1893 Miss Barton organized a relief corps which was sent to Russia to the relief of peasants during the famine of that year.

In 1898 she headed a party which went to Armenia after the Armenian massacre. And during the Spanish-American war Miss Barton, who was then nearly 80 years old and for years had borne a large share of the expenses of the organization, went to Cuba and directed the work of the society on the field.

HARRIET TUBMAN

ca. 1822–March 10, 1913

Harriet Tubman Davis, an ex-slave, known as the "Moses of her people," who before the Civil War took 300 slaves to Canada through her "underground railroad," died on Monday night at the home she founded for aged and indigent negroes at Auburn,

N.Y. She was said to be 91 years old, and her death was caused by pneumonia.

Harriet Tubman Davis was esteemed by such men as Ralph Waldo Emerson, William Lloyd Garrison, Phillips Brooks, Horace Mann, Frederick Douglas[s], Gerrit Smith, and John Brown, while on the other hand planters and slave owners offered rewards of from $12,000 to $40,000 for her capture during the fifties, at the time when she was taking slaves out of the United States. She had served as scout, nurse, and spy in the Union Army.

MARCUS GARVEY

August 17, 1887–June 10, 1940

LONDON, June 11—Marcus Garvey, West Indian Negro, who once set himself up as "Emperor of the Kingdom of Africa" in New York's Harlem and later appeared before the League of Nations as representative of "the black peoples of the world," died here yesterday.—*United Press*

Marcus Garvey was a short, stout, ebony-colored firebrand who styled himself a "world-famous orator." He was a promoter who sold hundreds of thousands of American Negroes on the idea of a nation for themselves, an African empire. He preached racial solidarity, racial enterprise and race segregation. Until some of his promotions landed him in jail, they paid him at least $22,000 a year, and probably much more.

Where Father Divine of a later day created "angels" and "archangels" among the colored population of Harlem, Garvey in his time sprinkled the area with princes and princesses, barons, knights, viscounts, earls and dukes, and kept for himself for a time the comparatively humble designation of "Sir Provisional President of Africa."

There was no evidence that he had ever set foot on that continent, and the Republic of Liberia was, by announcement of its government, closed to him and his followers. He blamed the British and French Governments for that. His proposed hegira of black men and women back to the continent of their origin remained to the last simply a proposal.

Exact information about the origins of Marcus Aurelius Garvey, as he sometimes proudly named himself, was never forthcoming. It appeared, however, that some time about 1887 he was born in Jamaica, B.W.I., which fact made him a British citizen. According to his own story he was the editor of a Catholic newspaper in Jamaica at the age of 15, and thereafter edited papers in Jamaica and Costa Rica. He also said that he spent a year traveling through Europe before coming to the United States as the World War was about to begin.

His career in this country began as a journalist and lecturer to Negro audiences. It appeared to him that the Negroes in this country were in a state of semi-serfdom and he proposed to do something about it. The first step was the formation, in July 1914, of the Universal Negro Improvement Association, with an original membership of 15.

The next five or six years were his firebrand period. He made inflammatory attacks upon white people; suggested that for every Negro lynched in the South a white man should be similarly treated by the Negroes in New York. The trickle of dues into his "parent body," as he began to call the U.N.I.A., swelled into a stream, and Garvey began to dream other dreams than race fighting. He had learned that small sums contributed by many persons may reach an impressive total.

So he organized the Black Star Steamship Line and the Black Star Steamship Company, to establish a world shipping firm staffed wholly by Negroes. He called a convention of his U.N.I.A. and offered some 5,000 Negroes who attended at Madison Square Garden an opportunity to buy stock at $5 a share. The money rolled in and he bought several ships. One was the Yarmouth, another the Kanawha, which had been the pleasure yacht of the late colonel Henry Huddleston Rogers.

The first job the Yarmouth had was to haul a $3,000,000 cargo of liquor from Brooklyn to Cuba for a firm that wanted to get it out of the country before Prohibition became effective on Jan. 15, 1920. All that whisky was too much temptation for the crew, who got drunk and put in at Norfolk, where the ship was seized under the Prohibition law. A total loss.

The black skipper of the Kanawha also had bad luck at Norfolk. On his first voyage he rammed a pier there, his boiler exploded, and the Kanawha, too, became a total loss.

Nothing, meanwhile, had happened in Harlem except the multiplication of Garvey's notions. He had organized the African Community League, incorporated at $1,000,000; the Negro Factories Corporation and, on the non-commercial side, the Order of the Nile; the Black Cross Nurses and the Universal African Legion.

In February, 1925, three years after he had been arrested on a charge of using the mails to defraud in soliciting funds for one of his ship companies, Garvey went to Atlanta penitentiary, where he stayed until the middle of 1927, when his sentence was commuted, so that he could be deported. Sent back to Jamaica, he tried to carry on with the mission he had inaugurated in the United States. Back within the British Empire, his pleas were less well received, financially, and, after a futile effort to raise funds to rescue Ethiopia from the Italians, he sank into obscurity.

MALCOLM X

May 19, 1925–February 21, 1965

By Peter Kihss

Malcolm X, the 39-year-old leader of a militant black nationalist movement, was shot to death yesterday afternoon at a rally of his followers in a ballroom in Washington Heights.

Shortly before midnight, a 22-year-old Negro, Thomas Hagan, was charged with the killing. The police rescued him from the ballroom crowd after he had been shot and beaten.

Malcolm, a bearded extremist, had said only a few words of greeting when a fusillade rang out. The bullets knocked him over backward.

Pandemonium broke out among the 400 Negroes in the Audubon Ballroom at 166th Street and Broadway. As men, women and children ducked under tables and flattened themselves on the floor, more shots were fired. Some witnesses said 30 shots had been fired.

The police said seven bullets had struck Malcolm. Three other Negroes were shot.

The police said the shooting had apparently been a result of a feud between followers of Malcolm and members of the extremist group he broke with last year, the Black Muslims.

As Hagan fired at Malcolm, a follower of Malcolm shot Hagan in the left thigh, and his left leg was broken, apparently by kicks. Two other Negroes, described as "apparent spectators," were shot.

Malcolm, a slim, reddish-haired six-footer with a gift for bitter eloquence against what he considered white exploitation of Negroes, broke in March, 1964, with the Black Muslim movement called the Nation of Islam, headed by Elijah Muhammad.

James X, New York spokesman for the Black Muslims, denied that his organization had had anything to do with the killing.

Just one week before the slaying, Malcolm was bombed out of the small brick home in East Elmhurst, Queens,

where he had been living. James X suggested that Malcolm had set off firebombs "to get publicity."

Assemblyman Percy Sutton, Malcolm's lawyer, said the murdered leader had planned to disclose at yesterday's rally "the names of those who were trying to kill him."

Gene Simpson, a WMCA newsman, said he was sitting in the front row when Malcolm was introduced. He said Malcolm gave the traditional Arabic greeting, "Salaam Aleikum"—"Peace be unto you."

"The crowd responded, 'Aleikum Salaam,'" Mr. Simpson said, "and then there was some disturbance about eight rows back. Everybody turned, and so did I, and then I heard Malcolm saying, 'Be cool now, don't get excited.'

"And then I heard this muffled sound, and I saw Malcolm hit with his hands still raised, and then he fell back over the chairs behind him. And everybody was shouting, and I saw one man firing a gun from under his coat behind me as I hit it [the floor] too.

"And he was firing like he was in some Western, running backward toward the door and firing at the same time."

Extra policemen were on duty in Harlem and upper Manhattan yesterday and last night.

By Philip Benjamin

He was Malcolm Little, alias Big Red, a marijuana-smoking, cocaine-sniffing, zoot-suited, hip-talking hoodlum when he went to prison in 1946.

When he went free seven years later he was Malcolm X, an ascetic, a Black Muslim, a highly articulate man who hated the white world—a world he never made, but by whose standards he said he had lived.

"Christianity took me to prison and Islam brought me out," Malcolm X used to say. He had no apologies for his criminal record, he said, "because it was all done when I was part of the white man's Christian world."

He was born in Omaha, on May 19, 1925, the son of the Rev. Earl Little, a 6-foot, 4-inch man who preached the back-to-Africa movement of Marcus Garvey, a Jamaican Negro who died in 1940.

His mother was a West Indian whose father was white. From this "white devil" grandfather Malcolm X got his reddish-brown complexion and reddish-brown hair.

"I hate every drop of that white rapist's blood that is in me," Malcolm once wrote.

The Little family, including 11 children, moved to Lansing, Mich. Malcolm's earliest vivid memory was seeing, at the age of four, his house being burned to the ground by white racists. When he was six his father was killed under the wheels of a streetcar. Malcolm always believed his father had been murdered—first bludgeoned and then laid across the tracks.

The family broke up and Malcolm was sent to a state institution and was enrolled in the local public school at Mason, Mich. He was the only Negro student and his grades were among the highest in his class.

But after the eighth grade he left school and took a bus to Boston to live with a sister. In Boston and later in New York he drifted into the "cool" world; he drank, smoked marijuana and had an affair with a white woman. He became a waiter at Small's Paradise, a Harlem night club.

He was Big Red because he stood well over 6 feet and his hair was rust-colored. Big Red steered white men to Negro prostitutes and Negro men to white prostitutes; he sold marijuana, ran numbers, carried a pistol—in short, he was a hustler.

His cocaine habit cost him $20 a day and to support it he became a burglar. He was arrested in Boston after a series of burglaries there and was sent to the state prison at Charlestown. He was not quite 21 years old.

While he was in prison his sisters and brothers wrote to him about a "new" religion, Islam, preached to black men in the United States by the Honorable Elijah Muhammad, formerly Elijah Poole. The core of his teaching was the superiority of the black man, who was the first man on earth; the whites came later, a "devil" race.

Malcolm began to correspond with Elijah Muhammad, and when he left prison he was a Black Muslim. He no longer bore the surname of Little, because, as with nearly all American Negro surnames, it belonged to the white slave owners.

He went to Chicago, where Elijah Muhammad had his headquarters, and as eagerly as he had entered the "cool" world he entered the ascetic world. He gave up pork, tobacco, alcohol, marijuana, cocaine, gambling, dancing, movies, sports and promiscuity.

Elijah Muhammad recognized almost at once that he had in Malcolm a man of intelligence and authority. He sent him on speaking tours, and eventually Malcolm came to New York to take over Mosque

No. 7, then a small, voiceless and ineffectual group.

In conversation he was quiet, pleasant, articulate and even humorous. His accent was Midwestern. On the public platform his quality was cold fury; his eyes burned behind horn-rimmed glasses. In a few years he built up Mosque Seven and in 1958 he married a member of the mosque, Sister Betty X, and they had four children.

By his own admission, he had once been a racist, an advocate of black separatism. But after he broke with Elijah Muhammad last year, he said he had turned away from racism. That break came after the assassination of President Kennedy. Malcolm X had said the assassination was a case of "chickens coming home to roost."

For this remark Elijah Muhammad suspended Malcolm X, and the break was never healed. Malcolm set up the Muslim Mosque, Inc., with headquarters at the Theresa Hotel at 125th Street and Seventh Avenue. Last year he went to Mecca as a pilgrim. There, he said, he had been impressed by the "brotherhood, the people of all races, all colors coming together as one."

Two weeks ago he visited Britain and went to Smethwick, a town near Birmingham with a large colored population. His tour of Smethwick was criticized by some residents as an attempt to fan racism.

His home in Queens was bombed a week ago, and he accused the Black Muslims of doing it.

Writing in the Saturday Evening Post last year he said: "Some of the followers of Elijah Muhammad would still consider it a first-rank honor to kill me. Also I know that any day, any night, I could die at the hands of some white devil racists....I dream that one day history will look upon me as having been one of the voices that perhaps helped to save America from a grave, even possibly fatal catastrophe."

CHE GUEVARA

June 14, 1928–October 9, 1967

By Paul Hofmann

VALLE GRANDE—The Army High Command officially confirmed today that Ernesto Che Guevara, the Latin revolutionary leader, was killed in a clash between guerrillas and Bolivian troops in southeastern Bolivia yesterday.

The Armed Forces commander General Alfredo Ovando Candia said Mr. Guevara, who was 39, had admitted his identity before dying of his wounds.

Mr. Guevara, a maverick Communist whom Moscow distrusted, gained a reputation as a political adventurer imbued with the notion that the lonely man of action could revolutionize a people and shape history. An Argentine of Spanish and Irish ancestry

who became a "natural-born" Cuban citizen by special law, he strove almost from adolescence to destroy what he saw as Yankee domination of Latin America.

Mr. Guevara's picture of himself was that of a successor to the 19th-century liberators, Simón Bolivar and José de San Martin, who broke Spanish dominance south of the Isthmus of Panama in dashing campaigns that started with daring attacks by ragtag troops and who suffered disastrous defeats before final triumph.

As a boy he was so puny that his family sent him to a resort in the Andes mountains to strengthen him. Asthmatic attacks left him exhausted and laboring for breath. Yet he braved hardship in his student days, battled the Buenos Aires police in street clashes, underwent secret military training in Mexico, survived the perilous rise to power in Cuba with Fidel Castro, directed guerrilla actions in the Sierra Maestra and rode into a delirious Havana at Mr. Castro's side.

He became one of the leaders of the Cuban revolutionary regime, repeatedly visited Moscow, Peking and African capitals, and addressed the United Nations.

After another voyage that started with a sojourn in New York in December, 1964, and that led him to Africa and Communist China, Mr. Guevara returned to Havana in March of 1965. A few days later, he gave a lecture at the Industries Ministry that was to be his last public appearance in Cuba. He then dropped out of sight.

Inevitably, rumors flitted around Havana. Mr. Guevara was said to have been confined in a sanitarium, deported to the Soviet Union or executed after a quarrel with Premier Castro.

Castro waited until October of 1965 before announcing that his former right-hand man was no longer in Cuba. The Premier told a Havana rally that Mr. Guevara left in April after having relinquished his posts in the Government.

Mr. Guevara was reported to have written in a letter to the Premier: "I have fulfilled my duty's role that tied me to the Cuban revolution. Other lands in the world demand my modest efforts. I can do what is denied to you because of your responsibility to Cuba, and the hour of parting company has come for us."

Those who accepted the theory that he had left the island voluntarily theorized that there had been mounting Soviet pressure to have him removed from economic posts and that his friendship with the Premier had cooled.

Mr. Guevara, who was born June 14, 1928, in Rosario, was married twice. His second wife was Aleida March, a Cuban and a former teacher. His first wife, a Peruvian leftist named Hilda Gadea, was once quoted as having said, "I lost a husband to a revolution."

By Reuters

VALLE GRANDE, Bolivia—The army high command officially confirmed today that Ernesto Che Guevara, the Latin revolutionary leader, was killed in a clash between guerrillas and Bolivian troops in southeastern Bolivia last Sunday.

The armed forces commander, Gen. Alfredo Ovando Candia, said Mr. Guevara had admitted his identity before dying of his wounds. General Ovando said at a news conference that the guerrilla leader had also admitted that he failed in the seven-month guerrilla campaign he organized in Bolivia.

The identification of the body was made after fingerprinting by the Eighth Army command.

[United States officials in Washington reacted cautiously to the Bolivian reports that Mr. Guevara had been killed, but there was an increasing tendency to regard them as true.]

The body was flown here yesterday, lashed to the landing runners of a helicopter that brought it from the mountain scene of the clash. The army said yesterday that it had received a report that Mr. Guevara had been killed near Higueras, but it declined to make immediate positive identification at the time.

After the body, dressed in bloody clothes, arrived here, it was fingerprinted and embalmed.

[The Guevara fingerprints are on file with the Argentine federal police. As an Argentine citizen, Mr. Guevara was required to be fingerprinted to obtain a passport when he left his homeland in 1952. These official records have provided the basis for comparison with the fingerprints taken by the Bolivians from the body said to be that of Mr. Guevara.]

The scanty beard, shoulder-length hair and shape of the head resembled the features of Mr. Guevara as shown in earlier photographs. He was 39 years old.

An Englishman in the crowd, which except for the press was kept away at bayonet point, said that he had seen Mr. Guevara in Cuba and that he was "absolutely convinced" it was the long-sought revolutionary leader.

The body appeared to bear wounds in at least three places—two in the neck and one in the throat.

It was dressed in a green jacket with a zippered front, patched and faded green denim pants, green woolen socks and a pair of homemade moccasins.

MARTIN LUTHER KING JR.

January 15, 1929–April 4, 1968

MEMPHIS—The Rev. Dr. Martin Luther King Jr., who preached nonviolence and racial brotherhood, was fatally shot here last night by a distant gunman who then raced away and escaped.

Four thousand National Guard troops were ordered into Memphis by Gov. Buford Ellington after the 39-year-old Nobel Prize–winning civil rights leader died.

A curfew was imposed on the shocked city of 550,000 inhabitants, 40 percent of whom are Negro.

But the police said the tragedy had been followed by incidents that included sporadic shooting, fires, bricks and bottles thrown at policemen, and looting that started in Negro districts and then spread over the city.

Police Director Frank Holloman said the assassin might have been a white man who was "50 to 100 yards away in a flophouse."

Chief of Detectives W. P. Huston said a late model white Mustang was believed to have been the killer's getaway car. Its occupant was described as a bareheaded white man in his 30's, wearing a black suit and black tie.

Dr. King was shot while he leaned over a second-floor railing outside his room at the Lorraine Motel. He was chatting with two friends just before starting for dinner.

Dr. King had come back to Memphis Wednesday morning to organize support once again for 1,300 sanitation workers who have been striking since Lincoln's Birthday. He was apparently still living when he reached the St. Joseph's Hospital operating room for emergency surgery. He was borne in on a stretcher, the bloody towel over his head.

It was the same emergency room to which James H. Meredith, the first Negro enrolled at the University of Mississippi, was taken after he was ambushed and shot in June, 1965, at Hernando, Miss., a few miles south of Memphis. Mr. Meredith was not seriously hurt.

The Rev. Andrew Young, executive director of Dr. King's Southern Christian Leadership Conference, recalled there had been some talk Wednesday night about possible harm to Dr. King in Memphis.

Mr. Young recalled: "He said he had reached the pinnacle of fulfillment with his nonviolent movement, and these reports did not bother him."—*Earl Caldwell*

By Murray Schumach

To many millions of American Negroes, the Rev. Dr. Martin Luther King Jr. was the prophet of their crusade for racial equality. He was their voice of anguish, their eloquence in humiliation, their battle cry for human dignity. He forged for them the weapons of nonviolence that withstood and blunted the ferocity of segregation.

And to many millions of American whites, he was one of a group of Negroes who preserved the bridge of communication between races when racial warfare threatened the United States in the nineteen-sixties, as Negroes sought the full emancipation pledged to them a century before by Abraham Lincoln.

To the world, Dr. King had the stature that accrued to a winner of the Nobel Peace Prize, a man with access to the White House and the Vatican; a veritable hero in the African states that were just emerging from colonialism.

In his dedication to nonviolence, Dr. King was caught between white and Negro extremists as racial tensions erupted into arson, gunfire and looting in many of the nation's cities during the summer of 1967.

Militant Negroes, with the cry of, "burn, baby burn," argued that only by violence and segregation could the Negro attain self-respect, dignity and real equality in the United States.

Floyd B. McKissick, when director of the Congress of Racial Equality, declared in August of that year that it was a "foolish assumption to try to sell nonviolence to the ghettos."

And white extremists, not bothering to make distinctions between degrees of Negro militancy, looked upon Dr. King as one of their chief enemies.

At the time he was assassinated in Memphis, Dr. King was involved in one of his greatest plans to dramatize the plight of the poor and stir Congress to help Negroes.

He called this venture the "Poor People's Campaign." It was to be a huge "camp-in" either in Washington or in Chicago during the Democratic National Convention.

In one of his last public announcements before the shooting, Dr. King told an audience in a Harlem church on March 26:

"We need an alternative to riots and to timid supplication. Nonviolence is our most potent weapon."

His strong beliefs in civil rights and nonviolence made him one of the leading opponents of American participation in the war in Vietnam. To him the war was unjust, diverting vast sums away from programs to alleviate the condition of the Negro poor in this country.

Inevitably, as a symbol of integration, he became the object of unrelenting attacks and vilification. His home was bombed. He was spat upon and mocked. He was struck and kicked. He was stabbed, almost fatally, by a deranged Negro woman. He was frequently thrown into jail. Threats became so commonplace that his wife could ignore burning crosses on the lawn and ominous phone calls. Through it all he adhered

to the creed of passive disobedience that infuriated segregationists.

The adulation that was heaped upon him eventually irritated some Negroes in the civil rights movement who worked hard, but in relative obscurity. They pointed out—and Dr. King admitted—that he was a poor administrator. Sometimes, with sarcasm, they referred to him, privately, as "De Lawd."

The doctrine of "black power" threatened to split the Negro civil rights movement and antagonize white liberals who had been supporting Negro causes, and Dr. King suggested "militant nonviolence" as a formula for progress with peace.

At the root of his civil rights convictions was an even more profound faith in the basic goodness of man and the great potential of American democracy. These beliefs gave to his speeches a fervor that could not be stilled by criticism.

Scores of millions of Americans—white as well as Negro—who sat before television sets in the summer of 1963 to watch the awesome march of some 200,000 Negroes on Washington were deeply stirred when Dr. King, in the shadow of the Lincoln Memorial, said:

"Even though we face the difficulties of today and tomorrow, I still have a dream. I have a dream that one day this nation will rise up and live out the true meaning of its creed: 'We hold these truths to be self-evident that all men are created equal.'"

For the poor and unlettered of his own race, Dr. King embraced the rhythm and passion of the revivalist and evangelist. It was said that so devoted was his vast following that even among illiterates he could, by calm discussion of Platonic dogma, evoke deep cries of "Amen."

Dr. King also had a way of reducing complex issues to terms that anyone could understand. Thus, in the summer of 1965, when there was widespread discontent among Negroes about their struggle for equality of employment, he declared:

"What good does it do to be able to eat at a lunch counter if you can't buy a hamburger?"

The enormous impact of Dr. King's words was one of the reasons he was in the President's Room in the Capitol on Aug. 6, 1965, when President Johnson signed the Voting Rights Act that marked the growth of the Negro as a political force in the South.

Dr. King's effectiveness was enhanced and given continuity by the fact that he had an organization behind him. Formed in 1960, with headquarters in Atlanta, it was called the Southern Christian Leadership Conference. Allied with it was another organization formed under Dr. King's sponsorship, the Student Nonviolent Coordinating Committee.

This minister, who became the most famous spokesman for Negro rights since Booker T. Washington, was not particularly impressive in appearance. There was little of the rabblerouser in his oratory. He was not prone to extravagant gestures or loud peroration. In private gatherings, Dr. King lacked that laughing gregariousness that often makes for popularity. He also did not have the cool strategic brilliance of Roy Wilkins, head of the National Association for the Advancement of Colored People.

What Dr. King did have was an instinct for the right moment to make his moves. It was this sense of timing that raised him in 1955, from a newly arrived minister in Montgomery, Ala., with his first church, to a figure of national prominence.

Negroes in that city had begun a boycott of buses to win the right to sit where they pleased instead of being forced to move to the rear of buses or to surrender seats to white people when a bus was crowded.

The 381-day boycott by Negroes was already under way when the young pastor was placed in charge of the campaign. However, it was Dr. King who dramatized the boycott by making it the testing ground of his belief in the civil disobedience teachings of Thoreau and Gandhi.

Even more dramatic, in some ways, was his reaction to the bombing of his home during the boycott. He was away at the time and rushed back fearful for his wife and children. They were not injured. But when he reached the modest house, more than a thousand Negroes had already gathered and were in an ugly mood. The police were jittery. Quickly, Dr. King pacified the crowd and there was no trouble.

Dr. King was even more impressive during the "big push" in Birmingham, which began in April, 1963. With the minister in the limelight, Negroes there began a campaign of sit-ins at lunch counters, picketing and protest marches. Hundreds of children were jailed.

The entire world was stirred when the police turned dogs on the demonstrators. Dr. King was jailed for five days. While he was in prison he issued a 9,000-word letter that created considerable controversy among white people, alienating some sympathizers who thought Dr. King was being too aggressive.

In the letter he wrote:

"I have almost reached the regrettable conclusion that the Negro's great stumbling block in the stride toward freedom is not the White Citizens Counciler or the Ku Klux Klanner, but the white moderate who is more devoted to order than to justice; who prefers a negative peace, which is the absence of tension, to a positive peace, which is the presence of justice."

The role of Dr. King in Birmingham added to his stature and showed that his enormous following was deeply devoted to him.

But some critics—Negroes as well as white—noted that sometimes, despite all the publicity he attracted, he left campaigns unfinished or else failed to attain his goals.

Dr. King was aware of this. But he pointed out, in 1964, in St Augustine, Fla., one of the toughest civil rights battlegrounds, that there were important intangibles.

"Even if we do not get all we should," he said, "movements such as this tend more and more to give a Negro the sense of self-respect that he needs. It tends to generate courage in Negroes outside the movement. It brings intangible results outside the community where it is carried out. There is a hardening of attitudes in situations like this. But other cities see and say: "'We don't want to be another Albany or Birmingham,' and they make changes. Some communities, like this one, had to bear the cross."

The enormous influence of Dr. King's voice in the turbulent racial conflict reached into New York in 1964. In the summer racial rioting exploded there and in other Northern cities with large Negro populations. There was widespread fear that the disorders, particularly in Harlem, might set off unprecedented racial violence.

At this point Dr. King became one of the major intermediaries in restoring order. He conferred with Mayor Robert F. Wagner and with Negro leaders. A statement was issued, of which he was one of the signers, calling for "a broad curtailment if not total moratorium on mass demonstrations until after Presidential elections."

The following year, Dr. King was once more in the headlines and on television—this time leading a drive for Negro voter registration in Selma, Ala. Negroes were arrested by the hundreds. Dr. King was punched and kicked by a white man when he became the first Negro to register at a century-old hotel in Selma.

Martin Luther King Jr. was born Jan. 15, 1929, in Atlanta. His father, the Rev. Martin Luther King Sr. was pastor of the Ebenezer Baptist Church.

Young Martin went to Atlanta's Morehouse College and decided, in his junior year, to be a clergyman.

He pursued his studies in the integrated Crozier Theological Seminary, in Chester, Pa. He was one of six Negroes in a student body of about a hundred. He became the first Negro class president. After winning a fellowship to study for a doctorate at the school of his choice, he enrolled at Boston College in 1951.

For his doctoral thesis he sought to resolve the differences between the Harvard theologian Paul Tillich and the neo-naturalist philosopher Henry Nelson Wieman. He took courses at Harvard, as well.

While he was working on his doctorate he met Coretta Scott, a graduate of Antioch College, who was doing graduate work in music. He married the singer in 1953. They had four children, Yolanda, Martin Luther King 3d, Dexter Scott and Bernice.

In 1954, Dr. King became pastor of the Dexter Avenue Baptist Church in Montgomery, Ala. Few of Montgomery's white residents seemed to realize how deeply the city's Negroes resented segregated seating on buses.

On Dec. 1, 1955, they learned, almost by accident. Mrs. Rosa Parks, a Negro seamstress, refused to give up her seat to a white passenger. She was arrested, convicted and fined $10 and costs, a total of $14. Almost as spontaneous as Mrs. Parks's act was the rallying of many Negro leaders in the city to help her.

From this protest Dr. King began his public career.

In 1959, he and his family moved back to Atlanta, where he became a co-pastor, with his father, of the Ebenezer Baptist Church.

As his fame increased, public interest in his beliefs led him to write books. It was while he was autographing one of these books, "Stride Toward Freedom," in a Harlem department store that he was stabbed by a Negro woman.

The possibility that he might someday be assassinated was considered by Dr. King on June 5, 1964, when he reported, in St. Augustine, that his life had been threatened. He said:

"Well, if physical death is the price that I must pay to free my white brothers and sisters from a permanent death of the spirit, then nothing can be more redemptive."

HELEN KELLER

June 27, 1880–June 1, 1968

WESTPORT, Conn.—Helen Keller, who overcame blindness and deafness to become a symbol of the indomitable human spirit, died this afternoon in her home here. She was 87 years old.

"She drifted off in her sleep," said Mrs. Winifred Corbally, Miss Keller's companion for the last 11 years.

She is survived by a brother and a sister.

By Alden Whitman

For the first 18 months of her life Helen Keller was a normal infant. Then, as she recalled later, "came the illness which closed my eyes and ears and plunged me into the unconsciousness of a newborn baby."

The illness, perhaps scarlet fever, vanished quickly, but it erased not only the child's vision and hearing but also, as a result, her powers of articulate speech.

Her life thereafter became a triumph over crushing adversity and shattering affliction. In time, Miss Keller learned to circumvent her blindness, deafness and muteness; she could "see" and "hear" with exceptional acuity; she even learned to talk passably. Her remarkable mind unfolded, and she was in and of the world, a full and happy participant in life.

What set Miss Keller apart was that no similarly afflicted person before had done more than acquire the simplest skills. But she was graduated from Radcliffe, she became a writer, she led a vigorous life, and she energized movements that revolutionized help for the blind and the deaf.

Her tremendous accomplishments and force of personality were released through the devotion and skill of Anne Sullivan Macy, the teacher through whom she largely expressed herself. Mrs. Macy was succeeded, at her death in 1936, by Polly Thomson, who died in 1960.

Miss Keller's life was so long and so crowded with improbable feats—from riding horseback to learning Greek—and she was so serene yet so determined that she became a legend.

Many found it difficult to believe that a person so handicapped could acquire the profound knowledge and the sensitive perception and writing talent that she exhibited when she was mature. Yet no substantial proof was ever adduced that Miss Keller was anything less than she appeared—a person whose character impelled her to perform the seemingly impossible.

Miss Keller always insisted that there was nothing mysterious or miraculous about her achievements. Her dark and silent world was held in her hand and shaped with her mind.

Tall, handsome, gracious, poised, Miss Keller exuded vitality and optimism. "My life has been happy because I have had wonderful friends and plenty of interesting work to do," she once remarked, adding, "I seldom think about my limitations, and they never make me sad. Perhaps there is just a touch of yearning at times, but it is vague, like a breeze among flowers."

Helen Adams Keller was born on June 27, 1880, on a farm near Tuscumbia, Ala. Her father was Arthur Keller, who had served in the Confederate Army. Her mother was the former Kate Adams.

After Helen's illness, her infancy and early childhood were a succession of days of frustration, manifest by outbursts of anger and fractious behavior. "A wild, unruly child" who kicked, scratched and screamed was how she afterward described herself.

A Baltimore eye physician put her parents in touch with Alexander Graham Bell, the inventor of the telephone and an authority on teaching speech to the deaf. Bell advised the Kellers to ask his son-in-law, Michael Anagnos, director of the Perkins Institution, about finding a teacher for Helen.

The teacher Mr. Anagnos selected was 20-year-old Anne Mansfield Sullivan, who was called Annie. Miss Sullivan had learned at Perkins how to communicate with the deaf and blind through a hand alphabet signaled by touch into the patient's palm.

"The most important day I remember in all my life is the one on which my teacher came to me," Miss Keller wrote later. "It was the third of March, 1887, three months before I was 7 years old."

It was days before Miss Sullivan, whom Miss Keller called "Teacher," could calm the child and begin to spell words into her hand. The problem was of associating words and objects or actions: What was a doll, what was water? Miss Sullivan's solution was a stroke of genius. Recounting it, Miss Keller wrote:

"We walked down the path to the well-house, attracted by the fragrance of the honeysuckle with which it was covered. Someone was drawing water and my teacher placed my hand under the spout.

"As the cool stream gushed over one hand she spelled into the other the word water, first slowly, then rapidly. I stood still, my whole attention fixed upon the motions of her fingers. Suddenly I felt a misty consciousness as of something forgotten—a thrill of returning thought; and somehow the mystery of language was revealed to me.

"I knew then that 'w-a-t-e-r' meant the wonderful cool something that was flowing over my hand. That living word awakened my soul, gave it light, hope, joy, set it free."

Once Helen began to learn, her hunger for knowledge was insatiable. Abstractions proved difficult, but her teacher's patience and ingenuity prevailed.

Helen's next opening into the world was learning to read. "As soon as I could spell a few words my teacher gave me slips of cardboard on which were printed words in raised letters," she recalled. "I quickly learned that each printed word stood for an object, an act or a quality."

Helen's progress was so rapid that in May, 1888, she made her first trip to the Perkins Institution in Boston, where she learned to read Braille. It was in the spring of 1890 that Helen was taught to speak by Sarah Fuller of the Horace Mann School.

"Miss Fuller's method was this," Miss Keller recalled. "She passed my hand lightly over her face, and let me feel the position of her tongue and lips when she made a sound. I was eager to imitate every motion and in an hour had learned six elements of speech: M, P, A, S, T, I. I shall never forget the surprise and delight I felt when I uttered my first connected sentence: 'It is warm.'"

At the same time the child learned to lip-read by placing her fingers on the lips and throat of those who talked with her. Her crude speech and her lip-reading facility further opened her mind.

Each of the young girl's advances brought pressure on her for new wonders and this inevitably fed public skepticism. This was intensified when, in 1892, a story appeared under her name that was similar to a published work. Although she denied the charge of plagiarism, the episode hurt Miss Keller.

When she was 14, with Miss Sullivan at her side and spelling into her hand, Miss Keller prepared herself for admission to Radcliffe, which she entered in the fall of 1900. Her acceptance was an amazing feat, but no more astonishing than her graduation cum laude in 1904, with honors in German and English.

While still in Radcliffe, Miss Keller wrote her first autobiography. "The Story of My Life" was published in 1902, as a book. It consisted largely of themes written for an English composition course.

Most reviewers found the book well written, but some critics scoffed. "All of her knowledge is hearsay knowledge," The Nation said. "Her very sensations are for the most part vicarious and she writes of things beyond her power of perception and with the assurance of one who had verified every word."

Miss Keller's defenders replied that she had ways of knowing things not reckoned by others. When she wrote of the New York subway that it "opened its jaws like a great beast," it was noted that she had stroked a lion's mouth and knew whereof she spoke.

In the twenties, Miss Keller, Miss Sullivan and her husband moved from Wrentham, Mass., to Forest Hills, Queens, in New York. Miss Keller used this home as a base for her fund-raising tours for the American Foundation for the Blind.

Miss Keller toured the world with Miss Sullivan in the years before World War II. Everywhere she went she lectured in behalf of the blind and the deaf.

In adulthood she was subjected to criticisms and crises that sometimes unsettled her. The most frustrating such episode occurred in 1916.

Miss Keller, then 36, fell in love with Peter Fagan, a Socialist and newspaperman who was her temporary secretary. The couple took out a marriage license, intending a secret wedding. But a Boston reporter found out about the license, and his article on the romance horrified Mrs. Keller, who broke up the affair.

"The love which had come, unseen and unexpected, departed with tempest on his wings," Miss Keller wrote in sadness.

JOHN L. LEWIS
February 12, 1880–June 11, 1969

Washington—John L. Lewis, a giant of the American labor movement and for decades a top figure on the American scene, died tonight at Doctors Hospital.

The president emeritus of the powerful United Mine Workers Union was 89 years old.

Through the nineteen-thirties and nineteen-forties few names were more frequently in headlines than Mr. Lewis's. Except for President Franklin D. Roosevelt, few in those years did more to shape the economic face of the United States.

Through formation of the Committee for Industrial Organization he changed the structure and orientation of the labor movement. His influence helped fashion much of the labor legislation enacted by Congress.

Mr. Lewis, a self-educated man, sharp of wit and tongue, lived in suburban Alexandria, Va. His wife, Myrta, died in 1942. A son survives him.—*The Associated Press*

By Alden Whitman

For 40 years, and especially during the turbulent nineteen-thirties, forties and early fifties, John Llewellyn Lewis, a pugnacious man of righteous wrath and rococo rhetoric, was a dominant figure in the American labor movement. He aspired to national political and economic power, but both largely eluded his grasp. He nudged greatness as a labor leader only to end in isolation from the mainstream of trade unionism.

But in his headline years Mr. Lewis, with his black leonine mane and outthrust-jaw stubbornness, was an idol to millions of workers and the symbol of blackest malevolence to millions in the middle and upper classes. As the thunderer for labor he was unexcelled.

Starting in 1935, when coal was the country's kingpin fuel and he was president of the United Mine Workers of America, Mr. Lewis shattered the complacent craft-union American Federation of Labor by setting up the Committee for Industrial Organization to organize workers into single unions for each big industry.

He went on to lead convulsive sitdown strikes, to humble the auto industry and Big Steel, to endorse and then break bitterly with President Roosevelt, to defy the Government in coal-mine disputes in World War II, and to battle President Harry S. Truman in two coal strikes in which he was twice held in contempt of court.

In the course of tumultuous labor politics, Mr. Lewis's wealthy and influential union left the American Federation of Labor and then rejoined it after leaving the Congress of Industrial Organizations. Finally, Mr. Lewis took his union out of the A.F.L. and went it alone. Addressing the miners, he summed up his efforts in their behalf:

"I have never faltered or failed to present the cause or plead the case of the mine workers of this country. I have pleaded your case not in the quavering tones of a mendicant asking alms, but in the thundering voice of the captain of a mighty host, demanding the rights to which free men are entitled."

Soot-smirched miners heeded Mr. Lewis without question. If he called for a shutdown, the pits were deserted. If he wanted the mines run on a three-day week, that was how they operated. For their unswerving loyalty the miners received wage increases, vacation pay, pensions at age 60, and improved mine safety.

A superb orator, Mr. Lewis swayed thousands of emotion-hungry audiences. With mine operators in wage negotiations Mr. Lewis was equally effective.

C. L. Sulzberger, in his book "Sit Down with John L. Lewis," described this Lewis speech during contract talks in the early thirties:

"'Gentlemen,' he said, speaking in a slow, tricky way. 'Gentlemen, I speak to you for my people. I speak to you for the miners' families in the broad Ohio Valley, the Pennsylvania mountains and the black West Virginia hills.

"'There, the shanties lean over as if intoxicated by the smoke fumes of the mine dumps....The little children are gathered around a bare table without anything to eat. Their mothers are saying, 'We want bread.'"

The operators, according to Mr. Sulzberger's book, squirmed, and one of them muttered, "Tell him to stop. Tell him we'll settle."

Mr. Lewis was often pictured as a radical. Basically, however, Mr. Lewis's economic and political views tended to be conservative. He supported President Roosevelt in 1936 and was on close personal terms with him until the outbreak of World War II in Europe in 1939.

Although much of the public may have equated Mr. Lewis with bellicosity, he was an amiable and courtly person, possessed of a nimble wit and a pleasant laugh.

John Lewis was born to the coal mines and to unionism. His father was Thomas Lewis, a miner who had emigrated from Wales to Lucas, Iowa. His mother, Louisa Watkins Lewis, was the daughter of a miner. John, their first child—there were, in all, six sons and two daughters—was born Feb. 12, 1880, in Lucas.

For his role in a Knights of Labor strike, Thomas Lewis was blacklisted for several years, and talk of militant trade unionism and the miners' hazardous lot filled John's childhood.

He left school after the seventh grade and was toiling in the mines at 15. He also read, guided by Myrta Bell, who later became his wife.

As a miner in Lucas, he was elected a delegate to the national convention of the United Mine Workers, which traced its history to 1849. The next move was to Panama, Ill., and in a year he was president of the local mine union.

In 1911, he was named general field agent for the A.F.L. by Samuel Gompers, then its president. Mr. Lewis built a large personal following in the mine union, for which he became chief statistician in 1917 and later that year vice president. In 1920 he became president, an office he held for 40 years.

The genesis of the C.I.O. was in the plague years of the Depression, when unemployment mounted to 15 million workers. Union working and wage standards were toppled, and the A.F.L. lost thousands of members. The mine union dropped to 100,000 members.

At the same time, it became evident that organization of workers by skilled crafts, which was the basis of the A.F.L., was unrealistic in most major industries, where unskilled or semiskilled workers constituted the bulk of employees. This situation led to the C.I.O.'s efforts to organize the unorganized.

The C.I.O. came into being after the A.F.L. convention of 1935, in which tensions between industrial and craft unions erupted in a fistfight between William Hutcheson of the Carpenters Union and Mr. Lewis. When the convention adjourned, Mr. Lewis met to form the C.I.O. with, among others, Charles P. Howard of the International Typographical Union, David Dubinsky of the International Ladies Garment Workers, Thomas McMahon of the Textile Workers, and Sidney Hillman of the Amalgamated Clothing Workers.

Subsequently these and other unions backing the C.I.O. were expelled from the A.F.L., but it was an empty gesture, for workers responded to the C.I.O. campaigns in the basic industries. First autos capitulated, then Big Steel, then others, until 4 million workers were enrolled in C.I.O. unions. The procession of successes was interrupted in late 1937 by Little Steel, representing the smaller fabricators.

The Little Steel strike was marked by violence. In Chicago on Memorial Day the police shot and killed 10 strikers and sympathizers. In the course of the strike, which was lost, President Roosevelt was asked what he thought of the dispute. "A plague on both your houses," he replied, a remark that enraged Mr. Lewis, whose union had contributed $500,000 to the President's 1936 campaign. His retort was:

"It ill behooves one who has supped at labor's table and who has been sheltered in labor's house to curse with equal fervor and fine impartiality both labor and its adversaries when they become locked in deadly embrace."

Mr. Lewis followed this excoriation with others equally acerbic in the campaign of 1940, in which he sought to rally organized labor against the Roosevelt third-term bid. After Mr. Roosevelt won the election Mr. Lewis resigned as head of what was then the Congress of Industrial Organizations, and Philip Murray, a Lewis lieutenant, took over. In 1942, Mr. Lewis broke with Mr. Murray, and the mine union left the C.I.O.

Four years later he and his union were back in the A.F.L., but their stay lasted less than two years. Again there was a battle of words, this time over a provision of the Taft-Hartley Act requiring union officials to swear they were not Communists. The A.F.L. was willing to comply, Mr. Lewis was not. To him the law was "damnable, vicious, unwholesome and a slave statute," and the mine union went its independent way.

Then in the spring of 1946 he called a soft-coal strike in a bid for royalties on each ton of coal mined, the money to go into the union's health and welfare fund. President Truman ordered the mines seized, and the strike ended on May 29 with a wage increase and a royalty arrangement. A hard-coal strike followed but ended on about the same terms.

Peace was short-lived. In November Mr. Lewis denounced the contract under which the Government had been running the mines. An order was issued restraining Mr. Lewis from maintaining the contract-termination notice. President Truman ordered the Justice Department to seek a contempt citation if Mr. Lewis disobeyed the court. When the union chief made no move to halt the walkout, the judge found him and the union guilty of contempt and fines were imposed.

Three days later, Mr. Lewis sent the miners back to work, pending appeal of the contempt ruling to the Supreme Court. That tribunal upheld the contempt judgment and the fine against Mr. Lewis, although the fine against the union was reduced.

In 1948, after the Government had returned the mines to the operators, Mr. Lewis was again in court. The miners were idle in a pension dispute, and Mr. Lewis and the union were ordered to end the walkout. He declined and both were fined.

By his flair for dramatizing the problem of his miners, Mr. Lewis also won a long struggle for Federal mine inspection in 1952. When 119 miners perished in a West Frankfort, Ill., mine explosion in 1951, he flew to the scene, inspected the shafts and assailed Congress for failing to enact safety legislation. In testimony before a Senate subcommittee, he called on Congress to give the Federal Government power to close unsafe mines.

The Federal Mine Safety Law was enacted, setting up a board of review of which the union's safety director was a member.

When Mr. Lewis announced in 1959 that he was preparing to retire, the operators expressed regret, praising him for his "outstanding ability" and as "an extraordinarily fine person."

In his farewell address to his union he said:

"The years have been long and the individual burdens oppressive, yet progress has been great.

"At first, your wages were low, your hours long, your labor perilous, your health disregarded, your children without opportunity, your union weak, your fellow citizens and public representatives indifferent to your wrongs.

"Today, because of your fortitude and your deep loyalty to your union, your wages are the highest in the land, your working hours the lowest, your safety more assured, your health more guarded, your old age protected, your children equal in opportunity with their generation and your union strong with material resources."

CESAR CHAVEZ

March 31, 1927–April 23, 1993

By Robert Lindsey

Cesar Chavez, the migrant worker who emerged from the poverty of an agricultural valley in Arizona to found America's first successful union of farm workers, died yesterday in San Luis, Ariz. He was 66.

Mr. Chavez, who lived in Keene, Calif., and was in Arizona on union business, died in his sleep, the police said.

Blending the nonviolent resistance of Gandhi with the organizational skills of his mentor, the social activist Saul Alinsky, Mr. Chavez captured worldwide attention in the 1960's. Leading an initially lonely battle to unionize the fields and orchards of California, he issued a call to boycott grapes that soon became a cause celebre.

Mr. Chavez, whom Robert F. Kennedy once called "one of the heroic figures of our time," was widely acknowledged to have done more than anyone else to improve the lot of the migrant farm worker.

Fighting growers and shippers who for generations had defeated efforts to unionize field workers, and later fighting rival unionists, Mr. Chavez for the first time brought a degree of stability and security to the lives of some migrant workers. Largely because of him, the California Legislature in 1975 passed the nation's first collective bargaining act outside Hawaii for farm workers, who are largely excluded from Federal labor law coverage. "For the first time," Mr. Chavez said of the union's achievement, "the farm worker got some power."

Asked what had motivated his stubborn fight, he said, "For many years I was a farm worker, a migratory worker, and, well, personally—and I'm being very frank—maybe it's just a matter of trying to even the score."

But he ultimately failed to realize his dream of forging a nationwide organization. In most of America, farm workers continue to toil for low wages, without job security, vulnerable to exploitation. Even in California, the union Mr. Chavez founded, the United Farm Workers of America, was unable to organize more than 20 percent of the state's 200,000 farm workers. The tactics he used so effectively in the 1960's and early 70's—strikes, boycotts and fasting—lost their magic. The United Farm Workers were no longer seen as a social cause but as a conventional labor union.

In 1965, when he formed the union, farm workers in California averaged less than $1.50 an hour. They had no fringe benefits and no way to challenge abuses by employers. Unionization brought sharp pay increases. For the first time, migrant workers were eligible for medical insurance, employer-paid pensions and unemployment insurance.

Cesar Estrada Chavez was born on March 31, 1927, near Yuma, Ariz., one of five children of Juana and Librado Chavez. His father's parents migrated from Mexico in 1880.

His early years were spent on the family's 160-acre farm. But in the seventh year of the Depression, when he was 10, the family fell behind on mortgage payments and lost its farm.

Along with thousands of other families in the Southwest, they sought a new life in California. They found it picking carrots, cotton and other crops.

Mr. Chavez never graduated from high school, and once counted 65 elementary schools he had attended "for a day, a week or a few months."

Unions had tried for decades to organize immigrant unskilled immigrant workers on whom California growers depended. But the field hands found themselves fighting both powerful growers and the police and government officials.

In 1939 Mr. Chavez's family settled in San Jose. After serving in the Navy in World War II, Mr. Chavez resumed his life as a migrant. He married Helen Fabela in Delano, which he later made famous far beyond its dusty corner of the San Joaquin Valley. He is survived by his wife, eight children, three brothers and two sisters.

The pivotal role in Mr. Chavez's emergence as a labor leader was played by Mr. Alinsky, the Chicago-based organizer who called himself a "professional radical." In the early 1950's he helped Mexican-Americans organize into a political bloc.

Mr. Alinsky sent an aide to recruit potential leaders, and among the first people he met was Mr. Chavez, then working in a San Jose apricot orchard.

Mr. Chavez joined Mr. Alinsky's Community Service Organization, helping Mexican-Americans deal with government agencies. But in 1958 he quit, went to Delano and formed the National Farm Workers Association.

By 1965 Mr. Chavez had organized 1,700 families and persuaded two growers to raise wages moderately. Eight hundred workers in a moribund A.F.L.-C.I.O. group, the Agricultural Workers Organizing Committee, struck grape growers in Delano, and some members of his group demanded to join the strike.

That was the beginning of five years of La Huelga—"the strike"—in which the labor leader became familiar to people in much of the world as he battled the economic power of the farmers and corporations in the San Joaquin Valley.

In 1968 Mr. Chavez began his most visible campaign, urging Americans not to buy table grapes produced in the San Joaquin Valley until growers agreed to union contracts. The boycott proved a huge success. A public opinion poll found that 17 million Americans had stopped buying grapes because of the boycott.

On July 30, 1970, growers agreed to sign the contracts.

But soon many of the largest growers, in an effort to stave off Mr. Chavez's union, invited the International Brotherhood of Teamsters to organize their workers. His gains in Delano seemed to be slipping away.

But two things kept Mr. Chavez's dream alive. First, the teamsters' leaders, smarting from charges of corruption, made a truce. Second, Edmund G. Brown Jr., a Democrat, won adoption of a landmark bill establishing collective bargaining for farm workers and granting the union various concessions.

The United Farm Workers subsequently signed occasional contracts with growers but never attained the dominance that Mr. Chavez envisioned. A decade after the Delano strike, fewer than 10 percent of the grapes in that community were harvested by his union's members.

MOTHER TERESA

August 26, 1910–September 5, 1997

By Eric Pace

Mother Teresa, the Roman Catholic nun who won the 1979 Nobel Peace Prize for her work among the poorest of the world's poor, died yesterday in Calcutta, India, where she had lived since her work with the destitute began five decades ago. She was 87.

Her physician in Rome said she suffered cardiac arrest during the evening at her convent in Calcutta. As her health deteriorated over the past year, Mother Teresa stepped aside and her order, the Missionaries of Charity, chose a new leader, Sister Nirmala, in March.

Mother Teresa, an ethnic Albanian born in what is now Macedonia, was revered in India, where she worked for 68 years. She also came to be honored around the world for the compassionate, effective way she set up and oversaw projects to provide care and comfort to the very poor and the very sick, orphans, lepers and the dying.

Traveling widely even in her later years, she became known to millions as a slight, brown-eyed figure—she was only 5 feet tall—dressed in the plain white sari with blue trim of her order.

The Nobel Committee said its award to her in 1979 was "for work undertaken in the struggle to overcome poverty and distress in the world, which also constitute a threat to peace."

But she came in for criticism, too. A British television documentary in 1994 contended that perceptions of her were colored by "hyperbole and credulity."

Mother Teresa, who had been a school administrator in a suburb of Calcutta, began working in the slums of that poverty-ridden city in 1948. She had received what she described as a divine "call within a call" two years earlier. "The message was quite clear," she recalled. "I was to help the poor while living among them."

In 1950 she established the Order of the Missionaries of Charity, becoming its Superior General. She went on to organize far-flung programs for the impoverished, eventually reaching more than 90 countries.

Her chief task, as she defined it, was to provide "free service to the poor and the unwanted, irrespective of caste, creed, nationality or race."

Mother Teresa set up orphanages, schools in slums and Pure Heart Homes for sick and dying homeless people. She set up mobile health clinics, centers for the malnourished, rehabilitation hospices for lepers, homes for alcoholics and drug addicts, and shelters for the homeless. Her centers in the United States included the Gift of Love Hospice for men with AIDS, in Greenwich Village.

By the time Mother Teresa won the Nobel Prize, her order had attracted 1,800 nuns and 120,000 lay workers, running more than 80 centers in India and more than 100 others elsewhere in the world. The order's patients included 53,000 lepers.

By 1988, her order was operating 600 mobile health clinics where almost 4 million people received treatment. That year Mother Teresa visited South Africa, which was still under apartheid rule, to set up a hostel in a black township. By early 1992, members of her order—4,000 nuns and novices, 400 priests and brothers and hundreds of thousands of lay volunteers—worked at 450 sites worldwide, including in Albania and Iraq.

Mother Teresa often paid tribute to the stricken people she cared for. Speaking to a gathering at the United Nations in 1975, she recalled a woman she had found dying on a Calcutta street.

"I knew she was dying," she said softly. "After I did what I could, she took my hand, gave me a beautiful smile and thanked me. She gave me more than I gave her."

Mother Teresa put particular emphasis on giving the deprived and the sick a sensation of dignity through personal contact. "Ours is a humble service," she once said. "We try to remain right down on the ground."

But she said pity did not help the poor. "They need love and compassion," she said.

On certain social questions, Mother Teresa adhered outspokenly to the doctrine of her church. She voiced strong opposition to contraception, abortion and divorce. In accepting the Nobel Prize, she declared: "To me the nations with legalized abortion are the poorest nations. The greatest destroyer of peace today is the crime against the unborn child."

Criticism of her came from various quarters. Christopher Hitchens, a columnist for Vanity Fair and The Nation, voiced particularly strong criticism of her in a 1995 book, "The Missionary Position: Mother Teresa in Theory and Practice." Her success, he said, "depends on the exploitation of the simple and the humble by the cunning and the single-minded."

Mother Teresa was born Agnes Bojaxhiu on either Aug. 26 or 27, 1910, to Albanian parents in Skopje, about 200 miles south of Belgrade. The city is today the capital of Macedonia, but was then ruled by Ottoman Turks, before becoming part of Serbia in 1913. An authorized biography of her published in Britain in 1992 said her father was a building contractor.

At the age of 12 she first felt the desire to become a nun. At 18 she decided to do so and got in touch with the Sisters of Loreto, an Irish Catholic order with missions in Bengal. She joined the order in Rathfarnham, a suburb of Dublin, in 1928 and spent more than a year in Darjeeling, north of Calcutta, where the order ran a girls' school.

She then became a teacher at St. Mary's High School, on the grounds of the Entally Convent outside Calcutta. In time she learned Bengali and Hindi and became the school's principal.

It was while riding on a train on Sept. 10, 1946, that she received her "call within a call," she said. She left her school and learned nursing skills from other nuns. Then she began her good works among Calcutta's poor.

In 1950 she won canonical recognition for her new order, the Missionaries of Charity. The religious sisters who joined took vows of chastity, obedience, poverty and service.

One day in 1952, as her longtime associate Sister Agnes recalled years later, "she found an old woman dying in the streets."

"We tried to get someone to take her to a hospital," Sister Agnes said, "but before we could, she died. Mother said there should be a place where people can die with dignity and know that they are wanted."

And so Mother Teresa set about establishing a home for the dying destitute. She persuaded Calcutta's municipal authorities to give her a shabby one-story building, which stood next to a complex of Hindu shrines. In that humble structure, she created a place where those who died would do so with dignity and the dying were cared for with compassion. The establishment was called Nirmal Hriday, the place for the pure of heart.

Mother Teresa's undertakings continued. There was a home for abandoned children, a leper colony and an old people's home. She went on to set up welfare institutions ranging from a family clinic to mobile leprosy clinics to nurseries for abandoned children.

One of her biographers, Eileen Egan, reported in the book "Such a Vision of the Street: Mother Teresa—the Spirit and the Work" that a Red Cross official who helped her observed later: "What stunned everyone was her energy. We didn't expect a saint to be so efficient."

In 1971 Mother Teresa's order opened its first house in the United States, in Harlem. It was soon moved to the Bronx, where, on a visit to the United States in 1980, she helped open a soup kitchen and declared her thanks to the poor people of New York "for allowing themselves to be taken care of" by her order.

Her work brought in donations. She recalled that when her order opened a house in New York, "Terence Cardinal Cooke was very anxious that he should give every month a maintenance for the sisters."

"I didn't want to hurt him," she said, "but I didn't know how to explain to him that our services are purely for the love of God and that we cannot accept maintenance. I expressed it the only way I could: 'Your Eminence, I don't think God is going to become bankrupt in New York City!'"

ROSA PARKS

February 4, 1913–October 24, 2005

By E. R. Shipp

Rosa Parks, a black seamstress whose refusal to relinquish her seat to a white man on a city bus in Montgomery, Ala., almost 50 years ago grew into a mythic event that helped touch off the civil rights movement of the 1950's and 1960's, died yesterday at her home in Detroit. She was 92 years old.

For her act of defiance, Mrs. Parks was arrested, convicted of violating the segregation laws and fined $10, plus $4 in court fees. In response, blacks in Montgomery boycotted the buses for nearly 13 months while mounting a successful Supreme Court challenge to the Jim Crow law that enforced their second-class status on the public bus system.

The events that began on the bus helped transform a young preacher named Martin Luther King Jr. into a major civil rights leader. It was Dr. King, the new pastor of the Dexter Avenue Baptist Church in Montgomery, who was drafted to head the Montgomery Improvement Association, the organization formed to direct the nascent civil rights struggle.

"Mrs. Parks's arrest was the precipitating factor rather than the cause of the protest," Dr. King wrote in his 1958 book, "Stride Toward Freedom," adding, "The cause lay deep in the record of similar injustices."

Over the years myth tended to obscure the truth about Mrs. Parks. One legend had it that she was a cleaning woman with bad feet who was too tired to drag herself to the rear of the bus. Another had it that she was a "plant" by the National Association for the Advancement of Colored People.

The truth, as she later explained, was that she was tired of being humiliated, of having to adapt to the byzantine rules, some codified as law and others passed on as tradition, that reinforced the position of blacks as something less than full human beings.

Mrs. Parks was very active in the Montgomery N.A.A.C.P. chapter, and she and her husband, Raymond, a barber, had taken part in voter registration drives. But as she rushed home from her job as a seamstress at a department store on Dec. 1, 1955, the last thing on her mind was becoming "the mother of the civil rights movement," as many would later describe her. She had to send out notices of the N.A.A.C.P.'s coming election of officers. And she had to prepare for the workshop that she was running for teenagers that weekend.

"So it was not a time for me to be planning to get arrested," she recalled years later.

On Montgomery buses, the first four rows were reserved for whites. The rear was for blacks, who made up more than 75 percent of the bus system's riders. Blacks could sit in the middle rows until those seats were needed by whites. Then the blacks had to move to seats in the rear, stand or, if there was no room, leave the bus. Even getting on the bus presented hurdles: If whites were already sitting in the front, blacks could board to pay the fare but then they had to disembark and re-enter through the rear door.

For years blacks had complained. "My resisting being mistreated on the bus did not begin with that particular arrest," Mrs. Parks said. "I did a lot of walking in Montgomery."

After a confrontation in 1943, a driver named James Blake ejected Mrs. Parks from his bus. As fate would have it, he was driving the Cleveland Avenue bus on Dec. 1, 1955. He demanded that four blacks give up their seats in the middle section so a lone white man could sit. Three of them complied.

Recalling the incident for "Eyes on the Prize," a 1987 public television series on the civil rights movement, Mrs. Parks said: "When he saw me still sitting, he asked if I was going to stand up, and I said, 'No, I'm not.' And he said, 'Well, if you don't stand up, I'm going to have to call the police and have you arrested.' I said, 'You may do that.'"

Her arrest was the answer to prayers for the Women's Political Council, which was set up in 1946 in response to the mistreatment of black bus riders, and for E. D. Nixon, a leading advocate of equality for blacks in Montgomery.

Blacks had begun to build a case around a 15-year-old girl's arrest for refusing to give up her seat, but when they learned that the girl was pregnant, they decided that she was an unsuitable symbol. Mrs. Parks, on the other hand, was regarded as "one of the finest citizens of Montgomery—not one of the finest Negro citizens—but one of the finest citizens of Montgomery," Dr. King said.

While Mr. Nixon met with lawyers and preachers to plan an assault on the Jim Crow laws, the women's council distributed handbills that urged blacks to boycott the buses on Monday, Dec. 5, the day of Mrs. Parks's trial. On Sunday, Dec. 4, the announcement was made from many black pulpits.

Some blacks rode in carpools that Monday. Others rode in black-owned taxis that charged only the bus fare, 10 cents. But most black commuters—40,000 people—walked, some more than 20 miles.

At a church rally that night, blacks unanimously agreed to continue the boycott until these demands were met: that they be treated with courtesy, that black drivers be hired, and that seating in the middle of the bus go on a first-come basis.

The boycott lasted 381 days, during which many blacks were harassed and arrested. Churches and houses, including those of Dr. King and Mr. Nixon, were dynamited.

Finally, on Nov. 13, 1956, the Supreme Court outlawed segregation on buses. The court order arrived in Montgomery on Dec. 20; the boycott ended the next day. But the violence escalated: snipers fired into buses as well as Dr. King's home, and bombs were tossed into churches and ministers' homes.

Early the next year, the Parkses moved to Hampton, Va. Then they moved to Detroit, where Mrs. Parks worked for a time as an aide to Representative John Conyers Jr. Mrs. Parks's husband, Raymond, died in 1977. There are no immediate survivors.

Rosa Louise McCauley was born in Tuskegee, Ala., on Feb. 4, 1913, the elder of Leona and James McCauley's two children. Although the McCauleys were farmers, Mr. McCauley also worked as a carpenter and Mrs. McCauley as a teacher.

Rosa McCauley dropped out of high school to care for her ailing grandmother. It was not until she was 21 that she earned a diploma.

Mrs. Parks was awarded the Presidential Medal of Freedom and the Congressional Gold Medal, but her final years were troubled. She was hospitalized after a 28-year-old man beat her in her home and stole $53. She had problems paying her rent, relying on a local church for support until last December, when her landlord stopped charging her rent.

Mrs. Parks often appeared uncomfortable with the near-beatification bestowed upon her by blacks. She would say that she hoped only to inspire others "to be dedicated enough to make useful lives for themselves and to help others."

CAREER AND WRITINGS OF THE FOUNDER

OF THE INTERNATIONAL ASSOCIATION.

LONDON, March 16.—Dr. Friederich Engel, an intimate friend of Karl Marx, says Herr Marx died in London, near Regent's Park. Dr. Engel was present at the time of his death, which was caused by bronchitis, abscess of the lungs, and internal bleeding. He died without pain. In respect to the wishes of Herr Marx, who always avoided a demonstration, his family have decided that the funeral shall be private. About 18 persons will be present, including a few friends who are coming from the Continent. The place of interment has not been announced. Dr. Engel will probably speak at the grave. There will be no religious ceremony. At the time of his death the third edition of Herr Marx's book, "Das Kapital," first published in 1864, was in preparation for the press.

PARIS, March 16.—*La Justice*, of which M. Longuet, son-in-law of Karl Marx, is one of the staff, says Herr Marx spent part of last Summer at Argenteuil, but returned to London in October.

Karl Marx, the German Socialist and founder of the International Association, was born in Cologne in 1818, and after studying philosophy and the law at the Universities of Bonn and Berlin became the editor of the *Rhenish Gazette*, in 1842. The opinions which he published were of so radical a character that the paper was suppressed the following year. He then went to France, where he devoted himself to the study of political economy and social questions, and published in the *Franco-German Year Book*, in 1844, " A Critical Review of Hegel's Philosophy" and "The Holy Family against Bruno and His Consorts," a satire on German idealism. Expelled from France on the demand of the Prussian Government, he went to Belgium. He afterward took part in the Working Men's Congress in London in 1847, and was one of the authors of

Book. in 1844. "A Critical Review of Hegel's Philosophy" and "The Holy Family against Bruno and His Consorts," a satire on German idealism. Expelled from France on the demand of the Prussian Government, he went to Belgium. He afterward took part in the Working Men's Congress in London in 1847, and was one of the authors of the manifesto of the Communists. He was in Paris during the revolution of February, 1848, and then returned to Cologne, where he founded a paper called the *New Rhenish Gazette*. After the dissolution of the Prussian Chambers, Marx advised the people to organize and resist the collection of the imposts, and for this his journal was a second time suppressed. He continued the agitation against the tax, and was arrested several times, but always acquitted by the jury on trial. He was finally banished from Germany, and returned to Paris, where he took part in the stormy scenes of the June disturbances, for which he was imprisoned.

THINKERS

London, where he established himself permanently. There, in 1864, he founded the Association of Working Men, since known as the "International." Herr Marx was the leading spirit of the first Central Council of that organization, which framed the laws which were adopted at the Geneva congress in 1866. He became the Corresponding Secretary for Germany and Russia, and from that time was the real Director of the International. In 1871 he was attacked by the English section of the association and pronounced an unfit man to be a leader of the working classes. The schism was broadened in 1872, at the congress held at The Hague, when the Central Council at London was repudiated and Marx was deposed from his office as Secretary. The Internationals then divided into two factions—the Centralists, with Marx at their head, who transferred the headquarters of the Central Council to this City, and the Federalists, who had thrown Marx overboard. Marx continued to reside in London, where he was for many years a correspondent of a New-York paper. Among the works published by him are "A Treatise on Free Exchange," "The Misery of Philosophy," which is an answer to Proudhon's "Philosophy of Misery," and "Capital: a Criticism of Political Economy," which is a complete exposi-

ALEXIS DE TOCQUEVILLE

July 29, 1805–April 16, 1859

The London Times announces the death of the distinguished author of "Democracy in America"; an event for which previous reports of his rapidly declining health had prepared us.

The intelligence will be of melancholy interest to the multitudes in this country, who have read that capital production, and of personal regret to the survivors of those who enjoyed the gratification of intercourse with him during his travels through the United States, more than a quarter of a century ago.

Alexis Clerel de Tocqueville, a great-grandson of the loyal and philosophic Malesherbes, was born at Verneuil, July 29, 1805. Having completed his legal studies at Paris, he was named, in 1826, Judge of Instruction at Versailles, and in 1830 Alternate Judge. The following year he was selected with his friend E. G. de Beaumont to visit the United States in order to report upon the penitentiary systems of the several States.

The first fruit of his expedition was the "Démocratie en Amérique," which he published in 1835. The work was received with extraordinary applause. Royer-Collard described it as "a continuation of Montesquieu"; it had numberless editions, was translated into nearly every European language, and in 1836 received the Montyon prize. The next year, M. de Tocqueville was elected to the Academy of Sciences, and in 1841 to a seat in the French Academy. With his journey to America, the judicial career of M. de Tocqueville closed.

In 1839 he was chosen to the Chamber of Deputies from Valogne, Department of La Manche, retaining his seat until 1848, aiding consistently the opposition to the Administration of Louis Philippe. The January of the latter year, he predicted the approach of the revolution, which actually broke out in the month following. The Department of La Manche chose him its representative in the Constituent Assembly, where he distinguished himself by his hearty reprobation of Socialism, but otherwise sustained the Republic.

Gen. [Louis-Eugène] Cavaignau, during his brief administration, selected M. de Tocqueville to represent France in the Brussels Conferences on Italian affairs. On his return from this mission, he was re-elected to his seat in the Deputies; and on the 3rd of June, 1810, received from the hands of President Louis Napoleon the portfolio of Foreign Affairs, and advocated the occupation of Rome, with all his powerful abilities.

The peculiar views, on this subject, announced in the President's Message of Oct. 31, led to the resig-

nation of the moderate members of the Cabinet, M. de Tocqueville among the number. In the Legislative Assembly the ex-Minister at once took position on the benches of the Opposition.

On the 2nd December 1851, he was one of the deputies who met to protest against the coup d'etat. Imprisoned, with his principal associates, he was presently set at liberty; and finally withdrew to private life.

His latest publication was "L'ancien Régime et la Révolution, 1856." His closing days have been spent in the South of France, chiefly at Lannes, the seat of Lord Brougham's Summer residence.

JOHN STUART MILL

May 20, 1806–May 8, 1873

LONDON—John Stuart Mill is dead. Intelligence of his death at Avignon, France, reached here at 3 o'clock this afternoon.

There are only two or three great thinkers in a century, and the loss of one of them is an incident notable in the world's history. Such an event occurred two days ago, when Mr. John Stuart Mill died at Avignon.

This remarkable man was from his birth placed in circumstances peculiarly favorable to the development of his genius. He was a conspicuous instance of hereditary talent. His father, James Mill, was, like so many other men eminent in philosophical science, a Scotchman. He took orders at the University of Edinburgh, where he gained great distinction.

In 1798 he was licensed to preach, but he turned his back upon the pulpit, and became one of the throng of literary aspirants in the English metropolis. He subsequently became editor of the Literary Journal and contributed to the Edinburgh Review, which had just burst upon the world.

It was in 1806, just when he had commenced his History of India, that his son was born and christened John Stuart, after a Scottish baronet who had befriended his father. Mr. James Mill's work on British India had a considerable bearing on the fortunes of his son, for the ability and knowledge displayed in it resulted in his appointment to a position in the East India Company's office.

It was the father's connection with this establishment which led to the son's entering it, and when only 17, John Stuart Mill entered upon his duties as a clerk in the India House.

The circumstance is noteworthy as showing what a remarkable man can do as compared with an ordinary one under the same circumstances. Hundreds, nay thousands, of young men have entered the India House but were never heard of afterward, while this one man, leading the life of what has been termed a man mummy—a clerk in a Government office—has made a reputation which may endure as long as a mummy itself.

In 1820 Mr. John Stuart Mill went to France, where he attained a perfect knowledge of the French language and formed a perfect acquaintance with the history, politics, and literature of that country. Returning thence, he in 1823 entered the India Office as a subordinate clerk, where he was destined to remain until the extinction of the old East India Company in 1858. He was then offered a seat in the new council, appointed on the reconstruction of the department, which passed into the hands of the Crown, but declined to enter on the service of a new mistress, and retired.

Thrown in his father's house among many of the most aspiring minds of the day, and running over with eager thought, it was to be expected that Mr. J. S. Mill should early have commenced to give utterance to his opinions on paper, and in 1830 the agitation in reference to the Reform bill offered a tempting opportunity for him to embark in the field of periodical literature. He began to write much in various newspapers and reviews, and it need not be said that his advocacy was persistently in the cause of liberalism.

It was about this time that he fell in with a young man several years his junior, on whom he exerted great influence and through whom he probably exercised much influence on others. This was Sir William Molesworth, a young baronet of family and fortune. In 1835 Sir William purchased the Westminster Review, which, conjointly with his friend, he edited, and it became the vehicle of many of those views which the editors desired to bring before the public.

In 1843 Mr. J. S. Mill published his Logic, which soon became a standard work. This was followed, in 1844, by Essays on Some Unsettled Questions of Political Economy, and, in 1848, by Principles of Political Economy. These works were only a few out of many, but they contributed to his lasting fame as a philosophic thinker.

In 1865 Mr. Mill made what many regard as the only error in a faultless life by entering Parliament. Men 50

times his inferior found themselves equal to him, if not superior, in the mere power of pouring out words and expressing themselves attractively. He was dubbed "a mere book in breeches," and the feeling was general that he was not the right man in the right place.

In 1868 he retired. His wife's death occurred soon after, a blow from which he never recovered, and most of his remaining days were spent in the charming old town of Avignon, where the couple had spent many of their happiest hours.

It is almost impossible to estimate the influence such a mind as that of Mill exercises over his contemporaries. Its immediate influence is felt by only such a narrow circle as may be compared to that formed by a stone thrown into a pond, but each circle forms another until the effect becomes enormous. The immense value of such a mind lies in its extraordinary suggestiveness, combined with absolute purity in the motives for making suggestions.

To him, indeed, may well be applied those words of a great man in regard to his brother philosopher, [Thomas] Hobbes: "His is a great name in philosophy, on account both of the value of what be taught and the extraordinary impulse he communicated to the spirit of free inquiry."

RALPH WALDO EMERSON

May 25, 1803–April 27, 1882

CONCORD—Ralph Waldo Emerson died this evening at 8:50 o'clock. His death was, after all, somewhat sudden, and when the crisis had nearly passed there was believed to be fair reason to expect that improvement would follow. He suffered little pain the early part of the day and had only very slight fever, but as the day advanced he grew weaker. At about noon the patient began to display increased difficulty in breathing and to suffer pain, which speedily grew so intense that ether was administered him. It was while unconscious of pain and of his surroundings that he passed away.

At 9:30 o'clock the news was announced to the townspeople by the 79 strokes being sounded—the bell of the Unitarian church tolling the years of his life. To the Concord people this death came as a personal loss. He was as beloved by the people about him for the sweetness of his disposition and his uniform kindliness as he was honored for the wealth of his intellect and the exalted position he held among thinkers and men of letters of two continents.

The disease from which he died is pronounced acute pneumonia.

Ralph Waldo Emerson was conspicuously of the best blood of New England. He was born in Boston, May 25, 1803, his father being the Rev. William Emerson, Pastor of the First (Unitarian) Church of that city. The boy lost his father when he was but eight—a loss he always deplored—and was then placed in a public grammar school until fitted to enter the Latin school, where he made his first ventures in composition. They were precocious verses, having reference to the purpose of life, the destiny of man, the mission of beauty, half-dreamy, half-mystical, unconventional, very much, it must be confessed, like many of the poems he produced in his maturity.

He was considered gifted but peculiar, and predictions were made—they were verified in his case—

of his future celebrity. He entered Harvard at 14 and was graduated at 18. One who knew him in those days has described him as "a slender, delicate youth, younger than most of his classmates, and of a sensitive, retiring nature." In the recitation room he did always well with Greek and Latin, but in philosophy he did poorly, and mathematics were "his utter despair."

Leaving college, and having little means, he followed the customary course of New England youth, and taught school, continuing for five years. At 23 he had qualified himself for the pulpit, and in his 29th year was chosen colleague of Henry Ware, Jr., of the Second Unitarian Church. He had been there scarcely three years when he began to cherish doubts as to his belief. Granted permission to withdraw from his office, and shaking off all traditions of creed and authority, he stepped, as he said, into the free air and open world to utter his private thought to all who were willing to hear it.

From that hour dates the untrammeled life of Ralph Waldo Emerson as the present and many of a past generation know and knew him. He was very slow to gain recognition as an author, and well-nigh any man might have been dispirited by the lack of appreciation which so long attended him. But he had invincible faith in himself, and he waited patiently until he had found his audience and his audience had found him.

No American or European has been so fastidious as he respecting publication. He believed that a book should have every reason for being; that nothing trivial, passing, or temporary should be introduced into it; that the sole excuse for a book should be the presentation of fresh thought; that its contents should be in some manner an addition to the common stock of knowledge. If he had less vanity than members of his craft generally, he had more pride, more regard for his reputation, more confident expectation of enduring fame. He published what was universal and abiding in interest and influence, and compressed his utterances into the smallest space. Had all writers followed his example how immeasurably libraries would have been reduced!

The lectures of the American Plato, as he has been termed, soon found admirers in Boston. It became the mode of certain highly cultured sets in that city to extol the new light, the young transcendentalist, and being the mode, some who raved about him failed to understand him. Still, the great majority of his hearers were in harmony with his thought, and were sincere in their enthusiasm. Many became his disciples. The cheap wits of the day ridiculed his mysticism and studied opacity, as they were pleased to regard it, and decried all admiration of Emerson as a transparent affectation.

Jeremiah Mason, who ranked, in his day, as one of the foremost of New England lawyers, was induced to attend a course of Emerson's lectures. Asked what he thought of them, he replied: "They are utterly meaningless to me, but my daughters, aged 15 and 17, understand them thoroughly." This was repeated far and wide as a jest, but it may have been, probably was, literally true. A purely legal mind like Mason's was not of the kind to appreciate the speculative, idealistic mind of the lecturer, and it is not at all unlikely that the imaginative, intuitive, poetic girls caught at once what eluded their father's perception.

Mr. Emerson's first publication was a thin volume entitled "Nature" (1836), in eight chapters, embracing "Commodity," "Beauty," "Language," "Discipline," "Idealism," "Spirit," and "Prospects." It was virtually a pamphlet, but such a pamphlet as has seldom been issued. It had a new voice and a new strength, and its introduction was a key to whatever its author said afterward. Here are the opening words:

"Our age is retrospective. It builds the sepulchres of the fathers. It writes biographies, histories, and criticism. The foregoing generations beheld God and nature face to face; we through their eyes. Why should not we also enjoy an original relation to the universe?…There are new lands, new men, new thoughts. Let us demand our own works and laws and worship."

The transcendentalists needed an organ, and a quarterly, the Dial, was started (1840), with Margaret Fuller as editor, assisted by Emerson. It was exceedingly clever, even brilliant; it represented faithfully its class; but its class was too restricted, too far removed from the ordinary concerns of life, to place it on a substantial basis. As its editor said, Pegasus is a divine steed, though he cannot be expected to draw the baker's cart to one's door. Consequently it died after four years.

In 1841 the poet philosopher's first volume of "Essays" appeared, treating such subjects as self-reliance, compensation, love, friendship, prudence, heroism, art, character, intellect, experience, and in so novel, eloquent, and sagacious a manner that the volume would have been eagerly sought had it not run counter to the theological prejudices of Beacon-street, and startled well-regulated conservatism from its propriety by audacious paradoxes and iconoclastic judgments.

In 1876 Mr. Emerson collected a dozen essays into "Letters and Social Aims," practically his last volume. The final essay is "Immortality," and in it occurs this passage: "Sixty years ago…we were all taught that we were born to die, and over that all the terrors that theology could gather from savage notions were added to increase the gloom. A great change has occurred. Death is seen as a natural event and is met with firmness. A wise man in our time caused to be written on his tomb, 'Think on living!' That inscription describes a progress in opinion. Cease from this antedating of your experience! Sufficient to to-day are the duties of to-day. Don't waste life in doubts and fears! Spend yourself on the work before you, well assured that the right performance of this hour's duties will be the best preparation for the hours that follow it.

'The name of death was never terrible
To him that knew to live.'"

Anyone who may turn over the pages of Emerson must be struck with the number of phrases, and especially with the forms of expression, he has given to our mother tongue. The speech and writing of many cultured persons are stamped with his individuality. His pages are laden with aphorisms, and they are so felicitously put, and on such a variety of themes, that the capturing memory declines to surrender them, and speedily claims them as its own. How incessantly are we hearing these and hundreds of others?

Consistency is the hobgoblin of little minds.
Every man is a quotation from all his ancestors.
The devil is an ass.
No great men are original.
To be great is to be misunderstood.

Emerson appears to have acted his own definition of a philosopher—he reported to his own mind the constitution of the universe. He looked calmly at everything, into it, through it; and when aught came to him from within or without he jotted it down, not mentally merely, but actually. At all times he followed the habit, in the street or in his study, at midnight or morning. His wife, as the story goes, sometimes asked him when he had arisen in the watches of the night, "Are you ill, Waldo?" "No, dear," from the self-poised husband, "only an idea."

He had been twice married, first, when 27, to Ellen L. Tucker, of Boston, who died a few months after; secondly, three years later, to Lidian Jackson, of Plymouth, Mass. He has had three children, a son and two daughters, who are clever and capable. His home at Concord is described as a "plain, square wooden house, standing in a grove of pine trees." It was along the road facing which Mr. Emerson's house stands that the British troops marched on the memorable 19th of April, 1775.

Apparently absorbed in transcendentalism, Mr. Emerson always managed his affairs with intelligence and thrift. No immersion in the mysticism of the Bhagavad Gita could render him unmindful of duty to his family, the keeping of an engagement or the advantage of an investment. Of worldly goods he naturally had little; but of the little he made the most, and always kept rigorously clear of debt. No preoccupation with the planets caused him to forget his individual obligations or the quantity of coal in the cellar. A man so rounded, so conscientious, apart from what he was as scholar and thinker, could not fail by example to enrich in some sort our national life, for to live as high as we think is rarer than the rarest genius.

KARL MARX

May 5, 1818–March 14, 1883

LONDON—Dr. Friederich Engel [Friedrich Engels], an intimate friend of Karl Marx, says Herr Marx died in London, near Regent's Park. Dr. Engel was present at the time of his death, which was caused by bronchitis, abscess of the lungs, and internal bleeding. He died without pain.

In respect to the wishes of Herr Marx, who always avoided a demonstration, his family have decided that the funeral shall be private. About 18 persons will be present, including a few friends who are coming from the Continent. The place of interment has not been announced. Dr. Engel will probably speak at the grave. There will be no religious ceremony. At the time of his death the third edition of Herr Marx's book, "Das Kapital," first published in 1864, was in preparation for the press.

Karl Marx, the German Socialist and founder of the International Association, was born in Cologne in 1818, and after studying philosophy and the law at the Universities of Bonn and Berlin became the editor of the Rhenish Gazette, in 1842. The opinions which he published were of so radical a character that the paper was suppressed the following year.

He then went to France, where he devoted himself to the study of political economy and social questions, and published in the Franco-German Tear Book, in 1844, "A Critical Review of Hegel's Philosophy" and "The Holy Family against Bruno and His Consorts," a satire on German idealism.

Expelled from France on the demand of the Prussian Government, he went to Belgium. He afterward took part in the Working Men's Congress in London in 1847, and was one of the authors of the manifesto of the Communists. He was in Paris during the revolution of February, 1848, and then returned to Cologne, where he founded a paper called the New Rhenish Gazette.

After the dissolution of the Prussian Chambers, Marx advised the people to organize and resist the collection of the imposts, and for this his journal was a second time suppressed. He continued the agitation against the tax, and was arrested several times, but always acquitted by the jury on trial. He was finally banished from Germany, and returned to Paris, where he took part in the stormy scenes of the June disturbances, for which he was imprisoned, but managed to escape to London, where he established himself permanently.

There, in 1864, he founded the Association of Working Men, since known as the "International." Herr Marx was the leading spirit of the first Central Council of that organization, which framed the laws which were adopted at the Geneva congress in 1866. He became the Corresponding Secretary for Germany and Russia, and from that time was the real Director of the International.

In 1871 he was attacked by the English section of the association and pronounced an unfit man to be a leader of the working classes. The schism was broadened in 1872, at the congress held at The Hague, when the Central Council at London was repudiated and Marx was deposed from his office as Secretary. The Internationals then divided into two factions— the Centralists, with Marx at their head, who transferred the headquarters of the Central Council to this City, and the Federalists, who had thrown Marx overboard.

Marx continued to reside in London, where he was for many years a correspondent of a New York paper. Among the works published by him are "A Treatise on Free Exchange," "The Misery of Philosophy," which is an answer to Proudhon's "Philosophy of Misery," and "Capital; a Criticism of Political Economy," which is a complete exposition of the author's doctrines.

FRIEDRICH NIETZSCHE

October 15, 1844–August 25, 1900

WEIMAR, GERMANY—Prof. Friedrich Wilhelm Nietzsche, the philosopher, died here today of apoplexy.

Prof. Nietzsche was one of the most prominent of modern German philosophers, and he is considered the apostle of extreme modern rationalism and one of the founders of the socialistic school, whose ideas have had such a profound influence on the growth of political and social life throughout the civilized world.

Nietzsche was largely influenced by the pessimism of [Arthur] Schopenhauer, and his writings, full of revolutionary opinions, were fired with a fearless iconoclasm which surpassed the wildest dreams of contemporary free thought. His doctrines, however, were inspired by lofty aspirations, while the brilliancy of his thought and diction and the epigrammatic force of his writings commanded even the admiration of his most pronounced enemies, of which he had many.

Of Slavonic ancestry, Nietzsche was born in 1844 in the village of Röcken, on the historic battlefield of Lützen. He lost his parents early in life, but received a fine education at the Latin School at Pforta, concluding his studies at Bonn and Leipsic. Although educated for the ministry, Nietzsche soon renounced all faith in Christianity on the ground that it impeded the free expansion of life. He then devoted his attention to the study of Oriental languages and accepted in 1869 a professorship at the University of Basel, Switzerland.

This position he held until 1876, when overwork induced an affection of the brain and eyes, and he had to travel for his health. During these years of suffering and while in distressed circumstances he wrote most of his works.

Since 1889 Nietzsche had been hopelessly insane, living in Weimar, at the home of his sister, Elizabeth Forster-Nietzsche, who has edited his works. For many years he was a close friend of Richard Wagner, the composer. His principal publications are "The Old Faith and the New," "The Overman," "The Dawn of Day," "Twilight of the Gods," and "So Spake Zarathustra," which is perhaps the most remarkable of his works.

SIGMUND FREUD

May 6, 1856–September 23, 1939

LONDON—Dr. Sigmund Freud, originator of the theory of psychoanalysis, died shortly before midnight tonight at his son's home in Hampstead at the age of 83.

Dr. Freud fled from Austria last year when the country was invaded by Germany and had been living with his son, Dr. Ernst Freud. He had been in ill health for more than a year and yesterday he passed into a coma from which he never rallied.

One of the most widely discussed scientists of the present day and originator of countless new ideas in the field of psychology, Dr. Sigmund Freud was a man who never compromised but often modified. In his long and stormy career he set the entire world talking about psychoanalysis, the method which he originated and in which he dramatized for mankind the hampering force of inhibitions.

"The mind is an iceberg—it floats with only one-seventh of its bulk above water" was one of his metaphorical statements on the vast preponderance of the subconscious element in human life. Another was, "The conscious mind may be compared to a fountain playing in the sun and falling back into the subterranean pool of the subconscious from which it rises."

Probably the most radical departure from the old psychology introduced in Dr. Freud's science of psychoanalysis was that man is a willing rather than a thinking animal. Previous to his time psychology had been overwhelmingly "intellectual," regarding images, perceptions and ideas as the fundamental factors in mental life. But Dr. Freud laid the main stress of his system on the element of will or desire, relegating intellect to the background.

It was under this new system that Dr. Freud was able to explain many of the old "mysteries" of life, particularly regarding the fantasies and delusions of the deranged mind, and to shed a ray of light on the significance of dreams. It was also natural that, with this new basis of desire, sex should occupy the focal point of the system and that a new vocabulary of "Freudian" words should arise, among them "complex, inhibition, neurosis, psychosis, repression, resistance and transference."

The early critics of Freud's theories were filled with violent prejudice and moral indignation and sought to tear to pieces his entire system. The later critics acknowledged many of his theories to be valuable and devoted themselves to critical studies of his plan with a view to perfection rather than destruction. Dr. Freud himself believed that his ideas were harmed by their excessive popularity, which led to a reckless use of his theory and an exaggeration of his doctrines.

Although known as a Viennese, Dr. Freud was a Moravian by birth. He was born in this old Austro-Hungarian province on May 6, 1856, in the town of Freiberg. His parents moved to Vienna while he was young and he took his degree of Doctor of Medicine at the university there in 1881. After his graduation he served in turn as demonstrator in the physiological institute, Vienna, assistant physician in the general hospital, and lecturer on nervous diseases.

After becoming intensely interested in psychiatry he went on to Paris in 1885 to study in the famous school of [Jean-Martin] Charcot and [Pierre] Janet, known as the founders of modern abnormal psychology. He plunged into a wholly new investigation of neurotic disorders and developed a method so new that he made Janet one of his bitterest professional enemies. Several of Dr. Freud's pupils in turn, among them C. G. Jung and Alfred Adler, diverged from him as widely as he did from his own teachers.

In forming his ideas about psychoanalysis Freud proceeded with an independence and uncompromising attitude which served either to alienate his associates completely or to win them over as virtual disciples.

After remaining in Paris a year he returned to Vienna, where he became a Professor Extraordinary of Neurology in 1902. He also used his apartment in Berggasse as a clinic and received daily many patients who came to him with all types and varieties of mental ailments. Later in life, age and illness forced him to cut down the number of his patients, but he continued to develop his theories and to write treatises on his chosen subject.

The Communist experiment in Russia was of great interest to the psychoanalyst, but the United States failed to attract him, even though he had visited this country in 1909, when he received an honorary degree from Clark University. Probably the only American whom he held in high esteem was William James, who he said was "one of the most charming men I have ever met." Professor James, however, was to him the one exception in a country which has produced only "an unthinking optimism and a shallow philosophy of activity."

The United States was scarcely more tolerant in many ways toward Dr. Freud, and many of his conceptions of this country were based on exaggerated or burlesqued writings on his principles. Probably the most predominant criticism in America of the Freudian theory is that the element of sex is grossly overplayed in his explanations of human actions and reactions.

Even the defenders of Dr. Freud have from time to time admitted that, like most specialists, he had carried many of his ideas too far and that he saw sex where its presence was debatable or even absent.

Dr. Freud was a prolific writer. His books have put before the world his wealth of ideas, startling and even sensational during the pre-war conservatism. His works on hysteria and the interpretation of dreams were probably his most widely known writings. In these he brought out the theory that hysteria is the result of a nervous shock, emotional and usually sexual in nature, and that the ideas involved have been suppressed or inhibited until they can no longer be recalled. By a use of the principle of psychoanalysis and the employment of the patient's free-will associations these ideas can be recalled, he wrote, and the cause of the hysteria removed.

One of his outstanding works was an incidental writing which appeared near the close of the war, entitled "Reflections on War and Death."

"The history of the world is essentially a series of race murders," he wrote. "The individual does not believe in his own death. On the other hand, we recognize the death of strangers and of enemies, and sentence them to it just as willingly and unhesitatingly as primitive man did."

Despite the ravages of cancer and infirmities of age, Dr. Freud continued to be active until after his 80th birthday on May 6, 1936. At that time, declining a request for an interview, he wrote: "What I had to tell the world I have told. I place the last period after my work."

Many who had been the bitterest critics of his psychoanalysis theories gathered in Vienna on his 80th birthday to do him honor. He himself was not there, but his wife and family were, and they wept as Dr. Julius Wagneur-Jauregg, president of the Viennese Psychiatrists Association, said in opening the meeting:

"Viennese psychiatrists followed the trail blazed by Freud to worldwide fame and greatness. We are proud and happy to congratulate him as one of the great figures of the Viennese school of medicine."

He still received a few patients after 1930, but most of the questioning was done by his daughter Anna, whom he recognized as his successor, the bearded, stoop-shouldered doctor merely nodding agreement from time to time. He received only a few old friends, who called on Wednesday nights to talk and on Fridays to play cards.

His last years also were disturbed by the pogroms against the Jews. When his books were burned by the Nazis in the bonfire which also consumed the works of Heine and other non-Aryan authors, he remarked, "Well, at least I have been burned in good company."

Although egotistical in his professional contacts— he told the story that a peasant woman had told his mother when he was born that she had given birth to a great man—Freud was described by his family and his friends as gentle and considerate, a delightful companion when not talking "shop."

Soon after his 81st birthday, when he was suffering from both cancer and a painful heart malady, he said despairingly, "It is tragic when a man outlives his body."

During his last years, when he was to taste the bitterness of exile, Dr. Freud had been in retirement, engaged upon writing books. He had retired into his library and was seeking, in the few years left to him, to make a pioneering study of the nature of religion. As the annexation of Austria appeared more and more a menace, he was urged by his friends to seek refuge abroad, but he refused to go. If the Nazis invaded the refuge of his library, he told them, he was prepared to kill himself.

He was ill, a shadow of his former self at 82, when Nazi Germany moved her army into Austria and absorbed his homeland. He remained in seclusion in his five-room apartment, "dreading insults if he emerged—because he is a Jew," friends said. A delegation of Netherlands admirers went to Vienna to offer him the hospitality of their country, but the authorities forbade him to go, refusing him a passport. Soon the reason was disclosed. The Nazis were demanding that he be ransomed.

A fund had been raised quietly by American admirers to pay his and his family's living expenses once they left Vienna, but it was inadequate to meet the demand. Princess George of Greece, who as Princess Marie Bonaparte had studied under Freud, induced the Nazi authorities to accept a quarter million Austrian schillings to restore his passport.

In June, 1938, he was able to leave with his family and some personal books and papers. He went to Paris and then to London, the Nazi press sending after him a parting gibe, calling his school a "pornographic Jewish specialty." Settling in London, he finished a book, "Moses and Monotheism," a study of the Moses legend and its relation to the development of Judaism and Christianity.

The book, a first effort to use his psychoanalytic system to explain the origins of the institution of religion, aroused a storm of controversy. But it was hailed by Thomas Mann, who said it showed that the Freudian theory had become "a world movement embracing every possible field of learning and science," as, for future generations, one of the most important foundation stones for "the dwelling of a freer and wiser humanity."

In London Dr. Freud spent a contented year in a house a few hundred yards north of Regent's Park. Leaving further development of his psychological theories to his daughter, Anna, and his disciples, he concentrated on his monumental study of the Old Testament, which he estimated would take him five years to complete.

He had stated its theme, that all religions only reflect the hopes and fears of man's own deepest nature, in "Totem and Taboo" 25 years before, but now he sought to buttress his speculations with supporting evidence. This work, which he believed would have a far-reaching effect on religion, is now left uncompleted, it is believed.

JOHN MAYNARD KEYNES

June 5, 1883–April 21, 1946

LONDON—John Maynard Lord Keynes, the distinguished economist, whose work to restore the economic structure of a world twice shattered by war brought him worldwide influence, died of a heart attack today at his home in Firle, Sussex. He was 63.

Exhausted by the strain of the International Monetary Conference at Savannah, Ga., he returned to Britain a fortnight ago, tired and ill. Lady Keynes was with her husband at his death.

Noted as a political and social economist who influenced both specialists and the general public, Lord Keynes's name was linked with that of Adam Smith. He was a protagonist of the theory that makes full employment the overriding aim of financial policy.

His genius expressed itself in many other spheres of activity. He was a Parliamentary orator of high order, a historian and devotee of music, drama and the ballet. A successful farmer, he was an expert on development of grass feeding stuffs. He also was a book collector, and his collection of unpublished Newton manuscripts on alchemy was noteworthy.

Lord Keynes at one period was the center of a literary circle that was known as "Bloomsbury"—Lytton Strachey, Virginia Woolf and their intimate friends.

Lord Keynes first won public attention through his resignation from the British Treasury's mission to the Paris Peace Conference and his prediction that the Treaty of Versailles would prove more harmful to the nations dictating it than to Germany. His reasons were set forth in his 1919 book, "The Economic Consequences of the Peace," which included his premise that the reparations clauses were too severe.

The book created a storm of controversy but was so widely in demand that it ran five editions the first year and was translated into eleven languages. Lord Keynes was not again associated with the British Government in any official capacity until the spring of 1940, by which time much of what he had prophesied had come true.

His place in economics and finance was formally recognized in 1942 with publication of the King's Birthday Honors naming him first Baron of Tilton.

Lord Keynes had participated in the first meeting of the governors of the World Bank and Fund, set up under the Bretton Woods agreements, in Savannah, and was elected a vice president of the World Bank and Fund.

Born on June 5, 1883, in Cambridge, Lord Keynes entered government service at the age of 23, but continued his association with Cambridge University throughout his life and became High Steward of the city of Cambridge. His father, John Neville Keynes, was Registrary Emeritus of the university and his mother was a one-time Mayor of Cambridge.

Lord Keynes's first position was as a minor official in the Revenue Department of the India Office, where he remained two years, then returned to Cambridge to teach and in 1912 became editor of The Economic Journal, a post he held throughout his life.

In 1915 he joined the Treasury Department, remaining until his resignation. In 1913–14 he had served as a member of the Royal Commission on Indian Finance and Currency.

His official designation at the peace conference was as the principal representative of the Treasury and Deputy for the Chancellor of the Exchequer on the Supreme Economic Council.

The sensation created by "The Economic Consequences of the Peace" was due in large part to its lucid literary style and its revelation of the inside story of the Paris conference.

Referring to that period, Kingsley Martin, editor of The New Statesman and Nation, a British publication, wrote: "Those who knew nothing of economics could appreciate, if only from quotations in the press, Mr. Keynes' brilliant picture of M. Clemenceau, Mr. Lloyd George and President Wilson at Versailles."

"It convinced us all that, whatever the other merits or evils of the treaty, its real vice was its failure to treat Europe as an economic whole and to reconstruct it for the benefit of the common people," Mr. Martin continued. "It was a treaty of strategy and national greediness—with the League of Nations thrown in to make it look pretty."

Lord Keynes's theories about why the treaty would fail were largely reflected in his sketches of the principal participants in the conference.

He described M. Clemenceau as "by far the most eminent member of the Council of Four," who alone knew "what he wanted—namely, to cripple Germany." He claimed that President Wilson lacked the intellectual equipment to match wits with either Clemenceau or Lloyd George in the give-and-take of the conference table.

His characterization of the principals was summed up as follows:

"Clemenceau, aesthetically the noblest; the President, morally the most admirable; Lloyd George, intellectually the subtlest. Out of their disparities and weaknesses the treaty was born, child of the least worthy attributes of each of its parents, without nobility, without morality, without intellect."

The book in a certain sense was the turning point in Lord Keynes's career. Thereafter he was no longer a mere economist but a prophet and pamphleteer, a journalist and the author of a best seller.

Although contemptuous of Wilson, Lord Keynes was lavish in his praise of President [Franklin D.] Roosevelt. He sought, without success, to get the British Government to launch a spending program similar to that which President Roosevelt had established in the United States. He asked for a $500 million-a-year employment fund to provide for 500,000 men, a $500 million housing plan and a $500 million public works fund.

Frequently when Britain has been faced with a perplexing financial issue, Lord Keynes's advice had been relied on heavily.

As a forerunner to matters taken up at Bretton Woods, N.H., in July, 1944, a White Paper, authored a year earlier by Lord Keynes and issued by the British Government, outlined a plan for a banking system between nations similar to a banking system within a nation.

He took a leading role in helping to crystallize the ideas for a world bank and stabilization of international currency at the monetary conference at Bretton Woods.

CARL JUNG

July 26, 1875–June 6, 1961

Zurich—Professor Carl Gustav Jung, one of the founders of analytic psychology, died today at his villa in Kuessnacht on Lake Lucerne. The famed psychologist, who was beset by heart and circulatory troubles, was 85.—*The Associated Press*

Dr. Jung was one of the great modern adventurers who sought to push back the dark frontiers of man's mind.

Before the coming of his great forerunner, Dr. Sigmund Freud, the world was little used to rummaging through man's subconscious to find the key to his peace and security. Before Freud and Jung, the Western world was inclined to think of man's conduct in terms of original sin. Dr. Jung was one of those who gave a tremendous impetus to 20th-century thinking by declaring that this explanation was not good enough.

To bring some definition to the subconscious mind, Dr. Jung created special terms that soon became part of the language of the educated. Jungian terms such as extrovert and introvert became dinner-conversation clichés.

After an early apprenticeship, Dr. Jung broke with the harsh psychological school established by Freud. Freud held that nearly all human mental troubles were the result of sexual conflicts in infancy, the most powerful being the infantile urge to parricide and incest—the Oedipus and Electra complexes.

While admitting this urge, Dr. Jung said that man's natural instinct toward religion was perhaps as strong as his sexual instinct.

Dr. Freud traced religion to the child's helplessness before the outer world and the child's need to cling to its parents in order to survive.

The Freudian world was a gloomy jungle in which man was forever stumbling over repressed emotional experiences. Freud and those who formed the hard core of his school believed that the only cure for man's dilemma was to locate and remove these stumbling-block emotional experiences.

Dr. Jung, by contrast, held that man was not necessarily doomed to be buffeted by traumas over which he could exercise little control. The Jungians derided the Freudian theory that God was nothing more than man's self-created vision of his father, and that good deeds and a desire to advance in the world were only devices to forget more primitive urges.

Freud's world was found by many to be almost hopeless. Dr. Jung's world was not exactly cozy, but he believed that man's unconquerable spirit could make it better. Man could do this, Dr. Jung taught, because, in addition to the experiences of each in-

dividual, as registered in his subconscious mind, each person had a second group of experiences. This group was the collective experience of the race recorded in his subconscious mind, a collective experience that included man's never-ceasing urge toward religion.

Freud, Dr. Jung and Dr. Alfred Adler were the three great figures in the age of psychology. They influenced Western man's thinking as it had not been influenced since the publication of the "Origin of Species" in 1859. Adler, who likewise broke with the harsher theories of Freud, died in 1937, and Freud died two years later.

Dr. Jung was born on July 26, 1875, in Kesswil, Switzerland. He was a son of Paul Jung, an Evangelical minister, and Emille Freiswerk Jung. The family moved to Basel, where the son obtained a medical degree in 1900.

Dr. Jung became a lecturer in psychiatry at the University of Zurich and with Dr. Eugen Bleuler, founded the "Zurich School" of depth psychology. This school came to be thought of as opposing the "Vienna School" established by Dr. Freud, although Drs. Jung and Freud agreed about many basic tenets of modern psychology.

The methods used by Dr. Jung in obtaining the cooperation of the nonconscious factors in the mind were similar to those used by Freud.

In 1909 some of the best work in the United States in this field was being done at Clark University in

Worcester, Mass., and in 1909 Dr. Jung, Dr. Freud and other world authorities on psychiatry went to Clark for a series of lectures and conferences. Here Dr. Jung gave his first extensive exposition of his "association method," a hitherto untried method of probing the subconscious mind.

In 1911 Dr. Jung and other authorities in his field founded the International Psychoanalytic Society. Dr. Jung used this society to further his views on new elements that he believed he had found in dreams and fantasies.

Critics of Dr. Jung's theories attacked him for showing too much interest in such unscientific matters as occultism and witchcraft. The Freudians held that he was betraying pure scientific research by digressions into Buddhism and Christianity. At this period, Dr. Jung also explored yoga, alchemy, folklore and tribal religious rites. All this was seen by his opponents as a betrayal of scientific principles.

Dr. Jung said that, on the contrary, since mankind had devoted so much thought to such matters, they formed part of man's consciousness of the race.

During Hitler's ascendency in Germany, Dr. Jung's theories about the consciousness of the race were borrowed by the Nazis. Dr. Jung hastened to say that the Nazi interpretation of his theories was largely wrong and his statements in this matter had been distorted out of their true meaning by Hitler's followers.

In 1948, the C. G. Jung Institute was established in Zurich to provide scholars with a place to do advanced research in analytical psychology.

Although Dr. Freud and Dr. Jung differed on many of the fundamentals of applied psychology, they remained friendly and once talked nonstop for 12 hours. Each would tell the other his dreams and they would give their interpretations of their findings.

The two great explorers of the mind differed in their methods of obtaining their material. Dr. Freud established the now generally accepted method of placing his subject on a couch and withdrawing himself to create the impression on the subject that he was not intruding. Dr. Jung usually placed his subject in a chair opposite him and made him feel that he, Dr. Jung, would share his subject's experiences with him.

In 1903 Dr. Jung married Emma Rauschenbush, heiress to a Swiss watch fortune, who died in 1955. He is survived by a son and four daughters.

Dr. Jung was a tall, large-boned man who in his later years had a scraggly white mustache and thinning white hair. He had a ruddy complexion and a crinkly and charming smile.

Over the door of his home in Kuessnacht is carved the Latin inscription:

Vocatus atqua non vocatus deus aderit. (Called or not called, God is present.)

KARL BARTH

May 10, 1886–December 10, 1968

By Edward B. Fiske

Karl Barth, the Protestant theologian, died in his sleep Monday night at his home in Basel, Switzerland, a family spokesman announced yesterday. He was 82 years old.

In 1919 an unknown Swiss country pastor gave the world a rather unpretentious-sounding book entitled "The Epistle to the Romans." He had had difficulty finding a publisher, but, as a fellow theologian later put it, the volume "landed like a bombshell in the playground of the theologians."

The young pastor was Karl Barth, and his commentary on Romans was one of those events that happen only rarely in a discipline such as theology— when a revolutionary idea falls into the hands of a giant who possesses the powers not only to utter it but also to control its destiny.

In this case the idea was the radical transcendence of God. At a time when theologians had reduced God to little more than a projection of man's highest impulses, Dr. Barth rejected all that human disciplines such as history or philosophy could say about God and man. He spoke of God as the "wholly other" who entered human history at the moments of His own choosing and sat in judgment on any attempt by men to create a God in their own image.

Forty years later Dr. Barth (rhymes with "heart") was to apply a "corrective" to this radical distinction between God and man. In the meantime, he would produce one of the monuments of 20th-century scholarship, "Church Dogmatics," and come to be widely regarded as the most important Protestant theologian since John Calvin. He was frequently compared with Augustine, Anselm and Martin Luther.

Dr. Barth's conclusions were sometimes radical; but his language was traditional, and it was the classic dogmas of the church that excited his imagination. His overriding concern was to spell out in large, bold letters the grand Trinitarian themes of the Christian faith.

Largely because of this he came to have as much influence in the Roman Catholic community as any contemporary Protestant thinker.

Years after the appearance of the commentary that made him into a major theological figure, Dr. Barth likened himself to "one who, ascending the dark staircase of a church tower and trying to steady himself, reached for the banister, but got hold of the bell rope instead.

"To his horror, he had then to listen to what the great bell has sounded over him and not over him alone."

Liberal theology of the 19th century had started out as a protest against the sterile dogmatism and Biblical literalism into which Protestant thought had degenerated in the centuries following the Reformation.

In contrast to Luther, who was preoccupied with the sinfulness and helplessness of man before a just God, liberal theologians emphasized reason, the scientific method and the establishment of the Kingdom of God on earth.

By the turn of the 20th century, however, such thinking had itself become sterile.

Ludwig Feuerbach had reduced theology to anthropology, and the "queen of the sciences" came to be measured not by its own standards but by those of philosophy, natural science and history. Jesus took on all the attributes of a European gentleman.

The man who rang in a new theological era was as Swiss as cheese fondue. Dr. Barth was rather tall, with a high forehead and cheekbones, craggy eyebrows and pale blue eyes. In his later years he looked like a casting agency's idea of a German professor—with a shock of wayward gray hair and horn-rimmed glasses that usually sat at the tip of his nose. His physique was rugged and showed the effects of much horseback riding and mountain climbing in his youth.

The ideas that led to "The Epistle to the Romans" were formed during a 10-year pastorate in Safenwil, a small village in north central Switzerland. Along with Eduard Thurneysen, a close friend who was pastor in a neighboring village, Dr. Barth began to entertain doubts about the tradition on which he had been reared.

The critical moments came in 1914, the year that hopes for establishing the Kingdom of God on earth were trampled into the European mud by the heels of marching troops.

The biggest shock occurred on what Dr. Barth later described as a "black day" in August when 93 German intellectuals, including almost all of his theological teachers, proclaimed their support of the war policy of Kaiser Wilhelm II. In "The Epistle to the Romans" in 1919 and in a completely revised second edition three years later, Dr. Barth set out, as he put it, "to turn the rudder [of theology] an angle of exactly 180 degrees."

The marker on which he set his sights can be illustrated by a picture that hung above his desk during this period, Matthias Grunewald's "Crucifixion." Dominating the darkened landscape is the agonizing figure of Jesus on the Cross. Just as the composition of Grunewald's painting sends the viewer's eyes repeatedly back to the central figure, so Dr. Barth's theology is built around the revelation of God in Jesus Christ.

The Scriptures, said Dr. Barth, contain "divine thoughts about men, not human thoughts about God." He saw this as the cure for doctrinal errors that had led to the divisions within Christendom.

His fidelity to the Bible as the Word of God led him to reject Calvin's idea that some men were "predestined" by God to eternal salvation or damnation. Dr. Barth once remarked, "Calvin is in Heaven and has had time to ponder where he went wrong. Doubtless he is pleased that I am setting him right."

Dr. Barth's views were the source of much controversy. Fundamentalists charged that despite his emphasis on the Bible, he had actually replaced the Scriptures with Christ as the ultimate authority for faith. He was also accused of being too rigid, and many maintained that his emphasis on the helplessness of man in the face of evil was too pessimistic.

If Dr. Barth was a revolutionary, his ideas were also deeply embedded in the traditions of the Calvinistic, or Reformed, branch of Protestantism. Many Barths before him, including his father, Fritz, had been Swiss Reformed pastors.

He was born May 10, 1886, in Basel, where his father had a church. When he was three, the family moved to Bern, where Fritz Barth had accepted a post as professor of New Testament and church history at the university. It was there that Karl, the oldest of five children, was reared and educated and acquired the local Swiss German dialect that caused German purists to shudder.

He began studying theology in 1904 at the age of 18 under his father, and was ordained in 1908. After a year as assistant to the editor of a liberal theological journal, he took his first pastorate in Geneva. Two years later he moved to Safenwil, where he first revealed his penchant for political debate that later led to his confrontation with the Third Reich and an international dispute over his attitude toward Communism.

Dr. Barth became a religious socialist and in 1915 joined the Social Democratic party.

Following the publication of "The Epistle to the Romans," Dr. Barth accepted in September, 1921, a post as professor of Reformed theology at the University of Gottingen. By 1927 his theological ideas had crystallized sufficiently for him to publish "The Doctrine of the Word of God: Prolegomena to Christian Dogmatics." He soon came to regard this work as an unsuccessful experiment, however, and repudiated it.

In 1930 Dr. Barth became professor of systematic theology at Bonn. It was there, in 1932, that he published the first half-volume of "Church Dogmatics." This exposition of his theological thinking eventually grew to more than 6 million words on 7,000 pages in 12 volumes. It still lacked several volumes when he retired in 1962 and abandoned the project.

Dr. Barth was willing to reverse himself at times, and he insisted that even his own "Church Dogmatics" was tentative and written only to be revised and refined by his students.

His confrontation with the Third Reich began in the summer of 1933, when Hitler started to establish "German Christian" churches in which National Socialist teachings were given dogmatic status. He refused to take the oath of allegiance that Hitler required of state employes or to begin his lectures with a salutation to the Fuehrer.

In 1934 about 200 leaders of German Protestantism signed the Barmen Confession, which asserted the freedom of the church from temporal powers. Dr. Barth was the chief author.

He was soon convicted by a Nazi court of "seducing the minds" of his students and was suspended from his teaching position. In October, 1935, he was escorted to the Swiss border at Basel and expelled from Germany.

After the war this outspoken critic of Nazism became a controversial defender of the German people. He visited Germany in 1945 and in the next two years spent two semesters teaching in Bonn.

In 1948 Dr. Barth visited Hungary, and in the years following he drew bitter criticism for his refusal to attack Communism with the same vigor with which he had protested Nazism. He regarded Communism, too, as idolatrous, but he saw it as the "natural result" of the failure of Western culture to solve some of its human problems.

After his retirement in 1962 at the age of 75, Dr. Barth surprised everyone by undertaking a trip to the United States, where his son Markus was a professor of New Testament at the University of Chicago. He gave a number of lectures, but the highlights of the visit for him were trips to the Civil War battlefields at Gettysburg and Richmond.

From childhood Dr. Barth's hobby had been military history, and he carried in his head the names of all the generals and battles of the Napoleonic and other wars. In later years he became an American Civil War buff.

Despite an ascetic workday that for years lasted from regular 7 A.M. lectures to post-midnight writing and study, he was always willing to take time out to play tin soldiers with his sons. "Dad had a collection of hundreds of soldiers," Markus said, "and he always insisted on being Napoleon. So he always won."

Dr. Barth was proud that two of his sons followed him into the field of theology. Markus, the eldest, now teaches at the Pittsburgh Theological Seminary, while Christop is a professor of Old Testament in Mainz, West Germany. A daughter, Franziska, is married to a businessman in Basel, where the third son, Hans Jakob, is a landscape architect. A fourth son died in a mountain-climbing accident.

Their mother, the former Nell Hoffman, was a violin student whom Dr. Barth married in 1913.

REINHOLD NIEBUHR

June 21, 1892–June 1, 1971

By Alden Whitman

The Rev. Reinhold Niebuhr, the Protestant theologian who had wide influence in the worlds of religion and politics, died last evening at his summer home in Stockbridge, Mass., after a long illness. He was 78 years old.

Throughout his long career he was a theologian who preached in the marketplace, a philosopher of ethics who applied his belief to everyday moral predicaments and a political liberal who subscribed to a hard-boiled pragmatism.

Combining all these capacities, he was the architect of a complex philosophy based on the fallibility of man and the absurdity of human pretensions, as well as on the Biblical precepts that man should love God and his neighbor.

The Protestant theology that Mr. Niebuhr evolved over a lifetime was called neo-orthodoxy. It stressed original sin, which Mr. Niebuhr defined as pride, the "universality of self-regard in everybody's motives, whether they are idealists or realists or whether they are benevolent or not."

It rejected utopianism, the belief "that increasing reason, increasing education, increasing technical conquests of nature make for moral progress, that historical development means moral progress."

Reinhold Niebuhr was the mentor of scores of men, including Arthur Schlesinger Jr., who were the brain trust of the Democratic party in the nineteen-fifties and sixties. George F. Kennan, the diplomat and adviser to Presidents on Soviet affairs, called Mr. Niebuhr "the father of us all" in recognition of his role in encouraging intellectuals to help shape national policies.

"The finest task of achieving justice," Mr. Niebuhr once wrote, "will be done neither by the Utopians who dream dreams of perfect brotherhood nor yet by the cynics who believe that the self-interest of nations cannot be overcome. It must be done by the realists who understand that nations are selfish and will be so till the end of history, but that none of us, no matter how selfish we may be, can be only selfish."

Mr. Niebuhr was himself active in politics, as a member first of the Socialist party, and then as vice chairman of the Liberal party in New York.

He was an officer of Americans for Democratic Action and active in numerous committees established to deal with specific social, economic and political matters. He was a firm interventionist in the years before United States entry into World War II. He was equally firm in opposing Communist goals after the war, but at the same time he was against harassing American Communists.

Much of Mr. Niebuhr's political influence was embodied in an outpouring of articles on topics ranging from the moral basis of politics to race relations to pacifism to trade unionism to foreign affairs.

Mr. Niebuhr had been associated with Union Theological Seminary, Broadway and 121st Street, since 1928. Hundreds of seminarians jammed lecture halls for his courses, and thousands of laymen heard him preach or lecture. He spoke at many colleges, preached at scores of churches and appeared on innumerable public platforms.

Mr. Niebuhr possessed a deep voice and large blue eyes. He used his arms as though he were an orchestra conductor. He wore his erudition lightly and spoke in common accents. When he preached, one auditor recalled, "he always seemed the small-town parish minister."

He looked outsized in his snug office on the seventh floor of the seminary. Its walls were so hidden by books, mostly on sociology and economics, that there was space for only one picture, a wood engraving of Jonah inside the whale. On his desk, amid a wild miscellany of papers, was a framed photograph of his wife, Ursula, and his son and daughter, who survive him.

When students dropped in, he liked to rock back in his swivel chair, cross his legs, link his hands on top of his head and chat. Mr. Niebuhr was "Reinie" to friends and acquaintances. His highest earned academic degree was Master of Arts, which he received from Yale in 1915, but he collected 18 honorary doctorates, including a Doctor of Divinity from Oxford.

For several years in the nineteen-thirties he edited and contributed to The World Tomorrow, a Socialist party organ; from the forties he edited and wrote for Christianity and Crisis, a biweekly magazine devoted to religious matters. In an ecumenical spirit, he wrote for The Commonweal, a Roman Catholic magazine; for Advance and Christian Century, Protestant publications; and for Commentary, a Jewish publication.

Because Mr. Niebuhr did not employ Biblical citations to support his political attitudes, some associates were skeptical of the depth of his faith.

"Don't tell me Reinie takes that God business seriously," a political co-worker once said.

The remark got back to Mr. Niebuhr, who laughed and said: "I know. Some of my friends think I teach Christian ethics as a sort of front to make my politics respectable."

Troubled agnostics, Catholics, Protestants and Jews often came to him for spiritual guidance. Only half facetiously, one Jew confessed: "Reinie is my rabbi."

Among Mr. Niebuhr's admirers was Supreme Court Justice Felix Frankfurter. After listening to one sermon, the late Justice said:

"I liked what you said, Reinie, and I speak as a believing unbeliever."

"I'm glad you did," the clergyman replied, "for I spoke as an unbelieving believer."

Although Mr. Niebuhr was acclaimed as a theologian, the closest he came to systematizing his views was in his two-volume "The Nature and Destiny of Man," published in 1943. He began an "intellectual biography" issued in 1956 by saying:

"I cannot and do not claim to be a theologian. I have taught Christian Social Ethics for a quarter of a century and have also dealt in the ancillary field of apologetics. My avocational interest as a kind of circuit rider in colleges and universities has prompted an interest in the defense and justification of the Christian faith in a secular age...

"I have never been very competent in the nice points of pure theology; and I must confess that I have not been sufficiently interested heretofore to acquire the competence."

There was, nonetheless, a Niebuhr doctrine. In its essence it accepted God and contended that man knows Him chiefly through Christ, or what Mr. Niebuhr called "the Christ event." The doctrine, in its evolved form, suggested that man's condition was inherently sinful, and that his original, and largely ineradicable, sin is his pride, or egotism.

He argued also that man deluded himself most of the time; for example, he believed that a man who trumpeted his own tolerance was likely to be full of concealed prejudices and bigotries.

"The Christian faith cannot deny that our acts may be influenced by heredity, environment and the actions of others," he once wrote. "But it must deny that we can ever excuse our actions by attributing them to the fault of others, even though there has been a strong inclination to do this since Adam excused himself by the words, 'The woman gave me the apple.'"

Mr. Niebuhr also insisted that "when the Bible speaks of man being made in the image of God, it means that he is a free spirit as well as a creature; and that as a spirit he is finally responsible to God."

Billy Graham, the evangelist, and the Rev. Dr. Norman Vincent Peale, the expositor of "the power of positive thinking," were among the clergymen Mr. Niebuhr contradicted. Their "wholly individualistic conceptions of sin," he said, were "almost completely irrelevant" to the collective problems of the nuclear age.

Mr. Niebuhr objected especially to the notion that religious conversion could cure race prejudice, economic injustice or political chicanery. The remedy, he believed, lay in societal changes spurred by Christian realism.

Reinhold Niebuhr was born June 21, 1892, in Wright City, Mo., the son of Gustav and Lydia Niebuhr. His father was pastor of the Evangelical Synod Church, a German Lutheran congregation, in that farm community. At the age of 10 Reinhold decided that he wanted to be a minister because, as he told his father, "you're the most interesting man in town." At that point his father set about teaching him Greek.

From high school Reinhold went, with his brother Richard, to Elmhurst College in Illinois, a small denominational school, and from there, after four years, to Eden Theological Seminary, near St. Louis. After the death of his father in 1913, Reinhold was asked to take his pulpit in Lincoln, Ill. He declined in order to enter Yale Divinity School on a scholarship. He received his Bachelor of Divinity degree there in 1914, and his Master of Arts a year later.

Mr. Niebuhr was a member of the American Academy of Arts and Letters. He received the Presidential Medal of Freedom in 1964.

Upon his ordination by the Evangelical Synod of North America, he was sent to his first and only pastorate, the Bethel Evangelical Church of Detroit. He remained there 13 years, nurturing the congregation from 20 members to 650, and becoming the center of swirling controversy for his support of labor, and later for his espousal of pacifism.

"I cut my eyeteeth fighting Ford," Mr. Niebuhr said. Whereas Henry Ford was usually praised in those days for his wage of $5 a day and the low price of his automobiles, he was condemned by Mr. Niebuhr as ravaging his workers by the assembly line, the speedup, periodic layoffs and dismissal of men in middle age.

"Mr. Ford typified for my rather immature social imagination all that was wrong with American capitalism," Mr. Niebuhr said years later. "I became a Socialist in this reaction. I became a Socialist in theory long before I enrolled in the Socialist party and before I had read anything by Karl Marx."

For years Mr. Niebuhr preached what was termed "the social Gospel," a jeremiad against the abuse of laissez faire industrialism. He was a founder, in 1930, of the Fellowship of Socialist Christians.

"Capitalism is dying and it ought to die," he said in 1933, when he was agitating for the Socialist party. Yet even then he was reassessing his beliefs. He had never been a thoroughgoing Marxist, an advocate of class struggle and revolution. His ultimate break with socialism was on religious and ethical grounds, and later on realistic grounds. It was idolatry, he thought, to suggest that human beings could bring forth the Kingdom of God on earth.

JEAN-PAUL SARTRE

June 21, 1905–April 15, 1980

By Alden Whitman

Jean-Paul Sartre, whose existentialist philosophy influenced two generations of writers and thinkers throughout the world, died of edema of the lung yesterday in Paris. He was 74 years old.

Long regarded as one of France's reigning intellectuals, Mr. Sartre contributed profoundly to the social consciousness of the post–World War II generation through his leftward political commitments, which took him away from his desk and into the streets. He had ideas on virtually every subject, which were developed in novels, plays, biographies, essays and tracts.

Mr. Sartre's points of view were less heeded in the 1970's as he became a maverick political outsider on the extreme left. His last substantial work was a biography of the 19th-century French novelist Gustave Flaubert.

Although Mr. Sartre was once closely allied with the Communist Party, he was for the last 15 years an independent revolutionary who spoke more in the accents of Maoism than of Soviet Communism. As an intellectual and a public figure, he used his prestige to defend the rights of ultra-leftist groups to express themselves, and in 1973 he became titular editor of Liberation, a radical Paris daily. In addition, he lent his name to manifestos and open letters in favor of repressed groups in Greece, Chile and Spain. He was a rebel with a thousand causes, a modern Don Quixote.

Twenty-five years ago Mr. Sartre, with Albert Camus and a few others, was an iridescent intellectual leader. But in recent times his stature was that of an ancestor figure whose generative conceptions had lost their force.

It was fashionable to say that his lasting contribution would be his plays, implying that his essays and novels would not survive. As a philosopher he was increasingly criticized for his unsystematic approach. Nonetheless, few denied him respect for his continued attempts to live his ideas, often at the cost of ridicule.

"I have put myself on the line in various actions," Mr. Sartre said several years ago. He had in mind his activity against the Gaullist regime and his sometimes lonely protests against the American involvement in Vietnam.

Much earlier in his career as a freewheeling leftist, during the Nazi occupation of France, Mr. Sartre had, he said, "indeed worked with the Communists, as did all Resistants who were anti-Fascist." His support lasted until the Hungarian uprising of 1956 and the intervention by Russian troops. "The French Communist Party supported the invasion of Hungary, so

I broke with it," he explained. After backing the Algerian nationalists in their struggles with France, he moved steadily more leftward, and after the French demonstrations and street fighting of May 1968 he was an active militant.

He was arrested for ultra-leftist causes, and his voice became more strident. "The task of the intellectual is not to decide where there are battles but to join them wherever and whenever the people wage them," he said. "Commitment is an act, not a word."

His sense of commitment precluded homage. He rejected the Nobel Prize in Literature, awarded him in 1964, on the ground that he did not wish to be "transformed into an institution."

Mr. Sartre's philosophical views developed and shifted. In "Words," the story of his youth published in the mid-60's, he criticized the social, philosophical and literary ideas with which he had been raised. Commenting on his autobiographical novel "Nausea" and his philosophical work "Being and Nothingness," he said that an attitude of aristocratic idealism lay behind their composition, which he now rejected. The core of his existentialism, however, was not condemned. Roughly expressed, this suggests that "man makes himself" despite his "contingency" in an "absurd world."

His existentialism seemed to express a widespread disillusionment with fixed ideas amid the revolutionary changes that flowed from World War II. Out of this existentialism came such diverse manifestations as the anti-novel, the anti-hero, and the notion of man's anguished consciousness. Also implicit in it was a call to action, in which man could assume some control of his destiny.

This was a far different set of values from those into which Jean-Paul Sartre was born in Paris on June 21, 1905. His father, Jean-Baptiste, was a naval officer who died shortly after his son's birth. His mother, Anne-Marie Schweitzer, was a cousin of Albert Schweitzer.

As Mr. Sartre described himself, he was an ugly "toad" of a boy, without friends his age. By pretending to read, he learned to read before he was 4. By plagiarizing, he learned how to write stories, a process that hastened his retreat from life into words, more real than the objects they denoted.

He became a very good student, and he entered the elite Ecole Normale Superieure when he was 20. There he began his lifelong companionship with Simone de Beauvoir, a fellow student who would become his longtime companion, with an agreement pledging mutual loyalty in times of need but allowing "contingent loves."

After taking a degree, he went to Germany in 1933 to study under Edmund Husserl and Martin Heidegger, two of the most influential European philosophers, interested in the nature of being and reality and the mysteries of perception.

Mr. Sartre's ideas were summed up by Frank Kappler, an American writer who, after quoting Mr. Sartre's famous formula—"Existence precedes essence"—wrote:

"Man comes into a totally opaque, undifferentiated, meaningless universe. By the power of his mysterious consciousness, which Sartre calls unmeant, man makes of the universe a habitable world. Whatever meaning and value the world has comes from his existential choice. These choices differ from one to another.

"Each lives in his own world, or, as Sartre also says, each creates his own situation. Frequently this existential choice is buried in a lower level of consciousness. But to become truly alive, one must become aware of oneself as an 'I'—that is, a true existential subject, who must bear alone the responsibility for his own situation."

In this predicament, Mr. Sartre believed, one can choose an "inauthentic existence," or one can commit oneself by a resolute act of free choice to a positive role in human affairs. Most of these ideas are elaborated in "Being and Nothingness," which he wrote during the Nazi occupation of France. In 1938, he had published "Nausea," a novel in which a character named Antoine Roquentin was seized with the horrors of existentialism while meditating in a public park.

The novel ends when Roquentin decides that if he can only create something, a novel perhaps, his creativity could mean engagement. The central character was almost certainly the author.

By the end of World War II, Mr. Sartre was well known in France for both his writings and his activity in the Resistance. His philosophy suited many of the younger generation of students, who saw in existentialism an opportunity for salvation through commitment to a "new" French culture.

Mr. Sartre and his disciples at first gathered at the Cafe de Flore on Paris's Left Bank. As the group grew, they moved to the roomier Cafe Pont-Royal.

After doing two plays during the war, including "No Exit," Mr. Sartre busied himself with the theater in a number of dramas of ideas. Mr. Sartre was also writing biographies of Baudelaire, the 19th-century poet, and Jean Genet, a writer with a long criminal record. Parts of these and other of his writings were published in Les Temps Modernes, his monthly review founded in 1945.

Mr. Sartre, a short, wall-eyed man who always seemed in a fury of creativity, lived simply, with few possessions other than his books, in a small apartment on the Left Bank. And although he betrayed a certain amiability, he remained until the end an angry man.

"As far as the state of French politics goes, I don't see a lot I can do," he wrote. "It's so rotten what's happening in France now! And there's no hope in the immediate future; no party offers any hope at all."

SUSAN SONTAG

January 16, 1933–December 28, 2004

By Margalit Fox

Susan Sontag, the novelist, essayist and critic whose impassioned advocacy of the avant-garde and equally impassioned political pronouncements made her one of the most lionized and polarizing presences in 20th-century letters, died yesterday morning in Manhattan. She was 71.

The cause was complications of leukemia, her son, David Rieff, said. Ms. Sontag had been ill with cancer intermittently for the last 30 years, a struggle that informed one of her most famous books, the critical study "Illness as Metaphor."

A highly visible public figure since the mid-1960's, Ms. Sontag wrote four novels, dozens of essays and a volume of short stories and was also an occasional filmmaker, playwright and theater director. For four decades her work was part of the contemporary canon, discussed everywhere from graduate seminars to the pages of popular magazines.

Ms. Sontag gleefully blurred the boundaries between high and popular culture. She advocated an aesthetic approach to the study of culture, championing style over content. She was concerned with sensation, in both meanings of the term.

"The theme that runs through Susan's writing is this lifelong struggle to arrive at the proper balance between the moral and the aesthetic," said Leon Wieseltier, literary editor of The New Republic and an old friend of Ms. Sontag's. "There was something unusually vivid about her writing. That's why even if one disagrees with it—as I did frequently—it was unusually stimulating."

Through four decades, public response to Ms. Sontag remained irreconcilably divided. She was described, variously, as original, derivative, approachable, aloof, condescending, populist, puritanical, sybaritic, sincere, posturing, ascetic, voluptuary, right-wing, left-wing, profound, superficial, ardent, bloodless, dogmatic, ambivalent, lucid, inscrutable, visceral, reasoned, chilly, effusive, humorous, humorless, deadpan and cantankerous. No one called her dull.

Ms. Sontag's best-known books include the novels "The Volcano Lover" and "In America"; the essay collections "Against Interpretation," "Styles of Radical Will" and "Under the Sign of Saturn"; the critical studies "On Photography" and "AIDS and Its Metaphors"; and the short-story collection "I, Etcetera." One of her most famous works was an essay, "Notes on Camp," published in 1964 and still widely read.

Unlike most serious intellectuals, Ms. Sontag was also a celebrity, partly because of her telegenic

appearance, partly because of her outspoken statements. She was undoubtedly the only writer of her
generation to win major literary prizes (among them
a National Book Critics Circle Award and a National
Book Award), to appear in films by Woody Allen and
Andy Warhol, and to be photographed by Annie Lei-
bovitz for an Absolut Vodka ad.

Through the decades her image—strong features,
wide mouth, intense gaze and dark mane crowned
in her middle years by a sweeping streak of white—
became an instantly recognizable artifact of 20th-
century popular culture.

Ms. Sontag tackled broad, difficult and elusive subjects: the nature of art, the nature of consciousness
and, above all, the nature of the modern condition.
Where many American critics before her had mined
the past, Ms. Sontag became an evangelist of the new,
training her eye on the culture unfolding around her.

For Ms. Sontag, culture encompassed a vast landscape. She wrote serious studies of popular art forms,
like cinema, that earlier critics disdained. She wrote
experimental novels, published painstaking critical
dissections of photography, dance, illness, politics
and, most famously, camp. Her work helped make
the study of popular culture a respectable academic
pursuit.

What united Ms. Sontag's output was a propulsive
desire to define the forces that shape the modernist
sensibility. In so doing, she sought to explain what it
meant to be human in the late 20th century.

Many critics found her work bold and thrilling.
The Mexican writer Carlos Fuentes once compared

Ms. Sontag to the Renaissance humanist Erasmus.
"Erasmus traveled with 32 volumes, which contained
all the knowledge worth knowing," he said. "Susan
Sontag carries it in her brain! I know of no other intellectual who is so clear-minded, with a capacity to
link, to connect, to relate."

Others were less enthralled. Some branded Ms.
Sontag an unoriginal thinker, a popularizer who could
boil down difficult writers for mass consumption. Some
saw her scholarly approach to popular art forms as
pretentious. (Ms. Sontag once remarked that she could
appreciate Patti Smith because she had read Nietzsche.)

In person Ms. Sontag could be astringent. But she
could also be warm and girlish, speaking confidingly
in her rich, low voice. When she discussed something
that engaged her passionately, her dark eyes often
filled with tears.

Ms. Sontag had a knack for getting into trouble.
She could be provocative to the point of being inflammatory, as when she championed the Nazi-era filmmaker Leni Riefenstahl in a 1965 essay; she would
later revise her position. After the attacks of Sept. 11,
2001, she wrote in The New Yorker, "Whatever may
be said of the perpetrators of Tuesday's slaughter,
they were not cowards."

Ms. Sontag was born Susan Rosenblatt in Manhattan on Jan. 16, 1933, the daughter of Mildred and
Jack Rosenblatt, a fur trader in China. When Susan
was five, her father died and her mother moved the
family to Arizona. There she married a World War II
veteran named Capt. Nathan Sontag.

For Susan, who graduated from high school before

her 16th birthday, the philistinism of American culture was a torment she vowed early to escape. "My greatest dream," she later wrote, "was to grow up and come to New York and write for Partisan Review and be read by 5,000 people."

She would get her wish—Ms. Sontag burst onto the scene with "Notes on Camp," which was published in Partisan Review—but not before she earned three degrees, married, had a child and divorced, all by the time she turned 26.

In 1951 Ms. Sontag received a bachelor's degree from the University of Chicago, where she wandered into a class taught by the sociologist Philip Rieff, then a 28-year-old instructor. They were married 10 days later; Ms. Sontag was 17.

Moving with her husband to Boston, Ms. Sontag earned two master's degrees from Harvard, in English and philosophy. In 1952 she and Dr. Rieff became the parents of a son, David Rieff, a journalist who was for years his mother's editor at Farrar, Straus & Giroux. He survives her, as does Ms. Sontag's sister.

Ms. Sontag was divorced from Dr. Rieff in 1958. In 1959 she arrived in New York with, as she later described it, "$70, two suitcases and a 7-year-old." She worked as an editor at Commentary, juggled teaching jobs and published her first essays and her first novel, "The Benefactor."

With "Notes on Camp," an essay that made its author an international celebrity, Ms. Sontag fired a shot across the bow of the New York critical establishment, which included eminences like Lionel and Diana Trilling, Alfred Kazin and Irving Howe. That essay illuminated a particular modern sensibility, one that had been largely the province of gay culture, which centered on artifice, exaggeration and the veneration of style.

"The experiences of Camp are based on the great discovery that the sensibility of high culture has no monopoly on refinement," Ms. Sontag wrote. "The man who insists on high and serious pleasures is depriving himself of pleasure; he continually restricts what he can enjoy; in the constant exercise of his good taste he will eventually price himself out of the market, so to speak. Here Camp taste supervenes upon good taste as a daring and witty hedonism. It makes the man of good taste cheerful, where before he ran the risk of being chronically frustrated."

In 1966 Ms. Sontag published her first essay collection, "Against Interpretation." The title essay, in which she argued that art should be experienced viscerally rather than cerebrally, helped cement her reputation as a champion of style over content.

It was a position she could take to extremes. In the essay "On Style," published in the same volume, Ms. Sontag offended many readers by upholding the films of Leni Riefenstahl as masterworks of aesthetic form, with little regard for their content. Ms. Sontag would reconsider her position in a subsequent essay.

Though she thought of herself as a novelist, it was through her essays that Ms. Sontag became known.

"On Photography," a collection of six essays that won the National Book Critics Circle Award in 1978, explored the role of the photographic image and the act of picture-taking in contemporary culture. The crush of photographs, Ms. Sontag argued, has numbed us to depictions of suffering.

In the mid-1970's Ms. Sontag learned she had breast cancer. Doctors gave her a 10 percent chance of surviving for two years. She underwent a mastectomy and two and a half years of radiation.

Out of her experience came "Illness as Metaphor," which examined the cultural mythologizing of disease and condemned the often militaristic language around illness ("battling" disease, the "war" on cancer) that Ms. Sontag felt simultaneously marginalized the sick and held them responsible for their condition.

In "AIDS and Its Metaphors" Ms. Sontag discussed the social implications of the disease, which she viewed as a "cultural plague" that had replaced cancer as the modern bearer of stigma. She returned to the subject of AIDS in her acclaimed short story "The Way We Live Now."

Although Ms. Sontag was strongly identified with the American left during the Vietnam era, in later years her politics were harder to classify. In 1982 she delivered a stinging blow to progressives in a speech at Town Hall in Manhattan, denouncing European communism as "fascism with a human face."

In 1992, Ms. Sontag published "The Volcano Lover," a novel that told the story of Sir William Hamilton, the 18th-century British envoy to the court of Naples; his wife, Emma; and her lover, Lord Nelson, the naval hero.

Ms. Sontag's final novel, "In America," was loosely based on the life of the 19th-century Polish actress Helena Modjeska, who immigrated to California to start a utopian community. Though "In America" received a National Book Award, accusations of plagiarism surfaced.

Ms. Sontag defended her method. "All of us who deal with real characters in history transcribe and adopt original sources in the original domain," she said. "I've used these sources and I've completely transformed them."

In a 1992 interview in which Ms. Sontag described the creative force that animated "The Volcano Lover," she identified the sensibility that would inform all her work: "I don't want to express alienation. It isn't what I feel. I'm interested in various kinds of passionate engagement. All my work says, be serious, be passionate, wake up."

s inspiration from the Kremlin.
Ethel, two years his senior, was a
plain-faced girl, petite without
being pretty. They met while both
were students at Seward Park
High School. She got a job as a
stenographer after graduation; he
went on to City College but became so engrossed in Communist
activities that he "flunked out" in
1937. He resolved to give more
attention to his classes, was reinstated at the college and won his
degree in electrical engineering in
February, 1939. A few months
later Julius and Ethel were
married.

He bounced from one engineering job to another until he got a
civil service appointment as a
junior engineer in the Army Signal
Corps on Sept. 3, 1940. That was
the period of the Hitler-Stalin
pact, when the Communists in this
country were doing everything
they could to obstruct our preparedness program, but there was
no testimony that reflected ad-
versely on Julius Rosenberg's performance of his job.

BEGINNING OF THE PLOT

After Pearl Harbor, with the
United States and Russia established as wartime allies, Julius
began to brood over the reluctance
of our Government to entrust all
its military secrets to the Soviet
Union. He decided that the Russians were entitled to know everything we knew and that it was his
responsibility to help them get any
information they could not get
through established channels of
military or diplomatic communi-

not to make any notes. She m
rized David's answers and c
them back to New York. In
uary David came home hims
a twenty-two day furlough.
asked him to turn over every
he knew about the bomb
might be of value to the So
Working from memory,
made sketches of a high-exp
lens, for which he had made
in his New Mexico machine
(The lens is a curve-shaped
explosive used to set off the
reaction that detonates the b

Greenglass had taken his
seriously. He was able to su
ment his sketches with a ma
technical material about the
and how it worked. He had
dered all over the top-secret
area" at Los Alamos, list
avidly to everything he could
and questioning people "wi
their knowing it" to get a c
idea of what they were o
Julius was jubilant when Dav
livered his information. He sa
sketches were "very good," a
got out a portable typewrit
Ethel could type up the da
the workings of the bomb. It
twelve pages to get it all

CONTACT WITH RUSSIANS

What did Julius do with th
terial he got from David?
cording to the Greenglasse
had microfilming equipment
cealed in a hollowed-out se

THE
NOTORIOUS

Avenue in Brooklyn and handed him two manila folders. One marked "doctor" contained the information the spy had got from Fuchs; the second marked "other" contained the Greenglass offering. Two weeks later Yakovlev told Gold that the material had been sent to the Soviet Union right away and that the data from Greenglass had proved "extremely excellent and very valuable."

Russian as Co-Conspirator

The indictment that led to the Rosenbergs' death named Yakovlev as a co-conspirator, but he never came to trial. He left the United States on Dec. 27, 1946, and vanished behind the Iron Curtain.

Rosenberg did not confine his professional interest to atomic information, according to the evidence at his trial. He confided to Greenglass that he had stolen the proximity fuse while he was working at the Emerson Radio Company on a Signal Corps project. He simply slipped the fuse into the brief case in which he had brought his lunch, and gave it to the Russians. His Communist ties cost him his civilian job with the Signal Corps on Feb. 9, 1945, even though he protested to his commanding officer that he had never belonged to the party. But neither his dismissal nor the end of the war brought a close to his career as a spy. In 1947 he told David about a fantastic "sky platform"

tary about the Ru_ the United Nation_ to take up a stand time beside a stat_ in Mexico City. _ a finger in a guide_ a man approached_ "That is a magnif_ am from Oklahom_ saw anything like_ the man was to re_ much more beaut_ Paris." Then the _ David money and _ would carry the Gr_ eventual haven in _

Preparations for _

_e thought of _ two-week-old infar_ peal to David and _ pretended to fall i_ Rosenberg gave th_ 000, wrapped in br_ later used the mo_ David's lawyer at _ In the meantime, _ were making prepa_ own to get out _ They had passport _ but they were still _ lius was arrested o_ Ethel was arreste_ month later.

The only one who_

MATA-HARI

August 7, 1876–October 15, 1917

PARIS—Mata-Hari, the Dutch dancer and adventuress, who, two months ago, was found guilty by a court-martial on the charge of espionage, was shot at dawn this morning.

The condemned woman, otherwise known as Marguerite Gertrude Zelle, who was 41, was taken in an automobile from St. Lazaire prison to the parade ground at Vincennes, where the execution took place. Two sisters of Charity and a priest accompanied her.

Mlle. Mata-Hari, long known in Europe as a woman of great attractiveness and with a romantic history, was accused, according to press dispatches, of conveying to the Germans the secret of the construction of the Entente "tanks," this resulting in the Germans rushing work on a special gas to combat their operations.

She was said to have left Paris last Spring and to have spent some time in the English town where the first "tanks" were being made, afterward traveling back and forth between England and Holland, and later going to Spain, where she aroused suspicion by associating with a man whom the French Secret Service had long suspected. When she reappeared in Paris she was arrested—a contributing circumstance, it appears, being the fact that she was seen there with a young British officer attached to the "tank" service.

AL CAPONE

January 17, 1899–January 25, 1947

MIAMI BEACH, Fla.—Al Capone, ex-Chicago gangster and Prohibition era crime leader, died in his home here tonight.

"Death came very suddenly," said Dr. Kenneth S. Phillips, who has been attending Capone since he was stricken with apoplexy Tuesday.

"All the family was present. His wife, Mae, collapsed and is in very serious condition."

Dr. Phillips said death was caused by heart failure.

—The Associated Press

Alphonse (Scarface) Capone, the fat boy from Brooklyn, was a Horatio Alger hero—underworld version. More than any other one man, he represented, at the height of his power, from 1925 through 1931, the debauchery of the "dry" era. He seized and held in thrall during that period the great city of Chicago and its suburbs.

Head of the cruelest cutthroats in American history, he inspired gang wars in which more than 300 men died by the knife, the shotgun, the tommy gun and the pineapple, the gangster adaptation of the World War I hand grenade.

His infamy made international legend. In France, for example, he was "The One Who Is Scarred." He was the symbol of the ultimate in American lawlessness.

Capone won great wealth; how much, no one will ever know, except that the figure was fantastic. He remained immune from prosecution for his multitudinous murders (including the St. Valentine Day Massacre in 1929, when his gunners, dressed as policemen, trapped and killed eight of the Bugs Moran bootleg outfit in a Chicago garage), but was brought to book, finally, on the comparatively sissy charge of evasion of income taxes amounting to around $215,000.

For this, he was sentenced to 11 years in Federal prison—serving first at Atlanta, then on The Rock, at Alcatraz—and was fined $50,000, with $20,000 additional for costs. With time out for good conduct, he finished this sentence in mid-January of 1939; but by then he was a slack-jawed paretic overcome by social disease, and paralytic to boot.

Capone was born in Naples on Jan. 17, 1899, the son of an impoverished barber. The family moved to New York and settled in the Mulberry Bend district near the Brooklyn Bridge. Here, after he quit school in the fourth grade to knock about the streets, he met Johnny Torrio, whom he was to succeed, many years later, as head of the bootleg and vice syndicate in Chicago.

The parents, devout people, moved to South Brooklyn, and Al, barely out of his teens, one day bullied one of the neighbors, an undersized, quick-tempered Sicilian, in a Fourth Avenue barber shop. His victim backed Capone into a corner and slashed him twice with a razor. He and Capone never crossed trails again, nor did Capone, on his infrequent visits to the old neighborhood after he reached great power, ever seek him out or order his destruction.

In 1910, John Torrio left the Five Points and Mulberry Bend to try his evil genius in Chicago. The advent of Prohibition in 1920 saw great expansion of the Torrio interests. He took to bootlegging in a big way.

Torrio needed more men, tough men. He sent for the fat boy, and Capone took the next train for Chicago to join Torrio at $75 a week. This was big money for him at the time. He had managed to stay out of the World War because he didn't like that type of fighting. Later he encouraged the legend that he had been a machine gunner in the AEF [American Expeditionary Forces], but this was Capone poppycock.

For three or four years after Capone's arrival in Chicago, he served as a "rod," or professional killer, for Torrio and at the same time proved himself unusually good at organizing the vice and bootleg phases of the Torrio chain.

Greed begets greater greed. Torrio wanted a hog's share of the "take" and shortchanged his men. This resulted in a split, the opposition taking form under the leadership of Dion O'Banion, a murderous fellow who, paradoxically, had an inordinate love for flowers.

Most of his men were Irish; most of Torrio's Italian, and the war took on a bitter racial angle. On Nov. 10, 1924, three Capone men walked into the florist shop opened by O'Banion more for a hobby than for profit. They riddled him with shot, and he fell back among his roses and carnations. Capone and Torrio attended the burial, sent loads of wreaths as a sentimental gesture and tried to look innocent.

Later in 1925, a gang caught up with Torrio and fired five shots into him. He decided, at this juncture, that he had had enough. He pulled out, and Capone was left in command.

Immediately Capone began a campaign of expansion. He established agents along the East Coast to handle his rum cargoes, he had men in Florida and in the Bahamas; he had men along the Canadian border. Capone caravans crisscrossed the nation with valuable loads of contraband to slake the thirst of the Middle West.

By the end of 1925, Capone was riding high. He had a magnificent home on Prairie Avenue, where he lived with his wife, Mae, and their Sonny, six years old. His brother Ralph (Bottles) Capone, was on his staff.

Word came to Chicago at this time that Peg-Leg Lonergan, head of the downtown Brooklyn waterfront bad men, was plaguing some of Capone's old friends. Peg-Leg's idea of sport was to lead a handful of longshoremen into the Adonis Social Club on 20th Street, near Fourth Avenue, and badger the Italian customers, all old neighbors of Capone's.

The Adonis Club had sentimental attachments for Capone. In the cellar of the club, in his teens, he had perfected his pistol work by shooting at beer bottles. He was in the place on Christmas night, 1925, with five furtive-looking men-at-arms from Chicago, when Peg-Leg and his boisterous crew came in a-whooping.

At 3 o'clock the next morning, police of the Fifth Avenue station reached the club on the run, attracted by a fusillade of gunfire. Peg-Leg lay dead near the door; Aaron Harms and Needles Ferry, two of his pals, lay dead under the piano, staring with unseeing eyes at the orange, red and green paper twists that bedecked the ceilings and fixtures. A fourth Lonergan man crawled on the sidewalk, badly wounded.

Capone and eight other men, together with a couple of girl patrons of the Adonis Club, were rounded up. The fat man from Chicago, blazing with diamonds, assumed an air of injured innocence. He insisted that he had come all the way from the Windy City to pay a Christmas call on his mother and that he had merely happened to be in the nightclub when the shooting started.

He was turned out with the rest because all the other witnesses, like himself, related that they did not happen to be looking when the guns opened fire. Without witnesses the police had no case. Capone, having paid his Christmas call and having delivered three neat homicides as gifts, returned to Chicago.

Emboldened, Capone came out in the open to sup-

port Big Bill Thompson in 1929, in what was known as the "pineapple" primary. Opposition candidates were subject to all the little violent tricks in the Capone bag, including the tossing of this iron fruit. His men had shot and killed William McSwiggin, State's Attorney for Cook County, and if they could get away with that (as they did) he felt he could get away with anything.

Before the pineapple primary, he had also staged the cruelest murder in the annals of American gangster crime. He had hired Fred (Killer) Burke of the Egan's Rats, a St. Louis gang, to perform this particular job. The Killer dressed three of his men in police uniforms, walked in on seven Moran men in the SMC Cartage Company Garage on St. Valentine's Day, 1929, and sprayed them with Thompson submachine guns and sawed-off shotguns until the last of the seven stopped twitching.

The Capone crowd lost the pineapple primary, in spite of terroristic tactics. Dissension, subsurface but sinister, got to work in the organization. The fat boy tried to stem it with a brutal show of power at a hotel banquet, where he brained the guests of honor—two defecting brothers who thought their plotting had been secret—with a baseball bat. He had also been warned of a double-cross by Frankie Uale, his Brooklyn agent, and Uale had been shot to death by Killer Burke and his crowd.

In May 1929, Capone surrendered to the police in Philadelphia to get a year's peace from the increasing threat of the Moran guns. The charge in the Philadelphia case was carrying concealed weapons.

In October 1931, he went on trial for income-tax evasion, guarded in the Federal court chamber by one of his own men. An attendant spotted the bodyguard's shoulder holster, and the thug was sentenced for contempt.

Capone's highly paid counsel tried to persuade a grim-lipped jury that their client was a persecuted man. The plea fell on deaf ears. When Judge Wilkerson pronounced sentence, the fat man's face went dark and the ugly scar went white.

Capone entered Atlanta penitentiary on May 5, 1932. In August 1934, he was chained and fettered and taken to forbidding Alcatraz. This was the beginning of the end for America's "Public Enemy Number One," a title in which he had gloried.

In February 1938, he became violent. Word came out of Alcatraz that the prison doctors had decided that the great Capone was done; "subject to intermittent mental disturbances."

In November 1939, Capone was released from prison and admitted to the Union Memorial Hospital in Baltimore to take treatment for paresis. Later he settled at Miami Beach.

ETHEL ROSENBERG

September 28, 1915–June 19, 1953

JULIUS ROSENBERG

May 12, 1918–June 19, 1953

By William R. Conklin

OSSINING. N.Y.—Stoic and tight-lipped to the end, Julius and Ethel Rosenberg paid the death penalty tonight in the electric chair at Sing Sing Prison for their war-time atomic espionage for Soviet Russia.

The pair, first husband and wife to pay the supreme penalty here, and the first in the United States to die for espionage, went to their deaths with a composure that astonished the witnesses.

Both executions of the death sentence had been advanced from the usual Sing Sing hour of 11 P.M. so that they would not conflict with the Jewish Sabbath. The last rays of a red sun over the Hudson River were casting a faint light when the double execution was completed.

By A. H. Raskin

The execution of Julius and Ethel Rosenberg on Friday night brought to an end a case that has stirred more worldwide interest than any American judicial proceeding since the Sacco-Vanzetti trial a quarter of a century ago. The Rosenbergs were sentenced to death for a new kind of crime in a new age—the age of atomic destruction. What follows is a narrative of the Rosenbergs' story as it was developed at their trial.

The depression brought Julius and Ethel Rosenberg to communism, and communism brought them to one another. Born on Manhattan's poverty-ridden East Side, they embraced the Communist movement in their teens while millions of Americans were out of work and Franklin D. Roosevelt was struggling to put a splintered economy back into one piece.

They met at Seward Park High School. She got a job as a stenographer after graduation; he went on to City College and won his degree in electrical engineering in February, 1939. A few months later Julius and Ethel were married.

He became a junior engineer in the Army Signal Corps on Sept. 3, 1940. After Pearl Harbor, with the United States and Russia established as war-time allies, Julius began to brood over the reluctance of our Government to entrust all its military secrets to the Soviet Union. He decided that the Russians were entitled to know everything we knew.

His first big opportunity to help the Russians came in August, 1944, when the Army assigned Ethel's brother, David Greenglass, a machinist, to work on the atomic bomb at Los Alamos, N.M.

In November, 1941, David's wife, Ruth, visited him and told him that she had had dinner with the Rosenbergs in their Knickerbocker Village apartment. They disclosed that they had joined the Communist underground—they were shunning open association with the party's activities, staying away from its meetings and not buying The Daily Worker.

Julius urged her to rush out to New Mexico and bring back facts about the bomb for transmission to the Russians. Resistant at first, she changed her mind. She told David of Julius's argument that Russia was fighting side by side with the United States and was not getting data she ought to have. David agreed to supply the information Julius wanted about the physical layout at Los Alamos, the number of people working there and the names of the key scientists supervising the project.

She memorized David's answers and carried them back to New York. In January David came home himself on a furlough. Working from memory, David made sketches of a high-explosive lens, for which he had made molds in his New Mexico machine shop. (The lens is a curve-shaped high explosive used to set off the chain reaction that detonates the bomb.)

Greenglass was able to supplement his sketches with a mass of technical material about the bomb. Julius was jubilant when David delivered his information. He said the sketches were "very good." Ethel typed up the data. It took 12 pages to get it all down.

What did Julius do with the material he got from David? According to the Greenglasses, he had microfilming equipment concealed in a hollowed-out section of a console table given to him by the Russians. Whenever he had a message or microfilm to turn over, he would leave it in the alcove of a movie theater.

When a meeting seemed in order, he would leave a note in the alcove, then rendezvous with his contacts in little-frequented spots on Long Island. Greenglass testified that on his visit to New York Rosenberg had arranged to have him meet a Russian, whose name David never learned, on First Avenue.

When David went back to his post, he took Ruth with him. He also took plans for supplying more information to Julius's Russian friends. Julius gave Greenglass an irregularly cut section of a Jell-o package and told him to have his information ready for transmission to a courier, who would present the matching part of the package as identification.

The courier was Harry Gold, a Swiss-born biochemist and a member of the Communist spy ring since 1935. He had no direct dealings with Rosenberg and he never made his identity known to Greenglass. Gold's contact was Anatoli A. Yakovlev, Soviet Vice Consul in New York. He gave Gold a double-barreled mission to New Mexico in June, 1945.

One task was to go to Santa Fe and get data from Dr. Klaus Fuchs, a high-ranking British atomic scientist, from whom Gold had obtained vital material before. The other part was to visit Greenglass in Albuquerque.

In Albuquerque, Gold went through the prescribed ritual of recognition signal and panel presentation. Greenglass walked across the parlor and fished the matching section out of his wife's pocketbook. The pudgy-faced courier introduced himself as "Dave from Pittsburgh."

Before departing with a fresh set of drawings and explanatory material from Greenglass, Gold gave the G.I. an envelope containing $500. The money came from Yakovlev. Two days later, Gold met the Russian in Brooklyn and handed him the information from Fuchs and Greenglass. Two weeks later Yakovlev told Gold that the material had been sent to the Soviet Union and that the data from Greenglass had proved "extremely excellent and very valuable."

Rosenberg did not confine himself to atomic information. He confided to Greenglass that he had stolen the proximity fuse while he was working at the Emerson Radio Company on a Signal Corps project and gave it to the Russians.

In 1948, he made contact with a former City College student, Morton Sobell, an electronics and radar expert, who worked on the classified Government contracts, and received a 35mm film can filled with secret information. Tried with the Rosenbergs, Sobell drew a 30-year jail sentence.

Rosenberg knew that the end was in sight for him when the British announced the arrest of Klaus Fuchs in February, 1950. He warned Greenglass that Gold would be taken into custody soon and he recommended that David leave the country.

When the F.B.I. jailed Gold on May 23, Rosenberg went into high gear. He gave Greenglass $1,000 and promised that the Russians would supply as much more as was needed to get David, his wife and their two small children out of the United States.

The thought of fleeing with a two-week-old infant did not appeal to David and Ruth, but they pretended to fall in with the plan. Rosenberg gave them another $4,000, wrapped in brown paper. In the meantime, the Rosenbergs prepared to get out of the country. But they were still here when Julius was arrested on July 17, 1950. Ethel was arrested less than a month later.

The only one who did leave after Fuchs and Gold had been apprehended was Sobell. He flew to Mexico City on June 21 with his family. He was deported from Mexico and arrested at the Texas border.

The Rosenbergs denied throughout their trial that they had anything to do with espionage. They denied everything the Greenglasses and Gold swore to. They refused to answer questions about membership in the Communist party or the Young Communist League on grounds of possible self-incrimination, but swore that they were loyal to the United States.

The defense argued that David Greenglass had perjured himself to save his wife at the expense of his sister. Efforts also were made to get across the idea that Greenglass was personally unstable and unreliable, that he had been coached by the F.B.I., and that he had a grudge against Julius Rosenberg because of a business row when they were partners in a machine shop after the war. Ruth Greenglass was not indicted.

The echoes of the case will be heard as long as the "cold war" goes on. The evidence that brought the jury's verdict and the judge's sentence will be lost in endless clouds of emotion, much of it politically generated.

ADOLF EICHMANN

March 19, 1906–June 1, 1962

By Lawrence Fellows

RAMLE, Israel—Adolf Eichmann was hanged just before last midnight for the part he played in rounding up millions of Jews and transporting them to their deaths in Nazi camps during World War II.

President Itzhak Ben-Zvi rejected Eichmann's appeal for mercy shortly before the execution.

Eichmann's body was cremated early today, as had been requested in his will. The ashes were scattered in the Mediterranean outside Israeli waters.

Cold and unyielding to the end, Eichmann rejected an appeal by a Protestant minister that he repent. His last words, spoken in German to a small group of witnesses in the execution chamber, were:

"After a short while, gentlemen, we shall all meet again. So is the fate of all men. I have lived believing in God and I die believing in God.

"Long live Germany. Long live Argentina. Long live Austria. These are the countries with which I have been most closely associated and I shall not forget them.

"I greet my wife, my family and friends. I had to obey the rules of war and my flag. I am ready."

The hanging was carried out in the gloomy, fogbound Ramle Prison only a few hours after Eichmann's final plea had been rejected by President Ben-Zvi.

During the day, the President had received hundreds of appeals for clemency. A delegation of Hebrew University professors, headed by the philosopher Martin Buber, urged him to prevent the execution.

But a brief announcement by the President's office last night said: "The President of the State of Israel has decided not to exercise his prerogative to pardon offenders or reduce sentences in the case of Adolf Eichmann."

On receiving this word, the Rev. William Hull, the Canadian missionary assigned by the Government to attend Eichmann, returned to the prison, where he had talked with the prisoner earlier.

The minister's wife, who served as his interpreter, said Eichmann had seemed hard and bitter after the Supreme Court rejected his appeal Tuesday.

Eichmann sat down at 7 P.M. to his last meal—regular prison fare of peas, bread, olives and tea. At 8 o'clock, the Commissioner of Prisons, Avraham Nir, notified him that the President had rejected his appeal.

Eichmann did not appear surprised, the commissioner said. At the prisoner's request, a bottle of dry red Israeli wine was brought. He drank about half of it. Two letters from a brother were brought to him and he read them.

Half an hour before midnight, Mr. Hull, head of the nondenominational Zion Christian Mission in Jerusalem, was taken to Eichmann. Again, Mrs. Hull interpreted.

Later, the minister said Eichmann "was not prepared to discuss the Bible—he did not have time to waste."

Mrs. Hull said Eichmann looked sad, but said he was ready to die.

Mr. Hull revealed that Eichmann had asked him: "Tell my wife to take it calmly. I have peace in the heart."

The minister led the 50-yard walk from the cell to the execution chamber. Eichmann, his hands bound behind him, walked erect and apparently calm. He coughed once.

The gallows—the first to be used in the history of Israel—had been set up in a small room that formerly served as living quarters for guards on the third floor of the prison.

Eichmann, who wore reddish brown trousers and a shirt open at the neck, was led to a black-painted trapdoor that had been cut in the floor.

Guards tied his ankles and knees. Eichmann asked them to loosen the bonds around his knees so that he could stand erect. He refused a black hood that was offered him.

Then, his eyes nearly shut, he stared slightly to the side and downward at the trap as he spoke his last words.

When he had finished, Commissioner Nir called, "Muchan!"—Hebrew for "Ready!" A noose was slipped over Eichmann's head. Again, the commissioner called "Muchan!"

There was a rustle behind a blanket partition in a corner of the room, where three men stood at controls so rigged that none could tell which was the one controlling the gallows.

The trap opened, and Eichmann plummeted to his death.

The minister cried, "Christ, Jesus Christ."

In unanimous judgment, five justices of the Supreme Court accepted Tuesday the reasons and conclusions of the specially composed district court that tried Eichmann a year ago and sentenced him to death last December.

"The man," the Supreme Court wrote, "who was entrusted by no lesser eminence than Reinhard Heydrich, Gestapo General, himself, with the task of dealing with the final solution of 11 million Jews is no mere screw, small or large, of a machine propelled by others. He is himself one of those who propel the machine."

Eichmann objected to these findings in his appeal. "The judges of Israel," he wrote, "made a basic mistake because they did not distinguish between the responsible leaders, those who gave the orders, and the men of the line who only carried the orders out."

The argument was knocked down repeatedly in court. The supreme court held:

"The appellant has never shown either repentance or weakness or any sapping of strength or any weakening of will in the performance of the task which he undertook.

"He was the right man in the right place and he carried out his unspeakably horrible crimes with genuine joy and enthusiasm to his own gratification and the satisfaction of all his superiors."

OSAMA BIN LADEN

March 10, 1957–May 2, 2011

WASHINGTON—Osama bin Laden, the mastermind of the most devastating attack on American soil in modern times and the most hunted man in the world, was killed in a firefight with United States forces in Pakistan on Sunday, President Obama announced.

In a dramatic late-night appearance in the East Room of the White House, Mr. Obama declared that "justice has been done" as he disclosed that American military and C.I.A. operatives had finally cornered bin Laden, the Al Qaeda leader who had eluded them for nearly a decade. American officials said bin Laden resisted and was shot in the head. He was buried at sea.

The news touched off an extraordinary outpouring of emotion as crowds gathered outside the White House, in Times Square and at the Ground Zero site, waving American flags, cheering, shouting, laughing and chanting, "USA, USA!"

Bin Laden's demise is a defining moment in the American-led war on terrorism, a symbolic stroke affirming the relentlessness of the pursuit of those who attacked New York and Washington on Sept. 11, 2001.

When the end came for bin Laden, he was found not in the remote tribal areas along the Pakistani-Afghan border, where he had long been presumed to be sheltered, but in a massive compound about an hour's drive north from the Pakistani capital of Is-lamabad. He was hiding in the medium-size city of Abbottabad, home to a large Pakistani military base and an Army academy.

The house at the end of a narrow dirt road was roughly eight times larger than other homes in the area, but had no telephone or television connections. When American operatives converged on the house on Sunday, bin Laden "resisted the assault force" and was killed in the middle of a gun battle, a senior administration official said, but details were still sketchy early Monday morning.

By Kate Zernike and Michael T. Kaufman

Osama bin Laden was a son of the Saudi elite whose radical, violent campaign to recreate a seventh-century Muslim empire redefined the threat of terrorism for the 21st century.

With the attacks on the World Trade Center and the Pentagon on Sept. 11, 2001, Bin Laden was elevated to the realm of evil in the American imagination once reserved for dictators like Hitler and Stalin. He was a new national enemy, his face on wanted posters. He gloated on videotapes, taunting the United States and Western civilization. He was generally believed to be 54.

Terrorism before bin Laden was often state-sponsored, but he was a terrorist who had sponsored a state. From 1996 to 2001 he bought the protection of the Taliban, then the rulers of Afghanistan, and used the time and freedom to make Al Qaeda—which means "the base" in Arabic—into a multinational enterprise for the export of terrorism. Groups calling themselves Al Qaeda, or acting in the name of its cause, attacked American troops in Iraq, bombed tourist spots in Bali and blew up passenger trains in Spain.

He waged holy war with modern methods. He sent fatwas—religious decrees—by fax and declared war on Americans in an e-mail beamed by satellite around the world. He styled himself a Muslim ascetic, a billionaire's son who gave up a life of privilege for the cause. But he was media savvy and acutely image-conscious.

His reedy voice seemed to belie the warrior image he cultivated, a man whose constant companion was a Kalashnikov rifle, which he boasted he had taken from a Russian soldier he had killed in the war in Afghanistan. While he built his reputation on his combat experience against Soviet troops, even some of his supporters questioned whether he had actually fought.

Bin Laden claimed to follow the purest form of Islam, but many scholars insisted that he was glossing over the faith's edicts against killing innocents and civilians. Yet it was the United States, bin Laden insisted, that was guilty of a double standard. "It wants to occupy our countries, steal our resources, impose agents on us to rule us and then wants us to agree to all this," he told CNN in 1997.

He sought to topple infidel governments through jihad, or holy war.

He modeled himself after the Prophet Muhammad, who in the seventh century led the Muslim people to rout the infidels, or nonbelievers, from North Africa and the Middle East.

In his vision, bin Laden would be the "emir," or prince, in a restoration of the khalifa, a political empire extending from Afghanistan across the globe. Al Qaeda became the infrastructure for his dream.

Osama bin Muhammad bin Awad bin Laden was born in 1957, the seventh son and 17th child, among 50 or more, of his father, people close to the family say.

His father, Muhammad bin Awad bin Laden, had in 1931 immigrated from Yemen to what would soon become Saudi Arabia. There he began as a janitor and rose to become owner of the largest construction company in Saudi Arabia. Bin Laden's mother, the last of his father's four wives, was from Syria.

Bin Laden was educated in Wahhabism, a puritanical, ardently anti-Western strain of Islam. By most accounts he was devout and quiet, marrying a relative, the first of his four wives, at age 17.

It was at King Abdulaziz University in Jidda that he shaped his militancy, and in 1979, when Soviet troops invaded Afghanistan, he arrived at the Pakistan-Afghanistan border within two weeks of the occupation. Later he brought into Afghanistan construction machinery and recruits. In 1984, he helped set up guesthouses in Peshawar, the first stop for holy warriors on their way to Afghanistan, and establish the Office of Services, which branched out across the world to recruit young jihadists, as many as 20,000.

The crucible of Afghanistan prompted the founding of Al Qaeda and brought bin Laden into contact with leaders of other Islamists, including Ayman al-Zawahiri, whose group, Egyptian Jihad, would merge with Al Qaeda.

Through the looking glass of Sept. 11, it seemed ironic that the Americans and Osama bin Laden had fought on the same side against the Soviets in Afghanistan—as if the Americans had somehow created the bin Laden monster by providing arms and cash to the Arabs.

Bin Laden himself said the resistance received training and money from the Americans. In truth, the Americans did not deal directly with bin Laden; they worked through the middlemen of the Pakistani intelligence service.

The triumph in Afghanistan infused the movement with confidence.

Bin Laden returned to Saudi Arabia, welcomed as a hero. But Saudi royals grew wary of him as he became more outspoken against the government. He opposed the Saudis' decision to allow the Americans to defend the kingdom during the Iraqi invasion of Kuwait in 1990. To him, it was the height of American arrogance.

Bin Laden fled to Sudan and set up legitimate businesses that would help finance Al Qaeda. It was during this time that it is believed he honed his resolve against the United States.

On Dec. 29, 1992, a bomb exploded in a hotel in Aden, Yemen, where American troops had been staying while on their way to Somalia. The troops had already left, and the bomb killed two Austrian tourists. American intelligence officials came to believe that it was bin Laden's first attack.

On Feb. 26, 1993, a bomb exploded at the World Trade Center, killing six people. Bin Laden later praised Ramzi Yousef, who was convicted of the bombing. That year, in Somalia, 18 American service members were killed—some of their bodies dragged through the streets—while on a peacekeeping mission; bin Laden was almost giddy about the deaths and their impact on Islamist fighters.

"The youth were surprised at the low morale of the American soldiers and realized more than before that the American soldier was a paper tiger and after a few blows ran in defeat," he told an interviewer.

By 1994, bin Laden had established training camps in Sudan. He called for guerrilla attacks to drive Americans from Saudi Arabia. In November 1995, a truck bomb exploded at a Saudi National Guard training center operated by the United States in Riyadh, killing seven people.

The next May, when the men accused of the bombing were beheaded, they were forced to confess the connection to bin Laden. The next month, June 1996, a truck bomb destroyed Khobar Towers, an American military residence in Dhahran. It killed 19 soldiers.

Bin Laden fled to Afghanistan that summer after Sudan expelled him under pressure from the Americans and Saudis, and he forged an alliance with the Taliban. In August 1996, he issued his "Declaration of War Against the Americans Who Occupy the Land of the Two Holy Mosques."

The imbalance of power between American and Muslim forces demanded a new kind of fighting, he wrote, "in other words, to initiate a guerrilla war, where sons of the nation, not the military forces, take part in it."

In February 1998, he called for attacks on Americans anywhere in the world, declaring it an "individual duty" for all Muslims.

On Aug. 7, 1998, the eighth anniversary of the United States order sending troops into the Gulf region, two bombs exploded simultaneously at the American Embassies in Nairobi, Kenya, and Dar es Salaam, Tanzania. The Nairobi bomb killed 213 people and wounded 4,500; the bomb in Dar es Salaam killed 11 and wounded 85.

The United States retaliated with strikes against what were thought to be terrorist training camps in Afghanistan and a pharmaceutical plant in Sudan, which officials contended—erroneously, it turned out—was producing chemical weapons for Al Qaeda.

Bin Laden had trapped the United States in a spiral of tension, where any defensive or retaliatory actions would affirm the evils that he said had provoked the attacks in the first place.

After Sept. 11, bin Laden eluded the allied forces in pursuit of him, moving, it was said, under cover of night, at first between mountain caves. Yet he was determined that if he had to die, he would die a martyr's death.

His greatest hope, he told supporters, was that if he died at the hands of the Americans, the Muslim world would rise up and defeat the nation that had killed him.

[M]ajor Gen. George A. Custer, who was [kill]ed with his whole command while attacking an [enc]ampment of Sioux Iudians, under command of [Sitt]ing Bull, was one of the bravest and most [wid]ely known officers in the United States Army. [He] has for the past fifteen years been known to the [cou]ntry and to his comrades as a man who feared [no] danger, as a soldier in the truest sense of the [wor]d. He was daring to a fault, gener[ous] beyond most men. His memory will [eve]r be kept green in many friendly [hea]rts. Born at New-Rumley, Harrison County, [Ohi]o, on the 5th of December, 1839, he obtained a [goo]d common education, and after graduating en[gag]ed for a time in teaching school. In June, [185]7, through the influence of Hon. John A. [Bin]gham. then member of Congress from Ohio, [he] obtained an appointment to the United States [Mili]tary Academy at West Point, and en[tere]d that institution on the 1st of July of [the] year named. He graduated on the 24th of [Ju]ne, 1861, with what was considered the fair [sta]nding of No. 34 in one of the brightest classes [tha]t ever left the academy. Immediately upon [lea]ving West Point he was appointed Second Lieu[ten]ant in Company G of the Second United States [Cava]lry, a regiment which had formerly [bee]n commanded by Robert E. Lee. He reported [to] Lieut. Gen. Scott on the 20th of July, the day [pre]ceding the battle of Bull Run, and the Com[man]der in Chief gave him the choice of accepting a [pos]ition on his staff or of joining his regiment, [the]n under command of Gen. McDowell, [in] the field. Longing for an 'opportunity [to] see active service, and determined [to] win distinction Lieut. Custer chose the latter [cou]rse, and after riding all night through a coun[try] filled with people who were, to say the least, [un]friendly, he reached McDowell's head-quarters [at d]aybreak on the morning of the 21st. Prepara[tion]s for the battle had already begun, and [afte]r delivering his dispatches from Gen. Scott and

Army, which th[e]
horses shot un[der]
the battle co[mmand]
attack the e[nemy]
to force its
destroyed mo[re]
Hagerstown, M[d.]
again had his
Waters, short[ly]
brigade the e[ne]
erate comman[d]
his command
two pieces of
some time aft[er]
gaged in skirm[ish]
the Winter
Rapidan betwe[en]
in the battle o[f]
9th of May of
he set out on
His brigade
Dam, burnec[d]
cars loaded
Union prisone[rs]
Pamunkey, he
ments. After
he did most
in command
that position
ever-memorab[le]
was on the rig[ht]
the morning,
field, after th[e]
one command
der was "Go i[n]
only waited fo[r]
out until the
yond the batt[le]
ers were car[ried]
eral. Forty-f[ive]
taken. For
a Brevet Maj[or]
as a further m[ark]
carry the ne[w]
battle-flag to
on his forty

WASHINGTON, Dec. 15.—Indian Commissioner
Morgan this evening received from Indian
Agent McLaughlin the following dispatch, dated
Fort Yates, North Dakota, Dec. 15:
"Indian police arrested Sitting Bull at his
camp, forty miles northwest of the agency,
this morning at daylight. His followers attempted his rescue and fighting commenced. Four policemen were killed and three
wounded. Eight Indians were killed, including Sitting Bull and his son, Crowfoot,
and several others were wounded. The police
were surrounded for some time, but maintained
their ground until relieved by United States
troops, who now have possession of Sitting Bull's
camp, with all the women, children, and property.
Sitting Bull's followers, probably 100 men, deserted their families and fled West up the Grand
River. The police behaved nobly, and great
credit is due them. Particulars by mail."
Commissioner Morgan showed this telegram
to the President late this evening. The President said that he regarded Sitting Bull as
the great disturbing element in his tribe, and
now that he was out of the way he hoped that a
settlement of the difficulties could be reached
without further bloodshed.
Gen. Schofield was asked for his opinion of the
effect on the other Indians of the killing of Sitting Bull, but he was disinclined to discuss the
matter, saying that it was not possible
to predict the result. He indulged the
hope expressed by others that this would
hasten the settlement of the Indian
trouble. He thought it would make more definite the line of division between the friendly
Indians and those determined to be hostile, but
just how numerous the latter might be could
not be told at this time. He had from the
start of the troubles in the Northwest hoped the
matter would be settled without conflict and
regretted that blood had been shed, but he
hoped for favorable results. Further than this,
Gen. Schofield declined to be interviewed.
When Secretary Proctor was asked concerning
the effect of the killing he said he did not think
it would have any bad effect on friendly Indians.
They had not been kindly disposed toward Sitting Bull and had no love for him. It was only
with the disaffected Indians that he held any in-

THE OLD WEST

CRAZY HORSE

ca. 1840–September 5, 1877

The Cheyenne Sun says: "The notorious Sioux Chieftain, Crazy Horse, died at Camp Robinson at midnight of the 5th inst. It is a coincidence worthy of note that the unconquered and atrocious chief received his death wound—a terrible bowie-knife cut in the side—at the hands of one of his former followers, a soldier Indian, who had stood side by side with the chief in the battle of the Rosebud, in the Custer massacre, and in other engagements of the Sioux war.

"When Crazy Horse essayed his escape, a few days before his death, the Indian soldiers who had been foremost in acts of brutality one year ago hunted him down like blood-hounds.

"The scene around and inside the Adjutant's office as the chief died, was in perfect keeping with his long years of thrilling adventure and unstinted revenge. His father, with one or two faithful followers, watched by his side, while crowds of savages hung around the building, giving vent to their feelings in the curdling whoop, and lending utter drear to the murky darkness with the ominous death chant. Indian soldiers and disarmed hostiles were there alike, the first glorying in their delegated peace-keeping power, and the others only harmless because helpless.

"When the chief was dead he was quickly borne down by the side of White Earth River, where four months ago he first knelt to the sway of the military, and there cared for with the customary savage ceremony by his few remaining friends. Crazy Horse was about 35 years old, a relative of Red Cloud, and an aborigine from head to foot. He was of medium height, slender and wiry build, and as mean a looking Indian as ever knocked for admission to the happy hunting ground.

"However, a bullet wound through his face, received in battle, added much to his brutal and treacherous look. He has known nothing but fight and marauding since boyhood, and was last seen at the agencies about 12 years ago. Among the hostiles, he has been considered the peer of Sitting Bull in influence, and vastly that old chieftain's superior in out and out bravery, devilishness, and unrest. He has done more to retard the settlement of this frontier, by his deeds of blood and pillage, than all other war chiefs combined. The taking off of such a savage will result in more real good than a decisive battle, for it is he who has sown continued dissension and inspired atrocity in others, even on the heels of defeat."

JESSE JAMES

September 5, 1847–April 3, 1882

ST. JOSEPH, Mo.—A great sensation was created in this city this morning by the announcement that Jesse James, the notorious bandit and train robber, had been shot and killed here.

The news spread with great rapidity, and crowds of people rushed to the quarter of the city where the shooting had occurred, anxious to view the body of the dead outlaw and learn the particulars.

In a small frame shanty in the southeast part of the city, Jesse James has lived with his wife since some time in November last. Robert and Charles Ford, two of his gang, have made their headquarters at his house. Charles, it is said, has lived with him in the shanty ever since November; Robert arrived about 10 days ago, and the three have been making preparations for a raiding expedition on which they were to start tonight.

James and the two Fords were in the front room about 9 o'clock this morning. James took off his belt and laid his pistols on the bed, preparing to wash himself, when Robert Ford sprang up behind him and sent a bullet through his brain. The ball entered the back of his head at the base of the right brain, coming out over the eye.

The Ford brothers at once made known what they had done and gave themselves up. They are now under guard at the Courthouse. The body of Jesse

James was conveyed to an undertaker's, where it was prepared for burial.

A look at the body, while it was being photographed at the undertaker's, showed that he was a fine-looking man, apparently 40 years old, with broad forehead, and his physiognomy was that of an intelligent as well as a resolute and daring man.

The house where James lived, and in which he was killed, has the appearance of an armory. A number of guns and pistols, including a repeating rifle, a needle-gun and Navy revolvers, with a good store of ammunition, were found there. Jesse was in the habit of wearing two belts, with a brace of very fine revolvers and 25 extra cartridges. In a stable near the house were discovered several horses, the property of James.

The Ford brothers claim that they are detectives, and that they have been on James's tracks for a long time. It is believed that they were with James in the Blue Cut train robbery, and that they were influenced in killing him by the hope of getting the big reward which has been offered for James, dead or alive.

As soon as the news of the killing of Jesse James was received in Kansas City, Police Commissioner Craig started for St. Joseph with a heavily armed posse of men to guard James's body and give protection to the man who killed him.

Robert Ford is about 22 years of age. In appearance he is a mere boy and is the last person in the world to be taken as the slayer of the famous outlaw.

The following are the particulars of the shooting of Jesse James yesterday: After having eaten breakfast, Jesse James and Charles Ford went to the stable to curry the horses, and, on returning to the room, where Robert Ford was, Jesse said: "It's an awfully hot day." He pulled off his coat and vest and tossed them on the bed. Then he said: "I guess I'll take off my pistols for fear somebody will see them if I walk in the yard." He unbuckled the belt in which he carried two .45-caliber revolvers, one a Smith & Wesson and the other a Colt, and laid them on the bed with his coat and vest. He then picked up a dusting-brush, with the intention of dusting some pictures which hung on the wall. In order to do this he got on a chair, his back being now turned to the brothers, who silently stepped between Jesse and his revolvers, and, at a motion from Charlie, both drew their guns. Robert was the quicker of the two. In one motion he had the long weapon on a level with his eye, with the muzzle not more than four feet from the back of the outlaw's head. Even in that motion, quick as thought, there was something which did not escape the acute ears of the hunted man. He made a motion as if to turn his head to ascertain the cause of that suspicious sound, but too late. A nervous pressure on the trigger, a quick flash, a sharp report, and the well-directed ball crashed through the outlaw's skull. There was no outcry—just a swaying of the body, and it fell heavily back upon the carpeted floor, the ball having entered the base of the skull and made its way out through the forehead over the left eye. It had been fired out of a Colt's "45" improved weapon, silver mounted and pearl-handled, which had been presented by the dead man to his slayer only a few days ago.

Mrs. James was in the kitchen when the shooting was done, separated from the room in which the tragedy occurred by the dining-room. She heard the shot and, dropping her household duties, ran into the front room. She saw her husband lying on his back, and his slayers, each holding his revolver in his hand, making for the fence in the rear of the house.

Robert had reached the enclosure and was in the act of scaling it, when she stepped to the door and called to him: "Robert, you have done this; come back." Robert answered: "I swear to God I did not." They then returned to where she stood.

Mrs. James ran to the side of her husband and lifted up his head. Life was not yet extinct, and when she asked him if he were hurt it seemed to her that he wanted to say something but could not. She tried to wash away the blood that was coursing over his face from the hole in his forehead, but it seemed to her that the blood came faster than she could wash it away, and in her arms Jesse James died.

SITTING BULL

ca. 1831–December 15, 1890

St. Paul, Minn.—A report has been received here to the effect that Sitting Bull, the Sioux chief, has been killed. It is stated that the Indian police started out this morning to arrest him, and meeting him three miles from camp tried to effect his capture. A fight ensued in which Sitting Bull was killed.

A dispatch stated that the Indian police understood that Sitting Bull proposed leaving [the Sioux reservation] for the Bad Lands at once. The police were followed by a troop of cavalry under Capt. Bouchet and infantry under Col. Drum.

When the police reached Sitting Bull's camp on the Grand River, about 40 miles from Standing Rock, they found arrangements being made for departure. The cavalry had not yet reached the camp, when the police arrested Bull and started back with him. His followers quickly rallied to his rescue and tried to retake him. In the melee that ensued, the wily old chief is said to have been killed, and five of the best of the Indian police were also killed.

The remainder of the band are now in retreat up the Grand River.

Sitting Bull, of all the Indians, was the most unrelenting, the most hostile, the most sagacious, the most cruel, and the most desperate foe of the whites of any chief of modern times. He never assented to the control of the United States Government over his people, but persistently fought the troops whenever they came in his way.

He claimed that the country belonged to the Indians; that they had a right to hunt or fish wherever they pleased; that the white man had wronged them, and thus appealing to the feelings of the younger portion of his race, he induced a large number to follow him, and for 20 years carried on his war of murder and rapine, until he finally surrendered to the United States forces on the 19th of July, 1881.

Sitting Bull began his career as a "medicine man." He was the son of Four Horns, one of the four supreme chiefs elected by the Sioux Nation more than a century ago. The Custer episode marked the zenith of Sitting Bull's fame and the beginning of his downfall. He was undoubtedly the most wily and astute Indian in the Sioux Nation. With no reputation as a warrior to aid him, he gained ascendancy as a "medicine man," a prophet, a preacher, a teacher, a politician.

He divided the chieftainship with Gall. Ever since the Little Big Horn fight there has been a bitter rivalry between the men. He commanded the Indians on that occasion, Sitting Bull remaining in his tent performing incantations, distilling "medicines," and indulging in the foolery that was supposed to exercise great influence over the fortunes of the battle. His influence had become so great and was working such deleterious effects among the agency Indians that finally the department at Washington was obliged to take prompt measures to prevent a general outbreak among the friendly Indian tribes, and to this end Sitting Bull and his followers were ordered to come into the reservation, or they would fall under the control of the military power. Sitting Bull laughed at these commands of the Indian Department and still continued his raids, and then followed the campaign of 1876, inaugurated by Gen. Sheridan, wherein three powerful columns of troops were to move simultaneously upon the enemy and force them either into civilization or extermination. Gen. Crook was repulsed, and Gen. Custer, in his eagerness to make an attack, without proper support, which could have been obtained, brought on a fight in which he and his men were all killed, leaving Sitting Bull and his warriors complete masters of the field.

After the battle the savages crossed into Canada. Then the old chieftain began again to commit depredations among the Americans, and finally a commission was appointed by the United States Government to cross the line and to effect by diplomacy what had failed by force of arms. Sitting Bull sneeringly rejected every overture for peace.

Matters now continued quiet with Sitting Bull for nearly one year and a half, when, in 1879, he broke out again, and commenced depredations upon the settlers. He was met by Gen. Miles, and a battle ensued, Bull being in command in person. Then followed the surrender of Rain in the Face, Crow Wing, Chief Gall, and many thousand Indians. For endeavoring to stir up the Indians at Standing Rock against his rival, Gall, Sitting Bull with his relatives were made prisoners and confined at Fort Randall. He was afterward released, and has since made his home in Grand River Valley.

GERONIMO

June 16, 1829–February 17, 1909

LAWTON, Okla.—Geronimo, the Apache Indian chief, died of pneumonia today in the hospital at Fort Sill. He was nearly 90 years of age, and had been held at the Fort as a prisoner of war for many years. He will be buried in the Indian Cemetery tomorrow by the missionaries, the old chief having professed religion three years ago.

As the leader of the warring Apaches of the Southwestern territories in pioneer days, Geronimo gained a reputation for cruelty and cunning never surpassed by that of any other American Indian chief. For more than 20 years he and his men were the terror of the country, always leaving a trail of bloodshed and devastation. The old chief was captured many times, but always got away again, until his final capture, in 1886, by a small command of infantry scouts under Capt. H. W. Lawton, who, as Major General, was killed at the head of command in the Philippines, and Assistant Surgeon Leonard Wood, today in command of the Department of the East, with headquarters at Governors Island.

The capture was made in the Summer, after a long and very trying campaign of many months, in which Lawton and Wood gained a reputation which will be long remembered in the annals of the army. Geronimo was at first sent to Fort Pickens, but was later transferred to Fort Sill. Until a few years ago he did not give up the hope of some day returning to the leadership of the tribes of the Southwest.

Geronimo was a Chiricahua Apache, the son of Chal-o-Row of Mangus-Colorado, the war chief of the Warm Spring Apaches, whose career of murder and devastation through Arizona, New Mexico, and Northern Mexico in his day almost equaled that of his terrible son. According to stories told by the old Indian during his last days, he was crowned war chief of his tribe at the early age of 16. For many years he followed the lead of old Cochise, the hereditary chief of the Apaches, who died in 1875 and was succeeded by Natchez, his son, who, however, was soon displaced by Geronimo with his superior cunning and genius for the Indian method of warfare.

After trailing the band led by Geronimo for more than 10 years, Gen. Crook would probably have captured him in 1875 had he not been transferred to duty among the Utes just as success seemed to be near at hand. For several years after this the situation in the Southwest was the worst ever faced by the settlers. Crook was sent back in 1882. A large body of troops was placed at his disposal, and in a month he had succeeded in driving Geronimo back to his reservation, capturing him and his men on the Mexican border.

In 1885 Geronimo broke out again, and this time was surrounded by Crook in the Cañon de los Embidos. But the Indians succeeded in slipping away, and Crook was removed and Nelson A. Miles placed in command. Miles had already gained a reputation as an Indian fighter, and while he did not exactly cut the field wires behind him to prevent interference from Washington, stories are told of the frequent disregard of troublesome messages.

Lawton and Wood were placed in command of the scouts late in the Summer of 1885. They asked permission to take a picked body of men into the hostile territory and endeavor to run down Geronimo. Gen. Miles finally sent them off with many misgivings. There followed months of privation and hardships which were never forgotten by the men who went with the two young officers. They were gone nearly a year, Gen. Miles often not knowing even where they were or whether or not they had been destroyed by the enemy. On the night of Aug. 20, 1886, the General was sitting at the telegraph instrument in the office at Wilcox, Ariz., waiting for dispatches, when the key suddenly clicked off the news that Geronimo and his men had been surrounded near the Mexican border. Miles hastened there and met the chief on his way north under guard of Lawton. The old warrior was surrounded by about 400 bucks, squaws, papooses, and dogs. They had little else than their blankets and tent poles, and as Gen. Miles afterward stated in his memoirs, "The wily old chief had evidently decided to give up warfare for a time and live on the Government until his tribes gained sufficient strength to return to the warpath."

Gen. Miles writes: "Every one at Washington had now become convinced that there was no good in the old chief, and he was, in fact, one of the lowest and most cruel of the savages of the American continent." The people of the West demanded that he be not allowed to go back to the reservation. He and his bucks were accordingly sent to Fort Pickens and the squaws and papooses to Fort Marion, Florida. It was finally decided to keep Geronimo confined as a prisoner of war. His desire to get back to the West was so pitiful, however, that he was transferred to Fort Sill, where he spent the remainder of his days.

Gen. Wood tells an interesting anecdote of an incident which occurred one afternoon when he was guarding the old chief: "About 2 o'clock in the afternoon the old Indian came to me and asked to see my rifle. It was a Hotchkiss, and he said he had never seen its mechanism. When he asked me for the gun and some ammunition I must confess I felt a little nervous, for I thought it might be a device to get hold of one of our weapons. I made no objection, however, and let him have it, showing him how to use it. He fired at a mark, just missing one of his own men who was passing. This he regarded as a great joke, rolling on the ground and laughing heartily and shouting, 'Good gun.'"

ANNIE OAKLEY

August 13, 1860–November 3, 1926

GREENVILLE, Ohio—Annie Oakley, champion markswoman, who in private life was Mrs. Frank Butler, died at the home of a relative here last night. She had been in ill health for some time.

Injuries received in a train accident in 1901 resulted in one side of her body being almost completely paralyzed. Some of her best records for straight and fancy shooting, however, were made after she recovered. At Pinehurst, N.C., in 1922, she broke 100 clay targets straight from the 16-yard mark.

Her husband, who was her manager, has been seriously ill in Detroit for several days. He is the only survivor. The funeral services Saturday will be private. (AP)

Annie Oakley was born in a log cabin in Ohio 66 years ago. Her father died when she was four years old and she soon helped out her mother by bringing in rabbits and other game that fell to her shotgun. At nine she was shooting so much game that she sent what the family did not need to town by stagecoach. For the rest of her life she supported herself with her keen eye and steady hand.

She was almost 16 years old when she met Frank Butler in her first public shooting match. Her husband lost the match and fell desperately in love

with his conqueror. They were soon married and nearly 50 years later Mrs. Butler remarked: "Frank really reared me. And we're not fashionable, either; we've never been to Reno."

She joined Buffalo Bill in the late 70's. The great Western scout and showman needed less than 15 minutes' observation before he signed up the young girl, whom he always called "Missie," and for the rest of his career they were firm friends and business associates. "I never had a written contract with Buffalo Bill," said Annie Oakley. "I didn't need any. Our outfit was more like a clan than a show or a business. Even with all the thousands of men and women, the cowboys and Comanches, the Cossacks and the Arab, we remained just one big family with Buffalo Bill at its head."

Touring Europe with the Buffalo Bill show, Annie Oakley met many crowned heads and one head that later wore a crown she came within four inches of hitting with a bullet. It was the head of William Hohenzollern. She was giving an exhibition of sharpshooting at Berlin and one of her tricks was the removal of the ashes from a cigarette held in a man's mouth. The Crown Prince stepped forward, cigarette in mouth, and asked to have the trick performed on him. Manager Butler was none too pleased at the prospect, but his wife coolly took aim and removed the ashes in the manner desired by the Prince, who later became Kaiser Wilhelm II. Edward VII of England told her she was "the best rifle shot in the world" and gave her a medal.

One of the picturesque friends she made was Sitting Bull, the Indian chief. He called her "Watanic Cicilia," or "Little Sureshot." He bequeathed her all his property.

Annie Oakley will be buried in the hills of Darke County, Ohio, where she learned to handle a gun. Last year she arranged for a final resting place at Woodland.

WYATT EARP

March 19, 1848–January 13, 1929

Los Angeles—The West lost another of its few remaining frontier gunfighters today with the death here of Wyatt Earp, once a peace officer at Dodge City, Kan., and at Tombstone, Ariz. Mr. Earp's colorful career led him through a dozen fatal conflicts with "bad men" of the Old West. He was 78 years old.

Earp and three brothers, Virgil, Morgan and Jim, together with Doc Holliday, were principal figures in the stormy days of Cochise County, Ariz., where Tombstone is located. Their conflict with the Clanton gang of cowboys, shortly after which Morgan Earp was killed from ambush, and during which two famous gunmen died, was followed by an investigation.

The Earps, led by Wyatt, then a Deputy United States Marshal, were exonerated on the ground that they had acted as peace officers.

Wyatt Earp gained further public notice when he was chosen as referee of the Tom Sharkey–Bob Fitzsimmons fight in San Francisco. He wore a six-shooter in the ring, and no protests were made at the time, although many were heard later.

Among the friends of Earp were Bat Masterson, Wild Bill Hickok and other famous figures of the early West. In Alaska, during the gold rush, Earp met Bill Hart, the motion-picture actor; Wilson Mizner, playwright, and the late Tex Rickard, all of whom were close friends.

Earp had been ill for some time. He left his bed the day before Rickard died to send a telegram to his sick friend in Florida. The exertion caused a relapse.

Earp left a widow and a niece. The funeral will be held Tuesday. —*Associated Press*

Point Pleasant, Ohio, 25 miles above Cincinnati on the Ohio River, was born Hiram Ulysses Grant, the eldest of the six children of Jesse R. and Hannah Simpson Grant. His great grandfather, Noah Grant, and Noah's brother Solomon, of Connecticut, commissioned officers in the French and Indian war, were killed in 1756. His grandfather, Noah Grant, served all through the Revolutionary War. His father and also his mother's father were born in Pennsylvania. The father of Ulysses was a tanner by trade, and removed, the year after his son's birth, to Georgetown, in the neighboring county, where the lad's boyhood was passed. At the age of 17 he received a cadetship in the Military Academy through the Congressman of his district, who erroneously registered him as Ulysses S. Grant and so his name remains in history.

Graduated from West Point in 1843, No. 21 in a class of 39 members, young Grant was attached as Brevet Second Lieutenant to the Fourth Infantry, which, after various garrison service, two years later joined Gen. Zachary Taylor's army, assembling in Texas. War with Mexico broke out in the Spring of 1846, and Grant, then a full Second Lieutenant, took part with his regiment in many of Taylor's operations and in Scott's campaign from the siege of Vera Cruz to the capture of the city of Mexico, being present at the battles of Palo Alto, Resaca de la Palma, Monterey, Cerro Gordo, Churubusco, Molino del Rey, and Chapultepec. For gallantry at Molino del Rey he was brevetted First Lieutenant, and for gallantry at Chapultepec Captain, while his brigade commander, Col. Garland, said of him: "I must not omit to call attention to Lieut. Grant, Fourth Infantry, who ac-

During this
will perhaps
its intrinsic in
first action f
on the field,
was near putt
the outset. W
or three hors
afterward s
other officers
men, yet Gra
soldier pres
found that,
transports,
to supervise.
alone, in ord
glancing at
covered a Co
50 yards of
Turning hi
back to t
ing down t
and trotting
the gangplar
to receive hi

FORTS H
The Tenn
emptying in
and 35 miles
advantages
naval adven
such an adv
on the right
Fort Donels
left bank of
between Ke
these forts,
and Bowling
defensive c
and other r
break the li
everywhere
ported to G.
pedition tha
was easy an
short work
January
Louis as fo
will take ar

Gen. George Smith Patton Jr.
as one of the most brilliant sol-
iers in American history. Auda-
ious, unorthodox and inspiring, he
ed his troops to great victories in
North Africa, Sicily and on the
Western Front. Nazi generals ad-
itted that of all American field
ommanders he was the one they
ost feared. To Americans he was
worthy successor of such hard-
tten cavalrymen as Philip Sheri-
an, J. E. B. Stuart and Nathan
edford Forrest.

His great soldierly qualities were
atched by one of the most color-
l personalties of his period.
bout him countless legends clus-
red—some true, some untrue, but
l testifying to the firm hold he
d upon the ...ations of
en. He went ...
o pearl-handled ...
ers on his hips. He was the mas-
r of an unprintable brand of elo-
ence, yet at times he coined
rases that will live in the Amer-
an Army's traditions.

"We shall attack and attack un-
we are exhausted, and then we
all attack again," he told his
oops before the initial landings
North Africa, thereby sum-
arizing the military creed that
n victory after victory along the
g road that led from Casablanca
the heart of Germany.

At El Guettar in March of 1943
won the first major American
ctory over Nazi arms. In July of
at year he leaped from a landing
rge and waded ashore to the
achhead at Gela, Sicily, thus benning a campaign that, as he
mself observed, out-blitzed the
ventors of Blitzkreig. In just
irty-eight days the American
venth Army, under his leader-
ip, and the British Eighth Army,
der Gen. Sir Bernard Montgom-
y, conquered all of Sicily.

of nazism from German life,
ten days later, on Oct. 2, 1945
was removed from the comm...
of his beloved Third Army.

Although reports were cur...
that he might retire, General
ton took his transfer in soldi...
silence. He assumed comman...
the American Fifteenth Army...
paper organization devoted t...
study of the tactical lessons t...
learned from the war just c...
pleted, and told friends that
was in line with what had been
favorite mental occupation s...
he was 7 years old: the study
war.

Although he customarily sig...
himself George Smith Patton
General Patton was actually
third in line of his family to
that name. The original Geo...
Smith Patton his grandfat...
his ...e of Virginia
and became
colonel in the Confederate Ar...
He was killed in action at the
tle of Cedar Creek.

Expert Horseman From Childh...

General Patton's father w...
through V. M. I., then studied
and moved west. He marrie...
daughter of Benjamin Wilson,
was the first Mayor of Los
geles, and for whom Mount Wil...
was named. The future gen...
was born on the family ranch...
San Gabriel, Calif., on Nov.
1885, and from childhood was
expert horseman.

At the age of 18 he came
and entered V. M. I., but afte...
year there he entered West P...
with the class of 1909. Ther...
a legend at the academy that
boasted at his entrance that
would be cadet captain, the h...
est post in the cadet corps,
that he would also be the f...
member of his class to becom...
general. Actually, he was c...
adjutant, the second highest
and was the second member...

WARRIORS

ROBERT E. LEE

January 19, 1807–October 12, 1870

Intelligence was received last evening of the death at Lexington, Va., of Gen. Robert E. Lee, the most famous of the officers whose celebrity was gained in the service of the Southern Confederacy during the late terrible rebellion.

A report was received some days ago that he had been smitten with paralysis, but this was denied, and hopes of his speedy recovery were entertained by his friends.

Within the last few days his symptoms had taken an unfavorable turn, and he expired at 9 o'clock yesterday morning of congestion of the brain, at the age of 63 years, 8 months and 23 days.

Robert Edmund Lee was the son of Gen. Henry Lee, the friend of Washington, and a representative of one of the wealthiest and most respected families of Virginia.

Born in January, 1807, he grew up amid all the advantages which wealth and family position could give in a republican land, and received the best education afforded by the institutions of his native State.

Having inherited a taste for military studies, he en-

tered the National Academy at West Point in 1825, and graduated in 1829, the second in scholarship in his class. He was at once commissioned Second Lieutenant of engineers, and in 1835 acted as Assistant Astronomer in drawing the boundary line between the States of Michigan and Ohio.

In the following year he was promoted to the grade of First Lieutenant, and in 1836 received a Captain's commission. On the breaking out of the war with Mexico, he was made Chief-Engineer of the army under the command of Gen. Wool.

After the battle of Cerro Gordo, in April, 1847, in which he distinguished himself by his gallant conduct, he was promoted to the rank of Major. He displayed equal bravery at Contreras, Cherubusco and Chapultepec, and in the battle at the last-mentioned place received a severe wound. His admirable conduct throughout this struggle was rewarded with the commission of a Lieutenant-Colonel and the title of Colonel.

In 1852 he was appointed to the position of Superintendent of the Military Academy at West Point, which he retained until 1855. On retiring from this position he was made Lieutenant-Colonel of the Second Calvary, and on the 16th of March, 1861, received the commission of Colonel of the First Calvary.

Thus far the career of Col. Lee had been one of

honor and the highest promise. In every service entrusted to him he had proved efficient, prompt and faithful, and his merits had always been readily acknowledged and rewarded by promotion. He was regarded by his superior officers as one of the most brilliant and promising men in the army of the United States.

His personal integrity was well known, and his loyalty and patriotism were not doubted. But he seems to have been imbued with that pernicious doctrine that his first and highest allegiance was due to the State of his birth.

When Virginia joined the ill-fated movement of secession from the Union, he immediately threw up his commission in the Federal Army and offered his sword to the newly formed Confederacy, declaring that his sense of duty would never permit him to "raise his hand against his relatives, his children, and his home."

In his farewell letter to Gen. Winfield Scott, he spoke of the struggle which this step had cost him, and his wife declared that he "wept tears of blood over this terrible war."

Probably few doubt the sincerity of his protestation, but thousands have regretted the error of judgment, the false conception of the allegiance due to his Government and his country, which led one so gifted to cast his lot with traitors and devote his splendid talents to the execution of a wicked plot to tear asunder the Republic.

He resigned his commission on the 25th of April, 1861, and immediately betook himself to Richmond, where he was received with open arms and put in command of all the forces of Virginia by Gov. Letcher. On the 10th of May he received the commission of a Major-General in the army of the Confederate States, retaining the command in Virginia, and was soon promoted to the rank of General in the regular army.

He first took the field in the mountainous region of Western Virginia, where he was defeated at Greenbrier by Gen. J. J. Reynolds on the 3rd of October, 1861. He was subsequently sent to take command of the Department of the South Atlantic Coast, but was later recalled to Virginia, and placed at the head of the forces defending the capital.

He engaged with the Army of the Potomac under his old companion-in-arms, Gen. McClellan, and drove it back to the Rappahannock. He afterward, in August, 1862, attacked the Army of Virginia, under Gen. Pope, and after driving it back to Washington, crossed the Potomac into Maryland, where he issued a proclamation calling upon the inhabitants to enlist under his triumphant banners.

Meantime, McClellan gathered a new army from the broken remnants of his former forces, met Lee at Hagerstown, and, after a battle of two days, compelled him to retreat. Reinforced by "Stonewall" Jackson, on the 16th of September, Lee turned to renew the battle, but after two days of terrible fighting at Sharpsburg and Antietam, was driven from the soil of Maryland.

Retiring beyond the Rappahannock, he took up his position at Fredericksburg, where he was attacked, on the 13th of December, by Gen. Burnside, whom he drove back with terrible slaughter.

Gen. Lee met with the same success in May, 1863, when attacked by Hooker, at Chancellorsville. Encouraged by these victories, in the ensuing Summer he determined to make a bold invasion into the territory of the North. He met Gen. Meade at Gettysburg, Penn., on the 1st of July, 1863, and after one of the most terrible battles of modern times, was driven from Northern soil.

Soon after this, a new character appeared on the battlefields of Virginia, and Gen. Lee gathered his forces for the defense of the Confederate capital against the onslaughts of Gen. Grant. In the Spring and Summer of 1864 that indomitable soldier gradually enclosed the City of Richmond as with a girdle of iron, which he drew closer and closer, repulsing the rebel forces whenever they ventured to make an attack.

In this difficult position, holding the citadel of the Confederacy, and charged with its hopes and destinies, Lee was made Commander-in-Chief of the armies of the South. He held out until the Spring of 1865, vainly endeavoring to gather the broken forces of the Confederacy, and break asunder the terrible line which was closing around them.

After a desperate and final effort at Burkesville, on the 9th of April, 1865, he was compelled to acknowledge his defeat, and surrendered his sword to Gen. Grant on the generous terms dictated by that great soldier.

Lee retired under his parole to Weldon, and soon after made a formal submission to the Federal Government. Subsequently, by an official clemency, which is probably without a parallel in the history of the world, he was formally pardoned for his part in the mad effort of the Southern States to break up the Union and destroy the Government.

Not long after his surrender he was invited to become the President of Washington University, at Lexington, Va., and was installed in that position on the 2nd of October, 1865. Since that time he has devoted himself to the interests of that institution, and by his unobtrusive modesty and purity of life, has won the respect even of those who most bitterly deplore his course in the rebellion.

GEORGE CUSTER

December 5, 1839–June 25, 1876

SALT LAKE CITY—The special correspondent of the Helena (Montana) Herald writes from Stillwater, Montana, under date of July 2, as follows:

Muggins Taylor, a scout for Gen. Gibbon, arrived here last night direct from Little Horn River, and reports that Gen. [George Armstrong] Custer found the Indian camp of 2,000 lodges on the Little Horn, and immediately attacked it. He charged the thickest portion of the camp with five companies. Nothing is known of the operations of this detachment, except their course as traced by the dead. Major Reno commanded the other seven companies, and attacked the lower portion of the camp. The Indians poured a murderous fire from all directions. Gen. Custer, his two brothers, his nephew, and brother-in-law were all killed, and not one of his detachment escaped. Two hundred and seven men were buried in one place. The number of killed is estimated at 300, and the wounded at 31.

The Seventh fought like tigers, and were overcome by mere brute force. The Indian loss cannot be estimated. The Indians got all the arms of the killed soldiers. There were 17 commissioned officers killed. The whole Custer family died at the head of their column. The Indians actually pulled men off their horses, in some instances.

This report is given as Taylor told it, as he was over the field after the battle. The above is confirmed by other letters, which say Custer has met with a fearful disaster.

Major Gen. George Armstrong Custer, who was killed with his whole command while attacking an encampment of Sioux Indians, under command of Sitting Bull, was one of the bravest and most widely known officers in the United States Army. He has for the past 15 years been known to the country and to his comrades as a man who feared no danger, as a soldier in the truest sense of the word. He was daring to a fault, generous beyond most men. His memory will long be kept green in many friendly hearts.

Born at New-Rumley, Harrison County, Ohio, on the 5th of December, 1839, he obtained a good common education, and after graduating engaged for a time in teaching school. In June, 1857, he obtained an appointment to the United States Military Academy.

He graduated on the 24th of June, 1861, with what was considered the fair standing of No. 34 in one of the brightest classes that ever left the academy. Immediately upon leaving West Point he was appointed Second Lieutenant in Company G of the Second United States Cavalry, a regiment which had formerly been commanded by Robert E. Lee.

He reported to Lieut. Gen. Scott on the 20th of July, the day preceding the battle of Bull Run, and the Commander in Chief gave him the choice of accepting a position on his staff or of joining his regiment, then under command of Gen. McDowell, in the field. Lieut. Custer chose the latter course, and after riding all night through a country filled with people who were, to say the least, not friendly, he reached McDowell's head-quarters at daybreak on the 21st.

Preparations for the battle had already begun, and after delivering his dispatches from Gen. Scott and hastily partaking of a mouthful of coffee and a piece of hard bread, he joined his company. It is not necessary now to recount the disasters of the fight that followed. Suffice it to say that Lieut. Custer's company was among the last to leave the field.

The young officer continued to serve with his company, and was engaged in the drilling of volunteer recruits in and about the defenses of Washington, when upon the appointment of Phil Kearny to the position of Brigadier General, that officer gave him a position on his staff.

With his company Lieut. Custer marched forward with that part of the Army of the Potomac which moved upon Manassas after its evacuation by the rebels. Our cavalry was in advance and encountered the rebel horsemen for the first time near Catlett's Station.

The commanding officer made a call for volunteers to charge the enemy's advance post. Lieut. Custer was among the first to step to the front, and in command of his company he shortly afterward made his first charge. He drove the rebels across Muddy Creek, wounded a number of them, and had one of his own men injured.

After this Custer went with the Army of the Potomac to the Peninsula and remained with his company until the Army settled down before Yorktown, when he was detailed as an Assistant Engineer. Acting in this capacity he planned and erected the earthworks nearest the enemy's lines. He also accompanied the advance under Gen. Hancock in pursuit of the enemy from Yorktown. Shortly afterward, he captured the first battle-flag ever secured by the Army of the Potomac.

From this time on he was nearly always the first in every work of daring. When the Army reached the Chickahominy he was the first man to cross the river; he did so in the face of the fire of the enemy's pickets, and at times was obliged to wade up to his armpits. For this brave act Gen. McClellan promoted him to a Captaincy and made him one of his personal aides. In this capacity he served during most of the Peninsula campaign, and participated in all its battles.

He performed the duty of marking out the position which was occupied by the Union Army at the battle of Gaines' Mills. He also participated in the campaign which ended in the battles of South Mountain and Antietam.

He was next engaged in the battle of Chancellorsville, and immediately after that fight he was made a personal aide by Gen. Pleasonton, who was then commanding a division of cavalry. Serving in this capacity, he marked himself as one of the most dashing, some said the most reckless, officers in the service.

When Pleasonton was made a Major General, he requested the appointment of four Brigadiers to command under him. Young Custer was made a Brigadier General and assigned to the command of the First, Fifth, Sixth, and Seventh Michigan Cavalry.

He did noble service at the battle of Gettysburg. He held the right of line, and was obliged to face Hampton's division of cavalry, and after a hotly contested fight, utterly routed the rebels. Custer had two horses shot under him.

Hardly had the battle concluded when he was sent to attack the enemy, which was trying to force its way to the Potomac. He destroyed more than 400 wagons.

At Hagerstown, Md., Custer again had his horse shot under him. At Falling Waters, shortly after, he attacked with his small brigade the entire rebel rear guard. The Confederate commander Gen. Pettigrew was killed and his command routed, with a loss of 1,300 prisoners.

Custer participated in the battle of the Wilderness in 1864, and on the 9th of May of the same year,

under Gen. Sheridan, he set out on the famous raid toward Richmond. His brigade led the column, captured Beaver Dam, burned the station and a train of cars loaded with supplies, and released 400 Union prisoners. After the battle of Fisher's Hill, he was placed in command of a division, and remained in that position until after Lee's surrender.

When the rebels fell back to Appomattox, Custer had the advance of Sheridan's command, and his share in the action is well described in the entertaining volume entitled "With Sheridan in His Last Campaign."

"When the sun was an hour high in the west, energetic Custer in advance spied the depot and four heavy trains of freight ears," the book says. "He quickly ordered his leading regiments to circle out to the left through the woods, and as they gained the railroad beyond the station he led the rest of his division pell-mell down the road and enveloped the train as quick as winking.

"At the head of the horsemen rode Custer of the golden locks, his broad sombrero turned up from his hard, bronzed face, the ends of his crimson cravat floating over his shoulder, gold galore spangling his jacket sleeves, a pistol in his boots, jangling spurs on his heels, and a ponderous claymore swinging at his side; a wild, dare-devil of a General."

On July 28, 1866, he was appointed Lieutenant Colonel of the Seventh United States Cavalry for service on the frontier.

ULYSSES S. GRANT

April 27, 1822–July 23, 1885

MOUNT McGREGOR, NY—Surrounded by all of his family and with no sign of pain, Gen. [Ulysses S.] Grant passed from life at six minutes after eight o'clock this morning. The end came with so little immediate notice as to be in the nature of a surprise. All night had the family been on watch, part of the time in the parlor, where he lay, rarely venturing further away from him than the porch on which the parlor opens.

The General did not speak even in a whisper after 3 o'clock this morning. It was soon evident that he was too far gone to be aided by stimulants. Then came the waiting for death. The General lay on the bed, his face leaden, yet with some warmth left in its hue. His eyes were closed. Power to open them had been restored to him, and it was occasionally invoked when some member of the family, or the doctor, or one of the attendants spoke to him. Then he would open his eyes. He could make no other recognition, but that of the eyes was clear. His lungs and pulse were failing, but there was yet no cloud on the brain.

The rays of the morning sun fell across the cottage porch upon a family waiting only for death. The doctor said he would inform them instantly of any change. [About 7:45] a change had come. Dr. Shrady sent for the family. The bed stood in the middle of the room. Dr. Douglas drew a chair to the head near the General. Mrs. Grant came in and sat on the opposite side. She clasped gently one of the white hands in her own.

When the Colonel came in, Dr. Douglas gave up his chair to him. The Colonel began to stroke his father's forehead, as was his habit when attending him. Only the Colonel and Mrs. Grant sat. Mrs. Sartoris stood at her mother's shoulder, Dr. Shrady a little behind. Jesse Grant leaned against the low headboard fanning the General. Ulysses junior stood at the foot. Dr. Douglas was behind the Colonel. The wives of the three sons were grouped near the foot. Harrison was in the doorway, and the nurse, Henry, near a remote corner. Between

them, at a window, stood Dr. Sands. The General's little grandchildren, U. S. Grant, Jr., and Nellie, were sleeping the sleep of childhood in the nursery room above stairs.

All eyes were intent on the General. His breathing had become soft, though quick. A shade of pallor crept slowly but perceptibly over this features. His bared throat quivered with the quickened breath. The outer air, gently moving, swayed the curtain at an east window. In the crevice crept a white ray from the sun. It reached across the room like a rod and lighted a picture of Lincoln over the deathbed. The sun did not touch the companion picture, which was of the General. A group of watchers in a shaded room, with only this quivering shaft of pure light, the gaze of all turned on the pillowed occupant of the bed, all knowing that the end had come, and thankful, knowing it, that no sign of pain attended it—this was the simple setting of the scene.

The General made no motion. Only the fluttering throat, white as his sick robe, showed that life remained. The face was one of peace. There was no trace of present suffering. The moments passed in silence. The light on the portrait of Lincoln was slowly sinking. Presently the General opened his eyes and glanced about him, looking into the faces of all. The glance lingered as it met the tender gaze of his companion. A startled, wavering motion at the throat, a few quiet gasps, a sigh, and the appearance of dropping into gentle sleep followed. The eyes of affection were still upon him. He lay without a motion. At that

instant the window curtain swayed back in place, shutting out the sunbeam.

"At last," said Dr. Shrady, in a whisper.

"It is all over," sighed Dr. Douglas.

Mrs. Grant could not believe it until the Colonel, realizing the truth, kneeled at the bedside clasping his father's hand. Then she buried her face in her handkerchief. There was not a sound in the room, no sobbing, no unrestrained show of grief. The example set by him who had gone so quietly kept grief in check at that moment. The doctors withdrew. Dr. Newman, who had entered in response to a summons just at the instant of the passing away, looked into the calm face, now beyond suffering, and bowed his head. There was a brief silence. Then Dr. Newman led Mrs. Grant to a lounge, and the others of the family sought their rooms.

The General had not been dead two minutes when the wires were sending it over the country. It was known in New York before some of the guests heard of it at the hotel, where it spread very quickly. Undertaker Holmes was on his way from Saratoga almost as soon as the family had withdrawn to their rooms. A special train which had waited for him all night was at once dispatched for him. Sculptor Gohardt was informed that he might take the death mask. The General's body still lay on the bed clad in the white flannel gown and the light apparel that he had last worn. The face seemed to have filled out somewhat, looking more as in familiar portraits of him.

It was yet early in the morning when dispatches of

condolence and offers of help began to come in on the family. One was from the Managers of the Soldiers' Home at Washington, offering for the place of interment a site in the grounds at the Home, carefully selected and on an eminence overlooking the city.

Col. Grant said that recently the General had written a note embodying his wishes in regard to the subject of removal from here. He was then anticipating death during this month. It would be too bad, he wrote, to send the family back to the city in the hot weather on account of his death. He proposed, therefore, that his body be embalmed and kept on this hill until the weather should become cool enough to let them go back to the city in comfort, and allow an official burial if one should be desired. The General's supposition in writing this note was that he would be buried in New York. Washington was not one of the places named.

He did not know that the family had been in correspondence with Gen. Sheridan, in April, about a burial place at Washington, or that Gen. Sheridan had selected a site on the grounds of the Soldiers' Home. It was urged this morning [that] the General might have preferred Washington above any other place, but that he had omitted to mention it because of modesty. The disposition of the family, however, was to follow his wishes.

[The note was written on June 24. Gen. Grant] stepped into the office room early in the evening and handed to Col. Grant a slip of paper on which was written substantially this:

"There are three places from which I wish a choice of burial place to be made:

"West Point.—I would prefer this above others but for the fact that my wife could not be placed beside me there.

"Galena, or some place in Illinois.—Because from that State I received my first General's commission.

"New York.—Because the people of that city befriended me in my need."

When he had delivered this slip to the Colonel he walked back into the sick room. In a few minutes he reappeared, walking round in front of the Colonel.

"I don't like this, father," the son said, holding out the slip.

"What is there about it you don't like?" asked the General, in his husky whisper.

"I don't like any of it. There is no need of talking of such things."

The General took the slip, folded it, tore it lengthwise, across, and again until the pieces were so small that hardly a word could have been made out from any of them, and throwing them in the waste basket went back to his room without speaking.

This was the first time the General indicated any wish in regard to his burial. The family, however, had done something toward it in April, when he was supposed to be dying. At that time, while some of them had not abandoned hope, the matter was discussed as a possibility. It was agreed that if he should die, there would be little time, in the confusion sure to prevail, to decide on that matter. Correspondence was accordingly opened with Gen. Sheridan, who thought, as did many others, that at the Soldiers' Home in Washington would be the best place for burial, because the General saved that city; and arrangements were made to take his body there.

In view of [Gen. Grant's] expressed wish, however, it is more than likely that he will be buried in New York. The spot selected, whether it be Central Park, as was talked of in the Spring, or elsewhere, will certainly be accepted by the family only on condition that Mrs. Grant may be laid beside him.

[The General's final weeks and days proved highly emotional for Mrs. Grant, yet she remained hopeful.]

One evening, as the General sat in the parlor with the family, the Colonel mentioned having that day received a letter from Webster & Co., the publishers of [his] memoirs, saying that subscriptions to the book already guaranteed $300,000 to the General. Taking up his pad, the General wrote:

"That will be all for you, Julia," and handed the slip over to Mrs. Grant.

She began to cry, and could not be calmed for some time. That evening she regained courage in prayer, and the next morning she talked as hopefully as ever of the General's recovery.

"I have seen the General in trouble before," she often said. "Those about me were despondent over him during the war. The newspapers and my friends did not believe he would take Vicksburg. They were skeptical about what he could do in Virginia. But no one knew him as I did. I was always confident that he would succeed. I am equally sure he will come out of this trouble, for the old faith sustains me."

Accompanying this news article was a biographical portrait of more than 40,000 words.

GEORGE PATTON

November 11, 1885–December 21, 1945

FRANKFORT ON THE MAIN, Germany—Gen. George S. Patton Jr., one of the most vivid figures among Allied combat leaders in World War II, succumbed at 5:50 P.M. (11:50 A.M., Eastern Standard Time) to a lung congestion brought on by paralysis of his chest, the result of his auto accident two weeks ago.

The end came for the former United States Third Army commander as he was sleeping in an Army hospital in Heidelberg. He was 60 years old. [Patton was buried in an American military cemetery in Luxembourg City alongside some of the fallen from the Third Army.]—*Kathleen McLaughlin*

Audacious, unorthodox and inspiring, Gen. George Smith Patton Jr. led his troops to great victories in North Africa, Sicily and on the Western Front. Nazi generals admitted that of all American field commanders he was the one they most feared.

He went into action with two pearl-handled revolvers in holsters on his hips. He was the master of an unprintable brand of eloquence, yet at times he coined phrases that will live in the American Army's traditions.

"We shall attack and attack until we are exhausted, and then we shall attack again," he told his troops before the initial landings in North Africa, thereby summarizing the creed that won victory after victory.

At El Guettar in March of 1943 he won the first major American victory over Nazi arms. In July of that year he leaped from a landing barge and waded ashore to the beachhead at Gela, Sicily. In just 38 days the American Seventh Army, under his leadership, and the British Eighth Army, under Gen. Sir Bernard Montgomery, conquered all of Sicily.

But it was as the leader of his beloved Third Army on the Western Front that General Patton staked his claims to greatness. In 10 months his armor and infantry roared through six countries—France, Belgium, Luxembourg, Germany, Czechoslovakia and Austria. It crossed the Seine, the Loire, the Moselle, the Saar, the Rhine, the Danube and a score of lesser rivers; captured more than 750,000 Nazis and killed or disabled 500,000 others.

There were times when not even Supreme Headquarters knew where his vanguards were. His advance units had to be supplied with gasoline and maps dropped by air.

His best-known nickname, "Old Blood and Guts," was one that he detested but his men loved. "His guts and my blood," his wounded veterans used to say. His explosive wrath and lurid vocabulary became legendary.

But General Patton had a softer side. He composed two volumes of poetry, which he stipulated were not to be published until after his death. He was an intensely religious man, who liked to sing in church and who knew the Episcopal Order of Morning Prayer by heart.

He seemed fated to be the center of controversy. Again and again, when his fame and popularity were at their height, some rash statement or ill-considered deed precipitated a storm. The most celebrated of these incidents was the slapping of a soldier whom he took to be a malingerer but who was actually suffering from battle fatigue.

This episode resulted in widespread demands for his removal from command and caused the Senate to delay his confirmation to the permanent rank of major general for almost a year. General [Dwight D.] Eisenhower sharply rebuked him, but insisted that his qualifications, loyalty and tenacity made him invaluable.

The turmoil had hardly died away when he caused another stir by a speech at the opening of a club for

American soldiers in London. The original version of his remarks quoted him as saying that the British and American peoples were destined to rule the world, but after this had evoked an outburst of criticism, Army press relations officers insisted that he had actually said, "we British, American and, of course, the Russian people" were destined to rule.

He caused a furor by an interview he granted American correspondents in Germany after the end of the war. Discussing conditions in Bavaria, where the military government was under his command, he said too much fuss was being made over denazification and compared the Nazi party to the losers in an election between Democrats and Republicans.

General Eisenhower promptly called him on the carpet. General Patton promised that he would be loyal to the Potsdam agreements prescribing the complete and ruthless elimination of Nazism, but on Oct. 2, 1945, he was removed from the command of his Third Army. He assumed command of the Fifteenth Army, a paper organization devoted to a study of the tactical lessons to be learned from the war.

Although he signed himself George Smith Patton Jr., General Patton was actually the third in line of his family to bear that name. The original George Smith Patton, his grandfather, was a graduate of Virginia Military Institute and became a colonel in the Confederate Army. He was killed at the battle of Cedar Creek.

General Patton's father went through V.M.I., studied law, and moved west. He married a daughter of Benjamin Wilson, the first Mayor of Los Angeles. The future general was born on the family ranch at San Gabriel, Calif., on Nov. 11, 1885, and from childhood was an expert horseman.

At the age of 18 he came east and entered V.M.I., but after a year there he entered West Point with the class of 1909. He was a poor student (all his life he was remarkably deficient in spelling) but an outstanding athlete. He excelled as a sprinter on the track team and was also an expert fencer, swimmer, rider and shot. He rose to cadet adjutant, the second highest post in the cadet corps.

On May 26, 1910, General Patton married Beatrice Ayer of Boston, who survives him. They had two daughters and a son.

In 1912 he represented the United States at the Olympic Games in Stockholm, competing in the modern pentathlon. He finished fifth among more than 30 contestants.

His first post was at Fort Sheridan, Ill., but in December, 1911, he was transferred to Fort Myer, Va., where he was detailed to design a new cavalry saber. In 1913 he went to France to study French saber methods, and on his return was made Master of the Sword at the Mounted Service School, Fort Riley, Kan.

He accompanied Gen. John J. Pershing as his aide on the punitive expedition into Mexico after the bandit Pancho Villa in 1916, and the next year he went to France with the general as a member of his staff. He attended the French Tank School and then saw action at the battle of Cambrai, where the British first used tanks on a large scale.

He was assigned to organize and direct the American Tank Center at Langres. For his service in that capacity he was subsequently awarded the Distinguished Service Medal. He took command of the 304th Brigade of the Tank Corps and distinguished himself by his leadership of it in the St. Mihiel offensive in September, 1918. Later that autumn, during the Meuse-Argonne offensive, he was severely wounded in the left leg. After the war, he served in various tank and cavalry posts in the United States.

When this country began to rearm in the summer of 1940 Patton was a colonel. He was sent to Fort Benning, Ga., as commander of a brigade of the Second Armored Division, then being formed. In April, 1941, he became division commander. Promoted to corps commander, he organized the Desert Training Center in California.

When the North African invasion was planned, General Patton was placed in command of the American forces scheduled to land in Morocco. After the American reverse at Kasserine Pass in February, he took command of the Second United States Corps, which forced the Nazis back into a corridor between the mountains and the sea, up which the British Eighth Army under General Montgomery pursued them.

On April 16 Gen. Omar Bradley succeeded him in command of the Second Corps.

There were rumors that General Patton had fallen into disfavor. Actually, General Eisenhower had withdrawn him from action to prepare the Seventh Army for the invasion of Sicily in July.

The invasion was brilliantly successful, and General Patton's troops cut clear across the island to Palermo, then fought their way along the north coast to Messina.

General Patton, who drove himself as hard as he drove his men, visited a hospital not far from the front when he had been under prolonged strain. There he encountered two men who showed no signs of visible wounds, but who had been diagnosed as suffering from battle neurosis.

General Patton called them "yellow bellies" and other unprintable epithets, and struck one so hard that his helmet liner flew off.

General Eisenhower castigated General Patton, although he did not formally reprimand him. General Patton made personal apologies to all those present at the time of the episode, and later sent public apologies to each division of the Seventh Army.

General Patton did not appear during the campaign on the Italian mainland that followed, and some observers thought he had been relegated to a secondary role. Actually, General Eisenhower had picked him for a key role in the invasion of Western Europe, and he was then in England preparing for it.

For almost two months after D-Day, June 6, 1944, General Patton's whereabouts remained a mystery. The fact that he was in England was well known, and the inability of the Nazi intelligence to locate him forced their High Command to retain the German 15th Army in the Pas de Calais area, far from the Normandy beachhead, lest he head a landing there.

Instead, the Third Army landed on the beachhead in great secrecy, and deployed behind the First Army. When the First Army broke the German lines between St. Lo and the sea on July 25, the Third Army poured through the breach to exploit it. General Patton's armor and motorized infantry smashed across France, all the way to the Moselle, with planes dropping supplies before lack of gasoline finally halted the chase.

In the bitter autumn that followed, General Patton's men made slow but steady headway. From Oct. 3 to Nov. 22, they carried on a sanguinary attack against Metz, which in 1,500 years of history had never before been taken by assault. They had to fight their way in, fort by fort and street by street, but they eventually took the city.

Early in December the Third Army began an attack on the Saar Basin, but the unexpected success of von Rundstedt's offensive against the First Army's lines to the north forced a swift change. General Patton was ordered to go to the rescue of the crumbling American positions on the south side of the "bulge."

He redeployed his forces with astonishing speed. Within three days the Third Army had begun to pound at the southern flank of the Nazi wedge. Some of its divisions had traveled 150 miles in open trucks. By Dec. 28 they had fought their way to the relief of Bastogne. For another month they hammered away at the bulge, until it was no more.

In February the Third Army broke through the Siegfried Line and crossed the Moselle, cutting to pieces the Nazi forces in the Saar-Palatinate region. On March 17 it seized Coblenz. On April 18 the Third crossed the border of Czechoslovakia and nine days later it entered Austria. Its advance units were in the vicinity of Linz when the shooting stopped.

DOUGLAS MacARTHUR

January 26, 1880–April 5, 1964

WASHINGTON—General of the Army Douglas MacArthur died today after a determined fight for life. He was 84 years old.

The general, who led the Allied victory over Japan in World War II and commanded the United Nations forces in the Korean War, died at 2:39 P.M. at the Walter Reed Army Medical Center, where he had been a patient since March 2. Death was attributed to acute kidney and liver failure.

The general's wife, Jean, and their son, Arthur, 26, were at the hospital at the end.—*Jack Raymond*

General MacArthur's evaluation of his role in history was probably most succinctly and characteristically voiced by him in 1950 in a protracted conversation with a newspaper correspondent who had known him for many years. Asked if he could explain his success, he puffed slowly at his corncob pipe and said, "I believe it was destiny."

Douglas MacArthur was born Jan. 26, 1880, at Fort Dodge, Little Rock, Ark. He was the third of three sons born to Capt. Arthur MacArthur and his Virginia-born wife, the former Mary Pinkney Hardy.

His eldest brother was Arthur, born in 1876, who graduated from the United States Naval Academy in 1896 and had a distinguished career. The second brother, Malcolm, died at the age of five.

General MacArthur's father was the son of Arthur MacArthur, a descendant of the MacArtair branch of the Clan Campbell. General MacArthur's grandfather, with his widowed mother, came to this country in 1825 and settled in Chicopee Falls, Mass. He became a lawyer.

General MacArthur's father was destined for West Point, but in August, 1862, a little more than a year after the outbreak of the Civil War, he joined the 24th Wisconsin Volunteer Infantry. He rose through the ranks, won the Medal of Honor in the Battle of Missionary Ridge in November, 1863, and was known as "the boy colonel."

In 1898, the elder MacArthur was ordered to the Philippines where, following the capitulation of Spain, he fought against Emilio Aguinaldo's revolutionaries. The elder MacArthur rose to major general commanding the Army of the Philippines, and retired as a lieutenant general.

Douglas MacArthur and his mother had remained in the United States. In 1898, Douglas took the examinations for the United States Military Academy. He passed with high marks and entered West Point in June, 1899.

His mother established a residence nearby. Her son visited her every day and graduated first in his class in 1903. As a new second lieutenant in the Corp of Engineers, he was posted to the Philippines and was involved in surveying the islands, where skirmishes with Moro dissidents were not uncommon. He once had his hat shot off.

With the outbreak of World War I, he helped to organize the 42nd (Rainbow) Division. As a brigade commander in France with the temporary rank of brigadier general, he directed actions that sometimes ran counter to grand strategy. On one occasion, with the capture of the French city of Sedan assigned to the French Army, he entered into competition with the French to be first in the town.

The prize was of particular significance to the French because it was the site of the surrender of the French to the Germans in 1870.

Orders for the operation had been drawn up by Col. George C. Marshall, an operations officer with the American Expeditionary Force. General MacArthur acted on his own interpretation of the orders. History recorded conflicting accounts of which forces first entered Sedan, but the French were listed officially as the first.

Having once told General MacArthur, "Young man, I do not like your attitude," Gen. John J. Pershing, commanding the American Expeditionary Force, nevertheless, pinned the Distinguished Service Cross and the Distinguished Service Medal on the bold young officer.

In 1919, General MacArthur was appointed Superintendent of West Point, whose curriculum he worked to broaden.

A former varsity football and baseball player, General MacArthur encouraged intramural athletics and wrote the motto that now stands in bronze on the inner wall of West Point's gymnasium: "Upon the fields of friendly strife are sown the seeds that, upon other fields, on other days, will bear the fruits of victory."

General MacArthur achieved his fourth star in 1930, when he was named Chief of Staff of the Army by President Herbert Hoover.

In the summer of 1932, several thousand unemployed men, many of them veterans of World War I, gathered in Washington to demand immediate payment of war bonuses. They camped in squalor on Washington's Anacostia Flats amid widespread sympathy for their plight, but to the vast embarrassment of the Hoover Administration.

WARRIORS

On July 29, President Hoover ordered Chief of Staff MacArthur to clear and destroy the camp. With Maj. Dwight D. Eisenhower at his side, General MacArthur directed the operation. In some newspapers General MacArthur was pictured as a beribboned military dandy directing his troops to shoot down hungry former soldiers.

When President Franklin D. Roosevelt succeeded Mr. Hoover, General MacArthur was re-appointed Chief of Staff of the Army, a post he held until 1935. But no rapport ever developed between the President and General MacArthur, who appeared unable to defer to a civilian politician.

President Roosevelt relieved General MacArthur as Chief of Staff on Oct. 3, 1935. Resuming his permanent rank of major general, General MacArthur was sent to the Philippines. For two years he worked at building a military force that might be capable of defending the islands with American help. On Aug. 6, 1937, he was notified that he would be returned shortly for duty in the United States. Stating that his task in the Philippines was not yet completed, he retired from the Army.

Manuel Quezon, the Philippines Commonwealth President, then appointed him Field Marshal of the Philippines. Exercising the privileges of rank, General MacArthur designed the gold leaf-encrusted garrison cap that, along with sunglasses and a corncob pipe, was to become his trademark.

As the possibility of war grew, the Philippine Army was merged with the United States Army under the command of General MacArthur, who was restored to duty with the American forces as a lieutenant general on July 27, 1941. In December he was made a full general 11 days after the Japanese attack on Pearl Harbor.

That attack was followed by a Japanese attack on military installations in the Philippines. A hardened, well-equipped Japanese force landed on Luzon and struck toward the fortified United States military base on Bataan Peninsula.

General MacArthur commanded 12,000 Philippine scouts and 19,000 United States troops. Added to this force were about 100,000 partly equipped Filipinos. The Japanese rolled the American forces into the Bataan Peninsula, where it was hoped they could hold out for 14 months.

General MacArthur assured his troops that aid would be forthcoming, although he had been given no such assurances by Washington. Word of his promises to his troops reached President Roosevelt, who was reportedly incensed.

Meanwhile, the Japanese tightened the noose around Bataan. As General MacArthur directed the defense from the labyrinthine, underground fortifications of Corregidor, orders came to him on Feb. 22 to leave his command in the hands of Lieut. Gen. Jonathan Wainwright and proceed to Australia.

Bidding farewell to the troops before boarding a PT boat, General MacArthur uttered a phrase that was to be added to his trademarks: "I shall return."

Arriving in Melbourne, the general began agitating Washington with demands for more men and equipment, seeming not to comprehend that the war in Europe held priority. He dreamed of relieving Corregidor up to the very moment of its capitulation on May 5, 1942.

As the initiative in the Pacific Theater swung toward the Americans, he longed to fulfill his pledge.

On Oct. 30, 1944, General MacArthur waded ashore at Leyte and proclaimed: "I have returned. By the grace of Almighty God, our forces stand again on Philippine soil."

On Dec. 18, 1944, he was promoted to the newly created rank of General of the Army. His forces went on to Manila, which fell Feb. 25, 1945. Okinawa fell in July. The next month, the doom of Japan was sealed with the dropping of the atomic bombs on Nagasaki and Hiroshima.

On Sept. 2, 1945, Japanese representatives boarded the battleship U.S.S. Missouri in Tokyo Bay to sign the unconditional surrender. Attired in morning coat and top hat, a representative of Emperor Hirohito walked to the document table. It appeared that he intended to read the surrender document before signing it.

"Show him where to sign," the General ordered Lieut. Gen. Richard K. Sutherland, his Chief of Staff.

In swift strokes, the occupation instituted reforms that shook the roots of an ancient class society. All precedent was shattered and Japanese traditionalists were appalled when the Emperor, believed by Japanese to be divine, went to pay his respects to the American general.

Of the occupation, General MacArthur made this observation:

"The pages of history in recording America's 20th-century contributions may, perchance, pass over lightly the wars we have fought. But, I believe they will not fail to record the influence for good upon Asia which will inevitably follow the spiritual regeneration of Japan."

But the apparent serenity of Asia was shattered on June 25, 1950, when North Korean troops who had been trained and equipped by Russians swept southward across the 38th parallel in a lightning effort to overwhelm the inadequate South Korean forces, who were being trained by a small United States military advisory team.

President Truman ordered General MacArthur to take whatever steps he thought necessary to evacuate the Americans from South Korea. The civilians were evacuated by sea and air. The advisory troops remained with the Korean units.

The unequal struggle between the highly trained North Korean Communist Army of 500,000 and the ill-prepared South Korean Army of slightly more than 100,000 men soon involved scattered units of American troops, swept up hastily from scattered bases in the Far East.

The United States appealed to the United Nations. Since the Soviet Union was at that moment boycotting the Security Council for other reasons and was not present to use its veto, the U.N. decided to join forces with the South Koreans and the United States.

On Sept. 12, 1950, General MacArthur executed a daring strike from the sea on the North Korean rear and flank with an amphibious landing at the western port of Inchon. North Korea's defense broke and the remnants of its army fled in disorder across the 38th parallel. General MacArthur announced that the war was virtually over, except for the need to pursue the enemy to the Yalu River, the border between Communist China and North Korea.

Unit commanders were in favor of pursuing the enemy northward without delay. However, orders were held in abeyance as word came that there was grave consternation at United Nations headquarters as to whether the intent of the combined effort had been to repel the invaders or rid the entire peninsula of Communist military forces.

On Oct. 10, President Truman, concerned with the General's propensity for independent action, flew to Wake Island for a meeting. General MacArthur said there was "very little" chance that the Chinese Communists or the Soviet Union would react to a venture into North Korea.

General MacArthur returned to Tokyo and began to "close out" the Korean War. Near the end of October, United States paratroopers were dropped at two points just north of the North Korean capital of Pyongyang to cut off fleeing and disorganized Communist units. United Nations ground troops slashed across the 38th parallel in a dash to the Yalu River.

But elements identified as Chinese Communist troops were found south of the 38th parallel. They had crossed the Yalu in mid-October. General MacArthur's intelligence officers had apparently failed to attach any significance to the reports of their presence.

By the second week in November full-scale warfare had begun and the United Nations forces were giving ground. General MacArthur let it be known that he was displeased with high decisions to refrain from attacking outside Korea lest the war spread.

In April, 1951, he was relieved of command by President [Harry S.] Truman. On April 17, the general, his wife and son arrived in San Francisco. In city after city, the General was greeted like a conquering hero.

Addressing Congress on April 19, he ended with a quotation from an old army song: "Old soldiers never die—they just fade away."

inking spell that developed soon after midnight, Wilbur Wright, aviator and aeroplane builder, died of typhoid fever at :15 A. M. to-day. Wright had been lingering for many days and though his condition from time to time gave some hopes to members of his family, the attending physicians, Drs. D. B. Conklin and Levi Spitler, maintained throughout the latter part of his sickness that he could not recover.

When the patient succumbed to the burning fever that had been racking his body for days and nights, he was surrounded by the members of his family, which included his aged father, Bishop Milton Wright, Miss Catherine Wright, Orville, the co-inventor of the aeroplane; Reuchlin Wright and Lorin Wright. All of the family reside in this city, except Reuchlin, who lives in Kansas.

The most alarming symptoms in Wright's sickness developed yesterday, shortly before noon, when his fever suddenly mounted from 104 up to 106 and then quickly subsided to its former stage. At this juncture of the crisis, the patient was seized with chills and the attending physicians were baffled by the turn of events.

The condition of the aviator remained unchanged throughout the rest of the day, and there was no improvement until last midnight. Then Wright began to show an improvement and the watchers at his bedside were reassured, but soon after midnight the patient suddenly became worse and Dr. D. B. Conklin was called. The doctor arrived at 3:25 and learned that Wright had breathed his last a few minutes before.

Wilbur Wright was seized with typhoid on May 4 while on a business trip in the East. On that day he returned to Dayton from Boston and consulted Dr. Conklin, the family physician. He took to his bed almost immediately, and it was several days before his case was definitely diagnosed as typhoid. Throughout the

school of Charcot and Janet, known
s the virtual founders of modern
bnormal psychology. The influence of his masters, however, was
argely one of provoking thought on
is own part. He plunged into a
holly new investigation of neurotic
isorders and deleveped a meth-
d so new that he made Janet one
f his bitterest professional ene-
ies. being accused by him of in-
oducing unwarranted assumptions
nto the orthodox doctrine. Several
f Dr. Freud's pupils in turn,
mong them C. G. Jung and Alfred
dler, diverged from him as widely
s he did from his own teachers.

GROUNDBREAKERS

n independence and uncompromis-
g attitude which served either to
ienate his associates completely
· to win them over as virtual dis-
ples.

After remaining in Paris a year
e returned to Vienna, where he
ecame a Professor Extraordinary
Neurology in 1902. He also used
s apartment in Berggasse as a
inic and received daily many pa-
ents who came to him with all
pes and varieties of mental ail-
ents. Later in life, age and ill-
ess forced him to cut down the
mber of his patients to a mini-
um and to make but few public
ppearances, but he continued to
velop his theories and to write
eatises on his chosen subject.

eeply Interested in Soviet Russia.

The Communist experiment in
ussia was of great interest to the

He himself was
wife and family we
as Dr. Julius
president of the
atrists Association
the meeting:
"Viennese psyc
the trail blazed b
wide fame and gr
proud and happy
him as one of the
the Viennese scho
One of Dr. Fre
was a revision in
for the Psychiatr
year earlier he ha
published his "Au
three years before
small book, "A N
troductory Lectu
after 1930, but mo
ing was done by h
whom he recogn
cessor, the aged,
shouldered doctor
agreement from t
made no public ap
ceived only a few
called on Wednes
and on Fridays to
To the last he
ant of criticism
with his theories
understand why
sured for his bitt
"What claims a
us in the name
wrote in his 1952
when somebody
opinion that we
mentally false
'Thanks for the
His last years a
by the pogroms

THOMAS H. GALLAUDET*

December 10, 1787–September 10, 1851

The public papers have already announced the deaths of several distinguished gentlemen in various parts of the country. Of Hon. Levi Woodbury and the Rev. Stephen Olin, D.D., extended notices have already been published. One or two others, however, have died, of whom adequate obituaries have not yet been given.

Among these was the Rev. Thomas H. Gallaudet, L.L.D., well-known as the pioneer of Deaf-Mute Instruction in this country, who died at his residence in Hartford, on Wednesday, the 10th inst., at the age of 64.

At an early period of his life, Mr. Gallaudet became interested in the cause of the Deaf and Dumb, and an accidental circumstance decided his future career. In the autumn of the year 1807, a child of Dr. Mason F. Cogswell, then residing in the city of Hartford, became, through the effects of a malignant fever, first deaf and then dumb. Mr. Gallaudet, a young man of talents, education and benevolence, interested himself in the case of this unfortunate child, and, with a strong desire to alleviate her condition, attempted to converse with and instruct her. His efforts were rewarded with partial success; and through the exertions of Dr. Cogswell, Mr. Gallaudet was commissioned to visit Europe for the purpose of qualifying himself to become a teacher of the Deaf and Dumb

* This is the first formal obituary to be published in The Times.

in this country. Seven gentlemen of Hartford subscribed a sufficient amount of funds to defray his expenses, and on the 25th of May, 1815, Mr. Gallaudet sailed for Europe.

Meanwhile, the friends of the project employed the interval of time in procuring an act of incorporation from the Legislature of Connecticut, which was accomplished in May, 1816. In May, 1819, the name of "the American Asylum at Hartford for the Education and Instruction of the Deaf and Dumb," was bestowed by the Legislature on the first institution for the Deaf-Mutes established in the United States.

After spending several months in the assiduous prosecution of his studies, under the Abbé Siçard and others, Mr. Gallaudet returned to this country in August, 1816. He was accompanied by Mr. Laurent Clerc, a deaf and dumb Professor in the Institution of Paris, and well-known in Europe as a most intelligent pupil of the Abbé. Mr. Clerc is now living in a vigorous old age, and is still a teacher in the American Asylum at Hartford.

The Asylum was opened on the 15th of April, 1817, and during the first week of its existence numbered seven pupils; it now averages 220 annually. Mr. Gallaudet became the Principal of the Institution at its commencement, and held the office until April, 1830, when he resigned, and has since officiated as Chaplain of the Retreat for the Insane at Hartford.

His interest in the cause of the Deaf-Mute Education has always continued unabated, and his memory will be warmly cherished by that unfortunate class of our fellow beings as well as by a large circle of devoted friends. The tree which was planted under his supervision and tended by his care, has borne good fruit.

SAMUEL F. B. MORSE

April 27, 1791–April 2, 1872

Prof. [Samuel F. B.] Morse died last evening at 8 o'clock, his condition having become very low soon after sunrise. [He was 80 years old.] Though expected, the death of this distinguished man will be received with regret by thousands to whom he was only known by fame.

Few persons have ever lived to whom all departments of industry owe a greater debt than the man whose death we are now called on to record. There has been no national or sectional prejudice in the honor that has been accorded to him, from the fact that the benefit he was the means of bestowing upon mankind has been universal, and on this account the sorrow occasioned by his death will be equally worldwide.

Prof. Morse was born in Charlestown, Mass., April 27, 1791. His father, Dr. Jedidiah I. Morse, was a prominent Congregational minister. At an early age Samuel was sent to Yale College, and was graduated from that institution in 1810. Passionately fond of art, he determined to become a painter, and for this purpose in the following year he sailed for England, in company with Washington Alston, in order to study under the direction of Benjamin West, at that time considered the leading artist in Europe. Within two years he had made such progress that he received the gold medal of the Adelphi Society, for a cast of the "Dying Hercules."

He returned to this country in 1815, and devoted himself entirely to his profession. While on a visit to Concord, N.H., in order to paint the portraits of several persons there, he formed the acquaintance of Lucretia Walker, who soon after became his wife.

In 1825, in connection with a number of other artists of this City, he organized an Art Association, which, a year later, was reorganized as the National Academy of Arts, a name it has ever since borne. In 1829 he made a second trip to Europe, for the purpose of still further pursuing his professional studies. During this trip, which lasted three years, he greatly improved himself in the technical branches of the art.

While abroad he was elected Professor of the Literature of the Arts of Design in the University of the City of New York, and it was on his return to accept the position that the invention that has since made his name illustrious suggested itself to him. While at college he had devoted much of his time to the study of chemistry, and even in after years the phenomena of electricity and of electromagnetism had been to him a source of considerable speculation, and during the present voyage, which was made from Havre to New York on the old packet-ship Sully, the conversation turned accidentally on this subject, in connection with a discovery that had shortly before been made in France, of the correlation of electricity and magnetism.

While one day conversing on this matter with a fellow-passenger, the thought flashed upon Morse's mind that this chemical relationship might be made practically useful. It would probably have been impossible even for the inventor to have said how the proper means for effecting this purpose suggested themselves to him; it was something almost superhuman, as will readily be seen, when it is said that he then conceived in his mind, not only the idea of the electric telegraph, but of the electromagnetic and chemical recording telegraph, substantially as they now exist.

On reaching home, he devoted the greater part of his time to making experiments on this subject. At first there was great difficulty in obtaining the proper instruments, though in 1835 he had succeeded in constructing an apparatus which enabled him to communicate from one extremity of two distant points, of a circuit of half a mile. Unfortunately, this did not allow him to communicate back from the other extremity, but two years more of persistent research was sufficient to overcome this difficulty, and the invention was now ready for exhibition.

This was done in the Autumn of 1837, the wires being laid on the roof of the University building, opposite Washington Square. A great many hundreds visited the place, and all expressed, as well they might, their unbounded astonishment.

In the Winter of the same year Prof. Morse went to Washington to urge upon Congress the necessity of making some provision to assist him in carrying out his invention. Yet to the minds of Congressmen, the invention seemed altogether too chimerical to be likely ever to prove of any worth; and so, after a futile attempt to induce the Congressional Committee to make a favorable report, Prof. Morse returned to New York, having wasted an entire Winter and accomplished nothing.

In the Spring of 1838, he determined to make an effort in Europe, hoping for better appreciation there than in his own country. It was a mistaken thought, however, for after a sojourn of four years he returned to New York, having succeeded in procuring merely a brevet d'invention [patent] in France, and no aid or security of any kind from the other countries.

A less energetic man would have given up after so many rebuffs, but a firm belief in the inestimable value of his invention prompted Prof. Morse to make still another effort at Washington. So faint were the chances of Congress appropriating anything that on the last night of the session, having become thoroughly wearied and disgusted with the whole matter, Prof. Morse retired to bed; but in the morning he was roused with the information that a few minutes before midnight his bill had come up, had been considered, and that he had been awarded $30,000 with which to make an experimental essay between Baltimore and Washington.

The year following the work was completed, and proved a complete success. From that time until the present the demands for the telegraph have been constantly increasing; they have been spread over every civilized country in the world, and have become, by usage, absolutely necessary for the well-being of society.

Prof. Morse was twice married; and his private life was one of almost unalloyed happiness. He resided during the Summer at Poughkeepsie, in a delightful country house on the banks of the Hudson, surrounded by everything that could minister comfort, or gratify his tastes. In the Winter he generally lived in New York. By those who have examined the question, it is reported that the first idea of a submarine cable to Europe emanated in the brain of Prof. Morse, in which case there is little connected with telegraphy of which he may not be said to be the author.

CHARLES DARWIN

February 12, 1809–April 19, 1882

The announcement that Charles Robert Darwin died on Wednesday at his residence, Down House, near Orpington, will be read by very few individuals who have not some degree of acquaintance with the physical theories formulated and taught by this distinguished naturalist, however scanty may be their actual knowledge of his works.

Darwin has been read much, but talked about more. Since the publication of his work "On the Origin of Species" in 1859, and particularly within the 11 years which have elapsed since his "Descent of Man" was given to the world, he has been the most widely known of living thinkers. Doctrines such as he set forth could not long remain the exclusive property of philosophers nor of educated people. They made their way at once into the reading and thought of the masses until the slightest allusion to Darwinism was sure of instant recognition.

It is not to be supposed that every country clergyman became profoundly versed in the doctrines of evolution, or that little laughing schoolgirls joking with each other about a monkey ancestry had followed Mr. Darwin very far in his speculations on differentiation of species, but the ministers somehow all knew that evolution was an abominable heresy, and the schoolchildren intuitively understood that if man is descended from the ape, he cannot be descended from Adam. All that part of the world which had never thought of such things before was aroused by the shock of the new idea.

There had been skeptics and atheists and deists and what not before, but what grave essayists call scientific unbelief sprang primarily from works of Charles Darwin, and is fed chiefly from the writings of other scientists who are at work extending and completing the framework be erected. Mr. Darwin, therefore, may be called an epoch-making man.

The qualities and natural bent of his clear mind were inherited. His father and grandfather were naturalists, though the latter, Dr. Erasmus Darwin, was a much more famous and productive man than his son, Dr. R. W. Darwin. Erasmus Darwin, a botanist of renown, is best known as the author of a remarkable poem called the "Botanic Garden," which, though destitute of the poetic feeling, shows its author to have been deeply versed in the Linnaean system of botany.

Charles Robert Darwin was born at Shrewsbury, England, Feb. 12, 1809. When he was 16 years old, he entered Edinburgh University, and remained there two years, going then to Christ's College, Cambridge, where he received the degree of Bachelor of Arts in 1831. In December of the same year he was selected as a naturalist to make a voyage of scientific exploration around the world on board the ship Beagle. Five years were spent in this way.

The opportunities for research, experiment, and study, particularly during his stay in South America, were fruitful in the material and hints out of which his later theories were evolved. Returning from this voyage in 1836, he began the preparation of a "Journal of Researches" into the geology and natural history of the countries visited by the expedition. Between 1844 and 1859 his publications were mostly brief monographs contributed to scientific publications or read before learned societies. But during this long period he occupied himself with untiring zeal and systematic regularity in the study of nature, making a series of observations upon the forms and habits of animals, plants and minerals and slowly accumulating that vast mass of facts and registered phenomena to which he was later on to apply his theory of evolution.

The publication in 1859 of his work, "On the Origin of Species by Means of Natural Selection; or, the Preservation of Favored Races in the Struggle for Life," was the announcement to his friends that he had at length passed over the sea of hypothesis to the firm ground of scientific assertion and to the world that it must revise or fortify its opinions on biological subjects. In 1871 appeared the best known of all his books, "The Descent of Man, and Selection in Relation to Sex," in two volumes; the following years saw the publication of half a dozen more. Each of these books has its place in the development of the theory which bears their author's name. But it is upon the "Origin of Species" and the "Descent of Man" that his fame chiefly rests.

Mr. Darwin made an extremely modest use of his great attainments. He did not construct a theory of the cosmos, and he did not deal with the entire theory of evolution. He was content to leave others to poke about in the original protoplasmic mire, and to extend the evolutionary law to social and political phenomena. For himself, he tried to show how higher organic forms were evolved out of lower. He starts with life already existing, and traces it through its successive forms up to the highest—man. His central principle—his opponents call it a dogma—is "natural selection," called by Herbert Spencer "the survival of the fittest," a choice which results inevitably from "the struggle for existence." It is a law and fact in nature that there shall be the weak and the strong. The strong shall triumph and the weak shall go to the wall.

The law, though involving destruction, is really preservative. If all plants and animals were free to reproduce their kind under like and equally favorable conditions, if all were equally strong and well equipped for obtaining sustenance and making their way in the world, there would soon be no room on the earth for even a single species. The limit of subsistence and the power of reproduction are the bounds between which the conflict rages. In this struggle the multitudes are slain and the few survive. But the survivors do not owe their good luck to chance. Their adaptation to their surroundings is the secret of their exemption from the fate which overtakes those less happily circumstanced. A variety of squirrels, for instance, which is capable of wandering far afield in pursuit of its food, which is cunning and swift enough to evade its enemies, and has a habit of providing a store of nuts for Winter use, will naturally have a better chance of survival than a variety deficient in these qualities.

But Mr. Darwin also discovered that natural selection created special fitness for given circumstances and surroundings. Climate, soil, food supply, and other conditions act in this way, and the result is the differentiation of species. A certain thistle grows in a kind of soil which is rich in the elements which go to produce the tiny hairs upon the surface of the plant. The seeds are thus furnished with downy wings longer than usual, and are wafted further off where they have plenty of space to grow, and they, in turn, reproduce and emphasize the changes to which they owe their existence. Seeds or nuts developing a thick covering for the kernel are thus protected from birds and animals, and live to germinate, producing also hard-shelled seeds, and thus the process goes on.

Varieties which do not develop a high degree of special adaptation to their surroundings fall out of the race. An infinitesimally minute variation of function or structure, repeated and becoming more marked through many successive generations, results ultimately in the production of a variety; or even of a species, quite unlike the parent individual.

Mr. Darwin was by no means the discoverer of the theory of evolution. That is at least as old as Aristotle, who supposed individuals to be produced, not by a simultaneous creation of a minute copy of the adult, with all the different organs, but by epigenesis—that is, by successive acts of generation or growth, in which the rudiment or cell received additions. Other philosophers have adopted and used this theory to a greater or less extent. But it never had a substantial basis of fact or a thoroughly scientific application until Mr. Darwin worked it out.

Within the limits he set for himself Mr. Darwin meets no rival claimant for the honors the scientific and thinking world have accorded him. The dispatch announcing his death says that he had been suffering for some time from weakness of the heart, but continued to work to the last. He was taken ill on Tuesday night with pains in the chest, faintness, and nausea. The nausea lasted more or less during Wednesday and culminated in death in the afternoon. Mr. Darwin remained fully conscious until within a quarter of an hour of his death.

LOUIS PASTEUR

December 27, 1822–September 28, 1895

PARIS—Prof. Louis Pasteur, the distinguished chemist and discoverer of the Pasteur treatment for the cure of rabies, is dead.

Louis Pasteur was pre-eminently a man of his time, of this very moment. His name and the names of the young physicians who became his pupils were synonyms of scientific progress, except to very conservative practitioners, and to these they were synonyms of at least restless research and patient labor.

He had implicit faith in science, and he gave the example of incessant investigating from which he knew the future would derive advantage. Even in later years, when adverse criticism that had pained him extremely had ceased, and marks of distinction had come to him from those whose esteem he valued, and a partial paralysis had rendered useless one side of his body, he was at work every day in his laboratory. His head was bent like a ripe sheaf of wheat, his steps were a painful shuffle, but he was always present with the punctuality of one disciplined to answer to a roll call.

His name is inseparable from any stage of the study of micro-organisms, he founded all the modern anti-surgical principles, he was the master of bacteriology, but his influence was more profound than these phrases indicate.

Pasteur gave to the world better methods of preventing and healing disease, an incalculable economy of lives, proofs against attractive hypotheses which were resulting in false philosophical forms, a revelation of the concealed operations of myriads of organisms, a link in the chain of evidence respecting the proof of the law of evolution.

Dr. Carpenter said of him, in a reference to the London Medical Congress of 1881: "There was none whose presence was more universally or more cordially welcomed than that of a quiet-looking Frenchman, who is neither a great physician nor a great surgeon, nor even a great physiologist, but who, originally a chemist, has done for medical science more than any savant of his day."

Pasteur demonstrated against all the savants who had preceded him that fermentation is life without air. He extracted the pure juice from the interior of the grape and proved that without contact with impure air it never fermented. He proved that the ferment of the grape is held for germination in the particles of saccharomyces which cling to its exterior and to the twigs of the vine.

In 1885 the silk culture of France produced a revenue of 130,000,000f.; in 12 years it fell, by disease in silkworms, to 8,000,000f. The chemist Dumas appealed to Pasteur, who had never handled a silkworm. Pasteur proved that independent mobile corpuscles, which caused the silk plague, were present in all states of the insect. He proved that when present in the egg they reappeared in all the cyclical alterations of the insect's life. He proved that they could be readily detected only in the moth. He suggested the selection of healthy moths, proved his views by experiments with others, prophesied results, and restored the silk industry.

Lister, inspired by Pasteur's work, studied lactic fermentation, verified the latter's researches into the influence of air in causing fermentation, and redemonstrated in his own field of inquiries the different causes operating in both fermentation and putrefaction. His practical application of the knowledge was in the perfect antiseptic dressing of wounds.

After suppressing the silk plague, preserving the vineyards and the vines, successfully vaccinating the cattle, and giving to Lister a new surgical system, Pasteur discovered the vaccine virus against the rabies, or hydrophobia.

In America the malady is comparatively not frequent, but in Europe, and especially in Russia, it has ever been a cause of mortal anguish.

Pasteur proved that the brain substance and the medulla of a rabid animal would cause rabies if injected hypodermically, and that the period of incubation was of about the same duration as that following the bite of a rabid dog. Then he established the fact that the period of incubation could be shortened almost to a definite time, and when he had triumphantly replied to all objections, began his amazing record of cures from hydrophobia.

A writer on the perfection of Pasteur's experimental methods has said:

"The caution exercised by Pasteur, both in the execution of his experiments and in the reasoning based upon them, is perfectly evident to those who, through the practice of severe experimental inquiry, have rendered themselves competent to judge of good experimental work. He found germs in the mercury used to isolate the air. He was never sure that they did not cling to the instruments he employed, or to his own person. Thus, when he opened his hermetically sealed flasks upon the Mer-de-Glace, he had his eye upon the file used to detach the drawn-out necks of his bottles; and he was careful to stand to leeward when each flask was opened. Using these precautions, he found the glacier air incompetent in 19 cases out of 20 to generate life, while similar flasks opened amid the vegetation of the lowlands were soon crowded with living things."

He was born at Dole, in the Department of the Jura [in eastern France], Dec. 27, 1822. He became at 18 a member of the university, in the situation of a supernumerary master of studies at the College of Besançon. At 21 he was admitted as a pupil to the Normal School. He was a graduate in the physical sciences in September, 1846, but he remained at the school two years longer as an assistant instructor in chemistry, obtained a doctor's degree, and received the appointment of Professor of Physics at the Lycée of Dijon. Then his long years of comparative poverty came to an end.

In 1849 he was a substitute at the Chali of Chemistry in the Strasburg Faculty of Sciences; in 1852 he was invested with this chair. At the end of 1854 he organized the newly created Faculty of Sciences at Lille. In 1857 he returned to Paris as science director at the Normal School.

He retained this office for 10 years, adding to his labor in 1863 the tedious, infinitely wearisome Professorship of Geology, Physics, and Chemistry at the Ecole des Beaux-Arts. He was professor at the Sorbonne from 1867 to 1875.

He varied his labors not by recreation, but, by changing their nature. He experimented when not teaching, and wrote when not doing either. He was the recipient of numerous honors, including the rank of Grand Officer of the Legion of Honor and the magnificent laboratories of the Pasteur Institute in Paris, built by popular subscription and a liberal contribution from the Czar of Russia.

He was kind to his assistants and pupils. They were profoundly devoted to him. His work is not finished by his death, but wherever there are lovers of science there will be reverently whispered a regretful comment, for it is a very pure and brilliant light that has gone out.

WILBUR WRIGHT

April 16, 1867–May 30, 1912

DAYTON, Ohio—Following a sinking spell that developed soon after midnight, Wilbur Wright, aviator and aeroplane builder, died of typhoid fever at 8:15 A.M. today.

When the patient succumbed at age 45 to the burning fever that had been racking his body for days and nights, he was surrounded by the members of his family, which included his father, Bishop Milton Wright, and brother Orville, the co-inventor of the aeroplane.

Wilbur was born near the Town of Dune Park, Indiana, on April 16, 1867. Four years later, after the family had moved to Ohio, Orville, was born in Dayton.

Instead of referring to any achievement as his own, Wilbur invariably referred to it as coming from "the Wright brothers."

ORVILLE WRIGHT

August 19, 1871–January 30, 1948

DAYTON, Ohio—Orville Wright, who with his brother, the late Wilbur Wright, invented the airplane, died here tonight at 10:40 in Miami Valley Hospital. He was 76 years old and had been suffering from lung congestion and coronary arteriosclerosis.

In the early fall of 1900 fishermen and Coast Guardsmen dwelling on that lonely and desolate spot of sand dividing Albemarle Sound from the Atlantic Ocean on the coast of North Carolina called Kitty Hawk discovered a new amusement. Trudging through the deep sand and beach grass to the side of the cone-shaped twin dunes known as the Kill Devil Hills, they watched two young men from Ohio try to break their necks.

These young men would launch themselves from the steep side of one of the hills lying flat down on the lower panel of what appeared to be a huge box-kite. His companion at one wing and a volunteer at the other would run and help the kite into the air. Then the kite would fly while the bird-man turned his body this way and that to maintain balance.

The real fun came when the kite would suddenly nose down and plow into the sand and the operator would hurtle out the front doubled up into a ball and roll in a cloud of sand and dust down the side of the hill.

The onlookers did not know it, but they were witnesses at the birth of aviation, and the two who provided so much entertainment were Orville and Wilbur Wright.

Orville was born at Dayton on Aug. 19, 1871, four years after the birth of Wilbur, the son of Bishop Milton Wright, a militant pastor and publicist of the United Brethren Church. There were seven children in the family, but only two others, Lorin and a sister, Katherine, were especially concerned with aviation.

As early as 1891, Orville and Wilbur had read of the experiments of Otto Lilienthal and other glider pioneers, but it was not until Lilienthal's death in 1896 in a glider accident that they took a definite interest in the problems of flight. Orville at that time was recovering from a bout with typhoid fever and Wilbur read aloud to him. From Lilienthal they went to Samuel P. Langley and his experiments. They read Marey on animal mechanism and by 1899 had progressed through the records of Octave Chanute and works obtained through the Smithsonian Institution.

From Lilienthal and Chanute they got the enthusiasm that decided them to attempt gliding. They sent for Langley's tables and Lilienthal's and watched the progress of Sir Hiram Maxim's experiments. Langley and Maxim represented the school of scientific research and Chanute and Lilienthal were the experimenters actually trying their wings. The Wrights were drawn to the fliers rather than the mathematicians and physicists.

Using the tables of Lilienthal and Langley, they constructed a series of gliders. The gliders did not function and so the Wrights changed them, still following the tables of their predecessors. Finally, they concluded that something was wrong with the tables. For one thing, a concave wing surface produced a resultant force when air passed across it utterly at variance with the theory of Langley and Lilienthal.

The Wrights had been contented before 1900 with wind currents on the flat Ohio terrain, but they knew that for the best results they must find steady, even winds blowing up over smooth hills. With the aid of the Weather Bureau they discovered Kitty Hawk.

While hundreds of attempts to "mount the machine" were made on the first Kitty Hawk visit, the brothers flew only a few minutes altogether. They returned to their home to study. The second glider they took to Kitty Hawk, in the summer of 1901, was

better than the first, but they were not satisfied. Again they returned to Dayton to experiment.

In the autumn of 1902 they were ready with a biplane with the adjustable trailing edges on the wings, the horizontal elevator and the vertical rudder. They connected all these to a single set of controls—the first time anything of the sort had been done.

In Kitty Hawk from late September until December 1903, they worked on the machine in a shed which nearly blew away, airplane and all, during a hurricane. Even after they were ready, bad weather set in again and they had strong winds day after day.

During the enforced idleness they invented and constructed an air-speed indicator and a device for measuring the distance flown in respect to the moving air itself. Finally a good day came. The two brothers flipped a coin to decide who should be the first and Wilbur won. The engine was started and the machine lifted after a short run along the track they had built for its skids.

But immediately one wing dipped. It stalled and was on the ground again after being in the air for three seconds. Pleased with the result, the brothers were still not willing to call it a flight. A skid was broken in the attempt and two days were consumed in fixing it. Finally on the evening of Dec. 16 everything was again ready and the flight was set for next morning.

It was Orville's turn. Into the teeth of a 27-mile-an-hour wind the plane was pointed. Orville released the wire that connected it to the track and it started so slowly that Wilbur was able to keep pace alongside, clinging to one wing to help steady the craft. Orville, lying flat on the lower wing, opened the engine wide. The plane speeded up and lifted clear.

It rose about 10 feet suddenly and then as suddenly darted toward the ground. A sudden dive 120 feet from the point it rose into the air brought it to earth again and man's first flight in a powered heavier-than-air machine was over. It had lasted 12 seconds, and allowing for the wind, it had made a forward speed of more than 33 miles an hour. Three more flights were made that day, with Wilbur up twice and Orville once, and on the fourth trial Wilbur flew 59 seconds, covered 852 feet over the ground and made an air distance of more than half a mile.

In July 1909, Orville won a government contract by attaining a speed of 42 miles an hour. His contract called for a plane that could make 40 miles an hour and the Government offered a bonus for speeds above that limit. Manufacturing began at Dayton. This period also was marked by a series of patent fights. Glenn Curtiss was starting his experiments and adapted principles that the courts finally ruled were the property of the Wright brothers.

After Wilbur died in 1912, Orville worked on quietly at Dayton. Although friendly and accessible to visitors he avoided the spotlight. The death of Wilbur had left him very much alone.

ALEXANDER GRAHAM BELL

March 3, 1847–August 2, 1922

SYDNEY, **Nova Scotia**—Dr. Alexander Graham Bell, inventor of the telephone, died at 2 o'clock this morning at Beinn Bhreagh, his estate near Baddeck.

Although the inventor, who was in his 76th year, had been in failing health for several months, the end was unexpected. Yesterday afternoon his condition, brought about by progressive anemia, became serious, and Dr. Ker of Washington, a cousin of Mrs. Bell, a house guest and a Sydney physician, attended him.

With Mr. Bell when he died were Mrs. Bell, a daughter, Mrs. Marion Hubbard Fairchild, and her husband. The inventor leaves another daughter, Mrs. Elise M. Grosvenor.

At sunset on Friday, on the crest of Beinn Bhreagh Mountain, the body of Dr. Bell will be buried at a spot chosen by the inventor himself. The grave of the venerable scientist, the immensity of whose life work was attested by scores of telegrams which came today to the Bell estate from the world's prominent figures,

is at a point overlooking the town of Baddeck, Cape Breton. The sweeping vista from the mountaintop, so admired by Dr. Bell, stretches far over the Bras d'Or Lakes. Sunset, chosen as the moment when the body will be committed to the sturdy hills, gilds the waters of the lakes until they are really what their name means—"the lakes of the arm of gold."

Dr. Bell asked to be buried in the countryside where he had spent the major portion of the last 35 years of his life. The inventor came to Cape Breton 40 years ago, and five years later purchased the Beinn Bhreagh estate. His last experiments, dealing with flying boats, were made on Bras d'Or Lakes.

American specialists who were rushing to the bedside of Dr. Bell were told of his death while aboard fast trains bound for Baddeck, and, being too late, turned back.

On learning of his death President Harding sent this telegram to Mrs. Bell:

"The announcement of your eminent husband's death comes as a great shock to me. In common with all of his countrymen, I have learned to revere him as one of the great benefactors of the race and among the foremost Americans of all generations."

President Thayer of the American Telephone and Telegraph Company ordered the Bell system throughout the country to half-mast flags on its buildings.

And Thomas A. Edison today paid the following tribute to his fellow-inventor, Alexander Graham Bell: "I am sorry to learn of the death of Alexander Graham Bell, the inventor of the first telephone. I have always regarded him very highly, especially for his extreme modesty."

Alexander Graham Bell lived to see the telephonic instrument over which he talked a distance of 20 feet in 1876 used, with improvements, for the transmission of speech across the continent, and more than that, for the transmission of speech across the Atlantic and from Washington to Honolulu without wires. The little instrument he patented less than 50 years ago, scorned then as a joke, was when he died the basis for 18,000,000 telephones used in every civilized country in the world. The Bell basic patent, the famed No. 174,465 which he received on his 29th birthday and which was sustained in a historic court fight, has been called the most valuable patent ever issued.

Although the inventor of many contrivances which he regarded with as much tenderness and to which he attached as much importance as the telephone, a business world which he confessed he was often unable to understand made it assured that he would go down in history as the man who made the telephone. He was an inventor of the gramophone, and for nearly 20 years was engaged in aeronautics. Associated with Glenn H. Curtiss and others whose names are now known wherever airplanes fly, he pinned his faith on the efficacy for aviation of the tetrahedral cell, which never achieved the success he saw for it in aviation, but as a by-product of his study he established an important new principle in architecture.

Up to the time of his death Dr. Bell took the deepest interest in aviation. Upon his return from a tour of the European countries in 1909 he reported that the Continental nations were far ahead of America in aviation and urged that steps be taken to keep apace of them. He predicted in 1916 that the great war would be won in the air. It was always a theory of his that flying machines could make ever so much more speed at great heights, in rarefied atmosphere, and he often said that the transatlantic flight would be some time made in one day, a prediction which he lived to see fulfilled.

The inventor of the telephone was born in Edinburgh, on March 3, 1847. Means of communication had been a hobby in the Bell family long before Alexander was born. His grandfather was the inventor of a device for overcoming stammering and his father perfected a system of visible speech for deaf mutes. When Alexander was about 15 years old he made an artificial skull of guttapercha and India rubber that would pronounce weird tones when blown into by a hand bellows. At the age of 16 he became, like his father, a teacher of elocution and instructor of deaf mutes.

When young Bell was 22 years old he was threatened with tuberculosis, which had caused the death of his two brothers, and the Bell family migrated to Brantford, Canada.

Soon after he came to America, at a meeting with Sir Charles Wheatsone, the English inventor, Bell got the ambition to perfect a musical or multiple telegraph. His father, in an address in Boston one day, mentioned his son's success in teaching deaf mutes, which led the Boston Board of Education to offer the younger Bell $100 to introduce his system in the newly opened school for deaf mutes there. He was then 24 years old, and quickly gained prominence for his teaching methods. He was soon named a professor in Boston University.

But teaching interfered with his inventing and he gave up all but two of his pupils. One of these was Mabel Hubbard of a wealthy family. She had lost her speech and hearing when a baby and Bell took the most acute interest in enabling her to hear. She later became Mrs. Bell.

Bell spent the following three years working, mostly at night, in a cellar in Salem, Mass. Gardiner G. Hubbard, his future father-in-law, and Thomas Sanders helped him financially while he worked on his theory that speech could be reproduced by means of an electrically charged wire. His first success came while he was testing his instruments in new quarters in Boston. Thomas A. Watson, Bell's assistant, had struck a clock spring at one end of a wire and Bell heard the sound in another room. For 40 weeks he worked on his instruments, and on March 10, 1876, Watson, who was working in another room, was startled to hear Bell's voice say:

"Mr. Watson, come here. I want you."

On his 29th birthday Bell received his patent. At the Centennial in Philadelphia he gave the first public demonstration of his instrument. He had not intended to go to the exposition. He was poor and had planned to take up teaching again. In June he went to the railroad station one day to see Miss Hubbard off for Philadelphia. She had believed he was going with her. As he put her on the train and it moved off without him, she burst into tears. Seeing this, Bell rushed ahead and caught the train, without baggage or ticket.

An exhibition on a Sunday afternoon was promised to him. When the hour arrived it was hot, and the judges were tired. It looked as if there would be no demonstration for Bell, when Dom Pedro, the Emperor of Brazil, appeared and shook Mr. Bell by the hand. He had heard some of the young man's lectures. Bell made ready for the demonstration. A wire had been strung along the room. Bell took the transmitter, and Dom Pedro placed the receiver to his ear.

"My God, it talks!" he exclaimed.

Then Lord Kelvin took the receiver.

"It does speak," he said. "It is the most wonderful thing I have seen in America."

The judges then took turns listening, and the demonstration lasted until 10 o'clock that night. The instrument was the center of interest for scientists the rest of the exposition.

The commercial development of the telephone dated from that day in Philadelphia.

While Alexander Graham Bell will be best remembered as the inventor of the telephone, a claim he sustained through many legal contests, he also became noted for other inventions. With Sumner Tainter he invented the gramophone. He invented a new method of lithography, a photophone, and an induction balance. He invented the telephone probe, which was used to locate the bullet that killed President Garfield. He spent 15 years and more than $200,000 in testing his tetrahedral kite, which he believed would be the basis for aviation.

The inventor was the recipient of many honors in this country and abroad.

Dr. Bell regarded the summit of his career as reached when in January of 1915 he and his old associate, Mr. Watson, talked to one another over the telephone from San Francisco to New York. It was nearly two years later that by a combination of telephonic and wireless telegraphy instruments the engineers of the American Telephone and Telegraph Company sent speech across the Atlantic.

In 1915 Dr. Bell said that he looked forward to the day when men would communicate their thoughts by wire without the spoken word.

"The possibilities of further achievement by the use of electricity are inconceivable," he said. "Men can do nearly everything else by electricity already, and I can imagine them with coils of wire about their heads coming together for communication of thought by induction."

In April of 1916 he declared that land and sea power would become secondary to air power. He expressed then the opinion that the airplane would be more valuable as a fighting machine than the Zeppelin and urged that the United States build a strong aerial fleet.

THOMAS EDISON

February 11, 1847–October 18, 1931

WEST ORANGE, N.J.—Thomas Alva Edison died at 3:24 o'clock this morning at his home, Glenmont, in the Llewellyn Park section of this city. The great inventor, the fruits of whose genius so magically transformed the everyday world, was 84 years and 8 months old.

The end came almost imperceptibly as the sick man's ebbing strength, sapped by long months of struggle against a complication of ailments, gradually receded until his heart ceased beating.

Through the long days when Mr. Edison calmly, cheerfully awaited the inevitable, amazing evidences of the world's affectionate concern for one of its most useful citizens were plentiful. Pope Pius XI, President Hoover, Henry Ford and a host of others kept in daily touch [about] his condition.

Anxiety for the man whose creative genius gave the world the electric light, the phonograph, the motion picture camera and a thousand other inventions ranging through all the various fields of science had been general since he collapsed in the living room of his home on Aug. 1.

Thomas Alva Edison was born in Milan, Ohio, on Feb. 11, 1847. He came of vigorous and independent-minded stock, originally coming to America from the Zayder Zee. His great-grandfather was Thomas Edison, a New York banker of prominence on the Tory side during the Revolutionary War. So much of a Loyalist was he that when the Colonies won their independence he went to Canada to live under the British flag. There his grandson, Samuel, became a rebel against the King, rose to the rank of Captain in Papineau's insurgent army in 1837 and fled to the States with a price on his head.

Samuel Edison settled at Milan, Ohio, where his son, Thomas, was born. Edison got most of his schooling there. He was always, as he remembered it later, at the foot of his class. In interviews he recalled his mother's indignation when one teacher told him that he was "addled," a fighting adjective in country districts. His mother, who had been a teacher, took him out of school and educated him herself. At the age of nine he had read or his mother had read to him "The Penn Encyclopedia," "Hume's History of England" and Gibbons's "Decline and Fall of the Roman Empire."

But the books which put the backward schoolboy of the tiny canal village on the way to become one of the greatest men of his time were popular works on electricity and chemistry. He and his mother performed some of the simple chemical experiments they found described in the books.

At the age of 12, to earn money for his experiments, he persuaded his parents to allow him to become a railroad newsboy. He set up a laboratory in the baggage car, along with a printing press, on which he published a weekly newspaper that gained as many as 400 paid subscribers.

One day a bottle containing phosphorus fell off a shelf and broke upon the floor. The phosphorus set fire to the car, which was with some difficulty saved from burning up, and the conductor put the boy and his belongings off the train and boxed his ears so soundly as to cause the beginning of the deafness with which he has ever since been afflicted.

The young man found work as a telegraph operator, drifted to New York, and began repairing stock tickers for a market reporting firm. Fortune began to smile on him at the age of about 22, when he worked out improvements in tickers and telegraph appliances and got $50,000 for one invention.

Almost entirely self-educated, Edison was never a profound student of physics, mathematics and theoretical chemistry, but he had a rich equipment for an inventor. To an enormous practical grasp of physics and electricity he joined wide general experience, reading and intellectual activity. He read books of every kind. He was a believer in vast and miscellaneous general information, as he demonstrated in 1921, when the Edison questionnaire became famous. He gave to his prospective employees the kind of examination which he himself could have passed when he was a youth. He wanted to find men of his own type, men of intellectual curiosity and general knowledge. His practical scientific knowledge, his original, penetrating mind and his invincible industry gave him the greatest output of invention of any living man.

When Edison was only 26 years old, in 1873, he made an agreement with the Western Union Telegraph Company to give them an option on all telegraph inventions that came out of his head. He then moved to Newark, N.J., into a bigger shop than his Manhattan working place. He completed an automatic telegraph, making possible the transmission of 1,000 words a minute between points as far distant as Washington and New York.

At the age of 29 Edison had become so famous that curious people crowded his workshop and he could not work satisfactorily. He moved further away from New York, to Menlo Park, N.J.

Before that time he had already experimented on an incandescent electric light. At the time, the arc lamp was already in existence in public squares in this city. Backed by a syndicate with a capital of $300,000, including men such as J. Pierpont Morgan, Edison extended his experiments. Finally, in 1879, he made the discovery which made the incandescent light a success.

One night in his laboratory, idly rolling between his fingers a piece of compressed lampblack, he realized that a slender filament of it might emit incandescent light if burned in a vacuum. So it did, and further experiments demonstrated that a filament of burned cotton thread would provide even greater incandescence. He placed the filament in a globe and connected it with the wires leading to the machine generating electric current. Then he extracted the air from the globe and turned on the electricity.

"Presto! A beautiful light greeted his eyes," in the words of a New York newspaper article. "He turned on more current, expecting the fragile filament immediately to fuse; but no. The only change was a more brilliant light. He turned on more current and still

more, but the delicate thread remained intact. Then, with characteristic impetuosity, and wondering and marveling at the strength of the little filament, he turned on the full power of the machine and eagerly watched the consequences. For a minute or more the tender thread seemed to struggle with the intense heat passing through it—heat that would melt the diamond itself. Then at last it succumbed and all was darkness. The powerful current had broken it in twain, but not before it had emitted a light of several gas jets."

On Jan. 1, 1880, the public was invited to go to Menlo Park and see the operation of the first lighting plant. Electricians, many of them, insisted that there was some trickery in the exhibition, but almost simultaneously the Edison lighting system spread all over civilization.

In 1877, while at work on a machine to improve the transmission of Morse code, Edison realized that its sounds made indentations on paper fitted to a rapidly rotating cylinder—"a musical, rhythmic sound resembling that of human talk heard indistinctly," as he later wrote in the North American Review in 1887. "This led me to try fitting a diaphragm to the machine which would receive the vibrations or sound waves made by my voice when I talked to it and register these vibrations upon an impressible material placed on the cylinder." He continued:

"The indentations on the cylinder, when rapidly revolved, caused a repetition of the original vibrations to reach the ear through a recorder, just as if the machine itself was speaking." Thus was born the phonograph.

Edison invented the motion picture machine in 1887. The Zoetrope and other machines were then in existence for throwing pictures from transparencies on a screen one after another and giving the effect of action. It occurred to Edison that pictures could be taken in rapid succession by the camera and later used to synthesize motion. He put his pictures on the market in the form of a peep-show. Put a nickel in the slot and you could see dances, prizefights, fencing matches and other bits of action.

Here Edison, for all his powers of forecasting the future, made his major failure as a prophet. For a long time he opposed the idea of projecting pictures on the screen. He thought that it would ruin the nickel-in-the-slot peep-show business. In spite of his creative imagination and his comprehensive genius, he seemed to have been lacking in showmanship.

Edison was married twice, in 1873 to Miss Mary G. Stillwell, by whom he had three children, and in 1886 to Miss Mina Miller, who is the mother of three more.

Mr. Edison relaxed a little in the latter years of his life. He spent his Winters at Fort Myers, Fla., where he experimented with a miniature rubber plantation. In spite of his deafness, he remained sunny and genial till the end of his days. Honors came to him from all sides. Edison's career was brilliantly summed up by Arthur Williams, Vice President of the New York Edison Company, who said:

"Entering this building [the Hotel Astor] tonight, we passed through that extraordinary area of public-ity by light, often called the brightest spot on earth—Times Square. Standing there, thinking of Edison and his work, we may well remember the inscription on the tomb of Sir Christopher Wren in St. Paul's, London, 'If you would see his monument, look around.'"

ALBERT EINSTEIN

March 14, 1879–April 18, 1955

PRINCETON, N.J.—Dr. Albert Einstein, one of the great thinkers of the ages, died in his sleep here early today.

A rupture of the aorta brought death to the 76-year-old master physicist and mathematician and practicing humanitarian. He died at 1:15 A.M. in Princeton Hospital.

The shy professor's exit was as unostentatious as the life he had led for many years in the New Jersey village, where he was attached to the Institute for Advanced Study.

The body was cremated without ceremony at 4:30 P.M. after the removal, for scientific study, of vital organs, among them the brain that had worked out the theory of relativity and made possible the development of nuclear fission.

President [Dwight D.] Eisenhower declared that "no other man contributed so much to the vast expansion of 20th-century knowledge." Eminent scientists and heads of state sent tributes from many nations, including Israel, whose establishment as a state he had championed, and Germany, which he had left forever in 1932 because of Nazism's rising threat against individual liberty and Jewish life.

In 1904, Albert Einstein, then an obscure young man of 25, could be seen daily in the late afternoon wheeling a baby carriage on the streets of Bern, Switzerland, halting now and then, unmindful of the traffic around him, to scribble down some mathematical symbols in a notebook that shared the carriage with his infant son, also named Albert.

Out of those symbols came the most explosive ideas in the age-old strivings of man to fathom the mystery of his universe. Out of them, incidentally, came the atomic bomb, which, viewed from the long-range perspective of mankind's intellectual and spiritual history may turn out, Einstein fervently hoped, to have been just a minor by-product.

With those symbols Dr. Einstein was building his theory of relativity. In that baby carriage with his infant son was Dr. Einstein's universe-in-the-making, a vast, finite-infinite four-dimensional universe, in which the conventional universe—existing in absolute three-dimensional space and in absolute three-dimensional time of past, present and future—vanished into a mere subjective shadow.

Dr. Einstein was then building his universe in his spare time, on the completion of his day's routine work as a humble, $600-a-year examiner in the Government Patent Office in Bern.

A few months later, in 1905, the entries in the notebook were published in four epoch-making scientific papers. In the first he described a method for determining molecular dimensions. In the second he explained the photo-electric effect, the basis of electronics, for which he won the Nobel Prize in 1921. In the third, he presented a molecular kinetic theory of heat. The fourth and last paper that year, entitled "Electrodynamics of Moving Bodies," a short article of 31 pages, was the first presentation of what became known as the Special Relativity Theory.

Neither Dr. Einstein, nor the world he lived in, nor man's concept of his material universe, were ever the same again.

The scientific fraternity recognized that a new star of the first magnitude had appeared on their firmament. By 1920 the name of Einstein had become synonymous with relativity, a theory universally regarded as so profound that only 12 men in the entire world were believed able to fathom its depths.

Albert Einstein was born at Ulm, Wuerttemberg, Germany, on March 14, 1879. His boyhood was spent in Munich, where his father, who owned electrotechnical works, had settled. The family migrated to Italy in 1894, and Albert was sent to a cantonal school at Aarau in Switzerland. In 1901 he was appointed examiner of patents at the Patent Office at Bern where, having become a Swiss citizen, he remained until 1909.

It was in this period that he obtained his Ph.D. degree at the University of Zurich and published his first papers on physical subjects.

These were so highly esteemed that in 1909 he was appointed Extraordinary Professor of Theoretical Physics at the University of Zurich. In 1913 a special position was created for him in Berlin as director of the Kaiser Wilhelm Physical Institute. He was elected a member of the Royal Prussian Academy of Sciences and received a stipend sufficient to enable him to devote all his time to research.

Dr. Einstein married Mileva Marec, a fellow-student, in Switzerland, in 1901. They had two sons. The marriage ended in divorce. He married again, in 1917, this time his cousin, Elsa Einstein, a widow with two daughters. She died in Princeton in 1936.

When the Institute for Advanced Study was organized in 1932 at Princeton, Dr. Einstein accepted the place of Professor of Mathematics and Theoretical Physics. He made plans to live there about half of each year.

These plans were changed suddenly. Adolf Hitler rose to power in Germany and essential human liberty, even for Jews with world reputations like Dr. Einstein, became impossible in Germany. In the late spring of 1933 Dr. Einstein learned that his two stepdaughters had been forced to flee Germany.

Not long after that he was ousted from the supervising board of the German Bureau of Standards. His home at Caputh was sacked by Hitler Brown Shirts on the allegation that Dr. Einstein, a pacifist, had a vast store of arms hidden there.

The Prussian Academy of Science expelled him and also attacked him for having made statements regarding Hitler atrocities. His reply was this:

"I do not want to remain in a state where individuals are not conceded equal rights before the law for freedom of speech and doctrine."

In September of 1933 he went into seclusion on the coast of England, fearful that the Nazis had plans upon his life. Then he journeyed to Princeton and in 1940 became a citizen of the United States.

Paradoxically, the figure of Einstein the man became more and more remote, while that of Einstein the legend came ever nearer to the masses of mankind. They grew to know him not as a universe-maker whose theories they could not hope to understand but as a world citizen, a symbol of the human spirit and its highest aspirations.

"Saintly," "noble" and "lovable" were the words used to describe him. He radiated humor, warmth and kindliness. He loved jokes and laughed easily.

Princeton residents would see him walk in their midst, a familiar figure, yet a stranger; a close neighbor, yet a visitor from another world. And as he grew older his otherworldliness became more pronounced, yet his human warmth did not diminish.

Outward appearance meant nothing to him. Princetonians soon got used to the long-haired figure in pullover sweater and unpressed slacks, a knitted stocking cap covering his head in winter.

"My passionate interest in social justice and social responsibility," he wrote, "has always stood in curious contrast to a marked lack of desire for direct association with men and women. I am a horse for single harness, not cut out for tandem or team work. I have never belonged wholeheartedly to country or state, to my circle of friends, or even to my own family."

It was this independence that made Dr. Einstein on occasions the center of controversy. In January 1953 he urged President Harry S. Truman to commute the death sentences of Julius and Ethel Rosenberg, the two convicted atomic spies who were executed five months later. Later that year he advised a witness not to answer any questions by Senator Joseph R. McCarthy, Republican of Wisconsin.

His political ideal was democracy. "I am convinced," he wrote in 1931, two years before Hitler came to power, "that degeneracy follows every autocratic system of violence, for violence inevitably attracts moral inferiors."

His love for the oppressed also led him to become a strong supporter of Zionism. In November, 1952, following the death of Chaim Weizmann, Dr. Einstein was asked if he would accept the Presidency of Israel. He replied that he was deeply touched by the offer but that he was not suited for the position.

On Aug. 6, 1945, when the world was electrified with the news that an atomic bomb had exploded over Japan, the significance of relativity was intuitively grasped by the millions. From then on the destiny of mankind hung on a thin mathematical thread.

Informed of the news by a reporter for The New York Times, Dr. Einstein asked, "Do you mean that, young man?" When the reporter replied "Yes" the physicist was silent for a moment, then shook his head.

"Ach! The world is not ready for it," he said.

Thereafter Dr. Einstein became the chairman of

the Emergency Committee of Atomic Scientists, organized to make the American people aware of the potential horrors of atomic warfare and the necessity for the international control of atomic energy.

He found recreation from his labors in playing the grand piano that stood in the solitary den in the garret of his residence. Much of his leisure time, too, was spent in playing the violin. He was fond of playing trios and quartets with musical friends.

While he did not believe in a formal, dogmatic religion, Dr. Einstein, like all true mystics, was of a deeply religious nature.

"The most beautiful and profound emotion we can experience," he wrote, "is the mystical. It is the source of all true art and science. He to whom this emotion is a stranger, who can no longer pause to wonder and stand rapt in awe, is as good as dead: his eyes are closed."

J. ROBERT OPPENHEIMER

April 22, 1904–February 18, 1967

PRINCETON, N.J.—J. Robert Oppenheimer, the nuclear physicist who has been called "the father of the atomic bomb," died here tonight at the age of 62.

A spokesman for the family said Dr. Oppenheimer died in his home at the Institute for Advanced Study. He had been suffering from cancer of the throat. Dr. Oppenheimer and his wife, Katherine, had a son and daughter.

Starting precisely at 5:30 A.M., Mountain War Time, July 16, 1945, J. Robert Oppenheimer lived his life in the blinding light and the crepusculine shadow of the world's first manmade atomic explosion.

That sun-like flash illuminated him as a scientific genius. It also led to his disgrace when, in 1954, he was described as a security risk. Publicly rehabilitated in 1963, this bafflingly complex man nonetheless never fully succeeded in dispelling doubts about his conduct.

Dr. Oppenheimer was a cultivated scholar, a humanist, a linguist of eight tongues and a brooding searcher for ultimate spiritual values. And, from the moment that the test bomb exploded at Alamogordo, N.M., he was haunted by the implications for man in the unleashing of the basic forces of the universe.

As he clung to one of the uprights in the desert control room that July morning and saw the mushroom cloud rising, a passage from the Bhagavad-Gita, the Hindu sacred epic, flashed through his mind: "If the radiance of a thousand suns were to burst into the sky, that would be like the splendor of the Mighty One."

And as the atomic cloud pushed higher above Point Zero, another line came to him from the same scripture: "I am become Death, the shatterer of worlds." Two years later, he was still beset by the moral consequences of the bomb, which, he told fellow physicists, had "dramatized so mercilessly the inhumanity and evil of modern war."

With the detonation of the first three atomic bombs and the Allied victory in World War II, Dr. Oppenheimer, at 41, reached the apogee of his career. Acclaimed as "the father of the atomic bomb," he was credited by the War Department "with achieving the implementation of atomic energy for military purposes." In 1946, he received a Presidential Citation and a Medal of Merit for his direction of the Los Alamos Laboratory, where the bomb had been developed.

From 1945 to 1952, Dr. Oppenheimer was one of the foremost Government advisers on atomic policy. He was the dominant author of the Acheson-Lilienthal Report [named for Secretary of State Dean Acheson and David Lilienthal, first chairman of the Atomic Energy Commission], which offered a plan for international control of atomic energy.

From 1947 to 1952, Dr. Oppenheimer headed the A.E.C.'s General Advisory Committee of top nuclear scientists, and for the following two years he was its consultant. Then, in December 1953, President Dwight D. Eisenhower ordered that a "blank wall be placed between Dr. Oppenheimer and any secret data," pending a hearing.

Up to then, Dr. Oppenheimer's big-brimmed brown porkpie hat was a frequent sight in Washington and the capitals of Western Europe. People were captivated by his charm, eloquence and sharp, subtle humor and awed by the scope of his erudition, the incisiveness of his mind, and his arrogance toward those he thought were slow or shoddy thinkers.

He was an energetic man at parties, where he was usually the center of attention. He was gracious as a host and the maker of fine and potent martinis.

J. Robert Oppenheimer (the "J" stood for nothing) was born in New York on April 22, 1904, the son of Julius and Ella Freedman (or Friedman) Oppenheimer. Julius Oppenheimer was a prosperous textile importer who had emigrated from Germany, and his wife was a Baltimore artist, who died when her elder son was 10. (The younger son, Frank, also became a physicist.)

Robert was a shy, delicate boy who was more concerned with his homework and with poetry and architecture than with mixing with other youngsters. After attending the Ethical Culture School, he entered Harvard College in 1922, intending to become a chemist.

In addition to studying physics and other sciences, he learned Latin and Greek and was graduated summa cum laude in 1925, having completed four years' work in three.

From Harvard, he went to the University of Cambridge, in England, where he worked in atomics under Lord Rutherford, the eminent physicist. Thence he went to the Georg-August-Universitat in Gottingen, Germany. He received his doctorate there in 1927.

In 1929, Dr. Oppenheimer joined the faculties of Caltech at Pasadena and the University of California at Berkeley. Magnetic, lucid, always accessible, he developed hundreds of young physicists. At that time, he recalled later, "I was not interested in and did not read about economics or politics. I was almost wholly divorced from the contemporary scene in this country."

But beginning in late 1936, his life underwent a change of direction that involved him in Communist, trade union and liberal causes. These commitments and associations ended about 1940, according to the scientist.

One factor in his awakening to the world about him was a love affair, starting in 1936, with a woman who was a Communist, now dead. (In 1940 he married the former Katherine Puening, who had been a Communist during her marriage to Joseph Dallet, a Communist who died fighting for the Spanish Republican Government.)

Dr. Oppenheimer also felt, as he put it, a "smoldering fury about the treatment of Jews in Germany," and he was deeply dismayed by the Depression. But he consistently denied that he was ever a member of the Communist party.

Dr. Arthur H. Compton, the Nobel Prize–winning scientist, brought Dr. Oppenheimer informally into the atomic project in 1941. Dr. Oppenheimer impressed Maj. Gen. Leslie R. Groves, in charge of the $2 billion Manhattan Engineer District, as the bomb project was code-named, who named him director despite Army Counter-Intelligence qualms over his past associations.

With General Groves, Dr. Oppenheimer selected the Los Alamos site for the laboratory and gathered a top-notch scientific staff, including Dr. Enrico Fermi and Dr. Niels Bohr. Dr. Oppenheimer displayed a special genius for administration and handling the sensitive prima-donna scientific staff. He drove himself at breakneck speed, and at one time his weight dropped to 115 pounds.

Because a security-risk potential was already imputed to him, he was dogged by Army agents. His phone calls were monitored, and his mail was opened. Then an overnight visit with his former fiancee—by then no longer a Communist—on a trip to San Francisco in June 1943 aroused the Counter-Intelligence Corps.

That August, for reasons that remain obscure, Dr.

Oppenheimer volunteered to a C.I.C. agent that the Russians had tried to get information about the Los Alamos project. George Eltenton, a Briton and a slight acquaintance of Dr. Oppenheimer, had asked a third party to get in touch with some project scientists.

In three subsequent interrogations Dr. Oppenheimer embroidered this story, but he declined to name the third party or to identify the scientists. (In one interrogation, however, he gave the C.I.C. a long list of persons he said were Communists or Communist sympathizers, and he offered to dig up information on former Communists at Los Alamos.)

Finally, in December, 1943, Dr. Oppenheimer, at General Groves's order, identified the third party as Prof. Haakon Chevalier, a French teacher at Berkeley and a longtime friend of the Oppenheimer family. At the security hearings in 1954, the scientist recanted his espionage account as a "cock-and-bull story," saying only that he was "an idiot" to have told it.

Neither Professor Chevalier nor Mr. Eltenton was prosecuted. Later, Professor Chevalier asserted that Dr. Oppenheimer had betrayed him out of ambition.

Another charge against Dr. Oppenheimer involved the hydrogen, or fusion, bomb and his relations with Dr. Edward Teller. At Los Alamos Dr. Teller, a vociferous proponent of the hydrogen bomb, was passed over for Dr. Hans Bethe as head of the important Theoretical Physics Division. Dr. Teller, meantime, worked on problems of fusion.

At the war's end, hydrogen bomb work was generally suspended. In 1949, however, when the Soviet Union exploded its first fission bomb, the United States considered pressing forward with a fusion device. The matter came to the A.E.C.'s General Advisory Committee, headed by Dr. Oppenheimer.

On the ground that manufacturing a hydrogen bomb was not technically feasible at the moment, the committee unanimously recommended that thermonuclear research be maintained at a theoretical level only.

In 1950 President Harry S. Truman overruled Dr. Oppenheimer's committee and ordered work pushed on the fusion bomb. Dr. Teller was given his own laboratory and within a few months the hydrogen bomb was perfected.

In late 1953, William L. Borden, former executive director of the Joint Congressional Committee on Atomic Energy, wrote to F.B.I. Director J. Edgar Hoover asserting that, in his opinion, Dr. Oppenheimer had been "a hardened Communist" and had probably "been functioning as an espionage agent."

President Eisenhower cut Dr. Oppenheimer off from access to secret material. Lewis L. Strauss, then chairman of the A.E.C., gave Dr. Oppenheimer the option of cutting ties with the commission or asking for a hearing. He chose a hearing.

The action against Dr. Oppenheimer dismayed the scientific community and many other Americans. He was widely pictured as a victim of McCarthyism.

It was charged at the security hearings that Dr. Oppenheimer had not been sufficiently diligent in furthering the hydrogen bomb and that he influenced other scientists. Dr. Teller testified that, apart from giving him a list of names, Dr. Oppenheimer had not assisted him "in the slightest" in recruiting scientists. Dr. Teller, moreover, said he was opposed to restoring Dr. Oppenheimer's security clearance.

Dr. Oppenheimer vigorously denied that he had been dilatory or neglectful in supporting the hydrogen bomb.

The three-member Personnel Security Board of the A.E.C. held hearings in Washington in April and May 1954. By a vote of 2 to 1, the board declined to reinstate Dr. Oppenheimer's security clearance, even though it called the scientist "a loyal citizen."

Dr. Oppenheimer returned to Princeton to live quietly until April 1962, when President John F. Kennedy invited him to a White House dinner. In December 1963, President Johnson handed Dr. Oppenheimer the highest award of the A.E.C., the $50,000 tax-free Fermi Award. In accepting it, Dr. Oppenheimer said, "I think it is just possible, Mr. President, that it has taken some charity and some courage for you to make this award today."

CHARLES A. LINDBERGH

February 4, 1902–August 26, 1974

Maui, Hawaii—Charles A. Lindbergh, the first man to fly the Atlantic solo nonstop, died this morning at his simple seaside home here. He was 72 years old.

The cause was cancer of the lymphatic system, according to Dr. Milton Howell, a longtime friend.

Mr. Lindbergh was buried about three hours later in the cemetery adjoining the tiny Kipahulu church. He was dressed in simple work clothing and his body was placed in a coffin built by cowboys employed on cattle ranches in the nearby town of Hana. Dr. Howell said that the aviator had spent the last weeks of his life planning his funeral.

In a tribute this evening to Mr. Lindbergh, President Ford said the courage and daring of his Atlantic flight would never be forgotten. He said the selfless, sincere man himself would be remembered as one of America's all-time heroes and a great pioneer of the air age that changed the world.

By Alden Whitman

In Paris at 10:22 P.M. on May 21, 1927, Charles Augustus Lindbergh, a one-time Central Minnesota farm boy, became an international celebrity. A fame enveloped the 25-year-old American that was to last him for the remainder of his life, transforming him in a frenzied instant from an obscure aviator into a historical figure.

The consequences of this fame were to exhilarate him, to involve him in profound grief, to engage him in fierce controversy, to turn him into an embittered fugitive from the public, to accentuate his individualism to the point where he became a loner, to give him a special sense of his own importance, to allow him to play an enormous role in the growth of commercial aviation, as well as to be a figure in missile and space technology, to give him influence in military affairs, and to raise a significant voice for conservation, a concern that marked his older years.

All these things were touched off when a former stunt flier and airmail pilot touched down the wheels of his small and delicate monoplane, the Spirit of St. Louis, on the tarmac of Le Bourget 33 1/2 hours after having lifted the craft off Roosevelt Field on Long Island. Thousands trampled through fences and over guards to surround the silvery plane and to acclaim the first man to fly the Atlantic solo nonstop from the United States to Europe—a feat that was equivalent in the public mind then to the first human step on the moon 42 years later. Icarus had at last succeeded, a daring man alone had attained the unattainable.

What enhanced the feat for many was that Lindbergh was a tall, handsome bachelor with a becoming smile, an errant lock of blond hair over his forehead and a pleasing outward modesty and guilelessness. He was the flawless El Cid, the gleaming Galahad, Frank Merriwell in the flesh.

The delirium that engulfed Paris swirled out over the civilized world. He was gushed over, adulated, worshiped, feted in France, Belgium and Britain. In New York, 4 million people spilled into the streets. Ticker tape and confetti rained on the Broadway parade. Lindbergh, at one point, was "so filled up with listening to this hero guff that I was ready to shout murder."

What the pandemonium obscured was that Lindbergh's epic flight was a most minutely planned venture by a professional flier with 2,000 air hours. "Why shouldn't I fly from New York to Paris?" he had asked himself in September, 1926. "I have more than four years of aviation behind me. I've barnstormed over half of the 48 states. I've flown my mail through the worst of nights."

There had been two previous Atlantic flights—both in 1919, the first when one of three Navy craft flew from Newfoundland to the Azores; and the second when John Alcock and Arthur Brown made it from Newfoundland to Ireland. But no one had made the crossing alone, or from continent to continent.

Lindbergh was conceived of as a nice young man, perhaps a little unpolished socially. He attracted new friends who were considerate of his strong individualism.

The conservative views that Lindbergh later articulated, the remarks about Jews that proved so startling when he was opposing American entry into World War II, his adverse opinion of the Soviet Union, his belief in Western civilization—these were all a reflection of a worldview prevalent among his friends, many rich and conservative. An engineer and aviator of genius, he was, however, not an intellectual, nor a consistent reader, nor a social analyst.

Lindbergh did not regard himself as an anti-Semite. Indeed, he was shocked a couple of years ago when this writer put the question to him. "Good God, no," he responded, citing his fondness for Jews he had known or dealt with. Nor did he condone the Nazi treatment of German Jews. On the other hand, he accepted as fact that American Jewish groups were among those promoting United States involvement in World War II.

He voiced these views in a speech in Des Moines, Iowa, on Sept. 11, 1941. He said of the Jewish people: "Their greatest danger to their country lies in their large ownership and influence in our motion pictures, our press, our radio and our government."

The speech evoked a nationwide outcry. Lindbergh never withdrew his remarks, which he considered statements of "obvious fact."

He also declined to repudiate the award to him of the Service Cross of the German Eagle, bestowed in 1938 by Hermann Goering, the Nazi leader, "at the direction" of Hitler. The medal plagued his reputation for the rest of his life.

Lindbergh's life, like his personality, was full of shadows and enigmas. Born Feb. 4, 1902, he was the son of C. A. Lindbergh, a prosperous Little Falls, Minn., lawyer and land speculator, and his second wife, Evangeline Lodge Land. Charles Augustus Lindbergh Jr. lived in Little Falls with few interruptions until he was 18.

His interest in flying was sparked in 1908 or '09, when, one day, he heard a buzzing in the sky and climbed onto the roof of his home to witness a frail biplane skimming through the clouds.

"Afterward, I remember lying in the grass and looking up at the clouds and thinking how much fun it would be to fly up there," he recalled later.

In 1921, he motorcycled to the Nebraska Aircraft Corporation in Lincoln, which was then producing an airplane and giving flying lessons to promote the product.

Lindbergh took his first flight April 9, 1922, and barnstormed over the Midwest. He was billed as "Daredevil Lindbergh" for his stunt feats.

However, he did not solo until April, 1923, when he purchased his first plane, a Jenny. Shortly afterward, he began to take up passengers in various towns at $5 a ride. He then attended an Army flying school and spent some time as an air circus stunt flier before being hired in St. Louis as the chief pilot on a mail run to Chicago.

On a flight in September, 1926, he was musing about the possibilities of long-distance trips, and he "startled" himself by thinking "I could fly nonstop between New York and Paris."

Ultimately, he persuaded a group of St. Louis businessmen to put up $15,000, which was one reason why the plane was called the Spirit of St. Louis.

For several years after the Paris flight, Lindbergh lived in the glare of publicity. He was regarded as a sort of oracle, and his opinion was solicited on every conceivable subject.

He was, moreover, linked falsely with a number of girls. His interest, however, was in Anne Spencer Morrow, the daughter of Dwight Morrow, then Ambassador to Mexico. They were married on May 27, 1929.

Their first child, Charles Augustus 3rd, was born June 24, 1930. Twenty months later, the baby was kidnapped from [the] nursery in his parents' home in Hopewell, N.J. The date was March 1, 1932. On May 12 the baby's body was found in a shallow grave not far from the house.

In between, there were false leads and sensations galore, through all of which Lindbergh bore himself with great public stoicism.

If public attention glared on Lindbergh during the hunt for his son, it positively poured down on him with the arrest of Bruno Richard Hauptmann, a Bronx carpenter, in 1934. After a six-week trial, in which a web of circumstantial evidence was woven about Hauptmann, he was found guilty and executed.

Lindbergh took his family to England to seek a safe, secluded residence. While there, he was invited to inspect the Luftwaffe and warplane factories in the Reich. By 1939 he had concluded that the power of the Luftwaffe was overwhelming. He sought to warn leaders of European countries, the Soviet Union excepted, of the perils they were facing.

Lindbergh returned to the United States shortly before World War II. He felt he ought to do all he could to prevent American involvement. Not a pacifist nor an isolationist, he was a non-interventionist.

"My opposition to World War II resulted from the growing conviction that such a war would probably devastate Europe, kill millions of men and possibly result in the end of Western civilization," he told this writer a few years ago.

In April 1941, Lindbergh joined the national board of the America First Committee, the country's principal antiwar group. He rallied millions to the cause with such effectiveness that President Roosevelt considered him a major threat.

With Pearl Harbor, America First collapsed and Lindbergh sought to join the armed forces. "Now that we are at war I want to contribute as best I can to my country's war effort," he wrote.

His bid to soldier was rebuffed, however, an action for which he blamed Roosevelt personally. Later in the war, he was a consultant to the United Aircraft Corporation. As a civilian he flew 50 missions. He had at least one close brush with death in a dogfight near Biak Island.

After the war, Lindbergh studied developments in Nazi aircraft and missiles. Earlier, he had given crucial assistance to the space flight pioneer Dr. Robert Goddard, whose basic rocketry patents were used in the development of United States missiles after the war.

For more than 15 years after the Allied victory, Lindbergh virtually disappeared from the news, though he was consultant to the Secretary of the Air

Force and took part in the reorganization of the Strategic Air Command.

In Africa, in 1964, he found an interest that was to bring him out of his public reclusiveness. The issue was conservation.

That cause led him to activity in conservation organizations, to having a large hand in saving the humpback and the blue whales, and to public advocacy of steps to save the world's environment.

Even though he was talking to a generation born long after his Paris flight, his person and his name evoked a tangible response. This was, perhaps, the ultimate enigma of his life; for beneath his outer coating was a man who kept more to himself (and perhaps to his wife) than he ever gave to the public.

JONAS SALK

October 28, 1914–June 23, 1995

By Harold M. Schmeck Jr.

Dr. Jonas Salk, who in the 1950's developed the first successful vaccine against poliomyelitis, the viral illness that had gripped a fearful nation with images of children doomed to death or paralysis, died yesterday at Green Hospital in the La Jolla section of San Diego. He was 80.

The cause was heart failure, said a spokeswoman for the Salk Institute, which Dr. Salk had established to carry out medical research.

As an intense 40-year-old scientist, Dr. Salk became a revered medical figure upon the announcement in 1955 that his new polio vaccine was safe and effective. It was a turning point in the fight against a disease that condemned some victims to live the rest of their lives in tanklike breathing machines called iron lungs and placed swimming holes off limits to children because of parents' fears of contagion.

The Salk vaccine changed medical history, preventing many thousands of cases of crippling illness and saving thousands of lives. In the United States, the vaccine soon ended the yearly threat of epidemics and the toll of paralysis and death.

In the five years before 1955, when mass inoculations with the vaccine began, cases of paralytic polio averaged about 25,000 a year in the United States. A few years after vaccination became routine, the annual number of cases dropped to a dozen or so. In 1969 not a single death from polio was reported in the nation, and now the disease is on the verge of being eradicated worldwide.

Success against polio was a critical event in the dawning of the modern era of vaccine development, which has been marked by effective preventatives against other infectious diseases, including influenza and measles.

In America, paralytic polio was never as widespread as influenza or measles. In the 1920's, 30's and 40's, however, outbreaks of the disease came in frightening epidemics. Many children and young adults died, were crippled or paralyzed.

In the epidemic of 1952, the worst on record, nearly 58,000 cases were reported in the United States; more than 3,000 died of the disease.

The turning point in the battle against polio was probably the day, April 12, 1955, when Dr. Thomas Francis Jr. of the University of Michigan announced the successful results of a field trial in which 440,000 American children had been injected with Dr. Salk's new vaccine.

In the light of earlier, smaller test projects, the polio vaccine had seemed likely to be safe and highly effective. The big field trial, which involved more than 1 million people, proved that it was worthy of the nation's hopes.

The news caused a public sensation probably unequaled by any health development in modern times. The chairman of the board of the American Medical Association, Dr. Dwight H. Murray, called it "one of the greatest events in the history of medicine."

But the successful development of a polio vaccine also led to a long scientific debate over the relative merits of Dr. Salk's version, which used killed virus, and one developed later by Dr. Albert Sabin, which used live virus. The Sabin vaccine, which is taken orally, eventually supplanted the Salk vaccine in the United States, and a sharp rivalry persisted between the two scientists.

The pinnacle of acclaim that Dr. Salk reached on the occasion of the successful field trials came to him through long years of hard work and a dedication to a principle that was less familiar then than it is now.

"My ambition," he said in 1980, "was to bring to bear on medicine a chemical approach. I did that by chemical manipulation of viruses and chemical ways of thinking in biomedical research."

Jonas Edward Salk was born in New York City on Oct. 28, 1914, the eldest of three sons of Daniel and Doris Press Salk. His father worked in New York's garment district.

After graduating in 1934 from City College, Mr. Salk enrolled in New York University's medical school. While there, he had a research fellowship in a virus laboratory, where he was first introduced to a field that that would shape his entire life. He received his medical degree in 1939.

That year he married Donna Lindsay, a social worker. The marriage ended in divorce in 1968. In 1970 he married Francoise Gilot, the French painter and former mistress of Picasso. She survives him, as do three sons from his first marriage.

In 1942 Dr. Salk went to the University of Michigan on a fellowship to study the influenza virus with Dr. Francis, an internationally known virologist. With him he helped develop commercial vaccines against flu. Many Americans could remember the devastating flu pandemic of 1918, which killed an estimated 20 million people.

When the University of Pittsburgh expanded its virus research program after World War II, Dr. Salk joined their staff and soon became director of virus research. There his scientific interests moved from influenza to the urgent effort to develop a polio vaccine. Polio seemed to be on the increase, and some means of coping with the disease was acutely needed.

A crucial factor in the ultimate success of polio vaccine was earlier research at Harvard University on methods of growing viruses in animal-cell tissue cultures in the laboratory. Dr. John Enders of Harvard later won a Nobel Prize for the work.

The Salk vaccine virus was grown on monkey kidney cells, then inactivated, or killed, by formaldehyde.

Some eminent virologists insisted that the killed virus vaccine should be withheld in favor of a live virus vaccine concurrently under development. The live virus vaccine, developed by Dr. Sabin, was first licensed in 1961. It is modified in the laboratory so that it stimulates immunity but causes no damage.

Shortly after the Salk vaccine came into use, a

manufacturing error left live virus in one batch. Several cases of polio resulted and use of the vaccine was halted until corrective measures were taken.

After the polio vaccine was proved successful in the field trials, an opinion poll ranked Dr. Salk roughly between Churchill and Gandhi as a revered figure of modern history.

But among scientists, Dr. Salk and his vaccine were controversial. The usefulness of the vaccine has been vindicated among millions of users, but the debate over the relative merits of the Salk vaccine and the Sabin vaccine has continued.

The live virus vaccine promised lifetime immunity, while the original Salk vaccine did not. But Dr. Salk never lost faith in killed virus polio vaccine. He pointed out that the live virus vaccine did, on rare occasions, produce the disease as well as immunity, while the killed virus vaccine, properly made, carried no such risk.

For his part, Dr. Sabin, who died in 1993 at age 86, remained exasperated at the mention of Dr. Salk's name. "It was pure kitchen chemistry," Dr. Sabin said of his rival's work. "Salk didn't discover anything."

In 1963 Dr. Salk fulfilled a long-held dream, the creation of an institute where scientists and brilliant people in other fields could work toward goals important to humanity. The Salk Institute for Biological Studies opened that year, housed in an architecturally grand group of buildings designed by Louis Kahn, on land overlooking the Pacific Ocean donated by the city of San Diego.

There Dr. Salk continued biomedical research. Over the last decade, he turned his attention to AIDS, trying to develop an immunization to help prevent those already infected with the AIDS virus from developing full-fledged AIDS.

BENJAMIN SPOCK

May 2, 1903–March 15, 1998

By Eric Pace

Dr. Benjamin Spock, the pediatrician who gently coached anxious postwar parents to trust their "own common sense," only to be blamed by some critics for the self-indulgence of those parents' children, the 60's generation, died on Sunday at his home in San Diego. He was 94.

Over half a century, Dr. Spock's homey handbook on child care, now titled "Dr. Spock's Baby and Child Care," became one of the best sellers of all time. Almost 50 million copies have been sold around the world, translated into 42 languages. Dr. Spock also became well known as an antiwar demonstrator in the 1960's, as he campaigned for nuclear disarmament and against the war in Vietnam. "There's no point in raising children if they're going to be burned alive," was how he made the connection between parents, pediatricians and politics.

Dr. Spock had already broken with authority in his child-rearing handbook, which he saw as giving "practical application" to the ideas propounded by two early 20th-century sages, Sigmund Freud and John Dewey, the American philosopher and educator.

"John Dewey and Freud said that kids don't have to be disciplined into adulthood but can direct themselves toward adulthood by following their own will," he observed in 1972. And so in the opening chapter of the book, first published in hardcover in 1946 with the title "The Common Sense Book of Baby and Child Care," Dr. Spock counseled his readers not to "take too seriously all that the neighbors say."

"Don't be afraid to trust your own common sense," he wrote. "What good mothers and fathers instinctively feel like doing for their babies is usually best."

Such relaxed advice, given in the practical, reassuring way that he had with parents, was light-years from the stern dictums of earlier standard works, like the 1928 book "Psychological Care of Infant and Child" by Dr. John B. Watson. "Never, never kiss your child," Dr. Watson commanded. "Never hold it in your lap. Never rock its carriage."

Dr. T. Berry Brazelton of the Harvard Medical School, another noted pediatrician-author, once said of Dr. Spock: "Before he came along, advice to parents was very didactic. He opened the whole area of empowered parenting."

Dr. Spock repeatedly revised his own book over the years, and, for the fifth and sixth editions, which appeared in 1985 and 1992, respectively, he had a co-author: Dr. Michael B. Rothenberg, a professor at the University of Washington's medical school.

In the 1960's and 1970's, Dr. Spock's views on child-rearing were sometimes blamed for the disorderliness of young people, many of whose parents had been devotees of his book.

It was in the 1960's that Dr. Spock became an antiwar activist and opponent of the draft, nuclear armaments and America's involvement in Vietnam. He was a co-chairman of the National Committee for a Sane Nuclear Policy from 1962 to 1967 and was arrested at protest demonstrations. In 1968 a Boston court convicted him of conspiring to counsel evasion of the draft, but the conviction was reversed in 1969.

In 1972 Dr. Spock was the Presidential candidate of the People's Party, a coalition of left-wing organizations, and in 1976 he was the party's candidate for Vice President. The Rev. Dr. Norman Vincent Peale, the author of "The Power of Positive Thinking" and a critic of Dr. Spock, said the doctor had gone "out in the streets with these babies raised according to his books, demonstrating with them for things they claim we should not deny them."

Dr. Spock said his critics had distorted what he had written. "I didn't want to encourage permissiveness, but rather to relax rigidity," he once observed. "Every once in a while, somebody would say to me, 'There's a perfectly horrible child down the block whose mother tells everybody that he's being brought up entirely by your book.' But my own children were raised strictly, to be polite and considerate. I guess people read into the book what they wanted to."

The doctor's was also criticized by the women's movement for what were called sexist passages in his writing.

Benjamin McLane Spock was born May 2, 1903 in New Haven. He was the eldest of the six children of Benjamin Ives Spock, a lawyer, and Mildred Louise Stoughton Spock.

After graduating from Phillips Academy in Andover, Mass., Dr. Spock entered Yale College. Six feet 4 inches tall and broad-shouldered, he was, literally and figuratively, a big man on campus as a member of the Yale crew that won in the Paris Olympics in 1924. He also worked summers in a home for crippled children. "I guess that's why I became a baby doctor, thinking of those kids," he said.

After graduating in 1925, he studied at the Yale Medical School and then Columbia University's College of Physicians and Surgeons, earning his M.D. in 1929. He was a resident in pediatrics at the New York Nursery and Child's Hospital. "Sometime during the pediatric residency years (1931–1932)," Dr. Spock wrote years later, "I conceived the idea that someone going into pediatrics should have psychological training." He spent 10 months as a resident in psychiatry at New York Hospital, and went on to part-time training at the New York Psychoanalytic Institute from 1933 to 1938.

In 1933 he also opened his pediatric practice, where his success was partly the result of his warmth and vitality. "All the young mothers had a great crush on him," a former patient recalled. "He was a gay and charming man."

Another reason he did well was that he took great pleasure in being with his little patients. He once said, "One of my faults as a pediatrician has always been that I whoop it up too much with children." Dr. Spock began writing "The Common Sense Book of Baby and Child Care" in 1943, ten years after the birth of his first son, Michael. He spent evenings dictating it to his first wife, the former Jane Davenport Cheney, who typed it up as he went along. Dictating the book helped to give it the conversational tone that was one of its attractions.

In the book, Dr. Spock wrote that a mother did not have to stick to a rigid feeding schedule for her baby and that it hurt a mother emotionally to have to wait for a fixed feeding time while her baby wailed. But he also stipulated: "This is not an argument against reasonable regularity. I do not think it is harmful for a baby or a mother to work toward a schedule. The mother has to run the rest of her household and when the baby is ready to fit in, it will help everybody."

On the question of crying, Dr. Spock took a balanced view: "I don't think it's good to let a baby cry miserably for long periods if there's a way to comfort him, not because it will do him any physical harm but because of what it might do to his and his mother's spirits.

"On the other hand, you don't have to rush and pick him up every time he whimpers. Plenty of babies fuss off and on and then go back to sleep again." In retrospect, it seemed inevitable that the book would become an enormous success, appearing as it did when the post–World War II baby boom was under way, and winds of change were stirring in the baby and child care field. Even Dr. Spock's flinty Yankee mother is said to have observed, after reading the book, "Why Benny, it's really quite sensible."

In 1976, he was divorced from his first wife and married Mary Morgan. In addition to his wife, Dr. Spock is survived by two sons, a stepdaughter, four grandchildren, one great-granddaughter and two sisters.

Dr. Spock, who gave up his New York practice in 1947 and went on to teach, continued to make changes in his baby and child care book, and the fourth edition in 1976 was revised largely, as he said in a preface, "to eliminate the sexist biases of the sort that help to create and perpetuate discrimination against girls and women." One change was to refer to the baby and child as "she" as well as "he."

Another was in descriptions of the parents' roles.

"I always assumed that the parent taking the greater share of young children (and of the home) would be the mother, whether or not she wanted an outside career," he said in the preface. "Yet it's this almost universal assumption that leads to women feeling a much greater compulsion than men to sacrifice a part of their careers in order that the children will be well cared for," he went on. "Now I recognize that the father's responsibility is as great as the mother's."

NEIL ARMSTRONG

August 5, 1930–August 25, 2012

By John Noble Wilford

Neil Armstrong, who made the "giant leap for mankind" as the first human to set foot on the Moon, died on Saturday. He was 82.

His family said the cause was "complications resulting from cardiovascular procedures." He had undergone heart bypass surgery this month in Cincinnati, near where he lived. His recovery had been going well, and his death came as a surprise to many close to him, including his fellow Apollo astronauts.

A quiet, private man, at heart an engineer and crack test pilot, Mr. Armstrong made history on July 20, 1969, as the commander of the Apollo 11 spacecraft on the mission that culminated the Soviet-American space race in the 1960s. President John F. Kennedy had committed the nation "to achieving the goal, before the decade is out, of landing a man on the Moon and returning him safely to Earth." It was done with more than five months to spare.

On that day, Mr. Armstrong and his co-pilot, Col. Edwin E. Aldrin Jr., known as Buzz, steered their lunar landing craft, Eagle, to a level, rock-strewn plain near the Sea of Tranquillity. It was touch and go the last minute or two, with computer alarms sounding and fuel running low. But they made it.

"Houston, Tranquillity Base here," Mr. Armstrong radioed to mission control. "The Eagle has landed."

"Roger, Tranquillity," mission control replied. "We copy you on the ground. You've got a bunch of guys about to turn blue. We're breathing again. Thanks a lot."

The same could have been said for hundreds of millions of people around the world watching on television.

A few hours later, there was Mr. Armstrong bundled in a white spacesuit and helmet on the ladder of the landing craft. Planting his feet on the lunar surface, he said, "That's one small step for man, one giant leap for mankind." (His words would become the subject of a minor historical debate, as to whether he said "man" or an indistinct "a man.")

Soon Colonel Aldrin joined Mr. Armstrong, bounding like kangaroos in the low lunar gravity, one-sixth that of Earth's, while the command ship pilot, Michael Collins, remained in orbit about 60 miles overhead, awaiting their return. In all, 12 American astronauts walked on the moon between then and the Apollo 17 mission in 1972.

Apollo 11 capped a tumultuous and consequential decade. The '60s in America had started with such promise, with the election of a youthful president, mixed with the ever-present anxieties of the cold war. Then it touched greatness in the civil rights movement, only to implode in the years of assassinations and burning city streets and campus riots. But before it ended, human beings had reached that longtime symbol of the unreachable.

The moonwalk lasted 2 hours and 19 minutes, long enough to let the astronauts test their footing in the fine and powdery surface and set up a television camera and scientific instruments and collect rock samples.

Charles F. Bolden Jr., the current NASA administrator, said, "As long as there are history books, Neil Armstrong will be included in them," and noted that in the years after the moonwalk, Mr. Armstrong "carried himself with a grace and humility that was an example to us all." The historian Douglas Brinkley described him as "our nation's most bashful Galahad." His family called him "a reluctant hero who always believed he was just doing his job."

Neil Alden Armstrong was born on Aug. 5, 1930, in the small town of Wapakoneta, Ohio, to Stephen Armstrong and the former Viola Louise Engel. His father was a state auditor, which meant the family moved every few years to a new Ohio town. At the age of 6, he and his father took a ride in a Ford Trimotor airplane, known as the Tin Goose. It must have made an impression, for by the time he was 15 Neil had learned to fly.

He became an Eagle Scout when the family moved back to Wapakoneta, where he finished high school. (The town now has a museum named for Mr. Armstrong.) From there, he went to Purdue as an engineering student on a Navy scholarship. His college years were interrupted by the Korean War, in which he was a Navy fighter pilot who flew 78 combat missions, including one in which he was forced to eject after the plane lost an aileron.

Back at Purdue after the Navy, Mr. Armstrong plunged more earnestly into aeronautical engineering studies, his grades rising and a career in sight.

By this time, he had also met Janet Elizabeth Shearon, a student in home economics from Evanston, Ill. Soon after his graduation, they were married, in January 1956.

They had two sons, Eric and Mark, who survive. A daughter, Karen, died of an inoperable brain tumor in 1962. The couple were divorced in 1994; in 1999, Mr. Armstrong married Carol Knight, a widow 15 years his junior; she also survives. They lived in Indian Hill, a suburb of Cincinnati. Other survivors include a stepson and stepdaughter; a brother, Dean; a sister, June Armstrong Hoffman; and 10 grandchildren.

Mr. Armstrong's first flight in a rocket plane was in the Bell X-1B (a successor to the plane that broke the sound barrier) as an experimental test pilot for the forerunner of the National Aeronautics and Space Administration. Later, he made seven X-15 flights at 4,000 miles per hour, reaching the edge of space, and piloted many of the most innovative and dangerous aircraft ever developed.

Before long he was tapped for NASA's astronaut corps. As he told his biographer, "I thought the attractions of being an astronaut were actually not so much the Moon, but flying in a completely new medium."

At Houston, the new astronaut began training for flights in the two-person Gemini spacecraft, the forerunner to the three-person Apollos. Mr. Armstrong became the first American civilian astronaut to fly in space, as commander of Gemini 8. In March 1966, he and his co-pilot, David R. Scott, performed the first successful docking of two vehicles in space, their Gemini linking with an unmanned Agena in an essential test for later operations on lunar flights.

In late 1968, Mr. Armstrong was the backup commander for Apollo 8, the first flight to circumnavigate the Moon, putting him in position to command Apollo 11; as the commander, NASA officials decided, he would be the first to walk on the Moon.

About six and a half hours after the landing, Mr. Armstrong opened the hatch of the four-legged lunar module and slowly made his way down the ladder to the lunar surface. A television camera followed his every step for all the world to see.

He and Colonel Aldrin left a plaque on the Moon that read: "Here men from the planet Earth first set foot upon the moon. July 1969 A.D. We came in peace for all mankind."

After leaving the space program, Mr. Armstrong was careful to do nothing to tarnish that image or achievement. He rarely gave interviews and avoided the spotlight.

In a biography, "First Man: The Life of Neil Armstrong," James R. Hansen noted, "Everyone gives Neil the greatest credit for not trying to take advantage of his fame, not like other astronauts have done." To which Janet Armstrong responded: "Yes, but look what it's done to him inside. He feels guilty that he got all the acclaim for an effort of tens of thousands of people." Then she added: "He's certainly led an interesting life. But he took it too seriously to heart."

For a time, Mr. Armstrong was an associate NASA administrator, but he tired of a Washington desk job. Ignoring many offers in business and academia, he returned to Ohio as a professor of aeronautical engineering at the University of Cincinnati and bought a farm near Lebanon, Ohio.

Almost as soon as Mr. Armstrong's death was announced, there was an outpouring on Web sites and social media, a reflection of the extraordinary public acclaim that came to a very private man.

"While we mourn the loss of a very good man," his family said, "we also celebrate his remarkable life and hope that it serves as an example to young people around the world to work hard to make their dreams come true, to be willing to explore and push the limits, and to selflessly serve a cause greater than themselves."

Arendt was the author [of at] least eight major books [in ad]dition to the last work. [Her r]eputation as a writer and [schol]ar became firmly estab[lished] with the publication of [The] Origins of Totalitarian[ism] in 1951.

[Th]at work analyzed the two [major] forms of 20th-century [totali]tarianism — Nazism and [Com]munism—and Dr. Arendt [trace]d their origins to the anti[Semi]tism and imperialism of [the 1]9th-century. It was widely [accla]imed, and even some of [those] who disagreed with the [author's] praised the professional [quali]ty of the work.

[A] reviewer in The New York [Time]s suggested that the book [was] "written throughout under [the s]tress of deep emotion" and [was] the "work of one who has [thou]ght as well as suffered."

[Dr.] Hans Jonas, a professor [at the] New School whose friend[ship] with Dr. Arendt dates to [y]ears ago in Germany, de[scrib]ed her yesterday as [a ver]y exceptional person, no[t only] intellectually but in the [inten]sity of her commitment [Ther]e was a supreme relevance [to] what she had to say [whe]ther you thought her righ[t or w]rong, what she had to say [was] invariably important."

Controversial Book

[Dr.] Arendt stirred the mos[t cont]roversy with the publica[tion] in 1963 of "Eichmann i[n Jeru]salem, a Report on th[e Banal]ity of Evil," which gre[w out] of her coverage for Th[e New] Yorker of the trial o[f Adolf Eichmann for his role i]

she became executive sec[re]tary. It succeeded in recaptu[r]ing and redistributing much [of] the cultural property looted [by] the Nazis from the Jews [of] Europe.

Before leaving Europe, [Dr.] Arendt was married to Hei[n]rich Bluecher, who became [an] art historian at Bard Colle[ge.] He died several years ago.

Despite her scholarship c[re]dentials, Dr. Arendt was una[ble] in her early years in this cou[n]try to find an academic po[si]tion. Then, in 1952, she w[as] awarded a Guggenheim Fello[w]ship. The next year she w[as] invited to deliver the Christi[an] Gauss lectures at Princet[on] University, beginning a tea[ch]ing career that included serv[ice] on the faculties of the Univer[si]ty of California at Berkel[ey,] the University of Chicago, C[o]lumbia, Northwestern, Corn[ell] and other universities bef[ore] joining the New School.

While at the University [of] Chicago, Dr. Arendt delive[red] a series of lectures that w[ere] later published in a book cal[led] "The Human Condition." Br[and] Blanshard, writing in [The] Times, called it a work [of] intense and brooding ref[lec]tion."

Mary McCarthy, in The N[ew] Yorker, said "the combinat[ion] of tremendous intellectual p[ow]er with great common se[nse] makes Miss Arendt's insig[ht] into history and politics s[eem] both amazing and obvio[us]

In the spring semester [of] 1959, Dr. Arendt returned [to]

den heart attack tonight
me in Carmel. He was 70
.
LINCOLN STEFFENS

m was his wife, Ella Win-
a writer. For the last
s Mr. Steffens had done
his writing at his home

---

less Search for Truth

Steffens was regarded as
e best reporters and one
nost relentless searchers
th in his generation by
hose who knew anything
.

himself was always one of
to admit that he had not
the truth there was, or
e had found was truth
shed the record of his
an understanding of
ehavior in a two-v
aphy in 1931, after
forty years.

t went on as long as Mr.
id, but his autobiography
ded as his last great con-
o the current record. It
gnized not as an oppor-
the world to look in at
ns so much as an invita-
the world to look out
Ir. Steffens's eyes.

volumes in which he re-
s lifetime were regarded
dinary in more ways than
the directness, intensity
e same time, the toler-
the personality they re-
the wide range of the
s related; in the insight
aled into human nature;
ingling of idealism with
y.

an unusual ability not
lling how things looked
in finding out how they
ough other men's eyes—
e eyes of Bill Haywood,
eodore Roosevelt, Harri-

THE
MEDIA

was dreadfully scared, he
confronted them and adde
to his list of friends.

Steffens was usually whe
news was. He covered wa
revolutions. He saw Mexic
sia and Italy at first han
attended the peace conferer
was sent on the famous secr
sion with William C. Bu
bring back the answers to qu
whereby the English and
cans hoped to bring the Fren
negotiations with Russia i
This was the mission which
terested powers were compe
repudiate as a matter of
ency, sending Mr. Bullitt in
rary diplomatic eclipse unt
sia was recognized in 1934
was made Ambassador.

Explained Mussolini

Steffens meanwhile went j
about his business looking
world. Some of his friends
him if he had backslid w
wrote calmly about Mussoli
explained that what he saw i
solini was what he had s
Lenin and in Stinnes in Ger
an attempt, conscious or oth
to make "the government o
ness and the business of g
ment" one. He thought suc
sion would make for more h
and less hyprocrisy.

At the end Mr. Steffens
the world with what he de
as "my optimistic grin,"
Russia and America, each ir
ferent fashion, approachir
goal of a state of society in
"not the cunning, graspin
sessors of things but the ge
industrious producers and th
imaginative leaders of the
shall be fit to survive."

He was married for the
time in 1924 to Miss Ella
in Paris, his first wife

JOSEPH PULITZER

April 10, 1847–October 29, 1911

CHARLESTON, S.C.—Joseph Pulitzer, proprietor of The New York World and St. Louis Post-Dispatch, died aboard his yacht, the Liberty, in Charleston Harbor this afternoon. The immediate cause of death was heart disease.

Mrs. Pulitzer, who had been sent for, reached the yacht shortly before her husband died.

Joseph Pulitzer's career was a striking example of the opportunities that have been found in the United States for advancement from penury and friendlessness to wealth and power. Few who have come here to find their fortunes have been more handicapped at the start. He was without funds, had no acquaintances in this country, did not know the language, and suffered from defective vision which harassed him all his life. Yet at 31, thirteen years after landing at Castle Garden, he was the owner of a daily newspaper and on the road to riches.

Mr. Pulitzer's influence on the development of modern American journalism has been large. In the first issue of The St. Louis Post-Dispatch he gave expression to those ideals as follows:

"The Post and Dispatch will serve no party but the people; will be no organ of Republicanism, but the organ of truth; will follow no caucuses but its own convictions; will not support the Administration, but criticise it; will oppose all frauds and shams wherever and whatever they are; will advocate principles and ideas rather than prejudices and partisanship."

In assuming proprietorship of The New York World, Mr. Pulitzer said:

"There is room in this great and growing city for a journal that is not only cheap but bright, not only bright but large, not only large but truly democratic—dedicated to the cause of the people rather than that of purse potentates—devoted more to the news of the New than the Old World; that will expose all fraud and sham; fight all public evils and abuses; that will serve and battle for the people with earnest sincerity."

Joseph Pulitzer was born in Budapest [in what was then Austria-Hungary] in 1847. His father was a businessman, but when he died, while Joseph was still a boy, it was found that the estate was very small. Joseph determined to enter the army, but he was rejected because of the defect in one eye.

The Civil War was in progress in this country, and he decided to come here. He landed at Castle Garden in 1864 practically penniless. He knew nobody in this country and could speak only a dozen words of English.

However, men were badly needed in the Union Army. The young Austrian was enrolled and served to the end of the war.

When he was mustered in New York City, another Austrian suggested that they go West to seek their fortunes. They went to a railroad ticket office, threw down all the money they had between them, and asked for passage as far West as their capital would take them. It was thus by chance that Mr. Pulitzer went to St. Louis.

He eventually began to study law, and in 1868 he was admitted to the bar. He practiced for a short time, but the profession was too slow for him. He looked about for some manner of life in which he could bring all his suppressed energies into immediate play. He found it in journalism.

He became a reporter for the Westliche Post, a German paper edited by Carl Schurz. His first appearance in this capacity was described by one who was at the time a reporter on an English paper:

"I remember his appearance distinctly, because he apparently had dashed out of the office upon receiving the first intimation of whatever was happening, without stopping to put on his coat or collar. In one hand he held a pad of paper and in the other a pencil. He did not wait for inquiries, but announced that he was the reporter for The Westliche Post, and then he began to ask questions of everybody in sight. I remember to have remarked to my companions that for a beginner he was exasperatingly inquisitive. The manner in which he went to work to dig out the facts, however, showed that he was a born reporter."

Mr. Pulitzer's chief ambition seemed to be to root out public abuses and expose evildoers. In this he was absolutely fearless.

This was 1868, and before the year was over he had risen to city editor and later to managing editor. Still later he became part owner of the paper. In the meantime he had begun taking an active part in politics. In 1869 he was elected to the Missouri Legislature, though but 22 years old, and only five years after he had landed here penniless and ignorant of the language.

In 1874 he sold his interest in the paper and went abroad to complete his education.

During the bitter contest that followed the Tilden-Hayes campaign, Mr. Pulitzer served The New York Sun at Washington as special correspondent and editorial writer. His articles were of vitriolic brilliancy and appeared over his own name, a departure that was rare in those days.

He continued this work until 1878. In the Fall of that year he went to St. Louis, where The Evening Dispatch was to be sold at auction after a precarious existence of several years. Mr. Pulitzer bought it for $2,500. When he entered the office the next morning he was unable to find as much as a bushel of coal or a roll of white paper.

By impressing into service everybody within reach, he managed to get out an issue of 1,000 copies. He set to work at once with characteristic energy to improve the situation. At that time the journalistic field in the West was occupied almost exclusively by morning papers. There were two other afternoon papers in St. Louis, The Post and The Star. Within 48 hours he had absorbed the Post, and the first number of The Post-Dispatch, which afterward became an enormous success, was issued.

During this period his political activities continued. In 1884 he was elected to Congress from a New York district, though he resigned after a few months.

It was at this time that he bought The New York World from Jay Gould. The World had been started in June 1880 as a penny paper of blameless features, eschewing intelligence of scandals, divorces, and even dramatic news. Its backing was ample, but it failed to make money. Mr. Pulitzer took possession May 10, 1883.

By the adoption of methods similar to those he had employed in St. Louis, Mr. Pulitzer soon had The World on a paying basis. Of these beginnings The World itself recently said:

"He was unable to expend large sums of money in the gathering of news, for the very excellent reason that he did not have it to spend. He did instill life and energy into every department of the paper on the very first day of his proprietorship, and in no part was the change in the character of matter printed more noticeable than in the news columns. But it is a fact, patent to anyone who will turn over the files for that year, that the first impetus given to the new World came from the editorial page. To this Mr. Pulitzer gave his personal and almost undivided attention, and by this agency first impressed upon the public mind the fact that a new, vigorous, and potent moral force had sprung up in the community."

Mr. Pulitzer had one of the most expensive households in America. He had a home on East 73rd Street, an estate at Bar Harbor, and another country place on Jekyll Island, off the Georgia coast. He also had a 1,500-ton steam yacht.

His blindness made it necessary for him to have a large personal staff. He could not read or distinguish the faces of those about him. He could only listen and think.

Mr. Pulitzer was married to Miss Kate Davis. He leaves five children.

Since attaining affluence, he gave considerable sums to philanthropy, chiefly in the cause of education. He gave to Columbia University an endowment of $1,000,000 for the establishment of a school of journalism, which it has been understood would be utilized after his death.

ADOLPH S. OCHS

March 12, 1858–April 8, 1935

CHATTANOOGA, Tenn.—Adolph S. Ochs, publisher of The New York Times, died here at 4:10 o'clock this afternoon amid the scenes of his first venture in publishing and his first professional triumphs. He was 77 years old.

Mr. Ochs suffered a cerebral hemorrhage while at lunch.

The end of the publisher's long career came after he had visited the staff of The Chattanooga Times, whose success under his direction made that of The New York Times possible.

Mr. Ochs is survived by Mrs. Ochs; a daughter, Mrs. Arthur Hays Sulzberger; a brother, three sisters, and four grandchildren, Marian, Ruth, Judith and Arthur Ochs Sulzberger.

The story of Adolph S. Ochs is one of a career which, in poverty and wealth, obscurity and eminence, was all of one piece. The qualities that his employers noted when he began his newspaper career as a printer's devil in Knoxville, Tenn., were qualities he manifested throughout his life. The principles he put into practice when at the age of 20 he took charge of a bankrupt small-town newspaper were the principles he put into practice 18 years later when he took charge of the bankrupt New York Times and carried it to influence and prosperity.

He believed in publishing only one kind of paper, and his great achievement was the proof that publishing that kind of paper—"clean, dignified, trustworthy and impartial," as he phrased it in his announcement in The Times on Aug. 18, 1896—could be both economically and ethically successful.

That he did so was due largely to the fact that he learned the newspaper business from the ground up. The poverty of his parents cut short his formal schooling; but the printing office was his high school and university, and something of the impress of the old-time printing shop and the old-school printers stayed with him all his life.

He was born in Cincinnati on March 12, 1858, eldest of the six children of Julius and Bertha Levy Ochs. Julius Ochs taught languages in various Southern schools.

After the war the family moved to Knoxville, but their fortunes did not prosper. Adolph, the oldest boy, went to work at the age of 11 as office boy to Captain William Rule, editor of The Knoxville Chronicle. He later became the paper's printer's devil, the old-time printer's term for the boy who did the odd jobs about the composing room. He learned about the printing trade, and he learned fast.

But his eye was on Chattanooga, which was served by a single struggling newspaper, The Times. Discovering that Chattanooga had no city directory, Mr. Ochs set to work on this, his first publication. The directory not only made Mr. Ochs acquainted with Chattanooga, but made Chattanooga acquainted with Mr. Ochs.

The editor of The Times offered to sell it to Mr. Ochs for $800 if he would assume the paper's debts. He borrowed $250 and bought a half interest in The Times, with the stipulation that he would have control of the paper. He became publisher on July 2, 1878.

The salutatory of the new publisher announced the theme around which his whole life was to be woven. The Times would get all the news it could, at home and abroad. But, it was added, "we shall conduct our business on business principles, neither seeking nor giving sops and donations."

The young man had a newspaper plant fit for nothing but the junk heap, publishing a four-page paper with a circulation of 250. There was one reporter and a business office staff of one, and the proprietor and publisher was also business manager and advertising solicitor.

But the paper became successful, and two years after the publisher had bought the control of The Times, he bought the other half interest in the paper.

On Feb. 28, 1883, Mr. Ochs was married to Miss Effie Miriam Wise. To this union was born a daughter, Iphigene Bertha, who was married in 1917 to Arthur Hays Sulzberger.

All sorts of people passed through Chattanooga in the late eighties and early nineties. One was Harry Alloway, a Wall Street reporter for The New York Times, to whom Mr. Ochs remarked casually that he thought The Times offered the greatest opportunity in American journalism.

In 1896 Mr. Ochs received a telegram from Mr. Alloway. Since 1890 The Times had declined and there was talk of a reorganization. Alloway wired Mr. Ochs that if he were interested in The Times it could probably be bought cheap.

Mr. Ochs went to New York to investigate the situation. George Jones, who had joined with Henry J. Raymond in founding The New York Times in 1851 and had conducted it since Raymond's death, had died in 1891. His heirs were now prepared to sell The Times.

As it turned out, only one purchaser was willing to pay the $1,000,000 they asked, a company under the presidency of Charles R. Miller, editor of The Times. Then the panic of 1893 struck. By the Spring of 1896 the circulation of The Times had dwindled to 9,000 and was losing $1,000 a day. A plan of reorganization was being formulated by Charles R. Flint and Spencer Trask, but the plan needed a man to work it.

In this situation the young publisher from Chattanooga came to town, and through Alloway arranged an interview with Mr. Miller. By the time the two men parted, Mr. Miller was convinced that The Times had found the man.

Mr. Ochs lacked the money to join the syndicate created by Mr. Flint and Mr. Trask. But Mr. Miller felt sure that Mr. Ochs could save the paper if he had a little time. A receiver kept The Times going while Mr. Ochs raised the needed funds, and the paper was transferred to him on Aug. 18, 1896.

Mr. Ochs himself bought $75,000 worth of bonds, carrying with them 1,125 shares of stock. Of the rest of the stock, 3,876 shares, enough to make an absolute majority, were put into escrow, to be delivered to the publisher when the paper had paid its way for three consecutive years. His control, however, was to be absolute from the first.

At the moment it seemed almost incredible that he could win. Dominating New York journalism of the period were The Herald, The World and The (morning) Journal, now The American; the former with a costly foreign service, the latter two wildly sensational, with immense circulations built up at a price of 1 cent, while the other morning papers, The Times included, sold for 3 cents.

To have imitated any of these competitors would have been suicidal; but Mr. Ochs would not have done it anyway. His salutatory announcement promised "to conduct a high-standard newspaper" for "thoughtful, pure-minded people," emphasized by the adoption on Oct. 25, 1896, of the motto "All the News That's Fit to Print," which The Times carries to this day.

This definition of The Times's purpose was Mr. Ochs's own, and the phraseology was an emphatic announcement that The Times would not be what the nineties called a yellow newspaper. In place of the comic supplements of the yellows, The Times soon offered a pictorial Sunday magazine, and shortly after Mr. Ochs took charge, the Saturday Review of

Books, later shifted to Sunday, became a permanent feature of the paper.

In the first year of Mr. Ochs's proprietorship the circulation more than doubled, and the deficit, which had been $1,000 a day when he took charge, averaged less than a fifth of that at the end of the year. But there was still a deficit.

The Times steadily gained in circulation and advertising. But the deficit in Mr. Ochs's second year was $78,000—larger than in the first year; the circulation had been pushed up to 25,000, but the advertising lineage of 1898 showed only a 10 percent gain over 1896. Something had to be done.

Mr. Ochs was advised to raise the price of the paper from 3 cents to 5 cents a copy. To the astonishment of all, Mr. Ochs proposed instead to cut the price to 1 cent.

This was to prove one of his most brilliant inspirations. Mr. Ochs believed that many people bought the "yellow journals" only because they cost a third as much as the other papers, and that they would buy a different sort of paper if they could get it for the same price.

The cut in price marked the beginning of victory. A year after the change the circulation of The Times had trebled, rising to 76,000, and for the most part it has been rising ever since.

Mr. Ochs's third year as publisher showed a profit of $50,000, and from then on the success of The Times was assured. The original agreement had stipulated that the 3,876 shares held in escrow should be turned over to Mr. Ochs when he had made the paper pay for three successive years. On July 1, 1900, he had fulfilled this condition and became the owner of a majority stock interest in The Times, which he retained ever afterward.

The great fight of Mr. Ochs's life was won, therefore, by 1900, and he won it by himself. He was the man who, as E. A. Bradford, a veteran of the editorial staff, put it, "found the paper on the rocks and turned them into foundation stones."

That it kept on going up was due largely, in Mr. Ochs's opinion, to the fact that most of the profits were plowed back into the business.

As The Times grew, Mr. Ochs seized upon every improvement in technique that would enable his paper to get the news more quickly and more fully and to get it to the reader in the best possible form and with the least possible lapse of time.

In 1896 The Times was still being published on Park Row. When this building became too small. Mr. Ochs resolved to build in what is now known as Times Square, and in January, 1905, the paper was moved uptown. In 1913, needing even more space, the paper migrated to the Times Annex at 229 West 43rd Street, just off the square.

In June, 1918, The Times received the first award of the Pulitzer Gold Medal for "disinterested and meritorious service" for publishing in full so many documents and speeches by European statesmen relating to the war. Advertising, circulation and the size of the paper had expanded greatly.

Mr. Ochs continued to direct The Times all his life. His town house was for many years at 308 West 75th Street, until in the Fall of 1931 he bought an estate in White Plains. He was a firm adherent of the reformed Jewish faith, and for many years he was a trustee of Temple Emanu-El in New York.

A charity close to Mr. Ochs's heart was the collection of funds, each year at the Christmas season, for "The Hundred Neediest Cases." This feature was inaugurated by him in 1912, when a fund of $3,630 was collected, to be distributed to persons chosen from lists furnished by the city's leading charitable organizations. The appeal still is made solely through the publication of brief individual narratives in The Times.

WILLIAM RANDOLPH HEARST

April 29, 1863–August 14, 1951

By Gladwin Hill

BEVERLY HILLS, Calif.—William Randolph Hearst, founder of a vast publishing empire, and one of the most controversial figures in American journalism and politics, died today of a brain hemorrhage at his home here. His age was 88.

Although an invalid for four years, the publisher had kept in intimate touch with the operation of his 18 newspapers and other enterprises virtually up to the time of his death.

Mr. Hearst lapsed into a coma Sunday from which he did not recover. He died at 9:50 A.M., Pacific daylight time, in the house at 1007 North Beverly Drive to which he had retired from his fabulous San Simeon castle and ranch in mid-California when illness overtook him.

At his bedside were his five sons, William Randolph Jr., publisher of The New York Journal-American; David, publisher of The Los Angeles Evening Herald and Express; Randolph, publisher of The San Francisco Call-Bulletin;

journalism, died today." The second version was: "William Randolph Hearst is dead. The greatest figure in American journalism, whose patriotism and wisdom had been a strongly guiding influence on the nation during a career that began more than a half century ago, died today."

Mr. Hearst's body was flown to his native San Francisco.

At the height of his career, William Randolph Hearst was one of the world's wealthiest and most powerful newspaper owners. His newspapers frequently fought the battles of the common man, for whose attention they competed by means of comic strips, scandal, society gossip, pseudo-science, jingoism and political invective.

The term "yellow journalism," generally believed to have derived from one of the early Hearst comic strips, "The Yellow Kid," was coined to apply to Mr. Hearst's newspaper practices.

At the peak of his influence he engendered the heat of controversy more than almost any other American. He bitterly opposed the participation of the United States in the European phases of both World Wars, and his sympathies until this country entered the conflicts seemed to lie with Germany.

Mr. Hearst led his newspapers in fights for many causes usually considered progressive. These included the eight-hour working day, direct election of United States Senators, woman suffrage, postal-savings banks, anti-trust legislation and municipal ownership of certain types of public utilities. He fought communism and government graft violently on all occasions.

Where his newspapers frequently were raucous and rowdy, Mr. Hearst himself was quiet and even shy. For years he lived in remote splendor after the manner of a feudal lord, but he liked to believe that he never lost the common touch.

Despite the great influence of his newspapers, Mr. Hearst never was able to achieve his ambition to hold high elective office. He had to be content with two uneventful terms in the House of Representatives.

Mr. Hearst's newspaper campaigns were spectacular and exercised a profound effect on measures before Congress. As much as any other single man he was responsible for the defeat of resolutions to make the United States a party to the World Court covenant.

When Mr. Hearst was a child, his father acquired great wealth, and when Mr. Hearst's mother was told at the beginning of her son's newspaper-owning career that he was losing a million dollars a year, she is reported to have replied:

"That's too bad; at that rate Willie can hold out for only 30 years."

Mr. Hearst was born on the southeast corner of California and Montgomery Streets, San Francisco, on April 29, 1863. It was the year of Gettysburg and Vicksburg in the East, but in the West the raw frontier that was to shape much of Mr. Hearst's thinking

George and John; also Martin F. Huberth, chairman of the board of the Hearst Corporation; Richard E. Berlin, president of the corporation, and Dr. Myron Prinzmetal, Mr. Hearst's physician.

They were joined by Marion Davies, former motion-picture star, who had long been a friend and confidante of the publisher.

Mr. Hearst's wife, Mrs. Millicent Willson Hearst, from whom he had been separated for more than two decades, was at her home in New York.

Mr. Hearst was credited with keeping in day-to-day touch with the content and operations of his transcontinental newspaper chain, rewarding accomplishments handsomely and meting out sharp and acute criticism of blunders. His surveillance was close enough so that within the last week the word had passed among his Los Angeles staffs that "the chief," as he was known among his employees, had waxed wrathful about something.

His interest in world affairs had remained equally lively. The last of the many campaigns and crusades he conceived, inspired and directed, a number of which have taken their place in American history, was his newspapers' leadership of the movement in defense of General of the Army Douglas MacArthur after his dismissal from his Pacific command.

It was also generally understood that the publisher had such a strong aversion to the anticipation of death that even the staffs of his downtown papers had hesitated to make detailed plans for the inevitability. Support was lent to this by the fact that The Herald and Express altered the introduction of its story of his death between editions.

The first said "William Randolph Hearst, whose career as a publisher spanned more than half a century and ushered in the modern era of American

was awaiting the Midas touch of such men as George Hearst, his father, who was to amass a fortune—much of it in gold mine speculations—and become a United States Senator.

As a boy and young man, William Randolph Hearst was a bit of a handful. His doting father called him Buster Billy. After leaving the local schools, the youth made a brief appearance at St. Paul's School, Concord, N.H., and private tutors completed his preparation for Harvard.

He already was interested in journalism, and he took the moribund college comic magazine, The Lampoon, and put it on its financial feet. When the university authorities failed to appreciate one of young Mr. Hearst's practical jokes, he left Harvard in 1885 without taking a degree.

On March 4, 1887, Mr. Hearst's name appeared on the editorial page of a newspaper for the first time, he, then 23, having persuaded his father to let him try his hand at running The San Francisco Examiner, which the elder Hearst had acquired for a bad debt.

The noisy battle later on in New York between Mr. Hearst and Joseph Pulitzer, publisher of The World, for circulation began when Mr. Hearst bought the failing Morning Journal on Oct. 7, 1896, with $180,000 of his mother's money. Mr. Pulitzer soon felt the weight of this 33-year-old Californian with the college clothes who had a habit of executing a few dance steps when he felt good.

In three months the circulation of The Journal jumped from 20,000 to 150,000. Mr. Hearst dropped The Journal's price to one cent, and Mr. Pulitzer was compelled to do the same. Not only did Mr. Hearst threaten The World's circulation, but he raided Mr. Pulitzer's high-class staff for some of his ablest craftsmen.

William McKinley became President on March 4, 1897, and war with Spain became a distinct possibility. Mr. Hearst saw in the insurrection then occurring in Cuba the makings of spectacular newspaper copy. In August, Karl Decker, a Hearst agent, engineered the escape of Evangelina Cisneros, a Cuban woman of 18, from a Cuban prison, and she was brought to New York as proof of Spanish brutality.

Mr. Hearst played the loudest horn in the war clamor that heated public frenzy to a cherry red. When the United States declared war on Spain on April 24, 1898, Mr. Hearst became a national figure.

In 1903 Mr. Hearst was elected to the House of Representatives, where he stayed for two terms. He was frequently absent from roll call.

Mr. Hearst was 41 years old in 1904, when his name was presented for the Presidential nomination at the Democratic National Convention in St. Louis. His nomination was seconded by Clarence Darrow, famous liberal attorney of Chicago. Mr. Hearst received 200 votes, 20 of them from California delegates. The nomination went to Judge Alton B. Parker, who got 658 votes and was then defeated decisively by Theodore Roosevelt.

Mr. Hearst ran unsuccessfully for Mayor of New York against George B. McClellan on the ticket of the Municipal Ownership League in 1905. Undaunted, Mr. Hearst ran for Governor of New York State in 1906 against Charles Evans Hughes, but lost after a bitter struggle.

In 1909 Mr. Hearst made his last attempt to win elective office when he ran for Mayor of New York against William J. Gaynor. He was decisively defeated.

Mr. Hearst's political prestige in New York received a blow from which it never recovered in 1922, when Alfred E. Smith refused to run on a Democratic ticket with him, his anger aroused by stories and cartoons picturing him as a tool of the milk trust.

Mr. Hearst enjoyed a brief moment of power in 1932 when he helped to clinch the nomination of Franklin D. Roosevelt for his first term as President at the Democratic national convention in Chicago. But scarcely had Mr. Roosevelt been installed in the White House the following March when political warfare broke out between the President and the publisher. The President's "New Deal" became the "Raw Deal" in all Hearst newspapers and was bitterly denounced.

Mr. Hearst was one of the first newspaper publishers to recognize the possibilities of motion pictures, though he was reported to have lost more than $2,000,000 in his ventures. In 1913 a company that he owned screened "The Perils of Pauline," an interminable cliff-hanger featuring Pearl White. Mr. Hearst's attempts to make a leading American movie star out of a striking New York blonde whose screen name was Marion Davies were successful.

In 1922 Mr. Hearst probably was at the height of his fame and power as a newspaper publisher. He owned 20 newspapers in 13 cities of the country and it is likely that at that time he was making more money than any publisher ever had made. His expenditures were fabulous. It is doubtful whether any American citizen ever had lived on so lavish a scale. His 240,000-acre ranch at San Simeon, with its 50 miles of oceanfront, was crowned by a great mansion and three vast guest houses, all of which at one time were filled with works of art and one of the world's greatest collections of curios.

On April 30, 1903, Mr. Hearst married Miss Millicent Willson in Grace Protestant Episcopal Church, New York. Five sons were born to the marriage—George, William Jr., John, David and Randolph.

Legends clustered about Mr. Hearst, but none was as strange as the truth. His achievements as a collector would have made him unique if he had done nothing else. He acquired Etruscan tombs, California mountain ranges, herds of yak, Elizabethan caudle cups, Crusaders' armor, paintings, tapestries, a knocked-down and crated Spanish abbey or two, 15th-century choir stalls, dozens of Mexican bridles, several Egyptian mummies and hundreds of other items, many of which he never saw.

H. L. MENCKEN

September 12, 1880–January 29, 1956

BALTIMORE—H. L. Mencken was found dead in bed early today.

The 75-year-old author, editor, critic and newspaper man had lived in retirement since suffering a cerebral hemorrhage in 1948.

Mr. Mencken, one of the leading American satirists, essayists and journalists of any day, exerted a tremendous influence on American letters between about 1910 and the middle Nineteen Thirties. The period of his strongest influence was relatively brief, but it had about it a quality of intensity that later generations found hard to understand.

Mr. Mencken blew a blast of fresh air into the somewhat musty American literary scene, particularly in the Nineteen Twenties. He directed the attention of the American reading public to a group of distinguished writers clamoring for greater recognition that included Sinclair Lewis, Theodore Dreiser, D. H. Lawrence, James Branch Cabell, Joseph Conrad, Ford Maddox Ford, Sherwood Anderson, Edgar Lee Masters and James Joyce.

Although not a formally trained scholar, Mr. Mencken made considerable contributions to philology by his studies in the American language. He used to say that he was not a scholar but a "scout for the scholars."

Appearing on the literary scene with menacing agility in the pre–World War I period, Mr. Mencken laid about him with a cudgeling style of writing calculated to inflict severe lacerations and contusions on the American middle classes. His admirers cared little if this style was one that practically precluded temperate and objective discussion. He once wrote:

"The plain fact is that I am not a fair man and don't want to hear both sides. On all subjects, from aviation to xylophone playing, I have fixed and invariable ideas."

At the height of his influence Mr. Mencken was the bright hero of the young intellectuals. They carried about with them as badges of distinction, first The Smart Set and somewhat later, The American Mercury, publications edited by Mr. Mencken and George Jean Nathan. A whole generation of young newspapermen cocked their feet on desks and roared with laughter as they read the green-covered Mercury, in which Messrs. Mencken and Nathan thwacked the residents of the so-called "Bible Belt."

Mr. Mencken's lively comment on American life was delivered in a tone of omniscience that was probably responsible for a decline in his vogue during the Depression of the Thirties. He frequently had used the Sinclair Lewis character of George F. Babbitt as the standard of the American bourgeois mind.

But when the Depression was under way it became apparent even to Mr. Mencken's stanchest admirers that while Babbitt did not have the answers, neither did Mr. Mencken.

The attention of the young intellectuals began to settle upon new prophets more versed in the idiom of economics. Also, Mr. Mencken was of German ancestry and was strong for the German ideas of discipline and political orderliness. These ideas had become associated in many minds with the activities of Adolf Hitler in the German Reich.

All his life Henry Louis Mencken remained steeped in the cultivated literary, musical, eating and drinking traditions of old Baltimore, where he was born Sept. 12, 1880. His father was August Mencken, a prosperous cigarmaker whose father had migrated from Saxony. His mother, Anna Margaret Abhau Mencken, was a celebrated Baltimore beauty of her day.

Mr. Mencken graduated from Baltimore Polytechnic Institute at the head of his class. Baltimore Poly was only a high school, and he never had a university education. On Jan. 16, 1899, he went to work as a police reporter on The Baltimore Morning Herald.

The young newspaper man spent his spare time discovering for himself such writers as George Bernard Shaw and Henrik Ibsen, and in writing supercharged short stories as well as verses in the manner of Rudyard Kipling.

By 1903 he was city editor of The Herald, and in 1906 he went to The Baltimore Sun, with which he was associated on and off during much of his career. He began to free-lance assiduously, and his name began to appear in print with fair regularity.

Theodore Dreiser, whose literary career was to owe much to Mr. Mencken at a later date, has left a keen word picture of the Mencken of this period. He recalled him as a "taut, ruddy, snub-nosed youth . . . whose brisk gait and ingratiating smile proved to be at once enormously intriguing and amusing. I had, for some reason not connected with his basic mentality, you may be sure, the sense of a small town roisterer or a college sophomore of the crudest yet most disturbing charm and impishness who, for some reason, had strayed into the field of letters."

Two important things happened to Mr. Mencken on May 8, 1908. He got a part-time job writing about books for The Smart Set, and he met Mr. Nathan, the new Smart Set dramatic critic with whom his literary life was to be linked for many years.

In 1914 Mr. Mencken and Mr. Nathan became co-editors of The Smart Set. During the period of their association with this magazine, many of the most important new writers in America made their first appearances in the publication. The two men-about-town conducted their collaboration in an atmosphere of highly literate horseplay.

It was not always easy sledding in the business department, however. When Joseph Conrad's literary agent in London cabled asking $600 for one of Conrad's stories, Mr. Mencken replied, "For $600 you can have Smart Set."

The entrance of the United States into World War I forced prices for newsprint and labor out of sight and dealt the coup de grâce to The Smart Set. Alfred A. Knopf backed Mr. Mencken and Mr. Nathan in The American Mercury, which appeared for the first time with the January, 1924, issue.

Nearly all the writing in The American Mercury was vivid and distinctive, and some of it was regarded by critics as distinguished. Mr. Mencken and his associates lavished loving care on "Americana," one of the departments brought over from The Smart Set.

This was a miscellany of notes and clippings from provincial newspapers. It was used to demonstrate Mr. Mencken's theory that the American middle-class mind was a dreadful affair.

A typical item might deal with the hearty and extroverted doings at a businessmen's luncheon in Kansas. Or perhaps a group of clergymen being presented with black cravats by a silk manufacturer while a choir sings "Blest Be the Tie that Binds."

Mr. Mencken's literary style was vivid and violent. He urged the intelligentsia to "have at" the "booboisie" of the "hinterland," and he delighted in the use of such words as "swinish" and "hoggish."

The Mercury printed articles by such non-professional writers as Ernest Booth, a convicted bank robber. The frequency with which unlikely persons had their writings printed in The Mercury inspired a magazine of humor to publish a picture of two tramps sitting on a park bench. One of them is saying to the other:

"I enjoyed your little piece in The Mercury."

Mr. Mencken, an implacable enemy of the New Deal, was a conservative Baltimorean all his life in spite of the lusty warfare that he waged on prudery and sham. His savage attacks on Prohibition caused those favoring these legal enactments to picture Mr. Mencken as a beer-guzzling rake. Actually, Mr. Mencken was a moderate drinker; most of his tippling was done in print rather than at the bar.

The quintessence of all that Mr. Mencken belabored in American life manifested itself in 1925 in Dayton, Tenn., when John Thomas Scopes went on trial for teaching high school students "certain theories that deny divine creation of man, as taught in the Bible; and did teach instead thereof that man was descended from the lower order of animals."

At the trial Mr. Mencken was in the press seats to report with savage joy the verbal mauling of William Jennings Bryan, special prosecutor, by Clarence Darrow, defense attorney. Mr. Scopes was convicted and fined $100.

Mr. Nathan dropped out of The American Mercury in 1930 and three years later Mr. Mencken severed his connections with the magazine. The magazine had less than 30,000 circulation when Mr. Mencken left. Its peak circulation under Messrs. Mencken and Nathan had been 90,000.

After reporting the 1948 election campaign for The Baltimore Sun papers, Mr. Mencken suffered a stroke from which he never fully recovered.

Mr. Mencken, a great lover of words, kept records during his career of many Americanisms that he later listed in what he called, "The American Language." It is generally agreed that these philological researches have formed an important basis for more exhaustive studies along the same lines.

Mr. Mencken long ago wrote this epitaph for himself:

"If after I depart this vale, you ever remember me and have thought to please my ghost, forgive some sinner and wink your eye at some homely girl."

EDWARD R. MURROW

April 25, 1908–April 27, 1965

Edward R. Murrow, whose independence and incisive reporting brought heightened journalistic stature to radio and television, died yesterday at his home in Pawling, N.Y., at the age of 57.

The former head of the United States Information Agency had been battling cancer since October, 1963.

The ever-present cigarette (he smoked 60 to 70 a day), the baritone voice and the high-domed, worried face were the trademarks of the radio reporter who became internationally famous during World War II with broadcasts that started, "This . . . is London." Later, on television, his series of news documentaries, "See It Now," on the Columbia Broadcasting System from 1951 to 1958, set the standard for all television documentaries on all networks.

Mr. Murrow, who lived on a 280-acre farm, is survived by his widow, Janet, a son, and two brothers.

Mr. Murrow's career with C.B.S., which spanned 25 years, ended in January, 1961, when President

Kennedy named him head of the United States Information Agency. In October, 1963, a malignant tumor made the removal of his left lung necessary, and three months later he resigned.

Mr. Murrow achieved distinction first as a radio correspondent, reporting from London in World War II, and then as a pioneer television journalist opening the home screen to the stimulus of controversy. No other figure in broadcast news left such a strong stamp on both media.

His independence was reflected in doing what he thought had to be done on the air and worrying later about the repercussions among sponsors, viewers and stations.

In the last war, Mr. Murrow conveyed the facts with a compelling precision. But he went beyond the reporting of the facts. By describing what he saw in detail, he sought to convey the moods and feelings of war. In one memorable broadcast he said that as he "walked home at 7 in the morning, the windows in the West End were red with reflected fire, and the raindrops were like blood on the panes."

Had a London street just been bombed out? The young correspondent was soon there in helmet, gray flannel trousers and sports coat, quietly describing everything he saw against the urgent sound patterns of rescue operations. Or he would be in a plane on a combat mission, broadcasting live on the return leg and describing the bombing he had watched as "orchestrated hell."

He flew 25 missions in the war, despite the opposition of top C.B.S. executives in New York, who regarded him as too valuable to be so regularly risked. In the endless German air raids on London, his office was bombed out three times, but he escaped injury.

For a dozen years, as radio's highest paid newscaster, he was known to millions of his countrymen by voice alone, a baritone tinged with an echo of doom. Then television added an equally distinctive face, with high-domed forehead and deep-set, serious eyes.

As the armchair interviewer on "Person to Person," Mr. Murrow carried out a gentlemanly electronic invasion of the homes of scores of celebrities in the nineteen-fifties, from Sophie Tucker through Billy Graham.

From 1951 to 1958 Mr. Murrow also did a series of news documentaries under the title "See It Now." In the 1953–54 season the telecast studied the impact of the emotional and political phenomenon known as "McCarthyism." Senator Joseph R. McCarthy, Republican of Wisconsin, was then conducting his crusade against alleged Communist influence, but television had given the matter gingerly treatment.

Mr. Murrow and his long-time co-editor, Fred W. Friendly, broke this pattern decisively on Tuesday evening, March 9, 1954. Using film clips that showed the Senator to no good advantage, the two men offered a provocative examination of the man and his methods. The program, many thought, had a devastating effect. "McCarthyism" lost public force in succeeding months.

Egbert Roscoe Murrow was born on April 25, 1908, at Pole Cat Creek, N.C. He changed his first name to Edward in college. His father, a tenant farmer, moved to Blanchard, Wash., where his son grew up.

In 1930 Mr. Murrow graduated from Washington State College, and in 1935, he was employed by C.B.S. as director of talks and education. Then in 1937, he received an unexpected call from headquarters asking if he would go to Europe.

His answer—"yes"—was the decisive turn of his career.

Mr. Murrow, then 29, became the network's one-man staff in Europe. He arranged cultural programs and interviewed leaders, and though his office was in London, he traveled extensively.

As war began to seem inevitable, he hired William L. Shirer, a newspaperman, to cover the Continent. He and Mr. Shirer were arranging musical broadcasts when Hitler marched into Austria.

Mr. Murrow flew to Berlin and chartered a Lufthansa transport to Vienna, arriving in time to watch the arrival of goose-stepping German troops. For 10 days he was allowed to broadcast, and he described the nation's swift transition to a subject state. At home, millions hung on his and Shirer's words.

As news chief for C.B.S. in Europe he hired the men who were to become the network's famous roster of war correspondents—among them Eric Sevareid, Charles Collingwood, Howard K. Smith and Richard Hottelet.

Mr. Murrow's wartime broadcasts from Britain, North Africa and finally the Continent gripped listeners by their firm, spare authority. He was the first Allied correspondent inside the Nazi concentration camp at Buchenwald. Near 300 bodies, he saw a mound of men's, women's and children's shoes.

"I regarded that broadcast as a failure," he said. "I could have described three pairs of those shoes— but hundreds of them! I couldn't. The tragedy of it simply overwhelmed me."

Returning to the United States in 1946, he became a vice president of C.B.S. in news operations. He was away from the microphone for 18 months. Then on Sept. 29, the former war correspondent went on the air with his evening radio report, "Edward R. Murrow with the News." It was carried by 125 network stations to an audience of several million people weeknights for 13 years.

His sign-off on both radio and television was a crisp "Good night, and good luck."

WALTER WINCHELL

April 7, 1897–February 20, 1972

LOS ANGELES—Walter Winchell, the fast-talking song-and-dance man who became a newspaper columnist and popular newscaster on radio, died today of prostate cancer at the U.C.L.A. Medical Center. He was 74.—*The Associated Press*

By Alden Whitman

In the 20 years of his heyday, from 1930 to 1950, Walter Winchell was the country's best-known and most widely read journalist as well as among its most influential.

Millions read "On Broadway," his daily syndicated column that appeared locally in the old Daily Mirror. More millions listened to his weekly radio broadcasts. "WW," as he often styled himself, purveyed a mélange of intimate news about personalities, mostly in show business and politics; "inside" items about business and finance; bits and pieces about the underworld; denunciations of Italian and German Fascism; diatribes against Communism; puffs for people, stocks and events that pleased him.

Although Mr. Winchell was often demonstrably inaccurate or hyperbolic, he was implicitly believed by many of his readers and auditors. In clumsier hands, his "news" might not have had much impact, but he imparted a certain urgency and importance to what he wrote and said by the frenetic and almost breathless style of his presentation.

In Winchellese, a person could start life as "a bundle from Heaven," attend "moom pitchers" in his youth, then be "on the merge" or "on fire" and "middle-aisle it" or be "welded" to a "squaw." Later on, the couple might "infanticipate" and be "storked."

Although Mr. Winchell was often thought lacking in taste, he had friends in high and low places. Among those in exalted places were President Franklin D. Roosevelt and J. Edgar Hoover, director of the Federal Bureau of Investigation.

Mr. Winchell kept the President supplied with the latest Broadway jokes, and Mr. Roosevelt countered with news tidbits and encouragement for the columnist's vitriolic attacks on the "Ratskis," his name for the German Nazis and their American followers.

These attacks infuriated the Nazis, who publicly excoriated their author as "a new hater of the New Germany." They also disquieted William Randolph Hearst, a Hitler admirer and Mr. Winchell's boss.

Mr. Hoover and Mr. Winchell were frequent companions at Sherman Billingsley's Stork Club, a restaurant the columnist single-handedly made famous.

In 1939, in one of the most spectacular episodes of his career, Mr. Winchell was able to arrange the surrender of Louis (Lepke) Buchalter, a New York gangster, to Mr. Hoover. The hoodlum was wanted in New York on capital charges and by the Federal Government for narcotics smuggling. He telephoned Mr. Winchell, offering to give himself up to Mr. Hoover if the columnist were present.

Mr. Winchell picked up the gangster on a Manhattan street corner and delivered him to Mr. Hoover a few blocks away.

"Mr. Hoover," said the columnist, "this is Lepke."

"How do you do," said Mr. Hoover.

"Glad to meet you," said the hoodlum.

In his prime, Mr. Winchell loved to respond to police and fire calls, often arriving at the scene first. His car, courtesy of the police, was outfitted with a siren and a red light.

At a crime scene, according to Bob Thomas's authoritative "Winchell," he "interviewed victims and interrogated suspects, some of whom spilled out confessions because of awe over meeting" the columnist.

Mr. Winchell lived and worked in a free-spending atmosphere to which he himself was immune. Save for a Westchester house he bought to please his wife, "he lavished money on nothing," Mr. Thomas reported, adding:

"He hadn't the slightest inclination to art and other possessions. He owned eight suits, no more. He lived with utmost simplicity in an apartment which was useful only for sleeping. Every restaurant and nightclub owner in New York was eager to entertain him."

He kept his money in cash in bank vaults. On becoming a millionaire in 1937, he had the Colony Club cater him an elegant meal, which he ate alone.

The plates and napery of that lunch were far removed from the poverty in which the columnist was reared. Born in Manhattan on April 7, 1897, Walter was the elder son of Jacob and Janette Bakst Winchel—the son later added a second "L" to the name. Jacob left the family when Walter was young.

Walter picked up his first money as a newsboy. When he was 12 he made his debut in the entertainment world after getting a tryout as a singer. For two years, he toured with the Edwards revues in company with young George Jessel, Eddie Cantor, Lila

Lee and Georgie Price. Walter had quit school in the sixth grade.

In 1915, Walter teamed in a vaudeville act with Rita Green. In World War I, Mr. Winchell served as an admiral's receptionist in New York. Returning to second-rate vaudeville after the war, he began posting bulletins with gossip of the other entertainers.

Mr. Winchell and Miss Green were married in 1920—the union lasted two years—and he began to submit show business gossip columns to Billboard, an entertainment weekly, and later to The Vaudeville News, for which he went to work in 1922 as a reporter and advertising salesman. His column, "Stage Whispers," attracted attention, and he became known around Broadway as a bright and eager and very brash hustler.

In his rounds, he met June Magee, a red-haired dancer, whom he married in 1923. She died in 1970, reunited with her husband after a long estrangement.

After about two years on The Vaudeville News, Mr. Winchell was hired by The Evening Graphic, a bizarre tabloid that had been founded in 1924 by Bernarr Macfadden, an eccentric millionaire, food faddist and physical culture advocate. He was paid $100 a week.

One day in 1925, Mr. Winchell sat down and typed out a clutch of gossip notes he had acquired. The first few items read:

"Helen Eby Brooks, widow of William Rock, has been plunging in Miami real estate. . . . It's a girl at the Carter de Havens. . . . Lenore Ulric paid $7 income tax . . . Fanny Brice is betting on the horses at Belmont . . . S. Jay Kaufman sails on the 16th via the Berengaria to be hitched to a Hungarian . . . Report has it that Lillian Lorraine has taken a husband again . . ."

It was the prototype of Winchell columns for almost 40 years. Shortly "Your Broadway and Mine," the column's title then, was the backbone of The Graphic's circulation.

Leaving The Graphic in 1929 after repeatedly clashing with editors, Mr. Winchell moved to The Mirror. His first column appeared there June 10, 1929, and he was paid $500 a week.

In later years, the columnist moved to the far right politically. He became a champion of Senator Joseph R. McCarthy and wrote screeching anti-Communist columns.

Mr. Winchell's power started to wane in the late forties. Executives became more wary of him because he devoted so much time to feuds and vendettas. His column slipped from 800 papers to 175, and it virtually disappeared with the demise in 1963 of The Mirror.

Mr. Winchell, who had few friends, moved west in 1965 and for the last several years stayed at the Ambassador in Los Angeles. His son, Walter Jr., committed suicide in 1967.

KATHARINE GRAHAM

June 16, 1917–July 17, 2001

By Marilyn Berger

Katharine Graham, who transformed The Washington Post from a mediocre newspaper into an American institution and, in the process, transformed herself from a lonely widow into a publishing legend, died today in Boise, Idaho, where she had been hospitalized since being injured in a fall over the weekend. She was 84.

Mrs. Graham was one of the most powerful figures in American journalism and, for the last decades of her life, at the pinnacle of Washington's political and social establishments—a position that this shy, diffident wife and mother never imagined she would, or could, occupy.

It was only after she succeeded her father and her husband as publisher that The Washington Post, a newspaper with a modest circulation and more modest reputation, moved into the front rank of American newspapers, reaching new heights when its unrelenting reporting of the Watergate scandal contributed to the resignation of President Richard M. Nixon in 1974. Mrs. Graham's courage in supporting her reporters and editors through the long investigation was critical to its success.

A year before Watergate, she gave solid backing to The New York Times in a historic confrontation with the federal government when she permitted her editors to join in publishing the secret revelations about the war in Vietnam known as the Pentagon Papers.

Mrs. Graham capped her career when she was 80 years old in 1998 by winning a Pulitzer Prize for biography for her often-painful reminiscence, "Personal History." Nora Ephron, in her review of this best-selling memoir in The New York Times Book Review, wrote of Mrs. Graham, "The story of her journey from daughter to wife to widow to woman parallels to a surprising degree the history of women in this century."

She was born in New York City on June 16, 1917. Her father, Eugene Meyer, made his fortune on Wall Street and became the first president of the World Bank. Her mother, the former Agnes Ernst, was a tall, self-absorbed woman of intellectual and artistic ambition. She was scathingly critical and often harsh with her daughter, the fourth of five children.

Mrs. Graham remembered a solitary and lonely childhood in palatial houses in Mount Kisco, N.Y., and in Washington. Neither parent attended her graduation from the University of Chicago in 1938.

When Katharine was 16, no one thought to tell her that her father had bid $825,000 at public auction to buy the bankrupt Washington Post, a paper with a circulation of 50,000 that was losing a million dollars a year.

Washington, in 1939, was full of young people converging on the capital to work for the New Deal. Among them was Philip L. Graham of Florida, a brilliant lawyer and a clerk at the Supreme Court. Shy and insecure, Katharine Meyer could not believe her luck when he asked her to marry him. Mr. Graham soon accepted his father-in-law's invitation to join The Post. He became associate publisher at 30 and publisher at 31. Mr. Meyer also arranged for him to hold more stock in the company than his daughter because, he explained to her, "no man should be in the position of working for his wife."

Mrs. Graham was belittled and silenced by a husband she adored, the man she called "the fizz" in her life. When he drank too much, gave vent to his rage or frequently became ill, she attributed it to the pressure of his work and not to a serious emotional affliction that had not yet been identified.

Mr. Graham had his first breakdown in 1957. His recovery was slow, but he re-emerged into Washington life. In 1961, he negotiated the purchase of Newsweek magazine. He also added television stations to the company's holdings.

Mrs. Graham was shattered when she discovered that her husband was having an affair with a Newsweek employee. But there was an added blow: she discovered he had developed a scheme to pay her off and take ownership of The Post, in which he already had controlling interest because her father had given him the majority of the Post's class A shares.

But she resolved not to give her husband a divorce unless he gave up enough controlling stock to give her majority interest.

Mr. Graham became increasingly ill. Finally, his illness had a name, manic depression. In August 1963 he shot himself to death at their farm in Virginia.

As Mrs. Graham mourned, she sought ways to hold on to The Post. She wrote that she was startled when her friend Luvie Pearson, the wife of the columnist Drew Pearson, told her to run the paper herself. "Don't be silly, dear. You can do it," Mrs. Pearson told her. "You've got all those genes. . . . You've just been pushed down so far you don't recognize what you can do."

Mrs. Graham met with the paper's directors and told them that The Post would not be sold and that it would remain in the family. She was elected president of the company, but she felt "abysmally ignorant" about how to proceed. She said she was embarrassed to talk to her own reporters, timid in dealing with the paper's executives and uncomfortable with balance sheets. Both at The Post and in the wider journalistic community, Mrs. Graham was usually the only woman at meetings and dinners. The men hardly knew what to make of her.

Two years after taking over The Post, she appointed Benjamin C. Bradlee, Newsweek's Washington bureau chief, as executive editor. They made a formidable team, propelling The Post into one of its most dynamic periods. It became a breezy, gutsy paper that investigated government with gusto. A saucy, impertinent Style section appeared. In 1969, still with trepidation, Mrs. Graham added the title of publisher to that of president of the Washington Post Company.

In June 1971, The New York Times started publishing the secret history of decision-making during the Vietnam War known as the Pentagon Papers. After a few days, a federal judge put The Times under a temporary restraining order, the first time in American history that an order of prior restraint was imposed.

The Post scrambled and got its own copy. There was a crisis atmosphere, for the Washington Post Company was preparing an initial public offering of its stock, raising concerns that it could face retribution from federal regulators if it published the Papers while The Times was enjoined. Lawyers suggested waiting, fearing that the whole company was at stake. Mrs. Graham later wrote: "Frightened and tense, I took a big gulp and said, 'Go ahead, go ahead, go ahead. Let's go. Let's publish.'"

When the issue got to the Supreme Court, the cases for The Times and The Post were heard together, and the justices voted, 6 to 3, against restraining publication on the ground of endangering national security. The vote is considered a major triumph for freedom of the press.

On June 17, 1972, five men were caught breaking into the headquarters of the Democratic National Committee in the Watergate complex in Washington. The Post began an intense investigation by two little-known reporters, Bob Woodward and Carl Bernstein, that eventually connected the break-in to the White House.

In the course of the investigation, the licenses of two of the company's television stations were challenged. Mrs. Graham was also threatened with unspecified retaliation if The Post published an article that said John Mitchell, when he was attorney general, had controlled a secret fund that was used to spy on the Democrats. Mr. Mitchell crudely warned Mr. Bernstein that "Katie Graham" would have a breast "caught in a big fat wringer if that's published."

Mrs. Graham did not back down, and The Post's reporting on Watergate was vindicated.

In time, Mrs. Graham became comfortable with her power. She started to entertain the political elite at her home in Georgetown. By her 70th birthday party her power was such that the humor columnist Art Buchwald said in his toast: "There is one word that brings us all together here tonight. And that word is 'fear.'"

With the help of the women's movement, Mrs. Graham said, she became more cognizant of the causes of her own insecurities and more aware of the problems of working women. She played a signal role in changing Washington mores when it became widely known that on one evening after dinner she had refused to join the ladies upstairs while the men discussed world affairs over brandy and cigars.

Besides her son, Donald, Mrs. Graham is survived by her daughter, Elizabeth Weymouth, known as Lally; her sons William and Stephen; a sister, Ruth Epstein; 10 grandchildren and one great-grandchild.

Mrs. Graham's resolve on editorial questions often contrasted with indecisiveness on business matters. In the 1970's, she remembered, she hired and dismissed top executives too often. But, to cut costs, she dealt firmly with The Post's mechanical unions, and in October 1975 the pressmen went on strike. All 72 of the newspaper's presses were vandalized to make it impossible to publish.

But Mrs. Graham won the battle, and by the end of 1981, The Post's daily circulation had soared to 984,000 from 771,000.

Donald Graham succeeded his mother as publisher in 1979 and chief executive of the company in 1991. By then it was valued at nearly $2 billion.

Mrs. Graham stepped down as chairwoman in 1993, again to be succeeded by her son, but remained on the board as chairwoman of the executive committee.

She was on her way to a bridge game this weekend when she collapsed and never recovered. Her life ended the way she said she had wanted it to. "The only thing I think any of us want," she once said, "is to last as long as we're any good. And then not."

A. M. ROSENTHAL

May 2, 1922–May 10, 2006

By Robert D. McFadden

A. M. Rosenthal, a Pulitzer Prize–winning foreign correspondent who became the executive editor of The New York Times and led the paper's global news operations through 17 years of record growth, modernization and major journalistic change, died yesterday in Manhattan. He was 84.

His death, at Mount Sinai Medical Center, came two weeks after he suffered a stroke, his son Andrew, who is the deputy editorial page editor of The Times, said. Mr. Rosenthal lived in Manhattan.

From ink-stained days as a campus correspondent at City College through exotic years as a reporter in Europe, Asia and Africa, Mr. Rosenthal climbed on rungs of talent, drive and ambition to the highest echelons of The Times and American journalism.

Brilliant, passionate, abrasive, a man of dark moods and mercurial temperament, he could coolly evaluate world developments one minute and humble a subordinate in the next. He spent almost all of his 60-year career with The Times.

As a reporter and correspondent for 19 years, he covered New York City, the United Nations, India, Poland and Japan, winning acclaim for his writing. The Pulitzer was for international reporting in 1960, for what the Communist regime in Poland, which had expelled him, called probing too deeply.

Returning to New York in 1963, he became an editor. Over the next 23 years, he served as metropolitan editor, assistant managing editor, managing editor and executive editor, enlarging his realms of authority by driving his staffs relentlessly, pursuing the news aggressively and outmaneuvering rivals for the executive suite.

Mr. Rosenthal directed coverage of the major news stories of the era—the war in Vietnam, the Pentagon Papers, the Watergate scandal and crises in the Middle East.

Publication of the Pentagon Papers in 1971 was a historic achievement for The Times. The papers, a 7,000-page secret government history of the Vietnam War, showed that every administration since World War II had enlarged America's involvement while hiding the true dimensions of the conflict. But publishing the classified documents was risky: Would there be fines or jail terms? Would it lead to financial ruin for the paper?

The Nixon administration tried to suppress publication, and the case led to a landmark Supreme Court decision upholding the primacy of the press over government attempts to impose "prior restraint" on what may be printed. Major roles were played by Times staff members, among them Neil Sheehan, who had uncovered the papers. But it was Mr. Rosenthal as editor, arguing strenuously for publication, and Arthur Ochs Sulzberger, the publisher, who made the crucial decisions.

After 17 years as a principal architect of the modern New York Times, Mr. Rosenthal stepped down as the top editor in 1986 as he neared his job's mandatory retirement age of 65. He then began nearly 13 years as the author of a column, "On My Mind," for the Op-Ed page, in which he addressed topics with a generally conservative point of view. He surrendered it reluctantly.

Mr. Rosenthal's life and career were chronicled closely, and his personal traits and private and professional conduct were analyzed with fascination in gossip and press columns, in magazines and books, and in the newsrooms and bars where those who had worked for or against him told their tales of admiration and woe.

The extraordinary interest was rooted only partly in the methods, achievements and faults of a powerful figure in journalism; it came, too, from the man himself: a table-pounding adventurer who shattered the stereotype of the genteel Times editor with his gut fighter's instincts and legendary bouts of anger.

A gravel-voiced man with a tight smile, a shock of black hair and judgmental gray-green eyes behind horn-rimmed glasses, he was regarded by colleagues as complex, often contradictory. He saw himself as the guardian of tradition at The Times; but he presided over more changes than any editor in the paper's history.

As managing editor from 1969 to 1977 and as executive editor until 1986, he guided The Times through a transformation that brightened its sober pages, expanded news coverage, launched a national edition, won new advertisers and new readers, and raised the paper's sagging fortunes to unparalleled profitability.

By the end of the 1960's, The Times, despite a distinguished journalistic history, had a clouded future. Its reporting and writing were regarded as thorough but ponderous. Revenues were declining, profits were marginal, and circulation was stagnant. Mr. Rosenthal's objective was to erase a stodgy image and to improve readability and profitability while maintaining the paper's character.

He expanded the weekday paper from two to four parts and inaugurated new weekday feature sections, innovations that were highly popular with readers and advertisers. He also began a series of Sunday magazine supplements and a national edition of The Times.

ham developed osteomyelitis, a bone-marrow disease, in his legs. It left him in acute pain, able to walk only with a cane or crutches. Because of the family's poverty, he received inadequate medical treatment, and while encased in a cast from neck to feet he was told he might never walk again.

He was forced to drop out of DeWitt Clinton High School for a year. Accepted as a charity patient by the Mayo Clinic in Minnesota, he underwent operations and eventually recovered almost completely.

He later enrolled at City College, joined the school newspaper and discovered that he liked, and was good at, reporting. In 1943, he became the campus correspondent for The Times. Editors eyed him as a promising young reporter, and in February 1944 he was hired as a staff reporter at 21. He quit City College to devote himself to his new job. After two years of local reporting, he was assigned to cover the United Nations, and his byline began to appear on the front page.

In 1954, Mr. Rosenthal was assigned to New Delhi and for the next four years covered the Indian subcontinent. He quickly established himself as an outstanding foreign correspondent. He was perceptive, aggressive, and could write on deadline with grace. In 1958, he was transferred to Warsaw and covered Poland and other nations of Eastern Europe for two years.

Mr. Rosenthal's writing style was disarmingly personal: it was as if he had written a letter home to a friend. An article for The New York Times Magazine based on a visit to the Nazi death camp at Auschwitz, was typical.

"And so," he wrote, "there is no news to report from Auschwitz. There is merely the compulsion to write something about it, a compulsion that grows out of a restless feeling that to have visited Auschwitz and then turned away without having said or written anything would be a most grievous act of discourtesy to those who died there."

The 1959 dispatch that led to Mr. Rosenthal's expulsion called the Polish leader, Wladyslaw Gomulka, "moody and irascible," adding: "He is said to have a feeling of having been let down—by intellectuals and economists he never had any sympathy for anyway, by workers he accuses of squeezing overtime out of a normal day's work, by suspicious peasants who turn their backs on the government's plans, orders and pleas."

His expulsion order charged: "You have written very deeply and in detail about the internal situation, party and leadership matters. The Polish government cannot tolerate such probing reporting." Those phrases were cited by the Pulitzer committee when Mr. Rosenthal was awarded the prize for international reporting.

In 1963, after a two-year stint covering Japan, Mr. Rosenthal became an editor. His first assignment was command of a large, tradition-bound city news staff, not with the usual title of "city editor" but as "metropolitan editor," reflecting new authority that he had demanded

While many newspapers were struggling to stay alive, The Times prospered under Mr. Sulzberger and Mr. Rosenthal. Between 1969 and 1986, revenues of The New York Times Company soared, and net income rose to $132 million from $14 million. The Times and its staff members won 24 Pulitzers during Mr. Rosenthal's years as editor.

Mr. Rosenthal, assisted by top lieutenants, including the deputy managing editor Arthur Gelb, who was his closest friend, decided which articles would appear on page 1, thus helping to shape the perceptions of millions of readers, government and corporate policy makers and news editors across the country. He came to be regarded as the most influential newspaper editor in the nation, perhaps the world, with only Benjamin C. Bradlee of The Washington Post as a possible rival.

Press critics chronicled his rising fortune and the growing success of The Times. But they also described Mr. Rosenthal personally and as an administrator in generally unflattering terms and characterized his staff as rife with low morale.

Abraham Michael Rosenthal was born on May 2, 1922, in Sault Ste. Marie, Ontario, the son of Harry and Sarah Dickstein Rosenthal of Byelorussia. His father migrated to Canada in the 1890's and became a fur trapper and trader.

The Rosenthals had six children, five of them girls. Abraham was the youngest. When he was a boy, the family moved to the Bronx.

In the 1930's, a series of tragedies enveloped the family. Abraham's father died of injuries suffered in a fall, and four of his sisters died. As a teenager, Abra-

over a previously independent cultural news staff and a mandate for change throughout the newsroom.

He transformed the staff. Ignoring seniority, he began favoring the best writers, regardless of age; he began emphasizing investigative journalism and sent reporters out to capture the flavor and complexity of neighborhoods.

He encouraged his staff to abandon the stiff prose that had long characterized local news in The Times, and invited articles written with imagination, humor and literary flair. He assigned pieces on interracial marriage and other topics atypical for The Times.

One article assigned by Mr. Rosenthal, on New Yorkers' fear of involvement in crime, recounted the murder of Kitty Genovese, a Queens woman whose screams were reportedly ignored by 38 neighbors while her killer attacked her on a street for 35 minutes.

Mr. Rosenthal was named assistant managing editor in 1966 and associate managing editor in 1968. Later, as managing editor and executive editor, he often traveled abroad and spoke publicly on freedom of the press.

He is survived by his first wife, Ann Marie Burke, from whom he was divorced, and their three sons. He is also survived by his second wife, Shirley Lord, and by a sister and four grandchildren.

Mr. Rosenthal's final column for The Times was a summation of his life and career. He closed by saying that he could not promise to right all wrongs.

"But," he wrote, "I can say that I will keep trying and that I thank God for (a) making me an American citizen, (b) giving me that college-boy job on The Times, and (c) handing me the opportunity to make other columnists kick themselves when they see what I am writing, in this fresh start of my life."

WALTER CRONKITE

November 4, 1916–July 17, 2009

By Douglas Martin

Walter Cronkite, who pioneered and then mastered the role of television news anchorman with such plain-spoken grace that he was called the most trusted man in America, died Friday at his home in New York. He was 92.

The cause was complications of dementia, said Chip Cronkite, his son.

From 1962 to 1981, Mr. Cronkite was a nightly presence in American homes and always a reassuring one, guiding viewers through national triumphs and tragedies alike, from moonwalks to war, in an era when network news was central to many people's lives.

He became something of a national institution, with an unflappable delivery, a distinctively avuncular voice and a daily benediction: "And that's the way it is." He was Uncle Walter to many: respected, liked and listened to.

Along with Chet Huntley and David Brinkley on NBC, Mr. Cronkite was among the first celebrity anchormen.

Yet he was a reluctant star. He was genuinely perplexed when people rushed to see him rather than the politicians he was covering. He saw himself as an old-fashioned newsman—his title was managing editor of the "CBS Evening News"—and so did his audience.

As anchorman and reporter, Mr. Cronkite described wars, natural disasters, nuclear explosions, social upheavals and space flights, from Alan Shepard's 15-minute ride to lunar landings. On July 20, 1969, when the Eagle touched down on the moon, Mr. Cronkite exclaimed, "Oh, boy!"

On the day President John F. Kennedy was assassinated, Mr. Cronkite briefly lost his composure in announcing that the president had been pronounced dead at Parkland Memorial Hospital in Dallas. Taking off his black-framed glasses and blinking back tears, he registered the emotions of millions. It was an uncharacteristically personal note from a newsman who was uncomfortable expressing opinion.

"I am a news presenter, a news broadcaster, an anchorman, a managing editor—not a commentator or analyst," he said in an interview in 1973.

But when he did pronounce judgment, the impact was large.

In 1968, he visited Vietnam and returned to do a rare special program on the war. He called the conflict a stalemate and advocated a negotiated peace. President Lyndon B. Johnson watched the broadcast, Mr. Cronkite wrote in his 1996 memoir, "A Reporter's Life," quoting a description of the scene by Bill Moyers, then a Johnson aide.

"The president flipped off the set," Mr. Moyers recalled, "and said, 'If I've lost Cronkite, I've lost middle America.'"

Mr. Cronkite sometimes pushed beyond the usual two-minute limit to news items. On Oct. 27, 1972, his 14-minute report on Watergate, followed by an eight-minute segment four days later, "put the Watergate story clearly and substantially before millions of Americans" for the first time, the broadcast historian Marvin Barrett wrote in "Moments of Truth."

"From his earliest days," David Halberstam wrote in "The Powers That Be," his 1979 book about the news media, "he was one of the hungriest reporters around, wildly competitive, no one was going to beat Walter Cronkite on a story, and as he grew older and more successful, the marvel of it was that he never changed, the wild fires still burned."

Walter Leland Cronkite Jr. was born on Nov. 4, 1916, in St. Joseph, Mo., the son of Walter Sr., a dentist, and the former Helen Lena Fritsche.

As a boy, Walter peddled magazines door to door and hawked newspapers. As a teenager, after the family had moved to Houston, he got a job with The Houston Post as a copy boy and cub reporter.

Mr. Cronkite attended the University of Texas for two years, working on the school newspaper and picking up journalism jobs with The Houston Press. He left college in 1935 without graduating to take a job as a reporter with The Press.

While visiting Kansas City, Mo., he was hired by the radio station KCMO to read news and broadcast football games under the name Walter Wilcox. He was not at the games but received summaries of each play by telegraph, which provided fodder for vivid descriptions of the action.

At KCMO, Mr. Cronkite met an advertising writer named Mary Elizabeth Maxwell. The two read a commercial together. One of Mr. Cronkite's lines was, "You look like an angel." They were married for 64 years until her death in 2005.

In addition to his son, Walter Leland III, known as Chip, Mr. Cronkite is survived by his daughters, Nancy Elizabeth and Mary Kathleen, and four grandsons.

After being fired from KCMO in a dispute over journalism practices he considered shabby, Mr. Cronkite, in 1939, landed a job at the United Press news agency, now United Press International. He reported from Houston, Dallas, El Paso and Kansas City, and eventually became one of the first reporters accredited to American forces in World War II. He gained fame as a war correspondent, accompanying the first Allied troops into North Africa, reporting on the Normandy invasion and covering the Battle of the Bulge.

In 1943, Edward R. Murrow asked Mr. Cronkite to join his wartime broadcast team in CBS's Moscow bureau. In "The Murrow Boys: Pioneers on the Front Lines of Broadcast Journalism," Stanley Cloud and Lynne Olson wrote that Murrow was astounded when Mr. Cronkite rejected his $125-a-week job offer and decided to stay with United Press for $92 a week.

That year Mr. Cronkite was one of eight journalists selected for an Army Air Forces program that took them on a bombing mission to Germany aboard B-17 Flying Fortresses. Mr. Cronkite manned a machine gun until he was "up to my hips in spent .50-caliber shells," he wrote.

After covering the Nuremberg war-crimes trials and then reporting from Moscow from 1946 to 1948, he again left print journalism to become the Washington correspondent for a dozen Midwestern radio stations. In 1950, Murrow successfully recruited him for CBS.

Mr. Cronkite was assigned to develop the news department of a new CBS station in Washington. Within a year he was appearing on nationally broadcast public affairs programs like "Man of the Week."

In February 1953 he narrated the first installment of his long-running series "You Are There," which recreated historic events, like the Battle of the Alamo, and reported them as if they were breaking news.

"What sort of day was it?" Mr. Cronkite said at the end of each episode. "A day like all days, filled with those events that alter and illuminate our times. And you were there."

In 1952, the first presidential year in which television outshined radio, Mr. Cronkite was chosen to lead the coverage of the Democratic and Republican national conventions. By his account, it was then that the term "anchor" was first used—by Sig Mickelson, the first director of television news for CBS, who had likened the chief announcer's job to an anchor that holds a boat in place.

The 1952 conventions made Mr. Cronkite a star, and he went on to anchor every national political convention and election night until 1980, except in 1964. That year he was replaced at the Democratic convention in Atlantic City by Roger Mudd and Robert Trout in an effort to challenge NBC's Huntley and Brinkley team.

Mr. Cronkite replaced Murrow as CBS's senior correspondent in 1961, and on April 16, 1962, he began anchoring the evening news, succeeding Douglas Edwards. As managing editor, Mr. Cronkite helped shape the nightly report.

The evening broadcast had been a 15-minute program, but on Sept. 2, 1963, CBS doubled the length to a half-hour. Mr. Cronkite interviewed President Kennedy on the first longer broadcast, renamed the "CBS Evening News with Walter Cronkite." He also broadcast from a real newsroom and not, as Edwards had done, from a studio set.

Mr. Cronkite retired in 1981 at 64, to be replaced by Dan Rather. He continued to be seen on CBS as the host of "Walter Cronkite's Universe," a science series that ran from 1980 until 1982. After he spent 10 years on the board of CBS, more and more of his broadcast work appeared on CNN, National Public Radio and elsewhere.

His long "retirement" was not leisurely. When Senator John Glenn went back into space on the shuttle Discovery in 1998, 36 years after his astronaut days, Mr. Cronkite did an encore in covering the event for CNN. He made some 60 documentaries.

On his 90th birthday, Mr. Cronkite told The Daily News, "I would like to think I'm still quite capable of covering a story." He promised at the time to continue to follow news developments "from a perch yet to be determined."

"I just hope that wherever that is," he added, "folks will still stop me, as they do today, and ask, 'Didn't you used to be Walter Cronkite?'"

BEN BRADLEE

August 26, 1921–October 21, 2014

By Marilyn Berger

Ben Bradlee, who presided over The Washington Post's Watergate reporting that led to the fall of President Richard M. Nixon and that stamped him in American culture as the quintessential newspaper editor of his era—gruff, charming and tenacious—died on Tuesday at his home in Washington. He was 93.

Backed by his publisher, Katharine Graham, Mr. Bradlee led The Post into the first rank of American newspapers, making it a thorn in the side of Washington officials.

When they complained, Mr. Bradlee shielded his underlings. "Just get it right," he would tell them. Usually, they did, but there were mistakes, one so big that the paper had to return a Pulitzer Prize.

Mr. Bradlee—"this last of the lion-king newspaper editors," as Phil Bronstein, a former editor of The San Francisco Chronicle, said—could be classy or profane, an energetic figure with a boxer's nose who wore white-collared, bold-striped Turnbull & Asser shirts, with the sleeves rolled up.

When not prowling the newsroom, he sat behind a glass office wall, through which he could see his reporters and editors and they him. "We would follow this man over any hill, into any battle, no matter what lay ahead," his successor, Leonard Downie Jr., once said.

A former Newsweek reporter, Mr. Bradlee became deputy managing editor of The Post in 1965. Within three months he was managing editor, the second in command; within three years he was executive editor.

The Post had been a sleepy newspaper. To wake it up, Mr. Bradlee transformed the "women's" section into Style, a brash and gossipy overview of Washington mores. He built up the staff, determined that a Post reporter "would be the best in town on every beat," as he wrote in a 1995 memoir, "A Good Life: Newspapering and Other Adventures." He added, "We had a long way to go."

That became painfully clear to him in June 1971, when The Post was scooped by The New York Times on the Pentagon Papers, a secret government history of United States involvement in Vietnam. After The Times printed excerpts for three days, a federal court enjoined it from publishing any more, arguing that publication would irreparably harm the nation. The Post, meanwhile, had obtained its own copy of the papers and prepared to publish.

But The Post was on the verge of a $35 million stock offering, and publishing could have scuttled the deal. At the same time, Mr. Bradlee was under pressure from reporters threatening to quit if he caved in. Mrs. Graham decided to publish.

The government tried to muzzle The Post, as it had The Times, but the Supreme Court ruled in favor of both papers. The publication of the Pentagon Papers "forged forever between the Grahams and the newsroom a sense of confidence within The Post, a sense of mission," Mr. Bradlee recalled.

In 1972, The Post embarked on its biggest, most dangerous mission after a break-in at the Democratic National Committee headquarters in the Watergate complex on June 17, 1972. The burglary caught the attention of two metropolitan reporters, Carl Bernstein and Bob Woodward.

With the support of Mrs. Graham and Mr. Bradlee, and despite denials and threats from the Nixon administration, the young reporters explored a trail of secret funds, espionage, sabotage, dirty tricks and illegal wiretapping. When the trail led to the White House, Nixon resigned in August 1974.

The episode became the basis of a best seller, "All the President's Men," by Mr. Woodward and Mr. Bernstein, and the book became, in 1976, the basis of a Hollywood box-office hit.

Consumed by Watergate, Mr. Bradlee had been spending most of his waking hours at The Post when he started receiving what he called anonymous "mash notes." By this time, his second marriage, to the former Antoinette Pinchot, was cooling.

In 1973, Sally Quinn, an irreverent Style reporter, let him know that she was his secret admirer. But after another divorce, Mr. Bradlee was leery of a third marriage, telling a colleague that he would marry Ms. Quinn when the Catholic Church elected a Polish pope.

On Oct. 16, 1978, Cardinal Karol Wojtyla of Poland became pope; four days later, the couple were married.

Ms. Quinn survives him, as do their son, Quinn; three children from his previous marriages, Dominic, Benjamin Jr. and Marina Murdock; 10 grandchildren; and a great-grandchild. (Antoinette Pinchot Bradlee died in 2011.)

The Post's Watergate coverage won the 1973 Pulitzer Prize for public service. The Pulitzer was the 18th The Post received during Mr. Bradlee's tenure. There would have been 19 if The Post had not been compelled to return one awarded to a young reporter, Janet Cooke, for an article, titled "Jimmy's World," about an eight-year-old drug addict. Only after Ms. Cooke was given the prize was it discovered that she had fabricated the story (and some of her credentials).

Mr. Bradlee offered to resign but received the same support from Mrs. Graham's son Donald, who had become the publisher, as he had from Mrs. Graham.

Benjamin Crowninshield Bradlee was born in Boston on Aug. 26, 1921, the second son of Frederick Josiah Bradlee Jr. and Josephine de Gersdorff Bradlee. With his brother, Freddy, and a sister, Constance, he learned French, took piano lessons and went to the symphony and the opera. He was at St. Mark's School when he was stricken with polio. He exercised rigorously at home, and when he returned to school the next fall he had noticeably strong arms and chest and could walk without limping.

Continuing a family tradition, he attended Harvard, where he joined the Naval R.O.T.C. On Aug. 8, 1942, he graduated ("by the skin of his teeth," he wrote of himself) as a Greek-English major, was commissioned an ensign and married Jean Saltonstall. A month later, he shipped out to the Pacific on a destroyer and saw combat for two years.

After the war, Mr. Bradlee and a group of friends started The New Hampshire Sunday News, a weekly. When the paper was sold, he snagged his first job at The Washington Post, as a cub reporter, in 1948.

In 1951 he accepted the job of press attaché at the American embassy in Paris and left for France with his wife and young Benjamin Jr. He moved to Newsweek in 1954 as European correspondent based in Paris.

Around that time, his marriage was falling apart. It disintegrated when he met Antoinette Pinchot Pittman, known as Tony. They were married in 1957. A year later, Mr. Bradlee took up his post as the low man in Newsweek's Washington bureau.

He also took up residence in a Georgetown house next door to John F. Kennedy, then a young senator from Massachusetts. Thus began a rewarding and sometimes uneasy friendship.

Mr. Bradlee fell under pressure to separate what he learned as a Kennedy intimate from what he could use as a reporter. But his inside track on the Kennedy campaign for the White House in 1960 elevated him at Newsweek. He later said that Kennedy had been aware that he was keeping notes of their encounters; Mr. Bradlee published them in the 1975 book "Conversations with Kennedy."

As journalism changed and private lives became fair game, Mr. Bradlee answered criticism that he never reported on Kennedy's proclivity to jump "casually from bed to bed with a wide variety of women," as he put it. He insisted in his memoir that he knew nothing of Kennedy's sex life at the time, and that he was "appalled" by the details that emerged.

Concerned about rumors that Newsweek might be sold, Mr. Bradlee called Philip Graham, the publisher of The Washington Post, late one night and urged him to buy the magazine. On March 9, 1961, The Post acquired Newsweek, and Mr. Bradlee, soon to become the magazine's Washington bureau chief, was rewarded with enough Post stock, as a finder's fee, to live as a wealthy man.

Philip Graham committed suicide in August 1963, leaving his widow, Katharine, in charge of the family business. Two years later she was still finding her way at a newspaper that had been losing $1 million a year when she proposed that Mr. Bradlee become deputy managing editor. Thus began the bond that lasted until Mrs. Graham's death in 2001.

Mr. Bradlee remained with the paper for 26 years, stepping down in 1991 at age 70. He was awarded the Presidential Medal of Freedom, the country's highest civilian honor, in 2013.

In his memoir Mr. Bradlee said he had no overarching prescriptions for the practice of journalism. He recalled the motto of one of his grade-school teachers: "Our best today; better tomorrow."

"Put out the best, most honest newspaper you can today," he said, "and put out a better one the next day."

the Fathers of the Republic. They were precocious verses, having reference to the purpose of life, the destiny of man, the mission of beauty, half-dreamy, half-mystical, unconventional, very much, it must be confessed, like many of the poems he produced in his maturity. They were significant and supremely characteristic, showing the bent of his mind and the hue of his temperament. Above all, they were individual, and possessed a certain strength which is very rare in juvenile rhymes.

He was considered gifted but peculiar, and predictions were made—they were verified in his case—of his future celebrity. He evidently had the start, through inheritance, of most of his fellow-pupils, and contained the material from which thinkers are developed. He entered Harvard at 14 and was graduated at 18, having more general culture than proficiency in routine studies. One who knew him in those days has described him as "a slender, delicate youth, younger than most of his class-mates, and of a sensitive, retiring nature." His brother was in the Senior Class when he entered the Freshman, but, in spite of this, he made acquaintances slowly. For the noisy ways of the many he had a positive dislike, and it was only the more studious who finally sought him out. These found him unusually thoughtful and well-read, knowing, perhaps, less than they about text-books, but far more about literature. He had already studied the early English dramatists and poets; had pored over Montaigne, of whom he was afterward to write in the "Representative Men," while Shakespeare he knew almost by heart. He belonged to a club which subscribed for the reviews, including the young and struggling *North American*, and eagerly devoured, as they came out, the novels of Sir Walter Scott. Out of "Rob Roy" Emerson extracted the passage where Roy's wife condemns Morris to death, and used it with such good results for a declamation that many who heard it remembered it for half a century. He received a Bowdoin prize in his Junior year for an essay on "The Character of Socrates," and in his

Globe," a chara
cally handled.

Emerson delive
months later, fi
"Michael Angelo
cles largely mad
appeared in the M
"George Fox," r
read at Cambri
Kappa Society,
saturated with th
but abounding
without flashes o
Concord about th
for the remainde
Winter of 1835 h
ten lectures on
in succeeding
"Philosophy of
"Human Life,"
Times," and div
these have never
having always be
he put into print
book as a sacred
purest and best of
to enter. No
been so superlativ
ing publication.
should have every
ing trivial, passi
introduced into it
book should be
thought; that its
manner an additi
knowledge. Mos
their lectures and
cause they had w
could gain someth
Emerson was c
guild in this part
than members of
more pride, more
more confident ex
It is said that he
in this, and that
was universal and
fluence, and comp
smallest space,
example how in
have been redu
would shrink to d
hope of a tireless

THE
LITERARY WORLD

JAMES FENIMORE COOPER

September 15, 1789–September 14, 1851

James Fenimore Cooper, known throughout the world as the first of American novelists, died at his residence, at Cooperstown, on the 14th inst., at the age of 62. Born in 1789, at Burlington, N.J., and graduated at Yale College in 1805, he entered the Navy as Midshipman the next year, but after six years left the service. In 1811, he was married to Miss Delancey, sister of the Episcopal Bishop of Western New York, and soon after published his first novel, "Precaution," a tale of English Society. It was, however, a failure; but, "The Spy," which followed it, gave him rank at once, as one of the most brilliant novelists of the day. The public is familiar with his subsequent literary history.

After having given to the world a series of truly American novels—American in scenery, character and tone, and exalted American literature to a rank in European estimation which it had never before approached—he incurred the enmity of the American public, by censures of American manners. He had spent some years in Europe and, returning to the United States, published two or three books in succession, in which he held up, for censure and reform, those faults of his own countrymen, to which residence abroad had called his attention. The lesson, however well meant, was not well received. His books were savagely reviewed, and he, personally, was unsparingly denounced. He carried the contest from print to courts of law, and waged active war with the whole newspaper press. The result, of course, without regard to verdicts, was injurious to him, and for the last few years he has not been a favorite in the United States.

In Europe, and especially on the Continent, no American name stands higher than that of Cooper. The attendant at the Castle of Chillon, on the northern shore of Lake Geneva, points to his name upon one of the pillars of Bonnivard's dungeon, before any of the rest, except Byron's, and in every part of the Continent his name is known and honored. In England, his reputation as a writer is second only to that of Irving. He was not only a novelist, but a man of strong intellect, clear and quick in his apprehensions. His genius is one of which America should be proud.

NATHANIEL HAWTHORNE

July 4, 1804–May 19, 1864

The telegraph brings us the mournful and unexpected news of the death of the most charming of American novelists, and one of the foremost descriptive writers in the language. NATHANIEL HAWTHORNE was found dead in his bed yesterday morning, at Plymouth, N.H., where, in the companionship of one or more of his earliest friends, he was spending some days for the benefit of his health. Mr. HAWTHORNE was all but 60 years of age, having been born at Salem, Mass., on the 4th of July, 1804. Of his ancestry, the current biographies profess to find records in the witch-burning era of Salem, and by the same authorities, he is affiliated to a line of seafaring colonists who combined the pursuits of agriculture and commerce on a scale of uncertain magnitude, but with steady perseverance. The salient points in his private and official life are briefly these: His father having died at Havana in 1810, young HAWTHORNE was shortly afterward put under the charge of a farmer near Sebago Lake, Maine, chiefly with a view to the recruitment of his health, which was delicate. He entered Bowdoin College, Maine (where FRANKLIN PIERCE and GEORGE B. CHEEVER were his fellow-students) in 1825, and at the close of his collegiate career he settled at Salem. Fortune some time later (in 1838) found him a Government position as gauger in the Boston Custom-house, under Mr. BANCROFT, then the collector at that port during the VAN BUREN Administration. When the Whigs came into power in 1841, HAWTHORNE lost his appointment, and, conceiving (probably like SOUTHEY, COLLERIDGE and LOVELL) the idea of a pantocracy, he joined the famous Brook Farm Association, returning, however, fully satisfied with his experience of "a perfect state of society" to Boston in 1843. Here he married and made his home; subsequently for some years in "the Old Manse," at Concord, Mass.

His party affiliations again brought him official position and promotion, on the accession of the Polk Administration, and he received the appointment of Surveyor of the port of Salem. When the Whigs returned to power, HAWTHORNE returned to his retreat, and to his studies among the hills of Berkshire. Once again, in 1842, he was tendered and accepted office under Government—the Consulate at Liverpool, one of the most lucrative appointments in the gift of the President being placed at his disposal by Mr. PIERCE, partly, no doubt, as a tribute of long-standing personal friendship, and partly as a reward also for important service as a party penman. His remaining days, after his return from Liverpool, were spent at Concord.

HAWTHORNE's literary life commenced at Salem on the close of his college days. Leading for several years almost the life of a recluse, he here produced a series of sketches, tales and romances, some of which were found worthy of revival in his maturer years, under the title of Twice-Told Tales. Then followed, after his retirement from the Boston gaugership, the papers called Mosses from an Old Manse, succeeded by the most widely known of all his works, The Scarlet Letter, in 1850; by The House of Seven Gables, in 1851; by The Blithesdale Romance, in 1852; by The Marble Faun, in 1859; and by Our Old Home, his last work, in 1863. His minor sketches would be difficult of enumeration. They continued to grace the pages of the best contemporary periodicals, occasionally, up to the time of his death.

HAWTHORNE, in his sudden and comparatively early death, was saved the most awful of miseries that can befall the aspirant for permanent renown—that of seeing the honor and glory of youth extinguished in his own presence. The Force of Beauty and of Reason were conspicuous in all he did to the last. A profound apprehensiveness of truth, a deep sincerity and unvarying kindness uniformly to the end, restrained and modulated his facile humor; and probably no class of his admirers will be more deeply touched with the sad intelligence of his death than our cousins of the Old Home, whose national and social foibles receive such humorous treatment in the last important effort of his pen.

CHARLES DICKENS

February 7, 1812–June 9, 1870

LONDON—The London Globe, in its last edition this evening, startled the community with the announcement that Charles Dickens had been seized with paralysis and was lying insensible at his residence at Gads-Hill, near Rochester, in Kent.

But the worst was still to come. Mr. Dickens was at dinner on Wednesday when he was seized with a fit. Dr. Steele, who was the family physician, was immediately called in, and remained till nearly midnight. This morning several London physicians arrived at Gads-Hill. The case was at once pronounced hopeless, and the patient died at 6 1/4 o'clock this evening.

The death of Mr. Dickens has plunged the nation into mourning. The Times says: "The ordinary expressions of regret are now cold and conventional. Millions of people feel the personal bereavement. Statesmen, savants and benefactors of the race, when they die, can leave no such void. They cannot, like this great novelist, be an inmate of every house."

The death of Mr. Charles Dickens creates a greater gap in English literature than the loss of any other man could have occasioned. He was incomparably the greatest novelist of his time. At Gads-Hill, he was surrounded with everything that ordinarily makes life pleasant. He had abundant means, especially since his recent visit to the United States. "Troops of friends" constantly surrounded him when he desired their company.

Save in a literary sense, the life of Dickens was not eventful. With the exception of his visits to the United States and occasional journeys to the continent, he passed his life either at the desk or in those curious perambulations by which his immense variety of experience of English life was gained.

His home during boyhood appears to have been a happy one. The father, John Dickens, was a navy pay agent, and on February 7, 1812, at one of the stations to which duty called him, Charles was born. The war between France and Great Britain closing in 1815, John Dickens retired and subsequently moved to London.

That the life which the family led was not marked by a fair measure of prosperity, there is every reason to believe. When the time arrived for choosing an occupation, he was engaged as a reporter by the True Sun, and then by the Morning Chronicle. It was to this paper that he contributed his first literary efforts. He had already acquired considerable reputation as an accurate and rapid reporter, and his ability as an author became speedily recognized.

The "Sketches by Boz," published in 1836 and 1837, attracted considerable notice by their original vein of thought and reflection, and the powers of observation and good-natured sarcasm which they evinced. The story has become familiar to all of how Mr. Chapman, of the firm of Chapman & Hall, proposed to the young author a new undertaking, the description of adventures by a party of Cockney sportsmen, and of how the scheme resulted in the "Pickwick Papers." The sensation which the book produced was extraordinary.

Mr. Pickwick, Sam Weller and the rest of its characters became familiar at every fireside.

The book was finished in 1837, and Dickens then assumed the editorship of Bentley's Miscellany, in which was published, in 1838, his second novel, "Oliver Twist." In this work, as in Pickwick, the writer developed one characteristic that never left him. He wrote not only to amuse his readers but to effect a distinct purpose—the purpose of reforming some abuse. Pickwick assailed imprisonment for debt, and Oliver Twist the work-house system; and both blows were aimed with telling effect.

Next, in 1839, came Nicholas Nickleby, wherein "Yorkshire schools" received so overwhelming an exposure that the worst of the class ceased to exist. The story is by many regarded as his best in point of constructive ability, force of description and powerful delineation of character.

The next effort of Dickens's genius was Master Humphrey's Clock, which was published in weekly and monthly parts. The first design of the work was to make it a collection of stories, but the author lapsed into his old method of producing complete novels. The Old Curiosity Shop, which nearly forms the first volume of the Clock, therefore, came next in the list of his fictions. The strong interest felt in this story was manifested in a very striking manner, the author receiving countless letters begging him "not to kill little Nell," a request with which the exigencies of the plot did not permit him to comply.

On Jan. 22, 1842, Mr. Dickens arrived in Boston after a voyage of 18 days. He had been much gratified by the number of letters written to him from America on the loss of his children, and resolved that he would visit a country the people of which had shown so much sympathy and appreciation. This intention he announced in a letter to Mr. L. Gaylord Clark, editor of the Knickerbocker Magazine.

Soon after Mr. Dickens's arrival, Mr. Clark invited a number of gentlemen to meet him. In response to this invitation there were present W. Cullen Bryant, Washington Irving, and other celebrated men of the world of literature and art. Mr. Dickens gathered material for his American Notes, which, however, was not at the time generally regarded as a very happy effort of his pen.

In 1843–44 appeared Martin Chuzzlewit, and the Christmas Carol was brought out at the end of the first of these years. Mr. Dickens wrote Dombey and Son in 1847–48, a work which was as successful as any of its predecessors. David Copperfield was concluded in 1850. This book is frequently alluded to as a partial description of its author's own experiences. Whether this is the case is difficult to judge, although some of David Copperfield's struggles in his literary career constitute a parallel to those of Dickens himself. Bleak House, Hard Times, Little Dorrit, Great Expectations, Our Mutual Friend, A Tale of Two Cities, several Christmas books and miscellaneous stories complete a library of works such as no other man but Sir Walter Scott ever produced.

The last of the works of Charles Dickens is The Mystery of Edwin Drood, the issue of which he was not destined to see completed.

It was on Thursday, the 13th of April, 1861, that Charles Dickens made his first appearance as a public reader in St. James's Hall, London. The following sketch of him then is from the pen of one who was present and communicated his impressions to Harper's Magazine:

"Mr. Dickens appeared about 8 o'clock, dressed in a sumptuous manner. Thus, the nosegay at his buttonhole was a size larger, and several hues brighter, than that pleasant conceit of nature in fashionable circles is apt to be. And the area of frilled linen presented by his bosom was in extent great, and in whiteness out of the reach of suspicion. It was, moreover, studded with doubtless expensive and certainly showy buttons. In addition to which there was that in the tie of his white cravat which bespoke faculties of mind not developed, so far as I am aware, in any of the published works of the author."

The series was found to be profitable as well as popular, and was continued at intervals during the next year in all the chief towns of England, Ireland and Scotland. People flocked eagerly to see the greatest living writer of fiction, and Mr. Dickens began to realize the hold he had obtained over the hearts of his countrymen.

The immense popularity of the works of Mr. Dickens in this country, in spite of the feeling excited by the American Notes and Martin Chuzzlewit, induced him to try the experiment of a reading tour over the chief cities of the Union. On Tuesday, the 19th of November, 1867, he landed in Boston harbor, and on Monday, the 2nd of December, he made his first appearance before an American audience as a reader, in the Tremont Temple, where his reception was of the most enthusiastic kind.

The scene was repeated when, on the Monday following, he made his bow before a New York audience in Steinway Hall. Precisely at 8 o'clock the gas was turned up and Dickens appeared. Walking rapidly up to the desk, amid the waving of handkerchiefs and many-tongued hurrahs, he gracefully acknowledged the cordiality of his reception, placed a book before him, and then said: "Ladies and gentlemen, I shall have the honor of reading to you tonight A Christmas Carol, in four parts, the first part being 'Marley's Ghost.'"

The pressure of incessant engagements told upon the health of Mr. Dickens, and during the early part of 1868 he was compelled to take his physician's prescription of "instant rest." On Saturday, the 18th of April, he was the recipient of a tribute of respect such as no other man of letters has received in this country from his brethren of the pen. The New York Press Banquet was the spontaneous utterance of the warmest feelings of esteem and admiration, and was deeply felt by Mr. Dickens, who stated his acceptance of the compliment "in grateful remembrance of a calling that was once my own, and in loyal sympathy toward a brotherhood that I have never quitted."

On Monday, the 20th of April, 1868, Mr. Dickens bade farewell to America in his reading in Steinway Hall of the Christmas Carol and the trial from Pickwick. The great hall was crowded long before the hour of opening, and hundreds who had tickets of admission were compelled to go away without reaching even the vestibule of the building.

His coming on the platform was the signal for a great outburst of applause. He had no sooner finished than the entire audience rose and joined in hearty cheers, while the ladies waved their handkerchiefs and loud calls were made for a speech from the retiring reader. Mr. Dickens in response spoke as follows:

"Ladies and Gentlemen: The shadow of one word has impended over me all this evening, but the time has at length come when the shadow must fall. It is a short word, but its weight is not measurable by its length. Last Thursday evening while I read the story of David Copperfield, I felt that there was another meaning than usual in the words of old Mr. Peggotty, 'My future life lies over the sea.' . . . There has been on my part the most earnest attention to the work of preparation to entertain you, and on your part the kindest sympathy, which cannot be forgotten forever. I shall often recall you by the Winter fire of my home, or in the pleasant Summer of Old England—never as a public audience, but always as dear personal friends."

A perfect tempest of applause succeeded this address, and Mr. Dickens retired forever from an American audience. On Wednesday, the 22nd April, Mr. Dickens departed for Europe, carrying with him, it was said, a substantial result of his tour in the shape of the equivalent for $200,000 in gold.

Imagination was the source and secret of his power. His persons and scenes seem to stand out from the page, so vividly are they painted, and so minutely is every detail of surroundings and accessories filled in. The middle and lower ranks of English life are his favorite studies. He delighted to depict strange, old-world corners of London, moldy staircases and musty, cobwebbed chambers, where the din of the city is subdued to a dull hum, and where one might expect to encounter one of the original tenants in tiewig and gaiters. He was wonderfully familiar with the habits and phraseology of that strange compound, the London street-boy.

Ostlers, waiters and strolling players were equally congenial to his facile pen, and he could always extract wisdom, pathos, and humor from the most unlikely materials, and never failed to reach the man underneath all the strange wrappages that habit, speech and association might have flung around him. No better describer can be found of English scenery, whether among the trim hedgerows or on the breezy downs, amid the shimmer and rustle of the Woodlands, on the dank, gloomy expanse of the marshlands, or around the rock-bound and storm-beaten coast.

Some of his characters are little more than the impersonations of some ruling passion or habit—sometimes scarcely human in their villainy, or altogether elfish in their oddity. As an example of the intense contrasts in which Dickens delighted, no better example can be found than the plot and personages of the Old Curiosity Shop.

The tender, unaffected sentiment that inspired the narration of the death of Little Nell may be taken as a sample of the highest qualities of Dickens's mind, and stands unexcelled by anything in modern fiction. The scene is simply painted and simply told. The language well befits the story, and may almost compare with Pilgrims' Progress, or the English version of the New Testament. There is a subtle art in the way in which the narrative reveals the death-bed scene only in the dim consciousness of the half-witted old man, throwing a veil of soft mystery over the details and leaving the pure heroic spirit to ascend in solitude and silence to its God.

The peculiar humor of Dickens is embodied in passages and characters familiar as household words. His wonderful insight into the dim hopes and imaginings of child life shows a delicacy of perception which no living novelist has approached. He has pilloried some of the most notorious shams and abuses of the age in a way that has not a little hastened their removal. No man will deny that he brought a sympathetic heart to every mood and feeling of our human nature and limned tenderly and honestly all that he thought made man and woman more noble, generous and true.

GUSTAVE FLAUBERT

December 12, 1821–May 8, 1880

The death is announced, from Paris, of Gustave Flaubert, the French novelist. He was born at Rouen Dec. 12, 1821.

He began the study of medicine, but soon abandoned it and turned his attention to literature. His first novel—"Madame De Bovary"—was published in 1857. This met with much success, partly because of legal proceedings taken against its author on the ground of its immorality. These proceedings, however, fell to the ground. He published, in 1862, "Salammbo," a novel which embodied the results of his explorations about Carthage. Among his later works is "L'Education Sentimentale, Histoire d'un Jeune Homme," in two volumes, published in 1869. He was made a Chevalier of the Legion of Honor in 1866.

GEORGE ELIOT

November 22, 1819–December 22, 1880

A dispatch from London announces the fact that Mrs. Cross (George Eliot), the distinguished novelist, died at 10 o'clock Wednesday night.

Mrs. Cross was seized with a sudden chill, which attacked her on Sunday last. The attack, however, did not give serious cause for alarm until 6 o'clock Wednesday evening, and she passed away quietly.

George Eliot's life was distinctively a literary and domestic one. Moreover, she always strived to keep herself in the background. There is, therefore, both little to tell, and a lack of authoritative information. But of gossip, there has of late years been an endless flood.

She was born in Warwickshire, England, about 1820, and her maiden name was Mary Ann (or Marian) Evans. Her father was a clergyman, and a graduate of Oxford. His means were insufficient to educate her liberally, but that obstacle was removed, according to one report, by his receiving a small legacy, and, according to another, by her virtual adoption by a wealthy clergyman.

She well repaid the efforts spent upon her. George Henry Lewes once noted that she was mistress of seven languages. In music she was an expert performer of both simple ballads and classical compositions. Of the range of her literary reading it is scarcely necessary to speak, while her proficiency in philoso-

phy and metaphysics was evidenced by her earliest labors as a writer.

At 23 she went to London. She was anxious to be independent of her benefactor, and she felt that she could and must write. She began her career as an essayist and translator, writing for the influential reviews, the Edinburgh, Fraser's, Blackwood's and especially the Westminster, of which, when she was barely 27, she was assistant editor under Dr. Chapman, under whose roof she lived.

Her first sustained work was a translation of Strauss's "Leben Jesu" ("Life of Christ"), which appeared in 1846. Meanwhile she continued her magazine work, and by it was brought into acquaintance with John Stuart Mill, Matthew Arnold, Herbert Spencer, and others. Doubtless to these friendships, as well as to her own strength of mind and studies of German theology, may be traced the emancipated views which gave her such freedom from the usually accepted dicta of society on such matters as religion and the relations of men and women.

Up to this time she had never ventured on fiction. "I wrote reviews for years," she once said, "because I knew too little of human nature to write a novel." She was 37 when she published in Blackwood's a series of stories bearing the heading "Scenes of Clerical Life," and the signature "George Eliot." They attracted attention at once, and curiosity was rife as to the author. The signature was believed to be a pen-name.

Charles Dickens was the only one who guessed the sex of "George" and he wrote to the publisher a private letter praising "her" genius. There then appeared in print the following letter, which asked:

"If the act of publishing a book deprives a man of all claim to the courtesies usual among gentlemen? If not, the attempt to pry into what is obviously meant to be withheld (his name), and to publish the rumors which such prying may give rise to, seems to me quite indefensible; still more so to state those rumors as ascertained truths. I have the honor to be, Sir, yours, &c., GEORGE ELIOT."

"Scenes of Clerical Life" was followed in 1859 by "Adam Bede," a book with nothing on the title-page to show the identity of the writer. "Adam Bede" fixed her status as a literary star, and she now added to her list of friends Dickens and Thackeray. Then followed, in rapid succession, "The Mill on the Floss" (1860), "Silas Marner" (1861), "Romola" (1863), "Felix Holt, the Radical" (1866), "Middlemarch" (1871), "Daniel Deronda" (1876), and "The Impressions of Theophrastus Such" (1879). Her poetical works are "The Spanish Gipsy" (1868) and the "Legend of Jubal" (1874).

Her writings have been very profitable. For "Scenes in Clerical Life" she received only $1,500. But for "Adam Bede" she got about ten times as much. For "The Spanish Gypsy" she got $20,000, which is rather more than her publishers got back from the public. Her entire earnings have been estimated at $250,000.

It now only remains to speak of her relations with Mr. Lewes and Mr. Cross, and of her personality. She was called Mrs. Lewes, and she lived with Mr. Lewes as his wife from shortly after "Adam Bede" appeared until his death in 1878. But she was never his wife. The reason usually given for the non-performance of the marriage ceremony is that Mr. Lewes was already married and a divorce was impossible.

But Mr. Moncure D. Conway has denied all this. According to him, the literary pair never felt any anxiety as to how the world viewed their unconventional conduct. After suddenly disappearing from London together to take a trip on the Continent, they returned to live under the same roof.

It is said that his love was purely platonic. Be that as it may, the union, from every point of view but a conventional one, was perfect, and their Sunday evening receptions were as well attended as any similar gatherings in London. When at Mr. Lewes's death she mourned as a wife for her husband, there was not one discordant note in the chorus of sympathy which was tendered her in this country.

Her widowhood was a brief one. Mr. Lewes died on Dec. 1, 1878, and in the London Times of May 7 of this year appeared the following: "On the 6th at St. George's Hanover-square, John Walter Cross, of Weybridge, Surrey, to Mary Ann Evans Lewes, of the Priory, North Bank, Regent's Park." She signed the marriage register "spinster."

Here was a double shock. The "High Priestess of Positivism" was married in the most fashionable church in London, and thus conclusively negatived any excuses which had been made for her earlier venture on the ground of her transcendental theories of marriage.

Mr. Cross was then under 40, and his wife about 60. He is a banker and is said to be handsome, attractive, and intelligent. It is safe to say that George Eliot received more sneers and harsh criticism for her marriage than for her dispensing with it.

Mrs. H. M. Field has given a description of George Eliot's home and personality perhaps as good as any other: "In this beautiful suburb (Regent's Park, London) stands the home of the author of 'Adam Bede.' Enter the gate and you see a square house of two stories, with no architectural pretensions, but yet which has about it an air of taste which is very attractive. There is nothing pretentious.

"The furniture is simple and modest, yet there is harmony of color which pleases the eye. All this the eye takes in at a glance before it rests on the mistress of this charming English home. No one who had ever seen her could mistake the large head (her brain must be heavier than most men's) covered with a mass of rich auburn hair. At first I thought her tall, for one could not think that such a head could rest on an ordinary woman's shoulders.

"Her manners are very sweet, because very simple and free from affection. Never did a sweeter voice fascinate a listener, so soft and low one must almost bend to hear.

"She does not engross the conversation, but is more eager to listen than to talk. She makes you forget the celebrated author and think only of the refined and highly cultivated woman.

"There is a singular earnestness about her, as if those mild eyes looked deep into the great, sad, awful truths of existence. To her, life is a serious reality, and the gift of genius a grave responsibility."

What has been written here is as full and accurate as can be furnished from any except personal sources of information. Nevertheless, much discredit attaches to everything which has appeared in print about the subject of this sketch, as will appear from the following letter:

THE PRIORY, Jan. 25, 1877

DEAR SIR: Mrs. Lewes never reads articles written about herself. In reply to your question, beg to assure you that every single detail in it is wholly Imaginary—birth, parentage, education, and history are not distorted or exaggerated, they are totally wide of all resemblance to the facts.

"One single point will suffice. Mr. Herbert Spencer is said to have been her instructor, and taught her languages. Had the writer troubled himself to make the slightest inquiry, he would have learned that Mr. H. S. knows very little of one language besides his own, whereas she, before she knew him, was mistress of seven. Yours truly, G. H. LEWES.

HERMAN MELVILLE

August 1, 1819–September 28, 1891

Herman Melville died yesterday at his residence, 104 East 26th Street, this city, of heart failure, aged 72. He was the author of "Typee," "Omoo," "Moby-Dick," and other seafaring tales, written in earlier years. He leaves a wife and two daughters, Mrs. M. B. Thomas and Miss Melville.

There has died and been buried in this city, during the current week, at an advanced age, a man who is so little known, even by name, to the generation now in the vigor of life that only one newspaper contained an obituary of him, and this was but three or four lines. Yet 40 years ago the appearance of a new book by Herman Melville was esteemed a literary event, not only throughout his own country, but so far as the English-speaking race extended.

To the quarterly British reviews of that time, the author of "Typee" was the most interesting of literary Americans, and men who made few exceptions to the British rule of not reading an American book not only made Melville one of them, but paid him the further compliment of discussing him as an unquestionable literary force.

Yet when a visiting British writer a few years ago inquired at a gathering in New York of distinctly literary Americans what had become of Herman Mel-ville, not one among them was able to tell him. In fact, scarcely one among them had ever heard of the man, albeit that man was then living within a half mile of the place of the conversation.

Years ago the books by which Melville's reputation had been made had long been out of print and out of demand. The latest book, now about a quarter of a century old, "Battle Pieces and Aspects of the War," fell flat, and he has died an absolutely forgotten man.

This speedy oblivion by which a once famous man so long survived his fame is almost unique, and it is not easily explicable. Of course, there are writings that attain a great vogue and then fall entirely out of regard. But this is almost always because either the interest of the subject matter is temporary, and the writings are in the nature of journalism, or the workmanship to which they owe their temporary success is the product of a passing fashion.

This was not the case with Herman Melville. Whoever turns back now to the books that were so much read and talked about 40 years ago has no difficulty in determining why they were then read and talked about. The difficulty will be rather to discover why they are read and talked about no longer. The total eclipse of what was then a literary luminary seems like a wanton caprice of fame.

Melville was a born romancer. One cannot account for the success of his early romances by saying that in the Great South Sea he had found and worked a new field for romance, since evidently it was not his experience in the South Sea that had led him to romance, but the irresistible attraction that romance had over him that led him to the South Sea. He was able both to feel and interpret that charm, as it never had been interpreted before, as it never has been interpreted since.

It was the romance and mystery of the great ocean and its groups of islands that made so alluring to his own generation the series of fantastic tales in which these things were celebrated. "Typee" and "Omoo" and "Mardi" remain for readers of English the poetic interpretation of the Polynesian Islands and their surrounding seas.

Melville's pictorial power was very great. It is this power which gave these romances such a powerful hold upon readers.

It is almost as visible in those of his books that are not professed romances, but purport to be accounts of authentic experiences—in "White Jacket," the story of life before the mast in an American man-of-war; in "Moby-Dick," the story of a whaling voyage. The imagination that kindles at a touch is as plainly shown in these as in the novels, and few readers who have read it are likely to forget Melville's poetizing of the prosaic process of trying out blubber in his description of the old whaler wallowing through the dark and "burning a corpse."

Nevertheless, the South Pacific is the field that he mainly made his own, and that he made his own beyond rivalry. That this was a considerable literary achievement there can be no question.

For some months a contemporaneous writer, of whom nobody will dispute that he is a romancer and a literary artist, has been working in the same field, but it cannot seriously be pretended that Mr. Stevenson has taken from Herman Melville the laureateship of the Great South Sea. In fact, the readers of Stevenson abandon as quite unreadable what he has written from that quarter.

WALT WHITMAN

May 31, 1819–March 26, 1892

PHILADELPHIA—Walt Whitman, the poet, died at 6:43 o'clock this evening at his home, 328 Michel Street, Camden, N.J.

The end was peaceful. The aged poet, when asked by the physician if he felt any pain, answered in an almost inaudible tone, "No."

Mr. Whitman, who was 72, had been in bed since the 17th day of last December, when he was taken sick with pneumonia.

The remains of the poet will be placed in the recently completed tomb in Harleigh Cemetery, on the outskirts of Camden, a spot selected by Mr. Whitman when he was well.

When asked why he selected such a spot, he replied: "I would rather go in the woods."

In his slender volume of verse and prose issued this year by David McKay in Philadelphia, Walt Whitman bade his strange, unromantic and yet imposing Muse farewell:

> Good-bye my Fancy!
> Farewell, dear mate. dear love!
> I'm going away I know not where.
> Or to what fortune, or whether
>   I may ever see you again.
> So good-bye, my Fancy.
> Now for my last—let me look back a
>   moment;
> The slower, fainter ticking of the clock is
>   in me.
> Exit, nightfall, and soon the heart-thud
>   stopping.

This is from what he called the second annex to "Leaves of Grass," for the old poet was prone to linger over what he felt to be his masterpiece and add to it touch after touch. With Whitman, indeed, inspiration did not come with a rush; he brooded on his matter, perhaps because of a defective early education, which made him a laborious composer, but the efforts he made to overcome his disadvantages of training brought him to a pitch of originality attained by few poets of the century.

In the passing away of a writer whom his admirers loved to call the Good Gray Poet, the City of New York has lost the most remarkable literary character since Washington Irving.

Whitman was a New York poet in more ways than one. His birthplace was Long Island; his home for many years alternately Brooklyn or New York, and his heart at all times was centerd on our great, vibrating hive of a city. But New York never cared for Walt Whitman or bought or read his books. Probably very few New Yorkers have seen the poem which speaks of

> Manhattan streets with their powerful
>   throbs, with the
>   beating drums, as now
> The endless, noisy chorus, the
>   rustle and clank of muskets,
>   (even the sight of the wounded,)
> Manhattan crowds,
>   with their turbulent musical chorus,
>   with varied chorus and light of the
>   sparkling eye.
> Manhattan faces and eyes forever for
>   me.

The reason was that Whitman, whose smooth early verses had pleased the crude literary tastes of the readers of newspapers in the early half of the century, sprang with a bound far beyond their comprehension when he learned to disdain the fetters of ordinary rhythms and the chains of rhyme.

Born at West Hills, L.I., in a farmhouse within sight and sound of the ocean, on the 31st of May, 1819, Walter Whitman received a strain of Holland blood from his mother and of English from his father, who was a carpenter and housebuilder.

In 1823 the Whitmans moved to Brooklyn, and in 1832 the boy was taken from school and put in the office of a lawyer, then in that of a physician and finally into a printing office to do errands and odd jobs. There he set type, an accomplishment that stood him in stead all his life; for it gave him the chance to reach the ear of the public when no publisher would issue his poems. He later began to teach school, thus getting an opportunity to learn something while posing as an instructor. After

two years of this he started at Huntington, L.I., a paper called the Long Islander.

In 1847 and 1848 he edited the Brooklyn Eagle, but quarreled with the proprietor on politics. By 1854 he had struck the peculiar vein which delights a comparative few, is not understood by the multitude, and proves a stumbling block to those who feel strongly on the subject of convention in literary and social matters.

Whitman seems to have been profoundly shocked by the hypocrisy of men and women of our race and time, and the revulsion showed itself in his style. From a dry, anxious, and colorless versification he turned to a turgid, warm, overloaded method, in which he sought to unite the best of prose and poetry, retaining the elasticity of prose, and yet not losing the artificial helps of verse. In so doing rhyme had to be sacrificed and rhythm changed to a largely unconventional movement.

The enormous size of the Union and the crude, turbulent life of the Commonwealths growing like magic along the tremendous waterways of North America fired his imagination. He appeared in his new phase—as champion of democracy and lover of all mankind—in the year 1855, when a slim quarto, called "Leaves of Grass," appeared in New York, including but 12 poems. Needless to say it was to a large extent printed by himself. The next edition was in 1856, with 384 pages and 32 poems, and the third in 1860, with 456 pages.

Whitman's first two editions were hardly noticed; the third was published at Boston by Eldridge & Co. But the outbreak of the rebellion gave little leisure for literary quarrels. True to the gospel he had begun to preach, and with too much Quaker blood in his veins to enlist as a soldier, sympathizing deeply with the spirit of the people in the first years of the war, Whitman in 1862 left New York to nurse and help the sick and wounded at the hospitals in and about Washington. He has left the record of his ministrations in later editions of "Leaves of Grass," but more particularly in the prose "Memoranda During the War," published in "Two Rivulets."

Friends of Whitman who knew him in Washington during the war, where he held clerkships in the Department of the Interior and the Attorney General's office, speak of him as a good comrade, who seemed anxious to make himself conspicuous by a peculiar dress—broad hat and semi-military cloak.

There was also in his mind the same impulse to throw aside conventions as well as clothes. Whitman sang his own body and liked to speak of the nude; he had a fixed idea that the hairy breast is the breast of the powerful man. It must be remembered that at that time the literary ideals of the United States ran toward pallor, stooping shoulders, and a minute learning in the classical tongues.

The dismay which such utterances cast among the fastidious and romantic who fed on Tennyson and Wordsworth and swooned at the sound of an Americanism may well be left to the imagination.

Whitman liked the incense of public recognition so well that his dress and behavior on the street often appeared to be calculated to ensure conspicuousness. But in his intercourse with men and women he impressed his own personality at all times, often rousing great affection, and in many cases lifelong friendships resulted.

His odd dress—wide-open flannel shirt, wide trousers, broad-brimmed soft hat, and thick stick—prejudiced against him many persons who thought that he was merely a vain fellow. Many, also, who took the trouble to read his verse were repelled by the apparent lawlessness of versification and the tremendous heaping up of epithets, repetitions, and eccentric grammar. And a goodly number of readers fell away when they came to read the passages in which Whitman contends like an inspired physiologist for the beauty, dignity and poetry of functions and organs not mentioned save in medical works.

Whitman's great strength and his great weakness was generalization. He strikes it in the first lines of "Leaves of Grass:"

One's self I sing—a simple, separate person.

But while these bards sang of old heroes and the tribal chief of the day, Whitman was under the influence of his own land and century.

The inchoate aspirations after freedom, the rude, unmannerly, boisterous behavior of youth, the tremendous reaching out after some nebulous but gigantic ideal of the future which characterized the town populace of these States up to the time that the Civil War made blood to flow are wonderfully reflected in the greater part of "Leaves of Grass." That book also explores the war fever of 1861, and here again Whitman responded to the national movement with the section called "Drum-Taps," in which are found lyrics of surpassing dignity, beauty, and thrilling grandeur, bearing that stamp of simplicity which is beyond all praise.

Whitman's bigness of heart is not merely claimed in a hundred poems, but shown in many moving passages, such as that describing the body of a fallen woman in the Morgue. The love of man for man, as well as man for woman, forms a striking element in his creed; but, indeed, with Whitman, love reaches out beyond humanity and embraces the cosmos with the same passionate affection with which he regards a blade of grass.

Since the rebellion Walt Whitman has occupied a strange position in letters. He contracted hospital malaria at Washington which in 1873 brought on a paralytic attack, from which he was long in recovering. But as early as 1864 the portions of his poems which were thought by many indecent got him into trouble. Secretary Harlan removed him from his clerkship while he was at work on one of his noblest efforts, "President Lincoln's Funeral Hymn," a most exquisite piece, beginning "When lilacs last in the dooryard bloom'd."

In 1865, 1866, 1867, and 1870 he reprinted "Leaves of Grass," continually adding, classifying, and changing the contents to suit his widening ideas.

But from 1855, when his first venture appeared, Whitman was attacked in the public press on the score of immorality. He clung to the idea of "telling all" and was not disheartened by the assaults of those who disbelieve in calling a spade a spade. In 1870 appeared the "Passage to India," poems, and "Democratic Vistas," prose.

Till 1873, when he was paralyzed, he retained his second clerkship at Washington, and after recovery in 1879 traveled in Colorado, Kansas, and Missouri. After the Osgood firm declined to go on with the printing of "Leaves of Grass," Whitman took the stereotyped plates and began to publish for his own account at Camden.

It is impossible to forecast what Whitman's place in American literature is going to be. He represents, as no college graduate and scholarly man has hitherto, the great bulk of the Nation educated in common schools. Yet the people will have none of him, unless it be a jewel from "Drum-Taps," or a rhapsody entirely free from physiological theories like that beginning, "Out of the cradle endlessly rocking," a threnody on a forsaken mockingbird, which ranks with the greatest productions of genius in English.

At any rate, posterity is not going to judge him as harshly as some of the virtuous of today have done, for how can the men of the future fail to be won over by a man who believes so rapturously in the essential goodness of all created things—even of that pit, the soul of man? In one of the notes which run in small type at the foot of the pages of "Two Rivulets," the poet, apparently staggered by the attempt to understand himself or his real object, hazards this opinion: "Probably, indeed, the whole of these varied songs, and all my writings, both volumes, only ring changes in some sort, on the ejaculation. How vast, how eligible, how joyful, how real, is a Human Being, himself or herself!"

ALFRED LORD TENNYSON

August 6, 1809–October 6, 1892

LONDON—Lord Tennyson died at his home, Aldworth, near Haslemere, Surrey, at 1:35 o'clock this morning.

Sir Andrew Clark, one of the physicians who attended the poet laureate, said that Lord Tennyson's death was the most glorious he had ever seen. There was no artificial light in the room, and the chamber was almost in darkness, save where a broad flood of moonlight poured in through a western window. The moon's rays fell across the bed upon which the dying man lay, bathing him in their pure pellucid light and forming a Rembrandt-like background to the scene. All was silent save for the soughing of the Autumn wind as it gently played through the trees surrounding the house, a fitting requiem for the poet who sang of love and the beauties of nature.

All the members of the family were by the bedside, and Sir Andrew Clark remained with him from the moment of his arrival yesterday until the poet breathed his last.

So gentle and painless was his passing away that the family did not know he had gone until Dr. Clark broke the news to Lady Tennyson, who bore the closing scenes of her great trial well, in spite of her extremely delicate health.

The Hon. Hallam Tennyson, the poet's son, says that his father's death was peaceful. He did not show a single trace of suffering to distress his sorrowing relatives and friends. Once or twice during the night he lifted his eyes to the faces of the watchers by his bedside and a beautiful smile played over his features. No doubt as to the future was in his wan face, and as the end came he appeared to fall asleep.

Lord Tennyson spoke to his wife about an hour before he died, and his words to her were the last he uttered. Lady Tennyson bent over her dying husband and he whispered a few words to her.

His features in death bear a look of absolute peace. The body lies on the bed in which he died. He looks 15 years younger than before death, the lines and wrinkles of the face being less apparent. The beard, which was unkempt in life, has been carefully trimmed; the hands are folded over the chest, a laurel wreath crowns the head and another lies at the feet. The coverlet over the body is almost hidden beneath the flowers which have been placed upon it. Burning wax tapers lend a subdued light to the chamber.

The Bishop of Winchester will preach the funeral sermon in the Haslemere Church on Sunday.

The Canon of Westminster Abbey has formally invited Hallam Tennyson to bury his father in Westminster Abbey.

ROBERT LOUIS STEVENSON

November 13, 1850–December 3, 1894

London—A dispatch to The Star, dated Apia, Samoa, Dec. 8, confirms the report that Robert Louis Stevenson, the novelist, died suddenly a few days ago from apoplexy at the age of 44. His body was buried on the summit of Paa Mountain, 1,300 feet high.

The Westminster Gazette says that there is little doubt that his untimely end was due to apoplexy, induced by the heat of the climate. He left a new novel half completed. The Gazette says he was among the most lovable of modern writers, and the news of his death will be heard with the keenest regret. Perhaps no author of recent years has enlisted so much personal interest on the part of his readers.

The Pall Mall Gazette says that in letters recently written Mr. Stevenson said he had two novels practically completed, but could not be induced to part with them until they had received finishing touches. One is entitled "The Chief Justice's Clerk," the plot of which was foreshadowed in "Catriona." Those who have read portions of this work regard it as his masterpiece. The other book, entitled "St. Ives," is the story of a French prisoner who made his escape from Edinburgh Castle and had stirring adventures in a ro-

mantic district of Scotland. Mr. Stevenson had many shorter tales sketched out. He loved Samoa better than any other place, except Scotland. His wife, interviewed recently, said: "We mean to live in Samoa always and leave our bones there."

Robert Louis Balfour Stevenson was a native of Edinburgh, Scotland, and the date of his birth was Nov. 13, 1850. For many years his father, Thomas Stevenson, was an Inspector of Lighthouses. When he died, in 1888, his son wrote a sketch of his life, and one of his son's books was dedicated to him.

Of his Scotch origin Stevenson was always proud. "You have to learn," he said, "the paraphrases and the Shorter Catechism; you generally take to drink; your youth, so far as I can find out, is a time of louder war against society, of more outcry and tears and turmoil than if you were born, for instance, in England. But, somehow, life is warmer and closer, the hearth burns more redly, the lights of home shine softer on the rainy street, the very names endeared in verse and music cling nearer round our hearts."

Stevenson's father intended him for a lawyer, and carefully educated him at private schools and at the University of Edinburgh. He went far enough with his legal studies to be entered at the Scottish bar, and then changed the whole course of his life. He began to travel for his health, and in this found such enjoyment that he took to writing of the things he saw.

His first published books, from 1878, immediately won him praise for their rare humor, great insight, refined feeling, and splendid powers of fresh description. But "Treasure Island," in 1883, widened and deepened his fame everywhere. The book is said to have had its origin in a suggestion made to the author by a small boy, who repeatedly had asked him why he did not write something interesting, like "Robinson Crusoe." Although especially a book for boys, this work gave quite as much pleasure to folks grown to man's estate.

Mr. Stevenson's first visit to America had been made before "Treasure Island" appeared. In the Summer of 1879 he determined to make a voyage from Liverpool to New York in the steerage, and on arrival here he concluded to continue the journey on land in an immigrant car as far as San Francisco. It was an odd mode of travel for one with Stevenson's refinement and sensitive spirit, but with him love of adventure has ever been one of the strongest passions. Out of the trip he got a series of magazine papers, and some years later a book, "The Silverado Squatters; a Sketch from a California Mountain," which had to do with a deserted mining camp in the southern part of the State. Mr. Stevenson's charming collection of verse relating to the inner life of childhood followed next. It was appropriately called "A Child's Garden of Verse."

His "Strange Case of Dr. Jekyll and Mr. Hyde," from 1886, has enjoyed the double reputation of great success on the stage as well as in book and story form. Mr. Stevenson has declared that the principal incident was dreamed by him many years before he wrote the story. In his dream he saw Hyde rush into a mysterious recess, take a drug, and then, by the terror that followed, was awakened. Such was the impression the dream made on him that it haunted him for years before he made a story out of it.

In the same year was published "Kidnapped," the tale of a boy who is kidnapped and cast away on a desert island, then escapes to further adventures in the West Highlands of Scotland. The workmanship was admired and the horrors were related with such charm and freshness, joined to refinement, that readers of fine taste found the work a source of genuine pleasure.

Stevenson's marriage was as romantic as any tale he ever told. Mrs. Stevenson was recently divorced from her husband, Samuel C. Osbourne, whom she had married in Indiana in 1858. In 1861 the couple, with a son and daughter, started for Arizona to invest, unsuccessfully, in a mine; they then went to San Francisco, and he so prospered as a court reporter that he sent his wife [Fanny] to Europe to educate the children.

In Paris Mrs. Osbourne, in 1883, met Stevenson, who had moved to France for his health. She fell in love with him, returned to San Francisco to obtain a divorce, and at once began arrangements to marry him. Osbourne was invited to the wedding and accepted. On the appointed day he presented himself in faultless attire with a lady on his arm, whom he introduced as Mrs. Osbourne. To this lady Osbourne had been quietly married as soon as the divorce was granted. Some newspaper stories have declared that the divorce broke Osbourne's heart, but his prompt second marriage hardly bears out the story. In any event, it is known that as Mr. and Mrs. Stevenson took up their abode in Samoa, so Mr. and Mrs. Osbourne took up theirs in Australia. Each couple went to a land where all the old ties might be forgotten.

HARRIET BEECHER STOWE

June 14, 1811–July 1, 1896

HARTFORD—Mrs. Harriet Beecher Stowe, the authoress of "Uncle Tom's Cabin," "Dred," and other works of worldwide reputation, died at her home, 73 Forest Street, at noon today at the age of 85 without regaining consciousness. She passed peacefully away, as though into a deep sleep, with members of her family by her bedside.

Mrs. Stowe's malady of many years' continuance,

a mental trouble, took an acute form on Friday, June 26, when congestion of the brain, with partial paralysis, appeared. Mrs. Stowe, until about seven years ago, was about the city and attended church regularly at the Windsor Avenue Congregational Church, of which her son, the Rev. Charles Edward Stowe, was then the pastor.

She first came to Hartford in 1824, as a schoolgirl, and had lived here permanently, with a Winter residence, an orange plantation, at Mandarin, Fla., since 1865.

Mrs. Stowe's funeral will be attended at her home at 5 o'clock tomorrow afternoon. Her body will be taken to Andover, Mass., and the burial will be in the cemetery connected with the Andover Theological Seminary, where Mrs. Stowe's husband, Prof. Calvin E. Stowe, and her son Henry, are buried.

The death of Harriet Beecher Stowe is more than the ending of a woman's life of whatever degree of fame. It is one of the closing leaves in an era of our century. Rarely is there so much in a single life so memorable or so interesting as in that of the writer of probably the most widely read work of fiction ever penned.

"Beecher on Intemperance" was a famous book in its day. Its author was the Rev. Lyman Beecher, father of Henry Ward and Harriet and the rest, who almost constitute a genus by themselves, so marked are they in their talents. The stern and eloquent old Calvinist parson was settled in Litchfield, Conn., and there the daughter, who was to surpass her father, was born on June 14, 1811.

They were the affectionate children of loving parents, yet they grew up in a home where feeling was repressed. Birthdays and family festivals and such little loving gifts and words as now pass between brothers and sisters were infrequent, if not actually discouraged in that family. Of Harriet's mental traits none was earlier or more fully developed than her memory. The bulk of the Bible and extended passages from most of the English classics were at her tongue's end. Her 15 years of childhood were spent in cultured society with lawyers, ministers, and professors, who were frequenters of her father's circle. Her mother died in her early youth, and she was still a slip of a girl when she went to help her sister Catharine, who was the head of a successful girls school at Hartford. Thus, prosily her life passed until in her 21st year, in January 1828, she married Calvin E. Stowe, Professor of Languages and Biblical Literature at Lane Seminary, Cincinnati. That was the turning point of her career.

Nowhere were the "underground railway" and pathetic incidents under the Fugitive Slave Law more familiar than on the border of Ohio. Nowhere was there a stronger anti-slavery agitation or more flourishing hotbed of abolition than at Lane Seminary. A majority of the students left the seminary because

the Trustees insisted upon their disbanding an anti-slavery debating society.

In anticipation of violence, the Stowe residence was armed and equipped with a large bell to summon help. In her husband's house many a fugitive was sheltered and many a thrilling tale rehearsed. Thus, in a sense, "Uncle Tom's Cabin" was not a freak of fancy. Its inspiration and its incidents came from actual life.

After leaving Cincinnati the Stowes lived for a time in Brunswick, Me., her husband being a professor at Bowdoin College. In 1852 they settled in Andover, in the famous theological seminary of which village he also held a chair. He was an ideal old-time New Englander, about 10 years older than his wife. His flowing white beard and silvery hair, falling from a fine head bald on top, suggested the reference to the "dear old rabbi" contained in a personal letter to his wife from George Eliot. His death preceded his wife's by about 10 years. Mrs. Stowe has left this picture of herself at the age when she wrote her most famous book:

"A little bit of a woman, rather more than forty, as withered and dry as a pinch of snuff, never very well worth looking at in my best days, and now a decidedly used-up article."

In Hartford the Stowes were members of a delightful coterie, including Charles Dudley Warner and Mark Twain as near neighbors. Their plain brick residence on Forest Street is remarkable chiefly for the portraits, souvenirs, and tributes which have come unsought from famous people all over the world, but the walls are also adorned with many paintings by Mrs. Stowe. She was an artist only in the second place, and if she had not become famous by her writings, her transcripts of natural scenes in color would have won her credit enough to satisfy most women.

Mrs. Stowe's literary life began shortly after marriage, and was long confined to fugitive tales and sketches, afterward printed under the title of "The Mayflower." She did nothing memorable until her maturity, and then leaped full-fledged into the company of the illustrious women of the century. Besides "Uncle Tom's Cabin," she did nothing better than "The Minister's Wooing" (1859), which pleased the critics at least as well as it did the public.

Possibly her least happy venture was "Lady Byron Vindicated." In 1853 she had visited England and formed the acquaintance of the unhappy wife of the poet, and upon what she then learned was based an unmentionable charge against him. Upon this tour was based "Sunny Memories of Foreign Lands." In 1856 appeared her second anti-slavery novel, "Dred." It was a powerful work, but marred by the sentiment inspired by the attack upon [Senator Charles] Sumner in the Senate Chamber. It was thus that the bitter, avenging spirit was given to Dred at the expense of the art of the story. She has written other works creditable enough, but they will not live.

America's greatest orator has said that true eloquence is very rare, because there go to make it up three things almost never found together—the man, the subject, and the occasion. Never was there a riper occasion than when the country was writhing in its death grip with slavery. Never was there a subject appealing more deeply to the tenderest sentiments of every human being.

In the English language the Bible and Shakespeare's works are the only rivals to "Uncle Tom's Cabin." Within five years a half-million copies were sold in the United States alone, a degree of success phenomenal, but far inferior to that recorded in England, where a million copies were sold in 1855 alone. In each year of the generation since gone by, the sale has steadily continued, in a host of languages, and every year the book in its dramatic form is seen upon the stage by many audiences.

It has already been hinted how the book came to be written. Escaping slaves were familiar to her. She heard their stories, she saw their wounds, she helped their flight. Uncle Tom was the husband of a domestic in her family, and his death was the chapter first written. Topsy was a pickaninny named Celeste who lived on Walnut Hills, Cincinnati. Eliza's escape across the ice floating in the Ohio was an incident recorded in the press of that period by a witness of it.

Thus she was brimming over with her topic when she was asked to write a story for The National Era. It was begun in the expectation that it would run through a month or so, but it was scarcely finished within a year. To say that it was not appreciated in serial form is to state the case mildly. Her publisher was anxious for her to stop. Her brother, Henry Ward, warned her to cut it short, lest its length should prevent printing it as a book. She answered them never a word. Her genius was in travail, and, whatever others might think, she could not stop or turn.

The death of Uncle Tom was conceived at the communion table, and when her little sons heard it they declared slavery was the wickedest thing in the world. After the chapter of Eva's death, the author was prostrated three days in bed. She was wholly beside herself and in the control of her idea. She did not consider the book hers. She belonged to the book. In her own phrase: "That wasn't mine; that was given to me."

At length the book was finished, and the next thing was to find a publisher for it. Mrs. Stowe at least hoped it would bring her a silk gown. Accordingly, her sister Catharine offered it to the publisher of one of her own books. Mr. Lee replied that he could not sell a thousand copies and, as it would ruin his trade with the South, he declined the project. John R. Jewett of Boston finally undertook to bring it out. That within a few months he should hand to her $10,000 as her share of the profits was beyond his wildest conceptions. How far it fell short of the reality is in some degree set forth above.

LEWIS CARROLL

January 27, 1832–January 14, 1898

London—The Rev. C. L. Dodgson, whose nom de plume was Lewis Carroll, the author of "Alice in Wonderland," is dead.

Mr. Dodgson was born in England in 1832 and was graduated from Christ Church, Oxford, as a first-class mathematician in 1854. He published "The Adventures of Alice in Wonderland" in 1865, having remained at Oxford as lecturer on mathematics, tutor, and student, and except for his books, his life was as uneventful as that of any man in the university. In 1869 he published "Phantasmagoria," a collection of humorous poems and parodies, and in 1871 children whose earliest recollections were of the delights of "Alice in Wonderland" were further charmed by "Through the Looking Glass and What Alice Found There." "The Hunting of the Snark, an Agony in Eight Fits," which has become almost as famous and familiar in the larger world as Alice is in the nursery, was published in 1876.

Mr. Dodgson's life was as grotesque in its contradictions as his most deliciously absurd conceptions. He was a profound student of mathematics and wrote ponderous books on that exact science, turning aside to put into orderly words and fascinating form the chaotic, queer ideas and dreams of a child's unformed and untrained mind, and to weave nonsense words and the wildest of imaginary things and events into irresistible humor.

In addition to his better-known works, he wrote such books as "A Syllabus of Plane Algebraical Geometry," "An Elementary Treatise on Determinants," "A New Theory of Parallels," and so on. He was also the author of "A Tangled Tale," "Alice's Adventures Underground," "Rhyme? and Reason?" "Doublets, a Word Puzzle," and "Euclid and His Modern Rivals."

He had no children of his own, having never married, but was devoted to children as they were to him, spending all his spare time with them and throwing aside his dignity when in their company. It is told of him that a company of dignified people at a London dinner table was once astonished by seeing a strange gentleman, evidently a clergyman, Mr. Dodgson having been ordained in 1861, enter the dining room on all fours. When matters were explained, it was found that the author of "Alice," having been invited to a children's party at a house nearby, had mistaken the place, and made before the wrong company the entrance with which he had intended to amuse his young friends. As the children grew to manhood and womanhood, he lost interest in them, and turned from them to the next generation.

The original of Alice, whose wonderful adventures have probably delighted more children than any other book that was ever written, is said to have been Alice Liddell, daughter of a former Dean of Oxford, who afterward became Mrs. Reginald Hargreaves. She and her sister Edith were Mr. Dodgson's favorite playmates in their day, and his first idea of "Alice in Wonderland" is said by tradition to have originated one drowsy Summer day as he lay in the bottom of a boat while the two little girls were zealously splashing and tugging with the oars along the shining and tranquil surface of the river.

His children's books were illustrated by Tenniel, and Henry Holiday drew the curious pictures for "The Hunting of the Snark."

STEPHEN CRANE

November 1, 1871–June 5, 1900

BADENWEILER, Baden—Stephen Crane, the American author and war correspondent, died here today, aged 30 years.

Stephen Crane stepped early into literary notice because of his power in word painting. "The Red Badge of Courage," his first published novel, drew approving comment from various quarters, and some speculation regarding the author. In England the opinion was advanced that he must be a veteran soldier, since no one who had not been under fire could so well describe a battle. Mr. Crane dismissed this theory by saying that he got his ideas from the football field.

After this introduction, in 1895, to book readers, Mr. Crane issued a book called "Maggie: A Girl of the Streets," which had been written by him when he was about 16 years old and printed privately. In the five years between these books he occupied himself with miscellaneous newspaper and sketch work in this city, printing among other things verses entitled "The Black Riders, and Other Lines." He printed "George's Mother" in 1896, and "The Little Regiment," a war story, and "The Third Violet," in 1897, his books by that time having vogue both here and abroad.

"The Red Badge of Courage" was written while he was in New York writing sketches for the various newspapers and in very indifferent financial circumstances. His inspiration for it came from an artist friend whose studio he was visiting. Crane had been reading a war story in a current magazine, which he finally tossed aside in disgust, saying that he could write a better story himself.

"Why don't you do it, then?" said his friend.

"I will," said Crane, snatching up his hat and leaving the room.

The next three days he secured all the books he could find on the Civil War in the various public libraries. He knew little or nothing about the Civil War when he started, but when he had finished his studies he was thoroughly imbued with local color. The story which he produced was refused by all the publishers, but was afterward accepted in a condensed form for $90 by a newspaper syndicate.

When the Graeco-Turkish war broke out he was in London. He went into the field as correspondent for The Westminster Gazette and The New York Journal. After that he started for Cuba with a filibustering expedition, which was wrecked off the American coast. He then went to Cuba as The Journal's correspondent and witnessed the operations at Santiago and Havana and afterward in Porto Rico.

After this experience he came to this city, intending to engage here and in London in book writing. While looking in the Tenderloin for "color" for a story of the seamy side of life he was arrested and had an experience with the police. In court the following day he pleaded his case so well that the Magistrate released him, and also the young woman arrested with him. He wrote in 1898 "The Open Boat" and "The Eternal Patience."

For the last 18 months Mr. Crane lived in England, having made his home on an estate in Essex since last Fall. He wrote, after leaving here, two novels and a volume of verse called "War Is Kind," all three books inspired by the Turkish war, and a volume of short stories entitled "The Monster." His last work, "Whilomville Stories," a series of tales of child life, is now in course of publication in American magazines.

Mr. Crane was born in Newark, N.J., in 1871, and was the son of the Rev. Dr. J. I. Crane. He attended Lafayette College and Syracuse University, but was not graduated from either.

OSCAR WILDE

October 16, 1854–November 30, 1900

PARIS—Oscar Wilde died at 3 o'clock this afternoon in the Maison du Perier, Rue des Beaux Arts, in the Latin Quarter. It is a small, obscure hotel, at which Wilde had been living for several months under the name of Manmoth.

Wilde was operated upon six weeks ago for meningitis, caused by an abscess in the ear, which the doctors were unable to locate. He is said to have been unconscious for two days, and before that time to have been received into the Roman Catholic Church. Lord Alfred Douglas was with him when he died at 46 years of age.

Le Journal says that it is rumored that Wilde committed suicide. Recent reports from Paris were to the effect that he was living in abject poverty.

Oscar Wilde was born in Dublin in 1854. He was the son of Sir William R. Wills Wilde, M.D., surgeon-oculist to Queen Victoria, antiquarian, statistician, and man of letters, and of Jane Francesca, Lady Wilde, who achieved considerable reputation as a poetess. Oscar's first schooling was at the Portora Royal School, Enniskillen, and later he studied at Trinity College, Dublin, and at Magdalen College, Oxford University.

In 1879 he went to London, and soon became a celebrity through the aesthetic fad which he started. His eccentricities of dress soon made him one of the most talked about persons in London. He clad himself in black velvet, with knickerbockers, and black silk stockings, and he wore a sunflower. He was caricatured and satirized. The advertising he received was just what he wanted. He took advantage of it to effect a contract for a lecture tour in America. The tour was not the success he had anticipated, but he made some money out of it.

On his return to England Wilde dropped all his eccentricities of dress, but his other affectations became greater than ever. In the high social circles of London, he was regarded as a brilliant conversationalist and poseur. Wilde was married to Constance, daughter of Horace Lloyd, barrister. They had two children, Cyril and Vivian, both of whom survive.

Wilde's first published book was his Newdigate prize poem, printed in 1879, and well received by the reviewers. After his return from the United States he applied himself industriously to literary work.

The most popular of Wilde's books was "The Picture of Dorian Gray," which has had an immense sale. It appeared first in Lippincott's Magazine, in 1895, and was afterward issued in book form. After the famous trial the London publishers withdrew it from circulation.

Among literary people "Intentions," published in 1894, is regarded as Wilde's finest prose work. It is a collection of essays, and, though full of the author's favorite paradoxes, contains much art criticism which shows evidences of careful thought.

Wilde's poems were first published in 1881, and a new edition was issued about 10 years later. Both editions were exhausted a very short time after publication. Many isolated stanzas and lines have been quoted to show that, had he possessed the necessary perseverance and steadfastness of character, Wilde could have been one of the great poets of the 19th century.

After Wilde's release from prison a poem was published anonymously, entitled "A Ballad of Reading Jail." It created a great deal of interest and favorable criticism, and is now known to have been written by Wilde.

Wilde was spoken of as an aspiring dramatist long before any piece signed by his name was acted. His "Salome" was cast in the dramatic form, and "Guido Ferranti," a tragic piece briefly acted here by Lawrence Barrett, was reputed to be his work. His first acknowledged play, however, was "Lady Windermere's Fan," produced by George Alexander at the St. James's Theatre, in London, in 1893, and acted here soon afterward at Wallack's (then Palmer's) without setting the town ablaze. There was much verbal smartness in this piece, and it was no strong accusation against its merit to say that its plot was antique and its stagecraft insufficient.

But its insincerity and diffusiveness were not to be denied. After the first performance in London, Wilde appeared on the stage of the St. James's smoking a cigarette, and responded to a "call" that was not altogether friendly with imperturbable good humor and assurance.

His next play, "A Woman of No Importance," was acted first at the London Haymarket, under Beerbohm Tree's direction, and in New York, at the Fifth Avenue Theatre, with Rose Coghlan in the principal role. It was indeed a play of no importance.

"The Importance of Being Earnest," frankly a farce and full of nimble wit, on the other hand, missed a long run at the Empire Theatre because it was too dainty and fragile to suit the taste and understanding of the ordinary theatergoer, and "An Ideal Husband," admirably acted by Daniel Frohman's company at the Lyceum, while it made no one's fortune and lacked vigorous dramatic spirit, was a clever piece of work.

Wilde was hampered by his utter lack of sincerity and his inability to master the technical side of playwriting. But his wit, his pleasing literary facility, and his droll views of life made some of his plays rather effective with a limited audience.

It was in 1895 that the great scandal broke. It came about through an action brought by the Marquis of Queensberry, whose motive was the protection of his son, Lord Alfred Douglas, over whom Wilde had exercised an evil influence. The evidence at Wilde's trial shocked the civilized world and covered him with disgrace. He was sentenced to prison for a term of years. At the expiration of his sentence he quitted England. From a pet of society he had become the most despised of social outcasts.

HENRIK IBSEN

March 20, 1828–May 23, 1906

CHRISTIANIA—Henrik Ibsen, Norway's greatest poet and dramatist, suffered a stroke of apoplexy last night, which rendered him unconscious. He died peacefully at 2:30 o'clock this afternoon. Mme. Ibsen, her son, Dr. Sigurd Ibsen, and the latter's wife were at his bedside. He was 78 years of age.

Although Ibsen's literary activity ceased some years ago when a seizure forced him to refrain from mental effort, he continued to be a familiar figure in the life of Christiania and was frequently seen driving in the streets with a companion.

King Haakon, upon receipt of the news, transmitted to the widow his own and Queen Maude's condolences. All the theaters were closed tonight. It is understood that the funeral will be a state function.

While there has been no actual indication in the last few years that the admiration for Henrik Ibsen's works has waned, there has been a decided falling off in the interest with which the man and his productions are regarded. A decade ago the Norwegian dramatist had not long been "discovered" by the English-speaking people, and Ibsen clubs were being founded all over the United Kingdom and the United States. One hears little about the doings of Ibsen clubs nowadays, and still less about private performances of Ibsen's works for the benefit of the "cultured few who can really appreciate them." Just why this phenomenon should be is a mystery.

Ibsen was born at Skien, a small town on the south coast of Norway, on March 20, 1828. His immediate ancestors were all seamen. The early youth of the dramatist was clouded by extreme poverty. His father, Knud Ibsen, failed when Henrik was 8 years old, and the latter left school at the age of 16 to begin life as an apothecary's apprentice in the seaport of Grimstad. His purpose was, however, to go to the University of Christiania to study medicine.

At Christiania he met Björnson and others who have since become famous. At that time Ibsen had written a good deal of verse. The revolutionary movement of 1848 had fired his imagination, and he produced 12 fiery sonnets in which he called upon the Norwegians to go to the help of their Danish brethren against the Germans. These sonnets served to call attention to Ibsen, but his sentiments were regarded as dangerous by most of his fellow-citizens.

Ibsen also wrote his first play at this period. It was entitled "Cataline," and was a defense of that famous conspirator. The play was published under a pseudonym, but few copies were sold, and at last the edition was disposed of as waste paper.

Ibsen might have ended his career as a physician had not a play by him been produced at Christiania just as he was about to enter the university. It was called "The Hero's Mound" and met with a most encouraging reception. Ibsen then definitely determined on a literary career, and he was appointed stage manager at the Bergen Theatre at a salary of $225 a year. He remained in Bergen seven years, and in 1857 was appointed artistic director at the Norwegian Theatre at Christiania.

In 1864, Ibsen left Christiania, and for many years resided in Rome, Ischia, and other places, but chiefly in Dresden and Munich, producing on average a drama every two years. It was at Ischia that he wrote "Peer Gynt," which some critics believe to be his greatest work, and which, although written amid the semitropical luxuriance of the Italian Summer, is the most exclusively Norwegian of his works in scenery and feeling.

Ibsen continued to live abroad until about 10 years ago, when he returned to and settled down in Christiania. Since then he had been regarded by tourists as much a sight of the Norwegian capital as the Castle of Agershuus, greatly to his own disgust.

Such is an outline of Henrik Ibsen's long but singularly uneventful career. It may be added that his earlier revolutionary opinions had given way, by the time he reached middle life, to conservatism of almost as extreme a character; and that whereas, as a young man, he addressed radical meetings and published a literary and revolutionary newspaper, in later life he was utterly unable to speak in public and hated journalism and journalists.

Ibsen's literary work divides itself naturally into the following three groups:

Historical and legendary dramas, chiefly in prose: "Cataline," "Dame Inger of Oestraat," "The Feast at Solhaug" (a historical play of the fourteenth century), "The Warriors of Helgeland" (a version of the Volsunga Saga), "The Pretenders" (dealing with 12th-century Norwegian history), and "Emperor and Galilean."

Dramatic poems: "Love's Comedy," "Brand," and "Peer Gynt."

Social dramas: "The Young Men's League," "The Pillars of Society," "A Doll's House; or, Nora," "Ghosts," "An Enemy of Society," "The Wild Duck," "Rosmersholm," "The Lady of the Sea," "Hedda Gabler," "The Master Builder," "John Gabriel Borkman," "Little Eyolf," and "When We Dead Awaken."

MARK TWAIN

November 30, 1835–April 21, 1910

DANBURY, Conn.—Samuel Langhorne Clemens, "Mark Twain," died at 22 minutes after 6 tonight. Beside him on the bed lay a beloved book—it was Carlyle's "French Revolution"—and near the book his glasses, pushed away with a weary sigh a few hours before. Too weak to speak clearly, "Give me my glasses," he had written on a piece of paper. He had received them, put them down, and sunk into unconsciousness.

For some time his daughter Clara and her husband, Ossip Gabrilowitsch, and the humorist's biographer and literary executor, Albert Bigelow Paine, had been by the bed waiting for the end.

Although the end had been foreseen by the doctors, the apparently strong rally of this morning had given basis for hope. The increasing sunlight seemed to bring ease to the patient, and by the time the family were about he was strong enough to sit up in bed and overjoyed them by recognizing all of them and speaking a few words to each.

For two hours he lay in bed enjoying the feeling of this return of strength. He read a little and then slowly put the Carlyle book down with a sigh. Soon he appeared to become drowsy and settled on his pillow. Gradually he sank and settled into a lethargy.

The family was called and gathered about the bedside watching in a silence which was long unbroken. It was the end. At 22 minutes past 6, with the sunlight just turning red as it stole into the window, in perfect silence he breathed his last. He was in his 75th year.

The people of Redding, Bethel, and Danbury say among themselves that he died of a broken heart. The man who has stood to the public for the greatest humorist this country has produced has in private life suffered overwhelming sorrows. The loss of an only son in infancy, a daughter in her teens and one in middle life, and finally of a wife who was a constant and sympathetic companion, has preyed upon his mind. The recent loss of his daughter Jean was the final blow.

THE LITERARY WORLD

One of the last acts of Mark Twain was to write out a check for $6,000 for the library in which the literary coterie settled near Redding have been interested for a year. The library is to be a memorial to Jean Clemens.

It is certain to be recalled that Mark Twain was for more than 50 years an inveterate smoker, and the first conjecture of the layman would be that he had weakened his heart by overindulgence in tobacco. Dr. Halsey said tonight that he was unable to say that the angina pectoris was in any way a sequel of nicotine poisoning. Yet it is true that since his illness began the doctors had cut down Mark Twain's daily allowance of 20 cigars and countless pipes to 4 cigars a day.

Mr. Paine said tonight that Mark Twain had put his affairs in perfect order and that he died well off, though by no means a rich man. He leaves a considerable number of manuscripts, in all stages of incompleteness and of all characters, many of them begun years ago and put aside as unsatisfactory.

Samuel Langhorne Clemens was known far beyond the boundaries where English is spoken as the greatest humorist using that tongue, if not actually the greatest humorist and satirist living. His famous telegram to a newspaper publishing a report of his death, when happily it was untrue, has been quoted and requoted almost everywhere. "The report of my death," he wired, "is greatly exaggerated."

The father of Mark Twain was John Marshall Clemens, who migrated from Virginia to Tennessee when a young man. There he married a young woman named Langhorne, who brought him family prestige and many broad acres. But with the prevalent spirit of unrest among pioneers, the couple crossed over into Missouri, settling at Florida, Monroe Country, where, on Nov. 30, 1835, their since famous son was born. Three years later, the family moved to Hannibal, Marion County. Hannibal has been described many times as a typical river town of that day, a sleepy place, filled with drawling, lazy, picturesque inhabitants black and white.

Young Clemens went to school there, and, so the record runs, studied just as little as he could. He had been painted in that period as an incorrigible truant, roaming the river banks and bluffs, watching the passing steamboats, and listening keenly to the trials that went on in the shabby office where the Justice of the Peace, his father, settled the disputes and punished the misdemeanors of his neighbors. In that period, while the ambition to be a pilot on the great river burned in him, was stored in Samuel's memory the material which in after years crystallized into "Tom Sawyer," "Huckleberry Finn," and "Pudd'nhead Wilson."

Mark Twain's school days ended when he was 12. The father died, leaving nothing behind save the reputation of being a good neighbor and an upright man, and his children at once became breadwinners. "Sam"

was apprenticed as a printer at 50 cents a week in the office of The Hannibal Weekly Journal. After three years, with a capital of a few dollars in his pocket, he became a familiar sight, a wanderer from one printing office to another. About this period he paid his first visit to New York, having been drawn here by stories of a great exposition then in progress.

He worked here for a while, then moved on to Philadelphia, and later, obeying always the wandering instinct which finally carried him around the world, to nearly all the larger cities of the South and West, including New Orleans. The trip down the river awakened the old desire to be a pilot. He paid in cash and promises of $500 to a Mississippi pilot to take him on as an assistant and "teach him the river." He became a pilot and stuck to it until the outbreak of the Civil War, earning $250 a month, but chief of all he got here his material for "Life on the Mississippi."

His experience as a Confederate soldier was brief and inglorious. Hardly had he enlisted before he was captured. Released on parole, he broke the parole and returned to the ranks, and soon was recaptured. He got away again, and stopped flight only on reaching Nevada. There several letters of his to The Virginia City Enterprise resulted in an offer of a place on the staff.

While employed on the Enterprise he first used the pen name "Mark Twain," a phrase commonly used by the leadsmen on Mississippi boats to indicate a certain depth of water. At this period, also, many of his short humorous sketches were written, including notably, "The Jumping Frog of Calaveras County."

From Nevada Mark Twain moved out to San Francisco where, after a brief service on the local staff of The Call, he was discharged as useless. Then he and Bret Harte were associated [with] The Californian, but both soon deserted the paper to make their fortunes mining if they could. Neither did, and Mark Twain was soon back in San Francisco penniless and ill. This was in 1866. The Sacramento Union sent him to the Sandwich Islands to write a series of letters on the sugar trade—an assignment which this time he filled to the editor's satisfaction—and returned restored to health.

That Winter, however, was one of "roughing it" for him. He could get little to do as reporter or editor and finally took to lecturing in a small way. He was a success from the start. He spoke in many of the small towns of California and Nevada earning more than a living, and meantime writing sketches for Eastern papers. These attracted considerable notice, and in March of 1867 he issued his first book, containing the "Jumping Frog" and other stories. Its reception was so cordial that Mark Twain decided to try his fortunes in the East. On reaching New York he learned that a select excursion was about to start for the Holy Land in the steamer Quaker City. He made the trip, which proved the beginning of his fortune, for "Innocents Abroad," his first famous book, had taken shape in his mind before his return.

Its success was instant and overwhelming. Edition after edition was sold in such rapid succession that the presses could not turn them out fast enough. Mark Twain had become a man of note overnight.

Among his friends on the Holy Land trip had been Judge Jervis J. Langdon of Elmira, N.Y., and his two children, Dan of the "Innocents" and Lizzie. Mark Twain fell in love with the latter. But Judge Langdon, who was rich, did not at first favor the union of his daughter and the nearly penniless journalist, and Miss Langdon twice rejected him before a third proposal was accepted. His father-in-law gave him a handsome home in Buffalo, but the young couple remained there but a year, going to Hartford, where they lived for many years and where Mark Twain did perhaps his most prolific work. In rapid succession appeared "Roughing It," in 1870; "The Golden Age," in 1873; "The Adventures of Tom Sawyer," in 1876; "A Tramp Abroad," in 1880; "The Prince and the Pauper," in 1882; and "Life on the Mississippi," in 1883.

These works were all issued by the American Company, his first publishers, but desiring larger royalties Mark Twain determined to become his own publisher, and joined with his nephew in establishing in this city the house of C. L. Webster & Co. The firm brought out "The Adventures of Huckleberry Finn," in 1885.

Two years later the firm failed and Mark Twain's fortune was swept away. Again he took to the lecture field, and everywhere was greeted by large and enthusiastic audiences. He made a new fortune and paid his debts.

Mark Twain had outlived most of his family. His wife died some years ago, and on the morning before Christmas, last year, his daughter Miss Jean Clemens was drowned in a bathtub in their home at Redding, Conn. Broken himself in health, and utterly crushed by this sudden affliction, he wrote on that day: "She was all that I had left, except Clara, who married Mr. Gabrilowitsch lately, and has just arrived in Europe."

In 1905 Mark Twain celebrated his 70th birthday with a notable gathering of literary folk. Two years later he was honored by Oxford University with the degree of Doctor of Laws. In nearly all his public appearances in the last five years he had worn white flannel, and even had a dress suit, clawhammer and all, made of this soft white material, whose evident cleanliness appealed so strongly to him.

LEO TOLSTOY

September 9, 1828–November 20, 1910

ASTAPOVA—In a low room, hung with pine branches, Tolstoy's body lies in the rude hut in which he died early this morning at 82 years of age. All the peasants in the district have flocked here. The silence at times was broken by orthodox chants for the repose of the soul of the dead.

Tolstoy left a written wish that he be buried without pomp, wreathes or rites, under "Poverty Oak," on a hillock where he played as a child and where the peasants were accustomed to congregate.

Around that house all last night while Tolstoy's life ebbed away and the doctors fought the losing battle with death, had pressed, waiting and watching and hoping, a motley crowd. There huddled together were relatives of the dying man, Tolstoy disciples, villagers, and many churchmen.

As the Sunday dawn dispelled the foggy-raw November night they still stood spellbound. Then a voice came quietly: "Leo Nikolavitch is dead."

A moment of silence and every head was bared. There were sounds of sobbing.

One called out: "His heart was broken by his boundless love for mankind." These and words like them ran from mouth to mouth through the little knot of weeping Russians.

The story of the life of Leo Tolstoy has yet to be written, but in its essentials it is the story of other great men who, through an inner awakening, have turned from the world to find their salvation in the life of the spirit.

With this difference: In Tolstoy's case the process, which with Loyola, St. Augustine and many other saints was sudden, was extended over many years, and in those years Tolstoy produced the works of genius which caused him, during the last two decades, to be regarded as the most famous writer of the Occidental world. He wrote more than one masterpiece before the process began and one after he had become a mystic, but the greater part of his literary work was accomplished during the period of transition. These books are already regarded as among the world's classics.

Count Leo Nikolavitch Tolstoy was born on the ancestral estate of his family Yasnaya Polyana in the district of Tula, Central Russia, 150 miles south of Moscow, on Aug. 28, 1828, according to the Russian calendar, and Sept. 10, according to the Gregorian calendar. His father was Count Nikolai Ilyvitch Tolstoy, a descendant of Count Peter Tolstoy, who was the companion and friend of Czar Peter the Great. Tolstoy is said to have sketched his father's portrait in the character of Peter Rostoff in "War and Peace."

As a youth Tolstoy entered the University of Kazan, but left to take charge of his ancestral estates, to which he had succeeded by the death of his parents. In 1851 he made a visit to the Caucasus. The rugged wildness of the country impressed him profoundly, and the study of its influence on the life and character of the people had a great effect on his later philosophy.

Tolstoy entered the Russian Army in the same year, and was appointed a subaltern of artillery. With merely perfunctory duties to perform, he began his long career as a novelist.

When the Crimean War began, Tolstoy was anxious to see active service. When aid was being rushed to the garrison at Sevastopol, Tolstoy went forward at the head of a battery and took part in the siege, distinguishing himself by numerous acts of personal bravery. He was wounded, and his firsthand experience with war was most valuable to him in his later work as a novelist.

At the close of the war Tolstoy resigned his commission and went to St. Petersburg. Here he had a most flattering reception as a nobleman, a returning hero, and a litterateur. But he soon became utterly disgusted with his life there. He returned to his estate, freed his serfs, dressed himself in peasant costume, and preached the gospel of what is now known as the simple life.

In 1862 Tolstoy met and wooed his wife, Sophia Berss. At the time he met her she was a young girl. He was by his own account a jaded man of the world. His strange religious ideas were just beginning to find expression. He knew the women of the Russian aristocracy well and had decided that there were no good women in the world and that he would never marry. So in his customary erratic way, he sold the lovely old mansion which had come to him through his grandfather.

Then he met the woman with whom he fell in love, and she changed the whole world for him. They were married soon afterward, and the Countess began her life of constant self-sacrifice by going out to a little hut on the Polyana estate—all that was left after the sale of the mansion. There she lived for 17 years in a lonely, deserted place, miles from any town. Tolstoy spent his time going up and down the great Russian Empire, studying social conditions, being absent from home a great deal of the time.

The couple were too poor to have any servants; she nursed each one of her 13 children, she dispensed with governesses and taught the children English, French, and German, gave them music lessons, made their clothes. Then, as soon as her husband commenced a book she began revising it, translating it from Russian into French or German, copying it in her clear handwriting, so the printers could read it.

With her help and constant inspiration Tolstoy wrote his great novels. He was appointed a magistrate of his district and devoted much time to the educa-tion of the peasantry and elaboration of plans for their material improvement. He realized the necessity of living the life of the people if he hoped to benefit them, and accordingly, even with his increased means, the house, in which he wrote textbooks for the poor and instructed classes of the peasantry of the neighborhood, was furnished with the rudest of chairs and tables, and the mode of life in his household was monastic in its simplicity.

The salvation of Russia, he declared, depended on the peasant ownership of land and the introduction of the single tax system of Henry George.

During these years Tolstoy wrote "Youth," "Two Hussars," "Albert," "Three Deaths," and "Family Happiness." His next work, issued in 1867, "War and Peace," won him his great reputation as a novelist. The work deals with Russia's great struggle against Napoleon Bonaparte.

Eight years later Tolstoy produced his even more celebrated "Anna Karénina," a study of one side of the marriage question, worked out to a conclusion of terrible tragedy. This work provoked discussion throughout the civilized world, and provoked Matthew Arnold to say: "This is less a work of art than a piece of life. But what it loses in art it gains in reality."

About the time of the publication of "Anna Karénina," Tolstoy accepted the doctrines of Jesus in a very literal way. He took as his text the Sermon on the Mount, and added to his work as teacher, physician, friend and adviser of his poor neighbors that of a cobbler and farm laborer. He made over his property to the members of his family.

Tolstoy's "The Kreutzer Sonata," a surprisingly frank novel dealing with the marital relation, was published in 1890. It caused much censure from the pulpits and was severely criticized in England and the United States.

In 1892, when a famine prevailed in Russia, Tolstoy established relief stations in Tula and Samara and published his volume "The Famine." In the next two years he produced "The Kingdom of God Within Us," "Christ's Christianity," "My Religion," and "Patriotism and Christianity."

Early in 1900 Tolstoy published the novel "Resurrection." The immediate object of its publication was to aid the Doukhobors, who were persecuted in Russia because of their religious beliefs. He devoted the funds he derived from the work to financing the emigration of members of the sect to land promised to them by the Dominion of Canada.

The publication of "Resurrection" led to Tolstoy's excommunication by the Holy Synod. Tolstoy replied by addressing an open letter to the Czar in which he denounced the State Church and governmental despotism in Russia.

HENRY JAMES

April 15, 1843–February 28, 1916

LONDON—Henry James died this afternoon at his residence, 21 Carlyle Mansions, Chelsea. He became unconscious on Friday afternoon and remained so until the end.

Mr. James had been ill for several months, but late in January his physicians reported that he was improving. The affliction from which he suffered, however, had been complicated by two strokes of apoplexy. About two weeks ago his condition became grave again, and his recovery was not looked for.

Internationally famous for his writings, Henry James most recently attracted attention when he renounced his American citizenship and swore allegiance to England. His sympathy with the cause of the Allies and his long residence in England are said to have impelled him to take this step.

The London Daily News, in editorial comment on his action, said: "The decision of one of the two greatest living novelists to seek British citizenship sets a dramatic seal upon the conclusion to which these things—the struggle of ideals between England and Germany—have long pointed."

Mr. James was one of the five children of the Rev. Henry James, and was born in New York City on April 15, 1843. Of his three brothers, William became a famous philosopher and Professor of Psychology at Harvard University. Another, Wilkinson James, was a gallant soldier in the Civil War. Their grandfather was an Irishman, William James, who came to this country and settled in Albany. When he died, he left a large fortune.

When Henry James was a child, his parents went to Germany and he spent a large part of his boyhood there. Before he reached his 20s the family returned to this country and eventually settled in Cambridge, Mass.

In 1862 he entered the Harvard Law School, although he gave no indication of adopting the law as his life's work. It was in this period that he first began contributing sketches to the magazines and began his literary career, which resulted in the production of nearly 100 novels and tales, together with critical essays and plays.

Henry James's first serious literary work was done for the Atlantic Monthly, with which he always maintained a close connection. His first contribution, entitled "The Story of the Year," appeared in March, 1865, and was founded on the Civil War. His first serial story, "Poor Richard," was followed by "Gabrielle de Bergerac" three years later. Then came "Watch and Ward," which was followed by a more ambitious effort, "Roderick Hudson." After this novel there were three others, "The American," "The Europeans," and "The Portrait of a Lady," all of which appeared in the Atlantic Monthly and attracted much attention and admiration.

Mr. James then wrote "Washington Square" for Harper's Magazine and "Confidence" for Scribner's.

After his first efforts, Mr. James wrote, in the order in which they are named: "The Siege of London," "The Tale of Three Cities," "The Bostonians," "The Reverberator," "A London Life," "The Tragic Muse," "The Lesson of the Master," "The Private Life," "Terminations," "The Spoils of Poynton," "What Maisie Knew," "The Two Magics," "In the Cage," "The Awkward Age," "The Soft Side," "The Sacred Fount," and "The Wings of the Dove."

Ranked as he was by the critics as one of the most masterful writers of the past generation, Mr. James's books were never so popular in this country as in England. His writings were of the analytical and metaphysical school of fiction. To understand Henry James was, in the popular idea, the gift of only a privileged few.

Being independent of the reading public for his income, since his private fortune was sufficient, Mr. James always adhered to his own principles of romance, regardless of how popular his works might become. Nevertheless he had, particularly in England, a host of readers who virtually formed a cult known as "The Jamesites."

It appeared to be Mr. James's belief that the story that could be told was not worth the telling, and it was his choice. as one of his critics declares, "to rigorously set himself to tell the story that cannot be told." The endless controversy was as to whether he was successful. He contended that it was of more interest to the author to paint the various aimless ways in which human beings are actually thrown together than to construct an artificial complication of circumstances.

While much has been written about Mr. James's books and his fame as an author, little has been published about the man himself. He was known to be very charitable in the most unostentatious manner. On one occasion, when a novelist died, his two little children were left alone in the world. One of his friends wrote to other literary men asking their help to save the babies from an orphanage. Henry James was appealed to, and his check for £50 was received by return mail.

During the eighties Mr. James lived in cozy bachelor's lodgings at 3 Bolton Street, just off Piccadilly, in London, and it was here that much of his best work was done. Of his manner of life a newspaper writer of the period said: "On rising he takes the continental breakfast of coffee and rolls in his rooms, and immediately sits down to his literary work, generally writing by the light of two candles, the London mornings being so dark.

"Mr. James composes slowly and painfully, rewriting and retouching his work continually, his strikingly artistic style being gained only at the expense of real toil. But by his system of working a regular length of time each day he turns out a great amount of manuscript in the course of a year—much more than most authors who compose readily, but only at regular intervals, when 'in the mood,' and then producing a goodly quantity of work at white heat. Mr. James writes until noon and then goes to his club for luncheon."

Mr. James was of a very retiring disposition and greatly disliked publicity. This was never more strikingly emphasized than at the opening performance of "The High Bid," which was produced at His Majesty's Theatre, Haymarket. At the urging of his friends Mr. James finally agreed to attend the performance and occupied a box on the second tier.

A most cultured and refined audience sat through the performance in silence, greeting its conclusion with well-modulated applause. As this was dying out, the cry "Author! Author!" was raised, and all eyes turned to Mr. James's box, expecting him to rise and bow his acknowledgments. There was a tense moment and then a loud thud. Mr. James had fainted.

Of recent years Mr. James made his home in Rye, an old-fashioned town in Sussex and a favorite spot for artists and authors, among them Ruskin, Turner, and J. E. Millais. Here he lived in a great 18th-century structure known as Lamb House at the end of a little street.

Mr. James used to tell his intimates of the "very active" ghost which had frequented Lamb House for many years. He was wont to tell the tale of how he waited and watched all one night for the ghost, which was due to appear on that date. All the night long he watched, while the wind, blowing in from the sea, made eerie noises about the house. When morning came, he found that instead of catching the ghost, he had caught a severe cold.

Before going to Rye he tried to spend a Summer at some retired country village and leased an old house there for the season. He did not remain long in peace. Some guidebook used by Americans came out with detailed directions of how to reach the "Home of Henry James, the Noted American Novelist," and a procession of touring Americans began to arrive. When Mr. James found out what had happened, he promptly packed up and returned to London.

MARCEL PROUST

July 10, 1871–November 18, 1922

The death of Marcel Proust at his home in Paris on Nov. 19 was not reported by cable. One reads in the Temps: "Poor Marcel Proust has proved by dying that he really was sick. One had begun to doubt it. He had announced his approaching end so often that one had got into the habit of expecting him to go on always hovering between life and death up to 90 or 100."

Although 51, it is only within the last few years that M. Proust became known to the English and American literary world. More than any of his contemporaries, M. Proust will go down to posterity as the author of one book. It includes five parts, which have appeared in French, and two others have been announced as being in press.

Described as an "anatomist of society," his series of connected works are marked by originality of thought in contemporary psychology, slow, relentless expositions and pitiless dissection of the human mind. His work has won passionate admirers and ardent disciples. The younger critics of France regard him as a master, and Marcel Proust societies have been formed in England and Holland.

Proust was fastidious in his tastes. He liked the best of everything—elegant women, aristocratic drawing rooms, great cosmopolitan gatherings. He was seldom seen before 9 o'clock in the evening, and then always in evening clothes. He lived at night and slept or rested during the day. He was solitary in his habits, and had a horror of noises and drafts. In order to deaden the sounds from the street and from neighbors, he had the walls and ceilings of his apartment covered with cork. The story is told that one of his friends on going to see him in his apartment remarked to a servant in a whisper upon entering that the place seemed like an asylum, and the servant replied, "It seems to suit the ideas of monsieur."

He published hardly anything until he was about 45. Then a volume appeared called "Pleasures and Days" (Plaisirs et les jours), illustrated by Madeleine Lemaire. A little before the outbreak of the war, his great work, "Memories of Things Past" (A la recherche du temps perdu), began to appear. This as it now stands includes five books, of which one is in three volumes; "Du côté de chez Swann," "A l'Ombre des jeunes filles en fleur," "Côté de Guermantes I et II," "Sodome et Gomorrhe I et II." "Sodome et Gomorrhe III et IV" and "Temps retrouvé" have been announced as being in press.

Much of M. Proust's writing has the form of improvisation. This is, however, consistent with the temperament of Marcel Proust. He was quite capable of having adopted this aspect of his writing as a sort of supreme elegance, exactly the touch necessary to give the most vivid impression of the quality he wished to convey to his readers. His works furnish an extraordinary collection of observations, sensations and images, presented with an acuteness and penetration; a style that is markedly unequal, sometimes loose, but often abounding in picturesque originality; a convincing power, a dynamic nervousness which makes one think of a Saint-Simon, esthetic and even a little feminine.

Marcel Proust concerned himself with the facts of mental life and with the behavior of individuals. He was therefore a psychologist. Victor Hugo said of Balzac that his stock in trade was observation and imagination. No one has yet added to that estimate, especially if the word "and" be sufficiently emphasized. Proust's great endowment was capacity for observation, and to this he conjoined capacity for notation. Only by slaving work did he acquire narrative. He has been compared to Balzac. He was more like Huysmans.

JOSEPH CONRAD

December 3, 1857–August 3, 1924

LONDON—Joseph Conrad, the novelist, died suddenly this morning at his house at Bishopsbourne near Canterbury. He was 67 years old.

In recent years Joseph Conrad had received such high titles as "the greatest living writer of English" and "the most arresting and the most romantic figure in English literature." And as his fame increased among the critical, so did his position with the general public, so that from being merely the idol of the discerning few when "Almayer's Folly" appeared in 1895, after the publication of "The Rover" last year, he became, or very nearly became, a popular favorite.

Teodor Josef Konrad Korzenlowski was born in the Ukraine on Dec. 6, 1857, the son of a Polish squire. Although the family fortunes suffered from his father's exile to Vologda, the boy was brought up in traditions of culture and refinement, and would no doubt have taken his place among other Polish gentlemen had there not stirred deeply within him a passion for the sea. At the age of nine, or thereabout, he one day struck his hand on a map of Africa, on the region marked "The Congo," and exclaimed: "I am going there."

The boy stuck to this idea and finally secured, through his father, a berth on a collier at Marseilles. (Conrad had since been particular to deny the story that he ran away to sea.) "Later," he says in a sketch of his career, "I shipped as an ordinary seaman at Newcastle, and since then I have served on many vessels in many seas, through all the grades—from able seaman to master of both sailing vessels and steamships.

The turning point in the composition and in the life of the author came when the manuscript, unfinished, faded and yellow, was submitted to the judgment of a Cambridge man, traveling to Australia for his health on the ship Torrens.

"We were in the open sea," as Conrad tells the incident, "and one evening after a longish conversation, the subject of which was the famous 13th chapter of Gibbons's 'Rome,' I asked, 'Would it bore you very much reading a manuscript in a handwriting like mine?'

"'Next day Jacques—that was his name—entered my cabin with the manuscript in his hand. He tendered it to me with a steady look, but without a word.

"'Well, what do you say?' I asked at length. 'Is it worth finishing?'

'Distinctly.'"

"'Is the story perfectly clear to you as it stands?'"

"'Yes, perfectly.'"

The book at once attracted attention and its author was urged to keep on writing He did not at once decide to abandon the sea, but in 1896 he published a second work, "An Outcast of the Islands."

Conrad had married in 1895 and he settled in England unreservedly as an author.

After calling upon Conrad in 1912 at his country home in Kent, James Huneker wrote for The New York Times this personal impression of the novelist:

"At the door of what he calls his 'farmhouse' I was met by a man of the world, neither sailor nor novelist, just a simple-mannered gentleman, whose welcome was sincere, whose glance was slightly veiled, faraway at times, whose ways were Polish, French, anything but bluff, or English, or 'literary.' He is not so tall as he seems. He is very restless. He paces an imaginary quarter deck and occasionally peers through, the little windows of his quaint house as if searching the weather. A caged sea lion, I thought. His shrug and play of hands are Gallic, or Polish, as you please, and his eyes, shining or clouded, are not of our race, they are Slavic; even the slightly muffled voice is Slavic. "When Mr. Conrad speaks English, which he does with rapidity and clearness of enunciation, you can hear, rather overhear, the foreign cadence, the soft slurring of sibilants so characteristic of Polish speech. In a word, he is more foreign looking than I had expected. He speaks French with purity and fluency and he often lapsed into it during our conversation. Like many another big man, he asked more questions than he answered mine, his curiosity being prompted by a boundless sympathy for all things human. He is as you must have surmised from his writings, the most human and lovable of men. Joseph Conrad, mirror of the sea and of the human heart."

"I have often been ill, and it was through one of these attacks that I came to be in Bangkok, Siam, when the Ortolan came in without a master. Thus it was that I took the first cargo of Siamese teakwood to Australia. The owners were inclined to sell or dismantle the Ortolan—she had never paid—but when I became master her luck turned, and for the two years I commanded her she made 20 percent. I was always a good businessman for others, never for myself."

In 1877 Conrad had joined an English steamer bound for the Azov Sea, and when the vessel brought the load of grain back home the young sailor first put foot on English soil. In 1884 he passed the examination for his master's "ticket," and in the same year became a naturalized subject of the British Crown. For 10 years he sailed in command, a contributing cause of his eventually leaving the sea being the effects of an attack of African fever contracted during the only visit he ever made to that Congo, his original inspiration.

He had mastered the English language to a degree attained only by a few who were native born, but so great was his shyness that he had kept secret the fact that in 1880 he began the composition of a novel, now known as "Almayer's Folly." The manuscript traveled with him from ship to ship and ashore. When his canoe upset in an especially awkward turn of the Congo River, it was the only bit of his luggage that was rescued.

EDITH WHARTON

January 24, 1862–August 11, 1937

PARIS—Edith Wharton, American novelist, died yesterday afternoon at her villa, Pavilion Colombes, near Saint Brice, Seine-et-Oise.

She had been in fairly good health until she suffered an apoplectic stroke early yesterday morning and did not recover consciousness. She died at 5:30 P.M.

She is survived by a niece.

Edith Wharton was the child as well as the author of "The Age of Innocence." In her 75 years of life she published 38 books, including that great love story, "Ethan Frome." But her reputation rested mostly upon her achievement as the chronicler of Fifth Avenue, when the brownstone front hid wealth and dignity at its ease upon the antimacassar-covered plush chairs of the Brown Decade.

As a child she lived within the inner circle of New York society that always thought of itself as spelled with a capital S. In her ancestry was a long succession of important names: The Schermerhorns, Joneses, Pendletons, Stevenses, Ledyards, Rhinelanders and Gallatins, who had led the social life of New York before men with strange new names from the West had descended on the town. Her own father, although not overly rich, was nevertheless able to live, as she said, "a life of leisure and amiable hospitality."

Besides Fifth Avenue, there was Newport. Beyond that was only Europe. When little Edith walked on the Avenue she passed nothing but brownstone. When she went on Bailey's Beach she shielded her skin from the sun with a black veil. When she went to Europe it was an escape from the crudities of American society. Innocence was the life of her childhood and it was the stuff of her better books.

Edith Wharton was born Edith Newbold Jones on Jan. 24, 1862. Her father was George Frederick Jones; her mother was the former Lucretia Stevens Rhinelander, and back of each were Colonial and Revolutionary ancestors. When she was four the family went abroad in pursuit of culture, health and economy.

Her early impressions were the international—New York and Newport, Rome, Paris and Madrid. Added to this was a vivid imagination, which found outlet in storytelling even before she could read. She was never sent to school, but was taught at home. She began writing short stories in her early teens, but they were never about "real people." Little happened to the real people she knew; what did "happen" was generally not talked about.

From this background Mrs. Wharton inherited the belief from which she never departed, that "any one gifted with the least creative faculty knows the absurdity of such a charge" as that of "putting flesh-and-blood people into books."

The young author wrote her first efforts on brown paper salvaged from parcels. She was not encouraged. "In the eyes of our provincial society," she was later to say, "authorship was still regarded as something between a black art and a form of manual labor." Her first acceptance was three poems which she sent to the editor with her calling card attached.

In her autobiography Mrs. Wharton gives a picture of her literary beginnings. Her first novel, written when she was 11, began: "'Oh, how do you do, Mrs. Brown?' said Mrs. Tompkins. 'If only I had known you were going to call I should have tidied up the drawing room.'" The child showed it to her mother, whose comment was: "Drawing rooms are always tidy."

Her first published book was a collaboration called "The Decoration of Homes." She was encouraged in her writing by such friends as Edward Burlingame, for many years editor of Scribner's Magazine.

But it was Henry James who was her closest friend and most worthwhile advocate. Although he disguised the severity of his judgments with his usual elaborate verbal courtesies, he managed to convey the meaning of his criticism. He remained her close friend until his death.

In 1899 Mrs. Wharton—she had been married in 1885 to Edward Wharton, a Boston banker—

THE LITERARY WORLD

published her first book: "The Greater Inclination." In this is found two of her best short stories, "The Pelican" and "Souls Belated." But not until 1905 did she gain a large public.

In 1905 she published her first of many best-sellers, "The House of Mirth," and its popularity established her as a writer. Its title came from the biblical assertion, "The heart of fools is in the House of Mirth," and it was a happy title for projecting, as Wilbur Cross once put it, "a group of pleasure-loving New Yorkers, mostly as dull as they are immoral, and letting them play out their drama unmolested by others."

Other novels came in rapid succession, but none attracted the attention in this country that was reserved for the book Elmer Davis once called "the last great American love story," "Ethan Frome."

"Ethan Frome," which was dramatized two seasons ago, was written in 1911. In it Mrs. Wharton most successfully blended the psychological refinements she had learned from Henry James with her own inimitable ability to tell a story with a beginning and an end. One critic has said it is comparable only to the work of Nathaniel Hawthorne as a tragedy of New England life. The book is considered a masterpiece of love and frustration, and is likely to stand as her most accomplished work.

Until 1906 Mrs. Wharton had divided her time between New York and her summer home at Lenox, Mass. In that year she went to live in France, in summer at Saint Brice and in winter at Hyeres in Provence.

When the World War broke out she was in Paris and she plunged into relief work, opening a room for women who were thrown out of employment by the closing of workrooms. She also fed and housed 600 Belgian refugee orphans.

"The Age of Innocence" was her next book and in terms of sales her most successful. Here she used the materials she had hitherto used only for background—the social life of the New York into which she had been born and bred.

Published here and abroad, it was widely read and was awarded the Pulitzer Prize for 1920. It showed Mrs. Wharton at her best, understanding the cramped society of her youth, unaware of the world beyond it. Four years later she followed it with four novelettes published under the title of "Old New York," a constricted panorama of society in the Forties, Fifties, Sixties and Seventies.

Shortly after the publication of this volume she returned to America, to be awarded the Gold Medal of the National Institute of Arts and Letters, the first woman to be so honored.

Since that time she had written other books, including "Twilight Sleep," a story of fashionable life in modern New York; "The Children," a study of the children of expatriated divorcees; "Hudson River Bracketed," a study of a modern writer, and "Certain People," a collection of short stories.

That generation which knew her best for "The Age of Innocence" flocked to see "Ethan Frome" when it was adapted for the stage. Presented on Broadway with Pauline Lord, Ruth Gordon and Raymond Massey in the leading roles, the grim tragedy proved to be as good theater as it had been a great book.

"Ethan Frome" was not the only one of her books to have been translated into plays. "The Age of Innocence" helped add to the luster of Katharine Cornell eight years ago, and one of her shorter pieces became "The Old Maid" of the theater, in which Judith Anderson and Helen Menken starred in 1935.

WILLIAM BUTLER YEATS

June 13, 1865–January 28, 1939

NICE, France—The death of William Butler Yeats, famous Irish poet and playwright, occurred yesterday. Mr. Yeats, who won the Nobel Prize for Literature in 1923, was 73 years old.

Mr. Yeats died in the little French Riviera town of Roquebrune, after a short illness, at a boarding house where he and his wife had been staying.

He will be buried tomorrow at Roquebrune. It was expected, however, that eventually the poet's body would be removed to his native Ireland.

Mr. Yeats arrived in Roquebrune early last month in ill health. He suffered repeated heart attacks, and was able to take only short walks in the gardens of the house where he stayed. He had been confined to his bed since Tuesday.—*The Associated Press*

When he labored at his chosen craft, that of writing poetry, essays and plays, Mr. Yeats frequently let his mind roam far afield in the realm of fancy, and it is for the gentle beauty of such works that he was hailed by many as the greatest poet of his time in the English language.

Yeats found time to crusade for worldly ends, but there his tactics were notable for tenacity and vigor. At

Yeats was born at Sandymount, near Dublin, on June 13, 1865, son of John Butler Yeats, well-known Irish painter. When 10 years old he was taken to London for training at the Godolphin School in Hammersmith, but much of his time, especially during the Summers, was spent in County Sligo, Ireland.

Three years directed to the study of painting failed to satisfy the young man's desire to express himself and, in 1886, he finally abandoned his father's profession in preference for a literary one and returned to London.

George Moore, his opponent in many a literary battle, wrote of him at this period: "Yeats was striding to and fro at the back of the dress circle, a long black cloak drooping from his shoulders, a soft black sombrero on his head, voluminous black silk tie flowing from his collar, loose black trousers dragging untidily over his long, heavy feet. His hair was black and his skin yellow."

It has been said his laughter was "the most melancholy thing in the world."

While yet in his 20s the Irish poet dwelt on the possibility of rejuvenating the intellectual life of his native land, faithfully holding to the hope of writing Irish plays in verse with Irish folklore as subject material and natives of Ireland sharing as actors and audience.

Lady Gregory and others answered his prayer for the organization of a national theatre in Dublin. With the opening of the Abbey Theatre, Yeats found opportunity to fulfill his passion for dramatic writing.

Yeats wrote more effectively in verse than prose, although there was frequently scant difference. Innumerable articles slipped from his pen and, as the years passed, he came to be synonymous with the Irish Movement in literature. Nevertheless, Sean O'Faolain, a countryman, notes:

"He began independently of Ireland. Some of his finest work was done under her inspiration. But his positively finest work of all—his later poems—are the work of a man who has again retired into himself and who writes clean out of his 'heart of darkness.'"

His contribution to Eire will grow out of the Abbey Theatre group, and far exceeded anything else Yeats accomplished in a non-literary field.

True, he defended divorce from the floor of the Dail, pleaded for a restricted use of Gaelic because he had utterly "failed to learn any language but English," given stump speeches on the tax question, and in every way conducted himself after the manner of public politicians.

"I am a Cosgrave man," Yeats once said, "but I believe that de Valera is dead right in his dispute with Great Britain. Whether or not Ireland can stand the racket is a ticklish question . . . We are a nation of believers. We produce anti-clerics, but atheists, never."

the turn of the century he shared in the establishment of the Abbey Theatre in Dublin, and for 10 years devoted himself almost exclusively to drama. The struggle of the Irish Free State likewise occupied his time. From 1922 until 1928 he was a Senator in the Dail Eireann.

John Masefield, poet laureate of England, on the occasion of Yeats's 70th birthday in June, 1935, called him "the greatest living poet," and unquestionably it will be for his verse that posterity will remember him. The high point in a life full with recognition came in 1923, when Yeats received the Nobel Prize for Literature.

Nearly 50 years ago he published his first verse in the Dublin University Review. The flow of words exhibited in that early composition indicated Yeats's natural command of language. Thus, he wrote:

I passed a little further on and heard a
*   peacock say:*
Who made the grass and made the
*   worms and made my feathers gay?*
He is a monstrous peacock, and he
*   waveth all the night*
His languid tail above us, lit with myriad
*   spots of light.*

In 1917 he married Georgia Hyde Lees of Wrexham, Wales, a woman who is said to possess powers as a spiritualist medium. They lived for many years with their two children in an ancient tower on the outermost coast of Ireland.

Three years ago to a day the poet suffered a heart attack at Palma, Mallorca. He rallied, however, and in May published a volume hailed as among the outstanding intellectual autobiographies of our time. "Dramatis Personae" continues the thread of reveries started in the Nineties and covers mi-

nutely the crowded years at the turn of the century when the Irish Dramatic Movement was conceived.

Today the words of Yeats's poem "The Shadowy Waters," written in 1900, come to mind:

> Could we but give us wholly to the dreams,
> And get into their world that to the sense
> Is shadow, and not linger wretchedly
> Among substantial things.

F. SCOTT FITZGERALD

September 24, 1896–December 21, 1940

HOLLYWOOD, Calif.—F. Scott Fitzgerald, novelist, short story writer and scenarist, died at his Hollywood home yesterday. His age was 44. He suffered a heart attack three weeks ago.—*The Associated Press*

Mr. Fitzgerald in his life and writings epitomized "all the sad young men" of the post-war generation. With the skill of a reporter and ability of an artist he captured the essence of a period when flappers and gin and "the beautiful and the damned" were the symbols of the carefree madness of an age.

Roughly, his own career began and ended with the Nineteen Twenties. "This Side of Paradise," his first

book, was published in the first year of that decade of skyscrapers and short skirts. Only six others came between it and his last, which, not without irony, he called "Taps at Reveille." That was published in 1935. Since then a few short stories, the script of a moving picture or two, were all that came from his typewriter. The promise of his brilliant career was never fulfilled.

The best of his books, the critics said, was "The Great Gatsby." When it was published in 1925, this ironic tale of life on Long Island at a time when gin was the national drink and sex the national obsession (according to the exponents of Mr. Fitzgerald's school of writers) received critical acclaim. In it Mr. Fitzgerald was at his best, which was, according to John Chamberlain, his "ability to catch the flavor of a period, the fragrance of a night, a snatch of old song, in a phrase."

This same ability was shown in his first book, and its hero, Amory Blaine, became as much a symbol of Mr. Fitzgerald's own generation as, two years later, Sinclair Lewis's Babbitt was to become a symbol of another facet of American culture. All his other books and many of his short stories (notably "The Beautiful and the Damned") had this same quality.

Francis Scott Key Fitzgerald (he was named after the author of the National Anthem, a distant relative of his mother's) was a stocky, good-looking young man with blond hair and blue eyes who might have stepped from the gay pages of one of his own novels. He was born Sept. 24, 1896, at St. Paul, Minn., the son of Edward and Mary McQuillan Fitzgerald.

At the Newman School, in Lakewood, N.J., where he was sent, young Fitzgerald paid more attention to extracurricular activities than to his studies. When he entered Princeton in 1913, he had already decided upon a career as writer of musical comedies. He spent most of his first year writing an operetta for the Triangle Club and consequently "flunked" in several subjects. He had to spend the Summer studying. In his sophomore year he was a "chorus girl" in his own show.

War came along in 1917, and Fitzgerald quit Princeton to join the Army. He served as a second lieutenant and then as a first lieutenant in the 45th and 67th Infantry Regiments and then as aide de camp to Brig. Gen. J. A. Ryan.

Every Saturday he would hurry over to the Officers' Club and there "in a room full of smoke, conversation and rattling newspapers" he wrote a 120,000-word novel on the consecutive weekends of three months. He called it "The Romantic Egotist." The publisher to whom he submitted it said it was the most original manuscript he had seen for years—but he wouldn't publish it.

After the war he begged the seven city editors of the seven newspapers in New York to give him a job. Each turned him down. He went to work for the Barron Collier advertising agency, where he penned the slogan for a Muscatine, Iowa, laundry:

"We keep you clean in Muscatine."

This got him a raise, but his heart was not in writing cards for streetcars. He spent all his spare time writing satires, only one of which he sold—for $30. He then abandoned New York in disgust and went back to St. Paul, where he wrote "This Side of Paradise." Its flash and tempo and its characters, who, in the estimation of Gertrude Stein, created for the general public "the new generation," made it an immediate success.

At the same time he married Miss Zelda Sayre of Montgomery, Ala., who has been called more than once "the brilliant counterpart of the heroines of his novels." Their only child, Frances Scott Fitzgerald, was born in 1921.

His next two books were collections of short stories: "Flappers and Philosophers" (1920) and "Tales of the Jazz Age" (1922). In 1923 he published a satirical play, "The Vegetable or, From President to Postman," and then for the next two years he worked on "The Great Gatsby." He had gathered material for it while living on Long Island after the war, and all its characters were taken compositely from life. He wrote most of it in Rome or on the Riviera, where he also wrote his most successful short stories. These, in 1926, were gathered under the title "All the Sad Young Men."

Only two other books were to follow: "Tender Is the Night" (1934) and "Taps at Reveille" (1935). After that, for several years, he lived near Baltimore, Md., where he suffered a depression of spirit which kept him from writing. He made several efforts to write but failed, and in an autobiographical article in Esquire likened himself to a "cracked plate."

"Sometimes, though," he wrote, "the cracked plate has to be retained in the pantry, has to be kept in service as a household necessity. It can never be warmed on the stove nor shuffled with the other plates in the dishpan; it will not be brought out for company, but it will do to hold crackers late at night, or to go into the ice-box with the left overs."

VIRGINIA WOOLF

January 25, 1882–March 28, 1941

LONDON—Mrs. Virginia Woolf, novelist and essayist, who had been missing from her home since last Friday, is believed to have been drowned at Rodwell, near Lewes, where she and her husband, Leonard Sidney Woolf, had a country residence.

Mr. Woolf said tonight:

"Mrs. Woolf is presumed to be dead. She went for a walk last Friday, leaving a letter behind, and it is thought she has drowned. Her body, however, has not been recovered."

The circumstances surrounding the novelist's disappearance were not revealed. The authorities at Lewes said they had no report of Mrs. Woolf's death.

It was reported her hat and cane had been found on the bank of the Ouse River. Mrs. Woolf, who was 59, had been ill for some time.

The Woolfs ran the Hogarth Press from 1917 to 1938, when Mrs. Woolf retired to devote her time to writing. Her last book was "Roger Fry, a Biography," published last year.

Mrs. Woolf was born in 1882. She was a daughter of Sir Leslie Stephen. James Russell Lowell was her godfather. She was granddaughter of Thackeray and relative of the Darwins, Symondes and Stracheys.

She grew up in a household that Stevenson, Ruskin, Lowell, Hardy, Meredith and other writers visited. As the wife of Leonard Woolf and the sister-in-law of Clive Bell, Mrs. Woolf had a literary circle of her own.

She was the author of 15 books of high quality, in which the critics met up with at least four different kinds of thinking and writing. This led to her being characterized as "the multiple Mrs. Woolf."

In the "Three Guineas" Mrs. Woolf replied to the question of a barrister: "How in your opinion are we to prevent war?" The keynote of this work was her remark that the inquiry must be unique in the history of human correspondence, "since when before has an educated man asked a woman how in her opinion war can be prevented."

Of one of her novels, "The Years," Ralph Thompson, book reviewer of The New York Times, said: "Mrs. Woolf is nearest perfection when dealing with the past or with a present that has already begin to lose itself in the past. Then she is near perfection indeed."

When not working on novels and longer essays, Mrs. Woolf frequently wrote for critical literary magazines, entering a number of literary controversies. One of her last tilts was with book reviewers in December, 1939.

She contended it was a "public duty" to abolish the book reviewer, holding that reviews were so hurriedly written that the reviewer was unable to deal adequately with the books his editor sent him. Mrs. Woolf declared no Act of Parliament would be necessary to abolish the reviewer, contending that the tendencies she deplored would soon condition him out of existence.

Commenting editorially on Mrs. Woolf's description of Augustine Birrell as a "born writer," The New York Times in August, 1930, described Mrs. Woolf as "one of the most subtle, original and modern of moderns, herself a born writer."

Mrs. Woolf's published works began with "The Voyage," in 1915, followed by "Night and Day," in 1919; "Jacob's Room," in 1922; "The Common Reader" and "Mrs. Dalloway," in 1925; "To the Lighthouse," in 1927; "Orlando" and "A Room of One's Own," in 1929; "The Waves," in 1931; "The Common Reader, Second Series," in 1932; "Flush," in 1933; "The Years," in 1937; "Three Guineas," in 1938, and "Roger Fry, A Biography," in 1940.

All her education was received at home from private tutors. Her favorite recreation was printing, in which she joined with her husband, Leonard Woolf, novelist and essayist, founder of the Hogarth Press, and former literary editor of The Nation.

The Associated Press

Dr. E. F. Hoare, Coroner at New Haven, Sussex, gave a verdict of suicide today in the drowning of Virginia Woolf, novelist. Her body was recovered last night from the River Ouse near her weekend house at Lewes.

The Coroner read a note that Mrs. Woolf had left for her husband, Leonard.

"I have a feeling I shall go mad," the note read. "I cannot go on any longer in these terrible times. I hear voices and cannot concentrate on my work. I have fought against it but cannot fight any longer. I owe all my happiness to you but cannot go on and spoil your life."

Her husband testified that Mrs. Woolf had been depressed for a considerable length of time.

When their Bloomsbury home was wrecked by a bomb some time ago, Mr. and Mrs. Woolf moved to another nearby. It, too, was made uninhabitable by a bomb, and the Woolfs then moved to their weekend home in Sussex.

Mrs. Woolf vanished March 28.

GERTRUDE STEIN

February 3, 1874–July 27, 1946

PARIS—Gertrude Stein, famed woman writer and one of the most controversial figures of American letters, died at 6:30 o'clock tonight at the American Hospital in Neuilly, a suburb of Paris. Her age was 72.

She had been suffering from cancer and had been in the hospital about a week. At the bedside were Miss Alice B. Toklas and Miss Stein's nephew and niece.

Although Gertrude Stein could and did write intelligibly, her distinction rested on her use of words apart from their conventional meaning. Her emphasis on sound rather than sense is illustrated by her oft-quoted "A rose is a rose is a rose."

Devotees of her cult professed to find her restoring a pristine freshness and rhythm to language. Medical authorities compared her effusions to the rantings of the insane. The Hearst press inquired, "Is Gertrude Stein not Gertrude Stein but somebody else living and talking in the same body?"

Born Feb. 3, 1874, in Allegheny, Pa., the daughter of Daniel Stein, who was vice president of a street railway, and Amelia Keyser Stein, she spent her childhood in Oakland and San Francisco. She was, in her own words, "an omnivorous reader, going through whole libraries, reading everything."

From 1893 to 1897 she was a student at Radcliffe College, where she was a favorite pupil of William James. When she sat down to write her final examination for him, she was tired, having been to the opera the night before. "Dear Professor James," she wrote on her paper, "I am so sorry but I do not feel a bit like an examination paper in philosophy today."

William James replied by postcard: "Dear Miss Stein, I understand perfectly how you feel. I often feel like that myself." He gave her the highest mark in the course.

During this period she published in a psychological journal a paper recording her experiments in spontaneous automatic writing—the method, according to some critics, by which her books were produced. She then studied medicine four years at Johns Hopkins University but took no degrees, explaining that she was bored by tests.

In 1903 she removed to Paris with Alice B. Toklas, a San Francisco friend, who was to be her lifelong secretary-companion.

On her arrival in Paris, she met the artists [Pablo] Picasso, [Henri] Matisse and [Georges] Braque. Possessed of an independent income, she became a patron of these men, was influenced by them and handed along that influence to younger artists and writers, among them Ernest Hemingway and Sherwood Anderson.

Her hobby was collecting the works of painters before they were famous. She claimed to have discovered Picasso, Juan Gris, Matisse and Braque and introduced them to the French and American public. Her shrewd connoisseurship is indicated by the fact that her collection of paintings was worth more than 10 times what she paid for it.

Her first book, "Three Lives," 1909, written in completely intelligible style, contained realistic tender portraits of two servant girls and a study of the unhappy love affair of a Negress. Carl Van Vechten, the critic, classed it with the greatest books of the age in his introduction to the Modern Library edition, which was a best seller.

Also written with more or less lucidity were her two biographies of herself, entitled "The Autobiography of Alice B. Toklas" and "Everybody's Autobiography," containing chitchat about Paris artists and American writers in Paris, with discourses on celebrities, art, literature, history, life in general and the genius of Gertrude Stein in particular.

During the First World War, Miss Stein drove a Ford down the lines distributing supplies to soldiers and visiting hospitals.

Her publications included "Making of Americans," 1926, and "Prayers and Portraits," 1934, the latter compared by John Chamberlain in The New York Times to "the Chinese water torture; it never stops and it is always the same."

Another critic once remarked that Miss Stein "elected to write in a manner which much of the time makes her concrete meaning inaccessible to the reader. . . . She pushed abstraction to its farthest limits." Clifton Fadiman dismissed Miss Stein as "the Mamma of Dada."

Perhaps the peak of her publicity was reached in 1934 when she came here on a lecture tour, and her opera "Four Saints in Three Acts," with music by Virgil Thomson, containing the famed line "Pigeons on the grass alas," was produced.

Her lectures went off well. Her audiences, if bewildered by her pronouncements, were also entertained by this roughly dressed woman with close-cropped hair that set off her strong features.

Among her most recent works were "Paris, France," "a love letter to France"; and "Wars I Have Seen," her experiences in occupied France. In it she follows life in a French village from day to day in defeat and after liberation. She wrote the book in Culoz beyond Grenoble, under the noses of the Nazis.

Writing of this book, Francis Hackett, The Times reviewer, concluded, "Hers is a powerful personality, but it needed the American Army to liberate her."

Miss Stein's latest book was published only a week ago under the title "Brewsie and Willie" and was described by Charles Poore in last Sunday's Times Book Review as a book about what the GI's talked of when they gathered around her feet in Paris, "or rather," Mr. Poore remarked, "what she would like to think they talked about, for Miss Stein is a very powerful character and things are apt to change dizzily when translated into Steinese."

GEORGE BERNARD SHAW

July 26, 1856–November 2, 1950

Ayot St. Lawrence, England—George Bernard Shaw, one of the modern age's greatest dramatists and its most caustic critic, died today at the age of 94. The white-bearded Irish-born sage, whose wit was renowned throughout the world for half a century, succumbed at 4:59 A.M.

His death was announced to newsmen by his housekeeper, Mrs. Alice Laden. Wearing black, she appeared at the gates of his cottage, Shaw's Corner, and told the reporters: "Mr. Shaw is dead."

The famed dramatist, who professed himself both a Communist and an atheist, was visited in his last hours by an Anglican clergyman, who said final prayers for the old sage's soul.

Shaw lapsed into his final coma yesterday morning and never regained consciousness. Operated on seven weeks ago for a broken thigh suffered when he slipped and fell in his garden, he grew steadily weaker. A bladder ailment aggravated his condition.

The reedy sage of Ayot St. Lawrence, never noted for modesty, proclaimed himself "the dramatic emperor of Europe," and many conceded him the title. He was the author of more than 50 plays. Many, like "Pygmalion," "Candida" and "Major Barbara," are world famous. Indeed, Shaw considered himself the rightful successor and perhaps the superior of Shakespeare.

Shaw ate only vegetables but spoke as if he fed only on raw meat. He gloried in his reputation as acknowledged world master of the studied insult. Even as death approached he continued to shoot vitriol-dipped barbs at the notions and foibles of his contemporaries.—*The Associated Press*

Goaded by the voice of Henry George and guided by the hand of Karl Marx, George Bernard Shaw stepped from the poverty of Dublin to flit across the Western world, the flaming, mocking, deadly serious messenger boy of the "new age." Tossing off sparks of wit and satire as his heels clicked against the pavement of conservatism, thumbing his nose at the smug and censorious, urging the world to read his books and reform, he never stopped his capers even when his red hair had turned white and his Mephistophelian eyebrows drooped with age.

He criticized the best-loved institutions of mankind—and "got away with it" because he was a supreme wit. Nothing escaped him, and those he pilloried the most flocked by the thousands to see his plays and helped make him rich by buying his books.

His huge energy and mental agility had made him an early controversialist. He moved from the benches of debating halls to the platform after being fired by the eloquence of Henry George.

"George switched me over to economics," he said. "I became very excited about his 'Progress and Poverty.'" Told that no one was qualified to discuss George until he read Karl Marx, the 26-year-old Shaw hied to the British Museum to read "Das Kapital." That, he told a biographer, "was the turning point in my career. Marx was a revelation. His abstract economics, I discovered later, were wrong, but he rent the veil."

Mr. Shaw was born in Dublin on July 26, 1856. He was the third child and only son of George Carr Shaw, an impecunious civil servant, and of Lucinda Elizabeth Shaw, daughter of a County Carlow landowner.

From his father, Mr. Shaw inherited his Irish gayety, wit and humor, but little else. A few years before the son's birth the father's public post had been abolished, and he had compounded his pension in a lump sum to engage in business as a corn merchant. He failed to make a go of it. Consequently, the family life of the Shaws was one of shabby gentility.

One of Mr. Shaw's pronounced traits can be traced to his father, who professed such a horror of alcohol that the young Shaw decided to become a teetotaler. Soon he discovered that "the governor" was a steady drinker.

"Even a quarrelsome or boastful drunkard may be found entertaining by people who are not particular," Mr. Shaw told a biographer. "But a miserable drunkard—and my father, in theory a teetotaler, was racked with shame and remorse even in his cups—is unbearable."

Mr. Shaw's mother was a singer who took part in amateur operatic performances in Dublin. Through her interests and associates, the Shaw children acquired a culture in music, drama and painting.

Mr. Shaw's formal education was extremely limited. In 1876, at the age of 20, he fled to London to take up a literary career. There he joined his mother, who had left her alcoholic husband and was earning her own living in that city as a music teacher.

It was at first a poverty-stricken existence, for in nine years Mr. Shaw was able to earn no more than the equivalent of about $30 with his pen. His efforts to become a novelist resulted in five books that garnered about 60 rejections from publishers.

In 1884 Mr. Shaw joined the Fabian Society of moderate socialists and became an ardent pamphleteer and a lecturer for the cause of socialism. He spoke at street corners, in parks, in halls in London and in the country.

About the same time, he embarked upon a notable career in journalism, serving as music critic for The World, where the initials "G.B.S." became famous, and as drama critic for The Saturday Review.

While still engaged in journalism, Mr. Shaw began his career as a dramatist. He wrote "Mrs. Warren's Profession" as a treatise on prostitution in its relation to the existing social order, in 1894. Under the British Censorship Law, the Lord Chamberlain refused a license for the performance of the play, and it was not produced until 1902. In 1905, when it played in New York, the actors were arrested and prosecuted.

Mr. Shaw suffered a breakdown from overwork in 1898, at the age of 42. This caused him to abandon journalism and most of his platform activities and to devote himself to the stage. In the same year he married Miss Charlotte Frances Payne-Townshend, of County Cork, a wealthy Irishwoman who shared his interest in social reform and the theater. She had nursed him back to health after his illness.

"Man and Superman," in 1905, established Mr. Shaw's fame with the public. What he was really driving at became clear to thousands who had not hitherto troubled to think of him otherwise than as a political fanatic or a buffoon. The doctrine of "creative evolution" which underlay this play was seen as the guiding social philosophy of all his work.

The First World War and its destruction of life and civilized standards made a profound impression upon Mr. Shaw. On one side, he returned to his old role as a pamphleteer. On the other side, he wrote fewer plays, and in them dealt with even more profound subjects than before, becoming more and more preoccupied with religious and philosophical themes.

His plays "Heartbreak House," "Back to Methuselah" and "Saint Joan" were accepted by the critics as formulating a Shavian philosophy based upon the idea that the Life Force (God) is an imperfect power striving to become perfect. All existence has been occupied in this struggle for perfection; man is still on probation, and will be scrapped as the mammoth beasts were if he fails to achieve God's purpose.

In 1925 Mr. Shaw received the Nobel Prize for Literature. He turned it down, calling the £7,000 award "a lifebelt thrown to a swimmer who has already reached the shore in safety." But under pressure he accepted the prize just long enough to turn the money over to the Anglo-Swedish Literary Alliance.

Mr. Shaw visited Russia in 1931, but until 1933 he refused all invitations to visit the United States. He ridiculed and scoffed at Americans.

In that year he made a world tour with Mrs. Shaw on the steamship Empress of Britain. Arriving in New York on April 11, 1933, he stayed only 26 hours, just long enough to make an incognito sightseeing tour and to deliver his only American lecture before a crowded audience at the Metropolitan Opera House. In a speech of 16,000 words, he advised the United States to scrap its Constitution, nationalize its banks, destroy the power of financiers and cancel all war indebtedness.

The speech failed to make a good impression.

For many years he would have no more to do with the movies or the radio than with the United States, and once refused an offer of $1,000,000 for exclusive movie rights to his works, but he finally succumbed. Late in life he talked frequently over the radio, including international hook-ups, posed and talked for newsreels, and in 1930 sold the movie rights to his plays.

During the early Thirties, a sensation was created by the publication in book form of some 300 letters which had passed between Mr. Shaw and Ellen Terry, the celebrated actress, for whom he had written the leading role in "Captain Brassbound's Conversion." Those of 1896 and 1897, just before Shaw's marriage, were passionate love letters in form. There was another sensation, typically Shavian in its paradoxical nature, when it was disclosed that the love affair was an entirely platonic one, and that Shaw and Miss Terry never met until 1905, except publicly in the theater. For years they purposely refrained from meeting lest it spoil their correspondence and end their "delicious flirtation."

Throughout the Second World War Mr. Shaw maintained his lifelong role of "general consultant to mankind," still unable to stay out of any controversy. He protested the closing of British theaters, and excoriated the British Government for dawdling, denouncing the party system of government, and, while steadfastly maintaining his love for democracy, found it, as practiced, a fraud on the people.

He was fatalistic about the prospect of peace under the benevolent guidance of an iron-fisted, powerful Big Four. Far from believing they could bring the world to peace, he even doubted if they could stick together. "We must still live dangerously, whether we like it or not," he said, refusing to celebrate V-E Day. He added: "The worst is yet to come."

His mordant wit, seemingly undulled, turned to any public question. He scoffed at projected war-guilt trials. He sent his japeries across the seas to America, which, he said, would soon lose Shaw and would then be in a devil of a fix.

Many have tried to anticipate the judgment of history upon the question whether Mr. Shaw is to take his place among the true geniuses of the world. To some authorities, there was no question as to his genius. Frank Harris, his close friend, thought he would survive like Dr. Johnson and Samuel Pepys, "two men in English literature whose personalities also were bigger than their works." Others held many different views, including the one that Mr. Shaw was just a charlatan, a mountebank, a buffoon, who was not to be taken seriously at all.

Whether he was genius or charlatan, Mr. Shaw's age did not know. It hated him, but it laughed at him and with him; it tried to stop him, but he wouldn't be stopped. He confounded his critics, both those who admired him and those who derided him. He would not give up the world. He grew old and was the last of his generation. If nothing else, he had made it think and had given it a good time; and if the "messenger boy of the new age" never found what he thought he was looking for, he and his thousands of admirers in two hemispheres lost nothing by reason of his long, tumultuous search.

EUGENE O'NEILL

October 16, 1888–November 27, 1953

BOSTON—Eugene O'Neill, the noted American playwright whose prolific talents had brought to him both Nobel and Pulitzer Prizes, died today of bronchial pneumonia.

Mr. O'Neill, who was 65, had been ill for several years with Parkinson's disease.

Mr. O'Neill, who died in a Boston apartment where he had been living recently, is survived by his third wife, Carlotta Monterey; a son, Shane, and a daughter, Oona O'Neill, the wife of the actor Charlie Chaplin.

Eugene Gladstone O'Neill was generally regarded as the foremost American playwright, his achievements in the theater overwhelming those of his ablest contemporaries. He came upon the scene at an opportune moment and remained active long after the American theater had come of age.

In the words of Brooks Atkinson of The New York Times, Mr. O'Neill shook up the drama as well as audiences and helped transform the theater into an art seriously related to life. The genius of Mr. O'Neill lay in raw boldness, in the elemental strength of his attack upon outworn concepts of destiny.

The playwright received the Pulitzer Prize on three occasions and was the second American to win the Nobel Prize for Literature.

The author of 38 plays, most of them grim dramas in which murder, disease, suicide and insanity are recurring themes, Mr. O'Neill was in recent years too wracked by illness to write. He lived in a house by the sea with his third wife, a former actress.

But his plays continued to be produced to acclaim here and abroad, and the fall of 1951 saw a O'Neill "revival" on Broadway. The American National Theatre and Academy scheduled his "Desire Under the Elms" to launch its new season. The New York City Theatre Company played "Anna Christie" as the second offering of its winter season.

A revival of "Ah, Wilderness!," the playwright's nostalgic comedy of first love, found its way to the television screen.

No modern playwright except the late George Bernard Shaw had been more widely produced than Mr. O'Neill. He was as well known in Stockholm, Buenos Aires, Mexico City and Calcutta as in New York.

There was as much color and excitement in his early life as there was in his plays. Indeed, much of his success was attributable to the fact that he had lived in and seen the very world from which he drew his dramatic material.

As a young man he spent his days as a sailor and his nights in dives that lined the water's edge. Out of these experiences came such plays as "The Hairy Ape," "Anna Christie" and "Beyond the Horizon," all of which have had a lasting life in the theater.

Mr. O'Neill was born on Oct. 16, 1888, in the Barrett House, a family hotel at 43rd Street and Broadway. His father was James O'Neill, who starred for so many years in "The Count of Monte Cristo." His mother was the former Ellen Quinlan. The first seven years of Eugene's life were spent trouping around the country with his parents.

On his eighth birthday he was enrolled in a Roman Catholic boarding school on the Hudson. In 1902, when he was 13, he entered Betts Academy in Stamford, Conn., then considered one of the leading boys' schools in New England.

He was graduated in 1906 and went to Princeton. After 10 months at the university, he was expelled for heaving a brick through a window of the local stationmaster's house. It marked the end of his formal education.

Shortly thereafter he went to Honduras with a young mining engineer, and the two spent several months exploring the country's jungles and tried their hand at prospecting for gold. The venture ended after Mr. O'Neill became ill with fever and was shipped home.

For a time the young man worked as an assistant stage manager for his father, who was touring in a play called "The White Sister." But he soon succumbed to the lure of far-off places and shipped as an ordinary seaman on a Norwegian freighter bound for Buenos Aires. This began his acquaintance with the forecastle that would stand him in good dramatic stead later on.

After Buenos Aires, he shipped again, this time for Portuguese East Africa. From there he sailed back to Buenos Aires, then worked his way to New York on an American ship.

In New York he lived at a waterfront dive known as Jimmy the Priest's, and acquired the locale for "Anna Christie." In August, 1912, he went to work as a reporter on The New London Telegraph in Connecticut. His newspaper career lasted for four months because, as he admitted, he was more interested in writing verse and swimming than in gathering news.

Just before Christmas in 1912 he developed tuberculosis and was sent to the Gaylord Farm Sanitarium at Wallingford, Conn., where he spent five months.

At Gaylord he began to read [August] Strindberg. "It was reading his plays," Mr. O'Neill later recalled, "that, above all else, first gave me the vision of what modern drama could be, and first inspired me with the urge to write for the theater myself."

After his discharge from the sanitarium he boarded with a family in New London for 15 months. During this period he wrote 11 one-act plays and two long ones. He tore up all but six of the one-acters. His father paid to have five of the six short plays printed in a volume called "Thirst," published in 1914.

The elder O'Neill also paid a year's tuition for his son at Prof. George Baker's famous playwriting course at Harvard. Afterwards, Mr. O'Neill returned to New York and settled in a Greenwich Village rooming house, where he proceeded to soak up more "local color" at various Village dives, among them a saloon known as The Working Girls' Home.

Mr. O'Neill lived in the Village until 1916, when he moved to Provincetown, Mass., and fell in with a group conducting a summer theatrical stock company known as the Wharf Theatre. He hauled out a sizable collection of unproduced and unpublished plays, one of which, a one-acter called "Bound East for Cardiff," was put into rehearsal. It marked Mr. O'Neill's debut as a dramatist.

At summer's end the Wharf Theatre set up shop in New York and called itself the Provincetown Players, a name that was to become famous. The company produced more of Mr. O'Neill's plays, and the budding playwright began to be talked about in theatrical circles farther afield. About the same time, three of his one-act plays, "The Long Voyage Home," "Ile" and "The Moon of the Carribbees," were published in the magazine Smart Set.

In 1918 Mr. O'Neill went to Cape Cod to live, occupying a former Coast Guard station on a lonely spit of land three miles from Provincetown. He started working on longer plays and, in 1920, had his first big year when he won the first of his three Pulitzer Prizes for "Beyond the Horizon." The play marked Mr. O'Neill's first appearance on Broadway. The other prize winners were "Anna Christie" in 1922 and "Strange Interlude" in 1928.

"Beyond the Horizon" established Mr. O'Neill as both a ranking playwright and a moneymaker. The play ran for 111 performances and grossed $117,071.

The Theatre Guild began producing his plays with "Marco Millions" in 1927 and staged all his plays thereafter. At least three of the plays, "Mourning Becomes Electra," "Strange Interlude" and "The Iceman Cometh," marked a new departure—they ran from four to five hours in length.

Mr. O'Neill's dramas ranged from simple realism to the most abstruse symbolism, but one play—"Ah, Wilderness!"—was more in the tradition of straight entertainment and interspersed with sentiment. The play ran for 289 performances.

Mr. O'Neill did not always meet with approval. At times he was the object of bitter denunciation, especially from persons who believed his works smacked of immorality. By his choice of themes he several times stirred up storms that swept his plays into the courts.

"All God's Chillun Got Wings" was fought by New York authorities on the ground that it might lead to race riots. "Desire Under the Elms" was almost closed in the face of mounting protests. It never did open in Boston. The play was permitted to go on in Los Angeles, but after a few performances the police arrested everybody in the cast.

"The Hairy Ape," which starred Louis Wolheim in the role of Yank, a powerful, primitive stoker, was one of the dramatist's most popular works. The play ran for 10 weeks, went on the road for a long tour and later was popular abroad.

Many critics felt that "Mourning Becomes Electra," which opened on Oct. 26, 1931, and had 14 acts, was Mr. O'Neill's masterpiece. Mr. Atkinson called it "heroically thought out and magnificently wrought in style and structure." Joseph Wood Krutch observed that "it may turn out to be the only permanent contribution yet made by the 20th century to dramatic literature."

After "Days Without End" was produced in 1934, a play that lasted only 57 performances, Mr. O'Neill was not represented on Broadway until 1946, when "The Iceman Cometh" was staged.

In 1936, he won the Nobel Prize but could not go to Stockholm to receive it because of an appendicitis operation.

In a letter to the prize committee, Mr. O'Neill said: "This highest of distinctions is all the more grateful to me because I feel so deeply that it is not only my work which is being honored but the work of all my colleagues in America—that the Nobel Prize is a symbol of the coming of age of the American theatre."

After "The Iceman Cometh," Mr. O'Neill wrote a play called "Long Day's Journey into Night," which will not be produced until 25 years after his death. He had shown the manuscript to a few friends, and it was reported that the play deals with his own family life.

Mr. O'Neill was stricken with Parkinson's disease about 1947. The disease caused his hands to jerk convulsively, making it impossible for him to write in longhand.

In 1909 the dramatist married the former Kathleen Jenkins, who bore him a son, Eugene O'Neill Jr. The son committed suicide on Sept. 25, 1950. The marriage ended in divorce in 1912, and six years later, Mr. O'Neill married the former Agnes Boulton. They were divorced in 1929. Shane and Oona were born to this marriage. Mr. O'Neill married Miss Monterey on July 22, 1929.

ERNEST HEMINGWAY

July 21, 1899–July 2, 1961

KETCHUM, Idaho—Ernest Hemingway was found dead of a shotgun wound in the head at his home here today. His wife, Mary, said that he had killed himself accidentally while cleaning the weapon.

Mr. Hemingway, whose writings won him a Nobel Prize and a Pulitzer Prize, would have been 62 years old July 21.

Frank Hewitt, the Blaine County Sheriff, said after a preliminary investigation that the death "looks like an accident," adding, "There is no evidence of foul play."

The body of the bearded, barrel-chested writer, clad in a robe and pajamas, was found by his wife in their modern concrete house in this village on the outskirts of Sun Valley. A double-barreled, 12-gauge shotgun lay beside him with one chamber discharged.

Mrs. Hemingway, the author's fourth wife, was at the time of the shooting the only other person in the house and was asleep in a bedroom upstairs. The shot woke her and she went downstairs to find her husband's body near a gun rack in the foyer. Mrs. Hemingway told friends that she had been unable to find any note.

Mr. Hemingway was an ardent hunter and an expert on firearms. His father, Dr. Clarence Edmonds

Hemingway, who was also devoted to hunting, shot himself to death in 1928 at the age of 57, despondent over a diabetic condition. The theme of a father's suicide cropped up frequently in Mr. Hemingway's short stories and at least one novel, "For Whom the Bell Tolls."

As an adult, he sought out danger. He was wounded by mortar shells in Italy in World War I and narrowly escaped death in the Spanish Civil War when three shells plunged into his hotel room. In World War II, he was injured in a taxi accident. He nearly died of blood poisoning on one African safari, and he and his wife walked away from an airplane crash in 1954 on another big-game hunt.

The author, who owned two estates in Cuba and a home in Key West, Fla., started coming to Ketchum 20 years ago. His house sits on a hillside near the banks of the Wood River.

Mr. Hemingway achieved worldwide fame and influence as a writer by a combination of great emotional power and a highly individual style that could be parodied but never successfully imitated. His lean and sinewy prose; his mastery of a laconic, understated dialogue; his insistent use of repetition, often of a single word, built up and transmitted an inner excitement to countless of his readers. In his best work, the effect was accumulative; it was as if the creative voltage increased as the pages turned.

Not all readers agreed on Mr. Hemingway, and his "best" single work will be the subject of literary

debate for generations. But possibly "The Old Man and the Sea," published in 1952, had the essence of the uncluttered force that drove his other stories. In it, man is a victim of, and yet rises above, the elemental harshness of nature.

The short novel won the Pulitzer Prize in 1953, and it unquestionably moved the judges who awarded Mr. Hemingway the Nobel Prize for Literature the following year. A great deal of Mr. Hemingway's work showed a preoccupation, frequently called an obsession, with violence and death. He loved guns, he was one of the great aficionados of the deadly bullfight, and he identified with the adventures of partisan warfare.

He wrote a great deal of hunting, fishing, and prizefighting, with directness, vigor, and the accuracy of a man who has handled the artifacts of a sport. He was at times a hard liver and a hard drinker, but he was also a hard and constant worker.

Mr. Hemingway's fascination with the calibers of cartridges and physical conflict in general brought a barb from the writer Max Eastman in 1937. "Come out from behind that false hair on your chest, Ernest," Mr. Eastman wrote. "We all know you."

Mainly by trial and error, Mr. Hemingway had taught himself to write limpid English prose. Of his apprentice days as a writer in Paris, he wrote:

"I was trying to write then and I found the greatest difficulty, aside from knowing truly what you really felt, rather than what you were supposed to feel, and had been taught to feel, was to put down what really happened in action; what the actual things were which produced the emotion that you experienced."

Ernest Miller Hemingway was born in Oak Park, Ill., a suburb of Chicago, on July 21, 1899, the second of six children. His father was a physician who was more devoted to hunting and fishing than to his practice and gave the boy a fishing rod when he was 3 and a shotgun when he was 10. His mother, Grace Hall Hemingway, was a religious-minded woman who sang in the choir of the First Congregational Church.

With his graduation from Oak Park High, Mr. Hemingway completed his formal education. He read widely, however, and had a natural facility for languages.

World War I was underway, and Mr. Hemingway managed to get to Italy, where he wangled his way into the fighting as a Red Cross ambulance driver with the Italian Army. He learned all about the great Italian rout at Caporetto, which he described brilliantly in "A Farewell to Arms," published in 1929.

On July 8, 1918, while he was passing out candy to frontline troops at Fossalta di Piave, Mr. Hemingway was wounded in the leg by an Austrian mortar shell and hospitalized for many weeks. He eventually drifted to the expatriate Left Bank world of Paris and was soon one of the writers who frequented Shakespeare & Co., the bookstore of Sylvia Beach. Here he met, among many others, André Gide and James Joyce.

It was in Paris that Mr. Hemingway began to write seriously. He wrote with discernment about the persons around him, his expatriate countrymen, together with the "Lost Generation" British and European post-war strays, and he limned them with deadly precision.

Before he was established as a writer, Mr. Hemingway underwent the privations that were almost standard for young men of letters in Paris. He lived in a tiny room and often subsisted on a few cents' worth of fried potatoes a day. With the publication in 1926 of "The Sun Also Rises" after three years of indifferent response to his work, he achieved sudden fame.

In 1928, Mr. Hemingway returned to the United States, where he lived for the next 10 years, mostly in Florida. He was still only 30 when he published his highly successful "A Farewell to Arms."

"Death in the Afternoon" was published in 1932, and the book's great success established its author as one of the great popularizers of bullfighting.

For several years Mr. Hemingway hunted big game in Africa and did much shooting and fishing in different parts of the world. "Winner Take Nothing" was published in 1933 and "The Green Hills of Africa" in 1935. The latter was one of the best contemporary accounts of the complex relationships between the hunter, the hunted and the African natives who are essential to the ritual of their confrontation.

Like many American intellectuals, Mr. Hemingway offered some degree of support to left-wing movements during the Nineteen Thirties. In "To Have and Have Not" (1937), one critic thought he had sounded "vaguely Socialist," although more readers will remember the work as a tale of action and tragedy in the Florida Keys, the love affair between the doomed boatman and his slatternly wife.

In 1936, Mr. Hemingway went to Spain and covered the war for the North American Newspaper Alliance. In 1940 his novel of the Spanish Civil War, "For Whom the Bell Tolls," showed that his own deepest sympathies were with the Loyalists.

The year World War II broke out, Mr. Hemingway took up residence in Cuba. But soon he was back in action in Europe, resuming the combat correspondence he had begun in Spain. He was with the first of the Allied armed forces to enter Paris, where, as he put it, he "liberated the Ritz" Hotel. Later he was with the Fourth United States Infantry Division in an assault in the Hurtgen Forest, winning the Bronze Star for his semi-military services in this action.

In 1950, critics were disappointed by "Across the River and into the Trees," the story of a frustrated United States infantry colonel who goes to Venice to philosophize, make love and die. But two years later "The Old Man and the Sea" pleased virtually everyone. It relied on the elemental drama of a fisherman who catches the greatest marlin of his life, only to have it eaten to the skeleton by sharks before he can get it to port.

On Jan. 23, 1954, the writer and the fourth Mrs. Hemingway, the former Mary Welsh, figured in a double crash in Uganda, British East Africa. First reports said both had been killed. In fact, after one light plane crashed, a second had picked up the couple unhurt. Both Mr. Hemingway and his wife suffered injuries in the crack-up of the rescue plane.

Mr. Hemingway's other published writings include "Three Stories and Ten Poems," "In Our Time," "The Torrents of Spring," "Men Without Women," and "The Fifth Column and First Forty-nine Stories."

Mr. Hemingway earned millions of dollars from his work, partly because many of his stories and novels were adapted to the screen and television. These included "The Killers," an early gangster story; "The Snows of Kilimanjaro" and "The Short Happy Life of Francis Macomber," both set in East Africa; "The Sun Also Rises," "A Farewell to Arms," "For Whom the Bell Tolls" and "The Old Man and the Sea."

Mr. Hemingway's first wife was the former Hadley Richardson, whom he married in 1919. They were divorced in 1926. The next year Mr. Hemingway married Pauline Pfeiffer. This marriage ended with divorce in 1940, and that year Mr. Hemingway married a novelist, Martha Gellhorn. In 1946, after their divorce, Mr. Hemingway married Miss Welsh. Along with his wife, Mr. Hemingway is survived by a sister and three sons.

WILLIAM FAULKNER

September 25, 1897–July 6, 1962

Oxford, Miss.—William Faulkner died of a heart attack today in this Mississippi town that he made famous in literature.

The author was 64 years old. His wife, Estelle, was at his bedside.

In recent years Mr. Faulkner had spent much of his time at the University of Virginia, where he was a lecturer on American literature. He and his wife returned last May to Oxford, a community of about 8,000 that Mr. Faulkner used as home base throughout his career.

President [John F.] Kennedy, leading the nation in tributes to the author, said: "Since Henry James, no writer has left behind such a vast and enduring monument to the strength of American literature."

Mr. Faulkner won the Nobel Prize for 1949 for a series of novels in which he created his own Yoknapatawpha County in northern Mississippi. There he set his Gothic saga of decadent sophisticates, greedy landlords, and shrewd and brutal tenant farmers.

Mr. Faulkner won a Pulitzer Prize for his 1954 novel, "The Fable."

His most famous novels were "Absalom, Absalom!" "Sartoris," "The Sound and the Fury," "As I Lay Dying," "Sanctuary" and "Light in August," and the trilogy "The Hamlet," "The Town" and "The Mansion." His most recent novel, "The Reivers," was published June 4 to critical acclaim.

In addition to his widow, survivors include his daughter and two brothers.

A key to Mr. Faulkner's genius was the faculty he possessed of thinking and writing in the vernacular of poor whites and Negroes of his section.

The tales of Yoknapatawpha, interwoven with rape, violence and sadism, repelled some readers to the extent that recognition in his homeland had to await acclaim from abroad.—*United Press International*

The storm of literary controversy that beat about William Faulkner is not likely to diminish with his death. Many of the most firmly established critics of literature were deeply impressed by the stark and somber power of his writing. Yet many commentators were repelled by his themes and his prose style.

To the sympathetic critics, Mr. Falkner dealt with the dark journey and the final doom of man in terms that recalled the Greek tragedians. They found symbolism in the frequently unrelieved brutality of the yokels of Yoknapatawpha County, the imaginary Deep South region from which Mr. Faulkner drew the persons and scenes of his most characteristic works.

Actually, Yoknapatawpha was Lafayette County and Jefferson town was the Oxford on the red-hill section of northern Mississippi where William Faulkner was reared and where his family had been deeply rooted for generations.

While admitting that Mr. Faulkner's prose sometimes lurched and sprawled, his admirers could point out an undeniable golden sharpness of characterization and description.

Of Mr. Faulkner's power to create living and deeply moving characters, Malcolm Cowley wrote:

"And Faulkner loved these people created in the image of the land. After a second reading of his novels, you continue to be impressed by his villains, Popeye and Jason and Joe Christmas and Flem Snopes: but this time you find more place in your memory for other figures standing a little in the background yet presented by the author with quiet affection: old ladies like Miss Jenny DuPré, with their sharp-tongued benevolence; shrewd but kindly bargainers like Ratliff, the sewing machine agent, and Will Varner, with his cotton gin and general store."

Mr. Faulkner was an acknowledged master of the vivid descriptive phrase. Popeye had eyes that "looked like rubber knobs." He had a face that "just went away, like the face of a wax doll set too near the fire and forgotten."

The apt phrases that Mr. Faulkner found for the weather and the seasons were cited by his admirers. There was the "hot pine-winey silence of the August afternoon," "the moonless September dust, the trees not rising soaring as trees should but squatting like huge fowl," "those windless Mississippi December days which are a sort of Indian summer's Indian summer."

Many critics contended that Mr. Faulkner served up raw slabs of pseudorealism that had little merit as serious writing. They said that his writings showed an obsession with murder, rape, incest, suicide, greed and depravity that existed largely in the author's mind.

William Faulkner was born in New Albany, Miss., on Sept. 25, 1897.

The first Faulkners—the "u" is a recent restoration by William Faulkner—came to Mississippi in the Eighteen Forties. William Faulkner was the oldest child of Murray Falkner and Maude Butler Falkner. Murray Falkner ran a livery stable in Oxford and later became business manager of the University of Mississippi at Oxford.

In William Faulkner's fiction the Sartoris clan is the Falkner family. The Sartorises are forced to make humiliating compromises with the members of the grasping and upstart Snopes family.

William Faulkner played quarterback on the Oxford High School football team but failed to graduate. Later he wrote: "Quit school to work in grandfather's bank. Learned medicinal value of his liquor. Grandfather thought it was the janitor. Hard on the janitor."

Oxford, where Mr. Faulkner grew up, is a typical Deep-South town. It has the traditional courthouse square flanked with statues of Confederate soldiers, and a quiet main street lined by one-story buildings and stores.

The 1949 motion picture "Intruder in the Dust," based on Mr. Faulkner's novel of that name, was filmed in Oxford.

The film depicted racial intolerance and bigotry in a small Southern community but had a "happy ending" in which an elderly, proud Negro accused of murder is saved from lynching by a white Southern lawyer with the help of a white boy and an elderly white woman. The movie was called "great" by Bosley Crowther, The New York Times critic.

Mr. Faulkner also said he had written a dozen movie scripts, most of them for his friend Howard Hawks, adding:

"He sent for me later to help adapt what Ernest Hemingway said was the worst book he ever wrote, 'To Have and Have Not.' Then I did another one, from that book by Raymond Chandler, 'The Big Sleep.' I also did a war picture, one I liked doing, 'The Road to Glory,' with Fredric March and Lionel Barrymore. I made me some money and I had me some fun."

Back home, he was briefly a student at the University of Mississippi.

One who knew Mr. Faulkner as a student at the University of Mississippi is George W. Healy Jr., editor of The New Orleans Times-Picayune.

"I first knew Bill when he was postmaster at the University of Mississippi post office in 1922," Mr. Healy said. "But Bill got fired as postmaster because he used the post office as a kind of men's club. One day a post office inspector came in while a bridge game was in progress and a little while later Bill told us he was leaving."

With the publication of "The Sound and the Fury" in 1929, Mr. Faulkner gave strong indications of being a major writer. The critics found in it something of the word-intoxication of James Joyce and the long, lasso-like sentences of Henry James.

"Sanctuary," published in 1931, was Mr. Faulkner's most popular and best-selling novel. It is about the harrowing experiences of a sensitive Southern girl, Temple Drake, who, like many Faulkner characters, reappears in another book, in this case "Requiem for a Nun." One of Mr. Faulkner's most memorable characters, Popeye, was created for "Sanctuary."

Among Mr. Faulkner's other notable books were "The Sound and the Fury" and "As I Lay Dying." The former, described by one critic as "one of the few original efforts at experimental writing in America," is told partly through the mind of an idiot named Benjy.

Mr. Faulkner lived and did most of his writing in Oxford in an old colonial house that he bought in 1930. He was a slightly built man who carried himself tensely, and when bothered or bored he could exhibit quick anger. He had thick iron-gray hair and a dark mustache. When he felt like it he could be charming and his manners were impeccable.

On one occasion, Bennett Cerf, head of Random House, Mr. Faulkner's publisher, had taken the bourbon-sipping author to task for not answering his mail. Mr. Faulkner was said to have replied:

"Mr. Cerf, when I get a letter from you, I open it and shake it and if a check doesn't fall out I tend to forget it."

ROBERT FROST

March 26, 1874–January 29, 1963

BOSTON—Robert Frost, dean of American poets, died today at the age of 88.

He was pronounced dead at Peter Bent Brigham Hospital at 1:50 A.M. The cause was listed as "probably a pulmonary embolism," or blood clot in the lungs.

Not long before his death, Mr. Frost had been dictating an article on Ezra Pound from his hospital bed when he fell asleep, according to his daughter, Leslie Frost.—*The Associated Press*

Robert Frost was beyond doubt the only American poet to play a touching personal role at a Presidential inauguration; to report a casual remark of a Soviet dictator that stung officials in Washington, and to twit the Russians about the barrier to Berlin by reading to them, on their own ground, his celebrated poem about another kind of wall.

But it would be much more to the point to say he was also without question the only poet to win four Pulitzer Prizes and, in his ninth decade, to symbolize the rough-hewn individuality of the American creative spirit more than any other man.

Finally, it might have been even more appropriate to link his uniqueness to his breathtaking sense of exactitude in the use of metaphors based on direct observations ("I don't like to write anything I don't see," he told

an interviewer in Cambridge, Mass., two days before his 88th birthday.)

Thus he recorded timelessly how the swimming buck pushed the "crumpled" water; how the wagon's wheels "freshly sliced" the April mire; how the ice crystals from the frozen birch snapped off and went "avalanching" on the snowy crust.

The incident of Jan. 20, 1961—when John F. Kennedy took the oath as President—was perhaps the most dramatic of Mr. Frost's "public" life.

Invited to write a poem for the occasion, he rose to read it. But the blur of the sun and the edge of the wind hampered him; his brief plight was so moving that a photograph of former President Dwight D. Eisenhower, Mrs. Kennedy and Mrs. Lyndon Johnson watching him won a prize because of the deep apprehension in their faces.

But Mr. Frost was not daunted. Aware of the problem, he simply put aside the new poem and recited from memory an old favorite, "The Gift Outright," dating to the nineteen-thirties. It fit the circumstances as snugly as a glove.

In 1962, Mr. Frost accompanied Stewart L. Udall, Secretary of the Interior, on a visit to Moscow.

A first encounter with Soviet children, studying English, did not encourage the poet. He recognized the problem posed by the language; it was painfully ironic, because he had said years before that poetry was what was "lost in translation."

But a few days later, he read "Mending Wall" at a Moscow literary evening. "Something there is that doesn't love a wall," the poem begins. The Russians may not have got the subsequent nuances. But the idea quickly spread that the choice of the poem was not unrelated to the wall partitioning Berlin.

On Sept. 7, the poet had a long talk with Premier Khrushchev. He described the Soviet leader as "no fathead"; as smart, big and "not a coward."

"He's not afraid of us and we're not afraid of him," he added.

Subsequently, Mr. Frost reported that Mr. Khrushchev had said the United States was "too liberal to fight." It was this remark that caused a considerable stir in Washington.

Explaining why he invited Mr. Frost to speak at his inauguration, President Kennedy said, "I think politicians and poets share at least one thing, and that is their greatness depends upon the courage with which they face the challenges of life."

The President was echoing a cry that Mr. Frost had long made—the higher role of the poet in a business society. "Everyone comes down to Washington to get equal with someone else," he told a Senate education subcommittee. "I want our poets to be declared equal to—what shall I say?—the scientists. No, to big business."

Many years before, he told young writers gathered under Bread Loaf Mountain at Middlebury, Vt.:

"Every artist must have two fears—the fear of God and the fear of man—fear of God that his creation will ultimately be found unworthy, and the fear of man that he will be misunderstood by his fellows."

These two fears were ever present in Robert Frost, with the result that his published verses were of the highest order and completely understood by thousands of Americans in whom they struck a ready response. To countless persons who had never seen New Hampshire birches in the snow or caressed a perfect ax he exemplified a great American tradition with his superb, almost angular verses written out of the New England scene.

His pictures of an abandoned cord of wood warming "the frozen swamp as best it could with the slow smokeless burning of decay," or of how "two roads diverged in a wood, and I—I took the one less traveled by, and that has made all the difference," with their Yankee economy of words, moved his readers nostalgically and filled the back pastures of their mind with memories of a shrewd and quiet way of life.

Strangely enough, Mr. Frost spent 20 years writing his verses about stone walls and brown earth, blue butterflies and tall, slim trees without winning any recognition in America. It was not until "A Boy's Will" was published in England and Ezra Pound publicized it that Mr. Frost was recognized as the indigenous American poet that he was.

In the years that followed, besides receiving the four Pulitzers, he was to be honored by institutions of higher learning and find it possible for a poet to earn enough money so that he would not have to teach or farm or make shoes or write for newspapers—all things he had done in his early days.

Like many another Yankee individualist, Mr. Frost was a rebel. He was the son of an ardent Democrat whose belief in the Confederacy led him to name his son Robert Lee. The father, William Frost, had run away from Amherst, Mass., to go West; Robert was born in San Francisco on March 26, 1874. His mother, born in Edinburgh, Scotland, emigrated to Philadelphia when she was a girl.

His father died when Robert was about 11. The boy and his mother, the former Isabelle Moody, went to live at Lawrence, Mass., with William Prescott Frost, Robert's grandfather, who gave the boy a good schooling. Influenced by the poems of Edgar Allan Poe, Robert wanted to be a poet before he went to Dartmouth College, where he stayed only through 1892.

In the next several years he worked as a bobbin boy in the Lawrence mills, as a shoemaker and as a reporter for The Lawrence Sentinel. He attended Harvard in 1897–98, then became a farmer at Derry, N.H., and taught there. In 1905 he married Elinor White, also a teacher, by whom he had five children. In 1912 Mr. Frost sold the farm and the family went to England.

He came home to find the editor of The Atlantic Monthly asking for poems. He sent along the very ones the magazine had previously rejected, and they were published. The Frosts went to Franconia, N.H., to live in a farm house Mr. Frost had bought for $1,000. His poetry brought him some money, and in 1916 he again

became a teacher. He was a professor of English, then "poet in residence" for more than 20 years at Amherst College. He spent two years in a similar capacity at the University of Michigan. Later Frost lectured and taught at The New School in New York.

In 1938 he retired temporarily as a teacher. Mrs. Frost died that year in Florida. Afterward, he taught intermittently at Harvard, Amherst and Dartmouth.

While critics heaped belated praise on his earthy, Yankee poems, there were also finely fashioned lyrics in which the man of the soil flashed fire with intellect. Such a poem was "Reluctance" with its nostalgic ending:

> *Ah, when to the heart of man was it ever*
> *   less than treason*
> *To go with the drift of things, to yield with*
> *   a grace to reason,*
> *And bow and accept the end of a love or*
> *   a season?*

Or:

> *Some say the world will end in fire,*
> *Some say in ice.*
> *From what I've tasted of desire*
> *I hold with those who favor fire.*
> *But if it had to perish twice,*
> *I think I know enough of hate*
> *To say that for destruction ice*
> *Is also great*
> *And would suffice.*

Asked about his method of writing a poem, Mr. Frost said: "I have worried quite a number of them into existence, but any sneaking preference [I have had] remains for the ones I have carried through like the stroke of a racquet, club or headsman's ax."

In another interview he observed: "If poetry isn't understanding all, the whole world, then it isn't worth anything. Young poets forget that poetry must include the mind as well as the emotions. Too many poets delude themselves by thinking the mind is dangerous and must be left out. Well, the mind is dangerous and must be left in."

T. S. ELIOT

September 26, 1888–January 4, 1965

LONDON—T. S. Eliot, the quiet, gray figure who gave new meaning to English-language poetry, died today at his home in London. He was 76 years old.

Eliot was an American who moved to England at the beginning of World War I and became wholly identified with Britain, even becoming naturalized in 1927.

The influence of Eliot began with the publication in 1917 of his poem "The Love Song of J. Alfred Prufrock." Perhaps his most significant contribution came five years later in the lengthy poem "The Waste Land."

Eliot, who won the Nobel Prize for Literature in 1948, was a convert to Anglo-Catholicism, and his religious belief showed up strongly in his later works.

This is the way the world ends
This is the way the world ends
This is the way the world ends
Not with a bang but a whimper.

These four lines by Thomas Stearns Eliot, written as the conclusion to "The Hollow Men" in 1925, are probably the most quoted lines of any 20th-century poet writing in English. They are also the essence of Eliot as he established his reputation as a poet of post–World War I disillusion and despair.

They were written by an expatriate from St. Louis, a graduate of Harvard College, who had chosen to live in London and who was working as a bank clerk.

Together with "The Waste Land," published three years earlier, these works established Eliot as a major poet. From there he went on to fame and financial independence, but he always remained, in the layman's view, the poet of gray melancholy.

Eliot's early poems did not represent the more mature conclusions of his later years about the state of mankind and the world, as stated in "The Four Quartets," or his delicious sense of humor, whose subjects included himself:

How unpleasant to meet Mr. Eliot!
With his features of clerical cut.
And his brow so grim
And his mouth so prim . . .

Whereas Eliot began his seminal "The Waste Land" with the line "April is the cruellest month" and ended it 434 lines later with "Shantih shantih shantih," his more seasoned reflections included these lines from "The Four Quartets":

And right action is freedom
From past and future also.
For most of us, this is the aim
Never here to be realized;
Who are only undefeated
Because we have gone on trying;
We, content at last
If our temporal reversion nourish
(Not too far from the yew-tree)
The life of significant soil.

Not only did Eliot shift his philosophic outlook, but his poetic accents also became almost conversational.

In appearance he was an unlikely figure for a poet. Eliot was a stooped man of just over 6 feet who had a prim appearance which mingled with a slight air of anxiety.

He lacked flamboyance or oddity in dress or manner, and there was nothing of the romantic about him. His habits of work were equally "unpoetic," for he eschewed bars and cafes for the bourgeois comforts of an office with padded chairs and a well-lighted desk.

Eliot's attire was a model of the London man of business. He wore a bowler and often carried a tightly rolled umbrella. His accent, which started out as pure American Middle West, became over the years quite upper-class British.

The poet was born on Sept. 26, 1888, into a family that had a good background in the intellectual, religious and business life of New England.

He entered Harvard in 1906 in the class that included Water Lippmann, Heywood Broun, and John Reed. He completed his undergraduate work in three years and took a Master of Arts degree in his fourth. Although he never took his doctorate, he completed the dissertation in 1916.

His Harvard classmates recall that he dressed with the studied carelessness of a British gentleman, smoked a pipe and liked to be left alone. This aspect of Eliot was hardly altered when he briefly returned to Harvard in the nineteen-thirties as a sort of poet in residence.

In that sojourn he lived in an undergraduate house near the Charles River and entertained students at teas. The tea was always brewed and he poured with great delicacy, his long fingers clasping the handle of the silver teapot. The quality of his tea, the excellence of the petit fours and the rippling flow of his conversation drew overflow crowds of students.

Eliot was an omnivorous reader. He consumed philosophy, languages and letters, and this lent his poetry an erudition and scholarship unmatched in this century. He footnoted "The Waste Land" as though it were a doctoral thesis.

He had a strong dislike for most teaching of poetry, and once recalled that he had been turned against Shakespeare in his youth by didactical instructors.

"I took a dislike to 'Julius Caesar' which lasted, I am sorry to say, until I saw the film of Marlon Brando and John Gielgud," he said, "and a dislike to 'The Merchant of Venice' which persists to this day."

In 1915 Eliot became a teacher in the Highgate School in London, and the next year went to work in Lloyds Bank, Ltd.

In London, Eliot lived in a comfortable apartment in Chelsea overlooking the Thames. In 1915, he married Miss Vivienne Haigh-Wood, who died in 1947. In 1957, Eliot married Miss Valerie Fletcher, his private secretary. He was then 68 and his bride about 30.

Eliot's association with the "little" magazines—those voices of protest against the Establishment—began when he was assistant editor of Egoist from 1917 to 1919.

He established The Criterion, a literary publication that never had a circulation exceeding 900. Later he was an editor for Faber & Faber.

The first poem that started Eliot's reputation was "The Love Song of J. Alfred Prufrock" in 1917. In it he assumed the pose of a fastidious, world-weary, young-old man, aging into ironic wit. The poem is full of exquisitely precise surrealist images and rhythms, but it also has everyday metaphors. Part of it goes:

> I grow old . . . I grow old . . .
> I shall wear the bottoms of my trousers
>   rolled.
> Shall I part my hair behind?
> Do I dare to eat a peach?
> I shall wear white flannel trousers and
>   walk upon the beach.

Eliot's strictures on applying concentrated efforts to the understanding of poetry could well apply to his next major poem, "The Waste Land." Heavily influenced by Ezra Pound, "The Waste Land" was an expression of gigantic frustration and despair.

The poem, a series of somewhat blurred visions, centers on an imaginary waste region, the home of the Fisher King, a little-known figure in mythology, who is sexually impotent. The work made his reputation.

Eliot was regarded as an important literary critic as well as a poet. His first book, "The Sacred Wood," was published in 1920.

It is possible that Eliot is most widely known through his drama "Murder in the Cathedral," a sardonic account of the murder of Thomas à Becket, Archbishop of Canterbury, in 1170.

Two of Eliot's plays enjoyed critical success in London and New York. "The Cocktail Party," published in 1954, was a story of deeply religious experience told against a background of highly literate and amusing British people. "The Confidential Clerk" told of bastardy and general unhappiness.

In his lighter moments Eliot was an unabashed ailurophile. He kept cats at home, bestowing upon them such names as Man in White Spats; he also wrote a book of poems called "Old Possum's Book of Practical Cats."

These lines from "The Naming of Cats" illustrate Eliot's profound insight into the narcissistic world of the feline:

> But I tell you, a cat needs a name that's
>   particular.
> A name that is peculiar, and more
>   dignified,
> Else how can he keep up his tail
>   perpendicular.
> Or spread out his whiskers, or cherish his
>   pride?
> . . . When you notice a cat in profound
>   meditation,
> The reason, I tell you, is always the
>   same:
> His mind is engaged in rapt
>   contemplation
> Of the thought, of the thought, of the
>   thought of his name;
> His ineffable effable
> Effeineffable
> Deep and inscrutable singular Name.

Those critical of Eliot's writing accused him of obscurity for its own sake. They found his verses full of coy and precious mannerisms. They accused him of loading down his writing with obscure references that could be known only by a few intimate friends.

Yet no man between the two World Wars so dominated his time as critic and creator. This expatriate American caught and expressed in his verse the sense of a doomed world, of fragmentation, of a wasteland of the spirit that moved the generation after the war.

It was a generation that felt tricked by the politicians, felt that the enormous bloodletting of World War I had been a fraud and saw in the disintegrating Europe of their time the symbol of their own lives. Their mood of spiritual despair was exquisitely rendered in Eliot's poetry.

The dry tone, the arid physical and spiritual landscape of his early poetry, and the bleakness that stared out of his verse summed up for a generation their own sense of defeat and barrenness. They echoed his words, "I have seen the moment of my greatness flicker."

LANGSTON HUGHES

February 1, 1902–May 22, 1967

By Thomas Lask

Langston Hughes, the noted writer of novels, stories, poems and plays about Negro life, died last night in Polyclinic Hospital [in Manhattan] at the age of 65.

Mr. Hughes, who died of congestive heart failure, was sometimes characterized as the "O. Henry of Harlem." He was an extremely versatile and productive author who was well known for his folksy humor.

In a description of himself written for "Twentieth Century Authors," Mr. Hughes wrote:

"My chief literary influences have been Paul Laurence Dunbar, Carl Sandburg and Walt Whitman. My favorite public figures include Jimmy Durante, Marlene Dietrich, Mary McLeod Bethune, Mrs. Franklin D. Roosevelt, Marian Anderson and Henry Armstrong."

"I live in Harlem, New York City," he continued. "I am unmarried. I like 'Tristan,' goat's milk, short novels, lyric poems, heat, simple folk, boats and bullfights; I dislike 'Aida,' parsnips, long novels, narrative poems, cold, pretentious folk, buses and bridges."

It was said that whenever Mr. Hughes had a pencil and paper in his hands, he would scribble poetry. He recalled an anecdote about how he was "discovered" by the poet Vachel Lindsay.

Lindsay was dining at the Wardman Park Hotel in Washington when a busboy summoned his courage and slipped several sheets of paper beside the poet's plate. Lindsay was annoyed, but he picked up the papers and read a poem titled "The Weary Blues."

As Lindsay read, his interest grew. He called for the busboy and asked, "Who wrote this!"

"I did," replied Langston Hughes.

Lindsay introduced the youth to publishers, who brought out such works as "Shakespeare in Harlem," "The Dream Keeper," "Not Without Laughter,' and "The Ways of White Folks" as well as the initial "The Weary Blues."

"My writing," Mr. Hughes said, "has been largely concerned with the depicting of Negro life in America."

In one of his many anecdotes Mr. Hughes explained that he became a poet when he was named "class poet" in grammar school in Lincoln, Ill.

"I was a victim of a stereotype," he observed wryly. "There were only two of us Negro kids in the whole class and our English teacher was always stressing the importance of rhythm in poetry.

"Well, everybody knows—except us—that all Negroes have rhythm, so they elected me class poet. I felt I couldn't let my white classmates down, and I've been writing poetry ever since."

James Langston Hughes, who dropped his first name, was born in Joplin, Mo., on Feb. 1, 1902. His mother was a schoolteacher and his father was a storekeeper.

After his graduation from Central High School in Cleveland, he went to Mexico and then attended Columbia University for a year. Mr. Hughes held a variety of jobs, including seaman on trips to Europe and Africa and busboy at the Washington hotel where he presented his poetry to Lindsay.

His first book, "The Weary Blues," was published by Alfred A. Knopf in 1925.

A scholarship enabled him to complete his education at Lincoln University in Pennsylvania.

His output was prodigious: poems, short stories, novels, librettos, lyrics, juveniles, pageants, anthologies, translations, television scripts. Between "The Weary Blues," his first book of poems, and "The Best Short Stories by Negro Writers," his last anthology, published in March, there were three dozen books.

His work lacked the power of the Negro writers who came after him. He felt as strongly as they did, but he was more amiable in expression. He was close to those he wrote about, and he captured their speech and their wry approach to life into his books.

No poetry of our day has caught the syncopated quality of jazz better than Mr. Hughes's "Dream Boogie," "Parade," and "Warning: Augmented." The plain speech of his verse and the ordinary subject matter often received as much criticism from Negroes as from those white people who couldn't see his writing as poetry. The Negroes felt it lacked the proper dignity that was their due. They were right. What the poetry had instead was life—a quality that has kept it fresh and spirited over the years.

Mr. Hughes will be recognized for what he was: an American writer of charm and vitality.

Despite the variety of form, Mr. Hughes's subject was nearly always the same: what it is like to be a black man in the United States. More gently than a younger generation of Negro writers would have preferred, Mr. Hughes always found the funny side of that life.

One of his most memorable characters, Jesse B. Semple, nicknamed Simple in the three books that Mr. Hughes wrote about him, spoke his mind with wry understatement.

"White folks," Simple said, "is the cause of a lot of inconvenience in my life."

Sometimes Mr. Hughes wrote about the adventures of Simple's cousin, Minnie, who was in Harlem during the riots of 1964. "My advice to all womens taking in riots is to leave your wig at home," said Minnie, who had lost hers.

This approach inevitably laid Mr. Hughes open to charges of clouding the bitter realities of racial strife with evasive humor.

He replied that he did not think the race problem was "too deep for comic relief."

"Colored people are always laughing at some wry Jim Crow incident or absurd nuance of the color line," he said. "If Negroes took all the white world's boorishness to heart and wept over it as profoundly as our serious writers do, we would have been dead long ago."

His defense was given more credence in light of the fact that Mr. Hughes's humor did not disguise a compassion for his people and their oppressors, best expressed in the title of a collection of his short stories: "Laughing to Keep from Crying."

Nor was Simple simply a clown. "Where do white folks get off calling everything bad black?" he once asked. "I would like to change all that around and say that the people who Jim Crow me have a white heart."

Simple, who in 1957 became the hero of a Broadway musical, "Simply Heavenly," may be Mr. Hughes's most lasting contribution to literature. But it was as a poet that he first came to public attention.

His best work was stripped, laconic, set to an unheard blues beat. His interest in rhythm made him a follower of the poetry of Carl Sandburg and Vachel Lindsay in the 1920s.

"Weary Blues," the poem Mr. Hughes showed Mr. Lindsay that fateful night at the Wardman Park Hotel, was full of the songs that Mr. Hughes had been hearing all his life—"gay songs, because you had to be gay or die; sad songs, because you couldn't help being sad sometimes," as he later said. "My best poems were all written when I felt the worst."

Mr. Hughes was born on Feb. 1, 1902, in Joplin, Mo. His mother, Carrie, had been a grammar school teacher in Guthrie, Okla., when she met his father, James, a storekeeper. His parents separated shortly after his birth and he lived with his grandmother in Lawrence, Kan., until he was 12.

Mary Sampson Patterson Leary Langston was a tough, self-reliant woman whose first husband had been killed in John Brown's raid on Harpers Ferry and whose second husband had been active in the underground railway.

His father financed a year's education for him at Columbia University. He found it a stale year, and decided to sign on as a freighter-hand and see the world.

The first freighter he could get was bound for Africa. "With that trip," he said, "I began to live." Impulsively, he threw all his books overboard and resolved to see things through his own eyes. Eventually he landed in Paris, where he lived for a year, supporting himself by washing dishes.

Mr. Hughes completed his formal education at Lincoln University, graduating in 1929.

The books that followed maintained his first success, particularly "Not Without Laughter," a novel; "The Ways of White Folks," short stories; "The Big Sea," an autobiography; "Shakespeare in Harlem," poems, and the Simple books: "Simple Speaks His Mind," "Simple Takes a Wife" and "Simple Stakes a Claim."

He also continued traveling, covering the Spanish Civil War for The Baltimore Afro-American, and visiting Cuba, Haiti, Africa, and the Soviet Union.

One of Mr. Hughes's poems provided the title for Lorraine Hansberry's play, "A Raisin in the Sun."

What happens to a dream deferred
Does it dry up
Like a raisin in the sun?
Or fester like a sore—
And then run?

Does it stink like rotten meat?

Or crust and sugar over—

Like a syrupy sweet?

Maybe it just sags

Like a heavy load.

Or does it explode?

The theater tempted him, and he had considerable success in it. He wrote the lyrics for Kurt Weill's "Street Scene," a play called "Mulatto," which had a successful run in New York though it was banned in Philadelphia because it dealt with miscegenation, and "Black Nativity."

Mr. Hughes, who is survived by a brother, an uncle and an aunt, was charged during the McCarthy era with having belonged to several so-called Communist front organizations in the nineteen-thirties, a charge he did not deny, although he said he had never been a Communist.

Far from expressing dismay that some of his earlier books had been removed from United States Information Agency libraries around the world, Mr. Hughes told investigators that he was surprised they had been on the shelves in the first place.

NOËL COWARD

December 16, 1899–March 26, 1973

By Albin Krebs

Sir Noël Coward, whose light sharp wit enlivened the English stage for half a century as actor, playwright, songwriter, composer and director, died of a heart attack as he was preparing to have morning coffee yesterday in his villa, Blue Harbor, on the coast of Jamaica in the West Indies. He was 73 years old.

Hailed here and in London in the nineteen-twenties as a master of sophisticated, then-daring comedy, Sir Noël also sounded patriotic themes in "Cavalcade" between the wars and in "In Which We Serve," a film about the Royal Navy in World War II. He was knighted by Queen Elizabeth in 1970.

"The world has treated me very well," Sir Noël once said, adding, "but then I haven't treated it so badly, either."

The remark, typically free of self-effacement, constituted fair comment. In his 63 years as a theatrical jack-of-all-trades (and master of most), the urbane Sir Noël gave the world unstintingly of what he called "a talent to amuse."

He wrote 27 comedies, dramas and musicals for the stage, the best-known of which were "Private Lives," "Blithe Spirit," "Cavalcade" and "Bitter-Sweet."

Among the 281 songs for which he provided words and music—that he could not read notes did not deter him—were several that have become standards, including "Someday I'll Find You," "I'll See You Again," "Mad About the Boy" and "Mad Dogs and Englishmen."

Of his films, the most memorable were the World War II epic of courage, "In Which We Serve," and "Brief Encounter," still considered one of the finest movies about romantic love.

In the last few years there has been an enormous revival of interest in the works of Sir Noël. Maggie Smith and Robert Stephens starred on the London stage in productions of "Design for Living" and "Private Lives." Two revues culled from Sir Noël's shows, songs and autobiographies are playing to capacity audiences.

The multitalented Sir Noël often acted in, directed and produced his own plays and films, and in the nineteen-fifties he turned to the new career of cabaret performer. By then, however, he had established himself as a major spokesman, in the dramatic arts, of an era—those two dazzling decades between two World Wars during which a generation of chic, smart-talking young people delighted in shocking their Victorian elders.

Because he often dealt with amoral characters who used mildly profane language and talked about sex, Sir Noël's plays ran into censorship troubles. There were also objections to the fact that most of his stage characters were rich, spoiled, neurotic, vain, snobbish and selfish, but he made them bearable and even attractive by putting into their mouths an endless string of witticisms.

Some critics said there was too much humor, too much glittering, effervescent polish in his writing. "Private Lives" contained such lines as "Certain women should be struck regularly, like gongs," which helped create the impression, for some, that the play was all sparkle and no fire.

On a deeper level, however, "Private Lives" and other Coward plays dealt with characters who almost continually said one thing while thinking another. The surface badinage was a cover. The relationships he repeatedly examined were those of people who couldn't live together yet couldn't live apart. In many ways, Sir Noël's personal life and his personality resembled those of his characters. He was witty, generous, jaded, mercurial, sophisticated, lonely, snobbish.

In conversations, he sprinkled quips like salt. When asked whether he had ever tried to enlighten his audiences as well as amuse them, he replied: "I have a

slight reforming urge, but I have rather cunningly kept it down."

Sir Noël gave the appearance of being a great bon vivant, inhabiting a world of celebrity in which he enjoyed the friendship of such persons as Sir Winston Churchill, Franklin D. Roosevelt, Lynn Fontanne, George Bernard Shaw, Cary Grant and Marlene Dietrich.

Born Noël Pierce Coward on Dec. 16, 1899, in Teddington, near London, the future actor, singer, dancer, playwright, author, composer, librettist, lyricist and director was the son of Arthur Sabin Coward, an organist who was forced to work as a piano and organ salesman to support his family.

Sir Noël's mother, the former Violet Agnes Veitch, was one of those doting stage mothers who relentlessly pushed their children forward in the theater. She remained the strongest influence in her son's life until she died in 1954 at the age of 91.

Young Coward learned to play the piano by ear, but his formal education, which ended when he was 14, was haphazard. At 10 he made his professional debut on the London stage as Prince Mussel in an all-child production of "The Goldfish." Soon he was bedeviling every producer in London for work.

"I was a brazen, odious little prodigy," he said, "overpleased with myself and precocious to a degree. I was a talented boy, God knows, and when washed and smarmed down a bit, passably attractive."

By 1914 he was touring as Slightly in "Peter Pan." In 1918, when he was 19, he wrote his first play, "The Rat Trap," which was not produced until 1926. Sir Noël developed a lifelong fondness for Ameri-

cans during a stay of several months in New York in 1921. From then on he shuttled between London and New York, and came to regard the latter city as his second home.

His first stage success was "The Vortex," which he wrote in 1923 and starred in the following year in London. The play was a melodrama and its central characters, a drug addict and his nymphomaniacal mother, shocked and titillated audiences.

At one point in 1925, three of London's biggest stage successes were Coward hits. While he was still appearing in "The Vortex," his revue "On with the Dance," for which he wrote the book and songs, opened to raves, and his comedy of bad manners, "Hay Fever," which he directed, was also successful. The same year marked the opening of his comedy "Fallen Angels."

Success piled on top of success as Sir Noël's plays were produced in New York, Paris and Berlin. In 1928 he turned out "This Year of Grace!," a revue, and the next year the sentimental operetta "Bitter-Sweet," which became an international hit. At the time he completed "Bitter-Sweet" he was appearing in "This Year of Grace!" in New York, and, he said, he composed the operetta's best-known song, "I'll See You Again," while his taxi was caught in a traffic jam.

The pace at which he worked and lived took its toll. In 1930 he suffered a breakdown and took a long voyage to the Orient to recuperate. He could not resist the urge to work, however, and in four days, propped up in bed in his Shanghai hotel, he wrote "Private Lives," the comedy that he had promised his friend, Gertrude Lawrence, to write for them to act in.

"'Private Lives' was described variously as 'tenuous, thin, brittle, gossamer, iridescent and delightfully daring,'" Sir Noël said, "all of which connotated to the public mind cocktails, evening dress, repartee and irreverent allusions to copulation, thereby causing a gratifying number of respectable people to queue up at the box office."

They did. "Private Lives" became the most popular and profitable Coward work. For himself and his friends the Lunts, Sir Noël wrote "Design for Living," in which they appeared in New York in 1933. Meanwhile, "Cavalcade" had been staged in London and filmed in Hollywood. His 1933 musical, "Conversation Piece," featured the songs "I'll Follow My Secret Heart" and "Don't Put Your Daughter on the Stage, Mrs. Worthington." Later in the thirties he wrote and appeared with Miss Lawrence in "Tonight at 8:30," a brace of short plays; "Present Laughter" and "This Happy Breed." His biggest hit in World War II was "Blithe Spirit."

"I behaved through most of the war with gallantry tinged, I suspect, by a strong urge to show off," Sir

Noël said. Actually, in addition to writing, producing, acting in and codirecting "In Which We Serve," an important contribution to British morale, he drove himself to a physical breakdown by entertaining troops in Asia and Africa.

After the war, there was a pronounced shift in Sir Noël's fortunes. The critics began to conclude that he and his work were outdated. In 1955 his bank overdraft was more than $60,000.

He fell back on two solutions to his problems: One was to take his cabaret act to the Desert Inn in Las Vegas, which paid him $40,000 a week to entertain what Sir Noël called "Nescafé Society." The other was to escape high taxes in England by taking up residence in Jamaica and Switzerland.

The climate of the theater and the temper of the times had changed sufficiently by 1966 that Sir Noël was able to write and act in his most intensely autobiographical play, "A Song at Twilight." The play concerns an aging homosexual writer who has not been able to write truthfully about himself in his work. Confronted by a blackmailer who upbraids him for having masked his homosexuality in his art and his life, the writer replies:

"Was that so unpardonable? I was young, ambitious and already almost a public figure. Was it so base of me to try to show to the world that I was capable of playing the game according to the rules?"

TENNESSEE WILLIAMS

March 26, 1911–February 25, 1983

By Mel Gussow

Tennessee Williams, whose innovative drama and sense of lyricism were a major force in the postwar American theater, died yesterday at the age of 71. He was found dead in his suite in the Hotel Elysee on East 54th Street.

Officials said that death was due to natural causes.

The author of more than 24 full-length plays, including "The Glass Menagerie," "A Streetcar Named Desire" and "Cat on a Hot Tin Roof," the last two works winners of Pulitzer Prizes, Tennessee Williams was the most important American playwright after Eugene O'Neill.

He had a profound effect on the American theater and on American playwrights and actors, and he wrote with deep sympathy and expansive humor about society's outcasts. Though his images were often violent, he was a poet of the human heart. His works, which are among the most popular plays of our time, continue to

provide a rich reservoir of acting challenges. Among the actors celebrated in Williams roles were Laurette Taylor in "The Glass Menagerie," Marlon Brando and Jessica Tandy in "A Streetcar Named Desire" (and Vivien Leigh in the movie version), and Burl Ives in "Cat on a Hot Tin Roof."

"The Glass Menagerie," his first success, was his "memory play." Many of his other plays were his nightmares. His plays were almost all intensely personal, torn from his own private anguishes and anxieties.

He once described his sister's room in the family home in St. Louis, with her collection of glass figures, as representing "all the softest emotions that belong to recollection of things past." But, he remembered, outside the room was an alley in which, nightly, dogs destroyed cats.

Mr. Williams's work, which was unequaled in passion and imagination by any of his contemporaries' works, was a barrage of conflicts, of the blackest horrors offset by purity. Perhaps his greatest character, Blanche Du Bois, the heroine of "Streetcar," has been described as a tigress and a moth. As Mr. Williams created her, there was no contradiction. His basic premise, he said, was "the need for understanding and tenderness and fortitude among individuals trapped by circumstance."

Just as his work reflected his life, his life reflected his work. A monumental hypochondriac, he became obsessed with sickness, failure and death. Several times he thought he was losing his sight, and he had four operations for cataracts. Constantly he thought his heart would stop beating. In desperation, he drank and took pills immoderately.

He was a man of great shyness, but with friends he showed great openness, which often worked to his disadvantage. He was extremely vulnerable to demands—from directors, actresses, the public, his critics, admirers and detractors. Unfavorable reviews devastated him.

Success arrived suddenly in 1945, with the Broadway premiere of "The Glass Menagerie," and it frightened him much more than failure.

He was born as Thomas Lanier Williams in Columbus, Miss., on March 26, 1911. His mother, the former Edwina Dakin, was the daughter of an Episcopal rector. His father, Cornelius Coffin Williams, was a traveling salesman who later settled down in St. Louis. There was an older daughter, Rose (memorialized as Laura in "the Glass Menagerie"), and in 1919 another son was born, Walter Dakin.

"It was just a wrong marriage," the playwright wrote of his parents. His mother was the model for the foolish but indomitable Amanda Wingfield in "The Glass Menagerie," his father for the brutish Big Daddy in "Cat on a Hot Tin Roof."

While his father traveled, Tom was mostly brought up, and overprotected, by his mother, particularly

after he contracted diphtheria at the age of five. By the time the family moved to St. Louis, the pattern was clear. Young Tom retreated into himself. He made up and told stories, many of them scary.

In the fall of 1929 he went off to the University of Missouri to study journalism, but soon dropped out and took a job as a clerk in a shoe company. It was, he recalled, "living death."

To survive, every day after work he retreated to his room and wrote—stories, poems, plays—through the night. The strain led to a nervous breakdown. Sent to Memphis to recuperate, he joined a local theater group.

In 1937, Mr. Williams re-enrolled as a student, this time at the University of Iowa. There and in St. Louis he wrote an enormous number of plays, some of which were produced on campus. He graduated in 1938.

Success seemed paired with tragedy. His sister lost her mind. The family allowed a prefrontal lobotomy to be performed, and she spent much of her life in a sanitarium.

At 28, Thomas Williams left home for New Orleans. There he changed his style of living as well as his name, to become Tennessee Williams, and there he discovered new netherworlds, soaking up the milieu that would appear in "A Streetcar Named Desire." He wrote stories, some of which later became plays, and entered a Group Theater playwriting contest. He won $100 and was solicited by the agent Audrey Wood, who became his friend and adviser.

"Battle of Angels," a play he wrote during a visit to St. Louis, opened in Boston in 1940, closed in two weeks and did not come to New York. Mr. Williams, however, brought it back in a revised version in 1957 as "Orpheus Descending" and as the Marlon Brando–Anna Magnani movie, "The Fugitive Kind."

To his amazement, Audrey Wood got him a job in Hollywood writing scripts for Metro-Goldwyn-Mayer at $250 a week. Disdainfully, he began writing an original screenplay, which was rejected. Still under contract, he began turning the screenplay into a play titled "The Gentleman Caller," which evolved into "The Glass Menagerie." On March 31, 1945, five days after its author became 34, it opened on Broadway and changed Mr. Williams's life and the American theater. He was inundated with success—the play won the New York Drama Critics' Circle award—and he fought to keep afloat.

"Once you fully apprehend the vacuity of a life without struggle," he wrote, "you are equipped with the basic means of salvation." Realizing that his art was his salvation, he wrote his second masterpiece, "A Streetcar Named Desire." Opening in 1947, "Streetcar" was an even bigger hit than "The Glass Menagerie." It won Mr. Williams his second Drama Critics' award and his first Pulitzer Prize.

For many years after "Streetcar," almost every other season there was another Williams play on Broadway. Soon there was a continual flow from the stage to the screen. For more than 35 years, the stream was unabated. He produced an enormous body of work, including more than two dozen full-length plays, all of them produced, a record unequaled by any of his contemporaries. There were successes and failures, and often great disagreement over which was which. In 1948 there was "Summer and Smoke," which failed on Broadway, was a huge success in a revival Off Broadway and made a star of Geraldine Page, one of many magnificent leading ladies in Mr. Williams's works (others were Laurette Taylor, Jessica Tandy, Vivien Leigh, Maureen Stapleton, Anna Magnani). There followed "The Rose Tattoo," "Camino Real," "Cat on a Hot Tin Roof" (his second Pulitzer), "Orpheus Descending," "Garden District" and "Sweet Bird of Youth."

He also wrote two novels, the film "Baby Doll," and his "Memoirs," in which for the first time he wrote in detail about his homosexuality.

As he became increasingly successful, Mr. Williams became somewhat portly and seedy. Gradually he found it harder and harder to write. The turning point, as he saw it, was 1955, and after "Cat on a Hot Tin Roof" there was a noticeable decline in his work. To keep going, he began relying on a combination of coffee, cigarettes, drugs and alcohol.

"The Night of the Iguana," in 1961, was his last major success. After "Iguana," Mr. Williams seemed to fall apart. But at the same time he discovered religion. In 1968 he was converted to Roman Catholicism, and his last plays, though still dealing with grotesques, also dealt with salvation.

"The Milk Train Doesn't Stop Here Anymore," which failed on Broadway and as an Elizabeth Taylor–Richard Burton movie entitled "Boom!," was an allegory about a Christlike young man and a dying dowager.

In recent years, Mr. Williams, who is survived by his brother and his sister, divided his time between his apartment in New York and his house in Key West.

"I always felt like Tennessee and I were compatriots," said Marlon Brando. "He told the truth as best he perceived it, and never turned away from things that beset or frightened him. We are all diminished by his death."

JORGE LUIS BORGES

August 24, 1899–June 14, 1986

By Edward A. Gargan

Jorge Luis Borges, the Argentine short-story writer, poet and essayist who was considered one of Latin America's greatest writers, died yesterday in Geneva, where he had been living for three months. He was 86 years old.

Mr. Borges died of liver cancer, said the executor of his estate, Osvaldo Luis Vidaurre.

While almost unknown outside Argentina before 1961, his stories, punctilious in their language and mysterious in their opaque paradoxes, attained a following that grew to international proportions. His writings explored the crannies of the human psyche, the fantastic within the apparently mundane, imaginary bestiaries and fables of obscure libraries and arcane scholarship. Many hailed him as the century's most important Latin American writer.

Among his works of fiction that have appeared in the United States are "Ficciones," "The Aleph and Other Stories" and "Labyrinths," all published in 1962, and "A Universal History of Infamy," in 1971. Among his collections of essays available in English are "The Book of Imaginary Beings" and "An Introduction to American Literature." "Selected Poems, 1923–1967" was published in 1972 and "In Praise of Darkness," consisting of poetry and short pieces, in 1974.

In 1975 John Updike wrote that Mr. Borges's "driest paragraph is somehow compelling."

"His fables are written from a height of intelligence less rare in philosophy and physics than in fiction," he said. "Furthermore, he is, at least for anyone whose taste runs to puzzles or pure speculation, delightfully entertaining."

For Mr. Borges, the short story was the most compelling form. "In the course of a lifetime devoted chiefly to books," he wrote, "I have read but few novels and, in most cases, only a sense of duty has enabled me to find my way to their last page. I have always been a reader and rereader of short stories."

Beginning in 1927, when he had a series of operations on his eyes, Mr. Borges was increasingly afflicted by blindness. While he called the condition a "slow, summer twilight," it did not impede his work.

Jorge Luis Borges was born in Buenos Aires on Aug. 24, 1899. His father "was a philosophical anarchist," Mr. Borges wrote, and a teacher of psychology. His mother translated American classics into Spanish.

At the age of six or seven, the young Borges began to write. "I was expected to be a writer," he recalled later in life. He confessed that his first writing was modeled on classic Spanish writers, mostly [Miguel de] Cervantes.

In 1914 the family moved to Europe so that Jorge could attend school in Geneva. In the College of Geneva he was immersed in Latin, and outside it he tackled German, eventually finding his way to [Arthur] Schopenhauer.

"Were I to choose a single philosopher, I would choose him," Mr. Borges wrote. "If the riddle of the universe can be stated in words, I think these words would be in his writings."

After Mr. Borges received his degree, his family moved to Spain, where his first poem, "Hymn to the Sea," was published. In 1921, he returned with his family to Buenos Aires, where he continued to write.

The "real beginning" of his career, Mr. Borges wrote, came in the early 1930's with a series of sketches called "A Universal History of Infamy." In these, which "were in the nature of hoaxes and pseudo-essays," Mr. Borges chronicled the lives of Lazarus Morell, who both freed and imprisoned slaves; of Tom Castro, an implausible prodigal son; of the widow Ching, a pirate who terrorized the seas of Asia; of Monk Eastman, a New York gunman and "purveyor of iniquities"; of Kotsuke no Suke, who refused to commit hara-kiri, "which as a nobleman was his duty."

With Mr. Borges's next story, "The Approach to al-Mu'tasim," written in 1935, the shape of many of his later stories was established. The story is a fictive review of a book purportedly published in Bombay. Mr. Borges invests the mythical volume with a genuine publisher and reviewer but, as he wrote later, "the author and the book are entirely my own invention."

In this story, many of the basic literary elements that came to characterize Mr. Borges's style were apparent: a concern for history and identity; the central role of an obscure scholarly work; a maze of discourse laden with elaborate and Byzantine detail;

footnotes; meticulous references to remote academic journals, and deliberately translucent paradox.

Mr. Borges took his first full-time job in 1937 as an assistant in a branch of the Buenos Aires Municipal Library; he remained there for nine years, completing his work each day in an hour and devoting the rest of his time to reading and writing. In this period, he wrote the short story "Pierre Menard, Author of the Quixote," which he described as a "halfway house between the essay and true tale."

"Pierre Menard" led to a story of a strange world that displaces our planet—"Tlon, Uqbar, Orbis Tertius"—and then to stories concerned with labyrinths and mirrors and encyclopedias that came to form the foundation of Mr. Borges's oeuvre. "The Garden of Forking Paths," an anthology of short stories, was published in 1941. Three years later "Ficciones," perhaps his most celebrated collection of short stories, went into print.

In 1946, Juan Domingo Peron—"a President," Mr. Borges wrote, "whose name I do not want to remember"—came to power. Soon afterward, Mr. Borges was named inspector of poultry and rabbits in the public markets, but later resigned.

After the Peron Government was overthrown in 1955, Mr. Borges was appointed director of the National Library in Buenos Aires. The next year he became a professor of English and American literature at the University of Buenos Aires.

By the late 1950's, Mr. Borges was completely blind. "One salient consequence of my blindness was my gradual abandonment of free verse in favor of classical metrics," he wrote later. "In fact, blindness made me take up the writing of poetry again. Since rough drafts were denied me, I had to fall back on memory. It is obviously easier to remember verse than prose and to remember regular verse forms rather than free ones."

Some have insisted that Mr. Borges's unwillingness to criticize the repression of post-Peronist regimes kept him from becoming a Nobel laureate. He was, however, sympathetic to the plight of mothers whose children were victims of death squads that were supported by Argentina's military Government. "I had my say about the disappeared," he once said. "But what can I do? I'm an old man. What can they do to me? Torture me, eh?"

Mr. Borges led a hermetic, unworldly life. Seemingly fragile in his last years, he relied increasingly on assistants to read to him and to write what he dictated.

"To me, reading has been a way of living," he once said. "I think the only possible fate for me was a literary life. I can't think of myself in a bookless world."

At the age of 68, Mr. Borges married a childhood sweetheart, Elsa Astete Millan, but they divorced three years later. A few weeks ago he married Maria Kodama, his secretary and longtime traveling companion.

In later life, Mr. Borges was less happy than he had been with Argentina and its capital. "Buenos Aires is a dreary city now," he said in 1982. "I don't understand my own country. But the world is not meant to be understood by men. Every night, I dream. I have nightmares—of being lost, of being in an unknown city. I don't remember the name of the hotel, or I can't find my way home in Buenos Aires. Maybe I feel very lost because the world is meaningless."

Yet Mr. Borges found meaning in his own work. "Through the years, a man peoples a space with images of provinces, kingdoms, mountains, bays, ships, islands, fishes, rooms, tools, stars, horses, and people," he once wrote. "Shortly before his death, he discovers that the patient labyrinth of lines traces the image of his own face."

JAMES BALDWIN

August 2, 1924–December 1, 1987

By Lee Daniels

James Baldwin, whose passionate, intensely personal essays in the 1950's and 60's on racial discrimination in America helped break down the nation's color barrier, died of cancer last night at his home in southern France. He was 63 years old.

At least in the early years of his career, Mr. Baldwin saw himself primarily as a novelist. But it is his essays that arguably constitute his most substantial contribution to literature.

Mr. Baldwin published his three most important collections of essays—"Notes of a Native Son" (1955), "Nobody Knows My Name" (1961) and "The Fire Next Time" (1963)—during the years the civil rights movement was exploding across the American South.

Some critics said his language was sometimes too elliptical, his indictments too sweeping. But Mr. Baldwin's prose, with its apocalyptic tone—a legacy of his early exposure to religious fundamentalism—and its passionate sense of advocacy, seemed perfect for a period in which blacks in the South lived under continual threat of racial violence and civil rights workers often faced brutal beatings and even death.

Mr. Baldwin had moved to France in the late 1940's to escape what he felt was the stifling racial bigotry of America. Nonetheless, although France remained his permanent residence, Mr. Baldwin in later years described himself as a "commuter" rather than an expatriate.

"Only white Americans can consider themselves to be expatriates," he said. "Once I found myself on the other side of the ocean, I could see where I came from very clearly, and I could see that I carried myself, which is my home, with me. You can never escape that. I am the grandson of a slave, and I am a writer. I must deal with both."

Despite the prominent role he played in the civil rights movement in the early 1960's, Mr. Baldwin rejected the labels of "leader" or "spokesman." Instead, he described himself as one whose mission was to "bear witness to the truth."

"A spokesman assumes that he is speaking for others," he told Julius Lester, a faculty colleague at the University of Massachusetts at Amherst, in an interview in 1984. "I never assumed that I could. What I tried to do, or to interpret and make clear was that no

society can smash the social contract and be exempt from the consequences, and the consequences are chaos for everybody in the society."

This sense of independence was an intrinsic part of Mr. Baldwin's personality.

"I was a maverick, a maverick in the sense that I depended on neither the white world nor the black world," he told Mr. Lester. "That was the only way I could've played it. I would've been broken otherwise. I had to say, 'A curse on both your houses.' The fact that I went to Europe so early is probably what saved me. It gave me another touchstone—myself."

Mr. Baldwin did not limit his "bearing witness" to racial matters. He opposed American military involvement in Vietnam as early as 1963, and in the early 1960's he began to criticize discrimination against homosexuals.

Mr. Baldwin's literary achievements and his activism made him a world figure and brought him many honors. Yet, Mr. Baldwin was also clearly disappointed that, despite his undeniable powers as an essayist, his novels and plays drew decidedly mixed reviews.

"Go Tell It on the Mountain," his first book and first novel, published in 1953, was widely praised. Partly autobiographical, it tells of a poor boy growing up in Harlem in the 1930's under the tyranny of his father, an autocratic preacher who hated his son.

Mr. Baldwin said in 1985 that in many ways the book remained the keystone of his career.

"'Mountain' is the book I had to write if I was ever going to write anything else," he remarked. "I had to deal with what hurt me most. I had to deal, above all, with my father. He was my model. I learned a lot from him. Nobody's ever frightened me since."

But the reception accorded his other works was at best lukewarm, and his frank discussion of homosexuality in "Giovanni's Room" (1956) and in "Another Country" (1962) drew criticism from within and outside the civil rights movement. In a celebrated polemic in the late 1960's, Eldridge Cleaver, then a member of the Black Panther Party, asserted that the novel illustrated Mr. Baldwin's "agonizing, total hatred of blacks."

Another assessment of Mr. Baldwin was offered by the poet Langston Hughes, who observed, "Few American writers handle words more effectively in the essay form than James Baldwin. To my way of thinking, he is much better at provoking thought in the essay than he is in arousing emotion in fiction."

Mr. Baldwin's other works included the novel "Tell Me How Long the Train's Been Gone," the stage plays "Blues for Mr. Charlie" and "The Amen Corner," and "The Evidence of Things Not Seen," an essay on the murder of 28 black children in Atlanta in 1980 and 1981.

James Baldwin was born in 1924 in Harlem and attended DeWitt Clinton High School in the Bronx.

He was a precocious writer, and by his early 20s was publishing reviews and essays in The New Leader, The Nation, Commentary and Partisan Review, and socializing with the circle of New York writers and intellectuals that included Randall Jarrell, Dwight Macdonald, Lionel Trilling, Delmore Schwartz and Irving Howe.

Yet Mr. Baldwin was among the last persons one would have initially marked for a leadership role in a national movement. Slight and soft-spoken, he long thought of himself as ugly, and wrote poignantly of his struggle to accept the way he looked.

SAMUEL BECKETT

April 13, 1906–December 22, 1989

By Mel Gussow

Samuel Beckett, a towering figure in drama and fiction who altered the course of contemporary theater, died on Friday at the age of 83.

He died of respiratory problems in a Paris hospital, and was buried yesterday at the Montparnasse cemetery after a private funeral.

Explaining the secrecy surrounding his hospitalization and death, Irene Lindon, representing the author's Paris publisher, Editions de Minuit, said it was "what he would have wanted."

Beckett's plays became the cornerstone of 20th-century theater, beginning with "Waiting for Godot," first produced in 1953. As the play's two tramps wait for a salvation that never comes, they exchange vaudeville routines and metaphysical musings—and comedy rises to tragedy.

Before Beckett there was a naturalistic tradition. After him, scores of playwrights were encouraged to experiment with the underlying meaning of their work as well as with an absurdist style. As the Beckett scholar Ruby Cohn wrote: "After 'Godot,' plots could be minimal; exposition, expendable; characters, contradictory; settings, unlocalized, and dialogue, unpredictable. Blatant farce could jostle tragedy."

At the same time, Beckett's novels, particularly his trilogy, "Molloy," "Malone Dies" and "The Unnamable," inspired by James Joyce, move subliminally into the minds of the characters. The novels are among the most experimental and most profound in Western literature.

For his accomplishments in drama and fiction, the Irish author, who wrote first in English and later in French, received the Nobel Prize in Literature in 1969.

At the root of his art was a philosophy of the deepest yet most courageous pessimism, exploring man's relationship with his God. With Beckett, one searched for hope amid despair and continued living with a kind of stoicism, as illustrated by the final words of his novel, "The Unnamable": "You must go on, I can't go on, I'll go on." Or as he wrote in "Worstward Ho," one of his later works of fiction: "Try again. Fail again. Fail better."

Though the word Beckettian entered the English language as a synonym for bleakness, Beckett was a man of great humor and compassion, in his life as in his work. He was a tragicomic playwright whose art was consistently instilled with mordant wit. Scholars and critics scrutinized his writing for metaphor and ulterior meaning, but he refrained from analysis or even explanation.

As he wrote to his favorite director, Alan Schneider: "If people want to have headaches among the overtones, let them. And provide their own aspirin." When Mr. Schneider asked Beckett who Godot was, the playwright answered, "If I knew, I would have said so in the play."

His greatest successes were in his middle years, in the 1950's with "Waiting for Godot" and "Endgame," and with his trilogy of novels. It was suggested that for an artist of his stature, he had a relatively small body of work, but only if one measures size by number of words. Distilling his art to its essence, he produced scores of eloquent plays and stories, many of those in his later years not strictly defined as full length. But in terms of the intensity of the imagery, plays like "Not I," "Footfalls" and "Rockaby" were complete visions.

He wrote six novels, four long plays and dozens of shorter ones, volumes of stories and narrative fragments, some of which were short novels. He wrote poetry and essays on the arts, radio and television plays, and prose pieces he called residua and disjecta.

Despite his artistic reputation, his ascension was slow and for many years discouraging. When his work began to be published and produced, he was plagued by philistinism, especially with "Waiting for Godot," which puzzled and outraged many theatergoers and critics, some of whom regarded it as a travesty if not a hoax.

From the first he had his ardent supporters, who included, notably, Jean Anouilh, the bellwether of French theatrical tradition. Anouilh greeted "Godot" at its premiere in Paris as "a masterpiece that will cause despair for men in general and for playwrights in particular." In both respects, he proved prescient.

Today "Godot" is generally accepted as a cornerstone of modern theater. It is performed worldwide in schools and prisons as well as on public stages. With "Godot" and his other plays, Beckett influenced countless playwrights who followed him, including

Edward Albee, Harold Pinter, Tom Stoppard and David Mamet.

The name "Godot" is part of international mythology. Godot, who may or may not be a savior, never arrives, but man keeps waiting for his possible arrival. For Beckett himself, waiting became a way of living—waiting for inspiration, recognition, understanding or death.

For more than 50 years the writer lived in his adopted city of Paris, for much of that time in a working-class district in Montparnasse. Though he wrote most of his work in French, he remained definably Irish in his voice, manner and humor. In no way could he be considered an optimist. In an often repeated story, on a glorious sunny day he walked jauntily through a London park with an old friend and exuded a feeling of joy. The friend said it was the kind of day that made one glad to be alive. "I wouldn't go that far," Beckett responded.

Samuel Barclay Beckett was born in Foxrock, a suburb of Dublin, on April 13, 1906. (That date is sometimes disputed.) His father, William Beckett Jr., was a surveyor. His mother, Mary Roe Beckett, had been a nurse.

Samuel and his older brother, Frank, were brought up as Protestants. They went to Earlsfort House School in Dublin. Samuel then continued his education at Portora Royal School in Enniskillen, County Fermanagh, and at Trinity College, Dublin. At school he excelled in both his studies and sports. He received his Bachelor of Arts degree in 1927 and his Master of Arts degree in 1931.

In the intervening time, he spent two years in Paris in an exchange program. In Paris, he met James Joyce and other members of the literary and artistic set. He became a close friend and aide to Joyce, reading to him when his eyes began to fail.

Returning to Ireland, Beckett taught Romance languages at Trinity but resigned in 1932 and left Ireland, moving permanently to Paris in 1937. By that time he had published "More Pricks Than Kicks," a collection of short stories; "Echo's Bones," a volume of poetry, and "Murphy," his first novel.

In Paris, Beckett became a familiar figure at Left Bank cafes, continuing his alliance with Joyce while also becoming friends with artists like Marcel Duchamp and Alberto Giacometti.

With a young piano student named Suzanne Deschevaux-Dumesnil, whom he met in 1938 and would marry in 1961, he chose to remain in France during World War II rather than return to the safety of Ireland. The couple became active in the French Resistance, and when forced to flee Paris, went to Roussillon near the Spanish border. While working as a farm laborer and running messages for the Resistance, Beckett wrote the novel "Watt." It was often said that his experiences in hiding during the war were an inspiration for "Waiting for Godot."

After "Watt," he began writing in French, which allowed him, as the Joyce biographer Richard Ellman observed, "a private liberation from the English tradition."

The five years starting in 1947 were his most creative period. In a little more than a year he finished "Waiting for Godot," his greatest play, as well as the first two parts of his trilogy of novels, "Molloy" and "Malone Dies."

Though he found a publisher for the trilogy (Jerome Lindon at Editions de Minuit, who remained his French publisher for the rest of his life), the plays were more difficult to place. Then Roger Blin, the French actor and director, agreed to present one. He chose "Godot" over "Eleutheria," Beckett's first play, partly because it had fewer characters. Only when "Waiting for Godot" was in rehearsal, with Beckett in attendance, did Blin fully realize the excitement of his discovery.

"En Attendant Godot," as the play was titled, opened on Jan. 5, 1953, at the Theatre de Babylone. The first review, written by Sylvain Zegel in La Liberation, said Beckett was "one of today's best playwrights," a fact that was not universally acknowledged. The first London production, using the playwright's English translation and directed by Peter Hall, received generally dismissive daily reviews. It was rescued by Harold Hobson, then the drama critic of The Sunday Times in London, who said the play might "securely lodge in a corner of your mind as long as you live."

In January 1956, Michael Myerberg opened the first United States production at the Coconut Grove Playhouse in Miami, with Bert Lahr and Tom Ewell as the Beckett tramps Estragon and Vladimir. Expecting a Bert Lahr comedy, the audience was mystified. As Alan Schneider, the director of that original production, said, doing "Godot" in Miami was like dancing "Giselle" in Roseland. With both the director and Mr. Ewell replaced, the play moved to Broadway in April. Most critics were confounded. Several were abusive. The play closed after 59 performances.

That "Waiting for Godot" became a contemporary classic can be attributed to the enthusiasm of its champions and the profundity of the work itself. "Godot" came to be regarded not only as a clown comedy with tragic dimensions but as a play about man coping with the nature of his existence in a world that appeared to be hurtling toward a self-induced apocalypse.

Before "Godot" was produced in London, Beckett completed a second play, "Fin de Partie," or "Endgame," as the title was translated. In this dramatic equivalent of chess, Hamm the master oppresses Clov the servant in a bunker looking out on the void of the world. "Endgame" was followed by the radio play "All That Fall" and by the monodrama "Krapp's Last Tape."

In 1961 after Beckett and Miss Deschevaux-Dumesnil were married, he finished "Happy Days," about a long and not always happy marriage, in which a woman is buried up to her neck in earth.

In 1969 he was awarded the Nobel Prize in Literature for a body of work that "has transformed the destitution of man into his exaltation."

He continued to write and to maintain his privacy. His plays and prose became shorter and even terser, as in "Not I," in which the play's principal character is a woman's heavily lipsticked mouth; "That Time," in which a spotlight shines on a man's head and his corona of white hair, and "Rockaby," in which an old woman rocks herself to death. Two of his prose pieces, "Company" and "Worstward Ho," were published as short novels.

On July 17 this year, Beckett's wife died. There are no immediate survivors.

About a year ago, he moved to a nursing home, where he continued to receive visitors, and he lived his last year in a small, barely furnished room.

THEODOR SEUSS GEISEL

March 2, 1904–September 24, 1991

By Eric Pace

Theodor Seuss Geisel, the author and illustrator whose whimsical fantasies written under the pen name Dr. Seuss entertained and instructed millions of children and adults around the world, died in his sleep on Tuesday night at his home in La Jolla, Calif. He was 87 years old.

"We've lost the finest talent in the history of children's books," Jerry Harrison, who oversees children's books for Random House, Mr. Geisel's longtime publishers, said, "and we'll probably never see one like him again."

Mr. Geisel's work delighted children by combining the ridiculous and the logical, generally with a homely moral. "If I start out with the concept of a two-headed animal," he once said, "I must put two hats on his head and two toothbrushes in the bathroom. It's logical insanity."

Mr. Geisel's first book, "And to Think That I Saw It on Mulberry Street," appeared in 1937. It was followed by such classics as "Horton Hatches the Egg" in 1940 and "The Cat in the Hat" in 1957.

Over the years, zany animal characters were the Dr. Seuss trademarks. There was "Yertle the Tertle" (1958), "Fox in Socks" (1965), "Mr. Brown Can Moo! Can You?" (1970) and others too improbable to mention.

But the archetypal Seuss hero, many connoisseurs felt, was Horton, a conscientious pachyderm who was duped by a lazy bird into sitting on her egg. Horton stuck to the job for many weeks, despite dreadful weather and other harassments, saying, "I meant what I said and I said what I meant; an elephant's faithful 100 percent." His virtue was finally rewarded when the egg hatched and out came a creature with a bird's wings and an elephant's head.

Mr. Geisel won the hearts and minds of children "by the sneaky stratagem of making them laugh," Richard R. Lingeman wrote in a review in The New York Times. He also charmed adults, especially with "Oh, the Places You'll Go!," a 1990 book he wrote for adult readers as well as children, which has been on the Times best-seller list for 79 weeks. Sales of books by Mr. Geisel totaled well over 200 million copies. His books have been translated into 20 languages.

In 1984, he won a special Pulitzer citation "for his contribution over nearly half a century to the educa-

tion and enjoyment of America's children and their parents."

Mr. Geisel—pronounced GUYS-ell—was also the founder and a longtime executive of Beginner Books, a publishing concern bought by Random House.

Mr. Geisel began using his middle name as a pen name for his cartoons because he hoped to use his surname as a novelist one day. But when he got around to doing a grown-up book—"The Seven Lady Godivas" in 1939—the grown-ups did not seem to want to buy his humor, and he went back to writing for children, becoming famous and wealthy.

"I'd rather write for kids," he later explained. "They're more appreciative; adults are obsolete children, and the hell with them."

When Mr. Geisel was interested or amused, which was very often, his eyes would light up with boyish warmth. With his lank hair, beaky nose and neat bow ties, he looked rather like the college professor he had originally set out to be. Though he never earned a doctorate, his alma mater, Dartmouth College, gave him an honorary one.

The world of Mr. Geisel's imagination was nourished by his childhood visits to the zoo in Springfield, Mass. He was born in Springfield on March 4, 1904, the son of Theodor R. Geisel, the Superintendent of Parks, and Henrietta Seuss Geisel. Superintendent Geisel, son of an émigré German cavalry officer who founded a brewery in Springfield, expanded the zoo and liked to show it off to his son.

"I used to hang around there a lot," Mr. Geisel recalled in an interview. "They'd let me in the cage with the small lions and the small tigers, and I got chewed up every once in a while."

After graduating from high school, he majored in English at Dartmouth, where he contributed cartoons to the campus humor magazine, Jack-O-Lantern, and became its editor. He graduated with a B.A. in 1925. Then followed a year of graduate work in English literature at Lincoln College of Oxford University, after which he spent a year traveling in Europe.

In 1927, Mr. Geisel married Helen Marion Palmer of Orange, N.J., a teacher he had met when they were studying at Oxford. She persuaded him to give up thoughts of teaching and make drawing a career.

"Ted's notebooks were always filled with these fabulous animals," she later recalled. "So I set to work diverting him; here was a man who could draw such pictures; he should be earning a living doing that."

In addition to serving as her husband's business manager and helping edit his books, she wrote children's books under her maiden name.

Mr. Geisel began contributing humorous material to Vanity Fair, Liberty, Judge and other magazines. But when he first became famous, it was for drawing the "Quick, Henry, the Flit!" insecticide advertisements.

Mr. Geisel also wrote for the movies. His documentary films "Hitler Lives" and "Design for Death" won Academy Awards in 1946 and 1947, and his cartoon short "Gerald McBoing-Boing" won an Oscar in 1951. He also designed and produced cartoons for television, including the Peabody Award–winning

"How the Grinch Stole Christmas" and "Horton Hears a Who!"

Among his later books were some on serious topics. In "The Butter Battle Book" (1984), he introduced young readers to the dangers of the nuclear arms race. In 1986, in "You're Only Old Once!," he addressed the problems of old age in a book for grown-ups. Edward Sorel, writing in The Times Book Review, said the book was illustrated with Mr. Geisel's "characteristic verve and imagination." But, he added, "there's something amiss in the blithe assumption that the sort of rhymes which delight a 4-year-old (or an adult reading to a 4-year-old) will still entertain when read alone through bifocals."

Admirers of Mr. Geisel said the universality of "Oh, the Places You'll Go!," which addresses the difficulties of finding one's way through life, accounted for its success last year. The book quickly became a popular graduation present, and more than a million copies are said to have been sold.

Helen Palmer Geisel died in 1967. She and Mr. Geisel had no children. In 1968, Mr. Geisel married Audrey Stone Dimond, who survives him.

RALPH ELLISON

March 1, 1913–April 16, 1994

By Richard D. Lyons

Ralph Ellison, whose widely read novel "Invisible Man" was a stark account of racial alienation that foreshadowed the attention Americans eventually paid to divisions in their midst, died yesterday in his apartment on Riverside Drive. He was 80.

The cause was pancreatic cancer.

"Invisible Man," which was written over a seven-year period and published by Random House in 1952, is a chronicle of a young black man's awakening to racial discrimination and his battle against the refusal of Americans to see him apart from his ethnic background, which in turn leads to humiliation and disillusionment.

"Invisible Man" has been viewed as one of the most important works of fiction in the 20th century, has been read by millions, influenced dozens of younger writers and established Mr. Ellison as a major American writer.

Mr. Ellison's short stories, essays, reviews and criticisms have also been widely published over the years; one collection was printed by Random House in 1964 under the title "Shadow and Act." The second and last collection, "Going to the Territory," came out in 1986.

Yet Mr. Ellison's long-awaited second novel proved to be a struggle and has yet to emerge.

His editor, Mr. Fox, said yesterday that the second novel "does exist."

"It is very long, I don't know the name, but it is not a sequel to 'Invisible Man,'" Mr. Fox said. "The book was started in the late 1950's. The initial work on the book was destroyed in a fire in his home upstate, and that was so devastating that he did not resume work on it for several years.

"Just recently Ralph told me that I would be getting the book soon, and I know that he had been working on it every day, but that he was having trouble with what he termed 'transitions.'"

"Invisible Man" was almost instantly acclaimed as the work of a major new author. It remained on the bestseller lists for 16 weeks, and millions of copies have been printed.

The book is the story of an unnamed, idealistic young black man growing up in a segregated community in the South, attending a Negro college and moving to New York to become involved in civil rights issues only to retreat, amid confusion and violence, into invisibility.

Hundreds of thousands of readers have felt themselves tingle to the flatly stated passion of the book's opening lines:

"I am an invisible man. No, I am not a spook like those who haunted Edgar Allan Poe; nor am I one of your Hollywood-movie ectoplasms. I am a man of substance, of flesh and bone, fiber and liquids—and I might even be said to possess a mind. I am invisible, understand, simply because people refuse to see me . . ."

And 572 pages later the unnamed narrator was to evolve into the spokesman for all races when he asks in the book's last line: "Who knows but that, on the lower frequencies, I speak for you?"

The author was born in Oklahoma City. His full name was Ralph Waldo Ellison, for the essayist Ralph Waldo Emerson. Mr. Ellison was the son of Lewis Ellison, a vendor of ice and coal who died accidentally when the boy was only three years old. He was raised by his mother, Ida, who worked as a domestic. "Invisible Man" is dedicated to her, and Mr. Ellison attributed his activist streak to a mother who had recruited black votes for the Socialist Party.

Mr. Ellison began playing the trumpet at age eight, played in his high school band and knew blues singer Jimmy Rushing and trumpeter Hot Lips Page. Also drawn to writing, Mr. Ellison was to say later that his early exposure to the works of Ernest Hemingway and T. S. Eliot impressed him deeply and that he began to connect such writing with his experiences "within the Negro communities in which I grew up."

However, his environment was not segregated. Mr. Ellison was to recall years later that, in the Oklahoma City society of that time, his parents "had many white friends who came to the house when I was quite small, so that any feelings of distrust I was to develop toward whites later on were modified by those with whom I had warm relations."

He studied classical composition at Tuskegee Institute in Alabama, which he reached by riding freight trains. He stayed at Tuskegee from 1933 to 1936, before moving to New York, where he worked with the Federal Writers Project.

During a stay in Harlem during his junior year in college, Mr. Ellison met the poet Langston Hughes and the novelist Richard Wright, who several years later published "Native Son."

Mr. Wright, six years older than Mr. Ellison, became a friend. Mr. Wright encouraged him to persevere with writing, and short stories followed, including, in 1944, "King of the Bingo Game" and "Flying Home."

During World War II, Mr. Ellison served in the Merchant Marine as a cook, and became ill from his ship's contaminated water supply. At the end of hostilities, he visited a friend in Vermont and one day typed, "I am an invisible man," and the novel started. He recalled later, however, he didn't know what those words represented at the start, and had no idea what had inspired the idea.

Yet the words and the ideas were to strike a resonant chord among the public, but also among American intellectuals. Over the years such authors as Kurt Vonnegut and Joseph Heller have credited Mr. Ellison with having influenced them.

Saul Bellow hailed "what a great thing it is when a brilliant individual victory occurs, like Mr. Ellison's, proving that a truly heroic quality can exist among our contemporaries . . . (the tone) is tragicomic, poetic, the tone of the very strongest sort of creative intelligence."

Mr. Ellison was to teach creative writing at New York University, while also serving as a visiting scholar at many other institutions such as the University of Chicago, Rutgers University and Yale University.

He is survived by his wife of 48 years, Fanny, and a brother, Herbert.

Mr. Fox said a small funeral service would be held early next week and that a memorial service would be held at a later date.

EUDORA WELTY

April 13, 1909–July 23, 2001

By Albin Krebs

Eudora Welty, whose evocative short stories, notable for their imagery, sharp dialogue and fierce wit, made her a revered figure in contemporary American letters, died yesterday at a hospital near her home in Jackson, Miss. She was 92.

Miss Welty was plagued by health problems and had been confined to her home, where she had lived since high school and where she wrote most of her stories, novels, essays and memoirs.

As a short-story master, Miss Welty is often mentioned by critics in the same breath as [Anton] Chekhov, but she was dismissed early in her career as a regionalist and earned widespread critical respect only when she was no longer young. When recognition came, she accepted it with the modesty and grace that had become her hallmarks.

She was awarded a Pulitzer Prize in 1973 for her novel "The Optimist's Daughter." She also received the National Book Critics Circle Award, the American Book Award and several O. Henry Awards.

In 1998 Miss Welty said she was "excited and delighted" to learn that she had become the first living writer to be included in the prestigious Library of America series of collected works by United States literary giants. The library's break with its long tradition of choosing only dead authors for its series of definitive collections ushered Miss Welty into a pantheon that includes Mark Twain, Walt Whitman, Henry James and William Faulkner.

For decades she was pigeonholed by critics who placed her with Faulkner, Katherine Anne Porter, Flannery O'Connor and Carson McCullers as a writer of the so-called Southern School. But her work, like that of those other Southern writers, possessed a universal relevance and appeal.

"It is not the South we find in her stories, it is Eudora Welty's South, a region that feeds her imagination and a place we come to trust," Maureen Howard said when she reviewed Miss Welty's "Collected Stories" in 1980. "She is a Southerner as Chekhov was a Russian, because place provides them with a reality—a reality as difficult, mysterious and impermanent as life."

Eudora Welty was born on April 13, 1909, in Jackson, the daughter of Christian Webb Welty and the former Chestina Andrews. The Weltys settled in Jackson shortly after their marriage, and Mr. Welty became an executive in a life insurance company.

The Weltys were devoted to books and learning. In a memoir, "One Writer's Beginnings," Miss Welty recalled the exhilaration she felt when she fell under the spell of books.

"It had been startling and disappointing to me to find out that storybooks had been written by people, that books were not natural wonders, coming up of themselves like grass," she wrote. "Yet regardless of where they came from, I cannot remember a time when I was not in love with them—with the books themselves, cover and binding and the paper they were printed on, with their smell and their weight and with their possession in my arms, captured and carried off to myself. Still illiterate, I was ready for them, committed to all the reading I could give them."

Miss Welty learned to read before starting school and began turning out stories as a child, discovering them in daily life.

"Long before I wrote stories, I listened for stories," she wrote in 1984. "Listening for them is something more acute than listening to them. I suppose it's an early form of participation in what goes on. Listening children know stories are there. When their elders sit and begin, children are just waiting and hoping for one to come out, like a mouse from its hole."

In 1929 Miss Welty earned a bachelor's degree from the University of Wisconsin. After college she told her parents that she wanted to be a writer, but her father insisted that she "learn something to fall back on" to support herself, so she took advertising courses at the Columbia University School of Business.

During the Depression she got a publicity job at the Works Progress Administration, which enabled her to travel throughout Mississippi. She was trou-

bled and fascinated by the people she saw and took hundreds of snapshots.

The pictures were exhibited in New York in 1936, the same year that Miss Welty, who had sent dozens of unsolicited stories to magazines, made her first sale. A small literary magazine called Manuscript accepted "Death of a Traveling Salesman," the recounting of the last day in the life of a lonely, ill and frightened shoe salesman who loses his way in rural Mississippi. Before he dies of a heart attack, he realizes how little he has understood about himself and others.

Miss Welty began to attract attention after The Atlantic Monthly published two of her stories destined to become classics: "Why I Live at the P.O." and "A Worn Path." The first is a first-person explanation by a small-town postmistress of why she is moving out of her eccentric family's home to live at the post office. The second won Miss Welty her first of eight O. Henry Awards.

Early admirers of her short stories pressed Miss Welty to try her hand at a novel, but she resisted for several years. Her first hardcover book was a 1941 short-story collection, "A Curtain of Green." Its 17 stories became widely known and valued through their inclusion in anthologies and textbooks.

The editor and critic James Olney said of "A Curtain of Green": "The volume's tonal variety is astonishing: from the somber 'Death of a Traveling Salesman' to the hallucinatory 'Flowers for Marjorie,' from the wonderment at the variety of human faces of 'Clytie' to the foreboding near-violence of the title piece, from the jazzy 'Powerhouse' to the satiric 'Petrified Man,' from the wildly comic 'Why I Live at the

P.O.' to the dignified 'A Worn Path' (the 'grave, persistent, meditative' sound of old Phoenix Jackson's cane tapping the frozen earth establishes the tone at the outset)."

"Why I Live at the P.O." combined Miss Welty's antic sense of humor with her pleasure in language. As the narrator prepares to leave her family's home, she says: "So I hope to tell you I marched in and got the radio. And they could of all bit a nail in two, especially Stella-Rondo, that it used to belong to, and she well knew she couldn't get it back, I'd sue for it like a shot . . . The thermometer and the Hawaiian ukulele were certainly mine, and I stood on the stepladder and got all my watermelon-rind preserves and every fruit and vegetable I put up, every jar."

In 1941 Miss Welty followed "A Curtain of Green" with "The Wide Net and Other Stories," and in 1942 she published the novella "The Robber Bridegroom." Her first full-length novel, "Delta Wedding," appeared in 1946.

Three years later, a group of stories set in Morgana, an imaginary small town on the Mississippi Delta, was published under the title "The Golden Apples." All of Miss Welty's gifts for compression, metaphorical language and poetic structure were on display, as was her genius for using the details of daily life to illuminate the mysteries of the heart.

During World War II, Miss Welty was briefly on the staff of The New York Times Book Review. But she returned to Jackson during the 1950's, when her mother and brothers fell seriously ill. For almost 15 years she published just a few short stories, some book reviews and a children's book, "The Shoe Bird." During this period she cared for her family and worked on two novels. After the deaths of her mother and brothers, she returned in the 70's with the novels "Losing Battles" and "The Optimist's Daughter."

"Delta Wedding," along with the short novel "The Ponder Heart" and her longest one, "Losing Battles," are examples of Miss Welty's preoccupation with family life. They focus on weddings, reunions and funerals, which all bring family members together to recall the past, criticize and praise one another and settle old scores.

Her novels and stories expose the foibles to which large clans are prone, their tendencies to resist change, squelch individuality and ostracize outsiders. In "The Ponder Heart" she demonstrates her extraordinary ear for dialect and a sense of the ridiculous as she tells the entire story as a comic monologue by a garrulous hotel manager.

Commenting on many critics' observations that her works carried a strong sense of place, Miss Welty said: "I think Southerners have such an intimate sense of place. We grew up in the fact that we live here with people about whom we know almost everything that

can be known as a citizen of the same neighborhood or town. We learn significant things that way."

And because she was in her particular place in the racially discordant 60's, she said, "I was one of the writers who received dead-of-night telephone calls, when I was harangued by strangers saying, 'Why are you sitting down there writing your stories instead of out condemning your society?'"

"I didn't need their pointers to know that there was injustice among human beings or that there was trouble," she continued. "I had been writing about that steadily right along, by letting my characters show this. I see as my privilege writing about human beings as human beings with all the things that make them up, including bigotry, misunderstanding, injustice and also love and affection and whatever else. Whatever else makes them up interests me."

Miss Welty, who leaves no survivors, made one notable exception to her rule against direct crusading when Medgar Evers, the black civil rights leader, was shot to death by a sniper in Jackson in 1963.

"I did write a story the night it happened," she said. "I was so upset about this, and I thought: I live down here where this happened and I believe I must know what a person like that felt like—the murderer. There had been so many stories about such a character in the stock manner, written by people who didn't know the South, so I wrote about the murderer intimately—in the first person, which was a very daring thing for me to do."

The story, "Where Is the Voice Coming From?," was rushed into print in The New Yorker days after Evers's killer was arrested and represented a chilling journey into the mind of a bigoted psychopath.

ARTHUR MILLER

October 17, 1915–February 10, 2005

By Marilyn Berger

Arthur Miller, one of the great American playwrights, whose work exposed the flaws in the fabric of the American dream, died Thursday night at his home in Roxbury, Conn. He was 89.

The cause was congestive heart failure.

The author of "Death of a Salesman," a landmark of 20th-century drama, Mr. Miller grappled with the weightiest matters of social conscience in his plays and in them often reflected or reinterpreted the stormy and very public elements of his own life, including a brief and rocky marriage to Marilyn Monroe and his refusal to cooperate with the red-baiting House Un-American Activities Committee.

"Death of a Salesman," which opened on Broadway in 1949, established Mr. Miller as a giant of the American theater when he was only 33. It won the triple crown of theatrical artistry: the Pulitzer Prize, the New York Drama Critics' Circle Award and the Tony.

But the play's enormous success also overshadowed Mr. Miller's long career. "The Crucible," a 1953 play about the Salem witch trials inspired by his hatred of McCarthyism, and "A View from the Bridge," a 1955 drama of obsession and betrayal, ultimately took their place as classics of the international stage, but Mr. Miller's later plays never equaled his early successes. Although he wrote 17 plays, "The Price," produced on Broadway during the 1967–68 season, was his last solid hit.

Mr. Miller also wrote successfully in other media. He supplied the screenplay for "The Misfits," a 1961 movie directed by John Huston and starring Monroe, to whom he was married at the time. He also wrote an autobiography, "Timebends: A Life."

But his reputation rests on a handful of his best-known plays, the dramas of guilt, betrayal and redemption that continue to be revived. These dramas of social conscience were drawn from life and informed by the Great Depression, the event that he believed had a more profound impact on the nation than any other except, possibly, the Civil War.

"In play after play," the drama critic Mel Gussow wrote in The New York Times, "he holds man responsible for his and for his neighbor's actions."

Elia Kazan, who directed "All My Sons," "Death of a Salesman" and "After the Fall," recalled in an interview, "In the 30's and 40's, we came out of the Group Theater tradition that every play should teach a lesson and make a thematic point."

Mr. Miller, a lanky, wiry man, retained the appearance of a 1930's intellectual whether he was wearing work boots and jeans while fixing his porch or seated at his word processor.

Writing plays was for him, he said, like breathing. He wrote in "Timebends" that when he was young, he "imagined that with the possible exception of a doctor saving a life, writing a worthy play was the most important thing a human being could do." He saw plays as a way to change America, and, as he put it, "that meant grabbing people and shaking them by the back of the neck."

He had known hard work firsthand in an auto-parts warehouse during the Depression and at the Brooklyn Navy Yard during World War II. But Mr. Miller called playwriting the hardest work of all.

"A playwright lives in an occupied country," he said. "He's the enemy. And if you can't live like that, you don't stay. It's tough. He's got to be able to take a whack, and he's got to swallow bicycles and digest them."

What Mr. Miller could not swallow was critics. At one moment he was hailed as the greatest living playwright and at another as a has-been. Even at the height of his success, Mr. Miller's work received harsh criticism from prominent critics.

Arthur Miller was born in Manhattan on Oct. 17, 1915, to Augusta and Isidore Miller. His father was a coat manufacturer and so prosperous that he rode in a chauffeur-driven car from the family apartment overlooking Central Park to the Seventh Avenue garment district. For a child, Mr. Miller recalled, life unfolded as "a kind of scroll whose message was surprise and mostly good news."

The Depression changed everything for the family and became a theme that etched its way through Arthur Miller plays, from "Death of a Salesman" and "The Price" to "After the Fall," "The American Clock" and "A Memory of Two Mondays." The crash meant the collapse of the coat business and a move to reduced circumstances in Flatbush, Brooklyn, where the teenage Arthur worked as a bakery delivery boy.

He graduated from high school in 1932, and then went to work in an auto-parts warehouse to earn money for his first year of college. Mr. Miller knew by the time he was 16 that he wanted to be a writer.

He went to the University of Michigan with the hope of writing a play good enough to win the school's Avery Hopwood Award, which carried a prize of $250, enough for a second year at college. He did not win the first year, but scraped together enough money to go back to school. He went on to win two Hopwood Awards as well as a $1,250 Bureau of New Plays Award from the Theater Guild.

Within two years of graduating, Mr. Miller had written six plays, all of them rejected by producers except "The Man Who Had All the Luck," which lasted only four performances on Broadway.

In 1940 he married his college sweetheart, Mary Grace Slattery, with whom he had two children. To support his family he worked in the navy yard and took a final shot at playwriting.

"I laid myself a wager," he wrote in his autobiography. "I would hold back this play until I was as sure as I could be that every page was integral to the whole and would work; then, if my judgment of it proved wrong, I would leave the theater behind and write in other forms."

That play was "All My Sons," which Brooks Atkinson, the New York Times drama critic, called "an honest, forceful drama about a group of people caught up in a monstrous swindle that has caused the death of 21 Army pilots because of defectively manufactured cylinder heads." It won two Tony Awards.

In 1949 Willy Loman, riding on "a smile and a shoeshine" and determined to be not just liked but well liked, made his way into American consciousness in "Death of a Salesman."

Acclaimed as a modern American masterpiece and translated into 29 languages, "Salesman" was no sooner a major success of the Broadway stage than it was savaged in intellectual journals as melodrama or Marxist propaganda. Nonetheless, "Death of a Salesman" stunned audiences. Atkinson called it "a rare event in the theater."

Lines from the play became hallmarks of the postwar era. "You can't eat the orange and throw the peel away," Willy bellowed, pleading with his young boss to keep his job. "A man is not a piece of fruit." Willy's careworn wife spoke for the inherent dignity of her husband's life, providing a stirring refutation of the cruelties of America's capitalist culture: "Attention must be paid."

In 1950, Mr. Miller wrote an adaptation of Ibsen's drama "An Enemy of the People." This 19th-century play, whose hero resisted pressure to conform to the ideology of the day, resonated in the McCarthyite climate of the mid-20th century.

"An Enemy of the People," in philosophy at least, served as a forerunner of "The Crucible," a dramatization of the Salem witch hunt of the 17th century that implicitly articulated Mr. Miller's outrage at McCarthyism. He once recalled that at one performance of "The Crucible," upon the execution of the leading character, John Proctor, people "stood up and remained silent for a couple of minutes" because "the Rosenbergs were at that moment being electrocuted in Sing Sing."

Mr. Miller said that when he wrote "The Crucible," he hoped it would be seen as an affirmation for keeping one's own conscience.

"The Crucible" was also the occasion of Mr. Miller's explosive rift with Kazan, the director of his greatest successes. Kazan's decision to name names at a House Un-American Activities Committee hearing incensed Mr. Miller, and the play was seen by some as a personal rebuke. Bypassing Kazan for the project, Mr. Miller turned to the director Jed Harris.

Mr. Harris's production was not well received. Nevertheless, the play won Mr. Miller another Tony Award in 1953 and became his most frequently produced work.

In 1956, Mr. Miller was himself called to appear before the House Un-American Activities Committee. He was applauded in Hollywood and theater circles when he refused to name names, a courageous act in an atmosphere of fear. He was cited for contempt of Congress, although he said he had never joined the Communist Party.

Of Mr. Miller's performance before the committee, Atkinson wrote in 1957: "He refused to be an informer. He refused to turn his private conscience over to administration by the state. He has accordingly been found in contempt of Congress. That is the measure of the man who has written these highminded plays." Two years later, the courts dismissed the contempt citation.

He and Monroe were married in 1956, less than a month after his divorce from his wife and two years after her divorce from Joe DiMaggio.

For most of the four years of that marriage, Mr. Miller wrote almost nothing except "The Misfits," composed as a gift to his wife, who was increasingly tormented by personal demons and drug abuse. The film had its premiere early in 1961, shortly after the couple divorced. A year later, Mr. Miller remarried, and six months after that, Monroe was found dead of a drug overdose.

"After the Fall," his most overtly autobiographical play, brought Mr. Miller a storm of criticism when it was produced in 1964, shortly after Monroe's death. The play, written soon after the collapse of their marriage, implies a search for understanding of her inability to cope and his failure to help her. He professed surprise when critics noted the resemblance between Monroe and Maggie, the play's drug-addicted, blond-wigged protagonist, and accused him of defiling Monroe's image.

"The play," he said at the time, "is a work of fiction." Almost no one took his explanations at face value.

But "After the Fall" did occasion Mr. Miller's reunion with Kazan, the most insightful director of his work. It was brought about by Robert Whitehead, an architect of the plan to create an American repertory theater company as part of the new Lincoln Center complex. In his autobiography, "A Life," Kazan wrote, "Once brought together, Art and I got along well—even though I was somewhat tense in his company, because we'd never discussed (and never did discuss) the reasons for our 'break.'"

"After the Fall" was the inaugural production of the Repertory Theater of Lincoln Center. Mr. Miller contributed a second play, "Incident at Vichy," to the following season, but it, too, was poorly received.

After his divorce from Monroe, Mr. Miller married Inge Morath, a photographer, with whom he had a daughter, Rebecca Miller, a filmmaker. She survives him, along with the children of his first marriage, a sister, four grandchildren and his companion, Agnes Barley, a painter.

In the late 1980's, Mr. Miller reflected in an interview on the course he had taken in life. Asked how he wanted to be remembered, he did not hesitate: "I hope as a playwright. That would be all of it."

SAUL BELLOW

June 10, 1915–April 5, 2005

By Mel Gussow and Charles McGrath

Saul Bellow, the Nobel laureate and self-proclaimed historian of society whose fictional heroes—and whose scathing, unrelenting and darkly comic examination of their struggle for meaning—gave new immediacy to the American novel in the second half of the 20th century, died yesterday at his home in Brookline, Mass. He was 89.

"I cannot exceed what I see," Mr. Bellow once said. "I am bound, in other words, as the historian is bound by the period he writes about, by the situation I live in." But his was a history of a particular and idiosyncratic sort. The center of his fictional universe was Chicago, where he grew up and spent most of his life, and which he made into the first city of American letters. Many of his works are set there, and almost all of them have a Midwestern earthiness and brashness. Like their creator, Mr. Bellow's heroes were all head and all body both. They tended to be dreamers, questers or bookish intellectuals, but they lived in a lovingly depicted world of cranks, con men, fast-talking salesmen and wheeler-dealers.

In novels like "The Adventures of Augie March," his breakthrough novel in 1953, "Henderson the Rain King" and "Herzog," Mr. Bellow laid a path for old-fashioned, supersized characters and equally big themes and ideas. As the English novelist Malcolm Bradbury said, "His fame, literary, intellectual, moral, lay with his big books," which were "filled with their big, clever, flowing prose, and their big, more-than-lifesize heroes—Augie Marches, Hendersons, Herzogs, Humboldts—who fought the battle for courage, intelligence, selfhood and a sense of human grandeur in the postwar age of expansive, materialist, high-towered Chicago-style American capitalism."

Mr. Bellow said that of all his characters Eugene Henderson, of "Henderson the Rain King," a quixotic violinist and pig farmer who vainly sought a higher truth and a moral purpose in life, was the one most like himself. But there were also elements of the author in the put-upon, twice-divorced but everhopeful Moses Herzog and in wise but embattled older figures like Artur Sammler, of "Mr. Sammler's Planet," and Albert Corde, the dean in "The Dean's December." All were men trying to come to grips with what Corde called "the big-scale insanities of the 20th century."

All his work was written in a distinctive, immediately recognizable style that blended high and low, colloquial and mandarin, wisecrack and aphorism, as in the introduction of the poet Humboldt at the beginning of "Humboldt's Gift": "He was a wonderful talker, a hectic nonstop monologist and improvisator, a champion detractor. To be loused up by Humboldt was really a kind of privilege. It was like being the subject of a two-nosed portrait by Picasso, or an eviscerated chicken by Soutine."

Mr. Bellow stuck to an individualistic path, and steered clear of cliques, fads and schools of writing. He was frequently lumped together with Philip Roth and Bernard Malamud as a Jewish-American writer, but he rejected the label, saying he had no wish to be part of the "Hart, Schaffner & Marx" of American letters. He spoke his own mind, without regard for political correctness or fashion, and was often involved in fierce debates with feminists, black writers, postmodernists. On multiculturalism, he was once quoted as asking: "Who is the Tolstoy of the Zulus? The Proust of the Papuans?" The remark caused a furor and was taken as proof, he said, "that I was at best insensitive and at worst an elitist, a chauvinist, a reactionary and a racist—in a word, a monster."

In his life as in his work, he was unpredictable. The most urban of writers, he spent much of his time at a farm in Vermont. He admired the Chicago machers—the deal-makers and real-estate men—and he dressed like one of them, in bespoke suits, Turnbull & Asser shirts and a Borsalino hat.

In a long and unusually productive career, Mr. Bellow dodged many of the snares that typically entangle American writers. He didn't drink much, and though he was analyzed four times, his mental health was as robust as his physical health. He never stopped writing. The Nobel Prize, which he won in 1976, was the cornerstone of a career that included a Pulitzer Prize, three National Book Awards and more honors than any other American writer.

This most American of writers was born in Lachine, Quebec, an immigrant suburb of Montreal, and named Solomon Bellow. His birth date is listed as either June or July 10, 1915. His parents had emigrated from Russia. In Canada, Solomon's father, Abram, failed at one enterprise after another. His mother, Liza, was deeply religious and wanted the youngest of her four children to become a rabbi or a violinist. But when at the age of eight he spent six months in the Royal Victoria Hospital, suffering from a respiratory infection and reading "Uncle Tom's Cabin" and the funny papers, he became certain, he said, that he had discovered his destiny.

When young Soloman was nine, the Bellows moved to Chicago. During his childhood, he was steeped in Jewish tradition. But eventually he rebelled against what he considered a "suffocating orthodoxy" and found in Chicago not just a physical home but a spiritual one.

Recalling his sense of discovery and belonging, he later wrote, "The children of Chicago bakers, tailors, peddlers, insurance agents, pressers, cutters, grocers, the sons of families on relief, were reading buckram-bound books from the public library and were in a state of enthusiasm, having found themselves on the shore of a novelistic land to which they really belonged, discovering their birthright talking to one another about the mind, society, art, religion, epistemology and doing all this in Chicago, of all places."

Chicago became for him what Dublin was for Joyce, the center of both his life and his work and almost a character in its own right.

In 1933 Mr. Bellow began college at the University of Chicago, but two years later transferred to Northwestern. Put off by the tweedy anti-Semitism of the English department, he graduated in 1937 with honors in anthropology and sociology, subjects that would instill his novels. But he was still obsessed by fiction. While doing graduate work in anthropology at the University of Wisconsin, he found that "every time I worked on my thesis, it turned out to be a story."

Mr. Bellow came to New York "toward the end of the 30's, muddled in the head but keen to educate myself." He was in training with the merchant marine when the atom bomb was dropped on Hiroshima. During his service, he finished writing "Dangling Man," about the alienation of a young Chicagoan waiting to be drafted. It was published in 1944, before the author was 30, and was followed by "The Victim," a novel about anti-Semitism.

In 1948, Mr. Bellow went to Paris, where he had a kind of epiphany. He remembered a friend from his childhood named Chucky, "a wild talker who was always announcing cheerfully that he had a super scheme," and he began to wonder what a novel in Chucky's voice would sound like. "The book just came to me," he said later. "All I had to do was be there with buckets to catch it." The resulting novel, "The Adventures of Augie March," was published in 1953, and it became Mr. Bellow's breakthrough, a best seller that also established him as a writer of consequence. The beginning of the novel announced a brand-new voice in American fiction—jazzy, brash, exuberant, with accents that were both Yiddish and Whitmanian:

"I am an American, Chicago born—Chicago, that somber city—and go at things as I have taught myself, free-style, and will make the record in my own way: first to knock, first admitted; sometimes an innocent knock, sometimes a not so innocent."

"Fiction is the higher autobiography," Mr. Bellow once said, and in later novels, he often adapted facts from his own life and the lives of people he knew. Humboldt was a version of the poet Delmore Schwartz; Gersbach, the cuckolder in "Herzog," was a Bard professor named Jack Ludwig, who seduced Mr. Bellow's wife at the time; and in one guise or another most of Mr. Bellow's many girlfriends turned up.

"What a woman-filled life I always led," says Charlie Citrine, the protagonist of "Humboldt's Gift." Those words could have been echoed by the author, who had almost innumerable affairs and was married five times. His wives were Anita Goshkin, Alexandra Tsachacbasov, Susan Glassman, Alexandra Ionescu Tulcea and Janis Freedman. All but Mr. Bellow's last marriage ended in divorce. In addition to his wife, Janis, his survivors include a daughter and three sons.

With "Henderson the Rain King" in 1959, Mr. Bellow envisioned an even more ambitious canvas than that of "Augie March," with the story of an American millionaire who travels in Africa in search of regeneration. "Henderson" was followed in 1964 by "Herzog," with the title character a Jewish Everyman cuckolded by his wife and his best friend. "He is taken by an epistolary fit," said the author, "and writes grieving, biting, ironic and rambunctious letters not only to his friends and acquaintances, but also to the great men, the giants of thought, who formed his mind." The novel won a National Book Award.

With "Mr. Sammler's Planet," in 1969, a novel about a Holocaust survivor living in New York, Mr. Bellow won his third National Book Award. "Humboldt's Gift," in 1975, proved one of his greatest successes. In it, Charlie Citrine, a Pulitzer Prize–winning writer, must come to terms with the death of his mentor.

Life imitated art, and "Humboldt" won the Pulitzer Prize for fiction. The Nobel Prize in Literature soon followed.

His books eventually became shorter and shorter, although he returned to longer fiction in 2000 with "Ravelstein," about a celebrated professor dying of AIDS.

In 1993 Mr. Bellow moved to Boston and began teaching at Boston University. Explaining why he continued to teach, despite his financial success, he said: "You're all alone when you're a writer. Sometimes you just feel you need a humanity bath. Even a ride on the subway will do that. But it's much more interesting to talk about books. After all, that's what life used to be for writers: they talk books, politics, history, America. Nothing has replaced that."

NORMAN MAILER

January 31, 1923–November 10, 2007

By Charles McGrath

Norman Mailer, the combative, controversial and often outspoken novelist who loomed over American letters longer and larger than any other writer of his generation, died early yesterday in Manhattan. He was 84.

The cause was acute renal failure, his family said.

Mr. Mailer burst on the scene in 1948 with "The Naked and the Dead," a partly autobiographical novel about World War II, and for six decades he was rarely far from center stage. He published more than 30 books, including novels, biographies and works of nonfiction, and twice won the Pulitzer Prize: for "The Armies of the Night" (1968), which also won the National Book Award, and "The Executioner's Song" (1979).

He also wrote, directed and acted in several low-budget movies, helped found The Village Voice and for many years was a regular guest on television talk shows, where he could reliably be counted on to make oracular pronouncements and deliver provocative opinions, sometimes coherently and sometimes not.

Mr. Mailer belonged to the old literary school that regarded novel writing as a heroic enterprise undertaken by heroic characters with egos to match. He was the most transparently ambitious writer of his era, seeing himself in competition not just with his contemporaries but with the likes of Tolstoy and Dostoyevsky.

He was also the least shy and risk-averse of writers. He eagerly sought public attention, and publicity inevitably followed him on the few occasions when he tried to avoid it. His big ears, barrel chest, striking blue eyes and helmet of seemingly electrified hair—jet black at first and ultimately snow white—made him instantly recognizable, a celebrity long before most authors were lured out into the limelight.

At different points in his life Mr. Mailer was a prodigious drinker and drug taker, a womanizer, a devoted family man, a would-be politician who ran for mayor of New York, a hipster existentialist, an antiwar protester, an opponent of women's liberation and an all-purpose feuder and short-fused brawler, who with the slightest provocation would happily engage in head-butting, arm-wrestling and random punch-throwing. Boxing obsessed him and inspired some of his best writing. Any time he met a critic or a reviewer, even a friendly one, he would put up his fists and drop into a crouch.

Along the way, he transformed American journalism by introducing to nonfiction writing some of the techniques of the novelist and by placing at the center of his reporting a brilliant, flawed and larger-than-life character who was none other than Norman Mailer himself.

Norman Kingsley (or, in Hebrew, Nachem Malek) Mailer was born in Long Branch, N.J., on Jan. 31, 1923. His father, Isaac Barnett Mailer, was a South African émigré and a largely ineffectual businessman.

The dominant figure in the family was Mr. Mailer's mother, the former Fanny Schneider, who came from a vibrant clan in Long Branch, where her father ran a grocery and was the town's unofficial rabbi.

When Norman was nine, the family moved to Crown Heights, in Brooklyn. Pampered and doted on, he excelled at both Public School 161 and Boys High School, from which he graduated in 1939.

That fall, he entered Harvard as a 16-year-old. By the time he was a sophomore, he had fallen in love with literature. He spent the summer reading and rereading James T. Farrell's "Studs Lonigan," John Steinbeck's "Grapes of Wrath" and John Dos Passos's "U.S.A.," and he began, or so he claimed, to set himself a daily quota of 3,000 words of his own, on the theory that this was the way to get bad writing out of his system.

Mr. Mailer graduated from Harvard in 1943, determined on a literary career. He was called up by the Army in the spring of 1944, after marrying Bea Silverman in January, and was sent to the Philippines.

Mr. Mailer saw little combat, but his wartime experience, and in particular a single patrol he made on the island of Leyte, became the raw material for "The Naked and the Dead," the book that put him on the map.

The novel is about a platoon fighting on a Pacific atoll. When it was published it was almost universally praised—the last time this would happen to him. Some critics ranked it among the best war novels ever written. It sold 200,000 copies in just three months—a huge number in those days.

His second book, "Barbary Shore" (1951), a political novel about, among other things, the struggle between capitalism and socialism, earned what Mr. Mailer called "possibly the worst reviews of any serious novel in recent years." A third, "The Deer Park" (1955), in part a fictionalized account of Elia Kazan's troubles with the House Un-American Activities Committee, fared only a little better.

For much of the '50s he drifted, frequently drunk or stoned or both. In 1955, together with two friends, Daniel Wolf and Edwin Fancher, he founded The Village Voice, and while writing a column for that paper he began to evolve what became his trademark style—bold, poetic, metaphysical, even shamanistic at times—and his personal philosophy of hipsterism.

The most famous, or infamous, version of this philosophy was Mr. Mailer's controversial 1957 essay "The White Negro," which seemed to endorse violence as an existential act and declared the murder of a white candy-store owner by two 18-year-old blacks an example of "daring the unknown."

In November 1960, drinking heavily at a party, Mr. Mailer stabbed his second wife, Adele Morales, with a penknife, seriously wounding her. Mr. Mailer was arrested, but his wife declined to press charges, and he was eventually released after being sent to Bellevue Hospital for observation. The marriage broke up two years later.

All told, Mr. Mailer was married six times, counting a quickie with Carol Stevens, whom he wed and divorced within a couple of days in 1980 to grant legitimacy to their daughter, Maggie. His other wives, in addition to Ms. Silverman and Ms. Morales, were Lady Jeanne Campbell, granddaughter of Lord Beaverbrook; Beverly Rentz Bentley; and Norris Church, with whom he was living at his death. Lady Jeanne died in June.

In the 1970s Mr. Mailer entered into a long feud with proponents of women's liberation, and in a famous 1971 debate with Germaine Greer at Town Hall in Manhattan he declared himself an "enemy of birth control."

He meant it. By his various wives, Mr. Mailer had eight children, all of whom survive him. Also surviving are an adopted son, by an earlier marriage of Ms. Church's, and 10 grandchildren.

For all his hipsterism, Mr. Mailer was an old-fashioned, attentive father. Starting in the 1960s, the financial burden of his offspring, as well as keeping up with his numerous alimony payments, caused him to take on freelance magazine assignments.

A series of articles for Esquire on the 1968 Republican and Democratic conventions became the basis for his book "Miami and the Siege of Chicago," and articles for Harper's and Commentary about the 1967 antiwar march on the Pentagon were the basis for the prizewinning book "The Armies of the Night: History as a Novel, the Novel as History."

The critic Richard Gilman said of the book: "In 'Armies of the Night,' the rough force of Mailer's imagination, his brilliant wayward gifts of observation, his ravishing if often calculated honesty and his chutzpah all flourish on the steady ground of a newly coherent subject and theme."

Somehow in this busy decade Mr. Mailer also managed to make his most famous movie, "Maidstone," during the filming of which he bit off part of an ear of the actor Rip Torn after Mr. Torn attacked him with a hammer, and to run for mayor of New York with Jimmy Breslin on his ticket. They campaigned to make the city the 51st state. (The Mailer team eventually lost in the Democratic primary to Mario Procaccino, who was beaten in the election by John V. Lindsay.)

His best book, he said in an interview in 2006, was "Ancient Evenings" (1983), a long novel about ancient Egypt. About the book that many critics consider his masterpiece, "The Executioner's Song," he said he had mixed feelings because it wasn't entirely his project.

The book, which is about Gary Gilmore, a convicted murderer who, after a stay on death row, asked to be executed by the State of Utah in 1976, was the idea of Lawrence Schiller, a writer and filmmaker who did much of the reporting, taping Mr. Gilmore and his family.

But Mr. Mailer recast this material in what was for him a new impersonal voice that rendered the thoughts of his characters in a style partly drawn from their own way of talking. He called it a "true-life novel."

Joan Didion, reviewing the book for The New York Times Book Review, said: "It is ambitious to the point of vertigo. It is a largely unremarked fact about Mailer that he is a great and obsessed stylist, a writer to whom the shape of the sentence is the story. His sentences do not get long or short by accident, or because he is in a hurry. I think no one but Mailer could have dared this book. The authentic Western voice, the voice heard in 'The Executioner's Song,' is one heard often in life but only rarely in literature."

Mr. Mailer was drawn to another convict. He championed Jack Henry Abbott, who was serving a long sentence in a Utah prison for forgery and for killing a fellow inmate. In 1977, Mr. Abbott began writing to Mr. Mailer. Mr. Mailer saw literary talent in Mr. Abbott's letters and helped him publish them in an acclaimed volume called "In the Belly of the Beast." He also lobbied to get Mr. Abbott paroled. A few weeks after being released, in June 1981, Mr. Abbott, now a darling in leftist literary circles, stabbed to death a waiter in a Lower East Side restaurant, and his champion became a target of national outrage.

This was the last great controversy of Mr. Mailer's career. Chastened perhaps, the former scourge of parties became a regular guest at black-tie benefits and dinners given by the likes of William S. Paley, Gloria Vanderbilt and Oscar de la Renta. His editor, Jason Epstein, said of this period, "There are two sides to Norman Mailer, and the good side has won."

In the '90s Mr. Mailer's health began to fail. But his productivity was undiminished. In 1997 "The Gospel According to the Son," a first-person novel about Jesus, was published. It gave some critics the opportunity they had been waiting for. Norman Mailer thinks he's God, they said.

Mr. Mailer's next novel, "The Castle in the Forest," was about Hitler, but the narrator was a devil, a persona the author admitted he found particularly congenial. "It's as close as a writer gets to unrequited joy," he said. "We are devils when all is said and done."

Interviewed at his house in Provincetown, Mass., shortly before that book's publication, Mr. Mailer, frail but cheerful, talked of his life as a writer.

"In two years I will have been a published novelist for 60 years," he said. "That's not true for very many of us." And he recalled something he had said at the National Book Award ceremony in 2005, when he was given a lifetime achievement award: that he felt like an old coachmaker who looks with horror at the turn of the 20th century, watching automobiles roar by with their fumes.

"I think the novel is on the way out," he said. "I also believe, because it's natural to take one's own occupation more seriously than others, that the world may be the less for that."

JOHN UPDIKE

March 18, 1932–January 27, 2009

By Christopher Lehmann-Haupt

John Updike, the kaleidoscopically gifted writer whose quartet of Rabbit novels highlighted a body of fiction, verse, essays and criticism so vast, protean and lyrical as to place him in the first rank of American authors, died on Tuesday in Danvers, Mass. He was 76 and lived in Beverly Farms, Mass.

The cause was cancer, according to a statement by Knopf, his publisher.

Of Mr. Updike's many novels and stories, perhaps none captured the imagination of the book-reading public more than his precisely observed tales about ordinary citizens in small-town and urban settings.

His best-known protagonist, Harry Rabbit Angstrom, first appears as a former high-school basketball star trapped in a loveless marriage and a sales job he hates. Through the four novels whose titles bear his nickname—"Rabbit, Run," "Rabbit Redux," "Rabbit Is Rich" and "Rabbit at Rest"—the author traces the funny, restless and questing life of this middle American against the background of the last half-century's major events.

"My subject is the American Protestant small-town middle class," Mr. Updike said in 1966. "I like middles," he continued. "It is in middles that extremes clash, where ambiguity restlessly rules."

From his earliest short stories, he found his subject in the everyday dramas of marriage, sex and divorce. He wrote about America with boundless curiosity and wit in prose so careful and attentive that it burnished the ordinary with a painterly gleam.

Here he is in "A Sense of Shelter," an early short story:

"Snow fell against the high school all day, wet big-flake snow that did not accumulate well. Sharpening two pencils, William looked down on a parking lot that was a blackboard in reverse; car tires had cut smooth arcs of black into the white, and wherever a school bus had backed around, it had left an autocratic signature of two V's."

The detail of his writing was so rich that it inspired two schools of thought on Mr. Updike's fiction: those who responded to his descriptive prose as to a kind of poetry, a sensuous engagement with the world, and those who argued that it was more style than content.

"He is a prose writer of great beauty," the critic James Wood wrote in 1999, "but that prose confronts one with the question of whether beauty is enough."

Astonishingly industrious and prolific, Mr. Updike turned out three pages a day of fiction, essays, criticism or verse, proving the maxim that several pages a day was at least a book a year—or more. He published 60 books in his lifetime; his final one, "My Father's Tears and Other Stories," is to be published in June.

"I would write ads for deodorants or labels for catsup bottles, if I had to," he told The Paris Review in 1967. "The miracle of turning inklings into thoughts and thoughts into words and words into metal and print and ink never palls for me."

His vast output of poetry, which tended toward light verse, and his wide-ranging essays and criticism filled volume after volume.

He never abandoned short stories, of which he turned out several hundred, most for The New Yorker. It was here that he exercised his exquisitely sharp eye for the minutiae of domestic routine and the conflicts that animated it for him—between present satisfaction and future possibility, between sex and spirituality, and between the beauty of creation and the looming threat of death.

Philip Roth, one of his literary peers, said Tuesday: "John Updike is our time's greatest man of letters, as brilliant a literary critic and essayist as he was a novelist and short story writer. He is and always will be no less a national treasure than his 19th-century precursor, Nathaniel Hawthorne."

John Hoyer Updike was born on March 18, 1932, in Reading, Pa., and grew up in the nearby town of Shillington. He was the only child of Wesley Russell Updike, a junior high school math teacher of Dutch descent, and Linda Grace Hoyer Updike, who later also published fiction in The New Yorker and elsewhere.

His was a solitary childhood, but isolation fired his imagination as well as his desire to take flight from aloneness. He aspired first to be either an animator for Walt Disney or a magazine cartoonist.

After graduating from high school as co-valedictorian and senior-class president, Mr. Updike attended Harvard on a scholarship; he majored in English and wrote for and edited The Harvard Lampoon. In 1953 he married Mary Entwistle Pennington, a Radcliffe fine arts major.

Graduating from Harvard in 1954 summa cum laude, he won a fellowship to study art in Oxford, England. In June of that year, his short story "Friends from Philadelphia" was accepted, along with a poem, by The New Yorker. It was an event, he later said, that remained "the ecstatic breakthrough of my literary life."

Following the birth of his first child, Elizabeth, the couple returned to America, and Mr. Updike went to work writing Talk of the Town pieces for The New Yorker.

By 1959 he had completed three books—a volume of poetry; a novel, "The Poorhouse Fair"; and a collection of stories—and placed them with Alfred A. Knopf, which remained his publisher throughout his career. From 1954 to 1959, he also published more than a hundred essays, articles, poems and short stories in The New Yorker.

The Updikes settled in Ipswich, Mass., a small town north of Boston that seemed to stimulate his memories of Shillington and his creation of its fictional counterpart, Olinger. All his early stories were set there or in a neighboring city modeled on Reading, as were his first four novels, "The Poorhouse Fair," "The Centaur," "Of the Farm" and "Rabbit, Run."

With "Couples" (1968), his fifth novel, Mr. Updike moved his setting to the fictional Tarbox, Mass. The novel, about coupling and uncoupling among young married men and women, was remarkably frank for its time, with long, detailed and often lyrical descriptions of sexual acts. It became a best seller.

With the Rabbit quartet, Mr. Updike cast his keen eye on a still wider world. "Rabbit, Run" and its three sequels, published at 10-year intervals, summon decades of American experience: the cultural turmoil of the 1960s; the boom years, oil crisis and inflation of the 70s; and what Rabbit calls "Reagan's reign," with its trade war with Japan, its AIDS epidemic and the terror bombing of Pan Am 103 over Lockerbie, Scotland.

"Rabbit Is Rich" and "Rabbit at Rest" both won Pulitzer Prizes. Reissued as a set in 1995, "Rabbit Angstrom: A Tetralogy" was pronounced by some to be a contender for the crown of great American novel.

Against the grain of his calling and temperament, Mr. Updike strove, like the German writer Thomas Mann, for a burgherly life. He took up golf, which he played with passionate enthusiasm and a writer's eye, observing the grace notes in others' swings and tiny variations in the landscape.

He was a tall, handsome man with a prominent nose and a head of hair that Tom Wolfe once compared to "monkish thatch." And though as a youth he suffered from both a stutter and psoriasis, he became a person of immense charm, unfailingly polite and gracious in public.

In 1976 the Updikes were divorced, and the following year he married Martha Ruggles Bernhard, settling with her and her three children first in Georgetown, Mass., and then in 1984 in Beverly Farms, both towns in the same corner of the state as Ipswich.

In addition to his wife, Martha, he is survived by two sons, two daughters, three stepsons, seven grandchildren and seven step-grandchildren.

By the 1980s, with the storehouse of his youthful experience emptying and his material circumstances enriched, Mr. Updike nevertheless determined to keep publishing a book a year.

Among the dozen or more novels he brought out in the next quarter century, some clicked, like "The Witches of Eastwick" (1984), celebrated by some as an exuberant sexual comedy and a satirical view of women's liberation. Others seemed schematic, like the author's three takes on Hawthorne's "Scarlet Letter"—"Roger's Version" (1986), "S" (1988) and "A Month of Sundays" (1975)—and received lukewarm reviews.

Some readers complained about his portrayal of women. In an interview with The Times in 1988, Mr. Updike acknowledged the criticism that "my women are never on the move, that they're always stuck where the men have put them." His "only defense," he said, "would be that it's in the domesticity, the family, the sexual relations, that women interest me. I don't write about too many male businessmen, and I'm not apt to write about too many female businessmen."

Whatever his flaws as a novelist, his mastery of the short-story form continued to grow. Reviewing Mr. Updike's sixth collection of stories, "Museums and Women and Other Stories" (1972), Anatole Broyard wrote in The New York Times, "His former preciousness has toughened into precision."

It was in a story collection—his fifth, "Bech: A Book" (1970)—that Mr. Updike created a counterself living a counter-life. His character Henry Bech is an unmarried, urban, blocked Jewish writer immersed in the swim of literary celebrity—"a vain, limp leech on the leg of literature as it waded through swampy times," as Bech himself put it in a later novel.

As Mr. Updike's opposite, Bech not only writes in a voice very different from his creator's—world-weary, full of schmerz and a touch of schmalz—he also undertakes tasks that Mr. Updike avoided, like attending literary dinners, working off grudges, murdering critics and interviewing John Updike for The New York Times Book Review.

Bech even wins the Nobel Prize for Literature, something that Mr. Updike never did, to the consternation of many Western writers and critics.

By contrasting so sharply with his creator, Henry Bech also defined Mr. Updike more distinctly, particularly his determination to stick to the essentials of his craft. As Mr. Updike told The Paris Review about his decision to shun the New York spotlight:

"Hemingway described literary New York as a bottle full of tapeworms trying to feed on each other. When I write, I aim in my mind not toward New York but toward a vague spot a little to the east of Kansas. I think of the books on library shelves, without their jackets, years old, and a countryish teenaged boy finding them, have them speak to him. The reviews, the stacks in Brentano's, are just hurdles to get over, to place the books on that shelf."

ALEKSANDR SOLZHENITSYN

December 11, 1918–August 3, 2008

By Michael T. Kaufman

Aleksandr Solzhenitsyn, whose stubborn, lonely and combative literary struggles gained the force of prophecy as he revealed the heavy afflictions of Soviet Communism in some of the most powerful works of the 20th century, died on Sunday at the age of 89 in Moscow.

His son Yermolai said the cause was a heart ailment.

Mr. Solzhenitsyn had been an obscure, middle-aged high school science teacher in a provincial Russian town when he burst onto the literary stage in 1962 with "One Day in the Life of Ivan Denisovich." The book, a mold-breaking novel about a prison camp inmate, was a sensation. Suddenly he was being compared to giants of Russian literature like Tolstoy, Dostoyevski and Chekhov.

Over the next five decades, Mr. Solzhenitsyn's fame spread throughout the world as he drew upon his experiences of totalitarian duress to write evocative novels like "The First Circle" and "The Cancer Ward" and historical works like "The Gulag Archipelago." "Gulag" was a monumental account of the Soviet labor camp system, a chain of prisons that by Mr. Solzhenitsyn's calculation some 60 million people had entered during the 20th century. The book, which led to his expulsion from his native land, was described by George F. Kennan, the American diplomat, as "the greatest and most powerful single indictment of a political regime ever to be leveled in modern times."

Mr. Solzhenitsyn was heir to a morally focused Russian literary tradition, and he looked the part. With his stern visage, lofty brow and Old Testament beard, he recalled Tolstoy while suggesting a modern-day Jeremiah, denouncing the evils of the Kremlin and later the mores of the West. He returned to Russia and deplored what he considered its spiritual decline, but toward the end of his life he embraced President Vladimir V. Putin as a restorer of Russia's greatness.

In almost half a century, more than 30 million of his books have been sold worldwide and translated into some 40 languages. In 1970 he was awarded the Nobel Prize in Literature.

Mr. Solzhenitsyn owed his initial success to the Soviet leader Nikita S. Khrushchev's decision to allow "Ivan Denisovich" to be published in a popular journal. Khrushchev believed its publication would advance the liberal line he had promoted since his speech in 1956 on the crimes of Stalin. Soon after the story appeared, Khrushchev was replaced by hard-liners, and they campaigned to silence its author. They stopped publication of his new works, denounced him as a traitor and confiscated his manuscripts.

But by then his works were appearing outside the Soviet Union, in many languages, and he was being compared not just to Russia's literary giants but also to Stalin's literary victims, like Anna Akhmatova and Boris Pasternak.

Mr. Solzhenitsyn succeeded in having microfilms of his banned manuscripts smuggled out of the Soviet Union. He rallied support among friends and artists, who turned his struggles into one of the most celebrated cases of the cold war period. Hundreds of well-known intellectuals signed petitions against his silencing.

Their position was confirmed when Mr. Solzhenitsyn was awarded the 1970 Nobel Prize. In his acceptance speech, he said that while an ordinary man was obliged "not to participate in lies," artists had greater responsibilities: "It is within the power of writers and artists to do much more: to defeat the lie!"

By this time, Mr. Solzhenitsyn had completed his own massive attempt at truthfulness, "The Gulag Archipelago." In more than 300,000 words, it told the history of the Gulag prison camps, whose operations and even existence were subjects long considered taboo. Publishers in Paris and New York had secretly received the manuscript on microfilm, and the book was published in Paris just after Christmas 1973. The Soviet government counterattacked with critical articles, including one in Pravda, the state-run newspaper, headlined "The Path of a Traitor."

On Feb. 12, 1974, Mr. Solzhenitsyn was arrested, and the next day he was told that he was being deprived of his citizenship and deported. Six weeks after his expulsion, Mr. Solzhenitsyn was joined by his second wife, Natalia Svetlova, and their three sons. The family eventually moved to the United States, settling in the hamlet of Cavendish, Vt.

There he kept mostly to himself for some 18 years, writing and thinking a great deal about Russia and hardly at all about his new environment, so certain was he that he would return to his homeland one day.

His rare public appearances could turn into hectoring jeremiads. Delivering the commencement address at Harvard in 1978, he called the country of his sanctuary spiritually weak and mired in vulgar materialism.

In the autumn of 1961, Aleksandr Solzhenitsyn was a 43-year-old high school teacher of physics and astronomy in Ryazan, a city south of Moscow. He had been there since 1956, when his sentence of perpetual exile in a dusty region of Kazakhstan was suspended. Aside from his teaching duties, he was writing and rewriting stories he had conceived while confined in prisons and labor camps since 1944.

One story, a short novel, was "One Day in the Life of Ivan Denisovich," an account of a single day in an icy prison camp written in the voice of an inmate named Ivan Denisovich Shukov. With little sentimentality, he recounts the trials and sufferings of the prisoners, peasants willing to risk punishment and pain as they seek seemingly small advantages like a few more minutes before a fire.

The day ends with the prisoner in his bunk. "Shukov felt pleased with his life as he went to sleep," Mr. Solzhenitsyn wrote. Shukov was pleased because, among other things, he had not been put in an isolation cell, his brigade had avoided a work assignment in a place unprotected from the bitter wind, he had swiped some extra gruel, and he had been able to buy a bit of tobacco from another prisoner.

"The end of an unclouded day. Almost a happy one," Mr. Solzhenitsyn wrote, adding: "Just one of the 3,653 days of his sentence, from bell to bell. The extra three days were for leap years."

Mr. Solzhenitsyn sent one copy to Lev Kopelev, an intellectual with whom he had once shared a cell. Mr. Kopelev realized that under Khrushchev's policies of liberalization, it might be possible to have the story published by Novy Mir, the Soviet Union's prestigious literary and cultural journal. Mr. Kopelev and his colleagues took the story to Aleksandr Tvardovsky, the editor, who was able to get Khrushchev himself to read "One Day in the Life." Khrushchev was impressed, and the novel appeared in Novy Mir in 1962.

Mr. Solzhenitsyn was not the first to write about the camps. Some Soviet writers had typed accounts of their own experiences, and these pages and their carbon copies were passed from reader to reader in a clandestine effort called zamizdat. Given the millions who had been forced into the gulag, few families could have been unaware of the camp experiences of relatives or friends. But few had had access to these accounts. "One Day in the Life" changed that.

Aleksandr Isayevich Solzhenitsyn was born in the Caucasus spa town of Kislovodsk on Dec. 11, 1918, a year after the Soviet Union arose from revolution. His father, Isaaki, had been a Russian artillery officer and was married to Taissa Shcherback. Shortly before his son's birth, he was killed in a hunting accident.

In 1941, just before Germany attacked Russia to expand World War II into Soviet territory, Mr. Solzhenitsyn graduated from Rostov University with a degree in physics and math. A year earlier, he had married Natalia Reshetovskaya, a chemist. When hostilities began, he joined the army and spent three years in combat.

In February 1945, he was arrested on the East Prussian front by agents of Smersh, the Soviet spy agency. The evidence against him was found in a letter in which he referred to Stalin—disrespectfully, the authorities said—as "the man with the mustache." He was sentenced to eight years in a labor camp. It was his entry into the vast network of punitive institutions that he would later name the Gulag Archipelago, after the Russian acronym for the Main Administration of Camps.

On July 9, 1947, Mr. Solzhenitsyn was moved to a prison outside Moscow, an institution for inmates who were trained scientists and whose forced labor involved scientific research. His experiences there provided the basis for his novel "The First Circle," which was not published outside the Soviet Union until 1968.

Mr. Solzhenitsyn tended toward outspokenness, and it soon undid him. He was banished to a desolate penal camp in Kazakhstan called Ekibastuz, which would become the inspiration for "One Day in the Life."

At Ekibastuz, any writing would be seized as contraband. So he devised a method that enabled him to retain even long sections of prose. After seeing Lithuanian Catholic prisoners fashion rosaries out of beads made from chewed bread, he asked them to make a similar chain for him, but with more beads. In his hands, each bead came to represent a passage that he would repeat to himself until he could recite it without hesitation. He later wrote that by the end of his prison term, he had memorized 12,000 lines in this way.

On Feb. 9, 1953, his term in the camps officially ended. On March 6, he was sent farther east, arriving in Kok-Terek, a desert settlement, in time to hear the announcement of Stalin's death. It was here that Mr. Solzhenitsyn was ordered to spend his term of "perpetual exile."

He taught in a local school and wrote secretly. He learned he had cancer. His life as a pariah struggling with disease would lead to his novel "The Cancer Ward," which also first appeared outside the Soviet Union, in 1969.

Mr. Solzhenitsyn recovered. In April 1956, a letter arrived informing him that his period of internal exile had been lifted. He resumed teaching and writing, reworking some of the lines he had once stored away as he fingered his beads. Then in 1962 came the publication of "One Day in the Life."

But when Leonid I. Brezhnev replaced Khrushchev as party leader in October 1964, it was apparent that Mr. Solzhenitsyn was being silenced, and his skirmishes with the state intensified. While the authorities kept him from publishing, he kept writing and speaking out, eliciting threats by mail and phone. He slept with a pitchfork beside his bed. Finally, government agents arrested him, took him to the airport and deported him.

Mr. Solzhenitsyn believed that his stay in the United States would be temporary. With that goal, he lived like a recluse in rural Vermont as he kept writing about Russia, in Russian. He devoted himself to a gigantic work of historical fiction that eventually ran to more than 5,000 pages. The work, called "The Red Wheel," focused on the revolutionary chaos that had spawned Bolshevism and set the stage for modern Russian history.

Mr. Solzhenitsyn returned to Russia on May 27, 1994, and he and his family journeyed by rail across Russia to see what his post-Communist country now looked like. On the first stop, his judgment was clear. His homeland, he said, was "tortured, stunned, altered beyond recognition."

In the final years of his life, Mr. Solzhenitsyn had spoken approvingly of a "restoration" of Russia under Mr. Putin. Mr. Putin, he said in an interview, "inherited a ransacked and bewildered country, with a poor and demoralized people. And he started to do what was possible—a slow and gradual restoration."

J. D. SALINGER

January 1, 1919–January 27, 2010

By Charles McGrath

J. D. Salinger, who was thought at one time to be the most important American writer to emerge since World War II but who then turned his back on success and adulation, becoming the Garbo of letters, famous for not wanting to be famous, died on Wednesday at his home in Cornish, N.H., where he had lived in seclusion for more than 50 years. He was 91.

Mr. Salinger's literary representative, Harold Ober Associates, announced the death.

Mr. Salinger's literary reputation rests on a slender but enormously influential body of published work: the novel "The Catcher in the Rye," the collection "Nine Stories" and two compilations, each with two long stories about the fictional Glass family: "Franny and Zooey" and "Raise High the Roof Beam, Carpenters and Seymour: An Introduction."

"Catcher" was published in 1951, and its very first sentence, distantly echoing Mark Twain, struck a brash new note in American literature: "If you really want to hear about it, the first thing you'll probably want to know is where I was born and what my lousy childhood was like, and how my parents were occupied and all before they had me, and all that David Copperfield kind of crap, but I don't feel like going into it, if you want to know the truth."

Though not everyone, teachers and librarians especially, was sure what to make of it, "Catcher" became an almost immediate best seller, and its narrator and main character, Holden Caulfield, a teenager newly expelled from prep school, became America's best-known literary truant since Huckleberry Finn.

With its cynical, slangy vernacular voice (Holden's two favorite expressions are "phony" and "goddam"), its sympathetic understanding of adolescence and its fierce if alienated sense of morality and distrust of the adult world, the novel struck a nerve in cold war America and quickly attained cult status, especially among the young.

The novel's allure persists to this day, even if some of Holden's preoccupations now seem a bit dated, and it continues to sell more than 250,000 copies a year in paperback. Mark David Chapman, who killed John Lennon in 1980, even said the explanation for his act could be found in the pages of "The Catcher in the Rye." In 1974, Philip Roth wrote, "The response of college students to the work of J. D. Salinger indicates that he, more than anyone else, has not turned his back on the times but, instead, has managed to put his finger on whatever struggle of significance is going on today between self and culture."

Many critics preferred "Nine Stories," which came out in 1953 and helped shape writers like Philip Roth, John Updike and Harold Brodkey. The stories were remarkable for their sharp social observation, their pitch-perfect dialogue and the way they demolished whatever was left of the traditional architecture of the short story—the old structure of beginning, middle, end—for an architecture of emotion, in which a story could turn on a tiny alteration of mood or irony.

Orville Prescott wrote in The New York Times in 1963, "Rarely if ever in literary history has a handful of stories aroused so much discussion, controversy, praise, denunciation, mystification and interpretation."

As a young man Mr. Salinger yearned ardently for just this kind of attention. But success, once it arrived, paled quickly for him. He told the editors of Saturday Review that he was "good and sick" of seeing his photograph on the dust jacket of "The Catcher in the Rye" and demanded that it be removed from subsequent editions. In 1953 Mr. Salinger, who had been living in Manhattan, fled the literary world altogether and moved to a 90-acre compound on a wooded hillside in Cornish.

He rarely left and his publications slowed to a trickle and soon stopped completely. "Franny and Zooey" and "Raise High the Roof Beam," both collections of material previously published in The New Yorker, came out in 1961 and 1963, and the last work of Mr. Salinger's to appear in print was "Hapworth 16, 1924," a 25,000-word story that took up most of the June 19, 1965, issue of The New Yorker.

He seldom spoke to the press. And yet the more he sought privacy, the more famous he became, especially after his appearance on the cover of Time in 1961. For years it was a sort of journalistic sport for newspapers and magazines to send reporters to New Hampshire in hopes of a sighting.

In 1984 the British literary critic Ian Hamilton approached Mr. Salinger with the notion of writing his biography. Not surprisingly, Mr. Salinger turned him down, saying he had "borne all the exploitation and loss of privacy I can possibly bear in a single lifetime."

Mr. Hamilton went ahead anyway, and in 1986, Mr. Salinger took him to court to prevent the use of quotations and paraphrases from unpublished letters. The case went to the Supreme Court, and to the surprise of many, Mr. Salinger won, though not without some cost to his cherished privacy.

Mr. Salinger's privacy was further punctured in 1998 and again in 2000 with the publication of memoirs by, first, Joyce Maynard—with whom he had a 10-month affair in 1973, when Ms. Maynard was a college freshman—and then his daughter, Margaret. Some critics complained that both women were trying to exploit their history with Mr. Salinger, and Mr. Salinger's son, Matthew, wrote in a letter to The New York Observer that his sister had "a troubled mind." Both books nevertheless added a creepy, Howard Hughesish element to the Salinger legend.

Mr. Salinger was controlling and sexually manipulative, Ms. Maynard wrote, and a health nut obsessed with homeopathic medicine and with his diet (frozen peas for breakfast, undercooked lamb burger for dinner). Ms. Salinger added a long list of other enthusiasms: Zen Buddhism, Vedanta Hinduism, Christian Science, Scientology and acupuncture. Mr. Salinger drank his own urine, she wrote, and sat for hours in an orgone box.

But was he writing? The question obsessed Salingerologists, and in the absence of real evidence, theories multiplied. Ms. Maynard said she believed there were at least two novels locked away in a safe, though she had never seen them.

Jerome David Salinger was born in Manhattan on New Year's Day, 1919, the second of two children. His sister, Doris, who died in 2001, was for many years a buyer in the dress department at Bloomingdale's. Like the Glasses, the Salinger children were the product of a mixed marriage. Their father, Sol, was a Jew, the son of a rabbi, but sufficiently assimilated that he made his living importing both cheese and ham. Their mother, Marie Jillisch, was of Irish descent, born in Scotland, but changed her first name to Miriam to appease her in-laws.

Never much of a student, Mr. Salinger attended the progressive McBurney School on the Upper West Side. But he flunked out and in 1934 was packed off to Valley Forge Military Academy, in Wayne, Pa., which became the model for Holden's Pencey Prep.

In 1937, after a couple of unenthusiastic weeks at New York University, Mr. Salinger traveled with his father to Austria and Poland, where he was to learn the ham business. Deciding that wasn't for him, he returned to America and drifted through a term or so at Ursinus College in Collegeville, Pa. Fellow students remember him announcing that he was going to write the Great American Novel.

Mr. Salinger's most sustained exposure to higher education was an evening class he took at Columbia in 1939, taught by Whit Burnett, and under Mr. Burnett's tutelage he managed to sell a story, "The Young Folks," to Story magazine. He subsequently sold stories to Esquire, Collier's and The Saturday Evening Post—formulaic work that gave little hint of real originality.

In 1941, after several rejections, Mr. Salinger fi-

nally cracked The New Yorker, the ultimate goal of any aspiring writer back then, with a story, "Slight Rebellion Off Madison," that was an early sketch of what became a scene in "The Catcher in the Rye." But the magazine then had second thoughts, apparently worried about seeming to encourage young people to run away from school, and held the story for five years before finally publishing it in 1946, buried in the back of an issue.

Meanwhile Mr. Salinger had been drafted. He served with the Counter-Intelligence Corps of the Fourth Infantry Division, whose job was to interview Nazi deserters and sympathizers. On June 6, 1944, he landed at Utah Beach, and he later saw action during the Battle of the Bulge.

In 1945 he was hospitalized for "battle fatigue"— often a euphemism for a breakdown—and after recovering he stayed on in Europe past the end of the war, chasing Nazi functionaries. He married a German woman, very briefly—a doctor about whom biographers have been able to discover very little.

Back in New York, Mr. Salinger resumed his career. "A Perfect Day for Bananafish," austere, mysterious and Mr. Salinger's most famous and still most discussed story, appeared in The New Yorker in 1948 and suggested, not wrongly, that he had become a very different kind of writer.

As a young writer Mr. Salinger was something of a ladies' man and dated, among others, Oona O'Neill, the daughter of Eugene O'Neill and the future wife of Charlie Chaplin. In 1953 he met Claire Douglas, who was then a 19-year-old Radcliffe sophomore; they were married two years later. Margaret was born in 1955, and Matthew, now an actor and film producer, was born in 1960. But the marriage soon turned distant and isolating, and in 1966, Ms. Douglas sued for divorce.

The affair with Ms. Maynard, then a Yale freshman, began in 1972, after Mr. Salinger read an article she had written for The New York Times Magazine titled "An 18-Year-Old Looks Back on Life." They broke up after 10 months. In the late 1980s, he married Colleen O'Neill, a nurse, who is considerably younger than he is.

Besides his son, Matthew, Mr. Salinger is survived by Ms. O'Neill and his daughter, Margaret, as well as three grandsons.

His literary agents said in a statement there will be no service. "Salinger had remarked that he was in this world but not of it," the statement said. "His body is gone but the family hopes that he is still with those he loves, whether they are religious or historical figures, personal friends or fictional characters."

GABRIEL GARCÍA MÁRQUEZ

March 6, 1927–April 17, 2014

By Jonathan Kandell

Gabriel García Márquez, the Colombian novelist whose "One Hundred Years of Solitude" established him as a giant of 20th-century literature, died on Thursday at his home in Mexico City. He was 87.

Mr. García Márquez, who received the Nobel Prize for Literature in 1982, wrote fiction rooted in a mythical Latin American landscape of his own creation, but his appeal was universal. His books were translated into dozens of languages.

"Each new work of his is received by expectant critics and readers as an event of world importance," the Swedish Academy of Letters said in awarding him the Nobel.

Mr. García Márquez was a master of the genre known as magical realism, in which the miraculous and the real converge. Storms rage for years, flowers drift from the skies, tyrants survive for centuries, priests levitate and corpses fail to decompose. And, more plausibly, lovers rekindle their passion after a half-century apart.

Magical realism, he said, sprang from Latin America's history of vicious dictators and romantic revolutionaries, of long years of hunger, illness and violence. In accepting his Nobel, he said: "Poets and beggars, musicians and prophets, warriors and scoundrels, all creatures of that unbridled reality, we have had to ask but little of imagination."

Mr. García Márquez viewed the world from a left-wing perspective, bitterly opposing Gen. Augusto Pinochet, the right-wing Chilean dictator, and unswervingly supporting Fidel Castro. Mr. Castro became such a close friend that Mr. García Márquez showed him drafts of his unpublished books.

No draft had more impact than the one for "One Hundred Years of Solitude." Mr. García Márquez's editor began reading it at home one rainy day, and as he read page after page by this unknown Colombian author, his excitement grew. Soon he called the Argentine novelist Tomás Eloy Martínez and summoned him urgently to the home.

Mr. Eloy Martínez remembered entering the foyer with wet shoes and encountering pages strewn across the floor by the editor in his eagerness to read through the work. They were the first pages of a book that in 1967 would vault Mr. García Márquez onto the world stage. He later authorized an English translation, by Gregory Rabassa. Readers were tantalized from its opening sentences:

"Many years later, as he faced the firing squad,

Col. Aureliano Buendía was to remember that distant afternoon when his father took him to discover ice. At that time Macondo was a village of 20 adobe houses built on the bank of a river of clear water that ran along a bed of polished stones, which were white and enormous, like prehistoric eggs. The world was so recent that many things lacked names, and in order to indicate them it was necessary to point."

"One Hundred Years of Solitude" would sell tens of millions of copies. The Chilean poet Pablo Neruda called it "the greatest revelation in the Spanish language since 'Don Quixote.'" But Mr. García Márquez grew to hate it, fearing that his subsequent work would not measure up.

He need not have worried. Almost all his 15 other novels and short-story collections were lionized by critics and devoured by readers.

Gabriel García Márquez was born in Aracataca, a small town near Colombia's Caribbean coast, on March 6, 1927, the eldest child of Luisa Santiaga Márquez and Gabriel Elijio García. His father, a postal clerk, telegraph operator and itinerant pharmacist, could barely support his wife and 12 children; Gabriel, the eldest, spent his early childhood living in the large, ramshackle house of his maternal grandparents.

His maternal grandfather, Nicolás Márquez Mejía, a retired army colonel, was "the most important figure of my life," Mr. García Márquez said. The grandfather bore a marked resemblance to Colonel Buendía, the protagonist of "One Hundred Years of Solitude," and the book's mythical village of Macondo draws heavily on Aracataca.

In his 2002 memoir, "Living to Tell the Tale," Mr. García Márquez recalled a river trip back to Aracataca in 1950, his first trip there since childhood: "The first thing that struck me was the silence. A material silence I could have identified blindfolded among all the silences in the world. The reverberation of the heat was so intense that you seemed to be looking at everything through undulating glass. As far as the eye could see there was no recollection of human life, nothing that was not covered by a faint sprinkling of burning dust."

Mr. García Márquez moved to Bogotá as a teenager. He studied law there but never received a degree; he turned instead to journalism. The late 1940s and early '50s in Colombia were a period of civil strife known as La Violencia, which became the background for several of his novels.

Mr. García Márquez eked out a living writing for newspapers in Cartagena and then Barranquilla. He scored a scoop when he interviewed a sailor who had been portrayed by the Colombian government as the heroic survivor of a navy destroyer lost at sea. The sailor admitted to him that the ship had been carrying a heavy load of contraband household goods, which unloosed during a storm and caused the ship to list. His report, in 1955, infuriated Gen. Gustavo Rojas Pinilla, the country's dictator, and the writer fled to Europe. He spent two years there as a foreign correspondent.

Mr. García Márquez was less impressed by Western Europe than many Latin American writers. Europeans, he said in his Nobel address, "insist on measuring us with the yardstick that they use for themselves, forgetting that the ravages of life are not the same for all, and that the quest for our own identity is just as arduous and bloody for us as it was for them."

Mr. García Márquez lost his job when his newspaper was shut down by the Rojas Pinilla regime. Stranded in Paris, he scavenged and sold bottles to survive, but he managed to begin a short novel, "In Evil Hour."

While working on that book he took time off in 1957 to complete another short novel, "No One Writes to the Colonel," about an impoverished retired army officer, not unlike the author's grandfather. It was published to acclaim four years later. ("In Evil Hour" was also published in the early 1960s.)

From 1959 to 1961 he supported the Castro revolution and wrote for the official Cuban press agency. In 1961 he moved to Mexico City, where he would live on and off for the rest of his life. It was there, in 1965, after a four-year dry spell, that he began "One Hundred Years of Solitude." The inspiration for it, he said, came to him while he was driving to Acapulco.

Returning home, he began an almost undistracted 18 months of writing while his wife, Mercedes, looked after the household. "When I was finished writing," he recalled, "my wife said: 'Did you really finish it? We owe $12,000.'"

With the book's publication in 1967, in Buenos Aires, the family never owed a penny again. Besides his wife, the writer is survived by his sons, Rodrigo and Gonzalo.

In 1973, when General Pinochet overthrew Chile's democratically elected Marxist president, Salvador Allende, who committed suicide, Mr. García Márquez vowed never to write as long as General Pinochet remained in power.

The Pinochet dictatorship lasted 17 years, but Mr. García Márquez released himself from his vow well before it ended. "What I was doing was allowing Pinochet to stop me from writing, which means I had submitted to voluntary censorship," he said in a 1997 interview with The Washington Post.

In 1975 he published his next novel, "The Autumn of the Patriarch," about a dictator in a phantasmagorical Latin American state who rules for so many decades that nobody can recall what life was like before him. Despite mixed reviews, it became a global best seller. He called it his best novel.

"Love in the Time of Cholera," published in 1985, was his most romantic novel, the story of the resumption of a passionate relationship between a recently widowed septuagenarian and the lover she had broken with more than 50 years before.

"The General in His Labyrinth," published in 1989, combined imagination with historical fact to conjure up the last days of Simón Bolívar. The portrait of the aging Bolívar as a flatulent philanderer, abandoned and ridiculed by his onetime followers, aroused controversy on a continent that viewed him as South America's version of George Washington. But Mr. García Márquez said that his depiction had been drawn from a careful perusal of Bolívar's letters.

As his fame grew, the author enjoyed a lifestyle he would have found inconceivable in his youth. He kept homes in Mexico City, Barcelona, Paris and Cartagena, on Colombia's Caribbean coast.

For more than three decades the State Department denied Mr. García Márquez a visa to travel in the United States, supposedly because he had been a member of the Colombian Communist Party in the 1950s but almost certainly because of his continuing espousal of left-wing causes and his friendship with Mr. Castro. The ban was rescinded in 1995 after President Bill Clinton invited him to Martha's Vineyard.

After receiving a diagnosis of lymphatic cancer in 1999, Mr. García Márquez devoted most of his writing to his memoirs. In July 2012, his brother, Jaime, was quoted as saying that Mr. García Márquez had senile dementia and had stopped writing.

Cristóbal Pera, the author's editor at Random House Mondadori, said at the time that Mr. García Márquez had been working on a novel, but that no publication date had been scheduled. Mr. Pera said the author seemed disinclined to have it published at all and had said: "This far along I don't need to publish more."

Randal C. Archibold contributed reporting from Mexico City.

MAYA ANGELOU

April 4, 1928–May 28, 2014

By Margalit Fox

Maya Angelou, whose landmark book of 1969, "I Know Why the Caged Bird Sings"—a lyrical, unsparing account of her childhood in the Jim Crow South—was among the first autobiographies by a 20th-century black woman to reach a wide general readership, died on Wednesday at her home in Winston-Salem, N.C. She was 86.

In a statement, President Barack Obama called Ms. Angelou "a brilliant writer, a fierce friend and a truly phenomenal woman," adding, "She inspired my own mother to name my sister Maya."

Though her memoirs, which eventually filled six volumes, garnered more critical praise than her poetry did, Ms. Angelou (pronounced AHN-zhe-low) probably received her widest exposure on a chilly January day in 1993, when she delivered her inaugural poem, "On the Pulse of Morning," at the swearing-in of Bill Clinton, the nation's 42nd president. He, like Ms. Angelou, had grown up in Arkansas.

It began:

A Rock, A River, A Tree

Hosts to species long since departed,

Marked the mastodon,

The dinosaur, who left dried tokens

Of their sojourn here

On our planet floor,

Any broad alarm of their hastening doom

Is lost in the gloom of dust and ages.

But today, the Rock cries out to us,

clearly, forcefully,

Come, you may stand upon my

Back and face your distant destiny,

But seek no haven in my shadow,

I will give you no hiding place down here.

Long before that day, as she recounted in "Caged Bird" and its sequels, she had already been a dancer, calypso singer, streetcar conductor, single mother, official of the Southern Christian Leadership Conference and friend or associate of some of the most eminent black Americans of the mid-20th century, including James Baldwin, the Rev. Dr. Martin Luther King Jr. and Malcolm X.

Afterward (her six-volume memoir takes her only to age 40), Ms. Angelou was a Tony-nominated stage actress; college professor of American studies at Wake Forest University in Winston-Salem; ubiquitous presence on the lecture circuit; frequent guest on television shows, from "Oprah" to "Sesame Street"; and subject of scholarly studies.

Throughout her writing, Ms. Angelou explored the concepts of personal identity and resilience through the multifaceted lens of race, sex, family, community and the collective past. Her work offered a clear-eyed examination of the ways in which the socially marginalizing forces of racism and sexism played out at the level of the individual.

"If growing up is painful for the Southern Black girl, being aware of her displacement is the rust on the razor that threatens the throat," Ms. Angelou wrote in "I Know Why the Caged Bird Sings."

Hallmarks of Ms. Angelou's prose style included a directness of voice that recalls African-American oral tradition and gives her work the quality of testimony. She was also intimately concerned with sensation, describing the world around her with almost palpable feeling for its sights, sounds and smells.

"I Know Why the Caged Bird Sings," published when Ms. Angelou was in her early 40s, spans only her first 17 years. But what powerfully formative years they were.

Marguerite Johnson was born in St. Louis on April 4, 1928. Her father, Bailey Johnson Sr., a Navy dietitian, "was a lonely person, searching relentlessly in bottles, under women's skirts, in church work and lofty job titles for his 'personal niche,' lost before birth and unrecovered since," Ms. Angelou wrote. "How maddening it was to have been born in a cotton field with aspirations of grandeur."

Her mother, Vivian Baxter, was variously a nurse, hotel owner and card dealer. As a girl, Ms. Angelou was known as Rita, Ritie or Maya, her older brother's childhood nickname for her.

After her parents' marriage ended, three-year-old Maya was sent with her four-year-old brother, Bailey, to live with their father's mother in the tiny town of Stamps, Ark., which, she later wrote, "with its dust and hate and narrowness was as South as it was possible to get."

Their grandmother, Annie Henderson, owned a general store "in the heart of the Negro area," Ms. Angelou wrote. An upright woman known as Momma, "with her solid air packed around her like cotton," she is a warm, stabilizing presence throughout "I Know Why the Caged Bird Sings."

The children returned periodically to St. Louis to live with their mother. On one occasion, when Maya was seven or eight (her age varies slightly across her memoirs, which employ techniques of fiction to recount actual events), she was raped by her mother's boyfriend. She told her brother, who alerted the family, and the man was tried and convicted. Before he could begin serving his sentence, he was murdered.

Believing that her words had brought about the death, Maya did not speak for the next five years. Her love of literature, she later wrote, helped restore language to her.

As a teenager, living with her mother in San Francisco, she studied dance and drama at the California Labor School and became the first black woman to work as a streetcar conductor there. At 16, after a casual liaison with a neighborhood youth, she became pregnant and gave birth to a son. There the first book ends.

"I Know Why the Caged Bird Sings"—the title is a line from "Sympathy," by the African-American poet Paul Laurence Dunbar—became a bestseller, confounding the stereotype that black women's lives were rarely worthy of autobiography.

The five volumes of memoir that follow were "Gather Together in My Name," "Singin' and Swingin' and Gettin' Merry Like Christmas," "The Heart of a Woman," "All God's Children Need Traveling Shoes" and "A Song Flung Up to Heaven."

They describe her struggles to support her son, Guy Johnson, through odd jobs.

"Determined to raise him, I had worked as a shake dancer in nightclubs, fry cook in hamburger joints, dinner cook in a Creole restaurant and once had a job in a mechanic's shop, taking paint off cars with my hands," she wrote in "Singin' and Swingin'." Elsewhere, she described her brief stints as a prostitute and a madam.

Ms. Angelou goes on to recount her marriage to a Greek sailor, Tosh Angelos. (Throughout her life, she was cagey about the number of times she married, although it appears to have been at least three.)

After the marriage dissolved, she embarked on a career as a calypso dancer and singer under the name Maya Angelou, a variant of her married name. A striking stage presence—she was six feet tall—she occasionally partnered in San Francisco with Alvin Ailey in a nightclub act.

Ms. Angelou later settled in New York, where she became active in the Harlem Writers Guild, sang at the Apollo and succeeded Bayard Rustin as the coordinator of the New York office of the Southern Christian Leadership Conference, the organization that he, Dr. King and others had founded.

In the early 1960s, Ms. Angelou became romantically involved with Vusumzi L. Make, a South African civil rights activist. She moved with him to Cairo, and after leaving him moved to Accra, Ghana.

In 1973, Ms. Angelou appeared on Broadway in "Look Away," a play about Mary Todd Lincoln and her seamstress. Though the play closed after one performance, Ms. Angelou was nominated for a Tony Award. On the screen, she portrayed Kunta Kinte's grandmother in the 1977 television mini-series "Roots."

Ms. Angelou's marriage in the 1970s to Paul du Feu, who had previously been married to the feminist writer Germaine Greer, ended in divorce. Survivors include her son, three grandchildren and a great-grandchild.

Some reviewers expressed reservations about Ms. Angelou's memoiristic style, calling it facile and solipsistic. Others criticized her poetry as being little more than prose with line breaks. But her importance as a literary, cultural and historical figure was borne out by the many laurels she received, including a spate of honorary doctorates.

She remained best known for her memoirs, a striking fact because she never set out to be a memoirist. Near the end of "A Song Flung Up to Heaven," Ms. Angelou recalls her response when Robert Loomis, who would become her longtime editor at Random House, first asked her to write an autobiography.

Still planning to be a playwright and poet, she demurred. Cannily, Mr. Loomis called her again.

"You may be right not to attempt autobiography, because it is nearly impossible to write autobiography as literature," he said. "Almost impossible."

Ms. Angelou replied, "I'll start tomorrow."

HARPER LEE

April 28, 1926–February 19, 2016

By William Grimes

Harper Lee, whose first novel, "To Kill a Mockingbird," about racial injustice in a small Alabama town, sold more than 40 million copies and became one of the most beloved works of fiction ever written by an American, died yesterday at an assisted living facility in Monroeville, Ala., where she lived. She was 89.

The instant success of "To Kill a Mockingbird," which was published in 1960 and won the Pulitzer Prize for fiction, turned Ms. Lee into a literary celebrity, a role she found oppressive.

"I never expected any sort of success with 'Mockingbird,'" Ms. Lee said in 1964. "I was hoping for a quick and merciful death at the hands of the reviewers, but, at the same time I sort of hoped someone would like it well enough to give me encouragement."

The enormous success of the film version of the novel, released in 1962 with Gregory Peck starring as Atticus Finch, a small-town Southern lawyer who defends a black man falsely accused of raping a white woman, added to Ms. Lee's fame and fanned expectations for her next novel.

But for more than half a century a second novel failed to turn up, and Ms. Lee gained a reputation as a literary Garbo, a recluse whose public appearances counted as news simply because of their rarity.

Then, in February 2015, long after the public had given up on seeing anything more from Ms. Lee, her publisher, Harper, announced plans to publish a manuscript—long thought to be lost and now resurfacing in mysterious circumstances—that Ms. Lee had submitted to her editors in 1957 under the title "Go Set a Watchman." Ms. Lee's lawyer, Tonja B. Carter, had found it, attached to an original typescript of "To Kill a Mockingbird," while examining Ms. Lee's papers, the publishers explained. It told the story of Atticus and his daughter, Jean Louise Finch, known as Scout, 20 years later, when Scout is a young woman living in New York. It included scenes in which Atticus expresses conservative views on race relations seemingly at odds with his liberal stance in the earlier novel.

The book was published in July with an initial printing of 2 million and leapt to the top of the fiction best-seller lists, despite tepid reviews. "To Kill a Mockingbird" was really two books in one: an often humorous portrait of small-town life in the 1930s, and a sobering tale of race relations in the Deep South during the Jim Crow era.

Looking back on her childhood, Scout, the narrator, evokes the simple pleasures of an ordinary small town in Alabama. At the same time, this stark morality tale of a righteous Southern lawyer who stands

firm against racism and mob rule struck a chord with Americans. Some reviewers complained that the perceptions attributed to Scout were too complex for a girl starting grade school, and dismissed Atticus as a Southern Judge Hardy, dispensing moral bromides. But by the late 1970s "To Kill a Mockingbird" had sold nearly 10 million copies, and in 1988 the National Council of Teachers of English reported that it was being taught in 74 percent of the nation's secondary schools. A decade later Library Journal declared it the best novel of the 20th century.

Nelle Harper Lee was born on April 28, 1926, in Monroeville, in southern Alabama, the youngest of four children. "Nelle" was a backward spelling of her maternal grandmother's first name.

Her father, Amasa Coleman Lee, was a lawyer and the model for Atticus Finch. Her mother was Frances Finch Lee.

Ms. Lee, like her alter ego Scout, was a tomboy who enjoyed beating up the local boys, climbing trees and rolling in the dirt. One boy on the receiving end of Nelle's thrashings was Truman Persons (later Capote), who spent summers next door to Nelle with relatives. The two became friends.

Mr. Capote later wrote Nelle into his first book, "Other Voices, Other Rooms," as the tomboy Idabel Tompkins. Ms. Lee in turn cast Mr. Capote as the little blond tale-spinner Dill in "To Kill a Mockingbird."

Ms. Lee attended Huntingdon College, a local Methodist school, then transferred to the University of Alabama to study law, primarily to please her father, who hoped that she might become a lawyer. Her own interests, however, led her elsewhere.

After college, she decided to go to New York and become a writer. Arriving in Manhattan in 1949, she worked as an airlines reservations agent and at night wrote on a desk made from a door. She developed a portfolio of short stories, which she took to an agent, Maurice Crain, who suggested she try writing a novel. Two months later she returned with 50 pages of a manuscript she called "Go Set a Watchman."

It told the story of a small-town lawyer who stands guard outside a jail to protect his client against an angry mob, a central incident in the novel-to-be, whose title Mr. Crain changed to "Atticus" and later, as the manuscript evolved, to "To Kill a Mockingbird."

The title refers to an incident in which Atticus, on giving air rifles to his children, tells them they can shoot at tin cans but never at a mockingbird. Scout learns from Miss Maudie Atkinson, the widow across the street, that there is a proverb, "It's a sin to kill a mockingbird," and the reason for it: the birds harm no one and only make beautiful music.

Editors at Lippincott encouraged Ms. Lee to revise. Eventually they assigned her to work with Tay Hohoff, an editor with whom she developed a close personal and professional relationship.

As the novel moved toward publication, Mr. Capote called with a proposal. He was going to Kansas to research the shocking murder of a farm family. Would Ms. Lee like to come along as his "assistant researchist"?

She jumped at the offer. For months, she accompanied Mr. Capote as he interviewed police investigators and local folk, and each night she wrote for him detailed reports on her impressions.

When the book, "In Cold Blood," was published in 1966 to much acclaim, Mr. Capote repaid Ms. Lee's help with a brief thank you on the dedication page and thereafter minimized her role in the book's creation. By then the friendship had cooled, and it entered a deep freeze after "To Kill a Mockingbird" became a best seller.

Signs of its success were visible almost immediately after its publication in July 1960. The Book-of-the-Month Club and the Literary Guild made the novel one of their selections, and Reader's Digest condensed it. A week after publication, the novel jumped to the top of the best-seller list, remaining there for 88 weeks.

But a next novel refused to come. "Success has had a very bad effect on me," Ms. Lee told a reporter. "I've gotten fat—but extremely uncomplacent. I'm running just as scared as before."

Ms. Lee lived a quiet but relatively normal life in Monroeville, where friends and neighbors closed ranks around her to fend off unwelcome attention by tourists and reporters.

News of the rediscovery of "Go Set a Watchman" threw the literary world into turmoil. Many critics found the timing and the rediscovery story suspicious, and questioned whether Ms. Lee was mentally competent to approve its publication.

It remained an open question, for many critics, whether "Go Set a Watchman" was anything more than the initial draft of "To Kill a Mockingbird," from which, at the behest of her editors, Ms. Lee had excised the scenes from Scout's childhood and developed them into a separate book. "I was a first-time writer, and I did what I was told," Ms. Lee wrote in a statement issued by her publisher in 2015.

Many readers, who had grown up idolizing Atticus, were crushed by his portrayal, 20 years on, as a defender of segregation.

"The depiction of Atticus in 'Watchman' makes for disturbing reading, and for 'Mockingbird' fans, it's especially disorienting," the critic Michiko Kakutani wrote in The New York Times. "Scout is shocked to find, during her trip home, that her beloved father, who taught her everything she knows about fairness and compassion, has been affiliating with raving anti-integrationist, anti-black crazies, and the reader shares her horror and confusion."

1821, discouraged with the treatment he received in the English theatre. There is no doubt that this Booth was a great actor, greater in many parts than his rival, Edmund Kean. But the British public had, after years of neglect, made Kean its idol, and there was no room for Booth. His genius closely resembled Kean's; they were of much the same temperament; they took very nearly the same point of view. Booth, like Kean, could depict blazing passion and thrill the souls of his hearers with fiery eloquence. That, in his early manhood, told against him. There might have been room on the London stage, even when Kean's fame was at the zenith, for another John Kemble, cold, formal, correct, of formidable dignity and irreproachable skill. Macready slowly worked his way to the front in those days of Kean's ascendency. But no place in the public heart could be found for another Kean while Kean lived.

Junius Brutus Booth had some of the faults of Edmund Kean, as well as similar artistic gifts. He was, in his later years, eccentric almost to the verge of insanity. He was given to fits of melancholy. He played fast and loose with the public. He was intemperate. But his nature was of a finer fibre than Kean's; he was a purer and a wiser man. He had a larger actual knowledge of his own art and kindred arts than Kean had. He was affectionate, as Kean was not. As for his acting, it is conceded to-day that it equaled Kean's.

Junius Brutus Booth's second wife, who came to America with him, had been Mary Ann Holmes of Reading, England. They had ten children, namely, Junius Brutus, Rosalie Anne, Henry Byron, Mary, Frederick, Elizabeth, Edwin Thomas, Asia Sydney, John Wilkes, and Joseph Addison. Of these the younger Junius Brutus became an actor, managed theatres in California and in the East, and finally kept a popular Summer hotel in Massachusetts; Asia married John Sleeper Clarke, the comic actor; John Wilkes took to the stage, but, because of his profligacy and lack of balance, such gifts as he had

The marb
gained for h
part many t
went to Sac
Amador, El
pathize wit
In January,
Legislature
That year h
Romeo, Pes
mento Thea

He appear
cisco, and w
the rising s
tle of the
man, who w
after-dinner
later at De
chair of M
afford to g
night on the
and listen
greeted the
Booth's fri
California c
newspaper
minister of
New-York.
added to hi
beth, Petru
with his fam

When he r
sence of t
1876, he re
queror. Th
played, enor
ets, and pub

HIS FI

In the Wi
to the East
star actor o
Street Thea
made a tour
west, and be
Theatre the

fanatics; one gave her empty whisky bottles to play with instead of dolls.

At another stage, she lived in a drought area with a family of seven. She spent two years in a Los Angeles orphanage, wearing a uniform she detested.

By the time she was 9 years old, Norma Jean had begun to stammer—an affliction rare among females.

Her dream since childhood had been to be a movie star, and she succeeded beyond her wildest imaginings. The conviction of her mother's best friend was borne out; she had told the little girl, day after day:

"Don't worry. You're going to be a beautiful girl when you get big. You're going to be a star. Oh, I feel it in my bones."

Nunnally Johnson, the producer and writer, decided that Miss Monroe was something special. Marilyn, he said, was "a phenomenon of nature, like Niagara Falls and the Grand Canyon.

"You can't talk to it. It can't talk to you. All you can do is stand back and be awed by it," he said.

This figure in the minds of millions was difficult to analyze statistically. Her dimensions—37-23-37—were voluptuous but not extraordinary.

She stood 5 feet 5½ inches tall. She had soft blonde hair, wide, dreamy, gray-blue eyes. She spoke in a high baby voice that was little more than a breathless whisper.

Heavy Fan Mail

Fans wrote her 5,000 letters a week, at least a dozen of them proposing marriage. The Communists denounced her as a capitalist trick to make the Amer-

litzer-prize winning playwr Arthur Miller.

She was 16 when she mar for the first time. The b groom was James Dough 21, an aircraft worker.

Mr. Dougherty said their divorce four years in 1946, that she had bee "wonderful" housekeeper.

Her two successive divo came in 1954, when she with Mr. DiMaggio after nine months, and in 1960, a four-year marriage to Miller.

She became famous with first featured role of any pr nence, in "The Asphalt Jung issued in 1950.

Her appearance was brief unforgettable. From the ins she moved onto the screen that extraordinary walk of people asked themselves: "W that blonde?"

In 1952 it was revealed Miss Monroe had been the ject of a widely distributed calendar photograph shot she was a notably unsucces starlet.

Revealed Her Wit

It created a scandal, bu was her reaction to the sca that was remembered. She interviewers that she was ashamed and had needed money to pay her rent.

She also revealed her sens humor. When asked by a wo journalist, "You mean didn't have anything on?" replied breathlessly:

"Oh yes, I had the radio One of her most exaspera quirks was her tardiness. was, during the years of fame, anywhere from on twenty-four hours late for

P. T. BARNUM

July 4, 1810–April 7, 1891

BRIDGEPORT, Conn.—At 6:22 o'clock tonight the long sickness of P. T. Barnum came to an end by his quietly passing away at Marina, his residence in this city.

Shortly after midnight there came an alarming change for the worse. Drs. Hubbard and Godfrey, who were in attendance, saw at once that the change was such as to indicate that the patient could not long survive.

Among the sorrowing group in the sick room were Mrs. Barnum, the Rev. L. B. Fisher, pastor of the Universalist church of this city, of which Mr. Barnum was a member; Mrs. D. W. Thompson, Mr. Barnum's daughter; Mrs. W. H. Buchtelle of New York, another daughter; C. Barnum Seeley, his grandson; Drs. Hubbard and Godfrey, his physicians; and W. D. Roberts, his faithful colored valet. The scene at the deathbed was deeply pathetic. All were in tears.

Throughout the city tonight there is the deepest sorrow. Day before yesterday Mr. Barnum was 80 years and nine months of age.

For more than 40 years, the great American showman toiled to amuse the public, and his life was filled with many remarkable adventures.

Phineas Taylor Barnum was born in Bethel, Connecticut, on July 5, 1810. His father, Philo Barnum, was a tailor, a farmer, and a tavern keeper.

The boy was early taught that if he would succeed in the world he must work hard. When he was only six years of age he drove cows to and from pasture, weeded the kitchen garden at the back of the humble house in which he was born, and as he grew older rode the plow horse, and whenever he had an opportunity attended school.

In arithmetic he was particularly apt, and he was also at a remarkably early age aware of the value of money. When he was six he had saved coppers enough to exchange for a silver dollar. This he "turned" as rapidly as he could, and by peddling homemade molasses candy, gingerbread, and a liquor made by himself called cherry rum, he had accumulated when he was not quite 12 a sum sufficient to buy a sheep and a calf.

For years the life of young Barnum was one of constant struggle. His father died when he was 15, and he was left almost penniless. He was by turns a peddler and trader, a clerk in Brooklyn and New York, the keeper of a small porter house, the proprietor of a village store, and editor of a country newspaper. After this he kept a boarding house, made a trip to Philadelphia and was married to a young tailoress, whom he years after described as "the best woman in the world."

Then in 1835, he found the calling for which he seems to have been born. In short, he went into "the show business."

Regarding this period in his life he later wrote: "By this time it was clear to my mind that my proper position in this busy world was not yet reached. I had not found that I was to cater for that insatiate want of human nature—the love of amusement; that I was to make a sensation in two continents, and that fame and fortune awaited me so soon as I should appear in the character of a showman. The show business has all phases and grades of dignity, from the exhibition of a monkey to the exposition of that highest art in music or the drama which secures for the gifted artists a worldwide fame Princes well might envy. Men, women, and children who cannot live on gravity alone need something to satisfy their gayer, lighter moods and hours, and he who ministers to this want is, in my opinion, in a business established by the Creator of our nature."

The first venture to which Mr. Barnum thus refers was a remarkable negro woman, who was said to have been 161 years old and a nurse of Gen. George Washington. The wonders of this person are set forth in this notice, from the Pennsylvania Inquirer of July 15, 1835:

"CURIOSITY.—The citizens of Philadelphia and its vicinity have an opportunity of witnessing at Masonic Hall one of the greatest natural curiosities ever witnessed, viz., Joice Heth, a negress, aged 161 years, who formerly belonged to the father of Gen. Washington. She has been a member of the Baptist Church 116 years, and can rehearse many hymns and sing them according to former custom. She was born near the old Potomac River, in Virginia, and has for 90 or 100 years lived in Paris, Ky., with the Bowling family."

For $1,000, Mr. Barnum bought the "wonderful negress," and, making money by the venture, he continued to follow the business of a showman. During the years which followed he traveled all over this country and in many other parts of the world.

Of all his enterprises, however, he regarded his connection with the American Museum and his management of Jenny Lind and Tom Thumb as the most important. On the 27th of December, 1841, he obtained control of the American Museum, on the corner of Ann Street and Broadway in New York, and for years afterward he continued to conduct that establishment.

It became one of the most famous places of amusement in the world. In it were exhibited "the Feejee Mermaid," "the original bearded woman," and giants and dwarfs almost without end.

It was in November, 1842, that Mr. Barnum engaged Charles S. Stratton, whom he christened Tom Thumb. With him he traveled and made large sums of money in different parts of the world.

Regarding a visit which he made with Tom Thumb to the Queen of England, Mr. Barnum wrote: "We were conducted through a long corridor to a broad flight of marble steps, which led to the Queen's magnificent picture gallery . . . The General familiarly informed the Queen that her pictures were 'first-rate.'"

Mr. Barnum regarded his engagement of Jenny Lind as one of the great events in his career. That engagement was entered into in 1850. It resulted in a fortune for Mr. Barnum, and in the payment to Jenny Lind for 95 concerts of the sum of $176,675.09.

After his engagement with Jenny Lind, Mr. Barnum was everywhere regarded as being "a made man." But, as the years went on, trouble fell upon him, and by unwise speculation he lost every penny he had in the world.

Still he did not give up the fight, but by the help of friends, the increase in value of certain real estate owned by him, and the great energy which was one of his chief traits, he again commenced in a small way, subsequently took Tom Thumb to Europe for a second visit, and repaired his broken fortunes. Later on he again undertook the management of the museum in New York, and upon its destruction by fire established "the new museum" further up Broadway. It was also burned, and he lost much money. But fortune again smiled upon him, and as a manager of monster circuses and traveling shows he met with much success in all parts of the country.

During all his life Mr. Barnum was a great believer in the power of advertising. No man knew better than he the value of printer's ink, and nothing was too ambitious for him to undertake.

One of the greatest chances of his life came with Jumbo. He had often gazed on that monster in the Zoological Gardens at London, but it had never occurred to him as possible to possess the English pet. One of his agents induced the manager of the garden to offer the animal for $2,000. Mr. Barnum snapped up the offer at once. There was a cry of protest from all England. Pictures of Jumbo, Jumbo stories and poetry, Jumbo collars, neckties, cigars, fans, polkas, and hats were put on the market and worn, sung, smoked, and danced by the entire English nation.

Mr. Barnum was importuned to name the price at which he would relinquish his contract and permit Jumbo to remain in London. He said he had promised to show the animal in America and had advertised him extensively. Therefore, $100,000 would not induce him to cancel the purchase.

When Jumbo and his movements became a matter of deep public interest, the newspapers printed all they could get about him. His untimely death was mourned by two nations.

Mr. Barnum published his will in 1883. He valued his share in the show at $3,500,000, and the Children's Aid Society was named as a beneficiary of a certain percentage of each season's profits. "To me there is no picture so beautiful as smiling, bright-eyed, happy children; no music so sweet as their clear and ringing laughter," the great showman explained. "That I have had power to provide innocent amusement for the little ones, to create such pictures, to evoke such music, is my proudest reflection."

EDWIN BOOTH

November 13, 1833–June 7, 1893

Edwin Booth, the well-known actor, died at the Players' this morning at 1:17 o'clock. For several days he had been growing weaker, and all hope of his recovery had been abandoned.

It was in a heavy, painless sleep that Mr. Booth's spirit passed away.

Mrs. Grossman, Mr. Booth's daughter, had maintained a silent vigil, and it was in her arms that her father died.

Within half an hour every club in New York knew of the great tragedian's death.

His father, Junius Brutus Booth, came to America in 1821, discouraged with the treatment he received in the English theater. There is no doubt that this Booth was a great actor, greater in many parts than his rival, Edmund Kean. But no place in the public heart could be found for another Kean while Kean lived.

Junius Brutus Booth's second wife, had been Mary Ann Holmes of Reading, England. They had 10 children. Of these John Wilkes took to the stage, but, because of his profligacy, such gifts as he had were wasted.

The elder Booth bought a farm near the town of Belair, near Baltimore, Md., and there Edwin was born, Nov. 13, 1833.

He was, almost from his infancy, his father's favorite. But the father did not want his favorite son to be an actor. He never dreamed that little Edwin, in whom he saw no traces of talent, would be for years the foremost actor of a Nation of 60 million, and in his time the wisest and most eloquent interpreter of Shakespeare on the English-speaking stage.

Edwin Booth made his first appearance on the stage Sept. 10, 1849, at the Boston Museum, in the insignificant part of Tressel in "Richard III." He made his first appearance in New York Sept. 27, 1850, at the old National Theatre, in "The Iron Chest," acting Wilford to his father's Mortimer.

Edwin Booth and his father went to California in June, 1852, and appeared in several plays at the American Theatre in Sacramento. The father died later that year.

Edwin Booth became a member of the stock company of the Sacramento Theatre in 1855. He played Richard III on Aug. 11, and was hailed as "a promising young actor." The next week, he appeared as Hamlet for the first time.

He was hailed as the rising star, upon whose shoulders the mantle of the elder Booth had fallen. Gen. William Tecumseh Sherman, who was then a Lieutenant, told in an after-dinner speech nearly 35 years later at Delmonico's, as he stood beside the chair of Mr. Booth, how, when he could not afford to go to the theater, he used to sit at night on the veranda of his hotel across the way and listen to the thunders of applause that greeted the young tragedian.

Mr. Booth's first New York engagement was at Burton's New Theatre. It began May 4, 1857. The young tragedian appeared as Richard III, King Lear, Hamlet, and Romeo. These engagements were not profitable, but the tide had turned in his favor Nov. 26, 1860, when he began another engagement at the same house, which had been renamed Winter Garden Theatre.

His Hamlet began to be spoken of seriously. The popular applause indicated that his Hamlet was already preferred to all other Hamlets.

Mr. Booth went to England for the first time in 1861 and acted in London. He was married that year to Mary Devlin, who had been an actress. She died on Feb. 21, 1863, when she was not yet 23, leaving an infant daughter, Edwina.

At Winter Garden Theatre Sept. 29, 1862, Mr. Booth reappeared and was cordially received. "Hamlet" and "The Merchant of Venice" drew large audiences. Mr. Booth's next engagement at Winter Garden Theatre began with "Hamlet" May 3, 1864. This theater was then leased by him and his brother-in-law, John Sleeper Clarke.

The manager, William Stuart, an energetic Irish adventurer, was a skillful advertiser, and spared no pains in trumpeting the merits of Edwin Booth. The posters on the fences bearing his name were big enough for a circus.

Public excitement about the actor was at fever heat. Critics who doubted "if the modern stage had anything to equal his Hamlet" were plentiful. The handsome face of the actor, shaded by dark flowing locks and bearing an expression of poetic melancholy, was impressed on the eye of the multitude. His beautiful voice was raved about. His hour of triumph was at hand.

The celebrated long run of "Hamlet"—100 nights—began at Winter Garden, Oct. 31, 1864. His "Hamlet" was transferred to the Boston Theatre on March 24, 1865.

Three weeks later the country received the dreadful shock caused by the assassination of President Lincoln by Edwin Booth's younger brother. Edwin suffered no indignity, but the shame of the family disgrace burdened his mind. He never afterward appeared in Washington.

He returned to the New York stage at Winter Garden Theatre, Jan. 3, 1866, as Hamlet. He was received with cheers which expressed the sympathy of the public and the confidence in his patriotism, but perhaps also indicated the delight of the crowd at the sight of the man who had inevitably become more conspicuous since his brother's dastardly crime.

Booth had now reached his zenith. He had never before acted with the firmness, repose, strength, and exquisite delicacy that then marked his work, and he never surpassed the portrayals of Shakespeare's heroes which he gave during that last year at Winter Garden Theatre. In December, 1866, he played Iago to the Othello of Bogumil Dawison, the renowned German actor. Each used his own native language, and this was the first of many similar performances on the New York stage.

The Hamlet Medal, testifying to public approbation of Booth's impersonation of the Prince of Denmark, was presented to him at Winter Garden, Jan. 22, 1867, after a performance of Shakespeare's most esteemed tragedy. The medal, now preserved among the treasures of The Players in their clubhouse in Gramercy Park, is of gold, oval in shape, surrounded by a golden serpent. In the center is the head of Booth as Hamlet.

Mr. Booth was now, in his 34th year, the most popular actor in the United States. An enormous fortune seemed to be within his grasp. He had long desired to own a theater in which Shakespeare should be fittingly represented.

The cornerstone of Booth's Theatre, at Sixth Avenue and 23rd Street, was laid April 8, 1868, and the house was opened to the public Feb. 3, 1869. The exterior was of stone, massive and imposing in appearance. The auditorium was spacious and handsome. The acoustics were perfect. There was a great crowd in the theater on opening night for "Romeo and Juliet."

"Romeo and Juliet" ran until April 12, when "Othello" was produced with equal magnificence, Mr. Booth playing the Moor to the Iago of Adams, and the young actress Mary McVicker playing Desdemona. She and Mr. Booth were married on June 2, 1869.

Mr. Booth came forward again on Jan. 5, 1870, in "Hamlet." Booth's Hamlet, as graceful, touching, and picturesque as ever, was then supported, none too well, by the Claudius of Theodore Hamilton, the Laertes of William E. Sheridan, and the Polonius of D. C. Anderson.

But the money went out faster than it came in. Booth had mortgaged the property heavily, and borrowed large sums to meet his expenses. His advisers and assistants were neither wise nor competent. The stage was neglected, and the plays badly mounted. After the performance June 21, 1873, Booth formally retired from the management.

In February, 1874, Mr. Booth filed a petition in voluntary bankruptcy. His assets were announced as $9,000; the liabilities were enormous. Jarrett & Palmer, the firm of theatrical speculators who had inflicted Boucicault's "Formosa, or the Railroad to Ruin," on New York at Niblo's, secured the lease of the theater at an annual rental of $40,000. Mr. Booth protested against their use of his name as a trademark, but they found another Booth, the owner of a printing house, who cheerfully lent his name to the theater, which was called Booth's to the end. The property was sold, in foreclosure, Dec. 3, 1874.

The theater passed through many vicissitudes. Clara Morris tried to act Lady Macbeth there and failed. Sarah Bernhardt there made her American début.

The ill-fated theater, the noblest home the drama ever had in New York, was sold in 1883 to the notorious James D. Fish and Ferdinand Ward, who rebuilt it for mercantile purposes.

In March, 1891, at the Broadway Theatre, Booth played Shylock to the Bassanio of Mr. Barrett. Although his acting had been listless in his later years, he had never before offered a performance so feeble. His speech was halting; he could not always he heard; he walked with difficulty. He had been ill, and he lacked the strength to continue his labors. The sudden death of Lawrence Barrett, March 20, 1891, caused an early close of the season.

Booth then appeared in Brooklyn, at the Academy of Music. The representation of "Hamlet" there Saturday afternoon, April 4, 1891, was generally regarded as his "farewell," and such, indeed, it proved to be.

The club known as The Players, designed to provide a social meeting place for actors, dramatists, managers, and persons interested in the welfare of the stage, and to get together a great theatrical library and preserve valuable dramatic mementos and works of art, was founded in 1888 by Edwin Booth and others. Mr. Booth bought the house at 16 Gramercy Park and paid for its redecoration under the direction of Stanford White. This he presented to The Players. He retained the use of rooms in the house, which he made his home. The clubhouse was opened to the members and their friends on Dec. 31, 1888.

In recognition of this splendid gift a supper was given at Delmonico's in Mr. Booth's honor, March 30, 1889. The following Wednesday Mr. Booth was seized with an alarming fainting fit on stage in Rochester, N.Y., during a performance of "Othello." His physicians said at the time of his last engagement in New York that he was afflicted with malaria, caused by the bad ventilation and imperfect plumbing of some of the theaters in which he had been acting.

SARAH BERNHARDT

October 22 or 23, 1844–March 26, 1923

PARIS—Sarah Bernhardt is dead. The "greatest actress" passed away at 7:59 P.M. in the arms of her son, Maurice. Death came in her home with windows open on the Boulevard Pereire. It was the sudden closing of these windows that gave the signal to those waiting and watching without that Bernhardt was dead.

Bernhardt's grandson, M. Grosse, brought the first flowers into the death chamber—mauve and white lilacs. Flowers came from many friends, and soon the room was heaped with them, those from the family and dearest friends being placed on the bed.

The actress's son, her granddaughter, Lysiane, and Mlle. Louise Abbema, who was Bernhardt's best friend, had remained close to the chamber where the patient lay.

Bernhardt suffered greatly in her last illness. From time to time she became delirious and declaimed passages from the tragedy "Phèdre" and "L'Aiglon," her two greatest triumphs.

Word of Bernhardt's death spread through Paris rapidly. At the Théâtre Sarah Bernhardt, where "L'Aiglon" was playing, the announcement was made in the middle of the first act. The play was stopped and the audience filed out sorrowfully.

Crowds collected outside the residence on the Boulevard Pereire, gazing at the shuttered windows and watching the carriages and automobiles bringing celebrities of the literary and dramatic world.

Mme. Bernhardt was 78 years old. An acute uremic condition was the cause of death.

"I dream of dying, like the great Irving, in the harness," said Mme. Bernhardt in September, 1910. That sentence sums up her whole life. Work was her fountain of youth. She was never idle; she never rested.

Sarah Bernhardt was the natural child of Julie Bernhardt and a merchant of Amsterdam, who died shortly after her birth, on Oct. 22, 1844. At the age of eight she was placed in Mme. Fressard's school at Auteuil, and two years later, in 1855, was a scholar at the Grandchamps Convent at Versailles. The religious atmosphere of the convent made a strong appeal to her emotional nature, and after being converted to the Catholic faith she decided to become a nun.

Here also she appeared in her first play, called "Toby Recovering His Eyesight." This was a miracle play, and Mme. Bernhardt appeared, as she wrote in her "Memoirs," in "heavenly blue tarletan, with a blue sash around my waist to help confine the filmy drapery, and two paper wings fastened upon each shoulder for celestial atmosphere."

Her mother was much alarmed when her daughter announced that she would become a nun, and a family council was called. She was taken to the theater every night, but she persisted in her wish to enter the nunnery. When 14 years old, she was taken to a performance of "Britannicus" at the Théâtre Français, and was so moved and impressed that her family decided to make her an actress.

Two years later she competed for the National Conservatoire, and at the public trials recited a simple fable of La Fontaine's, "The Two Pigeons." Her performance so astonished that she was immediately and unanimously entered.

In 1862 Edmond Thierry called her to the Comédie Francaise, and she made her professional début in a minor part on "Iphigenie." Then came four years of hard work done in obscurity.

She entered the Gymnase de Montigny in 1866. Duquesnel of the Odéon recognized her latent genius and engaged her, paying her first year's salary out of his own pocket.

In 1867 Mme. Bernhardt made her debut as Armande in "Les Femmes Savantes." This appearance is considered the real starting point of her career, and she began to be famous by the end of 1869.

Then came the Franco-Prussian war, and she became a nurse. She turned a Parisian theater into a hospital and for more than a year gave herself up to the care of the wounded and dying.

In 1872 Mme. Bernhardt signed a contract to become a life member of the Comédie Francaise and scored great successes in "Phèdre," as Berthe in "La Fille de Roland," and as Posthumia in "Rome Vaincue." Three years later she was elected a sharing life member of the Comédie Française.

Then came a period of clashes with M. Perrin, the managing director of the Comédie Française. Mme. Bernhardt received roles that were uncongenial. One day, after remonstrating with M. Perrin for assigning her the part of Clorinda in "L'Aventurière," she burst out of his office like a tempest and gave up the stage.

She returned to the Comédie Française, only to break with M. Perrin permanently shortly after. This last break was brought about by an incident typical of the Bernhardt temperament.

She insisted on going up in a balloon—this was during the Exposition of 1878—and M. Perrin was sure she would break her engagement to play at the matinée that day. She landed just in time to keep the appointment, but Perrin was furious and announced that she was fined 1,000 francs.

Mme. Bernhardt immediately resigned. She then played for the first time outside France, appearing in London in "Phèdre" and as Mrs. Clarkson in "L'Etrangère."

"The English people," she said after this invasion, "first among all foreign nations welcomed me with such kindness that they made me believe in myself."

On Nov. 8, 1880, she made her first appearance in New York at Booth's Theatre. Mme. Bernhardt's first American tour comprised 27 performances in this city and 136 in 39 other cities during a period of seven months. She played eight dramas, including "La Dame aux Camelias" and "Frou Frou."

Then came a tour of Russia and Denmark, and in 1882 she earned fresh triumphs at the Vaudeville in Paris. One year later she became the owner of the Porte Sainte-Martin Theatre and played in repertoire until 1886, when she made her second American tour. Her third American tour followed in 1888–1889.

Then in 1891–1893 Mme. Bernhardt made an extended tour covering the United States, South America and many capitals of Europe. On her return to Paris she undertook the management of the Theatre de la Renaissance.

Mme. Bernhardt made her fifth American tour in 1896, and that December was present at a festival given in her honor in Paris. She was crowned queen of the drama before 500 artists, actors and authors.

Her sixth American tour was made in 1901–1902, during which she gave 180 performances in the principal cities. Mme. Bernhardt returned to her playhouse in Paris and presented a number of new plays with brilliant success, and in 1905 made her seventh visit to this country under the management of the Shuberts.

She played in both North and South America, and in Quebec, Canada, she went through, an unpleasant experience. She was credited by the newspapers with making certain criticisms of French Canadians, and she and her company were attacked by a mob on their way to the station after the engagement. Eggs, stones, sticks and snowballs were thrown.

She played in halls, armories, skating rinks, and churches, and in Texas, owing to the fact that no theaters could he obtained, she played in a Barnum & Bailey tent.

In 1910 she returned to this country for the first of her "farewell tours." In 35 weeks she gave 285 performances.

Mme. Bernhardt returned to this country again in December, 1912. Her repertoire consisted of famous scenes from her great successes, and the tour was an unqualified success. When the war came, she converted her theater into a hospital, just as she had nearly a half-century before.

Then in the midst of her ministrations she was stricken with inflammation of the right knee and had to undergo an operation which cost her her right leg. The operation was performed in February, 1915. That she was acting again at the end of six months was typical of her indomitable will.

In November she returned to the Paris stage and acted in a dramatic sketch called "Les Cathedrales," in which the players represented the voices of the devastated cathedrals of France. Mme. Bernhardt was the voice of the Cathedral of Strasbourg, and when she recited the closing words, "Weep, Germans, weep: thy Prussian Eagles have fallen bleeding into the Rhine," the audience became wild with emotion.

Mme. Bernhardt arrived on her last visit here in October, 1916. She then set off on one of the most arduous tours of her career, playing first in legitimate theaters and then on the Keith vaudeville circuit. At the Palace in this city she invariably received an ovation, particularly for her performance as the young French officer in "Du Theatre au Champ d'Honneur." She closed her season in Cleveland in October, 1918.

In October, 1921, she presented at her own theater "La Gloire," a play written for her by Maurice Rostand. Admitted to be the greatest actress of all time, Mme. Bernhardt also won distinction as a sculptor, writer, and artist. Her group "After the Storm" received honorable mention at the Salon in 1878. Her book "Dans les Nuages," written in 1878, describing her balloon ascension, was widely read, as were her "Memoirs."

She was married in 1882 to Jacques Damala, a handsome Greek actor of her own company, but they parted after one year. Later, when he was dying of consumption, she removed him to her home and nursed him until the end.

For 40 years Mme. Bernhardt's residence in Paris was the old house on the Boulevard Pereire. Her natural son lived with her there.

Her best work was done where she was able to display her powerful emotions. She was never surpassed and never will be, her critics say, in the emotional school. She played more than 200 parts and created most of them.

She received honors without number. Public fêtes for her were given in London and Paris and other capitals, and in Vienna one night after playing "Hamlet" the audience tore the horses from her carriage and dragged her through the street shouting "Vive Bernhardt!" —*Associated Press*

HARRY HOUDINI

March 24, 1874–October 31, 1926

DETROIT—Harry Houdini, world famous as a magician, a defier of locks and sealed chests and an exposer of spiritualist frauds, died here this afternoon after a week's struggle for life.

Death was due to peritonitis, which followed an operation for appendicitis. A second operation was performed last Friday. Like a newly discovered serum, used for the first time in Houdini's case, it was of no avail. He was 52 years old.

The chapter of accidents that ended fatally for the man who so often had seemed to be cheating the jaws of death began early in October at Albany, N.Y. On the opening night of his engagement a piece of apparatus used in his "water torture cell" trick struck him on the foot.

A bone was found to be fractured and Houdini was advised to discontinue his tour. He declined.

On Tuesday, Oct. 19, while in Montreal he addressed a class of students on spiritualistic tricks. After the address he commented on the ability of his stomach muscles to withstand hard blows without injury.

One of the students without warning struck him twice over his appendix. After he had boarded a train for Detroit he complained of pain.

Upon his arrival, Dr. Leo Kretzka, a physician, told the patient there were symptoms of appendicitis. At his hotel after the performance the pain increased. The following afternoon he underwent an operation for appendicitis.

According to the physicians, one of the blows he received in Montreal caused the appendix to burst.

Whatever the methods by which Harry Houdini deceived a large part of the world for nearly four decades, his career stamped him as one of the greatest showmen of modern times. With few exceptions, he invented all his tricks and illusions. In one or two cases Houdini alone knew the whole secret.

Houdini was born on March 24, 1874. His name originally was Eric Weiss and he was the son of a rabbi. He did not take the name Harry Houdini until he had been a performer for many years.

Legend has it that he opened his first lock when he wanted a piece of pie in the kitchen closet. When scarcely more than a baby he showed skill as an acrobat and contortionist, and both these talents helped his start in the show business and his development as an "escape king."

At the age of nine Houdini joined a traveling circus, touring Wisconsin as a contortionist and trapeze performer. Standing in the middle of the ring, he would invite anyone to tie him with ropes and then free himself inside the cabinet.

In the ring at Coffeyville, Kan., a sheriff tied him and then produced a pair of handcuffs with the taunt, "If I put these on you, you'll never get loose."

Houdini, still only a boy, told him to go ahead. After a much longer stay in the cabinet than usual, the performer emerged, carrying the handcuffs in his hands.

That was the beginning of his long series of escapes from every known sort of manacle. For years he called himself the Handcuff King.

From 1885 to 1900 he played all over the United States, in museums, music halls, circuses, and medicine shows.

During a six-year tour of the Continent he escaped from dozens of famous prisons. He returned to America to find his fame greatly increased and a newly organized vaudeville ready to pay him many times his old salary.

In 1908 Houdini dropped the handcuff tricks for more dangerous and dramatic escapes, including one from an airtight vessel, filled with water and locked in an iron-bound chest. He would free himself from the so-called torture cell, his own invention. In this he was suspended, head down, in a tank of water. He would hang from the roof of a skyscraper, bound in a straitjacket, from which he would wriggle free to the applause of the crowd in the street below. Thrown from a boat or bridge into a river, bound hand and foot and locked and nailed in a box, doomed to certain death by drowning or suffocation, he would emerge in a minute or so, swimming vigorously to safety.

An evidence of the deep impression his work made on the public mind is the fact that the Standard Dictionary now contains a verb, "houdinize," meaning "to release or extricate oneself (from confinement, bonds, or the like), as by wriggling out."

Houdini, who lived at 278 West 113th Street and in 1894 married Wilhelmina Rahner of Brooklyn, for 33 years tried to solve the mysteries of spiritism. He told friends he was ready to believe because he would find joy in proof that he could communicate with his parents and friends who had passed on. He had agreed with friends and acquaintances that the first to die was to try to communicate from the spirit world to the world of reality. Fourteen of those friends had died, but none had ever given a sign, he said.

"Such an agreement I made with both my parents," Houdini said. "They died and I have not heard from them. I thought once I saw my mother in a vision, but I now believe it was imagination."

Houdini counted that he had had "four close-ups with death" in his career of more than 30 years as a mystifier. The closest was in California, where he risked his life on a bet. Seven years ago in Los Angeles he made a wager that he could free himself from a six-foot grave into which he was to be buried after being manacled.

"The knowledge that I was six feet under the sod gave me the first thrill of horror I had ever experienced," Houdini was wont to say. "The momentary scare, the irretrievable mistake of all daredevils, nearly cost me my life, for it caused me to waste a fraction of breath when every fraction was needed to pull through. I had kept the sand loose about my body so that I could work dexterously. I did. But as I clawed and kneed the earth my strength began to fail. Then I made another mistake. I yelled. Or, at least, I attempted to, and the last remnants of my self-possession left me. Then instinct stepped in to the rescue. With my last reserve strength I fought through, more sand than air entering my nostrils. The sunlight came like a blinding blessing, and my friends about the grave said that, chalky pale and wild-eyed as I was, I presented a perfect imitation of a dead man rising.

"The next time I am buried it will not be alive if I can help it."

D. W. GRIFFITH

January 22, 1875–July 23, 1948

By Seymour Stern

HOLLYWOOD, Calif.—David Wark Griffith, one of the first and greatest contributors to the motion picture art, died this morning in Temple Hospital after suffering a cerebral hemorrhage. His age was 73.

The producer of "The Birth of a Nation," and pioneer in such techniques as closeups, fade-outs and flash-backs, was stricken at the Hollywood Knickerbocker Hotel, where he lived. Mr. Griffith, who is survived by a brother, was divorced from his second wife, the former Evelyn Marjorie Baldwin.

Mr. Griffith had been inactive in recent years. But the name of D. W. Griffith, the master producer and director of silent motion pictures, is synonymous with "father of the film art" and "king of directors."

He produced and directed almost 500 pictures costing $23,000,000 and grossing $80,000,000. His most famous film, "The Birth of a Nation," has grossed more than $48,000,000.

Although Mr. Griffith did not originate all the technical devices credited to him, he originated many of them, and vastly improved others. Chief among his improvements was his development of the closeup, first used in 1895, into a dramatic psychological contribution that shaped the entire art of the cinema.

Among the multitude of advanced methods which he started were the long shot, the vista, the vignette, the iris or eye-opener effect, the cameo-profile, the fade-in and fade-out, soft focus, back lighting, tinting, rapid-cutting, parallel action, mist photography, high and low angle shots, night photography, and the moving camera.

He was the first director to depart from the standard 1,000-foot film. This caused a break between him and the old Biograph Company. He then made the first four-reeler. "Judith of Bethulia," which had instantaneous success. When Mr. Griffith ordered a close-up shot of a human face, his cameraman, Billy Bitzer, quit in disgust. At the first close-up there were hisses and cries of "Where are their feet?"

It was as a creator of significant content in the films themselves, however, that Mr. Griffith was a mighty force in the cinema. Even before "The Birth of a Nation," that epic of the Civil War and the Reconstruction Period, which, directed by a man whose family had been ruined by the fall of the Confederacy, was deeply biased but was filled with great sweep and movement, he had exercised his bold conception of the exalted purpose which the medium might serve.

Long before the names of Sergei Eisenstein, Fritz Lang, Alfred Hitchcock, and Frank Capra were heard of, Mr. Griffith brought to the screen important historical and philosophical themes, challenging social questions, visionary prophecies. His films were emotional, dramatic, intellectual and esthetic.

In 1916 his "Intolerance" appeared, with four parallel stories, a stupendous re-creation of the Ancient World and an apocalyptic image-prophecy of the Second Coming of Christ. In this film, Griffith used 16,000 "extras" in a single scene.

Mr. Griffith brought lyric poetry and high tragedy to the screen in 1919 in "Broken Blossoms," a passionate plea for a renewal of the Christian ideal in interracial relations. His "Way Down East," a folk-melodrama of New England in the Nineties, produced in 1920, used landscapes and natural backgrounds as vital psychological and dramatic elements of a story.

In "Orphans of the Storm," in 1922, Mr. Griffith combined magnificent spectacle with a social theme, using the French Revolution as a platform from which to attack communism and Soviet Russia.

In 1924, Mr. Griffith produced the mammoth "America," another great historical pageant, this time of the American Revolution.

His last important film, in 1925, was "Isn't Life Wonderful," a grim tale of Polish refugees in post–World War I Germany.

In the days of his greatest glory Mr. Griffith never used a shooting script. "Intolerance," although it was 22 months in production and consumed 125 miles of film, was photographed entirely from his "mental notes."

Mary Pickford and Lillian Gish were outstanding examples of his genius in choosing and training performers for the new art. He induced Douglas Fairbanks to leave the stage for the screen. Dorothy Gish, Mabel Normand, Lionel Barrymore, and the Talmadge sisters owed their film careers to him.

Born at La Grange, Ky., on Jan. 22, 1875, the son of Colonel Jacob Wark Griffith and Margaret Oglesby Griffith, David Wark Griffith started work at 16 on a local newspaper.

After seeing Julia Marlowe in "Romola," he decided to become an actor. After working in various stock companies, he won entry to moving pictures as an actor, working at the Edison studio and then at Biograph.

In July, 1908, he made his first film, "The Adventures of Dollie."

In 1919, with Pickford, Fairbanks and Charles Chaplin, he formed United Artists Corporation, under whose seal some of the screen's outstanding productions were released.

Is Griffith merely the remarkable director who in 23 years of filmmaking employed upwards of 75,000 persons; who discovered, trained and launched so many directors and "stars" that to list them is to compile a "Who's Who in Hollywood, Today and Yesterday"? Is he merely an inventor of cinematic devices and technical devices?

The central fact in the director's story is the monumental, single-handed fight Griffith waged for freedom of expression in a medium cursed with censorship and control. He was the one creative figure who fought alone against financial monopoly and cultural dictatorship.

His most important masterpieces, "The Birth of a Nation" and "Intolerance," were financed, produced and exhibited in entire independence of the Hollywood film industry, which refused backing for both films. Three other major works—"Way Down East," "Orphans of the Storm" and "America"—were financed and produced independently of the industry.

The last three films were produced not in Hollywood but at Mamaroneck, N.Y. Griffith stuck his flag at Mamaroneck in 1924, after he had made the small but powerful film "Isn't Life Wonderful."

Although he made films for eight more years, practically none of his later output reflects the greatness and originality of mind that conceived Belshazzar's feast in "Intolerance," the imagination that fashioned the ride of the Clansmen in "The Birth of a Nation," or the cinematic wizardry that flashcut Paul Revere's ride in "America."

JAMES DEAN

February 8, 1931–September 30, 1955

Paso Robles, Calif.—James Dean, 24-year-old motion picture actor, was killed tonight in an automobile accident near here.

A spokesman for Warner Brothers, for whom Mr. Dean had just completed "The Giant," said he had no details of the accident except that the actor was en route to a sports car meeting at Salinas. He was driving a small German speedster.

Mr. Dean was the star of Elia Kazan's film "East of Eden," released last April and taken from John Steinbeck's novel. It was his first starring role in films.

He also appeared in "Rebel Without a Cause," still unreleased.

In 1954 he attracted [the] attention of critics as the young Arab servant in the Broadway production of "The Immoralist." His portrayal won for him the Donaldson and Perry awards.

HUMPHREY BOGART

December 25, 1899–January 14, 1957

Hollywood, Calif.—Humphrey Bogart died in his sleep this morning in his Holmby Hills home. The 57-year-old movie actor, an Academy Award winner, had been suffering for more than two years from cancer of the esophagus.

Mr. Bogart leaves his wife, Lauren Bacall, the actress, whom he married in 1945, and who was his fourth wife. Mr. Bogart is also survived by a son, a daughter, and a sister.

Mr. Bogart was one of the most paradoxical screen personalities in the recent annals of Hollywood. He often deflated the publicity balloons that keep many a screen star aloft, but he remained one of Hollywood's top box-office attractions for more than two decades.

On screen he was most often the snarling, laconic gangster who let his gun do his talking. In private life, however, he could speak wittily on a wide range of subjects and make better copy off the cuff than the publicists could devise for him.

Mr. Bogart received an Academy Award in 1952 for his performance in "The African Queen." Still, he made it clear that he set little store by such fanfare. Earlier he had established a mock award for the best performance in a film by an animal, making sure that the bit of satire received full notice in the press.

But despite this show of frivolity, he was fiercely proud of his profession. "I am a professional," he said. "I have a respect for my profession. I worked hard at it."

Attesting to this are a number of highly interesting characterizations in such films as "The Petrified Forest" (1936), "High Sierra" (1941), "Casablanca" (1942), "To Have and Have Not" (1944), "Key Largo" (1948), "The Treasure of Sierra Madre" (1948), "The African Queen" (1951), "Sabrina," (1954), "The Caine Mutiny" (1954) and "The Desperate Hours" (1955). The actor's last film, "The Harder They Fall," was released last year.

Mr. Bogart's sense of responsibility toward his profession may have stemmed from the fact that both his parents were successful professionals. His mother was Maud Humphrey, a noted illustrator and artist. His father was Belmont DeForest Bogart, a surgeon. Their son, born on Christmas Day in 1899, was reared in fashionable New York society.

Mr. Bogart worked for a time with World Films and then as a stage manager for an acting group. It was an easy step to his first roles in the early 1920's. His rise to fame over the next 15 years, however, was a hard road, often lined with critical brickbats.

He appeared in "Swifty" and plugged on in drawing-room comedies, appearing in "Hell's Bells, "The Cradle Snatchers," "It's a Wise Child" and many others in which he usually played a callow juvenile or a romantic second lead.

He accepted a contract with Fox in 1931, but roles in a few Westerns failed to improve matters, and soon he was back on Broadway, convinced that his hard-bitten face disqualified him for close-ups as a matinee idol.

But toward the end of 1934 he used his granite-like face to rebuild, with enormous success, a new dramatic career. Having heard that Robert E. Sherwood's "The Petrified Forest" had a gangster role, he approached Mr. Sherwood for the part.

Mr. Bogart was asked to return in three days for a reading. When he reappeared he had a three-day growth of beard and was wearing shabby clothes. His reading and appearance brought him the supporting role of Duke Mantee, his most memorable Broadway role. Mr. Bogart later performed the same role for the movie to considerable critical acclaim.

This was the first of more than 50 pictures that Mr. Bogart made. A spate of crime dramas followed, including "Angels with Dirty Faces." "The Roaring Twenties," Bullets or Ballots," "Dead End," "San Quentin" and, finally, "High Sierra" in 1941.

Mr. Bogart then insisted on roles with more scope.

They were forthcoming in such films as "Casablanca," "To Have and Have Not" and "Key Largo," wherein Mr. Bogart's notorious screen hardness was offset by a latent idealism that showed itself in the end.

In "The Treasure of Sierra Madre," as a prospector driven to evil by a lust for gold, the range of his characterization won him new followers.

A further range of his talents was displayed in "The African Queen," wherein his portrayal of a tramp with a yen for gin and Katharine Hepburn won him an "Oscar." Another distinguished portrait was that of the neurotic Captain Queeg in the movie version of "The Caine Mutiny." His aptitude for romantic comedy became clear when he played the bitter businessman who softens under the charms of Audrey Hepburn in "Sabrina." Mr. Bogart also appeared in "The Barefoot Contessa," made in 1954.

The movie actor made no secret of his nightclubbing. He was also a yachting enthusiast. At one point in his career he reportedly made $200,000 a film, and he was for years among the top 10 box-office attractions.

CECIL B. DE MILLE

August 12, 1881–January 21, 1959

HOLLYWOOD, Calif.—Cecil B. De Mille died of a heart ailment today in his home on De Mille Drive here. He was 77 years old.

At his bedside when he died were a daughter, Cecilia, and her husband, Joseph Harper. Mrs. De Mille, who is 85 and has been ailing for several years, was not informed until later in the morning. They had been married for 56 years.

Although confined to his home since last Saturday, Mr. De Mille was preparing to start filming "On My Honor," a history of the Boy Scout movement and its founder, the late Lord Baden-Powell.

Cecil Blount De Mille was the Phineas T. Barnum of the movies—a showman extraordinary.

A pioneer in the industry, he used the broad medium of the screen to interpret in "colossal" and "stupendous" spectacles the story of the Bible, the splendor that was Egypt, the glory that was Rome. He dreamed in terms of millions, marble pillars, golden bathtubs and mass drama; spent enormous sums to produce the rich effects for which he became famous.

He produced more than 70 major films, noted for their weight and mass rather than for subtlety or finely shaded artistry.

In 1953 he won his first Academy Award, for "The Greatest Show on Earth." Since then he had been showered with honors. France named him a Knight of the Legion of Honor, the Netherlands inducted him into the Order of Orange Nassau, and Thailand conferred on him the Most Exalted Order of the White Elephant.

The fact that his first Oscar did not come until 40 years after he had produced one of the earliest four-reel feature films, "The Squaw Man," was brushed off with a characteristic De Millean gesture:

"I win my awards at the box office."

This was true. His pageants and colossals awed the urban, suburban and backwoods audiences. By 1946 his personal fortune, despite his regal spending habits, was estimated at $8,000,000.

The producer basked in publicity's intense glare in 1944–45 when he made a heroic issue of a demand by the union of which he was a member that he pay a $1 contribution to its political action fund. He had been in radio about a decade by that time, staging shows for a soap company at a reported salary of $5,000 a week.

Mr. De Mille carried the fight to the courts, was defeated, and then went on a one-man campaign against political assessments by unions. He later sought reinstatement in the union but failed to get it.

Mr. De Mille was born at De Mille Corners, a backwoods crossroads in Ashfield, Mass., on Aug. 12, 1881, while his parents were touring New England with a stock company. His father, Henry Churchill De Mille, was of French-Dutch ancestry; his mother, the former Matilda Beatrice Samuel, of English stock.

At 17 he went on the stage. In the cast of one play, "Hearts Are Trumps," was Constance Adams, daughter of a New Jersey judge. They were married in 1902.

In 1908 Mr. De Mille threw in his lot with the ambitious Jesse Lasky and with a newcomer in the theater, Sam Goldwyn. All three reached the top rung in the movie world, though along separate paths.

The first product of their movie company was "The Squaw Man." It was turned out in an abandoned stable in Los Angeles with crude equipment, but it bore Mr. De Mille's mark.

He was credited with many motion picture innovations. Indoor lighting was first tried out on an actor in "The Squaw Man." This picture, besides being the screen's first epic, was also the first to publicize the names of its stars.

On his first day as head of the Lasky-Goldwyn-De Mille combine, Mr. De Mille signed three unknowns—a $5 cowpoke named Hal Roach, an oil-field hand named Bill (Hopalong Cassidy) Boyd and a thin-nosed teenager who called herself Gloria Swanson. This was the nucleus around which he built his galaxy of screen stars.

To Mr. De Mille was attributed the inspiration for doing different versions of a popular picture. The so-called "sneak preview"—showing a film to a test audience—was another contribution.

The first "Ten Commandments," produced in 1923 at a cost of $1,400,000, made money. From that time on Mr. De Mille wallowed in extravagant props and super-gorgeous sets.

A second version, issued in 1956 and differing greatly from the first, grossed a reported $60,000,000 here and abroad.

Mr. De Mille, who gave the University of Southern California a theater in memory of his parents, was lavish with gifts to other institutions.

In June, 1958, he learned that plans to place translations of the hieroglyphics on the Egyptian obelisk in Central Park were being put aside for lack of funds. He offered to pay the cost of erecting four bronze plaques at the base of "Cleopatra's Needle," saying:

"As a boy, I used to look upon the hieroglyphics as so many wonderful pictures."

Two weeks ago, the Department of Parks announced that Mr. De Mille had donated $3,760 for the project.

CLARK GABLE

February 1, 1901–November 16, 1960

HOLLYWOOD, Calif.—Clark Gable, for 30 years "King" of Hollywood actors, died tonight of a heart ailment. He was 59 years old.—*The Associated Press*

Mr. Gable was one of the world's most popular actors. For many years he was among the 10 top box-office attractions. Theater marquees would announce simply, "This week: Clark Gable."

To millions the tall, handsome man with the mustache, broad shoulders, brown hair and gray eyes was the symbol of masculinity, "naughty but nice."

He did not think he was a great actor. "I can't emote worth a damn," he said. And when he was earning $7,500 a week, he hung in his dressing room reminders of the days when he was a struggling actor or piling lumber in Oregon for $3.20 a day. Across the mementos he wrote: "Just to remind you, Gable."

There were many Gable legends. One was that in "It Happened One Night" (1934) he had sabotaged the undershirt industry overnight by peeling off his shirt in the picture and revealing nothing underneath.

"I didn't know what I was doing to the undershirt people," he recalled, adding, "I hadn't worn an undershirt since I started to school."

Early in his career he was turned down by one top studio. He quoted an executive as saying: "Gable won't do. Look at his big ears." The executive later hired him.

William Clark Gable (he dropped his first name after he entered the theater) was born in Cadiz, Ohio, on Feb. 1, 1901. His father was an oil contractor. His mother died before he was one year old.

At 15, after his father had remarried, the family moved to Ravenna, Ohio. His father quit oil drilling for farming. Young Gable forked hay, fed hogs and wanted to be a physician. But when he saw his first play, he decided to be an actor, and he got a job with a troupe that played everything from "Uncle Tom's Cabin" to "Her False Step."

When the company closed in Montana, he took a freight train to Oregon, where he worked in a lumber company, sold neckties, and was a telephone company linesman.

In 1924 Mr. Gable joined a theater company in Portland. He made his first appearance on the screen in a silent film starring Pola Negri. He appeared in two Los Angeles stage productions and then headed for Broadway.

In three years, he portrayed mostly villains. Then he returned to Los Angeles, where he was a hit in the role of Killer Mears in "The Last Mile."

This led to a movie role in "The Painted Desert" in 1930. The story is that Mr. Gable was interviewed and asked if he could ride a horse. He said he could, got the job, then went out and learned how to ride.

His effort won him a contract with Metro-Goldwyn-Mayer. He first became a leading man in "Dance, Fools, Dance," with Joan Crawford. His first big hit was "A Free Soul," in which he slapped Norma Shearer.

Women by the thousands wrote in that they, too, would like to be slapped by Mr. Gable. "For two years I pulled guns on people or hit women in the face," he later recalled.

His pictures included "Hell Divers," "Susan Lennox," "Polly of the Circus" "Strange Interlude," "Red Dust," "No Man of Her Own," "The White Sister," "Hold Your Man," "Night Flight," and "Dancing Lady." His roster of leading ladies included Greta Garbo, Jean Harlow, Carole Lombard and Helen Hayes.

In 1934, he was loaned to Columbia Pictures, which starred him in a comedy, "It Happened One Night." Claudette Colbert played a runaway heiress and Mr. Gable a newspaperman, traveling by bus from Miami to New York. Both won Academy Awards for the best performances of the year.

The next year he played Fletcher Christian in "Mutiny on the Bounty," which won an Academy Award as the best film of the year.

In the next seven years Mr. Gable appeared in more than 25 films, including "China Seas," "San Francisco," "Saratoga," "Test Pilot," "Idiot's Delight," "Gone with the Wind," "Boom Town," "They Met in Bombay" and "Somewhere I'll Find You."

From 1932 through 1943, he was listed among the first 10 money-making stars in the yearly surveys by The Motion Picture Herald. After time out for military duty, he regained that ranking in 1947, 1948, 1949 and 1955.

Observers believe that his films have grossed more than $100,000,000, including $50,000,000 for "Gone with the Wind." He had roles in at least 60 pictures.

After his third wife, Miss Lombard, was killed in a plane crash during a bond tour in World War II in 1942, Mr. Gable enlisted in the Army Air Forces as a private. He was then 41. He rose to major, took part in bomber missions over Europe, filmed a combat movie and won the Distinguished Flying Cross.

After the war, he returned to Hollywood, and a Metro slogan, "Gable is back and Garson's got him" spread across the country. He starred with Greer Garson in "Adventure." Then followed such films as "The Hucksters," "Mogambo," "The King and Four Queens," "The Tall Men," "Soldier of Fortune," "Teacher's Pet," "Run Silent, Run Deep," and "But Not for Me."

"It Started in Naples," a comedy with Mr. Gable and Sophia Loren, opened in New York in September, 1960. In July, 1960, Mr. Gable had begun work with Marilyn Monroe on "The Misfits."

Mr. Gable married five times. His fifth wife was Mrs. Kay Williams Spreckels, a former model and actress, whom he married in 1955. Last Sept. 30, Mr. Gable announced that she was to have a child in the spring, making Mr. Gable a father for the first time.

GARY COOPER

May 7, 1901–May 13, 1961

HOLLYWOOD, Calif.—Gary Cooper died today of cancer at his home in the Holmby Hills section of Los Angeles. He was 60 years old last Sunday.

The tall, lean actor, whose cowboy roles had made him a world symbol of the courageous, laconic pioneer of the American West, had been critically ill for several weeks.

The seriousness of his illness was revealed on April 17 when the Motion Picture Academy of Arts and Sciences was bestowing its Oscars on artists and technicians. A special statuette was ready for Mr. Cooper for his contributions during his long career. He had previously won two Oscars for acting—in the title role of "Sergeant York" in 1941 and as the courageous sheriff in "High Noon" in 1953.

However, James Stewart, the actor, accepted the honor for his close friend and gave a short, emotional tribute. Reporters, who had accepted the explanation that Mr. Cooper was unable to attend the ceremony because of a pinched nerve in his back, later learned that he was critically ill with cancer.

To millions of Americans, Gary Cooper represented the All-American Man.

He was an American frontier hero in "The Plainsman," an O.S.S. hero in "Cloak and Dagger," a Naval hero in "Task Force," a homespun millionaire hero in "Mr. Deeds Goes to Town," a common-man political hero in "Meet John Doe," a baseball hero in "The Pride of the Yankees," a medical hero in "The Story of Dr. Wassell" and a national hero in "Sergeant York."

He was the strong, silent man not only of the great

outdoors, where he was one of its slowest-talking and fastest-drawing citizens, but also of powerful dramas and sophisticated comedies.

"Ungainly, ungrammatical, head-scratching, ineloquent men draw comfort and renewed assurance from Gary Cooper," a writer once said.

Long, lean and broad of shoulder, Mr. Cooper walked gingerly, off screen as well as on. His eyes were of chilly blue. He was handy with a shotgun or rifle.

One writer said that in only two major respects did Mr. Cooper differ markedly from his screen self: he didn't go around wearing a horse and he didn't say "They went that-a-way." Mr. Cooper reportedly would say, "Thet way."

The men who directed his pictures said he had an instinctive sense of timing, a quick intelligence, the wit to think a role through and get to the heart of a character.

"I recognize my limitations," he once said. "For instance, I never tried Shakespeare." He paused and grinned slowly. "That's because I'd look funny in tights."

Mr. Cooper was once asked to give the reasons for his success. He replied: "I don't really know but maybe it's because once in a while I find a good picture, the happy combination of director and actors, which gives me a fresh start. Mostly I think it's because I look like the guy down the street."

Mr. Cooper was born May 7, 1901, in Helena, Mont., and christened Frank James Cooper. His father, Charles Henry Cooper, was a British lawyer who had gone to Helena, married a Montana girl, managed a ranch while practicing law and became a justice of the Montana Supreme Court.

The family went to England when young Cooper was nine and returned to Montana four years later. He worked on the family ranch.

"Getting up at 5 o'clock in the dead of winter to feed 450 head of cattle and shoveling manure at 40 below ain't romantic," he once recalled.

After two years at Grinnell College in Iowa, he headed for Los Angeles in 1924. His first job there was door-to-door solicitation for a photography studio. One day he met two friends from Helena who told him the Fox Western Studios were looking for riders. He got a job—at $10 a day.

Then he heard that Tom Mix, the cowboy star, was making $15,000 a week. Mr. Cooper decided to devote a year to make good in the movies.

A friend from Indiana suggested that he change his name because there already were several Frank Coopers in pictures, and Gary was a city whose name always sounded poetic to her.

Mr. Cooper got several bit parts, and just before the year ran out, got his first big role, opposite Vilma Banky in the 1926 film "The Winning of Barbara Worth." Eventually he equaled, if not surpassed, Tom Mix's $15,000 a week, although he was generally paid by the picture—reportedly around $300,000 in recent years.

In April, 1960, he underwent prostate-gland surgery in Boston. A major intestinal operation was performed five weeks later in Hollywood.

After his recovery, the actor went to England to make his last film, "The Naked Edge," in which he portrayed a murderer opposite Deborah Kerr.

In 1933, Mr. Cooper married the socially prominent Veronica Balfe, who had a brief screen career as Sandra Shaw. The couple had one daughter, Maria.

In 1959, Mr. Cooper became a member of the Roman Catholic Church, of which his wife and daughter already were members.

Also surviving Mr. Cooper is his 85-year-old mother, Mrs. Alice Bracia Cooper of Los Angeles.

MARILYN MONROE

June 1, 1926–August 5, 1962

HOLLYWOOD, Calif.—Marilyn Monroe, one of the most famous stars in Hollywood's history, was found dead early today in the bedroom of her home in the Brentwood section of Los Angeles. She was 36 years old.

Beside the bed was an empty bottle that had contained sleeping pills. Fourteen other bottles of medicines and tablets were on the nightstand.

The impact of Miss Monroe's death was international. Her fame was greater than her contributions as an actress. Her marriages to and divorces from Joe DiMaggio, the former Yankee baseball star, and Arthur Miller, the Pulitzer Prize–winning playwright, were accepted by millions as the prerogatives of this contemporary Venus.

The events leading to her death were in tragic contrast to the comic talent and zest for life that had helped to make "The Seven Year Itch" and "Some Like It Hot" smash hits. Other of her notable films included "Gentlemen Prefer Blondes," "Bus Stop" and "How to Marry a Millionaire."

During the last few years Miss Monroe had suffered severe setbacks. Her last two films, "Let's Make Love" and "The Misfits," were box-office disappointments. After completion of "The Misfits," written by Mr. Miller, she was divorced from him.

The last person to see her alive was her housekeeper, Mrs. Eunice Murray, who had lived with her. Mrs. Murray told the police that Miss Monroe retired to her bedroom about 8 P.M. yesterday.

About 3:25 A.M. today, the housekeeper noticed a light under Miss Monroe's door. She called to the actress but received no answer. She tried the bedroom door, but it was locked.

The housekeeper telephoned Miss Monroe's psychoanalyst, Dr. Ralph R. Greenson. When he arrived at her two-bedroom bungalow, he broke a pane of the French window and opened it. Determining that the star was dead, he phoned Miss Monroe's physician. After his arrival, the police were called.

In the last two years Miss Monroe had become the subject of considerable controversy in Hollywood. Some persons gibed at her aspirations as a serious actress and considered it ridiculous that she should have gone to New York to study under Lee Strasberg. Miss Monroe's defenders, however, asserted that her talents had been underestimated by those who thought her appeal to audiences was solely sexual.

The life of Marilyn Monroe, the golden girl of the movies, ended as it began, in misery and tragedy. Her death closed an incredibly glamorous career and capped a series of somber events that began with her birth as an unwanted, illegitimate baby and was illuminated during the last dozen years by the lightning of fame.

The first man to see her on the screen, the man who made her screen test, felt the almost universal reaction as he ran the wordless scene, in which she walked, sat down and lit a cigarette.

"I got a cold chill," he said. "This girl had something I hadn't seen since silent pictures. This is the first girl who looked like one of those lush stars of the silent era. Every frame of the test radiated sex."

Billy Wilder, the director, called it "flesh impact," adding, "Flesh impact is rare. Three I remember who had it were Clara Bow, Jean Harlow and Rita Hayworth. Such girls have flesh which photographs like flesh. You feel you can reach out and touch it."

Fans paid $200,000,000 to see her project this quality. No sex symbol of the era other than Brigitte Bardot could match her popularity. Toward the end, she also convinced critics and the public that she could act.

During the years of her greatest success, she saw two of her marriages end in divorce. She suffered at least two miscarriages. Her emotional insecurity deepened, and her many illnesses came upon her more frequently.

In 1961, she was twice admitted to hospitals in New York for psychiatric observation and rest. On June 8 she was dismissed by Twentieth Century Fox after being absent all but five days during seven weeks of shooting "Something's Got to Give," in which she starred.

"It's something that Marilyn no longer can control," one of her studio chiefs confided. "Sure she's sick. She believes she's sick. She may even have a fever, but it's a sickness of the mind."

In her last interview, published in the Aug. 3 issue of Life magazine, she said: "I was never used to being happy, so that wasn't something I ever took for granted."

Miss Monroe was born in Los Angeles on June 1, 1926. The name on the birth record is Norma Jean Mortenson, the surname of the man who fathered her, then abandoned her mother. She later took her mother's last name, Baker.

Both her maternal grandparents and her mother were committed to mental institutions. Her uncle killed himself. Her father died in a motorcycle accident three years after her birth.

During her mother's stays in asylums, she was farmed out to 12 sets of foster parents. One family gave her empty whisky bottles to play with instead of dolls. She also spent two years in a Los Angeles orphanage.

Her dream since childhood had been to be a movie star, and the conviction of her mother's best friend was borne out; day after day she had told the child: "You're going to be a beautiful girl when you get big. You're going to be a movie star. Oh, I feel it in my bones."

Miss Monroe's dimensions—37-23-37—were voluptuous but not extraordinary. She had soft blonde hair and wide, dreamy gray-blue eyes. She spoke in a baby voice that was little more than a breathless whisper.

Fans wrote her 5,000 letters a week, at least a dozen of them proposing marriage. Her second husband, Mr. DiMaggio, and her third, Mr. Miller, were American male idols.

She was 16 when she married for the first time. The bridegroom was James Dougherty, an aircraft worker. They were divorced four years later, in 1946. Her two subsequent divorces came in 1954, when she split with Mr. DiMaggio after only nine months, and in 1960, after a four-year marriage to Mr. Miller.

Miss Monroe became famous with her first featured role of any prominence, in "The Asphalt Jungle," in 1950. Her appearance was brief but unforgettable. From the instant she moved onto the screen with that extraordinary walk of hers, people asked themselves, "Who's that blonde?"

In 1952 it was revealed that Miss Monroe had been the subject of a nude calendar photograph that was shot while she was an unsuccessful starlet. The news created a scandal, but it was her reaction to the scandal that was remembered. She told interviewers that she had needed the money to pay her rent.

She also revealed her sense of humor. When asked by a woman journalist, "You mean you didn't have anything on?" she replied breathlessly: "Oh, yes, I had the radio on."

One of Miss Monroe's most exasperating quirks was her tardiness. During the years of her fame, she was up to 24 hours late for appointments.

"True, she's not punctual," said Jerry Wald, head of her studio, "but I'm not sad about it. I can get a dozen beautiful blondes who will show up promptly in makeup at 4 A.M. each morning, but they are not Marilyn Monroe."

Speaking of her career and her fame, Miss Monroe once said wistfully: "It might be kind of a relief to be finished. It's sort of like I don't know what kind of a yard dash you're running, but then you're at the finish line and you sort of sigh—you've made it! But you never have—you have to start all over again."

WALT DISNEY

December 5, 1901–December 15, 1966

LOS ANGELES—Walt Disney, who built his whimsical cartoon world of Mickey Mouse, Donald Duck and Snow White and the Seven Dwarfs into a $100-million-a-year entertainment empire, died in St. Joseph's Hospital here this morning. He was 65 years old.

He had undergone surgery for the removal of a lung tumor that was discovered after he entered the hospital for treatment of an old neck injury received in a polo match.

Just before his last illness, Mr. Disney was supervising the construction of a new Disneyland in Florida, a ski resort in Sequoia National Forest and the renovation of the 10-year-old Disneyland at Anaheim. His motion-picture studio was turning out six new productions and several television shows.

Although Mr. Disney held no formal title at Walt Disney Productions, he was in direct charge. Indeed, with the recent decision of Jack L. Warner to sell his interest in the Warner Brothers studio, Mr. Disney was the last of Hollywood's veteran moviemakers who remained in personal control of a major studio.

He is survived by his wife, Lillian, two daughters and his brother Roy, who is president and chairman of Walt Disney Productions.

From his fertile imagination and industrious factory of drawing boards, Walt Elias Disney fashioned the most popular movie stars ever to come from Hollywood and created one of the most fantastic entertainment empires in history.

In return for the happiness he supplied, the world lavished wealth and tributes upon him. He was probably the only man in Hollywood to have been praised by both the American Legion and the Soviet Union.

Where any other Hollywood producer would have been happy to get one Academy Award, Mr. Disney smashed all records by accumulating 29 Oscars.

"We're selling corn," Mr. Disney once told a reporter, "and I like corn."

Mr. Disney went from seven-minute animated cartoons to become the first man to mix animation with live action, and he pioneered in making feature-length cartoons. His nature films were almost as popular as his cartoons, and eventually he expanded into feature-length movies using only live actors.

From a small garage-studio, the Disney enterprise grew into one of the most modern movie studios in the world, with four sound stages on 51 acres. Mr. Disney acquired a 420-acre ranch that was used for shooting exterior shots for his movies and television productions. Among the lucrative by-products of his output were many comic scripts and enormous royalties paid to him by toy-makers.

Mr. Disney's restless mind created one of the nation's greatest tourist attractions, Disneyland, a 300-acre tract of amusement rides, fantasy spectacles and re-created Americana that cost $50.1 million.

By last year, when Disneyland observed its 10th birthday, it had been visited by some 50 million people. Its international fame was emphasized in 1959 by the then Soviet Premier, Nikita S. Khrushchev, who protested that he had been unable to see Disneyland. Security arrangements could not be made in time.

Even after Disneyland had proven itself, Mr. Disney declined to consider suggestions to leave well enough alone: "Disneyland will never be completed as long as there is imagination left in the world."

Repeatedly, as Mr. Disney came up with new ideas, he encountered skepticism. For Mickey Mouse, the foundation of his realm, Mr. Disney had to pawn and sell almost everything because most exhibitors looked upon it as just another cartoon. But when the public had a chance to speak, the noble-hearted mouse with the high-pitched voice, red pants, yellow shoes and white gloves became the most beloved of Hollywood stars.

When Mr. Disney decided to make the first feature-length cartoon, "Snow White and the Seven Dwarfs," Hollywood experts scoffed that no audience would sit through such a long animation. It became one of the biggest money-makers in movie history.

Mr. Disney was thought a fool when he became the first important movie producer to make films for television. His detractors, once again, were proven wrong.

He was, however, the only major movie producer who refused to release his movies to television. He contended, with a good deal of profitable evidence, that each seven years there would be another generation that would flock to the movie theaters to see his old films.

Mickey Mouse would have been fame enough for most men, but not for Walt Disney. He created Donald Duck, Pluto and Goofy. He dug into books for Dumbo, Bambi, Peter Pan, The Three Little Pigs, Ferdinand the Bull, Cinderella, the Sleeping Beauty, Brer Rabbit, Pinocchio. In "Fantasia," he blended cartoon stories with classical music.

Though Mr. Disney's cartoon characters differed markedly, they were all alike in two respects: they were lovable and unsophisticated. Most popular were big-eared Mickey of the piping voice; choleric Donald Duck of the unintelligible quacking; Pluto, that most amiable of clumsy dogs, and the seven dwarfs, who stole the show from Snow White: Dopey, Grumpy, Bashful, Sneezy, Happy, Sleepy and Doc.

Mr. Disney seemed to have had an almost superstitious fear of considering his movies as art, though an exhibition of some of his leading cartoon characters was once held in the Metropolitan Museum of Art in

New York. "I've never called this art," he said. "It's show business."

From Harvard and Yale, this stocky, industrious man who had never graduated from high school received honorary degrees. By the end of his career, the list of 700 awards and honors that Mr. Disney received from many nations filled 29 typewritten pages, and included 29 Oscars, four Emmys and the Presidential Freedom Medal.

Toys in the shape of Disney characters sold by the many millions. One of the most astounding exhibitions of popular devotion came in the wake of Mr. Disney's films about Davy Crockett. In a matter of months, youngsters all over the country who would balk at wearing a hat in winter were adorned in 'coonskin caps in midsummer.

In some ways Mr. Disney resembled the movie pioneers of a generation before him. Like them, he insisted on absolute authority and was savage in rebuking a subordinate. An associate of many years said the boss "could make you feel one-inch tall, but he wouldn't let anybody else do it. That was his privilege."

He was not afraid of risk. One day, when all the world thought of him as a fabulous success, he told an acquaintance, "I'm in great shape; I now owe the bank only eight million."

Mr. Disney had no trouble borrowing money in his later years. Bankers, in fact, sought him out. Last year Walt Disney Productions grossed $110 million. His family owns 38 percent of this publicly held corporation, and all of Retlaw, a company that controls the use of Mr. Disney's name.

Mr. Disney's contract with Walt Disney Productions gave him a basic salary of $182,000 a year and a deferred salary of $2,500 a week, with options to buy up to 25 percent interest in each of his live-action features. It is understood that he began exercising these options in 1961, but only up to 10 percent. These interests alone would have made him a multimillionaire.

Once in a bargaining dispute with a union of artists, a strike at the Disney studios went on for two months and was settled only after Government mediation.

This attitude by Mr. Disney was one reason some artists disparaged him. Another was that he did none of the drawings of his most famous cartoons. Mickey Mouse, for instance, was drawn by Ubbe Iwerks, who was with Mr. Disney almost from the beginning.

Mr. Iwerks insisted that Mr. Disney could have done the drawings but was too busy. Mr. Disney did, however, furnish Mickey's voice for all cartoons. He also sat in on all story conferences.

Although Mr. Disney's power and wealth multiplied with his achievements, his manner remained that of some prosperous, Midwestern storekeeper. Except when imbued with some new Disneyland project or movie idea, he was inclined to be phlegmatic.

His nasal speech, delivered slowly, was rarely accompanied by gestures.

Walt Disney was born in Chicago on Dec. 5, 1901. His family moved to Marceline, Mo., when he was a child and he spent most of his boyhood on a farm, where he enjoyed sketching animals. Later, when his family moved back to Chicago, he went to high school and studied cartoon drawing at night at the Academy of Fine Arts. He did illustrations for the school paper.

When the United States entered World War I he was turned down by the Army and Navy because he was too young. So he went to France as an ambulance driver for the Red Cross. He decorated the sides of his ambulance with cartoons and had his work published in Stars and Stripes.

After the war, he worked as a cartoonist for advertising agencies. When he got a job doing cartoons for advertisements that were shown in theaters between movies, he was determined that that was to be his future. In 1920 he organized his own company to make cartoons about fairy tales. At times he had no money for food and lived with Mr. Iwerks.

In 1923 Mr. Disney left Kansas City for Hollywood, where he formed a small company and did a series of film cartoons. After several years of stops and starts, Mr. Disney, his wife, his brother and Mr. Iwerks decided on a mouse for a new series. Mrs. Disney named it Mickey.

One day, when Mr. Disney was approaching 60, he was asked to reduce his success to a formula. His brown eyes became alternately intense and dreamy. "I guess I'm an optimist," he said. "I'm not in business to make unhappy pictures. I love comedy too much. I've always loved comedy. Another thing. Maybe it's because I can still be amazed at the wonders of the world."

JOHN FORD

February 1, 1894–August 31, 1973

By Albin Krebs

John Ford, one of the greatest directors the American motion-picture industry has produced, died of cancer yesterday at his home in Palm Desert, Calif. He was 78 years old.

Imaginative, daring, sensitive, courageous, tough and, above all, durable, Mr. Ford was the only person to win Academy Awards for four feature films, of which he directed more than 130 in a four-decade career. He also won an Oscar for his direction of a documentary during World War II.

With his classic "The Informer," released in 1935, less than a decade after the movies had learned to talk, Mr. Ford almost single-handedly made the sound motion picture come of age.

Most of Mr. Ford's films had merit, but particularly excellent were those for which he won the director's award of the Academy of Motion Picture Arts and Sciences—"The Informer," plus "The Grapes of Wrath" (1940), "How Green Was My Valley" (1941) and "The Quiet Man" (1952). He was also the only director to be cited four times by the New York Film Critics.

Other Ford movies that have won positions on lists of important films worldwide were "Stagecoach," "The Lost Patrol," "Young Mr. Lincoln," "The Fugitive" and "Arrowsmith."

Last April, Mr. Ford was honored with the American Film Institute's first Life Achievement Award at lavish ceremonies in Beverly Hills attended by colleagues and by one of his biggest fans—President [Richard M.] Nixon.

"I've seen virtually all of the 140 Ford movies," Mr. Nixon proclaimed before presenting him with the Medal of Freedom, the nation's highest civilian honor.

The director was a nervous, twitchy man given to biting handkerchiefs. A six-footer, in recent years he appeared quite thin, almost frail. His once sandy hair had grayed and become wispy, but his still jaunty, arm-swinging gait belied his years. He always had a cup—often filled with a brew stronger than coffee or tea—and a cigar near while he worked.

John Ford was born Sean Aloysius O'Fearna on Feb. 1, 1894, in Cape Elizabeth, Me. His father, Sean, a seaman, and his mother, the former Barbara Curran, were immigrants from Galway, Ireland, who in time went along with the way their neighbors pronounced their last name and had it changed legally to O'Feeney. (Sean O'Feeney remained Mr. Ford's legal name.)

In 1914, having failed to win an appointment to Annapolis, he went to Hollywood "to sponge off my older brother, Francis." Under the stage name of Francis Ford, his brother had become a successful director and star of silent serials. He put Sean, who soon became known as Jack Ford, to work as a property man, stuntman, assistant cameraman and grip.

All the while, he was carefully studying filmmaking techniques. He learned to be his own cameraman and editor, often functioning as such throughout his career. He mastered what became a new technique for directors—"cutting" or editing the film "in the camera."

"The Tornado," released in 1917, was the first Ford-directed movie. The two-reeler, which he wrote and starred in and for which he did his own stunt work, was about a cowboy who rescues the banker's daughter from outlaws and uses the reward money to bring his dear old Irish mother to America.

Between 1917 and 1920 Mr. Ford ground out some two dozen cheapjack movies. "The Iron Horse," in 1924, brought him renown and is still considered a classic of filmed Americana.

In 1930, "Men Without Women," a vividly photographed drama about 14 men trapped in a submarine, was released. It marked the beginning of his long, and mutually profitable, association with the scenarist Dudley Nichols.

Internationally acclaimed to this day, "The Informer," made in 1935, holds down its place on every major list of "the greatest films of all time." Mr. Ford called it "the easiest picture I ever directed," adding:

"No wonder. I had been dreaming of it for five years."

It took only three weeks to shoot, on a budget of $218,000, roughly the cost of one of today's half-hour television shows.

Supposedly a "B" picture that Mr. Ford sneaked over the studio bosses' heads ("I told 'em vaguely it was about gangsters and stool-pigeons"), "The Informer" won the first New York Film Critics Award as best picture, and the Academy of Motion Picture Arts and Sciences singled it out for several Oscars, including one for Mr. Nichols.

The Ford-Nichols chemistry also produced what most critics call the greatest Western ever made, "Stagecoach," in 1939. Starring John Wayne, Claire Trevor and Thomas Mitchell, the film, about an odd assortment of characters thrown together in 1884 during a journey by stagecoach through Apache-inhabited New Mexico Territory, was notable for its deft character studies, splendid photography and slam-bang action scenes.

The following year, Mr. Ford competed with himself for a director's Academy Award. Both "The Grapes of Wrath," a trenchant film of social realism based on John Steinbeck's novel detailing the Okie migrations, and "The Long Voyage Home," based on four one-act plays by Eugene O'Neill, were released in 1940. "The Grapes of Wrath" won Mr. Ford his second Oscar.

During World War II Mr. Ford, as a commander, was in charge of the Navy's film documentary unit. He was at Midway Island in June, 1942, when the Japanese attacked the important naval base there. His "The Battle of Midway," a 20-minute documentary released a month after the fighting stopped, won an Oscar as the best short subject of 1942. Mr. Ford's souvenir of the battle was a machine-gun slug wound in his left arm, which he sustained while filming an aerial attack.

Among the director's postwar movies were his trilogy on the United States Cavalry: "Fort Apache," "She Wore A Yellow Ribbon" and "Rio Grande." Other notable Ford films were "Wagonmaster," "The Fugitive," "Mogambo," "The Searchers," "Mister

Roberts," "The Last Hurrah" and "The Man Who Shot Liberty Valance."

Although all of his Oscars were won for non-Westerns, Mr. Ford was perhaps best known for his outdoor pictures. He was, indeed, a master of the big scene who possessed an almost uncanny ability to depict the drama of human masses in a large landscape. His films abounded with magnificent pictures, yet they were not mere pictures, mere decorations, but instruments for telling the story.

His action sequences, like the chase in "Stagecoach," were famous for their vigor and their unrivaled ability to build and sustain tension. Contrastingly, he could slow the pace of a scene to a near-standstill to make the fullest use of pauses and silences. In "My Darling Clementine," a young boy stands motionless, watching his older brothers ride off to a gunfight. Their horses are moving, but straight away from the camera, and so the viewer gets the overall impression of looking at a still picture.

Mr. Ford's curmudgeonly personality came out in infrequent interviews, which he hated and which he used to contradict earlier interviews. When it was once pointed out that several of his films, such as "The Grapes of Wrath" and "The Long Voyage Home," were serious "message" pictures, he replied testily:

"Bull! I made those pictures because they had a great story to tell. I'm thoroughly apolitical and non-ideological. I don't think I ever even voted in a Presidential election."

The director was a quiet family man who disliked nightclubs and parties attended by people he did not know well. He and his wife, the former Mary McBryde Smith, whom he married in 1920, had two children.

He was, according to one of his cronies, "a great shambles of a man," who on the set wore "mangy old khaki pants, tennis shoes with holes at the toes, a sloppy old campaign jacket, a beat-up fedora and a dirty scarf around the neck."

Throughout his life, Mr. Ford suffered poor eyesight and had to wear thick, shaded glasses. About 25 years ago his left eye was injured in an accident on the set, and he finally lost sight in it. In recent years he wore a black eye patch.

Although he was the first to admit that he had more than one bad movie behind him, he seldom talked about his fame as a director. But Carroll Baker, the actress who starred for him in "Cheyenne Autumn" in 1964, told an interviewer that one day, while they were on location in Monument Valley, she mentioned the films of Ingmar Bergman to Mr. Ford.

"Ingrid Bergman?" Mr. Ford asked.

Miss Baker said no, "Ingmar Bergman—you know, the great Swedish director."

"Oh, Ingmar Bergman," Mr. Ford said. "He's the fella that called me the greatest director in the world."

SAMUEL GOLDWYN

August 17, 1879–January 31, 1974

By Albin Krebs

Samuel Goldwyn, one of the last of the pioneer Hollywood producers, died yesterday at his Los Angeles home at the age of 91. He had been in frail health since 1968.

In a career that spanned a half-century, Mr. Goldwyn became a Hollywood legend, a motion picture producer whose films, always created on a grand scale, were notable for those most elusive of traits—taste and quality.

One of the last tycoons—he even looked the part—Mr. Goldwyn was a driving perfectionist, a man with a titanic temperament whose great gift was the ability to bring together, for each production, the very best writers, directors, cinematographers and other craftsmen.

He would dominate their work and their lives like a benign tyrant, praising them, goading them, encouraging them, browbeating them, as he supervised even the tiniest details.

This quest for the excellent often enraged Mr. Goldwyn's employes, but more often than not it gave his productions that sheen of quality and good taste that became known in the motion picture industry as "the Goldwyn touch."

Among the more than 70 movies to which he imparted that touch were "The Best Years of Our Lives," "Wuthering Heights," "The Pride of the Yankees," "Arrowsmith," "Dodsworth," "Stella Dallas," "Dead End," "The Westerner," "The Little Foxes," "Street Scene," "Hans Christian Andersen," "The Secret Life of Walter Mitty," "Guys and Dolls" and "Porgy and Bess."

Although he was one of the flashiest and most controversial of the independent producers, he was probably best known for his "Goldwynisms," the malapropisms, mixed metaphors, grammatical blunders and word manglings that included the now classic "Include me out" and "I'll tell you in two words—impossible!"

In recent years Mr. Goldwyn insisted that he was not the originator of half the Goldwynisms attributed to him. Whether genuine or apocryphal, they became part of the legend. Among the more famous:

"An oral agreement isn't worth the paper it's written on."

"A man who goes to a psychiatrist should have his head examined."

"This atom bomb is dynamite."

Another one supposedly evolved from a director's complaint that a film script in which Mr. Goldwyn was interested was "too caustic," to which the producer replied:

"Never mind the cost. If it's a good picture, we'll make it."

He used his Goldwynisms to gain publicity for himself and his pictures.

"People say that whenever I have a picture coming out I always start a controversy about something that gets into the papers," he said. "Well, in all sincerity, I want to assure you that, as a general proposition, there's not a single word of untruth in that."

Among the controversies that swirled about Mr. Goldwyn's bald head were his campaign against double features and his efforts to persuade fellow producers to make fewer but better pictures. He once said that Hollywood was grinding out 600 pictures a year when "there are not brains enough in Hollywood to produce more than 200 good ones."

Mr. Goldwyn was born Aug. 27, 1882, in Warsaw. Little was known of his family background, but he was the son of poor parents who died when he was young. At the age of 11, he left Poland. After two years in England, he migrated to Gloversville, N.Y., where he took a job sweeping floors in a glove factory. By the time he was 17 he was the foreman of 100 workers, and six years later he became a partner in the company.

In 1910 he married Blanche Lasky, whose brother, Jesse, was a vaudeville producer. Mr. Lasky, at the urging of a lawyer, Arthur S. Friend, toyed with the idea of filmmaking and tried to entice his brother-in-law. Mr. Goldwyn, who had moved to New York, was cool to the idea until one cold day in 1913, when he stepped into a Herald Square movie house to warm up and saw a Western starring Broncho Billy Anderson. He was impressed not only with the movie but also with all the dimes the management was raking in.

Mr. Goldwyn took up the idea of forming a film company. He and Mr. Lasky each put up $10,000, and Mrs. Goldwyn and Mr. Friend pledged the rest of the $26,500 capitalization.

The company, with Mr. Goldwyn doing most of the work, set out to produce long films that told romantic stories. Most "flickers" at the time were two-reelers, lasting about 20 minutes.

The company's first movie, "The Squaw Man," was a five-reeler, the first feature-length movie, and one of the first to be made in Hollywood. It was directed by a young stage manager and unsuccessful playwright named Cecil B. De Mille, who had never worked on a movie before.

Halfway through the filming, the money ran out. "I felt like we were on the brink of the abscess," said Mr. Goldwyn, uttering what was probably the first recorded Goldwynism. He raised additional money by selling theater owners the exhibition rights of "The Squaw Man" and 11 future pictures.

The movie was a tremendous success and resulted in a sudden intense interest from Mr. Goldwyn's partners, exactly what he didn't want. Shortly after the company merged with Adolph Zukor's Famous Players Company, Mr. Goldwyn sold out his shares for nearly a million dollars.

In 1917 he joined with Edgar and Arch Selwyn, who as Broadway producers had built up a library of plays that might make good films.

Mr. Goldwyn's name was still Goldfish, the nearest equivalent to his Polish name that immigration officials could think of when he came to this country. Goldwyn Pictures Corporation took its name from the "Gold" in Goldfish and the "wyn" in Selwyn.

Mr. Goldwyn liked the name so much that he had his own name legally changed. When the bankrupt Goldwyn company was merged with Metro Pictures, out of which Metro-Goldwyn-Mayer grew, Mr. Goldwyn withdrew with a substantial financial settlement.

In 1922, Mr. Goldwyn became an independent producer, convinced that he would never be able to get along with partners or boards of directors. In 1926 he became a member of United Artists, a cooperative formed by independent producers to distribute their pictures. In 1939 he had a falling-out with Mary Pickford, one of the other members, and in 1941, after a bitter court fight, he sold his stock to the corporation at a reported loss of $500,000.

Mr. Goldwyn coddled actors, writers and directors, but when he felt they were not producing what he had expected of them, he heaped invective upon them. Ben Hecht, who worked on the script of "Wuthering Heights," compared Mr. Goldwyn's treatment of writers to "an irritated man shaking a slot machine."

Mr. Goldwyn always believed that the story was the thing that made good movies, and he spent lavishly on scripts by writers such as Moss Hart, Lillian Hellman and Robert E. Sherwood.

One of several great directors with whom Mr. Goldwyn did not get along was William Wyler, yet Mr. Wyler made some of his best films, including "The Best Years of Our Lives," under the Goldwyn banner.

Among the stars Mr. Goldwyn discovered were Tallulah Bankhead, Robert Montgomery and Gary Cooper.

Perhaps his worst talent-finding gaffe was his import of the Polish actress Anna Sten, upon whom he spent hundreds of thousands of dollars to build up as a star. Miss Sten, he felt, had an enigmatic beauty, or, as he put it, "the face of a spink." She failed to pass muster with the public, and he was forced to admit, "She's colossal in a small way."

But his judgment was much better with Miss Bankhead, whom he discovered in a beauty contest and starred in "Thirty a Week" long before she won Broadway fame, and with several of the "Goldwyn girls"—the leggy chorines, among them Betty Grable, he chose to decorate his musicals.

When Sam Goldwyn made a picture, he spent only his own money, and he kept his hand in every aspect of his productions.

"I am the producer," he said. "I do not shove the money under the door and go home." He spent freely, often on inefficient yes men. "I'll take 50 percent efficiency," he explained, "to get 100 percent loyalty."

When he wasn't haunting his sound stages, Mr. Goldwyn was out selling his pictures. "I've got a great slogan for the company," he once said—giving birth to another Goldwynism—"'Goldwyn pictures griddle the earth.'"

They surely girdled the earth. In a 20-year period, more than 200 million people paid to see Goldwyn productions. Many were nominated for Academy Awards, but Mr. Goldwyn did not receive an Oscar for best picture until 1947, when "The Best Years of Our Lives" won all the major awards. He was also presented, at that time, with the Irving Thalberg Memorial Award for his contributions to the film industry.

Mr. Goldwyn's films won dozens of Oscars in several categories—direction, writing, scenic design, music, color and acting. Five were winners for set design; he was the first producer to use realistic, three-dimensional sets rather than painted flats.

Mr. Goldwyn was divorced in 1915 from Blanche Lasky, by whom he had a daughter, Ruth. In 1925 he married the actress Frances Howard. They had a son, Samuel Jr., who is a movie producer.

Mrs. Goldwyn gradually became her husband's unofficial second-in-command at the studio. She also was splendid at keeping her husband's personal life in order. Whenever the couple went out, she paid for everything because Mr. Goldwyn never carried change or a wallet. He was an extremely careful dresser and believed that his conservatively tailored suits would look lumpy if he put anything in his pockets.

He came out of semiretirement in 1959 to make his last film, "Porgy and Bess." Although he was 78, he held his chesty six-foot-tall body erect, and his swinging walk seemed as always to be jet-propelled as he strode through his studio streets. His eyes, deep-set in his rather plain face, could still flash with anger, and his Polish-accented voice had lost little of its deep vibrancy.

In recent years, Mr. Goldwyn rented his studio to independent film and television productions, but he was not pleased with much of the product that emanated from there and other parts of Hollywood. He believed movies and TV had become trashy.

Summing up his career, Mr. Goldwyn said, "I was a rebel, a lone wolf. My pictures were my own. I financed them myself and answered solely to myself. My mistakes and my successes were my own. My one rule was to please myself, and if I did that, there was a good chance I would please others."

PAUL ROBESON

April 9, 1898–January 23, 1976

By Alden Whitman

Paul Robeson, the singer, actor and black activist, died yesterday at the age of 77 in Philadelphia. He had suffered a stroke on Dec. 28.

Mr. Robeson, who had been an all-America football star at Rutgers, where he also won letters in baseball, basketball and track and a Phi Beta Kappa key, was known internationally for decades as a concert artist, singing such songs as "Ol' Man River," and as a stage actor, perhaps best remembered in the role of Othello.

One of the most influential performers and political figures to emerge from black America, Mr. Robeson was under a cloud in his native land during the cold war as a political dissenter and an outspoken admirer of the Soviet Union. These circumstances combined to close many minds to his merits as a singer and actor.

However, in his 75th year, Mr. Robeson was the subject of high praise by Clayton Riley, the American cultural historian, who described him as "one of the nation's greatest men, an individual whose time on earth has been spent in the pursuit of justice for all human beings and toward the enlightenment of men and women the world over."

Although Mr. Robeson denied under oath that he was a Communist Party member, affiliation with it was generally imputed to him because he proudly performed for so many trade unions and organizations deemed "subversive" and for so many causes promoted in left-wing periodicals. This activity caused such agitation that one of his concerts in Peekskill, N.Y., was disrupted by vigilantes; professional concert halls were refused him, and commercial bookings grew scarce. His income dropped from $100,000 in 1947 to $6,000 in 1952.

Another result of Mr. Robeson's overt alliance between his art and his politics was the State Department's cancellation, in 1950, of his passport on the grounds that he had refused to sign the then-required non-Communist oath. He took the department to court, and in 1958, the Supreme Court ruled that passports could not be withheld because of applicants' "beliefs and association."

Mr. Robeson was given a passport. He toured Europe and Australia as a singer, and in 1959 he appeared as the Moor, one of his most celebrated stage roles, in "Othello" at Stratford-on-Avon.

On his 60th birthday, in 1958, celebrations were held in a number of countries. The same birthday was also an occasion for his first New York recital in 11 years, a sold-out house at Carnegie Hall.

"When Mr. Robeson made his appearance," Harold C. Schonberg wrote in The Times, "he was greeted with a long standing ovation," adding that the performer was "a burly, imposing figure with tremendous dignity."

In a concert in London later that year, he brought the house down with "Ol' Man River," the Oscar Hammerstein 2nd–Jerome Kern song with which Mr. Robeson had been identified since the late 1920's. Two other songs closely identified with Mr. Robeson were "Ballad for Americans" and "Joe Hill," a song about a union organizer executed for an alleged murder.

Standing 6 feet 3 inches tall and weighing 240 pounds in his prime, he was a man of commanding presence. He spoke slowly and deliberately. His bass baritone, in his best years, was vibrant and evocative.

Once asked why he did not live in the Soviet Union, which he visited frequently, he retorted, "Because my father was a slave, and my people died to build this country, and I am going to stay right here and have a part of it, just like you."

Born in Princeton, N.J., on April 9, 1898, Paul Robeson was the youngest child of the Rev. W. D. Robeson, a North Carolina plantation slave until he ran away in 1860. His mother, who died when Paul was nine, was a teacher.

A bright student, he won a scholarship to Rutgers in 1915, where he was the third black to attend the then-private college. He starred in football, baseball, basketball and track, winning a dozen varsity letters. Walter Camp, the college football arbiter who twice selected Mr. Robeson as an all-America, called him "the greatest defensive end that ever trod the gridiron."

After graduation in 1919 he received a degree from Columbia Law School but never practiced because Eslanda Cardozo Goode, a brilliant Columbia chemistry student whom he married in 1921, directed his career toward the theater and was his manager until her death in 1965.

She helped persuade him to take a role in "Simon the Cyrenian" at the Young Men's Christian Association in 1920. He repeated his performance at the Lafayette Theater in 1921, and the following year he appeared as Jim in "Taboo" at the Sam H. Harris Theater on Broadway. He joined the Provincetown Players, a Greenwich Village group that included Eugene O'Neill, in whose "All God's Chillun Got Wings" he starred as Jim Harris.

This led to his appearance as Brutus Jones in "The Emperor Jones." The critic George Jean Nathan described him as "one of the most thoroughly eloquent, impressive and convincing actors" he had ever come upon.

Mr. Robeson repeated his triumph in "The Emperor Jones" in London, returned to New York to play Crown in "Porgy" and went back to London in 1928 to play Joe in "Show Boat."

He lived mostly abroad until 1939, primarily in London. One of his spectacular successes there came in 1930, when he played the lead in "Othello," appearing with Peggy Ashcroft, Sybil Thorndike and Maurice Brown.

Afterward he toured the chief European cities as a recitalist, and played in "Plant in the Sun," "The Hairy Ape," "Toussaint L'Ouverture," "Stevedore," "Black Boy" and "John Henry." He also ventured seriously into the movies, starring in "Sanders of the River," "King Solomon's Mines," "Big Fella," "Proud Valley," "The Emperor Jones" and "Show Boat." In all, he made 11 pictures.

In 1934, passing through Germany on his first of many visits to the Soviet Union, he was the object of racial epithets from Hitler's storm troopers, and he was angered. Arriving in Moscow, where he was feted, he was impressed, he said, by the absence of racial prejudice among Soviet citizens. Later, he often publicly expressed "my belief in the principles of scientific Socialism, my deep conviction that for all mankind a Socialist society represents an advance to a higher stage of life."

In the late 1930's Mr. Robeson went to Spain to sing for the Republican troops and for members of the International Brigades who were battling the Franco revolt, which was backed by Hitler and Mussolini.

The climate of opinion in the United States was fairly congenial to Mr. Robeson in those years, and reviews became ecstatic when, on Oct. 19, 1943, he became the first black to play the role of Othello with a white supporting cast (Jose Ferrer and Uta Hagen) on Broadway in the Theater Guild production.

Meanwhile, Mr. Robeson stepped up his political activity. He became a founder and chairman of the Progressive Party, which nominated former Vice President Henry A. Wallace in the 1948 Presidential race.

Some of Mr. Robeson's troubles during the cold war were traceable to a remark he made at a World Peace Congress in Paris in 1949. "It is unthinkable," he declared, "that American Negroes will go to war on behalf of those who have oppressed us for generations against a country [the Soviet Union] which in one generation has raised our people to the full dignity of mankind."

His words were widely turned against him in the United States, and one consequence was an attack by veterans' groups and right-wing extremists on crowds arriving for an outdoor concert near Peekskill, N.Y., in August, 1949. The concert was canceled.

Mr. Robeson, who is survived by his sister and a son, was questioned several times by Congressional committees, starting in 1948. He was usually asked if he were a member of the Communist Party, a query he uniformly declined to answer under his Fifth Amendment rights.

CHARLIE CHAPLIN

April 16, 1889–December 25, 1977

By Bosley Crowther

Charlie Chaplin, the poignant little tramp with the cane and comic walk who almost single-handedly elevated the novelty entertainment medium of motion pictures into art, died yesterday at his home in Switzerland. He was 88 years old.

His wife, Oona, and seven of their children were at his bedside. A daughter, the actress Geraldine Chaplin, was in Madrid but left to join her family at the Chaplin's villa at Corsiersur-Vevey, a village near Lake of Geneva.

Sir Charles—he was knighted by Queen Elizabeth in 1975—had been in failing health for years. He was confined to a wheelchair and his speech, hearing and sight were impaired.

No motion picture actor so captured and enthralled the world as did Charles Spencer Chaplin, a London ragamuffin who became an immortal artist for his humanization of man's tragicomic conflicts with fate. In more than 80 movies from 1914 to 1967, he portrayed or elaborated (he was a writer and director as well as an actor) the theme of the little fellow capriciously knocked about by life, but not so battered that he did not pick himself up in the hope that the next encounter would turn out better.

His Everyman was the Little Tramp, part clown, part social outcast, part philosopher. He might stumble, but he always maintained his dignity and self-respect.

The essence of Chaplin's humor was satire, sometimes subtle as in "The Kid" and "The Gold Rush," sometimes acerbic as in "The Great Dictator" and "Monsieur Verdoux."

In ridiculing man's follies, Chaplin displayed a basic affection for the human race. He was simultaneously serious and funny, and this blend of attitudes elevated his comedy beyond film slapstick into the realm of artistry.

A serious theme in "The Gold Rush," for example, is man's inhumanity to man. The comedy arises from the hero's adversity, illustrated by his boiling and eating his shoe with the éclat of a gourmet. The element of contrast exemplified by that scene was at the root of Chaplin's comedy. This sense of comedy tickled the fancy of millions of Americans for half a century.

The Little Tramp, the comedy character that lifted its creator to enduring fame, was neatly accoutered in baggy trousers, outsize shoes, an undersize derby, a frayed short cutaway and a bamboo cane. A black mustache completed the costume, which became Chaplin's symbol for a lifetime.

Chaplin studied the structure of comedy meticulously.

"All my pictures are built around the idea of getting me into trouble and so giving me the chance to be desperately serious in my attempt to appear as a normal little gentleman," he wrote. "That is why, no matter how desperate the predicament is, I am always very much in earnest about clutching my cane, straightening my derby hat, and fixing my tie, even though I have just landed on my head."

In his early days in Hollywood Chaplin had little to say about how his movies were made. Later, he achieved artistic control, and took infinite pains in perfecting each scene, often shooting hundreds of feet of film for a few minutes of final screen action.

Entering motion pictures before the advent of feature-length films and of course sound, Chaplin had to rely on situational comedy and pantomime, the use of gestures and facial expressions to convey emotion. This form of body language permitted the actor to be readily understood by people everywhere.

After only two years on the screen, Theodore Huff wrote in "The Language of Cinema," Chaplin "was unquestionably the top figure in the motion picture industry." Audience demand for his pictures was phenomenal. His popularity at the box office won him a $1 million contract—a stupendous sum in 1917—for eight pictures over 18 months.

Few men in this century in any field attained his stature with the public. "Charlie," "Charlot"—his first name in any language bespoke affection amounting to idolatry.

One explanation for Chaplin's extraordinary success was that after 1917 his command of pictures was complete. He was the author, star, producer, director and chief cutter.

Born April 16, 1889, in south London, Charles Spencer Chaplin was the son of a vaudevillian and a music hall soubrette whose stage name was Lily Harley.

The elder Chaplin was a heavy drinker. The couple separated shortly after the son was born, and Mrs. Chaplin's voice lost its quality. "It was owing to her vocal condition," the son recalled, "that at the age of five I made my first appearance on the stage."

"I remember standing in the wings when mother's voice cracked and went into a whisper," he continued. The audience began to laugh, and his mother was obliged to walk off the stage. When she came into the wings, "the stage manager said something about letting me go on in her place."

The lad was greeted by cheers and applause.

The family passed through a series of workhouses, Mrs. Chaplin was committed briefly as insane, and there followed for Charles months of catch-as-catch-can existence.

"I (was) newsvender, printer, toymaker, doctor's boy, etc., but during these occupational digressions, I never lost sight of my ultimate aim to become an actor," Chaplin recalled. "So, between jobs I would polish my shoes, brush my clothes, put on a clean collar and make periodic calls at a theatrical agency."

At 12 he received a small stage part, then toured the provinces and performed in London in "Sherlock Holmes." Later came a run in "Casey's Court Circus," in which he impersonated a patent-medicine faker.

In this engagement Chaplin decided to become a comedian. He also learned the unimportance of the spoken word. "Once, while playing in the Channel Islands," Mr. Huff wrote, "he found that his jokes were not getting over because the natives knew little English. He resorted to pantomime and got the desired laughs."

His success landed him a job with the Fred Karno Company, and in 1913 Mack Sennett, then the producer of short film comedies, signed the actor for $150 a week. Chaplin made his debut in "Making a Living," a one-reeler that appeared in 1914. In those early Sennett comedies there was no scenario. "We get an idea, then follow the natural sequence of events until it leads up to a chase, which is the essence of our comedy," Sennett explained.

Chaplin changed that by adopting an identifiable character—the Little Tramp—which allowed the public to single him out from other comedians.

In his year with Sennett, Chaplin played in 35 films, including "Tillie's Punctured Romance," the screen's first feature-length comedy.

These films were shown around the world, and the renown they brought to Chaplin enabled him to shift to the Essanay Company, for which he made 14 films in 1915, including "The Tramp," his first generally recognized classic.

In the picture, Chaplin, a tramp, saves a farmer's daughter from a robber gang, for which he is rewarded with a job on the farm. Routing the gang again, he is shot in the leg and nursed by the daughter. The tramp's happiness is unbounded until the girl's sweetheart arrives. Realizing his fate, the tramp scribbles a farewell and departs.

In the fadeout, Chaplin's back is to the camera. He walks dejectedly down a long road. Then he pauses, shrugs his shoulders, flips his heels and continues jauntily toward the horizon.

Chaplin then went to the Mutual Company for $670,000 a year. He was 26, three years out of vaudeville and perhaps the world's highest-paid performer.

His dozen Mutual films were two-reelers and included "The Floorwalker," "The Fireman," "The Vagabond" and "Easy Street."

Chaplin then went to First National for $1 million for eight pictures. For the first time he was his own producer in his own studio. His work for First National included some of his greatest achievements—"A Dog's Life," "Shoulder Arms" and "The Kid."

During the preparation of "The Kid," Chaplin was embroiled in the first of several marital and extra-marital episodes that were to plague him. Good-looking and attractive to women, he was involved in a score or more of alliances, many with glamorous actresses, but these were usually discreetly handled. Not so with his first two marriages.

In 1918, when the actor was 29, he married 16-year-old Mildred Harris. They were divorced two years later. Four years afterward he married Lolita McMurry, also 16, whose stage name was Lita Grey. The union ended in 1927 after a sensational divorce case.

The actor's third wife was a chorus girl whose film name was Paulette Goddard. They met in 1931, when Miss Goddard was 20, and were married in 1936 and divorced in 1942.

Meantime, in 1941, the actor met Joan Berry, a 21-year-old aspiring actress known as Joan Barry. She later charged that he was the father of her daughter, and filed a paternity suit, in which blood tests demonstrated that Chaplin was not her child's father. Nonetheless, a jury found against him and he was ordered to support the infant.

In 1943, Chaplin, then 54, married 18-year-old Oona O'Neill, the daughter of the playwright Eugene O'Neill.

Chaplin's later films were made for United Artists, a company he founded in 1919 with Mary Pickford, Douglas Fairbanks Sr. and David Wark Griffith. Chaplin's initial picture for this concern was "A Woman of Paris," a comedy of manners that he produced and directed without starring in it.

Considered a milestone in screen history for its influence on movie style, it was based in part on the life of Peggy Hopkins Joyce, briefly Chaplin's mistress.

"The Gold Rush"—"the picture I want to be remembered by," Chaplin said—came out in 1925 and it once again confirmed his hold on the public.

Starting work on "City Lights" in 1928, the actor faced a crisis in the advent of talkies. He feared that spoken dialogue would impair the character of the Tramp. "City Lights" was produced as a silent picture with a musical score.

The tragicomic story of the blind flower girl, played by Virginia Cherrill, was an enormous triumph when it opened in 1931. Many critics rank "City Lights" as among Chaplin's greatest creations.

He then embarked upon "Modern Times," a satire on mass production, which at the time gave the actor a reputation as a radical.

With "The Great Dictator," a ferocious ridicule of Hitler and Mussolini, Chaplin joined the sound-picture ranks.

Despite "The Great Dictator," the nineteen-forties were difficult years for Chaplin. Representative John E. Rankin, a right-wing legislator from Mississippi, demanded his deportation, asserting that Chaplin's life "is detrimental to the moral fabric of America."

In 1952, when the actor, a British subject, was sailing to Britain on vacation, the Attorney General announced that he could not re-enter the country unless he could prove his "moral worth." Chaplin spent the rest of his life in Europe.

In 1972, Chaplin visited the United States to receive a special Oscar from the Motion Picture Academy. By this time the actor could do little more than bow and smile in response to expressions of affection for him and his art.

JOHN WAYNE

May 26, 1907–June 11, 1979

LOS ANGELES—John Wayne, the veteran Hollywood actor, died today at 5:23 P.M., Pacific daylight time, at U.C.L.A. Medical Center, a hospital spokesman said. The cause of death was given as complications from cancer.

Mr. Wayne, 72 years old, had been hospitalized since May 2, when he was admitted for his second cancer operation of the year. His lower intestine was partly removed in the operation.—*The Associated Press*

By Richard F. Shepard

In more than 200 films made over 50 years, John Wayne saddled up to become the greatest figure of one of America's greatest native art forms, the western.

The movies he starred in rode the range from out-of-the-money sagebrush quickies to such classics as "Stagecoach" and "Red River." He won an Oscar as best actor for another western, "True Grit," in 1969. Yet some of the best films he made told stories far from the wilds of the West, such as "The Quiet Man" and "The Long Voyage Home."

In the last decades of his career, Mr. Wayne became something of an American folk figure, hero to some, villain to others, for his outspoken views. He was politi-

STAGE AND SCREEN

cally a conservative and, although he scorned politics as a way of life for himself, he enthusiastically supported Richard M. Nixon, Barry Goldwater, Spiro T. Agnew, Ronald Reagan and others who, he felt, fought for his concept of Americanism and anti-Communism.

But it was for millions of moviegoers who saw him only on the big screen that John Wayne really existed. He had not created the western with its clear-cut conflict between good and bad, right and wrong, but it was impossible to mention the word "western" without thinking of "the Duke," as he was called.

By the early 1960's, 161 of his films had grossed $350 million, and he had been paid as much as $666,000 to make a movie—although in his early days on screen, his salary ran to no more than two or three figures a week.

It was rarely a simple matter to find a unanimous opinion on Mr. Wayne, whether it had to do with his acting or his politics. Film critics were lavish in praise of him in some roles and shrugged wearily as they candled his less notable efforts.

He was co-director and star of "The Green Berets," a 1968 film that supported the United States action in Vietnam. The movie was assailed by many critics on all grounds, political and esthetic, but the public apparently did not mind; in only six months, it had earned $1 million above its production cost of $7 million.

Mr. Wayne was a symbolic male figure, a man of impregnable virility and the embodiment of simplistic, laconic virtues, packaged in a well-built 6-foot-4-inch, 225-pound frame.

He had a handsome and hearty face, with crin-

kles around eyes that were too lidded to express much emotion but gave the impression of a man of action, an outdoor man who chafed at a settled life. When he shambled into view, one could sense the arrival of coiled vigor awaiting only provocation to be sprung. This screen presence emerged particularly under the ministrations of John Ford and Howard Hawks, the directors.

Appearances were not altogether deceiving. Mr. Wayne loved adventure and the outdoors. He did believe that things were either right or wrong, and he came back against great odds. In 1964, a malignant tumor was removed from his chest and left lung, and within several months he was on location making another movie.

Mr. Wayne made his last public appearance at the Academy Awards ceremony in April, where he drew an emotional standing ovation when he strode out on stage to present the Oscar for best picture.

He was recently presented with a special Congressional medal of the kind given to such national figures as the Wright Brothers.

Between his first starring role in "The Big Trail" in 1930, and his last one, as a celebrated gunslinger dying of cancer in "The Shootist," in 1976, Mr. Wayne changed little in style or personality. He had consciously adapted his posture for that first movie and retained it.

"When I started, I knew I was no actor and I went to work on this Wayne thing," he once recalled. "It was as deliberate a projection as you'll ever see. I figured I needed a gimmick, so I dreamed up the drawl, the squint and a way of moving meant to suggest that I wasn't looking for trouble but would just as soon throw a bottle at your head as not. I practiced in front of a mirror."

His entrance into films was as fortuitous as any made by a young fellow who grew up near the Hollywood badlands. But the Wayne saga actually started much farther east, in the small town of Winterset, Iowa, where he was born May 26, 1907, and was named Marion Michael Morrison.

His father, Clyde L. Morrison, a druggist, moved the family to Southern California when Marion was 6. There the young boy saw movies being made at the Triangle Studios, where they often shot outdoor scenes. Along the way he acquired the nickname "Duke." It came from an Airedale terrier he had had, he used to say as he debunked press releases that tried to explain the moniker as some sort of rubbed-off nobility.

He worked as truck driver, fruit picker, soda jerk and ice hauler and was an honor student and a member of an outstanding high school football team. He got a job, as other football players did, as a scenery mover at Fox Films. John Ford was attracted to the youth's hulking physique and made him a "fourth-assistant prop boy." When Mr. Ford was making a submarine film on location in the channel off Catalina Island, the regular stuntmen refused to go into the water because of rough seas. Mr. Ford asked the prop boy if he would. He did, immediately, and became part of the Ford team.

In an early film, Republic Pictures gave him a screen credit as Michael Burn and, in another, as Duke Morrison. When Raoul Walsh cast him as the star of "The Big Trail," his expensive $2 million western, the director thought that Marion was too sissified a name for a western hero, and "John Wayne" was born.

That movie was a flop, and between 1933 and 1939 Mr. Wayne made more than 40 Grade B or C westerns—short-order horse operas. Then, like a good guy riding in to relieve the oppressed, his old benefactor, Mr. Ford, came along to cast Mr. Wayne as the Ringo Kid in the Oscar-winning "Stagecoach," the 1939 movie that took westerns from the Saturday afternoon for-kids-only category and attracted the attention of more intellectual film critics. It was a turning point also for Mr. Wayne.

His next major role found him in a milieu far from the cactus sets. He played a simple Swedish lad in the crew of a freighter in "The Long Voyage Home," Mr. Ford's 1940 film based on the sea plays of Eugene O'Neill.

Later came "Fort Apache" and "She Wore a Yellow Ribbon." In 1952, Mr. Wayne showed off to best effect as the young Irish-American returned to Ireland in Mr. Ford's "The Quiet Man."

Mr. Wayne invested $1.2 million in 1960 to make "The Alamo," about the fight between the Americans—the good guys—and the Mexicans—the bad guys. He played Davy Crockett. He was bitterly disappointed when the film failed.

In 1969, however, he was almost universally hailed when he played Rooster Cogburn, a disreputable one-eyed, drunken, fat old Federal Marshal, in "True Grit." The Academy of Motion Picture Arts and Sciences awarded him an Oscar for his portrayal.

His anti-Communist sentiments led Mr. Wayne to help found the Motion Picture Alliance for the Preservation of American Ideals in 1944, and he was its president for two terms.

The organization, which eventually disbanded, was accused of giving the names of suspected Communists in the film industry to the House Committee on Un-American Activities, although Mr. Wayne said later that he had never been party to any such thing.

Once interviewed about civil rights, he said: "I believe in white supremacy until the blacks are educated to the point of responsibility. I don't believe in giving authority and positions of leadership and judgment to irresponsible people."

Mr. Wayne lived with his third wife, Pilar Pallette Wayne, in an 11-room, seven-bathroom, $175,000 house in Newport Beach, Calif., where he had a 135-foot yacht. His first two marriages, to Josephine Saenz and Esperanzo Bauer, ended in divorces. He had seven children from his marriages, and more than 15 grandchildren.

ALFRED HITCHCOCK

August 13, 1899–April 29, 1980

By Peter B. Flint

Alfred Hitchcock, whose mastery of suspense and of directing technique made him one of the most popular and celebrated of filmmakers, died yesterday at the age of 80 at his home in Los Angeles. Mr. Hitchcock, ailing with arthritis and kidney failures, had been in declining health for a year.

In a characteristically incisive remark, Mr. Hitchcock once summed up his approach to moviemaking: "Some films are slices of life, mine are slices of cake." The director of scores of psychological thrillers for more than half a century was the master manipulator of menace and the macabre, and the leading specialist in suspense and shock.

His best movies were meticulously orchestrated nightmares of peril and pursuit relieved by unexpected comic ironies, absurdities and anomalies. Films made by the portly, cherubic director invariably progressed from deceptively commonplace trifles of life to shattering revelations, and with elegant style and structure he pervaded mundane events and scenes with a haunting mood of mounting anxiety.

In delicately balancing the commonplace and the bizarre, he was the most noted juggler of emotions in the longest major directorial career in film history. His distinctive style was vigorously visual, always stressing imagery over dialogue and often using silence to increase apprehension. Among his most stunning montages were a harrowing attack by a bullet-firing crop-dusting plane on Cary Grant at a deserted crossroad amid barren cornfields in "North by Northwest," a brutal shower-slaying in "Psycho" and an avian assault on a sleepy village in "The Birds."

Hitch, as he was called by his friends and colleagues, doubtlessly frightened more audiences than any other director in movie history, and he was one of the few filmmakers who was a household name for many decades.

A trademark was the fleeting, nonspeaking appearances he made in his films.

As the leading British director of the 30's, he set the standard for international intrigue and espionage with such classic thrillers as "The 39 Steps" and "The Lady Vanishes."

After moving to Hollywood in 1939, he made such taut melodramas as "Rebecca," "Foreign Correspondent," "Suspicion," "Shadow of a Doubt," "Lifeboat," "Spellbound," "Notorious," "Strangers on a Train," "Rear Window" and "Vertigo." His later shockers mirrored his increasingly pessimistic view of most people and mounting evil in the world.

Reflecting his motif of a world in disorder, Mr. Hitchcock placed endangered protagonists in settings epitomizing order—citadels of civilization, the Statue of Liberty, United Nations headquarters, Mount Rushmore and Britain's Parliament.

Reviewers acclaimed his virtuosity in creating a rhythm of anticipation with understated, sinister overtones, innovative pictorial nuance and montage, brilliant use of parallel editing of simultaneous action, menacingly oblique camera angles and revealing cross-cutting of objective shots with subjective views of a scene from an actor's perspective.

Detractors accused Mr. Hitchcock of relying on slick tricks, illogical story lines and wild coincidences. Spinning his sophisticated yarns to create maximum tension, Mr. Hitchcock was not concerned with plausibility, which he regarded as no more important than the "MacGuffin," the term he used for the device about which his suspense revolved, whether it be the secret or documents or whatever the villains were seeking or trying to protect.

A favorite Hitchcock theme centered on "the wrong man" who was unjustly accused of a crime and hunted by both the villains and the police because of mistaken identity or incriminating information he inadvertently acquired.

His films were spiced with unusual peripheral characters and often shot on location in exotic settings. His heroines were usually "cool" classic beauties who "don't drip sex," he said. "You discover sex in them."

In Mr. Hitchcock's world, people may or may not be what they appear to be, but the audience sees and knows more than the protagonists. He invariably alerted viewers to imminent dangers such as a ticking time bomb, withholding the knowledge from imperiled characters, and identified the villains early on, eschewing the "whodunit" as "a sort of intellectual puzzle" that is "void of emotion."

His films had such consistent mass appeal that reviewers were sometimes condescending to them. But in the '50s, a group of young French filmmakers and critics associated with the film journal Cahiers du Cinema newly extolled his achievements.

François Truffaut, a leading director of France's

New Wave, lauded Mr. Hitchcock as a leading "artist of anxiety" with a "purely visual" style.

"Hitchcock is almost unique in being able to film directly, that is, without resorting to explanatory dialogue, such intimate emotions as suspicion, jealousy, desire and envy," he commented.

Detractors faulted his films for lacking substance, for moral opportunism and for being cynical, superficial and glib in their views of human nature. Admirers vehemently disagreed, terming him a compulsive storyteller who showed human nature as it is and not as it should be, and describing the psychological probing of much of his later work as profound in its foresight of an irrational and disordered world.

Resembling a pixieish gargoyle, the rotund director had a pudgy, basset-hound face with heavy jowls and pouting lips. He was a witty raconteur who became somewhat of a national institution in shaping a public image as a genially ghoulish cynic noted for barbed pronouncements about life and commercials in two popular weekly television series, "Alfred Hitchcock Presents" and the "Alfred Hitchcock Hour," which he supervised and was host of in the late 50's and early 60's.

Regarded as a shrewd businessmen, he became a multimillionaire and gained more control over his productions than any Hollywood director.

Mr. Hitchcock, who also produced many of his later films, was showered with laurels. He won the 1967 Irving G. Thalberg Memorial Award of the Academy of Motion Picture Arts and Sciences, and "Rebecca," his first American movie, won an Oscar as the best film of 1940. He was nominated for directorial Oscars five times, for "Rebecca," "Lifeboat," in 1944, "Spellbound" in 1945, "Rear Window" in 1954 and "Psycho" in 1960.

Alfred Joseph Hitchcock was born in London on Aug. 13, 1899, to a poultry dealer, greengrocer and fruit importer and the former Emma Whelan. He graduated from St. Ignatius College, a Jesuit school in London, where he studied engineering, and took art courses at the University of London.

In childhood incidents, he developed a lifelong fear of the police and punishment, major influences on his movies. At about the age of five, he was sent by his father with a note to a local police chief, who locked him in a cell for five minutes. In releasing him, the officer said, "That's what we do to naughty boys." Mr. Hitchcock later said he could never forget "the sound and the solidity of that closing cell door and the bolt."

Mr. Hitchcock attributed his fear of punishment to ritual beatings of the hands with a hard rubber strop, administered for infractions at St. Ignatius, that he recalled "was like going to the gallows."

In his teens, he was determined to break into filmmaking, and won a job in 1920 writing and illustrating title cards for silent pictures. He rose quickly, to scriptwriter, art director and assistant director.

By 1925, Mr. Hitchcock had become a director, making a melodrama called "The Pleasure Garden" on a shoestring budget in Munich, Germany. He began shaping his genre with "The Lodger," about Jack the Ripper. Early influences, he said, were German Expressionistic and American films.

In 1926, he married Alma Reville, his assistant, who collaborated on many of his movies as a writer, adviser and general assistant. Their daughter, Patricia, acted in a number of his movies and television thrillers.

The pictorial and technical innovations of Mr. Hitchcock's early melodramas garnered him increasing praise. In 1929, he directed "Blackmail," Britain's first widely successful talking feature. In the 30's, he won international acclaim for his pacesetting spy thrillers, including "The Man Who Knew Too Much"; "The 39 Steps"; "Secret Agent"; "Sabotage," called "The Woman Alone" in the United States; and "The Lady Vanishes."

David O. Selznick lured Mr. Hitchcock to Hollywood. In his early years there, he created a stir when he quipped that "all actors are children" and "should be treated like cattle." He later showed particular disdain for Method school actors. But Mr. Hitchcock never raised his voice on a set. A number of stars later described him as a vividly persuasive man who knew exactly what he wanted in a picture—and got it.

The director had a measured, courtly manner. He was a gourmet and wine connoisseur, and, with a 5-foot-8-inch frame, his weight once soared to 290 pounds, though he tried to keep it down by dieting to about 220 pounds. He avoided exercise and fiction, and voraciously read contemporary biographies, travel books and true-crime accounts. Mr. Hitchcock was a noted practical joker whose favorite prank was telling a tantalizing story in a loud voice to a companion in an elevator, perfectly timing his exit just before the punch line and then bowing politely to the intrigued but frustrated passengers.

ORSON WELLES

May 6, 1915–October 10, 1985

Orson Welles, the Hollywood "boy wonder" who created the film classic "Citizen Kane," scared tens of thousands of Americans with a realistic radio report of a Martian invasion of New Jersey, and changed the face of film and theater with his daring new ideas, died yesterday in Los Angeles, apparently of a heart attack. He was 70 years old and lived in Las Vegas, Nev.

Despite the feeling of many that his career was one of largely unfulfilled promise, Welles eventually won the respect of his colleagues. He received the Lifetime Achievement Award of the American Film Institute in 1975, and the Directors Guild of America gave him its highest honor, the D. W. Griffith Award.

His unorthodox casting and staging for the theater gave new meaning to the classics and to contemporary works. As the "Wonder Boy" of Broadway in the 1930's, he set the stage on its ear with a "Julius Caesar" set in Fascist Italy, an all-black "Macbeth" and his presentation of Marc Blitzstein's "Cradle Will Rock." His Mercury Theater of the Air set new standards for radio drama, and in one performance panicked thousands across the nation.

In film, his innovations in deep-focus technology and his use of long takes without close-ups created a new vocabulary for the cinema.

By age 24, he was already being described as a has-been. But at that very moment Welles was creating "Citizen Kane," generally considered one of the best movies ever made. His second film, "The Magnificent Ambersons," is also regarded as a classic.

For his failure to realize his dreams, Welles blamed his critics and the financiers of Hollywood. Others blamed what they described as his erratic, egotistical, self-indulgent and self-destructive temperament. But in the end, few denied his genius.

He was a Falstaffian figure, 6 feet 2 inches tall, weighing well over 200 pounds, with a huge appetite for good food and drink. He was by turns loud, brash, amusing and insufferable.

George Orson Welles was born in Kenosha, Wis., on May 6, 1915, the son of Richard Head Welles, an inventor and manufacturer, and the former Beatrice Ives. His mother was dedicated to the theater, and Welles said he made his debut at two as the child of "Madame Butterfly" in an opera performance.

According to "Orson Welles," an authorized biography by Barbara Leaming, Welles's genius was discovered when he was only 18 months old by his doctor, who, pronouncing the child a prodigy, began to furnish him with a violin, painting supplies, a magic kit, theatrical makeup kits and a conductor's baton.

His parents were divorced; Mrs. Welles died when he was 6. At 10, he entered the Todd School in Woodstock, Ill. His five years there were his only formal education.

Under the guidance of Roger Hill, the headmaster, young Orson steeped himself in student theater, staging and acting in a series of Shakespeare productions.

Shortly after his graduation, he sailed for Ireland. There, smoking a cigar to disguise the fact that he was only 16, he convinced the Gate Theater in Dublin that he was a Theater Guild actor on a holiday. He went on as the Duke in "Jew Suss" and even achieved a role at the eminent Abbey Theater.

Through Thornton Wilder and Alexander Woollcott, Welles was introduced to Katharine Cornell. When she opened "Romeo and Juliet" on Broadway in 1934, Welles, then 19, played Tybalt.

Welles's acting was a subject of controversy. Critics accused him of hamming and hogging the limelight, but many found his presence electrifying. "He has the manner of a giant with the look of a child," said Jean Cocteau, "a lazy activeness, a mad wisdom, a solitude encompassing the world."

Early in his Broadway career, Welles picked up extra income as a radio actor. He became familiar to millions as the sepulchral voice of "The Shadow," a wizard who turned virtually invisible to foil criminals.

To combat unemployment, the Roosevelt Administration had set up the Works Progress Administration, whose projects included the Federal Theater. With John Houseman as manager and Welles as director, it mounted striking productions, including a black "Macbeth," that excited the theater world.

The Federal Theater also stirred conservative wrath. The last straw came when a troupe featuring Howard da Silva and Will Geer prepared to stage "The Cradle Will Rock," a leftist musical by Marc Blitzstein, in 1937.

The authorities banned the production and locked the company out of the theater on opening night. Welles joined the cast and an audience of 2,000 in a march up Sixth Avenue to a rented theater, where the actors sang from seats in the auditorium.

Welles and Mr. Houseman went on to found the Mercury Theater, whose first production in 1937, a "Julius Caesar" in modern dress with overtones of Fascist Italy, was a hit. The Mercury also took in the banned production of "The Cradle Will Rock."

Chiefly to provide its actors with steady income, the company signed up with CBS Radio as the Mercury Theater of the Air. Its acting, dramatic tension and inventive use of sound effects set new highs in radio theater.

On Oct. 30, 1938, the Mercury Theater of the Air presented a dramatization of H. G. Wells's "War of the Worlds," in the form of news bulletins and field reporting from the scene of a supposed Martian invasion of New Jersey.

Many thousands of listeners tuned in after the introduction, heard the bulletins and panicked. Some armed themselves and prepared to fight the invaders; many more seized a few belongings and fled for the hills. Police switchboards around the country were flooded with calls.

Welles was already famous; a few weeks earlier, at age 23, he had appeared on the cover of Time magazine as the theater's "Wonder Boy." Now he was suddenly a household word, the target of indignation but also of amused admiration.

The Mercury Theater on Broadway was nevertheless a financial failure, and ended its theatrical existence in early 1939. The following season the company went to Hollywood under a contract with R.K.O. that granted Welles total artistic freedom.

The movie community was not entranced by the unconventional young interloper, and a Saturday Evening Post profile in 1940 reflected this view. "Orson was an old war horse in the infant prodigy line by the time he was 10," it said. "He had already seen eight years' service as a child genius. Some see the 24-year-old boy of today as a mere shadow of the 2-year-old man they used to know."

Welles was then directing "Citizen Kane," based on a scenario by Herman J. Mankiewicz, with himself in the title role. An impressionistic biography of a newspaper publisher strongly suggestive of William Randolph Hearst, it is now fabled for its use of flashback, deep-focus photography, striking camera angles and imaginative sound and cutting.

Kenneth Tynan has written, "Nobody who saw 'Citizen Kane' at an impressionable age will ever forget the experience; overnight, the American cinema had acquired an adult vocabulary, a dictionary instead of a phrase book for illiterates." Stanley Kauffmann called it "the best serious picture ever made in this country."

The making of "Kane" has been the subject of fierce polemics. Pauline Kael, in a New Yorker article in 1971, called it a "shallow masterpiece" and "comic-strip tragic," and accused Welles of trying to deny credit to Mr. Mankiewicz, Mr. Houseman and the cameraman, Gregg Toland. This has been rebutted in part by Mr. Houseman and by many Welles admirers.

It turned out that Miss Kael had not sought to question Welles. His defenders concede that he had thrown violent tantrums, leading to the departure of Mr. Houseman, but say he was frequently generous in praise of his collaborators.

More seriously, the Hearst newspaper chain was accused of seeking to block the showing of "Kane" and it long barred mention of Welles and his film in its publications.

"Kane" drew a mixed reception when it opened in 1941, and it was years before it turned into a profit maker. Welles won an Academy Award for writing the film, and was nominated for directing and acting awards.

Meanwhile, Welles was making Mercury's second movie, "The Magnificent Ambersons." An impatient R.K.O. did the final cutting of the film, asserting that Welles was unreliable on costs and completion dates. Welles retorted that his budgets were always low and that his shooting schedules were sometimes extraordinarily tight.

Welles returned to Broadway in 1941 to direct a dramatization of Richard Wright's "Native Son," produced and acted in the movie thriller "Journey into Fear" and starred as Mr. Rochester in the highly popular "Jane Eyre" in 1943.

He took part as a magician in a tour of the European Theater of Operations, in which his act was sawing Marlene Dietrich in half. After the war he adapted and staged a Cole Porter musical version of "Around the World in 80 Days" and produced, directed and co-starred with Rita Hayworth in "The Lady from Shanghai."

He and Miss Hayworth were married in 1943 and divorced in 1948. His first marriage, to Virginia Nicholson, also ended in divorce. In 1955, he married the Italian actress Paola Mori.

His acting talents enhanced such films—made by other directors—as "The Third Man," "Compulsion," "A Man for All Seasons" and "Catch-22."

He put together and starred in "Othello" and "Macbeth." The latter film, shot in three weeks, has been violently criticized. Beginning in 1955, he filmed the not yet completed "Don Quixote." He also wrote, directed and acted in "The Trial," based on the Kafka novel.

In 1970, he began a major project, "The Other Side of the Wind," which remains unfinished. His last directorial effort to be released was "The Immortal Story" in 1968; he also performed in it.

In 1958, Welles returned briefly to Hollywood to act with Charlton Heston in "Touch of Evil." Welles was also enlisted as director. Some admirers consider it one of his best films.

He refused to appear on Broadway after an unfortunate appearance in "King Lear," during which, having broken an ankle, he acted in a wheelchair. He vowed that he would never return to the New York stage while Walter Kerr was still a critic there. Writing for The New York Herald Tribune, Mr. Kerr had described Welles as "an international joke."

Welles's film "Falstaff" had been hailed in Europe under the title "Chimes at Midnight." When it appeared here in 1967, some critics panned it, one saying he made Falstaff "a sort of Jackie Gleason."

More recently, the Times's Vincent Canby wrote

that the picture "may be the greatest Shakespearean film ever made."

Welles, who is survived by his wife and three children, inspired harsh criticism. Yet there were no dissenters when, at the dedication of a Theater Hall of Fame in New York in 1972, his name was among the first to be chosen.

JAMES CAGNEY

July 17, 1899–March 30, 1986

By Peter B. Flint

James Cagney, the cocky and pugnacious film star who set the standard for gangster roles in "The Public Enemy" and won an Academy Award for his portrayal of George M. Cohan in "Yankee Doodle Dandy," died yesterday at his Dutchess County farm in upstate New York. He was 86 years old.

Mr. Cagney had an explosive energy and a two-fisted vitality that made him one of the great film personalities of Hollywood's golden age.

An actor who could evoke pathos or humor, he invested scores of roles with a hungry intensity, punctuated by breathless slang, curling lips and spontaneous humor.

A former vaudevillian and, in his youth, a formidable street fighter, the 5-foot-8 1/2-inch, chunky, red-haired actor intuitively choreographed his motions with a body language that projected the image of an eager, bouncy terrier. His walk was jaunty and his manner defiant.

But along with his belligerence he displayed a comic zest in inventive, sometimes outrageous actions. He could play a hoofer as adeptly as a gangster, and whether brutish or impish, he molded a character that personified an urban Irish-American of irrepressible spirit.

Mr. Cagney's streetwise mannerisms were a favored subject for caricature by stand-up comedians. But the actor's self-image was essentially that of a song-and-dance man.

He became the screen's top mobster in 1931 in "The Public Enemy," which included a bench-mark scene. Angered by his girlfriend's yearnings for respectability, he suddenly squashed half a grapefruit into Mae Clarke's incredulous face. Audiences were at first stunned, then intrigued by his brash performance, and he won instant stardom.

He followed "The Public Enemy" with a popular series of gangster movies interspersed with musicals, and, in 62 films over three decades, he went on to prove his versatility in a wide range of roles, later mostly within the law and including many military men. Some of the movies were inferior, but he was consistently praised by reviewers, who often described a movie as "all" or "essentially" Cagney.

His favorite role was in "Yankee Doodle Dandy" (1942), a patriotic wartime tribute to George M. Cohan, the showman, actor and songwriter. The performance won Mr. Cagney an Academy Award. Four years earlier, the New York Film Critics Circle voted him best actor for his portrayal of an eventually repentant killer in "Angels With Dirty Faces."

Will Rogers remarked of Mr. Cagney, "Every time I see him work, it looks to me like a bunch of firecrackers going off all at once."

The actor's "irresistible charm" was cited by the author Kenneth Tynan, who wrote in 1952 that "Cagney, even with a submachine gun hot in hand and corpses piling at his ankles, can still persuade many people that it was not his fault."

Exhibitors voted the actor one of the top 10 box-office moneymakers in the late 1930's and early 40's. After a series of disputes with Warner Brothers in which he charged he was overworked and underpaid, he became the studio's highest-paid star in 1938, earning $234,000. The next year he was listed as one of the 10 biggest-salaried Americans, with, the Treasury Department said, an income of $368,333.

Cagney the screen hoodlum contrasted sharply with Cagney the man. Offscreen, he was amiable, self-effacing and reflective, a confirmed family man. He did not smoke and rarely drank liquor.

He was much admired by colleagues, from directors to stagehands. In 1974, he became the first actor to receive the Life Achievement Award of the American Film Institute. Among his other honors was the Medal of Freedom, the Government's highest civilian award, in 1984.

The actor was self-taught and a keen observer who varied his roles with mannerisms and eccentricities of men he had known. He did all his own fight scenes, learned judo and occasionally used Yiddish humor he had learned in his youth. He was not impressed by adulation, believing, "One shouldn't aspire to stardom—one should aspire to doing the job well."

He dismissed Method acting with disdain. "You don't psych yourself up for these things, you do them," he said. "I'm acting for the audience, not for myself, and I do it as directly as I can." He made these observations in his 1976 autobiography, "Cagney by Cagney." He said he wrote it because of errors in unauthorized biographies.

His early characterizations included a dynamic vaudeville director speeding his cast from theater to theater and singing and tap-dancing with Ruby Keeler as Shanghai Lil in "Footlight Parade" (1933), the comic Bottom in Shakespeare's "Midsummer Night's Dream" (1935), a wharf-rat turned gang

leader in "Frisco Kid" (1935), a blinded boxer in "City for Conquest" (1940) and a naive dentist in "The Strawberry Blonde" (1941).

Other roles included a newsman turned counterspy in "Blood on the Sun" (1945), a psychopathic murderer with a mother fixation in "White Heat" (1949), a political demagogue in "A Lion Is in the Streets" (1953), a quirky Navy captain in "Mister Roberts" (1955) and Lon Chaney, the long-suffering silent-film star, in "Man of a Thousand Faces" (1957).

In 1961, Mr. Cagney starred in Billy Wilder's "One, Two, Three," a razor-sharp satire of East-West relations. Then, though at the top of his talent, he announced his retirement from the screen.

The actor was born and raised in Manhattan, but he was smitten with country living while on a childhood visit to the then pastoral Flatbush section of Brooklyn. Accordingly, he retired with his wife to their farm near Millbrook in Dutchess County, N.Y., and raised Morgan horses. In 1936 he had also bought a farm in Martha's Vineyard, Mass., where the Cagneys spent as much time as possible between films.

For two decades, the actor received many offers to return to the movies, including many from major directors, but he steadfastly refused them.

However, in 1981 Mr. Cagney ended his retirement. He had been increasingly troubled by several ailments, and his doctors advised him to be more active.

The director Milos Forman persuaded him to play a cameo role in the movie "Ragtime," based on the best-selling novel by E. L. Doctorow. The actor played a combative turn-of-the-century New York City police chief, prompting Vincent Canby of The Times to write that the Cagney "manner and the humor are undiminished." The actor, the critic said, "does a lot with very little."

James Francis Cagney Jr. was born July 17, 1899, on Manhattan's Lower East Side and grew up there and in the Yorkville section. His father was of Irish descent, a bartender and, briefly, a saloon owner who died in a flu epidemic in 1918. His mother, the former Carolyn Nelson, who was of Norwegian stock, was the mainstay of the family of five children.

Yorkville was then a street-brawling neighborhood, and Jimmy became a champion battler. As a catcher for a Yorkville amateur baseball team, he played a game in 1919 at Sing Sing prison, where five former schoolmates were serving terms. Eight years later, one was executed in the electric chair.

The Cagneys were poor, and from the age of 14 Jimmy worked simultaneously as an office boy for The New York Sun, stacking books at a library and doing odd jobs at the Lenox Hill Settlement House. On Sundays, he sold tickets for the Hudson River Day Line.

He graduated from Stuyvesant High School. Needing money, he soon drifted into vaudeville as a dancer at 19. He had to fake it at first, studying professionals, stealing their steps and modifying them to mold his own style. Unexpectedly, the street tough's first role was a "chorus girl" in a female-impersonation act.

In 1920 Mr. Cagney started in the chorus of a Broadway musical, "Pitter Patter," and graduated to specialty dancer. A co-player was Frances Willard (Willie) Vernon, whom he married in 1922. Two decades later they adopted two children, James Jr., who died in 1984, and Cathleen.

The actor toured in vaudeville with his wife and occasionally performed in short-lived Broadway shows. Through the 1920's, often out of work and money, he attended every cast call he could, occasionally being dismissed, he recalled, "because I had exaggerated my abilities."

But in 1930 he played a cowardly killer in a melodrama, "Penny Arcade," with Joan Blondell. Warner Brothers took the two to Hollywood to film the play as "Sinners' Holiday." They both won contracts and co-starred together in half a dozen movies.

After playing supporting roles in three movies, Mr. Cagney got the second lead in "The Public Enemy." However the keen-eyed director, William Wellman, insisted that the actor switch roles with the scheduled lead, Edward Woods, because Mr. Cagney could project what Mr. Wellman termed the "direct gutter quality" of the tougher of the two street chums who turn to crime. The picture was a commercial blockbuster that opened an era of realistic gangster movies.

Many of the actor's other early movies for Warner were made cheaply and quickly, within a few weeks, with the crews sometimes working 18 hours a day, 7 days a week.

"Talent was not nurtured, it was consumed," Mr. Cagney observed. "We did our job. If anyone was practicing art, I never saw it." Many of his directors, he wrote, were "pedestrian workmen, mechanics," some of whom "couldn't direct you to a cheap delicatessen."

But the young performers, led by Mr. Cagney, varied the formula scripts with clever improvisations. The actor's affectionate jabs on actresses' chins were gestures his father had used. In "The St. Louis Kid," weary of punching, he slammed antagonists with his forehead. In "Angels with Dirty Faces" he imitated a hoodlum neighbor in Yorkville, hitching up his trousers, twisting his neck, snapping his fingers and bringing his hands together in a soft smack.

Politically, the actor was a longtime New Deal Democrat who, in later years, became a conservative because of what he perceived as a moral confusion threatening Americans' values.

In 1940 he was accused of Communist sympathies by a Los Angeles politician before the House Committee on Un-American Activities. He appeared before the committee, which exonerated him. The issue arose from contributions he had made and his fund-raising activities, including providing food for striking California farm workers and an ambulance for the Loyalist side in the Spanish Civil War.

In retirement, Mr. Cagney read widely, wrote verse, painted, played classical guitar, satisfied his longtime zest for sailing and farming and limbered up by dancing a chorus or two to ragtime music.

"Absorption in things other than self," he observed, "is the secret of a happy life."

FRED ASTAIRE

May 10, 1899–June 22, 1987

By Richard F. Shepard

Fred Astaire, whose flashing feet and limber legs made him America's most popular dancer and set standards for motion picture musical comedies that have rarely been met and never exceeded, died of pneumonia yesterday at Century City Hospital in Los Angeles. He was 88 years old.

Mr. Astaire blithely danced his way into the heart of an America tormented by the Depression and edging toward World War II. His deceptively easy-looking light-footedness, warm smile, top hat, cane, charm and talent helped people to forget the world that nagged at them outside the movie house.

The Astaire legend, which spanned more than six performing decades on stage, screen and television, began before he was 10 years old when his mother paired him as a dancer with his sister, Adele, the partner with whom he first found success. Mr. Astaire starred in more than 30 film musicals between 1933 and 1968, 11 of which co-starred Ginger Rogers, his most durable dancing partner. The music they danced to was written by the cream of the popular-music world, including Cole Porter, Irving Berlin, Jerome Kern and George and Ira Gershwin. There were other famous dancers, but few could match the sophistication and inventiveness of Mr. Astaire in such films as "Flying Down to Rio," "The Gay Divorcee," "Top Hat," "Swing Time," "Follow the Fleet," "Blue Skies" and "Easter Parade. For all the lushness of his films, often in settings of splendor and champagne, Mr. Astaire projected a down-to-earth personality, that of a good-hearted fellow whose effortless steps, even at their most dazzling, matched his casual demeanor.

His dance numbers gave the illusion of being boundless, without regard for the laws of gravity or the limitations of a set. He danced atop a wedding cake ("You'll Never Get Rich"), on roller skates ("Shall We Dance?"), while hitting golf balls ("Carefree") and up walls and on the ceiling ("Royal Wedding"). He danced while airborne, aboard ships and in countless ballrooms.

He was popular and beloved, a thin, sandy-haired man who fretted and sweated off-camera and offstage to make his dance come across with a spontaneity few could equal. During a long career in which he went from vaudeville to Broadway to Hollywood to television—his 1957 special, "An Evening with Fred Astaire," won nine Emmy Awards—he never failed to delight audiences.

He was also a paragon among his professional peers. George Balanchine, the artistic director of the New York City Ballet, called him simply "the greatest dancer in the world."

Irving Berlin, in whose musical "Top Hat" Mr. Astaire wore the topper and tails that became the dancer's working hallmark, said: "He's not just a great dancer; he's a great singer of songs. He's as good as any of them—as good as Jolson or Crosby or Sinatra."

The Astaire seen in performance was a different Astaire from the one who lived out of the spotlight. He detested formal dress, and frequently told interviewers he regarded top hat and tails as no more than working dress.

The easygoing air that surrounded his own performance was developed by a dancer who was serious and painstaking about his work.

"Dancing is a sweat job," he once said. "You can't just sit down and do it, you have to get up on your feet. When you're experimenting you have to try so many things before you choose what you want, that you may go days getting nothing but exhaustion. This search for what you want is like tracking something that doesn't want to be tracked."

He added: "It takes time to get a dance right, to create something memorable. There must be a certain amount of polish to it. . . . I always try to get to know my routine so well that I don't have to think, 'What comes next?' Everything should fall right into line, and then I know I've got control of the bloody floor."

Mr. Astaire stopped dancing professionally about 1970, when he was already over 70 years old.

"I don't want to be a professional octogenarian," he said nearly a decade later, adding. "I don't want to look like a little old man dancing out there."

The Astaire dance story began not long after his birth, in Omaha on May 10, 1899. His name was

Frederick Austerlitz, the same as his father's, a brewery worker and an emigrant from Austria who during World War I Anglicized the family name to Astaire.

As a boy he toddled along with his mother to pick up his sister, who was 18 months older than Fred, at dancing school. She was outstanding as a dancer at the age of 6, and their mother, Ann Geilus Austerlitz, soon had Fred studying ballet there, too, at the age of 4.

A few years later, Mrs. Austerlitz took the children to New York, where they were enrolled in the performing-arts school run by Ned Wayburn, a pioneer in modern tap dancing. By the time Fred was seven, they had an act called Juvenile Artists Presenting an Electric Musical Toe-Dancing Novelty.

When Fred was 10, he and Adele, who would become one of the country's best-known dance teams, made their first professional appearance, in vaudeville, in a Keyport, N.J., theater. The teen-age brother and sister hoofed their way through the Middle West but climbed to the first rung of success in a Shubert Broadway revue, "Over the Top," in 1917. The Astaires were a hit, and they were immediately booked into "The Passing Show of 1918," in which a critic called Fred "an agile youth, and apparently boneless."

There followed more theater engagements and stardom in 1922 in "For Goodness' Sake," which had several songs by George and Ira Gershwin. In the New York production, the Astaires had sixth billing, but they stole the show.

The Astaires danced their way to Broadway triumphs in the 1920's, starring in 11 musicals, among them "Funny Face," "Lady, Be Good!" and "The

Band Wagon," their last big hit together in 1931. Adele married Lord Cavendish in 1932, retired from the stage and died in 1981.

Mr. Astaire found a new partner, Claire Luce, and in 1932 they starred in Cole Porter's "Gay Divorce," later filmed as "The Gay Divorcee," in which he introduced the song "Night and Day." In that year he took a screen test and was approved by David O. Selznick of RKO Pictures, who found that the dancer's charm was tremendous, even though he had "enormous ears and a bad chin line." His first movie was "Dancing Lady" (1933), with Joan Crawford and Clark Gable. This was followed by "Flying Down to Rio," in which he appeared with Ginger Rogers. The hit of the movie was their performance of Vincent Youmans's "Carioca," and they danced off with the laurels.

From that point on, they were the uncontestable stars of their films. Their string of successes at RKO included such hits as "Top Hat," "Roberta" and "Swing Time," ending in 1939 with "The Story of Vernon and Irene Castle."

From 1940 on, Mr. Astaire made movies with many dancing partners, among them Miss Hayworth ("You Were Never Lovelier"), Judy Garland and Ann Miller ("Easter Parade"), Cyd Charisse ("The Band Wagon" and "Silk Stockings") and Audrey Hepburn ("Funny Face").

Mr. Astaire's first wife, Phyllis Livingston Potter, died in 1954. In 1980, at 81, he married Robyn Smith, who survives him, as do three children.

In later years, his daily routine was little changed from the life he had always led: He woke up at 5 A.M. and breakfasted on a single boiled egg that kept his weight at a perpetual 134 pounds.

LUCILLE BALL

August 6, 1911–April 26, 1989

By Peter B. Flint

Lucille Ball, the irrepressible queen of television comedy for nearly a quarter-century, died yesterday at Cedars-Sinai Medical Center in Los Angeles a week after undergoing heart surgery there. She was 77 years old.

Miss Ball, noted for impeccable timing, deft pantomime and an endearing talent for making the outrageous believable, was a Hollywood legend: a contract player at RKO in the 1930's and 40's who later bought the studio with Desi Arnaz, her first husband.

The elastic-faced, husky-voiced comedian was a national institution from 1951 to 1974 in three series and many specials on television that centered on her

"Lucy" character. The first series, "I Love Lucy," was for six years the most successful comedy series on television. The series, on CBS, chronicled the life of Lucy and Ricky Ricardo, a Cuban band leader played by Mr. Arnaz, who was Miss Ball's husband on and off screen for nearly 20 years.

It was a major national event when, on Jan. 19, 1953, Lucy Ricardo gave birth to Little Ricky on the air the same night Lucille Ball gave birth to her second child, Desiderio Alberto Arnaz y de Acha 4th. The audience for the episode was estimated at 44 million, a record at the time, and CBS said 1 million viewers responded with congratulatory telephone calls, telegrams, letters or gifts. (Miss Ball's first child, Lucie Desiree Arnaz, was born July 17, 1951, three months before the show went on the air.)

The Ricardos were the best-known, best-loved couple in America, and the first "Lucy" series is still in syndication in more than 80 countries.

Miss Ball was an astute business executive. From 1962 to 1967, she headed Desilu Productions, one of the biggest and most successful television production companies. Also, starting in 1968, she and her second husband, Gary Morton, a former nightclub comic, headed Lucille Ball Productions.

She bought Mr. Arnaz's share of Desilu Productions in 1962 with a $3 million bank loan, and she sold the company to Gulf and Western Industries in 1967 for $17 million. Her share totaled $10 million.

Before entering television, Miss Ball appeared in more than 50 films, beginning in 1933 as an unbilled chorus girl in an Eddie Cantor musical farce, "Roman Scandals." Her other films included "Having Wonderful Time" (1938), "Room Service" (1938), "The Big Street" (1942), "Best Foot Forward" (1943), the title role in "Du Barry Was a Lady" (1943), "Without Love" (1945), "Sorrowful Jones" (1949) and "Fancy Pants" (1950).

In 1960 she also starred in a Broadway musical, "Wildcat."

In 1964 there was a Lucy Day at the New York World's Fair, and in 1971 she became the first woman to receive the International Radio and Television Society's Gold Medal. Her other awards included four Emmys, induction into the Television Hall of Fame and a citation for lifetime achievement from the Kennedy Center for the Performing Arts.

Lucille Desiree Ball was born on Aug. 6, 1911 in Celoron, outside Jamestown, N.Y. She was the daughter of the former Desiree Hunt, a pianist, and Henry Dunnell Ball, a telephone lineman, who died when she was three. As a girl she spent a great deal of time with her maternal grandparents.

She embarked on a show-business career at 15 by going to Manhattan and enrolling in John Murray Anderson's dramatic school. From the first, she was told she had no talent and should go home. She tried and failed to get into four Broadway chorus lines.

She worked variously as a waitress and as a soda jerk in a Broadway drugstore. She then became a hat model and modeled for commercial photographers. She won national attention as the Chesterfield Cigarette Girl in 1933. This got her to Hollywood as a Goldwyn chorus girl in "Roman Scandals."

Over two years, she played unbilled and bit roles in two dozen movies and made two-reel comedies with Leon Errol and the Three Stooges. She then spent seven years at RKO Radio Pictures, getting many leading roles in low-budget movies.

She was typed and mostly wasted in films, but several roles suggested her talents: a cynical young actress in "Stage Door" (1937), a temperamental movie star in "The Affairs of Annabel" (1938), a rejected lover in the 1939 melodrama "Five Came Back," a gold-digging stripper in "Dance, Girl, Dance" (1940), a handicapped egotist in "The Big Street" (1942) and a tough-talking secretary in "The Dark Corner" (1946).

"I never cared about the movies," she said later, "because they cast me wrong."

In radio, Miss Ball did regular stints on comedy-variety shows in the late 30's and 40's and, from 1947 to 1951, she played the precursor to Lucy: the hare-brained wife of a Midwestern banker in the CBS radio comedy "My Favorite Husband."

In 1950, she and Mr. Arnaz tried to sell the "I Love Lucy" television show to CBS. Network executives balked, saying the public would not accept the team of an American redhead and a Cuban bandleader with a heavy accent. To prove their case, the couple went on a nationwide vaudeville tour with a 20-minute act that included a "Cuban Pete–Sally Sweet" medley. They produced a 30-minute film pilot with $5,000 of their own money. The broadcast officials were won over.

"I Love Lucy" had its premiere on Oct. 15, 1951, and within a few months millions of Americans tuned in every Monday evening to watch the antics of the Ricardos and their best friends, Fred and Ethel Mertz (William Frawley and Vivian Vance).

"I Love Lucy" was one of the first shows to be filmed rather than performed live, making it possible to have a high-quality print of each episode for rebroadcast, compared with the poor quality of live-show kinescopes. The change eventually led to a shift of television production from New York to Hollywood. The series, the first to be filmed before an audience, won more than 200 awards, including five Emmys.

"The extraordinary discipline and intuitive understanding of farce gives 'I Love Lucy' its engaging lilt and lift," Jack Gould of The New York Times wrote.

Mr. Arnaz made a fortune for the couple by obtaining rerun rights. He later sold the rights to CBS, allowing the couple's production company, Desilu, to

buy a studio, the former RKO lot where Miss Ball's film career had languished and where they had met in 1940 while appearing together in "Too Many Girls."

Despite the continuing popularity of "I Love Lucy," the couple sought a less demanding schedule and ended the series in 1957 after making 179 episodes. The format persisted, however, for three more years through a series of around-the-world specials called "The Luci-Desi Comedy Hour." Their collaboration ended with their divorce in 1960. Mr. Arnaz died in 1986.

Two years after their divorce, Miss Ball revived "Lucy," playing a widow in "The Lucy Show" for 156 episodes until 1968, then did "Here's Lucy" for 144 episodes from 1968 to 1974.

In later movies, she co-starred with Bob Hope in two comedies, "The Facts of Life" (1961) and "Critic's Choice" (1963), and appeared with Henry Fonda in "Yours, Mine and Ours," a 1968 farce about a couple with nearly a score of children. In 1974 she starred in a film version of the stage hit "Mame."

Miss Ball also appeared in television specials and played a bag lady in a 1985 television movie, "Stone Pillow." John J. O'Connor of The Times said she was "as wily and irresistible as ever." In 1986, she returned to weekly television as a grandmother in a sitcom series called "Life with Lucy," but it failed to gain an audience.

Perhaps her style had become passe. Still, as CBS Chairman William S. Paley said in tribute, "Lucy's extraordinary ability to light up the screen and brighten our lives is a legacy that will last forever."

LAURENCE OLIVIER

May 22, 1907–July 11, 1989

By Mel Gussow

Laurence Olivier, hailed as one of the greatest classical stage actors of his time, died yesterday at his home near London. He was 82 years old. Lord Olivier died "peacefully in his sleep" in West Sussex, said his agent, Laurence Evans. His last professional appearance was a cameo in the 1988 movie "War Requiem," based on the oratorio by Benjamin Britten.

Lord Olivier was a performer of astonishing virtuosity and daring. If that were not enough to fill a career, he was also a movie star of the first magnitude, a film director whose Shakespearean adaptations are unmatched on the screen, a stage director with a breadth of accomplishment in both contemporary and classic plays, and the founder and first artistic director of the National Theater of Britain.

Knighted in 1947, raised to life peerage in 1970, he was, in art as well as title, a princely lord of his profession. Although his achievements and influences were many and varied, he was primarily an actor, and in a six-decade career onstage and in films, his performances—as Henry V, Hamlet, Richard III, Oedipus, Othello, Archie Rice in "The Entertainer," Heathcliff in "Wuthering Heights" and Maxim De Winter in "Rebecca"—won him artistic immortality.

He played kings, villains and occasionally clowns, the most challenging roles in the classical repertory and also some of the most popular romantic figures.

In the last decade of his life, he had still another career as a character actor in Hollywood movies.

Though he retired from the stage in 1974 because of illness, he never stopped working as a serious actor. Paralleling his renewed Hollywood renown, he acted on television—as Lord Marchmain in "Brideshead Revisited," as the barrister in John Mortimer's "Voyage Round My Father" and, for the second time in his career, as a thunderous "King Lear."

Lord Olivier, Sir John Gielgud and the late Sir Ralph Richardson were ranked as the three most eminent knights of the English theater. One could elevate Sir John for his poetic bearing and voice and Sir Ralph for his gift for eccentric characterizations, but neither they nor their contemporaries could match Olivier in matters of boldness and bravery.

Olivier was known for his feats of physical as well as emotional courage. In his film "Hamlet," he leaped from a 15-foot platform to catch the conscience of Claudius. In Strindberg's "Dance of Death," he fell to the floor with such conviction that audiences thought he had had a stroke.

In his 1982 autobiography, "Confessions of an Actor," he wrote that to be a successful actor one needed "an equal trinity of contributing qualities: talent, luck and stamina." In conversation, he stressed that of the three, stamina, "actual physical strength," was the most important of all.

Though in hindsight, Olivier was accepted as a natural actor, to a large extent he willed himself to his position of greatness. He learned how to use his voice and body in the interest of his art, perfecting accents, experimenting with makeup and challenging himself in his choice of roles.

But in films he came to be regarded as a quintessential romantic hero—his Heathcliff still makes hearts beat faster—even his looks were, to a certain extent, a tribute to the persuasiveness of his performance.

"He has never been a particularly handsome man," Sir Tyrone Guthrie wrote, "but he has always been able, on the stage, to suggest extreme good looks."

Not to be underestimated was his gift for comedy. As the critic James Agate wrote, Olivier was "a comedian by instinct and a tragedian by art." In 1945, he combined the sublime and the ridiculous on a single bill: after his famous eye-gouging performance in "Oedipus" he offered a cameo as Mr. Puff in Sheridan's "Critic," an evening commonly referred to as "Oedipuff."

Laurence Kerr Olivier was born in Dorking, Surrey, on May 22, 1907. His mother, Agnes Crookenden Olivier, died when he was 12. He and his brother and sister were brought up by their father, Gerard Olivier, an Anglican clergyman, schoolmaster and disciplinarian.

Laurence made his theatrical debut at nine, playing Brutus in "Julius Caesar" at All Saints Choir School in London. In the audience were Sybil Thorndike and her husband, Lewis Casson. As Dame Sybil recalled:

"He had been onstage for only five minutes when we turned to each other and said: 'But this is an actor—absolutely an actor. Born to it.'"

Enrolling at Elsie Fogerty's Central School of Speech Training and Dramatic Art, he received a lesson in acting that would last a lifetime. Miss Fogerty suggested that he had one physical weakness, and she pointed to a place under his brow and over his nose. Not only did that provoke the young man to lift his head and improve his bearing, but it also made him use false noses in performance.

As Noel Coward analyzed: "I cannot think of any other living actor who has used such quantities of spirit gum with such gleeful abandon."

Coward persuaded him to play the role of Victor Prynne in "Private Lives," and Jill Esmond, the first Mrs. Olivier, joined the company for the Broadway engagement. He and Gielgud alternated roles as Romeo and Mercutio in "Romeo and Juliet." Playing the apothecary was a young Alec Guinness, who admired Gielgud but had his doubts about Olivier: "He seemed a bit cheap—striving after theatrical effects."

The next year Guinness understudied Olivier as Hamlet at the Old Vic and was "outraged at the gymnastic leaps and falls required by his example." Looking back, he realized that Olivier's approach "laid the foundation for his becoming a truly great actor."

In a month at the Old Vic, Olivier played Hamlet, Sir Toby Belch and Henry V, followed by Macbeth and Iago to Ralph Richardson's Othello.

Carried away by the Freudian interpretation that Iago was in love with Othello, in rehearsal without warning he threw his arms around Richardson and kissed him on the lips. Richardson, recounted Lord Olivier, "coolly disengaged himself from my embrace," "and more in sorrow than in anger, murmured, 'There, there now, dear boy.'"

Olivier and Vivien Leigh first acted together in the film "Fire Over England" (1936). Each was married, Miss Leigh to Leigh Holman, Olivier to Miss Esmond. The romance became international gossip as both pursued careers as film stars. For each, 1939 was a life-changing year. Miss Leigh won an Academy Award as Scarlett O'Hara in "Gone With the Wind"; Olivier acted in "Wuthering Heights" and the next year in "Rebecca" and "Pride and Prejudice."

After Olivier's divorce in 1940, he and Miss Leigh began a marriage that endured for 20 years despite conflicts and Miss Leigh's eventual mental illness.

Next came "Pride and Prejudice" with Greer Garson and "That Hamilton Woman," as Lord Nelson opposite Miss Leigh's Lady Hamilton.

In 1944, Olivier returned to the Old Vic, as a co-director with Richardson and John Burrell, and among his first roles was Richard III. That turned out to be a banner season, with Olivier as an actor in "Richard III," as the director, producer and star of the film "Henry V," and as the director of the London production of Thornton Wilder's "Skin of Our Teeth."

His film "Henry V" began his trilogy of Shakespearean cinematic masterpieces, completed by "Hamlet" and "Richard III," all directed by and starring Olivier. "Hamlet" won two Academy Awards, as best film and for Olivier as best actor.

He and Miss Leigh continued working together in "Antony and Cleopatra" and "Caesar and Cleopatra." Both appeared in Peter Brook's production of "Titus Andronicus," and Olivier's titanic performance provoked Kenneth Tynan to proclaim that it "ushers us into the presence of one who is, pound for pound, the greatest actor alive."

For all of his success, Olivier felt a compulsion to break new ground, which he did, resoundingly, in John Osborne's "Entertainer." His director, Tony Richardson, said that Olivier's performance as the second-rate vaudevillian Archie Rice "summed up the cynicism, the seediness, the moral compromises of the late 50's and the early 60's."

"The Entertainer" also signified the end of his marriage with Miss Leigh and the beginning of his relationship with Joan Plowright, who later became a major English actress. In 1961, soon after he and Miss Leigh were divorced, Olivier married Miss Plowright.

Olivier's leadership at the Old Vic and his continuing role as an actor and manager made him a natural to be named the first artistic director of the National Theater. In his first season there, in 1963, he directed Peter O'Toole as Hamlet and played Astrov in "Uncle Vanya."

It was with Ibsen's "The Master Builder" in 1964 that he was suddenly overcome with stage fright. "It pursued me for five years and became a monster of a nightmare," he recalled. "The only thing to do was to wear it out." Beginning with "Sleuth" in 1972 he began expanding his movie career. Among his later films are "The 7 Percent Solution," "Marathon Man," "A Little Romance," "Inchon" and, in 1985, "Wild Geese II."

Olivier, who is survived by his wife, two sons and two daughters, was still eager to work in movies and in television films even in his 80s. Every new prospect excited him. As he said, "When anyone is frankly in the business of showing off—of self-presentation—with each appearance, you are bound to take a leap in the dark."

BETTE DAVIS

April 5, 1908–October 6, 1989

By Albin Krebs

Bette Davis, who won two Academy Awards and cut a swath through Hollywood trailing cigarette smoke and delivering drop-dead barbs, died of breast cancer Friday night at the American Hospital in Neuilly-sur-Seine, France. She was 81 years old and lived in West Hollywood, Calif.

For more than a half century, Bette Davis reigned as a Hollywood star in the grandest meaning of the term. With her huge and expressive eyes, her flamboyant mannerisms and distinctive speaking style, she left an indelible mark on her audiences.

Nominated for 10 Oscars, Miss Davis was a perfectionist whose tempestuous battles for good scripts and the best production craftsmen for her films wreaked havoc in Hollywood executive suites.

"I was a legendary terror," she once recalled. "I was insufferably rude and ill-mannered in the cultivation of my career. I had no time for pleasantries."

Few in the entertainment industry could deny that Bette Davis possessed all the legendary indestructibility of the New England Yankee that she was. Starting as a stage actress, she won spectacular fame as a screen star.

Miss Davis's two Oscars for best performance by an actress were won in 1935, for "Dangerous," and in 1938, for "Jezebel." But she is best recalled for her tour de force as Margo Channing, the tough-talking stage actress in "All About Eve," for which she was nominated for an Academy Award.

She made almost 100 films. Her 10 nominations for Oscars are the most any actress has received.

Although Miss Davis reached the apex of her popularity in films between the mid-1930's and the early 50's, her appeal swept across generations, due largely to her frequent appearances in made-for-television films and showings of her old, now-classic movies on television. These include "Of Human Bondage," "Dark Victory," "The Corn Is Green," "The Letter," "The Great Lie," "A Stolen Life," "Now, Voyager," "Mr. Skeffington," "The Little Foxes," "The Petrified Forest" and "Whatever Happened to Baby Jane?"

New generations of entertainers, many of them female impersonators, have found her distinct mannerisms and clipped speech irresistible material for their acts.

"What a dump!" such an impersonator will say, rolling widened eyes and puffing on a cigarette. And, inevitably, the line that Margo Channing utters as she walks drunkenly up the stairs at her party: "Fasten your seat belts; it's going to be a bumpy night."

Ruth Elizabeth Davis was born in Lowell, Mass., on April 5, 1908. Her mother was the former Ruth Favor; her father, Harlow Morrell Davis, an attorney. Her parents divorced when Miss Davis was seven.

Around 1917 "Betty" Davis took a more exotic-sounding name. A friend of her mother's who was reading Balzac's "La Cousine Bette" suggested the name-spelling change, telling her it would "set you apart, my dear."

Miss Davis's first professional acting job was with a stock company in Rochester. She made her New York debut in 1929, at the Provincetown Playhouse in Greenwich Village, in Virgil Geddes's "The Earth Between." Brooks Atkinson, critic for The New York Times, called her "an entrancing creature."

The actress, then only 21, was in her first Broadway hit, "Broken Dishes," followed by "Solid South," in which she played the beguilingly named Alabama Follensby, the first of many Southern-belle roles that would come her way.

The movies had learned to talk only a few years earlier. Hollywood was spiriting away talented Broadway performers, and it was inevitable that a young actress with some experience and good notices would be offered a screen test.

Miss Davis was given a $300-a-week contract by Universal Pictures, and went to Los Angeles in 1930. Her first movie role was in "Bad Sister," whose cinematographer, Karl Freund, mentioned to studio bosses that "Davis has lovely eyes." Her option was picked up for another 13 weeks.

By the end of 1932, having appeared in six lackluster movies and with no contract, Miss Davis prepared to return to New York. Then she got a call from George Arliss, the English actor, who hired Miss Davis as his leading lady in "The Man Who Played God," her breakthrough movie role.

The film was a success, and its producer, Warner Brothers, signed Miss Davis to her first contract. It was the start of a love-hate relationship with the studio that was characterized by Miss Davis's storming off sets, being suspended for refusing to act in what she considered inferior movies, and going to court to sever her ties with Warners. But in her first three years at Warners Miss Davis made 14 films.

From the start Miss Davis had no qualms about playing unsympathetic roles, and so was overjoyed in 1934 when she was lent by Warners to RKO studios to play the slatternly waitress Mildred in W. Somerset

Maugham's "Of Human Bondage," opposite Leslie Howard as the crippled hero, Philip.

"Every actor who becomes a star is usually remembered for one or two roles," she said. "Mildred in 'Of Human Bondage' was such a role for me. She was the first leading-lady villainess ever played on a screen for real."

Miss Davis was nominated for an Academy Award for her performance but failed to win, although she did receive an Oscar the following year for "Dangerous."

By now Warners was giving her movies like "The Petrified Forest," with Leslie Howard and Humphrey Bogart. But Miss Davis harbored resentment against what she called the studio's "contract slave system."

Deciding in 1936 to defy the strictures of her contract, she agreed to go to London with an English company to make two movies. Years later she confessed that before she left, Jack L. Warner, the studio head, had offered her a chance "to play one of the great screen roles of all time, but I didn't know it."

" 'Please don't leave. I just bought a wonderful book for you,' " she quoted Mr. Warner as saying. "And I said, 'I'll bet it's a pip!' and walked out of his office." The role was Scarlett O'Hara in "Gone with the Wind."

Once Miss Davis returned to the United States, Warners gave her a new contract calling for fewer pictures at a much higher salary.

They also gave her excellent, high-budget pictures, like "Jezebel," for which she won her second Oscar in 1938. In a single year, 1939, Warners released four blockbuster Davis movies: "Dark Victory," "Juarez," "The Old Maid" and "The Private Lives of Elizabeth and Essex."

"Jezebel" began her halcyon years. "In 1939 I secured my career and my stardom forever," she said. "I made five pictures in 12 months, and every one of them made money."

The memorable Davis roles continued in swift order: The murderous planter's wife in Maugham's "The Letter" in 1940, followed the next year by "The Great Lie" and "The Little Foxes," in which she played the scheming Regina Giddens. In 1942 she scored again in "Now, Voyager," as Charlotte Vale, a frumpish spinster who blossoms into a confident beauty and finds true love with Paul Henreid. The film is remembered for the scenes in which Mr. Henreid lights two cigarettes at once and gives one to Miss Davis.

There were other triumphs in the 1940's—"The Man Who Came to Dinner," "Watch on the Rhine," "Mr. Skeffington," "The Corn Is Green" and "A Stolen Life." But Miss Davis's luck began to run out with critical and box-office disasters like "Winter Meeting" and "Deception," and in 1949 Warner Brothers, after 19 years, released her from her contract while she was making the ludicrous melodrama "Beyond the Forest." In it Miss Davis uttered one of her celebrated "camp" lines, "What a dump!"

With the end of the Warners era, Miss Davis's third marriage, to William Grant Sherry, with whom she had a daughter, was also ending. Her previous husbands were Harmon Oscar Nelson Jr., a band leader, from whom she was divorced, and Arthur Farnsworth, a businessman, who died in 1943.

In 1949 Miss Davis was offered a role of a lifetime in "All About Eve." She was a last-minute replacement for Claudette Colbert, for whom the director, Joseph L. Mankiewicz, had written the role of Margo Channing, the fading Broadway star. Miss Colbert could not begin the film on schedule because she "hurt her back, thank God," as Miss Davis liked to recall it.

She played Margo brilliantly, and with the aid of a witty script, sharp direction by Mr. Mankiewicz, and a sparkling cast that included Anne Baxter, Celeste Holm, George Sanders, Marilyn Monroe and Thelma Ritter, the movie became one of the all-time great Hollywood films.

During the filming, Miss Davis became romantically involved with her leading man, Gary Merrill, and they were married in 1950. Soon afterward they adopted two children.

Miss Davis received another Oscar nomination for "The Star," released in 1953, but the film was unsuccessful. At the same time, her marriage disintegrated and the couple divorced in 1960.

Having settled into character acting, Miss Davis in 1961 scored a success as a gin-soaked "bag lady" in "Pocketful of Miracles." That same year she was praised for her performance on Broadway in Tennessee Williams's "The Night of the Iguana," which she left in April 1962 to film "Whatever Happened to Baby Jane?" a box-office winner.

The horror movie revolved around two show-business has-been sisters living in creepy seclusion in a Hollywood mansion. The role of the loony Baby Jane Hansen gave Miss Davis a chance to pull out all the acting stops.

Despite advancing age Miss Davis kept on working, appearing mostly on television. "It is only work that truly satisfies," she said. "No one has ever understood the sweetness of my joy at the end of a good day's work. I guess I threw everything else down the drain."

This included her personal life, she said, adding: "All my marriages were charades, and I was equally responsible. But I always fell in love. That was the original sin."

In 1985 there appeared a scandalous book about her by her daughter. In "My Mother's Keeper," B. D. Hyman portrayed Miss Davis as an abusive mother and a grotesque alcoholic.

Two years later Miss Davis shot back with her own bestseller, "This 'N That," in which she defended herself as the victim of a lying, ungrateful child.

"Indestructible," she once said. "That's the word that's often used to describe me. I suppose it means that I just overcame everything. But without things to overcome, you don't become much of a person, do you?"

JIM HENSON

September 24, 1936–May 16, 1990

By Eleanor Blau

Jim Henson, the puppeteer whose Kermit the Frog and other Muppet creatures became the playmates and teachers of millions of youngsters who grew up watching "Sesame Street" on television, died yesterday at New York Hospital.

He was 53 years old.

Hospital spokesmen said he had died of streptococcus pneumonia.

Mr. Henson's creatures first appeared on television in 1954. But it was on "Sesame Street," the program for preschoolers that began in 1969, that Kermit the Frog, Oscar the Grouch, the voracious Cookie Monster, Bert and Ernie, innocent Big Bird and the rest of the Muppet crew won the hearts of a generation.

With wit that also appealed to adults, the Muppets helped youngsters learn about everything from numbers and the alphabet to birth and death.

They were role models, and they imparted values. And they were more than just television pals. Muppets romped on lunch boxes and sheets, and were reincarnated as toys. As "Sesame Street" evolved in the hands of its creators, the Children's Television Workshop, and the scope of its subject matter increased, so did the Muppets.

It was "The Muppet Show," introduced in 1976, which starred Kermit and the egotistical Miss Piggy, that established Mr. Henson as a puppeteer for people of all ages. The show succeeded phenomenally, reaching an estimated 235 million viewers each week in more than 100 countries and winning three Emmys during a five-year run.

In 1979 Mr. Henson turned to the big screen with a feature film, "The Muppet Movie," followed in 1981 by "The Great Muppet Caper," in which he made his debut as a director, and in 1984 by "The Muppets Take Manhattan."

Two fantasy films—"The Dark Crystal" (1982), co-directed with Frank Oz, a long-time associate, and "Labyrinth (1986), directed by Mr. Henson—introduced new Muppet characters.

On television, his CBS animated series, "Muppet Babies," won four Emmy Awards and is broadcast in more than 50 countries. His live-action puppet series, "Fraggle Rock," is shown on cable television's TNT and broadcast in more than 40 countries.

Last year the Walt Disney Company announced an agreement to acquire Henson Associates Inc., which owns the Muppets, for a price estimated by Wall Street analysts at $100 million to $150 million.

For "Sesame Street," now seen in more than 80 countries, Mr. Henson not only created but was the voice and manipulator of Kermit, Ernie and Guy Smiley, a game-show host.

"He was our era's Charlie Chaplin, Mae West, W. C. Fields and Marx Brothers," said Joan Ganz Cooney, chairman and chief executive of the Children's Television Workshop, which produces "Sesame Street," "and indeed he drew from all of them to create a new art form that influenced popular culture around the world."

Although Mr. Henson was not the first television puppeteer, he was the first to adapt the ancient art to the modern medium.

Recalling the arrival of a television set as the biggest event of his adolescence, the tall, bearded and soft-spoken puppeteer once remarked on how impressed he had been with Burr Tillstrom's "Kukla, Fran and Ollie" and Bil and Cora Baird's "Life with Snarky Parker."

Mr. Henson coined the name Muppet to describe his own combination of marionette and foam-rubber hand puppets. Most Muppets' heads are basically hand puppets, but their hands and other parts of their bodies may be operated by controls, including strings and rods.

James Maury Henson was born in Greenville, Miss. When his father, an agronomist with the federal government, was transferred to Washington, the family moved to Hyattsville, Md.

In 1955, during his freshman year as a theater arts major at the University of Maryland, he was offered a five-minute late-night television show of his own called "Sam and Friends." He asked a fellow freshman, Jane Nebel, to join him in operating the puppets. They formed a legal partnership in 1957, were married in 1959, and had five children.

In 1956 he built a frog hand puppet and called him Kermit. "I suppose that he's an alter ego," Mr. Henson said. "But he's a little snarkier than I am— slightly wise. Kermit says things I hold myself back from saying."

His wife told an interviewer that Mr. Henson was "calm and unbelievably patient," so much so that "sometimes you want to kick him." Patience was probably helpful. It would be 20 years before Mr. Henson's view of the Muppets as "entertainment for everybody" would be accepted enough for them to have their own television series.

In the late 1950's the Muppets were seen in commercials, and in the 60's they appeared regularly on "The Ed Sullivan Show."

Then came "Sesame Street," which, oddly enough, held back Mr. Henson's career by labeling him as a children's entertainer. The Muppets' ability to help children remember letters, numbers and various concepts brought Emmys. But at first the networks only shrugged when he insisted that his Muppets' "satiric comment on society seems to delight all ages." The breakthrough was "The Muppet Show."

Mr. Henson once credited Mr. Oz for "much of what's funny about the Muppets," although perhaps the best comedy emerged from the interplay between the exuberant Mr. Oz and the more subdued Mr. Henson.

It was Mr. Oz who created the superstar Miss Piggy from a nondescript pig puppet for a pilot program.

"In one rehearsal, I was working as Miss Piggy with Jim, who was doing Kermit," Mr. Oz recalled, "and the script called for her to slap him. Instead of a slap, I gave him a funny karate hit. Somehow, that hit crystallized her character for me—the coyness hiding the aggression; the conflict of that love with her desire for a career; her hunger for a glamour image; her tremendous out-and-out ego."

FRANK CAPRA

May 18, 1897–September 3, 1991

By Peter B. Flint

Frank Capra, the Academy Award–winning director whose movies were suffused with affectionate portrayals of the common man and the strengths and foibles of American democracy, died yesterday at his home. He was 94 years old and lived in La Quinta, Calif., a suburb of Palm Springs.

He died in his sleep, said his son Tom, executive producer of NBC's "Today" show.

Mr. Capra, the son of illiterate Sicilian peasants who came to this country by steerage when he was six, was one of Hollywood's pre-eminent directors in the 1930's and 40's, one of the first whose name appeared on marquees and above the title in film credits.

He was the first to win three directorial Oscars—for "It Happened One Night" (1934), "Mr. Deeds Goes to Town" (1936) and "You Can't Take It With You" (1938). The motion picture academy voted the first and third movies the best of the year.

Capra movies were idealistic, sentimental and patriotic, and his major films embodied his flair for improvisation, buoyant humor and sympathy for the populist beliefs of the 1930's.

Generations of moviegoers and television viewers have reveled in the hitchhiking antics of Clark Gable and Claudette Colbert in "It Happened One Night," in Gary Cooper's whimsical self-defense of Longfellow Deeds at a hilarious sanity hearing in "Mr. Deeds Goes to Town," in the impassioned filibuster by James Stewart as an incorruptible Senator in "Mr. Smith Goes to Washington," in Mr. Cooper's battle to prevent a power-crazed industrialist from taking dictatorial control of the country in "Meet John Doe," and in Mr. Stewart's salvation by a guardian angel in "It's a Wonderful Life."

The typical hero in almost all later Capra movies was a homespun American crusader, an honest idealist threatened by evil forces. He eventually wins out because of his goodness, wit and courage—and the aid of a shrewd girlfriend.

Mr. Capra bluffed his way into silent movies in 1922 and, despite total ignorance of moviemaking, directed and produced a profitable one-reeler. He advanced from prop man to gag writer to director-producer.

He rose to fame at Columbia Pictures, at the time a minor production company headed by the tyrannical Harry Cohn, and he became the key director in making Columbia a major studio.

His first major success was "Lady for a Day," a rambunctious 1933 comedy based on a Damon Runyon tale. A year later, the comedy "It Happened One Night" became the first movie to win all five major Academy Awards: best film, director, screenplay, actor and actress.

"Mr. Deeds Goes to Town" centered on a hayseed hero who, inheriting $20 million, seeks to subsidize farms for the Depression's jobless.

Mr. Capra then gambled successfully on a costly filming of a mystical novel, "Lost Horizon," by James Hilton, about a remote Tibetan paradise called Shangri-la, starring Ronald Colman.

"You Can't Take It With You" was based on a Pulitzer-Prize play by George S. Kaufman and Moss Hart about an unconventional family.

"Mr. Smith Goes to Washington" evoked the wrath of the Senate and the Washington press corps for depicting a corrupt Senator and a tippling journalist. But the 1939 film was regarded by critics as one of Mr. Capra's most brilliant.

"Meet John Doe" drew criticism for what was seen as a "cop-out" happy ending. But Bosley Crowther of The Times said the 1941 film was "by far the hardest-hitting and most trenchant picture on the theme of democracy" Mr. Capra had yet made.

By the late 1940's, however, the director's optimism no longer coincided with the mood of Americans, and some reviewers described his films as naive and sentimental "Capra-corn." In his autobiography, "The Name Above the Title," he defended his "gee whiz" philosophy. "I always felt the world cannot fall apart as long as free men see the rainbow, feel the rain and hear the laugh of a child," he wrote.

Capra innovations included accelerated pacing with overlapping dialogue and conversational speech. He made stars of Jean Harlow and Barbara Stanwyck. Soft-spoken in private life, he could be a tough professional, matching wits and barbs with Harry Cohn and, as president of the Directors Guild, forcing major producers to grant concessions to the guild.

A competitive man with a short, wiry build and glistening teeth, Mr. Capra dressed casually, favoring flat caps and rumpled trousers.

Frank Capra was born on May 18, 1897, in Palermo. In 1903 his family came to America and settled in Los Angeles.

The boy read voraciously and won a scholarship to the California Institute of Technology, graduating in 1918. He then enlisted in the Army.

He tricked his way into movies by giving an aspiring producer the impression he was a director. For $75 he adapted and directed a Rudyard Kipling bar-room poem.

Mr. Capra became, successively, a prop man, film cutter, assistant director, title-frame writer and gag writer for Hal Roach's "Our Gang" comedies and Mack Sennett's Keystone Comedies.

At Columbia Pictures he made a comedy, "That Certain Thing," won a long-term contract and directed successes like "Platinum Blonde," with Jean Harlow, and "The Miracle Woman," with Barbara Stanwyck.

Hitting his stride, Mr. Capra turned to contemporary issues. In "American Madness" (1932), a banker (Walter Huston) lends money on the basis of character rather than collateral. The bank suffers a run, but the people he had trusted save the day.

In "The Bitter Tea of General Yen," Mr. Capra dealt daringly with racism and miscegenation. The movie, starring Miss Stanwyck and Nils Asther, opened at Radio City Music Hall in 1933. In the next eight years, Mr. Capra made an unbroken succession of hits.

When the Japanese attacked Pearl Harbor on Dec. 7, 1941, he rejoined the Army, But before going on active duty he filmed the Broadway farce, "Arsenic and Old Lace," starring Cary Grant.

During the war, Colonel Capra produced a series of acclaimed propaganda movies contrasting freedom and totalitarianism. The first, "Prelude to War," won the best-documentary Oscar in 1942.

After the war, Mr. Capra and several colleagues formed an independent production company, Liberty Films. In 1946, while at Liberty, he co-wrote and directed "It's a Wonderful Life," a quintessential Capra fantasy reflecting his conviction that no man who has friends is a failure. The film, starring James Stewart as a small-town battler who is saved from suicide by an angel, was faulted by some reviewers for sentimentality. Nonetheless, the movie won many admirers and is invariably telecast at Christmas.

He went on to direct a series of acclaimed films until, in 1961, he remade "Lady for a Day," retitled "Pocketful of Miracles," starring Bette Davis, a Prohibition-era lampoon that was widely regarded as dated. It was his last movie.

Mr. Capra's wife, Lucille, died in 1984, 52 years after their wedding. In addition to his son Tom, he is survived by another son, Frank Jr., a daughter, Lucille, and 10 grandchildren.

FEDERICO FELLINI

January 20, 1920–October 31, 1993

By Peter B. Flint

Federico Fellini, whose deeply personal films were vivid, sometimes bizarre portraits of the human condition, died yesterday at the Umberto I Hospital in Rome. He was 73.

The cause was cardiac arrest, the Reuters news agency reported.

Four of Mr. Fellini's movies won Oscars for best foreign-language film: "La Strada" in 1956, "The Nights of Cabiria" in 1957, "8 1/2" in 1963 and "Amarcord" in 1974. In March, he received an honorary Oscar in recognition of his accomplishments as a director and screenwriter.

Throughout his career, Mr. Fellini focused on his personal vision of society and his preoccupation with the relationships between men and women and between sex and love. An avowed anticleric, he was also deeply concerned with guilt and alienation.

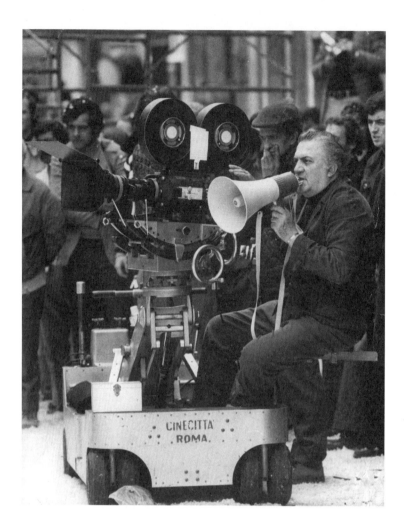

Fellini films are spiced with artifice (masks, masquerades and circuses), startling faces, the rococo and the outlandish, the prisms through which he sometimes viewed life. But as Vincent Canby, the chief film critic of The New York Times, observed in 1985, "What's important are not the prisms, though they are arresting, but the world he shows us: a place whose spectacularly grand, studio-built artificiality makes us see the interior truth of what is taken to be the 'real' world outside, which is a circus."

The concepts of all Fellini movies originated in the mind of "the Maestro," as his associates and compatriots fondly called him, in his memories, dreams, fantasies and fancies. He was often the protagonist of his films, and his most celebrated alter ego was Marcello Mastroianni, in "La Dolce Vita," "8 1/2" and "City of Women."

Mr. Fellini wrote all his scripts and supervised every creative detail, including the final editing. He was a perfectionist who repeatedly reshot scenes in a process that usually took two years. He kept producers away from his films until they were completed, explaining, "I do not need a producer. I need only a good production manager. I need only a man who will give me money."

He likened his craft to applying a thermometer to a troubled world and finding a high fever. "I'd like very much to make a confident picture," he once said.

"I would like to be as good as nature, which with a shower produces flowers and grass to cover the destruction. But we are surrounded by human fragmentation, by pessimism, and it is difficult to talk of other things."

Mr. Fellini said he sought to liberate viewers from "overidealized concepts of life." In a lighter vein, he remarked, "I make pictures to tell a story, to tell lies and to amuse."

Over the decades, Fellini films became increasingly original and subjective, and consequently more controversial and less commercial. His style evolved from neo-realism to fanciful neo-realism to surrealism, in which he discarded narrative story lines for freeflowing, freewheeling memoirs.

"When I start a picture," he said, "I always have a script, but I change it every day. I put in what occurs to me that day, out of my imagination. You start on a voyage; you know where you will end up, but not what will occur along the way. You want to be surprised."

His life centered on filmmaking. "When I am not making movies," he confided, "I feel I am not alive."

Fellini movies have many unexpected and indelible sequences. "La Dolce Vita" opens with a huge statue of Jesus, arms outstretched, being towed inexplicably by a helicopter above the rooftops of Rome. The film "8 1/2" ends with a quixotic film director leading all his contentious associates, real and imagined, alive and dead, in a dance of joyful reconciliation.

"I Vitelloni" ("The Loafers"), the third feature he directed, is an autobiographical tragicomic tale of five provincial youths who punctuate their aimless street life with pranks.

"La Dolce Vita" is a sensational and sobering scan of the decadent "sweet life" of Rome's cafe society, with its sexual promiscuity, search for exotic gratification and consuming boredom. The film shocked many Italians and was proscribed by the Roman Catholic Church, but it became a huge success in Italy and around the world.

"La Strada" ("The Road") is a poetic tragedy about a simple-minded waif who serves as the clown, cook and concubine for a boorish, brutish strongman.

"The Nights of Cabiria" deals with a sentimental prostitute who wistfully dreams of romance and respectability.

Mr. Fellini's most clearly autobiographical confession, "8 1/2," is an innovative romantic satire-fantasy about an egomaniacal filmmaker's moral and creative midlife crisis, his malaise and inability to make a movie. He titled it "8 1/2" because it was his seventh directorial feature in addition to three short films.

"Amarcord" ("I Remember") is a paean to youth and the memories of a year in the life of a provincial Italian town in the 1930's.

His other movies, also with evocative scores by Nino Rota, include "Juliet of the Spirits" (1965), his first color feature, which centers on a neglected wife obsessed by dreams and spirits; "Fellini Satyricon" (1969), an epic of decadence and the wanderings of a homosexual youth in ancient Rome's disintegrating society; "The Clowns" (1970), and "Fellini's Roma" (1972).

Others were "Fellini's Casanova" (1976), a saga of the 18th-century philanderer's conquests across Europe; "Orchestra Rehearsal" (1979), which uses an orchestra as a metaphor for a fragmenting society, and "City of Women" (1979), a feminist fantasy in which the hero searches for the perfect woman.

Later films also include "And the Ship Sails On" (1983), a flamboyant succession of mostly comic commentaries on art and self-absorbed artists; "Ginger and Fred" (1986), whose central characters are an Italian dance couple who are reunited on a television variety show, and "Intervista" (1987), a mock documentary described by Mr. Canby in a review as "a magical mixture of recollection, parody, memoir, satire, self-examination and joyous fantasy."

Mr. Fellini was impatient with interviewers who suggested that his films had been inspired by works he had not read and who pressed him with questions about the meanings of his imagery. "Meaning, always meaning!" he scoffed. "When someone asks, 'What do you mean in this picture?,' it shows he is a prisoner of intellectual, sentimental shackles. Without his meaning, he feels vulnerable."

Admirers said Fellini films were resplendent and exhilarating, and reflected a deepening and an enhancement of his art. They also believed that his later movies showed maturing, self-critical insights.

After the mid-1960's, his films often stressed the bizarre, the garish and the grotesque. Detractors praised some sequences, but variously termed the works excessive, simplistic and self-obsessed. Nonetheless, the consensus was that he made brave and original movies about important issues.

Mr. Canby praised Mr. Fellini for a dazzling inventiveness and skill and an "insatiable curiosity about and fondness for the human animal, especially those who maintain only the most tenuous holds on their dignity or sanity." At his top form, he "somehow brings out the best in us," Mr. Canby wrote. "We become more humane, less stuffy." Hailing Mr. Fellini's "very special, personal kind of cinema," the critic concluded, "one of Fellini's greatest gifts is his ability to communicate a sense of wonder, which has the effect of making us all feel much younger than we have any right to."

Federico Fellini was born on Jan. 20, 1920, in Rimini, an Italian port on the Adriatic. His father, Urbano, sold coffee and other foodstuffs, and his frequent travels left his wife, Ida, as the main parent for Federico and his brother and sister.

In 1985, he told a New York audience that his love of filmmaking originated in Rimini's primitive movie house, which, he said, had 200 seats and standing room for 500. Of 1930's American movies, he recalled, "I discovered there existed another way of life, a country of wide-open spaces, of fantastic cities that were a cross between Babylon and Mars."

At the age of 17 or 18, he left home for Florence, where he worked briefly as a proofreader and cartoonist. He went on to Rome, enrolling in the University of Rome's law school, but he did not attend classes and used his student status to avoid conscription while he worked as a cartoonist and short-story writer for a satirical publication.

At 19, he joined a vaudeville troupe, traveling across Italy and working primarily as a gag writer while performing utility tasks. The year, he recalled, "was perhaps the most important year of my life."

"I was overwhelmed by the variety of the country's physical landscape and, too, by the variety of its human landscape," he said. "It was the kind of experience that few young men are fortunate enough to have: a chance to discover the character of one's country and, at the same time, to discover one's own identity."

Back in Rome, he wrote radio scripts and started collaborating on film scripts. In 1943, after a four-month courtship, he married the actress Giulietta Masina, later the star of many Fellini films. A major inspiration for his life and work, she is his only survivor.

In 1944, after the Allies liberated Rome, Mr. Fellini and several friends opened the Funny Face Shop, an arcade that provided Allied troops with caricatures, portraits, photos and voice recordings for their families. The film director Roberto Rossellini visited the shop and asked Mr. Fellini to collaborate on a documentary about the Nazis' occupation of Rome. The venture evolved into "Open City" (1945), a neo-realistic movie that ignited Italy's postwar film renaissance.

Mr. Fellini was the assistant director of "Open City" and a co-writer and assistant director of Mr. Rossellini's second celebrated antiwar film, "Paisan" (1946), and his controversial religious film, "The Miracle" (1948), in which Mr. Fellini co-starred with Anna Magnani.

Mr. Fellini made his directorial debut in 1951, collaborating with Alberto Lattuada on "Variety Lights," a comedy-drama about a troupe of third-rate traveling vaudevillians.

His first solo directorial effort was the 1951 "White Sheik," a lampoon of Italy's adult comic-strip industry. Both movies were critical and commercial failures, but they were later re-released and praised.

Determined to direct films, Mr. Fellini struggled financially to complete his next project, "I Vitelloni," which became a major success in Italy and abroad. He consolidated his international prestige with "La Strada."

An exuberant, articulate, bearlike man, the director had an expressive face, a whimsical charm and a demonstrative manner. He often gestured with both hands, even while driving one of his favorite motor cars.

On movie sets, he savored his power as the ringmaster of a Felliniesque world. Wearing a wide-brimmed hat, he dominated the scene, alternately improvising, quipping and clowning. Some directors insist on silence on the set, but he preferred a touch of chaos.

Asked once by a friend when he planned to take a vacation, he replied: "Making a movie is my vacation. All the rest, the traveling about to premieres, the interviews, the social life, the endless arguments with producers who don't understand me, that is the work."

JIMMY STEWART

May 20, 1908–July 2, 1997

James Stewart, whose movie portrayals of decent, idealistic and naive small-town Americans made him a beloved national icon, died yesterday at his home in Beverly Hills, Calif. He was 89.

Mr. Stewart's performances in some 80 movies earned him every major award bestowed for his craft and acclaim and popularity for more than half a century. He was the last of that rare breed of male stars whose careers certified the star system as it operated virtually from the beginning of the sound era.

Actors like Mr. Stewart, Spencer Tracy, Gary Cooper, Clark Gable, Cary Grant, John Wayne and Henry Fonda were larger than life, and because the fusion of the performers' public and private personalities created something bigger than the sum of the two parts, something mythical.

The lanky actor with unruly hair and an ungainly stride had a boyish grin and an engaging manner. The Stewart way of speaking—laconic, with a hesitant, nasal drawl—is instantly recognizable by virtually every American. His early screen image, like his personal life, epitomized a Middle American ideal in a confusing, sophisticated world.

His archetypal role (and his own favorite) was that of George Bailey, the small-town banker in "It's a Wonderful Life," Frank Capra's moralistic fantasy in which the hero is rescued from suicide by a pixieish angel who shows him how much meaner life would have been in his hometown without him. The 1946 feature-length Christmas card was a failure among audiences, who dismissed it as overly sentimental, but in later decades it became one of the most popular movies ever made and a holiday staple on television.

But, as Mr. Stewart matured, the diffident innocents he played in the late 1930's and 40's gave way to more subtle and complicated roles—troubled, querulous protagonists torn between firmness and vulnerability, roles in conflict with his accepted image.

Mr. Stewart's subtle and seemingly effortless work prompted the critic Vincent Canby of The New York Times to hail him in 1990 as a great behavioral actor who absorbed each role into his own physical frame, shaping the mannerisms, the voice and even the intelligence to coincide with those of his own persona.

"This he does with such simplicity and ease that, for many years, the initial response was to say that what he does isn't acting, followed up by the damp, desperate criticism that he is always the same," Mr. Canby wrote.

The roles for which he was best remembered include a naively heroic young senator in "Mr. Smith Goes to Washington" (1939), a part that earned him major stardom; a forthright reporter redeeming a headstrong heiress (Katharine Hepburn) in "The Philadelphia Story" (1940) and a relentless defense attorney in "Anatomy of a Murder" (1959).

Also in the Stewart gallery of folk heroes were a gun-shy marshal who tamed a town in "Destry Rides Again" (1939); Monty Stratton, the Chicago White Sox pitcher who returned to the mound after losing a leg, in "The Stratton Story" (1949); a beloved big-band leader in "The Glenn Miller Story" (1954) and Charles A. Lindbergh, a boyhood hero, in his solitary 1927 trans-

Atlantic flight in "The Spirit of St. Louis" (1957).

Later in his career, a tougher, more worldly Stewart emerged in such Anthony Mann westerns as "Winchester '73," "The Far Country," "Bend of the River," "The Naked Spur" and "The Man from Laramie." Alfred Hitchcock used him against type in such films as "Rope" and "The Man Who Knew Too Much," and especially as a voyeur photographer in "Rear Window" and as a retired detective entranced by two forms of a mythic Kim Novak in "Vertigo."

When interviewed about his techniques, the self-effacing actor replied characteristically, "I don't act, I react."

His modest appraisal was challenged by Donna Reed, his co-star in "It's a Wonderful Life." She observed, "He's so natural, so realistic, that I never knew whether he was talking to me or doing the scene."

Weighing Mr. Stewart's work opposite such matchless actresses as Margaret Sullavan in Ernst Lubitsch's "Shop Around the Corner," Jean Arthur in Capra's "Mr. Smith," Ms. Hepburn in George Cukor's "Philadelphia Story," Marlene Dietrich in George Marshall's "Destry Rides Again" and Grace Kelly in "Rear Window," Mr. Canby said he "reveals a quality that at first seems out of sync with the shy, stammering personality favored by nightclub imitators."

"He is debonair," Mr. Canby said. "He has the same humor and lightness of touch that Fred Astaire expresses only through dance. . . . Mr. Stewart is best seen on the screen in full figure, with all of the lean 6-foot-3 1/2-inch man captured in a single frame. He acts with his whole body."

One of the actor's most admired performances was that of the gently eccentric tippler Elwood P. Dowd in "Harvey," whose companion was the title character, a giant, invisible rabbit. The actor played the film role in 1950 after appearing in the whimsical comedy on Broadway in 1947, then played the role again in a triumphant 1970 revival in New York and London that co-starred Helen Hayes.

Mr. Stewart appeared in half a dozen Broadway plays and in occasional television dramas. Also on television, he starred in two of his own series in the early 1970's, first as a family patriarch and college professor in "The Jimmy Stewart Show," a bucolic sitcom, and then as "Hawkins," a shrewd country lawyer.

Mr. Stewart received the American Film Institute's eighth life-achievement award in 1980, a Kennedy Center Honor in 1983 for contributions to the performing arts, a special 1984 Academy Award for "50 years of meaningful performances, for his high ideals, both on and off the screen," a 1985 Presidential Medal of Freedom and the 1990 annual tribute by the Film Society of Lincoln Center.

He had also won an Academy Award for the best performance by an actor in 1940 for "The Philadelphia Story" and four other Oscar nominations, for "Mr. Smith Goes to Washington," "It's a Wonderful Life," "Harvey" and "Anatomy of a Murder." Among many other honors were a Tony Award and the 1968 Screen Actors Guild Award.

After getting his start on Broadway, he honed his craft in Hollywood's big-studio era of the 1930's and 40's. He became a symbol of patriotism as the first top Hollywood actor to enter the service in World War II. Determined to become a combat pilot, he first logged 300 hours of flying because at the age of 33 he was too old to be an aviation cadet. He put on 10 pounds to meet the Army's minimum weight requirement for his tall, thin frame.

Mr. Stewart was inducted in March 1941. He qualified quickly as a pilot. Assigned to the Second Combat Wing of the Eighth Air Force in England, he was successively the operations officer, chief of staff and squadron commander.

He eventually led 20 bombing missions over Germany, hitting targets in Bremen, Frankfurt and Berlin. He won a cascade of decorations, including the Distinguished Flying Cross twice, one of them for piloting the lead plane in a spectacular raid on key aircraft factories in Brunswick, Germany.

When the war ended he was mustered out a colonel but remained in the Air Force Reserve and, in 1959, the Senate approved his promotion to brigadier general, making him the highest-ranking entertainer in the military. He retired from the Reserve in 1968.

Mr. Stewart was married in 1949, at the age of 41, to Gloria Hatrick McLean, a former model. They lived for decades in a Tudor-style house in Beverly Hills, at first with two boys from Mrs. Stewart's previous marriage, and then with their own twin girls, who were born in 1951.

One stepson, First Lieut. Ronald W. McLean, was killed in Vietnam in 1969. Mrs. Stewart died in 1994. Mr. Stewart is survived by his daughters and his other stepson.

James Maitland Stewart was born on May 20, 1908, in the western Pennsylvania town of Indiana, to Alexander Stewart and the former Elizabeth Ruth Jackson, who were of Scotch-Irish descent. The Stewart family had owned and managed a prosperous hardware store for half a century.

Jimmy and his two younger sisters were taught the value of responsibility, prudence and frugality. When not doing chores, the spindly, spectacled youth wrote and staged plays and played the accordion.

At prep school, the Mercersburg Academy in south-central Pennsylvania, he went out for football, track, dramatics and music. During summer vacations he was a construction laborer. Then, at Princeton, he joined the Triangle Club, rising from accordionist to leading roles in musicals. He graduated in 1932 with a bachelor's degree in architecture.

The Depression era offered little demand for architects, so he accepted an invitation from a college friend, Joshua Logan, to join the University Players on Cape Cod. The summer stock company included Henry Fonda, who became a lifelong friend even though Mr. Stewart was a conservative Republican and Fonda a liberal Democrat.

Mr. Stewart won his first major role on Broadway in 1934, as a gallant soldier-guinea pig in "Yellow Jack," Sidney Howard's drama about research on yellow fever, and then played a youth stunned by the adultery of his mother (Judith Anderson) in "Divided by Three." Brooks Atkinson of The Times acclaimed the neophyte's performance as "a minor masterpiece."

In 1935 he won a contract with MGM, where he made his feature debut as a cub reporter in "The Murder Man," a crime melodrama starring Spencer Tracy. Mr. Stewart's intelligent, deceptively casual acting in two dozen movies over the next five years earned him stardom.

Returning from war in late 1945, Mr. Stewart insisted that his military exploits not be publicized. He avoided studio contracts and freelanced, earning increasingly high salaries and becoming a pioneer of the percentage deal, under which he reportedly received up to half the profits of his movies. (An astute businessmen, he became a multimillionaire, with diversified investments and membership on corporate boards.)

On screen, he shook off his country-boy manner and assumed a new persona, a complex, sometimes cryptic image that was shaped in collaborations in the 1950's and 60's with directors like Hitchcock, Mr. Mann and John Ford. The actor played a cold bounty hunter in Mr. Mann's "Naked Spur" (1953),

a dedicated reporter in "Call Northside 777" (1948), a clown wanted for murder in "The Greatest Show on Earth" (1952), the photographer turned sleuth in Hitchcock's "Rear Window" (1954), the obsessive romantic in Hitchcock's "Vertigo" (1958) and a cynical marshal in Ford's "Two Rode Together" (1961).

Other later movies included "Broken Arrow," "The Far Country," "Strategic Air Command," "The F.B.I. Story," "How the West Was Won," "The Flight of the Phoenix" and "The Shootist," a 1976 valedictory to the career of a longtime friend, John Wayne.

He became a spokesman for conservative political and economic causes and a frequent campaigner for Republican political friends, including Ronald Reagan.

In 1989, the actor broke into print with "Jimmy Stewart and His Poems," a 32-page book of verse that became a best seller.

Nearing his 80th birthday, he was asked how he wanted to be remembered. As someone, he said, who "believed in hard work and love of country, love of family and love of community."

AKIRA KUROSAWA

March 23, 1910–September 6, 1998

By Rick Lyman

Akira Kurosawa, who personified Japanese movies to most of the world and who grew into one of the handful of truly important directors that the cinema has produced, died yesterday at his home in Tokyo. He was 88.

The cause was a stroke, his family said.

Although Mr. Kurosawa stumbled into filmmaking, he became one of the colossal figures in film history, an autocratic perfectionist with a painter's eye for composition, a dancer's sense of movement and a humanist's sensibility. Dozens of directors have acknowledged his enduring influence.

When Mr. Kurosawa's "Rashomon" reached Western audiences in 1951, little was known outside Japan about the country's cinema. That changed overnight with "Rashomon," a compelling study of ambiguity and deception that provides four contradictory accounts of a medieval rape and murder recalled by a bandit, a noblewoman, the ghost of her slain husband and a woodcutter. The characters, Mr. Kurosawa said, "cannot survive without lies to make them feel they are better people than they really are."

Mr. Kurosawa's blend of Japanese folklore with Western acting styles and storytelling techniques provided a link between the two worlds, reintroducing

Japanese culture to a postwar global audience and leading to an amazingly fertile decade that saw him produce several films that have widely been acclaimed as among the finest ever made, including "Seven Samurai," "Ikiru" and "Yojimbo."

"I suppose all of my films have a common theme," Mr. Kurosawa told the film scholar Donald Richie. "If I think about it, though, the only theme I can think of is really a question: Why can't people be happier together?"

Tall and large-boned, Mr. Kurosawa mixed a workingman's thick, powerful hands with the face of a professor, sometimes a very stern professor. He was known by colleagues, not always affectionately, as "the Emperor."

Stories of his perfectionism are plentiful. He once halted production to reconstruct a hugely expensive medieval set because he noticed that a nail head was barely visible in one shot. For the climax of "Throne of Blood," his 1957 samurai version of "Macbeth," he insisted that his star, Toshiro Mifune, wear a protective vest and perform the scene while being shot with real arrows.

Mr. Kurosawa rehearsed all of the scenes meticulously, sometimes for weeks, then shot them from beginning to end, using three cameras positioned at strategic points. "I put the A camera in the most orthodox positions, use the B camera for quick, decisive shots and the C camera as a kind of guerrilla unit," he said.

This is quite different from the way films are normally made, beginning with a "master shot" that is then augmented with close-ups and reverse-angle shots that are pieced together into a final version. Mr. Kurosawa wanted his scenes to be a record of a single performance.

"The editing stage is really, for me, a breeze," he said. "Every day, I edit the rushes together, so that by the time I am finished shooting, what is called the initial assembly is already completed."

While he was strict with his technical crew, Mr. Kurosawa was more patient with actors.

"It is really strange," said Shiro Miroya, one of Mr. Kurosawa's assistant directors. "Kurosawa, who can be a real demon at times, when he'll scream out, 'The rain isn't falling like I want it to,' or 'That damn wind isn't blowing the dust right,' is always so terribly gentle with actors."

Mr. Kurosawa described his approach this way: "Unless you can see, as an actor, what the director is trying to express simply by how he looks and acts himself, you are going to miss the finer points. When my cast and I are on location, we always eat together, sleep in the same rooms, are constantly talking together. As you might say, here is where I direct."

The approach paid off with an intense loyalty. Kyoko Kagawa, who starred in "The Lower Depths"

(1957) and the contemporary thriller "The Bad Sleep Well" (1960), told an interviewer, "It is only when I work with the Kurosawa group that I feel fulfilled as an actress—and coupled with that is the feeling of relief that I know when I see that Kurosawa is satisfied."

Perhaps the greatest loyalty was between Mr. Kurosawa and Toshiro Mifune, his most famous star. Mr. Kurosawa made 17 films between 1948 and 1965, and all but one of them starred Mifune. But the two had a falling-out following the making of "Red Beard" (1965), and never worked together again.

Mr. Kurosawa spent most of his time, when not working at his Tokyo studio, at the nearby home that he shared with his wife, Yoko Yaguchi, a former actress, who died in 1984. His son and daughter survive him.

Financial reversals following the release of "Dodeskaden" in 1970, combined with a painful ailment (later diagnosed as gallstones) led him to attempt suicide in 1971. Though he recovered, he seemed changed. After having made 19 films between 1946 and 1965, he made only 6 in the 28 years following "Dodeskaden," although two of them are considered among his finest works: the historical epics "Kagemusha" (1980), centered on a thief in feudal Japan who assumes a dead man's identity and becomes heroic, and "Ran" (1985).

His final films, "Rhapsody in August" (1990) and "Madadayo" (1993), struck many as containing a new, strident note of Japanese nationalism. But his influence on American filmmakers continued.

In 1960, Mr. Kurosawa's "Seven Samurai" was remade by the director John Sturges as "The Magnificent Seven." In 1964, "Rashomon" was remade by Martin Ritt as "The Outrage." In 1964, "Yojimbo" was remade by Sergio Leone as "A Fistful of Dollars," then remade again in 1996 by Walter Hill as "Last Man Standing."

And George Lucas has acknowledged "The Hidden Fortress," a 1958 adventure by Mr. Kurosawa in which a princess is escorted to freedom with the help of two bickering peasants, as one of the inspirations for his "Star Wars" series, in which he replaced the peasants with two bickering robots.

Akira Kurosawa was born in Tokyo in 1910. His father was a former military officer who had become an athletic instructor at the Imperial Army's Toyama Academy. His mother came from a well-to-do merchant family.

The Kurosawa family traced its lineage to a legendary 11th-century samurai. But by the time Akira was born they no longer had wealth or status.

While Mr. Kurosawa was a young child, a charismatic teacher inspired an interest in painting. Later he gravitated toward an older brother, Heigo, who shared his interest in art.

During his teens Akira spent much of his time with Heigo. What Akira remembered most about those years was going to the movies with his brother, who had taken a job as a silent-film narrator.

"We would go to the movies, particularly silent movies, and then discuss them all day," Mr. Kurosawa wrote. "I began to love to read books, especially Dostoyevsky, and I can remember when we went to see Abel Gance's 'La Roue' and it was the first film that really influenced me and made me think of wanting to become a filmmaker."

Akira enrolled in the Doshusha School of Western Painting in 1927 and tried to supplement the family's income with his work, but never made much money.

In 1936, he noticed an advertisement for Tokyo's P.C.L. Studios, which later became the Toho Film Production Company. It was looking for a half-dozen young men interested in becoming apprentice assistant directors.

All 500 applicants were asked to present themselves for an interview and bring along an essay each had written on "The Basic Defects of the Japanese Film Industry." A 26-year-old Mr. Kurosawa found himself facing Kajiro Yamamoto, then Japan's most prominent film director. Yamamoto took the young man under his wing.

Mr. Kurosawa worked as Yamamoto's assistant for seven years. Finally, in 1943, he was given the chance to direct his first film, "Sanshiro Sugata," a judo adventure that proved a box-office smash. Mr. Kurosawa followed it with "The Most Beautiful," about Japanese women working in factories, and "Sanshiro Sugata, Part II," another huge hit.

After the war, Mr. Kurosawa found traditional, stylized storytelling confining and hungered for realism, the kind of filmmaking he saw in the works of Roberto Rossellini and Vittorio De Sica.

In 1946 he directed "No Regrets for Our Youth," about persecutions in postwar Tokyo by elements in the Japanese right wing. "It was the first film in which I had something to say and in which my feelings were used," he said.

In 1950, Mr. Kurosawa released "Rashomon" in Tokyo. The film won the Venice Film Festival's grand prize and an Academy Award as best foreign-language movie. Its success made Mr. Kurosawa Japan's most famous and popular filmmaker.

"For the Japanese people, who had lost the war as well as their pride, this meant immeasurable encouragement and hope," he said.

His next film, an adaptation of "The Idiot" by Dostoyevsky, was followed, in 1952, by "Ikiru," which some consider his finest work. "Ikiru," which means "to live," is entirely unlike the later samurai epics that would cement his international reputation. Set in contemporary Tokyo, it follows a joyless, dying bureaucrat who decides to help slum parents build a playground. The film was immediately recognized as a great work.

In 1953, Mr. Kurosawa made "Seven Samurai," a four-hour epic, often referred to as among the greatest action films ever made. It tells the story of down-on-their-luck samurai who agree to defend a small village from bandits.

He had a major international success in 1974 with "Dersu Uzala," a Soviet production about the friendship between a Russian explorer and a Manchurian hunter that won the 1975 Academy Award for best foreign-language film.

The year 1980 brought the premiere of Mr. Kurosawa's "Kagemusha" at the New York Film Festival, and Mr. Kurosawa returned to the festival in 1985 with "Ran." Writing in The New York Times, Vincent Canby described "Ran" as "almost a religious experience—an epiphany" that "stands above all other 1985–1986 movies with the implacable presence of a force of nature."

Though Mr. Kurosawa often diverted the conversation when asked about his approach to filmmaking, he frequently described his attitude toward art in similar terms. "To be an artist," he once said, "means never to avert one's eyes."

KATHARINE HEPBURN

May 12, 1907–June 29, 2003

By Caryn James

Katharine Hepburn, the actress whose independent life and strong-willed movie characters made her a role model for generations of women and a beloved heroine to filmgoers for more than 60 years, died yesterday at her home in Old Saybrook, Conn. She was 96 and also had a home in Manhattan.

Her physical presence was distinctive, her often-imitated voice filled with the vowels of a well-bred New Englander, and her sharp-planed face defined by high cheekbones. In her youth she did not have classical leading-lady looks, but a handsome beauty. In old age she was a familiar figure with her hair, gradually changing from auburn to gray, in a topknot and her boyish figure in the trousers that she helped make fashionable.

Miss Hepburn played sharp-witted, sophisticated women with an ease that suggested that there was a thin line between the movie role and the off-screen personality. The romantic comedy "The Philadelphia Story"

and the screwball classic "Bringing Up Baby" were among her best, most typical roles. But through 43 films and dozens of stage and television appearances, she played comic and dramatic parts as varied as Jo in "Little Women," the reborn spinster Rosie in "The African Queen" and Eleanor of Aquitaine in "The Lion in Winter."

Her life and career were dominated by her love affair with Spencer Tracy, which created one of the great romantic legends and brilliant movie pairings of their day. Tracy was unhappily married and the father of two when they met, and he remained married until the end of his life. He and Miss Hepburn lived together for 27 years, until his death in 1967, and made nine films together. "Woman of the Year," "Adam's Rib" and "Pat and Mike" are typically bright and biting Tracy-Hepburn collaborations. She is wickedly smart and emotionally vulnerable. He is decent and down-to-earth. He manages to bring her down a peg; she never minds. Hepburn and Tracy, Vincent Canby wrote in The New York Times, "so beautifully complemented each other" that their relationship "never seemed to be a matter of capitulation." Rather, he added, it was "a matter of understanding and acknowledging each other's boundaries."

The frisson of their off-screen romance, always hinted at but never acknowledged during his lifetime, followed them on screen and became especially poignant when they played a married couple in their last movie together, "Guess Who's Coming to Dinner." Tracy died just 17 days after they had finished filming it.

Miss Hepburn, who is survived by a brother, a sister, nieces and nephews, was reticent about her personal life. But after the death of Tracy's wife, Louise, in 1983, she felt free to discuss the love affair. In later years she spoke openly about her life and career, especially in her 1991 autobiography, "Me: Stories of My Life."

Katharine Houghton Hepburn was born into a family whose comfortable social status and unconventional opinions fostered self-confidence and independence. Her father, Dr. Thomas Norval Hepburn, was a Hartford surgeon and a pioneer in fighting venereal disease. Her mother, Katharine Houghton, was a suffragist and a strong advocate of birth control.

In "Me," Miss Hepburn finally revealed her age. "I was born May 12, 1907," she wrote, "despite everything I may have said to the contrary." For years she had said she was two years younger and had given her birthday as Nov. 8.

After graduating from Bryn Mawr College in 1928, she had small parts in stock theater companies. She was dismissed from more than one play, but she retained supreme self-confidence. Late in life, she laughingly said of her younger self, "I am terribly afraid I just assumed I'd be famous." She was first noticed professionally in her role as Antiope in the play "The Warrior's Husband," a Greek fable in which she entered by descending a narrow staircase, carrying a stag over her shoulder.

That role led to a Hollywood screen test and her first film role, as John Barrymore's daughter in "A Bill of Divorcement" (1932). It was directed by George Cukor, who become one of her dearest friends and the director of many of her films, including "Little Women." He once recalled of her screen test: "She was unlike anybody I'd ever seen or heard. I was rather moved by the test, although the performance wasn't that good. But I thought, 'That girl is rather interesting.'"

Miss Hepburn became a movie star quickly. She won an Academy Award for her role as Eva Lovelace, the aspiring actress who learns a tough lesson about survival, in the 1933 film "Morning Glory," only her third movie. Over the years she was nominated for a dozen Oscars, and she won three more, for "Guess Who's Coming to Dinner," "The Lion in Winter" and "On Golden Pond."

When she was 84, she looked back at those early days and, with her trademark tough-mindedness, said: "In the beginning I had money; I wasn't a poor little thing. I don't know what I would have done if I'd had to come to New York and get a job as a waiter or something like that. I think I'm a success, but I had every advantage; I should have been."

She also credited her husband with helping her get started in her career. In 1928 she married Ludlow Ogden Smith, a member of a wealthy family. She made him change his name to S. Ogden Ludlow, partly because she didn't want to be known as Kate Smith.

They led separate lives long before their divorce in 1934, but they remained friendly. The town house they bought together in the Turtle Bay section of Manhattan was Miss Hepburn's home until the end of her life, along with the family home on the Connecticut River.

Despite her early success, reviewers in those days sometimes found her strident and mannered. In 1933 she returned to Broadway in a spectacular failure, "The Lake," which inspired Dorothy Parker to write her famous aphorism, "She ran the gamut of emotion from A to B."

Of those early years, Miss Hepburn said: "I strike people as peculiar in some way, although I don't quite understand why. Of course, I have an angular face, an angular body and, I suppose, an angular personality, which jabs into people."

Over time her screen presence softened and became more likable; meanwhile, society was catching up to her willful, independent style.

Many of her early films are now regarded as classics. Playing a tough, determined actress in "Stage Door" (1937), she read a line from a play—"The calla lilies are in bloom again"—that became the all-time favorite of Hepburn impersonators. Life magazine said that "Stage Door" proved that she was "potentially, the screen's greatest actress."

She played a free-spirited heiress in "Bringing Up Baby" (1938), opposite Cary Grant and a leopard. But the film, now treasured, was a box-office flop, and by then her career was in decline. In 1938 she appeared on a list of actors labeled "box-office poison" in a poll of movie exhibitors.

Rather than appear in a film called "Mother Carey's Chickens," she bought out her contract with R.K.O. She made "Holiday," another classic romantic comedy with Grant, in which she was another high-spirited socialite.

Then Miss Hepburn took charge of her career in a way few women dared in those days of the studio system. Philip Barry wrote the play "The Philadelphia Story" for her, modeling his heroine, Tracy Lord, on Miss Hepburn. Tracy Lord is a beautiful, high-spirited, rich woman, about to marry her second husband, when her first husband and a reporter who is covering the wedding arrive to create an unexpected romantic tangle.

The play was a hit, and Miss Hepburn owned the rights to it because Howard Hughes, a sometime beau, had bought them for her. She went to Louis B. Mayer, the head of the Metro-Goldwyn-Mayer studio, and sold him the property on the condition that she play the lead. She chose her friend George Cukor to direct. And she asked for Spencer Tracy and Clark Gable as her co-stars. She got Cary Grant as her former husband, James Stewart as the reporter, and a hit movie. She never lost control of her career again.

Soon she went back to Mayer with another script, "Woman of the Year," the story of the unlikely romance between a political columnist and a sportswriter. She asked for Tracy, whom she had never met, to play the sportswriter. This time she got him.

The success of "Woman of the Year" (1942) and the stars' off-screen relationship led to other Tracy and Hepburn films that followed a similar pattern. In "Adam's Rib" (1949), they are married opposing lawyers. In "Pat and Mike" (1952), she is a champion athlete, and he is her rough-hewn manager, with whom she falls in love.

It was in "Pat and Mike" that Tracy spoke the often-quoted line about Miss Hepburn's figure, "Not much meat on her, but what's there is 'cherce.'"

One of Miss Hepburn's most enduring films without Tracy was "The African Queen" (1952), in which she played the straitlaced Rosie opposite Humphrey Bogart for the director John Huston.

She wrote about it in her first book, published in 1987, whose title captures the direct, colloquial style of her writing: "The Making of the African Queen: Or, How I Went to Africa with Bogart, Bacall and Huston and Almost Lost My Mind."

Later she achieved one of her great artistic triumphs as the 12th-century Eleanor of Aquitaine in "The Lion in Winter" (1968).

Her versatility lasted well into her career. She played the drug-addicted Mary Tyrone in the 1962 film of Eugene O'Neill's "Long Day's Journey into Night." She was a fair match in toughness for John Wayne in the western "Rooster Cogburn" (1975). In "On Golden Pond" (1981) she starred opposite Henry Fonda as a feisty older woman coping with her husband's failing memory.

Her final screen appearance, in 1994, was in "Love Affair." Playing Warren Beatty's wise old aunt, she gave advice to the woman he loved, played by Annette Bening.

In 1994 she also appeared in the television movie "One Christmas," as yet another wise old aunt. Her tailor-made Hepburn lines included these: "I've always lived my life exactly as I wanted. I wouldn't change a single thing. No regrets."

Her most striking television appearance was in a 1986 tribute to Spencer Tracy. Speaking openly about their relationship at last, she read a letter she had written to him, which she later included in her autobiography. She recalled their last years together, when he was ill and had trouble sleeping, and she would sit on the floor by his side and talk. She wondered why he drank.

"What was it, Spense?" she asked. It was an elo-quent performance that distilled the way her public and private lives blended.

At the conclusion of "All About Me," her own television biography, she said: "In some ways I've lived my life as a man, made my own decisions. I've been as terrified as the next person, but you've got to keep a-going; you've got to dream." In typical Katharine Hepburn style, she faced the camera and, at the age of 85, tacitly acknowledged how close she had to be to the end.

"I have no fear of death," she said. "Must be wonderful, like a long sleep. But let's face it: it's how you live that really counts."

MARLON BRANDO

April 3, 1924–July 1, 2004

By Rick Lyman

Marlon Brando, the rebellious prodigy who electrified a generation and forever transformed the art of screen acting, but whose obstinacy and eccentricity prevented him from fully realizing the promise of his early genius, died on Thursday at a Los Angeles hospital. He was 80.

The cause was pulmonary fibrosis, said Jay Cantor, a family spokesman.

In the nearly 60 years since Mr. Brando first won acclaim, on Broadway and then in films, younger au-diences came to know him as a tabloid curiosity, an overweight target for late-night comics, not as what he once was: a truly revolutionary presence who strode through American popular culture like light-ning on legs.

Certainly among the handful of enduringly great American film actors—some say the greatest—he has also been, without question, the most widely im-itated. Virtually all of the finest male stars who have emerged in the last half-century, from Paul Newman to Warren Beatty to Robert De Niro to Sean Penn, contain some echo of Mr. Brando's paradigm.

Simply put, in film acting, there is before Brando, and there is after Brando. And they are like different worlds.

Yet, like Orson Welles—another famous prodigy who battled Hollywood only to balloon into a car-toon version of his early brilliance—Mr. Brando had a legend built on a surprisingly small number of roles.

There is his epochal Stanley Kowalski in Tennessee Williams's "Streetcar Named Desire," a role he cre-ated on Broadway in 1947, at age 23, and then played on film in 1951. And there is his performance as the fatally noble Mexican bandit in "Viva Zapata!" in 1952. And then two crucial roles, as the first in a long line of leather-clad mixed-up teenagers in "The Wild One" (1953) and in his Oscar-winning turn as Terry Malloy, the boxer who could have been a contender, in "On the Waterfront" (1954), which many consider his finest performance.

After that explosion of creative fire, there followed a huge gap of years filled with intermittently compel-ling but largely unmemorable roles—and more than a few outright disasters—before a stunning return to form with "The Godfather" in 1972 and "Last Tango in Paris" in 1973.

Through it all, he was an often combative and moody iconoclast, a polarizing and enigmatic figure who generally stayed out of the public eye.

He described himself as a lazy man, and he was notoriously lax about learning his lines. Yet no one was better at finding brilliant touches that brought a character to life. Many have pointed to a scene in "On the Waterfront" during which he delicately put on the dainty lace glove of the young woman he was awkwardly trying to court, a seemingly unconscious gesture that fills the moment with heartbreaking vulnerability.

Jack Nicholson termed him "a genius who was the beginning and end of his own revolution." In an interview yesterday, he said: "There's no one before or since like Marlon Brando. The gift was enormous and flawless, like Picasso."

Mr. Brando was not the first actor to bring to the screen the style known as the Method—an internalized acting technique promulgated in Russia by Konstantin Stanislavski in the 1920's and then popularized in New York in the 40's by evangelists like Lee Strasberg, Sanford Meisner and Stella Adler, Mr. Brando's beloved teacher. But Mr. Brando was the first to make clear how truly powerful and culture-shaking the Method could be, in the right hands.

To American audiences who first saw him in the late 40's, what was most apparent about Mr. Brando was that, compared with other actors of the period, he was brooding, muscular and intense. Detractors called him a slob. He appeared in tight blue jeans and torn T-shirts, grimy with sweat, alternately slack-jawed with stupidity and alive with feral cunning. And he was more openly sexual, in an animal way, than the actors who immediately preceded him. Often, Mr. Brando was accused of mumbling his lines, but audiences watching those early performances today would notice none of that, so complete has the Brando school of anti-glamour taken root.

Mr. Brando was born on April 3, 1924 in Omaha. In his 1994 autobiography, "Songs My Mother Taught Me," he described a painful childhood. His father, Marlon Brando Sr., a middle-class businessman, was an abusive alcoholic, he said, who never seemed to find anything good to say about his only son. His mother, Dorothy Pennebaker Brando, a disappointed actress, was also an alcoholic, he said, more interested in drinking than in caring for her family.

"I suppose the story of my life is a search for love," Mr. Brando said. "But more than that, I have been looking for a way to repair myself from the damages I suffered early on and to define my obligation, if I had any, to myself and my species."

In 1943, Mr. Brando arrived in New York. A bad knee exempted him from the draft. Mr. Brando enrolled in the Dramatic Workshop of the New School for Social Research. He seemed to understand the Method instinctively, how to use his own reservoir of memories and internalized emotions to find moments of truth. Indeed, some of his fellow students said that teaching him the technique was redundant.

"Marlon's going to school to learn the Method was like sending a tiger to jungle school," Elaine Stritch once said.

In 1947, Mr. Brando exploded onto the stage after a young director named Elia Kazan recommended him for the role of Stanley Kowalski in "A Streetcar Named Desire."

The inspiration for Mr. Brando's costume—torn T-shirt, extremely tight jeans—came from watching construction workers near the theater, said Lucinda Ballard, the play's costume designer. Mr. Brando painstakingly bulked up his muscles and then had a fitting for the specially made jeans, insisting that he wear no underwear for the fitting.

For three years, he parried offers from Hollywood until finally he accepted the lead role in "The Men," drawn by the character of a bitter and disabled war veteran.

The Hollywood establishment did not quite know what to make of Mr. Brando. It never did. In the early 50's, movie stars were expected to be models of glamour when they appeared in public. Mr. Brando went around in T-shirts and blue jeans. He was often spotted driving down Sunset Boulevard in a convertible wearing a fake arrow that seemed to penetrate his head.

"The Men" was followed in 1951 with the film version of "Streetcar," in which Mr. Brando had the same effect on movie audiences that he'd had on Broadway. Hollywood, however, kept its distance and he did not win an Academy Award.

After being passed over a few more times, he finally won his first Oscar in 1954 for his role as Terry Malloy in "On the Waterfront."

"If there is a better performance by a man in the history of film, I don't know what it is," said Mr. Kazan, his director again.

Hollywood had finally embraced Brando. At the Academy Awards ceremonies, he even joked with the emcee, Bob Hope, wrestling with him over the Oscar he had just won. It seemed to presage greater glories but proved to be the end of the most fertile period in Mr. Brando's professional life.

More and more, he seemed to be receding behind his makeup. And he developed a growing reputation for being difficult.

His fortunes were supposed to be revived by an expensive remake of "Mutiny on the Bounty." But the budget soared. Mr. Brando also ballooned, from 170 to 210 pounds. Nearly everyone blamed him for the film's trouble. The film, which opened in 1962, was a box-office disaster. It would be a long time before he would again star in an expensive production.

Mr. Brando seemed bored with acting and increasingly remote. He had fallen in love with Tahiti while making "Bounty," as well as with his co-star, Tarita Teriipia. So in 1966 he simply bought his own island—actually a small atoll—Tetiaroa, a sickle of palm and sand surrounding a green lagoon about 30 miles north of the island of Tahiti.

His first marriage, to Anna Kashfi, had dissolved in 1958 after a little more than a year. A subsequent child custody battle put Mr. Brando on the tabloid covers when his ex-wife publicly slapped him after a Santa Monica court hearing.

Movita Castenada, also an actress, married him in 1960, and that marriage, too, was over by 1962.

"Is Brando Necessary?" asked Film Comment magazine in 1969.

Hollywood didn't think so. By the time the director Francis Ford Coppola was casting about for an actor to play Vito Corleone in his 1972 adaptation of Mario Puzo's "Godfather," Mr. Brando wasn't on the studio's radar.

Paramount Pictures was considering Burt Lancaster, Orson Welles, George C. Scott, even Edward G. Robinson. When Mr. Coppola told them he wanted Mr. Brando, studio officials refused. Brando was trouble, they said.

But Mr. Coppola won out. The movie immediately became a classic and a reminder of Mr. Brando's powerful screen presence. So no one was surprised when he was nominated for a best actor Oscar.

Mr. Brando had frequently expressed disdain for awards in those years. Would he attend the Oscars? He refused to say until the last minute. He sent an American Indian actress, Sacheen Littlefeather, in his place.

When Mr. Brando's name was announced as the winner and the actor Roger Moore attempted to hand the Oscar statuette to Ms. Littlefeather, she brushed it aside and said that Mr. Brando "very regretfully cannot accept this very generous award" because of the way American Indians had been treated by Hollywood.

Onscreen, he followed up with one of his greatest performances, in Bernardo Bertolucci's "Last Tango in Paris," an X-rated sensation in its day. Many of his monologues, in particular one about being abandoned and humiliated, were drawn from his childhood experiences.

"'Last Tango' required a lot of emotional arm-wrestling," he wrote in his autobiography. "And when it was finished, I decided that I wasn't ever again going to destroy myself emotionally to make a movie."

Mr. Brando continued to recede into his private world. He reached a kind of oddball apogee in Mr. Coppola's "Apocalypse Now" (1979), playing a renegade Green Beret colonel in a surreal version of Vietnam.

In 1990, Mr. Brando found himself back on the tabloid front pages when his son Christian was accused of killing Dag Drollet, the son of a prominent Tahitian banker and politician who he thought had been abusing Cheyenne Brando, 20, his girlfriend. Suddenly, Mr. Brando's dysfunctional family became fodder for the gossip pages.

Christian Brando pleaded guilty to involuntary manslaughter and served nearly five years in prison. Cheyenne Brando later hanged herself in her mother's home in Tahiti.

In addition to his son Christian, Mr. Brando is known to be survived by at least two other sons, Miko and Simon, and three daughters, Rebecca, Petra and Ninna.

In the mid-90's, Mr. Brando made a pair of truly odd appearances on "Larry King Live" on CNN, kissing the host at one point and complaining that Hollywood was controlled by Jews who showed too little social conscience.

But the actor also told Mr. King why he loved the South Pacific so much and, in the process, explained something about himself.

He said: "When I lie on the beach there naked, which I do sometimes, and I feel the wind coming over me and I see the stars up above and I am looking into this very deep, indescribable night, it is something that escapes my vocabulary to describe. Then I think: 'God, I have no importance. Whatever I do or don't do, or what anybody does, is not more important than the grains of sand that I am lying on, or the coconut that I am using for my pillow.' So I really don't think in the long sense."

JOHNNY CARSON

October 23, 1925–January 23, 2005

By Richard Severo and Bill Carter

Johnny Carson, the droll, puckish comedian who dominated late-night television for 30 years, tucking millions of Americans into bed as the host of the "Tonight" show, died yesterday in Los Angeles. He was 79.

The cause was the effects of emphysema, family members said.

Mr. Carson took over the "Tonight" show from Jack Paar on Oct. 1, 1962, and surrendered it to Jay Leno on May 22, 1992. During those three decades, he became the biggest, most popular star in American television. Virtually every American with a television set saw a Carson monologue in those years. At his height, between 10 million and 15 million Americans slept better weeknights because of him.

Mr. Carson was often called "the king of late night," and he wielded an almost regal power. He was instrumental in changing some of the bedrock ways television operated. More than any other individual he shifted the nexus of power in television from New York to Los Angeles with his decision in 1972 to move his show from Rockefeller Center to NBC's

West Coast studios in Burbank, Calif. His move signified a realignment of American pop culture from Broadway to Hollywood.

And after the "Tonight" show ceased to be televised live from 11:30 p.m. to 1 a.m. and began being taped in the early evening, the practice of taping would become the norm.

In his monologue, Mr. Carson impaled the foibles of seven presidents as well as the doings of assorted nabobs and stuffed shirts from the private sector: secret polluters, tax evaders, preening lawyers, oily accountants, defendants who got off too easily and celebrities who talked too much.

All these oddments were sliced and diced so politely, so unmaliciously, that even the stuffiest conservative Republicans found themselves almost smiling at Mr. Carson's Nixon-Agnew jokes, and liberal Democrats savored his pokes at Lyndon B. Johnson and the Kennedys. Members of the public couldn't say whether they were on Johnny Carson's side or he was on theirs. All they knew was that they liked him and felt they knew him, a claim most of those who were close to him, including his wives, family and "Tonight" staff members, would not make with much confidence.

They knew Mr. Carson was intensely private, a self-described loner who shunned the spotlight when off camera. Still, Mr. Carson's scrubbed Midwestern presence was so appealing that he succeeded in unifying a fractious nation.

"Anyone looking at the show 100 years from now," said Tom Shales, the Washington Post television critic, when Mr. Carson retired from "Tonight" in 1992, "will probably have no trouble understanding what made Carson so widely popular and permitted him such longevity. He was affable, accessible, charming and amusing, not just a very funny comedian but the kind of guy you would gladly welcome into your home."

During his reign, Mr. Carson was the most powerful performer on television. He discovered or promoted new talent like Barbra Streisand and David Letterman, provided a spotlight for show business warhorses like Don Rickles and Buddy Hackett, and advanced the careers of emerging stars like Woody Allen, Steve Martin and his successor, Mr. Leno.

All the while he earned millions of dollars for himself and the National Broadcasting Company. In his heyday he generated 17 percent of the network's total profit, and his show was the biggest single money-maker in television history.

For a generation every performer of consequence made a visit to Mr. Carson's famous couch. He was a generous host, as long as he did not feel crossed. Those on the outs with him frequently saw their careers damaged, notably the comedian Joan Rivers, who dared to mount a late-night show to challenge his without first informing him.

In a celebrated New Yorker profile, Kenneth Tynan said of Mr. Carson that he practiced "the art of the expected." Americans were reassured when Doc Severinsen, the show's bandleader, would start up the show's bouncy theme song (written by Paul Anka and Mr. Carson himself), Ed McMahon, the jovial announcer, would intone "Heeeeere's Johnny," and the dapper host would appear to deliver his nightly monologue, a tour de force that the critic Les Brown called "America's bedtime story."

Mr. Carson's credibility with the public was such that his monologues were monitored by politicians mindful that no one who became a target of Johnny Carson could long survive in public life. It didn't help Richard Nixon when Mr. Carson produced some of the funniest Watergate jokes around.

His biggest single audience, an estimated 58 million viewers, tuned in on Dec. 17, 1969, to watch Tiny Tim, the falsetto singer, marry Vicki Budinger, a 17-year-old fan the singer called Miss Vicki.

Mr. Carson also portrayed a variety of characters, among them Carnac the Magnificent, an all-knowing seer, and Aunt Blabby, a gossipy old woman.

NBC occasionally tried to rein him in. In 1979 the network's president, Fred Silverman, began to complain that Mr. Carson took too much time off.

Mr. Carson thereupon announced his intention to quit the show when his contract expired, and a frightened network gave him the biggest salary in television, $5 million a year, and a total deal worth more than $50 million, an unheard-of amount in that era of television.

Mr. Carson also forced NBC to cut his show from 90 minutes to one hour, a decision that ushered in a new late-night time period, occupied first by Mr. Letterman and then Conan O'Brien.

John William Carson was born Oct. 23, 1925, in Corning, Iowa, son of Homer L. Carson, a manager for a power company, and Ruth Hook Carson, a homemaker with a flair for theatrics. In 1933, the family moved to Norfolk, Neb.

When Johnny was 12, he read "Hoffmann's Book of Magic" and sent away for a mail-order magic kit. Intrigued by stories about the great magician Harry Houdini, he decided he would be known as "the Great Carsoni." He made his professional debut, at 14, before the Norfolk Rotary Club, for which he earned $3.

When he graduated in 1943, a friend wrote in his yearbook, "John, if you don't get killed in the war you'll be a hell of an entertainer some day."

After serving in the Navy, Mr. Carson entered the University of Nebraska, where he was active in student theatrical productions. He also appeared on an early experimental television broadcast, which was seen by almost no one.

In 1951 he moved to Los Angeles, where he persuaded station KNXT-TV to give him a Sunday afternoon comedy show, "Carson's Cellar." During one telecast, a furtive figure ran by in the background. Mr. Carson told his viewers that it was Red Skelton.

As it happened, Mr. Skelton saw the show, enjoyed what he saw, and the next week showed up and demanded to appear. Mr. Skelton thought so highly of Mr. Carson's work that he hired him as a writer of his own CBS television show.

One day in 1954, Mr. Skelton injured himself before airtime. Producers, hard pressed to find a substitute, gave Mr. Carson a chance, and he did so well that CBS offered him his own show, but "The Johnny Carson Show" eventually folded.

Mr. Carson then moved to New York and made guest performances on shows, among them "Tonight," starring Mr. Paar. In March 1962, when Mr. Paar decided to leave the "Tonight" show, Mr. Carson was offered the job.

By 1969, Mr. Carson was earning about $20,000 a week. But he did not get to keep all that money. His several divorces were expensive. Joanna Holland, who was Mrs. Johnny Carson from 1972 to 1982, got more than $20 million in cash. Joanne Copeland, Ms. Holland's immediate predecessor, got a yearly "salary" of $100,000. His first wife was Jody Wolcott, who complained that she did not get enough. He is survived by his fourth wife, Alexis Maas, two sons, and a brother and sister.

Mr. Carson zealously guarded his private life. Betty Rollin once wrote that off camera he was "testy, defensive, preoccupied, withdrawn and wondrously inept and uncomfortable with people." Mr. Carson said of himself: "My bugging point is low. I'm not gregarious. I'm a loner."

His retirement in 1992 was another national event, though his show that preceded his finale on the air, which featured Bette Midler and Robin Williams as guests, was better remembered. Ms. Midler's version of "One for My Baby (and One More for the Road)" left the audience, and the host, in tears.

Someone once asked Mr. Carson what he would like his epitaph to be.

He thought for a moment and reached for the traditional line of a talk-show host:

"I'll be right back."

RICHARD PRYOR

December 1, 1940–December 10, 2005

By Mel Watkins

Richard Pryor, the iconoclastic standup comedian who transcended barriers of race and brought a biting, irreverent humor into America's living rooms, movie houses, clubs and concert halls, died Saturday. He was 65.

Mr. Pryor, who had been ill with multiple sclerosis, suffered a heart attack and died at a hospital in Los Angeles, his wife, Jennifer Lee Pryor, told CNN.

His health had been in decline for many years. Episodes of self-destructive, chaotic and violent behavior, often triggered by drug use, repeatedly threatened his career and jeopardized his life. "I couldn't escape the darkness," he acknowledged, but he was able to put his demons at the service of his art.

Mr. Pryor's brilliant comic imagination and creative use of the blunt cadences of street language were revelations to most Americans. He did not simply tell stories; he brought them to life, revealing the entire range of black America's humor, from its folksy rural origins to its raunchier urban expressions.

At the height of his career, in the late 1970's, Mr. Pryor prowled the stage like a restless cat. He was volatile yet vulnerable, crass but sensitive, streetwise and cocky but somehow still diffident and anxious.

"Pryor started it all," the director and comedian Keenen Ivory Wayans said. "He made the blueprint for the progressive thinking of black comedians, unlocking that irreverent style."

For the actor Eddie Murphy, Richard Pryor was simply "better than anyone who ever picked up a microphone." The playwright Neil Simon called him "the most brilliant comic in America."

Mr. Pryor's body language conveyed the ambivalence—at once belligerent and defensive—of the black male's provisional stance in society. He unleashed a galaxy of street characters who had traditionally been embarrassments to most middle-class blacks and mere stereotypes to most whites. And he presented them so truthfully and hilariously that he was able to transcend racial boundaries and capture a huge audience of admirers. In 1998, he received the Kennedy Center's award for humor, the Mark Twain Prize.

Some audiences were offended by his harsh observations and explicit language. But he insistently presented characters with little or no distortion. "A lie is profanity," he explained, adding, "Art is the ability to tell the truth, especially about oneself."

Richard Pryor, the only child of Leroy Pryor and Gertrude Thomas Pryor, was born in Peoria, Ill., on Dec. 1, 1940, and raised in a household where, as he wrote, "I lived among an assortment of relatives, neighbors, whores and winos—the people who inspired a lifetime of comedic material." His parents and grandmother ran a string of bars and bordellos.

A frail child, he learned how to use his quick wit and belligerent humor to gain respect from street gangs and bigger, more aggressive peers. But the antic behavior did not translate to the classroom, and he was expelled from school in the eighth grade. He worked as a truck driver, a laborer and a factory worker, then joined the Army, where he served in Germany until he was discharged after stabbing another serviceman during a fight.

He returned to Peoria, married, became the father of a son, Richard Jr., and, inspired by the television appearances of Redd Foxx and Dick Gregory, began performing in local nightclubs. In 1962, a variety act offered him a job as a master of ceremonies; leaving his wife and child behind, he began touring, appearing at small black nightclubs in East St. Louis, Cleveland, Chicago, Pittsburgh and Youngstown.

In 1963, after honing his craft on the "chitlin circuit," Mr. Pryor decided to take a crack at New York City. He felt ready to compete with the "big cats" and to try to emulate the success of Bill Cosby, the comedian he most admired. Soon, he was appearing at Greenwich Village clubs like Cafe Wha? and the Bitter End.

Big-time television appearances followed. He had, in his own words, "entered the mainstream," presenting "white bread," nonoffensive humor that freely copied the styles of other comedians. Yet despite his growing popularity, he was frustrated.

"There was a world of junkies and winos, pool hustlers and prostitutes, women and family screaming inside my head, trying to be heard," he wrote in his autobiography, "Pryor Convictions" (1995), adding, "The pressure built till I went nuts."

Despite resistance from club owners, booking agents and advisers, he began listening to those voices, developing new material during the next few years served straight from the black experience, even embracing the street vernacular use of the word "nigger."

When he returned to show business in Los Angeles, his comedy had changed radically. After seeing his revised act, Mr. Cosby said: "Richard killed the Bill Cosby in his act, made people hate it. Then he worked on them, doing pure Pryor, and it was the most astonishing metamorphosis I have ever seen. He was magnificent."

Mr. Pryor's 1974 album "That Nigger's Crazy" surprised record-industry executives with its appeal to young whites as well as blacks. The record sold more than a half-million copies and won the Grammy Award for best comedy album of the year. He was a popular host on "Saturday Night Live" in 1975, and two years later he agreed to do a series of television specials for NBC.

After returning from a trip to Africa in 1979, Mr. Pryor told audiences he would never use the word "nigger" again as a performer. While abroad, he said, he saw black people running governments and businesses, and realized that he did not see anyone he could call by that name.

He appeared in 40 films during a career that began with "Busy Bodies" in 1969 and concluded with a role opposite his frequent co-star Gene Wilder in "Another You" in 1992. His 1979 film "Richard Pryor, Live in Concert," in which he reflects on his own tumultuous life, remains the standard by which other movies of live comedy performances are judged.

Mr. Pryor was married six times and divorced five times. In addition to his wife, he is survived by six children.

If he used his misadventures to earn fame and fortune, Mr. Pryor also frequently undercut his career and his life with self-destructive behavior. In 1980, after a marathon drug binge, he was critically burned in an explosion that the police said was caused by the ignition of ether being used in conjunction with cocaine. Paramedics found him walking in a daze more than a mile from his home outside Los Angeles with third-degree burns over the upper half of his body. He was hospitalized for almost two months while undergoing a series of skin grafts.

Recovering, Mr. Pryor remained a top-box office attraction during most of the 1980's, but continued to be bedeviled by drug and health problems. In 1986, he received a diagnosis of multiple sclerosis, and as the years passed he experienced its cruelest symptoms: vertigo, tremors, muscle weakness and chronic fatigue.

Still, in 1992, he was back at the Comedy Store in Los Angeles polishing material for a concert tour. He was no longer able to stand on stage, and he delivered his monologue from an easy chair. But he was forced to cancel his tour early the next year.

"I realized that I had more heart than energy, more courage than strength," he said. "My mind was willing, but my feets couldn't carry me to the end zone."

INGMAR BERGMAN

July 14, 1918–July 30, 2007

By Mervyn Rothstein

Ingmar Bergman, the master filmmaker who found bleakness and despair as well as comedy and hope in his indelible explorations of the human condition, died yesterday at his home on the island of Faro, off the Baltic coast of Sweden. He was 89.

Mr. Bergman was widely considered one of the greatest directors in motion picture history. For much of the second half of the 20th century, he stood with directors like Federico Fellini and Akira Kurosawa at the pinnacle of serious filmmaking.

He moved from the comic romp of lovers in "Smiles of a Summer Night" in 1955 to the Crusader's death-haunted search for God in "The Seventh Seal" in 1957; from the harrowing portrayal of fatal illness in "Cries and Whispers" in 1972 to the alternately humorous and horrifying depiction of family life a decade later in "Fanny and Alexander."

Mr. Bergman dealt with pain and torment, desire and religion, evil and love. God is either silent or malevolent; men and women are creatures and prisoners of their desires.

For many filmgoers and critics, it was Mr. Bergman more than any other director who brought a new seriousness to filmmaking in the 1950s.

"Bergman was the first to bring metaphysics—religion, death, existentialism—to the screen," Bertrand Tavernier, the French film director, said. "But the best of Bergman is the way he speaks of women, of the relationship between men and women. He's like a miner digging in search of purity."

He influenced many other filmmakers, including Woody Allen, who once called Mr. Bergman "probably the greatest film artist, all things considered, since the invention of the motion picture camera."

Mr. Bergman made about 50 films over more than 40 years. He centered his work on two great themes, the relationship between the sexes and the relationship between mankind and God. Mr. Bergman found in film, he wrote in a 1965 essay, "a language that literally is spoken from soul to soul in expressions that, almost sensuously, escape the restrictive control of the intellect." He often acknowledged that his work was autobiographical, but only "in the way a dream transforms experience and emotions all the time."

He carried out a simultaneous career in the theater, becoming a director of Stockholm's Royal Dramatic Theater. He married multiple times and had highly publicized liaisons with his leading ladies.

Mr. Bergman broke upon the international film scene in the mid-1950s with four films that became symbols of his career—"Smiles of a Summer Night," "The Seventh Seal," "Wild Strawberries" and "The Magician."

He had been a director for 10 years but was little known outside Sweden. Then, in 1956, "Smiles" won a special prize at the Cannes International Film Festival. The next year, the haunting and eloquent "Seventh Seal," with its memorable medieval vision of a knight (Max von Sydow) playing chess with death in a world terrorized by the plague, won another special prize at Cannes. In 1959, "The Magician" took the special jury prize at the Venice Film Festival.

Audiences flocked to art cinemas all over the world to see Mr. Bergman's films. In 1960, "The Virgin Spring" told of a rape and its mysterious aftermath in medieval Scandinavia; it won the Academy Award as best foreign film. In only a few years, he had become both a cult figure and a box-office success.

Mr. Bergman often talked about what he considered the dual nature of his creative and private personalities. "I am very much aware of my own double self," he once said. "The well-known one is very under control; everything is planned and very secure. The unknown one can be very unpleasant. I think this side is responsible for all the creative work—he is in touch with the child. He is not rational; he is impulsive and extremely emotional."

Ernst Ingmar Bergman was born on July 14, 1918, in the university town of Uppsala, Sweden. His father, Erik, a Lutheran clergyman who later became chaplain to the Swedish royal family, believed in strict discipline, including caning and locking his children in closets. His mother, Karin, was moody and unpredictable.

Ingmar accompanied his father on preaching rounds of small country churches near Stockholm. His earliest memories, he once said, were of light and death.

"I also remember being forced to sit in church, listening to a very boring sermon, but it was a very beautiful church, and I loved the music and the light streaming through the windows," he said. "I used to sit up in the loft beside the organ, and when there were funerals, I had this marvelous long-shot view of the proceedings, with the coffin and the black drapes, and then later at the graveyard, watching the coffin lowered into the ground. I was never frightened by these sights. I was fascinated."

At the age of nine, he traded a set of tin soldiers for a battered magic lantern, a possession that altered the course of his life. Within a year, he had created a private world. He fashioned his own scenery, marionettes and lighting effects and gave puppet productions of [August] Strindberg plays in which he spoke all the parts.

He entered the University of Stockholm in 1937, but soon left university for a career in the theater and the movies. He became associated with the municipal theaters in the Swedish cities of Halsingborg and then Malmo, and in films he wrote as well as directed.

His name first appeared on the screen in 1944 in "Torment," which he wrote. The film, based on a story Mr. Bergman wrote about his final, torturous year at school, won the Grand Prix du Cinéma at Cannes. It made an international star of its leading actress, Mai Zetterling, who portrayed a shopgirl loved by a young student and shadowed by a sadistic teacher.

Mr. Bergman got his first chance to direct in 1945. Most critics agree that his first film of note was "Prison," the first all-Bergman production. It tells the story of a prostitute who committed suicide, and he made it in 18 days.

In the next few years, he made "Summer Interlude" (1951), a tragedy of teenage lovers; "Waiting Women" (1952), his first successful comedy; "Sawdust and Tinsel," set in a traveling circus; "A Lesson in Love" (1954), a witty comedy of marital infidelity; and, finally, his breakthroughs, "Smiles of a Summer Night" and "The Seventh Seal."

In 1957, the same year as "The Seventh Seal," Mr. Bergman also directed "Wild Strawberries," his acclaimed study of old age. In the film, the 78-year-old Isak Borg (played by Victor Sjostrom) drives through the countryside, stops at his childhood home, relives the memory of his first love and comes to terms with his emotional isolation.

"I had created a figure who, on the outside, looked like my father but was me, through and through," Mr. Bergman said. "I was then 37, cut off from all human emotions."

Mr. Bergman won his second Academy Award in 1962 for "Through a Glass Darkly," about a mentally ill woman who believes she is visited by God. Then came the turning point, "Winter Light," which he made in 1962, the second of his early-'60s trilogy, which ended with "The Silence."

"Winter Light" portrayed the loneliness and vulnerability of modern man, without faith or love. Many of his earlier films had been animated by an anguished search for belief, but "Winter Light," which shows a minister's own loss of faith, implies that any answers will be found on earth.

Mr. Bergman said his philosophical shift had occurred during a brief hospital stay. Awakening from the anesthesia, he realized that he was no longer scared of death. His films from then on, many critics have said, conveyed a kind of humanism in which love is the only hope of salvation.

Some critics attacked his films as obscure and pretentious. But every time he made a failure, he won back critics and audiences with films like "Persona," in which the personalities of two women break down and merge, and "Cries and Whispers," a stark portrait of three sisters.

Mr. Bergman often used what amounted to a repertory company, a group of actors who appeared in many of his films. They included Mr. von Sydow, Gunnar Bjornstrand, Ingrid Thulin, Bibi Andersson, Erland Josephson and, above all, Liv Ullmann, with whom he had a long personal relationship and a child. For many years he used the same cinematographer, Sven Nykvist.

The ideas for his films came to him in many ways, he said. Some were suggested by novels or music. In every case, he said, some outside event had turned the key on some deep-seated memory.

"I have maintained open channels with my childhood," he said. "I think it may be that way with many artists. Sometimes in the night, when I am on the limit between sleeping and being awake, I can just go through a door into my childhood and everything is as it was— with lights, smells, sounds and people. . . . I remember the silent street where my grandmother lived, the sudden aggressivity of the grown-up world, the terror of the unknown and the fear from the tension between my father and mother."

Mr. Bergman used his memories in many other films, including "Scenes From a Marriage," "Autumn Sonata," "From the Life of the Marionettes," "Hour of the Wolf," "Shame," "Face to Face" and his version of Mozart's "Magic Flute."

In 1982, Mr. Bergman announced that he had just made his last theatrical film, "Fanny and Alexander," a look at high society in a Swedish town early in the 19th century that was partly inspired by his own childhood.

"The time with 'Fanny and Alexander' was so wonderful," he said, "that I decided it was time to stop." The film won four Oscars, including the Academy Award for best foreign film.

Mr. Bergman's fifth wife, Ingrid Karlebo Bergman, died in 1995. He had many children from his marriages and relationships.

Many of his films could be said to reveal a preoccupation with death, but that concern, he said, had abated in later life. "When I was young, I was extremely scared of dying," he once said. "But now I think it a very, very wise arrangement. It's like a light that is extinguished. Not very much to make a fuss about."

PAUL NEWMAN

January 26, 1925–September 26, 2008

By Aljean Harmetz

Paul Newman, one of the last of the great 20th-century movie stars, died Friday at his home in Westport, Conn. He was 83.

The cause was cancer, said Jeff Sanderson of Chasen & Company, Mr. Newman's publicists.

If Marlon Brando and James Dean defined the defiant American male as a sullen rebel, Paul Newman recreated him as a likable renegade, a handsome figure of animal high spirits whose magnetism was impossible to resist, whether the character was Hud, Cool Hand Luke or Butch Cassidy.

He acted in more than 65 movies over more than 50 years, drawing on a physical grace, unassuming intelligence and good humor that made it all seem effortless.

Yet he was also an ambitious, intellectual actor and a passionate student of his craft, and he remained a major star into a craggy, charismatic old age even as he redefined himself as more than Hollywood star. He raced cars, opened summer camps for ailing children and became a nonprofit entrepreneur with a line of foods that put his picture on supermarket shelves around the world.

Mr. Newman made his Hollywood debut in the 1954 costume film "The Silver Chalice." Stardom arrived a year and a half later, when he inherited from James Dean the role of the boxer Rocky Graziano in "Somebody Up There Likes Me." Mr. Dean had been killed in a car crash before the screenplay was finished.

It was a rapid rise for Mr. Newman, but being taken seriously as an actor took longer. He was almost undone by his star power, his classic good looks and especially his brilliant blue eyes. "I picture my epitaph," he once said. "Here lies Paul Newman, who died a failure because his eyes turned brown."

Mr. Newman's filmography was a cavalcade of flawed heroes and winning antiheroes stretching over decades. In 1958 he was a drifting confidence man determined to marry a Southern belle in an adaptation of "The Long, Hot Summer." In 1982, in "The Verdict," he was a washed-up alcoholic lawyer who seeks to redeem himself in a malpractice case. In 2002, at 77, he was affably deadly as Tom Hanks's gangster boss in "Road to Perdition," his last onscreen role in a major movie.

Few major American stars have played so many imperfect men.

As Hud Bannon in "Hud" (1963), Mr. Newman was a heel on the Texas range who wanted the good life and was willing to sell diseased cattle to get it. As the self-destructive convict in "Cool Hand Luke" (1967), he was too rebellious to be broken by a brutal prison system. As Butch Cassidy in "Butch Cassidy and the Sundance Kid" (1969), he was an amiable bank robber, memorably paired with Robert Redford. In "The Hustler" (1961) he was the small-time pool shark Fast Eddie, a role he recreated 25 years later, now as a well-heeled middle-aged liquor salesman, in "The Color of Money" (1986).

That performance brought Mr. Newman his sole Academy Award, for best actor. He received eight Oscar nominations for best actor and one for best supporting actor, in "Road to Perdition." "Rachel, Rachel," which he directed, was nominated for best picture.

"When a role is right for him, he's peerless," the film critic Pauline Kael wrote in 1977. "Newman is most comfortable in a role when it isn't scaled heroically; even when he plays a bastard, he's not a big bastard— only a callow, selfish one, like Hud. He can play what he's not—a dumb lout. But you don't believe it when he plays someone perverse or vicious, and the older he gets and the better you know him, the less you believe it."

Performing was never enough for him. He became a racecar driver, winning several Sports Car Club of America national titles. In 1982 he decided to sell a salad dressing he had created and thus was born the Newman's Own brand, an enterprise he started with his friend A. E. Hotchner, the writer.

More than 25 years later the brand has expanded to include lemonade, popcorn, spaghetti sauce and other items. All its profits, of more than $200 million, have been donated to charity, the company says.

Much of the money was used to create a string of Hole in the Wall Gang Camps, named for the outlaw gang in "Butch Cassidy." The camps provide free summer recreation for seriously ill children.

Several years earlier, on Nov. 28, 1978, Scott Newman, the oldest of Mr. Newman's six children, died at 28 of an overdose of alcohol and pills. His father's monument to him was the Scott Newman Center, created to publicize the dangers of drugs and alcohol.

Mr. Newman's three younger daughters are the children of his 50-year second marriage, to the actress Joanne Woodward. Mr. Newman and Ms. Woodward both were cast in the Broadway play "Picnic" in 1953. Starting with "The Long, Hot Summer" in 1958, they co-starred in 10 movies, including "From the Terrace," "Harry & Son," which Mr. Newman also directed, produced and helped write; and "Mr. & Mrs. Bridge."

In 1968 he produced and directed "Rachel, Rachel" for Ms. Woodward. He also directed her in "The Effect of Gamma Rays on Man-in-the-Moon Marigolds" and "The Glass Menagerie." As a director his most ambitious film was "Sometimes a Great Notion."

In an industry in which long marriages are a rarity, Mr. Newman and Ms. Woodward's was striking for its endurance. As he told Playboy magazine, in an often-repeated quotation about marital fidelity, "I have steak at home; why go out for hamburger?"

Paul Leonard Newman was born in Cleveland on Jan. 26, 1925. His mother was the former Teresa Fetzer. His father, Arthur, owned a sporting goods store that enabled the family to settle in affluent Shaker Heights, Ohio.

In high school, the son acted in school plays. He served in the Navy Air Corps, and after the war entered Kenyon College in Ohio, where he acted in a dozen plays before graduating in 1949.

In 1950 Mr. Newman's father died, and he returned to Cleveland to run the sporting goods store. He brought with him a wife, an actress named Jacqueline Witte. But after 18 months Paul asked his brother to take over the business while he, his wife and their year-old son, Scott, headed for Yale University, where Mr. Newman intended to concentrate on directing.

He left Yale in 1952. Almost immediately, the director Josh Logan and the playwright William Inge gave him a small role in "Picnic," a play that would run 14 months on Broadway. Soon he was playing the second male lead and understudying Ralph Meeker as the sexy drifter who roils the women in a Kansas town.

Mr. Newman and Ms. Woodward were attracted to each other in rehearsals. But he was married, and Ms. Woodward has insisted that they spent the next few years running away from each other.

In the early 1950s Mr. Newman studied at the Actors Studio in New York alongside James Dean, Marlon Brando and, eventually, Ms. Woodward.

In 1954 Warner Brothers offered Mr. Newman

$1,000 a week to star in "The Silver Chalice," a film Mr. Newman would describe as the worst movie ever made. His antidote was to hurry back to Broadway. In Joseph Hayes's play "The Desperate Hours," he starred as an escaped convict who holds a family hostage. The play was a hit.

On his nights off Mr. Newman acted on live television. In one production, an adaptation of Ernest Hemingway's short story "The Battler," he took over the lead role after James Dean, who had been scheduled to star, was killed on Sept. 30, 1955.

Arthur Penn, who directed "The Battler," was sure that Mr. Newman's performance in that drama, as a disfigured prizefighter, won him the lead role in "Somebody Up There Likes Me," again replacing Mr. Dean. When Mr. Penn adapted the Billy the Kid teleplay for his first Hollywood film, "The Left Handed Gun," in 1958, he again cast Mr. Newman in the lead.

Even so, Mr. Newman was saddled for years with an image of being a "pretty boy" lightweight.

"Paul suffered a little bit from being so handsome—people doubted just how well he could act," Mr. Penn said.

By 1957 Mr. Newman and Ms. Woodward were discreetly living together in Hollywood. The couple were married in 1958.

That same year Mr. Newman played Brick, the husband of Maggie the Cat, in the film version of Tennessee Williams's "Cat on a Hot Tin Roof," earning his first Academy Award nomination, for best actor. In 1961, with "The Hustler," he earned his second best-actor Oscar nomination.

Many of his meaty performances during the early '60s came in movies directed by Martin Ritt. After directing "The Long, Hot Summer," Mr. Ritt directed Mr. Newman in "Paris Blues," a story of expatriate musicians; "Hemingway's Adventures of a Young Man"; "Hud," which brought Mr. Newman a third

Oscar nomination; "The Outrage," with Mr. Newman as a bandit, and "Hombre," in which Mr. Newman played a white man reared by Indians.

Among his other important films were Otto Preminger's "Exodus," Alfred Hitchcock's "Torn Curtain" and "Harper," in which he played Ross Macdonald's private detective Lew Archer.

In 1968, after he was cast as a racecar driver in "Winning," Mr. Newman was sent to a racing school. In midlife racing became his obsession.

When Mr. Newman turned 50, he settled into a new career as a character actor, playing the title role of Robert Altman's "Buffalo Bill and the Indians," an unscrupulous hockey coach in George Roy Hill's "Slap Shot" and the disintegrating lawyer in Sidney Lumet's "Verdict."

Most of Mr. Newman's films were commercial hits, probably none more so than "The Sting," in which he and Mr. Redford again teamed up to play a couple of con men, and "The Towering Inferno," in which he played an architect.

After his fifth best-actor Oscar nomination, for his portrait of a man discredited by the press in Sydney Pollack's "Absence of Malice," and his sixth a year later, for "The Verdict," the Academy of Motion Picture Arts and Sciences in 1986 gave Mr. Newman the consolation prize of an honorary award.

His best-actor Oscar, for "The Color of Money," came the next year. He earned his eighth nomination as best actor, for portraying a construction worker in "Nobody's Fool."

Besides Ms. Woodward, he is survived by his five daughters, a brother and two grandchildren.

Mr. Newman described his charitable work as his greatest legacy.

"We are such spendthrifts with our lives," he said. "The trick of living is to slip on and off the planet with the least fuss you can muster."

ELIZABETH TAYLOR

February 27, 1932–March 23, 2011

By Mel Gussow

Elizabeth Taylor, the actress who dazzled generations of moviegoers with her stunning beauty and whose name was synonymous with Hollywood glamour, died on Wednesday in Los Angeles. She was 79.

Her publicist, Sally Morrison, said the cause was complications of congestive heart failure. Ms. Taylor had had a series of medical setbacks over the

years and was hospitalized six weeks ago with heart problems.

In a world of flickering images, Elizabeth Taylor was a constant star. First appearing on screen at age 10, she grew up there, never passing through an awkward age. It was one quick leap from "National Velvet" to "A Place in the Sun" and from there to "Cleopatra," as she was indelibly transformed from a vulnerable child actress into a voluptuous film queen.

In a career of some 70 years and more than 50 films, she won two Academy Awards as best actress, for her performances as a call girl in "BUtterfield 8" (1960) and as the acid-tongued Martha in "Who's Afraid of Virginia Woolf?" (1966). Mike Nichols, who directed her in "Virginia Woolf," called her "one of the greatest cinema actresses."

When Ms. Taylor was honored in 1986 by the Film Society of Lincoln Center, Vincent Canby wrote in The New York Times, "More than anyone else I can think of, Elizabeth Taylor represents the complete movie phenomenon—what movies are as an art and an industry, and what they have meant to those of us who have grown up watching them in the dark."

Ms. Taylor's popularity endured throughout her life, but critics were sometimes reserved in their praise of her acting. In that sense she may have been up-staged by her own striking beauty. Could anyone as lovely as Elizabeth Taylor also be talented? The answer, of course, was yes.

Given her lack of professional training, her range was surprisingly wide. She played predatory vixens and wounded victims. She was Cleopatra of the bur-nished barge; Tennessee Williams's Maggie the cat; Catherine Holly, who confronted terror suddenly last summer; and Shakespeare's Kate.

Joseph L. Mankiewicz, who directed her in "Sud-denly, Last Summer" and "Cleopatra," saw her for the first time, in Cannes, when she was 18. "She was the most incredible vision of loveliness I have ever seen in my life," he said. "And she was sheer innocence."

Mankiewicz admired her professionalism. "What-ever the script called for, she played it," he said. "The thread that goes through the whole is that of a woman who is an honest performer. Therein lies her identity."

Marilyn Monroe was the sex goddess, Grace Kelly the ice queen, Audrey Hepburn the eternal gamine. Ms. Taylor was beauty incarnate. As the director George Stevens said when he chose her for "A Place in the Sun," the role called for the "beautiful girl in the yellow Cadillac convertible that every American boy, some time or other, thinks he can marry."

There was more than a touch of Ms. Taylor herself in the roles she played. She acted with the magnet of her personality. Although she could alter her look for a part—putting on weight for Martha in "Virginia Woolf" or wearing elaborate period costumes—she was not a chameleon, assuming the coloration of a character. Instead she would bring the character closer to herself. For her, acting was "purely intuitive."

More than most movie stars, she seemed to exist in the public domain. She was pursued by paparazzi and denounced by the Vatican. People watched and counted, with vicarious pleasure, as she became Eliz-abeth Taylor Hilton Wilding Todd Fisher Burton Burton Warner Fortensky—enough marriages to cer-tify her career as a serial wife. Asked why she mar-ried so often, she said, in an assumed drawl: "I don't know, honey. It sure beats the hell out of me."

In a lifetime of emotional and physical setbacks, serious illnesses and accidents, Ms. Taylor was a sur-vivor. "I've been lucky all my life," she said just before turning 60. "Everything was handed to me. Looks, fame, wealth, honors, love. I rarely had to fight for anything. But I've paid for that luck with disasters." At 65, she said: "I'm like a living example of what people can go through and survive. I'm not like anyone. I'm me."

Her life was played out in print: miles of newspaper and magazine articles, a galaxy of photographs and a shelf of biographies, each one painting a different portrait. Still, there was one point of general agreement: her beauty. As cameramen noted, her face was flawlessly symmetrical; she had no bad angle, and her eyes were of the deepest violet.

One prominent and perhaps surprising dissenter about her looks was Richard Burton, who was twice her husband. The notion of his wife as "the most beautiful woman in the world is absolute nonsense," he said. "She has wonderful eyes," he added, "but she has a double chin and an overdeveloped chest, and she's rather short in the leg."

On screen and off, Ms. Taylor was a provocative combination of the angel and the seductress. In all her incarnations she had a vibrant sensuality. But beneath it was more than a tinge of vulgarity, as in her love of showy jewelry. "I know I'm vulgar," she said, addressing her fans with typical candor, "but would you have me any other way?"

Even when her movies were unsuccessful, or, late in her career, when she acted infrequently, she retained her fame: there was only one Liz (a nickname she hated), and her celebrity increased the more she lived in the public eye. "The public me," she said, "the one named Elizabeth Taylor, has become a lot of hokum and fabrication—a bunch of drivel—and I find her slightly revolting."

Late in life she became a social activist. After her friend Rock Hudson died, she helped establish the American Foundation for AIDS Research and helped raise money for it. In 1997, she said, "I use my fame now when I want to help a cause or other people."

Twice she had leading roles on Broadway, in a 1981 revival of Lillian Hellman's "Little Foxes" and two years later in Noël Coward's "Private Lives," with Burton, then her former husband. In the first instance she won critical respect; in the second she and Burton descended into self-parody. But theater was not her ideal arena; it was as a movie star that she made her impact.

In a life of many surprises, one of the oddest facts is that as an infant she was considered to be an ugly duckling. Elizabeth Rosemond Taylor was born in London on Feb. 27, 1932, the second child of American parents with roots in Kansas. Her father, Francis Lenn Taylor, was an art dealer who had been transferred to London from New York; her mother, the former Sara Viola Warmbrodt, had acted in the theater in New York. At birth, her mother said, her daughter's "tiny face was so tightly closed it looked as if it would never unfold."

Elizabeth spent her early childhood in England. It was there, at three, that she learned to ride horseback, a skill that helped her win her first major role. Just before World War II, the family moved to the United States, eventually settling in Beverly Hills.

With the encouragement of her mother, who shared her love of movies, Elizabeth made her debut in 1942 in a forgettable film called "There's One Born Every Minute"; the casting director at Universal said of her: "The kid has nothing."

But the power of her attraction became evident in 1944, in "National Velvet," the story of a girl who is obsessed with horses and rides one to victory in Britain's Grand National Steeplechase. The 12-year-old Ms. Taylor gave a performance that, quite literally, made grown men and women weep. In The Nation, the tough-minded critic James Agee called her "rapturously beautiful."

The movie made her a star. Decades later she said "National Velvet" was still "the most exciting film" she had ever made. But there was a drawback. To do the movie she had to sign a long-term contract with MGM. As she said, she "became their chattel until I did 'Cleopatra.'"

At first she played typical teenagers and ingénues. That changed in 1951, when she made "A Place in the Sun," playing a wealthy young woman who is the catalyst for Montgomery Clift's American tragedy. To the astonishment of skeptics, she held her own with Clift and Shelley Winters.

Her role in "Raintree County" (1957), as a Civil War–era Southern belle who marries an Indiana abolitionist, earned her an Oscar nomination for best actress. It was the first of four consecutive nominations; the last resulted in a win for "BUtterfield 8."

Next was "Cleopatra," in which she was the first actress to be paid a million-dollar salary. Working overtime, she earned more than twice that amount. The movie cost so much ($40 million, a record then) and took so long that it almost bankrupted 20th Century Fox.

When "Cleopatra" was finally released in 1963 it was a disappointment. But the film became legendary for the off-screen affair of its stars—Ms. Taylor, then married to the singer Eddie Fisher, and Richard Burton, then married to Sybil Williams.

Taylor and Burton: it seemed like a meeting, or a collision, of opposites, the most famous movie star in the world and the man many believed to be the finest classical actor of his generation. What they had in common was an extraordinary passion for each other and for living life to the fullest. Their romantic roller coaster was chronicled by the international press, which referred them as an entity called Dickenliz.

Their life was one of excess. They owned mansions in various countries, rented entire floors of hotels and spent lavishly on cars, art and jewelry. After "Cleopatra," the couple united in a film partnership that gave the public glossy romances like "The V.I.P.s" and "The Sandpiper" and one powerful drama about marital destructiveness, the film version of Edward Albee's play "Who's Afraid of Virginia Woolf?"

As Martha, the faculty wife, a character 20 years older than she was, Ms. Taylor gained 20 pounds and made herself look dowdy. After she received her second Academy Award for the performance, Burton, who played Martha's husband, George, offered a wry response: "She won an Oscar for it, he said, bitterly, and I didn't, he said, equally bitterly."

After 10 high-living and often torrid years, the Burtons were divorced in 1974, remarried 16 months later, separated again the next February and divorced in 1976.

After that divorce, she wed John W. Warner, a Virginia politician, and was active in his winning campaign for the United States Senate. For five years she was a Washington political wife and, she said, "the loneliest person in the world." Overcome by depression, she checked into the Betty Ford Center in California, later admitting that she had been treated as "a drunk and a junkie."

Through the 1980s and '90s, Ms. Taylor acted in movies sporadically, did "The Little Foxes" and "Private Lives" on Broadway, and appeared on television in "Malice in Wonderland" in 1985 and as an aging actress in Tennessee Williams's "Sweet Bird of Youth" in 1989. In 1994 she played Fred Flintstone's mother-in-law in "The Flintstones," and in 1996 she made appearances on four CBS sitcoms.

In February 1997, after celebrating her 65th birthday at a party that was a benefit for AIDS research, she entered Cedars-Sinai Medical Center in Los Angeles for an operation on a brain tumor.

There were other medical trials. In 2009 she had surgery to address heart problems. This year she refused to undergo a back operation, saying she had already had a half-dozen and wasn't up to another. In February she entered Cedars-Sinai for the final time with congestive heart failure.

She is survived by two daughters, two sons, 10 grandchildren and four great-grandchildren.

Married or single, sick or healthy, on screen or off, Ms. Taylor never lost her appetite for experience. Late in life, when she had one of many offers to write her memoirs, she refused, saying with characteristic panache, "Hell no, I'm still living my memoirs."

NORA EPHRON

May 19, 1941–June 26, 2012

By Charles McGrath

Nora Ephron, an essayist and humorist in the Dorothy Parker mold (only smarter and funnier, some said) who became one of her era's most successful screenwriters and filmmakers, making romantic comedy hits like "Sleepless in Seattle" and "When Harry Met Sally . . . ," died Tuesday night in Manhattan. She was 71. The cause was pneumonia brought on by acute myeloid leukemia, her son Jacob Bernstein said.

In a commencement address she delivered in 1996 at Wellesley College, her alma mater, Ms. Ephron recalled that women of her generation weren't expected to do much of anything. But she wound up having several careers, all of them successfully and many of them simultaneously.

She was a journalist, a blogger, an essayist, a novelist, a playwright, an Oscar-nominated screenwriter and a movie director—a rarity in a film industry whose directorial ranks were and continue to be dominated by men. Her later box-office success included "You've Got Mail" and "Julie & Julia." By the end of her life, she had even become something of a philosopher about age and its indignities. "Why do people write books that say it's better to be older than to be younger?" she wrote in "I Feel Bad About My Neck," her 2006 best-selling collection of essays. "It's not better. Even if you have all your marbles, you're constantly reaching for the name of the person you met the day before yesterday."

Nora Ephron was born on May 19, 1941, on the Upper West Side of Manhattan, the eldest of four sisters, all of whom became writers. Her father, Henry, and her mother, the former Phoebe Wolkind, were Hollywood screenwriters who wrote, among other films, "Carousel" and "There's No Business Like Show Business." "Everything is copy," her mother once said, and she and her husband proved it by turning the college-age Nora into a character in a play, later a movie, "Take Her, She's Mine." The lesson was not lost on Ms. Ephron, who could make sparkling copy out of almost anything else: the wrinkles on her neck, her apartment, cabbage strudel.

She turned her painful breakup with her second husband, the Watergate journalist Carl Bernstein, into a best-selling novel, "Heartburn," which she then recycled into a successful movie starring Jack Nicholson and Meryl Streep. When Ms. Ephron was four, her parents moved from New York to Beverly Hills, where she grew up. At Wellesley, she began writing for the school newspaper, and in the summer of 1961 she was a summer intern in the Kennedy White House.

After graduation from college in 1962, she moved to

New York, intent on becoming a journalist. Her first job was as a mail girl at Newsweek. Soon she was contributing to a parody of The New York Post put out during the 1962 newspaper strike. Her piece of it earned her a tryout at The Post, where the publisher, Dorothy Schiff, remarked: "If they can parody The Post, they can write for it. Hire them." Ms. Ephron stayed at The Post for five years, covering stories like the Beatles, the Star of India robbery at the American Museum of Natural History, and a pair of hooded seals at the Coney Island aquarium that refused to mate.

In the late 1960s Ms. Ephron turned to magazine journalism, at Esquire and New York mostly. She quickly made a name for herself by writing frank, funny personal essays—about the smallness of her breasts, for example—and tart, sharply observed profiles of people like Ayn Rand and Helen Gurley Brown.

Her articles were characterized by humor and honesty, written in an understated style marked by an impeccable sense of when to deploy the punch line. (Many of her articles were assembled in the collections "Wallflower at the Orgy," "Crazy Salad" and "Scribble Scribble.")

Ms. Ephron made as much fun of herself as of anyone else. She was labeled a practitioner of the New Journalism, with its embrace of novelistic devices in the name of reaching a deeper truth, but she always denied the connection. "I am not a new journalist, whatever that is," she once wrote. "I just sit here at the typewriter and bang away at the old forms."

Ms. Ephron got into the movie business after her marriage to Mr. Bernstein in 1976. He and Bob Woodward, his partner in the Watergate investigation, were unhappy with William Goldman's script for the movie version of their book "All the President's Men," so Mr. Bernstein and Ms. Ephron took a stab at rewriting it. Their version was not used, but it brought her to the attention of people in Hollywood. Her first screenplay, written with her friend Alice Arlen and directed by Mike Nichols, was for "Silkwood," a 1983 film based on the life of Karen Silkwood, who died under suspicious circumstances while investigating abuses at a plutonium plant where she had worked.

Ms. Ephron followed "Silkwood" with a screenplay adaptation of her own novel "Heartburn," which was also directed by Mr. Nichols. But it was her script for "When Harry Met Sally . . . ," which became a hit Rob Reiner movie in 1989 starring Billy Crystal and Meg Ryan, that established Ms. Ephron's gift for romantic comedy and for delayed but happy endings that reconcile couples who are clearly meant for each other but don't know it.

"When Harry Met Sally . . ." is probably best remembered for Ms. Ryan's faked-orgasm scene with Mr. Crystal in Katz's Delicatessen on the Lower East Side, prompting a middle-aged woman sitting nearby to remark to her waiter, indelibly, "I'll have what she's having."

In many respects Ms. Ephron's films are old-fashioned movies, only in a brand-new guise. Her 1998 hit, "You've Got Mail," which she both wrote (with her sister Delia) and directed, is partly a remake of the old Ernst Lubitsch film "The Shop Around the Corner."

Her first effort at directing, "This Is My Life" (1992), with a screenplay by Ms. Ephron and her sister Delia, based on a Meg Wolitzer novel about a single mother trying to become a standup comedian, was a dud. But Ms. Ephron redeemed herself in 1993 with "Sleepless in Seattle" (she shared the screenwriting credits), which brought Tom Hanks and Meg Ryan together so winningly that they were cast again in "You've Got Mail."

Films Ms. Ephron also wrote and directed were "Lucky Numbers" (2000), "Bewitched" (2005) and, her last, "Julie & Julia" (2009), in which Ms. Streep played Julia Child.

Ms. Ephron earned three Oscar nominations for best screenplay, for "Silkwood," "Sleepless in Seattle" and "When Harry Met Sally. . ." But she never gave up writing in other forms. Two essay collections, "I Feel Bad About My Neck: And Other Reflections on Being a Woman" and "I Remember Nothing," were best sellers. With her sister Delia she wrote a play, "Love, Loss, and What I Wore," about women and their wardrobes, and by herself she wrote "Imaginary Friends," a play about the literary and personal quarrel between Lillian Hellman and Mary McCarthy. Ms. Ephron's first marriage, to the writer Dan Greenburg, ended in divorce, as did her marriage to Mr. Bernstein. In 1987 she married Nicholas Pileggi, the author of the books "Wiseguy" and "Casino." (Her contribution to "Not Quite What I Was Planning: Six-Word Memoirs by Writers Famous and Obscure," edited by Larry Smith and Rachel Fershleiser, reads: "Secret to life, marry an Italian.") In person Ms. Ephron—small and fine-boned with high cheeks and a toothy smile—had the same understated, though no less witty, style that she brought to the page. The producer Scott Rudin recalled that less than two weeks before her death, he had a long phone session with her from the hospital while she was undergoing treatment, going over notes for a pilot she was writing for a TV series. Afterward she told him, "If I could just get a hairdresser in here, we could have a meeting."

ROBIN WILLIAMS

July 21, 1951–August 11, 2014

By Dave Itzkoff

Robin Williams, the comedian who evolved into the surprisingly nuanced, Academy Award–winning actor, imbuing his performances with wild inventiveness and a kind of manic energy, died on Monday at his home in Tiburon, Calif., north of San Francisco. He was 63.

The Marin County sheriff's office said in a statement that it "suspects the death to be a suicide due to asphyxia." An investigation was underway. His publicist said in a statement that Mr. Williams "has been battling severe depression." The privileged son of a Detroit auto executive who grew up chubby and lonesome, playing by himself with 2,000 toy soldiers in an empty room of a suburban mansion, Mr. Williams, as a boy, hardly fit the stereotype of someone who would grow to become a brainy comedian, or a goofy one, but he was both. Onstage he was known for ricochet riffs on politics, social issues and cultural matters high and low; tales of drug and alcohol abuse; lewd commentaries on relations between the sexes; and lightning-like improvisations on anything an audience member might toss at him. His gigs were always rife with frenetic, spot-on impersonations that included Hollywood stars, presidents, prime ministers and popes. His irreverence was legendary and uncurtailable, and yet he never seemed to offend.

Almost from the moment that he first uttered the greeting "Nanoo, nanoo" as Mork from Ork, an alien who befriends a wholesome young Colorado woman (Pam Dawber), on the sitcom "Mork and Mindy," Mr. Williams was a comedy celebrity. "Mork and Mindy" made its debut on ABC in September 1978, and within two weeks had reached No. 7 in the Nielsen ratings. By the spring of 1979, 60 million viewers were tuning in each week to watch Mr. Williams drink water through his finger, stand on his head when told to sit down, and speak gibberish.

He went on to earn Academy Award nominations for his roles in films like "Good Morning, Vietnam," in which he played a loquacious radio D.J.; "Dead Poets Society," playing a mentor to students in need of inspiration; and

"The Fisher King," as a homeless man whose life has been struck by tragedy. He won an Oscar in 1998 for "Good Will Hunting," playing a therapist who works with a troubled prodigy played by Matt Damon.

Robin McLaurin Williams was born in Chicago on July 21, 1951, and raised in Bloomfield Hills, Mich., and Marin County, Calif. He studied acting at the Juilliard School, and rapidly ascended the entertainment industry's ladder. Soon after "Mork and Mindy" made him a star, Mr. Williams graduated into movie roles that included the title characters in "Popeye," Robert Altman's 1980 live-action musical about the cartoon sailor, and "The World According to Garp," the director George Roy Hill's 1982 adaptation of the John Irving novel.

He also continued to appear in raucous stand-up comedy specials like "Robin Williams: An Evening at the Met," which showcased his garrulous performance style and his ability to spontaneously free-associate.

Mr. Williams's acting career reached a new height in 1987 with his performance in Barry Levinson's film "Good Morning, Vietnam," in which he played a nonconformist Armed Forces Radio host working in Saigon in the 1960s. It earned Mr. Williams his first Oscar nomination. He earned another, two years later, for "Dead Poets Society," directed by Peter Weir and released in 1989, in which he played an unconventional English teacher at a 1950s boarding school who inspires his students to tear up their textbooks and seize the day. (Or, as Mr. Williams's character put it in the original Latin, "Carpe diem.")

In dozens of film roles that followed, Mr. Williams could be warm and zany, whether providing the voice of an irrepressible genie in "Aladdin," the 1992 animated Walt Disney feature, or playing a man who cross-dresses as a British housekeeper in "Mrs. Doubtfire," a 1993 comedy, or a doctor struggling to treat patients with an unknown neurological malady in "Awakenings," the 1990 drama adapted from the Oliver Sacks memoir.

Mr. Williams continued to keep audiences guessing. In addition to his Oscar-winning role in "Good Will Hunting," in which he played a gently humorous therapist, his résumé included roles as Teddy Roosevelt in the "Night at the Museum" movies and Dwight D. Eisenhower in the 2013 drama "Lee Daniels' The Butler."

He made his acting debut on Broadway in 2011 in "Bengal Tiger at the Baghdad Zoo," a play set amid the American invasion of Iraq.

Mr. Williams, who is survived by two sons and a daughter, was an admitted abuser of cocaine in the 1970s and '80s and addressed his drug habit in his comedy act. "What a wonderful drug," he once said. "Anything that makes you paranoid and impotent, give me more of that."

In 2006, he checked himself into the Hazelden center in Springbrook, Ore., to be treated for an addiction to alcohol. He later explained in an interview that this addiction had not been "caused by anything, it's just there," adding, "It lays in wait for the time when you think, 'It's fine now, I'm O.K.' Then, the next thing you know, it's not O.K. Then you realize, 'Where am I? I didn't realize I was in Cleveland.'"

MIKE NICHOLS

November 6, 1931–November 19, 2014

By Bruce Weber

Mike Nichols, one of America's most celebrated directors, whose long, protean résumé of critic- and crowd-pleasing work earned him adulation both on Broadway and in Hollywood, died on Wednesday in Manhattan. He was 83.

His death was announced by James Goldston, the president of ABC News. Mr. Nichols was married to the ABC broadcaster Diane Sawyer. A network spokeswoman said the cause was cardiac arrest.

Dryly urbane, Mr. Nichols had a gift for communicating with actors and a keen comic timing, which he honed early in his career as half of the popular sketch-comedy team Nichols and May. An immigrant whose work was marked by trenchant perceptions of American culture, he achieved—in films like "The Graduate," "Who's Afraid of Virginia Woolf?" and "Carnal Knowledge" and in comedies and dramas on stage—what few directors have: popular and artistic success in both film and theater.

An almost perennial prizewinner, he was one of only a dozen or so people to have won an Oscar, a Tony, an Emmy and a Grammy.

His career encompassed an entire era of screen and stage entertainment. On Broadway, where he won an astonishing nine Tonys, he once had four shows running simultaneously. He directed Neil Simon's early comedies "Barefoot in the Park" and "The Odd Couple" in the 1960s; the zany Monty Python musical, "Spamalot," four decades later; and, nearly a decade after that, an acclaimed revival of Arthur Miller's masterpiece, "Death of a Salesman."

From 1968 to 2000 his work included revivals of classics like Chekhov's "Uncle Vanya"; astringent dramas tied to world affairs like "Streamers," David Rabe's tale of soldiers preparing to be shipped out to Vietnam, and Ariel Dorfman's "Death and the Maiden," about the revenge of a former political prisoner; incisive social commentaries like "The Real Thing," by Tom Stoppard; and comedies, by turns acid (Mr. Rabe's "Hurlyburly"), sentimental ("The Gin Game," by D. L. Coburn), dark (Mr. Simon's "The Prisoner of Second Avenue") and light (his "Plaza Suite").

In 1984, as a producer, Mr. Nichols brought a talented monologuist to Broadway, supervising the one-woman show—it was called, simply, "Whoopi Goldberg"—that propelled her to fame. Alone or with the company he founded, Icarus Productions, he produced a number of well-known shows, including the musical "Annie," from which he earned a fortune.

The first time Mr. Nichols stepped behind the camera, in 1966, it was to direct Richard Burton and Elizabeth Taylor in an adaptation of Edward Albee's scabrous stage portrayal of a marriage, "Who's Afraid of Virginia Woolf?" The film was nominated for 13 Academy Awards, including one for best director. Though he didn't win, the film won five.

Mr. Nichols did win an Oscar for his second film, "The Graduate" (1967). The social satire lampooned the Eisenhower-era mind-set of the West Coast affluent and defined the uncertainty of adulthood for the generation that came of age in the 1960s.

The film also made a star of an unknown actor, Dustin Hoffman, who was nearly 30 when he played Benjamin Braddock, the 21-year-old protagonist, who sleeps with the wife of his father's best friend and then falls in love with her daughter. A small, dark, Jewish New York stage actor, Mr. Hoffman was an odd choice for an all-American suburban boy whose seemingly prescribed path has gone awry.

"There is no piece of casting in the 20th century that I know of that is more courageous than putting me in that part," Mr. Hoffman once said.

By the end of Mr. Nichols's career he was bravely casting another Hoffman—Philip Seymour—in the Broadway production of "Death of a Salesman." He cast Hoffman, then 44, to play Miller's tragic American in defeat, Willy Loman, a man in his 60s. In addition to Mr. Nichols's Tony Award for directing, the play won for best revival.

He has also turned his attention to television, winning Emmy Awards for directing adaptations of two celebrated plays for HBO: Margaret Edson's "Wit," about a woman dying of cancer, and Tony Kushner's AIDS drama, "Angels in America."

Stars flocked to work with him. He directed Julie Christie, Lillian Gish, George C. Scott and Morgan Freeman on Broadway. Off Broadway he directed Steve Martin and Robin Williams in Samuel Beckett's "Waiting for Godot." At the Delacorte Theater in Central Park, he directed Meryl Streep and Kevin Kline in Chekhov's "The Seagull."

When he directed Robert Redford and Elizabeth Ashley as bickering newlyweds in "Barefoot in the Park" (1963), they were largely unknown. When he directed Burton and Taylor in "Virginia Woolf," they were the world's biggest stars.

Romantic narratives were his main vehicle. He examined marriages—from the nascent, as in "Barefoot in the Park"; to the crumbling, as in his film adaptation of "Heartburn" (1986); to the unbearably brittle, as in "Virginia Woolf."

He examined courtship rituals in films like "Carnal Knowledge," which told the abrasively comic story of the sexual education of two men (Art Garfunkel and Jack Nicholson) who were college roommates, and "Closer," about seduction via the Internet; and in plays like "The Real Thing," Mr. Stoppard's excavation of the meaning of love, with Jeremy Irons and Glenn Close, and "The Gin Game," about the connection between an elderly pair of card players played by Jessica Tandy and Hume Cronyn.

"I think maybe my subject is the relationships between men and women," Mr. Nichols said in 1986, "centered around a bed." But he found equally rich material in gay relationships, as exemplified in "The Birdcage," a 1996 comedy about sexual identities.

And he often strayed to other kinds of stories, as in his adaptation of Joseph Heller's sardonic war farce,

"Catch-22"; "Silkwood," about a whistle-blower at a plutonium plant; "Working Girl," a revenge-of-the-working-class comedy about a secretary (Melanie Griffith) from Staten Island, and "Primary Colors," about a Clintonesque presidential candidate.

Especially consistent was his wry and savvy sensibility regarding behavior, derived in part from his early success in nightclubs and on television with Ms. May. Their program of satirical sketches depicting one-on-one moments of social interaction reached Broadway, where "An Evening with Mike Nichols and Elaine May" opened in 1960 and ran for more than 300 performances.

Developed through improvisation, written with sly verbal dexterity and performed with cannily calibrated comic timing, their best-known routines became classics of male-female miscommunication and social haplessness: a mother haranguing her scientist son for not calling her; teenagers on a date in the front seat of a car; a telephone operator and a desperate caller in a phone booth.

Mr. Nichols was born Mikhail Igor Peschkowsky in Berlin on Nov. 6, 1931. His father was a Jewish doctor from Russia who fled to America to escape the Nazis in 1938, Anglicizing part of his name—Nicholaiyevitch—to become Paul Nichols. Michael and his younger brother, Robert, joined him in New York the next year.

His mother, Brigitte Landauer, arrived in 1941, and Paul Nichols died the next year. Michael's sense of being a stranger in a strange land was aggravated by the loss of his hair at age four, the result of a reaction to an inoculation for whooping cough. He wore wigs the rest of his life.

As a student at the University of Chicago, he threw off what he had considered a lonely and difficult childhood. "I never had a friend from the time I came to this country until I got to the University of Chicago," he said.

It was in Chicago, in 1953, that he met Ms. May, the daughter of an actor in Yiddish theater. Both recalled that they loathed each other on sight. Then came a chance run-in at a train station, where Ms. May was seated on a bench. As Mr. Nichols recalled, "I went up to her and said, in a foreign accent, 'May I sit down?'

She said, 'If you vish.' We played a whole spy scene together." In 1955 the team of Nichols and May was born.

By 1959 they were in New York, playing clubs like the Village Vanguard and appearing on television. They stayed together until their show closed on Broadway, at which point the partnership ended, leaving Mr. Nichols floundering.

"When Elaine and I split up—that was a shattering year for me," he said in an interview. "I didn't know what I was. I was the leftover half of something."

The producer Arnold Saint-Subber changed that, hiring him in 1963 to direct a new comedy by a rising young playwright, Neil Simon. The play, "Nobody Loves Me," about Manhattan newlyweds in a sixth-floor walk-up, was subsequently retitled "Barefoot in the Park." It received ecstatic reviews, as did Mr. Nichols's direction.

Mr. Nichols won his first Tony for "Barefoot." He was awarded a second for his direction of two shows: Murray Schisgal's "Luv," a comedy about romantic misery that starred Alan Arkin, Eli Wallach and Anne Jackson, and Mr. Simon's celebrated portrait of mismatched roommates, "The Odd Couple," whose original cast included Art Carney as the neatnik Felix and Walter Matthau as the slob Oscar. Both were staged in the 1964–65 season.

More than 40 years later, in 2008, he directed a revival of Clifford Odets's "Country Girl" and left his penultimate mark on Broadway with his acclaimed "Death of a Salesman." In 2013, he directed Harold Pinter's "Betrayal," a drama about an adulterous affair, starring Daniel Craig and Rachel Weisz.

Mr. Nichols, who lived in Manhattan and Martha's Vineyard, married Ms. Sawyer, his fourth wife, in 1988. His first three marriages ended in divorce. In addition to Ms. Sawyer, he is survived by two daughters, a son, a brother and four grandchildren.

In 1999, when Mr. Nichols was honored at Lincoln Center for a lifetime of achievement, Ms. May offered a memorable encomium:

"So he's witty, he's brilliant, he's articulate, he's on time, he's prepared, and he writes. But is he perfect? He knows you can't really be liked or loved if you're perfect. You have to have just enough flaws. And he does. Just the right, perfect flaws to be absolutely endearing."

within a half hour of the final curtain on opening night, the news and meaning of her arrival had spread by the grapevine up to the cafes on the Champs-Elysées, where the witnesses of her triumph sat over their drinks excitedly repeating their report of what they had just seen. . . . Somewhere along the development, either then or it might have been a year or so later, as Josephine's career ripened, she appeared with her famous festoon of banana worn like a savage skirt around her hips. She was the established new American star for Europe."

Introduced 'Le Jazz Hot'

Miss Baker brought "le jazz hot" to Paris and was the personification there of black talent and moder black music. She led a long line of black American artists to Europe, mostly to Paris, where they sought, in her word, "freedom."

Asked many decades later if she had indeed found freedom in France, she said, "Yes, more or less, as an artist, as a human being."

Despite her success and love for France — she became a French citizen in 1937 — she never forgot her experiences with discrimination in the United States and never ceased her outspoken criticism.

She once told a Danish radio interviewer:

"I was born in America [June 3, 1906] and grew up in St. Louis. I was very young when I first went to Europe. I was 18 years old. But I had to go. I wanted to find freedom. I couldn't find it in St. Louis.

Monaco, and her own return to the stage, enabled Miss Baker to buy a $100,000 Rive villa at Roquebrune-Cap-Mart

The young Miss Baker rived in New York from Louis in the early ninetee twenties and was a chorus g in the revue "Shuffle Along which ran three years at Dal on 63d Street. She also a peared at the Cotton Club Harlem.

She went to Paris in " Revue Nègre," in which s scored her overnight triump The show starred Florence Mi and Sidney Bechet, the ja soprano saxophonist.

It was in the following ye that Miss Baker became a s herself, heading a revue at t Folies Bergère. There, weari her skirt of bananas, she int duced the Charleston to t French.

To the French public she w first "La Ba-kair" and th simply "Jasephine." She h difficulty in negotiating French "R," which lent a char ing lisp to her French. Throu the use of a rhinestone micr phone and with the moveme of her sleek body, she cou hold an audience entranced.

Her onstage charact changed with the years. At t outset of her long French care she represented Jazz Age Ha lem. Then she graduated Creole and later to Tonkine or something vaguely Orient with pagoda headdresses. I neath them her oval face loo ed like temple sculpture.

In 1930 she first sang a pla tive song by Vincent Scot "J'ai Deux Amours" ("I H

POPULAR MUSIC

electric amplifier—would
mble into a microphone,
g this, baby," as he ran
ough a repertory that in-
ded "Purple Haze," "Foxy
dy," "Let Me Stand Next to
ur Fire" and "The Wind Cries
ry."

mmediately, the performer
uld come to life, pulsating,
king his electric guitar be-
een his legs and propelling
with a nimble grind of his
s. Bending his head over
strings, he would pluck
m with his teeth, occasion-
y pulling away to take deep
aths, then, falling back and
g nearly supine, he pumped
guitar neck as it stood high
his belly, the while croon-
"Oh, baby." Then, now-
k it ...." now-
Suddenly, he would fix his
es on a girl in the front row
d cry in a sexually an-
shed voice, "I want you,
u, you!" and then would
k his tongue out at her. For
ymbolic finale, he would left
guitar high and send it
shing against the amplifiers.

Stressed the Music

f Mr. Hendrix was conscious
the explicit eroticism in his
formances, he did not admit
it. In an interview in 1968
The New York Times, he
lained it this way:

"Man, it's the music, that's
at comes first. People who
down our performance,
y're people who can't use
ir eyes and ears at the same
ie. They got a button on
ir shoulder blades that
ps only one working at a
e.

"Look, man, we might play
metimes just standing there;

as people understand that, the
better."

There are many who never
did understand, and Mr. Hendrix did not live long enough
to persuade them. But his fans
were numerous and vocal and,
during the last year, Mr. Hendrix and the various instrumentalists he appeared with were
reported to be earning $50,000
a performance.

Produced 'Space Music'

Despite all the energy ex-
pended during his concerts, Mr.
Hendrix made distinct contributions to progressive rock
music. His playing was fluid
and elastic. He seemingly could
bend and stretch a note, using
his fin-
lengths, yet keep his playing
within a solid form.

He was one of the main pop-
ulizers of the "fuzz box,"
whih extends notes, and the
"wa-wa pedal," which produces
a tone similar to a muted horn.

This style, combined with the
pyrotechnics and his sultry,
moaned tones, produced a
brand of rock occasionally
called "space music." It resembled almost nothing produced
by other rock musicians—just
a roar from the stage, with Mr.
Hendrix's notes floating above
it.

Much of the music Mr. Hen-
drex performed he wrote himself, but he also performed
many of the works of Bob Dylan.

James Marshall Hendrix was
born on Nov. 27, 1942, in
Seattle and quit high school for
the paratroopers at 16 ("Anybody could be in the Army,

STEPHEN FOSTER

July 4, 1826–January 13, 1864

STEPHEN C. FOSTER, the composer, died in this City on the 13th inst. [at 37 years old], and his funeral took place at Pittsburgh on Thursday, Jan. 21. He was born on the 4th of July, 1826. His father, W. B. FOSTER, Sen., was a native of Virginia, and settled in Pittsburgh in the year 1796. STEPHEN, at a very early age, manifested musical talents of an unusual order. At the age of seven years a flageolet was placed in his hands, and within a wonderfully short time he had, unaided, mastered its stops and sounds, so as to play with effect several familiar airs of the day. He never, however, aspired to greatness as a performer, either vocal or instrumental, though the taste and sweetness with which he brought forth the most touching tones of the piano and flute could fix his audience in rapt attention.

His first published song, called "Open thy Lattice, Love," was issued about the year 1842, by GEO. WILLIG, in Baltimore. "Old Uncle Ned" and "Oh, Susanna" were not long afterwards issued by W. C. PETERS in Cincinnati. No remuneration was asked or thought of by Mr. FOSTER for these, though they proved immensely profitable to the publisher. Returning to Pittsburgh, Mr. FOSTER produced successively the "Louisiana Belle," "Nelly was a Lady," "Camptown Races," "My Old Kentucky Home," "Master's in the Cold, Cold Ground," "Nelly-Bly," "Oh, Boys, Carry Me 'Long," and the world-renowned "Old Folks at Home"; together with a large number of other songs suitable for the performances of the Ethiopian Minstrels. He was induced to compose his songs at this time in the shape of negro melodies, on account of the wonderful interest all classes then took in that style of music.

For the past 10 years, however, he confined his productions to airs and words of a sentimental of devotional character. Among these are "Willie, We Have Missed You," "Ellen Bayne," "Maggie by My Side," "Come Where My Love Lies Dreaming," "Little Ella," "Jennie with the Light Brown Hair," "Willie My Brave," "Farewell, My Lillie Dear," "Oh, Comrades, Fill No Glass for Me," "Old Dog Tray," "Mollie, Do You Love Me?" "Summer Breath," "Ah, May the Red Rose Live Alway," "Come with Thy Sweet Voice Again," "I See Her Still in My Dreams," "Suffer Little Children to Come unto Me," "Ella Is an Angel," and some hundred others. There has been recently a book of hymns published in New York, with beautiful airs, composed by Mr. FOSTER expressly for each hymn.

As we previously remarked, Mr. FOSTER for a long period allowed his works to be published without thought of pecuniary compensation; but the demand for them became so great, and before long so many flattering offers were made to him, that he found himself impelled to abandon all other pursuits, and devote himself entirely to musical composition as a profession. He entered into an arrangement with FIRTH, POND & CO., the well known New York publishers, which continued many years, and was the source of immense income to Mr. FOSTER, and also of large profits to the publishers. The commissions paid Mr. F. by them on the "Old Folks at Home" alone amounted to over $15,000. Many other of his songs were nearly as profitable, but the "Old Folks at Home" reached a larger issue than any song ever published in America. For the privilege of having his name printed on one edition of this song, the late E. P. CHRIST paid Mr. FOSTER $500.

GEORGE GERSHWIN

September 26, 1898–July 11, 1937

HOLLYWOOD, Calif.—George Gershwin, 38-year-old composer, died today at 10:35 A.M. at the Cedars of Lebanon Hospital. He succumbed after being operated on for removal of a brain tumor.

Two weeks ago Mr. Gershwin collapsed at the Samuel Goldwyn studios, where he had been working on compositions for "The Goldwyn Follies."

Ira Gershwin, who wrote lyrics for his brother's music, was at his side when he died. Also surviving are his mother, Mrs. Rose Gershwin; a sister, Mrs. Leopold Godowsky Jr. and another brother, Arthur.

George Gershwin was a composer of his generation. What he wanted to do most, he said, was to interpret the soul of the American people. Thus in the tempo of jazz he jabbed at the dignities of American life while he won the plaudits of the musical élite with the classic qualities of "A Rhapsody in Blue." With his brother Ira and that master of gentle satire George S. Kaufman he set the nation laughing at the foibles of its government; but, in a more serious mood, he wrote music that the great conductors of his time were glad to present.

Mr. Gershwin was a child of the Twenties, the Age of Jazz. In the years after the war he was to music what F. Scott Fitzgerald was to prose. Four years after that decade began, Paul Whiteman sent the strains of his Rhapsody cascading far beyond Broadway, and the music they called Jazz had come of age. Serge Koussevitzky of the Boston Symphony Orchestra played his work and the capitals of Europe called for more.

For the musical comedy stage, the vaudeville act, the Hollywood lot, he made his music. He had grown up on the streets of Brooklyn and he had served his apprenticeship in Tin Pan Alley. He had woven the cadences of Broadway into his songs and he had given America the plaintive Negro music of "Porgy and Bess."

Some have claimed that his real contributions were his saucy, tuneful dance and musical comedy tunes. But upon one thing all are agreed—that his music will not soon be forgotten.

Mr. Gershwin was born in Brooklyn, Sept. 26, 1898. When he was 12 years old two important things happened. First, his mother bought a piano; second, he heard the violinist Max Rosen give a recital at school. This started young George on his musical career. The piano proved such an attraction that his parents arranged instruction with a woman teacher from the neighborhood. He later met Charles Hambitzer, whom some credit as having "discovered" Gershwin.

Mr. Hambitzer, teacher of piano, violin and cello, versatile orchestra musician and composer of light music, found his new pupil a genius. It was Mr. Hambitzer who gave Mr. Gershwin his first rudiments of harmony and initiated him to the wonder of the classics.

Mr. Gershwin's real learning came from experience, and his course therein started at Remick's music-publishing house. The boy was 16, and had passed two years in the High School of Commerce. His new position was that of "plugger," and it netted him $15 a week. His duties were to tour the haunts of Tin Pan Alley as a floor pianist to a song-and-dance performer, in order to note which songs were best received. It was about this time that he began to write tunes of his own.

After two years at Remick's he left to make his first contact with the theater. It was a job as rehearsal pianist for "Miss 1917," by Victor Herbert and Jerome Kern.

His ability was evident immediately and he was retained after the opening of the show by Ned Wayburn at a salary of $35 a week. It was at one of the Sunday concerts that were part of the run of "Miss 1917" that some of Gershwin's songs had first important hearings, for Vivienne Segal sang "You—Just You" and "There's More to a Kiss."

Then followed a rapid succession of events. He went on the Keith Vaudeville Circuit as accompanist to Louise Dresser; he was hired by the publishing firm of Harms as staff composer; he toured as pianist with Nora Bayes, and his songs were being heard in revues and other shows. When he was 20 he received his first musical comedy commission from Alex Aarons. The product was "La La Lucille," given in 1919. He was then introduced to George White, with the result that Gershwin wrote the music for the "Scandals" of five successive years, beginning in 1920.

His renown spread rapidly. In the next decade he was to turn out such musical comedy hits as "Our Nell" (1922), "Sweet Little Devil" (1923), "Lady Be Good," "Primrose" (1924), "Tip Toes," "Song of the Flame" (1925), "Oh, Kay!" (1926), "Strike Up the Band,"

"Funny Face," "Shake Your Feet" (1927), "Rosalie," "Treasure Girl" (1928), "Show Girl" (1929), "Girl Crazy" (1930), "Of Thee I Sing" (1931) "Pardon My English" (1932), and "Let 'Em Eat Cake" (1933).

America was ripe for "Of Thee I Sing" when its characters cavorted across a Boston stage for the first time just before Christmas, 1931. Washington had become a stuffy place and Mr. Kaufman and Mr. Gershwin hit upon the exact psychological moment to present Alexander Throttlebottom and the dancing graybeards of the Supreme Court.

To this satire of love in the White House, George Gershwin contributed the catchy tunes. His brother Ira wrote the lyrics, and many felt that it had at last developed the Gilbert and Sullivan of the new age. The music, especially that of the finale: "Of thee I sing—baby!" caught the spirit of the book exactly.

To some extent, Mr. Gershwin recaptured the vibrancy of this play in "Let 'Em Eat Cake," its successor, but critics felt, in the words of Mr. Brooks Atkinson, that there was more style than thought. Both scores, however, were hailed as masterpieces of modern light opera composition.

But Mr. Gershwin brought the artistic haut monde to his feet with the "Rhapsody in Blue," for piano and orchestra. It was written at the suggestion of Paul Whiteman and was first performed in the first concert of jazz music given by Mr. Whiteman's band on Feb. 12, 1924, in Aeolian Hall. Mr. Gershwin himself played the solo part.

The next large work was the orchestral piece "An American in Paris," first heard at the hands of the Philharmonic-Symphony, under Dr. Damrosch, in

Carnegie Hall. Koussevitzky and the Boston Symphony Orchestra, with Gershwin as soloist, introduced the Second Rhapsody in January, 1932.

Mr. Gershwin often appeared at the Lewisohn Stadium concerts of the Philharmonic-Symphony, as soloist, composer and conductor. One program devoted entirely to his own works, given Aug. 16, 1932, attracted an audience that set a record for the stadium. He appeared with all the leading orchestras in this country and many in Europe.

Perhaps his most ambitious work was the opera "Porgy and Bess," based on the dramatized novel of Dubose Heyward. Lyrics were by Ira Gershwin and Mr. Heyward. Described as something "between grand opera and musical comedy," it made a sensation at its world première performance in Boston, Sept. 30, 1935, by the Theatre Guild. It reached the Alvin Theatre in New York on Oct. 10 and repeated its triumph.

HANK WILLIAMS

September 17, 1923–January 1, 1953

OAK HILL, W. Va.—Hank Williams, singer and composer called "King of Hillbillies" by his followers, died today in his automobile on his way from Knoxville, Tenn., to fill an engagement in Marion, Ohio.

The 29-year-old one-time shoeshine boy, composer of "Jambalaya," was brought to Oak Hill Hospital by his chauffeur. The chauffeur, Charles Carr, said he became alarmed when he was unable to awaken Mr. Williams, who had been sleeping in a bed in the rear seat of the car.

Mr. Williams sang doleful mountain ballads in a nasal voice, accompanying himself on a guitar, which he began playing at the age of six years. His recording of "Lovesick Blues" was said to have sold more than a million copies. Other songs composed by him included "Cold, Cold Heart," "Wedding Bells," "Mansion on the Hill" and "Move It Over."

CHARLIE PARKER

August 29, 1920–March 12, 1955

Charlie Parker, one of the founders of progressive jazz, or be-bop, died [in Manhattan] last Saturday night.

The news of the death of the noted musician, known as "The Yardbird," spread quickly last night through Tin Pan Alley, where he was affectionately referred to as "The Bird." A virtuoso of the alto saxophone, Mr. Parker was ranked with Duke Ellington, Count Basie and other outstanding Negro musicians.

Mr. Parker had appeared several times in Carnegie Hall and had played in Europe. More than five years ago the Broadway jazz hall at 1678 Broadway was named Birdland in his honor.

Mr. Parker died while watching a television program in the apartment of the Baroness de Koenigswarter in the Hotel Stanhope, 995 Fifth Avenue. He had called last Wednesday on the Baroness on his way to Boston to fill an engagement. The Baroness, who is 40 years old, is the former Kathleen Annie Pannonica Rothschild of the London branch of the international banking family of Rothschild. She and Mr. Parker had been friends for many years.

Disturbed by Mr. Parker's appearance, the Baroness called Dr. Robert Freymann, with offices in the hotel. He urged the musician not to drive to Boston and advised him to enter a hospital immediately. Mr. Parker refused but the Baroness persuaded him to stay in her suite until he recovered.

At 7:30 o'clock Saturday evening Dr. Freymann found Mr. Parker in satisfactory condition. Forty-five minutes later he collapsed, and when the physician returned, Mr. Parker was pronounced dead.

Dr. Freymann, who notified the Medical Examiner, attributed death to a heart attack and cirrhosis of the liver. The body reached the Morgue at Bellevue Hospital at about 2 A.M. Sunday. Last night Chief Medical Examiner Milton Helpern said an autopsy had disclosed death was due to lobar pneumonia.

The police said Mr. Parker was about 35 years old. He lived with his wife, Chan, at 4 Barrow Street in Greenwich Village. They had three children, a son, who has just entered the Air Force; a daughter, 7, and a second son, 5.

BILLIE HOLIDAY

April 7, 1915–July 17, 1959

Billie Holiday, famed jazz singer, died yesterday in Metropolitan Hospital. Her age was 44. The immediate cause of death was given as congestion of the lungs complicated by heart failure.

Miss Holiday had lived at 26 West 87th Street. She had been under arrest in her hospital bed since June 12 for illegal possession of narcotics.

Miss Holiday set a pattern during her most fruitful years that has proved more influential than that of almost any other jazz singer, except the two who inspired her, Louis Armstrong and the late Bessie Smith.

Miss Holiday became a singer more from desperation than desire. She was named Eleanora Fagan after her birth in Baltimore. She was the daughter of a 13-year-old mother, Sadie Fagan, and a 15-year-old father who were married three years after she was born.

The first and major influence on her singing came when, as a child, she ran errands for the girls in a nearby brothel in return for the privilege of listening to recordings by Mr. Armstrong and Miss Smith.

Miss Holiday took her professional name from her father, Clarence Holiday, a guitarist who played with Fletcher Henderson's band in the 1920s, and from one of the favorite movie actresses of her childhood, Billie Dove.

She came to New York with her mother in 1928. They eked out a precarious living for a while, partially from her mother's employment as a housemaid. But when the Depression struck, her mother was unable to find work. Miss Holiday tried to make money scrubbing floors, and when this failed she started along Seventh Avenue in Harlem one night looking for any kind of work.

At Jerry Preston's Log Cabin, a nightclub, she asked for work as a dancer. She danced the only step she knew for 15 choruses and was turned down. The pianist, taking pity on her, asked if she could sing. She brashly assured him that she could. She sang "Trav'lin' All Alone" and then "Body and Soul" and got a job—$2 a night for six nights a week working from midnight until about 3 o'clock the next afternoon.

Miss Holiday had been singing in Harlem in this fashion for a year or two when she was heard by John Hammond, a jazz enthusiast, who recommended her to Benny Goodman, at that time a relatively unknown clarinet player who was the leader on occasional recording sessions.

She made her first recording, "Your Mother's Son-in-Law," in November, 1933, singing one nervous chorus with a band that included, in addition to Mr. Goodman, Jack Teagarden, Gene Krupa and Joe Sullivan.

Two years later Miss Holiday started a series of recordings with groups led by Teddy Wilson, the pianist, which established her reputation in the jazz world. On many of these recordings the accompanying musicians were members of Count Basie's band, a group with which she felt a special affinity. She was particularly close to Mr. Basie's tenor saxophonist, the late Lester Young.

It was Mr. Young who gave her the nickname by which she was known in jazz circles—Lady Day. She in turn created the name by which Mr. Young was identified by jazz bands, "Pres." She was the vocalist with the Basie band for a brief time during 1937, and the next year she signed for several months with Artie Shaw's band.

Miss Holiday came into her own as a singing star when she appeared at Cafe Society in New York in 1938 for the major part of the year. It was at Cafe Society that she introduced one of her best-known songs, "Strange Fruit," a biting depiction of a lynching written by Lewis Allen.

During that engagement, too, she established trademarks that followed her for many years—the swatch of gardenias in her hair, her fingers snapping lazily with the rhythm, her head cocked back at a jaunty angle as she sang.

In 1947, a cloud that had been gathering over Miss Holiday, and which was to cover the rest of her career, burst on her. She was arrested for a narcotics violation and, at her own request, was committed to a Federal rehabilitation establishment at Alderson, W. Va., for a year and a day in an attempt to rid herself of the habit.

Ten days after her release Miss Holiday gave a concert at Carnegie Hall to a packed house, but, although she appeared at concert halls in New York from time to time after that, she was not allowed to appear in New York nightclubs. As a result of her narcotics conviction, she could not get the necessary cabaret license.

During the 1950's Miss Holiday's voice began to lose its useful elasticity. This, combined with occasional brushes with narcotics agents, made her last years difficult, although she continued to record frequently.

Miss Holiday appeared in a film, "New Orleans," in 1946 and was featured in a Broadway revue for a short run a few years later. In 1954 she made a tour of Europe and was featured in a widely acclaimed television program, "The Sound of Jazz," in 1958.

She is survived by her husband, Louis McKay. A previous marriage, to Joe Guy, a trumpet player, ended in divorce.

JOHN COLTRANE

September 23, 1926–July 17, 1967

John Coltrane, the tenor saxophonist who was considered one of the most gifted modern jazz musicians of this decade, died yesterday at Huntington Hospital, Huntington, L.I. Mr. Coltrane, who was 40 years old, had entered the hospital for treatment for an inflamed liver.

Mr. Coltrane, who played the soprano as well as the tenor saxophone, was one of the most controversial instrumentalists since the late Charlie Parker. He developed a style in the late 1950's using what have been called "sheets of sound." Some more conservative critics referred to it as "honking" and "bleating."

Discussing the Coltrane style, John S. Wilson, jazz critic for the New York Times, wrote in 1961: "Until about five years ago, Mr. Coltrane appeared content to be a journeyman jazzman. Then, while he was a member of the Miles Davis Quintet, he began an exploration of the resources of his saxophone that led him to performances filled with long, hard-bitten, rapid, rising and falling runs that had the cumulative effect of an aural battering ram."

In 1965, Mr. Coltrane and his saxophone picked up just about all the formal jazz accolades. Down Beat, the jazz magazine, voted him the best jazz tenor saxophonist of the year, named him "Jazzman of the Year," elected him to the magazine's Hall of Fame, and chose his recording, "A Love Supreme," as the record of the year.

Mr. Coltrane (Trane to his friends) had come a long way from Hamlet, N.C., the small town where he was born on Sept. 23, 1926. His father, John William Coltrane Sr., was a tailor who loved music and played several instruments.

In high school, young John was in the band, starting with an E flat alto saxophone. For a time he played the clarinet, then switched to the tenor saxophone.

In his early years, he mostly played like the old-time New Orleans musicians. Sidney Bechet was one of his heroes, and he imitated him on the soprano saxophone.

Many years later, after Mr. Coltrane again turned to the soprano saxophone for some recordings, one critic observed that Mr. Coltrane "projects a passion and lyricism on the soprano saxophone that compare with the playing of Sidney Bechet, the only other jazz musician who has made major use of the instrument."

The Coltrane style was developed over a long period during which he played with some of the top jazz groups. He toured with Eddie (Clean Head) Vinson's rhythm and blues band in 1947 and 1948, and two years later joined Dizzy Gillespie's band. Mr. Coltrane also toured with Earl Bostic, Johnny Hodges and the Miles Davis Quintet.

For a time he played with Thelonious Monk's Quartet and he later formed the John Coltrane Quartet, whose original piano player was McCoy Tyner.

One of his most popular records was "Olé Coltrane," consisting of a long selection on one side and two shorter pieces. Some critics thought his selections were too long and boring, but a fellow jazz musician suggested that "you have to listen carefully to Trane, get involved with him."

Mr. Coltrane was a quiet man, described by one friend as "almost introspective and deeply religious." He studied the music and religions of the East, especially India, and the influence of Eastern music was often apparent in his compositions.

In an interview with Jazz magazine, Mr. Coltrane mused about his preoccupations with music and God. "I want to be a force for real good," he said. "In other words. I know that there are bad forces, forces that bring suffering to others and misery to the world, but I want to be the opposite force."

Mr. Coltrane, who had a home in Dix Hills, Huntington, and is survived by his widow, mother, and four children, made his last record, "Expression," for the Impulse label, last February. "He was almost as big a seller in France, Britain, Germany and Japan as he was here," said a spokesman for Impulse, "and that was big."

WOODY GUTHRIE

July 14, 1912–October 3, 1967

Woody Guthrie, the American folk singer and composer, died yesterday at Creedmoor State Hospital, Queens, following a 13-year illness. He was 55 years old.

Mr. Guthrie, who wrote more than 1,000 songs that echoed the glory and travail of American life, had been bedridden for the last nine years with Huntington's chorea, a rare hereditary disease that attacks the nervous system.

Harold Leventhal, the singer's agent and friend, said that in his last years Mr. Guthrie had been virtually immobile, unable to speak, read or use his hands.

For Woodrow Wilson Guthrie, his songs, his guitar and his humanism were his life. He was a wispy, raspy-voiced musical spokesman for the downtrodden who used his scarred guitar to sing out against injustice and sham.

He also sang of the beauty of his homeland—a beauty seen from the open doorway of a red-balling freight train or from the degradation of the migrant camps and Hoovervilles of the Depression years.

A small, weather-worn man with bushy hair, he was as simple and homespun as his songs. His grammar was often atrocious. But his vision of America was bursting with image upon image of verdant soil, towering mountains and the essential goodness and character of its people.

At a concert a few years ago in Connecticut, Odetta, the folk singer, told her audience that if she were in charge of things, one of Mr. Guthrie's songs, "This Land Is Your Land," would be the "national anthem."

The song, one of the balladeer's best known, shows Guthrie at his best:

> *This land is your land, this land is my land,*
> *From California to the New York Island,*

From the redwood forest to the
Gulfstream waters,
This land was made for you and me.

But Mr. Guthrie also stirred controversy with topical songs that were born in his radicalism and his impatience—songs deploring the Dust Bowl and the lot of its refugees, songs crying out against the misuse of migrant workers and extolling the virtues of labor unions. He also wrote talking blues, ballads and children's songs.

"I hate a song that makes you think that you're not any good; I hate a song that makes you think that you are born to lose," he once said, adding, "I am out to fight those kind of songs to my very last breath of air and my last drop of blood."

Woody Guthrie was born on July 14, 1912, in the Dust Bowl town of Okemah, Okla. His father, Charles Guthrie, was a professional guitarist and prizefighter who made his living at several trades.

The five Guthrie children—Roy, Clara, Woody, George and Mary Jo—were reared on the old songs and ballads sung to them by their mother, and on the Indian square dances and Negro blues shouted by their father.

As a boy, young Guthrie sold newspapers, sang and danced in the streets for pennies, and fought it out in gang brawls. His formal schooling ended in the 10th grade.

Life went sour for the Guthrie family in Okemah. Charles Guthrie's land-trading business went bankrupt, two of the family's houses were destroyed by fire, another by a cyclone. Young Guthrie's sister Clara was killed in an oil stove explosion. His mother developed Huntington's chorea and later died in a state asylum.

At the age of 15, he hit the road for Houston, working at odd jobs and playing the harmonica in barbershops and pool halls. He returned to Okemah, then joined his father in the Texas Panhandle town of Pampa, where an uncle taught him to play the guitar.

As the dust storms and the Depression pressed in on the Southwest, the balladeer left home again, heading for the West Coast by freight train, singing in saloons to eat. In California, he appeared regularly on radio, sang at union halls, gave support to striking farm laborers and wrote articles for the radical People's World.

From this exposure to America's social and economic ills came such songs as "So Long It's Been Good to Know You," "Hard Traveling," "Union Maid" and "Pastures of Plenty."

Mr. Guthrie rambled to New York City, where he sang his songs in waterfront taverns and in hobo jungles; to the lost men on the Bowery, to the upper classes in Town Hall and to the workingmen in Madison Square Garden.

Restless once again, he moved out for the South and the West. While in the Pacific Northwest, he composed 26 ballads for the Oregon Department of the Interior about Bonneville and Grand Coulee Dams, becoming a singing advocate of public power.

Later, he joined Pete Seeger, Lee Hays, Millard Lampell and others in the Almanac Singers, a group that sang to unionists and to audiences of farm and factory workers across the country.

In 1943, he and his close friend, the late folk singer Cisco Houston, joined the merchant marine. Mr. Guthrie took part in three invasions and was twice on ships that were torpedoed.

In 1943 he wrote "Bound for Glory," an odyssey of his life, a book that Orville Prescott, in The New York Times, said had "more triple-distilled essence of pure individual personality in it than any in years."

Mr. Guthrie recorded many of his songs on the Stinson, Folkways and Victor labels, giving whole new generations an opportunity to hear him. A result was that he had a profound influence on American folk singing, from the countless youngsters who sing out at Washington Square Park to such well-known performers as Bob Dylan, Tom Paxton, Logan English, Jack Elliott and Phil Ochs.

Realizing his voice did not sound "like dew dripping off the petals of the morning violet," Mr. Guthrie once said that "I had rather sound like the ashcans of the early morning, like the cab drivers cursing at one another, like the longshoremen yelling, like the cowhands whooping, and like the lone wolf barking."

The balladeer married twice, first in the early nineteen-thirties the former Mary Esta Jennings, and then in 1945 the former Marjorie Mazia Greenblatt. Both marriages ended in divorce.

Surviving are two daughters of his first marriage, two sons and a daughter of his second marriage, including Arlo, a folk singer, and a sister and a brother.

A family spokesman said Mr. Guthrie's body would be cremated and his ashes scattered in the waters off Coney Island, where he once lived.

JIMI HENDRIX

November 27, 1942–September 18, 1970

By George Gent

LONDON—Jimi Hendrix, the American rock star whose passionate, intense guitar playing stirred millions, died here today. He was 27 years old.

Mr. Hendrix was taken to St. Mary Abbots Hospital in Kensington after collapsing this morning at the home of friends. Unconfirmed reports said he had died of an overdose of drugs.

The pop star last performed at the Isle of Wight Festival last month.

Explosive and sensuous, Jimi Hendrix undulated his way into international popularity with young people on two continents while startling their elders with his frank sexuality.

During a typical performance, the singer-guitarist—dressed in tight black pants, a rainbow shirt and a black leather vest, his Afro looking as though it had been plugged into his electric amplifier—would mumble into a microphone, "Dig this, baby," as he ran through a repertory that included "Purple Haze," "Foxy Lady," "Let Me Stand Next to Your Fire" and "The Wind Cries Mary."

Immediately, the performer would come to life, flicking his electric guitar between his legs and propelling it with a grind of his hips. Bending over the strings, he would pluck them with his teeth. Then, falling back and lying nearly supine, he pumped the guitar neck as it stood high on his belly while crooning. "Oh, baby, come on now, sock it to me!"

Suddenly, he would fix his eyes on a girl in the front row and cry in an anguished voice, "I want you, you, you!" For a symbolic finale, he would send his guitar crashing against the amplifiers.

Mr. Hendrix seemingly could bend and stretch a note, using electronic distortions or his fingers, to almost impossible lengths. He was a main popularizer of the "fuzz box," which extends notes, and the "wah-wah pedal," which produces a tone similar to a muted horn.

This style, combined with the pyrotechnics and his sultry, moaned tones, produced a brand of rock that resembled almost nothing produced by other rock musicians—just a roar from the stage, with Mr. Hendrix's notes floating above it.

James Marshall Hendrix was born on Nov. 27, 1942, in Seattle and quit high school at 16. Musically, he came up the black route, learning guitar to Muddy Waters records, playing in Negro clubs in Nashville, begging his way onto Harlem bandstands, and touring as a backup guitarist with headliners like the Isley Brothers and Little Richard.

Of his time with Little Richard, he recalled: "I always wanted my own scene, making my music, not

playing the same riffs. Like once with Little Richard, me and another guy got fancy shirts 'cause we were tired of wearing the uniform.

"Richard called a meeting, 'I am Little Richard, I am Little Richard,' he said, 'the King, the King of Rock and Rhythm. I am the only one allowed to be pretty. Take off those shirts.' Man, it was all like that. Bad pay, lousy living, and getting burned."

The Jimi Hendrix Experience was born in October, 1966, and their first number, "Hey Joe," rose to No. 4 on the British pop charts. Shortly thereafter Mr. Hendrix was voted the world's top musician by readers of Melody Maker, an English pop-music paper.

Mr. Hendrix returned to this country in 1967 for a series of concerts. A year later, an overflow crowd of 18,000 turned out to hear him, Janis Joplin and others in Flushing Meadow Park, Queens.

His appearance at the Woodstock festival in August, 1969, is considered one of his most memorable. Mr. Hendrix brought the proceedings to a close in the early morning hours with a highly individualized, electronically amplified version of "The Star-Spangled Banner."

He reorganized his group that summer, calling it Jim Hendrix and His Gypsies. Appearing at Madison Square Garden last January for a Vietnam Moratorium concert, he threw down his guitar in the middle of a song, told the crowd, "I can't get it together," and walked off the stage.

In an interview more than a year ago, Mr. Hendrix, who was arrested in Toronto on drug possession charges but acquitted, gave a hint of the inner turmoil in his performances. "I tell you when I die I'm not going to have a funeral," he said. "I'm going to have a jam session. And, knowing me I'll probably get busted at my own funeral."

JANIS JOPLIN

January 19, 1943–October 4, 1970

HOLLYWOOD—Janis Joplin, the rock singer, was found dead in her Hollywood apartment tonight. She was 27 years old.

The cause of death was not immediately determined, but the police said she apparently died of an overdose of drugs. They said she had been dead for about two hours when she was found shortly after 10 P.M.

Miss Joplin was the second noted pop singer to die in less than three weeks. Jimi Hendrix, 27, died in London Sept. 18 after taking nine strong sleeping tablets.—*Reuters*

She would stand before her audience, microphone in hand, long red hair flailing, her raspy voice shrieking in rock mutations of black country blues. Pellets of sweat flew from her contorted face and glittered in the beam of footlights. Janis Joplin sang with more than her voice. Her involvement was total.

She lived that way, too. The girl from Port Arthur, Tex., who moved to stardom by way of the San Francisco rock upsurge, talked openly of the Southern Comfort she drank and of the joys of being inebriated. With the same abandon that she sang, she drove her Porsche through the hills of San Francisco, a fast-looking car, decorated with psychedelic butterflies.

"When I get scared and worried," she said at the time, "I tell myself, 'Janis, just have a good time.' So I juice up real good and that's just what I have."

By that time she was riding the crest of rock popularity, having soared into prominence with her rendition of "Love Is Like a Ball and Chain" and the 1967 Monterey Rock Festival. The song, said one critic, "was wrenched out of some deep dark nether region of her Texas soul."

Back home in Port Arthur she had been a misfit. "I read, I painted, I didn't hate niggers," she once recalled. "Man, those people back home hurt me. It makes me happy to know I'm making it and they're back there, plumbers just like they were."

She tried college several times, and a job as a computer programmer. She collected Leadbelly and Bessie Smith records, but she never really sang professionally until June of 1966. An old friend, Travis Rivers, had formed a band in San Francisco called Big Brother and the Holding Company. He sent for her and once again she left Port Arthur, this time for the Haight Ashbury section of San Francisco.

It was June of that year and the band was playing the Avalon, a ballroom. She had just arrived and the ambiance of the flailing, gyrating, burgeoning "youth scene" of San Francisco was heady.

"I couldn't believe it, all that rhythm and power," she said. "I got stoned just feeling it, like it was the best dope in the world. It was so sensual, so vibrant, loud, crazy. I couldn't stay still; I had never danced when I sang, but there I was moving and jumping. I couldn't hear myself, so I sang louder and louder. By the end I was wild . . ."

There followed performances at the Psychedelic Supermarket in Boston, the Kinetic Playground in Chicago, the Whisky A-Go-Go in Los Angeles and the Fillmore East in New York. There was "Cheap Thrills," the album that sold more than a million copies. And there was Miss Joplin screaming, "Take another piece of my heart, baby."

There were big money and rock festivals. And the tempo of her private life kept pace with the driving songs. The Southern Comfort distillery gave her a fur coat in recognition of the publicity she gave the company by drinking from a bottle at her concerts.

Her home in San Francisco was decorated in Rococo bordello style. She shared it with dog named George and a Siamese fighting fish named Charley whose aquarium was a wine bottle.

Her behavior was explosive. In November, 1969, she was arrested after a concert in Tampa, Fla., for screaming obscenities at a policeman in the audience. She was temperamental and demanded the same dedication of her backup musicians as she herself gave. She split from the Holding Company and formed her own band, the Janis Joplin Full Tilt Boogie Band.

And there were those who said that neither her voice nor her health could stand the demands she made upon them, on stage and off. Her answer: "Maybe I won't last as long as other singers, but I think you can destroy your now worrying about tomorrow."

JIM MORRISON

December 8, 1943–July 3, 1971

LOS ANGELES—Jim Morrison, the 27-year-old lead singer of "The Doors" rock group, died last Saturday in Paris, his public relations firm said today. His death was attributed to natural causes, but details were withheld pending the return of Mr. Morrison's agent from France. Funeral services were held in Paris today. —*United Press International*

In his black leather jacket and skin-tight vinyl pants, Jim Morrison personified rock music's image of the superstar as sullen, mystical sexual poet.

"The Doors," a quartet founded in 1964 in and near the film school at the University of California at Los Angeles, became by 1967 one of the most popular groups in the country, attracting the attention of serious critics who discussed their music's origins and meanings, as well as screaming, hysterical teen-agers who sometimes had to be peeled off the performers by stagehands at the group's frenzied concerts.

Their performances were invariably treated by reviewers as events of theater, for the Doors helped to take electronically amplified rock music that bloomed on the West Coast out of the sound studio and into the concert hall.

Their music was loud and distinctive, but perhaps the most attention was paid to the lyrics, written by Mr. Morrison, which were filled with suggestive and frequently perverse meanings abetted by Mr. Morrison's grunts, sneers and moans on stage.

"Think of us," Mr. Morrison once said, "as erotic politicians."

One critic echoed others when he called Mr. Morrison's presentations "lewd, lascivious, indecent and profane." Indeed, in one of his most famous episodes, he was arrested and later found guilty of indecent exposure at a rock concert in Miami in March of 1969.

It was this concert, which shocked even some of his teen-age fans, that led to a giant "Rally for Decency" in the Orange Bowl later that month, attended by 30,000 persons. Mr. Morrison was also forcibly removed from a New Haven stage in 1967 after he allegedly exposed himself.

Mr. Morrison's first two hits were "Light My Fire" and "People are Strange." One of his most important works was "The End," an 11 1/2-minute "extended popsong" that ended with a vision of violent death.

LOUIS ARMSTRONG

August 4, 1901–July 6, 1971

By Albin Krebs

Louis Armstrong, the celebrated jazz trumpeter and singer, died in his sleep yesterday morning at his home in the Corona section of Queens.

Death was attributed to a heart attack. Mr. Armstrong had been at home since mid-June, when he was discharged from Beth Israel Medical Center after 10 weeks of treatment for heart, liver and kidney disorders.

Tributes to Mr. Armstrong came from a number of leading musicians. Duke Ellington commented: "If anybody was Mr. Jazz it was Louis Armstrong. He was the epitome of jazz and always will be. He is what I call an American standard, an American original."

A master showman known to millions as Satchmo, Mr. Armstrong lived by a simple credo. Putting it into words a couple of years ago, he said:

"I never tried to prove nothing, just always wanted to give a good show. My life has been my music, it's always come first, but the music ain't worth nothing if you can't lay it on the public. The main thing is to live for that audience, 'cause what you're there for is to please the people."

Mr. Armstrong was first and most importantly a jazz trumpet player without peer, a virtuoso soloist who was one of the most vivid and influential forces in the development of American music.

But he was also known to delight millions around the world for his ebulliently sand-papery singing voice, his merry mangling of the English language and his great, wide grand-piano keyboard of a smile.

Jazz music, probably the only art form ever wholly originated in America, and Louis Armstrong grew up together in New Orleans. It was in a seamy slum there that Mr. Armstrong learned to love and play jazz in the company of gamblers, pimps and prostitutes.

Jazz experts, even the purists who criticized Mr. Armstrong for his mugging and showmanship, more often than not agreed that it was he, more than any other individual, who took the raw, gutsy Negro folk music of the New Orleans funeral parades and honky-tonks and built it into a unique art form.

Over the years, his life and his artistry changed radically. He left New Orleans for Chicago in the early nineteen-twenties, when he was still playing the cornet, and before 1930 made some of his most memorable recordings—with his Hot Five or Hot Seven groups.

Mr. Armstrong won his initial fame playing an endless grind of one-night stands. Under constant pressure to put on a show that made the customers tap their feet and cry for more, he did not hesitate to exploit a remarkable flair for showmanship. His mugging, his wisecracking and most of all his willingness to constantly repeat programs that had gone over well in the past won him the cheers of his audiences, along with the disapproving clucks of some of his fellow musicians and jazz specialists.

The criticism that he no longer improvised enough, innovated enough, mattered little to Mr. Armstrong. He dismissed the more "progressive" jazz approved of by some leading critics as "jujitsu music."

As his ability to play his horn exceptionally well waned with the years, Mr. Armstrong supplanted his trumpet solos with his singing voice. An almost phenomenal instrument in its own right, it has been compared to iron filings and to "a piece of sandpaper calling to its mate."

Just watching an Armstrong performance could be exhilarating. The man radiated a jollity that was infectious. Onstage he would bend back his stocky frame, point his trumpet to the heavens and joyfully blast out high C's. When he sang he fairly bubbled with pleasure. And as he swabbed away at the perspiration stirred up by his performing exertions, Satchmo grinned his famous toothy smile so incandescently that it seemed to light up the auditorium.

Mr. Armstrong's early years, spent in New Orleans, were marked by extreme poverty and squalor, but he emerged able to recall them without self-pity and even with good humor.

"I was a Southern Doodle Dandy," said Daniel Louis Armstrong. "My mother Mary Ann—we called her Mayann—was living in a two-room shack in James Alley, in the Back O' Town colored section of New Orleans. It was in a tough block, all them hustlers and their pimps and gamblers with their knives, between Gravier and Perdido Streets."

Mr. Armstrong's father, Willie Armstrong, who stoked furnaces in a turpentine factory, left Mrs. Armstrong when the boy was an infant. Leaving the child with his paternal grandmother, Mrs. Armstrong went to live in the Perdido-Liberty Street area, which was lined with prostitutes' cribs.

"Whether my mother did any hustling I can't say," Mr. Armstrong said. "If she did, she kept it out of my sight."

Dippermouth, as he was called as a child, and his friends often sang for pennies on the streets. Louis delivered coal to prostitutes' cribs and sold food plucked from hotel garbage cans.

The night of Dec. 31, 1913, Louis celebrated the New Year by running out on the street and firing a .38-caliber pistol. He was arrested and sent to the Colored Waifs Home for Boys.

"Pops, it sure was the greatest thing that ever happened to me," Mr. Armstrong said. "Me and music got married at the home."

Peter Davis, an instructor at the home, taught Louis to play the bugle and the cornet. Soon the boy became a member of the home's brass band. Louis was in the fifth grade when he was released from the home after spending 18 months there. He had no other formal education.

The youth worked as a junkman and sold coal, while grabbing every chance he could to play cornet in honky-tonk bands. The great jazz cornetist Joe (King) Oliver befriended him, gave him a cornet and tutored him.

"I was foolin' around with some tough ones," Mr. Armstrong recalled in 1969. "Get paid a little money, and a beeline for one of them gambling houses. Two hours, man, and I was a broke cat, broker than the Ten Commandments. Needed money so bad I even tried pimping, but my first client got jealous of me and we got to fussing about it and she stabbed me in the shoulder. Them was wild times."

In 1918, Mr. Armstrong married a 21-year-old prostitute named Daisy Parker. Since Daisy "wouldn't give up her line of work," Mr. Armstrong said, the marriage was stormy and short-lived.

The same year he was married, Mr. Armstrong joined the Kid Ory band, replacing King Oliver, who had moved to Chicago. In the next three years he marched with Papa Celestin's brass band and worked on the riverboat Sidney.

By then Mr. Armstrong's fame was spreading among New Orleans musicians, many of whom were moving to Chicago. In 1922 King Oliver sent for his protégé. Mr. Armstrong became second cornetist in Mr. Oliver's by then famous Creole Jazz Band. The two-cornet team had one of the most formidably brilliant attacks ever heard in a jazz group. Mr. Armstrong's first recordings were made with the Oliver band in 1923.

The pianist in the band was Lilian Hardin, whom Mr. Armstrong married in 1924. That year he joined Fletcher Henderson's orchestra at the Roseland Ballroom in New York.

For the first time, Mr. Armstrong found himself in the company of musicians of an entirely different stripe from those he had known who had fought their way up out of the back alleys. From these men, many of whom had conservatory educations, he learned considerable musical discipline.

Moving back to Chicago in 1925, Mr. Armstrong played with Erskine Tate's "symphonic jazz" orchestra at the Vendome Theater. It was at that point that he gave up the cornet for the trumpet.

"I was hired to play them hot choruses when the curtain went up," Mr. Armstrong recalled. "They put a spotlight on me. Used to hit 40 or 50 high C's—go wild, screamin' on my horn, I was crazy, Pops, plain nuts."

In that Chicago period, Mr. Armstrong began to make records under his own name, the first being "My Heart," recorded Nov. 12, 1925. Louis Armstrong's Hot Five (and later Hot Seven) recorded, over a three-year span, a series of jazz classics, with Earl (Fatha) Hines on the piano. These records earned Mr. Armstrong a worldwide reputation, and by 1929, when he returned to New York, he had become an idol in the jazz world.

While playing at Connie's Inn in Harlem, Mr. Armstrong also appeared on Broadway in the all-Negro review "Hot Chocolates," in which he introduced Fats Waller's "Ain't Misbehavin'," his first popular-song hit.

By 1932, the year he was divorced from Lil Hardin Armstrong, he had become so popular in Europe, via recordings, that he finally agreed to tour the Continent.

It was while he was starring at the London Palladium that Mr. Armstrong acquired the nickname Satchmo. A London music magazine editor inadvertently invented the name by garbling an earlier nickname, Satchelmouth.

One of Mr. Armstrong's pre–World War II European tours lasted 18 months. Over the years his tours took him to the Middle East and the Far East, to Africa and to South America. In Accra, Ghana, 100,000 natives went into a frenzied demonstration when he started to blow his horn, and in Léopoldville, tribesmen painted themselves ochre and violet and carried him into the city stadium on a canvas throne.

His 1960 African tour was denounced by Moscow as a "capitalist distraction," which made Mr. Armstrong laugh.

"I feel at home in Africa," he said. "I'm African-descended down to the bone, and I dig the friendly ways these people go about things. I got quite a bit of African blood in me from my grandmammy on my mammy's side and from my grandpappy on my pappy's side."

Before the war, Mr. Armstrong worked with several big bands, including the Guy Lombardo orchestra, concentrating on New Orleans standards such as "Muskrat Ramble" and "When the Saints Go Marchin' In." He did duets with Ella Fitzgerald and he accompanied Bessie Smith.

Mr. Armstrong lost track of the number of recordings he made, but it has been estimated there were as many as 1,500. Dozens have become collectors' items.

Some Negro militants criticized Mr. Armstrong for his earthy speech and his habit of rolling his eyes and flashing his toothy grin while performing. They said he was using stereotyped characteristics of the happy-go-lucky Negro and playing the Uncle Tom. Mr. Armstrong ignored the charges.

Nevertheless, Mr. Armstrong, on learning in 1965 that the police in Selma, Ala., had taken violent action against freedom-marching Negroes, told an interviewer:

"They would beat Jesus if he was black and marched. Maybe I'm not in the front line, but I support them with my donations. My life is my music. They would beat me on the mouth if I marched, and without my mouth I wouldn't be able to blow my horn."

For many years, Mr. Armstrong refused to perform in New Orleans, his hometown, because of segregation there. He did not return until 1965, after passage of the Civil Rights Act. On that occasion he triumphantly played with an integrated band in the city's Jazz Museum.

Reflecting on his music, Mr. Armstrong said: "There's three generations Satchmo has witnessed, the old cats, their children and their children's children, and they still all walk up and say, 'Ol' Satch, how do you do!' I love my audience and they love me and we just have one good time whenever I get up on the stage. It's such a lovely pleasure."

Mr. Armstrong is survived by his widow, the former Lucille Wilson, whom he married in 1942, and by an adopted son, Clarence Hatfield of New York. He also leaves a sister, Mrs. Beatrice Collins of New Orleans and two half-brothers, Henry and William Armstrong, both of New Orleans.

DUKE ELLINGTON

April 29, 1899–May 24, 1974

By John S. Wilson

Duke Ellington, who expanded the literature of American music with compositions and performances that drew international critical praise and brought listening and dancing pleasure to two generations, died yesterday at the age of 75.

He entered the Columbia Presbyterian Medical Center's Harkness Pavilion at the end of March for treatment of lung cancer, which was complicated when he developed pneumonia.

The phrase "beyond category," which Edward Kennedy Ellington had used as his highest form of praise for others, could be applied to the Duke himself, whose works were played and praised in settings as diverse as the old Cotton Club, Carnegie Hall and Westminster Abbey.

Mr. Ellington, whose innate elegance of manner won him his nickname of Duke while he was still a schoolboy in Washington, was tall, debonair and urbane, with a vitalizing sense of the dramatic and an ironic wit.

Amid the protests voiced in 1965 when a unanimous recommendation by the Pulitzer Prize music jury that Mr. Ellington, then 66, be given a special citation was rejected by the Pulitzer advisory board, he said, "Fate is being kind to me. Fate doesn't want me to be famous too young."

Mr. Ellington's work transcended the usual connotations of "jazz," a word that he consistently rejected in relation to his music.

"In the nineteen-twenties I used to try to convince Fletcher Henderson that we ought to call what we're doing 'Negro music,'" Mr. Ellington said in 1965. "But it's too late for that now. The music has become so integrated that you can't tell one part from the other so far as color is concerned."

As a composer and arranger, Mr. Ellington created an unusual and (as many other orchestra leaders found) inimitable style by building his works on the individualistic sounds of brilliant instrumentalists—the growling trumpets of Bubber Miley, Cootie Williams and Ray Nance, the virtuoso plunger mute effects of the trombonist Tricky Sam Nanton, the rich, mellow clarinet of Barney Bigard, the exquisite alto saxophone of Johnny Hodges, the huge, sturdy drive of Harry Carney's baritone saxophone. Billy Strayhorn, who was Mr. Ellington's musical right arm, his co-composer and co-arranger from 1939 until his death in

1967, explained that "Ellington plays the piano but his real instrument is his band."

The basis of the Ellington sound eluded other musicians. When Mr. Ellington's star was just beginning to rise and Paul Whiteman was the "King of Jazz," Mr. Whiteman and his arranger, Ferde Grofé, spent nights on end at the Cotton Club listening to the Ellington orchestra but, so legend has it, eventually abandoned their efforts to try to notate what the Duke's musicians were playing.

Although Mr. Ellington's basic working materials were almost invariably the blues and the voice-like manner in which a jazz musician plays his instrument, classically oriented musicians often found a relationship to Debussy, Delius and Ravel in his work.

Mr. Ellington was a pioneer in extending jazz composition beyond the customary chorus of 12 or 32 bars. His "Reminiscing in Tempo," written in 1934, was a 12-minute work. Four years later, Whiteman commissioned him to write a concert piece, "Blue Belles of Harlem," for the Whiteman orchestra. Mr. Ellington's first major effort at an extended composition came in 1943, when he wrote "Black, Brown and Beige," which ran for 50 minutes when it was introduced at Carnegie Hall.

His extended compositions also included "Harlem," "Night Creatures," "Suite Thursday," inspired by John Steinbeck's book "Sweet Thursday," and a Shakespeare suite, "Such Sweet Thunder."

In 1965, Mr. Ellington moved into a new musical field, presenting a Concert of Sacred Music of his own composition at Grace Cathedral in San Francisco. The performance, starting with the Biblical paraphrase "In the beginning, God . . .", was developed in typical Ellingtonian style with a company that included his full orchestra, three choirs, a dancer and several guest vocalists. Mr. Ellington considered the concert "the most important thing I've ever done."

But before Mr. Ellington became involved in extended composition, his songs, which included "Solitude," "Sophisticated Lady," "In a Sentimental Mood," "I Let a Song Go Out of My Heart" and "I Got It Bad," had become standards in the popular repertory. In addition, his short instrumental pieces—such as "Black and Tan Fantasy," "The Mooche," "Creole Love Call" and "Mood Indigo"—were established as part of the jazz repertory.

Mr. Ellington wrote more than 6,000 pieces, but one of the tunes most closely associated with him, "Take the 'A' Train," a signature theme for many years, was not written by him. It was composed by Mr. Strayhorn.

Mr. Ellington was born in Washington on April 29, 1899, the son of James Edward Ellington and the former Daisy Kennedy. His father was a blueprint maker for the Navy Department, who also worked occasionally as a butler, sometimes at the White House.

He wrote his first composition, "Soda Fountain Rag," while working after school as a soda jerk at the Poodle Dog Cafe. Piano lessons he had received at the age of seven were his only formal musical education. He learned by listening to the "two-fisted piano players" of the period, particularly Sticky Mack, Doc Perry, James P. Johnson and Willie (The Lion) Smith.

By the time he was 20 he was making $150 a week playing with his small band at parties and dances. Sonny Greer became Mr. Ellington's drummer and remained with him until 1950, setting a pattern that was to be followed by many Ellington sidemen.

In 1922 Wilbur Sweatman asked Mr. Greer to join his band in New York. Mr. Ellington and three others went along, too, but jobs in New York were so scarce that soon they were all back in Washington. However, Mr. Ellington had the opportunity to hear the Harlem pianists who became a prime influence—Willie (The Lion) Smith, James P. Johnson and Mr. Johnson's protégé Fats Waller.

At Mr. Waller's urging, Mr. Ellington's group returned to New York in 1923, playing at Barron's in Harlem with Elmer Snowden, the group's banjoist, as nominal leader. When they moved to a downtown club, Mr. Snowden left the group and Mr. Ellington took over.

During the four and a half years that Ellington's band remained there, the group made its first records and did its first radio broadcasts. Late in 1927, when the band had expanded to 10, the Cotton Club was in sudden need of an orchestra.

Mr. Ellington got the booking, but first he had to be released from a theater engagement in Philadelphia. This was arranged when the operators of the

Cotton Club asked some associates in Philadelphia to call on the theater manager with a proposition: "Be big or you'll be dead."

Mr. Ellington's unique use of growling brass (identified as his "jungle" style) and the rich variety of tonal colors that he drew from his band brought musicians of all schools to the Cotton Club.

In 1930 the Ellington band appeared in its first feature-length movie, "Check and Double Check," and in 1933 it went overseas for the first time, to Britain and Europe.

When the furor over swing bands rose in the late thirties, Ellington was overshadowed by Benny Goodman, Artie Shaw and Glenn Miller. But as the swing era faded, the Ellington band hit one of its peaks in 1941 and 1942.

In the fifties, when interest in big bands dropped so low that all but a handful gave up completely or worked part-time, Mr. Ellington kept his band together.

His fortunes started to rise again in 1956 when, at the Newport Jazz Festival, a performance of a composition Mr. Ellington had written 20 years before, "Diminuendo and Crescendo in Blue," propelled by a 27-chorus solo by the tenor saxophonist Paul Gonsalves, set off dancing in the aisles that reminded observers of the joyous excitement that Benny Goodman had generated at New York's Paramount Theater in the thirties.

During the next 15 years, Mr. Ellington's orchestra toured the Middle East, the Far East and the Soviet Union under the auspices of the State Department, playing in Africa, South America and Europe. Mr. Ellington wrote scores for five films—"Paris Blues," "Anatomy of a Murder," "Assault on a Queen," "Change of Mind" and a German picture, "Janus."

He composed a ballet, "The River," in 1970 for Alvin Ailey and the American Ballet Theater. In 1963 he wrote a pageant of black history, "My People," which was presented in Chicago.

Honors were heaped on him. In 1969, at a celebration of his 70th birthday at the White House, President [Richard M.] Nixon awarded him the Presidential Medal of Freedom. President Georges Pompidou of France in 1973 gave him the Legion of Honor. The Royal Swedish Academy of Music elected him a member in 1971. Chad and Togo issued postage stamps bearing his picture. In 1972, Yale University established the Duke Ellington Fellowship Fund "to preserve and perpetuate the Afro-American musical tradition."

Through all this, Mr. Ellington kept up his steady pace of composing and performing and traveling. Everywhere he went, his electric piano went with him, for there was scarcely a day in his life when he did not compose something.

"You know how it is," he said. "You go home expecting to go right to bed. But then, on the way, you go past the piano and there's a flirtation. It flirts with you. So, you sit down and try out a couple of chords and when you look up, it's 7 A.M."

Quite logically, Mr. Ellington called his autobiography, published in 1973, "Music Is My Mistress."

"Music is my mistress," he wrote, "and she plays second fiddle to no one."

Mr. Ellington married Edna Thompson in 1918. Their son, Mercer, was born the following year. The couple were divorced in 1930 and Mr. Ellington's second marriage, to Mildred Dixon, a dancer at the Cotton Club, also ended in divorce.

Surviving besides his son, Mercer, is his widow, Bea (Evie) Ellis; a sister and three grandchildren.

JOSEPHINE BAKER

June 3, 1906–April 12, 1975

PARIS—Josephine Baker, the American dancer and singer who became one of France's great music-hall stars, died early today in the Salpétrière Hospital. She was 68 years old and suffered a stroke Thursday, four days after opening a new revue celebrating her 50 years as an entertainer.

Josephine Baker went to Paris in 1925, tied a string of bananas around her waist and became first a local and then an international sensation.

Of the entertainer's electrifying opening night in 1925, Janet Flanner wrote in "Paris Is Yesterday," published in 1972:

"She made her entry [at the Théâtre des Champs-Elysées] entirely nude except for a pink flamingo feather between her limbs; she was being carried upside down and doing the split on the shoulder of a black giant. Midstage he paused, and with his long fingers holding her basket-wise around the waist, swung her in a slow cartwheel to the stage floor, where she stood, like his magnificent discarded burden, in an instant of complete silence. She was an unforgettable female ebony statue. A scream of salutation spread through the theater.

"Whatever happened next was unimportant. The two specific elements had been established and were unforgettable—her magnificent dark body, a new model that to the French proved for the first time that black was beautiful, and the acute response of the white masculine public in the capital of hedonism of all Europe—Paris.

"Within a half hour of the final curtain on opening night, the news and meaning of her arrival had spread by the grapevine up to the cafes on the Champs-Elysées, where the witnesses of her triumph sat over their drinks excitedly repeating their report of what they had just seen. . . . Somewhere along the development, either then or it might have been a year or so later, as Josephine's career ripened, she appeared with her famous festoon of banana worn like a savage skirt around her hips. She was the established new American star for Europe."

Miss Baker brought "le jazz hot" to Paris and was the personification there of black talent and modern black music. She led a long line of black American artists to Europe, mostly to Paris, where they sought, in her word, "freedom."

Asked many decades later if she had indeed found freedom in France, she said, "Yes, more or less, as an artist, as a human being."

Despite her success and love for France, she never forgot her experiences with discrimination in the United States.

"I was born in America [June 3, 1906] and grew up in St. Louis," she once said. "I was very young when I first went to Europe. I was 18 years old. But I had to go. I wanted to find freedom. I couldn't find it in St. Louis, of course."

The French applauded Miss Baker not only as a performer but also for her World War II activities. She served as an ambulance driver, intelligence agent and an entertainer with the Free French Air Force in North Africa.

"France made me what I am," she said. "They gave me their hearts. Surely I can give them my life."

In the nineteen-fifties, Miss Baker adopted a dozen orphans of various nationalities, races and religions, including a Korean, a Finn, an Israeli, a Venezuelan, an Algerian, a Japanese and a Colombian.

She called them her "rainbow tribe," and lived with them in a chateau, Les Milandes, in Southwestern France. The 300-acre estate was the centerpiece of a resort she tried to build and included a hotel, restaurant, swimming pool and theater.

But the cost of the project led her into debt. Her property and belongings were sold at auction in 1969, and Miss Baker had to be carried out into the rain by gendarmes. Financial help from friends, such as Princess Grace of Monaco, and her own return to the stage, enabled Miss Baker to buy a $100,000 Riviera villa.

The young Miss Baker arrived in New York from St. Louis in the early nineteen-twenties and was a chorus girl in the revue "Shuffle Along," which ran three years at Daly's on 63rd Street.

She went to Paris in "La Revue Nègre," in which she scored her overnight triumph. The following year Miss Baker became a star herself, heading a revue at the Folies Bergère. There, wearing her skirt of bananas, she introduced the Charleston to the French.

Her onstage character changed with the years. At the outset of her French career she represented Jazz Age Harlem. Then she graduated to Creole and later to something vaguely Oriental, with pagoda headdresses.

In 1930 she first sang a plaintive song by Vincent Scotto, "J'ai Deux Amours" ("I Have Two Loves")—the two loves being "my country and Paris." The song became her musical signature.

In the late twenties and through the thirties, she starred annually in revues at the Folies Bergère or at the Casino de Paris, becoming probably the outstanding popular performer of those years.

She came to Broadway in 1936 for the "Ziegfeld Follies," and she visited New York again in 1951. During that stay she charged that she had been a victim of discrimination at the Stork Club, served only after a long delay.

Miss Baker made triumphant return visits to perform in the United States in the last two years. She appeared at Carnegie Hall and at the Palace Theater in "An Evening with Josephine Baker."

Her marriage in the twenties to Count Heno Abatino, an Italian painter, ended in divorce. In 1935, she was married to Jean Lyon, a French industrialist, and they were divorced in 1940. Her next marriage was to Jo Bouillon, a jazz orchestra leader, from whom she had been separated since 1957.

ELVIS PRESLEY

January 8, 1935–August 16, 1977

By Molly Ivins

Elvis Presley, the first and greatest American rock-and-roll star, died yesterday at the age of 42. Mr. Presley, whose throaty baritone and blatant sexuality redefined popular music, was found unconscious in the bedroom of his home, called Graceland, in Memphis yesterday at 2:30 P.M.

He was pronounced dead an hour later at Baptist Memorial Hospital, after doctors failed to revive him.

Dr. Jerry Francisco, the Shelby County coroner, who conducted a two-hour examination of the body, said "preliminary autopsy findings" indicated that the cause of death was "cardiac arrhythmia," which a hospital spokesman defined as "an irregular and ineffective heartbeat." The coroner was not immediately able to determine the cause of the "cardiac arrhythmia."

Mr. Presley was once the object of such adulation that teen-age girls screamed and fainted at the sight of him. He was also denounced for what was considered sexually suggestive conduct on stage. Preachers inveighed against him in sermons, and parents forbade their children to watch him on television. In his first television appearance on the Ed Sullivan show, his act, tame by today's standards, was considered by the broadcasters to be so scandalous that the cameras showed him only from the waist up, lest his wiggling hips show.

Mr. Presley's early hit songs are an indelible part of the memories of anyone who grew up in the 50's. "Hound Dog," "Heartbreak Hotel" and "Blue Suede Shoes" were teen-age anthems. Like Frank Sinatra in the decade before and the Beatles a decade later, Mr. Presley was more than a singer—he was a phenomenon, with 45 gold records that sold more than one million copies each.

Mr. Presley was a show-business legend before he was 25 years old. At the age of 30 he was the highest-paid performer in the history of the business. He made 28 films, virtually every one of them frivolous personality vehicles, but they grossed millions.

In recent years, Mr. Presley, who used to carry about 175 pounds on a 6-foot frame, gained weight and appeared bloated on stage. A recently published book called "Elvis, What Happened?" by three of his former bodyguards alleged that the singer used amphetamines.

Asked repeatedly about whether the autopsy had revealed signs of drug abuse, Dr. Francisco, the coroner, said he had only detected drugs that had been prescribed by Mr. Presley's personal physician for hypertension and a blockage of the colon for which the singer had been hospitalized twice in 1975.

Elvis Aron Presley was born in a two-room house in Tupelo, Miss., on Jan. 8, 1935. During his childhood, he appeared with his parents, Gladys and Vernon Presley, as a popular singing trio at camp meetings, revivals and church conventions.

The family moved to Memphis when Mr. Presley was 13. He attended L. O. Humes High School and worked as an usher in a movie theater. After graduation, he got a job driving a truck for $35 a week. In 1953, Mr. Presley recorded his first song and paid $4 for the privilege; he took the one copy home and played it over and over.

A shrewd song promotor called "Colonel" Thomas A. Parker was impressed by the early records and took over the management of Mr. Presley's career. Mr. Presley toured in rural areas under the sobriquet "The Hill Billy Cat." Colonel Parker, a character of P. T. Barnum proportions, followed the credo, "Don't explain it, just sell it." He once observed, "I consider it my patriotic duty to keep Elvis up in the 90 percent tax bracket."

When Colonel Parker negotiated with 20th Century Fox on a film deal that would be Mr. Presley's screen debut, the studio executives dwelled on the singer's youth and inexperience. "Would $25,000 be all right?" one executive finally asked. Colonel Parker replied: "That's fine for me. Now, how about the boy?"

"Heartbreak Hotel," Mr. Presley's first song hit,

was released by RCA in January 1956. A blood-stirring dirge about love and loneliness, it burned up the jukeboxes and eventually sold 2 million copies.

A phenomenal string of hit songs followed, and Elvis Presley fan clubs sprouted [up] all over the world; membership rose to 400,000.

In 1957, he went to Hollywood to make his first film, "Love Me Tender." It opened to unanimous jeers from the critics and grossed between five and six times what it cost to make.

His later films were also panned by cineastes. One critic remarked of "Jailhouse Rock" that Mr. Presley had been "sensitively cast as a slob." Mr. Presley responded, "That's the way the mop flops."

In the spring of 1958, Mr. Presley was drafted into the Army as a private, an event that caused as much stir as an average Super Bowl. "The Pelvis," as he was known, was stationed in West Germany for two years and was given an ecstatic welcome home by his fans.

In 1967, Mr. Presley married Priscilla Beaulieu, the daughter of an Air Force colonel. They had a daughter named Lisa Marie, born on Feb. 1, 1968. The couple separated in February 1972. They were divorced in Santa Monica, Calif., in 1973.

Mr. Presley was said to have been a shy person, and rarely granted interviews. He seems to have been scarred by some of the early heavy publicity, and returned from his stint in the Army more withdrawn than he had been.

In the early 60's, he made no personal or even television appearances, but earned $5 million a year simply by cutting a few records and appearing in three movies a year. He made a picture called "Harem Holiday" in 18 days and was paid $1 million.

In the 70's Mr. Presley appeared frequently in Las Vegas nightclubs. Even when appearing overweight he was an excellent showman and audiences always loved him.

In his nightclub act, he would occasionally parody himself. "This lip used to curl easier," he joked, referring to his one-time trademark of singing with a sneer.

A generous and often sentimental man, he deeply mourned the death of his mother, and kept a suite for his grandmother, Minnie Presley, at his home in Memphis.

The house, Graceland, was an 18-room $1 million mansion with a jukebox at the poolside. Mr. Presley surrounded himself with a retinue of young men called the Memphis Mafia, who served as bodyguards, valets and travel agents. He had a passion for cars, especially Cadillacs, which he tended to acquire in multiples.

Mr. Presley also gave Cadillacs away with startling frequency. He would from time to time see some stranger, nose pressed against a car-showroom window, and invite the person to go inside and pick out a favorite color. Mr. Presley would then pay the entire cost of the purchase on the spot.

Mr. Presley's movie career ended in 1970, and in that year he made a successful television special. Critics remarked on how little he had aged. He kept in shape for years with karate, in which he had a black belt. But his penchant for peanut butter and banana sandwiches washed down with soda finally caught up. In one of his last appearances, his trademark skin-tight pants split open.

After his death became known yesterday, radio stations around the country began playing nothing but old Presley records. At his death, Mr. Presley had been an indelible part of the nation's musical consciousness for 20 years.

He is survived by his nine-year-old daughter, father and grandmother. His father and his daughter were reportedly at Graceland at the time of his death.

BING CROSBY

May 3, 1903–October 14, 1977

MADRID, Spain—Bing Crosby, whose crooning voice and relaxed humor entertained millions around the world for half a century, died of a heart attack today after a round of golf outside Madrid. He was 73 years old.

Mr. Crosby, an avid golfer, collapsed after finishing a game at the La Moraleja club with three Spanish champions. He was taken to the Red Cross hospital, where a spokesman said he was dead on arrival.

A few hours after learning of her husband's death, Kathryn Crosby told a news conference in Hillsborough, Calif., "I can't think of any better way for a golfer who sings for a living to finish the round."

Mrs. Crosby said she talked by phone with one of the men who had played golf with Mr. Crosby. "He told me that Bing had a very good round. I'd like that to be said," she stated, smiling with tears in her eyes.—*The Associated Press*

Harry Lillis Crosby parlayed a burbling baritone voice, a relaxed manner and a sense of business acumen into millions of dollars and a place in the front rank of world-famous entertainers.

A star performer for almost five decades, he delighted millions on radio, television, and in motion pictures and near World War II battlefields, where he entertained countless servicemen.

In all, Mr. Crosby sold more than 300 million records and in his later years, when he stopped making movies, he continued nonetheless to attract enormous public attention with appearances on television and at the Bing Crosby Pro-Amateur Golf Tournament in Pebble Beach, Calif.

Of more than a score of his recordings that sold above the million-disk mark, the most popular was "Silent Night," with "White Christmas" second. It has been said that there was not a moment during the year that the Crosby voice was not being heard somewhere in the world—on radio, phonograph or jukebox.

Mr. Crosby was born May 2, 1903, the fourth child in a Tacoma, Wash., bookkeeper's family. His father, Harry Lowe Crosby, worked for a local brewery to support his mother, the former Kate Harrigan, and his six siblings. His youngest brother, Bob, became well known as a singer and bandleader.

He acquired his nickname when he was seven or eight years old, the story goes, because of his fondness for a comic strip called "The Bingville Bugle." As a boy he was called Bing-o, but the "o" got lost along the way.

He attended Gonzaga University in Spokane, where he studied law and worked part time in a local law firm, but the entertainment world lured him from that and from his law studies.

In 1925, Mr. Crosby and Al Rinker, the band's piano player, left Spokane for Los Angeles, where Mr. Rinker's sister, Mildred Bailey, was a successful singer. The "Two Boys and a Piano," as they were billed, played engagements along the West Coast. Paul Whiteman, who caught their act in 1927, hired them as a singing act for his band.

Mr. Crosby's casual attitude did not go well with Mr. Whiteman, who dismissed him for not being serious enough about his work. The other members of the trio left with him. They played the Montmarte Cafe and the Cocoanut Grove in Los Angeles.

At the Montmartre, Mr. Crosby met Wilma Winifred Wyatt, a rising young film star known professionally as Dixie Lee. They were married on Sept. 29, 1930, and were to have four sons, all of whom became professional entertainers.

Shortly thereafter, Everett Crosby, a brother, sent a record of Mr. Crosby's crooning of "I Surrender, Dear" to William S. Paley, CBS president. The singer was put on the network from New York and became a sensation.

His swift success was as a practitioner of crooning, a singing style to which the teen-agers of the early 1930's and many of their elders were ecstatically addicted.

But as his fame blossomed, he became loved as more than just a deft practitioner of a single vocal style. He became a national institution.

Some historians of the Great Depression have maintained that what carried Mr. Crosby on to his expanding popularity was his espousal in song of the "don't worry" philosophy. Instead of concentrating on the woes of unrequited love, he brightened the idle moments of an impoverished or worried generation with songs about not needing a bundle of money to make life sunny or about pennies from heaven.

Mr. Crosby won a movie Oscar in 1944 as the year's best actor for his role as a priest in "Going My Way." Among the most popular of his half a hundred films were the "Road" comedies—"The Road to Singapore," "The Road to Zanzibar" and others—with Bob Hope and Dorothy Lamour.

His acting style was an embellishment, in a sense, of Mr. Crosby's own personality as a performer—relaxed, low-key and quietly charming. He almost never played a heavy. He once told an interviewer how he had recently turned down a film role as Scrooge.

"I don't think I would have been believable as Scrooge for a minute," he said. "Everybody knows I'm just a big good-natured slob."

The easy-going humor and the bizarrely loud sport shirts that were his trademarks were in evidence off stage as well. But they did not encompass the whole man, who knew trouble and anguish, too.

Dixie Lee Crosby died in 1952 after 22 years of marriage that had contained much heartbreak. Some of the unhappiness stemmed from her husband's iron-handed disciplining of their sons, who got into more than a modicum of trouble as young men.

In 1957, at the age of 53, Mr. Crosby married 23-year-old Kathryn Grant, an actress from Texas. The couple had two sons and a daughter. They appeared together on television in occasional Christmas specials and commercials.

Mr. Crosby made wise investments of most of the earnings his talent for entertainment brought him. Even his stable of racehorses, of whose slowness audiences were often reminded, paid off in the form of gags concocted by his scriptwriters.

His exhibition golf matches with Bob Hope, his

great friend with whom he also engaged in bantering exchanges of insults, raised thousands of dollars for charities.

In his later years, Mr. Crosby led the lifestyle of a man of wealth without much flamboyance. He continued his favorite hobbies—golf, fishing and hunting—and traveled with his family on safaris in Africa.

Last November, he and members of his family went on the CBS television network for a "White Christmas Special." On March 3 Mr. Crosby suffered a ruptured disk in his lower back when he fell 20 feet from a stage into an orchestra pit at a theater in Pasadena, Calif., where he was videotaping a television special. He lost his footing while acknowledging a standing ovation from the audience. The injury left him hospitalized for more than a month. Though still suffering from the effects of the fall, he completed his concert tour of Britain.

JOHN LENNON
October 9, 1940–December 8, 1980

By Les Ledbetter

John Lennon, one of the four Beatles, was shot and killed last night while entering the apartment building where he lived, the Dakota, on Manhattan's Upper West Side. A suspect was seized at the scene.

Mr. Lennon, 40, was shot in the back twice after getting out of a limousine and walking into an entranceway of the Dakota at 1 West 72nd Street, the police said. The suspect was identified as Mark David Chapman, 25, of Hawaii, who had been living in New York for about a week.

With the singer was his wife, Yoko Ono, who was not hurt.

Witnesses said the suspect paced back and forth in the entranceway after shooting the musician, arguing with the doorman and holding the gun in his hand pointing downward. The police said a .38-caliber revolver had been recovered.

Immediately after Mr. Lennon was shot, hundreds of people, some of them crying, began to gather at the site. Mr. Lennon was taken to Roosevelt Hospital, where he was pronounced dead. A crowd soon assembled outside the hospital.

Police Officer Anthony Palma, who drove Miss Ono to the hospital, described her as "very hysterical" and said she sobbed: "Tell me it isn't true."

Jack Douglas, Mr. Lennon's producer, said he and the Lennons had been at a midtown studio earlier in the evening and that Mr. Lennon had left at 10:30 P.M., saying he was going to get something to eat and then go home.

Lieut. John Schick of the 20th Precinct said the gunman let the Lennons pass him and enter the building's passageway. Lieutenant Schick said the man called out "Mr. Lennon" and then pulled a gun and started firing. Mr. Lennon struggled up six stairs and inside the alcove to a guard area where he collapsed.

Employees at the Dakota said someone resembling the suspect had obtained an autograph from Mr. Lennon earlier in the day.

A bystander said he saw the wounded Mr. Lennon being put into the back of a police car. He said the suspect was put into another police car and "had a smirk on his face" when he was taken away.

Mr. Lennon made his last Beatle album, "Abbey Road," in 1969. After the Beatles broke up in 1970, he continued writing songs and recording. But in 1975 he dropped out of the music business, saying he wanted to be with his son, Sean, and his wife.

John Lennon was born Oct. 9, 1940, in England's northern industrial seaport of Liverpool, the son of a porter father who deserted the family when John was three. When his father reappeared once Mr. Lennon reached stardom, the son slammed the door in his face. He later recalled, "I don't feel as if I owe him anything. He never helped me. I got there by myself."

Mr. Lennon attended secondary school in Liverpool and then went on to Liverpool College of Art, where he married a classmate, Cynthia Powell. They had a son, Julian, and were later divorced. In 1969, Mr. Lennon married Miss Ono, a Japanese-American artist, who was pregnant.

After the breakup of the Beatles, Mr. Lennon and Miss Ono lived in seclusion in New York for several years, but the couple were on the front page again in a messy deportation hearing. The United States Government contended that Mr. Lennon, a British subject, was ineligible for permanent residence because of a 1968 drug conviction in Britain. He eventually was allowed to stay in the United States.

The Beatles' music was as much a staple of the revolutionary 1960's as the Vietnam War, whose protesters sang their songs and let their hair grow long in imitation of the musicians.

By John Rockwell

The Beatles were without any question the most popular, most influential of all rock groups, and John Lennon was the most impassioned, and probably the most deeply talented, of all the Beatles.

In 1964, when the Beatles first reached America to appear on the Ed Sullivan program, bemused adult observers found it difficult to distinguish them. They all seemed similarly gray-suited, mop-topped mannequins; what seized their attention was that their songs—"I Want to Hold Your Hand" was the archetype—celebrated teen love in a way that teenagers

hadn't responded to since the days of Elvis Presley and Frank Sinatra.

But soon thereafter, as the Beatles began to define their generation, it became apparent that Mr. Lennon and Paul McCartney were actually the creative forces behind the band. Ringo Starr was cute and cuddly and George Harrison played eloquent lead guitar and helped channel the Beatles' energies into Eastern mysticism.

But it was Mr. Lennon and Mr. McCartney who counted. The two composed most of the band's songs and were the lead singers. At first they collaborated closely, sharing lyrics and music. Later they tended to compose separately, but for reasons of legality and personal loyalty the songs were still credited to both jointly.

Mr. Lennon and Mr. McCartney worked together in a classically complementary manner. Mr. McCartney was the sunny, bright one, the purveyor of lilting ballads and cheery love songs. Mr. Lennon was the harder, fiercer man, the true rocker of the foursome. He had the grittiest singing voice, and the deepest, most convoluted sense of rock's anger and potential triumph.

The Beatles' influence expressed itself first of all in the simple sociological dimensions of their success, unmatched in pop-music history to this day. But the band also managed almost single-handedly to transform the innocent entertainment of rock-and-roll into the artistically self-conscious pretensions of rock. Mr. Lennon, with his eager willingness to explore the ramifications of the psychedelic experience, led that transformation more than any other Beatle.

But, ironically, it was that very evolution away from the rude energy of early Beatles rock-and-roll that crystallized Mr. Lennon's dilemma for the 70's. He was once quoted as saying that the band had never made better, more intense music than it had in the cellar nightclubs of Hamburg in 1962. In the 70's, he tried to find a way to recapture the power of this youth and to reconcile it with his adulthood, but he had severe difficulties in so doing.

The dichotomy between Mr. Lennon's drive and Mr. McCartney's softness manifested itself ever more strongly after the band broke up in 1970, and ironically reaffirmed what each man had brought to the other. On his own, Mr. Lennon's solo albums sometimes reached real eloquence (above all, "Imagine"). But too often he degenerated into self-indulgent howling—frequently abetted by his wife, Yoko Ono. At the same time, Mr. McCartney, shorn of Mr. Lennon's toughening influence, drifted ever more thoughtlessly into frothy pop.

Throughout his life, from even before the Beatles came together, Mr. Lennon seemed a seeker. His first and perhaps ultimate way to salvation was rock music itself, which he mastered and conveyed with a passion and intensity rarely equaled in the genre. And he managed in the 60's to leaven that passion with a delightful wit.

But as the Beatles grew into the phenomenon they

became, Mr. Lennon appeared to grow troubled in his search, and to broaden it to include politics, religion and the self. In so doing he lost the focus his music had previously given him, and tended to rant emptily. All of the psychedelic adventures, sleep-in protests, nude album covers and primal screaming in the world could not replace the void that rock had once filled.

In the latter half of the 70's, Mr. Lennon withdrew almost completely into himself, and into the rearing of his young son, Sean. The recently released album that he and Miss Ono created, "Double Fantasy," was more an extension of that domestic introversion than a break from it. Mr. Lennon's songs on the record, even though they have done well commercially, represent a tired recycling of his youthful idioms—a sincere but misguided and slightly desperate fixation on domestic happiness that really doesn't suit rock at all.

As such, even in failure, he remained a spokesman for his generation, as true in personal retreat as he had been in the joyful assertion and tortured protests of his earlier years.

BENNY GOODMAN

May 30, 1909–June 13, 1986

By John S. Wilson

Benny Goodman, the King of Swing whose clarinet led a generation of music fans into the Big Band era in the 1930's, died yesterday at his Manhattan apartment, apparently of a heart attack.

The tall apple-cheeked bandleader with the horn-rimmed glasses, who brought jazz to Carnegie Hall and enthralled millions with renditions of "Sweet Georgia Brown" and "Stompin' at the Savoy," was 77 years old.

Lionel Hampton, the vibraphonist, recalled that Mr. Goodman was the first major music figure to put black and white musicians together on stage in the 1930's.

"The most important thing that Benny Goodman did," Mr. Hampton said, "was to put Teddy Wilson and me in the quartet. It was instant integration."

Mr. Goodman became the King of Swing the night of Aug. 21, 1935, at the Palomar Ballroom in Hollywood. In the following years, he drew throngs to nightclubs and theaters, toured the world and developed a band that was a training ground for such band leaders as Harry James, Gene Krupa, Mr. Hampton and Mr. Wilson.

But when he arrived at the Palomar in the summer of 1935 with a 14-piece band that he had formed a year before, no aura of success surrounded him. "I thought we'd finish the engagement in California and take the train back to New York and that would be it," he recalled. "I'd just be a clarinetist again."

On this night at the Palomar, Mr. Goodman brought out some of his favorite arrangements by Fletcher Henderson—of "Sugar Foot Stomp," "Blue Skies," "Sometimes I'm Happy" and "King Porter Stomp"—which had been his reason for recruiting a band that included such jazz specialists as the trumpeter Bunny Berrigan, the pianist Jess Stacy and the drummer Mr. Krupa.

As he beat out the tempo for "Sugar Foot Stomp," the band dug into the Henderson arrangement. Then Mr. Berrigan rose up and played a crackling solo. A roar went up from the listeners and they surged around the bandstand. That roar, Mr. Goodman said later, "was one of the sweetest sounds I ever heard in my life."

The crowd's roar would follow him for years both during the swing era, which lasted into the mid-1940's, and decades later when, in the 60's, he toured the Soviet Union with his band. He heard that same sound in March 1937, when he played at the Paramount Theater in New York. Teenagers were lined up around the theater to get into the morning show; more than 21,000 people jammed into the theater that day.

Mr. Goodman heard the roar again in January 1938, when, in white tie and tails, he led his orchestra in the first jazz concert ever given in Carnegie Hall.

Big bands had played swinging dance music before Mr. Goodman organized his orchestra. Henderson led a groundbreaking black jazz band in the mid-20's, and in his wake came Duke Ellington, Earl Hines and Jimmie Lunceford, all black.

But Mr. Goodman's band arrived at a moment when the public's ear had been attuned by these earlier bands. Mr. Goodman's blend of jazz and contemporary popular music filled this demand so successfully that jazz and popular music were briefly synonymous. His band also represented a blend of the freedom of jazz improvisation and the discipline that Mr. Goodman demanded from his musicians and from himself.

"With him, perfection was just around the corner," said Jess Stacy, the pianist. "I figure Benny will die in bed with that damn clarinet."

His discipline and his feeling for tempo produced performances that audiences found more exciting than the looser, more deeply jazz-flavored playing of Mr. Henderson's band.

"Benny was very conscious of tempos," said Willard Alexander, a booking agent. "I remember one time we dropped into the Roosevelt Grill when Guy Lombardo was playing there. Benny said to me, 'You know, this Lombardo's got something.' I thought he was putting me on. But he wasn't. 'You know his secret,' Benny said. 'He never plays a song in the wrong tempo.'"

Mr. Goodman was born in Chicago on May 30, 1909, one of 12 children in the family of an immigrant tailor. He was 10 when he got a clarinet on loan from a local synagogue, which provided music lessons.

By the time he was 14 he was earning $48 a week playing four nights in a neighborhood band. Still wearing short pants, he became part of a clique of teenage jazz musicians who were fascinated by the jazz sounds that flowed through Chicago in the 20's.

Leon Rappolo, clarinetist in the New Orleans Rhythm Kings, who leaned so far back in his chair when he played that he seemed to be lying down, influenced both Mr. Goodman's style and his posture. When Ben Pollack, the drummer in the Rhythm Kings, formed a band in California, he sent back to Chicago for "the kid in the short pants, the kid who played lying down, like Rappolo."

Mr. Goodman was 16 when he joined the Pollack band in Venice, Calif., in 1926. He remained in the band for four years, when Glenn Miller, Jack Teagarden, Bud Freeman, Jimmy McPartland and Mr. Goodman's brother, Harry, were in the group.

In the fall of 1929, Mr. Goodman left the band and began to freelance on radio and records. In 1933, he met a young jazz fan and jazz activist named John Hammond, whose enthusiasm, insight and energy would have a profound effect on the careers of Mr. Goodman, Billie Holiday and Count Basie.

Mr. Hammond had a commission to make some jazz records for release in England, and he asked Mr. Goodman to lead a band for this purpose. Mr. Goodman chose some of his freelance friends, a group that Mr. Hammond augmented by borrowing Mr. Krupa and Mr. Teagarden.

These records, released as by "Benny Goodman and His Orchestra," planted a seed that took root in 1934, when Mr. Goodman heard that Billy Rose was auditioning bands for a new club called the Music Hall. With Mr. Hammond's help, he started assembling a group with a tight small-band quality in which every man could be a soloist. The group included three musicians who remained with Mr. Goodman through the band's early days of glory—Red Ballard, trombonist, Arthur Rollini, saxophonist, and Hymie Schertzer, alto saxophone.

The band was eventually let go. But before that happened, it auditioned for a prospective radio program to be divided among Latin music, "sweet" music and "hot" music. Mr. Goodman's group was chosen as the "hot" band.

During the 26 weeks that he played on this program, he had a budget with which to buy eight arrangements a week at $37.50 each. Edgar Sampson's arrangement of "Stompin' at the Savoy" became a Goodman classic. Gordon Jenkins's arrangement of "Goodbye" became Mr. Goodman's closing theme. His opening signature, "Let's Dance," came from a "hot" arrangement of Carl Maria Von Weber's "Invitation to the Dance," written by George Bassman.

But the most important collection of arrangements came from Mr. Henderson, who in 1934 had given up the big band he had led for 11 years. "King Porter Stomp" and "Big John Special" provided Mr. Goodman with the basis for the library of what became known as "killer-dillers." Mr. Henderson also wrote arrangements of popular songs that established the melodic and swinging style of the Goodman band.

"Fletcher's ideas were far ahead of anybody else's at the time," Mr. Goodman said. "Without Fletcher, I probably would have had a pretty good band, but it would have been something quite different from what it eventually turned out to be."

After the program went off the air, Mr. Goodman's band was booked into the Roosevelt Grill as a summer replacement for Guy Lombardo, but lasted only two weeks. The trail of discouragement continued as the band headed west toward California and the triumph at the Palomar Ballroom.

Mr. Goodman stayed at the Palomar for two months. Then the band went to Chicago, where it spent six months in the Joseph Urban Room of the Congress Hotel and was billed for the first time as a "swing" band.

In December of 1935, some of Mr. Goodman's fans organized what may have been the first jazz concert, held in the Joseph Urban Room. The response was so enthusiastic that another concert was organized for Easter Sunday in 1936. This time Mr. Goodman flew Mr. Wilson, the pianist, out to Chicago from New York.

Less than a year before, Mr. Goodman had jammed with Mr. Wilson, accompanied on drums by Carl

Bellinger. This led to some recordings by a trio made up of Mr. Goodman, Mr. Wilson and Mr. Krupa, made just before Mr. Goodman's trip to the West Coast. This Chicago concert was the first time the trio performed in public, and the performance was so successful that Mr. Goodman decided to keep Mr. Wilson and the trio as a regular part of his troupe.

By making Mr. Wilson a part of his entourage, Mr. Goodman broke through the color barrier that had kept white bands white and black bands black. A few months later, while the band was in Hollywood making its first movie, "The Big Broadcast of 1937," Mr. Goodman heard Mr. Hampton leading a band at the Paradise Cafe and persuaded him to add his vibraphone to the trio, creating a quartet that was 50 percent black.

The eye of the Goodman whirlwind was the Hotel Pennsylvania in New York, where the band spent several months each year. When Mr. Goodman's mother heard his band for the first time, she asked in amazement, "This is the way he makes a living?"

In 1941, Mr. Goodman married Alice Duckworth, who died in 1979. He is survived by two daughters, four brothers, two sisters, and three stepdaughters.

Mr. Goodman had reorganized his band in 1940, luring away Mr. Ellington's trumpet star, Cootie Williams. He had a brilliant 18-year-old pianist, Mel Powell, and such veterans as Charlie Christian, Dave Tough, Billy Butterfield, Lou McGarity and Georgie Auld. Many Goodman fanciers considered this band his finest.

Mr. Goodman continued to lead a big band until 1950, and through the 50's, 60's and 70's, he formed small groups and big bands for concerts and tours.

IRVING BERLIN

May 11, 1888–September 22, 1989

By Marilyn Berger

Irving Berlin, the Russian-born minstrel whose songs like "Cheek to Cheek" and "White Christmas" became part of the fabric of American life, died yesterday at his home in Manhattan, just a few miles from the Lower East Side tenement he lived in when he wrote the first of his 1,500 songs. He was 101 years old.

A son-in-law, Alton E. Peters, said Mr. Berlin died in his sleep at his town house on Beekman Place.

Irving Berlin set the tone and the tempo for the tunes America played, sang and danced to for much of the 20th century. By the time he was 30 he was a legend, and he went on to write the scores for 19

Broadway shows and 18 Hollywood films.

The musical giant who never learned to read or write music composed his first major hit, "Alexander's Ragtime Band," in 1911. "With one song, the career of Irving Berlin and American music were intertwined forever," said Isaac Stern at Mr. Berlin's 100th-birthday celebration in May 1988, adding, "American music was born at his piano."

The last Berlin song to be noted by the American Society of Composers, Authors and Publishers was "An Old-Fashioned Wedding," the show-stopper he wrote for a 1966 revival of "Annie Get Your Gun."

In the intervening 55 years, besides "Cheek to Cheek" and "White Christmas," Mr. Berlin's outpouring of songs included "Always," "Remember," "Blue Skies," "Puttin' On the Ritz," "A Pretty Girl Is Like a Melody," "What'll I Do?" "How Deep Is the Ocean," "Easter Parade," "God Bless America," "Heat Wave," "Let's Face the Music and Dance," "This Is the Army, Mr. Jones," "Oh, How I Hate to Get Up in the Morning," "I Got Lost in His Arms," "The Girl That I Marry" and "There's No Business Like Show Business."

He often said there are only six tunes in the world. But from those six tunes he fashioned, according to his catalogue, 1,500 songs, and nobody knows how many more he may have stored somewhere. Not only did he compose the melodies, he also wrote the lyrics.

According to ASCAP, the American Society of Composers, Authors and Publishers, 25 Berlin songs reached the top of the charts. His songs were picked up again and again by top recording artists like Frank Sinatra, Barbra Streisand, Rosemary Clooney and Diana Ross and became hits all over again. "White Christmas" remains one of the most-performed standards in the ASCAP repertory.

The songwriter Sammy Cahn once said of Mr. Berlin's prodigious output: "If a man, in a lifetime of 50 years, can point to six songs that are immediately identifiable, he has achieved something. Irving Berlin can sing 60 that are immediately identifiable. Somebody once said you couldn't have a holiday without his permission."

That seemed accurate: "White Christmas" and "Easter Parade" were two Berlin songs that became holiday anthems.

Irving Berlin was a slender, dark-haired man with a quick smile and lively eyes topped by wide, prominent eyebrows. He never learned to play in any key but F sharp, but he could tap out tune after tune on the keys of a piano, leaving it to arrangers to write the harmony and transcribe his melodies. His songs were by turn romantic and tragic, feisty and sentimental, homespun and sophisticated.

His music evoked the mournful tunes of Russia, the land of his birth ("A Russian Lullaby"), and the rhythms of American rag ("Alexander's Ragtime Band"). The romance of the ballad was heard in his "Always" and "Remember," the romance of dance in "Cheek to Cheek" and "Let's Face the Music and Dance."

Mr. Berlin captured the rhythms of a young nation with songs that marked the country's wars and its prosperity and helped it to dance through the Depression. By 1924 he was already the subject of a biography. Alexander Woollcott wrote in "The Story of Irving Berlin" that Mr. Berlin was a "creative ignoramus," an unschooled genius.

"I really can't read music," Mr. Berlin once said. "Oh, I can pick out the melody of a song with one finger, but I can't read the harmony. I feel like an awful dope that I know so little about the mechanics of my trade." To overcome his inability to play in any key but F sharp, he used a specially built piano that had a hand clutch to change keys.

He was born Israel Baline near the Siberian border in the Russian village of Tyumen on May 11, 1888, one of eight children of Moses and Leah Lipkin Baline. His father was a cantor. A pogrom in 1893 persuaded Moses Baline to take his family to New York, and they settled on Cherry Street on the Lower East Side. Israel was eight years old when his father died, and the boy took to the streets to help support his family. This marked the end of his formal schooling.

Izzy, as he came to be known, found his first steady job on the Bowery, looking after Blind Sol, a singing beggar. He led him through the saloons, looked after his receipts and sang some sentimental ballads himself in his childish treble.

He was soon on his own, singing for tips at bars off the Bowery, plugging songs at Tony Pastor's Music Hall in Union Square and, in 1906, when he was 18, working as a singing waiter at the Pelham Cafe in Chinatown. When the bar closed for the night, young Berlin would sit at a piano in the back and pick out tunes.

Within a year, he published his first song, "Marie from Sunny Italy." He wrote the lyrics, and a friend, Nick Nicholson, composed the music. Because of a printer's error, the name of the lyricist on the cover of the sheet music appeared as "I. Berlin." He kept the name.

In the early days his grasp of the language was meager. But he made his shortcoming a virtue, writing lyrics in the American vernacular that were simple and direct: "I'll be loving you always . . . Not for just an hour/Not for just a day/Not for just a year/But always," and "How much do I love you?/I'll tell you no lie/How deep is the ocean?/How high is the sky?"

"My ambition is to reach the heart of the average American," Mr. Berlin once said, "Not the highbrow nor the lowbrow but that vast intermediate crew which is the real soul of the country. The highbrow is likely to be superficial, overtrained, supersensitive.

The lowbrow is warped, subnormal. My public is the real people."

Mr. Berlin even created songs out of his own sadness. In 1912, he married Dorothy Goetz, who died six months later of typhoid fever contracted during their honeymoon in Havana. The song he wrote to express his grief, "When I Lost You," was his first ballad. It was an immediate hit and sold more than a million copies.

His first complete score was written in 1914 for the revue "Watch Your Step." In 1916, he collaborated with Victor Herbert on the score of "The Century Girl." Aware of his technical limitations, he asked Mr. Herbert whether he should study composition.

"Learning theory might help you a little," Mr. Herbert told him, "but it could cramp your style."

Mr. Herbert was a moving force behind the creation of ASCAP. In 1914, Mr. Berlin joined with him to become a charter member of the organization, which protects the royalties of composers and writers.

Mr. Berlin was drafted in 1917 and stationed at Camp Upton, in Yaphank, L.I., where he was commissioned to write an all-soldier revue. The show, "Yip, Yip, Yaphank," is best remembered for Mr. Berlin's own rendition of "Oh, How I Hate to Get Up in the Morning," a song he repeated in his World War II revue "This Is the Army" and the movie that was made from it.

In the 1920's, in a story more romantic than his own ballads, Mr. Berlin fell in love with a young heiress. His courtship of Ellin Mackay was followed avidly by the newspapers, which found good copy in the romance of an immigrant from the Lower East Side and the daughter of Clarence Hungerford Mackay, the socially prominent head of the Postal Telegraph Cable Company.

The couple met in 1925, and Mr. Mackay opposed the match from the start. He hustled his daughter off to Europe, and Mr. Berlin wooed her over the airwaves with his songs "Remember" and "Always." When she returned to New York they were married.

Mr. Mackay threatened to disown his daughter. "I don't want your daughter for her money," Mr. Berlin told Mr. Mackay, according to breathless reports in the tabloids. "If you see fit to disinherit her, I'll probably have to make her a wedding present of a couple of million dollars."

Mr. Berlin did more. He gave her "Always" and other songs for which the royalties are still coming in. An inseparable couple until Ellin Berlin died in July 1988 at the age of 85, the couple had four children, three of whom survive.

In the mid-1920's, Mr. Berlin composed the songs for "The Cocoanuts," written by George S. Kaufman for the Marx Brothers. He wrote for the Ziegfeld Follies of 1911, 1919 and 1920, and for the Follies of

1927 he composed "Blue Skies."

He returned to Broadway in 1932 to collaborate with Moss Hart on "Face the Music," a production that included "Let's Have Another Cup of Coffee." He worked with Hart again in 1933 to create "As Thousands Cheer." "Heat Wave" and "Easter Parade" were two of the songs that made that show a box-office triumph.

During the Depression, Mr. Berlin was responsible for the scores of some of the most delightful screen musicals of the day, including three that starred Ginger Rogers and Fred Astaire—"Top Hat," "Follow the Fleet" and "Carefree."

In 1938, when Kate Smith asked Mr. Berlin to write a patriotic song for her, he reached into his files for a tune he had written 20 years earlier for "Yip, Yip, Yaphank" and had dropped from the show. He wrote new lyrics, and from the moment Kate Smith sang it on the radio, "God Bless America" became the nation's unofficial national anthem.

"White Christmas" was written for Bing Crosby in the 1942 movie "Holiday Inn." It won Mr. Berlin an Academy Award for best song, sold more than 50 million records and 4 million copies of sheet music and earned over $1 million in royalties.

After World War II Mr. Berlin wrote "Annie Get Your Gun" for Ethel Merman. This exuberant musical about Annie Oakley opened in 1946, ran for 1,147 performances and included such songs as "They Say It's Wonderful," "The Girl That I Marry," "Doin' What Comes Natur'lly" and "Anything You Can Do I Can Do Better." He enjoyed another triumph when he wrote "Call Me Madam" in 1950 for Miss Merman, who starred as "The Hostess with the Mostes' on the Ball."

For a while, "Call Me Madam" seemed to have been Mr. Berlin's farewell show, but in 1962, at 74, Mr. Berlin was back on Broadway with the score of "Mr. President."

A 100th-birthday celebration concert for him was held for the benefit of Carnegie Hall and ASCAP in May 1988. After the celebrating was over, Morton Gould, the president of ASCAP, said, in effect, that it would never be over.

"Irving Berlin's music will last forever," he said. "Not for just an hour, not for just a day, not for just a year, but always."

MILES DAVIS

May 26, 1926–September 28, 1991

By Jon Pareles

Miles Davis, the trumpeter and composer whose haunting tone and ever-changing style made him an elusive touchstone of jazz for four decades, died yesterday at St. John's Hospital and Health Center in Santa Monica, Calif. He was 65 years old.

He died of pneumonia, respiratory failure and a stroke, his doctor said.

Mr. Davis's unmistakable, voicelike, nearly vibratoless tone—at times distant and melancholy, at others assertive yet luminous—has been imitated around the world.

His solos, whether ruminating on a whispered ballad melody or jabbing against a beat, have been models for generations of jazz musicians. Other trumpeters play faster and higher, but more than in any technical feats Mr. Davis's influence lay in his phrasing and sense of space. "I always listen to what I can leave out," he would say.

Equally important, Mr. Davis never settled into one style; every few years he created a new lineup and format for his groups. Each phase brought denunciations from critics. "I have to change," he once said. "It's like a curse."

Mr. Davis came of age in the be-bop era; many successive styles—cool jazz, hard-bop, modal jazz, jazz-rock, jazz-funk—were sparked or ratified by his example. Throughout his career he was grounded in the blues, but he also drew on pop, flamenco, classical music, rock, Arab music and Indian music. Musicians he discovered often moved on to innovations of their own.

Mr. Davis had a volatile personality and a stage presence that could be charismatic or aloof. For a while, he turned his back on audiences as he played and walked offstage when he was not soloing. Yet his music was deeply collaborative: He spurred his sidemen to find their own musical voices and was inspired by them in turn.

Miles Dewey Davis 3rd was born May 25, 1926, in Alton, Ill., the son of an affluent dental surgeon, and grew up in East St. Louis, Ill. On his 13th birthday, he was given a trumpet and lessons with a local jazz musician, Elwood Buchanan.

Clark Terry, the trumpeter, one of his early idols, became Mr. Davis's mentor, and his local reputation grew quickly. In 1944 the Billy Eckstine band, which then included two men who were beginning to create be-bop— Charlie Parker and Dizzy Gillespie—arrived in St. Louis with an ailing third trumpeter. Mr. Davis sat in for two weeks. The experience made him decide to move to New York, the center of the be-bop revolution.

He enrolled in the Juilliard School of Music in September 1944 and studied classical music by day and jazz by night, in the clubs of 52nd Street and Harlem. Mr. Parker, who roomed with Mr. Davis for a time, and Mr. Gillespie introduced him to the coterie of be-bop musicians. From them he learned the harmonic vocabulary of be-bop and began to forge a solo style.

In the fall of 1945 he joined Charlie Parker's quintet and dropped out of Juilliard. With Parker's quintet, Mr. Davis recorded one of the first be-bop sessions in November 1945. His playing evolved into a pared-down, middle-register style that created a contrast with Parker's aggressive forays. He made his first recording as a leader on Aug. 14, 1947, with a quintet that included Parker on tenor saxophone.

But in 1948 he began to experiment with a new, more elaborately orchestrated style that would become known as "cool jazz." Working with the arrangers Gil Evans, John Lewis and Gerry Mulligan, Mr. Davis brought a nine-piece band to New York to play rich, ruminative ensemble pieces, with solos floating in diffuse clouds of harmony. The music helped spawn a cerebral cool-jazz movement on the West Coast.

Mr. Davis became a heroin addict in the early 1950's. But in 1954 he overcame his addiction and began his first string of important small-group recordings.

"Walkin'," a swaggering blues piece informed by the extended harmonies of be-bop, turned decisively away from cool jazz and announced the arrival of hard-bop.

Over the next year, he made a triumphant appearance at the Newport Jazz Festival and assembled his first important quintet, with John Coltrane on tenor saxophone, Red Garland on piano, Paul Chambers on bass and Philly Joe Jones on drums.

Like many of the Davis bands to follow, it seemed to be an incompatible grouping in prospect, mixing the suavity and harmonic nuances of Garland and Chambers with the forcefulness of Jones and the raw energy of Coltrane. But it brought Mr. Davis his first general popularity.

In 1957 Mr. Davis had a throat operation to remove nodes from his vocal cords. Two days later he began shouting at someone who, he once said, "tried to convince me to go into a deal I didn't want." His voice was permanently damaged, reduced to a raspy whisper.

During the late 1950's Mr. Davis alternated orchestral albums with Gil Evans arrangements—"Miles Ahead" (1957), "Porgy and Bess" (1958) and "Sketches of Spain" (1960)—with small-group sessions. He recorded the sound track for Louis Malle's film "Ascenseur Pour l'Echafaud" ("Elevator to the Gallows") with French musicians, then reconvened his quintet and added Julian (Cannonball) Adderley on alto saxophone. The sound track and the sextet's first album, "Milestones," signaled another metamor-

phosis, cutting back the harmonic motion of be-bop to make music with fewer chords and more ambiguous harmonies.

With "Kind of Blue" in 1959, that change was complete. Most of the pieces on "Kind of Blue" (composed by Mr. Davis or his new pianist, Bill Evans) were based on modal scales rather than chords. Mood and melodic tension became paramount, in music that was at times voluptuous and austere.

From this point onward, Mr. Davis would return often to music based on static, stripped-down harmonies. John Coltrane, among others, was to make modal jazz one of the definitive styles of the 1960's.

The Davis group's personnel fluctuated in the early 1960's until Mr. Davis settled on a new quintet in 1964, with Wayne Shorter on tenor saxophone, Herbie Hancock on piano, Ron Carter on bass and Tony Williams on drums. It was one of the most important ensembles in 1960's jazz, pushing tonal harmony to its limits.

On the albums "E.S.P.," "Miles Smiles," "The Sorcerer" and "Nefertiti," the group could swing furiously, then open up unexpected spaces or dissolve the beat into abstract waves of sound. The quintet defined an exploratory alternative to 1960's free jazz.

With the 1968 albums "Miles in the Sky" and "Filles de Kilimanjaro," he experimented with rock rhythms, repeating bass lines and electronic instruments. He also began to work with open-ended compositions, based on rhythmic feeling, fragments of melody or bass patterns and his own on-the-spot directives.

Mr. Davis expanded the group on "In a Silent Way" (1969) with three electric keyboards and electric guitar. Using static harmonics and a rock undercurrent, the music was eerie and reflective, at once abstract and grounded by the beat. "Bitches Brew" (1969), recorded by a larger group, was an aggressive, spooky sequel, roiling and churning with improvisations in every register.

The two albums, along with performances at the Fillmore East and Fillmore West rock auditoriums, brought Mr. Davis's music to the rock audience; "Bitches Brew" became a best-selling album. Musicians who had worked with Mr. Davis from 1968–70 went on to lead pioneering jazz-rock groups, including the Mahavishnu Orchestra and Weather Report.

Mr. Davis, meanwhile, was turning toward funk; in interviews at the time, he talked about reaching young black audiences. His bands in the 1970's were anchored by a bassist, Michael Henderson, who had worked with Stevie Wonder, and they moved percussion and syncopated bass lines into the foreground. Around them, keyboards, saxophone, guitars and Mr. Davis's trumpet (now electrified, and often played through a wah-wah pedal) supplied rhythmic and textural effects as well as solos.

"On the Corner" (1972) marked the change, and a pair of live albums, "Dark Magus" and "Pangaea," were even more jolting. The music was a thicket of rhythms and electronic textures. Those albums became an inspiration to the late-1970's "no wave" noise-rockers and a new generation of funk experimenters in the 1980's.

By the end of 1975 mounting medical problems—among them ulcers and bursitis—forced Mr. Davis into a five-year retirement. In 1981 he returned with an album, "The Man with the Horn," a Kool Jazz Festival concert in New York and a band featuring Robert Irving 3rd as keyboardist and co-producer.

Although Mr. Davis's technique was intact, the music seemed for the first time to involve commercial calculations and a look backward at Mr. Davis's previous styles. He recorded music layer by layer, like pop albums, instead of leading musicians in live interaction. But on stage and on record, there were still moments of the fierce beauty that is Mr. Davis's lasting legacy to American music.

ELLA FITZGERALD

April 25, 1917–June 15, 1996

By Stephen Holden

Ella Fitzgerald, whose sweet, silvery voice and endlessly inventive vocal improvisations made her the most celebrated jazz singer of her generation and won her the sobriquet "first lady of song," died yesterday at home in Beverly Hills, Calif. She was 79 and had suffered from diabetes for many years.

Bringing a classic sense of musical proportion and balance to everything she touched, Miss Fitzgerald earned the unqualified admiration of most of her peers.

"Man, woman or child, Ella is the greatest," Bing Crosby once said. Mel Torme hailed her as having "the best ear of any singer ever."

Until the 1970's, when physical problems began to impinge on her perfect technique, she seemed to loom as an immutable creative force in a musical world where everything else was crumbling.

Over six decades Miss Fitzgerald stood above the emotional fray of the scores of popular standards she performed. Stylistically she was the polar opposite of her equally legendary peer, Billie Holiday, who conveyed a wounded vulnerability. Even when handed a sad song, Miss Fitzgerald communicated a wistful, sweet-natured compassion for the heartache she described.

Where Holiday and Frank Sinatra lived out the dramas they sang about, Miss Fitzgerald, viewing them from afar, seemed to understand and forgive all. Her apparent equanimity and her clear pronunciation, which transcended race, ethnicity, class and age, made her a voice of profound reassurance and hope.

Miss Fitzgerald performed with big bands, symphony orchestras and small jazz groups. Her repertory encompassed show tunes, jazz songs, novelties (like her first major hit, "A-Tisket A-Tasket," recorded in 1938), bossa nova, and even opera ("Porgy and Bess" excerpts, recorded with Louis Armstrong).

At her jazziest, her material became a springboard for ever-changing, ebullient vocal inventions, delivered in a sweet, girlish voice that could leap, slide or growl anywhere within a range of nearly three octaves.

Miss Fitzgerald was renowned both for her delicately rendered ballads and her pyrotechnical displays of scat improvisation.

She was sometimes criticized for a lack of bluesiness and emotional depth. But her perfect intonation, vocal acrobatics, clear diction and endless store of melodic improvisations—all driven by powerful rhythmic undercurrents—brought her nearly universal acclaim.

Miss Fitzgerald recorded with Duke Ellington, Count Basie and Louis Armstrong. Her series of "Songbook" albums, celebrating such songwriters as Cole Porter, Harold Arlen, the Gershwins, Rodgers and Hart, and Ellington, helped to elevate the work of the best American songwriters.

"I never knew how good our songs were," Ira Gershwin once said, "until I heard Ella Fitzgerald sing them."

She was born on April 25, 1917, in Newport News, Va., the product of a common-law marriage between William Fitzgerald and Temperance Williams Fitzgerald. The couple separated within a year of her birth, and with her mother and a Portuguese immigrant named Joseph Da Silva, she moved to Yonkers.

Young Ella dreamed of being a dancer. But she also sang. As a teenager, she and a male friend developed a dance routine, which they performed in local clubs. When her mother died suddenly in 1932, she went to live with an aunt in Harlem.

On Nov. 21, 1934, she made her stage debut in an amateur contest at the Apollo Theater, singing two songs, "The Object of My Affection" and "Judy," in the style of Connee Boswell. She won first prize.

She caught the attention of Chick Webb, the band leader and drummer, who was reluctant to sign her to a contract because she was gawky and unkempt. But the audience's reaction to her won her a job, and

during the Webb band's residency at the Savoy Ballroom in Harlem her reputation blossomed.

Miss Fitzgerald made her first recording in 1935 ("Love and Kisses," with Chick Webb), and had her first hit with "A-Tisket, A-Tasket," a song she helped write, adapting the lyric, she later explained, from a childhood game.

The record made her a star. After Webb died in 1939, the young singer was the band's nominal leader until mid-1942, when it broke up. Between her recording debut in 1935 and 1942, Miss Fitzgerald recorded almost 150 sides, the majority of them novelties and disposable pop fluff.

During this period, she married Benjamin Kornegay, a shipyard worker and petty thief with a criminal record. The marriage ended in annulment after two years.

The singer was 30 when she fell in love with the bassist Ray Brown while they were on tour with Dizzy Gillespie's band. They were married in December 1947, set up housekeeping in East Elmhurst, Queens, and adopted the son of Miss Fitzgerald's half-sister, Frances. They named the boy Ray Jr. While Miss Fitzgerald concentrated on her career, her son was cared for by her aunt Virginia.

The marriage became a casualty of conflicting career schedules, and the couple divorced in 1953, although they continued to work together. Miss Fitzgerald is survived by Ray Brown Jr. and a grandchild.

As early as 1942 and 1943, Miss Fitzgerald began to be influenced by the experiments of such be-bop instrumentalists as Charlie Parker and Dizzy Gillespie. She incorporated elements of be-bop rhythm and harmony into her singing, and while on tour with the Gillespie band in 1946 she embraced the music wholeheartedly.

A year earlier, she had recorded what would become one of the most influential vocal jazz records of the decade, a version of "Flying Home," in which she indulged in the phonetic improvisation known as scat. While other singers, most notably Armstrong, had tried similar improvisation, no one before Miss Fitzgerald employed the technique with such dazzling inventiveness.

Two years later, when Decca released her sensational be-bop version of "Lady Be Good," Down Beat magazine proclaimed her "as great a master of bop as she has been of swing."

Between 1935 and 1955 she recorded for Decca Records. Under the producer Milt Gabler she was teamed with the vocal group the Ink Spots for several hits, including the million-selling "I'm Making Believe" and "Into Each Life Some Rain Must Fall." She also scored with novelty duets recorded with Louis Jordan, the most popular of which was "Stone Cold Dead in the Market."

Dictated largely by the fads of the moment, Miss Fitzgerald's pre-1955 pop recording career was an artistically mixed bag and stood distinct from her work as a swing and jazz singer in nightclubs. One artistic high point of the Decca years was a 10-inch long-playing record, "Ella Sings Gershwin," which she recorded with the pianist Ellis Larkins in 1950.

Miss Fitzgerald's life changed when Norman Granz, the impresario of the popular Jazz at the Philharmonic series, invited her to join the touring jam sessions in 1949 and later became her manager. One of her most popular numbers, "How High the Moon," evolved into the unofficial signature tune of the series.

Their relationship quickly developed into one of the most productive artist-manager partnerships in the history of jazz. When Miss Fitzgerald's contract with Decca expired, she became the first artist Mr. Granz signed to his new Verve label. Under his supervision she undertook the series of landmark "Songbook" albums that brought her voice to a large nonjazz audience.

"Norman came along, and he felt that I should do other things, so he produced 'The Cole Porter Songbook' with me," she recalled. "It was a turning point in my life."

"Ella Fitzgerald Sings the Cole Porter Songbook" became the prototype for a series of anthologies focusing on individual composers or composing teams, blending familiar standards and lesser-known first-rate songs.

From 1956 through the mid-1960's, Miss Fitzgerald's career soared. In 1957, she presented her own concert at the Hollywood Bowl. In April 1958 she gave a Carnegie Hall concert with Duke Ellington to celebrate the release of her four-disk set, "Ella Fitzgerald Sings the Duke Ellington Songbook."

Touring 40 to 45 weeks a year, Miss Fitzgerald showed the first signs of fatigue when she nearly collapsed on the stage during a concert in Munich in 1965. Five years earlier, Mr. Granz had sold Verve records to MGM, and when her contract came up for renewal in 1966, she was not re-signed to the label, but Mr. Granz moved her to Capitol, where her producer, Dave Dexter, promised to give her "a totally different sound." These albums, which included a religious record, an album of country music and a Christmas collection, found her groping for a new pop identity.

Signed briefly to Reprise Records, Miss Fitzgerald tried singing contemporary hits by the Beatles, Burt Bacharach and Marvin Gaye, but rock and soul proved almost as uncongenial to her style as had country.

She returned to jazz full time when Mr. Granz founded his label Pablo in 1973. Among her many Pablo recordings are four duet albums with the guitarist Joe Pass and another songbook album devoted to the music of Antonio Carlos Jobim. She also began performing with symphony orchestras, and in 1974 she teamed with Frank Sinatra and Count Basie for a two-week engagement in New York that grossed more than $1 million.

From the early 1970's, Miss Fitzgerald began to have eyesight problems complicated by diabetes, and in 1986 she had heart surgery, but she returned to the concert stage the next year. She continued to perform at least once a month into the early 1990's. Although her voice slowly deteriorated from the early 1970's, even at the end of her career her singing retained a remarkable rhythmic acuity.

Offstage, Miss Fitzgerald, who was shy and sensitive to criticism, lived quietly in a 13-room house in Beverly Hills. Her social life involved a small circle of old friends, including members of the Count Basie and Duke Ellington orchestras, and other singers.

Asked how she felt about being "a legend," she replied: "I don't think I noticed it at first. But when Norman Granz and I began recording the 'Songbook' series in the mid-50's, it just seemed that more people began to like my singing. The awards I started winning didn't make me feel important, but they made me realize people loved me."

Her awards included honorary doctorates at Yale and Dartmouth, the National Medal of Arts, and 13 Grammy Awards, including one in 1967 for Lifetime Achievement. In 1979 she was given a Kennedy Center Award for her lifetime in the performing arts.

Accepting an honorary doctorate of music at Yale, she said, "Not bad for someone who only studied music to get that half-credit in high school."

FRANK SINATRA

December 12, 1915–May 14, 1998

By Stephen Holden

Frank Sinatra, the singer and actor whose extraordinary voice elevated popular song into an art, died on Thursday night in Los Angeles. He was 82.

The cause was a heart attack, said his publicity agent, Susan Reynolds. Ms. Reynolds said his fourth wife, Barbara, his son, Frank Jr., and his daughters, Tina and Nancy, were at his side at Cedars-Sinai Medical Center.

Widely held to be the greatest singer in American pop history and one of the most successful entertainers of the 20th century, Sinatra was also the first modern pop superstar. He defined that role in the early 1940's, when his first solo appearances provoked the kind of mass pandemonium that later greeted Elvis Presley and the Beatles.

In a show business career of more than 50 years, Sinatra stood as a singular mirror of the American psyche.

His evolution from the idealistic crooner of the early 1940's to the sophisticated swinger of the 50's and 60's seemed to personify the country's loss of innocence. During World War II, Sinatra's tender romanticism served as the dreamy emotional link between millions of women and their husbands and boyfriends overseas. Reinventing himself in the 50's, he turned into the cosmopolitan man of the world, a bruised romantic with a tough-guy streak and a song for every emotional season.

In a series of brilliant conceptual albums, he codified a musical vocabulary of adult relationships with which millions identified. The haunted voice heard on a jukebox in the wee small hours of the morning lamenting the end of a love affair was the same voice that jubilantly invited the world to "come fly with me" to exotic realms in a never-ending party.

Sinatra appeared in 58 films, and won an Oscar as best supporting actor for his portrayal of the feisty misfit soldier Maggio in "From Here to Eternity" (1953). As an actor, he could communicate the same complex mixture of emotional honesty, vulnerability and cockiness that he projected as a singer.

It was as a singer that he exerted the strongest cultural influence. Following his idol Bing Crosby, who had pioneered the use of the microphone, Sinatra transformed popular singing by infusing lyrics with a personal, intimate point of view that conveyed a current of eroticism.

The skinny blue-eyed crooner, nicknamed The Voice, made hordes of bobby-soxers swoon in the 1940's with an extraordinarily smooth and flexible baritone.

After the voice lost its velvety youthfulness, Sinatra's interpretations grew more personal and idiosyncratic, so that each performance became a direct expression of his personality and his mood of the moment. In expressing anger, petulance and bravado—attitudes that had largely been excluded from the acceptable vocabulary of pop feeling—Sinatra paved the way for the unfettered vocal aggression of rock singers.

Almost single-handedly he helped lead a revival of vocalized swing music that took American pop to a new level of sophistication. Coinciding with the rise of the long-playing record album, his 1950's recordings were instrumental in establishing a canon of American pop song literature.

With Nelson Riddle, his most talented arranger, Sinatra defined the criteria for sound, style and song selection in pop recording during the pre-Beatles era. The aggressive uptempo style of Sinatra's mature years spawned a genre of punchy, rhythmic belting associated with Las Vegas, which he had helped establish and popularize as an entertainment capital.

By the late 1950's, Sinatra's life and art had become emblematic of the temper of the times. For years, he seemed the embodiment of the hard-drinking, he-

donistic swinger who could have his pick of women while leading a party-loving entourage.

On a deeper level, Sinatra's career and public image touched many aspects of American cultural life. For millions, his ascent from humble Italian-American roots in Hoboken, N.J., was a symbol of ethnic achievement. His change of allegiance from pro-Roosevelt Democrat in the 1940's to pro-Reagan Republican in the 1980's paralleled a seismic shift in American politics.

For decades his private life, with its many romances, feuds, brawls and associations with gangsters, was grist for the gossip columns. But he also had a reputation for spontaneous generosity, for helping singers who were starting out and for supporting friends who were in need. He gave hundreds of millions of dollars to various philanthropies.

Sinatra was born in Hoboken on Dec. 12, 1915, the only child of Martin Sinatra, a boilermaker and sometime boxer from Catania, Sicily, and his wife, Natalie Garavante, who was nicknamed Dolly. He decided to become a singer either after attending a Crosby concert or seeing a Crosby film sometime in 1931 or 1932.

In 1935, after two years of local club dates, he joined three other young men from Hoboken who called themselves the Three Flashes. The quartet renamed itself the Hoboken Four and won first prize on "Major Bowes's Original Amateur Hour."

After several months with the group, Sinatra decided to go it alone. Local radio exposure brought him to the attention of Harry James, the band leader. The singer made his first concert appearance with the James band in June 1939 and his first recording the next month.

Early that year, he married his longtime sweetheart, Nancy Barbato. They had three children: Nancy, Franklin Wayne (later shortened to Frank Jr.), and Christina (Tina).

Six months after Sinatra signed with Harry James,

Tommy Dorsey invited him to join his band, which was far more popular. Sinatra remained with Dorsey from January 1940 until September 1942. Three months after he left Dorsey, he made history at the age of 27 with his first solo appearance at the Paramount Theater in New York. It set off a public hysteria that made headlines. Within weeks he had signed lucrative contracts with Columbia Records, R.K.O. Pictures and the radio program "Your Hit Parade."

The adulation reached a high point on Oct. 12, 1944, the opening day of a three-week return engagement at the Paramount, when 30,000 fans—most of them bobby-soxers—formed a frenzied mob in Times Square.

In 1943, Columbia rereleased a recording he had made in 1939 with Harry James. The recording, "All or Nothing at All," which had sold 8,000 copies in its first release, sold over a million.

Sinatra's popularity remained at a peak through 1946, when he had 15 hit singles. Then it began a slide that hit bottom in 1952.

Part of the public disenchantment came after the columnist Robert Ruark denounced him in 1947 for having socialized with the deported gangster Lucky Luciano in Cuba. For the rest of Sinatra's career, stories of his relations with the underworld dogged him, and he reacted angrily to the charges.

While his career was in decline in the late 1940's, his marriage to Nancy Barbato also unraveled. In 1949 he began an affair with the movie star Ava Gardner and married her on November 7, 1951. Passionate but stormy, the marriage lasted just less than two years. They were divorced in 1957. (She died in 1990.)

Sinatra's resurgence began in 1953 with the release of "From Here to Eternity," the film about American G.I.'s in Hawaii on the eve of World War II. His Oscar-winning portrayal of Maggio, the combative Italian-American soldier, renewed public sympathy.

In April 1953, Sinatra, then 37, had signed with Capitol Records, just when his voice had lost most of its youthful sheen, but the move proved fortunate. Only five years earlier, the long-playing record had been introduced, and the longer form encouraged Sinatra to make cohesive album-length emotional statements.

He was teamed with Nelson Riddle, who pioneered in augmenting a big-band lineup with strings. He was the master of an elegant pop impressionism that enhanced Sinatra's vocal image of urbane sophistication.

The collaboration hit its artistic peak with three albums. "In the Wee Small Hours," a collection of classic torch songs sung in a quietly anguished baritone, was released in 1955. "Songs for Swingin' Lovers," released a year later, defined Sinatra in his adult "swinging" mode. It included what many regard as his greatest recorded performance: Cole Porter's "I've Got You Under My Skin." And "Frank Sinatra Sings for Only the Lonely," released in the summer of 1958, expanded on the mournful, introspective tone of "Wee Small Hours" by adding shadings that were at once jazzier and more operatic.

Sinatra's Capitol albums were among the first so-called concept albums in the way they explored different adult approaches to love and invoked varied aspects of the singer's personality, including the fun-loving hedonist ("Songs for Swingin' Lovers"), the jet-set playboy ("Come Fly with Me") and the romantic loner ("Where Are You?").

After "From Here to Eternity," Sinatra's movie career boomed. He played the perennial gambler Nathan Detroit in the musical "Guys and Dolls" (1955), a heroin addict in "The Man With the Golden Arm" the same year and an Army investigator tracking a would-be assassin in "The Manchurian Candidate" (1962).

Assessing his film career, the critic David Thomson said Sinatra had a "pervasive influence on American acting: he glamorized the fatalistic outsider; he made his own anger intriguing, and in the late 50's especially he was one of our darkest male icons."

At a time when restraints on sexual and social behavior had begun to loosen, the high-living Sinatra became in the popular press the embodiment of the swinger. In the 60's, Sinatra appeared to be America's quintessential middle-aged playboy.

He was surrounded by a hard-drinking clique—nicknamed the Rat Pack—that included Dean Martin, Peter Lawford, Sammy Davis Jr. and Joey Bishop. One of the Rat Pack's favorite playgrounds was Las Vegas, where in 1953 Sinatra bought a 2 percent interest in the Sands Hotel. He earned $100,000 a week in his frequent performances at the Sands.

Sinatra's recording career entered a new phase when he formed his own record company, Reprise, in 1960. He sold the company to Warner Brothers in 1963, retaining a one-third interest.

For two decades, Sinatra recorded more than 30 albums for Reprise. By this time, his voice had hardened and coarsened, which helped give his singing an extra rhythmic punch.

His 50th birthday in 1965 was celebrated with the release of two deliberately monumental albums, "September of My Years" and "A Man and His Music," an anthology of his career that he narrated and sang. In 1969 he had a substantial hit with "My Way." Along with "New York, New York," which he recorded in 1980, it was a signature song of his later years.

The moment when Sinatra and his style of music seemed the least fashionable was in the late 1960's, when the counterculture dominated popular music. Sinatra once dismissed rock-and-roll as music "sung, played and written for the most part by cretinous goons."

His surprise marriage in 1966 to the actress Mia Farrow, then 21 (30 years his junior), seemed in part to be a search for a youthful connection. They were divorced in 1968. In 1976 he married Barbara Blakely Marx. Besides her and his three children, he is survived by two grandchildren.

Sinatra's life was rocked in 1986 by the publication of "His Way," Kitty Kelley's best-selling unauthorized biography, which focused on his volatile personality, his personal feuds and his relationships with organized-crime figures. It was a harsh portrait that nevertheless acknowledged Sinatra's role as a musical icon.

His last concert was on Feb. 25, 1995 in Palm Desert, Calif.

Assessing his own abilities in 1963, Sinatra sounded a note that was quintessentially characteristic: forlorn and tough. "Being an 18-karat manic-depressive, and having lived a life of violent emotional contradictions, I have an overacute capacity for sadness as well as elation," he said. "Whatever else has been said about me personally is unimportant. When I sing, I believe, I'm honest."

JOHNNY CASH

February 26, 1932–September 12, 2003

By Stephen Holden

Johnny Cash, whose gravelly bass-baritone was the vocal bedrock of American country music for more than four decades, died yesterday in Nashville. He was 71 and lived nearby in Hendersonville, Tenn.

The cause was complications of diabetes, said Lou Robin, Mr. Cash's manager.

Known as the Man in Black, both for his voice, which projected the fateful gravity of a country patriarch, and for his signature look, which suggested a cowboy undertaker, Mr. Cash was one of the few performers who outlasted trends to become a mythical figure rediscovered by each new generation.

Beginning in the mid-1950's, when he made his first records for the Sun label, Mr. Cash forged a lean country-folk music that at its most powerful seemed to erase the lines between singing, storytelling and grueling life experience. Born in poverty in Arkansas, he was country music's foremost poet of the working poor. His stripped-down songs described the lives of coal miners and sharecroppers, convicts and cowboys, railroad workers and laborers.

His influence extended far beyond the sphere of country music; along with Elvis Presley, Jerry Lee Lewis and Carl Perkins, his peers on Sun Records in the mid-1950's, he is considered a pioneer of rock 'n' roll. Rockers embraced him after he and Bob Dylan recorded a duet, "Girl from the North Country," on Mr. Dylan's "Nashville Skyline" album.

In May, his wife, June Carter Cash, whom he married in 1968 and whom he credited with helping him stay off drugs, died. The marriage established them as the unofficial First Family of country music.

As Rich Kienzle observed in Country Music magazine, he "strengthened the bonds between folk and country music so that both sides saw their similarities as well as their differences.

"He helped to liberalize Nashville," Mr. Kienzle wrote, "so that it could accept the unconventional and the controversial, and he did as much as anyone to make the 'outlaw' phenomenon possible."

The sound of the slapped bass on his first major hit, "I Walk the Line," and the hard-edged boom-chigga beat of the early hits he recorded with the Tennessee Three, were primal rock 'n' roll sounds. And his deep vocals, with their crags and quavers, demonstrated that a voice need not be pretty to be eloquent.

Unable to read music, Mr. Cash would compose a song in his head and play it over and over until he was satisfied enough to put it on tape. He would often write lyrics while traveling from one engagement to another.

Mr. Cash's 1954 song about violent outcasts, "Folsom Prison Blues," has been described as a forerunner of gangsta rap. The song captured an essential ingredient of his mystique, the image of the reformed outlaw:

I hear that train a-comin'

Comin' round the bend.

I ain't seen the sunshine

Since I don't know when.

Well, I'm stuck in Folsom Prison

And time keeps draggin' on.

With its bare-bones realism, the song distilled the sepulchral grimness that often seemed to engulf Mr. Cash, who fought a long battle against addiction to drugs. But he spent only one day in jail, in El Paso, for possession of pills that would have been legal with a prescription.

"There is that beast there in me," he told The New York Times in 1994. "And I got to keep him caged, or he'll eat me alive."

In a career in which he recorded more than 1,500 songs, Mr. Cash applied his gritty voice, delivered in a near monotone, to blues, hymns, cowboy songs, American Indian ballads, railroad songs, children's songs, spoken narratives, patriotic songs and love songs.

His stoical singing about loneliness and death, love and humble Christian faith reflected the barren terrain of his upbringing. He was born in a shack on Feb. 26, 1932, in Kingsland, Ark., to Ray Cash and Carrie Rivers Cash. They named him J. R; it is not clear how John evolved, and the R is a mystery. But it was the record producer Sam Phillips of Sun Records who gave him the name Johnny.

When J. R. was three, the family, helped by the Depression-era New Deal, moved to 20 acres and a five-room house in Dyess Colony, in northeastern Arkansas. There he spent the next 15 years working in the fields and learning the plain-spoken stories of the sharecroppers. He was close to his three brothers and two sisters—Roy, Jack, Tommy, Reba and Joann—and was deeply influenced by his mother's devotion to the Pentecostal Church of God.

Following his high school graduation, he headed north and took a job at an auto body plant in Pontiac, Mich. The job lasted less than a month, and he enlisted in the Air Force in 1950. He was sent to Landsberg, Germany, where he wrote "Hey Porter," which would later be one side of his first single. Returning in 1954, he married Vivian Liberto, and they moved to Memphis, where he became a door-to-door appliance salesman.

Through his brother Ray, who worked in a garage, he met a pair of guitar-playing auto mechanics, Monroe Perkins and Marshall Grant, who with the steel guitarist A. W. Kernodle became the members of his first band, which performed at church socials and country fairs.

In late 1954, the band, minus Mr. Kernodle, auditioned for Mr. Phillips, and the following spring the group, the Tennessee Three, recorded five songs for Sun. One was Mr. Cash's ballad "Cry, Cry, Cry," which became the first country hit for the label. Mr. Cash was signed to a contract by Sun and began to tour the United States and Canada and appear on radio and television. His next successful disc was "Folsom Prison Blues."

In May 1956, Sun released Mr. Cash's biggest hit and signature song, "I Walk the Line," a stern avowal of sexual fidelity that eventually sold more than 2 million copies. By the summer of 1958, he had written more than 50 songs, and he had sold more than 6 million records for Sun. But when the label balked at letting Mr. Cash record gospel music, he moved to Columbia Records, where he remained for the next 28 years.

Mr. Cash did not shy away from social or political issues. He recorded several protest songs, including "The Ballad of Ira Hayes," about an American Indian who was one of the Marines who raised the American flag at Iwo Jima but descended into alcoholism after experiencing discrimination after the war.

The rigors of touring and Mr. Cash's own tendency toward depression contributed to a dependency on amphetamines and barbiturates, which began in the early 1960's and worsened. He began missing engagements. His wife sued for divorce.

After a drug binge in 1967, he was found, close to death, by a policeman in a tiny Georgia town. June Carter, the daughter of Mother Maybelle Carter of the Carter Family, persuaded him to get treatment and helped him to rediscover his Christian faith. After marrying in 1968, they toured together in a family show that often included Ms. Carter's sisters, Anita and Helen, as well as Mother Maybelle, Carl Perkins and the Statler Brothers.

Mr. Cash's drug problems, and treatment for them, recurred off and on.

His career took a sharp upswing in the late 1960's. He released two hugely successful albums, "At Folsom Prison" and "At San Quentin." His association with Mr. Dylan, whom he had befriended at the Newport Folk Festival in 1964, helped bring his music to a young rock audience.

By 1969, Mr. Cash was the host of his own network television show, appearing over the next two years with stars like Mr. Dylan, Glen Campbell, Ray Charles and the Carter Family. Also in 1969, his novelty song "A Boy Named Sue," written by Shel Silverstein, became his biggest pop hit.

By the 1980's, Mr. Cash and his family constituted one of the nation's most respected musical dynasties. Rosanne Cash, a daughter from his first marriage, and her husband at the time, the singer and songwriter Rodney Crowell, were leaders among the younger generation of country musicians who rejected the country-pop formulas of Nashville to blend elements of Southern California folk-rock with a more austere, new traditionalist country aesthetic.

Mr. Cash experienced some decline in record sales in the 1980's and 90's. But if his career flagged, his legend flourished. He and fellow country music performers Willie Nelson, Waylon Jennings and Kris Kristofferson toured and recorded as the Highwaymen. He received a Grammy Legend Award in 1990 and two years later was inducted into the Rock and Roll Hall of Fame.

Mr. Cash is survived by his daughters Rosanne, Tara, Cinda and Kathy, and a son, John Carter, who all performed with him at one time or another.

For all the grimness of his Man in Black persona, Mr. Cash insisted that he was not a morbid person. "I am not obsessed with death—I'm obsessed with living," he said in 1994, six years after heart surgery. "The battle against the dark one and the clinging to the right one is what my life is about."

RAY CHARLES

September 23, 1930–June 10, 2004

By Jon Pareles and Bernard Weinraub

Ray Charles, the piano man with the bluesy voice who reshaped American music for a half-century, bringing the essence of soul to country, jazz, rock, standards and every other style of music he touched, died yesterday at his home in Beverly Hills, Calif. He was 73.

The cause was complications of liver disease, his publicity agent, Jerry Digney, said.

Mr. Charles brought his influence to bear as a performer, songwriter, bandleader and producer. Though blind since childhood, he was a remarkable pianist, at home with splashy barrelhouse playing and precisely understated swing.

But his playing was inevitably overshadowed by his voice, a baritone steeped in the blues, strong and impure and gloriously unpredictable. He could belt like a blues shouter and croon like a pop singer, and he used the flaws and breaks in his voice to illuminate emotional paradoxes. Even in his early years he sounded like someone who had seen all the hopes and follies of humanity.

Leaping into falsetto, stretching a word and then breaking it off with a laugh or a sob, slipping into a whisper and then letting loose a whoop, Mr. Charles could sound suave or raw, brash or hesitant, joyful or desolate, earthy or devout. He projected the exuberance of a field holler and the sophistication of a bebopper; he could conjure exaltation, sorrow and determination within a single phrase.

In the 1950's Mr. Charles became an architect of soul music by bringing the fervor and dynamics of gospel to secular subjects. But he soon broke through any categories. By singing any song he prized— from "Hallelujah I Love Her So" to "I Can't Stop Loving You" to "Georgia on My Mind" to "America the Beautiful"—Mr. Charles claimed all of American music as his birthright. He made more than 60 albums, and his influence echoes through generations of rock and soul singers.

Mr. Charles influenced singers as varied as Elvis Presley, Aretha Franklin, Stevie Wonder, Van Morrison and Billy Joel. But he started out being influenced by a very different singer, Nat King Cole.

"When I started out I tried to imitate Nat Cole because I loved him so much," Mr. Charles said. "But then I woke up one morning and I said, 'People tell me all the time that I sound like Nat Cole, but wait a minute, they don't even know my name.' As scared as I was—because I got jobs sounding like Nat Cole—I just said, 'Well, I've got to change because nobody knows who I am.' And my Mom taught me one thing, 'Be yourself, boy.' And that's the premise I went on."

Ray Charles Robinson was born on Sept. 23, 1930, in Albany, Ga., and grew up in the small town of Greenville, Fla. He was five when he began losing his sight, possibly from glaucoma. He was completely blind by seven. But he began to learn piano from a local boogie-woogie pianist and soaked up gospel music at the Shiloh Baptist Church and rural blues from musicians like Tampa Red.

He would say years later that racism in the South affected him just as it had any other black person.

"What I never understood to this day, to this very day, was how white people could have black people cook for them, make their meals, but wouldn't let them sit at the table with them," he said. "How can you dislike someone so much and have them cook for you? Shoot, if I don't like someone you ain't cooking nothing for me, ever."

He attended the St. Augustine School for the Deaf and the Blind in Florida from 1937 to 1945. There he learned to repair radios and cars, and he started formal piano lessons. He learned to write music in Braille and played Chopin and Art Tatum; he also learned to play clarinet, alto saxophone, trumpet and organ. On the radio he listened to swing bands, country-and-western singers and gospel quartets. "My ears were sponges, soaked it all up," he told David Ritz, who collaborated on his bestselling 1978 autobiography, "Brother Ray."

He left school at 15, after his mother died, and went to Jacksonville, Fla., where he made a living as a sideman and solo act and called himself Ray Charles to distinguish himself from the boxer Sugar Ray Robinson.

After three years he moved to Seattle, where he formed the McSon Trio, named after its guitarist, Gosady McGee, and the "son" from Robinson. He also started an addiction to heroin that lasted 17 years.

After two years touring, he left and eventually signed to Atlantic Records; he also moved to New Orleans to work with Guitar Slim as pianist and arranger. Guitar Slim's "Things That I Used to Do," featuring Mr. Charles on piano, became a million-selling single in 1954 and convinced Mr. Charles to abandon his imitative style and free his own voice.

He then moved to Dallas and formed a band featuring the Texas saxophonist David (Fathead) Newman. After working with studio bands on his first Atlantic singles, he persuaded that label to let him record with his seven-piece touring band. "I've Got a Woman," recorded in Atlanta, became Mr. Charles's first national hit, in 1955.

He expanded his band in the 1950's to include the Raelettes, female backup singers, and they became a permanent part of his music. It was the beginning of the rock 'n' roll era, but Mr. Charles's songs were not geared to teenagers; they had the adult concerns of the blues. Nonetheless, his songs began showing up on the pop charts.

In 1959 a late-night jam session turned into "What'd I Say." It was a blues with an electric-piano riff, a quasi-Latin beat and cheerful come-ons that gave way to wordless call-and-response moans. Although some radio stations banned it, it became a Top 10 pop hit and sold a million copies. But his next album, "The Genius of Ray Charles," took a different tack: half of it was recorded with a lush string orchestra, half with a big band. He also recorded his first country song, a version of Hank Snow's "I'm Movin' On."

Mr. Charles left Atlantic for ABC-Paramount Records in 1959 and began to reach a larger pop audience with two No. 1 hits, his version of "Georgia on My Mind" in 1960 (one of his first songs to win a Grammy) and "Hit the Road Jack" in 1961. With increasing royalties and touring fees, Mr. Charles expanded his group to become a big band.

By the early 1960's Mr. Charles had virtually given up writing his own material to follow his eclectic impulses as an interpreter. He made an instrumental jazz album, "Genius + Soul = Jazz," playing Hammond organ with a big band featuring Count Basie sidemen. In 1962 he released the album "Modern Sounds in Country and Western Music" and his big-band version of the country standard "I Can't Stop Loving You" reached No. 1. Soon afterward he settled for good into an office and studio in Los Angeles.

Mr. Charles was arrested for possession of heroin in 1965 and spent time in a California sanatorium to shake his addiction, stopping performing for a year, the only break during his long career. When he emerged he resumed touring and releasing an album or two every year. He started his own label, Tangerine, and in the mid-1970's started another, Crossover.

His presence on the pop charts had dwindled, but he was still widely respected. In 1971 he joined Aretha Franklin for the concert she recorded as "Aretha Live at Fillmore West." His version of Stevie Wonder's "Living for the City" won a Grammy in 1975. In 1979 his version of "Georgia on My Mind" was named the official state song of Georgia, and in 1980 he appeared in the movie "The Blues Brothers."

In 1986 Mr. Charles was one of the first musicians inducted into the Rock and Roll Hall of Fame. He received a Grammy for Lifetime Achievement in 1987 and a dozen Grammys for his recordings. In 1990 he turned up in television ads for Diet Pepsi, singing, "You got the right one, baby, uh-huh!"

Mr. Charles was divorced twice and leaves behind 12 children, 20 grandchildren and 5 great-grandchildren. Among his numerous awards were the Presidential Medal for the Arts, in 1993, and the Kennedy Center Honors in 1986.

In the interview this year, Mr. Charles said that having aged he could sing only music that moved him in a way that he could not quite define. "I guess I'm kind of a strange animal," he said. "What works for me is songs that I can put myself into. It has nothing to do with the song. Maybe it's a great song. But there's got to be something in that song for me."

JAMES BROWN

May 3, 1933–December 25, 2006

By Jon Pareles

James Brown, the singer, songwriter, bandleader and dancer who indelibly transformed 20th-century music, died early yesterday in Atlanta. He was 73 and lived in Beech Island, S.C., across the Savannah River from Augusta, Ga.

Mr. Brown died of congestive heart failure after being hospitalized for pneumonia, said his agent, Frank Copsidas.

Mr. Brown sold millions of records in a career that lasted half a century. In the 1960s and 1970s he regularly topped the rhythm-and-blues charts, although he never had a No. 1 pop hit. Yet his music proved far more durable and influential than countless chart-toppers. His funk provides the sophisticated rhythms that are the basis of hip-hop and a wide swath of current pop.

Mr. Copsidas said Mr. Brown used one of his best-known slogans to convey his dedication to his fans:

"I'm the hardest working man in show business, and I'm not going to let them down."

Through the years, Mr. Brown did not only call himself "the hardest working man in show business." He also went by the "Godfather of Soul" and "Soul Brother No. 1," among other names.

His music was sweaty and complex, disciplined and wild, lusty and socially conscious. Beyond his dozens of hits, Mr. Brown forged an entire musical idiom that is now a foundation of pop worldwide.

"I taught them everything they know, but not everything I know," he wrote in an autobiography.

The funk Mr. Brown introduced in his 1965 hit "Papa's Got a Brand New Bag" was both deeply rooted in Africa and thoroughly American. Songs like "I Got You (I Feel Good)," "Cold Sweat," "Get Up (I Feel Like Being a) Sex Machine" and "Hot Pants" found the percussive side of every instrument and meshed sharply syncopated patterns into kinetic polyrhythms that made people dance.

Mr. Brown's innovations reverberated through the soul and rhythm-and-blues of the 1970s and the hip-hop of the next three decades. His stage moves—the spins, the quick shuffles, the knee-drops, the splits—were imitated by performers who tried to match his stamina, from Mick Jagger to Michael Jackson.

Mr. Brown was a political force, especially during the 1960s; his 1968 song "Say It Loud—I'm Black and I'm Proud" changed America's racial vocabulary. He was never politically predictable; in 1972 he endorsed the re-election of Richard M. Nixon.

Mr. Brown led a turbulent life, and served prison time as both a teenager and an adult. He was a task-master who fined his band members for missed notes or imperfect shoeshines. He was an entrepreneur who, at the end of the 1960s, owned his own publishing company, three radio stations and a Learjet.

Mr. Brown was born May 3, 1933, in a one-room shack in Barnwell, S.C. When his parents separated four years later, he was left in the care of his aunt Honey, who ran a brothel in Augusta, Ga. As a boy he earned pennies buck-dancing for soldiers; he also picked cotton and shined shoes.

He was imprisoned for petty theft in 1949 after breaking into a car. While in prison he sang in a gospel group. After his release in 1952, he joined a group led by Bobby Byrd, which eventually called itself the Flames, with Mr. Brown emerging as the frontman.

In 1955 the Flames recorded "Please Please Please" in Macon, Ga. A talent scout heard it on local radio and signed the Flames to a recording contract with King Records. A second version, in 1956, became a million-selling single.

Nine follow-up singles were flops until, in 1958, a gospel-rooted ballad, "Try Me," went to No. 1 on the rhythm-and-blues chart. Mr. Brown followed up with more ballads, although the Flames' stage shows would turn them into long, frenzied crescendos. His trademark routine of collapsing onstage, having a cape thrown over him and tossing it away for one more reprise, again and again, would leave audiences shouting for more.

Mr. Brown had his first Top 20 pop hit in 1963 with "Prisoner of Love," a ballad backed by an orchestra. That same year, his "Live at the Apollo," a recording of a 1962 concert at that Harlem theater, revealed what the rhythm-and-blues circuit already knew and became the No. 2 album nationwide.

By the mid-1960s, Mr. Brown was producing his own recording sessions. In February 1965, with "Papa's Got a Brand New Bag," he decided to shift the beat of his band: from the one-two-three-four backbeat to one-two-three-four.

"I changed from the upbeat to the downbeat," Mr. Brown said in 1990. "Simple as that, really."

Actually it wasn't that simple; drums, rhythm guitar and horns all kicked the beat around from different angles. "Papa's Got a Brand New Bag" won a Grammy Award as best rhythm-and-blues song, and it was only the beginning of Mr. Brown's rhythmic breakthroughs. Through the 1960s and into the '70s, he would make his funk ever more complex while stripping harmony to a bare minimum.

He didn't immediately abandon ballads; songs like "It's a Man's Man's Man's World," in 1966, mixed aching, bluesy lines with wrenching screams.

By the late 1960s Mr. Brown's funk was part of pop, R&B and jazz. It was also creating a sensation in Africa, where it would shape the Afrobeat of Fela Kuti, the juju of King Sunny Ade and the mbalax of Youssou N'Dour.

Musicians who left Mr. Brown's bands would also have a direct role in 1970s and 1980s funk; the saxophonist Maceo Parker, the trombonist Fred Wesley and the bassist Bootsy Collins were part of George Clinton's Parliament-Funkadelic, and Mr. Parker also worked with Prince.

Through the early 1970s Mr. Brown's songs filled dance floors. His self-described "super heavy funk" gave him No. 1 R&B hits and Top 20 pop hits, including "Give It Up or Turnit a Loose" and "Mother Popcorn" in 1969.

The rise of disco—a much simplified version of Mr. Brown's funk—knocked him out of the Top 40 in the late 1970s. But an appearance in the movie "The Blues Brothers" in 1980 started a career resurgence, and in 1985 Mr. Brown had a pop hit with "Living in America," the song he performed in the movie "Rocky IV." That year he was inducted into the Rock and Roll Hall of Fame as one of its first members.

Meanwhile hip-hop had arrived, and Mr. Brown's music often provided the beat. LL Cool J, Public Enemy, De La Soul and the Beastie Boys all sampled Clyde Stubblefield's drumming on "Funky Drummer."

Mr. Brown maintained a nearly constant touring schedule despite a tumultuous personal life. During the 1970s the Internal Revenue Service demanded $4.5 million in unpaid taxes; the jet and radio stations were sold. His oldest son, Teddy, died in a car accident in 1973.

In 1988, intoxicated on PCP, he burst into an insurance seminar adjoining his own office in Augusta, then led police on a car chase across the South Carolina border. He was sentenced to prison for carrying a deadly weapon at a public gathering, attempting to flee a police officer and driving under the influence of drugs, and was released in 1991.

In 1998, after discharging a rifle and another car chase, he was sentenced to a 90-day drug rehabilitation program. He was officially pardoned by South Carolina in 2003, but arrested again in 2004 on charges of domestic violence against his fourth wife, Tomi Rae Hynie, a former backup singer. "I would never hurt my wife," he said in a statement at the time. "I love her very much."

She survives him, along with their son, James Brown II, and at least five other children.

Despite the turmoil, Mr. Brown's status as an American archetype had long been assured. He received a Grammy Lifetime Achievement Award in 1992 and a Kennedy Center Honor in 2003, the same year that Michael Jackson presented him with a BET Award for lifetime achievement. In a 1990 interview with The New York Times, he said, "I was always 25 years ahead of my time."

MICHAEL JACKSON

August 29, 1958–June 25, 2009

By Brooks Barnes

LOS ANGELES—For his legions of fans, he was the Peter Pan of pop music: the little boy who refused to grow up. But on the verge of another attempted comeback, he is suddenly gone, this time for good.

Michael Jackson, whose quintessentially American tale of celebrity and excess took him from musical boy wonder to global pop superstar to sad figure haunted by lawsuits, paparazzi and failed plastic surgery, was pronounced dead on Thursday afternoon at U.C.L.A. Medical Center after arriving in a coma, a city official said. Mr. Jackson was 50, having spent 40 of those years in the public eye he loved.

The singer was rushed to the hospital, a six-minute drive from the rented Holmby Hills home in which he was living, shortly after noon by paramedics. A hospital spokesman would not confirm reports of cardiac arrest. He was pronounced dead at 2:26 p.m.

As with Elvis Presley or the Beatles, it is impossible to calculate the full effect Mr. Jackson had on the world of music. At the height of his career, he was indisputably the biggest star in the world; he has sold more than 750 million albums. Radio stations across the country reacted to his death with marathon sessions of his songs. MTV, which grew successful in part as a result of Mr. Jackson's groundbreaking videos, reprised its early days as a music channel by showing his biggest hits.

From his days as the youngest brother in the Jackson 5 to his solo career in the 1980s and early 1990s, Mr. Jackson was responsible for a string of hits like "I Want You Back," "I'll Be There" "Don't Stop 'Til You Get Enough" "Billie Jean" and "Black or White," all of which exploited his high voice, infectious energy and ear for irresistible hooks.

As a solo performer, he ushered in pop as a global product. He became more character than singer: his sequined glove, his whitened face, his moonwalk dance move became embedded in the cultural firmament.

His entertainment career hit high-water marks with the release of "Thriller," from 1982, which has been certified 28 times platinum by the Recording Industry Association of America, and with the "Victory" world tour, which reunited him with his brothers in 1984.

But soon afterward, his career started a bizarre disintegration. His darkest moment undoubtedly came in 2003, when he was indicted on child molesting charges. A young cancer patient claimed the singer had befriended him and then groped him at his Neverland estate near Santa Barbara, Calif., but Mr. Jackson was acquitted of all charges.

He had been an object of news media fascination since the Jackson 5's first hit, "I Want You Back," in 1969. His public image wavered between that of the musical naif, who wanted only to recapture his youth by riding on roller-coasters and having sleepovers with his friends, to the calculating mogul who constructed his persona around his often-baffling public behavior.

Mr. Jackson's brothers, Jackie, Tito, Jermaine, Marlon and Randy, have all had performing careers, with varying success, since they stopped performing together. His sisters, Rebbie, La Toya and Janet, are also singers, and Janet Jackson has been a major star in her own right for two decades. They all survive him, as do his parents, Joseph and Katherine Jackson, and three children: Michael Jr. and Paris, both born to Mr. Jackson's second wife, Deborah Jeanne Rowe, and Prince Michael Jackson II, the son of a surrogate mother. Mr. Jackson had been briefly married to Lisa Marie Presley, the daughter of Elvis Presley.

Michael Joseph Jackson was born in Gary, Ind., on Aug. 29, 1958. The second youngest of six brothers, he began performing professionally with four of them at the age of five in a group that their father, Joe, a steelworker, had organized. In 1968, the group, originally called the Jackson Brothers, was signed by Motown Records.

The Jackson 5 was an instant phenomenon. The group's first four singles—"I Want You Back," "ABC," "The Love You Save" and "I'll Be There"—all reached No. 1 on the pop charts in 1970, a feat no group had accomplished before. Michael handled virtually all the lead vocals and displayed a degree of showmanship rare in a performer of any age.

He began recording under his own name in 1971 while continuing to perform with his brothers. His recording of "Ben," the title song from a movie about a boy and his homicidal pet rat, was a No. 1 hit in 1972.

The brothers (minus Michael's older brother Jermaine, who was married to the daughter of Berry Gordy, Motown's founder and chief executive) left Motown in 1975 and, rechristened the Jacksons, signed to Epic, a unit of CBS Records.

Mr. Jackson's first solo album for Epic, "Off the Wall," released in 1979, yielded two No. 1 singles and sold 7 million copies, but it was a mere prologue to what came next. His follow-up, "Thriller," released in 1982, became the best-selling album of all time and helped usher in the music video age. The video for the title track, directed by John Landis, was an elaborate horror-movie pastiche that was more of a mini-movie than a promotional clip.

Seven of the nine tracks on "Thriller" were released as singles and reached the Top 10. The album sold an estimated 100 million copies worldwide. It also won eight Grammy Awards.

Mr. Jackson's next album, "Bad," released in 1987, sold 8 million copies and produced five No. 1 singles and another state-of-the-art video, this one directed by Martin Scorsese. It was a huge hit by almost anyone else's standards, but an inevitable letdown after "Thriller."

It was at this point that Mr. Jackson's private life began to overshadow his music.

Even with the millions he earned, his eccentric lifestyle took a severe financial toll. In 1988 he paid about $17 million for a 2,600-acre ranch in Los Olivos, Calif., 125 miles northwest of Los Angeles. Calling it Neverland, after the mythical island of Peter Pan, he outfitted the property with amusement-park rides, a zoo and a 50-seat theater, at a reported cost of $35 million. The ranch became his sanctum.

But Neverland, and Mr. Jackson's lifestyle, were expensive to maintain. Last year, Neverland narrowly escaped foreclosure after he defaulted on $24.5 million he owed on the property.

Mr. Jackson never recovered from the child molestation trial, which attracted news media from around the world. Each day, wearing a different costume, he appeared in a small courtroom in Santa Maria, Calif., to listen as witnesses spun a sometimes incredible tale.

The case turned on the credibility of his accuser, a 15-year-old cancer survivor who said Mr. Jackson had gotten him drunk and molested him several times. The boy's younger brother testified that he had seen Mr. Jackson groping his brother on two other occasions.

After seven days of deliberations, the jury returned not-guilty verdicts on all 14 counts against Mr. Jackson.

Despite the public relations blow of the trial, Mr. Jackson and his ever-changing retinue of managers, lawyers and advisers never stopped plotting his return. And despite his troubles, the press and the public never abandoned the star. A crowd of paparazzi and onlookers lined the street outside Mr. Jackson's home as the ambulance took him to the hospital.

DAVID BOWIE

January 8, 1947–January 10, 2016

By Jon Pareles

David Bowie, the infinitely changeable, fiercely forward-looking songwriter who taught generations of musicians about the power of drama, images and personas, died on Sunday, two days after his 69th birthday.

His publicist confirmed the death. No other details were provided. Mr. Bowie had been treated for cancer for the last 18 months, according to a statement on his social-media accounts.

Mr. Bowie wrote songs, above all, about being an outsider: an alien, a misfit, a sexual adventurer, a faraway astronaut. His music was always a mutable blend—rock, cabaret, jazz and what he called "plastic soul"—but it was suffused with genuine soul. He also captured the drama and longing of everyday life, enough to give him No. 1 pop hits like "Let's Dance."

In concerts and videos, Mr. Bowie's costumes and imagery traversed styles, eras and continents, from German Expressionism to commedia dell'arte to Japanese kimonos to spacesuits. He set an example, and a challenge, for every arena spectacle in his wake.

Mr. Bowie earned admiration and emulation across the musical spectrum—from rockers, balladeers, punks, hip-hop acts, creators of pop spectacles and even classical composers like Philip Glass, who based two symphonies on Mr. Bowie's albums "Low" and "Heroes."

Mr. Bowie's constantly morphing persona was a touchstone for performers like Madonna and Lady Gaga; his determination to stay contemporary introduced his fans to Philadelphia funk, Japanese fashion, German electronica and drum-and-bass dance music.

Yet throughout Mr. Bowie's metamorphoses, he was always recognizable. His message was that there was always empathy beyond difference.

Angst and apocalypse, media and paranoia, distance and yearning were among Mr. Bowie's lifelong themes. So was a penchant for transgression coupled with a determination to push cult tastes toward the mainstream.

Mr. Bowie was a person of relentless reinvention. He emerged in the late 1960s with the voice of a rock belter but with the sensibility of a cabaret singer, steeped in the dynamics of stage musicals.

He was Major Tom, the lost astronaut in his career-making 1969 hit "Space Oddity." He was Ziggy Stardust, the otherworldly pop star at the center of his 1972 album, "The Rise and Fall of Ziggy Stardust and the Spiders from Mars." He was the self-destructive Thin White Duke and the minimalist but

heartfelt voice of the three albums he recorded in Berlin in the '70s.

"The day will come when David Bowie is a star and the crushed remains of his melodies are broadcast from Muzak boxes in every elevator and hotel lobby in town," Nancy Erlich wrote in The Times.

The arrival of MTV in the 1980s was the perfect complement to Mr. Bowie's sense of theatricality and fashion. "Ashes to Ashes," the "Space Oddity" sequel that revealed, "We know Major Tom's a junkie," and "Let's Dance," which offered, "Put on your red shoes and dance the blues," gave him worldwide popularity.

Mr. Bowie was his generation's standard-bearer for rock as theater: something constructed and inflated yet sincere in its artifice, saying more than naturalism could. With a voice that dipped down to baritone and leapt into falsetto, he was complexly androgynous, an explorer of human impulses that could not be quantified.

He also pushed the limits of "Fashion" and "Fame," writing songs with those titles and also thinking deeply about the possibilities and strictures of pop renown.

He was born David Robert Jones on Jan. 8, 1947, in London, where as a youth he soaked up rock 'n' roll. He took up the saxophone in the 1960s and started leading bands as a teenager, singing the blues. He suffered a blow in a teenage brawl that caused his left pupil to be permanently dilated.

In the late 1960s, Lindsay Kemp, a dancer, actor and mime, became a lasting influence on Mr. Bowie, focusing his interest in movement and artifice.

Mr. Bowie's music turned toward folk-rock and psychedelia. The release of "Space Oddity," shortly before the Apollo 11 mission put men on the moon in 1969, gained him a British pop audience and, when it was rereleased in 1973 in the United States, an American one.

By then, with the albums "Hunky Dory," "The Rise and Fall of Ziggy Stardust and the Spiders From Mars" and "Aladdin Sane," Mr. Bowie had become a pioneer of glam rock and a major star in Britain, playing up an androgynous image. But he also had difficulties separating his onstage personas from real life and succumbed to drug problems, particularly cocaine use. In 1973, he abruptly announced his retirement—though it was the retirement of Ziggy Stardust, not of Mr. Bowie.

He moved to the United States in 1974 and made "Diamond Dogs," which included the hit "Rebel Rebel." In 1975, he turned toward funk with the album "Young Americans," recorded primarily in Philadelphia with collaborators, including a young Luther Vandross. John Lennon joined Mr. Bowie in writing and singing the hit "Fame." Mr. Bowie's 1976 album "Station to Station" yielded more hits, but drug problems were making Mr. Bowie increasingly unstable; in interviews, he made pro-fascist pronouncements that he would soon disown.

For a far-reaching change of environment, and to get away from drugs, Mr. Bowie moved in 1976 to Switzerland and then to West Berlin. Mr. Bowie shared a Berlin apartment with Iggy Pop, and he helped produce and write songs for two Iggy Pop albums, "The Idiot" and "Lust for Life."

He also made what is usually called his Berlin trilogy—"Low," "Heroes" and "Lodger"—working with Brian Eno and Mr. Bowie's collaborator over decades, the producer Tony Visconti. They used electronics and experimental methods, like having musicians play unfamiliar instruments, yet songs like "Heroes" conveyed romance against the bleakest odds.

As the 1980s began, Mr. Bowie turned to live theater, performing in multiple cities (including a Broadway run) in the demanding title role of "The Elephant Man." Yet he would also reach his peak as a mainstream pop musician in that decade—particularly with his 1983 album "Let's Dance." By 1989 Mr. Bowie was determined to change again; he recorded, without top billing, as a member of the rock band Tin Machine.

His experiments continued in the 1990s. In 1995, he reconnected with Mr. Eno on an album, "1. Outside"—influenced by science fiction and film noir—and toured with Nine Inch Nails in an innovative concert that had his band and Nine Inch Nails merging partway through. Mr. Bowie's 1997 album, "Earthling," turned toward the era's electronic dance music.

By the 21st century, Mr. Bowie was an elder statesman. He had been inducted into the Rock and Roll Hall of Fame in 1996. In 2001, he sang "Heroes" at the Concert for New York City after the Sept. 11 attacks.

His final albums were a glance back and a new excursion. "The Next Day," released in 2013, returned to something like the glam-rock sound of his 1970s guitar bands, for new songs suffused with bitter thoughts of mortality. And "Blackstar," released two days before his death, had him backed by a volatile jazz-based quartet, in songs that contemplated fame, spirituality, lust, death and, as always, startling transformations.

PRINCE

June 7, 1958–April 21, 2016

By Jon Pareles

Prince, the songwriter, singer, producer, one-man studio band and consummate showman, died on Thursday at his home, Paisley Park, in Chanhassen, Minn. He was 57.

The Carver County sheriff, Jim Olson, said deputies, responding to an emergency call, "found an unresponsive adult male in the elevator" and were unable to revive him. An autopsy was to be performed to determine the cause of death.

Prince was bursting with music—a wildly prolific songwriter, a virtuoso on guitars, keyboards and drums and a master architect of funk, rock, R&B and pop, even as his music defied genres. In a career that lasted from the late 1970s until his solo "Piano & a Microphone" tour this year, he was a sex symbol, a musical prodigy and an artist who shaped his career his way, often battling with music-business practices.

"When I first started out in the music industry, I was most concerned with freedom," he said when he was inducted into the Rock and Roll Hall of Fame in 2004. "Freedom to produce, freedom to play all the instruments on my records, freedom to say anything I wanted to."

A seven-time Grammy winner, Prince had Top 10 hits like "Little Red Corvette," "When Doves Cry," "Let's Go Crazy," "Kiss" and "The Most Beautiful Girl in the World"; albums like "Dirty Mind," "1999" and "Sign O' the Times" were full-length statements. Some of his songs became hits for others, among them "Nothing Compares 2 U" for Sinead O'Connor, "Manic Monday" for the Bangles and "I Feel for You" for Chaka Khan. With the 1984 film and album "Purple Rain," he told a fictionalized version of his own story: biracial, gifted, spectacularly ambitious. Its music won him an Academy Award, and the album sold more than 13 million copies in the United States alone.

Prince recorded most of his music entirely on his own, playing every instrument and singing every line. Performing those songs onstage, he worked as a bandleader in the polished, athletic, ecstatic tradition of James Brown, at once spontaneous and utterly precise, riveting enough to open a Grammy Awards telecast and play the Super Bowl halftime show. He would often follow a full-tilt arena concert with a late-night club show.

Prince sang passionately, affectionately and playfully about sex and seduction. With deep bedroom eyes and a sly, knowing smile, he was one of pop's ultimate flirts: a sex symbol devoted to romance and pleasure, not power or machismo. Elsewhere in his catalog were songs that addressed social issues and delved into mysticism and science fiction. He made himself a unifier of dualities—racial, sexual, musical, cultural—teasing at them in songs like "Controversy" and transcending them in his career.

Prince's music had a lasting influence: among songwriters concocting come-ons, among producers working on dance grooves, among studio experimenters and stage performers. He sang as a soul belter, a rocker, a bluesy ballad singer and a falsetto crooner. His most immediately recognizable (and widely imitated) instrumental style was a particular kind of pinpoint, staccato funk, defined as much by keyboards as by the rhythm section. But that was just one among the many styles he would draw on and blend, from hard rock to psychedelia to electronic music. His music was a cornucopia of ideas: triumphantly, brilliantly kaleidoscopic.

Prince Rogers Nelson was born in Minneapolis on June 7, 1958, the son of John L. Nelson, a musician whose stage name was "Prince Rogers," and Mattie Della Shaw, a jazz singer who had performed with the Prince Rogers Band. They were separated in 1965, and his mother remarried in 1967. Prince spent some time living with each parent and immersed himself in music, teaching himself to play his instruments.

He recorded with a Minneapolis band, 94 East, and began working on his own solo recordings. He was still a teenager when he was signed to Warner Bros. Records, in a deal that included full creative control. His first album, "For You" (1978), gained only modest attention. But his second, "Prince" (1979), started with "I Wanna Be Your Lover," a No. 1 R&B hit that reached No. 11 on the pop charts; during the 1980s nearly all his albums were million-sellers that reached the Top 10.

He also drew some opposition. "Darling Nikki," a song that refers to masturbation, shocked Tipper Gore, the wife of Al Gore, who was then a United States senator, when she heard her daughter listening to it, helping lead to the formation of the Parents' Music Resource Center, which eventually pressured record companies into labeling albums to warn of "explicit content." In a more religious phase, Prince decided not to use profanities onstage, but his songs never renounced carnal delights.

Friction grew in the 1990s between Prince and his label, Warner Bros., over the size of his output and how much music he was determined to release. By the mid-1990s, he was in open battle with the label, releasing albums as rapidly as he could to finish his contract; quality suffered and so did sales. He appeared with the word "Slave" written on his face, complaining about the terms of his contract, and in 1993 he changed his stage name to an unpronounceable glyph, only returning to Prince in 1996 after the Warner contract ended.

For the next two decades, Prince put out an avalanche of recordings. Hip-hop's takeover of R&B meant that he was heard far less often on the radio; his last Top 10 hit was "The Most Beautiful Girl in the World," in 1994. But he could always draw and satisfy a live audience, and concerts easily sustained his later career.

A trove of Prince's recordings remains unreleased, and it's likely that there are masterpieces yet to be heard.

having been born at Naples on Feb. 7, 1873. His origin was not so humble as it has been often represented. His father was a mechanic, but he was also an inventor and a man of considerable intelligence. Caruso himself had wit and brains, as well as a voice.

Caruso's early life was told by himself as follows:

"Had I followed the path that was chosen for me I should have been a mechanic, or possibly an engineer. My father was employed in Naples as a working mechanic and he had two sons—myself and a younger boy. I was a sad trial to my parents. I was very noisy and lively. I sang constantly and my voice then was pretty piercing.

"My father chastised me and tried to make me a sober, industrious mechanic, like himself. This did not attract me. I wanted to be a sailor and I haunted the docks for days. I swam there for hours at a time. I broke most of the rules and regulations at school and lived in constant disgrace.

"By the time I was 11 years old, I had developed a great love for singing and had, I believe, a fine contralto voice.

"One day the old organist of the Church of St. Anna, Naples, heard me singing some popular melody, and my youthful efforts delighted him so much that he engaged me to sing in his choir. And I received for my labors each Sunday the large sum of 10 pence weekly—the first money I ever earned.

"When I was 12 my schoolmaster sent me home in haste for refusing to obey certain rules. On the doorstep my father met me; chastisement followed as usual, after which he declared that I must be apprenticed at once to a mechanical engineer. I was, and I loathed my new work whole-heartedly. In fact, my only interest centred round mechanical drawing, and I promptly had

my brother volunteered time in my stead. On gaged for a season of and from this time career has simply been lifted from one round the next.

"After singing in after another, I went there back to Paris; an thence to the Argentin went to Rio Janeiro, ored by President C singing at a gala perf honor of the Presiden who was on an official From Rio I went to s

Caruso Becomes a

The late Maurice Gr tract that brought Ca but it was left to Heinrich Conried, to here. He was an und New York City from ance at the opening 1903, winning the popu three years later in t of Conried and Hamm peating with greater cesses in every season to many admirers. Car season were one and His first Metropolitan in "Rigoletto" Nov. was Mme. Sembrich.

One of the great istics was a childlike applause, a type of v vorced from megalom love which is mingle contempt for others. bounded admiration heart completely. T patriot and a cosmopo ly became fundamenta He numbered his war here by the thousands.

He spent most of years in Manhattan a On one of his arriva through a pretty ceren a handful of earth at ing it, by way of salu was so thoroughly M in 1919 he accepted Captain in the New

announcement was telegraphed all over the world last night of the sudden death, in Venice, of Richard Wagner. Great men who win their fame by their own efforts, who have not claimed consideration on account of the accident of birth or by reason of official favor, are in our day more certain of just recognition than ever before in the history of the world. With the spread of knowledge and general cultivation an additional meaning has been given to the axiom that "nothing succeeds like success." Pretenders in every department of the fine arts are now more certain to be estimated at their real worth than formerly, and when we see a man in these days who has never failed to believe in himself, has claimed to be moved by the influences of high purposes, and has asserted himself till he has commanded success, it is impossible to withhold the tribute of respect to his genius and energy. The life of Richard Wagner affords a notable illustration of the value of persistent effort in carrying out to its conclusion the inspiration of genius. In the face of mortifying failures and discouragements he apparently never lost confidence in himself. If he had been of common clay he would have early abandoned his theories and would have accepted the verdict passed upon him. He would then have been simply called by the few who had heard of him a conceited man who failed. But personal conceit is in his case shown to be a valuable quality when there is something to be conceited about, and loses its objectionable character in view of its subsequent justification. Whatever of opposition to his methods there was he certainly took no pains to remove by deviating from what thought to be the truth. He believed he was right, and possessed the force and ability to make a large and influential number of his contemporaries accept his authority. The result is that he has made for himself a niche in the temple of fame. "Wagnerism" is

DANCE AND CLASSICAL MUSIC

him, of which he h sian order of the Dre "Tannhäu theatre, bu later, in 184 voices and tel," and "Lohengri composed, in preparat the revolut Wagner ha ples, and w identified in the move pressed fle and becam he took up attacks conductors of all th sion. His musik" fo chief theor written a year he w and condu Drama" ories in aroused and unfav versy whic were unfo been colle der the t tungen," At Zuri ception o being a tri the Philha eight of was durin sical liter and held

RICHARD WAGNER

May 2, 1813–February 13, 1883

Without a word of warning the announcement was telegraphed all over the world last night of the sudden death, in Venice, of Richard Wagner [at the age of 69].

The life of Richard Wagner affords a remarkable illustration of the results of persistent effort in carrying out the inspiration of genius. In the face of mortifying failures and discouragements he never lost confidence in himself. If he had been of common clay he would have early abandoned his theories and accepted the verdict passed upon him. He would then have been simply called by the few who had heard of him a conceited man who failed. But personal conceit in his case proved a valuable quality when there is something to be conceited about.

He believed he was right, and possessed the force and ability to make a large and influential number of his contemporaries accept his authority. The result is that he has made for himself a niche in the temple of fame.

Like every reformer or man of positive character, he excited hostility, but there is now none of the ridicule which was at first used to crush him. The characteristics of a reformer do not make him lovable, and results in the division of people into but two classes. If one knows or cares anything of the matter he can hardly fail to be either a "Wagnerite" or an "anti-Wagnerite."

Among musicians Wagner's position is the most strongly disputed point. His adherents are a devoted band of followers, his opponents are uncompromising, but of late years the opposition to him has been tempered by respect, and they have admitted that though he was wrong, he was sincere, indomitable, and of mighty force.

Richard Wagner was born in Leipsic on the 22nd of May, 1813. He showed little aptitude for music in his earliest years, and was difficult to control, "preferring to hammer at tunes from the overture to 'Der Freisehütz' with monstrous fingering, to practicing his exercises," and was further said by his teacher to "torture the piano in a most abominable fashion." In 1824, at the age of 11, the boy was engaged in writing a drama, "a compound," he says himself, "of 'Hamlet' and 'King Lear.'

"The design was grand in the extreme. Forty-two people died in the course of the piece, and I was obliged to let most of them reappear as ghosts in the last act for want of living characters."

His most profound early musical impressions were received from hearing the orchestral compositions of Mozart and Beethoven, and at this time he received instruction from Theodor Weinlig, of the University of Leipsic. While a mere boy he wrote orchestral works which have been described as being "on a gigantic scale and full of unutterable aspiration," one of which, an overture, was performed at Leipsic and received with mortifying ridicule. The excellent result of this was that he then applied himself to the study of Gluck, Mozart, Bach, and Beethoven.

Heinrich Dorn said of him, "I doubt whether there ever was a young musician who knew Beethoven's works more thoroughly than Wagner in his 18th year." The influence of this study resulted in the reverence which Wagner always felt for Beethoven. He spoke of the Ninth Symphony as "that mystic source of my highest ecstasies."

In 1833 Wagner's first symphony was played in Leipsic, and the same year his opera the "Fairies" was brought out. In 1884 he was appointed musical director of the Magdeburg Theatre, where, in 1836, his second opera, "Das Liebes-verbot," was produced. These works have passed into oblivion, and the latter was such a failure that he had to resign, and left Magdeburg penniless and in debt. Also at Magdeburg he had unwisely married an actress, with whom he never lived happily.

In 1837 he became conductor at Riga, where he remained till 1839. There he conceived the plan for the first of his grand operas, "Rienzi," founded on Bulwer Lytton's novel. It was designed to be in five acts, but when he had completed two acts, he left his position in Riga, and in 1839, being 26 years of age, set out for Paris "without funds or friends or definite plan."

On his way he met [Giacomo] Meyerbeer, who was struck by the originality and character of the young aspirant's score, and gave him letters of introduction to the musical leaders of Paris. He obtained a commission to write an overture for the Société des Concerts, upon which he produced his "Faust" overture. This, however, was laid aside, the society not having the courage to produce so eccentric a work.

While in Paris Wagner wrote in the short space of seven weeks the music of his "Der Fliegende Holländer." After he had given up in despair his attempts to produce his "Rienzi" in Paris, he sent the score to the Court Theatre in Dresden, where it was accepted and brought out in 1842. It proved to be a great success, and suddenly Wagner, before he was 30 years old, found himself "the most popular man in Dresden."

In the following year "Der Fliegende Holländer" was produced. The success of these works was the turning point of his career. He was appointed Director of the Dresden Opera-house. In October, 1845, "Tannhäuser" was brought out by him at this theater. Two years later, in 1847, he produced a composition for male voices and orchestra, "Das Liebesmahl der Apostel," and soon afterward wrote his grand opera "Lohengrin." In 1849 "Die Meistersinger" was composed, and in that year also "Lohengrin" was in preparation for production at Dresden, when the revolutionary outbreak in Saxony took place.

Wagner had always been liberal in his principles, and was, even in 1830, identified with the Liberal Party. He was active in the movement as a leader, and when it was suppressed fled to Switzerland, where he remained until 1858.

At this period of his isolation he began "the great manifestation of his dramatic and operatic views in the composition, 'Der Ring des Nibelungen,'" and in 1857 wrote the poem and music of "Tristan and Isolde."

Wagner's relations with Liszt were of a particularly friendly character. Under Liszt's direction "Lohengrin" was produced for the first time in August, 1850, at Welmar. In 1859 and 1860 Wagner revisited Paris, giving three concerts in the latter year, and in 1861 "Tannhäuser" was brought out at the Grand Opera.

But the opera was "hooted and whistled off the stage by the members of the Jockey Club." Before the orchestra had played a dozen bars of the magnificent overture, the music was drowned in a chorus of hisses, yells, cat-calls, and whistles. After the curtain rose the same unseemly demonstrations continued. This disgraceful affair only reflected discredit on Paris.

In 1863 Wagner made what is styled "a triumphant professional tour through Austria and Prussia," conducting concerts, and "Tannhäuser" was produced with great success in Vienna and elsewhere, in marked contrast to the treatment it received in Paris. In 1864 he returned to Munich, where he gave satisfactory representations of his most important compositions, the first being" "Tristan and Isolde," which was brought out in 1865, followed by "Die Meistersinger von Nümberg" in 1868, "Das Rheingold" in 1869, and "Die Walküre" in 1870.

In the last named year he married his second wife, who was the daughter of Liszt.

The Bayreuth scheme which culminated in an imposing success in 1876 was doubtless the most remarkable event in the history of music. Such an opportunity was never before afforded an artist to give a complete performance under his own supervision. "Wagner societies" were formed in the cities of Europe and this country, a large sum of money collected to build the theater according to the ideas of the composer, at Bayreuth, and the four operas of the series of "Der Ring des Niebelungen," viz.: "Das Rheingold," "Die Walküre," "Siegfried," and "Götterdämmerung," were each performed three times during August, 1876.

The orchestra, composed of 119 musicians led by Hans Richter, was concealed from sight below the stage,

and all the preparations, under Wagner's own direction, were on the most elaborate and expensive scale.

The audience that assembled at this little out-of-the-way town was not the least remarkable part of the affair, the importance of which was recognized by the press all over the world. The Emperor of Germany, the Emperor of Brazil, a long list of Grand Dukes and other titled personages, the most eminent composers and musicians of this country and Europe, all gathered to hear Wagner's great work.

This undertaking was begun in 1871, the cornerstone of the theater was laid in 1872, and till 1876 the composer's energies were largely engaged in completing the requisite preparations.

For the past few years Wagner has lived at Bayreuth in a house of white marble built for him, and in which he has been surrounded with every luxury. The intense egotism of the man was suggested in everything about this gorgeous place, where everything was arranged for effect, from the busts of himself and pictures illustrative of his works, to the tomb within a stone's throw of the house in which he proposed to be laid, the inscription written by himself being already engraved and only awaiting the date of his death.

It is, of course, too early to decide the position of Wagner in musical history. Like Spencer, who was said to be the poet for poets, Wagner may be said to have been the musician for musicians. The number of his followers has steadily increased, and though there is still much of the incomprehensible about his operas to the average musically inclined listener, his instrumental works have continually grown in popular favor.

His originality, extravagant methods of handling the instruments of orchestra, and passionate effects require judgment on him to be made without comparison with others. He was a rule unto himself. Despite strong opposition and violent prejudices, no candid person can deny the great merit of his instrumental music.

As to his operas, opinions are more varied. The exceeding difficulty of any adequate production of them makes them comparatively unknown. The number of artists capable of singing them is a bar to their frequent performance.

The "Parsifal" in which Wagner took special pride will, of course, be ever famous as the last emanation of his genius. Such selections as have been heard in this country indicated that the great master was as powerful, earnest, and original as in his younger days.

The performance last year at Bayreuth attracted such an audience as only Wagner could collect and was made up of his admirers from every part of the civilized world. There was but one expression of opinion regarding the work, and when it is heard in its entirety there is no doubt that it will take rank with the immortal compositions that must live and grow in fame as the world advances in knowledge and cultivation.

FRANZ LISZT

October 22, 1811–July 31, 1886

BAYREUTH—Franz Liszt died at midnight last night. He attended the performances of "Parsifal" and "Tristan und Isolde" at the Wagner Theatre. He had been ailing for a long time but seemed to be in somewhat better health than usual.

Franz Liszt was born in the small town of Raiding, in Hungary, on Oct. 22, 1811. The lad's talent for music manifested itself at an early age, and induced his father, Adam Liszt, himself an amateur of no mean ability, to cultivate it. Adam Liszt was his son's first teacher and imparted to him his instruction for three years, until the nine-year-old lad played in public Ries's E flat major concerto with so much success that his father resolved to devote himself to the education and interests of his son.

The Liszts went to Vienna, where Czerny instructed Franz in piano playing and Salieri in composition. In 1823, in a concert in which Liszt took part, Beethoven embraced him. This incident produced a deep impression upon the youthful performer.

In the French capital he was acclaimed in 30 almost successive performances. His skill as a composer first revealed itself, and a one-act opera, "Don Sancho; or, The Castle of Love," was produced with encouraging consequences. Several piano compositions next made their appearance, and a profitable concert tour followed. All went well until 1827, when the sudden death of his father robbed Liszt of a tender parent

and valuable aid, and compelled him to look upon the practical side of life.

A brief period of poverty ensued, during which young Liszt, by composition and teaching, had to provide for his mother's wants and his own; at one time their needs were so pressing that he had to sell his piano. But the clouds soon broke, and the sunshine of fame and prosperity came forth, never to lose its brightness for half a century.

The principal salons of Parisian art and high life welcomed him. [Victor] Hugo, [Heinrich] Heine, and George Sand were his intimates, and Meyerbeer, for whom he retained a life-long friendship, and '[Frédéric] Chopin, whose biographer he was afterward to become, his musical associates.

The year 1834 proved an important epoch in his career. He met the Countess d'Agoult, and the liaison which commenced between the two lasted until 1844. A son and two daughters were born them. Liszt's son and one of his daughters have long since died; his daughter Cosima, who is married to Wagner, still lives. Liszt parted with the Countess, and, proceeding to Rome, took holy orders and was created an Abbé in partibus.

In Paris Liszt delighted audiences with his matchless fire and power, and his chivalric presence, his noble head, crowned with long, thick locks, his graceful bearing, his perfect manners, and his unparalleled personal magnetism carried everything before them. France, Spain, Italy, Germany, Russia, Norway, and Sweden rang with his praises.

Orders of knighthood and titles were lavished upon him; processions went forth to greet him; serenades made his every night melodious; honors and gold were showered upon him. The fair sex especially went wild in their enthusiasm; in Germany the broken strings of the pianos he played upon were made into bracelets and sold among his admirers. All this lasted until 1847.

And now the virtuoso reached a new phase of his existence. Choosing Weimar for his place of abode, he set about his new task. The mother of the Grand Duke was his steadfast friend; her son shared her regard for the composer, and soon Liszt was given complete control of affairs artistic in the Grand Duchy.

The 10 years of his abode in Weimar were divided between directing concerts and operatic performances, composing, imparting instruction to a favored few whose talent he deemed worthy of his attention, and adding an occasional chapter to the literature of music.

His crowning achievement was the representation of Wagner's operas, undertaken at a period when patronage of the composer of "Der Nibelungen Ring" called out the hostility and even violence of the better half of the musical world.

In 10 years hence what Liszt did toward establishing Wagner's celebrity will have passed out of mind. Yet but for his Weimar labors the "music of the future" might still be entitled to its scornful designation.

Liszt spent the last 20 years of his life between Weimar, Rome, and Pesth, in which latter city he was appointed, in 1875, Director of the Musical Academy. His latest appearance as an actor in events of marked public interest was recorded in 1876, during the representations of Wagner's trilogy in Bayreuth, where his doings and sayings attracted quite as much attention as those of Wagner.

His career as a composer may be divided into three epochs. In the first, by his settings, transcriptions, and reductions of orchestral scores he sought to assimilate the treasures of the past until they became an absolute part of himself. No one ever succeeded as he did in reproducing upon the piano every effect attainable by an orchestra. If the reader wishes to ascertain what Liszt could accomplish, let him glance at the pianist's arrangement of Paganini's "Twenty-four Studies," in which the peculiar characteristics of the violin are embodied with the utmost felicity.

His symphonic poems belong to the second epoch of his career. Whatever judgment posterity may pass upon Liszt's symphonic poems, no one can deny their magnificent and powerful tone-color. The somber splendor of the "Heroides Funèbres" and "Les Préludes," the wild rhythm and clangor of "Hungaria" and "Mazeppa," the highly characteristic "Faust Symphony," the poetry of the "mountain poem," and the tone-pictures in the "Dante Symphony" will sway the feelings of music-lovers in every clime.

Liszt's third period of productiveness was distinguished by a number of religious works, among them his "Graner Messe," his "Missa Solennis," and his "Christus," works of uncommon depth, significance and severity.

The full list of his musical compositions includes 179 opera, many of these containing 10 and 12 separate pieces. The symphonic poems proper, not including the "Dante" and "Faust" symphonies, are 12 in number. Two piano concertos and 15 "Hungarian Rhapsodies" stand forth prominently from the enormous work done during a long and industrious life.

Tremendous vigor and endurance, unexampled softness of touch, and an endless variety of tone were the chief elements of a style which appeared to vitalize everything that it touched. The uncommon personal magnetism of the man contributed largely to the influence of his playing, but his technique would have proved nothing short of marvelous.

In late years he was seldom heard in public, but in Weimar, where he allowed a small number of favored mortals to occasionally play in his presence, he often took his seat at the piano and evoked alternately its thunderous utterances and most crystalline harmonies. To the last, his feelings and sympathies could find expression in gradations of tone which, to those who heard them, will be as the "lost chord" of the poet forever. The magic which turned a soulless instrument of percussion into a mighty hand endowed with the vocal sweetness and pathos of strings was not to be imparted by man to man. Liszt leaves no pupil.

As a man there may have been some diversity of opinion as to his sincerity, and his relations with the opposite sex, in the judgment of his severest critics, more than once showed him to be vain and heartless. The reader who would seek enlightenment on this point will gather it from a small volume called "Mémoirs d'Une Pianiste," by Robert Franz, whose nom de plume thinly disguises one of the objects of the virtuoso's worship and subsequently one of his most bitter accusers.

But whatever censure his conduct in what the French call affairs of the heart may merit, there was no denying Liszt's numberless deeds of charity, his absence of petty jealousy, and his chivalric feats. He tried, by surrounding himself with youth, to keep young to the last, and a pretty face and bright smile were ever potent to charm and sway him.

From a portrait of Liszt, taken in the prime of life by Ary Scheffer, the musician's features must have been of the Dante type, while the subject's pose is decidedly Byronic. The face is not handsome, the forehead is lofty, but the nose and mouth are large. The long hair is combed straight back. The eyes are wonderfully fine and expressive.

Those who remember him by his latest appearances will recall him as a tall and slight figure, with the most mobile of faces, deep-set eyes, long, iron-gray hair, and thin Mephisthophelean lips, clad in a well worn priestly soutane, soft of speech, gentle in manner, and so courtly that he often seemed to belong to an age of romance rather than to the practical century in which he lived, labored, and died.

JENNY LIND

October 6, 1820–November 2, 1887

LONDON—Mme. Goldschmidt (Jenny Lind), the celebrated Swedish singer, is dead. She was 67 years of age and had been seriously ill for some weeks.

She was born in Stockholm on Oct. 20, 1820. Her father was in indifferent circumstances, and it was not until she was nine years of age that she entered the musical class attached to the Court Theatre.

The director of the theater was Count Puke. He gave the girl an opportunity to begin the study of her art, and when she was not quite 10 years old she made her first appearance on the stage as a genie in Mozart's "Il Flauto Magico."

Her début as an artist took place in Stockholm in 1838, when she sang Agatha in "Der Freischiitz." Her success was such that she subsequently sang the principal role in "Euryanthe," Alice in "Robert le Diable," and Julia in Spontini's "La Vestale," all with brilliant success.

She was the life of the Royal Theatre until 1841, when she went to Paris, where she studied under Manuel Garcia. Even in her childhood the tinge of melancholy, natural to most Swedes, gave to her singing a character which frequently brought tears to the eyes of her hearers.

Giacomo Meyerbeer was in Paris while she was pursuing her studies, and when he heard the young artist he predicted a brilliant future for her. Through Meyerbeer's influence she went to Berlin in 1844 and began the study of German. Again through the influence of Meyerbeer, who had written for her the leading role in his "Feldlager in Schlesien," better known as "L'Etoile du Nord," she obtained an engagement at the Opéra. Her first appearance took place on Dec. 15, when she sang "Norma," and was received with great enthusiasm. Afterward she sang with equal success her new role in the Meyerbeer opera.

While she was in Berlin she met Ignaz Moscheles, who, on Jan. 10, 1845, wrote of her performance in "L'Etoile du Nord": "Jenny Lind has fairly enchanted me; she is unique in her way, and her song, with two concertante flutes, is perhaps the most incredible feat in the way of bravura singing that can possibly be heard.

"What a glorious singer she is, and so unpretentious withal."

Her unpretentiousness was sadly belied by the management of Her Majesty's Theatre in London, where she appeared on May 4, 1847, as Alice in "Robert le Diable." All the artifices of sensational management were employed to excite public interest in her appearance. There were stories of broken contracts, special messengers, vacillation and hesitation continued through many tiresome months. Every trait of the young singer's character was advertised, and her domestic history was unfolded in detail.

After public curiosity had been more than sufficiently aroused, it was announced that the singer would not visit London after all.

But she did, and the result was what had been aimed at. People fought to hear her. Her hearers were prepared to worship her, and they did. Her triumph was by no means undeserved, for she sang and acted Alice magnificently. She sustained the high standard of excellence which she reached in "Robert" by her impersonation of Amina in "Sonnambula," in "Lucia," as Adina in "L'Elisir d'Amore," in "La Figlia del Reggimento," and as Julia in Spontini's "La Vestale."

In 1849 she announced her intention not to appear again on the operatic stage, but she sang on April 15 in Mozart's "Il Flauto Magico," on April 26 in "Sonnambula," and in three other operas. Her last appearance in opera took place on May 18, 1849, when she once more sang in "Robert." Thenceforth she was heard only on the concert stage.

In concert she made a special feature of northern music, which she had studied in her early days while an inmate of the household of Adolph Frederick Lindblad, a Swedish composer who died in 1878. His reputation rests in his melancholy Swedish songs, written mostly in minor keys, and these songs Jenny Lind sang with marvelous effect.

It was in 1848 that P. T. Barnum engaged her to visit this country, and she arrived here on Sept. 17, 1850, accompanied by Julius Benedict, the pianist. She gave her first concert here on Sept. 11, 1850, in Castle Garden, which was packed to its utmost capacity.

She subsequently made a tour of the principal cities of the United States. She had been engaged by Barnum for 150 concerts, but in Philadelphia, in 1851, she and her manager parted company. She subsequently continued the tour under her own management. She made £20,000 out of her tour, and on Feb. 5, 1852, was married in Boston to Otto Goldschmidt, a pianist, who had been imported from Hamburg after her separation from Benedict.

The receipts of her first two concerts in this city were $17,864 and $14,203. Her first concert in Boston, on Sept. 27, 1850, at the Tremont Temple, brought in $19,000, and her first in Philadelphia $12,000. Her tour through this country was a long succession of triumphs.

She went up the Mississippi in the steamer Magnolia, giving concerts at Natchez, Vicksburg, and Memphis, and going thence to St. Louis. Coming East, she gave three concerts in Louisville. She sang in Cincinnati and then at Pittsburgh and Baltimore. It was after singing at the National Theatre in Philadelphia that she parted company with Barnum, beginning under her own management at the hall. Her last concert in Philadelphia was given at the hall on Dec. 22, 1851. At her first concert in that city, at the Chestnut-street Theatre on Oct. 16, 1850, Roob, the daguerreotyper, paid $625 for the banner ticket.

She reappeared in New York on May 7, 1851, at Castle Garden and closed there June 6. At Utica, on July 14, 1851, she gave a concert in a church. In St. Louis, in March, 1851, the Polyhymnia Society presented her with a certificate of honorary membership enveloped in two satin flags, one American, one Swedish, While she was in this country Jenny Lind gave away about $90,000 to charities.

On her return to Europe, Mme. Jenny Lind-Goldschmidt, as she was now called, traveled through Holland and again visited Germany. In 1856 she returned to England, which she henceforth made her home. She sang in Exeter Hall, London, in the "Creation," in the "Elijah," and in the "Messiah," and she sang in Exeter Hall in her husband's oratorio, "Ruth."

She said once that her native land had little charm for her because it was never kind to her till the days of her prosperity. But that she had a warm spot for it in her heart is attested by the fact that she devoted the whole of her American earnings to founding and endowing art scholarships and other charities in Sweden. To Liverpool she gave a hospital, and she added a wing to one in London. She founded a scholarship in memory of her friend [Felix] Mendelssohn, and the first scholar elected to it was Sir Arthur Sullivan.

When she first visited London her voice showed some signs of early wear. It was a soprano of bright, penetrating, and extremely sympathetic quality. Its compass was two octaves, from D to D. A faculty of which she made most effective use was her wonderfully developed length of breath, which enabled her to execute long and difficult passages with astonishing ease and gradually diminish her most brilliant tones to the softest pianissimo. She made splendid use of this pianissimo in the largo in the last act of "La Sonnambula," singing it in a penetrating whisper as she strewed the flowers of her bouquet on the stage.

Her execution was marvelously facile. Her trills were unusually true and brilliant, her taste in ornamentation original and artistic, and she usually invented her own cadenza. In a song from "Beatrice di Tenda" she had a chromatic cadenza ascending to the high E, and returning to the note whence it had started, that could hardly be equaled for difficulty and perfection of execution. In the "Ah, non glunge," she sang at the end a cadenza in which she gave out the high C, D, and E in a manner positively startling.

She was one of the most conscientious singers [who] ever appeared before the public. Not a note was neglected, not a phrase lightly treated.

Thus it was that her best role was Julia in Spontini's "La Vestale." Both the story and the music call for constant effort. The faithless vestal is compelled to hide her secret love, and when her warrior returns from the field of victory, to her is confided the task of crowning him. She breaks her vows by admitting him to the temple at night, and during the passionate love duet between the two the sacred fire expires. She must offer herself as a sacrifice, and she is saved from the sepulchre by a miracle.

It was in these trying scenes that Jenny Lind shone with her greatest brilliancy; yet it is probable that her memory will be associated with the strange, plaintive songs of the North and the solemn oratorios in which she was so often heard on the concert stage. She leaves a daughter, also a singer, and now about 29 years of age.

PETER ILITSCH TCHAIKOVSKY

May 7, 1840–November 6, 1893

ST. PETERSBURG—Peter Ilitsch Tchaikovsky, the Russian composer, died in this city last night at the age of 53. He died of cholera, hours after he fell ill.

Tchaikovsky contracted cholera by drinking unboiled water in a restaurant.

This famous Russian musician was without much question the most strikingly original and forceful orchestral composer of the day, and his death at a time when his intellectual powers were, or ought to have been, at their maturity must be accounted a serious loss to music. The present is by no means richly productive in great orchestral works, and Tchaikovsky's masterpieces have the hall marks of real genius.

Tchaikovsky was the son of an engineer who held a post under the Government in the imperial mines of the Ural Mountain district. The musician was born at Wotkinsk, in the Province of Wiatka, on April 25, 1840. The boy was not intended by his parents to follow in the footsteps of the great composer Glinka. In 1840, his father, who was evidently a man of solid attainments, was appointed Director of the Technological Institute at St. Petersburg. The son was entered as a student in the School of Jurisprudence, which is open only to the sons of Government officials of the higher orders. It was the father's desire that the boy should enter the public service, and in 1859 he was appointed to a post in the Department of Justice.

In the meantime his love for music had declared itself, and while a law student he had made essays in composition. These attempts met with not a little opposition from his father, but music eventually prevailed over law, and the consent of the father was at length obtained. It was fortunate for Tchaikovsky that the great movement for the advancement of music in Russia had now begun. In 1862 Anton Rubinstein, the famous pianist and composer, established his now celebrated Conservatory of Music at St. Petersburg, where Tchaikovsky was one of the first of many gifted pupils.

He devoted himself diligently to study until 1865. His principal masters were Zaremba, who taught him harmony and counterpoint, and Nicolas Rubinstein, who taught him composition. In 1865 he was graduated with high honors.

In 1866 Rubinstein, then the head of the conservatory, offered him the post of Professor of Harmony, Composition, and the History of Music. As his heart was in the Russian musical movement, he accepted the chair, and for 12 years did admirable work as an instructor. In 1878 he resigned in order to devote himself more assiduously to composition. He lived at various times in St. Petersburg, Italy, Switzerland, and Kiev, in recent years his home.

Two years ago last May Tchaikovsky, at the invitation of Walter Damrosch, an enthusiastic admirer and performer of his works, visited America, and appeared in the series of festival concerts with which the Music Hall, at 57th Street and Seventh Avenue, was opened. The composer conducted his splendid third suite, his second piano concerto, in G. Opus 44, and two a capella choruses. The magnificent performance of the suite by the Symphony Orchestra under his electric leadership will long be remembered by music lovers.

He was so much pleased with his American experience that on meeting Damrosch in England last Summer he promised that conductor the manuscript of his new sixth symphony for its first public performance. It is not positively known whether the composer has left this symphony complete. Tchaikovsky's last notable public appearance was in the Summer just gone, when he conducted some of his own works at Oxford, and received the degree of Doctor of Music from the university.

Tchaikovsky was a prolific composer, yet given to somewhat close self-criticism. Only three or four years ago he threw into the fire the score of his early ballet, "Wojowode," produced in 1869. Although his name has been honored in this country for years, largely owing to the repeated performance of his music by Theodore Thomas and Walter Damrosch, his operas are, of course, wholly unknown here. In the dramatic field he was a consistent follower of the famous Glinka, and wrote his operas on Russian subjects and with Russian text. Preparations for the production of one of them, "Eugeny Onegin," have been lately going forward in London. Tchaikovsky's other stage compositions are "Opritschnik" (1874); "Wakula the Smith" (1876); "Schwanensee," "Snegowrotska," a drama with incidental music; "The Maid of Orleans" (1881), and "Mazeppa" (1884).

He is best known in this country by his grand fifth symphony in E minor, his scarcely less admirable fourth symphony in F minor, his third suite, his second piano concerto, his symphonic poem, "Francesca da Rimini," and his two great overtures, "Romeo and Juliet" and "Hamlet."

Tchaikovsky's orchestral music is remarkable for its fine employment of distinctly national melody, always closely resembling, when not directly borrowed from, the rich store of Russian folksong; for its deep and masterful melancholy, its overwhelming bursts of passion, sometimes verging upon barbaric rage; for its boldness of rhythm, its sharpness of modulation, and its splendor of orchestral color. Admiration for his work has been growing of late years, and critics who at first received his music coldly have recently given utterance to such praise as is bestowed only upon a genius.

JOHANNES BRAHMS

May 7, 1833–April 3, 1897

VIENNA—Johannes Brahms, the well-known musical composer, is dead. He had been ill for a long time. He suffered from jaundice last Autumn, and went to Carlsbad; but the cure was ineffective. The disease developed into cancer of the liver.

Johannes Brahms, who for many years was almost as great a subject for differences of opinion among musical persons as Wagner was among operagoers, was the eldest of three children of Johann Brahms, a double bass player at the Hamburg Opera. The boy was born at Hamburg on May 7, 1833. His father set him at the study of music in his early childhood.

At the age of 10 he became a pupil of Eduard Marxsen of Altona, and made rapid progress as a pianist. Marxsen soon began to instruct him in harmony, counterpoint, and theory, and the child showed evidences of his gifts in his earliest exercises in composition. At 14 he played in public works by Bach and Beethoven and original variations on a folksong.

In 1853 he was a master of the art of piano playing, and was permitted to go upon a concert tour with Remenyi, the violinist. In Hanover he met the famous violinist Josef Joachim, who was surprised by the lad's performance in transposing at sight a Beethoven sonata from A to B flat, and deeply impressed by the youth's original piano sonatas, his scherzo in E flat minor, and his first set of songs.

The head of the critical guild in Germany was at that time the great composer Robert Schumann, editor of the Neue Zeitschrift für Musik, and to him, at Düsseldorf, Joachim sent Brahms with a letter of introduction. Schumann published in his paper an article which served to apprise Germany of the advent of a new composer. Germany, however, was not yet prepared to be enthusiastic over a style so austere and intellectual as that of Brahms. Only a small circle of music lovers displayed a sympathetic interest in his productions.

He remained in Hanover a considerable time, making several concert tours with Joachim and Stockhausen, the noted singer. He published two or three works, and then devoted himself for several years to deep study. He became director of the orchestra and chorus at Detmold, and wrote a number of choruses and songs, two sextets, and two serenades for orchestra.

In January, 1859, he played his first piano concerto in Leipsic, but the criticism written at the time was evidence that Brahms's style was misunderstood even by those who did not resent it. In 1862 he made his first appearance in Vienna, where he was received with delight by the more cultivated musicians. He was appointed director of the Singakademie, but resigned after a year. For the next three years he was a nomad, giving concerts in cities of Germany and Switzerland. In 1867 he returned to Vienna, which became his home.

In 1866, after the death of his mother, he began his famous "German Requiem," a work which is still a bone of contention in the musical world. The whole was first given in the Bremen Cathedral in 1868. It was soon heard in other cities, where censure was mingled with admiration. While preparing this work for the press, Brahms stayed at Bonn, where he wrote two important works for solo, male chorus, and orchestra, "Rinaldo" and the "Rhapsodie," Opus 53.

In the years 1870 and 1871 he found inspiration in Germany's victories over France for his "Triumphlied," Opus 55, written for baritone solo, chorus, and orchestra, and first

performed at Bremen on Good Friday, 1871. Brahms now accepted the conductorship of the Society of the Friends of Music, and held the post until 1875.

After that year this famous master lived a quiet, almost secluded life in Vienna. He devoted himself almost exclusively to composition, and repelled all attempts at lionizing. He was, however, a genial and kindly man within his chosen circle of friends, and his conversation was far more varied than that of a musician usually is.

The opus number of Brahms's compositions is well up in the second hundred. The works best known in this country are the piano sonatas, the second concerto for piano and orchestra, the "German Requiem," his four symphonies, the "Academic Overture," the "Tragic Overture," the Hungarian dances, his variations on the "Chorale St. Anthony," the beautiful clarinet quintet, and other masterly pieces of chamber music, and a large number of songs that rank with those of Schubert and Schumann.

When he produced his first piano concerto at the Leipsic Gewandhaus, in 1859, the public was amazed and angered by the austere contours of a work devoid of the expected virtuoso passages, and the Leipziger Signalen dismissed it curtly as a "symphony with piano obbligato."

The critical war raged in German newspapers. The opponents of Brahms declared that his music was machine-made, without inspiration, while his advocates vowed that in structure his work was profound and that in feeling it was nobler than the tonal sensualisms of Berlioz and Wagner. The truth, as usual, lies between extremes.

Brahms was a master of musical construction. Although he wrote few symphonies, it is as a symphonist that he is best described. His melodic invention was happiest in the production of those fecund phrases which are big with possibilities of musical development.

It is true that many of his themes are somber in character, that they steady the musical fancy rather than excite it. It is equally true that the development of these themes is frequently difficult to follow at a first hearing. But in profound mastership of musical structure, no masters save Bach and Beethoven have excelled Brahms. His sonatas and symphonies withstand triumphantly the severest analytical examination.

The controversy that has raged about him has centered upon this point. His advocates have celebrated his brain power, and his opponents have condemned his want of heart. But year after year the general admiration of the world for Brahms has grown, and the musical public has come to appreciate the austerity and restraint of his style.

Some of his works will never be popular, but others, such as the second piano concerto and the symphonies in D and F, have long been accepted as the lineal successors of the products of Beethoven. When the world gets far enough away from Brahms to view him with a fair perspective, critical historians will probably award him a seat of honor among the Titans of music.

GIUSEPPE VERDI

October 9 or 10, 1813–January 27, 1901

By W. J. Henderson

MILAN—Giuseppe Verdi died this morning at the age of 87. The dispatch printed in the Patria of Rome announcing his death yesterday morning was premature.

The doctors were astounded that Verdi lived as long as he did. Several times yesterday a suspension of breathing gave the impression that he had expired, but animation slowly returned, and Verdi lifted his arm as though he wished to unbutton his shirt-collar.

The Pope telegraphed to inquire whether Verdi had received last sacraments. Crowds have been assembling to read the bulletins, which were posted in most of the towns.

The death of Giuseppe Verdi comes like the echo of a vast historical event out of a past epoch. For nearly 60 years Verdi has reigned over the domain of Italian opera. He was the leader and the representative man. He was the rejuvenator of an old style, the creator of a new one. He led Italian opera out of its dull and witless routine and made the human ear hum with a new musical life. In his later years, yet a quarter of a century ago, he hurried into the arena of art a new work, a new style, an utterly new creation. Men shook their heads and said he had drunk the virus of Wagnerism and gone mad. But he was still beautifully, serenely sane, purely and voluptuously Italian, a musician of musicians, a master of masters.

He sang with all the buoyant power of his first period, but with a new and more glorious purpose. And with his new song he founded a new school, for the children of his fancy are Mascagni and Leoncavallo, and Puccini. But a few days ago our Opera House ran with the pulsating rhythmic measure of his "Trovatore" and his "Aida," the choicest blossoms of his old and his new fruitfulness. Both of these works throb with power, and the day is far distant when the threadbare melodies of the former will cease to stir the multitudes. As for the latter, it will live its three-score years and ten and go the way of all operas, for the fashions of the Opera House change with the passing of centuries, and only Mozart lives forever.

All estimates of the position of Verdi as an artist based upon the works produced before "Aida" and "Otello" were rendered null and void by those two splendid achievements. Before writing these operas Verdi was essentially a popular composer. He wrote for the masses according to the formulas handed down to him by his predecessors in the field of Italian opera. It is undeniable, however, that he infused into these forms a new and masculine spirit in striking contrast to the dreamy lullabies with which Rossini soothed war-weary Europe to rest.

Verdi was called, after the brilliant works of his transition period, the "most nervous, theatric, sensuous composer of the nineteenth century," and the description was far from being unjust. He exhibited a singular misuse of power, coupled with a master's fund of melodic inventiveness. He gave the familiar elementary rhythms of the Neapolitan school a fresh and inviting aspect. He infused into the vocal score a new dramatic energy, not always truthfully significant, but rich in theatrical effectiveness.

His style in this period was often sadly meretricious, and his melodies of the cheapest kind, while sensationalism and violent outbreaks of meaningless noise were frequent. He astonished and overwhelmed the shallow, while he perplexed and grieved the judicious. If he had left it to posterity to award him his place among the immortals on the merits of "Rigoletto," "Il Trovatore," and "La Traviata," the frequency of false and pretentious conceits would probably have outweighed the influence of the few bursts of real genius—the quartet in the first, the death scene of the second, Azucena's narrative, the "Miserere" of the third—and Verdi might have been [relegated] to a secondary position.

But in "Aida," the great Italian revealed the existence of a genuine dramatic power. He constructed his melodies with an unexpected breadth and a convincing significance. The work was begun and sustained on a lofty level. Its dignity never flagged, and its coherency, elevation, and depth of dealing as a whole revealed not only novel methods, but a new purpose.

If these things are true of "Aida," how much more praise is due "Otello." The former is probably the more inspired work, but the latter is unquestionably the more sincere. It makes known in every scene an honest desire on this part of Verdi to produce something of universal worth. The aged composer was successful in demonstrating that he possessed unsuspected resources of eloquence and pathos. While it is true that Verdi in "Otello" frankly admitted the conquest of Teutonic ideas in music, he sacrificed not a jot of his individuality. Preserving a style distinctly Verdian, "Otello" impressed the unprejudiced hearer with the belief that it is one of the masterpieces of our time.

In his "Falstaff" Verdi departed still further from the hard and fast formulas of modern Italian opera, yet without losing either his nationality or his individuality. All vestiges of the old set forms disappeared in this work, and the composer wrote brisk, vivacious, eloquent musical dialogue. Grace, elegance, and subtlety alternate with brilliancy, abandon, and resistless vigor in this wonderful work, and it is safe to say that in writing it Verdi lifted himself out of the ranks of Italian opera composers and placed himself fairly beside Mozart and Wagner as one of the greatest lyric dramatists the world has known.

In the history of Italian opera there is no figure comparable to Verdi except Alessandro Scarlatti, but he possesses now only a historical importance. France has never produced a master who equaled Verdi in brilliancy and power. We are forced to go to Germany to find his compeers, and there we can count but two, or at best, three. The names of Mozart, Weber, and Wagner alone may stand on the page of musical history beside that of Verdi. And of these three we of today dare name but one as that of the master of all. The immortal Mozart, whose artistic children in a certain sense both Verdi and Wagner were, alone is entitled to stand in the center of this trio and lead the others by the hands.

With Verdi there passes from the world one of the Titans of music, one of the true geniuses. To us, the contemporaries of his later years, he has presented a beautiful and inspiring spectacle, that of a man of genius still laboring to advance, still seeking higher and chaster slopes of sunlit glory.

Verdi wintered in Genoa and summered at his villa St Agatha. He was a practical farmer, and he generally showed himself an excellent businessman. He rose early, walked in his garden, inspected every part of his little domain, indulged now and then in a game of billiards with a friend, and retired betimes. He composed at the piano, reading the libretto, the subject of which he habitually chose and the design of which was fashioned to his will, striking forth the themes as the perusal of the scenes suggested them, and changing and enriching them as he progressed. In person Verdi was rather tall, with a full beard, mustache, and whiskers, a deeply furrowed brow, a Roman nose, and a stern somewhat expressionless countenance.

GUSTAV MAHLER

July 7, 1860–May 18, 1911

BERLIN—Gustav Mahler, late conductor of the New York Philharmonic Orchestra, died in Vienna tonight after an illness which had prostrated him for the last eight weeks. The catastrophe was precipitated by the spread of his heart affection [sic] to his lungs, which developed a fatal pneumonic weakness during the last few days.

Mr. Mahler was taken to Vienna from Paris early in May, when his condition was already realized to be hopeless, in response to his urgently expressed wish to die in his native country.

The German press bestows unstinted tributes to Gustav Mahler's memory. He is praised as one of the towering musical figures of his day.

Gustav Mahler, who is equally well known as a composer and a conductor, was born July 7, 1860, at Kalisht, in Bohemia. He was educated at the Gymnasium at Iglau, at Prague, and at the University of Vienna, where he was also a pupil of the Conservatoire. From 1880 he conducted in various theaters in different towns in Austria, and in 1883 was appointed second conductor at Cassel, becoming first conductor at Prague as [Anton] Seidl's successor two years afterward.

In 1886 he went to Leipzig as [Arthur] Nickisch's assistant, in whose stead he conducted the opera for six months. In 1888 he undertook the direction of the opera at Pesth. In 1891 he went to Hamburg and remained there until 1897. In October of that year he was called to Vienna to direct the Hofoper, and he also succeeded Hans Richter as conductor of the Philharmonic concerts there. The post of Director of the Vienna Court Opera is the one most sought [after] by German musicians, and Mahler governed the opera with an iron hand for 10 years, only giving up this position to come to America in December, 1907.

Mahler is said to have given up his position in Vienna because his duties as conductor came into conflict with his ambitions as a composer. When Mahler undertook the direction of the Imperial Opera in Vienna, dull routine ruled there in everything, an indifference that is indescribable. The wonderful tale was repeated with shudders that the new conductor at one rehearsal had rapped to stop the orchestra 100 times. It was rumored that he had warned leading singers not to sing mezza voce at rehearsals; that he had taken parts away from prima donnas that they thought belonged to them, and crowded into the background singers with "influence" and "protection" at Court.

Mahler reformed everything—the orchestra, the company, the scenic decorations. Nothing escaped his notice. He even reformed the ballet. The day he began this reform people thought his fall was at hand, but he still maintained his position, with plenty of enemies, of course.

In addition to this, the anti-Semitic element in Vienna persecuted Mahler because he was a Jew. What he suffered from this need not be related.

It was Heinrich Conried who brought him to America in the Winter of 1907, where he made his first appearance at the Metropolitan Opera House on Jan. 1, 1908, conducting "Tristan und Isolde." He afterward conducted other works of Wagner, Mozart, Tchaikovsky's "Pique Dame," Smetana's "Prodana Nevasta," Beethoven's "Fidelio," and a few other works at this theater, where he remained for the season of 1908–9, and conducted a few performances during the season of 1909–10.

In his second season in New York he had been engaged by Walter Damrosch to conduct some special performances of the Symphony Society of New York, and it was with this organization that he made his American début as a symphony conductor.

The next season of 1909–10 found him at the head of the reorganized Philharmonic Society, and during the season just past he had devoted his time, until his illness came upon him, to this organization.

Several of Mr. Mahler's symphonies have been played here, in some instances conducted by the composer. The most recent of them, however, which was produced in Munich last Summer under the composer's direction, has not yet been given here. It calls for an enormous chorus and orchestra.

For his symphonic works in general it may be said that he demands not only a huge apparatus, but needs the most extreme length in which to develop and prepare his ideas. His second symphony occupies two hours and 40 minutes in delivery, his fifth an hour. He has employed themes, as set forth by his annotators, that are almost whole compositions in themselves.

Most of his work has been in symphonic form, he having left eight works of this description. However, he also wrote many songs.

ENRICO CARUSO

February 25, 1873–August 2, 1921

NAPLES, Italy—Enrico Caruso died here today. The great singer, whose ultimate recovery had been hoped for under the benign influences of his own Neapolitan skies, passed away at 9 o'clock this morning at the Hotel Vesuvius in this city.

It is recalled that when he lay gravely stricken in New York, he had expressed the wish that he might die in Italy, and now all Italy is mourning that this sad wish has come true.

Signor Caruso had been brought here hurriedly from Sorrento, on the Bay of Naples, where less than a week ago he avowed his returning strength and expressed the conviction that he would sing again as in the old days.

But soon afterward unfavorable symptoms, in the form of a high fever, manifested themselves, and his wife telegraphed to a Rome specialist to come to Sorrento. It was then discovered that a new internal abscess had developed.

Caruso's removal to Rome for an operation was advised, but he showed such weakness that it was impossible to transfer him further than Naples, where he arrived by sea Sunday evening. Four eminent physicians were called, and their examination showed the presence of a subphrenic abscess, accompanied by severe peritonitis.

Of the members of the family present at the death-bed, the most pathetic was his father's widow, who had always clung obstinately to her little home, despite her stepson's efforts to accustom her to the material comforts of life.

Present also were Caruso's wife, who was Dorothy, daughter of Park Benjamin of New York; their little daughter Gloria and Caruso's eldest son, Rodolfo, as well as the tenor's brother, Giovanni, several nephews, and Vincenzo Bellezza and Paolo Longone, two musicians. —*The Associated Press*

By The New York Times

Enrico Caruso was 48 years old, having been born at Naples on Feb. 27, 1873. His father was a mechanic, but he was also an inventor and a man of considerable intelligence. Caruso himself had wit and brains, as well as a voice.

Caruso's early life was told by himself as follows:

"Had I followed the path that was chosen for me I should have been a mechanic, or possibly an engineer. My father was employed in Naples as a working mechanic and he had two sons—myself and a younger boy. I was a sad trial to my parents. I was very noisy and lively. I sang constantly and my voice then was pretty piercing.

"My father chastised me and tried to make me a sober, industrious mechanic, like himself. This did not attract me. By the time I was 11 years old, I had developed a great love for singing and had, I believe, a fine contralto voice. One day the old organist of the Church of St. Anna, Naples, heard me singing some popular melody, and my youthful efforts delighted him so much that he engaged me to sing in his choir. I received for my labors each Sunday the large sum of 10 pence weekly.

"The turning point in my life came at the age of 15, when my dear mother died. Had she lived it is probable that I should have continued my mechanical studies to please her. But her death seemed to me to justify an alteration in my career before it was too late. Accordingly I announced my intention of devoting myself to art and music and left my father's house, following his furious ultimatum that I could 'be a mechanic or starve!'

"Somehow I managed to pick up a poor livelihood by singing at church festivals and private houses. I was often hungry, but never unhappy; and thus I went on until, at the age of 18, I was faced by this fearful problem, 'Was I a tenor or a baritone?' My voice at that time was so thin that it resembled the 'wind' whistling through a gaping window.

"The time came for me to serve my king and country, so away I went to be a soldato, registering a private vow that Naples should eventually acclaim me as 'El Tenore Caruso.' For a year I wore the uniform of the 13th Regiment of Artillery. One morning I was polishing the buttons on my tunic and singing for sheer joy. Suddenly Major Nagliati appeared, listened, and inquired: 'What is your profession?' Stammering, I muttered: 'I aspire to sing in opera.'

"Without a word he left me. But that same evening he told me he had found me a singing master, and that during my remaining 35 days in Rieti I could continue my studies.

"A little later my kind Major arranged that my brother should take my place, and thus it happened that in 1895, at the age of 22, I made by début in a new opera at the Teatro Nuovo, Naples.

"I was not a success nor was the opera, for in Naples there is a group of chronic dissentients whose presence makes that city a bad place for a début. Thus I failed; but though discouraged, determined to win success one day.

"My master, Vergine, to whose unfailing sympathy and endless patience I owe my deepest gratitude, encouraged me to go on studying and singing at every opportunity in various theaters. In this way my voice improved in timbre, strength and tone, and at last my great day dawned—though I nearly spoiled my own success through obstinacy.

"Sonsogno, Manager of the Teatro Liroco, Milan, asked me if I would study the role of Marcello in 'La Bohème' to sing at his theater. I began to study this role, but after a few days decided that it did not suit me.

"A little later I visited Milan and there Sonsogno came to me with a request that I would change my mind and consent to study the role, as he was certain it would suit me.

"I learned the role, and on Tuesday, Nov. 8, 1898, appeared as Marcello at the Teatro Liroco, Milan and made, if I may say so, my first success. On Nov. 9 I awoke to find press and public in agreement that I had not mistaken my vocation.

"After singing in one Italian city after another, I went to Egypt; from there back to Paris: and then to Berlin; thence to the Argentine. From there I went to Rio Janeiro, where I was honored by President Campos-Galles for singing at a gala performance given in honor of the President of Argentina. From Rio I went to sing in London."

Maurice Grau made the contract that brought Caruso to America, but it was left to Grau's successor, Heinrich Conried, to introduce him here. He was a success in New York City from his first appearance at the opening of the season of 1903, and repeating it with greater successes in every season since. His first Metropolitan role was the Duke in "Rigoletto" Nov. 23, 1903.

One of the great artist's characteristics was a childlike love of praise and applause. New York's unbounded admiration for him won his heart. Though an Italian patriot, he became fundamentally a New Yorker. He spent most of his last 18 years in Manhattan.

New York's regard for the great tenor was expressed in the ceremony at the Metropolitan Opera House in April of last year, when the thanks of the city were presented to him by Mayor Hylan. This was partly a tribute to the unique talent of the singer, partly to his good-natured personality, and partly to his generous dedication of his voice to good causes during the war.

Heavy penalties went with his fame. He could never appear in public without having every eye fixed on him. Crowds gathered around him on the streets, in railway stations, and at theater lobbies.

Once when asked for his own theory of his great success, he said, "I never refused an engagement."

Two of Caruso's children are Rodolpho and Enrico, Jr., the sons of Signora Giachetti, who was for years known as Mme. Caruso. Signora Giachetti and Caruso first met during a performance of "La Bohème," in which both took part.

They purchased a villa in Florence, where they made their home. Some years later Signora Giachetti left Caruso's home. In August, 1918, the singer married Miss Dorothy Park Benjamin. She and the daughter Gloria survive him.

In 18 successive seasons at the Metropolitan he appeared in at least 40 operas. Caruso came to be recognized by many critics as the "greatest voice of his century."

Giulio Gatti-Casazza, under whose management the greater part of his Metropolitan years were spent, was among his most outspoken admirers.

"I have heard all the great tenors of my time," he said. "Many of them were wonderful artists, with exceptional voices; and all sang some wonderful performances. Yet no one ever, in my judgment, sang any single role with the vocal or artistic consistency of Caruso, and certainly no other tenor I can think of remotely compares with Caruso in continuing to sing week after week and season after season, with the same unvarying achievement of supremacy, a man who almost never disappointed an audience through inability to appear. He has been a unique artist, with whom none other compared."

ISADORA DUNCAN

May 26 or 27, 1877–September 14, 1927

Paris—Isadora Duncan, the American dancer, tonight met a tragic death at Nice on the Riviera. Miss Duncan was hurled in an extraordinary manner from an open automobile in which she was riding and instantly killed by the force of her fall to the pavement.

Affecting, as was her habit, an unusual costume, Miss Duncan was wearing an immense iridescent silk scarf wrapped about her neck and streaming in long folds, part of which was swathed about her body with part trailing behind. After an evening walk along the

Promenade des Anglais about 10 o'clock, she entered an open rented car, directing the driver to take her to her hotel.

As she took her seat, neither she nor the driver noticed that one of the loose ends of the scarf fell over the side of the car and was caught in the rear wheel of the machine.

The automobile was going at full speed when the scarf suddenly began winding around the wheel and with terrific force dragged Miss Duncan, around whom it was securely wrapped, over the side of the car, precipitating her with violence against the cobblestone street. She was dragged for several yards before the chauffeur halted, attracted by her cries.

Medical aid was summoned, but it was stated that she had been strangled and killed instantly.

This end to a life full of many pathetic episodes was received as a great shock in France, where, despite her eccentric traits, Miss Duncan, who died at age 50, was regarded as a great artist. Her great popularity in France was increased by the nation's sympathy when in 1913 her two young children also perished in an automobile tragedy. The car in which they had been left seated started, driverless, down a hill and plunged over a bridge into the Seine.

Her love affair with the young poet laureate of Soviet Russia, Serge Essinin, terminated in divorce and Essinin's suicide two years ago.

In connection with her fatal accident it is recalled that Miss Duncan for years affected an unusual dress cult and, with her brother, Raymond, often appeared in the streets of Paris and elsewhere garbed in a Roman toga with bare legs and sandals.

The Petit Parisien tomorrow will say, in commenting on the tragedy:

"Sad news which will spread consternation through the world of arts and artists arrived today from Nice: Isadora Duncan has been killed in a frightful manner. This woman who throughout her life tried to shed grace and beauty about her met with the most tragic end imaginable.

"She danced as rarely, if ever, has been danced before her, with a fervor which seemed to raise her, transport her. Had she been practical she could have amassed an immense fortune, but she dies poor. Poor, and doubtless disillusioned, for what sorrows had she not suffered?"

ANNA PAVLOWA

February 12, 1881–January 23, 1931

THE HAGUE—Mme. Anna Pavlowa, the greatest dancer of her time, died of pleurisy at the Hotel des Indes here at 12:30 this morning.

Pavlowa, who was 49 years old, fell ill on Tuesday after she had come here on tour from Paris. With the dancer at the end was her husband and accompanist, Victor d'André, whom she married in 1924.

Anna Pavlowa was born in St. Petersburg, now Leningrad, Russia, on Feb. 12, 1881. Her rise to fame as one of Russia's leading ballerinas after a struggle against poverty, and later her worldwide triumphs, made her life story one of unusual interest.

During her sensational career as a dancer, she is said to have covered 350,000 miles in her tours. Her tours embraced the principal cities of the United States, Canada, Mexico, South America, South Africa, Europe and the Orient.

She was proclaimed by her admirers as the greatest of living dancers. The passage of time did not dim the luster of her name or the exquisite technique of her dancing. She received ovations of the sort seldom accorded anyone in the theater.

Before [World War I] she danced before Emperor Franz Josef of Austria and Emperor Wilhelm. King Alfonso of Spain and the King and Queen of the Belgians were among other royal personages who paid her homage.

Upon her return to Russia, after her first American tour, the late Czar Nicholas summoned her to the royal box and congratulated her. The dancer quotes the Czar as saying: "I so much regret that despite all I hear about your wonderful swan dance, I have never seen it. Yet I am called one of the absolute monarchs."

Pavlowa was always partial to the dance of the dying swan, and for years she kept swans in the garden of her home in Hempstead, London, so she could study their movements. The inspiration for the swan dance came first to her, she said, while watching the swans in a public park in Leningrad.

The dancer's last appearance in this country was during the season of 1924–25. She was due to return here next Fall for an extended tour, covering 75 cities.

As a child of 10 Pavlowa saw for the first time a ballet at the Imperial Ballet School, attached to the Marianski Theatre in Leningrad, and after that, she often said, dancing became the dream of her life. A year later she entered the school as a pupil on a year's trial. The Czar often visited the school and praised the little dancer's art even then.

After receiving instruction for eight years at the school, Pavlowa became prima ballerina of the Marianski Theatre, later appearing at the Imperial Opera House, Leningrad. At her first appearance in London in 1910, at the Palace Theatre, she scored an immediate success in "The Swan," "Butterflies," "Valse Caprice" and other divertissements. She was acclaimed in London as the sensation of a century.

After the London engagement she made a triumphal appearance in Paris with Diaghileff's Russian Ballet in "Les Sylphides," "Pavillon d'Armide" and "La Nuit Egyptienne."

Her American début was made on March 1, 1910, at the Metropolitan Opera House, in a revival of Delibes's ballet "Coppelia." The ballet did not commence until after 11, but before it was finished, about 1 A.M., the lithe, exquisitely formed little Russian had captured the Metropolitan audience.

After the début a New York critic declared such dancing had not been seen on the local stage during the present generation and praised the supreme ease with which Pavlowa executed the most difficult tricks of the dancer's art.

Pavlowa announced her marriage to her accompanist, Victor d'André, during her last American tour in 1924–25. Commenting on her marriage, the dancer said: "For an artist there is no husband. Pavlowa the artist and Pavlowa the wife, they are two very different persons, so I keep them separate. My dancing belongs to the world, but my husband to myself."

In 1929 it was reported that Pavlowa's aid to dancers in Soviet Russia was resented by the Bolsheviki. For 10 years Pavlowa had been sending an annual gift of $500 to help distressed dancers in London, where she resided, and an equal sum to the Marianski Theatre ballet in Leningrad. When this charity was discovered by the Communists, the committee that had administered the fund, it was said, was reprimanded for accepting aid from the emigré dancer, Pavlowa, "darling of wicked capitalist audiences in Europe and America."

RICHARD STRAUSS

June 11, 1864–September 8, 1949

GARMISH-PARTENKIRCHEN—Richard Strauss, whose music enriched the world for more than 70 years, died today at the age of 85. He succumbed to infirmities of the heart, gallbladder and kidneys which had kept him bedfast since mid-August. Uremia was given as the direct cause of death.

The life of the famous composer of such works as "Der Rosenkavalier" and "Salomé" was interwoven with triumphs and tragedies reaching from the unification of Germany by Bismarck through two World

Wars and the birth of a new West German Republic.

Strauss was an innovator whose realistic themes offended the classical tastes of Kaiser Wilhelm. But he patched up his differences with the Kaiser and set to music a war hymn written by the Emperor.

Surviving are his widow, Pauline; a son and a grandson. —*The Associated Press*

At a time when Wagner had "arrived" after great hubbub and dispute, Richard Strauss appeared in the musical world to upset still further the conventional rules of musical composition with works that were highly sensational.

Because of his versatility, Strauss, with his lyrical songs, fantastic operas and prankish tone-poems, found no imitator. Critics were baffled at the contrast of the melodious and romantic "Rosenkavalier" and "Till Eulenspiegel's Merry Pranks," with its abundance of impish and startling humor that borders on the grotesque.

Strauss was only four when he played the piano with much ability. When he was six he composed and when he was 10 he was studying music under F. W. Meyer. Born at Munich on June 11, 1864, he was the son of Franz Strauss, who played the Waldhorn, or French horn, and who was regarded as a virtuoso. The elder Strauss lost his wife and two children in a cholera epidemic in 1853. He later married Josephine Pschorr, and of that union Richard Strauss was born.

After passing through a local gymnasium and attending the University of Munich, where he studied science and literature, Strauss returned to his musical education. He became acquainted with Hans von Bülow, whom he succeeded as conductor of the Meiningen Orchestra in 1885.

Meanwhile his first relatively important work, a serenade for 13 wind instruments, had been played by von Bülow and had met with considerable approval. In 1894 he married Pauline de Ahna, a talented singer, who later interpreted many of his songs, and that same year he was appointed Hofkapellmeister at Munich.

By this time Strauss had composed a great many works, including the symphonic poems "Don Juan" and "Macbeth" (in 1888 and 1887, respectively) and his more sensational "Tod und Verklaärung."

His first opera, "Guntram," which was rather a la Wagner, was not an unqualified success when it was produced in 1894. But then came "Till Eulenspiegel," which was acknowledged to be one of the most remarkable and brilliantly clever scores ever to be penned. This tone-poem, if it can be classed as such, contains the most noteworthy example of the rondo in modern music.

Strauss became Hofkapellmeister in Berlin in 1899, but before that he had traveled in Egypt, Greece and Italy, gathering impressions everywhere, not least for his later opera "Die Aegyptische Helene" ("The Egyptian Helen"), which was first performed in 1928.

In 1907 began his collaboration with the poet Hugo von Hofmannsthal as librettist, and their first product was "Elektra." Long before that, however, Strauss had composed "Don Quixote" and "Also Sprach Zarathustra," both mature and imposing works which were instantly recognized.

It was with "Elektra" that he reached the height of his sensationalism. Its violence and weird discords caused enormous discussion, but this was mild in comparison with what was to follow with "Salomé."

Strauss next composed "Der Rosenkavalier," "Ariadne auf Naxos," "Josef's Legende," "Die Frau ohne Schatten" and "Schlagobers" ("Whipped Cream").

Strauss was director of the Vienna Opera from 1919 to 1924. He was popular in that musical center, and in 1927 he received a large grant of land from the Austrian Government in return for conducting gratuitously 20 operas each season for five years. The land and sumptuous villa that he received are in Belvedere Park, near the palace of Prince Eugene, which had last been occupied by Archduke Francis Ferdinand.

The latter years of the Meister's life were to be stormy ones. Growing old and feeble in a troubled world, he refused nevertheless to end his days in idleness. A month after his 73rd birthday he completed "Friedenstag," his 12th opera, and made arrangements for its performance in the summer of 1938 in the Munich State Opera.

His last previous work for the lyric stage had been "The Silent Woman," in 1935. The libretto of "The Silent Woman" was written by Stefan Zweig, a Jew. Practically all the librettos for Strauss's operas had been done by von Hofmannsthal, also a non-Aryan.

The association caused a furor in Nazi circles. Three weeks after the opera's première Strauss was removed from the office of president of the German Chamber of Culture.

After this encounter with the Nazis, Strauss disappeared from public view.

When the completion of "Friedenstag" was announced, Josef Gregor, a Viennese poet, was named as the author of its libretto. Although an Aryan, Gregor was one of the circle of literary men who were grouped around von Hofmannsthal. His choice, in some quarters, was seen as a capitulation in part to the Nazis' dislike of Strauss's usual choice of Jews or Jewish sympathizers as his librettists.

When Dr. Wilhelm Furtwaengler was "fired" as director of the Berlin State Opera in 1934, after violent attacks upon him by Nazi authorities because of his defense of Paul Hindemith, a young composer of Jewish descent, Strauss bowed to Hitler. Furtwaengler had long been his friend, but Strauss made no effort to defend him.

When American troops entered Garmisch, Germany, on May 1, 1945, they found the composer in a villa with his son, Franz, and Franz's wife. The composer reported that he was working on "Capriccio," a one-act opera. At the age of 81, he expressed the hope that the war would end and enable his later major works to get a wider hearing.

Even as late as 1947, when "Salomé" was performed in Berlin, a German newspaper berated him:

"Nobody seems to ask Richard Strauss to declare his position with respect to the Third Reich, whose favorite composer he has been and to which he dedicated his "Japanische Festmusik.""

In 1948 a denazification court in Munich cleared him of all charges. Evidence was introduced to show that he had devoted himself solely to music during the years of Nazi power.

VASLAV NIJINSKY

March 12, 1889–April 8, 1950

LONDON—Vaslav Nijinsky, world-famous Russian dancer, died here today at the age of 60, after a brief illness.

His wife, Romola, who for 30 years had devoted herself to trying to cure the mental illness that overtook him at the peak of his career in 1919, was at her husband's bedside.

Nijinsky was regarded as the finest male dancer in the history of ballet and was for eight years the idol of balletomanes all over the world. In the last few years he had shown signs of recovering from the schizophrenia that had brought his career to such a sudden and tragic end.

Nijinsky, the son of two ballet dancers, made his debut at the age of 17 in Moscow and was an immediate success. He danced opposite such famous ballerinas as Pavlova Karsavina and was largely responsible for bringing back the full vigor and reputation of male dancing.

His wife seldom left her husband's side after he was pronounced insane in 1919 and was for years the only person he would allow near him. Surviving also are a daughter and a sister.

Vaslav Nijinsky was born in Kiev on March 12, 1889. When he was nine years old, he was accepted by the school of the Imperial Ballet in St. Petersburg, and his talents as a dancer were early manifest.

In 1907, he made his professional debut at the famous Maryinsky Theatre in a pas de quatre in "Don Juan." At his graduation a year later, he began at once to perform solo roles, for his exceptional gifts had attracted the attention of the ballerina, Matilda Kshessinskaya, the Czar's favorite.

Nijinsky also won the admiration and devotion of Serge Diaghilev, connoisseur and advocate of the arts in Russia, and when Diaghilev borrowed members of the Imperial Ballet for a special season of modern ballets in Paris in 1909, Nijinsky was among the leading dancers. The success of that season was such that a new era for the ballet in Europe was clearly indicated, and much of Diaghilev's policy for the company in its annual seasons outside Russia was based

on the talents of Nijinsky.

The relationship with Diaghilev came to a bitter end when, in 1913, Nijinsky married a Hungarian dancer named Romola de Pulszky. The break with his artistic mentor was disastrous for his career.

When the First World War started in 1914, Nijinsky was interned with his wife in Budapest and later in Vienna. Two years later his release was effected through the efforts of the United States Government. In the meantime, the Metropolitan Opera Company had engaged the entire Diaghilev company for a New

York season and a national tour, and, since Nijinsky was one of the most famous of its stars, the directors of the Metropolitan were anxious for him to appear.

His first appearance here was at the Metropolitan Opera House, April 12, 1916, when he danced in "Spectre de la Rose" and "Petruchka," two of his most famous roles. At the close of the first American season, Diaghilev returned to Europe, leaving Nijinsky in charge of the company for its second season here. In October, 1916, Nijinsky produced his ballet, "Till Eulenspiegel," at the Manhattan Opera House, the only ballet of the Diaghilev organization to have its première in this country.

Already Nijinsky was beginning to show signs of his approaching mental disorder, which increased during the subsequent tours of Europe and South America. His final performance took place in Montevideo in 1917. Two years later he entered a private hospital for the insane at Kreuzlinger, Switzerland.

In 1940 the Nijinskys had arranged passage to the United States and arrived in Italy two days before Mussolini declared war. With that road blocked, they turned back to Romola's native Hungary. But Nijinsky could not stand the continual bombing of Budapest and they moved to a country inn on the Hungarian side of the Austrian border.

When the Russians arrived in 1945, Nijinsky heard his native tongue on every side again for the first time since 1911, when he left Russia. The dancer, who for years had spoken only in grunts and monosyllables, welcomed the first Russian he could halt in his native tongue.

Some days later Nijinsky came to a Russian barracks where Russian soldiers were singing around balalaikas and an accordion. The Russians offered him vodka. The music became louder and faster. Suddenly Nijinsky began dancing, leaping, twirling, executing ballet figures. The soldiers cheered and clapped.

The Russians assured Romola that Nijinsky would be welcomed in Russia as a hero of the Soviet Union. But Romola wanted to take him to Western Europe for treatment, and in 1947 they settled in Surrey, England.

Besides his great artistry as a dancer, Nijinsky was the choreographer of four ballets: "Till Eulenspiegel," "L'Après-midi d'un Faune," "Jeux," and "Le Sacre du Printemps." The first and the last of these precipitated major scandals at their premières, the former for its alleged immorality and the latter for its artistic iconoclasm.

IGOR STRAVINSKY

June 17, 1882–April 6, 1971

By Donal Henahan

Igor Stravinsky, the composer whose "Le Sacre du Printemps" exploded in the face of the music world in 1913 and blew it into the 20th century, died of heart failure yesterday.

The Russian-born musician, 88 years old, had been in frail health for years but had been released from Lenox Hill Hospital in good condition only a week before his death, which came at 5:20 A.M. in his newly purchased apartment at 920 Fifth Avenue.

Stravinsky's power as a detonating force and his position as this century's most significant composer were summed up by Pierre Boulez; who becomes musical director of the New York Philharmonic next season:

"The death of Stravinsky means the final disappearance of a musical generation which gave music its basic shock at the beginning of this century and which brought about the real departure from Romanticism.

"Something radically new, even foreign to Western tradition, had to be found for music to survive, and to enter our contemporary era. The glory of Stravinsky was to have belonged to this extremely gifted generation and to be one of the most creative of them all."

With Stravinsky at his bedside were his wife, Vera; his musical assistant and close friend, Robert Craft; Lillian Libman, his personal manager, and his nurse, Rita Christiansen.

The composer had returned in August, "much refreshed," after a vacation of two and a half months at Evian, France, Miss Libman said, but had entered Lenox Hill Hospital here with pulmonary edema on March 18. His stay there was extended somewhat, she said, because his new 10-room apartment overlooking Central Park was being decorated. He did not go home until March 30.

The last words Miss Libman could remember Stravinsky's saying, she said, were, "How lovely. This belongs to me, it is my home," as his nurse gave him a tour of the apartment in his wheelchair. He had moved around the world so much—Russia, Paris, Hollywood, New York—that his yearning for a home had been strong, she said.

Besides his widow, Stravinsky is survived by a daughter and two sons.

In accordance with Stravinsky's wish, burial will be in Venice, in the Russian corner of the cemetery of San Michele, where Diaghilev is buried. It was Diaghilev, the Russian ballet impresario, who produced the first performance of "Le Sacre du Printemps" on May 29, 1913, thereby giving Stravinsky his chance to turn music upside down.

During World War I, Igor Stravinsky was asked by a guard at the French border to declare his profession. "An inventor of music," he said.

It was a typical Stravinsky remark: flat, self-assured, flagrantly antiromantic. The composer who revolutionized the music of his time was a dapper little man who prided himself on keeping "banker's hours" at his work table. Let others wait for artistic inspiration; what inspired Igor Stravinsky, he said, was the "exact requirements" of the next work.

Between the early pieces, written under the eye of his only teacher, Nikolai Rimsky-Korsakov, and the compositions of Stravinsky's old age, there were more than 100 works: symphonies, concertos, chamber pieces, songs, piano sonatas, operas and, above all, ballets.

He was not unanimously honored during his lifetime. Three colorful works of his young manhood—"L'Oiseau de Feu" ("The Firebird"), "Petrushka" and "Le Sacre du Printemps" ("The Rite of Spring")—were generally admitted to be masterpieces.

But about his conversion to the austerities of neoclassicism in the nineteen-twenties, and his even more startling conversion to a cryptic serial style in the nineteen-fifties, there was critical disagreement. To some, his later works were thin and bloodless; to others, they showed a mastery only hinted at in the vivid early pieces.

To all, Stravinsky the man was a figure of fascination. The contradictions were dazzling. The composer marched through a long career with the self-assurance

of a Wagner—and was so nervous when performing in public that he thrice forgot his own piano concerto.

His Charles Eliot Norton lectures at Harvard in 1939–40 were dignified papers, delivered in French, on the high seriousness of the artist's calling. Three years later he wrote a polka for an elephant in the Ringling Brothers and Barnum & Bailey Circus.

He had many friends—Claude Debussy, Maurice Ravel, Pablo Picasso, Vaslav Nijinsky, André Gide, Jean Cocteau—and many homes. In every one he was restless at night unless a light burned outside his bedroom. That was how he slept, he explained, as a boy in St. Petersburg (now Leningrad).

Igor Feodorovich Stravinsky was born in a suburb of St. Petersburg on June 17, 1882: St. Igor's Day. He was the third of four sons born to Anna Kholodovsky and Feodor Ignatievitch Stravinsky. His father was the leading bass singer at the Imperial Opera in St. Petersburg.

The composer once described his childhood as "a period of waiting for the moment when I could send everyone and everything connected with it to hell." For his family he felt only "duties." At school he made few friends and proved only a mediocre student.

Music was a bright spot. At the age of two he surprised his parents by humming from memory a folk tune he had heard some women singing.

At nine, Igor started piano lessons and proved a good student, but no prodigy. Nevertheless, his interest in music grew. As a teen-ager he haunted his father's rehearsals at the Maryinsky Theater.

To his parents, the boy's interest in music was "mere amateurism, to be encouraged up to a point," he said. They agreed to let him study harmony with a private teacher—on the condition that he also study law at the University of St. Petersburg.

One of his classmates was a son of the great Russian composer Rimsky-Korsakov. In 1902 Stravinsky visited the elder man, gave him some of his early piano pieces for criticism and asked to become his pupil. The composer looked at the scores and replied noncommittally that the young man would need more technical preparation before he could accept him as a student.

After a year's outside study, he applied again to the master and was accepted. It was under the supervision of Rimsky-Korsakov that Stravinsky's first orchestral works—a symphony, a suite ("Le Faune et la Bergère"), the Scherzo Fantastique—were composed and performed.

In 1908, Stravinsky met Serge Diaghilev, then assembling a company of Russian dancers for a season in Paris. Impressed with the composer's first work, Diaghilev had a job for him: to orchestrate two piano pieces by Chopin for the ballet "Les Sylphides." The commission was gratefully accepted—Stravinsky now had a wife and two children—and impressively fulfilled.

A year later there was a more important Diaghilev commission: a ballet on a Russian folk tale, "The

Firebird," for the Russian Ballet's second season at the Paris Opera House.

The flashing, vigorous "Firebird" was a great success: so great that Stravinsky, in his later years, thought of it as an albatross around his neck. Arranged as an orchestral suite, it was played all over the world; the composer was asked to conduct it everywhere; it was the work the man-in-the-street most associated with the name Stravinsky. (On a train the composer met a man who called him "Mister Fireberg.")

While completing "The Firebird," Stravinsky had a daydream about a pagan ritual in which a young girl danced herself to death. This was the genesis of "The Rite of Spring," a revolutionary work whose premiere on May 29, 1913, caused one of the noisiest scandals in the history of music.

An open dress rehearsal had gone quietly, but protests against the music—barbarous, erotic, unlike anything Paris had ever heard—began almost as soon as the curtain went up on opening night.

Soon the Théâtre des Champs-Elysées was in an uproar. Stravinsky hurried backstage to find Diaghilev flicking the house lights in an attempt to restore order and Nijinsky, the choreographer, bawling counts at the dancers from the wings.

Stravinsky was furious; Diaghilev, who knew the value of publicity, said afterward that the crowd's reaction had been "exactly what I wanted."

World War I separated the composer permanently from his homeland (he did not see Russia again until a tour in 1962) and temporarily from Diaghilev. It also marked the start of a new style for Stravinsky—a leaner, more astringent, less colorful musical idiom that critics were to label "neoclassical."

In his middle years, Stravinsky turned more and more to purely instrumental music, including the "Dumbarton Oaks" Concerto for chamber orchestra (1938). His dogged productivity did not lessen with age. Having moved to the United States in 1939, Stravinsky arranged "The Star-Spangled Banner" for a performance in Boston—and brought in the police, who almost arrested him for tampering with the national anthem.

For years Stravinsky and Arnold Schoenberg were thought to divide the world of contemporary music between them. Stravinsky was head of the tonal camp: those whose works, dissonant or not, inhabited a universe of harmonic gravity; the world of "key."

Schoenberg and his disciples belonged to the 12-tone camp: a world where all notes of the scale were in free fall, none having more harmonic weight or status than another. It was a style of composition, Stravinsky had said, "essentially different" from his own.

Soon after "The Rake's Progress," however, Stravinsky himself became a 12-tone composer: more precisely, a "serial" composer, who based each work on a series of notes stated as a "tone row" in the opening measures.

Stravinsky's battles with music critics were legendary; he could not accept "the professional ignoramus, the journalist-reviewer pest." In 1929 he stated grandly that his music "was not to be discussed or criticized."

"One does not criticize somebody or something that is in a functional state. The nose is not manufactured. The nose is. Thus also my art," he said.

Stravinsky was a small, wiry man (5 feet 3 inches, 120 pounds) whose morning regimen, until he was 67, started with a set of "Hungarian calisthenics" (including walking on his hands). A renowned hypochondriac, according to his friends, the composer would visit his Los Angeles doctor almost every day—and then hike two miles home.

Stravinsky's remarkable face—long-lobed ears, hooded eyes, large nose, small mustache, full lips—tempted portraits from many artists. A straightforward Picasso sketch of the composer once caused a furor at the Italian border. A guard refused to let it out of the country on the suspicion that it was not a portrait at all but a mysterious, and probably subversive, "plan." "It is a plan of my face," Stravinsky protested. But the sketch had to leave the country in a diplomatic pouch from the British Embassy.

He worked like a craftsman in a room that looked like a laboratory, organized down to the very labels on the gum erasers and the pens for different colored inks. Unlike many composers, he worked directly at the piano.

Words fascinated Stravinsky. Besides Russian he could hold forth, and make puns, in French, German and English. "When I work with words in music, my musical saliva is set in motion by the sounds and rhythms of the syllables," he said.

Stravinsky wrote his own librettos for two works—"Renard" (1915) and "Les Noces"—and wrote several books as well.

Stravinsky married twice. His first wife, Catherine Nossenko ("my dearest friend and playmate"), was his first cousin. Married in 1906, they had four children: Theodore, Ludmilla, Sviatoslav Soulima and Maria Milena. Ludmilla died in 1938 and Mrs. Stravinsky in 1939, both of tuberculosis.

In 1940 Stravinsky married Vera de Bossett, a painter. They had no children.

PABLO CASALS

December 29, 1876–October 22, 1973

Pablo Casals, the celebrated cellist and conductor, died today in Auxilio Mutuo Hospital of complications from a heart attack suffered three weeks ago. He was 96 years old and lived in nearby Santurce with his wife Marta.

Not only a supreme musician, the Spanish-born Casals was also a dedicated humanitarian whose "Hymn to United Nations," with text by W. H. Auden was performed at the United Nations in New York two years ago. Receiving the United Nations Peace Medal then, he was hailed as a man who had "devoted your life to truth, to beauty and to peace."

A requiem mass will be offered at La Tiedad Church in San Juan tomorrow at 2 P.M., with Luid Cardinal Aponte Martinex as celebrant. Gov. Rafael Hernández Colón will deliver a eulogy.

By Alden Whitman

"I think it goes like this," a cello student struggling with a Johann Sebastian Bach suite once told Pablo Casals.

"Don't think," the master cellist replied. "It is better to feel."

With this emphasis on an inner sensitivity to a composer's intentions, Casals was able to demonstrate what luminescent and human music could be drawn from the strings of a rather awkward instrument. Over some 75 years, he provoked awe and applause for the profundity of his insights, the felicity of his playing and, above all, the soaring purity of his interpretations of baroque and classical composers. Bach was his specialty, but he was also at home with Boccherini, Mozart, Brahms, Beethoven, Schumann and Dvorak.

At the same time Casals (he pronounced the name Kaa-SAALS) won much acclaim as a man of principle for his humanitarianism, his personal musical "crusade for peace" and his one-man stand against the regime of Francisco Franco in his native Spain. Few musicians achieved in their own time the international renown accumulated by Casals.

Part of this fame, in the United States at least, came very late in life and rested on Casals's talents in conducting. Conducting gave him a sense of fulfillment, he said, because orchestras, with their human teamwork, are "the greatest of all instruments."

After a period of semiactivity in Europe starting in 1945, Casals went to Puerto Rico to live in 1956. He was then 79 years old and seemed spent. The next year, however, he started the Festival Casals, which became an annual springtime program of concerts. The concerts drew thousands of mainlanders to the island and introduced the post–World War II generation of music lovers to Casals.

Then in 1961 he joined Rudolf Serkin's Marlboro Music Festival in Vermont, where each July he conducted the orchestra and gave master classes in the cello. And, beginning in 1962, he conducted a choral work in New York every year.

In this period of resurgence, Casals gave a widely publicized cello recital at the United Nations in New York in 1958 to mark that organization's 13th anniversary. Three years later he played to a distinguished gathering at the White House on the invitation of President John F. Kennedy.

In the musical world, Casals's enduring reputation was associated with two accomplishments: his single-handed restoration to the repertory of Bach's cello music; and his innovations in bowing and fingering that gave the cello a new and striking personality in orchestral and solo works.

He greatly lightened the work of the left hand, for example, by changes of finger positions, thus adding to its mobility. He also showed that it was possible to attain fresh subtleties in tone by freer bowing.

Casals came upon the Bach suites by accident when he was 13 years old and browsing with his father in a Barcelona music shop.

"For me, Bach is like Shakespeare. He has known all and felt all," Casals told Bernard Taper in a profile published in The New Yorker in 1961. "He is everything. Everything except a professor. Professor Bach I do not know."

Casals was an ardent supporter of the Spanish Republican Government. He never reconciled himself to the Franco regime, which he considered tyrannical. With the Franco victory in 1939 he went into self-imposed exile, living until 1956 in Prades, France.

Up until 1958 he refused to visit the United States because it recognized Franco. But Casals bent his attitude sufficiently to play at the United Nations in 1958 because of "the great and perhaps mortal danger [of nuclear war] threatening all humanity."

Then in 1961 he relented further and played at the White House. In subsequent years he came to this country for regular yearly visits.

Pablo Carlos Salvador Defilló de Casals was born in the Catalan town of Vendrell, 40 miles from Barcelona, on Dec. 29, 1876, the second of 11 children of Charles and Pilar Defilló de Casals. His father was the town organist.

Shortly after Pablo's 10th birthday he heard a cello for the first time when José Garcia performed in Vendrell. After some coaxing, the elder Casals bought his son a cello and gave him a few lessons. Pablo proved so adept at it that he quickly exhausted his father's pedagogical abilities.

Pablo—not quite 12—went with his mother to Barcelona, where he enrolled in the Barcelona Municipal School of Music. To earn his living he played evenings for dances with a trio at the Café Tost, and later he persuaded the owner to devote one night a week to classical music.

That night attracted serious musicians to the bistro, including Isaac Albéniz, the composer and pianist. Albéniz gave him a letter of introduction to Count Guillermo de Morphy, a music patron who was an adviser to Queen Mother Maria Christina in Madrid.

The Count, taken with the young cellist, introduced him to Maria Christina, who was also charmed and who granted him a monthly stipend for his studies.

Casals lived in Madrid from 1894 to 1897, going to school at the Royal Conservatory of Music, playing duets with the Queen Mother (she was a fair pianist), chatting with the child who was to become Alfonso XIII and being guided in his general education by the Count de Morphy.

From Madrid, Casals and his mother went to Brussels and then to Paris, where he played at the Folies-Marigny at a wage barely sufficient to keep him and his mother from starvation. After a short time they returned to Barcelona, where Casals got a job teaching at the music school. For two years he taught cello, played it in the Barcelona Opera orchestra, gave concerts in churches and formed a string quartet, all the while saving money for a return to Paris.

In the fall of 1899, just before his 23rd birthday, he arrived in that city again, carrying a letter of introduction to Charles Lamoureux, the eminent conductor, from the Count de Morphy. When Casals presented himself for an audition, the conductor was annoyed by the intrusion. Nonetheless, the cellist sat down and began to play parts of the Lalo Cello Concerto. With the first notes, Lamoureux hoisted himself up from his desk and stood facing Casals until he finished playing, whereupon he embraced the young man and said, "My boy, you are one of the elect!"

Lamoureux immediately engaged him to play the Lalo concerto with his orchestra, and Casals made his Paris debut Nov. 12, 1899. He created a sensation there, as he did in London shortly afterward. In Britain he also played for Queen Victoria.

From then on his career was made, and he never lacked for engagements or for an audience. He commanded top fees, but lived economically.

For the next 20 years, until 1919, Casals, using Paris as his base, played in the principal cities of Europe and the Americas. Many of Casals's performances in those years were chamber music.

In 1914 Casals married Susan Metcalfe, the American lieder singer. It was his second marriage; the first, to Guilhermina Suggia, a Portuguese cellist, in 1906, had ended in divorce six years later. For several years Casals was the piano accompanist for Miss Metcalfe, a soprano, and at one point he considered dropping his career to further hers. However, the couple parted in 1920.

After World War I and with the breakup of his marriage, the cellist turned his energies to Barcelona, where, in 1920, he founded the Orquestra Pau (Catalan for Pablo) Casals and subsidized it for seven years until it became self-supporting. In these years (and afterward) he was its principal conductor.

When the Spanish Republic was proclaimed in 1931, Casals became one of its eager and hard-working supporters, all the more because the Republic restored many of his native Catalonia's ancient rights and granted the area a good deal of autonomy. He was president of Catalonia's music council, the Junta de Musica, and, during the Civil War, he gave hundreds of benefit concerts abroad for the Republic and put a large part of his personal savings at its disposal. The Government, in turn, named streets and squares for him and encouraged his exertions to bring great music to the common people.

Casals was in Barcelona in January, 1939, when the Franco forces burst into the city, but he made good an escape to France, vowing never to return to Spain while Franco was in power.

After several demoralizing weeks of despondency in Paris, he went to live in Prades among the thousands of Spanish exiles. There he helped to organize the care of the Catalans held in French camps and solicited funds for them from his friends all over the world. He continued to live in Prades in World War II.

Toward the end of the war he went on tour again. In the autumn of 1945, however, he cut short a concert trip in Britain and retired to Prades.

In explanation, he said he had assumed that an Allied victory would doom not only Hitler and Mussolini but also Franco. The democracies, he went on, had disillusioned him by not acting to topple Franco. He was therefore suspending his concert career until

Spain was freed. He said he could not separate his beliefs as a human being from his conduct as an artist.

Casals lived quietly and simply in Prades for close to 12 years. In 1950, however, he was prevailed upon to soften somewhat his vow of musical silence and take part in a Bach bicentenary festival. The event, which attracted hundreds of music lovers from many parts of the world, was held in the big Church of St. Pierre in Prades. The critics found that Casals's bow had lost none of its magic.

Some indication of a further shift in Casals's thinking came in 1951 in a colloquy with Albert Schweitzer, the humanitarian and philosopher. "It is better to create than to protest," Dr. Schweitzer said in urging the cellist to return to the concert stage. "Why not do both—why not create and protest both?" Casals replied. And he seemed to follow that course in his last years.

Appearing in New York last summer for a free Central Park concert with Mr. [Issac] Stern—it was cut short by rain before the cellist could perfom—Casals pronounced what could stand as his epitaph.

"What can I say to you?" he asked the assemblage. "I am perhaps the oldest musician in the world. I am an old man, but in many senses a very young man. And this is what I want you to be, young, young all your life, and to say things to the world that are true."

MARIA CALLAS

December 2, 1923–September 16, 1977

By Raymond Ericson and Harold C. Schonberg

Maria Callas, the soprano whose intensely dramatic portrayals made her the most exciting opera singer of her time, died of a heart attack yesterday at her home in Paris. She was 53 years old.

She once said, "Wherever I am, it is hectic." This may have been an understatement. Controversy, legend and myth surrounded the soprano throughout much of her career. Those who admired her felt that she was one of the greatest opera singers of all time. Others believed that her vocal inadequacies precluded any such claim.

Disputes and legal action seemed to arise wherever she sang. Her private life was seldom out of the limelight. Yet there was no denying that it was the magic of her personality that made her every move newsworthy.

Miss Callas sparked new interest in the largely forgotten bel canto operas of the 19th century, the works of Bellini, Donizetti and Rossini, which were considered too difficult and too uninteresting musically to be worth reviving. Miss Callas showed that they could be sung, that the melodies and the embellishments that were thought to be for virtuoso display could be turned to genuine dramatic use. A generation of singers followed her lead.

When Miss Callas was told that she was considered temperamental, her answer was, "I will always be as difficult as necessary to achieve the best." Everyone who worked with her agreed that she was a hard worker, willing to rehearse more than expected. She sang as many as 16 roles in one season. Her own interest in bel canto grew in 1948 in Venice, when she learned the difficult part of Elvira in Bellini's "I Puritani" in five days to substitute for an ailing singer.

More than any singer of the period after World War II, Maria Callas dominated opera. She was a prima donna assoluta in the old tradition, by virtue of voice, musicianship, a magnetic stage presence and a flaming temperament.

No singer of her time, and few in history, could so dominate an audience. Tall, slim, commanding, exotically beautiful, Miss Callas had a unique combination of electricity and brains, even if her voice was in some respects a flawed instrument, undependable in the high register.

Maria Anna Sofia Cecilia Kalogeropoulos was born Dec. 3, 1923 in Manhattan. Her Greek parents had arrived in the United States a few months earlier. Her father was a pharmacist. She attended public school in Washington Heights, and by the age of nine was singing for her schoolmates.

The family returned to Athens when Maria was

13. She won a scholarship to the Royal Academy of Music, and before she was 15 she was singing the dramatic role of Santuzza in Mascagni's "Cavalleria Rusticana." Four years later she made her official debut with the Athens Opera.

At the end of World War II, she went back to New York. She auditioned for the Metropolitan Opera and was offered the title roles in Puccini's "Madama Butterfly" and Beethoven's "Fidelio," but turned down both offers.

In 1947 she was given a contract to appear in Verona, and she sailed for Italy. She made her debut in the famous Arena in the title role of Ponchielli's "La Gioconda."

The goal of every opera singer in Italy then, as now, was La Scala in Milan. Miss Callas sang an Aida there in 1949, but she would not join the company officially until 1951, because, already independent minded, she would sing only leading roles in major operas and would not share a percentage of her salary with a powerful artist agency in Milan.

In the early 50's, Miss Callas sang in some rarely heard operas in Italian houses. These included Haydn's "Orfeo ed Euridice," Gluck's "Alceste" and Cherubini's "Medea."

She was offered a contract at the Met in 1952 by the general manager, Rudolf Bing, but she would not come to New York without her husband, Giovanni Battista Meneghini, who could not get a visa.

In this period, she had gained experience and a large measure of success not only in Italy, but also in South America, Mexico and Covent Garden in London. She took off 70 pounds, which left her at a slim 135 pounds. At 5 feet 8 inches and with a face made striking by her broad cheekbones, she became one of the handsomest women of the operatic stage.

She finally made her United States debut in 1954, with the Chicago Lyric Opera, in the role of Norma. Two years later, on Oct. 29, she sang the same part for her debut at the Metropolitan Opera. By this time her reputation was such that announcements of her appearances generated long lines outside the box office. Although critical reaction was usually mixed, she was ecstatically received for her musicianship, her personal appeal and the originality of her characterizations.

Having conquered many of the world's great opera companies, Miss Callas began to have trouble with them. In Chicago she was served with a lawsuit backstage during a performance, and she vowed never to sing there again. She was accused of breaking a contract with the Vienna State Opera over a question of fees. She canceled an engagement with the San Francisco Opera just before the season opened, pleading illness, and the company filed charges against her.

At the gala opening of one season in Rome, she sang the opening act of "Norma" and then refused to go on after that, because of laryngitis. At the Met, she quarreled with Mr. Bing, and he canceled their contract. She did not show up for scheduled performances at the Edinburgh Festival and at Athens.

All these actions made headlines, but Miss Callas was considered too valuable an artist and too great a box-office attraction to ignore.

As Mr. Bing said of her after he heard of her death: "She was a difficult artist, as many are, but she was one of the greatest artists of her time. We will not see her like again."

In fact, Miss Callas was re-engaged by the Met in 1965 to sing Tosca, and these became her last public opera performances.

In 1973, she and her close friend, the tenor Giuseppe di Stefano, decided to make a worldwide concert tour. It began in Hamburg, West Germany, in October, and the singers appeared at Carnegie Hall in February 1974. The audience was almost hysterical in its adulation, but the critics lamented that little was left of Miss Callas's voice. When the tour ended, it represented the soprano's last singing in public.

When she married Mr. Meneghini, 20 years her senior, in 1949, he, an Italian building-materials tycoon, gave her security and, it was said at first, affection. She called herself professionally Maria Meneghini Callas, and he became her manager and agent. They were separated in 1959 after she had become romantically involved with Aristotle Onassis, the Greek shipping magnate. The marriage was annulled six years later.

When Mr. Onassis married Jacqueline Kennedy, Ms. Callas said little about the matter except that she and Mr. Onassis remained good friends.

A celebrated feud between Miss Callas and the soprano Renata Tebaldi, who was her contemporary, was kept alive in the press and by their fans. At one time they were rival singers at La Scala. Miss Tebaldi refused to attend Miss Callas's performances, while Miss Callas went, with some ostentation, to those of Miss Tebaldi. Gossip writers hinted that she did so in order to make her nervous.

Dario Soria, former head of Angel Records, the label on which Miss Callas's recordings have been issued in this country, and now director of the Metropolitan Opera Guild, said yesterday that he had talked by phone to Miss Callas last summer, and that she sounded remote in spirit.

Asked what she was doing, she replied in a flat voice, "Nothing." "Without being able to perform," Mr. Soria said, "she apparently had nothing left to live for."

GEORGE BALANCHINE

January 22, 1904–April 30, 1983

George Balanchine, one of the greatest choreographers in the history of ballet and the co-founder and artistic director of the New York City Ballet, died yesterday.

Mr. Balanchine, who was 79 years old, died at Roosevelt Hospital of pneumonia.

In guiding the New York City Ballet to international pre-eminence, Mr. Balanchine established one of America's foremost artistic enterprises. As a 20th-century master, his personal contribution loomed even larger.

More than anyone else, he elevated choreography in ballet to an independent art. The plotless ballet became a synonym for Balanchine ballet. In an age when ballet had been dependent on a synthesis of spectacle, storytelling, decor, acting and music, and only partly on dancing, George Balanchine insisted that dance come first.

In his dictum that the material of dance is dance itself, he taught dancers and the public to look at ballet in a new way. In his attraction to the very essence of dance—movement, steps and combinations of steps—he enlarged the ballet vocabulary as had no other 20th-century choreographer.

And because his choreography was so closely related to the music, a Balanchine work, in his words, became an invitation to "see the music and hear the dancing."

Like Stravinsky and Picasso, the 20th-century modern artists with whom he has been ranked, Mr. Balanchine was an innovator who emerged from a classical tradition.

The hallmark of the Balanchine style was its conscious use of tradition as a base. The idiom in which Mr. Balanchine chose to work was the 400-year-old academic movement vocabulary he had learned as a child in his native Russia at the Maryinsky Theater. It was at this imperial theater in St. Petersburg that the 19th-century French-Russian choreographer Marius Petipa created his greatest works, including "The Sleeping Beauty."

Because of his return to Petipa's classical idiom at a time when ballet borrowed from freer-style movement, and because of his own foremost role in the development of a 20th-century neo-Classical style, Mr. Balanchine was often called Petipa's heir.

Yet in every sense George Balanchine was a modern artist. His dancers danced the same steps as Petipa's, but they were partnered at perilous angles undreamed of by Petipa and at a speed that could exist only in the 20th century.

The belief that radical innovation could come only from those steeped in tradition was central to Mr. Balanchine's work. It was reiterated in print by Lincoln Kirstein, the distinguished dance scholar who became Mr. Balanchine's patron and co-founder of the City Ballet and its precursor companies.

Together they established the School of American Ballet in 1934 and embarked on a venture that helped raise ballet to the highest status it has ever enjoyed in the performing arts.

It is likely that Mr. Balanchine's genius would have eventually flourished in any situation. But there is no doubt that Mr. Kirstein's invitation to Mr. Balanchine to come to the United States in 1933 made it easier.

The result was a creative output that raised the total of major Balanchine ballets to more than 200, most created during his time in America.

Throughout his career in the United States, the clarity of Mr. Balanchine's artistic vision remained remarkably consistent. The goal was a school and an American Classical company with its own new works rather than 19th-century classics and revivals.

Distinguished musical collaboration was a priority. "Whether a ballet has a story or none, the controlling image for me comes from the music," was the way Mr. Balanchine explained his own work, and he proved it in ballets that both "visualized" the structures of their scores and contributed a dimension of their own to the music.

Above all, a Balanchine ballet was more important than the individual dancer. The result was Mr. Balanchine's celebrated no-star policy. Consistently, however, he used dancers of star quality who helped create the image of a new kind of dancer. The speed and sharp attack with which City Ballet dancers performed were singular.

Balanchine was not for those who looked for spectacle or the dance-drama of the 20th-century psychological ballet. Yet while he was considered the great anti-Romantic, he produced many ballets with Romantic motifs. The theme of love thwarted by fate wove through "Serenade," "La Sonnambula," "La Valse" and other works.

In the same way, the choreographer for whom Stravinsky composed four ballets also turned to the marches of John Philip Sousa and cowboy tunes for his ballets. He choreographed more than 19 Broadway shows and four Hollywood films.

George Balanchine, whose original name was Georgi Melitonovitch Balanchivadze, was born in St. Petersburg, Russia, on Jan. 22, 1904. The surname of Balanchivadze was simplified by the impresario Serge Diaghilev in 1924, when the young dancer-choreographer joined Diaghilev's Ballets Russes.

Mr. Balanchine's mother, Maria Vasilyeva, was a bank employee. His father, Meliton Balanchivadze, was a composer who moved with his wife, daughter and younger son, Andrei, to Tiflis (now Tbilisi) in 1918 to be part of the Socialist Government of the independent Menshevik Georgian Republic. Mr. Balanchine's brother is his sole survivor.

Young Georgi was left behind in the Russian capital at the Maryinsky Theater's ballet school, where he had been enrolled in 1914.

He was seen in the classics at the State Academic Theater, as the Maryinsky was known after the Russian Revolution in 1917. (A knee injury in 1927 led him to mostly give up dancing by 1930.) He graduated from the ballet school in 1921.

A fellow student was Tamara Gevergeyeva, who later became known as Tamara Geva as an actress in America. The two were married in 1922. In 1936, Mr. Balanchine would create his celebrated dance sequence "Slaughter on Tenth Avenue" for her and Ray Bolger in the Broadway musical "On Your Toes."

In 1923, Mr. Balanchine presented the first of several concerts under the name "Evenings of the Young Ballet." He entitled the first program "The Evolution of Ballet from Petipa to Fokine to Balanchivadze."

He later agreed to be part of a small group of performers, which included Miss Geva, that would tour Germany in 1942. The Soviet authorities allowed the group out in June. A few weeks later, when they were ordered home, Mr. Balanchine and the dancers remained in the West.

Within a few weeks they had been hired by Diaghilev's Ballets Russes. Mr. Balanchine was taken on to dance and choreograph the ballets that Diaghilev had promised to provide the opera company at Monte Carlo. Bereft of a choreographer after the departure of Bronislava Nijinska, Diaghilev appointed the 21-year-old Mr. Balanchine to be choreographer of the world's most famous ballet company.

By the time Diaghilev died in August 1929, the 25-year-old choreographer had made an international name for himself. He had found his true self in the 1928 Stravinsky "Apollo," whose uncluttered

neo-Classical style pointed to the direction his work would take. "I regard this ballet as the crucial turning point in my artistic life," Mr. Balanchine said.

With Diaghilev's death, the members of the Ballets Russes faced an uncertain future. There were also changes in Mr. Balanchine's personal life. His marriage to Miss Geva had broken up in 1927.

The fact that Mr. Balanchine married four times—each time to a dancer for whom he created ballets—became a part of ballet lore. After he came to the United States, he married Vera Zorina in 1938, and later the City Ballet's Maria Tallchief, and then Tanaquil LeClercq, from whom he was divorced in 1969.

The years between 1929 and Mr. Balanchine's immigration to the United States in October 1933 were rootless ones. He was asked to become balletmaster of a new company, organized by Rene Blum in Monte Carlo, that became known as the Ballets Russes de Monte Carlo.

In 1933, he organized his own small company to create his own works. The troupe folded, but the all-Balanchine repertory convinced Mr. Kirstein to invite Mr. Balanchine to the United States to found a school and a company. On Jan. 2, 1934, the School of American Ballet opened in Manhattan on East 59th Street.

The first Balanchine-Kirstein company was named the American Ballet in 1935. Its repertory included "Serenade," the first Balanchine ballet choreographed in America. In a few months, however, the American Ballet's first tour suffered a financial collapse.

In the meantime, Mr. Balanchine choreographed Broadway shows including "Babes in Arms," "I Married an Angel" and "The Boys from Syracuse" in addition to "On Your Toes."

Mr. Kirstein, in 1936, had also founded a small touring company, Ballet Caravan, that concentrated on Americana and American folk themes. In 1941, the American Ballet Caravan, an amalgamation of the American Ballet and Ballet Caravan, was sent on a good-will tour to South America. For this occasion Mr. Balanchine created two of his most enduring ballets, the Tchaikovsky "Ballet Imperial" and the beautiful Bach "Concerto Barocco."

Mr. Kirstein established a new organization, Ballet Society, in 1946. For this group, Mr. Balanchine created two of his finest ballets, "The Four Temperaments" to Paul Hindemith's score of that title, and the Stravinsky "Orpheus.

Morton Baum, chairman of the City Center, invited Ballet Society to become a constituent of the center, which operated on West 55th Street, and the company was renamed the New York City Ballet.

Financially pressed, the City Ballet was often obliged to present its ballets without scenery or costumes. Mr. Balanchine stripped earlier ballets, such as "The Four Temperaments," of their elaborate costumes and put his dancers in practice clothes. A whole line of practice clothes ballets developed in the Balanchine repertory, among them "Agon," "Episodes" and "Ivesiana."

In this period Mr. Balanchine created some of his greatest works. Yet early critical reception was mixed or cool. Psychological ballet was in fashion, and it would be years before a larger public could accept the pure-dance ballets of which Mr. Balanchine was the master. Only in the mid-50's did he began to achieve wider recognition.

For the first time, Mr. Balanchine had found a permanent company that could serve as his creative instrument. An astonishing number of ballets from the City Center period remained long or permanently in the repertory.

When the City Ballet moved to its new home in the New York State Theater at Lincoln Center in 1964, the company reached a wider audience, and the Balanchine reputation was at its peak.

There was no doubt that Balanchine believed his own often-repeated remark that "ballet is woman." A galaxy of ballerinas would always be identified with his works. Speaking of his "Don Quixote," in which he had once cast himself as the Don and Suzanne Farrell as Dulcinea, he said:

"My interest in 'Don Quixote' has always been the hero's finding something to live for and sacrifice and serve. Every man wants an inspiration. For the Don, it was Dulcinea. I myself think that the same is true in life, that everything a man does he does for his ideal woman. You live only one life and you believe in something, and I believe in that."

VLADIMIR HOROWITZ

October 1, 1903–November 5, 1989

By Bernard Holland

Vladimir Horowitz, the eccentric virtuoso of the piano, whose extraordinary personality and skill overwhelmed six decades of concert audiences, died yesterday afternoon at his home in Manhattan, apparently of a heart attack.

Though standard biographies list his birth date as Oct. 1, 1904, Mr. Horowitz recently celebrated what he called his 86th birthday.

Held in awe by aficionados of the instrument, Mr. Horowitz virtually cornered the market on celebrity among 20th-century pianists. "He touched every musician who ever heard him," said the American pianist Murray Perahia. "He knew all the repertory and could play pieces he hadn't done in 20 years."

Emanuel Ax, another prominent American pianist, said: "I knew people who worshiped Horowitz, as I

did, and I knew people who hated him. But no one was indifferent. He brought the idea of excitement in piano playing to a higher pitch than anyone I've ever heard. For me the fascinating thing was a sense of complete control, and on the other hand, the feeling that everything was just on the verge of going haywire."

Mr. Horowitz's playing of such standards as Tchaikovsky's First Concerto and the Rachmaninoff Third electrified listeners. He was also famous for his high-powered versions of Mussorgsky's "Pictures at an Exhibition," Sousa's "Stars and Stripes Forever" and the Liszt Sonata.

Not everyone admired the Horowitz style. Some critics thought that his highly personalized interpretations ignored composers' intentions. The composer and critic Virgil Thomson called Mr. Horowitz "a master of distortion and exaggeration."

Mr. Horowitz was not overly worried by accusations of textual infidelity. "When I sit at the keyboard," he said, "I never know how I will play something. I play the way I feel at the moment. The head, the intellect, is only the controlling factor of music making. It is not a guide. The guide is your feelings. Chopin never played his own pieces the same way twice."

At another time Mr. Horowitz said: "I am a 19th-century Romantic. I am the last. I take terrible risks. Because my playing is very clear, when I make a mistake, you hear it. But the score is not a bible, and I am never afraid to dare. The music is behind those dots."

Into Mr. Horowitz's late 70's and early 80's, when he made a comeback in the concert world, he retained the ability to extract colors of extraordinary brilliance or extraordinary delicacy. In his concert appearances during the 1920's and 30's, his ability to create excitement in whatever he did on stage made him an almost mythical figure, a status enlarged by his personal eccentricities.

Even his frequent retirements from performing had a romantic appeal. A man known for his frail nerves, Mr. Horowitz quit playing in public four times—from 1936 to 1938, from 1953 to 1965, from 1968 to 1974 and from 1983 to 1985.

When he did play, he drove a hard bargain: his personal piano from his Manhattan living room accompanied him; concerts were at 4 P.M. and only on Sunday. Advance teams redecorated his hotel rooms to make him feel less estranged from the comfort of home.

In the last four years of his life, he became virtually a one-man industry in the concert business, with a much-publicized tour of the Soviet Union and performances in Europe and America, all linked with CD recordings, videotapes, television programs and films.

Mr. Horowitz was named Vladimir Gorowitz when he was born in Kiev, in the Ukraine, into a prosperous and cultured family. His father was an engineer. His mother and sister, Regina, were pianists, a brother, Georg, a violinist. Mr. Horowitz altered the first letter of the family name for his Berlin debut in 1926.

Piano lessons at home began at the age of three, formal training at six. He studied the piano and composition at the Kiev Conservatory, and his talent was apparent from early on.

The Bolshevik Revolution in 1917 pushed Mr. Horowitz onto the concert stage. In the political upheaval, his family members lost most of their possessions, and Mr. Horowitz began playing piano recitals to earn money for them. He performed 15 times in Kharkov during the 1922–23 season and subsequently went out on a 70-concert tour playing 200 different works.

In 1925, Mr. Horowitz induced the Soviet authorities to allow him a student's visa for foreign travel, but on arrival in Western Europe he plunged into a two-year tour of the continent. Audiences loved him and critics compared him to Anton Rubinstein. Mr. Horowitz was brought to America by Arthur Judson, the all-powerful impresario of the era. Early in 1928, Mr. Horowitz played the Tchaikovsky First with the New York Philharmonic under Sir Thomas Beecham.

Olin Downes, then a critic for The New York Times, described his reception as "the wildest welcome a pianist has received in many seasons in New York." The performance, wrote Downes, was "a whirlwind of virtuoso interpretation, amazing technique, irresistible youth, electrifying temperament."

This temperament contributed to his numerous retirements from the stage and the frequency with which he called off scheduled appearances. One frustrated manager described handling date changes and cancellations for Mr. Horowitz as a full-time job. The pianist, Hollywood actor and all-round wit Oscar Levant once proposed a full-page ad that would read: "Messrs. Horowitz and Levant wish to announce that they still have a few cancellations for next season."

The pianist insisted that he was not neurotic, only high-strung, and blamed his disaffection for concert performances on the rigors of travel.

"For me, playing the piano is the easiest thing in the world," he said in 1975. "It's all the things around playing that drive me crazy." About the same time, he said: "I could play every day. It is the moving that is the big deal for me."

The first of his several withdrawals from the concert stage was engendered by the 1935 season, in which Mr. Horowitz played nearly 100 recitals. Exhausted, he had a particularly slow recovery from an appendectomy. For the next two years, he lived in France and Switzerland. He began to play again in 1938, and in 1940 he returned to the United States and renewed his American career with a recital at Carnegie Hall.

In 1953, he celebrated the 25th anniversary of his American debut with a concert at Carnegie Hall. Then he went into a retirement that lasted 12 years.

Years later, Mr. Horowitz explained his disappearance to an interviewer: "The doctors said that I was overworked, that I needed a rest. I thought I would take a year's sabbatical. It was wonderful. When it was over, I thought I'd take another one. I saw friends and played cards and I talked philosophy and I read books and I listened to all kinds of music."

Ten years passed this way.

Mr. Horowitz began to consider a return to the stage in 1964. Finally he announced a date—May 9, 1965. Tickets went on sale at 10 A.M. on April 26. A line had begun to form the previous morning, and by 7:30 on the morning of the 26th, 1,500 people were waiting for tickets. The night before had been damp and cold, and Mr. Horowitz, touched by the devotion of his audience, had sent 100 cups of coffee to the waiting fans.

When Mr. Horowitz stepped out on the stage of Carnegie Hall, the audience rose to offer a stomping, cheering, standing ovation.

He played a few select concerts in the following years and recorded a television recital that was broadcast nationwide in 1968. Then he retired again.

Mr. Horowitz began to give concerts regularly in 1974. On Nov. 17 of that year, he played the first piano recital at the new Metropolitan Opera House at Lincoln Center.

He made his first recordings in 1928 for RCA Victor; he remained with the company until 1962, when he moved to Columbia Records. In 1975, he returned to RCA, where he remained until the mid-1980's, when he began to record for Deutsche Grammophon. This year, he returned to CBS (now called Sony Classical).

Mr. Horowitz's last appearances as a performer were in the spring of 1987 when he played in West Berlin, Amsterdam and Hamburg. His last American concerts were in the fall of 1986 when he played at Lincoln Center and helped celebrate the reopening of a refurbished Carnegie Hall.

Thomas Frost, who was Mr. Horowitz's record producer for many years, said yesterday that the last recording session with Mr. Horowitz was on Nov. 1.

"We had been working since Oct. 20—a Haydn sonata, some Chopin, and the Liszt-Wagner 'Liebestod' were some of the pieces," he said. "Though we probably needed two more sessions, I have a gut feeling there is enough more or less note-perfect material for a complete recording. We were very close to finishing."

Watching over Mr. Horowitz's health, as well as almost every aspect of his life, was his wife, Wanda Toscanini Horowitz, whom he met in 1933 after an invitation from her father, the conductor Arturo Toscanini, to be the soloist in the Beethoven "Emperor" Concerto. They married that year. A daughter, Sonya, born in 1934, died in 1975.

Isaac Stern, the violinist and president of Carnegie Hall, reached in Tokyo today, reflected on Mr. Horowitz's extraordinary career:

"How many musicians can say that they have created a standard against which others will be judged?" He added, "When you saw him playing close up, it was as if each of his 10 fingers had a separate intelligence. Each moved in its direction at the right time and with the right weight; and he sat apart, observing it and controlling it from a central organism, without great effort.

"He will be regarded as part of the pantheon of musicians who influenced their times, and who left a special legacy that will be remembered and thought about by anyone who cares about performance."

LEONARD BERNSTEIN

August 25, 1918–October 14, 1990

By Donal Henahan

Leonard Bernstein, one of the most prodigally talented and successful musicians in American history, died yesterday evening at his apartment at the Dakota on the Upper West Side of Manhattan. He was 72 years old.

Mr. Bernstein's spokeswoman, Margaret Carson, said he died of a heart attack caused by progressive lung failure.

His death followed by five days the announcement that Mr. Bernstein would retire from performing because of health problems. A heavy smoker for most of his life, he had been suffering from emphysema, pulmonary infections and a pleural tumor.

In recent months, Mr. Bernstein had canceled concerts in Japan and in Charleston, S.C., and a tour of Europe. He conducted his final performance at Tanglewood on Aug. 19, when he led the Boston Symphony in Britten's "Four Sea Interludes" and the Beethoven Seventh Symphony.

Long before Mr. Bernstein became, at the age of 40, the youngest music director ever engaged by the New York Philharmonic, the drama critic Harold Clurman sized up the flamboyant musician's future: "Lenny is hopelessly fated for success."

It was Mr. Bernstein's fate to be far more than routinely successful, however. His fast-burning energies, his bewildering versatility and his profuse gifts for both music and theater coalesced to make him a high-profile figure in a dozen fields, among them symphonic music, Broadway musicals, the ballet, films and television.

Still, his hydra-headed success did not please all his critics. While he was music director of the Philharmonic from 1959 to 1969, some friends and critics urged him to quit and compose theater music full time. Many regarded him as potentially the savior of the American musical, to which he contributed scores for "On the Town," "Wonderful Town," "Candide" and "West Side Story."

At the same time, others were deploring his continued activity in such fields, contending that to be a successful leader of a major orchestra he would have to focus on conducting.

Still other observers of the Bernstein phenomenon wished he would concentrate on the ballet, for which he had shown an affinity ("Fancy Free," "Facsimile"), or on opera and operetta ("Trouble in Tahiti," "Candide").

Or on musical education. His television programs on such subjects as conducting, symphonic music and jazz fascinated millions when he appeared on "Omnibus," the cultural series, and later as star of the Philharmonic's televised Young People's Concerts.

And still others, a loyal few, counseled Mr. Bernstein to throw it all over and compose more serious symphonic scores. His gifts along this line were apparent in such works as his Symphony No. 1 ("Jeremiah") of 1942, Symphony No. 2 ("The Age of Anxiety") of 1949 and Symphony No. 3 ("Kaddish") of 1963.

He played the piano well enough to have made a separate career as a virtuoso. He was a facile poet. He wrote several books, including the popular "The Joy of Music" (1959). He was a teacher of rare communicative talent, as television audiences discovered.

But Mr. Bernstein resolutely resisted pressure to restrict his activities. During his decade as the Philharmonic's musical director, he grew as an interpreter and as a technician.

His performances of Mahler's symphonies were almost universally conceded to be of the highest quality, and his recordings for Columbia Records of the complete set not only constituted the first such integral collection but also continue to be regarded as among the most idiomatic Mahler performances available.

The future Renaissance man of American music was born in Lawrence, Mass., on Aug. 25, 1918, the son of Samuel and Jennie Resnick Bernstein. His father, a beauty-supplies jobber who had come to the United States from Russia as a boy, wanted Leonard to take over the business when he grew up. For many years the father resisted his son's intention to be a musician.

The stories of how he discovered music became encrusted with legend, but all sources agree he was a prodigy. Mr. Bernstein's own version was that when he was 10 years old his Aunt Clara, who was in the middle of divorce proceedings, sent her upright piano to the Bernstein home to be stored. The child looked at it, hit the keys and cried: "Ma, I want lessons!"

Until he was 16, by his own testimony, he had never heard a live symphony orchestra, a late start for any musician, let alone a future musical director of the Philharmonic. Virgil Thomson, while music critic of

The New York Herald Tribune in the 1940's, commented on this:

"Whether Bernstein will become in time a traditional conductor or a highly personal one is not easy to prophesy. He is a consecrated character, and his culture is considerable. It might just come about, though, that, having to learn the classic repertory the hard way, which is to say after 15, he would throw his cultural beginnings away and build toward success on a sheer talent for animation and personal projection. I must say he worries us all a little bit."

These themes—the concern over Mr. Bernstein's "talent for animation" and over his penchant for "personal projection"—were to haunt the musician through much of his career.

In many aspects of his life and career, Mr. Bernstein was an embracer of diversity. The son of Jewish immigrants, he retained a lifelong respect for Hebrew and Jewish culture. His "Jeremiah" and "Kaddish" symphonies and several other works were founded on the Old Testament. But he also acquired a deep respect for Roman Catholicism, which was reflected in his "Mass," the 1971 work he wrote for the opening of the John F. Kennedy Center for the Performing Arts in Washington.

A similar catholicity was reflected throughout his music. His choral compositions include not only songs in Hebrew but also "Harvard Songs: Dedication and Lonely Men of Harvard." He was graduated in 1939 from Harvard, where he had studied composition with Walter Piston and Edward Burlingame Hill.

A sense of his origins, however, remained strong. Serge Koussevitzky, the music director of the Boston Symphony, proclaimed him a genius and a probable successor—"The boy is a new Koussevitzky, a reincarnation!"—but the older conductor urged Mr. Bernstein to improve his chances for success by changing his name. The young musician replied: "I'll do it as Bernstein or not at all!"

He pronounced the name in the German way, as BERN-stine, and could no more abide the pronunciation BERN-steen than he could enjoy being called "Lenny" by casual acquaintances.

Harvard played an important part in Mr. Bernstein's rise, providing a pinch of Brahminism. During his last semester at Harvard, he organized and led a performance of Marc Blitzstein's "Cradle Will Rock," a left-wing musical that had been banned in Massachusetts but that could not be proscribed within the academic walls. It was not his first fling as a producer. At age 16 he had starred in his own production of "Carmen" at a summer camp, playing the title role alluringly in wig and black gown.

It was as a result of another schoolboy production, at Camp Onota in the Berkshires, that he met Adolph Green, with whom he later collaborated in several Broadway musicals. Mr. Bernstein was a camp counselor and theater director and Mr. Green was in "The Pirates of Penzance."

Subsequently, when Mr. Bernstein was out of a job in New York City, he looked up Mr. Green, moved in with him in his East Ninth Street apartment in Greenwich Village, and began playing the piano at the Village Vanguard for a group called the Revuers. The ensemble included, besides Mr. Green, his musical comedy collaborator Betty Comden and the actress Judy Holliday.

Mr. Bernstein met Aaron Copland at Harvard in 1937, and through him came to know two other aspiring composers, Roy Harris and William Schuman. Admiring his intuitive grasp of modern music and his phenomenal skill at playing complex orchestral scores on the piano, the composers agreed that Mr. Bernstein should become a conductor. Dimitri Mitropoulos, the New York Philharmonic's music director, met Mr. Bernstein in 1938 and added to the consensus.

At that point, Mr. Bernstein "didn't know a baton from a tree trunk," as he later put it. Nevertheless, he had made up his mind. Because he had applied at the wrong time of the year and was turned down by the Juilliard School, he went to Philadelphia to audition for Reiner's conducting class at the Curtis Institute.

The initial offer from the New York Philharmonic came from the orchestra's music director, Arthur Rodzinski, who had heard Mr. Bernstein conduct a rehearsal at Tanglewood, remembered the young man and hired him as an assistant for the 1943–44 season. But the chance to conduct came without warning one Sunday afternoon in 1943. On Nov. 14, Bruno Walter, the guest conductor, fell ill and could not appear. The young assistant took over his program (works by Schumann, Rosza, Strauss and Wagner) and achieved a sensational success. Because the concert was broadcast over radio and a review appeared on page 1 of The New York Times the next day, the name of Leonard Bernstein suddenly became known throughout the country.

During the six-year tenure of Mitropoulos as music director of the Philharmonic, beginning in the 1951–52 season, Mr. Bernstein was a frequent guest conductor. In 1957–58, the two worked jointly as principal conductors of the orchestra. A year later, Mr. Bernstein was named music director.

The New York appointment would have been a severe test of any conductor. The orchestra's quality had gone downhill, its repertory had stagnated and audiences had fallen off. Orchestra morale was low and still sinking. Mr. Bernstein leaped in with his customary brio and showmanship and his willingness to try new ideas.

He designated the Thursday evening concerts as "Previews," at which he spoke informally to the audience about the music. He built his season around themes like "Schumann and the Romantic Movement" and "Keys to the 20th Century." Strange-sounding works by avant-garde composers like Elliott Carter, Milton Babbitt, Karlheinz Stockhausen, Gunther Schuller and John Cage began to infiltrate the Philharmonic's programs. He took the orchestra on tours to Latin America, Europe, Japan, Alaska and Canada.

Mr. Bernstein's life took a turn toward greater stability in 1951 when he married the actress Felicia Montealegre Cohn. Her American father had been head of the American Smelting and Refining Company in Chile, and she had been sent to New York City to study the piano. After several years of off-and-on romance, they were married in Boston. They had three children: a daughter, Jamie, a son, Alexander Serge (named for Serge Koussevitzky) and a second daughter, Nina.

Mr. Bernstein and his wife began a "trial separation" after 25 years of marriage. They continued, however, to appear together in concerts, one such occasion being a program in tribute to Alice Tully at Alice Tully Hall, where Mr. Bernstein conducted Sir William Walton's "Facade" with his wife as one of the two narrators. Mrs. Bernstein died in 1978 after a long illness.

Mr. Bernstein's private life, long the subject of rumors in the musical world, became an open book in 1987 when his homosexuality was brought to wide public attention by Joan Peyser's "Bernstein: A Biography."

Late in his extraordinarily restless and fruitful life, Mr. Bernstein defended his early decision to spread himself over as many fields of endeavor as he could master. "I don't want to spend my life, as Toscanini did, studying and restudying the same 50 pieces of music," he wrote in The New York Times.

"It would," he continued, "bore me to death. I want to conduct. I want to play the piano. I want to write for Hollywood. I want to write symphonic music. I want to keep on trying to be, in the full sense of that wonderful word, a musician. I also want to teach. I want to write books and poetry. And I think I can still do justice to them all."

AARON COPLAND

November 14, 1900–December 2, 1990

By John Rockwell

Aaron Copland, America's best-known composer of classical music and an impassioned champion of American music in every style, died yesterday evening at Phelps Memorial Hospital in North Tarrytown, N.Y. He was 90 years old.

Of many notable achievements, Mr. Copland's greatest gift was his ability to be both serious and popular, to adhere to the formal integrity and moral earnestness of modernism and to espouse the accessibility of the dominant political mores of the 1930's and 40's.

In ballet scores like "Billy the Kid" (1938), "Rodeo" (1942) and above all "Appalachian Spring" (1944), and in concert pieces like "El Salon Mexico" (1937), "Fanfare for the Common Man" (1942) and "Lincoln Portrait" (1942), Mr. Copland touched a chord in the American psyche reached by no other classical musician this country has produced.

Yet in less programmatic works, some of them embracing the supposedly elitist 12-tone system of Arnold Schoenberg, like the Piano Variations (1930), the "Short" Symphony (1934), the Third Symphony (1946) and "Connotations" (1962), Mr. Copland spoke with an uncompromisingly rigorous voice.

Attacked by admirers of his more popular style, the later works now increasingly seem the work of the same man, whose breadth of vision and warmth of spirit could unite Teutonic Serialism and all-American hoedowns.

Mr. Copland's industry as a concert organizer and promoter of new music was nearly as important a part of his legacy to American music as his compositions. Mr. Copland worked throughout the 1920's and 30's to organize concert series of new music and further the cause of the American composer in a time in which cultural fealty was still paid to Europe.

His most important steps as a promoter of new music included the founding, with Roger Sessions, of the Copland-Sessions Concerts in New York. For 25 years a leading member of the faculty at the Berkshire Music Center at Tanglewood, he helped make that festival a center for contemporary music.

In 1932, he directed the First Festival of Contemporary Music at Yaddo, the artists' colony in Saratoga Springs, N.Y., including a selection of songs by Charles Ives.

In an essay on Mr. Copland in his book "American Music Since 1910," Virgil Thomson observed of him: "He has never turned out bad work, nor worked without an inspiration. His stance is that not only of a professional but also of an artist—responsible, prepared, giving of his best."

Mr. Copland was the youngest of Harris and Sarah Copland's five children. His parents had come to this country in the 1870's and 80's from Russia.

In his book "Our New Music," the composer wrote: "I was born on Nov. 14, 1900, on a street in Brooklyn that can only be described as drab. It had none of the garish color of the ghetto, none of the charm of an old New England thoroughfare, or even a pioneer street. I mention it because it was there that I spent the first 20 years of my life. Also, because it fills me with mild wonder each time I realize that a musician was born on that street."

Mr. Copland's first musical training consisted of picking up scraps of musicianship from his older sister, an amateur pianist. He continued his piano studies with Leopold Wolfsohn, Victor Wittgenstein and Clarence Adler.

Graduating from Boys High School in 1918, Mr. Copland continued his musical studies under Rubin Goldmark. The young musician is said to have once glimpsed the score of Ives's "Concord" Sonata on the piano in Goldmark's studio, but his teacher kept it from him, lest his student become "contaminated."

Mr. Copland continued his musical studies in France.

"It was where the action seemed to be," he recalled. "Stravinsky was living there, and the whole new 'group of six' with Milhaud and Poulenc. And so I went to study at a new summer music school at the Palace of Fontainebleau. It's always said that I went to France to study with Nadia Boulanger, but I had never heard of her before I arrived."

Mr. Copland was the first in a distinguished line of American composers to train with Boulanger. Friendly with Serge Koussevitzky, who had recently been appointed music director of the Boston Symphony, Boulanger won a promise that he would lead a new symphony for organ and orchestra that Mr. Copland had agreed to write for her coming American tour.

Koussevitzky did conduct the Organ Symphony, but not until a month after its premiere, on Jan. 11, 1925, by the New York Symphony Society under Walter Damrosch. Addressing the audience afterward, Damrosch said, "If a young man can write a piece like that at the age of 24, in five years he will be ready to commit murder!"

"When he came home from Paris at 24, his study time with Nadia Boulanger completed, and began to be a successful young composer, it is said that he determined then to make no unnecessary enemies," Thomson wrote of Copland in "American Music Since 1910." "It is as if he could see already coming into existence an organized body of modernistic American composers with himself at the head of it, taking over the art and leading it by easy stages to higher ground."

Mr. Copland said in 1985: "Composers differ greatly in their ideas about how American you ought to sound. The main thing, of course, is to write music that you feel is great and that everybody wants to hear. But I had studied in France, where the composers were all distinctively French; it was their manner of composing. We had nothing like that here, and so it became important to me to try to establish a naturally American strain of so-called serious music."

He tried to do just that by incorporating jazz into "Music for the Theater" (1925) and then into the Piano Concerto (1927). There followed more expansive scores like the Symphonic Ode (1929) and the Dance Symphony (1930).

But his next phase, epitomized by the Piano Variations, the Short Symphony and the "Statements for Orchestra" (1934), constituted the culmination of the first phase of his more serious style, which he himself had trouble reconciling with his more popular works.

The problem was exacerbated by the political climate in the 30's, when so many artists and intellectuals became deeply sympathetic to left-wing ideology and its attendant populism. Although Mr. Copland himself never joined the Communist Party, he was, in the words of Vivian Perlis, a music historian, a "fellow traveler."

"It seemed to me," he wrote in "Our New Music," "that we composers were in danger of working in a vacuum. Moreover, an entirely new public for music had grown up around the radio and phonograph. It made no sense to ignore them and to continue writing as if they did not exist. I felt it was worth the effort to see if I couldn't say what I had to say in the simplest possible terms."

His first composition in this overt populist style was "El Salon Mexico," first played in Mexico City. It became one of the composer's best-known works and dramatized in sound his effort to bring American and Mexican composers and traditions under a common roof.

Mr. Copland quoted cowboy songs in his ballet "Billy the Kid" and other kinds of American folk tunes in "Rodeo." "Appalachian Spring," commissioned by the choreographer Martha Graham, evoked rural mysticism and the harmonies of country fiddlers and included a finale based on the Shaker hymn "The Gift to Be Simple." The suite from "Appalachian Spring" was awarded the Pulitzer Prize in 1944.

It was during this period that Mr. Copland had a flirtation with Hollywood, writing scores for "Our Town" (1944), "The Red Pony" (1948) and "The Heiress" (1948), for which he won an Oscar.

"Most of 'Appalachian Spring' and a good part of my Violin Sonata were composed at night at the Samuel Goldwyn studios in Hollywood," Mr. Copland recalled. "An air of mystery hovers over a film studio after dark. Its silent and empty streets give off something of the atmosphere of a walled medieval town. This seclusion provided the required calm for evoking the peaceful, open countryside of rural Pennsylvania depicted in 'Appalachian Spring.'"

There are no folk melodies in the Symphony No. 3 (1946), but it remains very much of a piece with the other music from this period. "The Tender Land," Mr. Copland's full-length opera, retains a thoroughly American identity through a simulation of folk styles.

Mr. Copland's adoption of the 12-tone system began gradually in the early 1950's. Leonard Bernstein was among many former friends and champions who lamented Mr. Copland's decision. In 1970, Bernstein wrote: "One of the sadnesses I recall in recent years occurred at the premiere of Copland's 'Inscape,' when he said to me, 'Do you realize there isn't one young composer here, there isn't one young musician who seems to be at all interested in this piece—a brand new piece which I've labored over?'"

After 1970, Mr. Copland virtually stopped composing.

"I'm amazed I don't miss composing more than I do," Mr. Copland told an interviewer in 1980. "You'd think if you had spent 50 years at it you'd have the feeling that something was missing, and I really don't. I must have expressed myself sufficiently. I certainly don't feel tortured or bitter, only lucky to have been given so long to be creative."

Mr. Copland was once described as a "tall, rather loosely knit man, who surveys the scene through plain spectacles with clear blue eyes." A lifelong bachelor, he lived for many years in the Empire Hotel near what is now Lincoln Center before moving to Westchester County. Survivors include a niece and two nephews.

"There was always a modesty about Copland, an attitude of not taking success for granted," his friend Minna Lederman Daniel once recalled. "Famous the world over, more than comfortably well off, there is still for him a modicum of wonder about it all."

MARTHA GRAHAM

May 11, 1894–April 1, 1991

By Anna Kisselgoff

Martha Graham, a revolutionary in the arts of this century and the American dancer and choreographer whose name became synonymous with modern dance, died yesterday at her home in Manhattan. She was 96 years old.

Frequently ranked with Picasso, Stravinsky and James Joyce for developing a form of expression that broke the traditional mold, Miss Graham was initially acclaimed as a great dancer. Yet ultimately her genius, universally recognized as she became the most honored figure in American dance, was embodied in her choreographic masterworks and her invention of a new and codified dance language.

The Graham technique, which is now used by dance companies throughout the world, became the first enduring alternative to the idiom of classical ballet. Powerful, dynamic, jagged and filled with tension, this vocabulary com-

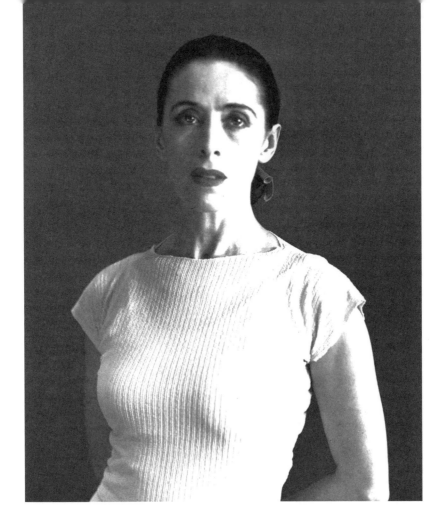

bined with Miss Graham's distinctive system of training to set her above other dance innovators.

Although such achievements were part of Miss Graham's pioneering role in helping to establish modern dance outside the older ballet tradition after the 1920's, she continued to amaze her public for more than 60 years. She choreographed more than 180 works, the most recent of which was her self-mocking "Maple Leaf Rag," which had its premiere on Oct. 2 with the Martha Graham Dance Company in New York.

Miss Graham's fundamental tenet was that dance should reach audiences through a visceral response rather than an objective image that registered upon the intellect. "Out of emotion comes form," she said, and then proved that out of form she could re-create the same emotion on stage.

She never wavered in her belief that movement could express inner feeling. Miss Graham sought to give "visible substance to things felt" and to "chart the graph of the heart." These celebrated Graham phrases became the metaphors central to her art.

Miss Graham's dances spoke eloquently against the crushing of the human spirit, and one of her frequent themes was the condemnation of intolerance, especially toward nonconformists.

Her own life as a creative artist epitomized the independent spirit with which she so frequently imbued her dramatic heroines. The figure conquering sexual fear in "Errand into the Maze," the woman looking deep into herself while preparing for an unnamed fate in "Herodiade," and the American pioneer brimming with optimism in "Frontier" could also be Clytemnestra or Jocasta, antiquity's queens who, in the Graham canon, emerged from crisis through the sheer force of self-understanding.

Miss Graham usually cast herself at the center of these works until 1969, when she gave her last performance and retired from the stage at the age of 75.

Miss Graham's highly intense dancing and choreography were not intended to soothe the spirit and did not find ready acceptance.

Like Picasso, she was concerned with an inner reality. "For me, dance is theater," she wrote. But she never resorted to a realistic theater. More often than not, her choreography presented a dancer's body as distorted or dislocated, an assemblage of forms aligned into maximum expressiveness.

Audiences throughout the world were often disturbed by Miss Graham's frank acknowledgment of human sexuality, especially in her famous cycle inspired by Greek myths. Miss Graham's Medea, Jocasta, Phaedra and Clytemnestra gave vent to their lust and hate, baring the passions that few humans liked to recognize in themselves but that Miss Graham exposed with unflinching scrutiny.

For Miss Graham, dance became a collective memory that could communicate the emotions universal to all civilizations: Mythology, she felt, was the psychology of the ancients.

Miss Graham's encyclopedic approach to dance—a creative wellspring from sources as varied as American Indian rituals and the Bible—often carried several levels of meaning and startled a public that defined dance in linear or pictorial terms. Miss Graham, for her part, said she wanted her dances to be "felt" rather than comprehended in the usual manner.

In general, Miss Graham saw art as a reflection of its time inseparable from life. "My dancing," she said, "is not an attempt to interpret life in the literary sense. It is an affirmation of life through movement."

Even the dance technique that she hammered out on her own body and then transferred to her school and company derived from the most organic aspect of human life: the act of breathing. That act was formalized and dramatized in the idiom's most basic principle, called contraction and release—intensified moments of exhalation and inhalation. Miss Graham said her aim was "to increase the emotional activity of the dancer's body so that you are teaching the body, not teaching the mind."

Above all, she said, "Dance is not representational." Miss Graham recalled in later years that as a young dancer about to embark upon an independent career in 1922, she had chanced upon a nonfigurative painting by Wassily Kandinsky—a slash of red against a field of blue. "I will dance like that," she said.

Like other modernists, Miss Graham rejected literal imagery in favor of abstraction. Form for form's sake, however, held no interest for her. Instead she focused on abstraction in its strict sense, that of extracting the essence of a quality of emotion. A celebrated example was "Lamentation," the 1930 solo in which Miss Graham, encased in a tube of stretch jersey, created sharply angular shapes on a bench. She did not dance about grief, but sought to be what she called "the thing itself" or the embodiment of grief.

The quintessential Graham could be found in "Frontier" (1935), one of the choreographer's pieces on overt American themes. The solo initiated her 32-year collaboration with the sculptor Isamu Noguchi.

The set for "Frontier" was a fragment of a fence seemingly anchored by a rope behind. It had the same spareness and economy of Miss Graham's solo and the score of her music director and mentor of that time, Louis Horst. Noguchi noted that he had found in Miss Graham "a drive that motivated her to strip the dance to its stark rudiment."

Among the composers who wrote scores for Miss Graham were Samuel Barber, William Schuman, Gian Carlo Menotti and Aaron Copland, whose score for her 1944 classic, "Appalachian Spring," won the Pulitzer Prize.

Martha Graham was born on May 11, 1894, in Allegheny, Pa., to George Graham, a physician, and the former Jane Beers, a descendant of Miles Standish.

In 1916, after graduation from a junior college, Miss Graham enrolled in the Denishawn school in Los Angeles and then joined the Denishawn Company. Den-

ishawn, organized by Ruth St. Denis and Ted Shawn, was then the only major dance company that worked outside the classical ballet tradition, and it became the incubating ground for such pioneering talents as Doris Humphrey, Charles Weidman and Miss Graham herself.

John Murray Anderson saw Miss Graham with Denishawn and hired her for his Greenwich Village Follies in 1923 and 1924. But in those two years Miss Graham realized that neither Denishawn nor the commercial theater was right for her. At the invitation of Rouben Mamoulian, she joined the dance division of the Eastman School of Music in Rochester, where she taught dance.

On April 18, 1926, she made her concert debut at the 48th Street Theater in New York with works that still showed the influence of Denishawn. "The idiom," the critic Robert Sabin recalled in 1953, "was still prevalently romantic and eclectic, but the spirit was new and as bracing as a salty sea wind."

Miss Graham taught in the early years in her studio at 66 Fifth Avenue and at the Neighborhood Playhouse. She assembled a company of women, who would work on new works for nine months, then give a few recitals in New York and go on tour.

From her group, augmented by men in 1938 to 1939, came the next generation of modern dancers, choreographers and teachers: Anna Sokolow, Sophie Maslow, Pearl Lang, May O'Donnell, Erick Hawkins, Merce Cunningham and later Paul Taylor and John Butler. Miss Graham, who had a long-term relationship with Mr. Horst, was married in 1948 to Mr. Hawkins, but they were later divorced.

In the early years, Miss Graham costumed herself and the women in her troupe in stretch jersey. She later referred to this time as her "long woolens" period. Her dances were spare and stark, testimony to her deep interest in ritual, and she was influenced by the ceremonial Indian dances she had witnessed in the Southwest.

In the 1930's, Miss Graham was known for her American themes. "We must look to America to bring forth an art as powerful as America itself," she said, and, besides "Appalachian Spring," she produced such works as "American Document," "American Provincials" and "Salem Shore."

After 1946, she immersed herself in Hebrew and Greek mythology, most powerfully in the full-evening "Clytemnestra" of 1958. She picked up historical personages with legendary qualities, the Bronte sisters for "Deaths and Entrances" and Joan of Arc for "Seraphic Dialogue."

Writing for The New York Times, Thomas Lask noted it was through her work "that she had, in William Faulkner's apt phrase, put a scratch on the face of eternity."

Martha Graham, who leaves no immediate survivors, was living proof of her own adage: "No artist is ahead of his time. He is his time; it is just that others are behind the time."

RUDOLF NUREYEV

March 17, 1938–January 6, 1993

By Jack Anderson

Rudolf Nureyev, one of the most charismatic ballet stars of the 20th century and an artist who was often called the greatest male dancer since Vaslav Nijinsky, died yesterday in a hospital near Paris. He was 54 and had homes in Paris, New York City and St. Bart's in the Caribbean.

He died of "a cardiac complication, following a grievous illness," his physician, Michel Canesi, said.

Mr. Nureyev's defection from the Soviet Union in 1961 made headlines around the world, and he remained in the public eye for nearly 30 years with a riveting stage presence that attracted millions of new fans to ballet.

During his career as a performer, Mr. Nureyev also choreographed, restaged many classics, served as the Paris Opera Ballet's artistic director and tried his hand as a ballet and orchestral conductor. Life and dance were one for Mr. Nureyev.

When he defected from the Kirov Ballet while it was on tour in Paris, American and Western European audiences were already familiar with great male dancers. Some were more elegant and precise than Mr. Nureyev, who was at the height of his powers. But when he burst on the scene, with his long hair, hollow cheeks and fiery expression, he performed with an intensity that startled and excited dancegoers.

At his peak, Mr. Nureyev combined a passionate, arrogant temperament with a perfectionist's standards. Upon his arrival in the West, he immediately became one of ballet's chief popularizers through his contemporary approach to the 19th-century classics and his legendary partnership with Dame Margot Fonteyn of the Royal Ballet. His personal obsession with dance inspired him to master a bewildering variety of styles and embark upon seemingly never-ending tours.

Mr. Nureyev was a stickler for classical technique, and his mastery of it made him a model for an entire generation of dancers. The standard of male dancing rose visibly in the West after the 1960's, largely because of Mr. Nureyev's inspiration. He showed dancers how to jump an extra measure higher and not to be afraid of the grand manner. The public flocked to see him, and he was often compared with rock stars.

Richard Buckle, the dance critic for The Sunday Times of London, described Mr. Nureyev in 1962 as "a pop dancer—that's what we've got—a pop dancer, at last," adding, "What the telly did for art, what Billy Graham did for religion, Nureyev has done for ballet."

Oleg Kerensky, another British critic, observed in 1970: "Part of Nureyev's sensational success is due to his animal magnetism and sensuality. He appeals to the mothering instinct in middle-aged women, the mating instinct in young ones and the desire of many male homosexuals."

The superstar's temperamental outbursts were a famous aspect of his career and personality. He walked offstage while partnering Merle Park of the Royal Ballet during a performance at the Metropolitan Opera

House in 1970. In 1973, Natalia Makarova accused him of deliberately dropping her onstage in Paris. Incidents in which Mr. Nureyev slapped his partners were widely reported.

Offstage, Mr. Nureyev was very much a night person who relished parties and discos, and was seen often in the company of prominent socialites. Nevertheless, he managed to keep details of his private life private. As he said in an interview: "Of course I have a personal life. Something goes on, I'm sure. But I don't think the public should know about that. Do you?"

Rudolf Hametovich Nureyev was born on March 17, 1938, on a train traveling in Siberia. His father, of Bashkir Muslim descent, was in the Soviet Army. His mother, Farida, was reportedly a Tatar from Kazan.

The Nureyevs lived in Moscow for part of World War II. The family then moved to Ufa, the capital of Bashkiria, a region within the Russian republic.

It was at the Ufa Opera that Mr. Nureyev first saw ballet performances. Enraptured, he began to work with folk-dance groups at his school and take ballet lessons with a local teacher, eventually becoming an apprentice member of the corps de ballet at the Ufa Opera House.

He appeared with other members of the Ufa Ballet in Moscow in 1955. After auditions, he was accepted by the schools of both the Bolshoi Ballet in Moscow and the Kirov Ballet in Leningrad. He chose the Kirov even though a teacher who auditioned him there said, "Young man, you'll become either a brilliant dancer or a total failure—and most likely you'll be a failure."

Mr. Nureyev was taken under the wing of one of the Kirov's best teachers, Aleksandr Pushkin. At his graduation in 1958, Mr. Nureyev joined the Kirov Ballet and was given solo roles from the outset.

He gained a reputation as an unpredictable individualist. He took little interest in politics but aroused the suspicion of Communist officials by his curiosity about the foreign attractions that visited Leningrad.

His defection occurred on June 17, 1961. The Kirov had just finished its season in Paris and was going on to London. But Mr. Nureyev was told that he was being sent to Moscow to dance at a gala. He suspected that once in the Soviet Union, he would no longer be allowed out.

When he arrived at Le Bourget airport with the rest of the company, Mr. Nureyev ran toward two French police inspectors and declared that he wished to remain in the West. He did not return to the Soviet Union until 1987, when he received a special visa to see his ailing mother.

Mr. Nureyev's first engagement with a Western troupe was in the De Cuevas Ballet's production of "The Sleeping Beauty." Americans first saw him on television on Jan. 19, 1962, on the "Bell Telephone Hour."

He made his New York stage debut at the Brooklyn Academy of Music on March 10, 1962, dancing the "Don Quixote" pas de deux with Sonia Arova during a performance by the Chicago Opera Ballet.

Mr. Nureyev made his British debut on Nov. 2, 1961, when Fonteyn invited him to participate in a charity gala, at which he partnered the American ballerina Rosella Hightower in the "Black Swan" pas de deux. Mr. Nureyev returned to London on Feb. 21, 1962, as a guest artist with the Royal Ballet.

This time, he was cast in "Giselle" and his ballerina was Fonteyn. Ballet history was made and Mr. Nureyev began his long association with the Royal Ballet as a "permanent guest artist."

It was widely assumed that Fonteyn was approaching the end of her performing career, but her new partner revitalized her. Mr. Nureyev said of Fonteyn in 1965: "I don't care if Margot is a Dame of the British Empire or older than myself. For me she represents eternal youth; there is an absolute musical quality in her beautiful body and phrasing. Because we are sincere and gifted, an intense abstract love is born between us every time we dance together."

Unwilling to confine himself to a single troupe, Mr. Nureyev became a globe-trotting guest artist. Early in his career in the West, he expressed a desire to work with George Balanchine, a co-founder of the New York City Ballet. But as Mr. Nureyev recalled in 1979, Balanchine told him: "My ballets are too dry for you. Go and dance your princes. When you're tired of them, come back."

Even as he was creating a sensation in the classical repertory, Mr. Nureyev was drawn to modern dance. He tried out a blend of modern and classical technique in 1970 in the Royal Ballet's production of "The Ropes of Time," by Rudi Van Dantzig, then appeared in Glen Tetley's "Field Figures," "Laborintus" and "Pierrot Lunaire."

Mr. Nureyev repeatedly appeared with the Martha Graham Dance Company. In 1975 he and Fonteyn starred in "Lucifer," a premiere by Graham, and in subsequent seasons he was seen in several Graham works, including, in 1987, "Appalachian Spring," when the cast included another Kirov defector and guest artist from the ballet world, Mikhail Baryshnikov.

Mr. Nureyev directed the Paris Opera Ballet from 1983 to 1989. His own choreography for the company included an adaptation of Henry James's "Washington Square" and a "Cinderella" set in Hollywood.

His film debut came in 1977 when he played the title role in Ken Russell's "Valentino."

Last October, in his last appearance on stage, to take a bow at the conclusion of the Paris premiere of his new production of "La Bayadère," he looked gaunt and blinked back tears as the audience gave him a 10-minute standing ovation.

Increasingly, he seemed unwilling to acknowledge that his dancing days were over. And the anti-Semitic remarks he had long made in private (he always re-ferred to Mr. Baryshnikov, who is not Jewish, as Moishe) surfaced in print.

After the late 1970's, it was increasingly acknowl-edged that Mr. Nureyev was dancing past his prime.

But he refused to announce his retirement. As he said in 1990, "The main thing is dancing, and before it withers away from my body, I will keep dancing till the last moment, the last drop."

MSTISLAV ROSTROPOVICH

March 27, 1927–April 27, 2007

By Allan Kozinn

Mstislav Rostropovich, the cellist and conduc-tor who was renowned not only as one of the great instrumentalists of the 20th century but also as an outspoken champion of artistic freedom in the Soviet Union during the last decades of the cold war, died yesterday in Moscow. He was 80 and lived in Paris, with homes also in Moscow, St. Petersburg, London and Lausanne, Switzerland.

Mr. Rostropovich had been in and out of hospi-tals in recent weeks, believed to be suffering from intestinal cancer. He was able to attend a celebration of his 80th birthday on March 27 at the Kremlin, where President Vladimir V. Putin presented him with a state medal, the Order of Service to the Fa-therland.

The author Aleksandr Solzhenitsyn, whom Mr. Rostropovich had sheltered from the Soviet author-ities in the 1970s, called the death a "bitter blow to our culture," the Russian news agency ITAR-Tass re-ported. "Farewell, beloved friend," he said.

As a cellist, Mr. Rostropovich played a vast reper-tory that included works written for him by some of the 20th century's greatest composers. Among them were Shostakovich's Cello Concertos; Prokofiev's Cello Con-certo, Cello Sonata and Symphony-Concerto; and Brit-ten's Sonata, Cello Symphony and three Suites.

Mr. Rostropovich was able to make his cello sing in an extraordinary range of musical accents. In the big Romantic showpieces—the Dvorak, Schumann, Saint-Säens and Elgar concertos, for example—he dazzled listeners with both his richly personalized interpretations and a majestic warmth of tone. His graceful accounts of the Bach Suites for Unaccompa-nied Cello illuminated the works' structural logic as well as their inner spirituality.

He could be a firebrand in contemporary works, and he seemed to enjoy producing the unusual tim-bres that modernist composers often demanded. He played the premieres of solo works by William Walton, Georges Auric, Dmitri Kabalevsky and Nikolai Miaskovsky, as well as concertos by Alfred Schnittke, Arvo Pärt, Krzysztof Penderecki and Lukas Foss.

As a conductor, he happily molded tempos, phrase shapes and instrumental balances to suit an inter-pretive vision that was distinctly his own. He was at his most eloquent, and also his most freewheeling, in Russian music, particularly in the symphonies of Tchaikovsky, Sergei Prokofiev and Dmitri Shostakov-ich.

In an interview in The New York Times last year, Mr. Rostropovich said of Shostakovich, "He was the most important man in my life, after my father."

He added: "Sometimes when I'm conducting, I see his face coming to me. Sometimes it's not really a happy face—I conduct maybe a bit too slow. So I conduct faster, and the face disappears."

Tall, heavyset and bald except for a halo of white hair, Mr. Rostropovich was a commanding presence. But he was also gregarious in an extroverted, Russian way. At the end of an orchestral performance, he often hopped off the podium and kissed and hugged every musician within reach.

He had a mischievous sense of humor that cut through the sobriety of the concert atmosphere. He sometimes surprised his accompanists by pasting cen-terfolds from men's magazines into the pages of their scores.

Mr. Rostropovich was the music director of the National Symphony Orchestra in Washington from 1977 to 1994 and remained close to it as its conductor laureate. He also had strong relationships with several of the world's great orchestras, including the London Symphony Orchestra, the Philadelphia Orchestra and the New York Philharmonic.

Mr. Rostropovich always said that one of the prin-cipal lures of the podium was that the orchestral repertory seemed so vast when compared with the cello repertory. But he did not confine himself to the classics. He commissioned regularly, and led the pre-mieres of more than 50 works.

Two pieces written for him during his National Symphony years—Stephen Albert's "Riverrun" Sym-phony and Morton Gould's "Stringmusic"—won Pulitzer Prizes. Leonard Bernstein, Jacob Druckman, Richard Wernick, Gunther Schuller and Ezra Lader-man were among the other composers who wrote for him or whose works had their world premieres under his baton.

Mr. Rostropovich, who was widely known by his diminutive, Slava (which means glory in Russian), was also an accomplished pianist. He was often the accompanist at recitals by his wife, the Russian soprano Galina Vishnevskaya, whom he married in 1955 and who survives him, as do two daughters.

When Mr. Solzhenitsyn came under attack by Soviet authorities in the late 1960s, Mr. Rostropovich and Ms. Vishnevskaya allowed him to stay in their dacha outside Moscow. He was their guest for four years, and Mr. Rostropovich tried to intercede on his behalf, personally taking the manuscript of "August 1914" to the Ministry of Culture and arguing that there was nothing threatening to the Soviet system in it. His efforts were rebuffed.

Mr. Rostropovich's own troubles began in 1970 when, out of frustration with the suppression of writers, artists and musicians, he sent an open letter to Pravda, the state-run newspaper, which did not publish it. Western newspapers did.

"Explain to me, please, why in our literature and art so often people absolutely incompetent in this field have the final word," he asked in the letter. After it was published, Mr. Rostropovich and Ms. Vishnevskaya were unable to travel abroad and faced dwindling engagements at home.

Occasionally, it would seem that the ban was lifted. In 1971, Mr. Rostropovich conducted and Ms. Vishnevskaya sang in Bolshoi Opera performances of Prokofiev's "War and Peace" in Vienna, and Mr. Rostropovich was allowed to travel to the United States for concerts. But the next year, appearances in Austria and Britain were canceled without explanation.

It was not until 1974 that they were allowed out of the country again and given two-year travel visas. In the West, Mr. Rostropovich told interviewers that he missed his homeland but would not return until artists were free to speak their minds.

The Soviet government's response was to revoke his and Ms. Vishnevskaya's citizenship in 1978. Thereafter they traveled on special Swiss documents.

With President Mikhail S. Gorbachev's program of increased openness, Mr. Rostropovich began to renew his contacts with his homeland. He met with Mr. Gorbachev and President Ronald Reagan at the White House in 1987. In November 1989, immediately after the fall of the Berlin Wall, he gave an impromptu concert there.

His Soviet citizenship was restored in January 1990. The next month, he took the National Symphony to Moscow and Leningrad (now St. Petersburg).

In 1991, when Communist hard-liners tried to topple the more open regime, Mr. Rostropovich went to Moscow to stand beside President Boris Yeltsin.

Two years later, during the siege of the Russian White House, Mr. Rostropovich, who was touring Russia again with the National Symphony, gave a free concert in Red Square, attended by 100,000 people. His soloist, for his 1993 Russian tour, was Ignat Solzhenitsyn, a pianist and the son of Aleksandr Solzhenitsyn.

Mstislav Leopoldovich Rostropovich was born in Baku, Azerbaijan, on March 27, 1927. His parents, Leopold Rostropovich and Sofiya Nikolaevna Fedotov, were both musicians, and his mother began teaching him the piano when he was four. When he was eight, he went to Paris to study the cello with his father, who had been a student of Pablo Casals.

In the mid-1930s, the family moved to Moscow, where Mstislav entered the Gnesin Institute. He made his debut at 13, playing a Saint-Saëns Concerto in Slavyansk, Ukraine, and in 1943, at 16, he entered the Moscow Conservatory as a student of Semyon Kozolupov.

He also studied composition with Shostakovich, and continued to do so even after the Soviet authorities condemned both Shostakovich and Prokofiev for "formalist perversions and antidemocratic tendencies."

By the late 1940s, he had won competitions in Moscow and, in his first trips outside the Soviet Union, in Prague and Budapest. He toured widely during the 1950s, and in 1956—the year he was appointed to a professorship at the Moscow Conservatory—he made his American debut at Carnegie Hall.

In 1987, President Reagan awarded him the Presidential Medal of Freedom, this country's highest civilian honor.

Mr. Rostropovich made his conducting debut in 1968, when he led a performance of Tchaikovsky's "Eugene Onegin" at the Bolshoi. He made his British conducting debut with the New Philharmonia Orchestra in 1974. His first American conducting performances were with the National Symphony and the San Francisco Opera in 1975.

In 1977 Mr. Rostropovich accepted the directorship of the National Symphony Orchestra, succeeding Antal Dorati. For one of his first concerts, Leonard Bernstein wrote "Slava!," a festive overture that captured the ebullience of Mr. Rostropovich's style.

The most frequent criticism of Mr. Rostropovich as a conductor was that he sometimes became so carried away with the music that he let the performance get out of his control. "If there is a choice," he told The Times in 1985, "I would rather have ideas and some difficulties of technique than a perfect technique and no ideas."

LUCIANO PAVAROTTI

October 12, 1935–September 6, 2007

By Bernard Holland

Luciano Pavarotti, the Italian singer whose ringing, pristine sound set a standard for operatic tenors of the postwar era, died on Thursday at his home near Modena, in northern Italy. He was 71.

In July 2006, he underwent surgery for pancreatic cancer and made no public appearances afterward.

Like Enrico Caruso and Jenny Lind before him, Mr. Pavarotti extended his presence far beyond the limits of Italian opera. He became a titan of pop culture. Millions saw him on television and found in his expansive personality, childlike charm and generous figure a link to an art form with which many had only a glancing familiarity.

Early in his career and into the 1970s he devoted himself with single-mindedness to his serious opera and recital career, quickly establishing his rich sound as the great male operatic voice of his generation—the "King of the High Cs," as his popular nickname had it.

By the 1980s he expanded his franchise exponentially with the Three Tenors projects, in which he shared the stage with Plácido Domingo and José Carreras. Most critics agreed that it was Mr. Pavarotti's charisma that made the collaboration such a success.

And in the early 1990s he began staging Pavarotti and Friends charity concerts, performing with rock stars like Elton John, Sting and Bono and making recordings from the shows.

Throughout these years, despite his busy and vocally demanding schedule, his voice remained in unusually good condition well into middle age.

Even so, as his stadium concerts and pop collaborations brought him fame well beyond what contemporary opera stars have come to expect, Mr. Pavarotti seemed increasingly willing to accept pedestrian musical standards. By the 1980s he found it difficult to learn new opera roles or even new song repertory for his recitals.

And although he planned to spend his final years performing in a grand worldwide farewell tour, he completed only about half the tour, which began in 2004. Physical ailments limited his movement on stage and regularly forced him to cancel performances. By 1995, when he was at the Metropolitan Opera singing one of his favorite roles, Tonio in Donizetti's "La Fille du Régiment," high notes sometimes failed him.

Yet his wholly natural stage manner and his wonderful way with the Italian language were completely intact. Mr. Pavarotti remained a darling of Met audiences until his retirement from that company's roster in 2004, an occasion celebrated with a string of "Tosca" performances. At the last of them, on March 13, 2004, he received a 15-minute standing ovation and 10 curtain calls.

In the late 1960s and '70s, when Mr. Pavarotti was at his best, he possessed a sound remarkable for its ability to penetrate large spaces easily. Yet he was able to encase that powerful sound in elegant, brilliant colors.

Mr. Pavarotti was perhaps the mirror opposite of Mr. Domingo. Five years Mr. Domingo's senior, Mr. Pavarotti had the natural range of a tenor, exposing him to the stress and wear that ruin so many tenors' careers before they have barely started. Mr. Pavarotti's confidence and naturalness in the face of these dangers made his longevity all the more noteworthy.

Mr. Domingo, on the other hand, began his musical life as a baritone and later manufactured a tenor range above it through hard work and scrupulous intelligence. Mr. Pavarotti, although he could find the heart of a character, was not an intellectual presence.

Yet in the late 1980s, it was Mr. Pavarotti who showed the dominant gift for soliciting adoration from large numbers of people. The most enduring symbol of Mr. Pavarotti's Midas touch, as a concert attraction and a recording artist, was the Three Tenors act, created with Mr. Domingo and Mr. Carreras. Some praised these concerts and recordings as popularizers of opera. But most classical music critics dismissed them as unworthy of the performers' talents.

Mr. Pavarotti had his uncomfortable moments in recent years. His proclivity for gaining weight became a topic of public discussion. He was caught lip-synching a recorded aria at a concert in Modena, his hometown. He was booed off the stage at La Scala in 1992.

His frequent withdrawals from prominent events at opera houses like the Met and Covent Garden in London, often from productions created with him in mind, caused administrative consternation. A series of cancellations at Lyric Opera of Chicago moved Lyric's general director in 1989, Ardis Krainik, to declare him persona non grata.

A similar banishment nearly happened at the Met in 2002. He was scheduled to sing two performances of "Tosca," one a gala concert with prices as high as $1,875 a ticket, which led to reports that the performances may be a farewell. Mr. Pavarotti arrived in New York barely in time for the dress rehearsal. On the day of the first performance, though, he had developed a cold and withdrew. That was on a Wednesday.

From then until the second scheduled performance, on Saturday, everyone debated the probability of his appearing. The New York Post ran the headline "Fat Man Won't Sing." The demand to see the performance was so great, however, that the Met set up 3,000 seats for a closed-circuit broadcast. Still, at the last minute, Mr. Pavarotti stayed in bed.

Luciano Pavarotti was born in Modena, Italy, on Oct. 12, 1935. His father was a baker and an amateur tenor; his mother worked at a cigar factory. As a child he listened to opera recordings, singing along with tenor stars.

He taught for two years before deciding to become a singer. His first breakthrough came in 1961, when he won an international competition at the Teatro Reggio Emilia. He made his debut as Rodolfo in Puccini's "Bohème" later that year.

In 1963 Mr. Pavarotti's international career began: first as Edgardo in Donizetti's "Lucia di Lammermoor" in Amsterdam and other Dutch cities, and then in Vienna and Zurich. His Covent Garden debut also came in 1963, when he substituted for Giuseppe di Stefano in "La Bohème." His reputation in Britain grew even more the next year, when he sang at the Glyndebourne Festival, taking the part of Idamante in Mozart's "Idomeneo."

A turning point was his association with the soprano Joan Sutherland. In 1965 he joined the Sutherland-Williamson company on an Australian tour during which he sang Edgardo to Ms. Sutherland's Lucia. He credited Ms. Sutherland's advice, encouragement and example as a major factor in the development of his technique.

Further milestones came in 1967, with Mr. Pavarotti's first appearances at La Scala in Milan and his participation in a performance of the Verdi Requiem under Herbert von Karajan. He came to the Metropolitan Opera a year later, singing with Mirella Freni, a childhood friend, in "La Bohème."

In his later years Mr. Pavarotti became as much an attraction as an opera singer. Hardly a week passed in the 1990s when his name did not surface in gossip columns. His outsize personality remained a strong drawing card, and even his lifelong battle with his circumference guaranteed headlines: a Pavarotti diet or a Pavarotti binge provided high-octane fuel for reporters.

In 1997 Mr. Pavarotti joined Sting for the opening of the Pavarotti Music Center in war-torn Mostar, Bosnia, and Michael Jackson and Paul McCartney on a CD tribute to Diana, Princess of Wales. In 2005 he was granted Freedom of the City of London for his fund-raising concerts for the Red Cross. He also was lauded by the Kennedy Center Honors in 2001, and he holds two spots in the Guinness Book of World Records: one for the greatest number of curtain calls (165), the other, held jointly with Mr. Domingo and Mr. Carreras, for the best-selling classical album of all time, the first Three Tenors album.

Mr. Pavarotti's health became an issue in the late 1990s. His mobility onstage was sometimes severely limited because of leg problems, and at a 1997 "Turandot" performance at the Met, extras helped him up and down steps. In January 1998, at a Met gala with two other singers, Mr. Pavarotti became lost in a trio from "Luisa Miller" despite having the music in front of him. He complained of dizziness and withdrew. Rumors flew alleging on one side a serious health problem and, on the other, a smoke screen for his unpreparedness. The latter was not a new accusation. In a 1997 review for The New York Times, Anthony Tommasini accused Mr. Pavarotti of "shamelessly coasting" through a recital.

It was a tribute to Mr. Pavarotti's box-office power that when, in 1997, he announced he could not or would not learn his part for a new "Forza del Destino" at the Met, the house substituted "Un Ballo in Maschera," a piece he was ready to sing.

Around that time Mr. Pavarotti left his wife of more than three decades, Adua, to live with his 26-year-old assistant, Nicoletta Mantovani. His divorce was finalized in October 2002, and he married Ms. Mantovani in 2003. She survives him, as do three daughters from his first marriage and a daughter with Ms. Mantovani.

The great tenor was on the mark in explaining his drawing power: "I think an important quality that I have is that if you turn on the radio and hear somebody sing, you know it's me. You don't confuse my voice with another voice."

Allan Kozinn contributed reporting.

JOAN SUTHERLAND

November 7, 1926–October 10, 2010

By Anthony Tommasini

Joan Sutherland, one of the most acclaimed sopranos of the 20th century, a singer of such power and range that she was crowned "La Stupenda," died on Sunday at her home in Switzerland, near Montreux. She was 83.

Her death was confirmed by her close friend the mezzo-soprano Marilyn Horne.

It was Italy's notoriously picky critics who dubbed the Australian-born Ms. Sutherland the Stupendous One after her Italian debut, in Venice in 1960. And for 40 years the name endured with opera lovers around the world. Her 1961 debut at the Metropolitan Opera in New York, in Donizetti's "Lucia di Lammermoor," generated so much excitement that standees began lining up at 7:30 that morning. Her singing of the Mad Scene drew a thunderous 12-minute ovation.

Ms. Sutherland's singing was founded on astonishing technique. Her voice was evenly produced throughout an enormous range, from a low G to effortless flights above high C. She could spin lyrical phrases with elegant legato, subtle colorings and expressive nuances. Her sound was warm, vibrant and resonant, without any forcing. Indeed, her voice was so naturally large that at the start of her career Ms. Sutherland seemed destined to become a Wagnerian dramatic soprano.

Following her first professional performances, in 1948, during a decade of steady growth and intensive training, Ms. Sutherland developed incomparable facility for fast runs, elaborate roulades and impeccable trills.

Her abilities led Richard Bonynge, the Sydney-born conductor and vocal coach whom she married in 1954, to persuade her early on to explore the early-19th-century Italian opera of the bel canto school. She became a major force in its revitalization.

Bel canto (which translates as "beautiful song" or "beautiful singing") denotes an approach to singing exemplified by evenness through the range and great agility. The term also refers to the early-19th-century Italian operas steeped in bel canto style. Outside of Italy, the repertory had languished for decades when Maria Callas appeared in the early 1950s and demonstrated that operas like "Lucia di Lammermoor" and Bellini's "Norma" were not just showcases for coloratura virtuosity but musically elegant and dramatically gripping works as well.

Even as a young man, Mr. Bonynge had uncommon knowledge of bel canto repertory and style. Ms. Sutherland and Mr. Bonynge, who is four years younger than she, met in Sydney at a youth concert and became casual friends. They were reacquainted later in London, where Ms. Sutherland settled with her mother in 1951 to attend the Royal College of Music. There Mr. Bonynge became the major influence on her development.

Ms. Sutherland used to say she thought of herself and her husband as a duo and that she didn't talk of her career, "but of ours."

In her repertory choices Ms. Sutherland ranged widely during the 1950s, singing lighter lyric Mozart roles like the Countess in "Le Nozze di Figaro" and heavier Verdi roles like Amelia in "Un Ballo in Maschera." Even then, astute listeners realized that she was en route to becoming something extraordinary.

In a glowing and perceptive review of her performance as Desdemona in Verdi's "Otello" at Covent Garden in London in late 1957, the critic Andrew Porter, writing in The Financial Times, commended her for not "sacrificing purity to power." This is "not her way," Mr. Porter wrote, "and five years on we shall bless her for her not endeavoring now to be 'exciting' but, instead, lyrical and beautiful."

She became an international sensation after her career-defining performance in the title role of "Lucia di Lammermoor" at Covent Garden—its first presentation there since 1925—which opened on Feb. 17, 1959. The production was directed by Franco Zeffirelli and conducted by the Italian maestro Tullio Serafin, a longtime Callas colleague, who elicited from the 32-year-old soprano a vocally resplendent and dramatically affecting portrayal of the trusting, unstable young bride of Lammermoor.

This triumph was followed in 1960 by landmark portrayals in neglected bel canto operas by Bellini: Elvira in "I Puritani" at the Glyndebourne Festival, the first presentation in England since 1887; and "La Sonnambula" at Covent Garden, the company's first production in half a century.

Ms. Sutherland's American debut came in November 1960 in the title role of Handel's "Alcina" at the Dallas Opera, the first American production of this now-popular work. Her distinguished Decca recording of "Lucia di Lammermoor" was released in 1961, the year of her enormously anticipated Metropolitan Opera debut in that same work, on Nov. 26.

Before she had sung a note, there was an enthusiastic ovation. Following the first half of Lucia's Mad Scene in the final act, which culminated in a glorious high E-flat, the ovation lasted almost five minutes. When she finished the scene and her crazed, dying Lucia collapsed to the stage floor, the ovation lasted 12 minutes.

At 5-foot-9, Ms. Sutherland was a large woman, with long arms and large hands, and a long, wide face. As her renown increased, she insisted that designers create costumes for her that compensated for her figure, which, as she admitted self-deprecatingly in countless interviews, was somewhat flat in the bust but wide in the rib cage. Certain dresses could make her look like "a large column walking about the stage," she wrote in "The Autobiography of Joan Sutherland: A Prima Donna's Progress" (1997).

Paradoxically, Mr. Bonynge contributed to the sometimes dramatically uninvolved quality of her performances. By the mid-1960s he was her conductor of choice, often part of the deal when she signed a contract.

Joan Alston Sutherland was born on Nov. 7, 1926, in Sydney, where the family lived in a modest house overlooking the harbor. Her mother, Muriel Sutherland, was a fine mezzo-soprano who had studied with Mathilde Marchesi, the teacher of the Australian soprano Nellie Melba, and was her daughter's principal teacher throughout her adolescence.

Ms. Sutherland's father, William, a Scottish-born tailor, had been married before. His first wife died during the influenza epidemic after World War I, leaving him with three daughters and a son. Ms. Sutherland was the only child of his second marriage. He died on the day of Ms. Sutherland's sixth birthday. Joan, along with her youngest half-sister and their mother, moved into the home of an aunt and uncle in the Sydney suburb of Woollahra.

At 16, facing the reality of having to support herself, Ms. Sutherland completed a secretarial course and took office jobs, while keeping up her vocal studies.

In 1951, with prize money from winning a vocal competition, she and her mother moved to London, where Ms. Sutherland enrolled at the opera school of the Royal College of Music. The next year, after three previous unsuccessful auditions, she was accepted into the Royal Opera at Covent Garden and made her debut as the First Lady in Mozart's "Zauberflöte."

In the company's landmark 1952 production of Bellini's "Norma," starring Maria Callas, Ms. Sutherland sang the small role of Clotilde, Norma's confi-dante. "Now look after your voice," Callas advised her at the time, adding, "We're going to hear great things of you."

"I lusted to sing Norma after being in those performances with Callas," Ms. Sutherland said in a 1998 interview. "But I knew that I could not sing it the way she did. It was 10 years before I sang the role. During that time I studied it, sang bits of it, and worked with Richard. But I had to evolve my own way to sing it, and I would have wrecked my voice to ribbons had I tried to sing it like her."

In 1955 she created the lead role of Jenifer in Michael Tippett's "Midsummer Marriage."

During this period Ms. Sutherland gave birth to her only child, Adam, who survives her, along with two grandchildren and Mr. Bonynge.

Ms. Sutherland was plain-spoken and down to earth, someone who enjoyed needlepoint and playing with her grandchildren. Though she knew who she was, she was quick to poke fun at her prima donna persona.

"I love all those demented old dames of the old operas," she said in 1961. "All right, so they're loony. The music's wonderful."

carried the vaudeville of esthetic nihilism to its logical conclusion. His exit was final, and the perfect complement to his output as an artist. Thus his life, as well as his much shorter career, was looked upon as esthetically significant (or insignificant, for some critics regarded the withdrawal of the Grand Dada as an escape from his own inadequacies as an artist).

But for the most part Duchamp maintained an aristocratic detachment and reserve from such speculations, politely nodding in acquiescence to the legend that he gave up art to play chess; or, with a thin smile crossing his sharply featured. ascetically gaunt face, describing his occupation of later years as that of "respirateur." He was, in the words of Lawrence Alloway, former curator of the Guggenheim Museum, "the Duke of Windsor of modern art." And even in his abdication he commanded the esteem of the avant-garde.

'Posterity Has to Decide'

"It is disastrous for an artist to declare—to defend his art," he said to a reporter late last year. "Posterity has to decide —and even if it is wrong all over the place it has the advantage of coming into being. I wish I could live another hundred years." "But," he added with a pensive smile and a moment's pause, "perhaps it would be better to be dead. You see, I find it perfectly acceptable to contradict myself."

Contradiction formed an important part of the ideological and artistic universe that Duchamp had created for himself. Finding scientific laws to

weeks were turned into critics by the 1913 Arm Show. At the center of pu ridicule, heaped primarily the cubist section of the e bition, Duchamp's "Nude scending a Staircase" stood the symbol of the insanity which modern art progressed.

The Association of Ameri Painters and Sculptors, org izers of the show, not only ticipated the clamor America's first exposure Europe's new, nonrepresen tional painting would gener they also helped to create circus atmosphere for its spection. Press releases delu the newspapers, which sponded enthusiastically v satirical cartoons and deri commentary. The "Nude" came an "explosion in a shin factory" and "a collection saddlebags." Big crowds f into the 69th Regiment mory, at Lexington Avenue 25th Street, and guards had restrain outraged art lov from damaging the painting

It was neither the nude the staircase, apparently, t had provoked them, but title, painted onto the canv which seemed to have little do with either—and the i of a nude descending instead traditionally reclining or sta ing.

'Time and Space'

Duchamp carefully explai the painting:

"It is an organization kinetic elements, an express of time and space through abstract presentation . of tion."

In trying to consider the tion of form through space

...last years, she continued to
be keenly observant of all that
went on around her. Until her
last birthday, Sept. 7, she rarely
failed to do a little painting
every day.

Grandma Moses is survived
by her daughter-in-law, Mrs.
Dorothy Moses; nine grandchildren and more than thirty
great-grandchildren.

A funeral service will be held
Saturday at 2 P. M. from the
painter's home. Burial will be
in the Maple Grove Cemetery
here.

_____

Crippled by Arthritis

Grandma Moses, whose paintings hang in nine museums in
the United St... in Vienna
and Paris, ...
picture when she was 76 years
old.

She took up painting because
arthritis had crippled her hands
so that she no longer could embroider. She could not hold a
needle, but she could hold a
brush, and she had been too
busy all her life to bear the
thought of being idle.

Two years later a New York
engineer and art collector, Louis
J. Caldor, who was driving
through Hoosick Falls saw
some of her paintings displayed
in a drug store. They were
priced from $3 to $5, depending
on size. He bought them all,
drove to the artist's home at
Eagle Bridge and bought ten
others she had there.

The next year, 1939, Grandma
Moses was represented in an exhibition of "contemporary un-

make us inclined to enjoy
simple and affirmative outlo...
of Grandma Moses."

As a self-taught "primitive
who in childhood began pain...
ing what she called "lam...
scapes" by squeezing out gra...
juice or lemon juice to get c...
ors, Grandma Moses has be...
compared to the great se...
taught French painter, Hen...
Rousseau, as well as to Bre...
ghel. Until the compariso...
were made, she had never hea...
of either artist.

Painted from Remembrance

Grandma Moses did all of h...
painting from remembrance ...
thing... ... She liked to
... ... she once sa...
and remember and imagi...
"Then I'll get an inspiration a...
start painting; then I'll forg...
everything, everything exce...
how things used to be and h...
to paint it so people will kn...
how we used to live."

She would sit on an old, ba...
tered swivel chair, perching ...
two large pillows. The Maso...
ite on which she painted wou...
lie flat on an old kitchen tab...
before her. There was no eas...
Crowding her in her "stud...
were an electric washer a...
dryer that had overflowed fr...
the kitchen.

For subject matter, Grandm...
Moses drew on memories of ...
long life as farm child, hir...
girl and farmer's wife. H...
first paintings had been se...
to the county fair along w...
samples of her raspberry ...

FREDERICK LAW OLMSTED

April 26, 1822–August 28, 1903

BOSTON—Frederick Law Olmsted, the famous landscape architect, died today at Waverly, Mass., aged 81 years. Death was due to weakness resulting from ill health and advanced age. His wife, two sons and a daughter, survive him.

For the last quarter of a century he had made his home at Brookline, near Boston, where for many years he had charge of the great system of suburban parks.

It is his work on Central Park, Manhattan, however, which placed Mr. Olmsted at the head of his profession and caused his services to be sought by many municipalities and persons. The formative period of his life work was passed in New York; but he found more general appreciation in New England and less opposition from city politicians.

Born at Hartford, Conn., in 1822, he studied at Phillips Academy, entered an importing house in New York, and followed the old track of adventurous youth in that period by shipping before the mast, thereby seeing something of China and the East Indies. On his return he studied engineering for a while at Yale, and determined to be a farmer.

After working on a farm in Connecticut, he took one of his own at Saybrook, moving later to Staten Island, where he farmed on the south side. At that time rich merchants of New York were beginning to lay out estates on Staten Island, as well as up the Hudson, and Olmsted's natural bent toward nature was exercised on the beautiful hills, forests, and views of Richmond County, as he saw attempts being made to introduce the art of the landscape gardener on a scale rarely seen on this side of the Atlantic.

In 1850, along with a brother and the late Charles Loring Brace, he crossed the ocean and made a pedestrian tour of Great Britain and parts of the Continent, observing the great English private parks and storing his mind with the results of the old landscape architecture as practiced by Dutch, French, and British artists. The trip was chronicled in a modest work in 1852 called "Walks and Talks of an American Farmer in England." Though spoken well of by British and American periodicals, this little book did not bring him money or fame.

It was in 1855 that failing health suggested a long tour on horseback through the Southern states. Henry J. Raymond, editor of The New York Times, printed a number of letters by Olmsted which were remarkable for their charming style, and owing to the growing excitement on the negro question excited the interest of all who were anxious to learn more of the situation of the black.

Olmsted was not a militant Abolitionist, but that made his criticism of slave labor from the economical side all the more powerful. "A Journey in the Seaboard Slave States, with Remarks on Their Economy," appearing in New York in 1856, made a great sensation throughout the United States and England.

It was followed next year by "A Journey Through Texas; or, A Saddle Trip on the Southwestern Frontier." He also edited T. H. Gladstone's "An Englishman in Kansas" and became one of the editors of Putnam's Magazine. A few years later, at the outbreak of the Civil War, appeared "A Journey in the Back Country," and in 1861 "Journeys and Explorations in the Cotton Kingdom," in two volumes.

Although the tremendous feeling at the outbreak of hostilities aided these publications, they are still most agreeable reading. Olmsted had graduated from farmer to publicist, but his most important life work was still before him. For this his previous career had prepared him in a most remarkable way.

In 1856 New York City had decided to forestall the inevitable northward movement by laying out a great park; a commission had been appointed, and chance threw one of the commissioners and Olmsted together at a watering place. Olmsted associated with him his friend, Calvert Vaux, and together they made a plan for Central Park, which in 1857 took the prize in a competition of 32 designs.

A partnership was formed, and it is to them we owe the beautiful breathing space of 800 acres, which has steadily grown more beautiful and more appreciated. In laying out Central Park, the narrowness of the plot, only from Fifth to Eighth Avenues, was a drawback. Another difficulty was the necessity of carrying transverse streets though the park without injury to its beauty and the feeling of seclusion necessary to the full enjoyment of the park.

It was owing to the art shown in this park that Olmsted was overwhelmed with commissions. Prospect and Washington Parks in Brooklyn, the parks of Montreal, Buffalo, Chicago, St. Louis, Milwaukee, Trenton, Detroit, and Bridgeport bear the stamp of his genius. The grand girdle of parks about Boston, the Capitol Park at Washington with the terraces, stairways, and approaches to the Capitol, are due to his initial effort.

It was he, indeed, who may be said to have created the title of landscape architect, now so worthily borne by many younger men, as opposed to the old title of landscape gardener or landscape engineer. Into the great polemic between the believers in formal gardening and those who think nature should be left as much as possible to herself he entered with no great zest.

During the Civil War Frederick Law Olmsted lived chiefly in Washington, where he was the leading spirit on the "Commission of Inquiry Regarding the Sanitary Condition of the Union Forces." Later he helped to organize the Southern Famine Relief Commission, still later the New York State Charities Aid Association.

He received from Yale, Harvard, and Amherst the degree of Master of Arts, followed 20 years later by the degrees of LL.D. from Harvard and Yale. He helped to found the Metropolitan Museum of Art and the American Museum of Natural History in Central Park.

In his later years he had been unable to work, but the pleasing characteristics of the man remained long after he had given up the practice of his profession. Personally Mr. Olmsted was a man who had great charm of manner, won perhaps in his long career as traveler and student of nature. His fine presence and handsome head will be sure to afford sculptors a grateful subject when Manhattan shall remember to erect his monument in or near Central Park.

STANFORD WHITE

November 9, 1853–June 25, 1906

Harry Kendall Thaw of Pittsburg, husband of Florence Evelyn Nesbit, former actress and artist's model, shot and killed Stanford White, the architect, on the roof of Madison Square Garden at 11:05 o'clock last night, just as the first performance of the musical comedy "Mamzelle Champagne" was drawing to a close.

Thaw, who is a member of a well-known and wealthy family, left his seat near the stage and in full view of the players and scores of persons shot White through the head.

Mr. White was the designer of the building on the roof of which he was killed. He it was who put Miss Nesbit, now Mrs. Thaw, on the stage.

Thaw, who was in evening clothes, had evidently been waiting for Mr. White, who entered the Garden at 10:55 and took a seat at a table five rows from the stage.

Thaw, who had a pistol concealed under his coat, placed it almost against the head of Mr. White and fired three shots. White's body tumbled from the chair.

On the stage a character was singing a song entitled "I Could Love a Million Girls." The refrain seemed to freeze upon his lips.

Then came the realization on the part of the audience that the farce had closed with a tragedy. A woman screamed. Many persons followed her example, and there was wild excitement.

In the meanwhile Thaw had reached the entrance to the elevators. Policeman Debes of the Tenderloin Station appeared and seized his arm.

"He deserved it," Thaw said to the policeman. "I can prove it. He ruined my life and then deserted the girl." Another witness said the word was "wife" instead of "life."

Mrs. Lizzie Hanlon, housekeeper for Mr. White at his residence, 121 East 21st Street, said: "Mr. White has been alone in the house for some time. Mrs. White has been away in the West for about three weeks or a month, but is now at her country residence at St. James, L.I."

Stanford White was born in this city on Nov. 9, 1853. He was the son of Richard Grant White and Alexina B. Mease. His father was well known as a critic, journalist, and essayist, and for more than 20 years served as Chief of the United States Revenue Marine Bureau for the District of New York. His mother was a daughter of Charles Bruton Mease.

The American head of the family was John White, who came to this country in 1632 from England and settled at Cambridge, Mass.

Stanford White was educated in the private schools of New York and by tutors, and received the degree of A.M. from New York College in 1883.

He began the study of architecture in the office of Charles T. Gabrill and Henry H. Richardson. From 1878 to 1881 he traveled and studied in Europe, and on his return formed a partnership with Charles F. McKim and William R. Mead, under the firm name of McKim, Mead & White.

The name of this firm is associated with some of the most notable architecture of the country, many examples of which were designed by Mr. White himself. He was the architect of the Villard house, on Madison Avenue, now the property of Whitelaw Reid; of the Madison Square Garden, the Century and the Metropolitan clubhouses, the Washington Arch, on Washington Square; the New York University, the University of Virginia, and many private residences throughout the country.

Among his most conspicuous works are the architectural features for the sculptures of Augustus Saint-Gaudens, notably the pedestal of the Farragut Statue, Madison Square; and the pedestals for the Lincoln and Logan Statues and the Adams Tomb, Washington, D.C.

He was the creator of interior designs which won great praise. Specimens of his work are shown in the Players and Metropolitan Club houses, the Villard residence, the Church of St. Paul the Apostle, and the Church of the Ascension, all of this city.

A work by which he will always be remembered, and which many of his friends consider the best specimen of his genius, is the Marble House, which he built at Newport for Mrs. William K. Vanderbilt. Its construction marked the zenith of his fame. He received carte blanche as to material and decoration. His bust now stands on a pedestal in the hall.

He had charge of the interior decorations for the Metropolitan Club. When the time came for building the University Club, the committee in charge told him that while the Metropolitan was superb they did not want him to copy it in the new structure. Although only a few years had elapsed since the Metropolitan was completed, he had discovered certain things which he thought he could improve, and these he embodied in what many call the handsomest clubhouse in the world.

In 1884 Mr. White married Bessie, daughter of Judge J. Lawrence Smith of New York. He leaves one son, Lawrence Grant White.

Mr. and Mrs. White have not been living together recently, and while the husband nominally retained his home at their house at Gramercy Park, he spent little time there.

Madison Square Garden, designed by him, and where he met his death, was known as his "pleasure house." When the Garden was nearing completion, he stipulated that he should have a suite of apartments in the tall tower.

For a busy man, who worked hard and achieved notable things, he devoted a great deal of time to the pleasures of friendship and sociability. He had a large acquaintance among actors and singers, lawyers and doctors and society folk. To them all he was known as "Stan."

He was never happier than when in the suite of apartments in Madison Square Garden, directly above the spot where he was killed. He was the supreme master and promoter of all the fun hatched there. It was an attractive place for suppers after the play or the horse show, and invitations to a function there were always highly prized.

AUGUSTE RODIN

November 12, 1840–November 17, 1917

PARIS—Auguste Rodin, the famous sculptor, died in his villa at Meudon, on the outskirts of Paris, after an illness of a few days.

Paul Laurens, the painter, said of Auguste Rodin: "He belongs to the race of those men who march alone."

And for most of the 77 years of his life the great sculptor marched alone, first battling the adversities of relentless poverty and hostile criticism and, in his latter years, alone at the head of an international army of enthusiastic admirers.

When Rodin presented one of his early pieces to the Academy of Fine Arts, he was told that his work did not "exhibit any evidence of talent." Some 50 years later critics were hailing him as the greatest sculptor of the world—save Michelangelo—since Phidias and Praxiteles. He faced starvation in his youth because he could not sell his statues, and in October, 1916, the French Chamber of Deputies accepted his gift of his works and art collections, valued at $400,000, and gave him for life the use of the Biron mansion in Paris, which became known as the Rodin Museum.

François Auguste Rodin was born in Paris on Nov. 12, 1840, of wretchedly poor parents. He entered a free drawing school in the Latin Quarter at 14 and, after several years of study, made a model in clay of one of his companions with which he tried to win entrance to the Academy of Fine Arts. He failed. Two more attempts resulted in failure. But he struggled on and submitted his work at every public examination that was held. Fortunately he came under the notice of Barye, the painter and sculptor of animals, who

carried Rodin's artistic education to the point from which he could pursue it alone.

At the age of 23 the future sculptor married. This move spurred him on in his task, for in less than 12 months he had produced his first masterpiece, entitled "L'homme au Nez Cassé."

This was submitted to the judges at the Salon in 1864 and promptly refused; he took it home and treasured it carefully. After his countrymen had recognized his talent, he had this bust cast in bronze, in which form it crossed the Channel and was shown at the Grosvenor Gallery in 1881.

After the Franco-German war, Rodin migrated to Brussels, where he executed a great deal of work, besides sending two busts to the Paris Salon: both were accepted, and placed on exhibition in 1875. Two years later he was further recognized with the "Age d'Airain," or "Primeval Man," which represents one of the first inhabitants of our world, physically perfect but in the infancy of comprehension. The claims of this amazing statue could not be overlooked by the Salon committee when Rodin brought the work to Paris. So realistic was it that some of the sculptor's critics hinted that the figure must have been molded from the living model.

But Rodin was not yet free from criticism and ridicule. The school of orthodoxy in sculpture was as hostile to him as were the orthodox musicians to Wagner. Rodin did not idealize his subjects, but aimed for realism, going to nature for his inspiration. He saw in the shaking form of an old man or woman, with bowed head and twisted limbs, something as worthy of artistic expression as a Venus or Apollo.

Even after he had won fame, Rodin's work was sometimes ridiculed. His statue of Balzac, for example, was received with jest and gibe. It was an extraordinary and unconventional conception of the great novelist, but the Parisian public became so worked up over the monument that the controversy for the time eclipsed interest even in the sensational Dreyfus trial.

Balzac was represented in a voluminous dressing gown, the features and figure roughly sketched. Critics exclaimed that it was "an enormous porpoise standing upright, draped in a thick bath wrapper." They called it grotesque and flippant; while on the other side there were those who saw in it "the incarnation of the great writer's soul." The society which had ordered it, however, found the work incomprehensible, if not ridiculous, and it gave the commission to the sculptor Falguière, who executed a more conventional work the following year.

Rodin's Victor Hugo was received with more appreciation, and by many is considered one of his masterpieces.

The sculptor was a tireless worker, the quantity of his work being as amazing as its quality. His greatest output in one year was in 1889. No less than 31 pieces of sculpture were put on view at the Georges Petit Gallery that year, among them some of the best of Rodin's life work, such as "Ugolino," "The Danaid," "The Thinker," "Bastien Lepage," and "The Bourgeois of Calais."

For years after the Balzac controversy Rodin devoted himself to a great decorative composition some

20 feet high, "The Portal of Hell," for the Museum of Decorative Arts. This work was inspired mainly by Dante's Inferno, the poet himself being seated at the top, while at his feet is the writhing of passion and [the] anguish of despair.

"The Thinker," one of the figures designed for "The Portal of Hell," has been exhibited in cast at the Metropolitan Museum of Fine Arts in New York. The Metropolitan has also obtained the largest single collection of the works of Rodin outside the artist's own studios. There are 40 examples of his works in the museum.

Rodin executed a deed of gift to the French Government of the entire collection of his own works, other art objects he had acquired, and the Hotel Biron, in which they were assembled for a museum.

Rodin's drawings are almost as wonderful as his sculpture. An album with 142 drawings was published by Messrs. Goupil. In more recent times the experiments the great sculptor made with his pencil were on behalf of friends. He illustrated Bergerat's "Engerrande" and Octave Mirabeau's "Jardin des Suppliers," and ornamented a copy of Baudelaire's "Fleurs de Mal."

MARY CASSATT

May 22, 1844–June 14, 1926

PHILADELPHIA—Miss Mary Cassatt, artist of international reputation, and sister of the late A. J. Cassatt, once President of the Pennsylvania Railroad, died yesterday at Mesnil-Theribus, Oise, a suburb of Paris. She had lived abroad for many years.

In pursuing her art talents, Miss Cassatt's subjects were almost invariably women and children. Among her best known paintings are "The Bath," "Breakfast in Bed," "Mother's Caress," "Children Playing with a Cat," "In the Garden" and "Maternity."

She is represented in the Metropolitan Museum of New York and the Corcoran Art Gallery in Washington. —*The Associated Press*

Mary Cassatt has been described by a French critic as perhaps, with the exception of Whistler, "the only artist of an elevated, personal and distinguished talent actually possessed by America." The comment was made some 30 years ago, and it shows the lamentable ignorance that we all show when we attempt to estimate the work of a foreign country.

But it shows also the deep impression made by Miss Cassatt's achievement upon a trained mind accustomed to French standards. The artist's mind in turn was deeply impressed by French art. The strain

of French blood in her ancestry may have had something to do with her dedication to France.

In an interview with the critic Achille Segard, she dwelt upon this inheritance. Telling him that her family was of French origin, that her great-great-grandfather was the grandson of a Frenchman called Cossart, who emigrated from France to Holland in 1662, she added that her mother, whose ancestry was Scotch, nevertheless grew up in an atmosphere of French culture, was taught by an American who had been in a school conducted chiefly for young girls of the French aristocracy, and continued all her life to correspond in French with those of her friends who used that language.

Mary Cassatt was taken to Paris when she was five or six years old and remained there for about five years, after which she returned to America and went on with her education in Philadelphia. In 1868 she decided to become a painter, and she spent several years in European cities studying the old masters and their methods at the source, in the museums.

In Italy she devoted much of her time to Correggio and his school. "Prodigious master!" she exclaimed, and there is evidence that she never forgot the lessons she learned from him. Rubens at the Prado so enchanted her that she hastened from Madrid to Antwerp to see more of him. She spent an entire summer at Antwerp to study Rubens, and it was there that she met the engraver Joseph Tourny, who later was to bring her to Degas.

Before Miss Cassatt came back to Paris in 1874 to settle there, she had had pictures accepted by the Salons, but in 1877 Degas persuaded her to send no more work to the Salon but to exhibit instead with his friends the Impressionists. She accepted with joy. "At last," she said to M. Segard, "I could work with absolute independence, without concerning myself with the final opinion of a jury. Already I had recognized my true masters. I admired Manet, Courbet and Degas. I hated conventional art. I commenced to live."

In her earlier work, "Dans la Loge," "On the Balcony" and other paintings, are found intimations of Manet and Degas, nothing of Renoir or the Rubens who dominated her Antwerp summer. Nothing of Correggio or any other ancient master. She sprang, technically armed, into the revolutionary art of her day. Her line was firm and direct, her planes well understood, her balance of dark and light unhackneyed. She worked with energy and buoyancy.

The early dark pictures have a peculiarly strong appeal; they are definitely the work of youth. Their accent is French, with none of the awkwardness of a foreigner in the use of unfamiliar idiom.

Three or four years after her entrance into the circle of the Impressionist, she was beginning to find herself. Her subjects then, as later, were almost altogether confined to women and children. In raising the key of her palette, letting air into her pictures, she avoided pointillism. She used strong color, her flesh tones were inclined to be bricky, the solidity of form was emphasized, accurate construction and explicit statement of anatomical facts were preferred to freedom of brushwork and subtleties of modeling.

Three or four years more found her in full possession of the style that would ripen and enlarge but not change. Any of her later paintings are immediately recognized as hers. Her clear, accurate vision and passion for truth-telling have made no compromise with charm, but charm has been added to the sum of her qualities as an artist.

A classic instinct for the beauty of health led her toward the Greek ideal. Her young mothers, often plain of feature, are radiant with wholesome normal beauty, expressed in their natural gestures, their ease and poise, their fine proportions. Their children have the same aspect of soundness and serenity. They are fresh, strong and good-tempered. Dedicated to this type of the Mother and Child theme, Mary Cassatt brought to it the science of her severe training.

Seldom in this century has there been so rich a flowering of sentiment supported by science. In her latest work the warm and gracious sentiment alone are apparent to the casual observer.

As a painter Miss Cassatt became widely known quite promptly in her career. Her prints even now are known to a comparatively restricted public.

Nevertheless she produced a considerable number, over 160 plates.

Her dry-points were made directly on the copper. Many are modeled fully so far as the head and shoulder are concerned, with the rest of the figure left in outline. Certain portrait heads done in this fashion are amazing in their realization of character. Amazing, because with so little salience of feature, the ordinary, rather inexpressive countenance of the subject has been probed for its exact measure of significance. To be at once so dull and so interesting is the supreme triumph of portraiture.

There are several plates of children past the age of infancy. One leaning wearily against the back of a chair, a heavy little head sagging on a thin childish neck, is especially rich in expression.

At one moment in her exploration of the graphic arts Miss Cassatt turned toward the color printing of Japan and produced a number of examples printed in color in the spirit of the Japanese, with exclusive concern for the contemporary scene.

It is none of these prints, however, admirable, vigorous and subtle as they are, that gives us the best account of Mary Cassatt's talents.

For the spirit of her invention, we must turn to plates upon which she has made rapid notations of children's heads, or to the aquatints upon which she has painted with a brushful of thick varnish. One of the latter shows an interior with a woman seated, her back to a window. The light pours in, touches the side of her face, her shoulder, her knee, and hounds to the glass doors of some bookshelves in the background. The light is the picture and the artist has pursued it with broad dashing strokes and masculine energy.

It is too soon for anything like a considered review of her achievement. At the moment one can say only that a vision, large and opulent and refined, has given us work that will live through all changes of sentiment and theory.

FRIDA KAHLO

July 6, 1907–July 13, 1954

Mexico City—Frida Kahlo, wife of Diego Rivera, the noted painter, was found dead in her home today. Her age was [47]. She had been suffering from cancer for several years.

She also was a painter and also had been active in leftist causes. She made her last public appearance in a wheelchair at a meeting here in support of the now ousted regime of Communist-backed President Jacobo Arbenz Guzman of Guatemala —*Associated Press*

Frida Kahlo began painting in 1926 while obliged to lie in bed during convalescence from injuries suffered

in a bus accident. Not long afterward she showed her work to Diego Rivera, who advised, "go on painting." They were married in 1929, began living apart in 1939, were reunited in 1941.

Usually classed as a surrealist, the artist had no special explanation for her methods. She said only: "I put on the canvas whatever comes into my mind." She gave one-woman shows in Mexico City, New York and elsewhere, and is said to have been the first woman artist to sell a picture to the Louvre.

Some of her pictures shocked beholders. One showed her with her hands cut off, a huge bleeding heart on the ground nearby, and on either side of her an empty dress. This was supposed to reveal how she felt when her husband went off alone on a trip. Another self-portrait presented the artist as a wounded deer, still carrying the shafts of nine arrows.

A year ago, too weak to stand for more than ten minutes, she sat daily at her easel, declaring: "I am happy to be alive as long as I can paint."

HENRI MATISSE

December 31, 1869–November 3, 1954

PARIS—The world of art today mourned Henri Matisse, one of France's greatest painters, who died in his apartment in Nice yesterday of a heart attack. He was 84 years old.

Death came swiftly to the aged artist, who had been a semi-invalid since undergoing an operation in 1940. At his bedside was his daughter, Mme. Marguerite Duthite.

Jean Cassou, director of the Museum of Modern Art in Paris, recalled that Matisse, bedridden much of the time after his operation, continued to work from his room.

"Henri Matisse is one of the last representatives of French genius," he said. "If the title of master suits any artist, it certainly suited him. All men deserving of this name, all men who think, can consider themselves as his disciples. His thinking has illuminated our era."

André Berthoin, Minister of National Education, in a statement on the death of the artist, said: "His was the most French of palettes. Intelligence, reason and the alliance of a sense of finesse and of simplifying geometry gave to all he painted the rare virtue of being truly French." Matisse's two sons, Jean and Pierre, arrived in Nice tonight to attend the funeral.

Henri Matisse, leader of young rebel artists who brought the modern art movement into being in Paris a half century ago, was a master of color, a supreme draftsman who imbued a relatively small range of subject matter with constant variety.

The artist's long career, begun with years of academic schooling, became set in its brilliant revolutionary course in 1905, when with Rouault, Derain, Dufy, Vlaminck and others, Matisse set Paris on its ears in the Autumn Salon. The painters were excoriated as fauves—wild beasts—and their flaming, defiant canvases were condemned.

On June 25, 1951, thousands of people crowded the small village of Vence in southern France to see the Bishop bless what Matisse had called his "masterpiece"—a chapel on which he had started work four years before.

Ailing and bedridden through much of this period, Matisse serenely progressed with his decorations for the chapel, drawing his designs with a long charcoal-tipped stick on the walls of his bedroom, later copying them on tiles and transferring them to stained glass. This was his last work, he announced: "My bags are packed."

Matisse held no common ground with those who considered modern art as a new mode. He once said that every art is a logical reflection of the time in which it is produced—an orderly and rational development of what had gone before.

The artist was born on Dec. 31, 1869, the son of a grain merchant in Le Cateau in Picardy. The law had been chosen as his profession, and it took some persuasion over parental objections for Matisse to begin the art studies he yearned for.

In Paris he studied under Gustave Moreau, and from 1893 to 1896 he produced sober still lifes and other quiet pictures influenced by Chardin and Corot. He copied old masters in the Louvre. In later years, telling about it, he said, "One must learn to walk firmly on the ground before one tries the tightrope."

In 1893 he married Amélie Moellie Parayre. The family was supported through the sale of all the painter's still lifes to a dealer who paid 400 francs apiece for them.

Matisse said later: "One day I had just finished one of my pictures. It was quite as good as the previous one and very much like it, and I knew that on its delivery I would get the money which I sorely needed. I looked at it, and then and there a feeling came over me that it was not I, that it did not express me or express what I felt." The artist destroyed the picture, counting his emancipation from that day.

Matisse would emerge as an artist of great powers, but sections of the academic world called his work "not art, but a dangerous and infectious disease." In 1908, excited comment had followed an exhibition of Matisse's paintings in the Stieglitz Gallery of New York; in 1913, at the famed Armory Show, the artist was the center of stormy debate.

Through the years the artist grew in stature. He never left his explorations, and age only increased his daring as a colorist and his brilliance and gaiety. Numbers of authoritative writers on Matisse and leading connoisseurs regard him as the foremost painter of the day.

Matisse settled permanently in Nice in 1917. When World War II started, the artist was in Paris. He made his way by taxi and train back to Nice.

In 1941, his son Pierre reported that Matisse had undergone a serious operation. Friends tried to persuade the aging artist to leave France, but Matisse said: "If all the talented people left France, the country would be much poorer. I began an artist's life very poor, and I am not afraid to be poor again. . . . Art has its value; it is a search after truth and truth is all that counts."

Around the time of his 83rd birthday, in a piece he wrote for the United Nations Educational, Scientific and Cultural Organization, Matisse said a little more of his theory of art.

"An artist has to look at life without prejudices, as he did when he was a child," he wrote. "If he loses that faculty, he cannot express himself in an original, that is, in a personal way."

By way of illustration he said there was nothing more difficult for a truly creative painter than to paint a rose.

"Because before he can do so," explained the artist, "he has first of all to forget all the roses that were ever painted."

JACKSON POLLOCK

January 28, 1912–August 11, 1956

SOUTHAMPTON, L.I.—Eight persons were killed and at least four others were injured in two separate automobile accidents near here tonight.

One of the dead was identified as Jackson Pollock, abstract painter. He was 44 years old.

A head-on collision on Montauk Highway at 10:43 P.M., four miles west of Southampton village, took the lives of six persons and injured three others.

The accident occurred when eastbound and westbound automobiles crashed at a curve on the two-lane highway in the Shinnecock Hills section of Southampton Town.

Mr. Pollock's convertible turned over three miles north of East Hampton, according to witnesses. The accident occurred shortly after 10 P.M. on Fireplace Road.

A woman riding in the car was killed and another woman, identified by Southampton hospital authorities as Ruth Kligman, was injured. The police were unable to determine the cause of the accident, but said the automobile had smashed into an embankment.

Traffic on the highway, also known as Route 27, was backed up for half a mile in both directions and was tied up for an hour and a half.

Mr. Pollock became known for an unorthodox painting technique of putting his canvas flat on the floor and dripping paint onto it. Some critics praised his paintings as "the most original art among the painters of his generation," while others dismissed his work as "unorganized explosions of random energy."

Once a student of Thomas Hart Benton, Mr. Pollock turned away from his teacher's "American Scene" realism and developed his own abstract style. After his one-man show in 1943, he had 10 solo exhibitions in New York within 11 years and won recognition in Europe as a leading abstract expressionist.

Mr. Pollock was married to Lee Krasner, an established painter in her own right. Acquaintances here said that she was now in Europe. For the last 10 years the couple had been living near East Hampton, where Mr. Pollock converted a nearby barn into a studio.

Mr. Pollock was born in 1912 on his father's farm near Cody, Wyo. He grew up in Wyoming, Arizona and California. Showing an aptitude for painting, he left Los Angeles High School at 17 to travel to New York, where he studied at the Art Students League for two years.

It was there, Mr. Pollock once said, that Benton gave him the "only formal instruction" he ever had.

In the early Forties he reacted against his earlier naturalistic approach and began painting in a semi-abstract, expressionist idiom.

By 1947 he had evolved the "dripped paint" technique that characterized the best-known period of his work.

A retrospective show covering 18 years of his work opened at the Sidney Janis Gallery in November, 1955. The exhibition comprised 16 canvases representing the artist's different artistic periods.

The New York Times critic commented at the time on "the ruthless steps he has taken to shatter the conventions of art and introduce, for the first time in art, raw and naked, the elemental and largely subconscious promptings of his creative nature."

CHRISTIAN DIOR

January 21, 1905–October 23, 1957

MONTECATINI, Italy—Christian Dior, for many years the leader in the world of fashion design, died here early today of a heart attack. His age was 52.

M. Dior, who tended to conservative suits and ties for his own attire, died at the Hotel La Place. He had been vacationing in northern Italy for the last week.

M. Dior's greatest feat was the "New Look" in 1947, when he seized and held for France the style leadership of the world after it had threatened to pass to the United States in the post-war years. For his achievement the French Government awarded the Legion of Honor to him.

He always denied any intention of making fashion sensations. "Changes just come about and many things contribute when everybody is ready for them," he once said.

In a book, he wrote that styles go in cycles, with a complete revolution about every seven years. The post-war year 1947, he said, was the psychological time to bring back femininity.

One of his precepts was "to make elegant women more beautiful; to make beautiful women more elegant." M. Dior once credited the fame of his creations to this credo: Please the ladies by enabling them to please their men.—*The Associated Press*

"Cri-cri," as he was called by his intimates, was by his scope as well as by his styles Designer Number One in the world of high fashion. He branched out faster and farther than any other couturier ever had.

The Dior interests at his death included not only the original Maison Dior on the Avenue Montaigne in Paris—a business structure of mirrored and chandeliered elegance—but also Dior enterprises in 24 countries, reporting grossing $15,000,000 a year.

His creation of the long hemline and full skirt in 1947—called the "New Look"—set off an international controversy, but clearly re-established Paris on its fashion throne.

But behind the vast Dior enterprises was always the plump, pink-cheeked master, who twice each year went into seclusion to create the newest designs. And much of that time he spent in the bathtub. There he soaked, and pondered a new line, and sketched his ideas on scraps of paper.

Other Dior innovations included the Zigzag (generous decollete), the Vertical (high value on the bosom, leaving to the legs their length and elegance) and the Tulip (high bosom).

M. Dior saw more than mere cloth-cutting in his world of fashion. "In a machine age," he once declared, "dressmaking is one of the last refuges of the human, the personal, the inimitable. In an epoch as somber as ours, luxury must be defended inch by inch."

He had no intention, as a young man, to become a dressmaker. The son of a wealthy chemical fertilizer manufacturer, young Dior—born at Granville, France, on Jan. 21, 1905—was expected to go into diplomacy.

But at the age of 23, influenced by friendships he had formed with a number of artists, he became an art dealer. His gallery was said to have been among the first to exhibit surrealist paintings, displaying pictures by such friends of his as Salvador Dali, Christian Berard and Jean Cocteau.

In 1934, Mr. Dior became ill and was forced to give up the gallery. After convalescing, he returned to Paris. The Figaro Illustrated engaged him as an illustrator of haute couture. His designs for hats quickly captured feminine fancies in Paris.

When war broke out, he was mustered into the French Army in the Engineers. In 1941, he became a designer for Lucien Lelong, and in 1946, he set up his own salon.

It was almost big business from the start, operated on terms of big business unknown to other firms in the fashion world. The organization includes general statistical surveys and a program against copying that permitted the immediate identification of dresses sold in France and overseas.

A Dior presentation was one of the high points of the fashion world, but M. Dior once described the opening of his shows this way: "The dressing room is a picture of hell, whereas to the public it has to appear as a bouquet."

FRANK LLOYD WRIGHT

June 8, 1867–April 9, 1959

PHOENIX—Frank Lloyd Wright, regarded by many as the greatest architect of the 20th century, died early today in St. Joseph's Hospital. He was 91 years old.

Mr. Wright, who considered himself "the greatest living architect," was admitted to the hospital Monday night for emergency surgery to remove an intestinal obstruction. His physician said he was "getting along satisfactorily and then suddenly died."

From his estate, Taliesin West, northeast of Phoenix, Mr. Wright designed a new Capitol for Arizona. He proposed an "oasis in the desert, its fountains and greenery contrasting with the sand and rocks around it." The plan created a controversy and was rejected.

When a group of architects proposed a skyscraper type of building for a Capitol, Mr. Wright looked at the drawing and described it as "a sidewalk-happy chimneypot with a derby hat on top, a poor version of a poor original—the United Nations Building in New York."

This was typical of Mr. Wright's comments, for which he was almost as well known as his buildings. He condemned retiring at 60 as a "murderous custom" and pleaded for a curb to America's "lust for ugliness."

A gradual change in the architect's fame, fortune and attitude might have been marked on May 28, 1953, when he received the Gold Medal Award of the National Institute of Arts and Letters. He then said:

"A shadow falls; I feel coming on me a strange disease—humility."

During his lifetime Mr. Wright was in turn the great radical of American architecture and the acknowledged leader of a flourishing modern school of building.

This change in status did not evolve through any relaxation of his uncompromising theory that form in building should follow function, but rather in the public's gradual acceptance of his doctrine and deviations.

Hailed in Europe in his early years as the creator of an American architecture, he did not so readily gain acceptance in his own country, where the skyscraper was king. Although trained by Louis Sullivan, who was known as the "father of the skyscraper," Mr. Wright was strong in his condemnation of that peculiarly American architectural phenomenon.

He scathingly condemned the topless towers of New York. He had no use for the great steel and stone cities; he denounced the "box" house in this country, calling the design "a coffin for the human spirit."

His own philosophy was enunciated in low terrain-conforming homes that became known as "prairie architecture"; in functional office buildings of modest height utilizing such materials as concrete slabs, glass bricks and tubing; in such monumental structures as the Imperial Hotel in Tokyo that withstood the great earthquake of 1923.

Mr. Wright was born on June 8, 1867, at Richland Center, Wis., the son of William Cary Wright and the former Anna Lloyd-Jones. His father became a minister, and gave young Frank a religious training. From his mother, who was a school teacher, it was said that he developed the idea of being an architect. From both parents he developed a strong individuality and the rebellious quality that characterized him and his work.

As a boy he attended public school in Wisconsin and then was sent to the University of Wisconsin to study civil engineering. Deciding he wanted to be an architect, Mr. Wright left college in his last year and headed not for Paris and the École des Beaux Arts, but, with his typical individuality, for Chicago.

There he found work in the drafting room of Louis Sullivan, the French-Irish Bostonian who had rebelled against classic architecture. Although he and Sullivan were inevitably to disagree, they had in common an opposition against the classic form.

Sullivan taught the young apprentice the ground rules of architecture and instilled in him his ideas for radical design. After four years they quarreled and Mr. Wright set up his own office. But throughout his life he referred to Sullivan, who died in 1927, as "der Meister."

Mr. Wright naturally took to rebellion. From the very beginning his designs were different from anything that had been built before—"designed-for-living" bungalows. He built the first one for himself and his bride, the former Catherine Tobin, whom he married when he was 21. She was 19. They had met at a church social.

The couple went to live at Oak Park, a Chicago suburb noted for its many churches. There the Wrights' six children were born: Lloyd and John, who became architects; Catherine, David, Frances and Llewellyn.

The architect's Oak Park houses were low bungalows, free of fancy woodwork, dormer windows, corner towers or towering chimneys. The horizontal planes of the structures were accentuated. They "hugged the earth."

Among architects the houses created a sensation. Soon Mr. Wright's designs became known as "prairie architecture" because they fitted so snugly into the flat landscape for which they were made. In Europe they were widely hailed; America, for the most part, still chose to ignore both the builder and his creations.

When Mr. Wright gained fame in his own country, it was not through his already substantial contribution to modern American architecture, but through scandal and tragedy.

In 1909 he went to Germany to arrange for publication of the portfolio of his work and some essays on architecture. A short time before, he had built a house for E. H. Cheney, a neighbor at Oak Park. When the architect sailed for Germany, Mrs. Cheney went with him.

When they returned, Mr. Wright built perhaps his most famous structure, his own home, Taliesin ("Shining brow" in his ancestral Welsh), in Spring Green, Wis., on a commanding site overlooking the Wisconsin River. It was to be a "refuge" for Mrs. Cheney, whose husband had divorced her.

On Aug. 15, 1914, tragedy struck Taliesin. Mrs. Cheney, her two children and four other persons were killed by a crazed servant, who also burned the house to the ground. Mr. Wright later rebuilt Taliesin, determined, as he said, "to wipe the scar from the hill."

Meanwhile, publication in Germany of Mr. Wright's work had come to the attention of the Emperor of Japan, who in the fall of 1915 sent a delegation of officials and architects to ask him to submit plans for a $4,500,000 hotel in Tokyo. The architect made sketches, which were accepted, and went to Japan to superintend the building of the hotel.

His greatest problem was to foil the earthquakes that periodically brought destruction and death to Japan. The Imperial Hotel was an elastic structure, the walls and floors having a sliding quality never before attained. Its plumbing was designed so that pipes would not break, and the electric wiring was placed so that temblors would not cause short circuits and charge the building with high-voltage death.

It was completed in 1922. A year later fierce quakes rocked Tokyo and Yokohama. Nearly 100,000 persons died under collapsing walls and falling roofs or were burned to death in the holocaust that followed. Days later, when communication between Tokyo and the outside world was re-established, word went out that the Imperial Hotel was the only large structure that had survived the disaster.

In the next few years domestic trouble continued to harass the architect. He had been estranged from his first wife, who finally consented to divorce him after his return from Tokyo. His second marriage, to Miriam Noel, a sculptor, was brief. They were married in 1923 and divorced in 1927. The next year Mr. Wright married Olga Lazovich. They had a daughter, Iovanna.

Through controversy and criticism the architect rose steadily. His critics declared he was not only ahead of his time, but also ahead of all time; his disciples and admirers made extravagant claims for his work.

Gradually he began to gain vogue and commissions. Among the structures for which he became famous were the Midway Gardens in Chicago, the

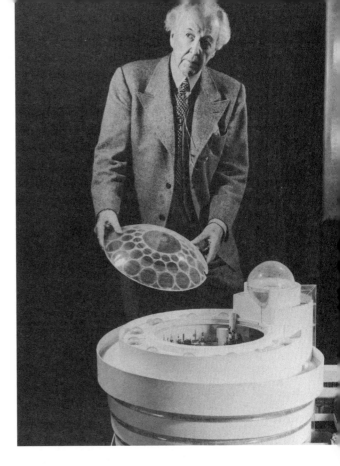

Larkin Company administration building in Buffalo, the S.C. Johnson Company building at Racine, Wis.; the Falling Water House of Edgar J. Kaufmann at Bear Run, Pa., which he built above a waterfall, and the Price Tower at Bartlesville, Okla.

There also was the circular Friedman house near Pleasantville, N.Y., in a cooperative development known as Usonia Houses. Usonia was the descriptive word used by Mr. Wright to typify what he considered to be the ideal American architectural style.

Even as an octogenarian who had received many prizes and honors, including election to the American Academy of Art and Letters, the white-haired individualist was still capable of stirring up the critics.

His plans for a building in Yosemite National Park were rejected ("politics," he snorted); and Venice turned down his plans for a glass and marble palace on the Grand Canal ("the tourists have won," he said).

And so he continued to live his later years, much as the earlier ones, hard at work and deep in discussion with his fellowman. At 89 he continued his teaching at Taliesin with 65 architectural students. Working a full day, he emerged often to make a public appearance in flowing tie, white hair under porkpie hat, and to make a characteristic utterance.

Besides his wife and children, Mr. Wright leaves a sister, nine grandchildren and eight great-grandchildren. His daughter Frances died last February. One of his grandchildren is Anne Baxter, the film actress.

One of Mr. Wright's favorite targets for caustic comment and criticism was New York's forest of skyscrapers. It was not until 1945 that he received his first commission in the city—the new home of the

Solomon R. Guggenheim Museum, on Fifth Avenue at 88th Street.

"For the first time art will be seen as if through an open window, and, of all places, in New York," he said. "It astounds me."

When the design was published, an avalanche of cheers and derision was loosed. The "little temple" was hailed by Wright partisans; by others it was called, variously, a "washing machine," a "hot cross bun," a "marshmallow."

Even some of the stanchest supporters of the gifted architect "shuddered" to envision the museum—cylindrical in shape—in its environment of staid, decades-old apartment buildings. Mr. Wright was imperturbable.

He stood firm on disputed specifications, such as a plexiglass dome for the building and glass doors. The plans to start building were delayed several times but, finally, the museum was in construction in 1956. It is expected to be completed in a month or two.

GRANDMA MOSES

September 7, 1860–December 13, 1961

Hoosick Falls, N.Y.—Grandma Moses, the spry, indomitable "genuine American primitive" who became one of the country's most famous painters in her late 70s, died here today at the age of 101.

She died at the Hoosick Falls Health Center, where she had been a patient since August. Her physician, Dr. Clayton E. Shaw, said the best way to describe the cause of death was to say, "She just wore out."

The simple realism, nostalgic atmosphere and luminous color with which Grandma Moses portrayed homely farm life and rural countryside won her a wide following. She was able to capture the excitement of winter's first snow, Thanksgiving preparations and the new, young green of oncoming spring.

Gay color, action and humor enlivened her portrayals of such simple farm activities as maple sugaring, soap-making, candle-making, haying, berrying and the making of apple butter.

A tiny, lively woman with mischievous gray eyes and a quick wit, she could be sharp-tongued with a sycophant and stern with an errant grandchild. Until her last birthday, Sept. 7, she rarely failed to do a little painting every day.

Grandma Moses is survived by her daughter-in-law, Mrs. Dorothy Moses; nine grandchildren and more than 30 great-grandchildren.

Grandma Moses, whose paintings hang in nine museums in the United States and in Vienna and Paris, turned out her first picture when she was 76 years old. She took up painting because arthritis had crippled her hands so that she no longer could embroider.

Two years later a New York engineer and art collector, Louis J. Caldor, saw some of her paintings displayed in a Hoosick Falls drugstore. They were priced from $3 to $5. He bought them all, drove to the artist's home at nearby Eagle Bridge and bought 10 others she had there.

The next year, 1939, Grandma Moses was represented in an exhibition at the Museum of Modern Art in New York. A show of her paintings was held in New York in 1940, and other one-man shows abroad followed. Her paintings were soon reproduced on Christmas cards, tiles and fabrics here and abroad. She was the guest of President and Mrs. Harry S. Truman in 1949 at a tea at which the President played the piano for her.

Governor [Nelson] Rockefeller proclaimed the painter's 100th and 101st birthdays "Grandma Moses Days" throughout the state, declaring this year that "There is no more renowned artist in our entire country today."

But to say that she was an American painter was less than the full portrait of Grandma Moses; European critics called her work "lovable," "fresh," "charming," "adorable" and "full of naive and childlike joy." A German fan offered his explanation for her wide popularity:

"There emanates from her paintings a light-hearted optimism; the world she shows us is beautiful and it is good. You feel at home in all these pictures, and you know their meaning. The unrest and the neurotic insecurity of the present day make us inclined to enjoy the simple and affirmative outlook of Grandma Moses."

As a self-taught "primitive," who in childhood began painting what she called "lamb-scapes" by squeezing out grape juice or lemon juice to get colors, Grandma Moses has been compared to the great self-taught French painter, Henri Rousseau, as well as to Breughel.

Grandma Moses did all of her painting from remembrance. She liked to sit quietly and think, she once said, and remember and imagine. "Then I'll get an inspiration and start painting; then I'll forget everything, everything except how things used to be and how to paint it so people will know how we used to live."

She would sit on an old, battered swivel chair, perching on two large pillows. The Masonite on which she painted would lie flat on an old kitchen table before her. There was no easel. Crowding her in her "studio" were an electric washer and dryer.

She would paint for five or six hours, and preferred the first part of the session because, as she said, her hand was fresher and "stiddier." At night, after dinner, she liked to watch television Westerns, not for the drama but because she liked to see horses.

Grandma Moses spent a lot of her time on what she called her "old-timey" New England landscapes: "First the sky, then the mountains, then the hills, then the trees, then the houses, then the cattle and then the people." Her tiny figures, disproportionately small, cast no shadows. They seem sharply arrested in action.

She learned to observe nature when her father took the children out for walks. He was a Methodist, but never went to church, and he allowed his children to believe what they wanted. Instead of going to church, they went for long walks in the woods.

During her lifetime she painted more than 1,000 pictures, 25 of them after she had passed her 100th birthday. Her oils have increased in value from those early $3 and $5 works to $8,000 or $10,000 for a large picture.

Grandma Moses, the former Anna Mary Robertson, was born at Greenwich, N.Y., in 1860, one of 10 children of Russell King Robertson and the former Margaret Shannahan. What little formal education she had was obtained in a one-room country school.

At the age of 12, she left home to work as a hired girl. At 27, she married Thomas Salmon Moses, the hired man on the farm where she was doing the housework.

The couple took a wedding trip to North Carolina. On the way back, they decided to invest their $600 savings in the rental of a farm near Staunton, Va.

They remained in Virginia for 20 years. They had 10 children, five of whom died in infancy. The couple returned to New York State and began farming at Eagle Bridge. Mr. Moses died there in 1927. For several years his widow operated the farm with the help of a son. She had to give up farm chores when arthritis attacked her hands.

In "My Life's History," her 1951 autobiography, she expressed her philosophy: "I look back on my life like a good day's work, it was done and I feel satisfied with it. I was happy and contented, I knew nothing better and made the best out of what life offered. And life is what we make it, always has been, always will be."

LE CORBUSIER

October 6, 1887–August 27, 1965

ROQUEBRUNE CAP-MAR-TIN, France—Le Corbusier, the architect, died of a heart attack today while swimming off this Riviera resort. He was 77 years old.

The architect is survived by a brother living in Switzerland. His wife wife died in 1957. They had no children. —*The Associated Press*

Charles-Edouard Jeannert-Gris, whose professional name was Le Corbusier, was as contentious in his manner as he was influential in his architectural ideas. "I am like a lightning conductor: I attract storms," he said.

Disputes swirled about him and his conceptions for more than 40 years, and in them he was almost always a temperamental participant, for he regarded himself, especially in his later years, as beset by red tape, politics and underappreciation.

Nevertheless, his influence was so enormous and so persuasive that there are few areas in modern building and city planning in which it is not reflected. Le Corbusier, according to Arthur Drexler of the Museum of Modern Art, was one of the three greats in modern

architecture, the others being Ludwig Mies van der Rohe and the late Frank Lloyd Wright.

Le Corbusier's output was not large—fewer than 100 buildings—yet it was distinctive. Among outstanding examples of his work are the Visual Arts Center at Harvard University in Cambridge, Mass.; the Ronchamp Chapel at Vosges, France; the capital buildings for the Punjab at Chandigarh, India; an apartment house at Marseilles and another in Berlin; a 10-story glass-walled office building in Moscow; a Salvation Army center in Paris, and the Ministry of Education building in Rio de Janeiro. That structure, a honeycomb of sun-shading, breeze-admitting vanes at the windows, was widely copied in South America, notably in Brasilia.

There are no examples of pure Le Corbusier in New York. The overall conception of the United Nations Secretariat Building, at 43d Street and the East River, was his, but the bold design was toned down, much to his annoyance. When the structure was finished, he complained:

"A new skyscraper, which everyone calls the 'Le Corbusier Building,' has appeared in New York. L-C was stripped of all his rights, without conscience and without pity."

The Lever Building on Park Avenue, which appears to be built on stilts, also incorporates one of Le Corbusier's fundamental notions—that the massive bulk of a big building should be offset by placing it on uprights and that pedestrians should be allowed to pass underneath the main structure.

In his early days, before he saw New York, Le Corbusier praised American skyscrapers, but he took one look at the city's slab buildings and crowded canyons and announced:

"Your skyscrapers are too small!"

Not only was Manhattan a jungle of masonry, he said, but the Hudson and East Rivers were also hidden and New York Harbor was lost. Nonetheless, Le Corbusier liked some aspects of the United States.

He said in 1935: "New York is the most beautiful manifestation of man's power, courage, enterprise and force, but it is utterly lacking in order and harmony and the comforts of the spirit. The skyscrapers are little needles all crowded together. They should be great obelisks, far apart, so that the city would have space and light and order. Those are the things that men need just as much as they need bread or a place to sleep."

The architect was quick to see hostility toward him. "For 50 years I have gotten kicks in the rear," he said last April.

He enunciated his architectural credo in the nineteen-twenties, saying: "Architecture has nothing to do with the various 'styles.' The styles are to architecture what a feather is on a woman's head; it is something pretty, though not always, and never anything more. Architecture has graver ends . . . Mass and surface are the elements by which it manifests itself."

Structure, Le Corbusier went on, is what makes a building beautiful, and he singled out the "great primary forms"—cubes, cones, spheres, cylinders and pyramids. These, he said, are always beautiful, and what can be reduced to these basic shapes is good architecture.

In the theories of Le Corbusier, the notion of "ma-

chine" has an important place. Just as he considered that, in relation to printing, "the picture is a machine of emotion," so he was the inventor of the phrase "a house is a machine to live in," and it reflected his iconoclastic, experimental attitude. Some critics thought it also represented a too austere and even inhuman view of man.

Yet Le Corbusier had always represented himself as the pioneer of an essentially gracious architecture. Thus, in order of importance, he ranked the "raw materials" of the urbanist: the sky, trees, iron, cement; he wished to bring man the "essential joys" to which all have right—the sun, space, verdure.

From this state of mind stem his principles of architecture: primal importance of the site; its exposure to the sun; the support wall, made useless by the steel framework and replaced by a glass sheet; the street belongs to the pedestrian (automobile and rail traffic go underground or overhead); construction on piles (the house is healthier and the ground disencumbered); pure air, cleansed of the toxic fumes of the city and obtained from a system of ventilation incorporated in the building, etc.

On such principles Le Corbusier, an enthusiastic town planner, drew up plans for Paris, Antwerp, Algiers, Buenos Aires, Montevideo and towns in India.

His masterpiece was his predominant share in making Chandigarh, the new city built from scratch on the plains of the Punjab, India, from 1951 to 1957. In this great work, Le Corbusier softened the rigidity of some of his characteristic forms.

He bowed to the Indians' objection that their lack of elevator technicians precluded skyscraper construction. Chandigarh is a sprawling bungalow city.

The buildings for which he was primarily responsible—the Government center at its heart—contained numerous innovations to cope with India's scorching sun, and were built in undecorated, rough-finished concrete for reasons of economy.

Charles-Edouard Jeanneret-Gris was born Oct. 6, 1887, in La Chaux-de-Fonds, Switzerland. His father was an enameler of watch faces.

After studying at the School of Fine Arts of his native town from 13 to 18, he studied in the ateliers of several eminent architects in Vienna, Paris and Berlin.

He moved to Paris in 1917. From 1920 to 1925 he wrote a series of articles in the magazine L'Esprit Nouveau that expressed his architectural philosophy and made him famous.

He was co-founder with the painter Amédée Ozenfant of this magazine, which propagated "purist" theories. Derived from cubism, it was the aim of "purism," which preached plastic severity, to react against the tendency to decoration, which at that time certain cubists seemed to be slipping into.

One important result was to establish his identity under the name Le Corbusier. He had chosen the pseudonym, the family name of his maternal grandmother, to keep his identity as architectural propagandist separate from that as aspiring painter. But Le Corbusier the architect eclipsed Jeanneret the artist.

A tireless international lecturer, he was also a trenchant writer. He originated the dictum that design should proceed "from within to without; the exterior is the result of an interior." He also wrote of New York and Chicago as "mighty storms, tornadoes, cataclysms, they are so utterly devoid of harmony."

The titles of the works in which Le Corbusier expressed his ideas reflect his humanistic modernism: "A House—A Palace" (1928), "The Radiant City" (1935), "When Cathedrals Were White" (1937) and "The House of Men" (1942).

The architect received several commissions after World War II when Europe badly needed rebuilding. His plan was adopted for the reconstruction of La Pallice, the port of La Rochelle. His "Maison Radieuse," a 17-story apartment house on stilts at Nantes-Rezé, Marseille, was constructed after difficulties with planning authorities and a suit by the Society for the Protection of Esthetic Beauty in France.

Le Corbusier's all-concrete chapel to replace a church destroyed by the war in the tiny town of Ronchamp, in the Vosges Mountains, caused a stir in 1955. The building had not a single straight line; its walls sloped inward or outward and the ceiling seemed to sag.

In 1930, Le Corbusier married Yvonne Gallis, a Monagesque. She was reputed to be a splendid cook and a calming influence on her volatile husband, although she was not enthusiastic over the walls of glass he built into their Paris apartment.

"I am tearing my hair out by the roots! All this light is driving me crazy!" she said shortly after they were wed, but she put up with it nonetheless.

DOROTHEA LANGE

May 26, 1895–October 11, 1965

SAN FRANCISCO—Dorothea Lange, whose documentary photographs captured the despair and hope of the nineteen-thirties, died Monday of cancer. She was 70 years old.

She leaves her husband, Dr. Paul Schuster Taylor, former chairman of the department of economics at the University of California at Berkeley; and two sons, Daniel Rhodes Dixon and John Goodness Dixon, children of a previous marriage to the late Maynard Dixon, an artist. —*United Press International*

Miss Lange used a knowing eye to record on film the plight of the "Oakies," the men, women and children who fled the Dust Bowl of the Middle West and Southwest more than 30 years ago. Her skill with a camera awakened the nation to a problem that it had ignored for years.

How she happened to apply her talents to these people interested observers long after her photographs were published in newspapers, magazines and books and shown in exhibitions at museums. She once explained it to an interviewer:

"Pictures are a medium of communication, and the subject must be something that you truly love or truly hate. Moreover, you have to know what you are going to do with the pictures afterwards."

Then she recounted the experience. She had been working in a studio turning out routine portraits, she recalled, when Roy Stryker began organizing a special group for the Farm Security Administration in the nineteen-thirties to tell the story of migratory workers. She was selected to join the group.

Miss Lange lived with the "Oakies" and suffered with them. Two of the photos she took, "White Angel" and an untitled view of a woman and her two children at a farm, have been shown repeatedly in exhibitions of memorable prints.

With Dr. Taylor, Miss Lange produced a book of pictures and text, "An American Exodus," that depicted what they had seen in the Dust Bowl. A reviewer noted:

"You see these American faces, strong, spare, anxious. Farmers with rugged idle hands. You see their covered wagons, their camps, the fields they have left. You will find it hard to forget this material of human erosion."

Miss Lange became interested in photography at an early age and spent more than half a century developing new techniques while continuing to work in the field. She had studied with Clarence White at Columbia University before opening a studio in San Francisco.

Her portrait "Migrant Mother" is in the Library of Congress. In 1960 it was selected by a University of Missouri panel as one of the 50 most memorable pictures of the last 50 years.

She enjoyed telling newcomers how to improve their work. "Pick a theme and work it to exhaustion," she advised them. "Then pick another, or handle several themes at a time. Let yourself loose on a theme. It is the only way to make the most of it."

Miss Lange had prepared a one-woman exhibition of her photography of the last half century. It will be shown at the Museum of Modern Art as a posthumous tribute, beginning Jan. 24.

EDWARD HOPPER

July 22, 1882–May 15, 1967

Edward Hopper, the celebrated painter of the American scene who was characterized as the painter of loneliness, died Monday, May 15, in his studio at 3 Washington Square North. He was 84 years old.

His widow, the former Josephine Nivison, who was also a painter, was with him. There are no other survivors.

Mr. Hopper attained a reputation as one of America's most distinguished and most individualistic painters. He remained resolutely determined to paint everyday subjects realistically throughout a long career that spanned numerous changes in contemporary art.

"My aim in painting," Mr. Hopper once observed. "has always been the most exact transcription possible of my most intimate impressions of nature."

"In general," he added, "it can be said that a nation's art is greatest when it most reflects the character of its people."

His city people sitting at the all-night lunch stand, his apartment dwellers reading newspapers in barren rooms, his plain-bodied girls dressing in the morning light, his usherettes trapped in the cheap and plushy gloom of the movie palace were painted by Mr. Hopper with a respect for their right to inner privacy in the face of mass living.

Mr. Hopper, who would study a subject for months and then paint it from memory, produced only a few paintings a year. Living simply in his Washington Square quarters, which contained two studios, a bedroom and a kitchen, he was secretive about his work. He painted in solitude in his bare, white-walled studio. Asked what he was painting, he would reply, "Go to my dealer."

Mr. Hopper hated ostentation, dressed simply in tweeds and ate frugally, sometimes eating with his wife in local restaurants and sometimes from cans in his apartment.

While contemporaries like Rockwell Kent and George Bellows gained swift fame when American art began to veer away from conservatism early in the 20th century, Mr. Hopper declined to follow the trends and labored for years in obscurity. He was 43 years old before recognition came to him.

The loneliness he probably felt as he worked aloof from dominant trends and influences pervades all of his work, and has become his hallmark. His carefully detailed Victorian houses, city streets, roadside lunch counters, theater interiors and New England cottages are typical parts of the American scene.

His reflective and personal style was modern in spirit without being quite attachable to any modern school; he put his faith neither in tradition nor in innovations but in his own vision.

Writing at the time of the retrospective exhibition of Mr. Hopper's work at the Whitney Museum of American Art in 1964, John Canaday, art critic of The New York Times, characterized the artist as "a rangy, big-boned man whose appearance suggests that he might have been a member of his college crew around the year 1900."

"Nothing suggests the wiry compactness of the long-distance runner," the critic continued "but a long-distance runner is what Edward Hopper has always been. His steady pace does not decrease from year to year, although today he is so far ahead of the field that you would think he might slow down a little."

Edward Hopper was born in Nyack, N.Y., on July 22, 1882. He came to New York to study art in 1900, and lived and worked here the rest of his life, except for summers in New England and short periods abroad.

His parents, Garrett Henry Hopper and the former Elizabeth Griffiths Smith, sent him to a private day school in Nyack, and he graduated from the local high school. During the winter of 1899–1900, he studied commercial illustration in New York. Shortly afterward he enrolled at the New York School of Art, where his fellow students included Mr. Bellows and Mr. Kent. For five years he worked under Kenneth Hayes Miller and Robert Henri, the latter a leading pioneer in the movement from idyllic to realistic painting scornfully dubbed the "Ash Can" school.

In 1913 the artist exhibited with other nonacademic painters at the revolutionary "Armory Show," and achieved his first sale, a canvas entitled "The Sailboat."

In 1915 Mr. Hopper turned to etching, and his etchings were hailed as lasting contributions to

American art. But heartened by an exhibition of his watercolors at the Rehn Galleries here in 1924, Mr. Hopper resumed painting in oils. Critical interest and admiration for his work began to grow, and in 1933 he was the subject of a one-man exhibition at the Museum of Modern Art.

At that time, Mr. Hopper had sold only two canvases, one of them bought in 1931 by the Metropolitan Museum of Art, which had previously been indifferent, if not hostile, to "modern" painters.

The Depression brought the attention of the abstractionists back to the American scene. They began to paint it realistically again, many in anger because of the poverty and suffering they saw. The revival of realism brought fresh admiration to Mr. Hopper, who had been painting this world all along, with steadily improving technique, deepening perception and a poet's sense of mood.

A 6-foot 5-inch lumbering man with a quietly brooding face, Mr. Hopper accepted his belated success calmly. He continued to live and work in his top-floor apartment studio on Washington Square North or at his summer home in Truro, Mass.

Another retrospective exhibition devoted to Mr. Hopper was held in 1950 at the Whitney Museum in New York. "In the main his view of life is searching, compassionate and profound," the critic Robert Coates commented. "At his best he can invest the simplest subjects with a magic and mystery it would be hard to duplicate."

In 1961, Mr. Hopper's painting "House of Squam Light, Cape Ann" was selected by Mrs. John F. Kennedy, along with 10 other works from the Boston Museum of Fine Arts, to be displayed at the White House to help broaden appreciation of American artists and craftsmen.

A retrospective exhibition of Mr. Hopper's work that was held at the Whitney Museum in 1964 covered 55 years of his painting.

"In the face of nature, or what is left of it," Mr. Canaday once observed of his work, "Hopper always checks himself well this side of lyricism and reminds us—for instance, by showing us the road-side gasoline pump in front of a pine forest—that nature in an urbanized century is only a relative concept.

"He can paint, as few painters can, the purity of the sky, the freshness of morning near the sea, the soft clarity of the light that strikes across dunes or grass and onto white clapboards," Mr. Canaday continued. "But nature is never an ineffable mystery for Hopper; he has no interest in the ineffable—or at least, by the evidence, he does not regard painting as a medium for expression of the ineffable.

"Nature for him is reduced in scale by the presence of men, by their cottages and lighthouses. The people who sit on porches or by open windows are warmed by the sun and refreshed by the air, but are inspired to no philosophical ponderings."

MARCEL DUCHAMP

July 28, 1887–October 2, 1968

By Alexander Keneas

PARIS—Marcel Duchamp, one of the most influential artists of the century, died last night in his studio in the Paris suburb of Neuilly. He collapsed just after having had dinner with his wife and friends.

Duchamp, who was 81 years old, was a naturalized American citizen. He maintained homes here and in New York.

Like the smile of the Mona Lisa, which he retouched with mustache and goatee, Marcel Duchamp remained an enigma.

Thrust into the international limelight by the 1913 Armory Show, he abandoned his career a decade later, at the age of 36. Yet in half a century the enfant terrible who had thumbed his nose at the pantheon of art grew up to become the spiritual father of the pop generation.

"I'm afraid I'm an agnostic in art." Duchamp once said. "I just don't believe in it with all the mystical trimmings. As a drug, it's probably very useful for a number of people—very sedative—but as religion it's not even as good as God."

Duchamp was the quintessence of the Dada spirit. Unlike other figures in the movement who after World War I would become serious painters, he carried the vaudeville of esthetic nihilism to its logical conclusion.

For the most part Duchamp maintained an aristocratic detachment about his work.

"It is disastrous for an artist to declare—to defend his art," he once said. "Posterity has to decide—and even if it is wrong all over the place it has the advantage of coming into being."

Contradiction formed an important part of the ideological and artistic universe that Duchamp had created for himself. In his universe an apple might not choose to "condescend" to the laws of gravity; the act of love

might—in mock deference to 20th-century science—exist as a fourth-dimensional ritual of machines.

It was all very seriously tongue in cheek, yet it was also appealing to more than a generation of intellectuals who felt that science had stripped them of traditional values and left them spiritually bankrupt. If Duchamp did not provide the cure for spiritual malaise, he at least offered wit, absurdity and the humor of paradox.

Yet Duchamp's works also pointed to more positive concepts of art that would be articulated by generations to come: the illusionism of painting giving way to the reality of the three-dimensional object, the self-effacement of the artist, the object competing and merging with its environment.

Duchamp was in some respects the star of the much-reviled Armory Show. At the center of public ridicule, heaped primarily on the cubist section of the exhibition, Duchamp's "Nude Descending a Staircase" stood as the symbol of the insanity to which modern art had progressed.

The Association of American Painters and Sculptors, organizers of the show, anticipated the clamor that America's first exposure to Europe's new, non-representational painting would generate, and newspapers responded with satirical cartoons and derisive commentary. The "Nude" became an "explosion in a shingle factory." Crowds filed into the 69th Regiment Armory on Lexington Avenue, and guards had to restrain outraged art lovers from damaging the painting.

It was neither the nude nor the staircase, apparently, that had provoked them, but the title, which seemed to have little to do with either—and the idea of a nude descending instead of traditionally reclining or standing.

Duchamp carefully explained the painting: "It is an organization of kinetic elements, an expression of time and space through the abstract presentation of motion."

In trying to consider the notion of form through space, in a given time, he said it was necessary "to enter the realm of geometry and mathematics."

"Now if I show the ascent of an airplane, I try to show what it does," he continued. "I do not make a still-life picture of it. When the vision of the 'Nude' flashed upon me, I knew that it would break forever the enslaving chains of naturalism."

The picture, valued at more than $250,000, now hangs in the Philadelphia Museum of Art.

Marcel Duchamp was born in Blainville, near Rouen, on July 28, 1887, the third son of a family remarkable for its contribution to art of this century. His eldest brother, Gaston (Jacques Villon), achieved international renown as a painter before his death in 1963. Another brother, Raymond (Duchamp-Villon), had been one of the most gifted sculptors of his generation; a younger sister, Suzanne, also became a painter.

With the blessings of his parents, Eugène Duchamp, a notary, and Lucie Nicolle Duchamp, Marcel left home at the age of 17 to pursue a career in art. He arrived in Paris at the twilight of an epoch. In just a few years, Braque and Picasso would shatter the conventions of representational art with cubism; soon futurism would compete with cubism for the attentions of the avant-garde, and Dada would sweep away established values.

The young painter had already demonstrated a technical grasp of Cézanne and Matisse when he began to experiment with the geometry and muted colors of cubism. But like the futurists, he used a succession of flat overlapping planes to depict spatial movement of machine-like forms.

In 1912, after making several preliminary studies of the "Nude," he submitted it to the Puteaux circle's exhibition at the Salon des Indépendants. The painting's futuristic elements angered the members of the group, and he withdrew the work.

"I put the painting under my arm, got into a taxi and went home," he recalled.

In the years before the war, he and the artist Francis Picabia became close friends. Both had been familiar with earlier practitioners of the genre: Alfred Jarry, the playwright who, suffering from malnutrition, on his deathbed had asked for a toothpick, and Erik Satie, the composer who, criticized for writing shapeless music, offered a work entitled "Three Pieces in the Form of a Pear."

In this spirit, Duchamp developed a "playful physics." Dissatisfied with the meter as a fixed unit of measurement, he created his own, painstakingly scientific unit. He cut pieces of thread exactly one meter in length and dropped them on painted canvas from a height of exactly one meter. He then varnished them in the chance positions they had assumed and had wooden rulers cut from them. Later he used the rulers to trace lines in his big unfinished work on transparent glass, "The Bride Stripped Bare by Her Bachelors, Even."

In 1913 he produced the first of his "ready-mades," the everyday objects he elevated by mere selection to the stature of art. These works would become the altarpieces of pop artists and junk sculptors.

In 1917 Duchamp resigned from the Society of Independent Artists after it had reversed its policy of accepting for exhibition any work accompanied by a $6 entry fee. The object of the controversy was "Fountain," a porcelain urinal turned upside down and signed by a Philadelphia sculptor, "R. Mutt." "Fountain," of course, was Duchamp's contribution to the exhibition.

In 1919 he visited a Paris in the full bloom of Dada as a hero of the movement, then returned to New York. By this time he had begun piecing together "The Bride Stripped Bare by Her Bachelors, Even."

The year 1923 marked his departure from the formal practice of art. In the years that followed, he devoted a good deal of his time to playing chess. He lived in a brownstone on 10th Street with his wife, the former Alexina (Teeny) Sattler, whom he married in 1954.

Duchamp attributed his longevity to "not much liquor but all the women you want," and, after smoking a pipe for many years, turned to inexpensive Philippine cigars. He also gave up chess.

"I don't play very much any more," he said last year. "I have a hard time winning, even from the wood pushers as we call them. Once or twice a year I go to the Marshall Chess Club across the street, but that's all. You can forget about something you love very much. It's a Zen concept. When I put my 'Nude' under my arm and went home, it was my first Zen experience. Don't cry."

MIES VAN DER ROHE

March 27, 1886–August 17, 1969

CHICAGO—Mies van der Rohe, one of the great figures of 20th-century architecture, died in Wesley Memorial Hospital here last night. He was 83 years old.

Mr. van der Rohe had entered the hospital two weeks ago.

He is survived by two daughters, five grandchildren and six great-grandchildren.

By Alden Whitman

Ludwig Mies van der Rohe, a man without any academic architectural training, was one of the great artist-architect-philosophers of his age, acclaimed as a genius for his uncompromisingly spare design, his fastidiousness and his innovations.

Along with Frank Lloyd Wright and Le Corbusier, this German-born master builder who was universally known as Mies (pronounced mees) fashioned scores of imposing structures expressing the spirit of the industrial 20th century.

"Architecture is the will of an epoch translated into space," he remarked in a talkative moment. Pressed to explain his role as a model for others, a matter on which he was shy, as he was on most others, he said, "I have tried to make an architecture for a technological society."

A building, he was convinced, should be "a clear and true statement of its times"—cathedrals for an age of pathos, glass and metal cages for an age of advanced industrialism.

He thought the George Washington Bridge an outstanding example of a structure expressing its period. He was fond of the bridge because he considered it beautifully proportioned and because it did not conceal its structure. Mies liked to see the steel, the brick, the concrete of buildings show themselves rather than be concealed by ornamentation.

Mies's stature rested not only on his lean yet sensuous business and residential buildings, but also on the profound influence he exerted on his colleagues and on public taste. As the number of his structures multiplied in the years since World War II, and as their stunning individuality became apparent, critical appreciation flowed to him, and his designs and models drew throngs to museums where they were exhibited. It became a status symbol to live in a Mies house, or to work in a Mies building.

The Mies name had already been established among architects long before he came to the United States in 1937. In 1919 and 1921 in Berlin he designed two steel skyscrapers sheathed in glass from street to roof. Although never executed, the designs are accepted as the originals of today's glass-and-metal skyscrapers.

In 1922 Mies introduced the concept of ribbon windows, uninterrupted bands of glass between the finished faces of concrete slabs, in a design for a German office building. That has since become the basis for many commercial structures.

Mies, in 1924, produced plans for a concrete villa that is now regarded as the forerunner of the California ranch house. He is also said to have foreshadowed the return of the inner patio of Roman times in an exhibition house built in 1931; to have started the idea of space dividers, the use of cabinets or screens instead of walls to break up interiors; and to have originated the glass house, to permit outside greenery to form the visual boundaries of a room.

Apart from simplicity of form, what struck students of Mies's buildings was their painstaking craftsmanship, their attention to detail.

In this respect the buildings reflected the man, for Mies was fussy about himself. He dressed in exquisitely hand-stitched suits of conservative hue, dined extravagantly well on haute cuisine, sipped the correct wines from the proper goblets, and chain-smoked hand-rolled cigars.

Rather than live in a contemporary building or one of his own houses, he made his home in a high-ceilinged, five-room suite on the third floor of an old-fashioned apartment house on Chicago's North Side.

The apartment contained armless chairs and furniture of his own designs as well as sofas and wing chairs. The walls were stark white; but the apartment had a glowing warmth, given off by the Klees, Braques and Schwitterses that dotted its walls. Paul Klee was a close friend, and Mies's collection of Klees was among the finest in private hands.

Mies's chairs were almost as well known as his buildings, and they were just as spare. He designed his first chair, known as the MR chair, in 1926. It had a caned seat and back, and its frame was tubular steel. There followed the Barcelona chair, an elegant armless leather and steel design of which the legs formed an X; the Tugendhat chair, an armless affair of leather and steel that resembled a square S; and the Brno chair, with a steel frame and leather upholstery that looked like a curved S.

Mies did not receive wide public recognition in the United States until he was over 50 years old. Up to 1937 he lived in Germany, where he was born, at Aachen, on March 27, 1886. Emigrating to Chicago, he had to wait for the postwar building boom before many of his designs were translated into actuality. At his death, examples of his work were in Chicago, Pittsburgh, Des Moines, Baltimore, Detroit, Newark, New York, Houston, Washington, Sao Paulo, Mexico City, Montreal, Toronto and Berlin. All his buildings were dissimilar, although the same basic principles were employed in each.

"The long path through function to creative work has only a single goal," he said, "to create order out of the desperate confusion of our time."

One Mies structure, accounted among his outstanding ones, is the 38-story dark bronze and pinkish-gray glass Seagram Building in New York. Designed with Philip C. Johnson, it has been called the city's most tranquil tower and "the most beautiful curtain-wall building in America." It emphasizes pure line, fine materials and exact detailing outside and in.

The Seagram Building ranked third in Mies's offhand list of his favorites, chosen to illustrate his most notable concept "Less is more."

First was the Illinois Institute of Technology's Crown Hall. This is a single glass-walled room measuring 120 feet by 220 feet and spanned by four huge trusses. The structure appears to do no more than to enclose space, a feeling reinforced by its interior movable partitions. Crown Hall is as good an example as any of Mies's "skin-and-bones architecture," a phrase that he once used to describe his point of view.

The Chicago Federal Center, Mies's largest complex of high- and low-rise buildings, was his second favorite. He considered its symmetry symbolic of his lifelong battle against disorder.

Ludwig Mies, who added the "van der Rohe" from his mother's name because of its sonority, learned the elements of architecture from his father, a German master mason and stonecutter, and from studying the medieval churches in Aachen.

"Now a brick, that's really something," he once said. "That's really building, not paper architecture."

For him the material was always the beginning. He used to talk of primitive building methods, where he saw the "wisdom of whole generations" stored in every stroke of an ax, every bite of a chisel.

At Aachen, Mies attended trade school and became a draftsman's apprentice before setting off for Berlin at 19 to become an apprentice to Bruno Paul, Germany's leading furniture designer. Two years later he built his first house, a wooden structure on a sloping site in suburban Berlin. Its style was 18th century.

In 1909 Mies apprenticed himself to Peter Behrens, then the foremost progressive architect in Germany, who had taught Le Corbusier, and Walter Gropius.

Mies opened his own office in 1913, but with the outbreak of the war in 1914 his life was dislocated for four years in the German Army, during which he built bridges and roads in the Balkans.

After the war, with his own style coming into definition, he directed the architectural activities of the Novembergruppe, an organization formed to propagandize modern art, and became one of the few progressive architects of the time to employ brick.

The peak achievement of Mies's European career was the German Barcelona pavilion. It consisted of a rectangular slab roof supported by steel columns, beneath which free-standing planes of Roman travertine, marble, onyx and glass of various hues were placed to create the feeling of space beyond.

In 1930 Mies took over direction of the Bauhaus, a laboratory of architecture and design in Dessau, Germany. It was closed three years later after the Nazis attacked the architect as "degenerate" and "un-German."

Mies emigrated to the United States to head the School of Architecture at the Armour (now Illinois) Institute of Technology in Chicago. He retired from the post in 1958.

Mies was well-to-do, but not wealthy. He received the usual architect's fee of 6 percent of the gross cost of a building, but he was not a very careful manager of his income, according to his friends. He was considered generous with his office staff and on spending for designs that were unlikely to see the light of day.

COCO CHANEL

August 19, 1883–January 10, 1971

By Enid Nemy

PARIS—Gabrielle (Coco) Chanel, one of the greatest couturiers of the 20th century, died tonight in her apartment at the Ritz Hotel. She was 87 years old.

The death of Coco, as she was known the world over, was announced by friends. The cause was not immediately known.

Chanel dominated the Paris fashion world in the 1920's and at the height of her career was running four business enterprises—a fashion house, a textile business, perfume laboratories and a workshop for costume jewelry—that altogether employed 3,500 workers.

It was perhaps her perfume more than her fashions that made the name Chanel famous. Called simply "Chanel No. 5"—she had been told by a fortune-teller that five was her lucky number—it made Coco a millionaire.

An intense woman with a scalding tongue, hair-trigger wit, unbounded immodesty and ineffable charm, Gabrielle Chanel was a free spirit who used fashion as her pulpit. Her message was carried to millions through the medium of the Paris haute couture, a world over which she reigned for much of six decades.

The darling of French society, a friend of dukes and dandies, a confidante of the rich and famous, she was impatient of pretense, intolerant of restrictions, incapable of self-deception. "There is no time for cut-and-dried monotony," she once said. "There is time for work. And time for love. That leaves no other time!"

Chanel was the fashion spirit of the 20th century, a Pied Piper who led women away from complicated, uncomfortable clothes to a bone-simple, uncluttered and casual look that became synonymous with her name.

She emancipated her sex from the tyrannies of fashion. Her strong convictions and independent opinions, her unswerving belief in simplicity and elegance, freed women of unnecessary constrictions and what she called "ludicrous trimmings and fussy bits and pieces."

Slim and dark-haired, with piercing black eyes, Chanel always believed she was right, and often was. She was responsible for many of the timeless fashions that look as current today as they did when she introduced them, in some cases more than half a century ago.

Among her innovations, most considered revolutionary at the time, were jersey dresses and suits, tweed suits with jersey blouses, bell-bottom trousers, trench coats, pea jackets, turtleneck sweaters, sailor hats, bobbed hair, costume jewelry and the little black dress, often collared and cuffed in white.

The Chanel suit, with its collarless, braid-trimmed cardigan jacket and graceful skirt, has probably been copied more, in all price ranges, than any other single garment designed by a couturier.

Chanel's handbag—soft, quilted leather with a chain handle—was copied so widely that it became one of the most universal accessories of the sixties.

The customers who went to the House of Chanel, a six-story building at 31 rue Cambon in Paris, included Marlene Dietrich, Françoise Sagan, Colette, Mrs. Georges Pompidou, and Diana Vreeland, editor in chief of Vogue.

For Chanel, the great changes in fashion stemmed from great changes in the manner and requirements of daily life. She explained her philosophy in 1957 when she traveled to the United States to receive, from Neiman-Marcus in Dallas, an award as the most significant designer of the last 50 years. She told a reporter that she inspired women to take off their bone corsets and cut their hair, in 1925, because they were just beginning to work in offices.

"Women drive autos, and this you cannot do with a crinoline skirt," she said. "But the grand problem, the most important problem, is to rejuvenate women, to make women look young. Then their outlook on life changes. They feel more joyous."

Chanel created an empire. In the twenties, at a time when she employed 2,400 people in her workrooms, her personal fortune was rumored to be $15 million. The financial basis of the empire was Chanel No. 5, introduced in 1922. This unorthodox blend of fragrances soon became the most familiar perfume in the world.

Chanel became increasingly temperamental, willful and, at times, vitriolic, as she grew older. She never stopped speaking her mind, yet she left untouched the myths that swirled around her. "What do I care what people write about me?" she once said. "Each year they will invent a new story."

Her age was never proved, but it is generally accepted that she was born on Aug. 19, 1883, near Issoire in the Auvergne, a region of south central France. She was baptized Gabrielle Bonheur—Gabrielle Happiness.

When she was six years old, her mother died of tuberculosis and her father abandoned his four daughters. Coco went to live with two aunts, who were relentless disciplinarians. They raised horses, and Coco became an expert horsewoman at an early age. She also learned how to sew.

Before her 16th birthday, she showed signs of the indomitable spirit that remained with her. On a visit to her grandfather, a Vichy blacksmith, she escaped from her aunts by persuading a young cavalry officer to take her away. The officer provided an entry into another world. Etienne Balsan was a member of a wealthy family of industrialists who owned fine stables, and it was during this liaison that Chanel learned the habits and tastes of the wealthy.

The career that made her name began in 1913 in Deauville, when she opened a tiny hat boutique. It was the heyday of elaborate and grotesque hats, and she detested them.

"How can the brain function under those things?" she asked, and went on to provide millinery that offered nothing but simplicity and line.

The next year she returned to Paris and opened a shop at 31 rue Cambon, where she sold hats, then sweaters and a few clothes. Within five years she was a force in the world of fashion. She began to impress wealthy, influential women with her originality. She was the first designer to use ordinary jersey for clothes; the September, 1917, issue of Vogue magazine referred to the Maison Chanel as "the jersey house."

A little later, she started the "poor-girl look," and rich women playfully wore clothes based on the garments of the humble.

Despite World War I, her social life was brilliant and hectic. Balsan was succeeded in her life by Arthur Capel, who was nicknamed Boy, an immensely rich, polo-playing Englishman. His lavish presents started her astonishing collection of jewels.

A dashing aristocrat, he was also credited, perhaps apocryphally, with being the inspiration for one of Chanel's most famous fashions. Her boxy suit jacket, with its practical pockets, was said to have been born after she had borrowed Capel's blazer on chilly days at polo games. Boy Capel, described by friends as "the only man she really loved," was killed in an automobile accident.

In the mid-twenties, Chanel's name grew luminous. By 1924, well-dressed women on both sides of the Atlantic were taken with a Chanel costume of a beige jersey blouse worn with a single strand of pearls, and a tweed suit with a cardigan jacket.

Chanel's first period of professional pre-eminence, from the mid-twenties to the late thirties, coincided, in part, with her most famous alliance, with Hugh Richard Arthur Grosvenor, the second Duke of Westminster, one of Europe's wealthiest man.

Chanel's friendship with the Duke ended by 1934. But she remained impressed by the clothes worn by Englishmen. One of the engineering secrets of the Chanel jacket was its high, tight armhole. It could have been tailored in Savile Row.

"The armhole was never high enough. She'd reset a sleeve six times," recalled Jackie Rogers, who modeled for Chanel in 1963. "The high armhole gave the jacket the cleaner, closer fit she wanted."

Unlike most couturiers, Chanel never made a drawing or linen prototype of her clothes. The only way she could work was by taking the material in her hands.

Chanel at one time entertained frequently at the splendid house she kept on the Faubourg St. Honoré. She also kept a small bedroom suite at the Ritz, where she often slept and dressed.

The Ritz was the scene of one of the few verified episodes in her life. It resulted in the fashion for bobbed hair. One night, some gas in the hot water heater exploded, spraying her with soot. Chanel cut off her long black hair so there would be less to shampoo. She washed it and tied a ribbon around it. That night she appeared at the opera in a white dress and short hair. The effect became an immediate fashion craze.

In the late thirties, when the fashionable world deserted Chanel for Elsa Schiaparelli, the Italian designer, and World War II broke out, Chanel shut her couture house and went across the street to hibernate at the Ritz. Chanel then went on to Vichy and to Switzerland, but the record of her life for 15 years is more blurred than usual.

Chanel's comeback, on Feb. 5, 1954, was a turning point in the fashion world. She showed a suit in heavy navy jersey with two patch pockets, worn with a white muslin blouse and a sailor hat. The critics' reaction was not ecstatic; however, women bought it. It was the forerunner of a style that evolved with increasing success.

Chanel, in her 80's and perhaps at the peak of her career, continued to rule her salon like a royal court.

Anne Chamberlin, writing in The Ladies Home Journal in October, 1963, said, "The weeks preceding the opening of a new collection are, next to the Bastille Day fireworks, one of the great pyrotechnic spectacles in Paris, witnessed by only a privileged few.

"Mademoiselle takes up her station on one of the gold ballroom chairs in the big showroom, with a pair of scissors hanging from a rope around her neck and a box of straight pins on the chair beside her ('I want every single pin in this house changed, not one is long enough'), asks to see the first dress, and the fun begins.

"She suffers from rheumatism and arthritis. Yet she still literally attacks each fitting with her bare hands, clawing and pushing at the fabric, jamming in pins, tearing out seams, sending seamstresses off in tears behind the fitting screens, where they get revenge by jabbing pins into the models."

Chanel outlived many of her closest friends. She never married, not because she preferred solitude but, according to one quotation, because she "never wanted to weigh more heavily on a man than a bird."

PABLO PICASSO

October 25, 1881–April 8, 1973

MOUGINS, France—Pablo Picasso, the titan of 20th-century art, died this morning at his hilltop villa of Notre Dame de Vie here. He was 91 years old.

The death of the Spanish-born artist was attributed to pulmonary edema, by Dr. Jean-Claude Rance, who was summoned to the 35-room mansion.

With Picasso when he died was his second wife, the 47-year-old Jacqueline Roque, whom he married in 1961. In the last few years, Picasso rarely left his 17-acre estate. He had been in exile from his native land since 1939, when Generalissimo Francisco Franco defeated the Republican Government of Spain in the three-year Civil War.

In addition to his wife, Picasso leaves four children: a son born to his late first wife, the dancer Olga Khoklova; a daughter born to his mistress Marie-Therese Walter, and a son and daughter born to Françoise Gilot, another mistress.

By Alden Whitman

There was Picasso the cubist; Picasso the surrealist; Picasso the modernist; Picasso the ceramist; Picasso the lithographer; Picasso the sculptor; Picasso the superb draftsman; Picasso the exuberant; Picasso the surly; Picasso the faithful and faithless lover; Picasso the cunning financial man; Picasso the publicity seeker; Picasso the smoldering Spaniard.

Pablo Picasso remains without doubt the most original, protean and forceful personality in the visual arts in the first three-quarters of this century. With his prodigious gift he transformed the universe of art. A man of many styles, his artistic life revealed a continuous process of exploration.

"For me, a picture is neither an end nor an achievement but rather a lucky chance and art experience," he once said. "I try to represent what I have found, not what I am seeking. I do not seek—I find."

Picasso's fecundity of imagination permitted him to metamorphize a mood or an idea into a work of art with bewildering quickness. He was, in André Malraux's phrase, "the archwizard of modern art," a man who, as a painter alone, produced well over 6,000 pictures.

In 1969, his 88th year, he produced a total of 165 paintings and 45 drawings, which were shown at the Palace of the Popes in Avignon, France. The exhibition moved Emily Genauer, the critic, to say, "I think Picasso's new pictures are the fire of heaven."

The painter was so much known for works that blurred or obliterated conventional distinctions between beauty and ugliness that he was accused of being an antihumanist. That appraisal disturbed him, for he regarded himself as having created new insights into a seen and unseen world.

"What is art?" a visitor once asked him. "What is not?" he replied. He once substantiated this point by combining a bicycle seat and a pair of handlebars to make a bull's head.

"Whatever the source of the emotion that drives me to create, I want to give it a form that has some connection with the visible world, even if it is only to wage war on that world," he explained to Miss Gilot. "Otherwise, a painting is just an old grab bag for everyone to reach into and pull out what he himself has put in. I want my paintings to be able to defend themselves, to resist the invader, just as though there were razor blades on all surfaces so no one could touch them without cutting his hands."

In the long course of upending traditionalism, Picasso became a one-man history of modern art. He worked in oils, watercolors, pastels, gouaches, pencil and ink drawings and aquatints; he etched, made lithographs, sculpted, fashioned ceramics, put together mosaics and constructed murals.

One of his masterpieces was "Guernica," painted in 1937. An oil on canvas 11 1/4 feet high and 25 1/2 feet long, it is a majestic indictment of the destructiveness of modern war. By contrast, another masterpiece was a simply and perfectly drawn white pigeon, "The Dove," which was disseminated around the world as a symbol of peace.

Exhibitions of his work, especially in his later years, were sure-fire attractions. Reproductions were nailed up in homes all over the Western world, a certain mark of the owner's claim to culture. Originals were widely dispersed, both in museums and in the hands of collectors wealthy enough to meet Picasso's prices. And they were steep. In 1965 he charged London's Tate Gallery $168,000 for "Les Trois Danseuses," a painting he did in 1925.

As Picasso's fame grew, so did his income, and he was canny about money. But he also gave large sums to the Republican side in the Spanish Civil War, and then to refugee groups that cared for the defeated Republicans who had fled to France.

All his studios and homes, even the 18-room rambling La Californie at Cannes, were crammed and cluttered with junk—pebbles, rocks, pieces of glass, a hollow elephant's foot, African drums, wooden crocodiles, ancient newspapers, broken crockery, bullfight posters, old hats. In later years this villa became a weekend residence, while his main home was Notre Dame de Vie in nearby Mougins.

Despite the disorganization with which he surrounded himself, Picasso was a methodical man. He arose late, devoted several hours to friends, conversation, business letters and lunch; then, at 3 or 4, he would go to his studio to work in Trappist silence, often for 12 hours at a stretch, breaking off only for dinner. He sometimes worked until 2 or 3 in the morning.

Photographs from his younger years showed a handsome man with jet-black hair. Apart from the absence of hair, the description of him by Fernande Olivier, his first long-term mistress, could have applied to the artist of later years.

"Small, dark, thickset, unquiet, quieting, with somber eyes, deep-set, piercing, strange, almost fixed," she wrote. "Awkward gestures, a woman's hands, ill-dressed, careless. A thick lock of hair, black and glossy, cut across his intelligent, obstinate forehead."

Women were one of Picasso's most persistent preoccupations. Seven women were significant in his personal and artistic life. He married two of them, but his relationships with the five others were well recognized.

In Picasso's early days in Paris, Miss Olivier, a young painter and teacher, lived, as he did, in a building in Montmartre.

"I met Picasso as I was coming home one stormy evening," she recalled. "He had a tiny kitten in his arms, which he laughingly offered me, at the same time blocking my path."

Their liaison lasted until 1912, when Picasso met Marcelle Humbert, the mistress of a sculptor friend. The two ran off together, and there followed a series of superb canvases expressing the artist's happiness. She died in 1914.

In 1917, he met Miss Khoklova, a ballerina with Sergei Diaghilev's Ballets Russes. They were married in 1918. The marriage broke up in 1935, and she died 20 years later. At the time of the separation, Picasso's mistress was his blond model Miss Walter.

Dora Maar, a young Yugoslav photographer, was the painter's next mistress. Their companionship lasted until 1944. That year, when Picasso was 62, he began an 11-year liaison with Miss Gilot.

Picasso's final attachment was to Jacqueline Roque, who became his mistress in 1955, and his wife in 1961, when she was 35 and he was 79.

Picasso maintained a strong emotional bond with the country of his birth. It influenced his painting and, after 1936 and the Spanish Civil War, propelled him into politics. The connection was romantic and passionate, and the fact that he shunned Generalissimo Franco's Spain yet kept his Spanish nationality was an expression of his feeling for the country.

There were two principal consequences of this bond. One was "Guernica." The other was his membership in the French Communist party, which he joined in 1944.

"Up to the time of the Spanish Civil War, Picasso was completely apolitical," Daniel-Henry Kahnweiler, his agent, recalled. "The Civil War changed all that."

With the outbreak of conflict in his homeland, Picasso became an aroused partisan of the Republican Government. But it took the bombing of the Basque town of Guernica y Luno on April 26, 1937, to drive Picasso to the heights of his genius. The carnage was enormous, and news of it appalled the world.

Picasso had been engaged by the Loyalist Government to do a mural for its pavilion at a Paris fair. The outrage at Guernica gave him his subject, and in a month of furious work he completed his great and stunning painting.

The monochromatic mural, stark black, gray and white, was to be given to Spain when it became a republic again.

When the artist joined the Communist party, many thought at first that the action was another of Picasso's caprices. He responded with a statement that said in part:

"What do you think an artist is? An imbecile who has only his eyes if he a painter, or his ears if a musician?

"On the contrary, he is at the same time a political being, constantly alert to the heart-rending, burning, or happy events in the world, molding himself in their likeness.

"How could it be possible to feel no interest in other people and, because of an ivory-tower indifference, detach yourself from the life they bring with such open hands?

"No, painting is not made to decorate apartments. It is an instrument of war, for attack and defense against the enemy."

One day in 1949 Matisse came to visit Picasso, bringing a white pigeon for his friend's cote. Picasso made a naturalistic lithograph of the newcomer, and Louis Aragon, the Communist poet and novelist, who saw it shortly thereafter, immediately realized its possibilities. The lithograph, signed by the artist, was first used as a poster at a World Peace Conference. From that introduction it flew around the world, reproduced in all sizes and in all media as a peace symbol.

Pablo Picasso was born on the night of Oct. 25, 1881, in Málaga, on Spain's south coast. His father was José Ruiz, who taught at the local school of arts and crafts. His mother was Maria Picasso. Pablo could draw as soon as he could grasp a pencil.

As a child, Picasso often accompanied his father to the bullfights. These made an indelible impression, for throughout his life bullring scenes were a significant part of his work.

In 1895 the family moved to Barcelona. By that time the youngster's talent was truly Mozartean, so obviously so that his father presented him with his own palette and brushes. This confidence was justified when Pablo, at 15, was admitted to classes at the art school. He remained there for a year before going to Madrid for further study.

The young artist, who dropped his father's name from the signature "P. Ruiz Picasso" in 1898, settled in Paris in 1904.

Meanwhile, his "blue" pictures had established him as an artist with a personal voice. This period was characterized by his use of the color blue to depict the haunting melancholy of dying clowns and agonized acrobats. "La Mort d'Arlequin" is one of the most widely known of these.

When the artist moved into the building in Montmartre, his studio became an important meeting place for persons later to be famous in arts and letters. One of Picasso's lifelong habits, painting at night, started during this time, for the simple reason that his day was frequently absorbed by visitors. It was also the time of his two-year "rose period," generally dated from 1904 to 1906 and so-called because hues of that color dominated his pictures.

Near the rose period's close, he was taken up by the Steins, American expatriates in Paris. Leo and Gertrude did not so much discover the painter as popularize him. He, in turn, did a portrait of Gertrude with a face far from representational. When Miss Stein protested that she didn't look like that, Picasso replied, "But you will."

The year 1907 was a milestone for the painter for it marked the birth of cubism in an oil of five distorted nudes called "Les Demoiselles d'Avignon." With cubism, Picasso—along with Braque—rejected light and perspective, painting not what he saw but what he represented to himself through analysis.

"When we painted as we did," Picasso said later, "we had no intention of creating cubism, but only of expressing what was inside us.

"Cubism is neither a seed nor a fetus, but an art which is primarily concerned with form, and, once a form has been created, then it exists and goes on living its own life."

This was also the case when Picasso added a new dimension to cubism in 1911 or 1912 by inventing the collage by gluing a piece of imitation chair caning to a still life.

In 1929 Picasso returned to sculpture. But he was soon attacking his easel, this time with variations within a distinctive, generally surrealistic framework. With these and other similar pictures, the artist's renown and income reached new heights.

In 1940 came the fall of Paris. Picasso remained in the city throughout World War II, painting industriously amid considerable personal hardship.

After the war, Picasso painted scores of portraits of his wife in a variety of poses. They gave the impression of a man of unlimited vitality in a perpetual state of creation. As if in confirmation of this, Picasso told a visitor who admired the vigor of the works:

"A painter never finishes. There's never a moment when you can say, 'I've worked well and tomorrow is Sunday.' As soon as you stop, it's because you've started again. You can put a picture aside and say you won't touch it again. But you can never write THE END."

NORMAN ROCKWELL

February 3, 1894–November 8, 1978

By Edwin McDowell

Norman Rockwell, the artist whose nostalgic evocations of small-town America appeared on hundreds of Saturday Evening Post covers, died Wednesday night at his home in Stockbridge, Mass., at the age of 84. He had been in failing health.

Mr. Rockwell painted in a converted carriage house in Stockbridge, a town whose New England charm he captured in his paintings.

"My worst enemy is the world-shaking idea," he once said, "stretching my neck like a swan and forgetting that I'm a duck." That assessment was characteristically modest, for Mr. Rockwell neglected to add that if he was a duck, he was an important duck in a very big pond.

There is hardly an American adult who has not experienced a wave of nostalgia while gazing at a Rockwell magazine cover, Boy Scout calendar or advertisement. "He has been America's most popular

artist for half a century," Thomas S. Buechner, director of the Brooklyn Museum, wrote in 1970. "In fact, his big work has been reproduced more often than all of Michelangelo's, Rembrandt's and Picasso's put together."

Mr. Rockwell was best known for his covers for The Saturday Evening Post, 317 of them between 1916 and 1963. A former Post editor observed that in the 1950's and early 60's a Rockwell cover was good for an extra 50,000 to 75,000 newsstand sales.

This was no doubt because a typical Rockwell cover tended to evoke emotions of sentiment, reverence or poignancy: a family gathered in thanksgiving around a holiday table; barefoot boys in tattered overalls carrying makeshift fishing poles; the kindly doctor preparing to inoculate a child's bare bottom; a runaway boy at a lunch counter confiding in an understanding policeman; a tomboy with a black eye in the doctor's waiting room.

And always Boy Scouts. Mr. Rockwell was associated with the Boy Scouts of America ever since the Scouts took over Boys' Life magazine in 1913 and hired him to do covers and story illustrations.

Mr. Rockwell was quick to agree that the virtues he celebrated on canvas were not necessarily the way things always were. In 1960 he said: "Maybe I grew up and found the world wasn't the perfectly pleasant place I had thought it to be, I unconsciously decided that if it wasn't an ideal world, it should be, and so painted only the ideal aspects of it, pictures in which there were no drunken fathers, or self-centered mothers, in which, on the contrary, there were only foxy Grandpas who played baseball with the kids, and boys fished from logs and got up circuses in the backyard. If there were problems, they were humorous problems."

This vision of America endeared Mr. Rockwell to millions of his countrymen, but it was not uniformly admired. Critics complained that his serene America—a land unpopulated by ethnic or black Americans, or untroubled by controversy more serious than youthful peccadillos—existed solely in the imagination.

After his relationship with the Post ended in 1963, in part because the magazine was about to embark on "sophisticated muckraking" and was anxious to jettison its old image, Mr. Rockwell went to work for Look magazine. In a belated attempt to keep abreast of the social turbulence that was sweeping America, he drew one cover depicting United States marshals escorting a solitary black girl to school in Little Rock, Ark.

Critics also tended to disparage Mr. Rockwell, referring to him as an illustrator rather than as an artist and saying that his work lacked subtlety, nuance and depth.

Mr. Rockwell finally achieved formal recognition as an artist with a 1968 exhibition of 50 of his oil paintings at a Madison Avenue gallery that drew large crowds. Four years later, a Rockwell retrospective at the Brooklyn Museum drew equally enthusiastic crowds.

Yet not even Mr. Rockwell's severest critics faulted his painstaking craftsmanship or his eye for detail. Near Hannibal, Mo., where he was preparing to illustrate special editions of "Tom Sawyer" and "Huckleberry Finn," he swapped his trousers and $4 for a pair of weather-beaten—and therefore "authentic"—trousers worn by a farmer who was plowing a field.

Mr. Rockwell sometimes worked from photographs, posing his models just long enough to capture them on camera. But for the first 25 years of his career, he used live models exclusively, mostly friends and neighbors. He once said that he had moved to New England—to Arlington, Vt., in 1940, then in 1953 to Stockbridge, the picturesque village in the Berkshires that could well have been designed by Mr. Rockwell himself—because guileless New Englanders were the best models for the ideas he wanted to portray.

Several neighbors turned up repeatedly in his illustrations, and modeling for the tall, thin celebrity in their midst became something of a cottage industry around Arlington and Stockbridge. Willie Gillis, the imaginary G.I. whose progress Mr. Rockwell recorded through basic training to service in India, was actually a Vermont sawmill worker.

Other friends and acquaintances showed up in the "Four Freedoms" posters that appeared first on the cover of the Post and were reproduced by the millions by the Office of War Information. Mr. Rockwell's other famous World War II magazine cover was "Rosie the Riveter," a rotund defense worker with overalls who appeared on a May 1943 Post cover, and who immediately became synonymous with the home defense effort.

Mr. Rockwell was born in New York on Feb. 3, 1894, the elder of two sons. His father, J. Waring Rockwell, managed the New York office of a Philadelphia textile company. The family moved to Mamaroneck, N.Y., when Norman was 10 years old.

At 17, he was drawing illustrations for several publications owned by Condé Nast, and four years later he scored with his first Saturday Evening Post cover, depicting a disconsolate boy shoving a baby carriage past jeering friends who were suited up for baseball.

GEORGIA O'KEEFFE

November 15, 1887–March 6, 1986

By Edith Evans Asbury

Georgia O'Keeffe, the undisputed doyenne of American painting and a leader, with her husband, Alfred Stieglitz, of a crucial phase in the development and dissemination of American modernism, died yesterday at St. Vincent Hospital in Santa Fe, N.M. She was 98 years old, and had lived in Santa Fe since 1984, when she moved there from her longtime home and studio in Abiquiu, N.M.

As an artist, as a reclusive but overwhelming personality and as a woman in what was long a man's world, Georgia O'Keeffe was a key figure in the American 20th century and made the American public aware that a woman could be the equal of any man in her chosen field.

As an interpreter and manipulator of natural forms, as a strong and individual colorist and as the lyric poet of her beloved New Mexico landscape, she left her mark on the history of American art and made it possible for other women to explore a new range of symbolic and ambiguous imagery.

Miss O'Keeffe was strong-willed, hard-working and whimsical. She would wrap herself in a blanket and wait, shivering, in the cold dark for a sunrise to paint; would climb a ladder to see the stars from a roof, and hop around in her stockings on an enormous canvas to add final touches before the paint dried.

Miss O'Keeffe burst upon the art world in 1916 via a one-woman show of her paintings at the famous "291" gallery of Alfred Stieglitz, the world-renowned pioneer in photography and sponsor of newly emerging modern art.

From then on Miss O'Keeffe was in the spotlight, shifting from one audacious way of presenting a subject to another. Her colors dazzled, her erotic implications provoked, her subjects astonished.

She painted the skull of a horse with a bright pink Mexican artificial flower stuck in the eye socket. She painted other animal skulls, horns, pelvises and leg bones that gleamed white against brilliant skies, spanned valleys and touched mountaintops, all with serene disdain for conventional notions of perspective. She also painted New York skyscrapers, Canadian barns and oversized flowers.

The artist painted as she pleased, and sold as often as she liked, for good prices. She joined the avant-garde inner circle of modern American artists around Stieglitz, whom she married in 1924. Stieglitz took more than 500 photographs of her, pictures that some have called the greatest love poem in the history of photography.

Her beauty aged well to another kind—weather-beaten, leathery skin wrinkled over high cheekbones and around a firm mouth. And long after Stieglitz had died, in 1946, after Miss O'Keeffe forsook New York for the mountains and deserts of New Mexico, she was discovered all over again and proclaimed a pioneering artist of great individuality, power and historic significance.

Miss O'Keeffe had never stopped painting, never stopped winning critical acclaim. But her paintings were so diverse, so uniquely her own and so unrelated to trends or schools that they had not attracted much close attention from New York critics.

Then, in 1970, when she was 83, a retrospective exhibition of her work was held at the Whitney Museum of American Art. The New York critics and collectors and a new generation of students and artists made an astonishing discovery. The artist who had been joyously painting as she pleased had always been a step ahead of everyone else.

Strolling through the Whitney show, one could think Miss O'Keeffe had made some "very neat adaptations of various successful styles of the 1950's and 1960's in her own highly refined and slightly removed manner," wrote John Canaday, art critic of The New York Times.

With no thought of resting on her laurels, the indomitable octogenarian went right on working. She painted new pictures, wrote an autobiography illustrated with her paintings that sold out immediately at $75 a copy and cooperated in the production of an award-winning film about herself and her work.

Despite the affinity of Miss O'Keeffe's work to paintings of other modern American artists, her paintings show surprisingly little evidence of the European influence seen in other American art. "She escaped the fate of remaining thrall to a European model by taking possession of her American experience and making that the core of her artistic vision," Hilton Kramer wrote in The Times in 1976 in his review of her book.

Miss O'Keeffe's career embraced virtually the whole history of modern art, from the early years of the century, when Stieglitz exhibited the new art to a shocked New York, to its eventual acceptance as a part of our culture. At 89, when her book was published, Miss O'Keeffe remained "a vital figure first of all as a painter of remarkable originality and power but also as a precious link with the first generation of American modernists," Mr. Kramer wrote.

Georgia O'Keeffe was born on a wheat farm near Sun Prairie, Wis., on Nov. 15, 1887. Her father, Francis Calixtus O'Keeffe, was Irish; her mother was the former Ida Totto. Georgia was named for her maternal grandfather, Giorgio Totto, who came to the United States from Hungary, where he had gone from Italy.

When Miss O'Keeffe was 14, the family moved to Williamsburg, Va. Three years later she graduated from Chatham Protestant Episcopal Institute in Virginia. She went immediately to Chicago, where she studied at the Art Institute.

Miss O'Keeffe had decided in Sun Prairie that she was going to be an artist when she grew up although, she wrote in her book, "I hadn't a desire to make anything like the pictures I had seen." For 10 discouraging years, she studied and painted, supporting herself by doing commercial art for ad agencies and by teaching. She attended art classes at the Art Students League in New York, the University of Virginia Summer School and Teachers College of Columbia University.

She was supervisor of art in the public schools of Amarillo, Tex., from 1912 to 1916, and then became head of the art department of West Texas Normal College.

Miss O'Keeffe's early pictures were imitative, but as she developed her technique, a ruggedly individual style began to assert itself. The results were out of step with the popular taste and accepted style of the early 1900's, but they encouraged her to concentrate boldly on expressing her own ideas.

"One day," Miss O'Keeffe recalled, "I found myself saying to myself, 'I can't live where I want to. I can't even say what I want to.' I decided I was a very stupid fool not to at least paint as I wanted to."

A friend, Anita Pollitzer, showed a group of Miss O'Keeffe's drawings and watercolors to Stieglitz in 1916. Miss Pollitzer, later to become a champion of equal rights for women and chairman of the National Woman's Party, had been a classmate of Miss O'Keeffe's at Columbia.

"At last, a woman on paper!" Stieglitz exclaimed when he saw the pictures. He hung them in his gallery, and the unknown Miss O'Keeffe created an immediate stir in the art world.

"Mabel Dodge Luhan brought strings of psychiatrists to look at them," Stieglitz recalled. "The critics came. There was talk, talk, talk." Some of the talk hinted at erotic symbolism.

Miss O'Keeffe stormed up from Texas and upbraided Stieglitz for showing her work without her permission. His answer was to persuade her to move to New York, abandon her teaching and devote herself to painting. He presented one-woman shows of her work almost annually thereafter until 1946, the year of his death. He and Miss O'Keeffe had been married 21 years.

After moving to New York, Miss O'Keeffe divided her time between New York City and Lake George, N.Y. After 1929, she also spent a great deal of time in New Mexico. She made her permanent residence at Abiquiu after the death of her husband.

Stieglitz's vigilant and canny management was a major factor in her rise to fame and fortune.

Miss O'Keeffe continued to wear what she pleased and to paint as she pleased. Spare and dark-skinned, she had dark hair drawn severely back and knotted into a bun in those years. No makeup softened the angularity of her face with its high cheekbones. Her clothes were usually black, loose-fitting and shapeless.

Miss O'Keeffe's paintings hang in museums throughout the United States—including, in New York, the Metropolitan, the Whitney and the Museum of Modern Art—and in most major private collections.

Miss O'Keeffe was elected to membership in the National Institute of Arts and Letters, the American Academy of Arts and Letters and the American Academy of Arts and Sciences.

In Abiquiu, she had the help of a young protege, Juan Hamilton, a potter. He supervised production of her book, and assisted with the film about her. He traveled with her and managed her business affairs. Their companionship was so close, there were rumors of marriage.

In 1978 Mr. Hamilton, then 33, came to New York alone on two missions. One was to put the finishing touches on the Metropolitan's exhibition of Stieglitz photographs of Miss O'Keeffe.

The other was to mount his own exhibition of the sculptured pots that Miss O'Keeffe had prodded him into producing. A gala party celebrating the opening of the show was interrupted by a process server bearing a notice that Mr. Hamilton was going to be sued for "malicious interference" with the business relationships of Doris Bry. Miss Bry, Ms. O'Keeffe's longtime New York representative, had been dismissed when Mr. Hamilton arrived on the scene, and Miss Bry tried to fight that

dismissal with a suit against him for $13.25 million. The suit was settled out of court.

Miss O'Keeffe, who is survived by a sister, Catherine Klenert, traveled to New York to visit friends and see art exhibitions until recent years, when poor eyesight and failing health kept her at home.

ANDY WARHOL

August 6, 1928–February 22, 1987

By Douglas C. McGill

Andy Warhol, a founder of Pop Art whose paintings and prints of Presidents, movie stars, soup cans and other icons of America made him one of the most famous artists in the world, died yesterday. He was believed to be 58 years old.

The artist died at the New York Hospital–Cornell Medical Center in Manhattan, where he underwent gallbladder surgery Saturday. His condition was stable after the operation, according to a hospital spokeswoman, but he had a heart attack in his sleep.

Though best known for his earliest works—including his silk-screen image of a Campbell's soup can and a wood sculpture painted like a box of Brillo pads—Mr. Warhol's career included successful forays into photography, moviemaking, writing and magazine publishing.

He founded Interview magazine in 1969, and in recent years he and his work were increasingly in the public eye—on national magazine covers, in society columns and in television advertisements for computers, cars, cameras and liquors.

In all these endeavors, Mr. Warhol's keenest talents were for attracting publicity, for uttering the unforgettable quote and finding the single visual image that would most shock and endure. That his art could attract and maintain the public interest made him among the most influential and widely emulated artists of his time.

Although shy and quiet, Mr. Warhol attracted dozens of followers who were anything but quiet, and the combination of his genius and their energy produced dozens of notorious events throughout his career. In the mid-1960's, he sometimes sent a Warhol lookalike to speak for him at lecture engagements. His Manhattan studio, "the Factory," was a legendary hangout for other artists and hangers-on.

In 1968, however, a would-be follower shot and critically wounded Mr. Warhol at the Factory. After more than a year of recuperation, he returned to his career, which he increasingly devoted to documenting, with Polaroid pictures and large silk-screen prints, political and entertainment figures. He started his magazine and became a fixture on the fashion and jet-set social scene.

In the 1980's, after a relatively quiet period in his career, Mr. Warhol burst back onto the contemporary art scene as a mentor and friend to young artists, including Keith Haring, Kenny Scharf and Jean-Michel Basquiat. With Mr. Basquiat, Mr. Warhol collaborated on a series of paintings in which he shunned mechanical reproduction techniques and painted individual canvases for the first time since the early 1960's.

He never denied his obsession with art as a business and with getting publicity; instead, he proclaimed them as philosophical tenets.

"Being good in business is the most fascinating kind of art," he said on one occasion. On another, he said: "Art? That's a man's name." As widely known as his art and his own image were, however, Mr. Warhol himself was something of a cipher.

The earliest facts of his life remain unclear. He was born somewhere in Pennsylvania in either 1928, 1929 or 1930, according to three versions of his life. (The most commonly accepted date is Aug. 6, 1928.) The son of immigrant parents from Czechoslovakia, his father a coal miner—the family's name was Warhola—he attended the Carnegie Institute of Technology (now Carnegie-Mellon University), from which he graduated with a degree in pictorial design in 1949.

He immediately set out for New York, where he changed his name to Warhol and began a career as an illustrator and a commercial artist, working for Tiffany's, Bonwit Teller's, Vogue, Glamour, The New York Times and other publications and department stores.

By the late 1950's he was highly successful, having earned enough money to move to a town house in Mid-

Warhol had dispensed with the brush altogether. Instead, he turned to hard-edged images using the medium of silk-screen print, which made a depersonalized image. It became Mr. Warhol's trademark.

"Painting a soup can is not in itself a radical act," the critic Robert Hughes wrote in 1971. "But what was radical in Warhol was that he adapted the means of production of soup cans to the way he produced paintings, turning them out en masse—consumer art mimicking the process as well as the look of consumer culture."

In 1964 Mr. Warhol was taken on by the Castelli Gallery, which remained his art dealer until his death. His experimentation with underground films began around that time—an interest that culminated in widespread notoriety if not box-office acclaim.

"Eat," a 45-minute film, showed the artist Robert Indiana eating a mushroom. "Haircut" showed a Warhol groupie having his hair cut over 33 minutes. "Poor Little Rich Girl" showed Edie Sedgwick, a Warhol follower who became a celebrity on the New York social circuit, talking about herself.

In the 1970's Mr. Warhol settled down to a sustained creative period in which his fame as a society figure leveled off but his output, if anything, increased. Working most often in silk-screen prints, he made series of pictures of political and Hollywood celebrities, including Mao, Liza Minnelli and Jimmy Carter.

In 1975, he published "The Philosophy of Andy Warhol (From A to B and Back Again)," a collection of statements and epigrams that elucidated his contrary views on art.

In his glancing and elliptical style, Mr. Warhol wrote about subjects ranging from art to money and sex. "Checks aren't money," he wrote in one section of the book. In another he said: "Fantasy love is much better than reality love. Never doing it is very exciting."

After the news of his death was publicized yesterday, artists, celebrities and politicians who knew Mr. Warhol spoke of his influence on culture and on their lives.

Mr. Castelli said Mr. Warhol, more than practically any artist of the last two decades, seemed to have a continuing and strong influence on today's emerging artists. "A real guru," Mr. Castelli said.

Mr. Warhol is survived by two brothers.

In his book, "The Philosophy of Andy Warhol," the artist wrote a short chapter, entitled "Death," that consisted almost entirely of these words: "I'm so sorry to hear about it. I just thought that things were magic and that it would never happen."

town. Despite his success, however, he increasingly considered trying his hand at making paintings, and in 1960 he did so with a series of pictures based on comic strips, including Superman and Dick Tracy, and on Coca-Cola bottles.

Success was not immediate. Leo Castelli, the art dealer best known for discovering the artists Jasper Johns and Robert Rauschenberg, saw Mr. Warhol's paintings but declined to show his work, since the gallery already represented Roy Lichtenstein, who also painted pictures taken from comic strips. Ivan Karp, a talent scout for Castelli who discovered Mr. Warhol, tried to help him find a New York gallery, with no success.

In 1962 the dam broke, with Mr. Warhol's first exhibition of the Campbell's soup cans at the Ferus Gallery in Los Angeles, and his show of other works at the Sidney Janis Gallery in New York. Other Pop artists, including Mr. Lichtenstein, James Rosenquist and Tom Wesselman, also began to achieve prominence, and the movement was born.

Though some of Mr. Warhol's first Pop Art paintings had drips on them—evidence that the painter's hand had left its mark on the work—by 1963 Mr.

WILLEM DE KOONING

April 24, 1904–March 19, 1997

By Michael Kimmelman

Willem de Kooning, who came to New York City from his native Rotterdam and radically altered the shape of American art after World War II, died yesterday at his home in East Hampton, L.I.. He was 92.

A near-mythic figure in American art, Mr. de Kooning became the embodiment of its heyday in the 1950's, when the movement that he epitomized, Abstract Expressionism, rose to international prominence. Even before then he was a charismatic presence on the New York art scene, a regular at the old Cedar Bar, the famous art-ists' hangout in Greenwich Village, where he became legendary for his choirboy good looks, soft-spoken charm and hard drinking.

Late in life, he remained a striking man, half Dutch sailor, half Charlie Chaplin in baggy trousers, with his thick Dutch accent, clear blue eyes and shock of white hair. His off-again, on-again marriage to the painter Elaine de Kooning lasted until she died in 1989 and his own health had declined.

Mr. de Kooning was known, among other things, for his "Woman" paintings. The female figure became the tonic note to which he returned again and again in his long career, and from this preoccupation came many of his most hotly contested works: the toothy, blowzy images of the late 1940's, 50's and 60's, which have been described as sexist and pornographic, affectionate and funny, or all these things at once. They are garish high-heeled figures with puckered lips and fuchsia nails, bulging eyes and breasts, painted with an almost vicious enthusiasm.

"They look vociferous and ferocious, and I think it had to do with the idea of the idol, the oracle and above all the hilariousness of it," Mr. de Kooning once said. "I do think that if I don't look upon life that way, I won't know how to keep on being around."

These icons of modern painting have continued to touch some nerve at the core of American consciousness. Long before Andy Warhol thought of silk-screening Marilyn Monroe, Mr. de Kooning culled sources from as far afield as tobacco advertisements and fashion spreads in women's magazines. "I always seem to be wrapped in the melodrama of vulgarity," he said.

He had suffered from Alzheimer's disease since at least the late 1980's, and much debate has focused on the nature of his art from the years immediately preceding, specifically, to what extent his paintings of the 1980's may have been affected by his illness. But a traveling show of late pictures proved that, nearly to the end, Mr. de Kooning worked as he always had, improvisationally and episodically.

Over the years critics contended that his decline began as early as 1950. In the 1960's, Mr. de Kooning became Public Enemy No. 1 for many young American artists clamoring for change, though painters who built their reputations partly in opposition to Abstract Expressionism, like Robert Rauschenberg, relied heavily on Mr. de Kooning's example.

They could hardly avoid it. Mr. de Kooning attracted countless imitators who could not begin to match the fluency, wit, sexual energy and sheer invention of his art, and they tarnished "Action Painting," as the critic Harold Rosenberg termed the style with which Mr. de Kooning was inextricably linked.

By consensus, his works from the late 1940's and early 50's are touchstones of 20th-century American art. After that, Mr. de Kooning's development can be said to have had an ebb and flow, with significant works emerging during nearly every phase of his career.

From his first mature paintings, of male figures in the 1930's, through his black-and-white paintings and "Woman" series, to the abstract cityscapes of the 50's, Mr. de Kooning progressively piled on pigment along with detail.

The early works from the 30's were flat, almost discreet images of contained emotion, with the remains of his constant revisions incorporated like worry lines in the final canvases. Gradually this style gave way to master-pieces like "Attic" (1949) and "Excavation" (1950), which were maelstroms of weaving lines and roiling forms. By the time Mr. de Kooning got to bravura canvases like "Gotham News" (1955) and "Saturday Night" (1956), his art had become a near-volcano of raucous, nervous energy.

By the early 1960's his art seemed to empty out. Mr. de Kooning had left Manhattan to live full time in East Hampton in 1963. His new paintings, with their big brushstrokes crisscrossing large canvases, also suggested the flat stretches of potato fields and beaches at his new home.

The works he produced in the early 60's became clean slates for another round of building up images. The process reached orgiastic extremes by the 1970's. The ocean seemed to be in those fluid 70's pictures, with their splashes and cascades of pigment and forms. So were human references. Mr. de Kooning never lost touch with the world of figures and landscapes. An often repeated story has it that the critic Clement Greenberg, who championed pure abstraction, insisted that it had become "impossible today to paint a face," to which Mr. de Kooning replied, "That's right, and it's impossible not to."

In the 80's heavy impasto gave way to sanded and scraped surfaces, rainbows of color yielding to red, orange and blue bands twisting on bare backgrounds. Sometimes he blanketed areas with white, leaving only a fragment of previous detail to bob up from beneath the fresh covering.

The best early 80's pictures can be lyrical and elegiac. But there is in some of them an icy silence that is hard to dissociate from Mr. de Kooning's mental decline.

Willem de Kooning was born on April 24, 1904, in Rotterdam to Leendert de Kooning and Cornelia Nobel. His father was a wine, beer and soft-drink distributor. His mother ran a bar. They divorced when Willem was young, and when he was 12, his mother sent him out to apprentice at a commercial art and decorating firm.

The firm recommended him to the Rotterdam Academy of Fine Arts and Techniques, where he took classes in painting and learned about Picasso and other modernists. He spent 1924 in art school in Brussels, then returned to complete his degree in Rotterdam in 1925.

He immigrated to the United States in 1926, a stowaway. As a boy, he had developed a romantic fascination with America, reading about Walt Whitman, Frank Lloyd Wright and the Wild West. He wanted to find a job as a commercial artist.

"Being young, I really didn't understand the nature of painting," he said years later. "I really intended to become an applied artist. I mean, it was more logical to be a designer or a commercial artist. I didn't intend to become a painter. That would come later."

In 1927 he moved to a studio on West 44th Street, and for the next eight years he worked at odd jobs, painting only on weekends.

When the Federal Art Project of the Works Progress Administration was established in 1935, Mr. de Kooning joined its mural division. Harold Rosenberg, who as a critic would become one of his great advocates, served as his assistant on a proposed mural for the Williamsburg Federal Housing Project in Brooklyn. The work was never completed, but the project allowed the artist to devote himself full time to painting.

"After the project I decided to paint and do odd jobs on the side," he said. "The situation was the same, but I had a different attitude."

He was given his first one-man show in 1948, at the Egan Gallery, when he was already 44. None of his work sold during the show.

Mr. de Kooning's poverty has been often recounted. His wife, Elaine, said they were so short of money that whenever they cobbled a few cents together, they had to decide between cigarettes and food.

After the Egan show, Mr. de Kooning's work received increasing attention. Clement Greenberg hailed him as "one of the four or five most important painters in the country," and he was included in international surveys like the 1950 Venice Biennale.

By 1956, when Jackson Pollock died, opinion was split over who was the pre-eminent New York School painter, Mr. Pollock or Mr. de Kooning. (At Pollock's funeral, Mr. de Kooning famously conceded that it was Mr. Pollock who "broke the ice" for Abstract Expressionism.)

Mr. de Kooning had met his wife, then an art student, in 1938. For a time, they lived on 22nd Street in a loft with a hot plate and chairs salvaged from the trash. In 1944, they moved to a cold-water flat on in Greenwich Village. Their relationship was tumultuous and unconventional, and they separated in 1955. Mr. de Kooning's daughter, Lisa, was born to the artist Joan Ward the next year. Through the 1960's and 70's various women moved in and out of his life.

These were rough years for him. He drank more and more, suffering blackouts. His wife re-entered his life in the late 1970's, helped him stop drinking and cared for him until her own death at 68.

Mr. de Kooning had moved to East Hampton partly to escape the endless interruptions that attended his growing fame. He designed his own studio, a space with huge glass walls and white terrazzo floors. The studio was once compared to both a chemist's workshop and a vast kitchen, filled as it was with his neat array of house painter's brushes, scrapers, spatulas, knives and the salad bowls in which he is said to have mixed oil paints with ingredients like kerosene.

Since the 1950's, Mr. de Kooning had had major exhibitions of his work around the world, among them the Guggenheim Museum, the Whitney Museum of American Art, the National Gallery of Art in Washington, the Tate Gallery in London and the Metropolitan Museum in New York. By the boom years of the 1980's, prices for his art had skyrocketed: "Interchange," a 1955 painting, sold at Sotheby's in 1989 for $20.7 million.

The artist is survived by Ms. de Kooning and their three daughters.

Of painters working into old age, Mr. de Kooning once observed that Titian, at 90, was so badly afflicted by arthritis that his assistants had to tie on his paint brushes. "But he kept on painting Virgins in that luminous light, like he'd just heard about them," he said. "Those guys had everything in place, the Virgin and God and the technique, but they kept it up like they were still looking for something. It's very mysterious."

HENRI CARTIER-BRESSON

August 22, 1908–August 3, 2004

By Michael Kimmelman

Henri Cartier-Bresson, who used his tiny, hand-held 35-millimeter Leica camera to bear humane witness to many of the 20th century's biggest events, from the Spanish Civil War to the German occupation of France to the partition of India to the Chinese revolution to the French student uprisings of 1968, died on Tuesday at his home in Southwest France. He was 95.

Mr. Cartier-Bresson seemed to know everyone and to see everything of importance throughout the middle decades of the last century. Even in his later years, when he more or less abandoned photography to draw, he remained an astonishing live wire who liked to say that his approach to life had been shaped by Buddhism. His wife, the photographer Martine Franck, described him to the Dalai Lama as "a Buddhist in turbulence."

He photographed dozens of luminaries: his pictures of a convalescent Matisse during World War II, of Sartre as a boulevardier and of Mahatma Gandhi minutes before he was killed have become icons of photographic portraiture. But he was also the archetype of the itinerant photojournalist during the heyday of photojournalism immediately after the war, when millions of people still learned what was happening in the world through the pictures that ran in magazines like Life and Paris-Match.

It was Mr. Cartier-Bresson's prestige, along with that of Robert Capa, George Rodger and David Seymour, known as Chim, that established Magnum Photos, which they founded in 1947, as the world's premier photo agency. Under its aegis, Mr. Cartier-Bresson went to China, India, Indonesia, Egypt, Cuba, the Soviet Union.

But he was far more than a gifted photojournalist. He combined a Rabelaisian appetite for the world with a clarity of vision and intellectual rigor that linked him to French masters like Poussin. His wit, lyricism and ability to see the geometry of a fleeting image and capture it in the blink of an eye created a new standard for photography. His best photographs are among the best works of 20th-century art.

In 1932, he stuck his camera between the slats of a fence near the St.-Lazare railway station in Paris at precisely the right instant and captured a picture of the watery lot behind the station, strewn with debris. A man has propelled himself from a ladder that lies in the water.

Photographs of puddle jumpers were clichés then, but Mr. Cartier-Bresson brings to his image layer on layer of fresh and uncanny detail: the figure of a leaping dancer on a pair of posters on a wall behind the man mirrors him and his reflection in the water; the rippling circles made by the ladder echo circular bands of discarded metal debris; another poster, advertising a performer named Brailowsky, puns with the railway station and the ladder, which, flat, resembles a railroad track.

No wonder other photographers couldn't believe Mr. Cartier-Bresson's luck, much less his skill. The term that has come to be associated with him is "the decisive moment," the English title of "Images à la Sauvette" ("Images on the Run" might be a closer translation), a book of his photographs published in 1952. Mr. Cartier-Bresson described "the simultaneous recognition in a fraction of a second of the significance of an event, as well as the precise organization of forms that give that event its proper expression."

Walker Evans reviewed "The Decisive Moment" when it was published. "What Cartier-Bresson has is a more or less dependable ability to snap a picture," he wrote, "just when a child takes off into an ecstatic state of being as he skips beside a wall that is covered with an unearthly design of some lunarlike patina." The photograph to which Evans referred shows a boy in Valencia, Spain, in 1933, his upturned face giving him the surreal look of someone in a trance. In reality the boy was waiting to catch a ball he had tossed in the air.

It was Mr. Cartier-Bresson's genius to see instantaneously how the child's expression would take on new meaning if the ball were not visible in the picture.

Nicolas Nabokov, the composer and writer, once described Mr. Cartier-Bresson as having a "blond and pink head" and "gently mocking smile." His eyes, Nabokov said, were "like darts, sharp and clever, limpidly blue and infinitely agile."

He tried to immerse himself in places before photographing them, to blend into and learn about their cultures. Photographers and others who saw him work talked about his swift and nimble ability to snap a picture undetected. They also admired his coolness under pressure. The director Louis Malle remembered that despite the turmoil at the peak of the student protests in Paris in May 1968, Mr. Cartier-Bresson took photographs at the rate of only about four an hour.

Mr. Cartier-Bresson insisted that his works not be cropped, but otherwise disdained the technical side of photography; the Leica was all he ever wanted to use; he wasn't interested in developing his own pictures.

Henri Cartier-Bresson was born in Chanteloup, not far from Paris, on August 22, 1908, the oldest of five children in a wealthy family. His father was a textile manufacturer; on his mother's side were cotton merchants and landowners in Normandy.

He was educated in Paris, and he read, among other things, Proust, Dostoyevsky, Nietzsche and a book on Schopenhauer, which he said led him to Romain Rolland and to Eastern philosophy.

He also recalled being struck, while still a teenager, by Martin Munkacsi's photographs:. "I said to myself: 'How can one do that?'—that combination of plastic beauty and vitality. When I saw those photographs, I said to myself: 'Now here's something to do.'"

But his first love was drawing and painting. In 1927 he began to study painting with André Lhote, an early exponent of Cubism. Mr. Cartier-Bresson would credit Lhote with teaching him "everything I know about photography."

Next he studied English literature and art at Cambridge University, then in 1930 was inducted into the French Army. Once out of the Army, he headed for Africa to hunt boar and antelope.

The metaphor of shooting became a familiar one in writings about his photography. Mr. Cartier-Bresson used it often himself: "approach tenderly, gently on tiptoe—even if the subject is a still life," he said. "A velvet hand, a hawk's eye—these we should all have." He also said: "It's like being a hunter. But some hunters are vegetarians—which is my relationship to photography."

With a Brownie that he had received as a gift, he began to snap photographs in Africa, but they ended up ruined. And having contracted blackwater fever, he nearly died.

Recuperating in Marseilles in 1931, he acquired his first Leica. "I prowled the streets all day, feeling very strung-up and ready to pounce, determined to 'trap' life—to preserve life in the act of living," he recalled. "Above all, I craved to seize the whole essence, in the confines of one single photograph, of some situation that was unrolling before my eyes."

The photographs he took during the next decade were groundbreaking. He had his first show in Madrid in 1933, another in 1934 in Mexico City, and yet another in 1935 at the Julien Levy Gallery in New York City.

In New York he met the photographer Paul Strand. Making movies at the time, Strand inspired Mr. Cartier-Bresson to think about doing the same, and after his return to France, Mr. Cartier-Bresson got a job with Jean Renoir, the director, as an assistant on "A Day in the Country" and "The Rules of the Game."

He directed his first film, "Return to Life," in 1937, a documentary about medical aid to the Loyalists in the Spanish Civil War.

In 1937 he married Ratna Mohini, a Javanese dancer. They divorced after 30 years, and in 1970 he married Ms. Franck, who survives him, along with their daughter.

When the Germans invaded France, Mr. Cartier-Bresson became a corporal in the Army's Film and Photo Unit, but was captured in June 1940 at St. Dié in the Vosges Mountains and spent 35 months in prisoner-of-war camps.

He escaped twice and was recaptured, then succeeded on a third try and obtained false papers that allowed him to travel in France. During this time he photographed Matisse, Bonnard and Braque for the publisher Pierre Braun. As a member of the Resistance, he established a photo division.

After the war he visited New York City for a retrospective of his photographs at the Museum of Modern Art, one that had been planned when he was rumored to have been killed by the Germans. The exhibition was conceived as a posthumous tribute.

The columnist Dorothy Norman interviewed him when he arrived in the city on assignment for Harper's Bazaar to photograph the Brooklyn Bridge. During the war, Mr. Cartier-Bresson told her, "I became increasingly less interested in what one might call an 'abstract' approach to photography."

"In whatever one does, there must be a relationship between the eye and the heart," he said, adding, "There must be time for contemplation, for reflection about the world and the people about one. If one photographs people, it is their inner look that must be revealed."

Shortly after that, in 1948, Mr. Cartier-Bresson was in Delhi, India, to see Mahatma Gandhi, and he photographed him. Fifteen minutes after they parted, Mr. Cartier-Bresson heard shouts that Gandhi had been killed. He sped back. His photo essay on the death of Gandhi for Life magazine shows vast, swirling pools of mourners at the funeral, the potential melodrama of the scene held in check, as always, by strict form.

Critics have sometimes complained about the intrusiveness of photojournalists like Mr. Cartier-Bresson. John Malcolm Brinnin, who traveled across the United States with him in 1946, later called him "a humanitarian indifferent to people."

Mr. Cartier-Bresson heard this criticism and replied: "There is something appalling about photographing people. It is certainly some sort of violation; so if sensitivity is lacking, there can be something barbaric about it." He quit Magnum in 1966.

He had always carried a little sketch pad with him, and he committed himself to drawing with an enthusiasm that people around him found remarkable. He still took photographs, but now only occasionally.

A few years ago, Mr. Cartier-Bresson went to the Pompidou Center in Paris to sketch a Matisse portrait. Balanced on his favorite shooting stick, nose buried in his drawing, he paid no attention to the tourists who snapped his picture; they seemed unaware of who he was but were charmed simply by the sight of an old man sketching.

When he got up to leave, he noticed a couple sitting side by side on a bench, a child resting on the man's shoulder. "A perfect composition if you cut out the woman," Mr. Cartier-Bresson said, and made a brisk, chopping gesture toward her. The woman looked baffled. "Why didn't I bring my camera?" he asked. Then he clicked an imaginary shutter and left.

GORDON PARKS

November 30, 1912–March 7, 2006

By Andy Grundberg

Gordon Parks, the photographer, filmmaker, writer and composer who used his prodigious, largely self-taught talents to chronicle the African-American experience and retell his own personal history, died yesterday at his home in Manhattan. He was 93.

Gordon Parks was the first African-American to work as a staff photographer for Life magazine and the first black artist to produce and direct a major Hollywood film, "The Learning Tree," in 1969.

He developed a large following as a photographer for Life for more than 20 years, and by age 50 he ranked among the most influential image makers of the postwar years. In the 1960's he began to write memoirs, novels, poems and screenplays, which led him to directing films. In addition to "The Learning Tree," he directed the popular action films "Shaft" (1971) and "Shaft's Big Score!" (1972), prototypes for what became known as blaxploitation films.

No matter what medium he chose, Mr. Parks sought to challenge stereotypes while still communicating to a large audience. In finding early acclaim as a photographer despite a lack of professional training, he became convinced that he could accomplish whatever he set his mind to. To an astonishing extent, he succeeded.

Gordon Parks developed his ability to overcome barriers in childhood, facing poverty, prejudice and the early death of his mother. He came close to being claimed by urban poverty and crime. But his nascent talent was his exit visa.

His success as a photographer was largely due to his persistence and persuasiveness in pursuing his subjects, whether they were socialites or an impoverished slum child in Brazil.

Mr. Parks's years as a contributor to Life, the largest-circulation picture magazine of its day, lasted from 1948 to 1972, and cemented his reputation as a humanitarian photojournalist and an artist with an eye for elegance. He specialized in subjects relating to racism, poverty and black urban life, but he also took exemplary pictures of Paris fashions, celebrities and politicians.

"I still don't know exactly who I am," Mr. Parks wrote in his 1979 memoir, "To Smile in Autumn," adding, "I've disappeared into myself so many different ways that I don't know who 'me' is."

Much of his literary energy was channeled into memoirs. His talent for telling vivid stories was used to good effect in "The Learning Tree," a coming-of-age story about a young black man whose childhood resembled the author's, which he wrote first as a novel and later converted into a screenplay. Mr. Parks wrote, produced and directed the film, wrote the soundtrack, and was the cinematographer.

"Gordon Parks was like the Jackie Robinson of film," said Donald Faulkner, the director of the New York State Writers Institute. "He broke ground for a lot of people—Spike Lee, John Singleton."

As a photographer Mr. Parks combined a devotion to documentary realism with a knack for making his own feelings self-evident. The style he favored was derived from the Depression-era photography project of the Farm Security Administration, which he joined in 1942.

Perhaps his best-known photograph, titled "American Gothic," was taken during his time with the agency; it shows a black cleaning woman standing stiffly in front of an American flag, a mop in one hand, a broom in the other. Mr. Parks wanted the picture to speak to the existence of racial bigotry and inequality in the nation's capital.

Anger at social inequity was at the root of many of Mr. Parks's best photographic stories, including his most famous Life article, which focused on a desperately sick boy living in a Rio de Janeiro slum.

Mr. Parks credited his first awareness of the power of the photographic image to the pictures taken by his predecessors at the Farm Security Administration, including Dorothea Lange and Ben Shahn. He first saw their photographs of migrant workers in a magazine that he picked up while working as a waiter in a railroad car. "I saw that the camera could be a weapon against poverty, against racism, against all sorts of social wrongs," he said. "I knew at that point I had to have a camera."

Mr. Parks made his mark mainly with images within his essays, like "American Gothic." His portraits of Malcolm X, Muhammad Ali and Eldridge and Kathleen Cleaver evoked the styles and strengths of black leadership in the turbulent transition from civil rights to black militancy.

But at Life magazine Mr. Parks also used his camera for less politicized ends, photographing the socialite Gloria Vanderbilt and the actress Ingrid Bergman and the director Roberto Rossellini at the start of their notorious love affair.

Much as his best pictures aspired to be metaphors, Mr. Parks shaped his own life story as a cautionary tale about overcoming racism, poverty and a lack of formal education. The first version of his autobiography was "A Choice of Weapons," which was followed by "To Smile in Autumn," "Voices in the Mirror: An Autobiography" and "Half Past Autumn."

Gordon Roger Alexander Buchanan Parks was born on Nov. 30, 1912, in Fort Scott, Kan. He was the youngest of 15 children born to a tenant farmer, Andrew Jackson Parks, and the former Sarah Ross. Although mired in poverty and threatened by segregation and the violence it engendered, the family was bound by Sarah Parks's conviction that dignity and hard work could overcome bigotry.

Young Gordon's security ended when his mother died. He was sent to St. Paul, Minn., to live with the family of a sister. But during a quarrel a few weeks later, Mr. Parks's brother-in-law threw him out of the house. Mr. Parks learned to survive on the streets, using his untutored musical gifts to find work as a piano player in a brothel and later as the singer for a band. He never graduated from high school.

In 1933 he married Sally Alvis, and they had a child, Gordon Jr.

Mr. Parks traveled widely to find work during the Depression. He joined the Civilian Conservation Corps, toured as a semi-pro basketball player and worked as a busboy in addition to a dining car waiter.

In 1938 Mr. Parks purchased his first camera at a Seattle pawn shop. Within months his pictures were exhibited in the windows of the Eastman Kodak store in Minneapolis, and he began to specialize in portraits of African-American women.

After moving to Chicago, he turned to documenting the slums of the South Side. His efforts gained him a Julius Rosenwald Fellowship, which he spent as an apprentice with the Farm Security Administration's photography project in Washington.

In 1943, the project was transferred to the Office of War Information (O.W.I.). Mr. Parks became a correspondent for the O.W.I., photographing the 332nd Fighter Group, an all-black unit based near Detroit.

In 1944 Alexander Liberman, then art director of Vogue, asked Mr. Parks to photograph women's fashions, and his pictures appeared regularly in the magazine for five years.

Life often assigned Mr. Parks to subjects that would have been difficult or impossible for a white photojournalist to carry out, such as the Black Muslim movement and the Black Panther Party. But he also enjoyed making definitive portraits of Barbra Streisand, Alberto Giacometti and Alexander Calder.

In 1962 Mr. Parks began to write a story based on his memories of his childhood in Kansas. The story became the novel "The Learning Tree," and its success opened new horizons, leading him to write "A

Choice of Weapons," his first memoir; to combine his photographs and poems in a book called "A Poet and His Camera," and to become a film director, beginning with the adaptation of "The Learning Tree."

Mr. Parks's second film, "Shaft," was a hit of a different order. Ushering in an onslaught of movies in which black protagonists played leading roles in violent, urban crime dramas, "Shaft" was both a commercial blockbuster and a racial breakthrough. Its hero, John Shaft, was a private eye whose success came from operating in the interstices of organized crime and the law.

Mr. Parks's marriages to Sally Alvis, Elizabeth Campbell and Genevieve Young ended in divorce. Survivors include two daughters and a son.

"I'm in a sense sort of a rare bird," Mr. Parks said in 1997, adding, "I had a great sense of curiosity and a great sense of just wanting to achieve. I just forgot I was black and walked in and asked for a job and tried to be prepared for what I was asking for."

LIZ CLAIBORNE

March 31, 1929–June 26, 2007

By Eric Wilson

Liz Claiborne, the designer of indefatigable career clothes for professional women entering the workforce en masse beginning in the 1970s, died Tuesday in Manhattan. She was 78.

Her death, at New York–Presbyterian Hospital, was caused by complications of cancer, said Arthur Ortenberg, her husband.

Before she became the most successful women's apparel designer in America, Ms. Claiborne had worked for 20 years in the backrooms of Seventh Avenue sportswear houses like Youth Guild and Juniorite, making peppy dresses.

A strong-willed designer with an acute sense for business, she defied the male-dominated ranks of the fashion industry by starting her own company in 1976 with Mr. Ortenberg, a textiles executive. In an apt reversal of roles, she gave him the corporate title of secretary.

Ms. Claiborne correctly anticipated a market for affordable, professional-looking clothes that women could wear to compete on an equal footing with men in corporate professions. She became something of a role model, and her label an inspirational emblem, to those who, like her, were looking to break through glass ceilings.

When Ms. Claiborne retired from active management of Liz Claiborne Inc. in 1990, it was the nation's largest women's apparel maker, with $1.4 billion in sales.

The company remains among the largest in fashion with $4.85 billion in sales in 2005 and a portfolio of brands that now includes Dana Buchman, Juicy Couture, Ellen Tracy and Lucky Brand jeans.

Ms. Claiborne's company was the first founded by a woman to enter the rankings of the Fortune 500, in 1986, and she was one of only a handful of women who were chief executives of companies on that list.

As a designer, Ms. Claiborne placed practical concerns over the glamour of the catwalks and the prestige of designer prices. Her arrival as a fashion brand caught the beginning of a great change in American society as women headed to the workplace in large numbers.

She created a new foundation for a modern working woman's wardrobe. Her creative expressions were made of colorful tailored separates that could be mixed with other pieces to create many outfits.

As women made headway in corporate America, Ms. Claiborne expanded with office-friendly sportswear that conveyed a potent blend of intelligence, strength and femininity.

"I wanted to dress busy and active women like myself, women who dress in a rush and who weren't perfect," Ms. Claiborne said in a 1989 interview. "But loving clothes, I knew clothes could do a certain thing for you from a flattering point of view."

Her strategy was to provide an alternative to the expensive options facing women. Her designs, she said, were "businesslike, but not too pinstripe, more casual, more imaginative, less uptight."

The formula was an instant success. Starting with an initial investment of $50,000 in savings and $200,000 raised from friends, Liz Claiborne Inc. grossed $2.6 million in its first year. The company went public in 1981, with net income of $10 million on sales of $117 million. By its 10th anniversary, sales exceeded $560 million, its payroll had grown to 2,200 people, and its operations included showrooms at 1441 Broadway and warehouses in Secaucus, N.J. In 1990, the company shipped over 35 million items.

Ms. Claiborne, with her close-cropped black hair and oversized glasses, was an imposing boss to her staff, presiding over design meetings with a glass bell she rang to maintain order.

After retiring, she and Mr. Ortenberg set off on travels to remote corners of the world. They founded a charitable foundation for environmental conservancy projects, among them a wildlife preserve in northeastern Tibet and efforts to rescue elephants in Myanmar and European brown bears in the Carpathian mountains of Romania.

Anne Elisabeth Jane Claiborne was born March 31, 1929, in Brussels, the daughter of Omer Villere, a banker, and Louise Carol Fenner Claiborne. As a teenager, she and her mother followed her father around Europe.

When she was 19, Ms. Claiborne, who had studied painting in Brussels and Nice but never completed high school, won a design contest advertised in Harper's Bazaar magazine and was inspired to pursue a career in fashion. Her parents did not approve. According to Irene Daria's 1990 book "The Fashion Cycle," the family was driving through Manhattan two years later when Ms. Claiborne declared, "I'm staying." Her father let her out of the car, handed her $50 and said, "Good luck."

Ms. Claiborne stayed with her grandmother while looking for a job. Tina Leser eventually hired her to work at her dress house as a sketcher and fit model.

She went on to work for a few other dress companies and later the Rhea Manufacturing Company, where she met her second husband, Mr. Ortenberg, in 1954. Although both were married at the time—she to Ben Schultz—they began an affair and left the company because of it, Mr. Ortenberg said. They divorced their spouses and were married in 1957.

Jonathan Logan, another large dress manufacturer, later hired Ms. Claiborne as the designer of its Youth Guild division, where she worked for 16 years. When the label folded, she and Mr. Ortenberg started Liz Claiborne Inc.

In addition to Mr. Ortenberg, she is survived by a son from her first marriage, Alexander G. Schultz, and by Mr. Ortenberg's children from his prior marriage, Neil Ortenberg and Nancy Ortenberg.

YVES SAINT LAURENT

August 1, 1936–June 1, 2008

By Anne-Marie Schiro

Yves Saint Laurent, who exploded on the fashion scene in 1958 as the boy-wonder successor to Christian Dior and endured as one of the best-known and most influential couturiers of the second half of the 20th century, died on Sunday at his apartment in Paris. He was 71.

His death was confirmed by Dominique Deroche, a spokeswoman for the Pierre Bergé–Yves Saint Laurent Foundation.

During a career that ran from 1957 to 2002 he was largely responsible for changing the way modern women dress, putting them into pants both day and night, into peacoats and safari jackets, into "le smoking" (as the French call a man's tuxedo jacket), and into leopard prints, trench coats and, for a time in the 1970s, peasant-inspired clothing in rich fabrics.

Mr. Saint Laurent often sought inspiration on the streets, bringing the Parisian beatnik style to couture runways and adapting the sailors' peacoats he found in Army-Navy stores in New York into jackets that found their way into fashionable women's wardrobes around the world. His glamorous evening clothes were often adorned with appliqués and beadwork inspired by artists like Picasso, Miró and Matisse. Above all, he was a master colorist, able to mix green, blue, rose and yellow in one outfit to achieve an effect that was artistic and never garish.

Among the women of style who wore his clothes were Catherine Deneuve, Paloma Picasso, Nan Kempner, Lauren Bacall, Marella Agnelli and Marie-Hélène de Rothschild.

Mr. Saint Laurent achieved instant fame in 1958 at the age of 21 when he showed his Trapeze collection, his first for Christian Dior following the master's death. But unlike many overnight sensations, Mr. Saint Laurent managed to remain at the top of his profession as fashion changed from an emphasis on formal, custom-made haute couture to casual sportswear.

His influence was at its height during the 1960s and '70s, when it was still normal for couturiers to change silhouettes and hemlines drastically every six months.

Among his greatest successes were his Mondrian collection in 1965, based on the Dutch artist's grid-like paintings, and the "rich peasant" collection of 1976, which stirred so much interest that the Paris show was restaged in New York for his American admirers. "The clothes incorporated all my dreams,"

he said after the show, "all my heroines in the novels, the operas, the paintings. It was my heart—everything I love that I gave to this collection."

Originally a maverick and a generator of controversy—in 1968, his suggestion that women wear pants as an everyday uniform was considered revolutionary—Mr. Saint Laurent developed into a more conservative designer, a believer in evolution rather than revolution. He often said that all a woman needed to be fashionable was a pair of pants, a sweater and a raincoat.

"My small job as a couturier," he once said, "is to make clothes that reflect our times. I'm convinced women want to wear pants."

By 1983, when he was 47, his work was recognized by fashion scholars as so fundamentally important to women's dress that a retrospective of his designs was held at the Costume Institute of the Metropolitan Museum of Art, the first time the museum had honored a living designer.

That exhibition could be considered the peak of Mr. Saint Laurent's career, for after that he settled into a classical mode of reinterpreting his earlier successes. The boy wonder had turned into the elder statesman.

Yet because so many of his early designs seeped into the public domain (and into many other designers' collections), he managed to retain his stellar position through his retirement in 2002.

Yves Henri Donat Mathieu-Saint-Laurent was born in Oran, Algeria, on Aug. 1, 1936, to Charles and Lucienne Andrée Mathieu-Saint-Laurent. His father was a lawyer and insurance broker, his mother

a woman of great personal style. He grew up in a villa by the Mediterranean with his two younger sisters, Michelle and Brigitte.

His mother and sisters, all of Paris, survive him.

The young Yves was said to be a quiet and retiring child (as an adult he was often described the same way) who developed a love for fashion and the theater. As a teenager, he designed clothes for his mother, who had them whipped up by a local seamstress. (His mother became his greatest fan, sitting in the front row at all his shows and wearing no one else's designs.)

He went to Paris at 17 to try his luck in theatrical and fashion design. He won first prize in an International Wool Secretariat design competition for his sketch of a cocktail dress. This led to an interview with Dior, who noted an uncanny resemblance between Mr. Saint Laurent's cocktail dress and one he himself was working on, and hired him on the spot as his assistant.

For three years, Mr. Saint Laurent worked closely with Dior, who called him "my dauphin." After Dior died suddenly in 1957, the House of Dior named Mr. Saint Laurent its head designer. At 21, he found himself at the head of a $20-million-a-year fashion empire.

His first collection in his new position, shown on Jan. 30, 1958, was based on the trapeze, a youthful silhouette that started with narrow shoulders and a raised waistline, then flared out gently to a wide hemline. The collection was received with great enthusiasm, and Yves Saint Laurent would soon become a household name.

He was credited with rejuvenating French fashion and securing his country's pre-eminent position in the world of haute couture. Newsboys shouted his triumph across the streets of Paris, while he waved to the crowds below the balcony of the House of Dior on the Avenue Montaigne. The dauphin was crowned king.

In September 1960, Mr. Saint Laurent was called up for 27 months of compulsory military service in France's war in Algeria. About three weeks after his induction, he was hospitalized for a nervous collapse. In October, the House of Dior gave his job to Marc Bohan, his former assistant.

In November, Mr. Saint Laurent was discharged from the army and entered a private clinic near Paris. In later years, he suffered from depression and an alcohol and drug dependency that he attributed to the drugs he had been given in a military psychiatric hospital. But he almost always recovered in time to take the ritual walk down the runway, however unsteadily, at the finale of his shows.

In January 1961, Mr. Bohan's collection for Dior was a huge success. Mr. Saint Laurent sued Dior after the house refused to reinstate him after his army discharge. He was awarded 680,000 francs by the court, equivalent then to about $140,000.

In September 1961, Mr. Saint Laurent announced plans to open his own haute couture house in partnership with his lover, Pierre Bergé. Mr. Bergé remained his lifelong business partner and was responsible for the company's financial success, although they split up as a couple in the early 1980s.

The first Yves Saint Laurent collection was shown on Jan. 19, 1962. It was the beginning of a success story that led to a ready-to-wear line sold in the designer's own Rive Gauche boutiques around the world; to hundreds of licenses for scarves, jewelry, furs, shoes, men's wear, cosmetics and perfumes, and even cigarettes; and to a host of awards, including the French Legion of Honor in 1985.

The House of Saint Laurent had various owners over the years. In 2000, Gucci Group bought the ready-to-wear and fragrance divisions, while Mr. Bergé and Mr. Saint Laurent retained the haute couture business. Under Gucci, to Mr. Saint Laurent's vocal displeasure, the YSL ready-to-wear line was designed by the American fashion star Tom Ford.

"The poor guy does what he can," Mr. Saint Laurent said of his successor.

When Mr. Saint Laurent announced his retirement in January 2002, many fashion editors and teary-eyed friends considered the possibility that he had felt pressured to resign. He and Mr. Bergé denied that.

The designer managed several times to create controversy during his career with, of all things, his fragrances. In 1971, he appeared nude in an advertisement for his men's cologne YSL. Then, in 1977, he named one of his women's perfumes Opium, which led to charges that he was glamorizing drug use.

Mr. Saint Laurent lived elegantly. All his homes—including famous ones in Deauville, France, and Marrakech, Morocco—which he shared with a succession of French bulldogs, always named Moujik, were lavishly decorated and filled with antiques and artwork by Picasso, Cocteau, Braque and others.

"Every man needs aesthetic phantoms in order to exist," Mr. Saint Laurent said at the announcement of his retirement. "I have known fear and the terrors of solitude. I have known those fair-weather friends we call tranquilizers and drugs. I have known the prison of depression and the confinement of hospital. But one day, I was able to come through all of that, dazzled yet sober."

ver left the line-up again until
s voluntary resignation fourteen
ars later. Perhaps that story is
t cut from the whole cloth. Geh-
g has denied it, but Pipp insists
st as vehemently that it is true.
 any rate, it is an interesting side-
ht on how a spectacular career
as begun.

Slipped in 1938

The beginning of the Gehrig play-
g days was abrupt but the ending
as a much slower process. In 1937
e Iron Horse batted .351, his
elfth successive season over the
0 mark. But in 1938 the Yankee
ptain slipped to .295, the same
gure he had established in his
25 campaign.

Not only his hitting but his field-
g had lost much of its crispness.
atted balls that the Gehrig of old
d gobbled up easily skidded past
m for base hits. In fact, the
tuation had developed to such an
tent that there was continual
lk in Spring training in 1939 that
e endurance record was approach-
g its completion.

This became even more obvious
 the early games of the campaign.
ankee followers were amazed to
e how badly Gehrig had fallen
om the peak. He was anchored
rmly near first base and only the
elding wizardry of Joe Gordon to
s right saved Gehrig from looking
ry bad. The second sacker over-
ifted to cover the hole between
m and his captain. Lou couldn't
 to his right any more.

At bat Gehrig was not even a pale
adow of his former self. Once he
d the outfielders backing up to
e fences when he stepped to the
ate. But this time he could hard-
 raise the ball out of the infield.
 one occasion when he caromed
 looping single to left—a certain

At his desk in t
new duties as a mem.

mond stalwarts had
join in the tribute t
team-mate, who had
carry on long after
tirement from the g

The group included
immortals as Babe
Hoyt, Bob Meusel,
Joe Dugan, Tony
Koenig, Benny Ber
Schang, Everett Sco
George Pipgras and

Overcome by this
reception, Gehrig fir
his emotions, and,
most remarkable va
delivered in a sport
poured his heart ou
throng of listeners,
for their appreciatio
them, with charac
that he still consi
"the luckiest fellow
much to live for."

From then until t
season Gehrig stuck
retired field captai
every day on the b
companied the club
trips, and at the fin
all four of the 193
games in which
crushed another Na
rival.

With the close of
Lou retired himself
circle of close frienc
time in fishing, a sp
to baseball in its
him, and on Oct. 11
other surprise move
La Guardia announc
ment to a ten-year t
ber of the three-n
Parole Commission
$5,700 a year.

ATHLETES

died late tonight of
r. His age was 59.
of Johnson's family
bedside when the end

wife, Hazel, died in
five children, three
s.

Great Popularity

not been a pitcher in
who had a greater hold
rican baseball public
Johnson. Following
Christy Mathewson,
attained popularity
fans of the country
lly to that of "Big
ways than on
oth were great pitch
re sterling characters
vere idols of young
1936 Johnson was one
five men named to
ll of Fame at Coop-
Y., the others being
ty Cobb, Honus Wag-
hewson.
coming to the big
veral years after
but contemporary
en Christy was fading
gster was at his peak,
time to wait for his
tined to be with a sec-
club, Johnson waited
ng seasons before he
first world's series.
hance came, however,
d, and his feat of win-
Senators in the decid-
th the Giants in 1924,
ng classic, earned for
secure in the baseball

than any other hurler in histor
That mark was 313. made in 191
These are only a few of forty
five records. His twenty-one year
with one club and his pitching 80
games for Washington constitut
another. He led the America
League in most complete game
for the greatest number of year
six, in 1911, 1913, 1914, 1915, 19
and 1918. He led his league
earned-run averages for six year
In addition to his 3,497 strik
out record, he held the big leagu
record for the greatest number
consecutive scoreless innings, fi
ty-six, and he scored three conse
utive shut-outs in four playin
days. On April 15, 1911, he struc
for the in the inning.

No-Hit, No-Run Game

Not until 1920 did Johnson pitc
his way into the baseball hall
fame reserved for no-hit, no-ru
games. On July 1 of that year
turned the trick against the Bo
ton Red Sox. In his major leagu
career he won 414 games and lo
276. His best season was in 191
when he won thirty-six games a
lost only seven. He led the Ame
ican League in games won for
years. His longest winning stre
was sixteen, in 1912. He was vot
the most valuable player in t
American League in 1924.
Johnson was born in Humbol
Kan., on Nov. 6, 1887. Drifti
out to the Pacific Coast in 19
Johnson was discovered by a T
coma (Wash.) scout and offered
job with that club, then in the
Northwestern League. For so
reason Johnson did not fancy
ing to Tacoma and, though

OLD TOM MORRIS

June 16, 1821–May 24, 1908

LONDON—"Old Tom" Morris, a veteran professional golfer, who was known by golfing men all over the world, died today at St. Andrew's from concussion of the brain, caused by falling down a flight of stairs in the clubhouse.

KNUTE ROCKNE

March 4, 1888–March 31, 1931

WICHITA, Kan.—Knute Rockne, Notre Dame football coach, and seven others, were killed at 11 o'clock this morning when a ten-passenger Trans-Continental & Western Airways plane dived into a pasture in the Flint Hills cattle country near Bazaar in Southeastern Kansas.

In a hazy drizzle, which gave poor flying visibility, the tri-motored Fokker left Kansas City at 9:15, three-quarters of an hour late after waiting for mail connections. It was due in Wichita at 10:25 under the regular schedule.

Witnesses heard the drone of the motors above the clouds, heard them sputter and stop and soon saw the big craft flash down through the cloud bank with a trail of smoke fluttering out behind. A wing tore loose and swirled away like a falling leaf, to land half a mile from where the plane plowed itself into the soft earth of a pasture.

Rockne was on his way to Los Angeles. He had waited at Kansas City for a chat with his sons, Billy Rockne, 11 years old, and Knute Rockne Jr., 14 years old, but missed them by minutes because he had to leave the railroad station before they arrived in order to get to the airport on time.

The boys, who had been visiting their mother at Coral Gables, Fla., were returning to Pembroke School, Kansas City. When news of the accident came, Dr. D. M. Nigro, president of the Notre Dame Club of Kansas City and a close friend of Rockne, got into telephone communication with Mrs. Rockne. He brought the sons here by automobile tonight. The news was told to them only after their arrival. They showed the strength of their father in bearing the blow.

By Robert F. Kelley

From his days as a player, Knute Rockne made his influence felt on the trend of football. As captain of the 1913 Notre Dame team, he figured, at end, in the most successful exhibition of forward passing the game had seen up to that time; and from that date on the forward pass grew steadily to its present importance in the game.

As a coach he brought the shift play to its highest state of perfection and made it such an important factor in offensive football that the rules committee finally passed legislation designed to take some of its power away.

That shift development, the backfield hop, was the most important of his contributions to the coaching of the game, but he added others, notably the reshaping of the line. Prior to Rockne, linemen were big men inevitably. Rockne brought the idea of using linemen, particularly guards, in interference, and demonstrated that the small, fast lineman could hold his own with the big man and outplay him where the big man was not as fast.

He worked for the perfection of a team as a whole and his last two teams won game after game through the successful application of what came to be called "the perfect plays." In these, every individual carried out a part of the blocking, and when no man failed to carry out his job the play often went for a touchdown.

In coaching he tried always for perfection and spent hours in teaching the art of blocking. Simple plays, well executed, were his idea of the way to win football games. He had small use for any so-called trick plays. There were only seven places in a line to send a man with a ball, he said, and there ought not to be many more than seven plays.

"The best thing I ever learned in life," he said, "was that things have to be worked for. A lot of people seem to think there is some sort of magic in making a winning football team. There isn't, but there's plenty of work."

As a player and captain of the 1913 Notre Dame team, Rockne began his shaping of football's destinies by bringing the forward pass suddenly and dramatically into the front of the game. Army that season had scheduled Notre Dame as a "breather" game on its schedule. Only a small crowd turned out, and they stood amazed as Notre Dame defeated Army, 35 to 13.

Gus Dorais threw 17 passes in that game and 13 were completed, and a great majority of these went to the short, chunky end, Knute Rockne. The forward pass had been more or less of a haphazard thing until that time. The success of this Western team with it amazed the football world. Dorais and Rockne remained behind at West Point for a few days after that game to show the Army how it was done.

That game was the direct result of the Summer before. Dorais and Rockne had obtained vacation jobs together at a mid-West beach and included a football in their baggage. All that Summer they got out on the beach and threw passes.

As a coach, of course, Rockne's record is one of the most remarkable that any coach of any sport has ever piled up. Nearly all of his teams have been in the front rank of the game, despite the fact that they always played hard schedules. Five of them were undefeated.

Taking over the head coach job, after helping instruct in the chemistry department of Notre Dame, in 1918, Rockne had almost immediate success. His 1919 team was undefeated and his 1920 team was one of the greatest that he had.

So successful were his teams with the backfield shift that three years ago the football rules committee, fearing the offense of the game would overbalance the defense, began ruling against it and this last year finally insisted that a full second, in which an official might count five, must come between the close of the shift and the start of the ball.

Rockne never was reconciled to this. Legislating against the shift, he said, was like taking the feinting out of boxing and leaving in only the slugging.

Rockne organized coaching schools. He assisted with Summer schools all over the country and in 1928 even conducted one at sea when he chartered a ship and took a party of coaches and athletes to the Olympic Games of that year.

Perhaps his greatest teams came in 1920, 1924, 1929 and 1930. On the first was George Gipp, who was named by Rockne as the greatest player he ever had. The coach told the story of seeing Gipp, who was not trying for the team, throwing and kicking a ball on the campus and of inducing him to join the squad. Gipp died a few weeks after the close of the 1920 season of a throat infection, with Rockne at his bedside.

The 1924 team was the one of the famous Four Horsemen: Harry Stuhldreher, Jimmy Crowley, Don Miller and Elmer Layden. As a combination they have not been excelled in modern backfields, and they had a great line in front of them.

If there were any doubt of the influence of Rockne on football, the list of head coaches for the past year might remove it. There were, throughout the country, North, South, East and West, 23 head coaches of football from Notre Dame without naming the assistants here and there.

The mere record of his work fails to bring out the incisive, clear-cut character and personality of the man. He gave words to the vocabulary of the sport as well, some of which fit people who criticize players and coaches after a defeat. "Sunday morning coaches" was Rockne's name for them.

JAMES NAISMITH

November 6, 1861–November 28, 1939

LAWRENCE, Kan.—Dr. James A. Naismith, inventor of basketball, died at 1:50 A.M. (Central Standard Time) today of a heart ailment following a cerebral hemorrhage. His age was 78.

Dr. Naismith was professor emeritus of physical education at Kansas University.—*The Associated Press*

By The New York Times

"The father of basketball," Dr. James A. Naismith had the distinction of originating the only major sport created in the United States, with the possible exception of baseball, about which there is much controversy.

The game, called Naismith ball when he devised it in 1891 at the Springfield (Mass.) Y.M.C.A. College for the delectation of Gay Nineties youths, has been streamlined and speeded up so that it appears to be quite different from the original sport. The fast, sprightly, colorful basketball of today, enjoyed in many lands by the young of both sexes in college, school, club, association and society gymnasiums and on professional courts, bears the same resemblance to the early game as that of a modern airliner to the Wright brothers' first "flying machine."

Dr. Naismith was on the staff of the Y.M.C.A. College when he was asked by Dr. Luther Gulick, head of the physical training department, to develop something to employ the energy of the young men of the college who found dumbbells and Indian clubs too tame between the football and baseball seasons.

The placing of the players as forwards and guards was suggested by lacrosse, with which he, an American citizen of Canadian birth, was familiar. Soccer, English rugby and other sports contributed to the game.

The original 13 rules were typed and handed to young Springfield students. The first game was played at Springfield College, with peach baskets tacked up in the gymnasium and with a soccer ball as the missile. It was played either in December, 1891, or January, 1892, according to different accounts.

At first it was not unusual for from 40 to 50 to play on a side, and for a time seven, eight and nine men composed a team. Now, under American men's rules, five men are on a team, with a girls' team numbering six. In 1936, basketball received a place at the Olympic Games.

Dr. Naismith played basketball only twice, in 1892 and 1898. Years later he explained that he "just didn't get around to playing." He committed many fouls. "I guess my early training in wrestling, boxing and football was too much for me," he said. "My reflexes made me hold my opponents. Once I even used a grapevine wrestling clamp on a man who was too big for me to handle."

Dr. Naismith was born in Almonte, Ont., Nov. 6, 1861, the son of John and Margaret Young Naismith. He received an A.B. degree from McGill University in 1887 and graduated from Presbyterian College, Montreal, in 1890 and from the Springfield Y.M.C.A. College in 1891. He received an M.D. degree from the University College in 1898 and an M.P.E. degree from Springfield in 1910.

In 1887–90 he was director of physical education at McGill, and in 1890–95 he held the same post at Springfield College. From 1895 to 1898 he was physical director of the Y.M.C.A. at Denver. He became physical director at the University of Kansas in 1898.

Dr. Naismith remained on the Kansas faculty until 1937, when he became Professor Emeritus. He did military service with the First Kansas Regiment for four months in 1916 and served the Y.M.C.A. in France in 1917–19.

In 1894 Dr. Naismith married Miss Maude E. Sherman. They had five children. His first wife died in 1937. He married Mrs. Florance Kincaid last Spring.

LOU GEHRIG

June 19, 1903–June 2, 1941

Lou Gehrig, former first baseman of the New York Yankees and one of the outstanding batsmen baseball has known, died at his home, 5204 Delafield Avenue, in the Fieldston section of the Bronx, last night. Death came to the erstwhile "Iron Man" at 10:10 o'clock. He would have been 38 years old on June 19.

Regarded by some observers as the greatest player ever to grace the diamond, Gehrig, after playing in 2,130 consecutive championship contests, was forced to end his career in 1939 when an ailment that had been hindering his efforts was diagnosed as a form of paralysis.

The disease was chronic, and for the last month Gehrig had been confined to his home. He lost weight steadily during the final weeks and was reported 25 pounds under weight shortly before he died.

Until his illness became more serious Gehrig went to his office regularly to perform his duties as a member of the New York City Parole Commission, a post he had held for a year and a half following his retirement from baseball. Ever hopeful that he would be able to conquer the rare disease—amyotrophic lateral sclerosis, a hardening of the spinal cord—although the ailment was considered incurable by many, Gehrig stopped going to his desk about a month ago to conserve his strength.

He was conscious until just before the end. At the bedside when he died were his wife, the former Eleanor Twitchell of Chicago; his parents, Mr. and Mrs. Henry Gehrig; his wife's mother, Mrs. Nellie Twitchell, and Dr. Caldwell B. Esselstyn.

When Gehrig stepped into the batter's box as a pinch hitter for the Yankees on June 1, 1925, he started a record that many believe will never be equaled in baseball. From that day on he never missed a game until April 30, 1939—fifteen seasons of Yankee box scores with the name of Gehrig always in the line-up. He announced on May 2, 1939, that he would not play that day, and thus his streak came to an end.

But as brilliant as was his career, Lou will be remembered for more than his endurance record. He was a superb batter in his heyday and a prodigious clouter of home runs. The record book is liberally strewn with his feats at the plate.

Only in his first season, 1925, and in his last full campaign, 1938, did he fail to go over the .300 mark. Once he led the American League in hitting with .363, but on three occasions he went over that without winning the batting crown—.373, .374 and .379.

But baseball has had other great hitters before and other great all-around players. It was the durability of Gehrig, combined with his other qualities, that lifted him above the ordinary players and put him in a class all his own.

Columbia Lou's string of consecutive games began, innocently enough, when the late Miller Huggins sent him up to bat for Peewee Wanninger on June 1, 1925. The husky 22-year-old promptly singled.

Huggins was impressed, but, according to the tale that is told, he had no notion of using him as a first baseman. The Yankees had a star at the initial sack in those days, Wally Pipp. But Pipp was troubled with frequent headaches.

On June 2 he was bothered by pains in his head.

"Has anyone an aspirin tablet?" asked Pipp.

Huggins overheard him and, on a sheer hunch, decided to use the "kid"—Gehrig—at first base. He never left the line-up again until his voluntary resignation 14 years later.

Perhaps that story is not cut from the whole cloth. Gehrig has denied it, but Pipp insists just as vehemently that it is true. At any rate, it is an interesting sidelight on how a spectacular career was begun.

The beginning of the Gehrig playing days was abrupt but the ending was a much slower process. In 1937 the Iron Horse batted .351, his 12th successive season over the .300 mark. But in 1938 the Yankee captain slipped to .295, the same figure he had established in his 1925 campaign.

Not only his hitting but his fielding had lost much of its crispness. Batted balls that the Gehrig of old had gobbled up easily skidded past him for base hits. In fact, the situation had developed to such an extent that there was continual talk in Spring training in 1939 that the endurance record was approaching its completion.

On April 30, 1939, he played his last big league game against the Washington Senators. The Bombers lost and Gehrig realized that he was a detriment to his team. When the Yanks took to the field again in Detroit on May 2, Gehrig—his batting average down to .143—withdrew from the line-up, his first missed game after 2,130 straight.

On June 12, when the Yankees engaged in an exhibition game in Kansas City, Lou played the last three innings, did nothing and promptly left for the Mayo Clinic. He was there a week, determined to discover just what was the matter with him. That something was wrong he was certain.

On June 21 the diagnosis was made. It was that he had a mild attack of paralysis. His career thus was brought to an abrupt conclusion. And an amazing career it had been.

The public's reaction to Gehrig's swift retirement gave rise to one of the most inspiring and dramatic episodes in sport when on July 4, in ceremonies preceding the afternoon's holiday double-header, a crowd of 61,808 joined in the Lou Gehrig Appreciation Day exercises at the Yankee Stadium and thundered a "hail and farewell" to baseball's stricken Iron Horse.

Overcome by this spontaneous reception, Gehrig finally mastered his emotions, and, in perhaps the most remarkable valedictory ever delivered in a sport arena, literally poured his heart out to his great throng of listeners, thanking them for their appreciation and assuring them, with characteristic pluck, that he still considered himself "the luckiest fellow on earth, with much to live for."

From then until the end of the season Gehrig stuck by his guns as retired field captain, and spent every day on the bench.

With the close of the campaign, Lou retired himself within a small circle of close friends, spent much time in fishing, and on Oct. 11 figured in another surprise move when Mayor La Guardia announced his appointment to the three-man Municipal Parole Commission at a salary of $5,700 a year.

Gehrig was born in New York on June 19, 1903. He starred on the High School of Commerce nine in New York, then matriculated at Columbia, pitching, outfielding and playing first base.

He quit before he had been long at Morningside Heights, joining the Yankees in 1923, shuttling for two years between the major league team and Hartford in the Eastern League.

Recalled by the Yankees in 1925, Gehrig batted .295 in 126 games and then he began to rocket through the baseball firmament. His first full season showed him with .313, but after that his successive batting averages were .373, .374, .300, .379, .341, .349, .334, .363, .329, .354, .351 and finally he was back to .295 in his last full campaign.

The .363 average gave him the batting championship in 1934, but signal honors had come to him before that. In 1927, his second full campaign with the Yankees, he was voted the most valuable player in the American League.

Seven times he participated in world series and, oddly enough, was a star on the Yankees of 1926–27–28 and with the all-star contingent of 1936–37–38. Each of these groups has its supporters as the greatest baseball team of all time. Ruth–Gehrig–Meusel, the famed "Murderers' Row," or DiMaggio–Gehrig–Dickey? Those were the batting fulcrums around which the teams revolved. Columbia Lou was the lone tie between the two.

His series deeds have been awe-inspiring. His lifetime average in world series games was .361—his full regular average .340—and twice he hit over the fantastic mark of .500, with .545 in 1928 and .529 in 1932. Babe Ruth, however, holds the series record of .625 in 1928.

That is an oddity in itself, Gehrig with two terrific averages but still behind the Babe. Yet for the better part of his career the Iron Horse was to be in the shadow of Ruth. Lou entered baseball when the Babe was riding high, straddling the sport such as no man has straddled it before or since.

Gehrig never left that shadow. For one thing, he did not have the flamboyant Ruth personality. They were teammates but far apart, one quiet, reserved and efficient and the other boisterous, friendly and efficient. Let it not be deduced that the Iron Horse was not of the friendly type. He was pleasant at all times, but unlike Ruth he never considered the world at large as his particular friend. Whereas the Babe would greet all and sundry with a booming "Hiya, kid?" Lou's was a more personalized welcome.

What a pair they made at the plate, coming up to bat in order! Each was likely to drive the ball out of the park. Frequently either or both did just that.

In spite of the shadow, so firm was Gehrig's place in the Yankee scheme of things that Manager Joe McCarthy refused to break the first baseman's string even when there was a clamor to the effect that the Iron Horse himself would benefit from it. Marse Joe shook his head to that.

"Gehrig plays as long as he wants to play," he said. Not many ball players would be granted such a privilege.

The day before he entered the Mayo Clinic for the examination, baseball celebrated its centennial at Cooperstown and the Hall of Fame was dedicated. Ruth already had been elected to it and within a short time another bronze plaque joined the Babe's as Henry Louis Gehrig took his proper place among the all-time greats that this sport had produced.

For though Baseball's Hall of Fame committee decided to hold no elections for new candidates in 1939, it chose, upon recommendation of the Baseball Writers Association of America, to make an exception and name Gehrig as the lone Hall of Fame award for the year.

WALTER JOHNSON

November 6, 1887–December 10, 1946

WASHINGTON—Walter Johnson, former strikeout king of the American League and a member of baseball's official Hall of Fame, died late tonight of a brain tumor. His age was 59.

Members of Johnson's family were at the bedside when the end came. Johnson's wife, Hazel, died in 1930, leaving five children, three of them boys. —*The Associated Press*

There has not been a pitcher in recent years who had a greater hold on the American baseball public than Walter Johnson. Following the immortal Christy Mathewson, "Big Barney" attained popularity among the fans of the country equal virtually to that of "Big Six."

Both were great pitchers. Both were sterling characters and both were idols of young America. In 1936 Johnson was one of the first five men named to baseball's Hall of Fame at Cooperstown, N.Y., the others being Babe Ruth, Ty Cobb, Honus Wagner and Mathewson.

Johnson, coming to the big leagues several years after Mathewson, but contemporary with him when Christy was fading and the youngster was at his peak, had a longer time to wait for his triumph. Destined to be with a second-division club, Johnson waited 17 long seasons before he played in his first world series.

When the chance came, however, he made good, and his feat of winning for the Senators in the deciding game with the Giants in 1924, a 12-inning classic, earned for him a place secure in the baseball Hall of Fame.

When he retired as a player in 1927, after 21 consecutive years with one club—a record in itself—he went for a time to the minors as a manager and then returned to Washington to become the leader of the team with which he had started as a major leaguer in 1907. He was manager of the Senators for 1929, 1930, 1931 and 1932.

He retired in 1932, but in midsummer of 1933 returned to the big leagues to become manager of the Cleveland team. "The Big Train," as he was also called, piloted the Indians until he resigned early in August, 1935.

Johnson received much publicity on Feb. 22 of the following year when he hurled two silver dollars across the Rappahannock River—a span of 272 feet—in connection with the annual Washington's Birthday celebration at Fredericksburg, Va. He thus duplicated a feat said to have been performed by George Washington in the latter's boyhood days.

The Presidential campaign of 1936 found Johnson taking an active interest in politics, and his Maryland farm was the scene of a rally for Alf Landon, Governor of Kansas and the Republican party's candidate for President. (Johnson was born in Humboldt, Kan., on Nov. 6, 1887.)

In 1938 Johnson was the lone Republican elected to the Board of Commissioners in Montgomery County, Md. Two years later he was the Republican nominee to represent Maryland's Sixth Congressional District, but was defeated by his Democratic opponent.

Between games of a Yankee-Washington doubleheader at Yankee Stadium on Aug. 23, 1942, Johnson and George Herman (Babe) Ruth came out of retirement to thrill 69,136 fans in a benefit program which enriched the Army-Navy Relief Fund by more than $80,000.

The assemblage gave a tremendous ovation as Johnson walked out to the mound and the Sultan of Swat stepped to the plate. Then the Big Train tossed them up, perhaps not so fast, but with the same effortless motion, while Ruth swung with all his old-time fervor.

Looking over his record, one finds it a veritable mine of wonderful feats. In his major league career he won 414 games and lost 276. His best season was in 1913, when he won 36 games and lost only seven. He held the world's shut-out record, having registered 113 shut-outs since 1907. He also struck out more batters than any other pitcher. His total, including his last season as a hurler, 1927, when he was ill and unable to pitch very many times, was 3,497 for 802 games.

In 1926, when Johnson celebrated his 20th year with the Washington club, a Walter Johnson Day was held in Washington on Aug. 2. A letter from President Coolidge was read. "I am sure that I speak for all when I say that he (Walter Johnson) has been a wholesome influence in clean living and clean sport," the President wrote.

BABE RUTH

February 6, 1895–August 16, 1948

By Murray Schumach

Babe Ruth died last night. The 53-year-old baseball idol succumbed to cancer of the throat at Memorial Hospital.

The home-run king's death ended nearly two years of fighting a disease that had sent him repeatedly to hospitals. Among those at the deathbed were his wife, Claire, his two daughters and his sister.

The powerful six-footer who had once electrified Americans with 60 homers in a season had wasted away. The once black hair seen when the Babe doffed his cap rounding the bases was almost white.

Probably nowhere in all of fiction could one find a career more dramatic than that portrayed in real life by George Herman Ruth. Known the world over as the Babe, he rose from the obscurity of a charitable institution in Baltimore to be the leading figure in professional baseball. He was also its greatest drawing-card, its highest salaried performer—at least of his day—and the idol of millions of American youngsters.

It has always been debatable whether Ruth owed his fame and the vast fortune it brought him to his ability to smash more home runs than any other player in the game's history or to a personality that was intensely real and "regular."

He made friends by the thousands. Affable, boisterous and good-natured to a fault, he could scarcely recall a name, but he overcame this deficiency with consummate skill. If you looked under 40, it was "Hello, kid, how are you?" If you appeared above 40, it was "Hello, doc, how's everything going?"

Single-handed, he tore the final game of the 1928 world series in St. Louis to shreds with his mighty bat by hitting three home runs over the right-field pavilion. That night, returning to New York, he went on a boisterous rampage and no one on the train got any sleep.

Such was the blending of qualities that made Babe Ruth a figure unprecedented in American life. He was a born showman off the field and a marvelous performer on it.

Of his early days in Baltimore even Babe himself was, or pretended to be, somewhat vague. However, the following account of his boyhood years appeared in a national magazine under Ruth's own "by-line":

"In the first place I was not an orphan. My mother, whose maiden name was Schanberg, lived until I was 13. My father, George Herman Ruth, lived until my second year in the majors.

"On June 13, 1902, when I was 7 years old my father and mother placed me in St. Mary's Industrial School in Baltimore. It has since been called an orphanage and a reform school. It was, in fact, a training school

for orphans, incorrigibles, delinquents, boys whose homes had been broken by divorce, runaways picked up on the streets of Baltimore and children of poor parents."

According to this account, he was in and out of St. Mary's until 1914. "The last item on my 'record' at St. Mary's," he wrote, "was a single sentence, written in the flowing hand of one of the teachers. It read: 'He is going to join the Balt. Baseball Team.'"

Then began a train of circumstances that would carry this raw-boned youngster to fame and a fortune that has been estimated as close to $1,000,000. Brother Benedict, an instructor at St. Mary's, was a great lover of the national pastime. He encouraged the youngster to play as much as he could, and later recommended him to his friend Jack Dunn, owner of the Baltimore Orioles of the International League, and Ruth received a trial. That was in 1914. The same summer he was sold to the Boston Red Sox for $2,900.

Ruth rapidly developed into one of the most talented left-handed pitchers in the majors. He had tremendous speed and a baffling cross-fire curve, which greatly impressed Ed Barrow, later associated with Colonel Jacob Ruppert as general manager of the Yankees. Barrow became the leader of the Red Sox in 1918 and gave much time to Ruth's development.

Even then Ruth also displayed unmistakable talent for batting a ball with tremendous power and unusual frequency, and Barrow decided to convert Ruth into an outfielder on the theory that a great hitter could be built into a greater attraction than a great pitcher.

It was a momentous decision, for in the 1918 world's series against the Cubs Ruth turned in two masterful performances on the mound for the Red Sox, winning both his games. He had also turned in one victory for the Red Sox against Brooklyn in the world's series of 1916.

Barrow had also seen Ruth, in 1918, hit 11 home runs, an astonishing number for that era.

The next year—1919—Ruth cracked 29 home runs. This total surpassed by four the major league record for home runs in a season.

The year 1920 marked the turning point in Babe Ruth's career and in the course of organized baseball. Baseball men generally agree that Babe Ruth practically single-handedly diverted the game into new channels that would reap an unprecedented golden harvest.

The first sensation came that winter when Ruth was sold to the Yankees for a reported price of $125,000, a record sum.

The Babe did not disappoint. The Yankees were

then playing their home games at the Polo Grounds, home of the Giants, and before the close of the season they were giving their more affluent rivals and landlords a stiff run for the city's baseball patronage.

Ruth surpassed all expectations by crashing out the unheard-of total of 54 home runs, and crowds which had lavished their attention on the Giants now jammed the historic Polo Grounds to see the marvelous Bambino hit a homer.

By the 1921 season, the nation's attention was centered on an even greater demonstration of superlative batting skill by the amazing Babe Ruth. Home runs began to scale off his bat in droves, crowds jammed ball parks in every city in which he appeared, and when he closed the season with a total of 59 circuit clouts, surpassing by five his own record of the year before, the baseball world lay at his feet.

The Yankees that year also captured the first pennant ever won by New York in the American League. The Yankees won again in 1922 and in 1923, in addition to winning the world's championship that year.

Also in 1923 came into being the "House That Ruth Built," the great Yankee Stadium that seated more than 70,000. The right-field bleachers became "Ruthville." Homers soared into them in abundance, and the exploitation of Babe Ruth, the greatest slugger of all times, was at its height.

Money was now pouring upon the Babe and being poured out as speedily. In 1921 he had drawn $20,000 and the following season he signed a five-year contract at $52,000 a season. He was also collecting royalties on various ventures.

But money meant nothing to the Babe, except as a means for lavish entertainment. He gambled recklessly. The Ruthian waistline began to assume alarming proportions. Training had become a bore.

There seemed to be no limits to his vitality or stamina. It was no trick for him to spend an evening roistering with convivial companions right through sun-up and until game time the next afternoon and then pound a home run.

In the 1924 season Colonel Ruppert began to fear he had made a mistake in having signed the Babe to that long-term contract at $52,000 per season, which ran from 1922 to 1926. The Yankees lost the pennant that year, and there came rumblings that Miller Huggins, the manager who had piloted the Yankees through three successful pennant years, was not in harmony with the Babe.

In 1925 the crash came. Ruth collapsed at the railroad station at Asheville, N.C., spent weeks in a hospital, and did not appear in a Yankee line-up until June 1.

Then a change came over the Babe. He trained faithfully in 1926, hammered 47 homers, and started the Yankees on another pennant-winning era. Sixty homers, a new record, sailed off his bat in 1927.

Another pennant followed that year and another in 1928, on top of which the Yankees swept through two world series triumphs in those two years without losing a single game.

In the Spring of 1929, after his first wife, from whom he had been estranged, died, the Babe married Mrs. Claire Hodgson, formerly an actress.

In 1927 he had become the highest salaried player of his time with a three-year contract at $70,000 a year. In 1930 he signed a two-year contract at $80,000 per season, but in 1932 accepted a $75,000 stipend for one season.

At the close of his baseball career it was estimated that in his 22 years in the major leagues he had earned in salaries $896,000. In addition, he was reputed to have made $1,000,000 from endorsements, tours, movies and radio appearances.

When he retired the Babe was able to live in comfort, maintaining a large apartment on New York's West Side.

Ruth came to the parting of the ways with the Yankees after the 1934 season, and in 1938 was named coach of the Dodgers. Burleigh Grimes, the manager of the team, recommending the move, said, "You can't keep a man like that out of baseball." But the Babe was not re-engaged as coach at the close of the season.

April 27, 1947, was designated as "Babe Ruth Day" at the Yankee Stadium, where a crowd of 58,339 turned out. That May Ruth established the Babe Ruth Foundation, devoted to the needs of underprivileged youth.

He went to Hollywood to help with the filming of his life story. While there, he was informed that the Yankees were planning to celebrate the 25th anniversary of the Yankee Stadium, on June 13, 1948.

For the occasion, the Babe donned his old uniform with the No. 3 on the back. When he was introduced and walked slowly to home plate, a thunderous ovation from 49,641 fans greeted him.

It was the last time No. 3 was worn by a Yankee player. The Babe turned his uniform over to the Hall of Fame, which sent it to the baseball shrine at Cooperstown, N.Y., to be placed among the Ruth collection there.

JIM THORPE

May 22, 1887–March 28, 1953

LOS ANGELES—Jim Thorpe, the Indian whose exploits in football, baseball and track and field won him acclaim as one of the greatest athletes of all time, died today after suffering a heart attack in his trailer home in suburban Lomita. His age was 64.

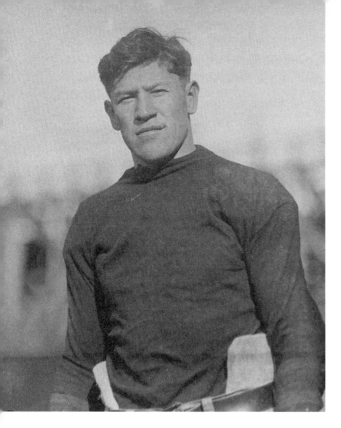

Hero of the 1912 Olympic Games at Stockholm and a towering football figure, Jim Thorpe was probably the greatest natural athlete the world had seen in modern times.

King Gustaf V of Sweden said to the black-haired Sac and Fox Indian as he stood before the royal box, "Sir, you are the greatest athlete in the world."

That was after Thorpe almost single-handedly gained the Olympic honors for the United States, setting a point-total record never before approached and dominating the games as no other figure. Thorpe came back from Stockholm with $50,000 worth of trophies. They included a Viking ship presented to him by the Czar of Russia, and gifts from King Gustaf.

A month later the new American sports idol was toppled from his high pedestal when the Amateur Athletic Union filed charges of professionalism against him, accusing him of receiving pay for playing summer baseball in the Eastern Carolina League. The amount of money was negligible, helping to tide him over at school, but the American Olympic Committee offered its apologies and sent back the gifts and medals lavished upon the young man to whom President Theodore Roosevelt had cabled long messages of congratulation.

Thorpe had won four of the five events in the Pentathlon and finished third in the other, a record unequaled to this day, and in the decathlon he scored 8,412 out of a possible 10,000 points, also unequaled.

Thorpe's decathlon feats in the Olympics have since been surpassed by Bob Mathias, who won the event for the second straight time last year. However, another Olympic great—Finland's Paavo Nurmi—declared that "Jim Thorpe could still beat them all."

Even if Thorpe never could beat Mathias in his prime, most experts still place the Indian ahead as an all-around athlete.

In 1950 Thorpe's athletic prowess won for him selection as the greatest athlete of the 20th century and the greatest football player in an Associated Press poll of sportswriters and broadcasters.

Before leaping into worldwide fame as the star of the Olympics, Thorpe had become a national sports figure as a member of the famous Carlisle Indians football teams, coached by Glenn S. (Pop) Warner. In 1911 and 1912 he was chosen as halfback on Walter Camp's All-America teams.

Thorpe played professional football for almost 15 years and in his prime at Carlisle and as a pro he never had to leave the field because of an injury, such was his courage and stamina. In his last year at the Indian school he won letters in five major sports, and he was proficient in others.

He could run the 100-yard dash in 10 seconds flat, the mile in 4:35, and the 220-yard low hurdles in 24 seconds. He broad-jumped 23 feet 6 inches and high-jumped 6 feet 5 inches. He pole-vaulted 11 feet, put the shot 47 feet 9 inches, threw the javelin 163 feet, the hammer 140 feet and the discus 136 feet.

Thorpe was born on a farm at Prague, Okla., the son of Hiram Thorpe, a ranchman. Dutch, Welsh and Irish blood were understood to flow in his veins, but he was predominantly Indian.

Young Jim was sent to the Haskell Indian School at Lawrence, Kan., and then to the Carlisle School at Carlisle, Pa. Warner persuaded him to come out for football in 1907. The next year he became a regular and attracted attention as a ball-carrier and kicker. He weighed around 178 pounds.

In the spring of 1908 Jim made the track team. Jumping and hurdling were his specialties. By the time he finished his five-year term at Carlisle in the spring of 1909 he had developed into a track star.

Thorpe returned to his home and played baseball in North Carolina. In 1911 he came back to Carlisle. That year he won All-America honors in football, as he did in 1912, performing sensationally.

President Eisenhower can attest to Thorpe's hitting power. When the general was a cadet at the United States Military Academy, the Army team played Carlisle, the Indians winning, 27–6. Thorpe stopped General Eisenhower time after time, and in the process the general injured his knee and never played again.

In his track days Carlisle was booked to meet the Lafayette team at Easton. A welcoming committee was puzzled when only two Indians got off the train.

"Where's your team?" they asked.

"This is the team," replied Thorpe.

"Only two of you?"

"Only one," Jim said with a smile. "This fellow's

the manager."

After his suspension as an amateur athlete, following his return from Stockholm, Thorpe left Carlisle in 1913 and signed with the New York Giants.

Although he never could be considered a star in the major leagues, having trouble hitting a curveball, Thorpe was good enough to last for seven seasons. In his last year, 1919, he batted a highly creditable .327, playing first base and the outfield for the Boston Braves.

Meanwhile, he went into the game he loved best—football—as a professional.

In 1915 he organized the famous Canton (Ohio) Bulldogs, which beat most of the good teams. Later he played with the Cleveland Tigers, the LaRue (Ohio) Indians and the Rock Island Independents. Jim got heavier and found it more difficult to keep in shape and he was appearing in New York at the Polo Grounds in a drop-kicking contest with Charley

Brickley as an extra attraction to the game. He played with other teams in Hammond, Ind., and Portsmouth, Ohio, and finally his competitive days ended.

Thorpe fell upon hard days. He went to California in 1930 as master of ceremonies for C. C. Pyle's cross-country marathon, known as the bunion derby. He settled down in Hawthorne, Calif., and got work as an extra in motion pictures, appearing in Western serials and in short football features, but things got worse for him.

After an operation for cancer of the lip in 1951, Thorpe had been discovered to be nearly penniless and groups throughout the country raised thousands of dollars for him.

In 1949, Warner Brothers started work on a motion picture entitled "Jim Thorpe—All American," with Burt Lancaster in the athlete's role. The picture reached Broadway in the summer of 1951.

BILL TILDEN

February 10, 1893–June 5, 1953

HOLLYWOOD, Calif.—William Tatum (Big Bill) Tilden 2nd, former world tennis champion, died late today, apparently of a heart attack, in his Hollywood apartment. He was 60 years old.—*The Associated Press*

William T. Tilden 2nd won a place among the great American heroes of sport. At the height of his re-

markable career, in sport's golden age of the Twenties, his name was a national and international byword, along with Jack Dempsey, Bobby Jones, Babe Ruth and Tommy Hitchcock.

Mr. Tilden was an amateur in those days and, great as was his fame, he won even more superlatives as a professional at an age when tennis players and athletes in other fields of endeavor had long since closed their competitive careers. His victories, in his 40s, established him as one of the real miracle men of sport.

Mr. Tilden's record shows that:

> He won the national amateur championship seven times, from 1920 through 1925, inclusive, and in 1930.

> He was the first American to win the men's championship at Wimbledon, in 1920, and that he triumphed there twice again.

> He was ranked as the No. 1 player of his country as an amateur ten times from 1920 through 1929.

It was as the ace of the American Davis Cup team that Mr. Tilden gained his greatest prestige, though from 1920 through 1925 he was so invincible that no player the world over stood a chance against him in any competition.

In 1928, Mr. Tilden was the captain of the team that went to Europe seeking to win back the cup. Out of that trip arose the most celebrated of the many dramatic episodes in his career.

While in France he was declared ineligible to play because of his violation of the player-writer provision of the amateur rule. That provision had been written into the rule as the aftermath of the controversies between Mr. Tilden and the United States Lawn Tennis Association over his writing activities.

The United States defeated Italy without his services and qualified to meet France in the challenge round. When the French realized that he was not to be allowed to play against their team, their indignation knew no bounds.

This was the first time they were to have the honor of staging a Davis Cup challenge round. For the occasion, they had built a beautiful new stadium at Auteuil, indirectly a monument to the drawing power of Tilden, just as is the stadium of the West Side Tennis Club at Forest Hills, Queens. To put on the show without Big Bill was unthinkable to them. It was like putting on Hamlet without the Melancholy Dane.

The outcry was so great, feeling ran so high, that Ambassador Myron T. Herrick found it necessary to intercede for the sake of international unity. Upon his request, the United States Lawn Tennis Association restored Tilden to the team at the 11th hour.

To add to the drama, Tilden threw a scare into the French by defeating the great Rene Lacoste. Upon his return home with the team, which was beaten by the French, Tilden was brought up on charges of violating the amateur rule and was barred from competing in the national championships that year, 1928.

Except for that year and 1926, Mr. Tilden was in every national championship final from 1918 through 1929.

It was on the private court of the family country home that Bill Tilden had his introduction to tennis. There and at Germantown, Philadelphia, where he was born on Feb. 10, 1893, he was playing the game when he was barely able to hold a racquet.

In 1920 Tilden was named on the Davis Cup team that went to England for the qualifying rounds, and with his victory at Wimbledon began the most absolute sway tennis has known. From the age of 27 to 33 he bestrode the court like a colossus. In the autumn of 1922, he suffered the amputation of the upper joint of his right middle finger as the result of an infection.

That might have ended the career of some, but Mr. Tilden overcame it, as he did physical frailties in his boyhood days and a knee injury later in his career. In December, 1930, Tilden said good-bye to amateur tennis. Like Bobby Jones, he made his exit by way of the motion pictures. He signed a contract to appear in a series of short films devoted to tennis, automatically disqualifying himself for amateur competition.

The next February, Mr. Tilden launched his career as a professional at the age of 38.

On Feb. 3, 1950, he was named the greatest tennis player of the first half of the 20th century by an overwhelming vote in a poll taken by The Associated Press.

In 1947, Mr. Tilden was sentenced to the county jail in Los Angeles for contributing to the delinquency of a minor. He was released after seven and one-half months. Arrested again in 1949 for violation of his probation, he remained in jail from February until December of that year.

CY YOUNG

March 29, 1867–November 4, 1955

NEWCOMERSTOWN, Ohio—Denton True (Cy) Young, one of baseball's great pitchers, died today at the age of 88.

A member of baseball's Hall of Fame, Mr. Young was stricken while sitting in a chair in the home of Mr. and Mrs. John Benedum, with whom he made his home near here. —*The Associated Press*

Traded to the majors from the minors for a suit of clothing, Cy Young thrilled the baseball world from 1890 to 1911 with a blazing fastball that set pitching records still unequaled.

Six feet two inches tall and weighing 210 pounds, this Ohio farmer pitched and won more games than any major leaguer. When he retired at the age of 45 because his legs had weakened, he had won 511 of 826 decisions in both leagues and for five teams. In all, he hurled in 906 games.

As the starting pitcher for the Boston Red Sox in 1903, Mr. Young threw the first pitch in a world series game. Fifty years later, as a guest at the opening game of the world series between the Brooklyn Dodgers and New York Yankees, he stood in the pitcher's box and threw a ceremonial strike to the Yankee catcher, Yogi Berra, to open the series. He was 86 at the time.

During his career, he was a 30-game winner five seasons; a 20-game victor 16 times. He pitched one perfect game, two other no-hit shutouts and performed the "iron man" feat of hurling and winning complete games of a doubleheader.

One of the early members of the baseball Hall of Fame at Cooperstown, N.Y., Mr. Young pitched for the Cleveland Nationals, St. Louis Cardinals, Cleveland Indians and Boston Braves, in addition to the Red Sox. He won 291 National League games and 220 in the American.

For 14 consecutive years, beginning in 1891, Mr. Young won 20 or more games. The 1892 season, when he posted a 36–10 record, was his best.

Mr. Young's feat of pitching 23 consecutive hitless innings over a four-game span early in 1904 still stands as a major league record. His total of 2,836 strikeouts was surpassed only by the late Walter Johnson's 3,497.

He was born on a farm in Gilmore, Ohio, on March 29, 1867. While pitching for the Canton (Ohio) club of the old Tri-State League in 1890, Mr. Young was nicknamed Cy. "I thought I had to show all my stuff," he recalled years later, "and I almost tore the boards off the grandstand with my fast ball. One of the fellows called me 'Cyclone,' but finally shortened it to 'Cy,' and it's been that ever since."

The league disbanded during the 1890 season and the pitcher joined the Cleveland Nationals early in August of that year.

Still a gawky country boy, he made his major league debut against Cap Anson's Chicago White Stockings and won the game. Mr. Young won 10 and lost 7 for Cleveland during the late stages of the season. Two of those victories were obtained on Oct. 4, when he captured both ends of a doubleheader against Philadelphia.

In his first complete major league campaign the next year, Mr. Young won 27 and lost 22 games. For the next 13 seasons he stayed above the .500 mark. He pitched his first major league no-hit, no-run contest on Sept. 18, 1897, blanking Cincinnati, 6 to 0. His affiliation with Cleveland ended after the 1898 campaign and he played with the St. Louis Cardinals in 1899 and 1900.

Mr. Young began eight years with the Red Sox in 1901. While blanking Philadelphia on May 5, 1904, he did not permit an opposing runner to reach first base. It was the third perfect game in major league history. On June 30, 1908, he won his third no-hit, no-run decision in the majors by shutting out New York, 8 to 0.

He was traded to the Cleveland Indians in 1909, and in the middle of the 1911 campaign was traded to the Braves. He retired to his farm near Peoli, Ohio, after that season.

BABE DIDRIKSON ZAHARIAS

June 26, 1911–September 27, 1956

GALVESTON, Tex.—Mrs. Mildred (Babe) Didrikson Zaharias, famed woman athlete, died of cancer in John Sealy Hospital here this morning. She was 45 years old.

Mrs. Zaharias had been under treatment since 1953, when the malignant condition was discovered after she had won a golf tournament. The tournament was one named for her—the Babe Zaharias Open of Beaumont, Tex., where she was reared.

Mrs. Zaharias is survived by her husband, George, a professional wrestler, along with three brothers and three sisters.

From the time she made the headlines during the 1932 Olympic Games at Los Angeles, winning the javelin throw and 80-meter hurdles, Mrs. Zaharias reigned as the world's top all-around woman athlete. In 1949 she was voted the greatest female athlete of the half century by the Associated Press, a selection that surprised no one.

She was born on June 26, 1911, in Port Arthur, Tex. Her father was a Norwegian ship carpenter who had sailed 19 times around Cape Horn.

She was an athlete almost from the time she could lift a baseball bat. As a youngster she excelled at running, swimming, diving, high-jumping, baseball and basketball, in addition to being adept with the javelin and at going over hurdles.

She beat the boys at mumblety-peg and outsped them in foot races. Her nickname of "Babe," after Babe Ruth, was acquired after she had hit five home runs in a baseball game. Instead of "wasting time with dolls," she conditioned

herself by using a backyard weightlifting machine built of broomsticks and her mother's flatirons.

At least part of Mrs. Zaharias's success could be attributed to her powers of diligence. When she decided to center her attention on golf, a game she began to play in 1935, she drove as many as 1,000 golf balls a day. She developed an aggressive, dramatic style, hitting down sharply and crisply on her iron shots and averaging 240 yards off the tee with her woods.

She began winning titles in 1940. In that year she captured the Western and Texas Open Championships. By the end of 1950 she had won every available golf title.

Asked whether she thought of retiring, Mrs. Zaharias answered: "As long as I am improving I will go on, and besides, there's too much money in the business to quit."

She turned professional in 1947, after her triumph in the British Amateur championship, a distinction that she was the first American to earn. In 1948 she won the world championship tournament and the National Open. She repeated her victory in the "world" event the next three years, and she won the Nationals in 1950.

The athlete from Texas was a constant source of colorful stories for newspapermen. She once pitched for the St. Louis Cardinals in an exhibition baseball game. She toured the United States giving billiard exhibitions and showed her versatility with a demonstration of needlework and typing—86 words a minute.

She met her future husband on a golf course in 1937. They eventually set up house in Tampa, Fla., where Mrs. Zaharias designed a modern push-button kitchen and made chintz curtains.

In April, 1953, she underwent an operation for cancer. Ten months after the surgery she won the $5,000 Serbin Women's Open Tournament at Miami Beach.

She regarded her comeback as complete when she won the 1954 Women's United States Open, recapturing the title she had held twice previously.

"It will show a lot of people that they need not be afraid of an operation and can go on and live a normal life," she commented after this triumph.

Early in 1955, however, a hip pain sidelined Mrs. Zaharias, and her physicians found that she was again suffering from cancer. Her condition worsened, and she was in and out of the hospital.

Mrs. Zaharias accepted stoically the news that the disease had returned. "Well, that's the rub of the greens," she told her husband. Together they established the Babe Didrikson Zaharias Fund to support cancer clinics and treatment centers.

During the latter stages of her career as a golfer it was estimated that she was earning more than $100,000 a year for exhibitions, endorsements and other activities connected with sports.

While she captivated many with her versatile stunts as a youngster, it was her achievements and deportment later in life that gained for her the most popularity. As a young girl she had disdained lipstick, plastered her hair back and talked out of the side of her mouth.

But as a top player and drawing power in golf, her attitude and demeanor changed. The once lonely tomboy became a social success. She developed into a graceful ballroom dancer and became the life of many a social gathering. At times she would take out a harmonica and give a rendition of hillbilly tunes she had learned as a youngster.

This change was the cause of a more convivial feeling toward her by rivals. In her younger days her desire to win had served to toughen her as far as any opponent was concerned. But in her later days, instead of goading her rivals with, "Yep, I'm gonna beat you," she began encouraging the younger girls on the golf circuit.

TY COBB

December 18, 1886–July 17, 1961

ATLANTA—Ty Cobb, the No. 1 player elected to baseball's Hall of Fame and probably the greatest star in the game's history, died today.

The famed Georgia Peach, a giant in the major leagues almost from the start of his career in 1905, died at the age of 74 in Emory University Hospital.

Cobb, one of the most feared players because of his daring and his short-fused temper, had suffered from cancer of the prostate gland, diabetes and chronic heart disease.

After playing 22 years with the Detroit Tigers and two years with the Philadelphia Athletics, Cobb was chosen in 1936 to the Hall of Fame. He beat out Babe Ruth, who was still playing at the time, by seven votes.

Sixteen of the major league records he set still stand.

Tall (6 feet), tough and fiery, Cobb was noted for the deadly use of his spikes on the base paths, his dramatic base stealing and his batting skill. His numerous records include the highest career batting average (.367); most batting championships (12); most stolen bases (829).

During 14 of his years in the major leagues he batted when the old "dead" ball was still in use and when there was virtually no limit on the tricks a pitcher could use.

Cobb started with Detroit on Aug. 30, 1905, at the age of 18. The Tigers had paid between $700 and $750 to get him from Augusta in the South Atlantic League. Cobb hit a double off Jack Chesbro in his first time at bat.

His first-year batting average was .240 for 41 games, but from then until he called it quits in 1928 he never fell below .322. Three times, he batted more than .400. He had 4,191 hits in 11,429 times at bat.

Batting left-handed and throwing right-handed, the center field star played in 3,033 games, scored 2,244 runs, hit 297 triples and nine times made more than 200 hits in a season. In 1915 he stole 96 bases.

A master of the hook and fall-away slide, Cobb raised base stealing to a height it has never regained. Several times Cobb stole second, third and home in one inning. One manager reportedly asked his catcher:

"What do you do when Cobb breaks for second?"

The catcher replied: "I throw to third."

Cobb was once home-run champion of his league, with nine in 1909, helping Detroit win its third straight American League pennant.

It was not only his ability that inspired fear and respect in his foes, but also his temper. Often called the "stormy petrel," as well as less printable epithets, he played every game as if it were the deciding contest in the world series.

He was frequently embroiled in fights with other players and with fans. In 1912 the Tigers went on strike after he was suspended for attacking a heckler who happened to be a cripple. In another famous scrap, Cobb squared off with George Moriarty, an umpire, under the stands.

In a soft-spoken way he liked to make jokes about his days as a "difficult player," and it was a habit of his to attend many of the old-time affairs and reminisce.

He continued to take long hikes and to go hunting, activities that he credited with developing his endurance and quick awareness.

As a manager, as well as a player, Cobb gave fans repeated thrills and excitement. In the off-season of 1920, he signed to manage Detroit. He brought the Tigers home second in 1923, but that was his best.

In his last years as player-manager, Cobb drove fans and opposition to distraction by jogging back

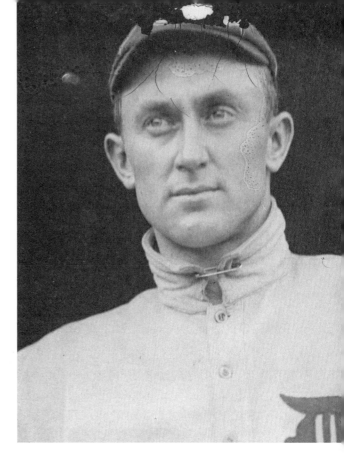

and forth from center field to talk to his pitcher, shift his infield, or otherwise evolve strategy. He resigned as manager in 1926.

Soon afterward he figured in a potential scandal that threatened to become another "Black Sox" affair. With Tris Speaker, another of baseball's heroes, he was accused by Dutch Leonard, a former Tiger pitcher, of figuring in an agreement to throw a game in 1919—the year of the crooked series between Cincinnati and Chicago.

But on Jan. 27, 1927, they were exonerated by Judge Kennesaw Mountain Landis, and Cobb said at once he felt "honor bound" to put in at least one more "big year."

Connie Mack signed him for the Athletics for a reported $75,000, and Cobb promptly predicted a pennant. But Mack's line-up of stars—he had signed Eddie Collins and Zach Wheat as well—lost to the Yankees.

Waspish as he was on the field, Cobb was a quiet man off it. Known to have invested his money wisely, he became a millionaire, largely on the investments he had made in a soft-drink stock.

After he quit, he rarely went to a ball park. He insisted that the game that he had played in the era of the multiple steal, the squeeze bunt and the dead ball was not matched in contemporary baseball.

In November, 1953, Cobb, who never went to college, donated a reported $100,000 to establish the Cobb Educational Foundation for promising Georgia students. His father had wanted him to become a lawyer or physician instead of a ballplayer.

Cobb was playing baseball when he was nine years old. A picture of the Royston (Ga.) Midgets, taken in 1895, hardly indicated, however, that of the whole squad of unsmiling youngsters, a dwarfed half-pint with torn stockings sitting at the left end of the front row would be the only one to make the picture worth reprinting.

Cobb was one of the first major leaguers to get into military service during World War I. He became a captain with the Army's Chemical Warfare Division and served overseas.

Cobb was divorced twice. His first wife was the former Charlie Lombard of Augusta. They had five children. In 1955, Cobb divorced his second wife, Mrs. Frances Cass Cobb.

The nickname Georgia Peach was given to Cobb by Grantland Rice, the sportswriter, who was impressed with the daring, talented youngster in action with Augusta. The name stuck.

BOBBY JONES

March 17, 1902–December 18, 1971

ATLANTA—Bobby Jones, the master golfer who scored an unparalleled grand slam by winning the United States and British Open and Amateur Tournaments in 1930, died today at his home. He was 69.

Mr. Jones, a lawyer by profession, who competed only as an amateur, had suffered from a progressive disease of the spinal cord since 1948. By the middle of last December he was no longer able to go to the offices of his firm, Jones, Bird & Howell. Death came from an aneurysm in his chest.

By Frank Litsky

In the decade following World War I, America luxuriated in the Golden Era of Sports and its greatest collection of super-athletes: Babe Ruth and Ty Cobb in baseball, Jack Dempsey and Gene Tunney in boxing, Bill Tilden in tennis, Red Grange in football and Bobby Jones in golf.

Many of their records have been broken, but one, sports experts agree, may outlast them—Bobby Jones's grand slam of 1930.

Jones, an intense, unspoiled young man, started early on the road to success. At the age of 10 he shot a 90 for 18 holes. At 11 he was down to 80, and at 12 he shot a 70. At 14 he competed in a major men's tournament, and at 21 he was United States Open champion.

At 28 Jones achieved the grand slam victories in one year—in the United States Open, British Open, United States Amateur and British Amateur championships. At that point, he retired from tournament golf.

A nation that idolized him for his success grew to respect him even more for his decision to treat golf as a game rather than a way of life.

"First come my wife and children," he explained. "Next comes my profession, the law. Finally, and never as a life in itself, comes golf."

His record, aside from the grand slam, was magnificent. He won the United States Open championship four times (1923, 1926, 1929 and 1930), the British Open three times (1926, 1927 and 1930) and the United States Amateur five times (1924, 1925, 1927, 1928 and 1930).

Though Jones appeared cool and calculating outwardly, he seethed inside. The best his stomach would hold during a major tournament was dry toast and tea.

The pressure of tournament competition manifested itself in other ways. Everyone expected Jones to win every time he played, including Atlanta friends who often bet heavily on him. He escaped the unending pressure by retiring from competition.

"Why should I punish myself like this over a golf tournament?" he once asked.

Jones was convivial in a quiet way. He was a good friend and always the gentleman, though he had full command of strong language when required. He had a fine sense of humor, and he laughed easily. He smoked cigarettes and drank bourbon.

He was besieged by people who wanted to play a social round of golf with him. And he learned to put up with the name of Bobby, which he hated (he preferred Bob).

As a youngster, he had a reputation for throwing clubs when everything was not going right. When Jim Barnes, the 1921 United States Open champion, watched him let off steam, he said: "Never mind that club-throwing and the beatings he's taking. Defeat will make him great."

Jones matured, so much so that O. B. Keeler, an Atlanta sportswriter and his long-time Boswell, once wrote, "He has more character than any champion in our history."

He also had a picture swing, though he never took a golf lesson; he learned by watching and mimicking Stewart Maiden, a Scottish professional at the Atlanta Athletic Club course.

His putting was famous. So was his putter, a rusty, goose-necked club known as Calamity Jane. He was an imaginative player, and he never hesitated to take a chance. In fact, he seldom hesitated on any shot, and he earned an unfair reputation as a mechanical golfer.

When he was an infant, doctors were not sure that he would survive. He had a serious digestive ailment until he was five. In his later years, he was crippled by syringomyelia, a chronic disease of the spinal cord, and he had circulation and heart trouble.

Robert Tyre Jones Jr. (named for his grandfather) was born on St. Patrick's Day, 1902, in Atlanta. His father was a star outfielder at the University of Georgia, and the youngster's first love was baseball. At the age of nine he settled down to golf.

He was 14 when he journeyed to the Merion Cricket Club near Philadelphia for his first United States Amateur championship. He was a chunky lad of 5 feet 4 inches and 165 pounds and somewhat knock-kneed. He was wearing his first pair of long trousers.

After qualifying for match play, he defeated Eben M. Byers, a former champion, in the first round. He beat Frank Dyer, a noted player at the time, in the second round, after losing five of the first six holes. Then he lost to Robert A. Gardner, the defending champion, 5 and 3 (down 5 holes with 3 to play).

Through all his success, golf was a sidelight to education. He earned bachelor's and master's degrees in engineering at Georgia Tech. Then he decided to become a lawyer. He went to Harvard and earned an-other bachelor's degree, then to Emory University in Atlanta for a Bachelor of Laws degree. In 1928, he joined his father's law firm in Atlanta.

In 1924, Jones decided that he was worrying too much about his opponent in match-play (man against man) competition. He vowed to play for pars and forget about his opponent.

That year, at Merion, Pa., he won the United States Amateur for the first time.

Also in 1924, he married Mary Malone, his high school sweetheart.

In 1929 Jones had a close call in the United States Open at the Winged Foot Golf Club, Mamaroneck, N.Y. He sank a 12-foot sloping sidehill putt on the last green to tie Al Espinosa. The next day, Jones won their 36-hole title playoff by 23 strokes.

Then came 1930 and the grand slam.

First came the British Amateur. In the final he beat Roger Wethered, 7 and 6. Next was the British Open at Hoylake, England, and his 72-hole score of 291 won.

Jones got his sternest test in the United States Open at Interlachen near Minneapolis. There were 15,000 spectators as he played the par-4 18th hole. He got a birdie 3 by sinking a 40-foot undulating putt, and his 287 won by two strokes.

The last of the grand-slam tournaments, the United States Amateur at Merion, was almost anti-climactic. No one doubted for a moment that Jones would win. After his victory, the crowd surged around him so wildly that it took a detachment of United States Marines to get him out safely.

Soon after, he retired from tournament play and made a series of golf motion pictures, the only time he ever made money from the game.

"Golf is like eating peanuts," he said about his re-tirement. "You can play too much or too little. I've become reconciled to the fact that I'll never play as well as I used to."

A few years later, Jones and the architect Alister Mackensie designed the Augusta National Golf Course in Georgia. In 1934 the Masters tournament was started there.

He was a close friend of Dwight D. Eisenhower. In January 1953, three months after a heart attack, Jones was honored at Golf House, the United States Golf Association headquarters in Manhattan.

A highlight was the reading of a letter from the President.

"Those who have been fortunate enough to know him," the letter said, "realize that his fame as a golfer is transcended by his inestimable qualities as a human being. . . . His gift to his friends is the warmth that comes from unselfishness, superb judgment, nobility of character, unwavering loyalty to principle."

Bobby Jones listened and cried.

JACKIE ROBINSON

January 31, 1919–October 24, 1972

By Dave Anderson

Jackie Robinson, who made history in 1947 by becoming the first black baseball player in the major leagues, suffered a heart attack in his home in Stamford, Conn., yesterday morning and died at Stamford Hospital. He was 53 years old and had been in failing health for several years.

For sociological impact, Jack Roosevelt Robinson was perhaps America's most significant athlete. His skill and accomplishments resulted in the acceptance of blacks in other major sports.

His dominant characteristic, as an athlete and as a black man, was a competitive flame. Outspoken, controversial, combative, he created critics as well as loyalists. But he never deviated from his opinions.

In his autobiography, "I Never Had It Made," he recalled standing for the National Anthem at his 1947 debut with the Brooklyn Dodgers and reflecting that "I have learned that I remain a black in a white world."

His belligerence flared throughout his career. "I was told that it would cost me some awards," he said last year. "But if I had to keep quiet to get an award, it wasn't worth it. Awards are great, but if I got one for being a nice kid, what good is it?"

Monte Irvin, who played for the New York Giants while Robinson was with the Dodgers and who now is an assistant to the commissioner of baseball, said yesterday:

"Jackie Robinson opened the door of baseball to all men."

"He meant everything to a black ballplayer," said Elston Howard, the first black member of the New York Yankees, who is now on the coaching staff. "He did it for all of us, for Willie Mays, Henry Aaron, Maury Wills, myself."

After a career as a clutch hitter and daring base runner while playing first base, second base, third base and left field at various stages of his 10 seasons with the Brooklyn Dodgers, he was elected to baseball's Hall of Fame in 1962, his first year of eligibility.

Despite his success, he minimized himself as an "instrument, a tool." He credited Branch Rickey, the Brooklyn Dodger owner who broke professional baseball's color line and whom Robinson called "the greatest human being I had ever known."

Mr. Rickey signed him for the 1946 season, which he spent with the Dodgers leading farm, the Montreal

Royals of the International League. "I think the Rickey Experiment, as I call it, the original idea, would not have come about as successfully with anybody other than Mr. Rickey," Robinson said.

Among Jackie Robinson's disappointments was the fact that he never was afforded an opportunity to be a major-league manager. "I had no future with the Dodgers because I was too closely identified with Branch Rickey," he once said. "After the club was taken over by Walter O'Malley, you couldn't even mention Mr. Rickey's name in front of him."

Robinson kept baseball in perspective. Ebbets Field, the Brooklyn ballpark that was the stage for his drama, was leveled shortly after Mr. O'Malley moved the Dodger franchise to Los Angeles in 1958. Apartment houses replaced it. Years later, asked what he felt about Ebbets Field, he replied: "I don't feel anything. They need those apartments more than they need a monument to the memory of baseball. I've had my thrills."

He also had his heartbreak. His son, Jackie Jr., died in 1971 at the age of 24 in an automobile accident three years after he was arrested for heroin possession. His addiction had begun while he served in the Army in Vietnam, where he was wounded. He was convicted and ordered to undergo treatment. Cured, he worked helping other addicts.

"You don't know what it's like," Robinson said, "to lose a son, find him, and lose him again." For the rest of his life, he was active in national campaigns against drug addiction.

Robinson's arrival with the Dodgers in 1947 prompted insults from some opponents, an aborted strike by the St. Louis Cardinals, an alleged deliberate spiking by Enos Slaughter of the Cardinals and stiffness from a few teammates. Robinson had been warned by Mr. Rickey to expect insults and to hold his temper. He complied. But the following season, he began to argue with the umpires and duel verbally with opponents.

As the years passed, Robinson developed a close relationship with many teammates. "After the game we went our separate ways," he explained. "But on the field, there was that understanding. No one can convince me that the things that happened on the ball club didn't affect people. The old Dodgers were something special, but of my teammates, over all, there was nobody like Pee Wee Reese for me."

In Boston once, some Braves players were taunting Robinson during infield practice. Reese, the popular shortstop, who came from Louisville, moved to the rescue.

"Pee Wee walked over and put his arm on my shoulder, as if to say, 'This is my teammate, whether you like it or not,'" Robinson said.

In Robinson's 10 seasons, the Dodgers won six National League pennants—1947, 1949, 1952, 1953, 1955 and 1956. They lost another in the 1951 playoff with the New York Giants, and another to the Philadelphia Phillies on the last day of the 1950 season.

In 1949, when he batted .342 to win the league title and drove in 124 runs, he was voted the league's Most Valuable Player Award. In 1947, he had been voted the rookie of the year.

Robinson had a career batting average of .311. Primarily a line drive hitter, he accumulated only 137 home runs, with a high of 19 in both 1951 and 1952. But on a team with such famous sluggers as Duke Snider, Gil Hodges and Roy Campanella, he was the cleanup hitter, fourth in the batting order.

His personality flared best as a base runner. He had a total of 197 stolen bases. He stole home 11 times, the most by any player in the post–World War II era. In the 1955 World Series, he stole home against the New York Yankees in the opening game of Brooklyn's only World Series triumph.

Pigeon-toed and muscular, wearing No. 42, he ran aggressively, typical of his college football training as a star runner and passer at the University of California at Los Angeles in 1939 and 1940. He ranked second in the Pacific Coast Conference in total offense in 1940 with 875 yards—440 rushing and 435 passing.

Born in Cairo, Ga., on Jan. 31, 1919, Robinson was soon taken to Pasadena, Calif., by his mother with her four other children after his father had deserted them. He competed in basketball and track in addition to baseball and football.

After attending U.C.L.A., he entered the Army and was commissioned a second lieutenant. After his discharge, he joined the Kansas City Monarchs of the Negro National League.

If he had quit the black leagues without having been signed by Mr. Rickey, what would he have done? "I more than likely would have gone to coach baseball at Sam Houston College," he said. "My minister had gone down there to Texas as president of the college. That was about the only thing a black athlete had left then, a chance to coach somewhere at a small black college."

The essence of Robinson's competitive fury was displayed in a 1954 game at Ebbets Field with the Giants. Sal Maglie, the Giants' ace who was known as "The Barber" because of his tendency to "shave" a batter's head with his fastball and sharp-breaking curve, was intimidating the Dodger hitters. In the Dodger dugout, Reese, the team captain, spoke to the 6-foot, 195-pound Robinson.

"Jack," said Reese, "we got to do something about this."

Robinson soon was kneeling in the on-deck circle as the next Dodger batter. With him was Charlie Di-Giovanna, the team's adult batboy, who was a confidant of the players.

"Let somebody else do it, Jack," DiGiovanna implored. "Every time something comes up, they call on you."

Robinson agreed, but once in the batter's box, he changed his mind. Hoping to draw Maglie toward the first-base line, Robinson bunted. The ball was fielded by Whitey Lockman, the first baseman, but Maglie didn't move off the mound. Davey Williams, the second baseman, covered the base for Lockman's throw.

"Maglie wouldn't cover," Robinson recalled. "Williams got in the way. He had a chance to get out of the way but he just stood there right on the base. It was just too bad, but I knocked him over. He had a Giant uniform on. That's what happens."

In the collision, Williams suffered a spinal injury that virtually ended his career. Two innings later, Alvin Dark, the Giants' captain and shortstop, retaliated by trying to stretch a double into a third-base collision with Robinson. Realizing that Dark hoped to avenge the Williams incident, Robinson stepped aside and tagged him in the face. But his grip on the ball wasn't secure. The ball bounced away. Dark was safe.

"I would've torn his face up," Robinson once recalled. "But as it turned out, I'm glad it didn't happen that way. I admired Al for what he did after I had run down Williams. I've always admired Al, despite his racial stands. I think he really believed that white people were put on this earth to take care of black people."

After the 1956 season, Robinson was traded to the Giants, but he chose to retire. He joined Chock Full O'Nuts, the lunch-counter chain, as an executive. He later had a succession of executive posts with an insurance firm, a food-franchising firm and an interracial construction firm. He also was chairman of the board of the Freedom National Bank in Harlem and a member of the New York State Athletic Commission.

His wife, Rachel, a fellow U.C.L.A. student whom he married in 1946, is an associate professor of psychiatric nursing at the Yale School of Medicine. Mr. Robinson is also survived by a son, a daughter, a sister and two brothers.

Jackie Robinson's struggle predated the emergence of "the first black who" in many areas of society. Even though he needed a Branch Rickey to open the door for him, Branch Rickey needed a Jackie Robinson to lead other blacks through that door.

JESSE OWENS

September 12, 1913–March 31, 1980

By Frank Litsky

Jesse Owens, whose four gold medals at the 1936 Olympic Games in Berlin made him perhaps the greatest and most famous athlete in track and field history, died of lung cancer yesterday in Tucson, Ariz. He was 66 years old.

Mr. Owens, a pack-a-day cigarette smoker for 35 years, had been hospitalized on and off since last Dec. 12. He died at the University of Arizona Health Sciences Center.

The White House issued a statement in which President Carter said, "Perhaps no athlete better symbolized the human struggle against tyranny, poverty and racial bigotry."

In Berlin, Mr. Owens, who was black, scored a triumph that would come to be regarded as not only athletic but also political. Adolf Hitler had intended the Berlin Games to be a showcase for the Nazi doctrine of Aryan supremacy.

A member of what the Nazis mockingly called America's "black auxiliaries," Mr. Owens achieved a feat unmatched in modern times in Olympic track competition. The year before, with a wrenched back so painful that he could not dress or undress without help, he broke five world records and equaled a sixth, all within 45 minutes.

But the Jesse Owens best remembered by many Americans was a public speaker with the ringing, inspirational delivery of an evangelist. Later in his life, he traveled 200,000 miles a year making two or three speeches a week, mostly to sales meetings and conventions, and primarily to white audiences. With his own public relations and marketing concern, he earned more than $100,000 a year.

James Cleveland Owens was born Sept. 12, 1913, in Danville, Ala., the son of a sharecropper and the grandson of slaves. The youngster picked cotton until he and his family moved to Cleveland when he was 9. There a schoolteacher asked the youth his name.

"J.C." he replied.

She thought he had said "Jesse," and he had a new name.

He ran his first race at age 13. He became a nationally known sprinter at East Technical High School in Cleveland, slim and lithe at 163 pounds. He ran with fluid grace. There were no starting blocks then; sprinters merely dug holes at the starting line in tracks of cinder or dirt.

After high school, he went to Ohio State University, paying his way as a $100-a-month night elevator operator because he had no athletic scholarship. As a sophomore, in his first Big Ten championships, he achieved a harvest of records even greater than the Olympic glory he would attain a year later.

A week before the Big Ten meet, which was held in Ann Arbor, Mich., Mr. Owens and a fraternity brother were wrestling playfully when they tumbled down a flight of stairs. Mr. Owens's back hurt so much that he could not work out all week. Coach Larry Snyder and teammates had to help him in and out of the car that drove him to the track for the meet.

There, in a vain attempt to lessen the back pain, he sat for half an hour in a hot tub. He did not warm up or even stretch. At the last minute, he rejected suggestions that he withdraw from the meet and said he would try, event by event.

On May 25, 1935, from 3:15 to 4 P.M., Jesse Owens successively equaled the world record for the 100-yard dash (9.4 seconds), broke the world record for the broad jump, now called the long jump, with his only attempt (26 feet 8 1/4 inches, which remained the record for 25 years), broke the world record for the 220-yard dash (20.3 seconds, which also bettered the record for 200 meters) and broke the world record for the 220-yard low hurdles (22.6 seconds, which also bettered the record for the 200-meter low hurdles).

The next year, with the Italians occupying Ethiopia, the Japanese in Manchuria, the Germans moving into the Rhineland and a civil war starting in Spain, the Olympic Games were held in Berlin. Despite pleas that the United States boycott the Olympics to protest Nazi racial policies, American officials voted to participate.

The United States Olympic track team, of 66 athletes, included 10 blacks. The Nazis derided the Americans for relying on what the Nazis called an inferior race, but of the 11 individual gold medals in track won by the American men, six were won by blacks.

The hero was Mr. Owens. He won the 100-meter dash in 10.3 seconds, the 200-meter dash in 20.7 seconds and the broad jump at 26 feet 5 1/2 inches, and he led off for the United States team that won the 400-meter relay in 39.8 seconds.

His individual performances broke two Olympic records and, except for an excessive following wind, would have broken the third. The relay team broke the world record. His 100-meter and 200-meter times would have won Olympic medals through 1964, his broad jump performance through 1968.

Mr. Owens had not been scheduled to run in the relay. Marty Glickman and Sam Stoller were, but American Olympic officials, led by Avery Brundage, wanted to avoid offending the Nazis. They replaced Mr. Glickman and Mr. Stoller, both Jews, with Mr. Owens and Ralph Metcalfe, both blacks.

Hitler did not congratulate any of the American black winners. "It was all right with me," Owens said years later. "I didn't go to Berlin to shake hands with him, anyway."

Besides, Mr. Owens faced snubs at home: "I came

back to my native country, and I couldn't ride in the front of the bus. I had to go to the back door. I couldn't live where I wanted."

Having returned from Berlin, he received no telephone call from President Franklin D. Roosevelt. Official recognition from his own country did not come until 1976, when President Gerald R. Ford presented him with the Presidential Medal of Freedom. Three years later, President Carter gave him the Living Legends Award.

Nor were there any lucrative contracts for an Olympic hero after the 1936 Games. Mr. Owens became a playground janitor because he could not find a better job. He ended his career as an amateur runner and accepted money to race against cars, trucks, motorcycles, horses and dogs. He toured with the Harlem Globetrotters basketball team.

"Sure, it bothered me," he said later. "But at least it was an honest living. I had to eat."

In time, the four gold medals changed his life. "They have kept me alive over the years," he once said. "Time has stood still for me. That golden moment dies hard."

He became a disk jockey, then ran his public relations and marketing concern, first in Chicago and then in Phoenix.

He also became celebrated as a speaker, using about five basic speeches with interchangeable parts. Each speech praised the virtues of patriotism, clean living and fair play. His delivery was old-fashioned spellbinding, a far cry from the days when he stuttered.

Even in casual conversations, he spoke in sweeping tones.

During the 1968 Olympics in Mexico City, when Mr. Owens attempted to mediate with militant American black athletes on behalf of the United States Olympic Committee, critics called him "Uncle Tom." He wrote a 1970 book, "Blackthink," decrying racial militancy, and a 1972 book, "I Have Changed," saying the ideas in his first book were wrong.

Yet he was uneasy with American black athletes who questioned the value of their gold medals: "Any black who strives to achieve in this country should think in terms of not only himself but also how he can reach down and grab another black child and pull him to the top of the mountain where he is. This is what a gold medal does to you."

"Regardless of his color, a man who becomes a recognized athlete has to learn to walk 10 feet tall," Mr. Owens once said. "But he must have his dignity off the athletic field."

As for riches, he observed: "Material reward is not all there is. How many meals can a man eat? How many cars can he drive? In how many beds can he sleep? All of life's wonders are not reflected in material wealth."

JOE LOUIS

May 13, 1914–April 12, 1981

By Deane McGowen

Joe Louis, who held the heavyweight boxing championship of the world for almost 12 years and the affection of the American public for most of his adult life, died yesterday of cardiac arrest in Las Vegas, Nev. He was 66 years old and had been in failing health for years.

Mr. Louis, who was champion from 1937 until 1949, collapsed in his home and was pronounced dead at a hospital soon afterward. His wife, Martha, was with him.

Slow of foot but redeemingly fast of hands, Joe Louis dominated heavyweight boxing from 1937 to 1948. He defended his title 25 times, facing all challengers and fighting the best that the countries of the world could offer. In the opinion of many boxing experts, the Brown Bomber, as he was known for his crushing left jab and hook, was probably the best heavyweight fighter of all time.

The 6-foot-1 1/2-inch, 197-pound Louis won his title on June 22, 1937, in Chicago, by knocking out James J. Braddock in eight rounds, thus becoming the first black heavyweight champion since Jack Johnson, who had reigned earlier in the century.

Before Louis retired undefeated as champion on March 1, 1949, his last title defense had been against Jersey Joe Walcott, whom he knocked out on June 25, 1948, in New York.

His fights had grossed more than $4.6 million, of which he received about $800,000. Since Louis wasted little time in dispatching his opponents, his earnings per round were extraordinarily high. Of the 25 title defenses, only three went the full 15 rounds.

Excluding exhibitions, Louis won 68 professional fights and lost only three. He scored 54 knockouts, five in the first round. After retiring, he continued to appear in exhibitions and in 1950 decided to make a comeback, but he was beaten by Ezzard Charles in 15 rounds. His final professional bout took place on Oct. 26, 1951, when he lost to Rocky Marciano in New York.

The most spectacular victim of Louis's robust punches was Max Schmeling, the German who was hailed by Adolf Hitler as a paragon of Teutonic manhood. Schmeling, who had knocked out Louis in 12 rounds in 1936, was given a return bout on June 22, 1938, in Yankee Stadium. He was knocked out in 2 minutes 4 seconds of the first round.

"He stepped in and started a lightning attack," John Kieran wrote of Louis in The New York Times. "Schmeling reeled into the ropes on the first-base side of the ring and clung like a shipwrecked soldier to a lifeline."

"Swaying on the ropes, Max peered out in a bewildered manner," the reporter continued. "He pushed himself off and Louis struck like dark lightning again. A ripping left and a smashing right. The right was the crusher. Schmeling went down. He was up again and then, under another fusillade, down again. Once more, and barely able to stand, and then down for the third and final time."

There was no Joe Louis behind any facade. He was the same slow-spoken, considerate person in a close social group as he was to the vast crowds that surged in on him to clutch his every word when he was at the apogee of the boxing world.

Louis was born Joseph Louis Barrow on May 13, 1914, in the cotton field country near Lafayette, Ala., the eighth child of Munn and Lilly Barrow, share-croppers.

His boyhood was one of want and little schooling. In his teens, he did odd jobs to help his family until they moved to Detroit. He worked as a laborer there in the River Rouge plant of the Ford Company.

Louis attended a vocational school for a time to learn cabinet-making, before turning to amateur boxing. He made his debut in an amateur tournament in Detroit as a light heavyweight. He lost the decision, getting knocked down three times by Johnny Miler in a three-rounder. However, he persevered and, in 1934, won the national Amateur Athletic Union light-heavyweight title.

His amateur record of 43 knockout victories in 54 bouts brought him to the attention of Julian Black and John Roxborough, who engaged the late Jack Blackburn, one of the ring's great competitors, to polish the rough spots in the young fighter's style.

On July 4, 1934, Louis appeared as a professional fighter for the first time and knocked out Jack Kracken in one round in Chicago. Louis had 11 more fights in 1934 and 14 in 1935. By then, his prowess had attracted the attention of the New York promoter Mike Jacobs, and Louis soon joined him.

On June 25, 1935, Louis appeared for the first time before New York fans, knocking out Primo Carnera in six rounds. Fans clamored for a match between him and Max Baer, who had lost the heavyweight championship to Braddock only two weeks earlier.

Louis and Baer met on Sept. 24, and the young fighter pounded Baer into helplessness in four rounds. Altogether Louis had 14 bouts in 1935 and earned $368,037, an almost incredible sum then for a fighter in his second year as a professional.

On June 19, 1936, Louis had his first meeting with Schmeling in New York. Schmeling told reporters before the bout that he had seen faults in Louis's style. After the bout, Schmeling disclosed that Louis had a habit of lowering his left shoulder and arm, leaving his chin open for a right-hand counterpunch.

Schmeling floored Louis with that weapon in the fourth round, and finally knocked him out with more of the right-hand blows in the 12th. Schmeling was promised a title bout against Braddock after he stopped Louis, but Mr. Jacobs wanted Louis to get the chance. After stalling Schmeling, Braddock agreed to meet Louis.

They fought in Chicago and Louis knocked out Braddock in the eighth round to win the heavyweight title. In 1938 the new champion had only three bouts, but one of those was his second against Schmeling. Germany was then expounding its superman propaganda, and Hitler had made it known that Schmeling was one of those supermen.

When Louis and the challenger met on June 22, 1938, in New York, the champion was in a rage. Louis cut his opponent down with terrific head and body punches.

The 2-minute-4-second time span was a record for turning back a challenger in a heavyweight title bout. The bout was the first million-dollar gate Louis attracted.

After that, he had things his own way in the ring, during his so-called "bum-of-the-month campaign." Beginning in December 1940, he met challengers at the rate of one a month, a performance that no other heavyweight champion ever attempted.

Louis came close to losing his crown in the first fight with Billy Conn of Pittsburgh on June 18, 1941, at the Polo Grounds. Conn, the light-heavyweight king, relinquished his title to meet Louis.

Many boxing writers had said that Conn would be too speedy and would outbox Louis. The champion had the perfect answer: "He can run but he can't hide." For 12 rounds Louis received a lesson in boxing from the stylish challenger. However, in the 13th, Conn foolishly tried to slug it out with Louis. Louis knocked him out with two seconds left in the round.

Louis went into the Army as a private in 1942. As a soldier, he traveled more than 21,000 miles and staged 96 boxing exhibitions. He came out of the Army on Oct. 1, 1945, and shortly afterward signed to defend his title against Conn. The bout drew the largest purse of his career, $625,916.44. The champion stopped Conn in the eighth round at Yankee Stadium on June 19, 1946.

Louis defended his title three more times, the last two against Jersey Joe Walcott, and officially retired on March 1, 1949.

When Louis tried a comeback, Ezzard Charles outpointed him in 15 rounds at Yankee Stadium on Sept. 27, 1950. Louis's career came to an end on Oct. 26, 1951, when Rocky Marciano knocked him out in the eighth round at Madison Square Garden.

Although Louis made a lot of money, it passed through his fingers quickly. The Internal Revenue Service calculated that his delinquent taxes amounted to $1.25 million. In the mid-1960's, an accommodation was reached and the boxer was able to pay off his obligations.

Louis and Marva Trotter were married on Sept. 24, 1935, hours before his fight with Max Baer. The couple divorced in 1945, remarried a year later and divorced again in 1949. A daughter, Jacquelin, was born to the couple on Feb. 8, 1943, and a son, Joe Jr., on May 28, 1947. The boxer's third marriage was to Rose Morgan; his fourth was to Martha Jackson.

Out of the ring for good, Louis wrestled briefly and engaged in various sports and commercial promotions. In 1969, he collapsed on a Manhattan street and was rushed to a hospital with what was described as "a physical breakdown." In 1970, he spent several months in Denver hospitals, suffering from paranoia.

In a 1971 book, "Brown Bomber: The Pilgrimage of Joe Louis," by Barney Nagler, Louis said his collapse in 1969 had been caused by cocaine, and that his hospitalization had been prompted by his fear of a plot to destroy him.

In a 1970 article in Ebony magazine, Chester Higgins wrote: "When Joe Louis fought, blacks in ghettos across the land were indoors glued to their radios, and when Louis won, as he nearly always did, they hit the streets whooping and hollering in celebration. For Joe's victory was their victory, a means of striking back at an oppressive and hateful environment. Louis was the black Atlas on whose broad shoulders blacks were lifted."

SATCHEL PAIGE

July 7, 1906–June 8, 1982

By Joseph Durso

Leroy (Satchel) Paige, one of the folk heroes of baseball's old Negro leagues who became a rookie pitcher in the major leagues at the age of 42, died yesterday at his home in Kansas City, Mo.

He was believed to be 75 years old when he died after a long siege of heart trouble and emphysema. But his exact age was one of the mysteries in the legend that accompanied him into the big leagues in 1948 with the Cleveland Indians, and it was still a mystery when he pitched his final three innings for the Kansas City A's in 1965 when he was admitting to 59.

By then, he was viewing the world from a rocking chair in the bullpen, a tall, thin man with a thin mustache who had lived one of the phenomenal careers in sports: 22 years as a barnstorming pitcher in the era before black players were admitted to the big leagues, then five seasons with three clubs in the American League.

In the barnstorming days, he pitched perhaps 2,500 games, completed 55 no-hitters and performed before crowds estimated at 10 million persons in the United States, the Caribbean and Central America. He once started 29 games in one month in Bismarck, N.D., and he said later that he won 104 of the 105 games he pitched in 1934.

By the time Jackie Robinson signed with the Brooklyn Dodgers in 1947 as the first black player in the majors, Mr. Paige was past 40. But Bill Veeck, the impresario of the Cleveland club, signed him to a contract the following summer, and he promptly drew crowds of 72,000 in his first game and 78,000 in his third game.

His career in the big leagues was spread over 18 years but, because he retired twice during that span, it totaled only five full seasons with these statistics: 28 victories, 31 defeats, 476 innings, 290 strikeouts and an earned-run average of 3.29.

Despite the uncertainty about his age, there was general agreement that he was the oldest player ever to appear in a major league game when he pitched three innings against the Boston Red Sox on Sept. 25, 1965.

Leroy Robert Paige was born in Mobile, Ala., the son of John and Lula Page. The family name became "Paige," he remembered, because "my folks later stuck in the 'i' to make themselves sound more high-toned."

He teased people about the date of his birth, saying that the certificate had been placed between the pages of a Bible that was eaten by the family's goat. But later he did not argue with evidence that he had been born on July 7, 1906.

He said he got his nickname as a boy hustling baggage at the railroad depot in Mobile. "I rigged up ropes around my shoulders and my waist, and I carried a satchel in each hand and one under each arm," he said. "I carried so many satchels that all you could see were satchels."

He took up pitching during four years spent at the Alabama Reform School for Boys. In 1924, he presented himself to Candy Jim Taylor, the manager of the Mobile Tigers, a black semiprofessional team, and fired 10 fastballs past the manager in an audition. He had a job, and soon a career.

For the next two decades, he traveled around the hemisphere with black teams. He also pitched in exhibition games against white major league stars. Once he outpitched Dizzy Dean, 1–0. Another time, he struck out Rogers Hornsby five times in one game. Joe DiMaggio called him "the best I've ever faced, and the fastest."

He was a lean but imposing figure on the mound, 6 feet 3 1/2 inches tall and 180 pounds, with a mean fastball, numerous curveballs and pinpoint control. One year after Jackie Robinson broke the color line, Mr. Veeck signed him as a pitcher, and a drawing card, on a Cleveland team headed for the championship. The date was July 7, 1948.

Lou Boudreau, the Indians' manager, introduced his new pitcher carefully, using him six times in relief before starting him in a game. In his first start, he defeated the Washington Senators, 5–3, before 72,434 fans in Cleveland's Municipal Stadium. Then he pitched two shutouts against the Chicago White Sox. By then he had pitched before combined crowds of 201,829 in three starts.

His record after less than three months showed six victories and one loss, and he made one brief appearance in the World Series that October against the Boston Braves. But after one more season with Cleveland, he was released after Mr. Veeck sold his controlling interest. However, two years later, Mr. Veeck bought the St. Louis Browns and promptly signed his former rookie, who now was at least 45 years old. Mr. Paige won 12 games in 1952 and was selected for the league's All-Star team.

After the 1953 season, he was released once more. He pitched in the minor leagues, then took the barnstorming route again. Another baseball showman, Charles O. Finley, drew him back to the big leagues briefly in 1965 with the Kansas City A's. Mr. Paige made his last public appearance last Saturday in ceremonies at a Kansas City baseball park that was named for him.

Satchel Paige offered these "master's maxims" as his guide to longevity: 1. Avoid fried meats, which angry up the blood. 2. If your stomach disputes you, lie down and pacify it with cool thoughts. 3. Keep the juices flowing by jangling around gently as you move. 4. Go very light on the vices, such as carrying on in society. The social rumble ain't restful. 5. Avoid running at all times. 6. Don't look back. Something might be gaining on you.

JACK DEMPSEY

June 24, 1895–May 31, 1983

By Red Smith

Jack Dempsey, one of the last of a dwindling company whose exploits distinguished the 1920's as "the golden age of sports," died yesterday. The former heavyweight boxing champion, known as the Manassa Mauler, was 87 years old and had been suffering from a heart ailment.

The police, who were called to the Dempsey apartment at 211 East 53d Street, said his wife, Deanna, had found him on the bedroom floor at about 4 P.M. He was pronounced dead shortly after 5.

Mr. Dempsey's contemporaries were Babe Ruth in baseball, Red Grange in football, Bobby Jones in golf, Bill Tilden and Helen Wills Moody in tennis, and Man o' War, the racehorse.

But none of the others enjoyed more lasting popularity than the man who ruled boxing between 1919 and 1926.

Strangely, though, Mr. Dempsey's popularity never approached its peak until he had lost the championship. He was reviled as a slacker during World War I, and although a jury exonerated him of a charge of draft-dodging, the odium clung to him until one night in Philadelphia when Gene Tunney punched him almost blind and took his title.

"Lead me out there," Jack told his trainer after that bout. "I want to shake his hand."

Back in their hotel, Estelle Taylor Dempsey was appalled by her husband's battered face. "Ginsberg!" she cried, using her pet name for him. "What happened?"

"Honey," the former champion said, "I forgot to duck."

From that day on, the gallant loser was a folk hero whose fame never diminished.

To many, Mr. Dempsey always remained the champion, and he always comported himself like one. He was warm and generous, a free spender when he had it and a soft touch for anybody down on his luck. After retirement from the ring, he made his headquarters in New York in Jack Dempsey's Restaurant, first at the corner of 50th Street across Eighth Avenue from the old Madison Square Garden and later at 1619 Broadway.

At almost any hour, Mr. Dempsey was on hand to greet friends and strangers with a cordial, "Hiya, pal," in a voice close to a boyish treble. (He wasn't much better at remembering names than Babe Ruth, who called people "kid.") He posed for thousands of photographs with an arm around a customer's shoulders or—if the customer preferred, and many males did—squared off face to face.

Grantland Rice said Mr. Dempsey was perhaps the finest gentleman, in the literal sense of gentle man, he had met in half a century of writing sports.

In the ring, he was a tiger without mercy who shuffled forward in a bobbing crouch, humming a barely audible tune and punching to the rhythm of the song. He was 187 pounds of unbridled violence. That isn't big by heavyweight standards, yet in the judgment of some, this black-browed product of Western mining camps and hobo jungles was the best of all pugilists. In 1950, a poll by The Associated Press named Mr. Dempsey the greatest fighter of the half-century.

Certainly nobody surpassed him in color and crowd appeal. Managed by Jack "Doc" Kearns, he drew boxing's first million-dollar gate in fighting Georges Carpentier and boxing's largest paid attendance in his first bout with Tunney.

Dempsey was less than two weeks past his 24th birthday but had been through more than 80 professional fights when he burst upon the championship scene like a mortar shell. It was July 4, 1919, a blistering day on the shore of Maumee Bay outside Toledo, Ohio. Awaiting the opening bell as challenger for the heavyweight title, the 6-foot-1-inch contender was tanned and fit at 187 pounds. But he looked no more than half the size of Jess Willard, the champion, a pale tract of meat measuring 6 feet 6 1/2 inches tall and weighing 245 pounds.

Three minutes later Willard looked like a case for the coroner. He had been down seven times, and one left hook had broken his cheekbone in 13 places. After two more rounds the helpless Willard was spared further damage.

The destruction of Willard convinced boxing men of the new champion's greatness, but the public was slow to accept Dempsey because of his war record. Ostensibly doing essential work in a Philadelphia shipyard, he had posed for a news photograph holding a riveting gun and wearing overalls, with patent-leather shoes. The fancy footgear raised noisy doubts about his contribution to the war effort.

To those who saw it, the Dempsey-Firpo bout of 1923 was the most wildly exciting ever fought for the heavyweight title. Luis Angel Firpo of Argentina, unpolished and untamed, dazed the champion with a right to the jaw seconds after the opening bell. Only half-conscious, Dempsey dropped Firpo four times. Firpo knocked the champion into the press row, where reporters instinctively raised hands and shoved to protect themselves. Thus aided, Dempsey got back in the ring and put Firpo down once more before the bell. Two more knockdowns finished the Argentine in the second round.

The Firpo fight was Dempsey's fifth title defense. Three years later he made his sixth and last against Tunney, the Shakespeare-loving veteran of the Marine Corps, in the huge horseshoe in Philadelphia then called Sesquicentennial Stadium.

Jabbing and circling through a drenching rainstorm, Tunney won going away.

One day less than a year later, the pair met again in Soldier Field in Chicago in a match that would make Dave Barry the world's most widely known referee. In the seventh round Tunney was knocked down for the first time in his life.

Gracious outside the ring, Dempsey in battle was no slave to the rules. With Tunney on the floor, it did not occur to Dempsey to retire to a neutral corner until Barry stopped the count and led him across the ring. Returning, the referee started the count all over. Tunney got up at "9"—it was established that he had had about 14 seconds to recuperate—and won a clear decision, scoring a knockdown in the eighth round.

To this day, the Dempsey cult believes Tunney was saved by the long count; Tunney always insisted he was in full control throughout.

That was the last time around for Dempsey as a fighter of importance.

Thirty-two years had passed since his birth on June 24, 1895, in Manassa, Colo., to Hyrum and Celia Dempsey, who had paused there with their brood on a meandering journey from Mudfork, W.Va.

Hyrum Dempsey was a tough, restless descendant of Irish immigrants who had quit a job as a schoolteacher to venture west. They named the baby William Harrison Dempsey and called him Harry, but at 16 he went his own way, adopted his own names and soon began to box.

Between saloon bouts he worked in the mines, shined shoes, picked fruit and hustled, riding the rods on trains and sleeping in hobo jungles. Meanwhile, his older brother, Bernie, was boxing as Jack Dempsey, having borrowed the name of an oldtime middleweight. One night in Denver, Harry substituted for Bernie and was introduced as Jack Dempsey. The name stuck.

Soon he and Mr. Kearns became partners. By the time of the rendezvous with Willard in 1919, Dempsey's record included 21 first-round knock-outs. There wasn't a heavyweight of repute Dempsey hadn't beaten, except Willard.

After taking care of that oversight, the new champion took his time about defending his title.

Like John L. Sullivan, Jim Corbett and other champions before him, he gave the stage at least as much attention as he bestowed on the ring. He accepted a featured role on Broadway in a play called "The Big Fight," directed by David Belasco. The feminine lead was Estelle Taylor, his wife.

He had learned that fighters suffer many distractions. "Some night," he told a young boxer, "you'll catch a punch between the eyes and all of a sudden you'll see three guys in the ring against you. Pick out the one in the middle and hit him, because he's the one who hit you."

Mr. Dempsey and Miss Taylor were divorced. He married twice after that.

After retirement, he remained identified with the ring, as a referee of boxing and wrestling and a participant in various promotions.

In the early days of Joe Louis's reign as champion, Mr. Dempsey lent his name and restaurant facilities to a "white hope" tournament, a term that had survived in boxing long after its racial implications had evaporated. Dropping into Dempsey's, John Lardner, the writer, saw a horde of young males devouring steak and chops.

"Finest bunch of white hopes ever assembled," the proprietor said proudly. "What about him?" Mr. Lardner asked, indicating a husky young black in the middle of the pack. Mr. Dempsey fetched him a slap on the shoulder.

"You got a good eye for a fighter," he said. "He's the best prospect in the bunch."

BEAR BRYANT

September 11, 1913–January 26, 1983

By Joseph Durso

Bear Bryant died of a heart attack yesterday in Tuscaloosa, Ala., only 37 days after he had retired as head football coach at the University of Alabama with the most victories in college football history.

Mr. Bryant, who was 69 years old, died after suffering a massive heart attack at Druid City Hospital in Tuscaloosa, where he was being treated for chest pains.

He created national headlines only a month ago when he ended his 38-year career as the most successful football coach on any American campus, and one of the most colorful. He quit with a record of 323 victories, 85 losses and 17 ties at four schools: Maryland, Kentucky, Texas A&M and, for the last 25 years, at his alma mater, Alabama.

Six of his teams at Alabama were rated No. 1 by the wire-service polls. And, when Alabama defeated Auburn, 28–17, on Nov. 28, 1981, for his 315th victory, he surpassed the record set early in the century by Amos Alonzo Stagg.

Mr. Bryant's impact on football everywhere was assured through the scores of men who had played or coached under "the Bear." In his time, he developed star quarterbacks such as Joe Namath, George Blanda, Babe Parilli and Ken Stabler. More than 40 of his former players became head college coaches, including Jerry Claiborne at Kentucky, Howard Schnellenberger at Miami and Ray Perkins, Mr. Bryant's successor at Alabama.

He also became instrumental in recruiting black athletes for Alabama. His first black player was Wilbur Jackson, a running back, in 1971. In his final season, 54 of the 128 football players at Alabama were black. Later, he remembered that he had wanted to recruit black football players at Kentucky, and said:

"They wouldn't let me. Then, at Alabama all those years, my hands were tied. To tell you the truth, Sam Cunningham did more for integration at Alabama than anybody else. He was a black running back for Southern Cal. Came down here in 1970 and ran all over my skinny little white boys."

The Bryant era ended on Dec. 29, when Alabama defeated Illinois in the Liberty Bowl, 21–15. It was the eighth victory of the season for Alabama after four defeats, the first time in 13 years the team had lost as many as four games. It was the last appearance in a stadium for the craggy-faced figure roaming the sidelines in the houndstooth hat.

Paul William Bryant was born Sept. 11, 1913, in Moro Bottom, Ark., which he described as "a little piece of bottom land on the Moro Creek, about seven miles fourth of Fordyce." He was one of 11 children in a poor family, and he remembered that he had an inferiority complex and "wasn't very smart in school, and lazy to boot."

But he was big, eventually growing to 6 feet 4 inches. And he recalled that he acquired his nickname as a teenager when he accepted a dare to wrestle a bear.

"It was outside the Lyric Theater," he said. "There was a poster out front with a picture of a bear, and a guy was offering a dollar a minute to anyone who would wrestle the bear. The guy who was supposed to wrestle the bear didn't show up, so they egged me on. They let me and my friends into the picture show free, and I wrestled this scrawny bear to the floor. I went around later to get my money, but the guy with the bear had flown the coop. All I got out of the whole thing was a nickname."

As an aggressive tackle on the Fordyce High School football team, Mr. Bryant lived up to his nickname by winning all-state honors. Recruited by Alabama, he played right end. His principal assignment, he remembered, was doing the blocking while Don Hutson, the left end, was the star pass receiver. But they thrived, winning 23 games and losing only 3, and they defeated Stanford in the 1935 Rose Bowl game, 29–13.

After his class had graduated, Mr. Bryant stayed at Alabama as an assistant coach. Four years later, he switched to Vanderbilt as an assistant to Red Sanders. But two years later, in 1941, he joined the Navy and served in World War II. He was discharged in 1945, in time to become head coach at Maryland, where he opened his long and sometimes stormy career.

He was an instant success. In his first game, Maryland whipped Guilford College, 60–6. That first season, Maryland won six games, lost two and tied one.

But he was also an instant center of controversy. He suspended a player for breaking training rules, was overruled by the school's president and promptly quit and took over as coach at Kentucky.

He stayed eight seasons, and his teams won 60 games and lost 23 and won the school's only Southeastern Conference championship. The highlight was a 13–7 victory in the Sugar Bowl in 1950 that broke a 31-game winning streak for Oklahoma.

After he left in 1954, Mr. Bryant conceded that one problem had been a conflict of personalities with Adolph Rupp, the highly successful basketball coach.

"The trouble," he said, "was that we were too much alike. He wanted basketball to be No. 1, and I wanted football No. 1. In an environment like that, one or the other has to go."

The next stop was Texas A&M, where Mr. Bryant stayed four seasons with a record of 25 victories and 14 defeats and a Southwestern Conference title in 1956. He also developed John David Crow, a running back who won the Heisman Trophy as the nation's best player. But more controversy arose when the school was placed on probation for violating the recruiting rules, and Mr. Bryant acknowledged later that some players had been paid, though not by him.

Finally, he went "home" in 1958 to his alma mater, Alabama. "It was like when you were out in the field, and you heard your mama calling you to dinner," he said, explaining his joy at returning. "Mama called."

Alabama had won only four games in three years. But in his first season, the Crimson Tide won five and lost four. And in 1961, he received his first No. 1 ranking nationally. His Alabama teams never suffered a losing season.

Controversy followed him home, however. An article in The Saturday Evening Post said that he and Wally Butts, the coach at Georgia, had arranged to fix a game in 1962. Alabama won the game, 35–0. Mr. Butts won a libel suit, and Mr. Bryant won a substantial out-of-court settlement.

Although he acknowledged an obsession for winning, he was a forbidding figure when it came to training rules. Not even Namath escaped his discipline. In 1964, he removed Namath for breaking training and kept him on the sidelines during the Sugar Bowl game.

Mr. Bryant was a tireless worker who customarily rose at 5 A.M. and did not stop until late in the evening. He often supervised practice from a tower overlooking two fields. One of his quarterbacks, Steadman Shealy, once said: "There's something about him up in that tower that makes you want to run through a wall."

He was married to his college sweetheart, Mary Harmon Black, who had been a campus beauty queen when he played at Alabama. They had two children, Paul William Jr. and May Martin Tyson, and four grandchildren.

Mr. Bryant's stature at Alabama was so great that his salary became something of a protocol problem. Eventually, it reached $120,000. But, for years, the university made an effort to keep the football coach's salary below that of the school's president. The president made $100,000 a year; Mr. Bryant was paid $99,999.99.

Mr. Bryant's funeral will be Friday in Tuscaloosa, with members of his 1982 team serving as honorary pallbearers.

RED GRANGE

June 13, 1903–January 28, 1991

By Gerald Eskenazi

Harold (Red) Grange, whose dramatic exploits as a football running back for the University of Illinois and the Chicago Bears more than 60 years ago made him an idol of his age and a legend to later generations, died yesterday at Lake Wales (Fla.) Hospital. He was 87 years old.

His wife of 49 years, Margaret, his only survivor, said he died of complications from pneumonia.

Red Grange belonged to the group of superstars who helped elevate the 1920's into a golden age of sports in the United States. He outlived the other larger-than-life heroes of that decade: Babe Ruth, Bill Tilden, Johnny Weissmuller, Jack Dempsey and Bobby Jones.

Mr. Grange became a charter member of the Professional Football Hall of Fame in 1963 and was a member of the National Football Foundation's College Football Hall of Fame.

The Grange legend flowered in 1924, when his Illinois team was facing undefeated Michigan. It was dedication day for Illinois Memorial Stadium. While many of the 66,609 fans were still finding their seats, Grange took the opening kickoff 95 yards for a touchdown. Then, on the Illini's first play from scrimmage, he broke through for a 67-yard touchdown. He followed that with touchdown runs of 54 yards and 44 yards. He astounded everyone by rushing for 265 yards and 4 touchdowns in the first 12 minutes of the game.

After a breather, he scored his fifth touchdown, on a 13-yard run. He tossed a 20-yard scoring pass in the fourth quarter as Illinois won, 39–14. In 41 minutes of play, he was responsible for 402 yards of offense, including 64 yards as a passer.

For this performance and others on other golden afternoons, Grange became known as the Galloping Ghost, in tribute to his elusive yet barreling running style. He was given that nickname by one of the era's primary sports chroniclers, Grantland Rice.

Grange was a three-time all-American, continually producing feats that seemingly could not be topped. His jersey number, 77, took on mythic proportions.

Red Grange's collegiate career mark of 2,071 yards rushing over three seasons was actually bettered several times by other Illini runners, but he accomplished that figure with only 388 carries—an average of 5.3 yards a carry. The last of his many records at Illinois, 31 touchdowns, was broken last year when Howard Griffith ended his Illini career with 33.

In 1925, he joined the Chicago Bears on Thanksgiving Day to begin a remarkable tour that helped lift pro football into the American consciousness. His abrupt departure from college football had a long-lasting effect on the relationship between colleges and the National Football League.

The Bears were owned and coached by George Halas, himself a former Illinois player. Coach Bob Zuppke of Illinois, angered by Mr. Halas's luring his star player away, told the Bear coach that such actions could jeopardize the college game. Mr. Halas came to agree and eventually persuaded the N.F.L. to adopt a draft of collegians and not take any of them before their class graduated.

Red Grange's professional tour started with 8 games in 12 days, and by the time it ended, in February 1926, he had earned $100,000. He helped to attract big crowds, like the 66,000 fans in the Polo Grounds for a meeting with the Giants, and almost instantly gave the N.F.L. the credibility it had lacked in its first five years.

He played two more seasons with the New York Yankees football team, and then returned to the Bears to play from 1929–34. After a brief career as an assistant coach, he tried a variety of pursuits, including acting. He returned to football as a radio and television analyst and announcer, broadcasting college games and Bear games from 1947 to 1961. He then retired to Indian Lake, Fla., where he owned an orange grove and an insurance agency and was involved in real estate.

Harold Grange, who was born on June 13, 1903, in Forksville, Pa., and raised in Wheaton, Ill., was a perfect football figure for the age of hyperbole in American sports. Yet, when he was asked for his fondest college football memory, he did not cite his five-touchdown performance against Michigan. Instead, it was a game at Iowa won when Earl Britton, his prime blocker on runs, kicked a 55-yard field goal.

"I held the ball for him," Mr. Grange recalled.

ARTHUR ASHE

July 10, 1943–February 6, 1993

By Robin Finn

Arthur Ashe, a tennis champion who spent his years in the sport fighting discrimination and then spent the final year of his life seeking to broaden public awareness of AIDS, died Saturday. He was 49.

A New York Hospital administrator, Judith Lilavois, said Ashe died of pneumonia, a complication of AIDS. He was admitted to the hospital on Friday.

Gov. L. Douglas Wilder of Virginia said Ashe's body would lie in state at the executive mansion in Richmond tomorrow. Ashe's wife, Jeanne Moutoussamy-Ashe, said the funeral would be Wednesday at the Arthur Ashe Youth Center in Richmond, his native city.

Ashe was the only black man to win Wimbledon, the United States Open and the Australian Open. Militant in his convictions but mild in his manner, this slim, bookish and bespectacled athlete never thought himself a rebel and preferred information to insurrection.

Since he believed his singular success carried inherent responsibilities, Ashe dedicated himself to dismantling the barriers of poverty, privilege, racism and social stereotyping. When his own mortality became a cause célèbre, Ashe, in the headlines again, conducted his final campaign against the ravages of AIDS.

Ashe said he believed he contracted H.I.V., the virus that causes AIDS, through a transfusion of tainted blood during his second round of heart-bypass surgery in 1983. He first learned of his infection after he entered New York Hospital for emergency brain surgery in September 1988. He was hospitalized after he suffered paralysis of his right arm, the one that served up 26 aces the day he became the 1968 United States Open champion. The surgery and a biopsy revealed toxoplasmosis, a parasitic infection linked to AIDS.

In recent weeks Ashe had been hospitalized with pneumocystis pneumonia. Two weeks ago he stayed in Manhattan, where he lived, rather than travel to Boston to receive an award.

He appeared short of breath in a videotape shown in the place of his appearance. But Ashe was as passionate as ever, speaking of a visit to South Africa in which a young boy told him he was the first free black man the child had ever seen.

Ashe chose not to publicize his condition, preferring to protect his family's privacy. Only in April 1992, after being told that USA Today intended to publish an article about his illness, did Ashe disclose it publicly.

As an avid golfer, prominent speaker, occasional columnist for The Washington Post, television commentator for HBO and ABC, author of a three-volume history of the black athlete in America, and a noted participant in countless civic projects and protests, Ashe hardly went into retreat in the four years that followed his diagnosis.

Ever in icy control on the tennis court, Ashe was just as assiduous about remaining in control of himself and his emotions in his off-court life.

Last August, Ashe assembled tennis luminaries at the United States Open to begin a 15-month, $5 million fund-raising effort on behalf of his namesake foundation to combat AIDS. With that project safely in the works, he traveled to Washington, where he and others were arrested while protesting the government's treatment of Haitian refugees. Later that week he suffered a mild heart attack, his third.

For Ashe, handcuffs were nothing new; this longtime friend to Nelson Mandela had been arrested in 1985 as he protested South Africa's policy of apartheid. (In 1973 he was the first black athlete to be granted a visa—but not hotel accommodations—to compete in South Africa.)

But becoming a human billboard in the fight against AIDS was something Ashe understood he would eventually accept with his usual poise.

Only the fact that the timing was beyond his control bothered him. As the father of a daughter—Camera, now 6—he didn't want his limited time to be spent working overtime on a public campaign.

But once the announcement was made, Ashe's initial anger dissipated and he seemed almost relieved. "The foundation was something I always knew I wanted to do, long before I went public on April 8," he said. On Dec. 1, World AIDS Day, he addressed the United Nations General Assembly on the need for greater awareness of the disease.

Shy yet eloquent, Ashe was the only prominent black male tennis player of his era, a position that left him feeling ostracized at times by both blacks and whites.

But Ashe served as a beacon for future generations of black tennis players.

"He's always been for black players someone to look up to and someone who says, 'You can do it, it doesn't matter where you come from or how you look,'" said Zina Garrison, a product of Houston's public parks system who reached a world ranking of No. 4 in 1989.

Pam Shriver, a many-time Grand Slam doubles champion, said Ashe's example was not lost on women campaigning for equality in tennis. "He was a voice for all the minorities, and that goes for women, too," she said.

Arthur Ashe, the son of a parks policeman, was born in Richmond on July 10, 1943. His mother died when he was six. His father died in 1989.

He played his first tennis at the age of seven on the courts at Brookfield Park, the segregated playground adjacent to his home. By age 14, he had found a patron in Dr. Walter Johnson, a physician with two decades of experience in assisting black tennis prodigies.

Ashe reached the semifinals of the junior national championships on his first attempt in 1958. He won the indoor singles title in 1960 and 1961, and transferred to Sumner High School in St. Louis to train full time with Richard Hudlin.

In 1962, as the fifth-ranked junior in the nation, Ashe received a full scholarship to U.C.L.A. There he attracted the attention of Gonzalez and Pancho Segura, both of whom helped refine Ashe's serve-and-volley game and the unshakable temperament that vaulted him to three Grand Slam tournament singles titles. They also encouraged his penchant for experimentation: At one time, his repertory included 16 variations of the backhand stroke.

In 1963 he joined the United States Davis Cup team, and by 1966, the year he graduated from U.C.L.A. with a degree in business administration, he was described by the renowned tennis teacher Harry Hopman as "the most promising player in the world."

Ashe won the 1968 United States Open at Forest Hills while still a 25-year-old amateur fulfilling a three-year Army stint. He defeated Tom Okker in the final, marking the first time a black man had won a Grand Slam event, one of the sport's four major tournaments. In 1970 he won the Australian Open.

In 1975 he defeated Jimmy Connors in the Wimbledon final, making his opponent even more manic than usual by calmly closing his eyes and meditating through every changeover.

The Grand Slam titles and ensuing endorsement contracts helped make Ashe tennis's first black millionaire, with $1,584,909 in prize money. He played on the Davis Cup team for 10 years, won three championships, and later served as its captain from 1981–84 after heart problems forced his retirement in 1980.

Ashe suffered his first heart attack in July 1979, just after conducting a clinic for underprivileged children in New York City. In December of that year, he underwent a quadruple bypass operation, and in 1983 a double bypass.

Also in 1988, Ashe helped create inner-city tennis programs for youths in Newark, Detroit, Atlanta, Kansas City and Indianapolis. He was inducted into the International Tennis Hall of Fame in Newport, R.I., in 1985, and last year Mayor David N. Dinkins proclaimed Aug. 30, the date of Ashe's kickoff for his $5 million AIDS fund-raiser, Arthur Ashe Day in New York City.

WILMA RUDOLPH

June 23, 1940–November 12, 1994

By Frank Litsky

Wilma Rudolph, who grew from a sickly child unable to walk into a statuesque athlete of 20 who won three gold medals as a sprinter in the 1960 Olympics in Rome, died yesterday at her home in Brentwood, Tenn., near Nashville. She was 54.

Her sister, Charlene Rudolph, said Rudolph had a malignant brain tumor.

Rudolph was a handsome, regal woman, 6 feet tall, charming, graceful and gracious. Over seven days, she became the first American woman to win three gold medals in track and field in one Olympics. She also became America's greatest female sports hero since Babe Didrikson Zaharias a generation earlier.

Rudolph competed in an era in which Olympic sports such as track and field were completely amateur, and for years later, as a frequent spokeswoman for Olympic-family organizations and causes, she preached the idealism of that bygone era.

"I love what the Olympics stand for," she said. "They'll always be a part of me."

Rudolph's life story was so dramatic that in 1977 it became a two-hour prime-time television movie. The movie was written, produced and directed by her friend

Bud Greenspan, the Olympic historian. "She was the Jesse Owens of women's track and field, and like Jesse, she changed the sport for all time," he said. "She became the benchmark for little black girls to aspire."

Wilma Glodean Rudolph was born on June 23, 1940, in Clarksville, Tenn., 45 miles north of Nashville, and grew up in Clarksville. She was the 20th of 22 children of Ed Rudolph, a railroad porter, from two marriages. Her mother, Blanche, was a domestic.

Wilma weighed four and a half pounds at birth. At age four, she contracted double pneumonia and scarlet fever simultaneously and almost died. The illnesses left her left leg paralyzed, and once a week, on her mother's day off, the mother made a 90-mile round trip with her to Nashville for heat and water treatment.

At 6, Wilma started to hop on one leg. At 8, she started to walk with a leg brace. Later, an orthopedic shoe replaced the brace. One day, when she was 11, her mother found her playing basketball in her bare feet. That was the end of the special shoe and the beginning of a fabled sports career.

"My father pushed me to become competitive," Rudolph wrote in "Wilma," her 1978 autobiography. "He felt that sports would help me overcome the problems."

At 13, she went out for the high school basketball team and twice made the all-state team. She would sometimes skip school to run on a track across the street. Her talent intrigued Ed Temple, the renowned coach at Tennessee State University in Nashville, and at his invitation she attended his summer track camps.

In 1956, a 16-year-old stringbean of 89 pounds, Rudolph ran in the Melbourne Olympics. To her dismay, she was eliminated in the 200-meter heats. She did win a bronze medal in the 400-meter relay.

When she graduated from high school, Temple gave her an athletic scholarship at Tennessee State. Bulked up to 130 pounds, she made the 1960 Olympic team. Temple was the women's coach.

The day before the 100 meters in the Rome Olympics, she stepped into a hole in the infield of the practice track and twisted an ankle. It became swollen and discolored. The next day, the ankle held up, and with her fluid running style she won her semifinal in 11.3 seconds, equaling the world record. She won the final easily in 11.0 seconds, but the following wind of 6.15 miles an hour (the allowable limit is 4.47) precluded recognition as a world record.

In the 200 meters, she set an Olympic record of 23.2 seconds in the heats and won the final easily in 24.0 seconds into a stiff wind. In the 400-meter relay, with college teammates running the first three legs, she helped set a world record of 44.4 seconds in a heat. In the final, after a bad baton pass to her, she turned a two-yard deficit into a three-yard victory in 44.5 seconds.

Rudolph returned to college and earned a degree in education in 1961. She was voted the 1961 Sullivan Award as America's outstanding amateur athlete, male or female.

But there was no money for amateurs then and no professional track, so she set out to make a living. She taught second grade and coached high school basketball and track in Tennessee, all for $400 a month. Then she ran a community center in Indiana for $600 a month.

Rudolph married William Ward in 1961 and was divorced the next year. In 1963, she married Robert Eldridge. They were divorced in 1976. She is survived by her two sons and two daughters with Mr. Eldridge, five sisters and two brothers, and seven grandchildren.

At DePauw University in Indiana, Rudolph coached briefly and recruited minority-group students. She established the Wilma Rudolph Foundation, working with youngsters and sending tutors to schools with books on American heroes.

She last raced in 1962. She quit, she said, because "I couldn't top what I did, so I'll be remembered for when I was at my best."

MICKEY MANTLE

October 20, 1931–August 13, 1995

By Joseph Durso

Mickey Mantle, the most powerful switch-hitter in baseball history and the successor to Babe Ruth and Joe DiMaggio as the symbol of the long reign of the New York Yankees, died of cancer yesterday in Dallas. He was 63.

Mantle died at 2:10 A.M. Eastern time at Baylor University Medical Center, succumbing to the disease that had spread from his liver to most of his other vital organs. His wife, Merlyn, and son David were at his bedside.

On June 8, Mantle underwent a transplant operation to replace a liver ravaged by cancer, hepatitis and cirrhosis. At the time, doctors said he would die within two to three weeks if he did not receive a new organ. On July 28, he re-entered Baylor Medical Center for treatment of cancerous spots in his right lung. On Aug. 9, the hospital said the cancer had spread to his abdomen.

"This is the most aggressive cancer that anyone on the medical team has ever seen," said Dr. Goran Klintmalm, medical director of transplant services at Baylor. "But the hope in this is that Mickey left behind a legacy. Mickey and his team have already made an enormous impact by increasing the awareness of organ donation. This may become Mickey's ultimate home run."

Mantle, who said he was "bred to play baseball," traveled from the dirt-poor fields of Oklahoma to reach Yankee Stadium in the 1950's and the Baseball Hall of Fame as one of the superstars of the second half of the 20th century.

He commanded the biggest stage in sports as the center fielder for the most successful team in baseball, and he did it at a time when New York was blessed with three great center fielders: Willie Mays of the Giants, Mantle of the Yankees and Duke Snider of the Brooklyn Dodgers. Renowned as "Willie, Mickey and the Duke," they captivated the public in the 1950's as the leaders of memorable teams.

Mantle outlived the family curse of Hodgkin's disease, which had contributed to the death by heart attack of his son Billy, at 36, and the early deaths of his father, at 39, his grandfather and two uncles. He was separated from Merlyn, his wife of 43 years, although they remained friendly. He was an alcoholic, which doctors said was at least partly responsible for causing his liver cancer.

Through all the adversity, he exhibited a quiet but shrewd wit that he often unfurled in an Oklahoma drawl. Of his fear of dying early, he once said: "I'll never get a pension. I won't live long enough." And after years of drinking and carousing with his teammates Whitey Ford and Billy Martin, he joked, "If I knew I was going to live this long, I'd have taken better care of myself."

In the end he had a more poignant message. In a news conference on July 11, a remorseful Mantle told the nation, especially its children: "Don't be like me. God gave me a body and the ability to play baseball. I had everything and I just . . ."

He was the storybook star with the storybook name, Mickey, or simply Mick. He was the blond, muscled switch-hitter who joined the Yankees at 19 in 1951 as DiMaggio was winding down his Hall of Fame career. Wearing No. 7, he led the team through 14 years of the greatest success any baseball team has known before he endured four more years of decline.

He not only hit the ball, he hammered it. He could drag a bunt, too, with runaway speed, and he played his role with a kind of all-American sense of destiny. He became wildly famous for his strength, his dash, his laconic manner and his heroic performances on damaged knees.

Long after the cheers faded, so did Mantle, although he revived his image as a kind of fallen hero who carried his afflictions with grace and humor. He acknowledged that some were self-inflicted, especially drinking, a habit that had seemed harmless enough when crowds were cheering and he was playing and hitting home runs despite an occasional hangover.

His transplant revived a debate over whether an alcoholic, even a recovering one, deserves a new liver, and whether his celebrity status had increased his chances of getting one.

Frail, and humbled by the sad events of his later life, Mantle received thousands of letters of support after his transplant operation and discovered that the public could forgive and forget. People chose instead to remember his baseball feats.

Mantle was the anchor of the Yankees for 18 seasons, first in center field and later, when his knees couldn't take the stress anymore, at first base. He played in 2,401 games and went to bat 8,102 times—more than any other Yankee—and delivered 2,415 hits for a .298 batting average. He hit 536 home runs (373 left-handed, 163 right-handed), and he knocked in 1,509 runs.

Mantle led the American League in home runs four times (in 1955, 1956, 1958 and 1960) and led the league in almost everything in 1956, when he won the triple crown with these totals: a .353 batting average, 130 runs batted in and 52 home runs. He was named the league's most valuable player in 1956, 1957 and 1962. He also hit a record total of 18 home runs in 12 World Series, and 2 more in 16 All-Star Games.

He took such an all-out swing at the ball that he struck out regularly and broke the record set two generations earlier by Ruth. It was a record that Mantle put into perspective when he was inducted into the Hall of Fame on Aug. 12, 1974. "He struck out only 1,500 times," he said. "I did it 1,710 times."

During their empire years, the Yankees built on the mountains of success they had fashioned in the days since Ruth joined them in 1920. With Mantle established in the lineup in 1951, they won the pennant seven times and the Series five times in his first eight years. And from 1960–64, with the addition of Roger Maris, they won five pennants and two World Series.

Not only that, but in their championship year of 1961, Mantle and Maris provided a seasonlong drama in their chase of Ruth's home run record; Mantle, sidelined by an abscessed hip, dropped out

in mid-September with 54, while Maris finished with a record 61.

Mickey Charles Mantle was born in Spavinaw, Okla., on Oct. 20, 1931. His father, Elvin, nicknamed Mutt, worked in the zinc mines. But he was also a part-time baseball player who had such a passion for the game that he named his son in honor of Mickey Cochrane, the great catcher for the Philadelphia Athletics and player-manager for the Detroit Tigers.

Playing for a semipro team, the Baxter Springs Whiz Kids, as a teenager, Mantle was discovered by a Yankee scout named Tom Greenwade. He started at Independence, Kan., in 1949, at a Class D minor league club. The next summer, at 18, he played Class C ball in Joplin, Mo., and the following spring, he joined the Yankees.

Ford remembered how shy and inarticulate the young Mantle seemed when he reported.

"Everything he owned was in a straw suitcase," he said. "No money, none of those $400 suits he got around to buying a couple of years later. Just those two pairs of pastel slacks and that blue sports coat that he wore every place."

Mantle closed his rookie season hitting .267 with 13 home runs in 96 games. That year, he tore ligaments in his knee in the World Series, and other injuries followed. He became one of the damaged demigods of sport, but he played with such natural power that his strength as a hitter became legendary. In 1956, and again in 1963, batting left-handed each time, he smashed a ball into the third deck of Yankee Stadium, within a few feet of the peak of the facade in right field. No one has come closer to driving a fair ball out of the park.

In 1956, he hit 16 home runs in May. He hit three home runs in the 1956 World Series, three more in the 1960 Series and three more in the 1964 Series, running his total to 18 and breaking Ruth's record.

The Yankees stopped winning pennants after the 1964 season, and Mantle stopped playing after the 1968 season.

In addition to his former wife and son David, he is survived by two other sons, Danny and Mickey Jr.

After retirement, he reported, he was living in a steady haze induced by all-day and all-night drinking. "When I was drinking," he said, "I thought it was funny—the life of the party. But as it turned out, nobody could stand to be around me. "

Mantle admitted that drinking had become a way of life even while he was playing. But it finally became a nightmare that undermined his life. He checked into the Betty Ford Center in 1994, and after leaving it he seemed to be a revived person.

"Everywhere I go," he said, "guys come up and shake hands and say, 'Good job, Mick.' It makes you feel good. It's unbelievable. They give a damn now."

BEN HOGAN

August 13, 1912–July 25, 1997

By Larry Dorman

Ben Hogan, the flinty-eyed Texan who was perhaps the most creative shotmaker in the history of golf and one of its most accomplished players, died yesterday morning in Fort Worth. He was 84.

He had been in poor health since undergoing surgery for colon cancer two years ago, according to Valerie Hogan, his wife of 62 years and his only survivor.

Hogan's influence on the game was profound and his legacy far-reaching. When he was at the peak of his powers, winning nine major championships—four United States Opens, two Masters, two P.G.A. championships and one British Open—from 1946 to 1953, he was considered by many to be the finest player in the game.

He is one of only four players to win all four major professional championships, and his 63 career victories rank third behind Sam Snead (81) and Jack Nicklaus (70). In 1953, probably the greatest year any professional golfer has had, he won the Masters, the United States Open and the British Open, the first three legs of the modern Grand Slam, a feat no other player has accomplished.

His indelible mark on the game stemmed not merely from his ability to control a golf ball, perhaps with more precision than anyone before or since, but also from his enormous will—a determination that forced him to remake his entire golf game, to come back from a near-fatal automobile accident and to set standards of excellence that were previously only imagined.

It was that steely sense of purpose and the impeccable technique he developed throughout his career that engendered legions of admirers, many of whom never saw him play. His legendary work ethic and quiet demeanor, combined with an aversion to interviews and public appearances, created what was known as the Hogan mystique, an aura that impressed even the most callous observers.

"All I know is, I've seen Jack Nicklaus watch Hogan practice," the great Texas golfer Tommy Bolt once said. "I've never seen Hogan watch Nicklaus practice."

Hogan was a taciturn man. He earned the nickname Bantam Ben because at 5 feet 8 inches he was short but aggressive, like a bantam. He was also known as the Wee Ice Mon for his steely-eyed approach to the game. But mostly he was called, simply, Hogan.

Although his life and game will be remembered as straightforward and indomitable, Hogan nonetheless had a flair for the dramatic on the golf course. And his ability to overcome a swing flaw that nearly drove him from the game is an achievement that amazed both his contemporaries and those who followed him.

He was born William Benjamin Hogan on Aug. 13, 1912, in Dublin, Tex., the son of a blacksmith, Chester Hogan, and his wife, Clara. Chester Hogan committed suicide nine years after Ben's birth, and Clara Hogan moved the family to Fort Worth, where the young Hogan began caddying at the age of 12.

Hogan turned professional in 1929, and for the first 16 years of his career, he fought a tendency to hit a hook, a dreaded golf shot that curves uncontrollably from right to left for a right-hander. A professional golfer afflicted with a hook is much like a professional baseball player who cannot hit a curveball. Both are destined to fail. Hogan knew that well, and once said of the hook: "It nauseates me. I could vomit when I see one. It's like a rattlesnake in your pocket."

To behead the rattlesnake, Hogan developed a technique that was mysteriously dubbed "the secret" by the golf cognoscenti. It was a formula that Hogan never revealed in full, but near the end of his life he said "the secret" was "in the dirt," meaning it was simply a repeating stroke that was born of countless hours of practice. He defeated the hook, turning it into a more manageable power fade by beating it into submission, thus becoming the greatest ball-striker of his, and perhaps any, era.

Ben Crenshaw, the accomplished touring professional and golf historian, once wrote of Hogan: "No one swung at a golf ball with more force and authority than Hogan."

Crenshaw spoke with awe of watching Hogan hit iron shots that would hit the middle of the green and then spin left or right, depending on the pin placement.

"They really couldn't hide a pin from Hogan," Crenshaw said.

Perhaps because of his determination to subdue golf by working at it harder than anyone else, Hogan is identified with the United States Open more than any other tournament. With brutally thick rough and slick greens, the Open is the tournament that demands more than any other of its winners, and it was an accepted fact of the 1940's and 50's that no one met its demands better than Hogan. No one prepared for a United States Open the way he did, nor could any player analyze a course the way he did.

The principal chronicler of the United States Open, the author Robert Sommers, wrote that Hogan "seemed to know every flat spot on a golf course and how a ball would bounce wherever it landed." This was the key to an amazing streak in which Hogan competed in 16 United States Opens from 1940 to 1960 and never finished out of the top 10. It was how he won four United States Open championships, with perhaps the most memorable of them being the 1950 victory at Merion Golf Club in Ardmore, Pa.

That victory came just one year and four months after Hogan's automobile accident in 1949 on a dark desert highway outside Van Horn, Tex., some 110 miles west of El Paso. In a head-on collision with a Greyhound bus, Hogan was hurt so badly that it was widely assumed he would never play competitive golf again.

His life probably was saved because he dived across the seat to shield his wife from the impact. The steering wheel column was driven through the driver's side seat, but the diving Hogan avoided it. Still, he suffered a double fracture of the pelvis, a fractured collarbone, a fractured left ankle and a chipped rib.

He spent the better part of a year in rehabilitation, and returned to competition at the 1950 Los Angeles Open, where he shot four-under-par 280 and ultimately lost in a playoff to Sam Snead. He was back, but he still had difficulty walking six months later during the Open at Merion. Each day after his rounds, Hogan loosened the bandages covering his ankles and thighs, and soaked his legs to relieve the pain.

But he tied for the lead after 72 holes with perhaps his most famous shot, a 1-iron to the 18th green that set up a par and a playoff. He won that by shooting 69 to Lloyd Mangrum's 73 and George Fazio's 75.

"Merion meant the most," he once said, "because I proved I could still win."

His comeback was dramatized in the 1951 film "Follow the Sun" in which Glenn Ford played Hogan.

Hogan never again played without some pain, but his greatness only increased. In 1953, he came closer than anyone has to winning golf's modern Grand Slam, capturing the Masters, the United States Open and the British Open in Scotland. He was unable to compete in the P.G.A. championship because the dates for the P.G.A. and British Open overlapped.

Hogan's last victory was in 1959, and by the mid-1960's he was semi-retired. His last great hurrah came in the 1967 Masters when, at age 54 and hobbled by ever-increasing pain, he shot a 66 in the third round, including a 30 on the back nine.

After he stopped playing competitive golf, Hogan had no use for testimonials, and he took care to maintain his reputation.

He once told a writer that any endorsement that bore his name would be associated only with unassailable value. That disposition had to do with something his mother told him when he was a boy. "Your name is the most important thing you own," Hogan said. "Don't ever do anything to disgrace it or cheapen it."

In a game that never quite allows perfection, the name Hogan was synonymous with the quest to achieve it.

HELEN MOODY

October 6, 1905–January 1, 1998

By Robin Finn

Helen Wills Moody, arguably the most dominant tennis player of the 20th century and the first American-born woman to achieve international celebrity as an athlete, died Thursday in Carmel, Calif. She was 92.

She was affectionately known as Little Miss Poker Face for her dispassionate on-court behavior. Wills, who never appeared for a match without her signature white visor, won 31 Grand Slam titles in her 15 years of competition.

She held the No. 1 world ranking for eight years and did not lose a set while amassing a 180-match winning streak from 1927 to 1933.

Her concentration was legendary. According to her biographer Larry Engelman, her mantra during a match was: "Every shot, every shot, every shot."

She won the first of her 19 Grand Slam singles titles as a pigtailed 17-year-old in 1923 at the national championships in Forest Hills, N.Y. She retired from tennis in 1938 after winning a record eighth Wimbledon title at age 32. That record remained until 1990, when Martina Navratilova captured her ninth singles championship at Wimbledon.

Wills seemed never to have lost her competitive edge. "She admired Martina Navratilova greatly as a tennis player who broke her record," said Jeanne Cherry, a Los Angeles tennis historian. "I once asked her how she felt about Martina breaking her record, and she said, "Well, you know, she pumps iron."

In addition to her eight Wimbledon singles titles, Wills captured seven United States singles titles, won the French championships four times and earned gold medals in singles and doubles at the 1924 Olympics. Moody also won 12 United States, French and Wimbledon doubles and mixed doubles titles.

"She hit the ball harder than most, except maybe Steffi Graf," said Don Budge, one of those who teamed with her in mixed doubles. "Her footwork didn't have to be great. She would control the play because she hit the ball so hard."

Reclusive by nature and dubbed the Garbo of the tennis tour by Alice Marble, one of many opponents who felt ignored by her, Wills nonetheless lived a most public and, at times, storybook existence. She took tea with the British Prime Minister, was the subject of poetry by Louis Untermeyer and counted Charlie Chaplin among her admirers. In 1930 Chaplin described "the movement of Helen Wills playing tennis" as the most beautiful sight he had ever seen.

Wills, an artist by avocation who painted throughout her life, also became a champion of fashion, particularly on the tennis court. Like her flamboyant

European role model, Suzanne Lenglen—the first of a new breed of female tennis players who abandoned the long skirts dictated by the era—Wills advocated sensible garb on the courts and always wore a knee-length pleated skirt during play.

Born in Centerville, Calif., on Oct. 6, 1905, Wills spent her childhood in Berkeley and received her initial tennis tutelage from her father, Dr. Clarence Wills. For her 14th birthday, her parents gave her a membership in the Berkeley Tennis Club. Wills played every day, and in 1921, at age 15, she won the national junior championship.

Two years later, at 17, she became the second-youngest United States national champion by de-throning Molla Mallory, the defending champion. Wills began a lengthy tenure at the top by receiving the No. 1 United States ranking after their match at Forest Hills.

In 1924 she lost the Wimbledon final to Britain's top player, Kitty McKane, but prevailed in all eight of her other Wimbledon finals.

Perhaps Wills's most infamous match was her only meeting with Lenglen in a much ballyhooed show-down at Cannes in 1926.

Tickets were scalped at a then-shocking rate of $50 each, and an international gallery of spectators included King Gustaf, a group of French schoolboys in a eucalyptus tree at one end of the court, and Wills's future husband, Frederick Moody, who introduced himself to her after the match.

Wills liked to note that although she lost the match, she gained a husband. She and Moody divorced in 1937, and two years later she married Aidan Roark, a film writer and polo player. She leaves no survivors.

"Whatever Helen did, she had to be the best at it," said Edward Chandler, a San Francisco attorney and a lifelong friend. "She stopped playing at 82, but she was outspoken in her admiration for Chris Evert, she despised Jimmy Connors for the way he behaved, and she was very happy to see Pete Sampras come along, because he seemed a throwback to the older school."

JOE DIMAGGIO

November 25, 1914–March 8, 1999

By Joseph Durso

HOLLYWOOD, Fla.—Joe DiMaggio, the flawless center fielder for the New York Yankees who, along with Babe Ruth and Mickey Mantle, symbolized the team's dynastic success across the 20th century and whose 56-game hitting streak in 1941 made him an instant and indelible American folk hero, died early today at his home here. He was 84 years old.

DiMaggio died nearly five months after undergoing surgery for cancer of the lungs and then battling infections and pneumonia. His illness generated a national vigil as he was reported near death several times.

In a country that has idolized and even immortalized its 20th century heroes, from Charles A. Lindbergh to Elvis Presley, no one more embodied the American dream of fame and fortune or created a more endur-ing legend than Joe DiMaggio. He became a figure of unequaled romance and integrity in the national mind because of his consistent professionalism on the baseball field, his marriage to the Hollywood star Marilyn Monroe, his devotion to her after her death, and the pride and courtliness with which he carried himself throughout his life.

DiMaggio burst onto the baseball scene from San Francisco in the 1930's and grew into the game's most gal-lant and graceful center fielder. He wore No. 5 and became the successor to Babe Ruth (No. 3) and Lou Gehrig (No. 4) in the Yankees' pantheon. DiMaggio was the team's superstar for 13 seasons, beginning in 1936 and ending in 1951, and appeared in 11 All-Star Games and 10 World Series. He was, as the writer Roy Blount Jr. once observed, "the class of the Yankees in times when the Yankees outclassed everybody else."

He was called the Yankee Clipper and was acclaimed at baseball's centennial in 1969 as "the greatest living ball-player," the man who in 1,736 games with the Yankees, had a career batting average of .325 and hit 361 home runs while striking out only 369 times, one of baseball's most amazing statistics. (By way of comparison, Mickey Mantle had 536 homers and struck out 1,710 times; Reggie Jackson slugged 563 homers and struck out 2,597 times.)

But DiMaggio's game was so complete and elegant that it transcended statistics.

He moved across the vast expanse of center field at Yankee Stadium with such incomparable grace that long after he stopped playing, the memory of him in full stride remains evergreen. The writer Wilfrid Sheed wrote, "In dreams I can still see him gliding after fly balls as if he were skimming the surface of the moon."

His batting stance was as graceful as his outfield stride. His swing was pure and flowing with an incredible follow-through. Casey Stengel, the Yankee manager for DiMaggio's last three seasons, said, "He made the rest of them look like plumbers."

ATHLETES

At his peak, he was serenaded as "Joltin' Joe DiMaggio" by Les Brown and saluted as "the great DiMaggio" by Ernest Hemingway in "The Old Man and the Sea." Years later, he was remembered by Paul Simon, who wondered with everybody else: "Where have you gone, Joe DiMaggio? A nation turns its lonely eyes to you."

He was private and remote. Yet he could be proud, reclusive and vain in such a composed, almost studied way that his reclusiveness contributed to his mystique. In the book "Summer of '49," David Halberstam wrote that DiMaggio "guards his special status carefully, wary of doing anything that might tarnish his special reputation. He tends to avoid all those who might define him in some way other than the way he defined himself on the field."

DiMaggio played his final year in 1951, when Mickey Mantle arrived to open yet another era in the remarkable run of Yankee success. In his 13 seasons, DiMaggio got 2,214 hits, knocked in 1,537 runs and reached base just under 40 percent of the time.

For decades, baseball fans argued over who was the better pure hitter, DiMaggio or Williams. Long after both had retired, Williams said: "In my heart, I always felt I was a better hitter than Joe. But I have to say, he was the greatest baseball player of our time. He could do it all."

In the field, DiMaggio ran down long drives with a deep range. In 1947, he tied what was then the American League fielding record for outfielders by making only one error in 141 games.

He also had one of the most powerful and precise throwing arms in the business and was credited with 153 assists in his 13 seasons.

His longtime manager, Joe McCarthy, once touched on another DiMaggio skill. "He was the best base runner I ever saw," McCarthy said. "He could have stolen 50, 60 bases a year if I let him. He wasn't the fastest man alive. He just knew how to run bases better than anybody."

Three times DiMaggio was voted his league's most valuable player: in 1939, 1941 and 1947. He entered the Hall of Fame in 1955.

Joseph Paul DiMaggio was born on Nov. 25, 1914, in Martinez, Calif., a fishing village 25 miles northeast of the Golden Gate. He was the eighth of nine children born to Giuseppe Paolo and Rosalie DiMaggio, who had immigrated to America in 1898 from Sicily. His father was a fisherman who moved his family to North Beach, the heavily Italian section near the San Francisco waterfront, the year Joe was born.

Three sons became major league outfielders by way of the sandlots of San Francisco. Vince played 10 seasons and led the National League in strikeouts six times. Dominic played 11 seasons with the Boston Red Sox, hitting .298 for his career. Of the three, Joe was the natural.

He dropped out of high school after one year and joined Vince on the San Francisco Seals of the Pacific Coast League, the highest level of minor league baseball. It was 1932, and Joe was still 17 years old.

He tore up the league and, after signing with the Yankees in 1935, he was brought up to New York in 1936 to join a talented team that included Lou Gehrig. It was two years after Babe Ruth had left, and an era of success had ended.

But now the rookie from California was arriving, and a new era was beginning. He played in 138 games, got 206 hits with 29 home runs, batted .323 and drove in 125 runs. In the World Series, he hit .346 against the Giants and made a spectacular catch in deepest center field in the Polo Grounds before a marveling crowd of 43,543, including President Franklin D. Roosevelt.

DiMaggio's luster was sometimes dimmed by salary disputes. After hitting 46 home runs in 1937, he held out for $40,000, but was forced to sign for $25,000. DiMaggio's holdout lasted a couple of weeks into the season; when he returned, he was booed.

He also had to endure the casual bigotry that existed when he first came up. Life magazine, in a 1939 article intending to compliment him, said: "Although he learned Italian first, Joe, now 24, speaks English without an accent, and is otherwise well adapted to most

U.S. mores. Instead of olive oil or smelly bear grease he keeps his hair slick with water. He never reeks of garlic and prefers chicken chow mein to spaghetti."

But he energized the fans by leading the league in hitting in 1939 (at .381) and again in 1940 (.352). Then, in 1941, he put together what has since been known simply as the Streak, and fashioned perhaps the most enduring record in sports.

The Streak began on May 15, 1941 and finally ended on the steamy night of July 17 in Cleveland. The stopper was the Indians' third baseman, Ken Keltner, who made two dazzling backhand plays deep behind third base to rob DiMaggio. It is sometimes overlooked that DiMaggio was intentionally walked in the fourth inning, and that he promptly started a 16-game streak the next day.

DiMaggio was passing milestones in his personal life, too. In 1939, he married an actress, Dorothy Arnold. In October 1941, his only child, Joseph Jr., was born. In addition to his son, he is survived by his brother Dominic; two granddaughters, Paula and Cathy; and four great-grandchildren.

On Dec. 3, 1942, DiMaggio enlisted in the Army Air Forces and taught baseball in the service, returning to the Yankees in 1946.

His most dramatic moments came in 1949, after he was sidelined by bone spurs on his right heel and did not play until June 26. Then he flew to Boston to join the team in Fenway Park, hit a single and home run the first two times he went to bat, hit two more home runs the next day and another the day after that.

The Yankees entered the final two days of that season trailing the Red Sox by one game. They had to sweep two games in Yankee Stadium to win the pennant, and they did. There were poignant moments before the first game when 69,551 fans rocked the stadium and cheered their hero, who was being honored with a Joe DiMaggio Day. He was almost too weak to play because of a severe viral infection, but he hit a single and double before removing himself from center field on wobbly legs.

After the Yankees won yet another World Series, in 1951, he retired and eased into a second career as Joe DiMaggio, legend. He spent many evenings at Toots

Shor's restaurant in Manhattan, where he hid out at a private table far in the back while Shor protected him from his public.

But his legend took a storybook turn in 1952, the year after he retired from the Yankees, when DiMaggio, whose marriage to Dorothy Arnold had ended in divorce in 1944, arranged a dinner date with Marilyn Monroe in California. They were married on Jan. 14, 1954, and spent nine months trying to reconcile their differences before they divorced in October.

DiMaggio always seemed tortured by Monroe's sex goddess image. He protested loudly during the making of Billy Wilder's "The Seven Year Itch" when the script called for her to cool herself over a subway grate while a sudden wind blew her skirt up high.

Still, they remained one of America's ultimate romantic fantasies: the tall, dark and handsome baseball hero wooing and winning the woman who epitomized Hollywood beauty, glamour and sexuality.

When the actress seemed on the verge of an emotional collapse in 1961, DiMaggio took her to the Yankees' training camp in Florida for rest and support. And when she died of an overdose of barbiturates at age 36 on Aug. 4, 1962, he took charge of her funeral, and for the next 20 years he sent roses three times a week to her crypt in the Westwood section of Los Angeles.

In retirement, he seemed to relish the invitations back to Yankee Stadium, where he frequently threw out the first ball on opening day, dressed elegantly, as always, in a dark business suit.

It was there on the day the season ended last year that he was acclaimed on yet another Joe DiMaggio Day, the timeless hero and the symbol of Yankee excellence, acknowledging the cheers of Yankee players and fans.

It was the kind of cheering that accompanied him through life and that he had quietly come to expect. It recalled the time when he and Monroe, soon after their wedding, took a trip to Tokyo. She continued on to entertain American troops in Korea, and said with fascination when she returned, "Joe, you've never heard such cheering."

And Joe DiMaggio replied softly, "Yes, I have."

WILT CHAMBERLAIN

August 21, 1936–October 12, 1999

By Frank Litsky

Wilt Chamberlain, whose size, strength and intimidation made him probably the most dominant player in basketball history, and whose 100-point game stands as one of the towering records in sport, was found dead yesterday in his home in the Bel-Air section of Los Angeles. He was 63.

Jim Wells, a Fire Department spokesman, said there were indications that Chamberlain had suffered a heart attack.

At 7 feet 1 inch and 275 pounds, Chamberlain was an awesome offensive force, and while he scored many points with gentle finger-roll shots, he also became the game's first monster dunker.

Before he came along, basketball had such big centers as 6-10 George Mikan and 7-foot Bob Kurland. But Chamberlain was bigger and stronger, with a more potent inside game, so overpowering that the National Basketball Association widened the free-throw lane to force him farther from the basket.

He helped usher in an era of dominant centers that included Bill Russell of the Boston Celtics, his antagonist in so many playoff and championship series, and continued with the 7-2 Kareem Abdul-Jabbar and the 7-1, 315-pound Shaquille O'Neal of the Lakers. They, like Chamberlain, were effective not just because of their height, but because they combined strength with agility and the ability to play above the rim.

Chamberlain's name overwhelms the pro basketball record book the way his presence on the court overwhelmed everyone else on it. He not only holds the record for most points in a game—the 100 he scored against the Knicks on March 2, 1962—but also for the highest scoring average in a season, 50.4, and the most rebounds for a career, 23,924. In some categories the list of top performances has only his name.

His physique and skills earned him not just one nickname but two—Wilt the Stilt, which he disliked, and the Big Dipper.

In the N.B.A., Chamberlain played five and a fraction seasons with the Warriors, first in Philadelphia and then in San Francisco. The Warriors traded him to the new Philadelphia team, the 76ers, and he played for them for three and a fraction seasons. His last five seasons were with the Lakers.

Over all, he scored 31,419 points, the N.B.A. career record until Abdul-Jabbar broke it, and averaged 30.1 points and 22.9 rebounds a game over his career. He never fouled out of a game.

His teams reached the playoffs 13 times, but only two won championships—the Philadelphia 76ers in 1967 and the Lakers in 1972. Four of his teams lost in playoff finals. In three of those finals, Russell and the Celtics won the seventh and final game by 1 or 2 points.

His 100-point night against the Knicks has become one of the most famous performances ever and gave rise to a legion of false boasts by fans who swear they were there at Madison Square Garden when Wilt scored 100. The game, however, was played in Hershey, Pa.

Chamberlain seemed almost irritated over the fuss made over his 100-point game at the expense of other accomplishments.

"I was hot that night," he said. "They were feeding me and it was just one game."

The N.B.A. records he liked best were his records of 50.4 points a game in the 1961–62 season, 48.5 minutes a game the same season (including overtimes) and 27.2 rebounds a game in 1960–61. He also holds the single-game record for rebounds, 55, set against Boston in 1960.

"I give Kareem full credit for breaking my all-time scoring record," Chamberlain said in an interview in 1994. "It's a record of longevity, not a flash in the pan."

Records aside, Chamberlain is forever linked with Russell. It was Chamberlain, the extrovert, against Russell, the introvert; Chamberlain, the bull, against Russell, the smoothie.

Their rivalry through the 1960's and 70's captivated fans and helped build the N.B.A. into the attraction it is today.

"Bill Russell was probably the most influential player," Leonard Koppett, the basketball historian, said, "but one on one, Wilt overwhelmed him like anybody else. There has been nothing like Wilt since."

When he started playing pro basketball, the 24-second clock (under the rule that requires a team to shoot within 24 seconds of gaining possession) had been introduced only five years earlier. The public was fascinated by scorers. So when Chamberlain entered the N.B.A., Eddie Gottlieb, who owned the Philadelphia Warriors, wanted to maximize that appeal. If others could score 30 points a game, Gottlieb wanted Chamberlain to score 40 or 50 or more.

Chamberlain obliged, but once he had averaged 50 points a game for an entire season, the thrill was gone. The team wanted him to pass more, and he soon became the league leader in assists. The team wanted him to play defense more, and he became even more of a terror. Whatever the team needed, he did it, and better than almost anyone else.

Wilton Norman Chamberlain was born Aug. 21, 1936, in Philadelphia. At Overbrook High School, he was such an outstanding basketball player that most of the major basketball-playing colleges strained to convince him to accept an athletic scholarship. The University of Kansas won him.

Soon after he arrived at Kansas, his freshman team beat the varsity behind his 42 points and 24 rebounds. Forrest C. (Phog) Allen, the celebrated Kansas coach, said that performance came from "the greatest player in the world." Chamberlain said he had an off night.

Chamberlain's college career, as expected, was outstanding, with one major disappointment. In his junior year, he led Kansas to the championship game of the National Collegiate Athletic Association tournament, only to lose to North Carolina in triple overtime.

That turned out to be his last college game. He was tired of the triple-team defenses and zones designed to foil him, and he gave up his last year of eligibility. He still had to wait a year to play in the N.B.A., so he signed a one-year contract with the touring Harlem Globetrotters for $65,000, the richest basketball contract to that time. Years later, Michael Jordan would earn $35 million in one season.

While basketball was his business, Chamberlain loved many sports. For many years after retirement, he was an elite-level volleyball player. When Muhammad Ali was in his prime, Chamberlain talked of challenging him to a fight. Chamberlain even carried boxing gloves with him, but when an airline ticket clerk asked him if he was serious about fighting, he replied, "No. It's just good publicity."

He received publicity of another sort when he wrote in his autobiography that he had had sexual relations with 20,000 women. Many people criticized him as promiscuous.

Chamberlain never married. In addition to his sister, Barbara, he is survived by three other sisters, Margaret Lane, Selina Gross and Yvonne Chamberlain; and two brothers, Wilbert and Oliver Chamberlain.

Chamberlain was elected to the Naismith Memorial Basketball Hall of Fame in Springfield, Mass., in 1978. His role in history was secure, but he knew he would never be judged without blemish.

"Nobody," he said, "roots for Goliath."

TED WILLIAMS

August 30, 1918–July 5, 2002

By Richard Goldstein and Robert McG. Thomas Jr.

Ted Williams, the tempestuous slugger of the Boston Red Sox who was the last man to bat .400 and was perhaps the greatest hitter in baseball history, died yesterday in Inverness, Fla. He was 83.

Williams was in cardiac arrest when he was brought to Citrus County Memorial Hospital from his home in Crystal River. After several strokes in the 1990's, he had a pacemaker implanted in November 2000 and underwent open-heart surgery two months later.

Williams's death comes close to concluding an era of larger-than-life baseball stars who began their careers in the days when the likes of Honus Wagner and John McGraw were still household names.

He was the ultimate perfectionist at the plate, gifted with extraordinary eyesight and possessed of supreme devotion to his craft. He was ranked with Ty Cobb, Babe Ruth and Joe DiMaggio as pre-eminent figures in the history of the game.

Yesterday, his fellow Hall of Famers remembered Williams as a marquee figure.

"Knowing Ted, everyone was hanging on to yesteryear through him," Willie Mays said.

In 1941, his third season in the major leagues, Williams batted .406, the last time anyone has exceeded .400. He won the American League batting championship six times during his 19 seasons with the Red Sox.

From the moment the 20-year-old rookie they never stopped calling the Kid got his first look at Fenway Park on April 22, 1939, to the overcast day he bid his Fenway fans farewell with his 521st home run in his last at-bat on Sept. 28, 1960, Williams made an argument for recognition as baseball's most accomplished hitter.

Despite missing three full seasons while serving as a Navy pilot in World War II and losing most of two seasons while a Marine pilot in the Korean War, he led the American League in runs batted in and in home runs four times, in walks and in slugging average eight times. He captured the triple crown twice and won two Most Valuable Player awards.

In 1957, at the age of 39, Williams became the oldest man to win a batting title, with a spectacular .388 average. He won the title again the next year (.328).

Then, after a preseason neck injury in 1959 led to his most dismal season and his only sub-.300 average (.254), Williams, angered that the Red Sox were urging him to retire, came back for a defiant final season in 1960. He underlined the magnificence of his career by turning in his second-lowest average—a not-so-low .316.

That brought his career average to .344, sixth-highest since 1900 and unsurpassed since.

Nobody brought such a studied intensity to hitting, a craft Williams once called an art but one he clearly saw as a science. A left-handed batter who did everything else right-handed, he was noted for never going after a pitch outside the strike zone. Start swinging at bad balls, he figured, and you would be sure to see more of them.

By his own account he played much of his career in a rage, often over what he saw as a vicious, unfair or downright fabricated blast from the Boston press.

He was an admittedly thin-skinned man who read his critics religiously and could pick out a single boo from a torrent of cheers. Williams, who early on tagged Boston fans as fickle front-runners, became known for his refusal to tip his cap to their cheers.

The very combativeness that stirred their disdain was a reflection of the intensity that made him such a dangerous hitter. As Williams himself pointed out, he never hit better than when he was mad.

Teddy Samuel Williams was born in San Diego on Aug. 30, 1918. His house was a modest bungalow on Utah Street but his home was the North Park playground a block and a half away.

After completing high school in June 1936, he began his professional career in the Pacific Coast League, accepting $150 a month to play for the San Diego Padres. The Red Sox exercised an option on Williams in December 1937.

At his first spring training, the teenaged rookie took no guff from the veterans. When he ran into

Bobby Doerr, a former Padres teammate, who had become impressed with the great slugger Jimmie Foxx, the following conversation took place:

Doerr: "Wait until you see this guy Foxx hit."

Williams: "Wait until Foxx sees me hit."

After another year in the minors, he made the Red Sox in 1939. It was an exuberant season. Williams, the darling of the Boston fans, hit .327 with 31 home runs and a league-leading 145 R.B.I. But his honeymoon with Boston came to an end before his second season, when a newspaper columnist chided him for not visiting his mother during the winter.

Williams began to hear boos for the first time, and he didn't like it. At one point he became so upset, he said he might quit baseball to become a fireman. The next time the team visited Chicago, the White Sox appeared in fire helmets. Other teams greeted him with clanging fire bells.

Many regard the 1941 season as the greatest ever, and Williams wouldn't argue. Although Joe DiMaggio got most of the headlines with a 56-game hitting streak, Williams had the nation's full attention when he entered the last doubleheader of the season, in Philadelphia, with his average at .39955, .400 by the usual rounding.

No one had hit .400 since 1930, and manager Joe Cronin would have allowed Williams to sit out the two final games to protect the rounded mark. But Williams never considered it. He went 6 for 8 in the doubleheader, ending up at .40570 (185 for 456).

Nor was there much mystery about who might surpass .400 again after 1941: the very man they variously called (besides the Kid) the Splendid Splinter (he was thin for a power hitter), No. 9 (his uniform number) or, as initially articulated by a little boy asked to name his favorite player, Teddy Ballgame.

And he might have, too, if not for World War II. After the 1942 season, Williams enlisted in the Navy as an aviator and did not return to the Red Sox until 1946, a year in which he led the team to the American League pennant. (He had a miserable World Series against the St. Louis Cardinals, hitting just .200 as Boston lost, 4 games to 3.)

Aside from photo finishes in 1948 and 1949, his Red Sox were never again in serious contention, and he was plagued by periodic injuries.

He also missed most of the 1952 and 1953 seasons while flying 39 missions in Korea as a Marine fighter pilot. His plane was hit on one early mission and he barely escaped a fiery crash landing.

Williams returned to the Red Sox in late 1953 and continued to pile up hits and controversy, most notoriously in 1956, when he celebrated his 400th home run by spitting in the direction of the press box, a gesture he repeated a couple of days later. The "great expectorations" led to a $5,000 fine.

His celebrated departure came on a gray day at

Fenway Park on Sept. 28, 1960. On his last at-bat in the eighth inning, Williams drove the ball to center field. It landed where the bullpen met the wall and disappeared.

John Updike, writing in The New Yorker, described the home run and its aftermath in his article "Hub Fans Bid Kid Adieu." After Williams circled the bases, the fans—"wailing," Updike wrote—beseeched him to leave the dugout for a curtain call. "The papers said that the other players and even the umpires on the field begged him to come out and acknowledge us in some way, but he never had and did not now. Gods do not answer letters."

In 1969, three years after his induction into the Hall of Fame, Williams, who had long before proclaimed managing "the worst job in the world," was persuaded by the lure of a five-year, $1.25 million contract to take over the Washington Senators.

He managed the team, which had finished last in 1968, to a winning record, and was voted the American League's manager of the year.

But the Senators couldn't hold their gains. Williams followed the team to Texas when it became the Rangers in 1972, then left after a last-place season. After that, he stuck to his second love, fishing, which he mastered with the same obsession he had brought to his hitting.

Williams, who was married and divorced three times, is survived by a daughter, Bobbie Jo, by his first wife, Doris Soule; and a son and a daughter by his third wife, Dolores Wettach.

On May 11, 1991, Williams and DiMaggio were brought together at Fenway Park in a ceremony marking the 50th anniversary of the season that spawned their greatest feats. They embraced at home plate.

The following December, Williams had a stroke that affected his right side and his right visual field; a more severe stroke, in 1994, left him in a wheelchair.

But Williams was at center stage for the 1999 All-Star Game at Fenway Park. As soon as he emerged in center field, riding in a green golf cart, the fans rose to salute him and he raised his white cap.

After he was brought to the mound to throw out the ceremonial first pitch, the All-Stars and former players assembled on the field edged toward him.

Tony Gwynn, like Williams the best hitter of his era, leaned in to shake his hand. Williams wiped away tears. Then, using Gwynn to support his left side, he tossed the pitch 40 feet to Carlton Fisk, the former Red Sox catcher. The crowd roared again.

As the novelist George V. Higgins, a Red Sox devotee, had written in 1991: "Time in its habitual cruelty occasionally lets up a bit and forgives us all our lapses, and as Ted Williams and the rest of us have become three decades older, it's rewarding to us spectators to see the now-elder statesman of the batted ball savoring at least somewhat the approbation and gratitude he neither got nor enjoyed fully while he was engaged in doing what he did so well."

To those who claimed that DiMaggio or Mickey Mantle or Hank Aaron was the greatest ballplayer of all time, Higgins continued, New Englanders "have an advantage over all who have made competing claims: When we say that of Number 9, we are speaking God's own truth."

ALTHEA GIBSON

August 25, 1927–September 28, 2003

By Robert McG. Thomas Jr.

Althea Gibson, a rough-hewn product of Harlem who emerged as a most unlikely queen of the tennis lawns of Wimbledon and Forest Hills in the 1950's and became a pre-eminent figure in her sport, died yesterday in East Orange, N.J. She was 76.

Gibson, who had been in poor health for years, died in a hospital where she was being treated for an infection and respiratory illness, a doctor said.

Gibson stood 5 feet 10 1/2 inches. Lean and muscular, she had a dominating serve and a long, graceful reach. She won 56 tournaments, including five Grand Slam singles titles—the United States nationals and Wimbledon twice, in 1957 and 1958, and the French championship in 1956. She was the first black player to win Wimbledon and the United States national championship.

Yet for all her ability, her success was remarkable, given her background as an eighth-grade dropout who had grown up far removed from the era's two genteel worlds of tennis: the white country club set and the network of black doctors, lawyers and other professionals who pursued tennis on private courts of their own.

Born in a sharecropper's shack in Silver, S.C., on Aug. 25, 1927, she was brought to New York by her parents when she was a few months old. By chance, the family moved into an apartment on a West 143rd Street block between Lenox and Seventh Avenues that was a designated play street.

When the Police Athletic League closed the block to traffic and set up recreation equipment, the spot marked off as a paddle tennis court was in front of the Gibsons' front stoop. Gibson took up paddle tennis at 9 and won a citywide championship when she was 12.

In 1941 Buddy Walker, a Harlem bandleader and part-time P.A.L. supervisor, bought her two rackets and introduced her to friends at a predominantly black tennis club just a few blocks and yet a world removed from the neighborhood she had known. Gibson was coached there by the club pro and taken up by the club's members, who taught her some more important lessons.

As she put it in her 1958 autobiography, "I Always Wanted to Be Somebody," the club attracted "the highest class" of Harlem residents, people who "had rigid ideas about what was socially acceptable."

"I'm ashamed to say," she wrote, "that I was still living pretty wild." Gibson would come home late (sometimes the next day) and her father, a garage attendant, would beat her. To escape him, she finally sought refuge in a Catholic home for girls and eventually received a welfare grant to get her own apartment while she worked at menial jobs.

In 1942 she won her first tournament, the New York State girls' championship, sponsored by the American Tennis Association, which had been organized in 1916 by black players as an alternative to the United States Lawn Tennis Association.

In 1946, when she lost in the final of her first A.T.A. women's championship, she caught the eye of two men who changed her life, Hubert A. Eaton of Wilmington, N.C., and R. Walter Johnson of Lynchburg, Va.

The men, both physicians and leaders of a cadre of black enthusiasts determined to crack the racial barriers of mainstream tennis, saw Gibson's potential. She lived with Eaton and his wife during the school year, practicing on his court and attending high school, and spent the summer traveling on the A.T.A. circuit with Johnson.

Gibson was 19 when she started at Wilmington Industrial High School, but finished in three years, graduating 10th in her class, and enrolled as a scholarship student at Florida A&M, receiving a degree at 25.

In 1947, she won the first of her 10 straight A.T.A. national championships. In 1949, a year after Dr. Benjamin Weir had become the first black to play in a United States Lawn Tennis Association title event, the 1948 National Indoor Championships, Gibson took her first steps beyond the world of black tennis, making it to the semifinals of the Eastern Indoor Championships and then to the semifinals of the national championships.

But even after she had won the 1950 Eastern Indoor Championship and a clamor had begun to let her play in the National Grass Court Championships at Forest Hills in Queens, the precursor of the United States Open, the powers of tennis seemed to close ranks to keep her out.

To qualify for an invitation to the 1950 nationals, she was required to make a name for herself at one of the major preliminary events. But no invitations were forthcoming.

Alice Marble, a former champion, rallied support for Gibson. "If tennis is a game for ladies and gentlemen," she wrote in a letter to American Lawn Tennis magazine, "it's time we acted a little more like gentlepeople and less like sanctimonious hypocrites."

Finally, Gibson received an invitation to the Eastern Grass Court Championships at the Orange Lawn Tennis Club in South Orange, N.J. She made it to the second round, good enough to win a bid to Forest Hills. On Aug. 28, 1950, Gibson became the first black player to compete in the national tennis championship.

On a remote court at the West Side Tennis Club in Forest Hills, she dispatched Barbara Knapp of England, 6–2, 6–2. The next day, she faced the Wimbledon champion, Louise Brough. After losing the first set, 6–1, Gibson took the second, 6–3, then fell behind by 3–0 in the third before surging to a 7–6 lead. She was on the verge of victory when a thunderstorm halted play. When play resumed the next day, Brough won three straight games to win the match.

Over the next half-dozen years, Gibson became a fixture in tennis, playing Wimbledon for the first time in 1951. But she became so disenchanted with her failure to break through to the top that she considered abandoning the sport.

In the fall of 1955, the State Department selected her for a goodwill tennis tour of Asia and the Far East, and the experience inspired her game. In 1956 she won 16 of her first 18 tournaments, including the French championship at Roland Garros.

After losing to Shirley Fry of the United States in the singles final of the Australian Open in 1957, she did not lose another match all year. At Wimbledon, she defeated Darlene Hard in the final. Then she rolled through the national championship at Forest Hills. In the final, she defeated Brough, who had eliminated her in her first national seven years before. Gibson repeated her Wimbledon and Forest Hills singles victories in 1958.

Then, under pressure from her family to make some money, she retired from amateur tennis. At a time when the professional game was little more than a sideshow, she went on an exhibition tour with the Harlem Globetrotters, playing tennis at halftime.

In the early 1960's she became the first black player to compete on the women's golf tour, but she never won a tournament.

Gibson lived in East Orange, where she served as recreation director. She was married twice and had no children.

Althea Gibson resisted attempts to portray her as a sort of female Jackie Robinson. But when another black woman, Zina Garrison, made it to the Wimbledon final in 1990 before losing to Martina Navratilova, Gibson was there to cheer her on. Then she receded from the limelight.

YOGI BERRA

May 12, 1925–September 22, 2015

By Bruce Weber

Yogi Berra, one of baseball's greatest catchers and characters, who as a player was a mainstay of 10 Yankees championship teams and as a manager led both the Yankees and the Mets to the World Series—but who may be more widely known as an ungainly but lovable cultural figure, issuing a seemingly limitless supply of unwittingly witty epigrams known as Yogi-isms—died on Tuesday. He was 90.

Berra lived for many years in Montclair, N.J., before moving in 2012 to an assisted-living facility in nearby West Caldwell, where he died.

In 1949, early in Berra's Yankee career, his manager, Casey Stengel, said, "Mr. Berra is a very strange fellow of very remarkable abilities."

And so he was. Universally known simply as Yogi, Berra was not exactly an unlikely hero, but he was often portrayed as one: an All-Star for 15 consecutive seasons whose skills were routinely underestimated; a well-built, appealingly open-faced man whose physical appearance was often belittled; and a prolific winner and a successful leader, whose intellect was a target of humor if not outright derision.

That he triumphed on the diamond was certainly a source of his popularity. So was the delight with which his famous, if not always documentable, pronouncements—somehow both nonsensical and sagacious—were received.

"You can observe a lot just by watching," he is reputed to have said about his strategy as a manager.

"If you can't imitate him," he advised a young player who was mimicking the batting stance of a great slugger, "don't copy him."

"When you come to a fork in the road, take it," he said, giving directions to his house. Either path, it turned out, got you there.

"Nobody goes there anymore," he said of a popular restaurant. "It's too crowded."

Whether Berra actually uttered those things, or phrased them precisely the way they were reported, is a matter of speculation. Berra himself published a book in 1998 called "The Yogi Book: I Really Didn't Say Everything I Said!"

The character Yogi Berra may even have overshadowed the Hall of Fame ballplayer Yogi Berra, obscuring what a remarkable athlete he was. He was fearsome in the clutch and the most durable and productive Yankee during the team's most successful era.

Stengel compared Berra favorably to star catchers of previous eras like Mickey Cochrane, Gabby

Hartnett and Bill Dickey. "You could look it up" was Stengel's catchphrase, and indeed the record book declares that Berra was among the game's greatest catchers, if not the greatest.

Berra's career batting average, .285, was not as high as that of his Yankees predecessor, Dickey (.313), but Berra hit more home runs (358 in all) and drove in more runs (1,430). Berra led the American League in assists five times and from 1957 through 1959 went 148 consecutive games behind the plate without making an error, a major league record at the time.

On defense, he surpassed Mike Piazza, the best-hitting catcher of recent vintage. On offense, Berra and the great Johnny Bench of the Cincinnati Reds were comparable, except that Bench struck out three times as often. Berra whiffed a mere 414 times in more than 8,300 plate appearances over 19 seasons—an astonishingly small ratio for a power hitter.

Only Roy Campanella, who played for the Brooklyn Dodgers and faced Berra in the World Series six times before his career was ended by a car accident, equaled Berra's total of three Most Valuable Player Awards.

Berra's career was punctuated by storied episodes. In Game 3 of the 1947 World Series, against the Dodgers, he hit the first pinch-hit home run in Series history, and in Game 4 he was behind the plate for what was almost the first no-hitter and was instead a stunning loss. With two outs in the ninth inning and two men on base after walks, the Yankees' starter, Bill Bevens, gave up a double to Cookie Lavagetto that cleared the bases and won the game.

In September 1951, with the Yankees once again on the brink of a no-hitter, this one by Allie Reynolds against the Boston Red Sox, Berra made one of baseball's famous errors. With two outs in the ninth inning, Ted Williams hit a towering foul ball between home plate and the Yankees' dugout. It looked like the end of the game, which would seal Reynolds's second no-hitter of the season. But the ball was caught in a gust of wind; Berra lunged backward, and the ball deflected off his glove. On the next pitch, Williams hit an almost identical pop-up. This time, Berra caught it, preserving Reynolds' no-hitter.

In the first game of the 1955 World Series against the Dodgers, the Yankees were ahead, 6–4, in the top of the eighth when the Dodgers' Jackie Robinson stole home. The plate umpire called him safe, and Berra went berserk. The Yankees won the game although not the Series—it was the only time Brooklyn got the better of Berra's Yankees—but Berra never forgot. More than 50 years later, he signed a photograph of the play for President Obama, writing, "Dear Mr. President, He was out!"

During the 1956 Series, again against the Dodgers, Berra was at the center of another indelible image, when he leapt into the arms of Don Larsen, who had just struck out Dale Mitchell to end Game 5 and

complete the only perfect game (and only no-hitter) in World Series history.

From 1946 to 1985, as a player, coach and manager, Berra appeared in 21 World Series. He starred on World Series winners in 1947, '49, '50, '51, '52, '53, '56 and '58. He was a backup catcher and part-time outfielder on the championship teams of 1961 and '62. He also played on World Series losers in 1955, '57, '60 and '63. He still holds Series records for games played, plate appearances, hits and doubles.

Lawrence Peter Berra was born on May 12, 1925, in the Italian enclave of St. Louis known as the Hill, which also fostered the baseball career of his boyhood friend Joe Garagiola. Berra was the fourth of five children. His father, Pietro, a construction worker and bricklayer, and his mother, Paulina, were Italian immigrants.

As a boy, Berra was known as Larry, or Lawdie, as his mother pronounced it. As recounted in "Yogi Berra: Eternal Yankee," a 2009 biography by Allen Barra, one day young Larry went with some friends to the movies and were watching a travelogue about India when a Hindu yogi appeared on the screen. His posture struck one of the friends as how Berra sat as he waited his turn at bat. From that day on, he was Yogi Berra.

Berra dropped out of school after the eighth grade. He played American Legion ball and worked odd jobs. As teenagers, he and Garagiola tried out with the St. Louis Cardinals and were offered contracts. But Garagiola's came with a $500 signing bonus and Berra's just $250, so Berra declined to sign.

The St. Louis Browns also wanted to sign Berra but were not willing to pay any bonus. Then, the day after the 1942 World Series, in which the Cardinals beat the Yankees, a Yankee coach offered Berra a minor league contract—along with the elusive $500.

Berra's professional baseball life began in Virginia in 1943 with the Norfolk Tars of the Class B Piedmont League, but World War II put his career on hold. Berra joined the Navy. He took part in the invasion of Normandy and, two months later, in an Allied assault on Marseilles in which he was bloodied by a bullet and earned a Purple Heart.

In 1946, after his discharge, he was assigned to the Newark Bears, then the Yankees' top farm team. He played outfield and catcher and hit .314 with 15 home runs and 59 R.B.I. in 77 games. That September, in his first big league game, he had two hits, including a home run.

Berra became a fan favorite, because of his superior play and because of his humility and guilelessness. In 1947, honored at Sportsman's Park in St. Louis, a nervous Berra said, "I want to thank everyone for making this night necessary."

Berra was a hit with sportswriters, too, although they often portrayed him as a baseball idiot savant. When writers kidded him about his girlfriend, Carmen

Short, saying he was too unattractive to marry her, he reportedly responded, "I'm human, ain't I?"

Berra married Carmen in 1949, and the marriage endured until her death in 2014. He is survived by their three sons—Tim, who played professional football for the Baltimore Colts; Dale, a former infielder for the Yankees, the Pittsburgh Pirates and the Houston Astros; and Lawrence Jr.—as well as 11 grandchildren and a great-grandson.

As the earlier jousting over signing bonuses had demonstrated, Berra was a canny negotiator. His salary as a player reached $65,000 in 1961, substantial for that era.

"He has continued to allow people to regard him as an amiable clown because it brings him quick acceptance, despite ample proof, on field and off, that he is intelligent, shrewd and opportunistic," Robert Lipsyte wrote in The New York Times in October 1963.

At the time, Berra had just concluded his career as a Yankees player, and the team had named him manager. The aging Yankees played listlessly through much of the summer of 1964. A squabble on the bus after a tough loss made it seem to some as if Berra had lost control. Although the Yankees won the pennant, Ralph Houk, the general manager, fired Berra after the team lost a seven-game World Series to St. Louis.

In a bizarre move, Houk replaced him with the Cardinals' manager, Johnny Keane. Keane's Yankees finished sixth in 1965. Berra, meanwhile, took a job as a coach for the Mets under Stengel. The team floundered until 1969, when the so-called Miracle Mets, with Gil Hodges as manager—and Berra coaching first base—won the World Series.

After Hodges died, before the start of the 1972 season, Berra replaced him. That summer, Berra was inducted into the Hall of Fame. But the Mets finished third in 1972. The following season, they were well under .500 and in sixth place when Berra supposedly uttered perhaps the most famous Yogi-ism of all.

"It ain't over till it's over," he said (or words to that effect).

Lo and behold, the Mets got hot and won the National League's Eastern Division title. They beat the Reds in the League Championship Series before losing to the Oakland Athletics in the World Series.

Berra was rewarded with a three-year contract, but the Mets finished fifth in 1974. The following August, with the team in third place, Berra was fired.

He returned to the Yankees as a coach, and in 1984 the owner, George Steinbrenner, named him to replace Billy Martin as manager. The team finished third that year, but during spring training Steinbrenner promised him that he would finish the 1985 season as manager. But after a 6–10 start, Steinbrenner fired Berra, bringing back Martin. Not only did Steinbrenner break his word, but he sent an underling to deliver the news.

For 14 years, Berra refused to set foot in Yankee Stadium. In January 1999, Steinbrenner tried to make amends, admitting that he should at least have had the decency to fire Berra face to face.

To welcome him back into the fold, the Yankees held a Yogi Berra Day on July 18, 1999. Don Larsen threw out the ceremonial first pitch, which Berra caught.

Incredibly, David Cone of the Yankees pitched a perfect game that day. It was, as Berra may or may not have said in another context, "déjà vu all over again."

MUHAMMAD ALI

January 17, 1942–June 3, 2016

By Robert Lipsyte

Muhammad Ali, the three-time world heavyweight boxing champion who helped define his turbulent times as the most charismatic and controversial sports figure of the 20th century, died on Friday in a Phoenix-area hospital. He was 74.

The cause was septic shock. Ali, who lived near Phoenix, had had Parkinson's disease for more than 30 years. He had been admitted to the hospital with a respiratory problem.

Ali was the most thrilling if not the best heavyweight ever, carrying into the ring a physically lyrical, unorthodox boxing style that fused speed, agility and power more seamlessly than that of any fighter before him.

But he was more than the sum of his athletic gifts. An agile mind, a buoyant personality, a brash self-confidence and an evolving set of personal convictions fostered a magnetism that the ring alone could not contain. He entertained as much with his mouth as with his fists, narrating his life with a patter of inventive doggerel. ("Me! Wheeeeee!")

Ali was as polarizing a superstar as the sports world has ever produced—both admired and vilified in the 1960s and '70s for his religious, political and social stances. His refusal to be drafted during the Vietnam War, his rejection of racial integration at the height of the civil rights movement, his conversion from Christianity to Islam and the changing of his "slave" name, Cassius Clay, to one bestowed by the separatist black sect he joined, the Lost-Found Nation of Islam, were perceived as serious threats by the conservative establishment and noble acts of defiance by the liberal opposition.

Loved or hated, he remained for 50 years one of the most recognizable people on the planet.

In later life Ali became something of a secular saint, a legend in soft focus. He was respected for having sacrificed more than three years of his boxing prime and untold millions of dollars for his antiwar principles after being banished from the ring; he was extolled for his un-self-conscious gallantry in the face of incurable illness, and he was beloved for his accommodating sweetness in public.

In 1996, he was trembling and nearly mute as he lit the Olympic caldron in Atlanta.

That passive image was far removed from the exuberant, talkative, vainglorious 22-year-old who bounded out of Louisville, Ky., and onto the world stage in 1964 with an upset victory over Sonny Liston to become the world champion. The press called him the Louisville Lip. He called himself the Greatest.

Ali also proved to be a shape-shifter—a public figure who kept reinventing his persona.

As a bubbly teenage gold medalist at the 1960 Olympics in Rome, he parroted America's Cold War line, lecturing a Soviet reporter about the superiority of the United States. But he became a critic of his country and a government target in 1966 with his declaration "I ain't got nothing against them Vietcong."

"He lived a lot of lives for a lot of people," said the comedian and civil rights activist Dick Gregory. "He was able to tell white folks for us to go to hell."

But Ali had his hypocrisies, or at least inconsistencies. How could he consider himself a "race man" yet mock the features of other African-Americans, most notably Joe Frazier, his rival in three classic matches? Ali called him "the gorilla," to Frazier's enduring bitterness.

The traditionalist fight crowd was appalled by his style; he kept his hands too low, the critics said,

and instead of allowing punches to "slip" past his head by bobbing and weaving, he leaned back from them.

Over 21 years, he won 56 fights and lost five. His Ali Shuffle may have been pure showboating, but the "rope-a-dope"—in which he rested on the ring's ropes and let an opponent punch himself out—was the stratagem that won the Rumble in the Jungle against George Foreman in 1974, the fight in Zaire (now the Democratic Republic of Congo) in which he regained his title.

His personal life was paradoxical. Ali belonged to a sect that emphasized strong families, yet he had dalliances as casual as autograph sessions. A brief first marriage to Sonji Roi ended in divorce after she refused to dress and behave as a proper Nation wife. (She died in 2005.) While married to Belinda Boyd, his second wife, Ali traveled openly with Veronica Porche, whom he later married. That marriage, too, ended in divorce.

Ali was politically and socially idiosyncratic as well, known for telling ethnic jokes at fund-raisers for the Muhammad Ali Center, a museum in Louisville dedicated to "respect, hope and understanding."

But Ali generated so much good will by that there was little he could say or do that would change the public's perception of him.

"We forgive Muhammad Ali his excesses," an Ali biographer, Dave Kindred, wrote, "because we see in him the child in us, and if he is foolish or cruel, if he is arrogant, if he is outrageously in love with his reflection, we forgive him because we no more can condemn him than condemn a rainbow for dissolving into the dark. Rainbows are born of thunderstorms, and Muhammad Ali is both."

Cassius Marcellus Clay Jr. was born in Louisville on Jan. 17, 1942, into a family of strivers that included teachers, musicians and craftsmen. Some of them traced their ancestry to Henry Clay, the 19th-century representative, senator and secretary of state, and his cousin Cassius Marcellus Clay, a noted abolitionist.

Ali's mother, Odessa, was a cook and a house cleaner, his father a sign painter and a church muralist who blamed discrimination for his failure to become a recognized artist. Cassius started to box at 12, after his bicycle was stolen off a downtown street. He reported the theft to Joe Martin, a police officer who ran a boxing gym. When Cassius boasted what he would do to the thief when he caught him, Martin suggested that he first learn how to punch properly.

For all his ambition and willingness to work hard, education—public and segregated—eluded him. The only subjects in which he received satisfactory grades were art and gym. He was never taught to read properly; years later he confided that he had never read a book.

In boxing he found boundaries, discipline and

stable guidance. Martin, who was white, trained him for six years. It was Martin who persuaded Clay to "gamble your life" and go to Rome with the 1960 Olympic team despite his fear of flying. Clay won the Olympic light-heavyweight title and came home a professional contender. Of course, few journalists followed Clay home to Louisville, where he was publicly referred to as "the Olympic nigger."

Clay turned professional by signing a six-year contract with 11 local white millionaires, the so-called Louisville Sponsoring Group. He was groomed by Angelo Dundee, a top trainer, in Miami.

At a mosque there, Clay was introduced to the Nation of Islam, known to the news media as "Black Muslims." Elijah Muhammad, the group's leader, taught that white people were devils genetically created by an evil scientist.

Years later, after leaving the group and converting to orthodox Islam, Ali gave the Nation of Islam credit for offering African-Americans a black-is-beautiful message at a time of low self-esteem and persecution.

Clay enjoyed early success against prudently chosen opponents. In 1963, at 21, after only 15 professional fights, he was on the cover of Time magazine. The winking quality of the prose—"Cassius Clay is Hercules, struggling through the twelve labors. He is Jason, chasing the Golden Fleece"—reinforced the assumption that he was just another boxer being sacrificed to the box office's lust for fresh meat. It was feared he would be seriously injured by the baleful slugger Liston, a 7-to-1 betting favorite to retain his title in Miami Beach, Fla., on Feb. 25, 1964.

But encouraged by his assistant trainer and "spiritual adviser," Drew Brown, known as Bundini, Clay mocked Liston as the "big ugly bear" and chanted a battle cry: "Float like a butterfly, sting like a bee, rumble, young man, rumble."

To the shock of the crowd, Clay, taller and broader than Liston at 6 feet 3 inches and 210 pounds and much faster, took control of the fight, dancing away from him and peppering his face with jabs, opening a cut over his left eye. Two rounds later, Liston, slumped on his stool, gave up.

Clay, the new champion, capered along the ring apron, shouting at the press: "Eat your words! I shook up the world! I'm king of the world!"

The next morning, Clay affirmed his membership in the Nation of Islam. A few weeks later he became Muhammad Ali, which he said meant "Worthy of all praise most high."

On Feb. 17, 1966, Ali learned that he had been reclassified 1A by his selective service board. The timing was suspicious to some; the contract with the Louisville millionaires had run out, and Nation members were taking over as Ali's managers.

On April 28, 1967, Ali refused to be drafted and requested conscientious-objector status. He was stripped of his title by boxing commissions around the country. Several months later he was convicted of draft evasion, a verdict he appealed. He did not fight again until he was almost 29.

Afterward, Ali supported himself on the college lecture circuit and starred in a short-lived Broadway musical, "Big Time Buck White." There was a fast-food chain called Champburger.

As Ali's draft-evasion case made its way to the United States Supreme Court, he returned to the ring on Oct. 26, 1970, heading for a showdown with Frazier, the new champion. "The Fight," as the Madison Square Garden bout with Frazier on March 8, 1971, was billed, lived up to expectations as an epic match, and Frazier won a 15-round decision. Both men suffered noticeable physical damage.

Ali was the underdog, smaller and seven years older than George Foreman, a bigger, more frightening version of Liston, when they met on Oct. 30, 1974, in Zaire. As the fight progressed, the crowd chanted, "Ali, bomaye!" ("Ali, kill him!"). In the eighth round, in a blur of punches, Ali knocked out Foreman to regain the title. He leaned down to reporters and said, "What did I tell you?"

Ali successfully defended his title 10 times over the next three years, at increasing physical cost. He knocked out Frazier in their third match, the so-called Thrilla in Manila in 1975, but the punishment of their 14 rounds, Ali said, felt close to dying. He retired in 1981, and soon learned he had Parkinson's disease. His wife, Lonnie, said it had been brought on by Ali's exposure to toxic chemicals at his training camp in Deer Lake, Pa.

In recent years, Parkinson's disease and spinal stenosis, which required surgery, limited Ali's mobility and ability to communicate. He spent most of his time at his home in Paradise Valley, Ariz.

"But he loved the adoration of crowds," his wife said. "Even though he became vulnerable in ways he couldn't control, he never lost his childlike innocence, his sunny, positive nature. Jokes and pranks and magic tricks. He wanted to entertain people, to make them happy."

ACKNOWLEDGMENTS

Editing down more than 300 historical obituaries of well more than half a million words to fit within the covers of a book, even one as hefty as this, takes some doing, and it was done largely and expertly by a platoon of editors, all of them lately retired from The New York Times after long and successful careers with the newspaper. (Indeed, their cumulative length of service probably exceeds the number of years that The Times itself has been in operation: 165 and counting.) So a warm thanks to Constance Rosenblum, Dave Smith, David Stout, Paul Winfield, David Corcoran and Charles Strum.

Finding and selecting photographs from a trove of hundreds (if not thousands) of them was also a challenge, and it was ably met by The Times photo editors Evan Sklar and William P. O'Donnell, as well as by Jeff Roth, who provided research as the head of The Times's archive known as "the morgue." The striking results of their labor can be seen throughout this book.

Any ambitious endeavor like this almost invariably has a guiding spirit, and at The Times it was Alex Ward, the editorial director of book projects. The book would plainly not have happened without his enthusiasm and dedication in seeing it through to completion.

At Black Dog & Leventhal, the senior editor Lisa Tenaglia was the patient and creative guiding force in realizing J.P. Leventhal's original vision for this book.

She was backed by a superb team: Ankur Ghosh in book production, Mike Olivo in managing editorial, and Neil DeYoung, Marcy Haggag and Lukas Fauset in designing and developing the impressively rich and deep website of historical obituaries that accompanies the book. Their work, aided by Evan Sandhaus, a technology director at The Times, helped make "The Book of the Dead" such a singular publishing enterprise—one that only begins between these covers before reaching even more widely into the past.

PHOTO CREDITS

INDEX